BOOKS

GENERAL EDITOR
LUCY DANIEL

BOOKS

CASSELL
ILLUSTRATED

A CASSELL BOOK

An Hachette Livre UK Company

First published in the UK 2007 by
Cassell Illustrated, a division of
Octopus Publishing Group Ltd.
2-4 Heron Quays,
London E14 4JP

Text, design and layout © 2007 Octopus Publishing Group Ltd.

A CIP catalogue record for this book is available from the
British Library.

ISBN-13: 978-1-84403588-5 (UK Edition)
ISBN-10: 1-84403-588-3 (UK Edition)

Distributed in the United States and Canada by
Sterling Publishing Co., Inc
387 Park Avenue South, New York, NY 10016-8810

ISBN-13: 978-1-84403605-9 (U.S. Edition)
ISBN-10: 1-84403-605-7 (U.S. Edition)

10 9 8 7 6 5 4 3 2 1

Commissioning Editor: Laura Price
Project Editor: Jenny Doubt
Designer: John Round

Printed in China

CONTENTS

CONTRIBUTORS

Jad Adams is an independent historian, author, and television producer. He specializes in "the decadence" and radical characters from the 19th and 20th centuries. His books include *Kipling; Madder Music, Stronger Wine: The Life of Ernest Dowson*, and *Hideous Absinthe: A History of the Devil in a Bottle*.

Letizia Alterno has recently completed an introductory volume on the novelist Raja Rao. She is Editor-in-Chief of the Raja Rao Project and director of Rao's official website (www.rajarao.com). She is planning to write a biography of Rao with Rao's wife Susan, and is working on the translation of his novels into Italian.

M.K. Asante, Jr. is a professor and award-winning author & filmmaker. He is the author of the books *Like Water Running Off My Back, Beautiful. And Ugly Too*, and *It's Bigger than Hip-Hop*. He teaches at Morgan State University.

Simon Avery is Senior Lecturer at the University of Hertfordshire. He specializes in 19th and 20th century literature and history and is currently writing a critical study of Thomas Hardy and a biography of Elizabeth Barrett Browning.

Maggie Awadalla works at Imperial College London. She has extensive publications in the field of Arabic literature and culture and is particularly interested in women's writing in the Arab world.

Sophie Baker lives in Newcastle upon Tyne and works at *Mslexia*, the magazine for women writers. She is currently studying for her MA in Creative Writing.

Charles Beckett is the author of several unpublished poems, and one novella. After leaving university, where he read literature, he joined the Arts Council of England. He is Community Literature Officer for the London regional office.

Nimrod Ben-Cnaan was recently teaching fellow in European cultural studies at University College London, where he completed a PhD on postwar French and British cultural pessimism. Formerly with the Jerusalem Spinoza Institute and the Van Leer Jerusalem Institute, he continues to research modern European history of ideas.

Cathy Benson lives in Edinburgh where she teaches overseas students at the university and occasionally works as a translator. She has also lived in Spain, Portugal, Catalonia, Mexico, and Berlin.

Kiki Benzon is an assistant professor in English Literature at the University of Lethbridge. She specializes in contemporary fiction, mental health literature, and text-image dynamics.

Matthew Birchwood is lecturer in English Literature at Kingston University where he teaches Renaissance literature and culture. His most recent work focuses on English engagement with Islam in the drama and polemic of the period and is the subject of a book, *Staging Islam: Drama and Culture 1640–1685*.

Sarah Birchwood is an English teacher and freelance journalist and copywriter, living in Singapore. She previously lived in Osaka, Japan where she was awarded the Swadesh De Roy Scholarship by the Foreign Correspondents' Club of Japan. Her interests lie in East Asian culture and literature, particularly Japanese.

Rosie Blau is Books Editor of the *Financial Times*.

Kasia Boddy teaches in the English Department at University College London.

Helen Brown is a book critic for the *Daily Telegraph, Waterstones Quarterly*, and BBC5 Live. She also contributes regularly to the *Independent* and BBC Radio London.

Sylvia Brownrigg is the author of the novels *Pages for You* and *The Delivery Room*, and a collection of stories, *Ten Women Who Shook the World*. Her reviews have appeared in many British and American publications, including the *New York Times* and the *Times Literary Supplement*.

Nuzhat Bukhari is a Fellow in English at Fitzwilliam College, University of Cambridge.

Margaret Busby was born in Ghana, West Africa, and was educated in Britain. She co-founded the publishing house Allison & Busby Ltd, of which she was editorial director for 20 years. She now works as a writer, editor, critic, consultant, and broadcaster. She is the editor of *Daughters of Africa: An International Anthology of Words and Writing by Women of African Descent*, has contributed to many national and international publications, and has written drama for the stage and radio.

Scott Button is CEO of Unruly Media, an internet technology firm.

Terry Castle has taught at Stanford University since 1983. She has published eight books on diverse subjects, including *Masquerade and Civilization, The Apparitional Lesbian*, and the prize-winning collection, *The Literature of Lesbianism: A Historical Anthology from Ariosto to Stonewall*. She is also a well-known essayist and has written frequently for the *London Review of Books, Atlantic, New Republic, Times Literary Supplement, New York Times Book Review*, and other periodicals.

Lesley Chamberlain is a writer, critic, and occasional broadcaster. Her books include *Nietzsche in Turin, Girl in a Garden* (a novel), and *In the Communist Mirror*.

Sarah Churchwell is a Senior Lecturer in American Literature at the University of East Anglia. She is the author of *The Many Lives of Marilyn Monroe*. She has published on Sylvia Plath and Ted Hughes, F. Scott Fitzgerald and Ernest Hemingway, Anita Loos' *Gentlemen Prefer Blondes*, and Janis Joplin biography. She writes regularly for the *Times Literary Supplement* and the *New York Times*, and frequently appears on television and radio.

James Clements is a PhD student at Hughes Hall, University of Cambridge, writing on Mysticism and Ethics in the work of Iris Murdoch, Patrick White, and Saul Bellow. He has delivered papers on both White and Murdoch, and has published on the songs of Bob Dylan.

Laura Coffey is Postdoctoral Teaching Fellow in the School of English and Humanities at Birkbeck, University of London. She has research interests in the British novel of the mid-20th century, and has published articles on Evelyn Waugh and Patrick Hamilton.

Josh Cohen is Reader in English and Comparative Literature at Goldsmiths University of London, and the author of *Spectacular Allegories, Interrupting Auschwitz,* and *How to Read Freud*, as well as numerous articles on modern literature and philosophy.

Jason Cowley is a senior editor and writer on the *Observer*, and a contributing editor of the *New Statesman*.

Matthew Creasy is a Teaching Fellow at the University of St Andrews. He has degrees from Cambridge and Oxford, and was a Kennedy Scholar at Harvard in 2000. He is currently completing a book about James Joyce.

Ian Crofton is a writer and editor, specializing in popular and cultural history. With John Ayto he co-authored *Brewer's Britain and Ireland*, and the 2nd edition of *Brewer's Dictionary of Modern Phrase and Fable*. As sole author, his publications include *Brewer's Curious*

Titles, *Brewer's Cabinet of Curiosities*, *The Kings and Queens of England*, and *A Dictionary of Art Quotations*. Ian Crofton was editor-in-chief of *The Guinness Encyclopedia*. He lives in Crouch End with his family and three whippets.

David Cross studied English and American literature at Oxford and London. He now works at Arts Council England.

Lucy Daniel is a freelance writer and editor.

Jerome de Groot is a Lecturer at the University of Manchester. He is the author of *Royalist Identities* and numerous articles, chapters, and reviews on subjects ranging from Oscar Wilde to *Medal of Honour*.

Helen May Dennis is an Associate Professor at the University of Warwick, where she specializes in North American Literature. She has published on Elizabeth Bishop, Willa Cather, H.D., Ezra Pound, Adrienne Rich, medieval Provençal poetry, gender in American literature and culture, and Native American literature. She is mother of three grown children, a grandmother, a poet, and author of *Native American Literature: Towards a Spatialized Reading*.

Thomas Dymond is a PhD student at the University of Sheffield. He is researching gay and lesbian drama in post-war British theater and is attached to the AHRC British Library & University of Sheffield Theatre Archive Project. Other research interests include Shakespeare, crime novels, and musical theater.

Ashraf A. Eissa is Media Adviser at the Foreign and Commonwealth Office; he is an Associate Member of the European Studies Research Institute, University of Salford, UK, and was lecturer in Arabic & Comparative Literature at University of Salford, University of Exeter, and SOAS, University of London.

Cecilia Enjuto Rangel is Assistant Professor of Spanish at the University of Oregon. She studied her BA at the University of Puerto Rico, and her PhD in Comparative Literature at Yale University. She has published on Paz, Eliot, Neruda, Cernuda, and Baudelaire, and is working on her book project, "Cities in Ruins in Modern Poetry."

Joseph Farrell is Professor of Italian Studies in the University of Strathclyde. He is author of *Leonardo Sciascia* and *Dario Fo and Franca Rame: Harlequins of the Revolution*. He has edited volumes of essays on Carlo Goldoni, Dario Fo, Primo Levi, and the mafia. He has produced editions of *Accidental Death of an Anarchist* and of *Six Characters in Search of an Author*. His translations include novels by Sciascia, Consolo, and Del Giudice, and plays by Fo, Baricco, De Filippo, and Goldoni.

Adam Feinstein is the author of the biography, *Pablo Neruda: A Passion For Life*. He writes on Latin America and autism for a number of publications, including the *Guardian* and the *Times Literary Supplement*. He is editor of two autism-related websites, *AutismConnect* (www.autismconnect.org) and *Awares* (www.awares.org), as well as a monthly international autism newsletter, *Looking Up* (www.lookingupautism.org).

Pierce Freelon is an African American Studies fellow in the Pan-African Studies Masters Program at Syracuse University. Freelon is the founder of *Blackademics* (http://www.blackademics.org), a web site and blog page for young scholars. He is co-founder of the Hip-Hop group *Language Arts*.

Maureen Freely is author of seven novels, including *Enlightenment*, set in Istanbul. She has been a regular contributor to *The Guardian*, *The Observer*, *The Independent*, and the *Sunday Times* for two decades, writing on feminism, family and social policy,

Turkish culture and politics, and contemporary writing. She is deputy director of the writing program at the University of Warwick. She is the translator of *Snow*, *The Black Book*, and *Istanbul: Memories of a City* by Turkish novelist and Nobel Laureate Orhan Pamuk.

Andrew Gallix edits *3:AM Magazine* and teaches at the Sorbonne in Paris. His fiction and reviews have appeared in a wide range of publications. He is not currently working on his first novel.

Pedro García-Caro obtained his doctorate in American Studies at the University of London and is currently an Assistant Professor at the University of Oregon. His research concentrates on nationalist discourses in the Americas, particularly the U.S. and Mexico, and their postcolonial relations with Europe.

Gretchen Gerzina is the author of several books, including *Carrington: A Life*, *Black England: Life Before Emancipation*, and *Frances Hodgson Burnett: The Unpredictable Life of the Author of The Secret Garden*. She is professor of English at Dartmouth College, and an Honorary Fellow at the University of Exeter.

Alice Goldie is a former Editor with the University of Edinburgh and now a freelance author/researcher who has worked on many publications. She is currently writing a children's book while growing organic fruit, flowers, vegetables, and raising one small, non-organic child.

David Gooblar is currently finishing a PhD on the works of Philip Roth at University College London.

Ángel Gurría-Quintana is a historian, translator, and literary journalist. He has contributed to *The Economist*, *The Observer*, *Prospect Magazine*, and *The Paris Review*, and writes regularly for the arts and books pages of the *Financial Times*.

Alexandra Hamlyn is a graduate of St Andrews with an MA Honours English Literature and Art History. For the last three years she has traveled in South America and Europe whilst working as a freelance writer from her base in Hong Kong.

Reyhan Harmanci is a staff writer for the *San Francisco Chronicle*, where she reports on arts, culture, trends, and (most importantly) reviews young adult novels.

Kate Harris is working on a PhD in early post-war British theater at the University of Sheffield. Her PhD is attached to the AHRC University of Sheffield British Library Theatre Archive Project.

Doug Haynes lectures in American Literature at the University of Sussex. He has published on Surrealism, Hegel, and black humor in American writing; a particular interest is the role of humor in both avant-gardism and critical theory. Doug is also a visual artist.

Natalie Haynes is a stand-up comedian, a regular panellist on TV and radio shows, and writes for *The Times* and *The Sunday Telegraph*. She has toured nationally and internationally on her sell-out stand up show. She has written and presented two Radio 4 documentaries; "Laughing Matters" and "Classical Comedy" about how modern comedians stole all their jokes from Aristophanes, Juvenal, and Martial. Natalie was a regular panellist on More4's "The Last Word" and appears frequently on *Newsnight Review*.

Stewart Home was born in south London in 1962. When he was sixteen he held down a factory job for a few months, an experience that led him to vow he'd never work again. After dabbling in rock journalism and music, in the early Eighties he switched his attention to the art world. Now Home writes novels as well as cultural commentary, and continues to make films and exhibitions. He has long been an underground legend in Europe, North America, and Brazil.

Jon Hughes is Senior Lecturer in German at Royal Holloway, University of London, where he teaches and researches modern German literature and culture. He is the author of a recent monograph on the work of Joseph Roth.

Kathryn Hughes is the author of three biographies, the most recent of which is *The Short Life and Long Times of Mrs Beeton*. She writes a weekly column for *The Guardian* and is Visiting Professor at the University of Kingston.

Rowland Hughes is a lecturer is English Literature at the University of Hertfordshire, where he teaches literature from the Renaissance to the present day. His research interests lie in 18th- and 19th-century American literature, literature of the American West, and Anglo-American cinema.

Miki Iwata is Assistant Professor of English at Tohoku University and the author of *The Lion and Hamlet: A Study of the Dramatic Works of W.B. Yeats*.

Emily Jeremiah studied Modern Languages at Exeter College, Oxford, and gained a PhD in German Studies from Swansea University; her thesis was published as *Troubling Maternity*. She is the author of articles, reviews, and translations, and recently completed an MA in Creative and Life Writing.

Julia Jordan is a writer and academic specializing in the mid-20th-century novel. She lives in Glasgow.

Alison Kelly holds an MA from Oxford University and a PhD from the University of Reading, where she teaches English literature. She is a postdoctoral fellow of the Rothermere American Institute, University of Oxford.

Christian Kerr is a part time writer living and working in the North East of England. He shares his home with his girlfriend, Lizzie, and a dog called China.

Jake Kerridge reviews fiction for *The Daily Telegraph*.

Kate Kerrigan works in community education in Edinburgh.

Michael Kerrigan is a freelance writer who lives in Edinburgh. He reviews regularly in the *Times Literary Supplement* and *The Scotsman*.

James Kidd was educated at the universities of Liverpool and London, and is a freelance writer.

Nick Lawrence teaches American writing and culture at the University of Warwick. He has written on Whitman, Hawthorne, Frank O'Hara, and American gothic, and is the co-editor of *Ordinary Mysteries: The Common Journal of Nathaniel and Sophia Hawthorne*.

Sophie Lewis is the first UK director of American publishing house Dalkey Archive Press, seeking out great literature to publish from all over the world. She also translates French literary fiction and prose into English.

Monifa Love Asante teaches at Morgan State University in Baltimore. She has written four books, and recently completed a cultural memoir, *Romancing Harlem*, with visual artist Charles Mills. She is at work on a critical companion to Langston Hughes, and a new collection of poetry.

Timothy Lovering is a Research Fellow at the University of the West of England. He is a specialist in the history of southern Africa, and is currently responsible for a major collection of Zimbabwean archives at the British Empire and Commonwealth Museum, Bristol.

Graeme Macdonald is Associate Professor in the Department of English and Comparative Literary Studies at the University of Warwick, England.

Royce Mahawatte is an Associate Lecturer at the University of the Arts, London. He writes for the *Times Literary Supplement* and the *Financial Times* magazine.

Jamal Mahjoub is a British/Sudanese novelist. He has published a number of novels including *The Drift Latitudes* and *Travelling With Djinns*. His work has been widely translated and has won several awards.

Mariarita Martino is studying for a PhD on Intersemiotic Translation, between Italian cinema and contemporary Italian literature, at the University of Warwick. Her research interests include film studies, feminist film theory, and translation studies.

Ruth Maxey is a Lecturer in Modern American Literature at the University of Nottingham. She has published on postcolonial literature, Edwardian writing, and contemporary American and British fiction.

Bruce Millar is a freelance journalist and editor who lives in London.

Rajeshwar Mittapalli is Associate Professor of English in Kakatiya University, Andhra Pradesh, India. His works of criticism include *The Novels of Wole Soyinka*, and *Indian Women Novelists and Psychoanalysis*. He edited the New Delhi based quarterly *Atlantic Literary Review* for 6 years, apart from 23 anthologies of critical articles on a variety of literary subjects.

Michael Munro is a freelance editor/lexicographer/writer. He is the author of *The Patter-A Guide to Current Glasgow Usage*; *The Complete Patter*; *Clichés and How to Avoid Them*, and *Chambers Desktop Guide to Report Writing*.

Mayako Murai is Associate Professor in English and Comparative Literature at Kanagawa University, Japan. She has written on Angela Carter, the fairy tale, and postmodern orientalism.

Murrough O'Brien is a regular contributor to the *Independent on Sunday*. He has also worked for the *Daily Telegraph* and the *Erotic Review*. He trained as an actor.

Federica G. Pedriali is Reader in Modern Italian Literature at the University of Edinburgh. She is the

author of *La farmacia degli incurabili. Da Collodi a Calvino*, and editor of *A Pocket Gadda Encyclopedia*. She is founder and director of the *Edinburgh Journal of Gadda Studies*. Her second Gadda monograph is in press. Her early work on Gadda is forthcoming in English as *Symmetries of Closure. Gadda Surveyed*.

Frances Powell was born in London and grew up in South Devon. She studied English at University College London, and worked in publishing before joining the BBC where she is now part of the Science Radio Unit. She lives in London with her husband.

Robin Purves is a lecturer in English Literature at the University of Central Lancashire. He has co-edited (with Sam Ladkin) *the darkness surrounds us: American Poetry* and a special issue of *Chicago Review* on New British Poets and published essays on contemporary poetry. He runs a small press, Object Permanence, with Peter Manson.

Rossella Riccobono is Lecturer in Italian at the University of St Andrews. Her research interests span from 20th-century poetry and narrative, to contemporary Italian cinema. She has published on Eugenio Montale and Cesare Pavese. With Doug Thompson she was co-editor of *Onde di questo mare Reconsidering Pavese*. She co-edited *Vested Voices, Literary Trasvestism in Italian Literature* with Ermina Passannanti. Her monograph *Montale's Worlds of Poetry* is due in 2007. She is a published poet, and directs the St Andrews Poetry Forum.

Dinah Roe is an independent scholar and freelance writer whose interests include 20th-century American fiction, the 19th-century novel, Victorian poetry, and women's writing. She recently published Christina Rossetti's *Faithful Imagination*. She is currently editing and introducing the forthcoming Penguin Classics edition of *Christina Rossetti's Selected Poems*.

Christopher Rollason (PhD, York University) has been a member of the

Department of Anglo-American Studies at Coimbra University (Portugal), and a Visiting Professor with Jawaharlal Nehru University, Delhi. He co-edited the anthologies *Modern Criticism* (with Rajeshwar Mittapalli), and *Postcolonial Feminist Writing* (with Dora Sales Salvador). His numerous publications include several articles on José Saramago.

Robert Rollason was educated at a Midland Grammar School and Cambridge University where he worked on the newspaper *Varsity*. He has been employed by *The Sunday Times* and *The Observer*. His travel writing has appeared in *The Guardian* and *The Independent*. He contributes to a number of literary society magazines.

Elizabeth Rosen is Visiting Assistant Professor of 20th-century American literature and culture at Lafayette College. She is the author of *Apocalyptic Transformation: Apocalypse and the Postmodern Imagination*, and a professional and creative writer for television, magazines, and fiction journals. She is non-fiction editor of a New York webzine called *Ducts.org*.

Amy Rosenthal is author of the plays *Sitting Pretty*, *Henna Night*, and *Jerusalem Syndrome*. Her radio play, *Little Words*, was broadcast on BBC Radio 4 and her 4-part adaptation of her father's autobiography, *Jack Rosenthal's Last Act*, aired on BBC Radio 4 in summer 2006. She is under commission to the Manchester Royal Exchange and Hampstead Theatre, London.

Tom Rutter is Lecturer in Renaissance Literature at Sheffield Hallam University

Dora Sales is Lecturer in Information and Documentation Studies at the University Jaume I of Castellón, Spain. She is author of *Puentes sobre el mundo*, on José María Arguedas and Vikram Chandra. She is a professional literary translator of Indian fiction from English to Spanish and has translated Vikram Chandra, Manju Kapur, and Vandana Singh.

Anne Schwan has a PhD from the University of London. She teaches at Keble College in Oxford. Anne has published in the areas of contemporary and historical gender studies; she is working on a book on women and prison writing in 19th-century England.

Francesca Segal is an author and freelance journalist. She writes for *The Telegraph*, *The Financial Times*, *The Observer*, *Jewish Chronicle*, and *Jewish Quarterly* magazine amongst others.

Stephen Shapiro is an Associate Professor of American Writing and Culture at the University of Warwick.

Felicity Skelton is an Associate Lecturer in English and Creative Writing at Sheffield Hallam University. She is also a writer, mainly of short stories, including a collection of stories, *Eating A Sandwich*.

Tim Stafford is Associate Lecturer in Literature at the University of Hertfordshire. Prior to this he was a primary school teacher and lectured in the university's School of Education. His areas of interest are masculinities and comic book fiction.

Jason Starr is the Barry and Anthony Award-winning author of eight acclaimed crime novels which are published in nine languages. His latest thriller is *The Follower*.

Andrew Stevens is Editor of *3:AM Magazine*. He edited its fifth anniversary anthology *The Edgier Waters* and lives in London, where he writes for an array of other publications.

Peter Swaab teaches English at UCL, and is most recently the editor of the *Collected Poems of Sara Coleridge* and *Selected Nonsense and Travel Writings of Edward Lear*.

Elisabetta Tarantino teaches Italian language at the University of Warwick. She is co-editor of *Il romanzo contemporaneo: voci italiane* (with Franca Pellegrini), and of *Nonsense and Other Senses: Dysfunctional Communication and Regulated Absurdity in Literature* (with Carlo Caruso).

David Taylor is Associate Professor of English at Tokyo Medical and Dental University. He has published on Asian travel writing, Bruce Chatwin, and the English literary ballads. He is currently working on a study of Samuel Beckett.

Susan Tomaselli is the founder and editor of *Dogmatika.com*, as well as a contributing editor to *3:AM Magazine*, where she writes a graphic novel-focused column called *The Funnies*.

Anna Tripp is a Senior Lecturer in Literature at the University of Hertfordshire. She teaches and researches 20th-century and contemporary poetry, children's literature, and gender theory.

Anastasia Valassopoulos has been teaching at Manchester since 2004. Her main area of research is in the postcolonial literature and culture of the Middle East and North Africa. She is the author of *Contemporary Arab Women Writers* and has written on a variety of authors, filmmakers, and musicians from the Arab world.

Paul Vlitos is lecturer in English at Tohoku University in Sendai, Japan. His recent writing includes work on V.S. Naipaul, Joseph Conrad, and Mrs Beeton. His first novel, *Welcome to the Working Week* was published in 2007.

Neil Wallington gained his PhD in English literature from University College London in 2005. He currently lives and works in London.

Kathy Watson read English at Oxford. She left an editor's job in women's magazines to write biographies. Her two books are *The Crossing: the curious story of the first man to swim the Channel* and *The Devil Kissed Her: the story of Mary Lamb*. She is the Royal Literary Fund fellow at City University.

Pat Wheeler is Principal Lecturer in Literature at the University of Hertfordshire. She has published on British and Irish fiction, science fiction, and representations of dystopia in literature and film. Forthcoming publications include books on science fiction and edited collections of essays on the work of Pat Barker.

Elizabeth Whyman writes regularly for *Mslexia*, a magazine for women writers. Her poems have been widely published in the UK and U.S. and her debut collection of poetry was launched in September 2007 at the Bristol Poetry Festival.

Juliet Wightman has taught English Studies for several years. Her research focuses on the relationship between language and violence, with particular reference to Renaissance literature and drama.

Sarah Wood is the author of *Quixotic Fictions of the USA 1792-1815*, and is currently writing a novel set in 1790s Philadelphia, USA.

Gerard Woodward's first collection of poetry, *Householder* (1991) won the Somerset Maugham Award. His first novel, *August*, was shortlisted for the Whitbread First Novel Award. His second, *I'll Go To Bed at Noon*, was shortlisted for the Man Booker Prize in 2004. A fourth collection of poetry, *We Were Pedestrians*, appeared in 2005, and was shortlisted for the T.S.Eliot Prize. He is currently lecturer in creative writing at Bath Spa University. His third novel, *A Curious Earth*, appeared in 2007.

Tomonao Yoshida is Associate Professor of English at Tokyo Medical and Dental University. His chief research areas are the history of literary criticism and aesthetic theory. He is currently preparing studies of Marshall McLuhan and Kenneth Burke.

Jennifer Young is a lecturer in Creative Writing at the University of Hertfordshire. Her research interests are experimental writing, metaphor theory, and the work of American novelist Harry Mathews. She is completing her PhD at the University of Southampton. She has written for an array of publications.

INTRODUCTION

An emblem of seduction, or perhaps something more akin to Pandora's box, this fascinating book is unlike any other: a unique directory brimming with past and potential pleasures and temptations. Within the pages readers will find 1,000 of the most astonishing moments in twentieth- and twenty-first-century literature from around the world, laid out decade by decade. Here are authors and books that inspired movements, and ones that simply moved us. Here are great slices of dialogue; unforgettable scenes of passion, astounding philosophical leaps. Here too are real events that became enshrined as works of art; moments of personal despair and public adulation, of loneliness and addiction, of friendship and celebration. All the most dashing heroes, antiheroes and heroines are here, from Astro Boy to Zeinab, and here also is an evolution of literary types – dandies and serial killers, New Women and femmes fatales.

Over and over again this book captures that joyful moment when something truly new is born, or a great truth is encountered for the first time; the inscrutable occasion that makes it so the world can never be quite the same again. Putting these authors, books, characters, passages, and events back in context gives us back something of their revolutionary nature, lets us know again their extraordinary creative energy. From this vantage point the century of books becomes a mind-boggling pageant; an outrageous World's Fair, a tragi-comic carnival of characters human, nonhuman, superhuman, and subhuman. A princess, assorted ghosts, and one particularly well-connected bird have lined up to join this motley parade, this diverse panorama sprung from the minds of the world's most inventive writers. Here they are as they first appeared to the world, old friends who once were

strangers, and perhaps too some strangers who might become new friends. Along the way we discover remarkable stories of authorship: love affairs that inspired legends; stories that grew from journeys into exile or freedom; books written in the hardest of conditions, lost for decades and unearthed gleaming into the light. Here are tales of persecution and censorship, infatuations, murders, disappearances, epiphanies, manifestoes. There are books whose aim was scandal, subversion, and sabotage, but also gentler innovations, inspirational meetings and relationships, unrequited and lost loves, forbidden loves, forbidden words, and their clamor to be heard.

This is both a story of the century's books and a picture of the century through its books. Reading the century through its books gives us an insight into social changes, technological breakthroughs – from cinema and the motor car to cloning and the internet. Using literature as a lens, the contours and preoccupations of the century come into focus. Many of these books have themselves been crucial in forming our idea of modern humanity; they opened up whole other worlds of experience. From this perspective our book also looks like a map of the century's social upheavals, its wars, revolutions, and struggles for equality. Through oppression and imprisonment, books have taken stock, held out hope, borne witness. All the writers invoked within these pages stood apart from the herd; pioneers, provocateurs, simply, in some way or another, they mattered. Their works still matter – not always as part of a canon of greatness or worthiness, though there are many great and worthy writers here; they might be bestsellers or works of propaganda. They may have shocked us or seduced us, but made an indelible imprint on their times, for good or bad.

Opposite Malcolm McDowell as Alex in *A Clockwork Orange*

One of the things I most enjoyed about compiling this bumper literary almanac was seeing how books rub up against one another – to know that *Lord Jim* was born at the same time as The *Wizard of Oz*, that *Love Story* came into the world at almost precisely the same moment as *Skinhead*, and to chance upon other such strange bedfellows. How pleasing it is to notice that in 1969, for example, three modern icons of masculinity swaggered into existence; that in 1930 both Sam Spade and Miss Marple were on the case for the first time, or in 1928 Macunaíma in Brazil and Mack the Knife in Germany were both on the prowl; how treacherous a year was 1910, when the world lost two of the greatest storytellers it has ever known; and that at the exact time when Russian literary artists were subjected to the iron rule of Socialist Realism, over in th U.S. the Black Mountain College experiment blossomed – or just as the House Un-American Activities Committee was clamping down in Hollywood, in Paris Olympia Press was springing up to confound attempts at censorship. Though freedoms have been temporarily removed, literature has ultimately found a way to grasp them back. Incidentally, we learn where exactly such terms as "hard-boiled," "stream of consciousness," or "Surrealism" come from. Here are the beginnings of the *nouveau roman*, the Harlem Renaissance, the Hindi New Story movement, the Japanese I-novel. Seeing where these tags originated helps us evaluate their usefulness. Herein too lies the growth of new ways of writing fiction: graphic novels, short stories, campus novels, cyberpunk, science fiction, children's fiction, hyperfiction.

The contributors who have supplied these compact capsules of wit, style, and erudition are novelists, critics, filmmakers, academics, poets, journalists, literary editors, broadcasters, publishers, playwrights, biographers, and translators from all around the world, who bring an eclectic international perspective to this century of books. They have

packed into each entry much more than plots and facts – this is not a litany of recommended reading. Instead they've taken the longer view, and explored what makes each moment so important, to show how the impact of each first great leap onto the page has reverberated down the years. Such a huge and endlessly unraveling subject must be forever contingent, incomplete, and tantalizing; winnowing down the infinite connections and possibilities has given a particular shape to the century, but with many happily unclassifiable outcrops. As we move closer to our own times, it becomes harder to discern who will be the key figures, and what will be the defining moments of our age. Some of them are here. I can't think of another book that's ever provided such an alluring compendium of the great moments in modern literature, which is why I have been so happy to be part of this one.

It is a great pleasure to thank all the eager, versatile, accomplished contributors and to reflect on the array of minds and personalities brought together here, like a very engaging party at which all the guests are scintillating. My greatest thanks are due, as always, to my parents Annette and Terry Daniel for their love and support and, once again, to Kasia Boddy, whose knowledge alone could fill this book. Thanks to Cathryn Stone and Ann Fraser and families, Ros Coward, and most especially José Enrique Martinez Yabar, my constant companion. Thanks also to Sylvia Brownrigg and Margaret Busby for judicious suggestions, and to Cathy Benson, Rosie Blau, Rowland Hughes, James Kidd, Michael Munro, Anastasia Valassopoulos, and Paul Vlitos for their generosity. Finally thank you to Laura Price for her unflagging professionalism, which has made everything possible, and Jenny Doubt for her extraordinarily perceptive solutions and attention to detail, and to all the above for the care and energy they have put into this book.
Lucy Daniel

Opposite Playwright, poet, and Nobel Laureate Derek Walcott

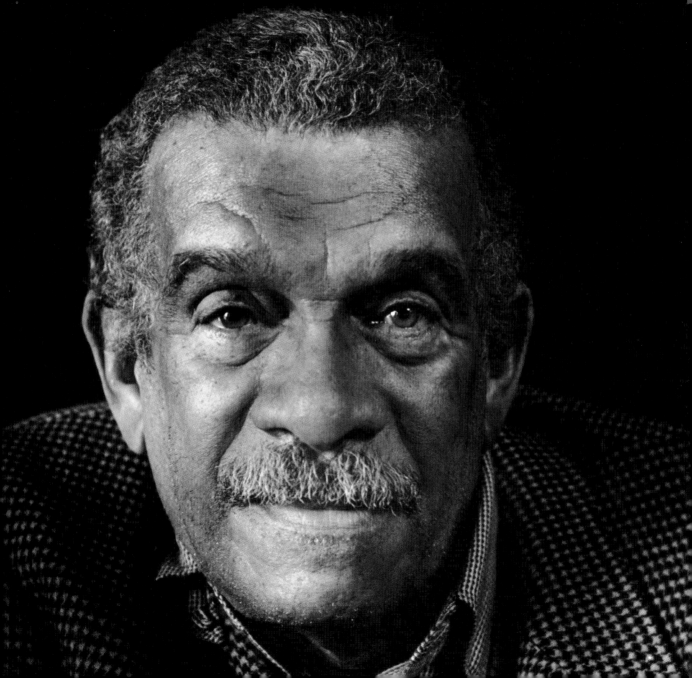

Key Book
The Time Machine

The Time Machine is one of Wells' most terrifying novels in its vision of the future. Initially set in London at the end of the nineteenth century, it focuses on an amateur scientist, known only as the Time Traveller, who develops a machine which enables him to journey through the fourth dimension to the year 802,701 AD. Here he finds that humans have divided into two discrete, but inter-dependent species: the beautiful, frail, and childlike Eloi who occupy a seemingly paradisal upper world and live a life of idleness and apathy; and the terrifying Morlocks, white ape-like creatures who live underground and are forced to work to supply the Eloi with food and clothing. In return, the Morlocks emerge from wellshafts at night and abduct the Eloi as their own food.

The novel offers Wells' socialist vision of what might become of the nineteenth-century class structure with the middle classes becoming lazy and ignorant, and the working classes being pushed underground in a devolved state. (The idea of the cannibalistic Morlocks has influenced various depictions of threatening, subterraneous species, as in J.R.R. Tolkien's *Lord of the Rings*, the *X Men* comic books, and the 1995 horror film, *The Descent*.)

Finally escaping this dystopia, the Time Traveller journeys further into the future only to find the dying earth occupied by giant crabs and later, solely by lichens, humankind having been obliterated altogether. As a warning about human arrogance and the illusory notion of "civilization" and progress, The Time Machine is a chilling vision of a possible future. The novel helped establish Wells as one of the fathers of the genre and is a principal text in the history of science fiction. It has been filmed several times and inspired several sequels, including K.W. Jeter's *Morlock Night* (1979) and Steven Baxter's *The Time Ships* (1995).

Simon Avery

Date 1895 (publication)

Author Herbert George Wells (1866–1946)

Nationality UK

Why It's Key Wells' first novel has been hugely influential in the development of science fiction. Since its publication, time travel has become a fundamental concept of SF narratives, as has the idea of the heroic time-traveller and the use of time travel to reflect upon the politics of so-called "civilization."

Opposite *The Time Machine*

14

Key Character **Herminia Barton**
The Woman Who Did

Herminia Barton, a Cambridge University-educated "New Woman" is preoccupied with the faults of the institution of marriage and the sexual double standard that judged men and women separately. She is inspired by the possibility of acting on principles alone, declaring "I have wrought it all out in my mind beforehand, covenanted with my soul that for woman's sake I would be a free woman."

She deliberately eschews marriage to enter into a "free union" with another advanced thinker, Alan Merrick, but he dies suddenly, leaving her with an illegitimate child. Herminia refuses to be ashamed and instead projects all her idealistic hopes for the future of women on her daughter, Dolores. Born free of marriage, she is to be the female messiah of a new age. In a thoughtful working out of the novel, as Dolores grows up she reverts to conventional feminine type, respecting propriety and looking forward to marriage.

Only now does Herminia tell her daughter the truth about her illegitimacy, about which Dolores is horrified and disgusted. She declares she will never marry while her mother is alive. Herminia feels she has no choice, she "put on a fresh white dress, as pure as her own soul, like the one she had worn on the night of her self-made bridal with Alan Merrick," and kills herself by drinking prussic acid.

Grant Allen's obvious affection for his heroine prevents the book from being a cruel satire on the pretensions of moral philosophy and turns it into a tragedy of idealism.

Jad Adams

Date 1895

Author Grant Allen (1848–1899)

Nationality UK

Why It's Key The most influential of the "New Woman" novels, *The Woman Who Did* expresses the anxieties and aspirations of the time more directly than more "literary" books because of its easily accessible combination of social criticism and romantic fiction.

Key Passage
The Red Badge of Courage

"Once the line encountered the body of a dead soldier. He lay upon his back staring at the sky. He was dressed in an awkward suit of yellowish brown. The youth could see that the soles of his shoes had been worn to the thinness of writing paper, and from a great rent in one the dead foot projected piteously. And it was as if fate had betrayed the soldier. In death it exposed to his enemies that poverty which in life he had perhaps concealed from his friends."

Stephen Crane's *The Red Badge of Courage* is one of the great novels about war. It is a startlingly modern work, in both style, with the terse, charged, yet ironically understated sentences that influenced Hemingway, and in its preoccupation with psychology, with the war that is fought as much inside one's head as it is in battle.

Henry Fleming, the protagonist of the novel, dreams of glory, of the heroic act – yet when tested on the battlefield as a Union recruit in the American Civil War he flees from the advancing Confederate forces. This is the moment to which he keeps returning as he seeks to redeem himself and find meaning through an existential moment of action. There is nothing sentimental or grandiose in Crane's vision of war. But there is considerable insight and pathos, even though Crane had no actual experience of war when he wrote the novel. What he did have, however, was experience of life – and when, with characteristic concision, he writes of the thinness of the dead soldier's shoes, his poverty exposed in death as perhaps it never was in life, you are moved not only by the empathy and detail of the writing but by the knowledge that Crane himself, like the soldier, died far too young. As a reader one is haunted by what he might have achieved had he lived longer. As it is, *The Red Badge of Courage* remains one of the most influential of all American realist novels.
Jason Cowley

Date 1895

Author Stephen Crane (1871–1900)

Nationality USA

Why It's Key Crane's American Civil War story was one of the most influential war stories ever written. His realistic psychological approach to warfare was groundbreaking.

Key Passage
Jude The Obscure

"'Done Because We Are Too Menny'
At signs of this Sue's nerves utterly gave way, an awful conviction that her discourse with the boy had been the main cause of the tragedy, throwing her into a convulsive agony which knew no abatement."

This suicide note from Jude Fawley's eldest son is perhaps one of the most poignant lines in English literature. Old Father Time – the nickname given to the prematurely adult child – has hanged himself and his two half-brothers. The trigger is a recent conversation with his stepmother Sue Bridehead in which she explained that having so many children was a bar to the family finding decent lodgings and well-paid employment.

This terrible scene represents the final nail in the coffin of the doomed relationship between Jude and Sue. For several years they have been "living in sin," a consequence of the fact that they are both still married to other people. This feeling of illegitimacy has set them on a peripatetic downward course in which they are forced to keep one step ahead of inquisitive employers and disapproving landladies. It is this dismal sense of hopelessness that has communicated itself to the child.

Feeling that God has punished her for her sins by taking away her children, Sue now returns to her husband, despite loving Jude. He, in turn, stumbles back to his wife Arabella, who is the mother of Old Father Time. Jude dies a broken man, having failed to achieve his dream of an Oxford education, far less a happy domestic life.
Kathryn Hughes

Date 1896

Author Thomas Hardy (1840–1928)

Nationality UK

Why It's Key Readers were shocked by the novel's "indecency," a large part of which concerned the harrowing scene of child suicide. Modern readers, less worried by such theological niceties, still find the scene unbearably pessimistic. Deeply upset by the reaction to the book, Hardy never wrote another novel, but turned instead to poetry.

Key Character **Count Dracula**
Dracula

The most perverse of fictional monsters, Dracula appeared in 1897 in Stoker's epistolary Gothic novel. Taking a creature from mediaeval folklore that could appear variously as human, bat, dog and even vapor, Stoker breathed into his thirsty Transylvanian a sinister charm and exotic sexuality that has easily survived the years. Indeed, the character has multiplied in our culture like a virus, cinema, in particular, drawn repeatedly to it, from Murnau's magnificent *Nosferatu* (1922) through the fruity décolletage of '60s British Hammer films to the overburdened Coppola epic of 1992. Clearly, something in Dracula speaks to us as much as it did to Victorians. Perhaps his ancient lusts, stemming from deep in his aristocratic past, vicariously invigorate us: "dwellers in the city," the Count, a denizen of the edges of Europe, suggests, "cannot enter into the feelings of the hunter." Or perhaps it is the barely masked sense of sexual transgression he embodies. Not only does he represent fantasies of violence, women under his spell are altered: beautiful Lucy Westenra in the Stoker text becomes a wanton when bitten; even virtuous angel of the household Mina Murray is forced to suck his open wound, if not go the whole way.

Dracula has been read as a metaphor for everything from fear of syphilis to the isolation of the monopoly capitalist, the latter suggested by Karl Marx's description of capital as "vampire-like" dead labor. Ever the shape-shifter, the Count will undoubtedly continue to solicit interpretations for generations to come.
Doug Haynes

Date 1897 (publication)

Author Bram Stoker (1847–1912)

Nationality Ireland

Why It's Key Not immediately a success, Stoker's caped crusader has gradually permeated our culture on every level, from children's cartoons to novels, theme parks, and Hollywood blockbusters.

Key Event
War of Canudos

Bloodshed heralded Brazil's twentieth century. In a remote corner of the north-eastern province of Bahia, a messianic figure preached the return of legendary king Sebastião and the end of the newly installed republic. Grizzled, charismatic, and nursing a private grievance against local tax authorities, Antônio Conselheiro (the Counsellor) settled in the abandoned farm of Canudos with some 8,000 followers in 1893. Canudos was soon a bustling village and, it was feared, a hub of insurrection.

In November 1896 a column of federal troops was routed by the Counsellor's supporters armed only with primitive weapons. Two further punitive expeditions sent early in 1897 were repelled by Canudos' villagers, whose number had risen to almost 30,000. During the government's final offensive, in October 1897, the village was razed to the ground with heavy artillery. Surviving men were decapitated, children shot, women raped. 25,000 people are thought to have died at Canudos.

Euclides da Cunha, a reporter for a São Paulo newspaper, offered the most authoritative account of the massacre in *Os Sertões* (*The Backlands*, 1901). It was, in his view, a battle between barbarism and civilization in which roles were reversed as forces of order became perpetrators of horror. "That campaign," he wrote, "was a throwback to the past. It was, in the whole sense of the word, a crime." His book inspired master works of twentieth century literature: *Verdict in Canudos*, by Hungarian novelist Sándor Márai (first published in Canada in 1970), and Peruvian Mario Vargas Llosa's *The War of the End of the World* (1981) both explore this historical episode as a devastating parable about the tenuous limit between good and evil.
Ángel Gurría-Quintana

Date 1897

Place Canudos, Brazil

Why It's Key At stake, at Canudos, was the rationalism of the new republic, against which stood a primitive mystic capable of rousing the dispossessed. Reason became an excuse for inhumanity. Literature helped preserve the memory of the conflagration.

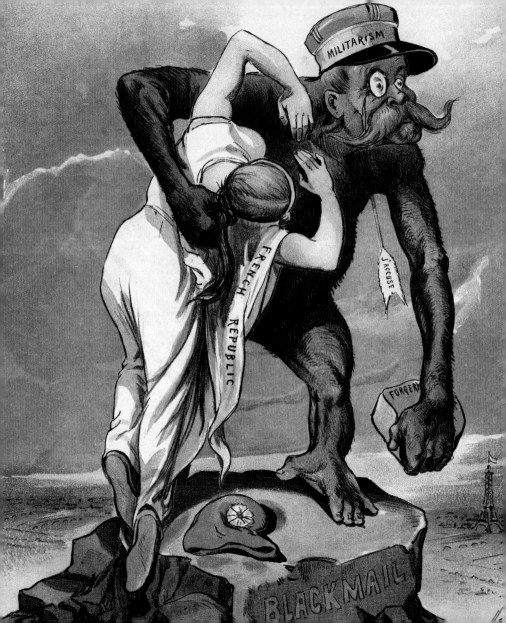

Key Event **End of the Spanish-American War and the naming of "Generation of '98"**

The nineteenth century ended in crisis for Spain: 1895 saw the uprising in Cuba and the following year that of the Philippines – Spain's last remaining colonies. Total defeat came in 1898, when Spain was forced to sign the Treaty of Paris granting Cuba independence, while the Philippines and Puerto Rico were placed under United States control. This shattering blow provoked a wave of indignation and protest in Spain which saw its literary manifestation in the writers of what came to be known as the Generación del '98 (Generation of '98).

The main representatives were Miguel de Unamuno, Ramon del Valle-Inclán, Pío Baroja, Azorín, and Antonio Machado. All were born between 1864 and 1875, and all were concerned with finding the true essence of Spain and a meaning to life, in the face of the apathy into which the country had been plunged. They looked to previous great writers – including Cervantes and Quevedo – to history, to the austere landscape of Castille, the poverty and simplicity of its people and the extremes of its climates. They rebelled against Spain's backwardness, and proposed the rebuilding of its education, culture, agriculture, and economy, as well the country's integration into Europe.

Their desire for reform saw them adopt a specific literary style which could be characterised by simple, expressive language – marking a distinct break from the rhetoric in vogue at the time – with a cultured vocabulary, sprinkled with foreign and colloquial words.

Unamuno and Valle-Inclán both died in 1936, while Machado – who read the closing speech at the anti-fascist Second International Writers' Congress in Valencia in July 1937 – fled to France in 1939 where he died that same year. Baroja died in 1956 while Azorín (José Martínez Ruiz) – an influential essayist, theorist and literary critic who is thought to have coined the term "Generation of '98" – died as late as 1967.

Adam Feinstein

Date 1898

Why It's Key Machado – one of the greatest Spanish poets – bore witness to the battle between what he saw as "the two Spains." Unamuno, a novelist and essayist, was haunted by metaphysical anguish, while Baroja's novels depict a pessimistic vision of Spanish reality, tempered by humor. The dramatist Valle-Inclán's concerns were fundamentally aesthetic – he was uninterested in most of the Generation of '98's ideological problems.

Key Event **"J'Accuse" is published on the front page of French newspaper *L'Aurore***

In 1894 Captain Alfred Dreyfus, a Jewish army officer, was accused of handing over secret documents to the Germans. He was sentenced to life imprisonment on Devil's Island, the notorious penal colony off the coast of French Guiana. In 1896 evidence emerged that another officer was the true culprit, but anti-Semitic elements in the army and the Roman Catholic Church mounted a virulent, sometimes even violent, campaign against a retrial.

At this point Émile Zola, one of the giants of French letters, waded into the fray. No stranger to controversy – his series of naturalistic novels had looked the harsh realities of French society unflinchingly in the face – he risked everything in a thundering denunciation of the miscarriage of justice. On 13 January 1898 the newspaper *L'Aurore* carried an open letter from Zola to President Faure, under the headline "J'Accuse… !" (I accuse). "The truth is on the march," wrote Zola, "and nothing shall stop it." He was charged with libel, and sentenced to a year's imprisonment, although he evaded his sentence by escaping to England.

The affair rumbled on. Dreyfus was subjected to another trial, but was again found guilty. The government issued a pardon in 1899, and in accepting it Dreyfus was obliged to accept his guilt. It was not until 1906 that the French appeal court quashed his sentence, and restored Dreyfus to his position in the army. Zola did not live to see his campaign vindicated: he had died on 29 September 1902, in what some believe were suspicious circumstances.

Ian Crofton

Date 1898

Author Émile Zola (1840–1902)

Why It's Key The great novelist Zola helped to turn the tables in the Dreyfus Affair, an issue that split French society down the middle between reactionaries and radicals.

Opposite Political cartoon of the Dreyfuss Affair

Key Author **Henrik Ibsen**
When We Dead Awaken

Widely regarded as "the Father of Modern Drama," Henrik Ibsen (1828–1906) began his career writing verse plays on subjects drawn from Norwegian history and folklore. Only his last two verse plays, *Brand* (1866) and *Peer Gynt* (1867), are now performed with any regularity. When he turned to prose drama, however, Ibsen revolutionized nineteenth-century theater. The subject matter of his later plays, particularly *A Doll's House* (1879) and *Ghosts* (1881), scandalized contemporary critics and audiences by exposing the dysfunctional nature of marriage and prevailing sexual double standards.

Most shocking perhaps, was the rigor with which the playwright attacked the illusions of his audiences, undermining moral certainties about the rewards of virtue, truth, and an ethical approach to life. Mrs Alving of *Ghosts* endures the infidelities of her husband, presenting a façade of marital respectability, only to watch her son Osvald suffer the physical and mental deterioration of inherited syphilis. Nora Helmer, the heroine of *A Doll's House*, is bullied and infantilized by the husband she steadfastly supports, until she makes the momentous decision to abandon her home and family. In *An Enemy of the People* (1882), Dr Stockmann suffers public opprobrium for alerting the inhabitants of his spa town to the damaging effects of the waters, as the people's only concern is the loss of tourist revenue.

While his later plays became increasingly symbolic, Ibsen's commitment to provocative themes and psychological realism never faltered. To the end of his career, he continued to repudiate hypocrisy in its many forms and to challenge conventional moral tenets, making theater a forum for debate and intellectual and moral enquiry.

David Cross

Date 1899 (publication)

Nationality Norway

Other Key Works *The Wild Duck* (1884), *Hedda Gabler* (1890), *The Master Builder* (1892), *Little Eyolf* (1894)

Why It's Key The plays of Ibsen's maturity now form part of the staple repertoire of theater companies around the world.

20

Key Passage **"The Dream Work"**
The Interpretation of Dreams

"Every dream will reveal itself as a psychological structure, full of significance, and one which may be assigned to a specific place in the psychic activities of the waking state."

Freud's "discovery" of the unconscious mind was an incalculably important moment for art and literature, giving rise at first to works dealing with psychological complexity, and then, especially within aesthetic modernism, to ideas of the fragmentation of the self. No work by Freud, then, has had a greater impact upon literature or literary theory than *The Interpretation of Dreams*, where he first proposed the notion of the unconscious and designated dreams the "royal road" by which it might be known.

What seems most exciting about Freudian dream theory appears in the passage, "The Dream Work." Here he describes how "dream-content," or the overt images of dreams are in fact the coded residue of "latent dream content," or "dream-thoughts." "The dream-content," he writes, "is, as it were, presented in hieroglyphics, whose symbols must be translated, one by one, into the language of the dream-thoughts." By proceeding from manifest images to the unconscious material they have radically transformed, one illuminates the unconscious mind.

So, while dreams may sometimes seem sensible, they are never significant at the level of aesthetic or semantic coherence. Latent content hides itself using what he calls condensation and displacement. Condensation is the process whereby dream-content contains multiple associations; displacement describes the shift whereby the real subject of a narrative is outside the story. Both radically estrange their subject. But the point is, any text can be viewed like this: behind apparent coherence lies a whole different world.

Doug Haynes

Date 1899 (publication)

Author Sigmund Freud (1856–1939)

Nationality Austria

Why It's Key Freud's work marks the proposal of his idea of the unconscious and thus helps usher in the modern notion of humanity.

Opposite Sigmund Freud

SPOILER

1890–1909

Key Passage
The Awakening

"The voice of the sea is seductive"

Kate Chopin's second and last novel, *The Awakening*, is set in late-nineteenth-century New Orleans, and centers on the twenty-eight-year-old Edna Pontellier, who rejects her stifling position as wife and mother for a new life of emancipation and self-discovery. Defying her husband, she initiates her awakening through a combination of independent thinking, painting, music, a new appreciation of her own body, and two illicit affairs. Most importantly, however, she seeks freedom and power through learning to swim in the sea at Grand Isle.

In the final lyrical scene of the novel, Edna, having realized the seeming impossibility of ever totally escaping convention, returns to the beach where she sees a bird with a broken wing flying erratically, a symbol of her own limited life. Walking to the water's edge, she removes her bathing suit, a representation of the shedding of imposed identity, and stands naked in the sun and air, feeling for the first time like "some new-born creature." Swimming out into the seductive water, her mind fills with fleeting memories of her life – her husband and children, her lovers, her own childhood – until she can swim no more and she succumbs to the water and drowns.

This closing scene has been interpreted in markedly opposing ways: as Edna's final bid for liberation or her resigned suicide. However we read it, it is clear that there is no place for Edna in the society of the time and that she has nowhere else to go if she is to be true to herself and maintain her "courageous soul." This is a beautifully written depiction of the emerging New Woman at the end of the nineteenth century.
Simon Avery

Date 1899

Author Kate Chopin (1851–1904)

Nationality USA

Why It's Key Originally condemned for its representation of a woman rejecting conventional marriage and motherhood for physical, psychological, and sexual freedom. Chopin's masterpiece was recovered by feminist criticism in the 1960s and subsequently heralded as a classic of women's writing and American literature.

22

Key Passage
The Theory of the Leisure Class

"Conspicuous consumption of valuable goods is a means of reputability to the gentleman of leisure."

Written at the turn of the twentieth century, and revised again in 1912, Veblen's work is a document of staggering prescience. Coining the term "conspicuous consumption," he hits on the notion, now a staple of sociology, that goods and services are consumed not just from necessity but to demonstrate one's social position to others. In other words, years before the advent of mass consumerism, he developed a theory of "branding" that foresaw even the magical desirability of the logo.

The cultivation of refined tastes and manners in his late nineteenth-century bourgeois subjects, however, was more than just an amalgam of display and group-solidarity. Their behavioral prowess represented in fact a considerable labor, a self-fashioning transforming into the genteel protocol of the drawing room the hard labor of those from whom capital was originally extracted. "Conspicuous" signs, that is, can be as convoluted and mysterious as a Freudian displacement.

In his passage describing "waste," we have something that speaks directly to the serious modern shopper. "It frequently happens that an element of the standard of living which set out with being primarily wasteful," he writes, "ends with becoming, in [the] apprehension of the consumer, a necessary of life," citing luxuries like silver table service, silk hats, and starched linen, a list to which we could now add plasma TVs, four-wheel drives, or cocaine. Rejecting the kinds of judgement we might make about what is genuinely useful, all objects of consumption, he suggests, shockingly, derive their value, at least in part, from the degree to which others want them.
Doug Haynes

Date 1899

Author Thorstein Veblen (1857–1929)

Nationality USA

Why It's Key Economist Thorstein Veblen's term "conspicuous consumption" has passed into everyday language and many of his hugely influencial theories, which anticipate later sociologists like Pierre Bordieu, are now regarded as common sense.

Key Passage
Heart of Darkness

In London looking across the Thames, at the center of the greatest empire the world has known, the narrator Marlow tells how he went upstream of an African river to a trading settlement to bring back ivory collected by the trader Kurtz. He finds that Kurtz has "collected, bartered, swindled or stolen more ivory than all the other agents together" and that his methods have been brutal to the point of the barbaric – his hut is ringed with human heads on sticks.

The phrase in common use was "darkest Africa," but Conrad adroitly reverses this – the darkness is in the hearts of the Europeans directing the unspeakable cruelty of which man is capable. It was based in part on Conrad's four-month journey up the Congo river in 1890 where he witnessed the realities of Belgian colonialism and (like Marlow) found the traders were oblivious to the cruelties inflicted on native workers.

Conrad's genius was to make Kurtz, who gains a realization of this horror, not a naturally wicked man but an altruistic one who entered into the spirit of empire-building with a belief in his innate moral superiority and the religious idealism of Europe. He had wanted to suppress savage customs and write a treatise on his work. That illusion has been torn away scrap by scrap until, at the point of death, all Kurtz can see is what is left: "he cried out twice, a cry that was no more than a breath – 'The horror, the horror.'"

Jad Adams

Date 1899 (serialization – published in book form in 1902)

Author Joseph Conrad (1857–1924)

Nationality Poland (naturalized UK)

Why It's Key *Heart of Darkness* has inspired creative artists from T.S.Eliot who uses it in "The Waste Land" to Francis Ford Coppola for whom it supplied the framework for his Vietnam film *Apocalypse Now*.

1890-1909

23

Key Author **Gabriele d'Annunzio**
The Flame of Life (Il Fuoco)

Gabriele d'Annunzio (1863–1938) was the leading interpreter of European decadence in Italy; his sensuous and erotically charged work had great influence on modern Italian literature.

In a career that started with his first publication of poems at the age of sixteen, he was already famous by the time his best-known novel, *The Triumph of Death*, was published in 1894 (English version 1896). His stories of provincial Italian life have a vivid realism; his novels are often semi-autobiographical representations of an amoral Nietzschean superman.

He wrote plays for the actress Eleonora Duse with whom he had a relationship which he recounted, after they had parted, in the novel *The Flame of Life* (1900). This contributed to his reputation as the greatest lover in Europe – or perhaps just the best publicized.

He became a hero during World War I, deliberately volunteering for dangerous assignments. After the war, angry that Italy had lost the Dalmatian port of Fiume in the Versailles settlement, he gathered some supporters and occupied the town. He ruled the territory as dictator for eighteen months in which time he developed techniques that were to be taken up by Italian fascism: the Roman salute, emotive public events, the blackshirt uniform, and the corporatist state.

D'Annunzio's powerful writing was celebrated while he was alive but he was always considered morally questionable, as he left readers with the disturbing impression that fascism was the natural political expression of artistic theories. His literary reputation in post-war Europe has also been clouded by his fascist associations.

Jad Adams

Date 1900

Nationality Italy

Key Works Poetry *New Song* (1882), *In Praise of Sky, Sea, Earth and Heroes* (1899)

Key Works Novels *The Child of Pleasure* (1889), *The Triumph of Death* (1894)

Why It's Key He showed a world used to drawing-room intellectuals that a poet could also be a man of action.

Key Character **Lord Jim**
Lord Jim

"Jim," a young Englishman about to make a career at sea, after a diet of adventure stories, sees himself as a hero, yet all too soon, and twice over on his first ship, he fails the test of bravery in other men's eyes. There is something blind and dogged about his conduct, which both leads him astray and makes him a victim, and yet also confirms him as a superior creature, because of the quality of his dreams. The actual crime pinned on Jim is unjust, but he has the inner resource to start his life again.

And so the strange moral life of this idealist blind to the ways of other men, and their view of him, continues. He begins a new life as a trader in a tropical outpost, where equally those ignorant of his past, and those who learn of it, like Conrad's famous narrator, Marlow, want to help a charming and sincere young man. Driven by his exacting desire to purge himself of his past error and become the great man he potentially is, he flees from place to place until finally on a remote island where he becomes loved by the local people and heralded as their strong leader, "Tuan" or "Lord" Jim, he marries and finds personal happiness. But this is a time of false respite and the plot hastens on to its inevitable denouement.

Jim, romantic and realist, hero and coward, innocent and experienced, has been seen as a model study of the fate of youthful ambition in the world, and Conrad's rich, ironic, multi-faceted treatment of the subject means we come away from Jim fascinated by the perils of self-perception. There must be drive, conviction, self-belief, and these are qualities which can both feed off social isolation and lead to self-destruction.

Lesley Chamberlain

Date 1900 (publication)

Author Joseph Conrad (1857–1924)

Nationality Poland (naturalized UK)

Why It's Key Winning approval from a broad swathe of the reading public, many critics objected to the circuitous narrative technique which Conrad used brilliantly to convey how other people saw the young romantic idealist consumed by his own vision.

1890-1909

25

Key Event
Oscar Wilde dies

Though disgraced, impoverished, and mortally ill in a cheap hotel in Paris, the city to which he exiled himself after serving two years' hard labor in Her Majesty's Prisons for homosexual offences, Oscar Wilde still couldn't resist camping it up. "My wallpaper and I are fighting a duel to the death," he opined: "One or the other of us has to go." It was a last show of gaiety from the once-fêted Irish poet, wit, novelist, and playwright – the nineteenth century's most famous proponent of Beauty, boys, and "the love that dare not speak its name." The wallpaper won. "At 5:30 A.M.," writes Wilde's biographer, Richard Ellmann, "a loud, strong death rattle began, like the turning of a crank. Foam and blood came from his mouth during the morning, and at ten minutes to two in the afternoon Wilde died. He had scarcely breathed his last breath when the body exploded with fluids from the ear, nose, mouth, and other orifices. The debris was appalling."

A ghastly emblem, this last. The Aesthetic Movement – that final strange effusion of late Romantic style – would likewise expire with Wilde: Putrefaction rather than Beauty was to be the watchword of the new century, as an army of corpses in Flanders' fields would soon testify.

Closer to home Wilde's persecution spooked and mortified a generation of homosexual writers and artists. James, Proust, Firbank, Owen, Sassoon, Gide, Forster, Coward, Maugham, Auden, Isherwood, and Ackerley: each exhibits the same arch, self-concealing circumspection. The truth could not be told so artifice and obliquity had to take its place. That twentieth-century phenomenon known as gay style – witty, ironic, irresistibly chic – is Wilde's lasting monument, one conceived in deception and pain.

Terry Castle

Date 1900 (death)

Place Paris, France

Nationality Ireland

Why It's Key Wilde's death seemed emblematic of the death of the fin-de-siècle world of the Aesthetic Movement, of which his art was the greatest flowering.

Opposite Oscar Wilde

Key Character **Sandokan** *The Tigers of Mompracem (Le Tigri di Mompracem)*

Sandokan is one of the first and foremost creations of Emilio Salgari, a prolific fantasist who never visited the countries he wrote about, though his stories are painstakingly researched. Sandokan's adventures, set in Borneo in the mid-nineteenth century, first appeared as a newspaper serial in 1883–1884 but the 1960s saw his popularity flourish, and Sandokan featured as the hero of a series of American films starring Steve Reeves and Ray Danton.

The hero, also known as the Tiger of Malaysia, is a prince turned pirate out of hatred for the colonialists who have destroyed his family and stolen his throne. A fierce critic of European colonialism in Asia, Salgari nevertheless often depicted relationships that cross the East-West divide, such as the friendship between Sandokan and his level-headed Portuguese blood brother, Yanez, while also giving his protagonist non-white enemies, such as archetypically evil Suyodhana, head of a dangerous Indian sect.

In fact, while Salgari's attitude towards race would fall short of today's idea of political correctness, he saluted absolute values such as courage, strength, loyalty, and independence wherever they manifested themselves. Sandokan (who has been linked to the hero of the Italian unification process, Giuseppe Garibaldi) possesses these masculine virtues to the highest degree, just as his woman, half-Italian, half-English Lady Marianna, the Pearl of Labuan, is a paragon of feminine charm. Both induce in their admirers an unflinching determination to sacrifice their lives for them: a quality that most seems to excite Salgari's thrilled awe. This underlying parallelism, and tension, between the power of love and the power of war could explain the great hold that Salgari's stories have had on female as well as male readers.
Elisabetta Tarantino

Date 1900 (publication)

Appears in *The Pirates of Malaysia* (1896), *The Two Tigers* (1904), *The King of the Sea* (1906), *Quest for a Throne* (1907), *Sandokan Fights Back* (1907), *Return to Mompracem* (1908)

Author Emilio Salgari (1862–1911)

Nationality Italy

Why It's Key Salgari's legendary heroes have been seen both as "proto-Fascist" icons of warlike prowess, and as iconic champions of liberal values.

26

Key Event
Sister Carrie is withheld from circulation

Polite society in the United States at the turn of the nineteenth century was simply not ready for *Sister Carrie*. It was seen as unacceptable that a woman, coming from a decent if lowly background, should be seen to prosper through being the successive mistress of two men, the second of them already married with a family. The conventions of the time demanded that virtue should be rewarded and transgressions from the moral code punished. However, at the end of the novel Dreiser's heroine has become rich and famous through pursuing a stage career, having abandoned her married lover, Hurstwood, to a descent into criminality, destitution, and eventual suicide. Dreiser's attempt to show Carrie as being finally unsatisfied and unhappy was not considered to be retribution enough for the immorality of her life.

The novel had been accepted for publication by the New York house of Doubleday Page & Co. when the senior partner, Frank Doubleday (or, as some say, his wife), strongly objected both to the morality of the tale and the daringly explicit account of the sexuality of a young unmarried woman.

Dreiser made many cuts but could not be persuaded to incorporate an ending in which the sinful Carrie would meet with just punishment. While contractually obliged to publish the book, Doubleday did little to publicize it and restricted its circulation, with the result that the novel flopped. It was not until 1981 that a scholarly edition of the novel, with Dreiser's cuts restored, was published.
Michael Munro

Date 1900

Author Theodore Dreiser (1871–1945)

Nationality USA

Why It's Key The publisher, Frank Doubleday, was so troubled by *Sister Carrie*'s naturalistic description of a woman's sexuality and ambition that he tried to limit its publication, with the result that it was not widely circulated. It is now seen as a major work of American naturalism.

Key Book
The Wizard of Oz

The Wizard of Oz is considered by some to be the most important and influential children's book of the last two hundred years. The first of a continuing series of books about Oz, it differs a great deal from the 1939 film. The book was made into numerous films, some by Baum himself, before the successful MGM musical version. However in Frank Baum's lifetime, it was the Oz books that followed that were known around the world, and which continue to be written today.

Illustrated by W.W. Denslow, the book has several major differences from the film. In it an old witch – not the glamorous Glinda – sends Dorothy on her way with a protective kiss on Dorothy's forehead, and gives her the silver shoes – not ruby slippers – of the dead witch. In the Emerald City, everyone must wear green sunglasses, an indication that all is not what it seems. The wizard becomes a real magician in subsequent books, and Dorothy moves back to Oz and becomes a princess. In an age of exploration before air travel, it was easy for children to imagine that Oz could exist.

The book has had several dubious interpretations, including one that sees it as a battle between the gold and silver standards (Yellow Brick Road), and another that sees it as the battle between agrarian (Scarecrow) and industrial (Tin Woodman) forces. Baum himself, married to a strong feminist, saw it as an imaginative story for children in which a feisty girl adventurer leads the way.

Gretchen Gerzina

Date 1900

Author L. Frank Baum (1856–1919)

Nationality USA

Why It's Key As well as being one of the most popular works of modern children's fiction, Baum's story has been seen as an allegory of the working man against the establishment. It's also an iconic gay text and a story of exile.

Key Author **Frank Norris**
The Octopus

Son of a successful entrepreneur father and actress mother, Frank Norris (1870–1902) was educated in Paris, Berkeley (where he left without a degree) and Harvard where his writing career began in earnest. At Berkeley he became heavily influenced by French literature, especially the work of Emile Zola, whose programmatic philosophy of literary naturalism Norris transposed into his series of novels confronting the post-Civil War American context. A time of massive urban, commercial, industrial, and demographic change required a new form of fiction detailing the harsh social, economic, and physical reality of life in street, field, and factory.

Norris also published adventure novels and worked as a war correspondent writing dispatches from the Boer and Spanish-American Wars. As assistant editor of *The Wave*, a San Francisco literary review, he wrote a series of vignettes and powerful essays about San Francisco life – the key city and region for his fiction. These columns were prototypically naturalist in their descriptive frankness and social commitment. His ensuing fiction mirrored their sociological and political intent, as well as Norris' revolutionary artistic ethos.

His most (in)famous novels such as *McTeague*, *The Octopus*, and *The Pit* were deeply controversial in their powerful assertion of an epic determinism and a conflict between civility and inner degeneration. In using unsentimental depictions of greed, sex, violence, poverty, and death, Norris believed that a novel should serve a moral function. "The novel with a purpose," he argued, "brings the tragedies and griefs of others to notice" and "prove(s) that injustice, crime, and inequality do exist." *The Pit* was the second volume in a planned trilogy, *Epic of the Wheat*, and was published posthumously after he died tragically young at 32, of kidney failure and a ruptured appendix.

Graeme Mcdonald

Date 1901 (publication)

Nationality USA

Key Works *McTeague* (1899), *The Pit* (1903)

Why It's Key Norris' works are central to the American naturalist canon. Together with writers such as Theodore Dreiser, he helped provide a literature that engaged with changing social issues and inspired a new tradition in the American novel.

Key Book
Up from Slavery

Washington's mother was a slave in Virginia when she bore him to a white father. As slavery was not abolished in the United States until 1863 with President Abraham Lincoln's Emancipation Proclamation, this meant that Washington himself was born a slave. His autobiography recounts his journey through the joy of liberation, self-education, and qualification as a teacher to his political life as a spokesman for black America. He was in favor of accommodation with white society, believing that black people could advance themselves best by learning practical skills and being industrious and thrifty so as to achieve both financial independence and status in society.

Up from Slavery became a bestseller and was seen as inspirational by black readers, a model of how to improve one's own life by hard work allied with ambition and determination not to be kept down. As Washington says in one passage: "I have learned that success is to be measured not so much by the position that one has reached in life as by the obstacles which he has overcome while trying to succeed." For white readers the book added fuel to the argument for racial equality. How could a man who had begun so low and risen so high belong to a race that was inherently inferior, as the segregationists continued to claim? *Up from Slavery* inspired black Americans throughout the twentieth century, even when its gradualist and accommodating message was sidelined by the rise of black militancy in the 1960s.

Michael Munro

Date 1901

Author Booker Taliaferro Washington (1856–1915)

Nationality USA

Why It's Key This autobiography was an inspiration to many black Americans. For non-black readers it was a revealing account of how far the life of most African-Americans had changed since slavery was abolished and how much remained to be done in achieving true racial equality.

Opposite Booker T. Washington

28

Key Book *Buddenbrooks, The Decline of a Family*

The Bildungsroman, usually the story of an individual finding his place in the world, was transformed by Thomas Mann's long, leisurely tale of a family dying out. Mann lovingly portrayed the grand life of the north German merchant class but broke spectacular new ground for the provincial German novel by introducing universal themes. The role of art and philosophy in undoing social convention was pivotal.

Himself the scion of a long line of Hamburg bankers, but with the huge success of this novel able to liberate himself to read the Schopenhauer and Nietzsche and listen to the Wagner he loved, Mann was highly self-conscious about having turned out "an artist."

Disease both real and figurative became one of his preoccupations. Writing on the cusp of the new century, he brilliantly captured the shift in values that heralded the end of grandiose middle-class stability and the arrival of a disquieting, individualistic modernity. He brought alive the links that the new science of sociology would explore between the Protestant work ethic and capitalism, only to show they were already dying. The last male Buddenbrook, Hanno, famously rules a line under the century-long family chronicle.

The realism of *Buddenbrooks* and the affection it exuded for old-style middle-class life made it Mann's most readable work, although uncharacteristic compared with what was to come. The symbolism was light, the characters three-dimensional and the homoeroticism muted. Irony, later to become the stylistic device that secured Mann's reputation as a modernist, was confined to the overall theme of decline.

Lesley Chamberlain

Date 1901

Author Thomas Mann (1875–1955)

Nationality Germany

Why It's Key Twenty-five-year-old Thomas Mann's first novel changed the course of German literature. Subtitled *The Decline of a Family*, *Buddenbrooks* reflected fashionable ideas of degeneration in its portrait of three generations of affluence and respectability.

EQUALITY

Key Character **Kim**
Kim

Kimball O'Hara is the orphaned child of an Irish sergeant and a nursemaid of indeterminate race. Fending for himself in the bazaar of Lahore, he is known as "friend of all the world" because he can move with facility across race, caste, religious, and class boundaries. His self-reliance and resourcefulness lead to his being used as a courier for documents by a British spy who has befriended him.

Kim wanders across India in the company of a Buddhist lama who seeks the Way while Kim is seeking (though he does not understand it except in symbols) the old regiment of his dead father. They come across the regiment and Kim is taken in by army chaplains. He is sent to the Anglo-Indian school at Lucknow where Kim is offered the chance to be made into a sahib if he stays. He sees more value in a shape-shifting, multi-lingual identity as a spy, a role to which he has been introduced by a spymaster who instructs boys in clandestine arts for the British Empire.

For this, Kipling's most sophisticated long work, he was paid the largest sum yet given to an author for serial rights. Intellectuals such as Henry James who had despaired of Kipling as a drum-banging patriot returned to extravagant praise for him when they read *Kim*. Kipling characters in other books such as Mowgli (not to mention Kipling himself) were faced with similar choices but *Kim* is remarkable for the sustained sympathy and understanding of India presented through the eyes of the character.
Jad Adams

Date 1901

Author Rudyard Kipling (1865–1936)

Nationality UK (born India)

Why It's Key In Kipling's best novel we see Kim choosing between two worlds: Indian and European, action and contemplation in the form of a hybrid character – part Indian part British.

Opposite **Kim**

Key Character **Sybylla Penelope Melvyn**
My Brilliant Career

"I rebel with all my lung force against sitting down under life as it is… " A typical outburst from Sybylla Penelope Melvyn, the irrepressible, independent heroine of *My Brilliant Career*. A born malcontent, she rails against filial pieties which require her to respect her vindictive mother, alcoholic father, and nondescript siblings, baulking at her social circumstances as a bush farmer's daughter. Artistic and precocious, frustrated by the endless grind of housekeeping and animal husbandry, she is also a staunch feminist (long before the term was recognized), repudiating contemporary models of feminine behavior, the "trap" of romantic love, and the narrow confines of domesticity. Buoyed only by a sense of her own potential, she struggles with her ungovernable feelings and against her attraction to her sometime fiancé, Harold Beecham.

My Career Goes Bung is frequently called the "sequel" to *My Brilliant Career*, but is a more self-reflexive work than this term implies. In this novel, we witness another version of Sybylla Melvyn – now an only child with a sober, sympathetic father – write a fictional autobiography of a young girl living in the Australian bush, only to be catapulted to literary notoriety and the bright lights of Sydney, where she remains largely unimpressed by the representatives of high society and the Australian literary scene she encounters.

Appalled at innumerable letters from young readers professing fervent identification with the original Sybylla, Miles Franklin wrote her second book as a "corrective" to the first. Though more self-possessed, atheistic, outspoken, and inured to the blandishments of the opposite sex, the "real" Sybylla happily retains the vivid character of the "fictional" one.
David Cross

Dates 1901 (and 1946)

Author Miles Franklin (born Stella Maria Sarah Miles Franklin) (1879–1954)

Nationality Australia

Why It's Key Considered one of the first novels with a distinctly Australian voice, pioneering spirit, and advocacy of Australian culture *My Brilliant Career* is now regarded as a feminist classic. Gillian Armstrong's 1979 film adaptation was seminal.

Key Character **A.J. Raffles**
The Black Mask

Handsome, charming, public school-educated, and one of England's finest cricketers, A.J. Raffles moves in the highest social circles; but he is also a thief. Although clearly working within a tradition of outlaw heroes, Hornung attracted some criticism for making his hero a criminal. Raffles is no Robin Hood; he usually keeps his ill-gotten gains for himself, and sometimes seems to steal purely for the thrill of it. His flaws are masked by the adoring narration of his partner in crime, Bunny, whose infatuation with Raffles borders on the homoerotic.

For Bunny, Raffles is eternally the golden figure of his schooldays, "when he was captain of the eleven, and I his fag." But though capable and daring, Raffles does not possess Holmes' almost superhuman abilities, and constantly flirts with disaster – Bunny ends the first book in prison, with Raffles disgraced and apparently dead. This vulnerability is crucial to Raffles' appeal. He is an outsider: unable to fund the lifestyle for which he has been educated, he steals partly out of resentment towards the idle rich, bitterly acknowledging that it is only his sporting prowess that gains him entry to the social elite. Intensely patriotic, his crimes are governed by a strict, eclectic code of honor that is increasingly out of step with the world around him. The stories are suffused with a sense of nostalgia for a Victorian world rapidly being overtaken by modernity, represented by Raffles' reluctant transition from "amateur cracksman" to professional thief.

Hornung was the brother-in-law of Arthur Conan Doyle, and openly acknowledged that Raffles and his companion Bunny were a criminal reflection of Holmes and Watson, but Raffles has endured in his own right, and persisted in popularity for over a century.
Rowland Hughes

Date 1901 (*Black Mask* published)

First Appearance "The Ides of March" (short story printed in Cassell's Magazine). First book publication in *The Amateur Cracksman* (1899)

Other Appearances *A Thief in the Night* (1905), *Mr. Justice Raffles* (1909)

Author E.W. Hornung (1866–1921)

Nationality UK

Why It's Key A landmark in the development of crime fiction.

32

Key Event **Emile Zola dies from carbon monoxide poisoning**

Emile Zola's (1840–1902) literary fame today rests primarily on the connected series of novels that he called *Les Rougon-Macquart* (1871–93), including such well-known individual titles as *Nana* (1879), *Germinal* (1885), and *La Terre* (1887). In these he wanted to demonstrate his theories of naturalism by showing the operation of heredity and environment on successive generations of two linked families, the Rougons and the Macquarts, under the French Second Empire.

Like other naturalist writers, Zola looked on the writing of fiction as being almost akin to a science. He believed that truth to life was important and could best be shown by the accumulation of detail and precise description of characters and settings. He aimed to let his readership see exactly how other people lived, especially those of a lower class, hoping that they would be inspired to press for social change. This is not to say that his novels were drily didactic. Rather, he was blessed by a powerful imagination, able to create stories on an epic scale, allied to a prose that could be wonderfully lyrical.

In political terms, Zola is remembered for his intervention in the *cause célèbre* of the Dreyfus Affair, especially his famous open letter "J'accuse." Zola was found guilty of libel and sentenced to a year's imprisonment (which he avoided by fleeing to England). He was eventually pardoned and returned to France as a hero, but he had made powerful enemies and it was suspected by many that the chimney that produced the carbon monoxide that killed him had been blocked deliberately by agents of the anti-Dreyfusard faction.
Michael Munro

Date 1902

Place Paris

Why It's Key The leading exponent of naturalism in fiction, Emile Zola died of carbon monoxide poisoning, resulting from a blocked chimney, in Paris. Zola was perceived not only as the greatest writer of the age, but as a dauntless crusader for truth and justice, and the streets of Paris were crowded as his funeral procession passed.

Key Character **Crichton**
The Admirable Crichton

Crichton is butler to Lord Loam, and is among a party who are shipwrecked on a desert island. While His Lordship is seen to have progressive views on class divisions, his butler disagrees, seeing the current set-up as the natural order of things. However, once beyond the pale of civilization, the hapless patricians find that they are forced to depend increasingly on the resourcefulness of their imperturbable manservant. Crichton, drawing on his own natural abilities, soon achieves a position in which he must be acknowledged by all as the true leader of their little marooned community.

Barrie, who borrowed the title from the name given to the sixteenth-century Scottish poet and scholar James Crichton, quietly sends up contemporary social attitudes by showing that the member of a so-called inferior class is actually the better man. If society were a true meritocracy, he suggests, then people like Crichton would soon rise to the top. Barrie, as the son

of a weaver who became a world-famous playwright and novelist, was living proof that this could happen.

Crichton is no revolutionary, however. While he becomes comfortable in his role and enjoys the trappings of power – he is even on the point of marrying Lord Loam's daughter – when the party are rescued he is content to return to his former status. The old order has been challenged by Crichton through his own practical abilities and inborn qualities, but while the possibility of upward social mobility based on talent has been mooted, it is the old order that is finally restored when the characters return to civilization.
Michael Munro

Date 1902 (publication)

Author James Matthew Barrie (1860–1937)

Nationality UK

Why It's Key In an era when class and social divisions were still of crucial importance, Barrie turned the current social stratification on its head in this comedy in which a butler proves himself to be the natural leader among a group of castaways on a desert island. A film version was made in 1957 with Kenneth More in the title role.

33

Key Character **Sherlock Holmes**
The Hound of the Baskervilles

Sherlock Holmes is one of those extraordinarily vivid fin-de-siècle literary characters who – like Bram Stoker's Dracula or Robert Louis Stevenson's Dr Jekyll – appear to have risen from the page and gained an independent existence in the popular imagination. He was first introduced by his creator, Arthur Conan Doyle, in *A Study in Scarlet* in 1887, but such is his reality effect that, over the years, hundreds of letters asking for his assistance have arrived at 221B Baker Street, the petitioners apparently under the impression that he is a real consulting detective. The Sherlock Holmes Museum in London is a reconstruction of his flat, set up as if he's still living there but has just stepped out for a moment.

His apparently superhuman abilities are based on techniques of close observation and logical deduction. In the opening scenes of *The Hound of the Baskervilles*, Holmes demonstrates his methods via a virtuoso reconstruction of the absent Dr Mortimer's entire

career from close reading of his walking stick. In stories like this, Holmes is seen working to maintain the status quo in the highly stratified and inequitable society of the late Victorian age. The working-class errand boy Cartwright is treated little better than a faithful dog; the vast Baskerville fortune which Holmes protects from the upstart Stapleton and his monstrous hound is a morally dubious mixture of the old money of aristocratic inheritance and new money made in a "South African speculation." It has been suggested that this role as protector of the property of the privileged classes is echoed in his name: Sure Lock Homes.
Anna Tripp

Date 1902

Author Arthur Conan Doyle (1859–1930)

Nationality UK

Why It's Key Sherlock Holmes is the archetypal fictional detective, instantly recognizable by his deerstalker hat and curved pipe. In 1893 Doyle tired of his popular creation and unsuccessfully attempted to kill him off – but Holmes cheated death to make further appearances in the first years of the twentieth century.

Key Book
The Tale of Peter Rabbit

When Peter Rabbit hopped into the middle-class nursery and took up residence there, it changed very young children's reading forever. *The Tale of Peter Rabbit* was the first of what Beatrix Potter called her "little books." These exquisitely illustrated narratives, which tell the adventures of a whole host of English farm and country animals, would become the most popular series of children's literature of all time.

Potter was an experienced naturalist and the figure of her hero is anatomically exact, from the way he hops to the way he hides. All the same, Peter is elevated from mere bunnyhood by his blue coat, a garment which in time became almost as famous as its wearer. The garden setting, too, recognisably belongs to the cottage plots of Potter's beloved Lancashire.

It is the story, however, that elevates *The Tale of Peter Rabbit* from being simply a charming picture book for children learning to read. Spare and elegant, it fuses rabbit psychology with that of a small child. It is Peter's curiosity, and his insistence on doing precisely what his mother tells him not to, that makes him such a delightfully sympathetic hero for any young reader. Nor are there any easy or consolatory endings. Although Peter makes it safely home after his adventure in Mr McGregor's garden, Potter does not flinch from explaining that his father was not so lucky. Mr Rabbit ends up in a pie, made by none other than Mrs McGregor.

Kathryn Hughes

Date 1902

Author Beatrix Potter (1866–1943)

Nationality UK

Why It's Key An immediate best-seller, *The Tale of Peter Rabbit* was the first of thirty or so that Beatrix Potter wrote for Frederick Warne & Co. After Peter came the equally loved Mrs Tiggy-Winkle. Potter was quick to exploit her intellectual property rights. Peter and co. can still be seen in nursery rooms around the world.

Opposite Peter Rabbit

Key Character **Kate Croy**
The Wings of the Dove

When we are first introduced to Kate Croy, standing in her father's shabby rooms and waiting for him to appear, we glimpse immediately the hopelessness of her situation. She is responsible for her reprobate and dishonest father, as well as her widowed sister, and her nephews and nieces. Taken under the wing of her wealthy aunt, Mrs. Lowder, Kate is in love with the penniless journalist Merton Densher, but unable to marry him. When she is introduced to the American heiress Milly Theale, rich and beautiful but also terminally ill, Kate begins to imagine a terrible way in which she can break free of her aunt and her background.

In the hands of a lesser talent, Kate would appear simply as an archetypal scheming villainess. Certainly, she is not too complex a character, but that is because James is determined instead to suggest through her the complexities of the human consciousness. In James' later novels, thought takes the place of action, and the reader follows the processes of thought with the same care as the plot. James' narrator aims to capture every subtle nuance of Kate's consciousness in his long, twisting, sinuous sentences, so that we can see how her dreadful plan gradually evolves in her mind. The technique preserves an element of ambiguity around Kate, and leaves room for doubt regarding her motivation. The effect is to show that she is not wholly evil, yet, while we never condone her actions, we continue to sympathize, allowing us to appreciate the full tragedy of her situation.

Neil Wallington

Date 1902

Author Henry James (1843–1916)

Nationality USA

Why It's Key Kate Croy, strong and intelligent, is a transitional character with a traditional predicament presented in a modern manner. She is one of the first characters in English fiction through whom an author suggests the workings of the conscious and unconscious mind.

Key Event *The Story of Mary MacLane* causes a nationwide scandal in the USA

Nineteen-year-old Mary MacLane's memoirs caused one of the greatest scandals in American literary history. With the melodramatic self-absorption to which only a teenage imagination can really do justice, she begins, "I of womankind and of nineteen years, will now begin to set down as full and frank a Portrayal as I am able of myself, Mary MacLane, for whom the world contains not a parallel." Her egotistical determination to chronicle every part of herself, right down to her gastric juices, is nothing short of astonishing. She alerts the reader to her photo in the frontispiece ("not all flesh – some of it is handkerchief") and kisses the pages of her "Portrayal" as she writes them.

The most notorious passage was MacLane's litany to the devil, asking him to deliver her of such pestilential things as "tape-worms… a nice young man… side-saddles"; she confesses to stealing, and graphically fantasizes about throwing herself down a well. Convinced of her own genius yet scared her femininity gets in the way of it, there is a plaintive edge to her lonely, if outrageous, desires. Uninterested in marriage, unless to either Napoleon or Satan (MacLane's original title was *I Await the Devil's Coming*), she also describes, with fascinating frankness, being in love with another woman.

The New York Herald declared: "She should be put under medical treatment, and pens and paper kept out of her way until she is restored to reason" (at the time a not unheard-of "cure" for transgressive women writers). There is indeed a delirious quality to her outpourings. There is also great poignancy to the fact that, despite the bombast, she was already mapping out the sources of her future wistfulness. Her "genius" never exceeded this autobiographical excrescence. She has been called "the first flapper," but that hardly begins to cover the fierceness of her rebellion, or her unique brand of lurid and desperate self-advertisement.
Lucy Daniel

Date 1902

Author Mary MacLane (1881–1929)

Nationality USA

Why It's Key The book was front-page news across the United States. "MacLaneism" manifested itself in societies set up by women in McLane's honour, cocktails named after her, general copycat mischief perpetrated by previously respectable young ladies, and, apparently, suicides.

36

Key Passage *The Virginian*

"When you call me that, *smile!*"

By the early twentieth century, the American frontier was officially declared to have vanished, but the mythology of the Wild West was still evolving. Three men – all friends, and all, ironically, born and educated in the East – were particularly influential in its development: the immensely popular President Theodore Roosevelt, who brought his "cowboy" persona and values to the forefront of American public life; the artist Frederic Remington, whose images cemented much of the iconography of the West; and Owen Wister, whose popular novel *The Virginian* performed a similar role in literature.

The novel's narrator is a "tenderfoot" Eastern gentleman who mediates between the alien culture of the frontier and Wister's more "civilized" readers. Throughout, he celebrates the chivalric conduct of the eponymous Southern hero, an uneducated but dignified cowboy who exemplifies Wister's (quintessentially American) faith in inherent nobility.

The Virginian is a deeply conservative text, morally, politically, and socially; set during Wyoming's Johnson County War in the 1890s, it endorses the methods (including lynching) used by large ranch-owners to displace smaller competitors. The Virginian himself speaks the most famous line from this urtext of the Western genre, after Trampas, the villain of the piece, has called him a "son of a ——" during a poker game, (an epithet that he has recently accepted from a friend); in this instance, however, he pulls out his pistol and faces Trampas, teaching the narrator that "the letter means nothing till the spirit gives it life."
Rowland Hughes

Date 1902

Author Owen Wister (1860–1938)

Nationality USA

Why It's Key Wister's romantic tale of Western adventure was the first significant fictional depiction of cowboy culture, other than in mass-produced dime novels. It established many of the conventions of the popular Western that subsequently proved so enduring in both popular fiction and film.

"How the Camel Got his Hump"

"In the beginning of years, when the world was so new-and-all, and the Animals were just beginning to work for Man, there was a Camel, and he lived in the middle of a Howling Desert because he did not want to work."

Kipling's teasing *Just So Stories* are written in a tone that veers between child-like language and pompous didacticism. They mock Darwinian theory by providing comic explanations for evolutionary events: "How the Leopard got his Spots," "How the Alphabet was Made," "The Beginning of the Armadilloes." The stories are full of fragments of Eastern mythology, of magicians, afrits and djinns. They parody the *Arabian Nights* as well as scientific discourse and reverse the usual expectations of children's stories that so often have glib moral messages. Thus for example, the elephant is rewarded for his curiosity when he goes to the Limpopo river "all set about with fever trees" to find out what the crocodile has for dinner.

The *Just So Stories* developed from tales Kipling told small audiences of children, his own and those of nephews and nieces. There was a ritual that laid down that the stories should be told with no change in wording or intonation from previous recitations. The phrase that they should be "just so" was that of Kipling's daughter Josephine, who died at the age of six. The book was completed and prepared for publication in 1902 with Josephine very much in mind; "I thought I knew something of what grief meant till that came to me," he wrote. Kipling lavished care on the book, with twelve stories, twelve poems, and accompanying pictures; it was the only book he illustrated himself. Many of the pictures are disturbing: of monstrous, menacing sea creatures, or of brooding men sitting alone.

Jad Adams

Date 1902

Author Rudyard Kipling (1865–1936)

Nationality UK (born India)

Why It's Key Of *Just So Stories*, G.K. Chesterton wrote: "Just as we are in the afterglow of a certain indignation against this stale, bitter modernity which had begun to appear in Mr. Kipling's work, we come upon this superb thing. He has written new legends."

Key Author **Frank Wedekind**
Pandora's Box (Die Büsche der Pandora)

The playwright Frank Wedekind is a crucial and influential figure within modern German drama, whose controversial plays proved influential in more than one way: they bridge the gap between the analytical, socially critical Naturalism of the late nineteenth century and the passionate Expressionism of the early twentieth, and confront the prevailing hypocrisy of patriarchal Wilhelmine society by addressing social, psychological, and sexual themes unflinchingly. His work frequently reflects his interest in contemporary social, scientific, and philosophical ideas, including Darwinism, Nietzschean nihilism, and biological vitalism.

His early play *Spring Awakening* (*Frühlings Erwachen*, 1891), which presents a damning portrait of contemporary parenting and schooling methods, represented an artistic breakthrough for Wedekind. The powerful story of a group of adolescents, whose sexual "awakening" becomes a source of anxiety, scandal, trauma, and death, highlights tensions between the "natural" and the "nurtured" and, in part because of its inclusion of explicitly sexual scenes, for many years was considered too shocking to perform. Internationally, Wedekind is probably best known as the author of the Lulu plays, *Earth Spirit* (*Erdgeist*, 1895) and *Pandora's Box* (*Die Büchse der Pandora*, 1902). The plays, like *Spring Awakening* hugely controversial and divisive, are daring in their portrayal of a passionate and liberated female protagonist; the character of Lulu, who ultimately becomes the victim of social and sexual machinations of powerful men, may be considered an embodiment of Wedekind's belief in the inherent vitality and value of childlike "innocence," impulse, and freedom.

Jon Hughes

Date 1902

Author Frank Wedekind (1864-1918)

Nationality Germany

Why It's Key A major playwright of the fin de siècle, Wedekind was the author of confrontational dramas challenging social and sexual taboos. His Lulu plays have been particularly influential, inspiring G.W. Pabst's 1929 film, *Die Büchse der Pandora* (*Pandora's Box*), starring Louise Brooks, and Alban Berg's opera *Lulu* (1937).

Key Event **Helen Keller's first book brings the story of her education to the world**

If Helen Keller had not lost her sight and hearing after suffering a high fever, at the tragically young age of nineteen months, then she would probably have remained unknown to most of the world's population. The following five frustrating years were spent in a dark, isolated world and as she was unable to see or hear, Helen also became mute.

In desperation, her parents consulted the Scottish inventor and expert on deafness, Alexander Graham Bell, who by divine intervention recommended Anne Sullivan (Macy) as a suitable teacher for Helen. As she had also been partially blind during her short life, Sullivan had a loyal empathy with Helen and would spell the words of objects on to Helen's palms. Ravenous for more knowledge, Keller learned to "hear" conversations by placing her hands on the face and throat of the speaker. She was soon reading Braille and using a specially adapted typewriter to write.

Having developed communication skills never previously achieved by any similarly disabled person, Helen began to write on many subjects for journals, and later published several books about her life.

Keller's publications and the subsequent fund-raising by both Keller and Sullivan were beneficial in preventing the practice of automatically placing all blind and deaf children in institutions for life. As an influential example of what an educated disabled person could achieve, Keller was able to convince powerful members of society of the value of appropriate education for disabled children and thus dramatically improve their futures and quality of life. In her own words, "Once I knew only darkness and stillness… but a little word from the fingers of another … and my heart leaped to the rapture of living."

Alice Goldie

Date 1903 (publication)

Title *The Story of My Life*

Author Helen Keller (1880–1968)

Nationality USA

Why It's Key By publishing her autobiography, *The Story of My Life*, deaf-blind Helen Keller became an international celebrity. This, her first book, documents her extraordinary achievement in learning to communicate and acquire a thorough education.

Key Book
The Way of All Flesh

Samuel Butler, son of a clergyman and grandson of a bishop, refused to follow in the family tradition and take religious orders; instead he became preoccupied with the ideas of Darwin. Religion and evolution were to dominate his writing life, culminating in this great semi-autobiographical novel.

Through an examination of four generations of the male side of a family, *The Way of All Flesh* demonstrates the potential for suffering generated by inherited traits and attitudes. Ernest Pontifex attempts to break free from his family background: as a student he is influenced in turn by a religious zealot and a freethinker before he attempts to break free from religion with sex. Unfortunately he accosts a respectable girl, thinking her a prostitute, and is imprisoned. This disgrace frees him from his faith and his class but despite his attempts to liberate himself from his past by conscious choices, his unconscious choices lead him back to grief.

His solution is to farm out his children, to spare them the tyranny of paternal influence, and then to live a solitary, literary life as did Butler.

Butler started writing the novel in 1873, and was still working on it in 1885 when the model for one of the "nice" characters died and he stopped revising it. *The Way of All Flesh* was published posthumously in 1903. The book helped to turn the tide against excessive parental dominance and religious rigidity in its corrosive exposure of the hypocrisies and cruelties of Victorian family life.

Jad Adams

Date 1903

Author Samuel Butler (1835–1902)

Nationality UK

Why It's Key A key early work in the rejection of Victorian values in the twentieth century. *The Way of All Flesh* also influenced a generation of new writers including G.B. Shaw and E.M. Forster.

Key Book
Such is Life

Sprawling, discursive, by turns philosophical and comic, *Such is Life* is unique in Australian literature, at once reminiscent of Lawrence Sterne's eighteenth-century oddity *Tristam Shandy* and an unacknowledged forerunner of such early twentieth-century monuments as Joyce's *Ulysses* and Proust's *Remembrance of Things Past*. The book arrived in 1897 apparently out of nowhere, when Joseph Furphy, an autodidact and voracious reader then in his mid-50s, sent his manuscript to the *Bulletin*, Australia's leading literary journal. Publication followed in 1903, but the author's achievement was not properly recognised until the 1940s, more than 30 years after his death.

Furphy himself spent much of his life as a "bullocky," transporting goods in a cart drawn by teams of bullocks in the Riverina, along the border between New South Wales and Victoria. *Such is Life* is set among a group of bullockies, chatting and exchanging yarns around the campfire: it is presented as transcripts of eight entries taken apparently at random from the diaries of Tom Collins, a minor government official traveling among the bullockies in 1883–4. In a letter to the Bulletin, Furphy described the book succinctly, as "temper, democratic; bias, offensively Australian," and non-Australian readers may find his rendering of accent and dialect difficult to penetrate.

The title is taken from the last words attributed to Ned Kelly, the bushranger hanged at Melbourne jail in 1880 who became a national icon, but they also refer to Furphy's claim to be presenting a sample of life as it actually is.

Bruce Millar

Date 1903 (publication)

Author Joseph Furphy (1843–1912)

Nationality Australia

Why It's Key Furphy reworked chapters cut from the original manuscript of *Such is Life* into stories entitled "Rigby's Romance" and "The Buln-Buln and the Brolga," both published after his death. He never wrote another major work, and soon after the publication of *Such is Life* joined his son in Western Australia.

Key Event **Weininger's suicide heightens the vogue for his infamous work**

The brilliant young philosopher Otto Weininger shot himself at the age of twenty-three shortly after publishing his masterpiece. Son of a Jewish goldsmith in Vienna, Weininger studied at the university there and received his PhD in 1902; shortly afterwards he converted to Christianity. *Sex and Character* was published the next year. Partly the study of sexology (then in its infancy), partly philosophical treatise, the book was "an attempt to place sexual relations in a new and decisive light."

At a time when female emancipation movements in northern countries were encouraging equality between men and women, *Sex and Character* aimed decisively to answer the "woman question" and to answer it by emphasising difference. "A man possesses sexual organs, a woman's sexual organs possess her," Weininger wrote.

While characterizing the ideal man and the ideal woman, Weininger emphasized that all living things combine both male and female elements, and was prepared to propose that homosexuals were people with the outer characteristics of one sex but the inner characteristics of another.

Even more controversially, he asserted that Judaism was feminine and cowardly as opposed to Christianity which was masculine and upright. His assertion that modern life was feminine, and overtly Jewish, was later seized upon by the Nazis who mined his book for supportive theories while disregarding others.

Weininger chose to kill himself in the house where Beethoven had died; the tragic death of the young writer secured immense success for his only book and inspired several imitation suicides.

Jad Adams

Date 1903

Title *Sex and Character* (1903)

Author Otto Weininger (1880–1903)

Nationality Austria

Why It's Key This was a period when "racial science" filtered out of medical literature into fiction: Gertrude Stein based her approach to character on Weininger's theories. James Joyce, D.H. Lawrence, and Jack London were among those also influenced by *Sex and Character*.

Key Character **Buck**
The Call of the Wild

SPOILER

The opening sentence of Jack London's *The Call of the Wild* announces that "Buck did not read the newspapers, or he would have known that trouble was brewing." This is not the way that animals are usually described, but Buck is so rational and thoughtful that it is a genuine surprise that he does not read (London does not say that he cannot). When Theodore Roosevelt complained about anthropomorphism, London responded by reminding the President of evolutionary theory.

Buck's journey is one from domestic comfort (his puppyhood is that of a "sated aristocrat" on a Californian ranch) to the "heart of things primordial" in Alaska. There he learns to abandon civilized notions of fair play and to fight like his forbears, the wolves. Chasing rabbits, and killing a rival called Spitz, Buck experiences "an ecstasy that marks the summit of life." But then he falls in love. Buck's love for his "ideal master" John Thornton is "feverish and burning." It is

"madness," "adoration." Only when Thornton is killed can the "domesticated generations" finally fall away forever. Buck gives in to the howl of the wild and goes off to join the pack of "wolf brothers." In 1905 London wrote a companion piece about the domestication of a wolf called White Fang. It takes a while but eventually the "love-master" wins him over with some "long, caressing strokes." And "having learned to snuggle, White Fang was guilty of it often." Perhaps Mark Seltzer is right to describe these dogs as "men in furs."

Kasia Boddy

Date 1903 (publication)

Author Jack London (1876–1916)

Nationality USA

Why It's Key One of the great dog heroes of modern literature.

Opposite Jack London

41

1890-1909

Key Author **W.E.B. Du Bois**
The Souls of Black Folk

By the time he published his landmark collection of essays *The Souls of Black Folk* (1903), W.E.B. Du Bois (1868–1963) was already among the most prominent of black Americans. The first black child to graduate from his Massachusetts high school, he attended black college Fisk University in Tennessee, experiencing first-hand the racial antagonisms of the South. He was later admitted to Harvard University and became the first African-American scholar to gain a PhD there. In 1897, crowning many other achievements, he took up a professorship in economics and history at Atlanta University.

A widely published essayist and campaigner on black issues, in many ways by 1903 Du Bois had achieved his ambition: to provide, like his hero Frederick Douglass, intellectual leadership for black Americans; his essay of that year, "The Talented Tenth," advocates just this responsibility for the ablest members of the black community.

The Souls of Black Folk popularised his views on race and respectfully upbraids the accommodating approach of Booker T. Washington. Key to *Souls* is the notion of "double consciousness," wherein, "One ever feels his two-ness, – an American, A Negro; two souls, two thoughts [...] two warring ideals." To be American and black, Du Bois suggests, is somehow dichotomous, a situation that must change. And over the following years, Du Bois' role as paterfamilias of black America cannot be overstated. Editor of the NAACP's journal, *The Crisis*, chafed against by the upstarts of the Harlem Renaissance and a founding member of the Pan-African movement, his influence is gargantuan, a constant wish to promote political progress and positive images for blacks, his legacy.

Although less well known, he ranks alongside Martin Luther King Jr., Marcus Garvey, and Malcolm X as an agent of social change.

Doug Haynes

Date 1903

Nationality USA

Key Works "The Talented Tenth" (1903), *Black Reconstruction* (1935), *The World and Africa* (1945), *The Black Flame* (trilogy of novels, 1976).

Why It's Key A tireless campaigner for black civil rights, an intellectual, and writer, Du Bois made among the greatest contributions to twentieth-century black American life.

Key Passage *Man and Superman: A Comedy and a Philosophy*

"Women … have a purpose which is not their own purpose, but that of the whole universe, a man is nothing to them but the instrument of that purpose."

Man and Superman is George Bernard Shaw's response to a friend who suggested that he should write "a Don Juan play," although in a typical Shavian inversion the Don Juan character is "the quarry instead of the huntsman," pursued by a young woman intent on marriage. This is more than a joke: Shaw seriously suggests that, although romantic convention has it that men pursue women, it is actually the other way round, because women are guided by a "Life Force" that compels them to seek out a suitable breeding-partner in order to perpetuate the human race. As Shaw's mouthpiece character Jack Tanner puts it, the purpose of marriage is not the woman's happiness, or her husband's, but Nature's.

Tanner goes on to claim that artists and thinkers are also governed by the Life Force, as their raison d'être is to teach humanity how to understand itself, to create "new mind as surely as any woman creates new men." The result, he says, is that artists use women for inspiration or comfort as selfishly as women use men for breeding.

Tanner's speech is meant as a warning to his poet friend Octavius against marrying the dynamic Ann Whitefield, but it turns out that Ann is after Tanner himself and by the end of the play he finds himself reluctantly engaged to her: the Life Force is too strong for him. Nietzschean philosophy in a drawing-room comedy proved too much for some people: John Murray refused to publish the play on the grounds that it was "wicked."

Jake Kerridge

Date 1903 (first performed 1905)

Author George Bernard Shaw (1856–1950)

Nationality Ireland

Why It's Key Shaw's theory of the "Life Force" was both inspired by, and a parody of, Nietzsche's idea of the Superman (Übermensch), and helped introduce Nietzsche's ideas to the English-speaking world.

Opposite G.B. Shaw

42

Key Play *The Cherry Orchard (Vishniovy sad)*

The Cherry Orchard was Chekhov's last play, written the year before his death. It tells the story of generous, irresponsible Madame Ranyevskaya and her family, whose estate and cherry orchard are to be auctioned to pay off their debts. Incapable of accepting this fate or suggesting an alternative, the family procrastinate until the decision is taken from their hands. At the close of the play they are scattered by the forces of a changing society as their beloved cherry orchard is felled. But despite its underlying melancholy, it was the author's intention that the play should be viewed as a comedy, "in places even a farce."

Directed by Stanislavski in 1904, the play met with great success, but Chekhov detested the ponderous, elegiac production. He understood that humor can be more dramatically effective than all the weighty passion in the world, and his interest lay in the drama of everyday life, in which comedy and tragedy are inextricably twinned.

The Cherry Orchard, like all his plays, is driven by character rather than action, and its humor derives from the endearing fallibility of his protagonists. Eschewing traditional heroes and villains, Chekhov instead created good-hearted characters, passionate in conviction but lacking in motivation, unable to make decisions or take action and totally at the mercy of the societal forces that surround them.

Chekhov was an actor's writer, who provided rich characterization for even the slightest role and ensured that every character, from Ranyevskaya to old Firs the footman, has their moment of self-expression. His warmth, economy of style, and skillful use of subtext have subsequently influenced generations of writers, directors, and actors.

Amy Rosenthal

Date 1903

Author Anton Chekhov (1860–1904)

Nationality Russia

Why It's Key Chekhov's plays were initially ill-received by an audience who couldn't fathom his desire to put ordinary life and naturalistic speech on stage. But his later works, particularly *The Cherry Orchard*, won the heart of his native Russia. After his death, his fame spread worldwide.

Key Author **O. Henry**
Cabbages and Kings

O.Henry (1862–1910) was the nom de plume of William Sidney Porter, a native of North Carolina. While working as a bank teller he started up a humorous weekly magazine called *The Rolling Stone*, filling it with his own stories and satirical pieces, but it was only when he was serving a five-year prison term for embezzlement that he began the career of short story writing that would make his name. He made his home in New York City, which he christened "Baghdad-on-the-Subway," and set many of his best-known stories there. His work was very much rooted in its time and taken together his short stories give us a vivid and detailed picture of daily life in the United States in the early twentieth century.

Henry's characteristic use of unexpected endings led to his being compared to French writer Guy de Maupassant, who also used this device, and was one of the aspects of his work that his wide readership most enjoyed. However, while Henry's endings could be ironic, they tended not to be completely disastrous and would usually leave the characters involved with something to hope for. Typical of this is one of his most popular short stories, "The Gifts of the Magi," in which a young wife sells her hair in order to buy her husband a watch chain as a Christmas present only to find that he has sold his watch to buy her fancy combs for her hair. As the author observes in this story, "Life is made up of sobs, sniffles and smiles, with sniffles predominating."

Michael Munro

Date 1904

Nationality USA

Why It's Key *Cabbages and Kings* rapidly established what would become O. Henry's trademark style of unexpected plot twists and surprise endings. So famous were these that they became known as the "O. Henry twist." He is also often credited with having coined the term "banana republic," in his case referring to Honduras.

Key Author **M.R. James**
Ghost Stories of an Antiquary

Montague Rhodes James (1862–1936) was, during his lifetime, more famous as a scholar and academic head than as a writer of ghost stories. He spent almost all his life in close association with Eton College and King's College Cambridge, first as pupil and student, then as Fellow and Dean of King's and later as Provost of Eton. James' scholarly interests centered upon the arcane of medieval and earlier history. He published distinguished works on the Biblical apocrypha, painstakingly classified the mutilated statuary of Ely Cathederal, and catalogued the forgotten medieval manuscripts that lingered in the vaults of the college libraries. It is easy to see how these interests fed into the ghost stories he began publishing in the 1890s.

James' stories combine meticulous scholarly (though fanciful) detail with a love of the English countryside. The typical James protagonist is a scholar or archaeologist, innocent and unworldly, whose researches bring them up sharply against a supernatural terror. Stories like "Whistle and I'll Come" and "Casting the Runes" place the medieval world of ghosts and demons in a contemporary setting of railway carriages and tram conductors. Or, rather like Agatha Christie's murder mysteries, they contaminate an idyll of vicarages and village greens with the stench of malevolent spirits.

James wrote many of his stories for the "entertainment" of the choristers at Kings and the scouts at Eton. Their understated power, where demons are mistaken for overcoats and the railway porter holds open the door for a companion who isn't there, still reverberates a century later.

Gerard Woodward

Date 1904 (publication)

Nationality UK

Why It's Key M.R. James' ghost stories brought Gothic horror into the modern world. James is now recognized as a master of the art of the ghost story.

Key Book
The Golden Bowl

The Golden Bowl is both an examination of the relations between the New World and the Old – a common theme in Henry James – and, in the manner of his last period, a minutely worked dissection of the consciousnesses and moral duplicities of its central characters, delivered in passages of immense length and complexity that leave many readers in a state of bewilderment.

A young American heiress, Maggie Verver, has come to Europe with her father, Adam Verver, to marry an impoverished Italian prince, Amerigo. In London, Amerigo encounters a former mistress, Charlotte Stant, and together the two search for a wedding present for Maggie. They find the eponymous golden bowl (in fact gilded crystal) in an antique shop, but Amerigo suspects a hidden flaw beneath the perfect surface – and so the bowl becomes a symbol of the moral imperfections that lurk under the polished surface of the haute monde of society.

Although Maggie and Amerigo marry, the latter resumes his relationship with Charlotte, while Maggie seems unable to abandon her close bond with her father. Eventually she lands upon the notion of arranging the marriage of her father to Charlotte, which would end what she believes is his loneliness. It is not until the golden bowl is deliberately broken that Maggie's innocence ends, and she becomes aware of Amerigo's infidelity. She dispatches her father and Charlotte off to America, and determines to work to create a more genuine marriage with her husband.

James drew the potent image of the golden bowl from Ecclesiastes: "Or ever… the golden bowl be broken… Then shall the dust return to the earth as it was… Vanity of vanities, saith the preacher; all is vanity."

Ian Crofton

Date 1904

Author Henry James

Nationality USA

Why It's Key James' last completed novel, and some say his greatest – although others would agree with Philip Guedalla: "The work of Henry James has always seemed divisible by a simple dynastic arrangement into three reigns: James I, James II, and the Old Pretender."

Key Event **First performance of *A Paulownia Leaf* opens a new path for kabuki plays**

First performed at the Tokyo Theatre in 1904, *A Paulownia Leaf* reflects its author's engagement in the Japanese dramatic reform movement of the time. Tsubouchi maintained that for modern audiences the traditional kabuki theater, famously mannered and stylized, was too fantastical and bombastic, and that a new type of historical drama had to be created. For that purpose, Tsubouchi combined traditional kabuki with an interest in complexity of character and motivation inspired by Shakespeare. Depicting the fall of Toyotomi family during the Siege of Osaka in 1614, the play focuses on describing the complex human psychology of characters such as Yodogimi and the Ophelia-like Kagero rather than on an aragoto (rough business)-style presentation of the battle.

In besieged Osaka Castle, Katagiri Katshumoto, a loyal retainer of the Toyotomi family, strives to manage negotiations with the besieging Tokugawas, who established the Edo Shogunate in 1603. He accepts their demand for Yodogimi, concubine of the late head of the Toyotomi family, as a hostage. Yodogimi herself is haunted by the ghosts of those whose deaths she has caused. However, informed of Katshumoto's decision, she resolves to kill him and urges her son Hideyori to do so. Although Katshumoto's ally tries to rescue him, Katshumoto finally has no choice but to retire to his own castle.

The actor Nakamura Shikan, who took the role of Yodogimi in the first performance of the play (all female characters in kabuki are portrayed by male actors), commented that he had never acted a part with such a complicated personality as hers. Despite attracting critical praise, the rest of the Japanese theatrical world of the day was indifferent or resistant to the play. However, *A Paulownia Leaf* opened up the closed kabuki world and provided a breath of fresh air.

Miki Iwata

Date 1904 (performance)

Original Title *Kiri Hitocha*

Author Shoyo Tsubouchi (1859–1935)

Nationality Japan

Why It's Key Regarded as the first of the new wave of kabuki plays that sought to connect with a modern audience by combining the traditional Japanese theatrical form with innovative and more character-focused elements.

Key Event **The advent of cinema inspires Kipling's short story "Mrs Bathurst"**

"Mrs Bathurst" has been described as the first modernist text in English and is certainly the most perplexing of Rudyard Kipling's stories. First published in the volume *Traffics and Discoveries*, it is based on Kipling's own recollection of a barmaid that he met on his travels. He said, "All I carried away from the magic town of Auckland was the face and voice of a woman who sold me beer at a little hotel there."

The story is ostensibly about a barmaid and her clients, and about the death by lightning strike of a naval warrant officer called Vickery. The narrator and some cronies are talking about Vickery who had seen the beloved barmaid Mrs Bathurst in a newsreel. As was common at the time, newsreels showed simple scenes of ordinary life such as London Bridge, or of a train arriving at a station. Mrs Bathurst is in one such street scene and the love-struck Vickery repeatedly sees the same clip of film.

Kipling uses the fragmentary structure of a newsreel for the story and gives a haunting picture of a world in which mechanized transport in ships and locomotives allows people to travel great distances while another technological advance, the cinema, makes immediate "Home and Friends" (as the newsreel is called). Kipling's short story is one of the earliest and most complex literary reactions to the power of the new medium of cinema.

Some early readers thought it too compressed and all but unintelligible; more recently it has been seen by Elliot L. Gilbert as "an elaborate puzzle game in which the reader must try to determine from artfully concealed clues, what the characters in the story are really up to."

Jad Adams

Date 1904

Author Rudyard Kipling (1865–1936)

Nationality UK (born India)

Why It's Key "The first modernist text in English. Deliberate obliqueness, formal fragmentation, absence of a privileged authorial point of view, intense literary self-consciousness, lack of closure – all the defining qualities of modernism were present and correct." (Harry Ricketts, *The Unforgiving Minute*)

46

Key Event **Henry James tours the United States *The American Scene***

"... if I had had time to become almost as 'fresh' as an inquiring stranger, I had not on the other hand had enough to cease to be... as acute as an initiated native."

Henry James (1893–1916) thus characterized his sense of being simultaneously an outsider and insider on returning to the United States in 1904 after an absence of nearly a quarter of a century. His trip partially funded by delivering his lecture, "The Lesson of Balzac," in several cities, James traveled down the Eastern seaboard, revisiting, among other places, New York, Boston, Philadelphia, and Washington. *The American Scene* would mark the beginning of an extraordinary ten-year period of reflection and looking backward in which James would also publish volumes of autobiography and revise the majority of his novels.

James' ambivalence towards his country of origin suffuses his narrative: he gently mocks New York's early skyscrapers; he deplores the decline in American manners, the standards of speech, and the loss of privacy in domestic life. His tone is nostalgic, discursive and ironic, and he satirizes himself as an awkward figure. Written in the tradition of Frances Trollope's *Domestic Manners of the Americans* (1832) and Dickens' *American Notes for General Circulations* (1842), contemporary U.S. reviewers had little patience with the rhetorical complexities of his late style and criticized his discriminations as snobbish and meaningless to the average American citizen.

In recording his impressions, James doubtless had a vested interest in affirming the wisdom of his choice to lead an expatriate life. He returned to the United States only once more when his brother, William, was dying. In 1915, ostensibly to express his disapproval of American reluctance to enter World War I, he became naturalized as a British citizen.

David Cross

Date 1904–05 (tour)

Nationality USA

Why It's Key James' survey of the American character and social scene generally accentuates the negative. Though some of his comments on immigration and the "leveling" tendencies of democracy are reactionary to the modern reader, his disturbance at the relentless consumerism of America resonates today.

Opposite Henry James and William James

Key Author **Natsume Soseki**
I Am a Cat

Soseki (1867–1916), a man unwilling to acknowledge his own defeat. Characteristically self-deprecating, Natsume Kinnosuke's choice of pen-name belies his acclaimed status and widespread popularity. But for Soseki, success did not come without sacrifice.

Born in Tokyo as the old Edo period made way for the Meiji Restoration, Soseki bore witness to important changes in Japanese society. Hurtling towards industrialization, the rise of modern Japanese language was accompanied by a decline in classical Japanese, Chinese, and English studies. Surprisingly, Soseki's early career is marked by relative ambivalence towards English and it is largely by virtue of timing that he was to become one of the remaining Japanese writers of the period with a mastery of the English language.

Studying English Literature at Tokyo's formidable Imperial University, Soseki forged a friendship with haiku master Masaoka Shiki, dabbling in Japanese and Chinese poetry. However, his greatest challenge was yet to come. 1900 saw Soseki leave a pregnant wife and daughter for a two-year sabbatical in London. Languishing in poverty amid London's run-down boarding houses, he suffered disillusionment and social isolation. Rumored to have "gone insane," Soseski's creative talents lay dormant, incubating in obscurity. Returning to Japan, he emerged from his chrysalis to pen the satirical masterpiece *I am a Cat* for serialization in 1904. The creativity of the following ten years proved to be unprecedented in Japanese literature. With his talent galvanised, Soseki produced celebrated works such as the rebellious *Botchan*, progressing to the dark and philosophical *Kokoro*. His sojourn in London provided rich material and the modern Japanese novel was born. Ever the rebel, Soseki declined the government's offer of an honorary Doctorate of Letters, dying aged 49 leaving *Light and Darkness* unfinished.
Sarah Birchwood

Date 1905

Nationality Japanese

Key Works The most widely translated Japanese authors, his legacy remains embedded in Japanese culture and beyond.

Why It's Key Highly revered Meiji-era novelist who has inspired songs, anime, and films. He was in mass circulation until recently as the figurehead on the 1000 Yen note.

Opposite **Natsume Soseki**

Key Passage
A Modern Utopia

"Down the mountain we shall go and down the passes, and as the valleys open the world will open, Utopia, where men and women are happy and laws are wise, and where all that is tangled and confused in human affairs has been unravelled and made right."

This novel is a classic utopian text that has its roots in Wells' social, political, and philosophical ideas. This passage is part of "Chapter the First," which is broken down into seven sections, with each containing a discursive, philosophical approach to what follows in the main narrative. The novel is typically utopian in that it contains one of the most recognized features of the genre – an imagined visit to a fictional place that is a "good" place.

Two men are travelling in the Swiss Alps when they are transported to a corresponding "other" world that is a far distant planet, identical to Earth and whose people are genetically the same. In another typical utopian development, protagonists from both worlds exchange ideas. The narrator and his identical "other" both learn from each other's worlds: "He is now in possession of some clear, general ideas about my own world, and I can broach almost at once the thoughts that have been growing and accumulating since my arrival in this planet of my dreams." In his philosophical contemplation of utopia Wells engages in a discussion of what makes a good place. This includes liberty, advanced technology, and freedom of expression among other things. He envisions a structured social order, hierarchical in configuration and with a ruling elite, who in Wells' "other" world are the samuari.

Wells said of the novel, "I have done my best to make the whole of this book as lucid and entertaining as its matter permits." *A Modern Utopia* despite containing rather controversial ideas remains among the most important of Wells' works.
Pat Wheeler

Date 1905

Author H.G. Wells (1866–1946)

Nationality UK

Why It's Key It had great impact not only for its rational scientific discourse, but also for its engagement with mystical and spiritual beliefs. It is a work of fiction, but, rather controversially, it frequently engages in discussions of the merits of other utopian writers. It influenced such works as Aldous Huxley's *Brave New World*, which was in part its parody.

Key Book
Doctor Glas

Prostitution, divorce, sexual disgust, conjugal rape, adultery, abortion, suicide, euthanasia, ethical murder: these are some of the subjects broached in Söderberg's masterpiece. The novel posed questions which were fervently debated in Sweden for many years; it bristles with moral dilemmas, and is spiced with a good pinch of devil's advocacy.

During a heatwave, a pretty young woman comes to Doctor Glas' surgery asking for help avoiding the relentless sexual attentions of her husband, an unappealing, aging vicar. She has taken a lover, but Glas, a 30-odd-year-old virgin and flâneur, also becomes obsessed with her. The novel is presented as Doctor Glas' diary, allowing the immediate relation of events as the plot coils itself meticulously around a little pot of cyanide pills which Glas keeps in his cabinet, along with the "secret poison in my soul."

Most controversial of all was Glas' argument that euthanasia, now criminal, should be accepted by "civilized people" as a moral duty. In the most famous passage he states, "The day will come, must come, when the right to die is recognized as far more important and inalienable a human right than the right to drop a voting ticket into a ballot box." His arguments are persuasive; but he is also riddled with misanthropy, self-hatred, and loneliness and sees himself, in a late diary entry, as empty as "a punctured boil." His description was so free, and his idea of morality as a "merry-go-round" so flagrant that combined with the directness of the diary form the book was at once shocking and compelling; these same qualities also hide the cogs of its great artistry. It is a novel of bold ideas which grips and unsettles until the final page.
Lucy Daniel

Date 1905

Author Hjalmar Söderberg (1869–1941)

Nationality Sweden

Why It's Key *Doctor Glas* caused a scandal because it was seen to advocate euthanasia, abortion, and even possibly murder. Söderberg is widely recognised as a literary icon in Sweden, but *Doctor Glas* was not widely available in English until 1963.

1890–1909

Key Character **The Scarlet Pimpernel**
The Scarlet Pimpernel: A Romance

We first see Sir Percy Blakeney through the bemused eyes of onlookers: "tall, above the average, even for an Englishman… he would have been called unusually good-looking, but for a certain lazy expression in his deep-set blue eyes, and that perpetual inane laugh…. " Blakeney is the richest man in England and married to the most beautiful and intelligent young Frenchwoman, Marguerite St. Just. There is a mystery here crying out to be solved, for how did "that demmed idiot Blakeney" ever captivate such a woman?

These are difficult times between the French and English – for aristo heads are claimed daily by Madame La Guillotine and it is rumored that a band of daring Englishman have begun to snatch those they can and carry them to safety in England. Who could possibly be the head of that brave band and what superb disguise could possibly dupe the sharp eyes both of revolutionaries and his charming wife? Suffice to say that by the end of the story, the scales have fallen at least from the eyes of Marguerite. She at last sees and understands "the whole aspect of the man, of indomitable energy, hiding, behind a perfectly acted comedy, his almost superhuman strength of will and marvellous ingenuity."

With his impenetrable disguises, his self-sacrificing care for the oppressed and his breathtaking acts of courage, this perfect type of noble Englishman set the pattern for decades of spy fiction and even superhero stories to follow – even down to his taste for fine attire, laconic attitude, trusty followers, and weakness for the woman he adores. Indeed such was the success of Orczy's character that she wrote thirteen sequels, two prequels, and several volumes of stories in order to supply more of the famously elusive gentleman to her readers.
Sophie Lewis

Date 1905 (publication)

Author Baroness Emmuska Orczy (1865–1947)

Nationality UK (born Hungary)

Why It's Key *The Scarlet Pimpernel* drew on the strength of romanticised fictions of the 1789 French Revolution but embodied something entirely contemporary to his English readers: the epitome of the English patriot and hero.

Opposite The Scarlet Pimpernel

Key Character **Lily Bart**
The House of Mirth

SPOILER

Lily Bart, the 29-year-old protagonist of Edith Wharton's first popular and critical success *The House of Mirth*, is a beautiful but impoverished member of New York's society elite who needs to marry money in order to maintain her social position. The novel traces Lily's fortunes as her plans for achieving security are repeatedly foiled and she consequently slides down the social scale towards eventual annihilation.

"Fashioned to adorn and delight," Lily is continually at conflict with herself, caught between playing the social game for marriage and being true to her ethical ideals and the search for a meaningful relationship. Whilst the world she occupies appears genteel and civilized, in reality it is based on corruption, materialism, and bribery, where individuals constantly manipulate one another for their own personal ends. Lily struggles in this environment, used and let down by a series of potential suitors, and ends up with nowhere to go but to drop out of society altogether. Reduced to taking on increasingly menial jobs in order to pay the rent, she eventually dies of an overdose of a sleeping draught, the victim of an exploitative world without humanity or social conscience.

Through the figure of Lily, Wharton was able to transform the traditonal novel of manners into a powerful exploration of the limited opportunities available for women and an insightful social-realist depiction of class struggle. A new voice for the new century, Wharton would have a major influence on the development of both American literature and women's writing.

Simon Avery

Date 1905 (publication)

Author Edith Wharton (1862–1937)

Nationality USA

Why It's Key Examining the transition from Old New York Society to the modern materialist world, the novel interrogates class, social, and gender issues, and (along with Pulitzer Prize-winning *The Age of Innocence* [1920]), would make Wharton influential on the development of twentieth-century fiction.

Opposite Lily Bart

1890–1909

53

Key Event **Thursdays at Gordon Square are the beginnings of the Bloomsbury Group**

In 1905 Thoby Stephen began hosting "Thursday Evenings" at 46 Gordon Square, the Bloomsbury address he shared with his sisters Virginia and Vanessa. These gatherings became the unofficial meeting ground for a whole generation of young men who, like Thoby, had recently graduated from Cambridge. Over time, core Bloomsbury members would come to include literary critic Lytton Strachey, art critics Roger Fry and Clive Bell, artist Duncan Grant, economist John Maynard Keynes, and political journalist Leonard Woolf, whom Virginia Stephen eventually married.

At these evenings – which transferred two years later to nearby 29 Fitzroy Square – the tone was both bawdy and intellectual, childish and arcane. "If you could say what you liked about art, sex, or religion," Vanessa Stephen recalled later, "you could also talk freely and very likely dully about the ordinary doings of daily life." Sexual candor, especially concerning male homosexuality, became a keynote of Bloomsbury conversation. However, there was also serious intellectual and creative work to be done. In 1907 Woolf began to write her first novel "Melymbrosia," which was later published as *The Voyage Out* (1915) while Vanessa established herself as a painter.

Over the next twenty years, thanks to the impact of both cataclysmic public events and quieter private ones, the Bloomsbury Group would drift apart, re-form, and take on several different shapes. What bound all these different manifestations together was a continuing tone of scepticism, irreverence, and iconoclasm, especially towards social and intellectual sacred cows.

Some critics, however, have dared to suggest that the "Bloomsberries" were self-indulgent aesthetes whose lives and works became irrelevant as the economic and political events of the 1930s unfolded.

Kathryn Hughes

Date 1905

Place London, UK

Why It's Key Thanks to the work of biographers Michael Holroyd and Frances Spalding over the past few decades, the Bloomsbury Group has become something of a cottage industry. Houses where members once lived are reverently preserved, while their dizzying network of love affairs and emotional alliances are diligently plotted.

Key Event **Henryk Sienkiewicz wins the Nobel Prize for Literature**

Henryk Sienkiewicz was born into an estate-owning family in the Russian-ruled part of Poland. His family were actively involved in the struggle for Polish independence and as punishment for their revolutionary actions, the family estate was confiscated. Sienkiewicz's early stories demonstrate a strong social conscience which is probably a result of his family's political activities, as well as of his own university studies.

His novels were all originally written as serials (he was a freelance journalist) and it was the publication of his trilogy of historical novels – *With Fire and Sword*, *The Deluge*, and *Pan Michael* – that established his reputation as an outstanding writer with great narrative powers. All of these novels discuss the social upheavals caused by the political instability in seventeenth-century Poland.

After writing on more contemporary subjects such as a vivid psychological study of a cultivated but debauched man in the novel *Without Dogma*, Sienkiewicz returned to the familiar area of historical fiction. His most famous and successful work, *Quo Vadis?*, is the story of Christian persecutions in Rome during Nero's reign. This best-selling novel set Sienkiewicz's international reputation as the most outstanding Polish writer in the second half of the nineteenth century and certainly influenced the Nobel judges in their decision-making.

As well as being regarded as a serious and important author, Sienkiewicz was an immensely popular and prolific one. In celebration of his 30-year writing career, the Polish government (with the approval of its people) presented Sienkiewicz with the estate where he and his ancestors had lived prior to its appropriation.
Alice Goldie

Date 1905

Author Henryk Sienkiewicz (1846–1916)

Nationality Poland

Why It's Key Author who achieved international fame after writing *Quo Vadis?* (1896). Other major works include *In Vain* (1876), *The Old Servant* (1880), *With Fire and Sword* (1884), *The Deluge* (1886), *Pan Michael* (1888), *Without Dogma* (1891), *The Knights of the Cross* (1900), *Whirlpools* (1910).

54

Key Event **Gertrude Stein holds her first literary and artistic salons**

Gertrude Stein (1874–1946) was born in Allegheny, Pennsylvania, the daughter of German-Jewish immigrants. As a young child, she lived in Vienna and Paris, as well as in the States, but grew up in California. After her studies, she went to Paris, where, from 1903, she lived with her brother Leo at 27 rue de Fleurus. The siblings collected art; their walls were covered with paintings by such luminaries as Matisse and Picasso, of whom Gertrude was an early champion. They also held dinner parties. Artists, writers, and critics were frequent callers. Stein's brilliant conversation drew many.

The influence of Parisian culture on Stein was profound, as she later noted: "And so I am an American and I have lived half my life in Paris, not the half that made me but the half in which I made what I made." Stein was inspired by, among other things, Cubism, Dadaism, and Surrealism. Her artistic judgements were influential. She had a large circle of friends and tirelessly promoted herself. By the 1920s her salon attracted writers like Ezra Pound, Thornton Wilder, Sherwood Anderson, and Ernest Hemingway, whom she mentored.

Stein coined the term "Lost Generation" for such expatriate Americans. The term, popularized by Hemingway, refers to those American writers who lived in Europe from the end of World War I to the beginning of the Great Depression. Members of the "Lost Generation" were said to be disillusioned by the carnage of the war and scornful of Victorian conventions. Many sought inspiration from European culture, claiming that American culture lacked breadth. Nevertheless, this period saw a flowering of American literature and art; Stein helped foster this.
Emily Jeremiah

Date 1905

Place Paris

Nationality USA

Why It's Key The salons held by Gertrude Stein were sites of lively artistic exchange. They were attended by numerous notable writers and artists of the time, and have consequently become legendary, epitomizing Paris' status as an artistic ex-pat haven.

Opposite Gertrude Stein (left)

Key Author
Jules Verne

Jules Hetzel's popular scientific magazine launched Jules Verne's (1828–1905) writing career and set the pattern for his popular "scientific romance" stories. His first publications appeared in 1850 but it was not until 1863, when he published *Five Weeks in a Balloon: A Journey of Discovery in Africa by Three Englishmen*, that he became acclaimed as a writer. Verne had a vivid imagination, but, more significantly, his work was underpinned by serious academic research.

In his stories he mapped the scientific developments of his day onto the fantastic exploits of a range of male protagonists. In *From the Earth to the Moon*, *20,000 Leagues Under the Sea*, *Journey to the Centre of the Earth*, and *Around the World in 80 Days* Verne describes variously the space race, powered flight, helicopters, guided missiles, and submarine technology. He is seen as one of the great prophetic writers of the era, but his "predictions" are careful meditations on contemporary scientific and technological debates, many of which could be found in the scientific journals of his day. Indeed his "Extraordinary Voyages" were initially published as part of an attempt to encourage children to study the sciences.

It was Verne's desire to create a new sort of reading experience that set him apart. His attention to scientific matters in his novels and stories was a relatively new phenomenon in the mid-nineteenth century and it was his propensity to chart what was then modern man's quest for the unknown that made him such a popular writer. He has an enormously important place in the history of the genre of science fiction and his fantastic adventure novels have influenced many writers who came after him.
Pat Wheeler

Date 1905 (death)

Nationality France

Key Works *Five Weeks in a Balloon* (1863), *Journey to the Centre of the Earth* (1864), *From the Earth to the Moon* (1865), *20,000 Leagues Under the Sea* (1869), *Around the World in Eighty Days* (1873)

Why It's Key Jules Verne is one of the "fathers of science fiction."

Opposite Illustration from *20,000 Leagues Under the Sea*

Key Author **Alexander Kuprin**
Junior Captain Rybnikov

Alexander Kuprin shot to fame with a long short story called "The Duel," set in the Russo-Japanese war and published the same year as Russia's military defeat prompted the Revolution of 1905. His earlier time in the army and the relevance of the war theme also informed *Junior Captain Rybnikov*, hailed by some critics as the pinnacle of his art and ignored by others.

An oddly sympathetic type, apparently a wounded Russian officer back from the East and looking for compensation for his injuries, Rybnikov hangs about government offices in St. Petersburg and frequents a restaurant where the city's top journalists hang out. He wants to hear anything about the war. Ace pressman Shchavinsky baits him but can't get a hold on him. The captain's appearance, including a yellowish skin tone and Mongol eyes, suggests two faces in one. Shchavinsky then organizes an evening drinking and whoring that eventually proves to be Rybnikov's undoing.

Nabokov called Kuprin a Russian Kipling for his stories about pathetic adventure-seekers. Here perhaps Shchavinsky, "the writer," is one such adventurer and the petty-criminal and chancer Len'ka, darling of the brothel girls, another. Their unheroic curiosity forces the much more likeable captain to betray himself. Yet his real secret he takes to the grave.

The vivid petit-bourgeois Russian setting, not a common one in the Russian literature of world renown, the straightfoward narrative and the fascination with moral psychology recalls early Simenon. *Junior Captain Rybnikov* has been called a spy thriller by a rare Russian writer uninterested in politics. Kuprin's work declined when he fell foul of the Bolsheviks and fled to France, only returning to Stalin's Russia to die.
Lesley Chamberlain

Date 1905

Nationality Russia

Key Works *Moloch* (1896), *The Duel* (1905), *Junior Captain Rybnikov* (1905), *The Garnet Bracelet* (1911)

Why It's Key Kuprin made his name as a popular writer in the period between 1900 and the Revolution, choosing topical, sensational subject matter for his stories and longer fiction.

Key Event **Wilde's letter to Lord Alfred Douglas is published as *De Profundis***

With his 1895 trial and conviction for gross indecency, Wilde went from feted playwright and society darling to, in the words of *De Profundis*, a "pariah." He had been led handcuffed from the courts, heard the jeers of a mob, brought disgrace on his family and, the worst pain of all, frittered away his talent.

De Profundis is Oscar Wilde's prison art. It was written in Reading Gaol when he was at his lowest ebb, and published posthumously. Conceived as a letter to his former lover, Lord Alfred Douglas, it burns with a sense of humiliation and anguish that makes it universally relevant. Though he identifies with Christ, the supreme sufferer, this essay is not about discovering God or religious salvation; instead it's a clear-eyed analysis of the ruin he has made of his life and an attempt to find some meaning in the mess.

Out of his experiences, he hopes to create a piece of writing that validates his life as an artist. The truth was, he already had. Wilde is remembered for his witty plays, in particular the comedy *The Importance of Being Earnest*. He was not the first professional funny-man who yearned to be taken more seriously: *De Profundis* is Wilde's true voice – sorrowful, loving, angry, and forgiving. This is Wilde dropping the brittle defences of wit and epigram, writing his truth because he had nothing left to lose. He stood, he writes, "in symbolic relation to the art and culture of the age" and, with his fall, the aesthetic movement died too.

Kathy Watson

Date 1905 (publication)

Author Oscar Wilde (1854–1900)

Nationality Ireland

Why It's Key Prison rules prevented Wilde from sending *De Profundis* to Lord Alfred Douglas. Douglas always claimed he never received it. Wilde's case, which received salacious press coverage, brought homosexuality into public view.

Key Passage **"The Great American Novelist"**

"The Great American Novel is not extinct like the Dodo, but mythical like the Hippogriff."

Frank Norris' essay on "The G.A.N." at once revivified the debate on the Great American Novel and defined the term's modern usage. He hints at such a work's necessarily hybrid provenance. America, the great melting pot, could only be represented by a novel successfully cross-pollinated by disparate, though co-existing, elements, such as romance and reportage, philosophy and gossip, wistfulness and skepticism – the "highs" and the "lows" coming together to create something truly unique and capturing the essence of the cultural mélange that makes up that country.

In DeForest's usage, the Great American Novel denoted an encapsulation of the mores, values, and themes prevalent in the culture of the time, so that the work could be held up and examined in the light of these things to yield a true picture of the American spirit as it was at that moment. In this sense, there have been many contenders for the Great American Novel, including John Steinbeck's *The Grapes of Wrath* and J.D. Salinger's *The Catcher in the Rye*.

For Norris, however, the Great American Novel has the mythical quality of something doubly impossible and, indeed, in an era when the question "what is 'American'?" is increasingly at the heart of cultural discourse it seems like the Great American Novel is as elusive a beast as ever it has been. It is Norris' figurative usage that endures, representing a literary Holy Grail, an ideal to strive for and a source of inspiration. The term "Great American Novel" represents in itself a search for America's true cultural identity. As Norris put it, "It all depends what you mean by Great, what you mean by American."

Christian Kerr

Date 1903 (publication)

Title *The Responsibilities of the Novelist*

Author Frank Norris (1870–1902)

Nationality USA

Why It's Key The term "Great American Novel" can be attributed to an essay, published in 1869 by American Civil War novelist, John William DeForest. But it was Norris who elaborated on the concept of a work that perfectly represents the spirit of America.

Key Author **E. Nesbit**
The Railway Children

For Edith Nesbit (1858–1924), writing children's books was more than a hobby – it was her livelihood. Her father had died when she was three, and her mother brought up the family in genteel poverty, leading a wandering life in France and Germany before settling in Halstead, Kent, the setting for *The Railway Children*. Through her elder sister Mary she mingled with a somewhat bohemian crowd, including the Rossettis, Swinburne and William Morris, and her interest in socialism led her to help found the Fellowship of the New Life, which later evolved into the Fabian Society, itself a precursor of the Labour Party.

Edith was already heavily pregnant when she married Hubert Bland, a fellow socialist, in 1880. Bland believed in open marriage, and Nesbit raised his two children by his mistress alongside her own. A combination of poor health and business failure meant that Bland was unable to support the family, so Edith had to turn to writing to bring in some income.

She wrote scores of books for both children and adults, although now only a handful are still read. The best-known of these – thanks to a television series and two film adaptations – is *The Railway Children* (1906), but perhaps more influential on subsequent children's authors, from C.S. Lewis' Narnia books to J.K. Rowling, are such classics as *Five Children and It* (1902) and *The Phoenix and the Carpet* (1904), in which children suddenly find their everyday lives transformed when they are confronted by the appearance of a character or object from another world.

Ian Crofton

Date 1906 (publication)

Nationality UK

Why It's Key Created a new genre of children's novel, in which the everyday world is sometimes touched by magic.

Key Author **John Galsworthy**
The Man of Property

The quality of John Galsworthy's (1867–1933) ten-volume *Forsyte Saga* declined after *The Man of Property*, its first instalment. What intervened was World War I, which, although Galsworthy's experience was restricted to working in a French hospital, intensified his melancholy. In one respect the catastrophe virtually destroyed the upper-middle-class English habitat of his books and weakened his will to criticize it. He also came to doubt his own talent. The rise of literary modernism, with its stylistic experimentation, further detracted from his serious reputation, although he won the Nobel Prize in 1932.

A stately melodrama, *The Man of Property* remains an old-fashioned classic. It is a memorable portrait of late Victorian London and respectable English foibles. Galsworthy had passed through years of ostracism by his own class because of love for a married woman. The failed marriage of Soames and Irene drew on the marriage she abandoned and gave his writing a

satirical bite. Uncannily, the novel also reflected great themes from the contemporary European novel. For instance the failure of the materialistic, hyper-conventional Forsyte clan to understand true art and passion suggests that weakness Thomas Mann explored in *Buddenbrooks*, another saga of a bourgeois family in decline. Irene also faintly resembled Tolstoy's *Anna Karenina*, trapped in a loveless marriage. However Galsworthy did not exploit his material so powerfully. He failed to strike the moral note that contemporary critics like Joseph Conrad required. Like young Jolyon, the hero-in-waiting of *The Man of Property*, he saw people as comic or pathetic, rather than good or bad.

Lesley Chamberlain

Date 1906

Nationality UK

Why It's Key Critics gave up on Galsworthy as a novelist before the war. Later generations have been encouraged to see the 1960s televised version of *The Forsyte Saga* as the progenitor of the modern soap more than a work of art.

Key Works *The Forsyte Saga* (1922), *A Modern Comedy* (1929)

Key Event *The Jungle* sparks a government investigation

After reading Upton Sinclair's novel *The Jungle*, Americans were sick to their stomachs. Looking at their dinner plates, readers saw their meals as the nauseating product of fouled goods doctored with chemical coloration. Sinclair's description of the unhealthy conditions of processed meat packaging directly led to the creation of the federal Food and Drug Administration (FDA) that continues to regulate dietary and medical standards in the United States.

A novel about the Chicago slums of immigrant housing, and working conditions in the meat factories, *The Jungle* matches a description of a living farm animal's slaughter and the carcass' dissection into parts for canning and other industrial uses with the breakdown of a Lithuanian immigrant family's disintegration into alcoholism, debt, prostitution, homelessness, and premature death as a result of their proletarian conditions.

Different from other muckraking journalists who reveal the official fraud and violence of American capitalism, Sinclair did not want to shock his middle-class readers into recognizing the presence of labor exploitation so much as encourage his working-class ones into socialist awareness. The novel ends, somewhat heavy-handedly, with a romantic call to "strike, strike, strike" against the various owners of big business.

As the American Zola, Sinclair's numerous books about industrial corruption were tied to his active participation in socialist politics and a 1934 candidacy for state governor promising to "End Poverty in California." A forerunner to eco-criticism, *The Jungle* represents the start of an American movement of the arts in self-consciously left directions on themes of labor.

Stephen Shapiro

Date 1906 (publication)

Author Upton Sinclair (1878–1968)

Nationality USA

Why It's Key *The Jungle* had immediate political impact when Theodore Roosevelt read it and ordered an investigation into the meat-packing industry it described in such horrific detail. Sinclair used the novel's proceeds to build a socialist meeting house and went on to write more than 100 books about industrial corruption.

Key Character **Pelle the Conqueror**
Pelle the Conqueror

There is no other literary hero quite like Pelle Karlsson. When we first meet them Pelle and his father Lasse stand penniless immigrants on the quayside, the old man almost in tears, but Pelle convinced "that the whole world would become theirs, with all that it contained in the way of wonders." As Pelle turns "an open, perspiring, victor's brow towards the world," he is already on his way to conquering it. By the end, Pelle's victory, his great success story, has become that of his fellow workers. He is the people's "conqueror."

Lasse and the child Pelle leave Sweden in 1877, migrating labourers who end up working on a farm. The story concerns the growth of Pelle's political consciousness, but because Nexö was himself born into poverty this is more than a political work – it is born of passion and love for his people, which shows in the compelling characterisation and scores of minor characters, fighting, loving, and committing small acts

of heroism. The story is so rich in incident and easily digested because this is poverty told from the inside, with the unsentimental voice of truth. Young Pelle, hungry, faithful, has a highly developed sense of injustice. With dignity and courage, after living in a poor Copenhagen tenement, becoming involved with trade unions, enjoying fatherhood and the love of three women, Pelle becomes a fighter and a leader of men.

Pelle's story was heralded as momentous; the *New York Tribune* wrote, "The book is world-wide in its significance. It is the chronicle of the growth of labour to consciousness of its rights and its strength to win them." While the socialist criteria have now all but vanished, this story of migrant workers, in the simplicity of its greatness, and its appeal to common humanity, is still – perhaps now more than at any time since it was written – internationally relevant.

Lucy Daniel

Date 1906 (four volumes completed in 1910)

Author Martin Andersen Nexö (1869–1954)

Nationality Denmark

Why It's Key Pelle's story was published in four parts, each of which can be read separately, although the most popular is the first, which tells of Pelle's rural childhood, and is the one used for the Oscar-winning film version (1987), for which the stately charisma of Max Von Sydow in the role of Lasse, Pelle's father, was perfectly suited.

Key Book
The Secret Agent

The Secret Agent, one of the earliest novels about terrorism, bears comparison with Dostoevsky's *The Devils*, though Conrad, who hated Russia, never acknowledged his debt.

A London detective investigates a bombing in Greenwich Park, an event which had a real precedent. In the course of his inquiries he conflicts with his boss, who takes him off the case. Yet these details only serve to give movement to Conrad's intense and thrilling psychological drama, in which the dubious profession of her husband, Mr Verloc, is slowly revealed to his wife Winnie.

The text is too rich in symmetry and allusion for any summary of events to do justice to the subtlety of Conrad's study of all his characters' moral attitudes. What shocked the public of his day was his radical view of a morally compromised, self-interested ruling class, set alongside the vices of the anarchists and revolutionaries gathered around the greasy Verloc.

In this book every character counts, from the shady, unnamed patrons of Verloc's pornography shop, to the now docile former revolutionary writing his memoirs in the country, living off bread and milk, to the poignant figure of Winnie's backward brother who is hypersensitive to violence and compassionate to the point of madness. With this ultra-modern, ironic text, into which he put much personal torment, Conrad, scornful of all establishments, including the organizations and programs of revolutionaries, became a kind of reluctant prophet of twentieth-century violence and political corruption.

Lesley Chamberlain

Date 1907 (publication)

Author Joseph Conrad (1857–1924)

Nationality Poland (naturalized UK)

Why It's Key In 1920 Conrad apologized to the public for his story of "utter desolation, madness and despair." "I have not intended to commit a gratuitous outrage on the feelings of mankind." *The Secret Agent* was his masterpiece, alongside *Nostromo*.

1890–1909

61

Key Event **Synge's comedy causes riots when first performed**

Alongside his fellow Protestants, W.B. Yeats and Lady Gregory, Synge was a key figure in the Irish Literary Revival, the movement that sought literary inspiration in the ancient folk culture of Ireland. Synge himself had spent five summers on the Irish-speaking Aran Islands, absorbing the stories of the peasants and the cadences of their speech. It is the latter, rendered into Synge's poetic English, that helps to give *The Playboy of the Western World* its almost Shakespearian power.

The play's story concerns the arrival of Christy Mahon in a small village in Connacht, the "Western World" of the title. He impresses the local women, especially Pegeen Mike, the publican's daughter, by boasting that he has killed his father in an argument. Conservative Irish nationalists, whose mindset was dominated by the Catholic Church, were outraged at the suggestion that such a deed could increase the attraction of a man to an Irish woman. At the first

performance at the Abbey Theatre in January 1907 things came to a head at Christy's line: "It's Pegeen I'm seeking only, and what'd I care if you brought me a drift of chosen females, standing in their shifts itself, maybe, from this place to the eastern world?" The image of a harem of Irish women in their underwear was too much for the narrow-minded in the audience, and the resulting riots lasted for a week. Yeats himself berated the crowd with the words: "You have disgraced yourselves again. Is this to be the recurring celebration of the arrival of Irish genius?"

Half a century later things had calmed down: in 1968 the Abbey company presented Pope Paul VI with a copy of the play bound in white leather.

Ian Crofton

Date 1907

Place Dublin

Title *The Playboy of the Western World*

Author J.M. Synge (1871–1909)

Why It's Key The riots provoked by the first production signalled a deep split in Irish culture, between Catholic conservatives and more secular nationalists.

Key Passage
"Matilda"

SPOILER

"Matilda told such Dreadful Lies,
It made one Gasp and Stretch one's Eyes"

P ublished in the same period as *The Railway Children*, *The Wind in the Willows*, and other wholesome stories, Belloc's *Cautionary Tales* appealed to the baser instincts of Edwardian children, satisfying those who wanted their literature spiked with mayhem, cruelty, and death. They are morality tales in verse in which children who do naughty things, such as "Henry King who chewed bits of string" or "Jim, who ran away from his nurse," end up dead.

One of the funniest is "Matilda," who summons the fire brigade to her aunt's house as a joke (the aunt "had to pay / To get the Men to go away!"– adults in Belloc's universe are all as greedy and unpleasant as the children). Subsequently, a real fire breaks out but Matilda's cries are ignored: "And therefore when her aunt returned, / Matilda, and the House, were burned."

For a child's death to be described in such a jaunty manner must have shocked some Edwardian parents, whose childhood reading would have included Dickens, in whose works the death of a child is the cue for pages of tear-jerking lamentation. Belloc's practice of describing children's gruesome fates with frivolity has influenced not just Roald Dahl and other children's authors but adult fiction too – he surely inspired the brilliantly offhand manner in which Evelyn Waugh detailed the death of little Lord Tangent in *Decline and Fall*. And his verses are still remembered today, with three "updated" versions of the *Cautionary Tales* being published in 2006.
Jake Kerridge

Date 1907 (publication)

Title *Cautionary Tales for Children*

Author Hilaire Belloc (1870–1953)

Nationality UK

Why It's Key In the first golden age of children's literature, a politician and poet introduces the elements of black humour and satire.

62

Key Passage
Father and Son

"This book is the record of a struggle between two temperaments, two consciences and almost two epochs. It ended, as was inevitable, in disruption. Of the two human beings here described, one was born to fly backward, the other could not help being carried forward. There came a time when neither spoke the same language as the other, or encompassed the same hopes, or was fortified by the same desires. But, at least, it is some consolation to the survivor, that neither, to the very last hour, ceased to respect the other, or to regard him with sad indulgence."

S o wrote Edmund Gosse at the beginning of a memoir describing the relationship between himself and his father, the eminent naturalist Philip Henry Gosse. Gosse senior combined an encyclopedic knowledge of Britain's flora and fauna with an abiding belief in the literal truth of the Bible. At a time when the scientific establishment had adopted Darwin's theories

of evolution, Gosse still clung to the belief that God created the world in six days, followed by a day of rest.

Brought up by his father in an isolated Devon village (his mother having died when he was eight), Edmund Gosse initially imbibed his father's dour religiosity and became something of a prig. In adolescence, however, he broke away from the Protestant sect in which he had been raised and started the long journey towards becoming a polished, urbane – and quite possibly bisexual – Edwardian man of letters.

In *Father and Son* Edmund Gosse turns a naturalist's eye on himself and his father. Despite all the empirical evidence to the contrary, Philip Henry Gosse insists on clinging to an outmoded interpretation of the earth's origins. His son, by contrast, belongs to the age of science and so "could not help being carried forward" into the future.
Kathryn Hughes

Date 1907

Author Edmund Gosse (1849–1928)

Nationality UK

Why It's Key Gosse initially published *Father and Son* anonymously, worried that it would seem like an act of gross filial impiety. Gosse summed up a whole generation's struggle to free itself from the clammy clutch of the Victorian values in which it had been schooled.

Opposite Edmund Gosse

Key Author
J-K. Huysmans

Joris-Karl Huysmans (1848–1907) spent a year at the University of Paris then began writing, notably in praise of the Impressionist artists of whom he was an early admirer and influential critic. Under the influence of Zola and naturalism his first novel, in 1876, was *Marthe: The Story of a Whore*, the first time such a theme had been written about explicitly in French literature. He had it printed abroad for fear of the authorities, and copies of the first edition were duly confiscated by the censors at the French border.

After other realistic works, he turned to more symbolic writing, the most important fruit of which was *Against the Grain* (*A Rebours*) in 1884, a novel without a plot about the classic decadent anti-hero Des Esseintes in his romantic agony. It is often referred to as the supreme expression of the decadent spirit. His *Over There* (*Là-bas*) of 1891 describes a character who arrives at Catholicism by way of Satanism.

Huysmans' writing is strange and exotic, full of black-clad, jewel-encrusted, or velvet-draped scenes and characters. He defined the decadent mood and provided inspiration for the work of Aubrey Beardsley and the British decadents. Oscar Wilde's *The Picture of Dorian Gray* refers to *A Rebours* and such critics as Arthur Symons and Max Beerbohm rated him highly. Huysmans' working out of the conflict that occurs between his sensual and spiritual natures led to a conversion to Roman Catholicism and he wrote novels about his retreat to a Trappist monastery and other religious subjects.

Jad Adams

Death 1907 (death)

Nationality France

Why It's Key The influential British critic Cyril Connolly wrote, in *The Modern Movement*, that "Mallarmé and Huysmans almost created the modern sensibility between them."

Key Book
The Old Wives' Tale

In his preface to his masterpiece, *The Old Wives' Tale*, Arnold Bennett recalled the genesis of his novel, watching a "fat, shapeless… ridiculous" old woman in a Parisian restaurant and pondering "the extreme pathos in the mere fact that every stout ageing woman was once a young girl with the unique charm of youth in her form and movements and in her mind." He resolved to write the history of two sisters, Constance and Sophia Baines, from their adolescence to their deaths, taking as his model the realism of Guy de Maupassant's novel, *Une Vie*.

The novel traces the fortunes of the sisters growing up together above their father's draper's shop in St. Luke's Square, Bursley in Staffordshire, then separated by marriage, Constance wedding Samuel Povey and remaining in the shop, while the more spirited Sophia elopes to Paris with the disreputable Gerald Scales, only to encounter the troubles of the 1870–71 Seige and to be abandoned by her husband.

Though the events of their lives are widely dissimilar, time – the great leveler – softens their differences and when the sisters are reunited in old age, they find comfort in each other's company and the consonances of their characters.

Bennett's commitment to the realistic portrayal of quotidian life and the passing of time resonates throughout the novel. His narrative voice is unremittingly ironic but suffused with sympathetic compassion for the foibles of ordinary people. As he did in *Anna of the Five Towns* (1902) and later in the *Clayhanger* trilogy (1910–1918), Bennett invests the industrial landscape of the Potteries towns (subsequently becoming the city of Stoke-on-Trent) with a distinctive aesthetic quality of their own.

David Cross

Date 1908

Author Arnold Bennett (1867–1931)

Nationality UK

Why It's Key Bennett's reputation faltered for much of the twentieth century – perhaps as a result of his traditional style and his unabashed admission of the financial motivation behind his considerable output – but is now regarded as a regional novelist second only to Thomas Hardy in achievement.

Key Book
The House on the Borderland

William Hope Hodgson was an extremely prolific writer of short stories and novels, who has attracted praise for his successful spanning of the different, though related, genres in his work, namely fantasy, horror, adventure, and science fiction. His short novel, *The House on the Borderland*, is a mélange of gothic horror, mystery tale, and ghost story, centered around the discovery of the diary of a man who once lived in a strange, old house in a remote Irish fishing village, the tattered pages of which hint at an unspeakable evil lurking just beyond the veil of normality.

The book marked a departure from the "realist" tendency in supernatural fiction, employing the traditional models of the ghost story and gothic fiction, but following through with a newer kind of "cosmic horror" that hinted at other realities governed by preternatural forces. H.P. Lovecraft cited Hodgson as a major influence, saying that "but for a few touches of commonplace sentimentality [*The House on the Borderland*] would be a classic of the first water."

Hodgson's power of expression in evoking not only a sense of terror but of a pervasiveness of potential terror, has been emulated in many forms of popular culture, from Hitchcock to *The Twilight Zone* and the magazine, *Weird Tales*, not to mention the EC horror comics of the 1950s. In fact, Hodgson's legacy can be traced in nearly every work of supernatural horror produced since the beginning of the twentieth century. He was truly the progenitor of the "weird tale."
Christian Kerr

Date 1908

Author William Hope Hodgson (1877–1918)

Nationality UK

Why It's Key Hodgson's work is characterized by the overlapping and blending of genres such as fantasy, horror, and science fiction. He was tragically killed by an artillery shell at Ypres on April 17, 1918.

Key Event **Nietzsche's "autobiography"**
Ecce Homo **is published**

Ecce Homo, blasphemous in title and bewildering in its layers of mischief and parody, was Nietzsche's last work, written in 1888, just before tertiary syphillis destroyed his reason, but not published until twenty years later. Scarcely an autobiography, it subverted an established humanistic genre and showed what Nietzsche meant by his famous "transvaluation of all values." The brief chapters, headed "Why I am So Wise," "Why I am a Destiny" and so on, provided a definitive judgement of his own work and illustrated the meaning of the subtitle "How I Became What I Am."

Nietzsche became himself by purging his being of Christian dualism and pathos. He loathed the classic moral virtue of selflessness and taught self-overcoming, which meant strength, openness, and sense of one's own path. The way of transcendent self-celebration was clearly revealed in the way he treated the influences of Socrates, Schopenhauer, and Wagner on his make-up. Self-overcoming was a philosophical response to the illness that dogged his life, as was the highly condensed writing, and the dithyrambic pursuit of undivided joy that ran through all the works. Aware of being at the peak of his powers in 1888, and threatened by collapse, Nietzsche responded by reviewing the whole of rational-Christian western culture as a decadent illness and showing how he for one escaped its dreary hold.

Critics who have associated Nietzsche's cheaply borrowed "superman" with Nazism have been quick, and crudely wide of the mark, to attribute the self-aggrandizing tone of *Ecce Homo* to incipient madness.
Lesley Chamberlain

Date 1908

Author Friedrich Nietzsche (1844–1900)

Nationality Germany

Why It's Key Nietzsche, with Freud and Marx, gave the western twentieth century its modern cultural character, pitching individualism and irony against rationalism and collectivism. His posthumously published "autobiography" coincided with the tidal wave of interest in his diatribe against Christianity and evocation of individual will.

Key Author
Kafu Nagai

Over the course of an enduring literary career lasting from 1908 to the end of the 1950s, and encompassing novels, short stories, drama, and one of history's greatest journals, Kafu Nagai was widely acclaimed for his humorous, detached accounts of the colorful and gradually disappearing habitués of old downtown Tokyo's floating world. Before and after his travels to the West, he was acquainted and at ease with the ways of the capital's libertines, geishas, courtesans, and artists.

Together with Junichiro Tanizaki, Kafu is often regarded as a representative figure of Japan's anti-naturalist aesthetic movement. However, he was unique in his lifelong critique of Japan and its social and political mores, and was outspoken in his opposition to the government's ultra-reactionary policies after the High Treason Incident of 1910 – a mass arrest of leftists accused of plotting the assassination of the Meiji Emperor,

ultimately resulting in the execution of twelve of the alleged conspirators.

Kafu's independent, irreverent voice, extraordinary for the time, was the result of youthful studies and employment in the United States and France from 1903 to 1908, and is already in evidence in the early works *American Stories* (1908, *Amerika Monogatari*) and *French Stories* (1908, *Fransu Monogatari*) published shortly after his return to Japan. From 1910 Kafu chose to immortalize the exquisite but passing beauty of traditional Japanese culture, his masterpiece being *A Tale of the River Sumida* (1937, *Bokuto Kidan*), in which the narrator recounts a nostalgic, tender love for a prostitute. Kafu's elegant, celebratory fiction also conveys an implicit disenchantment with the militarist and capitalist directions of twentieth-century Japan.
David Taylor and Tomonao Yoshida

Date 1908 (Kafu returns from his travels in the United States)

Author Kafu Nagai (1879–1959)

Nationality Japan

Key Works *American Stories* (1908), *A Tale of the River Sumida* (1937), *Dancho-Tei's Diary* (1917–1959)

Why It's Key Kafu Nagai's publication of his copious diary (1917 to 1959) provided an unmatchable, vivid record of Japan's modern social history.

Key Passage
The Wind in the Willows

"Toad sat straight down in the middle of the dusty road, his legs stretched out before him, and stared fixedly in the direction of the disappearing motor-car. He breathed short, his face wore a placid, satisfied expression, and at intervals he faintly murmured 'Poop-poop!'"

Kenneth Grahame's classic of children's literature, *The Wind in the Willows*, can be read in many different ways; as a wry commentary on the class system of Edwardian England, as a warning of the threat of social change and the destruction of rural values, as an oblique manifesto of Grahame's own views on politics, religion, and social reform.

Like E.M. Forster's *Howards End* (which also features an important early appearance of the motor car) it centers around the destiny of an English country house, which, in this case, has to be won back from the usurping, proletarian weasels.

In this scene from chapter two, Mr Toad, after nearly being killed by a passing motorist, falls in love with the idea of speed, "Villages skipped, towns and cities jumped – always somebody else's horizon! O bliss! O poop-poop! O my! O my!" The motor car here is a force of chaotic, destructive energy that sunders the arcadian world of the river bank, and Mr Toad, transfixed as he sits in the middle of the road watching the machine recede into the distance, stands for the point at which the human spirit is seduced by the folly of its own desires. The motor car changed their lives, and ours, for ever.
Gerard Woodward

Date 1908

Author Kenneth Grahame (1859–1932)

Nationality UK

Why It's Key Publication of *The Wind in The Willows* established Mr Toad as one of the most popular and memorable characters in children's literature. In 1929 *The Wind in the Willows* was dramatized by A.A. Milne as *Toad of Toad Hall*.

Opposite *Wind in the Willows*

Key Passage
Three Weeks

"A bright fire burnt in the grate, and some palest orchid-mauve silk curtains were drawn in the lady's room when Paul entered from the terrace. And loveliest sight of all, in front of the fire, stretched at full length, was his tiger – and on him – also at full length – reclined the lady… one white arm resting on the beast's head, her back supported by a pile of the velvet cushions… while between her red lips was a rose not redder than they – an almost scarlet rose. Paul had never seen one as red before. The whole picture was barbaric… It was not what one would expect to find in a sedate Swiss hotel."

The preposterous plot of *Three Weeks* concerns an unnamed northern European noblewoman, and Paul, "a splendid English young animal." No doubt one reason for the book's massive popularity was the inversion of the expected scene of sexual conquest: the heroine seduces the hapless virgin Paul to provide an heir to her throne. She mockingly calls him a "baby" and "sleeping beauty" – and finally summons him to her boudoir. In a scene which became the most iconic in all romantic fiction, the lady tells her young protégé, "love is a purely physical emotion," writhes around on the tiger skin, then reads him a passage (in Latin) about Cupid and Psyche, plays a quick tune on the guitar, and announces, "sweet Paul, I shall teach you many things, and among them I shall teach you how – to – LIVE."

These days readers will be lucky if it evinces even a slight erotic frisson – yet what raptures it must have stirred in the Edwardians' breasts, because they bought two million copies of the book. The scene made Glyn notorious, giving rise to the popular poem: Would you like to sin/With Elinor Glyn/On a tiger skin?/Or would you prefer/To err with her,/On some other fur?

Glyn later went to Hollywood, where she gave Rudolph Valentino kissing lessons.
Lucy Daniel

Date 1908

Author Elinor Glyn (1864–1943)

Nationality UK

Why It's Key *Three Weeks* made Glyn notorious, particularly for the famous scene on the tiger skin. Glyn's many novels exerted a huge and direct influence on romantic fiction and film. She later made it big in Hollywood's silent movie industry, as scriptwriter, director and actress.

Key Event **Mills & Boon is founded by Gerald Mills and Charles Boon**

Mills & Boon romances are renowned for their strapping, handsome male leads and lonely female protagonists desperate for love.

When Gerald Mills and Charles Boon created Mills & Boon in 1908 the company published novels of all sorts, including fiction by P.G. Woodhouse and Gaston Leroux's *Phantom of the Opera*. But by the 1930s, romance had become the preferred genre and Mills & Boon is now the biggest publisher of romance novels in the UK: they sell 200 million books every year, and the works have been translated into 25 languages.

The books were initially sold as hardbacks through weekly "two-penny libraries." In the 1950s the company brought the titles to a wider market by cutting the price and making them available in newsagents nationwide. Unusually for the book world, each Mills & Boon romance is sold only for a limited time period.

The basic template of a Mills & Boon romance has remained consistent. Loving woman meets seemingly unattainable man, usually within a page or two of the book's opening. They face obstacles. Will they ever find happiness? In the end, love inevitably – and always – wins the day.

These are "stories that capture the timeless adventure of falling in love," in the words of the publisher, but the books have kept track with the times. In the 1970s, true love was forced to navigate its way with the help of condoms and contraception. More recently, Mills & Boon has diversified into five brands, including the "Sensual" series with "hot, sizzling romance."
Rosie Blau

Date 1908

Author More than 1,500 authors have written for Mills & Boon

Nationality UK

Why It's Key The leader in the romance fiction market, Mills & Boon was one of the first companies to brand its products and make cheap books available through newsagents and subscription.

Key Author **Vicente Blasco Ibáñez**
Blood and Sand (Sangre y Arena)

In his youth Vicente Blasco Ibáñez (1867–1928) was imprisoned 30 times for republican politics, which also led him into duels and eventual exile; he died in France a rich man who had enjoyed enormous international popular success. *Blood and Sand (Sangre y arena* [1908]) was the tale of the equally passionate and vigorous romantic and sporting careers of a matador whose transient success in both bloody arenas, along with vivid depiction of aficionados from all walks of life, influenced Hemingway's perceptions of the bullring. Blasco Ibáñez had an eye, trained in early adoration of Balzac and Zola, for the human panorama. His best work was in his earlier, naturalistic novels set in his native Valencia – *Flor de Mayo (The Mayflower* [1895]), a family tragedy which told the lives of Valencian fishermen, and *Arroz y tartana* (1894), which depicted a bourgeois family struggling to show the world a respectable face. He excelled at showing social ambition and its disappointment, in all its bitter

ramifications, and also presented a rich dissection of the customs of many layers of Spanish society, from the luxury and vanity of middle class life to grinding poverty. Internationally his most popular work by far was his novel of World War I and its effect on the strata of European society, *The Four Horsemen of the Apocalypse (Los cuatro jinetes del Apocalipsis* [1916]) which with its anti-German sentiment became an important piece of propaganda, and a bestseller in the U.S. in 1919. On the strength of *Four Horsemen* he became perhaps the most internationally well-known Spanish author of the century. He also wrote novels of adventure, psychological novels, and novels addressing particular social "theses," as well as travel books. Hard to categorize, his short stories are classed among the best works of Spanish realism; he has been seen as the most widely read European novelist of the first decades of the twentieth century.

Lucy Daniel

Date 1908 (publication)

Nationality Spanish

Other Key Works *Cuentos Valencianos (Tales of Valencia* [1896]); *Cañas y barro (Reeds and Mud* [1902]); *La catedral (The Shadow of the Cathedral* [1903])

Why It's Key A hit on the silver screen, the 1921 film of *Four Horsemen* starred Rudolph Valentino; in 1922 Valentino again starred in *Blood and Sand*; other interpretations of the book include Blasco Ibanez's own, as early as 1916.

1890–1909

69

Key Character **Ann Veronica**
Ann Veronica

SPOILER

Ann Veronica is an entirely plausible and sympathetic picture of a young girl who yearns to free herself from her family and face life independently. She is the embodiment of the turn of the century interest in women's rights to education, to work, and to a satisfactory sex life.

Ann is clever enough to be enrolled in a science degree in London, but she is not intellectual. She thinks about her life all the time but is unable to make any progress by rational analysis: when her situation is difficult, she does something wilful and reckless.

Ann runs away from home twice in the novel, once because her father refuses to let her go to a bohemian ball; and then to be with her married boyfriend. She joins a suffragette demonstration and is imprisoned in Holloway while having only a minimal interest in gaining the vote. She accepts money and treats from a rich older man without apparently realizing that he is going to want sex with her.

Ann Veronica therefore acts as real people do, in spurts and jumps, not as characters in a novel manipulated in order to advance the plot.

The book's grounding in reality is doubtless because much of it was drawn from life, it is a roman à clef with many characters recognizable as Fabian Society members or others in public life. Ann is based on Wells' young lover Amber Reeves whom the writer impregnated and who went on from early excitement to a dull married content, as Ann does.

Jad Adams

Date 1909 (publication)

Author H.G. Wells (1866–1946)

Nationality UK

Why It's Key "It attracted attention not only in England and America but abroad. Advanced young people in Sweden, Bulgaria, Russia, and Austria learned to their amazement that there were young people like themselves in England." (Preface to Atlantic edition of *Ann Veronica*)

Key Author
Algernon Charles Swinburne

Algernon Swinburne (1837–1909) was a poet of moral, physical, and spiritual rebellion whose work shocked in its blasphemous yearning for a pre-Christian age of pagan sensuality. He was born into an aristocratic family and was educated at Eton (to which he was asked not to return after too visibly enjoying the floggings) and Balliol, Oxford which he left without a degree. There he made the acquaintance of the pre-Raphaelite artists including Rossetti. In the early 1860s he wrote plays, including a trilogy of dramas about Mary Queen of Scots. His notoriety began with *Poems and Ballads* (1866) with hymns to such idols as Dolores, a flagellatory embodiment of sexual love. Guy de Maupassant called him "the most extravagantly artistic person alive in the world."

Predictably, the work was excoriated by the Victorian middle class, *Punch* called the writer "swine-born"; but Oxford students linked arms and chanted its lyrics in the streets in open defiance of convention.

The evocative and rhythmic verse forms and daring subject matter made a revolutionary break with the righteous verse of the mid-Victorian period and led directly towards the literary experiments of the 1890s.

In 1879 Theodore Watts Dunton took the seriously alcoholic poet to live with him at his home in Putney and weaned him from brandy to wine then beer, thus saving the man from alcoholic demise but sacrificing the poet. Swinburne's best qualities had their drawbacks – his effortless erudition means his writing is often obscure to a modern reader, with its overwhelming accumulation of classical references.
Jad Adams

Date 1909 (death)

Nationality UK

Why It's Key His outspoken sexuality and hedonistic lifestyle make him a precursor of many literary and personal trends in the twentieth century.

Opposite *Algernon Swinburne*

70

Key Event **Italian poet and novelist Marinetti publishes his futurist manifesto**

First published on the front page of French newspaper *Le Figaro*, *The Futurist Manifesto* of the Italian poet Marinetti and his friends marked the first positive leap of aesthetics and sensibility into the technological twentieth century. Casting aside nineteenth-century bourgeois and sentimental traditions, the aggressive, self-liberating Futurist spirit was contemptuous of all that was not fast, automated, and transient. *The Futurist Manifesto* marked a new coalescence of interests between poetry and daily life, and was espoused by musicians and painters as well as writers.

A supremely lyrical document, it bore witness to the reinvention of art out of the arrival of the motorcar and the airplane, the combustion engine and electric light. At the same time, hovering on the brink of Marinetti's latent Fascism, it was linked to a desire to regenerate Italy and worshipped energy, courage, and revolt in a Nietzschean spirit. "Aggressive action… the

mortal leap, the punch and the slap" were among its unfortunate goals. Marinetti made a harsh, muscular, right-wing romance out of the industrial-technological future, rather than worrying about it as a cause of human misery.

As an artistic movement Futurism stimulated avant-garde movements like Constructivism in Russia, Vorticism in England, and its noisy self-publicizing inspired the Dadaists; in poetry it was far less profound than what sprang out of it in Russia. However in its innocent aspect its massive influence on modern lifestyle continues to be evident in everything from décor to food to typefaces. Influenced by early film, Marinetti's own futurist scenarios belonged to a world of television and advertising that was still yet to come.
Lesley Chamberlain

Date 1909

Title *The Futurist Manifesto*

Original Title *Manifeste de Futurisme*

Author Filippo Tommaso Marinetti (1876–1944)

Nationality Italy

Why It's Key The Futurist movement to which Marinetti gave wing with a series of innovative manifestos before World War I helped determine the aesthetic ambitions and visual impact of the twentieth century.

Key Event **Lagerlöf – the first woman to win the Nobel Prize for Literature**

When Selma Lagerlöf was awarded the 1909 Nobel Prize in literature "in appreciation of the lofty idealism, vivid imagination and spiritual perception that characterize her writings," the only other female Nobel Laureates at the time were Marie Curie and Baroness Bertha von Suttner, winning the Physics and Peace Prizes respectively. At a time when interest in the status of women and stories of protest and suffrage had lulled, this was a symbolic and powerful gesture by an internationally esteemed body.

Lagerlöf included in her stories a rich vein of fantasy that has led many to regard her as a writer mainly of children's books. Nevertheless, her eschewing of the dominant realist tendency in literature made her achievement all the more remarkable. *The Wonderful Adventures of Nils Holgersson* was originally commissioned by the Primary School Board as an aid to teaching Swedish geography. Despite its somewhat utilitarian genesis, the book has been acclaimed by many esteemed authors and critics, including the 1994 Nobel Laureate, Japanese novelist Kenzaburo Oe, who, upon visiting Stockholm, cited it as a favorite of his youth. The philosopher, Karl Popper, said, "For many, many years I reread this book at least once a year and in the course of time probably read everything by Selma Lagerlöf more than once." Lagerlöf is to this day highly regarded as an author of romantic, imaginative stories about the peasants of rural Sweden, though her popularity has waned, undeservedly, in English-speaking countries.

Christian Kerr

Date 1909

Author Selma Lagerlöf (1858–1940)

Nationality Sweden

Why It's Key Selma Lagerlöf was the first woman to win the Nobel Prize in Literature.

Key Character **Martin Eden**
Martin Eden

Martin Eden is a sailor who through hard grind and determination powers himself into becoming an astonishingly successful writer. The novel was, however, London's anti-success story, as all Martin's hard work and struggle leads only to the conclusion that success ain't what it's cracked up to be.

There are several autobiographical elements; Martin has huge literary success, as London himself did with *White Fang* and *The Call of the Wild*, as a young man. Martin is inspired to write to make himself worthy of his bourgeois sweetheart, who looks on his rough sailor's exterior with disdain; London's first love was a woman from a middle-class family, and he too was intently preoccupied with bettering himself. Martin loves Ruth not just for herself but for what she represents, and tries to shed the class from which he comes to move into hers.

London was a socialist, and in *Martin Eden* he tried to impose a political message. He interrogates the idea of fierce individualism and finds it lacking. In the book, Martin is disillusioned with the world he conquers; its choking conformism; its arid, false intellectualism; the shallowness of the accolades it bestows. In the book, Martin commits suicide by drowning himself when he realizes these things.

Yet the book, and in particular the character of Martin, has come to be seen as inspirational. Initially a critical failure, *Martin Eden* was a slow-burning success. It could be called the archetypal American Künstlerroman of the period: the story of the artist's rise. Martin Eden and Jack London have become bound into one image of the toiling writer who succeeds through his own pure will; they have somehow managed to confound their own disillusionment, and disprove their own most determined and noblest intentions.

Lucy Daniel

Date 1909

Author Jack London (1876–1916)

Nationality USA

Why It's Key Martin Eden, the hero of London's autobiographical novel, is a poor sailor who tries to become a member of the middle class through education, so he can be worthy of his bourgeois sweetheart. He ends tragically, but was nevertheless taken by many as an inspirational image of self-improvement and upward mobility.

Key Passage
Three Lives

"From the time that Melanctha was twelve until she was sixteen she wandered, always seeking but never more than very dimly seeing wisdom. All this time Melanctha went on with her school learning: she went to school rather longer than do most of the coloured children. Melanctha's wanderings after wisdom she always had to do in secret and by snatches… "

Three Lives contains a triptych of stories about working class American women. The first and last stories describe the lives of immigrant German servants. The long, central story tells the story of Melanctha, a "mulatta." Its style marks a transition from fairly conventional prose to the highly experimental texts of Stein's mature writing. "Melanctha" reworks an early work, *Q.E.D.* (1903) – a novel about a lesbian triangle – transforming it into the story of Melanctha's various, inconclusive friendships, romances, and affairs.

In its use of repetition, disruptions of conventional diction and syntax, and fluid use of the continuous present, "Melanctha" was radically innovative. These qualities make the narration indeterminate in places. Yet at the same time it does have a developing plot, as the reader follows Melanctha through stages of her erotic and personal life. Stein also repeats key words and phrases, in a technique she named "insistence," the effect of which is to build up strong sexual innuendo using the most innocuous words. This passage introduces the notion of "wandering" after "wisdom," something that Melanctha does throughout her life.

Richard Wright said that when he read "Melanctha" he "began to hear the speech of [his] grandmother, who spoke a deep, pure Negro dialect." The African American poet Claude McKay disagreed: "I found nothing striking and informative about Negro life. Melanctha, the mulatress, might have been a Jewess."
Helen May Dennis

Date 1909

Author Gertrude Stein (1874–1946)

Nationality USA

Why It's Key Like the artist Picasso, Stein sought to create portraits of people that focused on what is seen, not what is assumed or remembered. "Melanctha" was influenced by Stein's time spent as a medical student working in the "Negro" district of Baltimore.

1890–1909

73

Key Author
Futabatei Shimei

Though crucial to Japan's literary history, Futabatei Shimei's (1864–1909) career as a novelist was but one element in a short but strenuous life, spanning the era of huge social turmoil from the Meiji Restoration of 1868 to the Russo-Japanese War (1904–1905). An outstanding Meiji intellectual, Futabatei had the highest social concerns, and was deeply opposed to the war with Russia, attempting to mediate between the two countries after the conflict, and finally dying of pneumonia while returning to Japan from St Petersburg. His exceptional talent for foreign languages, especially Russian, led to roles as official interpreter for the Japanese government and correspondent for the *Asahi Shimbun* newspaper in St Petersburg, but also lay behind his great contribution to Japanese literature.

In the late 1800s, the highly conventional and inflexible forms of written Japanese made for hard reading, even incomprehension; but *The Drifting Clouds* (*Ukigumo*), under the influence of the Russian novel, brought an epoch-making clarity to Japanese prose. Futabatei's work was sophisticated but colloquial, literary but eminently readable. *The Drifting Clouds* is regarded as the very first attempt at literary realism in Japan, seminal in its objective representation of the ordinary citizen.

This pivotal achievement behind him by the age of 23, he gave up writing fiction temporarily to become one of the greatest translators of the Russian novel, his versions of Turgenev, Andreyev, Gogol, Gorky, and Belinsky having as influential an effect upon Japanese fiction as his own novels. He is also remembered as the first Japanese to create a guide to Esperanto.
David Taylor and Tomonao Yoshida

Date 1909 (death)

Nationality Japan

Key Works *The Drifting Clouds* (1887), *A Remembered Face* (1906), *The Mediocrity* (1907)

Why It's Key Futabatei Shimei's invention of "Genbun-Ichi," a semi-colloquial Japanese style, provided a highly influential prototype for modern fiction.

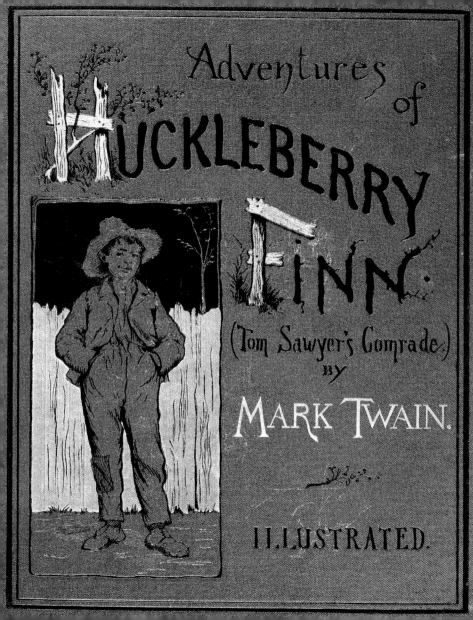

Key Author
Leo Tolstoy

Count Lev Nikolayevich Tolstoy (1828–1910) has maintained a formidable reputation as a writer of unusually voluminous fiction. *War and Peace*, an epic treatment of the Napoleonic invasion, and *Anna Karenina*, the story of a woman's adultery and eventual suicide, are expansive novels that examine the trenchant political issues of the periods they describe and the nuances of the intimate relationships that unfold within these contexts. Tolstoy's great skill lies in his ability to provide a panoramic representation of the historical moment, accurately reflecting the aspirations and anxieties of the people. And from this bigger picture of the socio-economic conditions, he is able to zoom in, bringing the realities of personal relationships sharply into focus. In this effortless modulation, he explores the determining social and ideological forces that shape history. Like his famous countryman, Karl Marx, he believed that individual consciousness was determined by wider social conditions, rather than the other way around. Tolstoy ascribed an altogether more providential explanation for this, however, and clearly believed that the lives of individuals are always subordinate to the inexorable progression of an overarching "history."

Tolstoy's works have been hugely influential in the development of the modern European novel. Passages from *Anna Karenina*, which portray Anna's increasingly troubled mind, deploy something akin to a "stream of consciousness," a narrative technique associated with modernist fiction. Indeed, in many ways he anticipated significant aspects of the modernist novel.

Quite apart from this, Tolstoy influenced his contemporaries and many of the subsequent greats of Russian literature. In addition, his lesser-known later works inspired by his Christian belief in non-violence impacted upon key twentieth-century thinkers as diverse as Wittgenstein and Gandhi.

Juliet Wightman

Date 1910 (death)

Nationality Russia

Key Works *War and Peace* (1863-9), *Anna Karenina* (1873-7)

Why It's Key Lauded as the author of two of the greatest European novels, Tolstoy is a writer of unrivalled perspicuity. The unprecedented scope, historical complexity, philosophical integrity, and structural sophistication of his work demonstrated exactly what the form was capable of.

1910–1919

Key Author
Mark Twain

When it comes to dying, there are those who go with a whimper and those who go with a bang. Mark Twain (1835–1910) wanted to go with a comet. In 1909, he was quoted as saying: "I came in with Halley's Comet in 1835. It is coming again next year, and I expect to go out with it. It will be the greatest disappointment of my life if I don't go out with Halley's Comet. The Almighty has said, no doubt: 'Now here are these two unaccountable freaks; they came in together, they must go out together.'" And go out together they did, when Mark Twain died on April 21, 1910.

Dubbed "the father of American literature" by William Faulkner, Mark Twain authored the picaresque *Adventures of Huckleberry Finn*, a raft-riding race down the Mississippi that retains its status as one of the Great American Novels. One of the first American novels to be written in the vernacular and to be narrated by a child, the book follows young Huck and a runaway slave, Jim, as they flee from the diseased and degenerate "sivilization" of the slave-holding South and steer their raft towards Ohio and freedom.

The book opens with a "Notice," a warning to readers that "Persons attempting to find a motive in this narrative will be prosecuted; persons attempting to find a moral in it will be banished; persons attempting to find a plot in it will be shot." For over a century now, this Polite Notice has been studiously ignored by critics and authors alike, and the various themes that the book explores – the relationship between Man and Nature, illusion versus reality, masculine identity and the possibilities for escape, freedom, and self-fulfilment – would go on to dominate twentieth-century American fiction.

Sarah Wood

Date 1910 (death)

Nationality USA

Key Works *The Adventures of Tom Sawyer* (1876), *The Prince and the Pauper* (1882)

Why It's Key Ernest Hemingway wrote that "all modern American literature comes from one book by Mark Twain called *Huckleberry Finn*… it's the best book we've had. All American writing comes from that. There was nothing before. There has been nothing as good since."

Opposite *Huck Finn* jacket

Key Passage
Howards End

"Only connect!... Only connect the prose and the passion, and both will be exalted… Live in fragments no longer."

*H*owards End, Forster's fourth novel, focuses upon three interconnected families – the rich capitalist Wilcoxes, the liberal middle-class Schlegels, and the working-class Basts – and through them explores ideas of Englishness, class conflict, gender relations, tradition, and the transition to modernity.

The "Only connect" passage in chapter 22 is one of the most famous in all Forster's work. Margaret Schlegel has just agreed to marry Henry Wilcox and, with some reservations about his worldview, attempts to encourage him to develop a wider, more empathetic consideration of things outside his immediate sphere. The novel is based upon a range of seemingly antagonistic oppositions – middle versus working class, materialism versus culture, repression versus spontaneity, pragmatism versus romance, male versus female – and the word "connect" is repeated throughout as a call for greater harmony and the need to heal the fractures inherent in modern life. Indeed, Forster used "Only connect… " as the epigraph to the novel as a whole.

As a search on the internet will show, the phrasing "Only connect" has escaped Forster's novel and entered mainstream language in a variety of contexts, emphasizing the need for greater tolerance and the opportunities to bring seemingly disparate ideas together and to think creatively.

In 1992, *Howards End* was made into a Merchant Ivory film starring Emma Thompson, Anthony Hopkins, and Helena Bonham Carter. More recently, it has inspired Zadie Smith's Orange Prize-winning novel, *On Beauty* (2006).
Simon Avery

Date 1910

Author Edward Morgan Forster (1879–1970)

Nationality UK

Why It's Key Calling for greater tolerance and understanding and the need for opposites to "connect," this novel revived the Condition of England novel, strongly influenced the development of the country house novel, and secured Forster's position as one of the most insightful social and political writers of the early twentieth century.

Key Event
Mexican Revolution

It began with the aim of removing an ageing tyrant from the presidency. It turned into a civil war lasting for seven years, in the course of which over one million people were killed. Official history hails it as the twentieth century's first social revolution.From the embers of the Mexican Revolution a new generation of storytellers came forth. Their emphasis was on social realism. They brought the tools of journalism to bear on their fiction. Each in his own way, they set out to tell the tales that emerged from the greatest debacle the country had known in its independent history.

In *The Underdogs* (1915), published while cannon-fire still rattled the country, Mariano Azuela, a doctor who rode with insurgents in the north, explained how even non-partisan peasants were unwittingly dragged into the fray: "You ask me why I follow the revolution. The revolution is a hurricane, and the man who surrenders to it is no longer a man, but the miserable dry leaf blown about by the gale."

Martín Luis Guzmán invented the Mexican political novel in books like *The Caudillos' Shadow* (1929), a vivid representation of the revolutionary ideals' degradation into opportunistic power-wrangling. Agustín Yáñez's *Al Filo del Agua* offered glimpses of small-town life on the brink of the cataclysm, while Mauricio Magdaleno shed light on how the country's downtrodden classes were poorly served by a revolution carried out in their name. Collectively, they were laying the groundwork for the birth of the modern Mexican novel.
Ángel Gurría-Quintana

Date 1910–1917

Why It's Key Mariano Azuela signaled the beginning of a literary movement with *The Underdogs*' naturalistic representations of the effects of war on the most vulnerable. His successors, including Martín Luis Guzmán, Rafael Muñoz, Agustín Yáñez, Mauricio Magdaleno, Gregorio López y Fuentes, and Francisco Urquizo contributed to both the creation and the erosion of the Mexican Revolution's myths.

Key Author **Ambrose Bierce**
The Devil's Dictionary

He was known as "The Wickedest Man in San Francisco." Some called him "Bitter Bierce." Perhaps he had good reason to be. He witnessed two of the bloodiest episodes of the American Civil War, lost two sons (suicide and pneumonia), and was cuckolded by his wife. His business ventures (he tried managing a mine) failed. Hardly surprising that his *Devil's Dictionary* (1911) defines a year as "A period of three hundred and sixty-five disappointments."

Born in Meigs County, Ohio, Ambrose Bierce's, (1842 –1914) first contact with journalism occurred when, at the age of fifteen, he began working for an abolitionist newspaper. When the Civil War broke out in 1862 he joined the Unionists. He took part in the battle of Shiloh (over 23,000 dead) and the battle of Chickamauga (over 16,000 dead). When promotions did not come, he resigned and settled in the City by the Bay. There began his career as journalist, priest-baiting polemicist, scourge of politicians and self-important scribblers.

In the San Francisco journal, *Wasp*, he began publishing the acrid, misanthropic entries for his *Devil's Dictionary* ("Self esteem, n, An erroneous appraisement"). In the pages of William Randolph Hearst's *San Francisco Examiner* he exorcised the ghosts of war through brutally succinct stories that would be collected in *Tales of Soldiers and Civilians* (he did not believe in longer fiction: "Novel, n. A short story padded"). San Francisco's wickedest man was one of the United States' most recognized writers when, in the winter of 1913, he crossed the Mexican border, never to be heard from again.

Ángel Gurría-Quintana

Date 1911 (publication)

Nationality USA

Why It's Key In short stories like "An Occurrence at Owl Creek Bridge" Bierce captured the anxieties of the American Civil War with clarity and directness. In *The Devil's Dictionary*, he defined optimism as "an intellectual disorder, yielding to no treatment but death."

1910-1919

Key Character **The Phantom of the Opera**
The Phantom of the Opera

Beneath the grandeur and extravagance of the Paris Opera House, something dark and sinister has made its home.

In the course of Gaston Leroux's Gothic masterpiece, the figure of the Phantom slowly begins to materialize. At first he seems only to exist as a superstition: someone to blame when events go wrong. The new managers of the Opera House, Monsieurs Richard and Moncharmin, are reluctant, as the reader is, to believe in a ghost. However as developments unfold – missing horses, threatening letters, and the loss of a Diva's singing voice – they are forced to comply with the Phantom's many demands.

The phantom manages to avoid the direct spotlight throughout the tale but his obsession with Christine Daaé, a young chorus girl, provokes him to stage manage proceedings in order to further her musical career.

The Phantom's mask is the chief metaphor of the piece, encompassing the idea of illusion and reality that Leroux centres the book upon. Emphatic evidence of the Opera Ghost's existence is hard to come by; the narrative is strung together from second-hand reports and hearsay. But finally the illusion of the ghost gives way to the reality of Erik, a circus freak with deformed facial features who is nevertheless gifted with a beautiful singing voice and a talent for trickery.

The novel combines a traditional Gothic style with nuances of the detective genre that Leroux favored in his other work, inventing an inimitable hybrid that is both entertaining and, in places, poignant. He creates a prototype thriller, mystery and suspense building to a dramatic conclusion, the reader never quite certain who to believe and how to distinguish reality and illusion.

Thomas Dymond

Date 1911

Author Gaston Leroux (1868–1927)

Nationality France

Original Title *Le Fantôm de L'Opéra*

Why It's Key Perhaps the most remarkable figure of late Gothic literature, *Phantom* has been the focus of many film versions. Andrew Lloyd-Webber's musical version has run for over twenty years in London's West End and has recently opened in a specifically built theater in Las Vegas.

Key Character **Peter Pan**
Peter Pan and Wendy

The archetypical figure of Peter Pan, clad in skeleton-leaves and flashing his eternal milk teeth in a cocky grin, first took flight in J.M. Barrie's 1904 stage play *Peter Pan, or The Boy Who Refused To Grow Up*. In 1911 Barrie turned the play into a novel. Peter and Wendy, whose opening sentence, "All children, except one, grow up," encapsulates both the appeal of Peter Pan and the distinction which isolates him from the world.

As an infant, Peter ran away to live amongst the fairies, returning to find the window barred and another boy asleep in his bed. He absconded to the Never Land, where he rules over the Lost Boys and battles his nemesis, Captain Hook. But Peter's experience has left him with a profound mistrust of adulthood, enabling him to wreak mischief on the adult world without compunction. When he breaks into the Darling family's nursery and entices Wendy and her brothers to fly away, they (and we) are seduced by his enchanting arrogance.

But Barrie's playful tone belies Peter's darkness and complexity. He is scarred by his early rejection, troubled by a shadowy understanding of his loneliness, yet unable to submit to being loved. However, whilst he feels fear, pain, and jealousy, notably when Wendy returns to the real world, his memory is short and he has no sense of time. Gloriously unfettered by nostalgia, guilt, or responsibility, Peter Pan speaks to the adventurous child in all of us, and equally to the wistful and compassionate adult.

J.M. Barrie was captivated by the character and eventually bequeathed the rights to his story to London's Great Ormond Street Hospital so that, in more senses than one, Peter Pan does indeed live forever.
Amy Rosenthal

Date 1911

Author James Matthew Barrie (1860–1937)

Nationality Scotland

Why It's Key Since his earliest inception, Peter Pan has resonated with adults and children alike. He has featured in countless film, television, and literary adaptations of the story and has become the psychological archetype for the charming, uncommitted man who resists the pressures of adulthood.

Opposite Depiction of Peter Pan with the Darling children

Key Book
Tales of the Uneasy

Violet Hunt's genius was to take the idea that supernatural activity is caused by strong emotion, and fuse the ghost story with the sentimental romance. In fashionable London houses, her frivolous, frilly, flippant women are "daylight people," immune to the world's darkness – until persuaded of it. A flirtatious belle has a guilty conscience over a spurned suitor; in Hunt's world this metaphorical haunting easily shifts into a real one. Or a frustrated young woman finds her lover behaving coldly towards her – could that be because he is a corpse? Admiring herself in the mirror in her new frock, a character is bent double in pain, possessed by her husband's ex-wife (but still vainly watching her own agony in the looking-glass).

The supernatural power entering the heart of this feminine dominion is exquisitely subversive. The other "uneasiness" here is that of unseated emotions, unloosened social strictures, the discomposure of seemingly perfect lives. Grim, definitely impolite, details

intrude; a murdered woman complains, "I was disgracefully cut up. I couldn't possibly have worn a low dress again!" The socially uncomfortable becomes apparent as the supernatural – where the unconventional, as much as the uncanny, is to be feared.

Hunt understands that affairs of the heart (about which she offers useful pointers) transport us to the realms of the unreasonable. Her men are desirable, elusive wraiths, with the power to make a woman "shiver over her chocolate mousse," in both passion and fear. The image of kissing a dead man recurs; Hunt's women are uniformly unsatisfied. "The uneasy" is also a metaphor for nervousness and hysteria. Surreptitiously, these stories contain female morphine addicts and alcoholics, and women who are already deceased. In one story, a male ghost steps up to a recently dead girl and most charmingly introduces himself with the words, "You are the lady we killed, I think?"
Lucy Daniel

Date 1911

Author Violet Hunt (1862–1942)

Nationality UK

Why It's Key The prolific, glamorous Hunt was known for her supernatural tales, her biography of Elizabeth Siddal (1932), and her relationships with Ford Madox Ford, W. Somerset Maugham, and H.G. Wells. She was the model for Florence in Ford's *The Good Soldier* and Nora Nesbit in Maugham's *Of Human Bondage*.

Key Character **Zuleika Dobson**
Zuleika Dobson

Date 1911

Author Max Beerbohm
(1872–1956)

Nationality UK

Zuleika (pronounced zoo-lee-ka) is a devastatingly beautiful girl whose uncle is the Warden of Judas College, Oxford. One summer, she pays a visit to her uncle and wreaks havoc on the undergraduate population of the university. Her looks, and her idiosyncratic charm (she is a conjuror) attract many suitors, but she spurns them all, causing mass suicide among Oxford's young bachelors, including the hapless Duke of Dorset. At the end of the book, Zuleika is seen boarding a train for Cambridge, where, it is supposed, she will have exactly the same effect.

She epitomizes and at the same time undermines the stereotype of the femme fatale, as her impenetrable hauteur and powers of attraction reach comic proportions. Any young man who sets eyes on her is instantly overcome. Eventually, all the undergraduates of Judas throw themselves into the river after the annual "Bumps" races. They cannot endure Zuleika's rejection. But their deaths do not move her, beyond a childish sense of loneliness, and nor do they affect the college dons, who enjoy the peace and quiet of an empty dining hall.

Beerbohm, or, "The Incomparable Max," as his friends liked to call him, married twice, but never had any children. He was equally famous, in his lifetime, for the witty caricatures he drew of friends and colleagues, as for his books. *Zuleika Dobson* is his only novel. But its enduring popularity has assured his reputation, and inspired devotion among generations of readers who enjoy the supreme gracefulness of the writing and the wry humor of the satire on naïve love.

Charles Beckett

Why It's Key *Zuleika Dobson* belongs to a type of frivolous, whimsical storytelling that has as much in common with fairy tale and mythology as it does with social commentary. The story has a kind of delicate and innocent beauty which has hardly been replicated in the novel since.

Key Character **Father Brown**
The Innocence of Father Brown

Date 1911

Author Gilbert Keith Chesterton (1874–1936)

Nationality UK

Introducing the Roman Catholic priest and amateur detective in the short story collection, *The Innocence of Father Brown*, G.K. Chesterton emphasizes the deceptiveness of appearances. His descriptions of the diminutive cleric stress his apparent lack of intellectual penetration: his face is "as round and dull as a Norfolk dumpling"; his eyes "as empty as the North Sea"; he has an air of "moon-calf simplicity." While his ecclesiastical dress and unworldly demeanor certainly serve to put adversaries off their guard, Father Brown is anything but innocent. On the contrary, years of hearing confession have given him a profound understanding of criminal instincts. "Has it never struck you," he asks the master criminal, Flambeau, "that a man who does next to nothing but hear men's real sins is not likely to be wholly unaware of human evil?"

This knowledge does not, however, dampen his predisposition to seek the good in people and he eventually succeeds in reforming Flambeau, threatening him not with a prison sentence, but with eternal damnation. Flambeau turns private detective, and acts as unlikely sidekick to Brown as they investigate a series of thefts and murders.

What distinguishes Father Brown from professional law-enforcers are his methods and priorities: he relies on psychology and intuition rather than the process of elimination and, more radically, is less concerned with prosecution than with the state of criminals' souls, always ready to offer his services as confessor. As Chesterton is unusual in including more philosophy than is common in detective fiction, his creation is unique in giving precedence to eternal, rather than worldly, justice and in regarding solution as incidental to salvation.

David Cross

Why It's Key Gilbert Keith Chesterton is now chiefly remembered for his *Father Brown* stories, of which he would write another four volumes. His priest detective arguably paved the way for later generations of unlikely sleuths with no professional connection to the police force or criminal justice system.

Key Event **Everyman Library publishes *Pinocchio***

The Adventures of Pinocchio was first published in instalments in a children's magazine in 1881. The novel was translated into English for the first time in 1892, but it became widely known after the 1911 Everyman's Library edition. "Once upon a time, there was… 'A king!' My little readers will say right away. No, children, you are wrong. Once upon a time there was a piece of wood": from the opening sentence the reader is made aware of the uniqueness of this story, and its departure from traditional fairy tales. Carved out of a piece of wood by his destitute father Geppetto, the puppet magically comes to life but turns into a very naughty child, particularly given to lying. In the course of the story, Pinocchio, with his mythic hat made out of bread, will be forced to leave the constraints of his small world and undertake a journey of self-discovery into the land of adulthood.

The stages of this journey are both gripping adventures and mythical and symbolic events, as Pinocchio is almost cooked and eaten by the grotesque Fire Eater, cheated by the Fox and the Cat, repeatedly rescued by the Blue Fairy, employed as a guard dog, and swallowed by a big fish.

The frightening metamorphoses, bizarre encounters, and surreal circumstances to which Pinocchio is exposed represent the inevitable steps towards maturity. The finale, in which the underlying goodness of this puppet-turned-child is finally allowed to emerge, communicates a heart-warming feeling while reinforcing the pedagogical implications of the story.
Mariarita Martino

Date 1911 (publication)

Title *The Adventures of Pinocchio* (*Le avventure di Pinocchio*, 1883)

Author Carlo Collodi (1826–1890)

Nationality Italy

Why It's Key The wooden puppet who came alive and whose nose grew when he told a lie has become a fixture of our collective imagination, through the story's countless adaptations in fiction, music, cinema, and television.

Key Character **Fantômas** *Fantômas*

From his first appearance in 1911, Fantômas seized the imagination of readers in France and beyond. The first thirty-two titles in the series appeared at monthly intervals and were eagerly snapped up by devotees who couldn't wait to read about his latest fantastical evil scheme and learn exactly how he would escape justice by a hair's breadth at the end (as he inevitably did). He was a new type of villain, one who gloried in acts of appalling cruelty and killed and maimed innocent people seemingly for no reason other than sociopathic sadism. A typical stunt was to replace the perfume in dispensers in a Paris department store with sulphuric acid. He did, of course, carry out audacious and inventive robberies, for example crashing a bus through the wall of a bank, but he seemed to derive most satisfaction from crimes without any apparent profit to himself, such as releasing a horde of rats infected with plague on board a passenger ship.

The lurid covers of the books were part of their appeal and the image of a masked man in a dinner suit looming in giant size over the skyline of Paris became an iconic image.

Fantômas was popular not only with the public at large but among the avant-garde artists and writers of belle-époque Paris. Among these fans was the poet Apollinaire, who founded a Society of Friends of Fantômas. The character spawned imitators, and many villains of the twentieth century, from comics to James Bond movies, owe a largely unacknowledged debt to his creators.
Michael Munro

Date 1911

Author Marcel Allain (1885–1970) and Pierre Souvestre (1874–1914)

Nationality France

Why It's Key Fantômas is a master criminal and arch-villain who is the protagonist of a series of highly popular and sensationalist crime novels. His sadism, treachery, ruthlessness, and mastery of disguise have become stock characteristics of many villains in comics, novels, films, and television dramas.

Key Book
The Secret Garden

Frances Hodgson Burnett had been a famous author for much of her life when she sat down to write *The Secret Garden* in her later years. The novel tells the story of Mary Lennox, whose parents die in a cholera epidemic in India, causing her to be sent to live with her uncle Archibald Craven in his lonely mansion on the Yorkshire moors. Although left on her own by nearly everyone, she is befriended by the maid, Martha Sowerby, who tells her that ten years earlier Craven locked a garden and threw away the key after his wife's death. Mary finds the garden and brings it back to life with the help of Martha's brother Dickon, and when she discovers Craven's invalid son Colin, the children bring him to the garden too, and he is eventually healed. It is a story of regeneration, hope, and healing.

Although its author was more famous in her lifetime for *Little Lord Fauntleroy*, and for dozens of adult novels and plays, *The Secret Garden*, written when she was 62, endured and eventually became one of the most beloved and influential children's books ever written. The term "the secret garden" has been widely used ever since – even, for example, as a popular name for bookshops and restaurants, and assured Frances Hodgson Burnett's fame for generations to come.

Gretchen Gerzina

Date 1911

Author Frances Hodgson Burnett (1849–1924)

Nationality UK (and USA)

Why It's Key *The Secret Garden* was the first children's book ever published in an adult magazine. Quickly republished as a book, it achieved enormous success and popularity.

Opposite from *The Secret Garden* film adaptation

1910–1919

Key Event "Wring the Neck of the Swan" marks a turning point in Mexican literature

Writing during the convulsed time of the Mexican Revolution (1910-1920), poet Enrique González Martínez is said to have critically revisited the cosmopolitan and sensual imagery that had overflowed poetry in Spanish since the publication of Nicaraguan poet Rubén Darío's influential *Azul* (1888), and *Prosas Profanas* (1896).

The question is still open to debate whether the opening verse from González's sonnet "Wring the Neck of the Swan" ("Tuércele el cuello al cisne") could actually turn or upset an entire literary trend which came to be known as modernism throughout the Spanish-speaking world. In an interview in his later years, González confessed that his intentions were not to attack his admired Darío, but to contribute further to the kinds of aesthetic and spiritual discussions that Darío had invited poets to engage in. In turn, by inviting the initiated poet to suspect the "deceiving plumage" of the swam and to look for the owl's more learned

advice, Gonzalez sought to direct poets towards a less sensual and more philosophical understanding of modernist aesthetics.

His "ars poetica" should also be seen as part of the turn-of-the-century liberal penchant for occultist and revelatory forms of knowledge that would transcend the crass and much reviled tenets of materialistic positivism.

Pedro García-Caro

Date 1911

Author Enrique González Martínez (1871–1952)

Nationality Mexico

Why It's Key The poem was seen as a poetic manifesto against the stylistic excesses of modern poetry – "Wring the neck of the swan with the deceiving plumage," it began provocatively. The sonnet called for a sincere language and form that echoed the cadences and depths of real life.

Key Event **The 11th edition of *The Encyclopaedia Britannica* is published**

The Encyclopaedia Britannica, one of the most notable products of the Scottish Enlightenment, was first published in Edinburgh in 1768–71. Many editions followed, the 10th edition of 1902–3 being sponsored by *The Times*. Cambridge University Press became the publishers of the 11th edition, and most of the work was undertaken in London under the editorship of Hugh Chisholm, although there was also considerable North American input via an editorial office in New York.

Previous editions of Britannica had sought to offer a comprehensive and scholarly presentation of the sum of human knowledge, but by the turn of the twentieth century the pace of scientific development and the expansion of other areas of knowledge had made such an aspiration unattainable. It was also undesirable if the encyclopaedia was to be made more accessible for a wider market, so it was decided to break up the previous massive treatises into many more articles. In the end, the 11th edition had 40,000 articles, compared to the 17,000 of the 10th, although the overall amount of text remained about the same. For the first time, biographies of living persons were also included.

Another innovation was the employment of female contributors, over thirty in all. Also among the contributors were many well-known names, including Edmund Gosse, Algernon Charles Swinburne, T.H. Huxley, G.K. Chesterton, Ernest Rutherford, and Bertrand Russell. Chisholm allowed a degree of subjectivity to his writers, and the 11th edition is particularly celebrated for its literary quality – although its Edwardian-era imperialist world-view is now very much at odds with today's values.
Ian Crofton

Date 1911

Editor Hugh Chisholm (1866–1924)

Nationality UK

Why It's Key Regarded by some as the finest edition of the leading multi-volume encyclopaedia, with contributions from many notable figures.

Key Event **Cicily Isabel Fairfield changes her name to Rebecca West**

Born Cicely Fairfield, the young critic changed her name to Rebecca West in 1911, after a character from an Ibsen play; it was a typical act of self-definition by a woman who was from the start outspoken, humane, fearless, and a brilliant critic.

West has been claimed as a feminist heroine both for her fearsome intellectual independence and for her defiance of convention in her personal life. For years the lover of H.G. Wells, she raised their son Anthony out of wedlock, and it wasn't until 1945 that West found happiness in marriage to banker Henry Andrews. By then she was one of the most celebrated writers in London for her plays, novels, and critical writings; in 1947 she was on the cover of *Time* magazine, hailed as "indisputably the world's No. 1 woman writer." In 1959 she was made a Dame of the British Empire.

Of West's novels, the family saga *The Fountain Overflows* (1957) has proved the most popular, but her reputation now rests more on her non-fiction. Her fascination with guilt and treason gave rise to two enduring works, *The Meaning of Treason* (1947, updated in 1964) as well as *A Train of Powder* (1955), but her indisputable masterpiece is her passionate encounter with Yugoslavia, *Black Lamb and Grey Falcon* (1942). A genre-defying work that encompasses history, travelogue, personal anecdote, and of course politics, the book has the sharp prose and dry humor that characterize all of West's best work, along with an intelligence that is stunningly broad and deep. One of many of West's distinctive judgments delivered in that work: "It is sometimes very hard to tell the difference between history and the smell of a skunk."
Sylvia Brownrigg

Date 1911

Editor Rebecca West (1892–1983)

Nationality UK

Why It's Key A bold, acerbic, highly intelligent writer whose career spanned the range of twentieth-century upheavals, social, and political, West was celebrated for her novels, her works on treason, and her masterwork on Yugoslavia, *Black Lamb and Grey Falcon* (1942).

Opposite Rebecca West

Key Event **Robert Falcon Scott sets off on his doomed polar expedition**

Scott had already led one expedition to the Antarctic when on 24 October 1911 he left his winter base at Cape Evans and headed for the South Pole. Before long Scott found that neither his motor sledges nor his ponies were any use, and he and his team – Wilson, Bowers, Oates, and Evans – continued on skis, hauling their sledges behind them. It took them a total of 81 days to reach the Pole. "Great God!" Scott wrote in his journal, "this is an awful place." Scott's bitterness was justified: when they arrived at the Pole, they found the Norwegian flag flying there, planted by a rival expedition led by Roald Amundsen.

The return journey, eloquently documented by Scott in his journal, turned into a nightmare. They were short of food, and the weather was appalling. Evans was the first to die, then Oates, who, realizing that his frostbitten foot was holding the others up, walked out of the tent into a blizzard, saying, "I am just going outside and may be some time." The remaining three men pressed on, but were confined to their tent when another blizzard struck, only 11 miles from a food depot.

Six months later a search party found their bodies, with Scott's journal, which contained a message to the public: "Had we lived I should have had a tale to tell of the hardihood, endurance and courage of my companions, which would have stirred the heart of every Englishman. These rough notes and our dead bodies must tell the tale."

Scott's journal was published the following year, as *Scott's Last Expedition*, and immediately became a bestseller, embodying as it did the British love of heroic failure.

Ian Crofton

Date 1911

Title *Scott's Last Expedition* (1911–12, published posthumously in 1913)

Author Robert Falcon Scott (1868–1912)

Nationality UK

Why It's Key A moving contribution to the misguided iconography of heroic sacrifice that was to see so much blood spilt in World War I.

Key Event
Thomas Mann takes a trip to Venice

If liberal societies become any more liberal future readers will have difficulty discerning the point of *Death in Venice*, which is premised on the classic inter-relationship of self-denial, social order, and high artistic achievement. The writer Gustav von Aschenbach has based his life and art on the extreme formal discipline which holds bourgeois society together, but in mid-life begins to tire of the effort and simultaneously falls in love with a beautiful, exotic boy in Venice. The same morbid fascination with eroticism, death, and decay, inspired by Mann's reading of Schopenhauer and Nietzsche, pervades this as many of his other works. Aschenbach travels in spirit from the dignified Apollonian ideal of beauty towards the dissolute Bacchic-Dionysian.

Mann's story announced the precarious nature of social order fourteen years before Freud's famous essay *Civilization and its Discontents*. Its chiselled, somewhat overwrought style is replete with leitmotivs and symbols drawn from classical mythology, juxtaposed with the sights and smells of Venice. The heavy sense of foreboding climaxes with an outbreak of cholera.

The novella is also indirectly autobiographical. Mann's struggle to repress his homosexuality was a feature of his posthumously published diaries. The difficulty for the relaxed and cosmopolitan modern reader is to care about the collapse of formal constraints. Perhaps this is best done by regarding all Mann's best work as a worry about the future of a once great European bourgeois artistic tradition, which set beauty, goodness, and truth at the center of its world, without realizing that these values were profoundly unstable.

Lesley Chamberlain

Date 1911

Title *Death in Venice* (1912)

Author Thomas Mann (1875–1955)

Nationality Germany

Why It's Key In "A Sketch of My Life" Mann described how "nothing was invented" in *Death in Venice*. Tadzio, the focus of the writer's infatuation, was based on the future Baron Moes, then aged ten, who in later life remembered being looked at by an "old man" on the beach.

Key Book
Mrs Spring Fragrance

Sui Sin Far is seen as the first Asian American fiction writer of note. Of Chinese and English parentage, she was also the first to explore the "Eurasian" experience in America. She wrote during a trend in American fiction for exoticized Orientalism; Lafcadio Hearn, Rudyard Kipling (then living in the United States), even Willa Cather were at it. Chinatown literature was particularly in vogue. But for the first time in Sui Sin Far's work, Chinese characters, particularly Chinese women and children, took a central role. Seattle and San Francisco were her two main settings. Although the stories she wrote for magazines from the 1890s onwards were very popular during her lifetime, Sui Sin Far later fell into obscurity, so Asian American fiction developed independently of her early groundbreaking work.

In her autobiographical "Leaves from the Mental Portfolio of an Eurasian" (1909) she wrote of a double consciousness stemming from her eastern and western heritage. Her stories are sometimes seen as contributing to a stereotypical view of Chinese America, partly because of their comedy. She was writing for both American and Chinese readers, and even her criticisms of American attitudes had to be couched in terms which appealed to a white readership, to gain publication. But she does discuss racism and the perturbed consciousness of the recent immigrant; in "The Wisdom of the New," a Chinese mother poisons her child rather than see him robbed of his Chinese culture. The character of Mrs Spring Fragrance embodies in her name the fusion of Chinese and American identity. In stories such as "The Americanising of Pau Tsu" and "In the Land of the Free" her trademark irony confronts issues of assimilation, and explores the traditions of a Chinese America that was still being formed.

Lucy Daniel

Date 1912

Author Sui Sin Far (also known as Edith Maude Eaton, 1865–1914)

Nationality Canada/USA (born UK)

Why It's Key *Mrs Spring Fragrance* was Sui Sin Far's only book-length collection of stories. She gave the first literary voice to Chinese Americans, at a time when they were subject to racism. The Chinese Exclusion Act had been passed in 1882, and was only repealed in 1943.

1910–1919

87

Key Author **Saki**
The Unbearable Bassington

According to Penguin's *Saki: The Complete Short Stories*, H.H. Munro found his *nom de plume* in the last stanza of *The Ruba'iyat of Omar Khayam*. A rival hypothesis suggests the source was the saki monkey, quite possibly the same cheeky primate that spreads havoc in the short story, "The Remoulding of Groby Lington." Seemingly "gentle, half-shy, half-trusting," the saki kills a parrot, pelts Miss Wepley with throat lozenges, and plays practical jokes across the county. Tenuous as this explanation is, it has the advantage of being both entertaining and apt. Superficially, Saki's (1870–1916) stories are refined, amusing, and fun. Masterful with one-liners ("The cook was a good cook, as cooks go; and as cooks go she went"), his anecdotal plots proceed like well-told shaggy dog stories and end with twists in the tale. These lead frequently to laughter: discovering "The Secret Sin of Septimus Brope," for instance. Yet, they can also unsettle, as Saki's refined surfaces are disturbed with darker undercurrents: animals hell-bent on destroying humans, emotionally stunted men, women, and children capable of calculation, coldness, and cruelty.

Some aspects of his writing have dated: Saki's world occasionally feels very small, and his depictions of Jews, women, and working class characters leave something to be desired. Other facets, however, feel uncannily fresh: the sharpness of his wit, or "Sredni Vashtar's" emotionally cool mix of the mundane and the macabre.

The effect is akin to P.G. Wodehouse collaborating with the brothers Grimm. In this, Saki's most obvious descendant is Roald Dahl, whose grisly short fiction loves to shock and subvert. Other offspring might include such diverse talents as Jeffrey Archer and Iain Banks, whose *Wasp Factory* owes something to "Sredni Vashtar's" matter-of-fact narration, juvenile sociopath, and nightmarish private religion. Saki's death on the battlefields of France in 1916 robbed Britain of one of its most curious and brilliant writers.

James Kidd

Date 1912 (publication)

Nationality UK

Other Key Works *Reginald* (1904), *The Chronicles of Clovis* (1911), *When William Came* (1914)

Why It's Key One of the finest exponents of the short story, Saki bridges Oscar Wilde's fizzy fin-de-siècle wit and Dorothy Parker's acid pen. Urbane and sardonic, his prose satirizes the hypocrisy and follies of upper crust Edwardian England.

Key Author
August Strindberg

Perhaps it was the long, dark winters and buttoned-up society of Lutheran Sweden that turned Strindberg (1849–1912) into a raving, neurotic, misogynist, deeply pessimistic genius. His father was an impoverished aristocrat who became a shipping agent and married his housekeeper after she had borne him three sons – hence the title of Strindberg's autobiography, *The Son of a Servant*. In this he rants against his miserable upbringing: "Family!… the home of all social evil… a hell for children." Misery continued into young adulthood, when he failed to qualify as either a pastor or a physician, and saw his first significant play, *Master Olof*, rejected by the Royal Theatre.

Strindberg was no more successful as a husband or father: he married and divorced three times, losing custody of all five of his children. Believing himself to be persecuted by women, he also struggled with alcoholism, writer's block, and madness. Yet out of all this turmoil there burst, like pus out of a lanced boil, tense, aggressive dramas such as *The Father* and *Miss Julie*, the latter incorporating all Strindberg's neuroses about women and class. These plays combine naturalistic dialogue with a concentration on pathological states of mind. Strindberg's later plays, such as *A Dream Play* and *Ghost Sonata*, replace realism with phantasmagoria and a search for salvation, although still concentrating on underlying themes of class and gender. Such works had a direct influence on German Expressionism and the later Theatre of the Absurd, as well as on less classifiable playwrights such as Eugene O'Neill, Sean O'Casey, and Luigi Pirandello.

Ian Crofton

Date 1912 (death)

Nationality Sweden

Why It's Key Strindberg was one of the fathers of modern theater.

Key Book
Riders of the Purple Sage

In the opening pages of Zane Grey's 1912 bestseller, *The Solitary Gunmen*, Lassiter, clad in black leather and riding a blind horse, comes riding out of the sage, with the sun at his back, to the aid of the novel's heroine, the Mormon Jane Withersteen. It is the first of several iconic moments in the book that have become staples of the genre that Grey did much to popularize and define. Though he did not invent the popular Western, he was certainly the most widely read practitioner of the form in the early twentieth century, producing nearly sixty novels by the time of his death, all of which were enthusiastically embraced by the reading public.

Riders of the Purple Sage was his first major success, and remains his best-known work. How, then, can we account for the novel's staggering popularity? Grey's writing, though sentimental and largely ahistorical, is often richly evocative of place, and his scenes of horseback pursuit are breathlessly effective. Nor should we overlook certain quirks that make the book distinctive – not least Grey's intense (but vague) distrust of Mormons, portrayed here as villainous, patriarchal gangsters. Its plot of captivity and redemption is highly formulaic and certainly indebted to precursors such as James Fenimore Cooper, but its vision of the transformative power of nature and the American landscape spoke urgently to an increasingly urban, modern audience for whom Grey's mythic West was becoming ever more remote.

Rowland Hughes

Date 1912

Author Zane Grey (1872–1939)

Nationality USA

Why It's Key Hugely influential in shaping the popular Western genre, *Riders of the Purple Sage* was also the book that firmly established Grey as the master of the genre, and one of the most popular authors of the twentieth century.

Opposite *Riders of the Purple Sage*

Key Event **Mallarmé's poem inspires a scandal, and the birth of modern ballet**

Mallarmé's poem, "L'après-midi d'un faune" was a high point of French Symbolist poetry in the nineteenth century. In the twentieth, it became the inspiration for one of the most scandalous and shocking premieres ever staged, and a ground breaking moment in the history of performance.

Mallarmé gave his poem the subtitle *églogue*: a short pastoral poem. In it, a lascivious faun struggles, against the soporific midday sun, to recreate the delicious fun he just had surprising and chasing two nymphs. But is he inventing the whole scenario? He begins: "These nymphs that I would perpetuate: so clear / And light… Did I love a dream?" The mystery remains unsolved.

Claude Debussy, a great admirer of the poet's work, intended to write a three-part composition on it, but only completed the Prelude. He consented reluctantly to Nijinsky making it the score for his first ballet choreography. The dancer was celebrated for his ethereal and virtuosic leaps but chose this opportunity instead to incarnate a creature of the earth and of classical antiquity.

Nijinsky himself danced the role of the faun as a brutal, lustful creature. His abrupt and stylized movements were set against rather than in time with Debussy's more fluid, dreamy music, and worst of all the faun's final gesture clearly mimed triumphant masturbation. The national newspaper *Le Figaro* began a campaign against Nijinsky's ballet, but artists including Auguste Rodin and Odilon Redon rushed to the dancer's defense. *L'après-midi d'un faune* so polarised opinion that it vanished from the repertoire only a couple of years after its premiere, despite its distinguished artistic origins. It was recovered in the 1980s and is now recognized as the first modern ballet.
Sophie Lewis

Date 1912 (Ballet first performed)

Place Paris, France

Performer Choreographer and star dancer Vaslav Nijinsky (1890–1950)

Nationality Russia

Why It's Key This performance so shocked its first audience that its patron-producer Serghei Diaghilev commissioned a repeat performance on the spot – and it was danced through again before anyone could protest.

Opposite Stéphane Mallarmé

Key Character **Mr Pooter** *The Diary of a Nobody*

The middle-aged, suburb-dwelling Charles Pooter – dutiful City clerk and chronically mortified hero of George and Weedon Grossmith's *The Diary of a Nobody* (1892) – might be dubbed the English Quixote. He is quixotic in the distinctive English manner: one in a long and risible line of upwardly-mobile comic fantasists – Mr Collins, Wemmick, and Basil Fawlty are others – whose pompous hankering after bourgeois respectability produces nothing but farce and fiasco. He is also, like the Don, a figure of considerable pathos. The more disastrous his efforts – at cutting a dash in local society, carrying out stylish home improvements, dealing with impertinent tradesmen – the more he elicits our tenderness. We love poor Pooter for his pretentiousness – his railway-abutting residence in unfashionable Holloway is named "The Laurels" – but also for his sweetness and optimism.

Along with Carrie, his put-upon wife, and Lupin, his layabout son, Pooter was the joint invention of the writer-actor George Grossmith (associate of Gilbert and Sullivan) and his brother Weedon. George produced the text; Weedon the Cruikshank-ian – and still very droll – illustrations. After appearing serially in *Punch* to great acclaim, the *Diary* was published in full in 1892. The hapless Pooter became a comic talisman and "Pooterism" a catchword for social climbing of the most inept and amusing sort.

Yet *The Diary of a Nobody* also has its serious aspect. Most important, it marks – with some ambivalence – the unfolding of a new and distinctly modern English type: the anxious, ambitious "self-made" man from the lower-middle classes. Eliot's Prufrock, Forster's Leonard Bast, and Woolf's unpleasant Charles Tansley are all Pooters of a sort; likewise, somewhat later, the more resentful heroes of Waugh, Osborne, Amis, and Pinter.
Terry Castle

Date 1912 (death of George)

Authors George Grossmith (1847–1912), Weedon Grossmith (1852–1919)

Nationality UK

Why It's Key Brothers George and Weedon Grossmith collaborated in the creation of Mr Pooter, which first appeared in *Punch*. Weedon also supplied the illustrations. Hilaire Belloc called Pooter "an immortal achievement."

Key Event **Harriet Monroe founds** *Poetry: A Magazine of Verse*

By introducing readers to new schools of poetry, parameters of American poetry could be extended. Harriet Monroe (1860–1936) established Chicago poet and critic, convinced 108 patrons to invest in this, her vision. Mailing potential subscribers and contributors, telling them, "of a chance to be heard in their own place, without the limitations imposed by a popular magazine,"she assured, "We shall read with special interest poems of modern significance, but the most classic subject will not be declined if it reaches a high standard of quality."

With her innovative approach, *Poetry* quickly became the principal forum for modern poetry of the English-speaking world, showcasing local populists Carl Sandburg, Edgar Lee Masters, and Vachel Lindsay during the Chicago Literary Renaissance and presenting new formalist movements alongside experimental ones. Early work by Wallace Stevens, Marianne Moore, D.H. Lawrence, Robert Frost, and William Carlos Williams appeared in early issues and Ezra Pound, the magazine's foreign correspondent, introduced an unknown and unpublished T.S. Eliot to its pages in 1915.

Believing that poets deserve both public and private support, Monroe's policy was to pay contributors from the offset, and her long-term correspondence with writers documents the thoughts and frustrations of those who would become central to the modernist movement. The magazine's open-door policy extended to the hospitality writers experienced when visiting Chicago.

She was editor for 26 years until her death in 1936. Today the magazine enjoys a rare longevity under The Poetry Foundation – undoubtedly due to the strong principals upon which is was founded.
Elizabeth Whyman

Date October 1912

Place USA

Why It's Key "*Poetry* magazine transformed the way that poetry and poets are recognized and read worldwide, and it continues to flourish as a major cultural influence." (Special Collections Research Center, University of Chicago).

Key Event **Ezra Pound creates a modernist movement**

Three short, elliptical poems published by Hilda Doolittle (known as H.D.) in *Poetry* magazine during 1912 have come to represent a significant moment in the emergence of modernist poetry. Arriving from America in 1911, H.D. met up in London with the American poet Ezra Pound and a young man called Richard Aldington, who she married in 1913. Aldington and H.D. used to meet Pound in a teashop near the British Museum to show him their poems. Pound took a unilateral decision that they had enough in common to become a movement, "Imagism." Arranging to publish their poems in *Poetry*, he added the word "Imagiste" to H.D.'s signature and published a manifesto outlining their beliefs:

1. Direct treatment of the "thing" whether subjective or objective.

2. To use absolutely no word that does not contribute to the presentation.

3. As regarding rhythm: to compose in the sequence of the musical phrase, not in sequence of a metronome.

In practice, this meant short poems with one or two central "images." Imagists favored blank or free verse over conventional rhyme schemes.

Pound also arranged for the publication of an anthology *Des Imagistes* (1914) which also included poems by William Carlos Williams, James Joyce, and Ford Madox Ford. As a movement, Imagism was mostly held together by Pound's say so and energy as a publicist. Yet it was instrumental for poets of the twentieth century in making a decisive and explicit break from the forms and subject matter of the nineteenth century.
Matthew Creasy

Date 1912

Title *Des Imagistes* (1914)

Authors Ezra Pound (1885–1972), Hilda Doolittle (1886–1961)

Nationality USA

Why It's Key Pound's involvement with Imagism did not last long. He took umbrage at the intervention of Amy Lowell, a wealthy American poetess, and distanced himself from Imagism in favor of a new movement, "Vorticism."

Opposite Ezra Pound

Key Book
Le Grand Meaulnes

Once upon a time in a remote corner of la France profonde in a golden age before the slaughter of World War I… that is the setting for *Le Grand Meaulnes*, an elegiac, fictionalized memoir of adolescence by young writer Henri Alban Fouriner, who took the pen name Alain-Fournier, because he shared his real name with an admiral and a racing driver. It was to be his only completed novel, and was based on his own unfulfilled love for a young woman called Yvonne de Quievrecourt. He himself was killed in action on the Meuse in September 1914.

The narrator of the novel is François Seurel, the son of a schoolmaster, a somewhat detached figure whose great friend is an impetuous, compelling boy called Augustin Meaulnes. Meaulnes tells how, playing truant from school, he becomes lost and stumbles across a mysterious and decrepit chateau one summer's night where a party of young people are holding a masquerade. It is as if some *fête galante* of Watteau had come to life in contemporary France. At the party Meaulnes meets and falls in love with a beautiful girl called Yvonne, but the festivities break up in confusion and Meaulnes finds himself once more in the prosaic world of everyday rural life. Meaulnes spends months trying to return to the lost chateau and the girl, but his quest proves in vain. "How can a man," the book asks, "who has once strayed into Heaven ever hope to make terms with the Earth?" And thus we are left with an inconsolable yearning for an irrecoverable world.

Ian Crofton

Date 1913

Title Originally translated into English as *The Lost Domain*, and also as *The Wanderer and The End of Youth*, but the French title is now generally used.

Author Alain-Fournier (1886–1914)

Nationality France

Why It's Key An achingly tender evocation of a lost world of adolescence. In terms of its stature, *Le Grand Meaulnes* is the French equivalent of *The Great Gatsby*.

Key Event **Robert Frost meets and mentors Edward Thomas**

When Robert Frost (1874–1963) and Edward Thomas (1878–1917) met in October 1913 both were writers in their late thirties, though neither had achieved the recognition they craved; both were family men who suffered bouts of depression.

In the Spring of 1914 Frost brought his family to England to establish himself as a poet, settling in the Gloucestershire village of Dymock. When Thomas, a critic and literary journalist, and his family moved into the neighboring house, the friendship blossomed, strengthened by long walks in the countryside together. Frost later referred to 1914 as "our year," writing, "We were together to the exclusion of every other person and interest."

Thomas helped Frost gain recognition in Britain and, with Frost's encouragement, began to write poetry in December 1914. Frost found a publisher for Thomas' poems when he returned to America, selling some to the esteemed *Poetry* magazine. Thomas' first collection was published in 1916 under the pseudonym Edward Eastaway. In *New Bearings in English Poetry* (1932) F.R. Leavis wrote, "He was exquisitely sincere and sensitive and he succeeded in expressing in poetry a representative modern sensibility."

After deliberating on whether to live near Frost in America or join the army, Thomas enlisted, aged 37. On April 9, 1917, the first day of the Battle of Arras, he was killed by a shell blast. Frost grieved deeply, later writing, "Edward Thomas was the only brother I ever had." Thomas, like Frost, would later be esteemed as one of the most influential poets of the twentieth century.

Elizabeth Whyman

Date 1913

Why It's Key The brief, intense friendship between two likeminded, virtually unknown poets led to the recognition of both as two of the most influential writers of the twentieth century.

Key Character **Eliza Doolittle**
Pygmalion

Phonetician Professor Higgins makes a bet with a friend that he can transform a cockney flower girl into a well-spoken lady who could pass for a Duchess. However, in Shaw's feisty heroine, Eliza Doolittle, he gets rather more than he expects.

Eliza rises admirably to the challenge, picking up the necessary standard speech and social niceties with ease. Along the way she begins to realize that Higgins sees her as a component in a social experiment rather than a fellow human being: "How the devil do I know what's to become of you? What does it matter what becomes of you?" (Higgins to Eliza, Act Four). Eliza strikes a blow for female independence by rebelling against the values of the man who has allegedly rescued her and choosing her own path in both life and love. Her direct and open nature highlights the artificiality and pretence on which the other characters' class distinctions are based. Eliza's telling observations about her new life as a "Lady" emphasize both the value of her old life and the unequal position of women in society: "I sold flowers. I didn't sell myself. Now you've made a Lady of me I'm not fit to sell anything else."

By the end of the play there is a strong sense that she has taught her "social betters" much more than they have ever taught her. Shaw disparaged any suggestion of a romantic connection between Higgins and Eliza by writing an epilogue which confirmed her decisive choice of an alternative husband.
Kate Harris

Date 1913

Author George Bernard Shaw (1856–1950)

Nationality Ireland

Why It's Key The part of Eliza Doolittle was specifically written for the famous actress Mrs. Patrick Campbell who was then in middle age and considered by many critics to be too old for the part. Today the character of Eliza enjoys worldwide fame as the rather more traditional romantic heroine of the musical *My Fair Lady* which is based on Shaw's play.

1910–1919

95

Key Character **Chandrakanta**
Chandrakanta

Devaki Nandan Khatri assured his place in literary history by writing what has become known as the first modern novel in the Hindi language. He was a historian who while researching the fort of Chunar (in the novel *Chunargarh*) was inspired to envelop it in his own version of fantastical events that might have taken place there. The result was *Chandrakanta*, the magical romance between prince Virendra Singh and the very beautiful neighboring princess, the eponymous Chandrakanta.

The novel was phenomenally successful. The story goes that thousands of people learned Hindi just so they could read it. As each chapter was released, huge crowds gathered outside the press, and the latest instalment was sold to the highest bidder. And no wonder it caused such a stir: *Chandrakanta* is a melee of magic and intrigue, with new twists in the story at every turn of the page, and a strong element of miraculousness. The scheming rival for Chandrakanta's love employs two ace detectives to intervene on his behalf. Their ability to change their faces is a major new weapon in the fictional spy's artillery, and leads to all manner of escapades and convoluted switching of identities among mountain hideouts and royal palaces, at the center of which is treasure hidden in a magical maze. Chandrakanta, with her dynamic troupe of maidservants, carries a dagger and thinks nothing of felling an enemy in the cause of true love. Kidnap and plotting, rescues and beheadings, enchantment and various other antics, as well as romantic adventures, keep the novel packed with incident, with seemingly inexhaustible cunning and invention.

Devaki Nandan Khatri's work was part of a mythologizing of India's past and a focus on magic and romance that became the staple theme of much Hindi fiction in his wake, until the groundbreaking realism brought to Hindi literature by Premchand in the 1920s.
Lucy Daniel

Date 1913 (death)

Author Devaki Nandan Khatri (1861-1913)

Nationality India

Title *Chandrakanta* (1888–1891)

Why It's Key Devaki Nandan Khatri, phenomenally successful author of the first Hindi novel, followed up the success of *Chandrakanta* with *Chandrakanta Santati*, a much longer and more ambitious sequel.

Key Passage
O Pioneers!

"When the road began to climb the first long swells of the Divide, Alexandra hummed an old Swedish hymn, and Emil wondered why his sister looked so happy. Her face was so radiant that he felt shy about asking her. For the first time, perhaps, since that land emerged from the waters of geologic ages, a human face was set toward it with love and yearning. It seemed beautiful to her, rich and strong and glorious. Her eyes drank in the breadth of it, until her tears blinded her. Then the Genius of the Divide, the great, free spirit which breathes across it, must have bent lower than it ever bent to a human will before. The history of every county begins in the heart of a man or a woman."

O Pioneers! was the first novel in which Willa Cather felt she had "walked off on my own feet" – a phrase which characteristically brings together the kind of independence equally necessary for artists and other cultural pioneers. The passage reproduced here catches something of the grandeur and depth with which she invests the history of American settlement. It leaves out some of the other, darker notes which complicate and enrich the novel. The story does not stint on the harshness and austerity – and sometimes the meanness – of life in late nineteenth-century Nebraska. And it is shadowed by the elegiac structure intrinsic to narratives of American progress: the virtues of the pioneers – their enterprise, courage, independence – are the very qualities that are no longer needed once the economic progress they enable has arrived.

O Pioneers! represents this elegiac strain in its tragic story of doomed young lovers: their romance is a casualty of this period of American life. Like Whitman, from whom she borrows her title, Cather implies that the vigor of American democracy often came from racial and sexual outsiders.

Peter Swaab

Date 1913

Author Willa Cather (1873–1947)

Nationality USA

Why It's Key *O Pioneers!* was Cather's first important novel, a work that celebrates the frontier spirit that was central to American identity.

Key Author
Rabindranath Tagore

When the Bengali poet Rabindranath Tagore won the Nobel Prize for literature in 1913 he was the first non-European to do so. It was a recognition of this mystic poet's influence in introducing Indian culture to the West. He also introduced western culture to Bengali literature; his first major collection, *The Ideal One* (*Manasi*) uses western verse forms. It contains his first political verse, presaging the passionate struggle for Indian independence in which Tagore was involved.

His work managing his father's estates brought him close to the poor about whose "humble lives and their small mysteries" he wrote short stories, thus making village folk the center of literature. Similarly, his friend Gandhi was to elevate the poor in Indian political life.

His poetry about human tragedies such as the death of his wife, of a son, and a daughter appealed internationally, to common humanity. His mystical collection of poems, *Song Offerings* (*Gitanjali*) won him the Nobel Prize and he was later awarded a knighthood, though he retuned it as an anti-imperialist gesture after the Amritsar Massacre. Lyrics from his poems became the national anthems both of India and of Bangladesh.

Tagore's influence spread through his lecture tours of Europe, the Americas, and Asia; and through his educational reforms. He founded a school that later became a university, aiming to blend the best of western and Indian traditions. Towards the end of his life a reaction against the adulation he had previously enjoyed led to a critical backlash, but his position as a figurehead of Indian literature is secure.

Jad Adams

Date 1913 (Nobel Prize awarded)

Author Rabindranath Tagore (1861–1941)

Nationality India

Other Key Works Stories *Gulpa Guccha* (*Bunches of Tales*, 1912) **Plays** *Raja* (*The King of the Dark Chamber*, 1910)

Why It's Key Tagore's work in translation has been influential throughout the world, particularly in Spanish literature.

Opposite Rabindranath Tagore

Key Passage *Swann's Way* (*Du Côté de Chez Swann*)

"No sooner had the warm liquid, and the crumbs with it, touched my palate than a shudder ran through my whole body, and I stopped, intent upon the extraordinary changes that were taking place. An exquisite pleasure had invaded my senses, but individual, detached, with no suggestion of its origin. And at once the vicissitudes of life had become indifferent to me, its disasters innocuous, its brevity illusory – this new sensation having had on me the effect which love has of filling me with a precious essence; or rather this essence was not in me, it was myself. I had ceased now to feel mediocre, accidental, mortal."

This passage from "Swann's Way," the first volume of *Remembrance of Things Past* (*A la Recherche du Temps Perdu*) describes how "Marcel," the narrator of Marcel Proust's epic novel, feels upon drinking a mouthful of herbal tea mixed with crumbs of "madeleine" – a small buttered cake. The sensation takes him back to the period in his childhood when he would serve his great aunt with the same tea and madeleine. This experience is the origin of his theory of "involuntary memory." Put simply, conscious memory is a poor tool for accessing the past. The only way to regain time is through such unforeseen moments of sensory evocation. Proust's lengthy novel is dedicated to recreating this process and exploring the implications for art. "Marcel" is an aspiring artist and the novel traces his life, loves, and acquaintance over the course of several decades, until he recognizes "involuntary memory." This achievement allows him to begin the book that will become *A la Recherche*.

Matthew Creasy

Date 1913

Title *Remembrance of Things Past* (1913–27)

Author Marcel Proust (1871–1922)

Nationality France

Why It's Key Proust published *Swann's Way* at his own expense after André Gide turned it down without reading it because he thought Proust was just a snob. Gide later relented and the book became famous and influential across the English-speaking world as well as in France.

Key Character **Pollyanna** *Pollyanna*

Like Judy Garland as Dorothy in *The Wizard of Oz* or Audrey Hepburn as Holly Golightly in *Breakfast at Tiffany's*, Hayley Mills' portrayal of Pollyanna in the 1960 movie *Pollyanna* has forever tied that actress to that personality, obscuring the literary roots of the character. Written in 1913 by Eleanor H. Porter, the children's novel told of a young girl named Pollyanna Whittier whose father dies. She is reluctantly adopted by her wealthy aunt, Miss Polly Harrington, but her breathless charm and trademark optimism lift the spirits of everyone who encounters her. She charms the whole town, manages to make a sick woman feel pretty, and brings out the sunny side of even the old rich town grump John Pendleton.

Even her illness and the specter of never walking again didn't get Pollyanna down: she kept playing the Glad Game (later a board game made by Parker Brothers from 1915–1967 in an early attempt at cross-marketing) and eventually got back on her feet. Her adventures continued in succeeding volumes, published by Elizabeth Borton.

But while the books contained not a trace of sarcasm or critique of her jubilant attitude, a backlash was inevitable. Take, for example, this passage, where Pollyanna gives a representative point of view on the human race: "'Oh, no, I don't mind it at all,' she explained to Nancy. 'I'm happy just to walk around and see the streets and the houses and watch the people. I just love people. Don't you, Nancy?'"

Guileless, full of cheer, able to conquer fear and prejudice with a dash of hope and a big smile – it's enough saccharine to make one gag. To call someone a "Pollyanna" is a veiled insult. But Pollyanna was onto that. She was an orphan, she suffered polio. She knew how the world works. She just chose another reality and brought several generations of children and adults with her.

Reyhan Harmanci

Date 1913

Author Eleanor H. Porter (1868–1920)

Nationality USA

Why It's Key While calling someone a "Pollyanna" these days is a borderline pejorative, only the coldest of hearts can resist the preternaturally positive heroine of the 1913 book. In the original novel, Pollyanna charmed a town and successfully fought polio; now she represents naive hope in the face of adversity.

Opposite *Pollyanna*

Key Author **D.H. Lawrence**
Sons and Lovers

The son of a Nottingham coal miner, much of Lawrence's early work, notably *Sons and Lovers* was influenced by his intense love for his mother and the conflict between her genteel aspirations and his father's working class conservatism. His work showed an earthy realism, the vibrant presence of a newly educated working class. Through Lawrence this class was able to show to the finely tuned literati that emotional turmoil and moral challenge were not merely the preserve of the better off, but were the common heritage of humanity.

His marriage to Freida (daughter of Baron von Richtofen) coincided with his greatest success as a novelist and with his exploration of sexual themes. A major novel, *The Rainbow* (1915) was condemned as obscene and all copies confiscated. Another book which developed the same characters, *Women in Love*, did not find a publisher until 1921 with some changes dictated by censorship. Lawrence also wrote plays,

essays and several volumes of short stories that are highly regarded.

In 1919 the couple left England, where Lawrence had been persecuted for being anti-war and Freida as a German. His last great work, *Lady Chatterley's Lover*, was first published in Florence in 1928 but not in England (in an unexpurgated version) until 1961. Just as shocking as its sexually explicit descriptions was the portrayal of a relationship between a working class man and an aristocrat. In place of class, Lawrence postulated an aristocracy of feeling which transcended other categories. After living in Italy, Ceylon, Australia, and Mexico, Lawrence returned to Europe, finally dying in France of tuberculosis at the age of 44.
Jad Adams

Date 1913

Author David Herbert Lawrence (1885–1930)

Nationality UK

Why It's Key Though born in the Victorian and growing up in the Edwardian period, Lawrence's concentration on sex and relationships made him a fiercely modern writer, who pushed the boundaries of fiction to the limit and beyond.

Key Event
Ambrose Bierce vanishes

There are conflicting reports regarding the mysterious disappearance of one of the United States' most notorious journalists and writers. In May of 1913, the author of *The Devil's Dictionary* had written to a friend: "I mean to go into Mexico – where, thank God, something is doing." That "something" was the Mexican Revolution, which had been raging for almost three years. Bierce (1842–1914?), a veteran of the United States' own civil war, had seen his share of combat. Was he now, at 71, hoping that his once glittering journalistic career might be rekindled by bearing witness to new conflicts?

In autumn he toured the battlefields where he served in his youth, and then – so it is believed – crossed into Mexico at El Paso. He is presumed to have joined the troops of Pancho Villa, the outlaw-turned-revolutionary general, and to have died during Villa's attack on the town of Ojinaga. His last known letter, dated December 1913 and addressed to his secretary,

is thought to have been posted from the Mexican city of Chihuahua: "If you hear of my being stood up against a Mexican stone wall and shot to rags please know that I think it a pretty good way to depart this life. It beats old age, disease, or falling down the cellar stairs. To be a Gringo in Mexico – ah, that is euthanasia!"

In *Old Gringo* (1985), Mexican novelist Carlos Fuentes fictionalizes the infamous curmudgeon's final fate: a washed out man, more romantic than cynical, waiting for death at the hands of a Mexican bullet.
Ángel Gurría-Quintana

Date 1913

Place USA

Why It's Key Despite federal agents' efforts to track him down at the time, the vanishing of the famously acid-tongued writer is still unsolved. Today there are (at least) two gravesites, one on either side of the United States – Mexico border, allegedly containing his remains.

Key Event *Zeinab* is acclaimed as the first fully-fledged novel in Arabic literature

Since its publication in episodes in *Al-Liwaa*,' the literary supplement of a daily nationalist newspaper, *Zeinab* has withstood many attempts to depose it from its throne as the first Arabic novel.

Set in a village in the Egyptian countryside, dealing with contemporary issues, Zeinab put its readers in touch with their hopes, dreams, and expectations in an unprecedented way. The novel engaged critics in myriad debates about a nascent sense of a unified national dream, and heralded an ever growing sense of national identity set against the background of an ailing feudal monarchy, the presence of a colonial power, and the rapid growth of an educated population that could read and write.

The novel signalled a change in poetic sensibility amongst its Arab readers who started to develop a taste for "real" heroes, in "real" settings and the artistic joys of a style distinct from the decorum of poetic verse or mediaeval rhymed narrative. The novel crystallized issues of gender inequality, social injustice, and economic deprivation and presented them in a new art form alien to the canon of traditional Arabic Literature where the *Qasidah*, the folktale, the *Maqamah* were the dominant genres. This novel was a clean break from the romantic and heroic traditions that dominated Arabic literature since its inception.

Zeinab also became Egypt's first silent narrative film in 1925. The eponymous heroine became the archetypal female protagonist in Egyptian and Arab cinema for decades. Her tragic depiction broached issues of gender inequality in Egyptian and wider Arab society, and heralded the beginning of women's emancipation movement with leading figures such as Qasim Amin and Huda Sha'rawi. The many similarities between Haykal's Zeinab and Hardy's Tess make this a pivotal intersection between the Arabic novel and its western forebears.

Ashraf Eissa

Date 1914 (serialized)

Publication Egypt

Written c. 1911 (Paris)

Author Muhammad Husayn Haykal (1888–1956)

Nationality Egypt

Why It's Key *Zeinab* heralded the emergence of a new readership with modernist sensibilities and a shift from romance to realism in narrative discourse. It also affirmed national identity based on the nation-state and influenced Arabic cinema.

1910-1919

101

Key Character **Stephen Dedalus**
A Portrait of the Artist as a Young Man

It took James Joyce at least two attempts to get the mixture of pathos and arrogance in Stephen Dedalus just right. Perhaps this was because the life of this character was modelled upon his own. Like Joyce, Stephen is born into a privileged middle-class Dublin family, but soon experiences a descent into poverty. He excels at school and considers becoming a priest, before rejecting a religious vocation for the life of an artist. Stephen is sexually precocious too and in one chapter visits a prostitute for sex while still young. Frightened by a sermon on hellfire, his feelings of guilt lead him towards intense Catholic piety. Thus, Stephen's life is one of extremes. When he finally chooses to become an artist, there are hints he may not succeed.

Joyce began his novel as an essay on biography in 1904 and then worked on a first version called *Stephen Hero* until 1907, when he began drafting the novel as we know it. This second, published draft is much more experimental and innovative in form. It begins with Stephen's babytalk as a young child and ends with scraps of his diary. Joyce also cut explicit reference to the idea of "epiphany" from this second draft. Stephen explains that art should capture "delicate and evanescent" moments which crystallize a sudden truth or flash of self-awareness. The theory is still relevant to his experience in the published novel, but its omission may contribute to uncertainty about Stephen's chances of success.

Matthew Creasy

Date 1914

Author James Joyce (1882–1941)

Nationality Ireland

Why It's Key Novelist H.G. Wells felt that *Portrait* was too fixated upon the sordid details of Stephen's experiences. He accused Joyce of having a "cloacal obsession" with the seedy side of life. Although many readers still find the hellfire sermon impressive, Joyce himself joked about it and turned it into a limerick in a letter to Ezra Pound.

Key Passage
"The Soldier"

"If I should die, think only this of me:
That there's some corner of a foreign field
That is for ever England."

Rupert Brooke, physically beautiful and personally charming, was the golden boy of the Georgian poets, adored by the Bloomsbury set as much for himself as for his poetry. Like virtually everybody else in Britain, he had no doubts about the justice of his country's cause when war broke out in August 1914, and shortly after penned a series of war sonnets, including "The Soldier."

The opening lines, quoted above, give the theme of the sonnet – that wherever in the world an English soldier dies will be transfigured by the values of dear old England, its flowers, its air, its rivers, its sun. The tone is elegiac, eagerly embracing the prospect of a hero's death. There is no argument in the poem, no complexity – and absolutely no comprehension of the actual realities of war or any questioning of its righteousness.

Brooke did not live long enough to have second thoughts. On his way to serve in the Dardanelles in 1915 he died of blood poisoning after being bitten by a mosquito. He was indeed buried in the corner of a foreign field, on the Greek island of Skyros. It was left to other young men – to Edward Thomas, Isaac Rosenberg, Siegfried Sassoon, Wilfred Owen – to experience the hell of war at first hand, and to transform it into a poetry more authentic than Brooke's febrile fantasy.

Ian Crofton

Date 1914 (written)

Published *New Numbers* (1915)

Author Rupert Brooke (1887–1915)

Nationality UK

Why It's Key A poem whose fevered patriotism and glorification of sacrifice inspired many young men as they went to their doom on the Western Front.

Key Event **Wyndham Lewis launches**
BLAST, the magazine of Vorticism

The periodical *BLAST* had a brief, violent, punky life. There were only two issues, the first published at the start of June 1914, just before the outbreak of war, the second a year later. They were edited by Wyndham Lewis, the novelist and painter, and the leading figure of the English Vorticist movement. Notice of *BLAST* was given in a publicity flier promising that the first number would contain a manifesto, a story by Lewis, poems by Ezra Pound (Lewis' main collaborator), and reproductions of artworks by artists including Epstein, Wadsworth, Gaudier-Brzeska, and Lewis himself. The magazine became a gathering of aesthetic forms under the umbrella of an emerging Modernism, with a drastic programme of cultural renewal filling its sails.

The flier promised "Discussion of Cubism, Futurism, Imagisme and all Vital Forms of Modern Art. / THE CUBE. THE PYRAMID. / Putrifaction of Guffaws Slain by Appearance of / BLAST. / NO Pornography. No Old Pulp. / END OF THE CHRISTIAN ERA." There is a kind of high-spirited grotesquerie in this Manichean grand narrative. The "Old" is clearly bad, so is a certain brand of humor. So, it seems, is misdirected sexual energy, whether under the banner of Pornography or the Christian Era. The manifesto as published in the first number kept up the work of "Blasting and Blessing." Contributors to *BLAST* included T.S. Eliot, Ford Madox Hueffer, and Rebecca West, as well as the artists already mentioned. The magazine meant to offend, and it did. Pound recalled that he had been dropped by another London journal because, according to its editor, G.W. Prothero, appearance in *BLAST* "stamps a man too disadvantageously."

Peter Swaab

Date 1914

Edited by Wyndham Lewis (1882–1957)

Nationality UK

Why It's Key *BLAST* was avant-garde in layout and content. T.S. Eliot's first publication was in the second issue. There were only two issues.

Key Book
The Married Woman (Parineeta)

Sarat Chandra Chattopadhyay, better known to his readers as Sarat Babu, was a towering literary figure who enjoyed a popularity rivaling that of the Nobel Laureate Rabindranath Tagore. His chief appeal lay in his masterful depiction of social reality during the Bengali renaissance and his sympathetic insight into the minds of his female characters.

Set in Calcutta of the early twentieth century *Parineeta* presents a realistic picture of the Bengali society as it went through the painful transformation from tradition to modernity. Both men and women were then unwitting victims of outmoded customs and unfriendly traditions. Fathers of marriageable girls were required to offer dowries beyond their means and young girls were routinely married off when they were hardly into their teens. Against this background *Parineeta* can be read both as a social document and as a portrait of the complexity of a sentimental young woman's mind. Social compulsions oblige Gurucharan,

the guardian of the teenage protagonist Lalita, to borrow heavily from his neighbor Nabin Roy and finally convert to Brahmoism. Fear of social censure prevents Roy's son Shekar from acknowledging his "marriage" with Lalita. Bowing to tradition and ruled by sentiments Lalita treats herself as married to Shekar when in fact she merely exchanged a garland of flowers during a game of doll's wedding. The situation is however not entirely hopeless. Gurucharan finds his deliverance in religious conversion; Lalita attains her goal through service, sacrifice, and steadfastness; and Shekar overcomes his vacillation when his despotic father dies, and accepts Lalita as his wife.

Rajeshwar Mittapalli

Date 1914

Author Sarat Chandra Chattopadhyay (1876–1938)

Nationality India

Why It's Key *Parineeta* marked an important turning point in the history of Indian fiction by reaching a wide readership. Almost a century after its publication it continues to have a powerful appeal to readers across India. It proved to be a prototype for innumerable adapted novels in India's many national languages.

1910–1919

Key Author **Natsume Soseki**
Kokoro

Soseki (1867–1916), a man unwilling to acknowledge his own defeat. Characteristically self-deprecating, Natsume Kinnosuke's choice of pen-name belies his acclaimed status and widespread popularity. But for Soseki, success did not come without sacrifice.

Born in Tokyo as the old Edo period made way for the Meiji Restoration, Soseki bore witness to important changes in Japanese society. Hurtling towards industrialization, the rise of modern Japanese language was accompanied by a decline in classical Japanese, Chinese, and English studies. Surprisingly, Soseki's early career is marked by relative ambivalence towards English and it is largely by virtue of timing that he was to become one of the remaining Japanese writers of the period with a mastery of the English language.

Studying English Literature at Tokyo's formidable Imperial University, Soseki forged a friendship with haiku master Masaoka Shiki, dabbling in Japanese and Chinese poetry. However, his greatest challenge was

yet to come. 1900 saw Soseki leave a pregnant wife and daughter for a two-year sabbatical in London. Languishing in poverty amid London's run-down boarding houses, he suffered disillusionment and social isolation. Rumored to have "gone insane," Soseki's creative talents lay dormant, incubating in obscurity. Returning to Japan, he emerged from his chrysalis to pen the satirical masterpiece *I am a Cat* for serialization in 1904. The creativity of the following ten years proved to be unprecedented in Japanese literature. With his talent galvanised, Soseki produced celebrated works such as the rebellious *Botchan*, progressing to the dark and philosophical *Kokoro*. His sojourn in London provided rich material and the modern Japanese novel was born. Ever the rebel, Soseki declined the government's offer of an honorary Doctorate of Letters, dying aged 49 leaving *Light and Darkness* unfinished.

Sarah Birchwood

Date 1914

Nationality Japan

Why It's Key Highly revered Meiji-era novelist who has inspired songs, anime, and films. He was in mass circulation until recently as the figurehead on the 1000 Yen note. The most widely translated Japanese author, his legacy remains embedded in Japanese culture and beyond.

Key Character **Tarzan**
Tarzan of the Apes

Tarzana in California is one of very few towns named after a fictional character. It is a measure of the impact that Tarzan has had on the popular imagination since his first appearance in Edgar Rice Burroughs' 1914 adventure fantasy, *Tarzan of the Apes*. Burroughs was one of the first writers to plan the multimedia exploitation of his new "property," not only following up the first novel with many sequels, but also envisaging films, cartoons, and all sorts of merchandizing. On screen, Tarzan was first played in a 1918 silent movie by Elmo Lincoln, but the most popular Tarzan was undoubtedly Johnny Weissmuller, the muscle-bound U.S. Olympic swimming champion who played the hero in a long-running series starting in 1932.

Tarzan is the son of an English aristocrat who was abandoned in the African jungle as a baby, and has been brought up by apes. This has given him not only considerable strength and agility to swing through the trees, but also an ability to communicate with all sorts of animals: In Burroughs' invented "monkey language" his name means "white skin." In the course of Burroughs' stories, Tarzan meets and marries Jane, and has a series of unlikely adventures. Tarzan himself, though bright, is a straightforward sort of a chap, morally spotless, faithful to his wife, reserved in a way appropriate to his caste, and at all times behaving like a gentleman – apart from the yodelling, and, of course, the skimpy loincloth, which wouldn't get you past the doormen of the better clubs in London.

Ian Crofton

Date 1914 (publication)

Author Edgar Rice Burroughs (1875–1950)

Nationality USA

Why It's Key Tarzan was the first and one of the most durable of the twentieth-century superheroes, and featured not only in further books by Burroughs, but in numerous films, comics, television and radio series.

Opposite Weissmuller as Tarzan in the film adaptation

Key Event **Delmira Agustini is shot dead by her husband**

The Uruguayan poet, Delmira Agustini (1886–1914), gave a feminine and a feminist voice to the Latin American aesthetics of Modernismo. Agustini came from a privileged family, who treated her as a child, the over-protected "nena" (girl). However, Agustini's poetry challenges stereotypical female roles, and explores multiple representations of desire. From her first book, *The White Book* (*El libro blanco*, 1907), her poetry reveals a shocking eroticism; with poems like "Intimate" ("Íntima") and "The stranger" ("El intruso") where metaphors of blooming flowers and opening doors portray a female body who willingly writes herself in the text. *Songs of the Morning* (*Cantos de la mañana*, 1910) merges religious and spiritual symbols with acute, erotic imagery.

The celebrated Nicaraguan poet Rubén Darío, who was impressed by Agustini's originality and passion, compared her visions of ecstasies to Saint Teresa's work. By 1913, Agustini published her most revolutionary, vanguard book, *The Empty Chalices* (*Los cálices vacíos*, 1913). Her famous meta-literary poem, "The Swan" ("El cisne") responds to Darío's poem of the same title, and graphically traces the sexual relationship between the speaker and her swan/lover. The animalization of the lover responds to the speaker's desires, and her desire that we see them in her lake, in her mirror, in the "crystal clear page" of the poem. Agustini's text stands on its own, in a rebellious feminine eroticism that joins pleasure and pain.

Agustini, who always evaded marriage, finally got married to Enrique Job Reyes, but after just two months of marriage she went back to her parents' house. After many quarrels, Agustini was convinced that she wanted a divorce, and in 1914 in a fatal encounter, her husband Reyes killed her, and then committed suicide. In 1924 her posthumous work, *The Rosary of Eros* (*El rosario de Eros*), was published.

Cecilia Enjuto Rangel

Date 1914 (death)

Place Uruguay

Why It's Key Agustini's death at the age of 28 silenced one of Latin America's most potent poetic voices.

Key Event **Publication of Tressell's novel exposes the hardships of working men**

Robert Tressell (1870–1911) began writing his novel *The Ragged Trousered Philanthropists* in 1906 when concerns about class relations in the workplace and existing class struggle were very topical. The consciously socialist perspective that Tressell brings to the novel makes a very different form of socially aware writing to what had gone before – Charles Dickens, George Gissing, Arthur Morrison, and Jack London all approach similar subject matter but here we have a different perspective. Tressell uses the Dickensian trope of characters representing the system, with names such as Nimrod, Hunter, Misery, Slyme, Grinder, Sweater, and Crass. The novel's originality lies partly in Tressell's use of extra-literary devices such as diagrams and public addresses, political speeches, meetings, and official forms of address. *The Ragged Trousered Philanthropists* was unique in that respect when it was published (although originally it appeared in a heavily edited form). Tressell does not merely describe the harsh conditions of the working people; he seeks to inform of the reasons for the poverty and exploitation. The novel's didactic purpose was to show workers they hold the means to change things.

According to Tressell, the novel is a fundamental critique of capitalism and in writing it he attempts to pierce the class façade which he sees is a barrier to fulfillment. His subject matter is not just the social conditions but the system that creates the conditions and impoverishes lives. Tressell gives the reader knowledge of causes – he shows what lies beneath the naked and unremitting exploitation on which capitalism is built. That is what makes the novel so important in the history of twentieth-century, working-class writing. Published three years after his death, the author signed his name using the pseudonym "Robert Tressel" because he feared recriminations.

Pat Wheeler

Date 1914

Why It's Key The portrayal of the housepainters of Mugsborough had a great impact when published, as it shows how complicit the establishment is in the oppression of the working people. The novel was a landmark work of British socialism and became a key text for trade union activists. A later edition is said to have played a part in Labour's landslide victory in 1945.

Opposite *The Ragged Trousered Philanthropists*

Key Passage **"The Dead"** *The Dubliners*

SPOILER

"His soul swooned slowly as he heard the snow falling faintly through the universe."

Few passages in Joyce reveal his ambivalent relation to Ireland with greater poetry than the closing paragraphs of "The Dead." The sense of a country trapped between Anglicized modernity and a romanticized Celtic past, an Ireland both colony and backwater, is painfully conveyed through the distress of central protagonist Gabriel Conroy.

In the small hours following his aunts' annual Christmas dance in Dublin, Gabriel, a successful writer, modern man and loving husband discovers, catastrophically, that his Galway-born wife, Gretta, actually reserves her tenderest emotions for the memory of doe-eyed Michael Furey, a "delicate" local boy she courted in her youth but who died at seventeen. If, the story asks, Gabriel has never properly known his wife, a child of the far west, how can he know himself? And how can modern Ireland, which he as a sophisticated "West Briton" typifies, reconcile itself with its ancient, but atavistic traditions?

Dismayed, Gabriel imagines himself ridiculous, inauthentic and possibly, like many characters here, spiritually paralyzed. But the image of snow, "general all over Ireland," provides an ambiguous finale for the tale. Entering a "grey impalpable world," Joyce writes, Gabriel "watched sleepily the flakes, silver and dark, falling obliquely against the lamplight. The time had come for him to set out on his journey westward." Will his voyage mean chilly death or Celtic rebirth? Or neither? As ever in *Dubliners*, Joyce reserves judgement and the future remains profoundly uncertain.

Doug Haynes

Date 1914

Author James Joyce (1882–1941)

Nationality Ireland

Why It's Key Unlike the sweeping, allusive and poetic riddles of *Ulysses* and *Finnegans Wake*, Joyce's earlier collection of stories renders Dublin in a subdued, melancholy fashion, the conventional prose style of his troubled vignettes allowing hints of the deep malaise into which he feels his country has fallen.

Key Author **Miguel de Unamuno**
Mist (Niebla)

Owlish in appearance, and peppery in manner, Miguel de Unamuno (1864–1936) may have looked professorial, yet he abhorred the idea of "professional" philosophy, and expressed his preoccupations – chief among them the human longing for existence after death, despite the absence of a rational basis for it – in poetry, drama, and idiosyncratic fiction as much as in his highly admired essays.

He learned Danish to read Kierkegaard, and like him is a forerunner of Existentialism, a sceptic longing for the lost certainties of faith. His short novel *San Manuel Bueno, Mártir* (*St. Manuel the Good, Martyr*) (1931) dramatizes this dilemma in the story of a priest who has lost his belief in God, yet maintains appearances for the sake of his peasant parishioners, whom he feels could not live without the solace of faith.

His greatest novel, *Mist (Niebla)* appeared in 1914, and narrates the unrequited love story of Antonio Pérez. The novel culminates in the hero's journey to meet his maker, where he pleads with Unamuno not to be allowed to die. This may surprise readers who assume this sort of thing only came in with Parisian postmodernism, but it is an entirely consistent development of Unamuno's thought, which drew parallels between fictional creation and reality.

Ever the contrarian, Unamuno resigned his rectorship of Salamanca University in 1936 at the start of the Civil War after publicly denouncing the bloodthirsty slogans of one of Franco's generals. This heroic act might have cost him his life, had he not died naturally shortly afterwards.

Cathy Benson

Date 1914 (publication)

Nationality Spain/Basque

Key Works *En torno al casticismo* (1905), *The Life of Don Quixote* (1905), *The Tragic Sense of Life* (1913), *Abel Sánchez* (1917)

Why It's Key Caught between the old world of faith and certainty, and the new one of doubt, Unamuno's passionate commitment to rationality expressed itself in novels which prefigure the literary strategies of postmodernism.

Opposite Miguel de Unamuno

108

Key Character **Josef K.**
The Trial

"Someone must have been telling lies about Josef K., he knew he had done nothing wrong but, one morning, he was arrested." With the same spare prose we find in "Metamorphosis," so begins Kafka's stifling account of a man's entombment within the maze of the law. K. is arrested on his thirtieth birthday for a crime never specified and, over the ensuing year, encounters no meaningful judgement or contact with a court. Ever deferred, yet ever oppressive, the law appears instead in the form of tricksy lawyers, gossip, inference, waiting rooms; everyone he meets has a different theory about how to influence his intangible, undisclosed case: his frustration mounts, but never culminates. Close to the book's end, a priest tells him a parable about a man who waits his whole life to enter the doorway of the law, a story that, understandably, "captivates" K. as he begins to suspect the law is in fact, "the lie made into the rule of the world."

Although not yet the fully abbreviated "K" of *The Castle*, Josef K. is nevertheless a character stripped to the essentials. Before his arrest he is a succesful bank official with one or two envious colleagues. He has affairs with women, described in the oblique, abject manner only Kafka knows how. He is a model of "normality," even blandness. There is apparently nothing in the case of this modern young bureaucrat that might attract the personalized hell set aside for him. And in this problem lies the novel's enigma.

Doug Haynes

Date 1915 (written, first published 1925)

Author Franz Kafka (1883–1924)

Nationality Czechoslovakia

Why It's Key Although, as the end of the novel shows and is perhaps appropriate, *The Trial* was never really finished, it joins Kafka's other texts in helping define a particular, inscrutable kind of modernism, one that some critics see presaging the totalitarian Europe of later in the century.

The love that lifted a man to paradise . . . and hurled him back to earth again!
LESLIE
HOWARD
"OF HUMAN BONDAGE"
WITH
BETTE DAVIS
FRANCES DEE
KAY JOHNSON
REGINALD DENNY
DIRECTED BY JOHN CROMWELL
A PANDRO S. BERMAN PRODUCTION
W. SOMERSET MAUGHAM
OF HUMAN BONDAGE
RKO Radio PICTURES

Key Author **William Somerset Maugham**
Of Human Bondage

"Willie" Maugham (1874–1965) was orphaned at the age of ten and brought up by an uncle. He studied medicine and turned his experiences of practising in the London slums into his first book, *Liza of Lambeth* (1897). He gave up on medicine and began to travel, first living a bohemian life in Paris and making his way as a writer. He wrote seven novels but was first successful as a playwright; he had four plays running simultaneously in the West End in 1908. The plays, mainly social comedies, made him financially secure but soon dated.

Despite his popularity, he yearned to be successful as a novelist and he took two years to write *Of Human Bondage* (1915), a largely autobiographical account of a medical student's travails in life and love. Other novels followed: *The Moon and Sixpence* (1919) is an account of the cruel and selfish life of an artist based on that of Paul Gauguin; *Cakes and Ale* (1930) is a social satire on a famous novelist supposedly based on Thomas Hardy.

His was the cynical gaze of the perpetual outsider, an authorial pose that was emulated though rarely bettered. The effortless narrative style of his short stories taught a generation how to write prose.

Maugham settled permanently on the French Riviera in 1927. He was criticized in later life for not lending his name and considerable reputation to calls to reform the draconian British anti-homosexuality law, particularly as he lived outside of Britain and was in no danger of prosecution.

Jad Adams

Date 1915 (publication)

Nationality UK

Why It's Key Maugham's narrative skill and power of cynical observation are a model of storytelling but he described himself as "second rate," as if to out-flank his later critics who have valued him less than did his contemporaries.

Opposite *Of Human Bondage* film poster

1910–1919

111

Key Passage
Pointed Roofs

"Tranquil moonlight lay across the room. It surprised her like a sudden hand stroking her brow. It seemed to feel for her heart. If she gave way to it her thought would go. Perhaps she ought to watch it and let her thoughts go. It passed over trouble like mother did when she said, 'Don't go so deeply into everything, chickie. You must learn to take life as it comes. Ah-eh, if I were strong I could show you how to enjoy life….' Delicate little mother, running quickly downstairs clearing her throat to sing. But mother did not know. She had no reasoning power."

Pointed Roofs – the first part of *Pilgrimage*, Richardson's thirteen-part novel sequence – is the first novel in English to use the technique of "stream of consciousness." Richardson believed that the novel should be a "reconstruction of experience focused from within the mind of a single individual" and that the reader should incessantly watch "the conflict of human forces through the eye of a single observer." She preferred the term "interior monologue" to describe her narrative technique, which also involved unconventional use of punctuation and syntax to produce "feminine prose."

Pilgrimage was a type of fictionalized life-writing, closely matching Richardson's own experiences. This extract occurs as Miriam tries to deal with her fevered wish to return home to England. Despite the homesickness, her stream of consciousness reflects her choice of a different female role from that of her mother. She tends to despise both her mother and the German schoolgirls she teaches for not having intellectual or political ambition. While moonlight is a conventional feminine symbol, it is used here to empower the lonely protagonist and reinforce her resolve to create an avant-garde, modern, urban version of femininity.

Helen May Dennis

Date 1915 (publication)

Author Dorothy Richardson (1873–1957)

Why It's Key *Pointed Roofs* is seen as the first novel in English to use the method of "stream of consciousness" narrative, the revolutionary method of describing a character's internal thought processes which has become a familiar feature of the modern novel, but which at the time was seen as avant-garde.

Key Character **The golem**
The Golem

The golem of legend has taken on many forms. "Golem" can mean an embryo, an unformed body, a statue, or a puppet. The golem is sometimes a gentle man wrought of clay, and brought into being by a holy rabbi to protect the Jews of Prague. In other versions, it is something less cosy, given to fits of destructive rage, controllable only by kabbalistic magic. But Gustav Meyrink's golem represents the greatest leap from tradition. Here, the creation seeking a soul becomes a spirit craving a host. The Renaissance legend of old Prague is transmuted into a deeply modern tale of spiritual angst, identity loss, and narcotic hallucination.

In *The Golem*, Athanasius Pernath, an artist from Prague, is being followed by a strange figure with oriental eyes. It is his alter ego; it also the golem. Hounded by his mysterious doppelgänger, Pernath undergoes a series of terrifying visions and visitations. The legend of the golem is being discussed at a gathering of friends. Someone produces a doll and

hands it to him: he looks at the doll, sees it take on the features of his pursuer and then, horribly, finds himself in the doll's body, seeing from the doll's eyes. His wanderings take him to a disused attic, a room without windows, in the corner of which a tarot pack lies. He remembers that the golem was supposed by tradition to sleep in a room without windows. Before his horror-stricken gaze, the harlequin card rises up from the paper to menace him.

Hillel, the saintly kabbalist, shows Pernath that his demons are all internal. There is no golem. But certain images abide, a slant-eyed man scribbling a cryptic note, a group of old bearded men in a room proffering mysterious pills, an attic with no windows, no means of escape.

Murrough O'Brien

Date 1915

Author Gustav Meyrink (1868–1932)

Nationality Austria

Why It's Key *The Golem* had a vast influence on Expressionist literature and cinema. More, it showed how urban legends, no less than rural myths, could be adapted to modern spiritual dilemmas.

Key Book
Herland

Herland's status as the progenitor of feminist science fiction has endured throughout the twentieth century. The novel uses the typical utopian technique of estrangement (it has a geographical displacement) and shows an all-female society that has developed independently from the existing world. The novel charts the adventures of three men who travel to the cut-off world (located somewhere in South America). On entering the land the men exclaim, "why this is a civilized country… there must be men." They are swiftly captured and imprisoned by the women inhabitants and are forcibly educated in the ways of the society they have penetrated.

Each man holds a stereotypical view of women and each view is gradually undermined. They come to realize that in this society being a man is of no importance as women are capable of all functions, including reproduction through parthenogenesis. Gilman's remarkable satire provides an intellectually

rigorous critique of society and challenges many assumptions made about women. It is especially meaningful as it affords the opportunity for women to imagine a world where there are no constraints placed on their lives. Gilman's alternative world allows the limitations of the prevailing society to be seen and along with them, the possibilities of change.

Herland's influence is seen in many women's science fiction works of the 1960s and 1970s and in particular in the lesbian separatist societies found within the genre. Writers such as Joanna Russ, Marge Piercy, and Ursula Le Guin are the progenies of Gilman, and *Herland* holds an unassailable position as one of the most influential novels in feminist science fiction writing.

Pat Wheeler

Date 1915

Author Charlotte Perkins Gilman (1860–1935)

Nationality USA

Why It's Key *Herland* is one of the most influential feminist utopian novels of the twentieth century. In this important work Charlotte Perkins Gilman uses the utopian form both as a critique of patriarchal, capitalist society and to foreground the lives of women.

Opposite Charlotte Perkins Gilman

Key Passage
"Metamorphosis"

"Gregor Samsa awoke from uneasy dreams one morning to find himself changed into a giant insect."

This odd, blunt first line sets the tone for all that follows in Kafka's pathetic tale. Aside from his "uneasy dreams," that is, we receive no explanation at all for Gregor's transformation; insecthood, it seems, is simply his unfortunate predicament. And sustaining this apparently straightforward register, Gregor's chief wish is thus to dress and get to the office, his metamorphosis only as worrying as the fact he has overslept. Likewise, later, his family, although disgusted by his appearance, nevertheless automatically assume this altered shape is still their boy.

The remainder of the opening passage reinforces a sense of embattled normality. Gregor lies pitifully on his back and can see his "dome-shaped brown belly banded with what looked like reinforcing arches, on top of which his quilt, while threatening to slip off completely at any moment, still maintained a precarious hold." His tiny legs "thrash ineffectually." Like a horrible comedy, the struggle merely to exist will detain him in a world that, including his own body, seems an inflexible carapace. This sense of constraint seems suggestive: a lonely traveling salesman, Gregor works for a martinet boss to whom his over-strict father is in debt; only his wages support the family. "What if all this peace, all this prosperity... were to end in terror?" he eventually wonders, exuding anxieties at once economic, Oedipal, political, and existential. Even though an insect, is Gregor's existence all that changed?

Doug Haynes

Date 1915 (publication)

Author Franz Kafka (1883–1924)

Nationality Czechoslovakia

Why It's Key This short story is one of the few works Kafka published in his lifetime, admired in the small literary circle that he inhabited although not widely read. It has since become a canonical, benchmark text for representations of the alienated modern consciousness.

Opposite Franz Kafka poster

1910–1919

115

Key Character **Richard Hannay**
The Thirty-Nine Steps

John Buchan's Richard Hannay is often regarded as the first modern action adventure hero, and the books in which he appeared as the forerunners of the espionage thrillers of writers like Ian Fleming and John Le Carré. While the theme of the international conspiracy undermined by the work of a single, undercover agent was ahead of its time in many ways, the character of Hannay could hardly be more different from James Bond. A gentleman adventurer, easily bored, shy of women, morally upright though with a fox-like cunning (especially in the area of disguise) and able to use his fists if necessary, he, like his author, is very much a product of the colonial age.

Buchan's keen interest in history and politics (he worked in intelligence during World War I, later entered parliament and ended his career as Governor-General of Canada) lend the sometimes improbable plots of the Hannay novels a convincing authenticity. *Greenmantle*, for instance, offers an intriguing picture of Germany's relationship with the Ottoman Empire and the Islamic peoples of the Near East during World War I. It is in this novel (written and published during the early years of the war) that Buchan contrived a brief meeting between Hannay and Kaiser Wilhelm, who is portrayed with daring sympathy. Buchan's reputation suffered through being too closely identified with his most famous creation. In the context of Buchan's work as a whole however (he wrote over a hundred books, including historical fiction, history, and biography), Hannay can be seen as something of a parody of the blunt, unimaginative hero stereotype.

Gerard Woodward

Date 1915 (publication)

Author John Buchan (1875–1940)

Nationality UK

Why It's Key Richard Hannay, the archetype of the early action hero and forerunner of the modern spy, makes his first appearance in *The Thirty-Nine Steps*. The other novels in which Hannay appears as a main character are: *Greenmantle* (1916), *Mr. Standfast* (1919), *The Three Hostages* (1924) and *The Island of Sheep* (1936).

Key Event **The final part of Frazer's anthropological work is published**

Anthropologist James Frazer applied himself to the rule of succession of the priesthood of Diana in the ancient grove at Aricia about sixteen miles from Rome. This is where a priest lived in fear for his life, for his place could be taken by anyone who could pluck a twig from the golden mistletoe bough growing on an oak in the grove and kill him.

"When I first set myself to solve the problem more than thirty years ago" Frazer wrote in his preface to the 1922 edition, "I thought that the solution could be found very briefly." In fact the initial enquiry branched out and filled two and then twelve volumes, published between 1890 and 1915.

The book is the nearest thing the nineteenth century came to "the key to all mythologies" that was long the grail of scholars, for Frazer's work expanded to cover similar customs of killing the priest-king in other countries and cultures, connecting ritual death with regeneration and fruitfulness.

It was written into a scheme of human intellectual evolution from the magical to the religious and then to the scientific. This is no longer accepted as a satisfactory model, but the expansiveness of thought and willingness to encompass all human activity, from primitive to civilized, set the tone for future scholarship. Frazer's distinction between magic (where the world can be controlled by charms) and religion (relying on an appeal to superior beings) has been the basis of much subsequent anthropological writing.

Jad Adams

Date 1915 (final volume published)

Title *The Golden Bough*

Author Sir James Frazer (1854–1941)

Nationality UK

Why It's Key T.S. Eliot remarked that *The Golden Bough* "has influenced our generation profoundly" and acknowledged he used its insights in *The Waste Land*. Pound, Joyce, Yeats, Lawrence were also influenced by this comparative study of world myths and religions.

Key Book
The Good Soldier

The poet John Rodker remarked that *The Good Soldier* was "the finest French novel in the English language": it was Ford's first serious attempt at breaking away from the mainstream of English fiction and trying to write something in the "impressionistic" style of continental writers such as Zola and de Maupassant.

His major innovation was to have his narrator, the rich American John Dowell, tell the story through non-chronological flashbacks, so that the reader is shuttled backwards and forwards through time. Dowell apologizes for telling his tale "in a very rambling way" but maintains that "real" stories are best told in the meandering manner of the oral storyteller: "They will then seem most real." This fragmentary narrative form allows Ford to relate key events in the wrong order, so that, at first, the reader is not always able to account for why characters behave as they do: this is appropriate because Dowell himself is incapable of

reading other people's emotions and motivations. He trusts in appearance and convention, so is unable to realize that his English friend Edward Ashburnham, regarded by society as a "good soldier" and honorable man, has been conducting a long affair with his wife. As Dowell relates the series of tragedies that results from this affair, it gradually becomes clear that he is as far from experiencing and comprehending human passion as ever and has learned nothing from his ordeal; the reader cannot trust him because he cannot – or dare not – try to understand even himself.

Jake Kerridge

Date 1915

Author Ford Madox Ford (1873–1939)

Nationality UK

Why It's Key Questioning whether human beings really can understand one another, Ford created an early example of the "unreliable narrator."

Key Author **Sol Plaatje**
Native Life in South Africa

Solomon Thekiso Plaatje (1876–1932) was an influential writer, but also a figure of great significance in South Africa's political history. In his lifetime, Sol Plaatje published two books, *Native Life in South Africa* (1916) and *Mhudi* (1930), the latter making him the first Black South African to publish a novel in English. He was editor of three Tswana language newspapers, a contributor to many others, and translated a number of Shakespeare's works into Tswana (he was fluent in eight languages). On the political stage, Plaatje was a founder in 1912 of the South African Native National Congress, forerunner of the ANC, and its first Secretary General.

The publication of *Native Life in South Africa* marked Plaatje's reaction to the Native Land Act of 1913, legislation which deprived Black Africans of the right to own land outside "reserves"; a precursor of apartheid. Plaatje began the book in 1914 as he traveled to Britain as part of a SANNC delegation protesting against the new law. It was intended to provide powerful evidence of the iniquities of segregationist policies, for a British audience. Plaatje's own resistance to these was founded upon his experience of Cape Colony's "color-blind" franchise, and a firm belief in the natural justice of racial equality.

Plaatje was a member of the Cape's black elite, yet in *Native Life* he describes the suffering of ordinary Africans with passion. Predating the apartheid policy by 33 years, *Native Life* can justly be regarded as the precursor of black anti-apartheid literature.
Tim Lovering

Date 1916 (publication)

Nationality South Africa

Key Works *Mafeking Diary: A Black Man's View of a White Man's War* (1973)

Why It's Key Plaatje was the first black South African to publish an English language novel, and one of the founders of the African Nationalist movement, who brought the plight of South Africa's black population to international attention through his writing.

1910–1919

117

Key Book
Petersburg

Andrei Bely was known in the years prior to the Bolshevik revolution of 1917 as a Symbolist poet and mystical thinker. Had the innovative value of *Petersburg* been grasped when it first appeared, it would have redrawn the literary map of the twentieth century. *Petersburg*'s involvement in language and consciousness relates it to Joyce's *Ulysses* and reflects the same intertwining of symbolic imagination and spiritual disinheritance as Eliot's *The Waste Land*. All three were works of art, contemporaneously conceived, about modern cities: St Petersburg, Dublin, and London. Driven by a powerful awareness of "cerebral play," Bely was fascinated by the discontinuity and interplay of multiple human consciousnesses. At the same time mystical philosophy gave him an animistic awareness of objects and led to *Petersburg* leading its own brooding, whimsical life from page to page.

The novel's nominal action, a terrorist attempt to blow up a high government official by recruiting his son to place the bomb, is filtered and fragmented by an account, spread over ten days, of the moods and routines of the characters going about a city often described as either dark or foggy. The text has been read as an essay in Russia's perennially tortured cultural position, torn between east and west, a problem especially palpable in an unnatural city arbitrarily required to exist by its founder-tyrant. The shifting text fell foul both of Soviet censorship and poor translation, and made its impact abroad only with an authoritative English version in 1979.
Lesley Chamberlain

Date 1916

Author Andrei Bely (1880–1934)

Nationality Russia

Why It's Key Bely's modernist masterpiece, still little known in both Russia and the West, was said by Vladimir Nabokov to be a profound influence on his own work. It relies on wordplay to evoke a sense of living in St Petersburg near the time of the 1905 Revolution.

Key Event
The Easter Rising

The Easter Rising of 1916 was an attempt by Irish Republicans to seize control of the British-ruled city of Dublin and therefore stage a coup within the entirety of Ireland itself. The rising was led by the Irish Republican Brotherhood, whose armed officers took the Post Office on O'Connell Street and announced an independent Irish Republic. Their rebellion lasted six days and was largely unpopular, but public opinion changed once the British dealt with the populace brutally and executed the leaders at Kilmainham Gaol.

More than any other event, the rising began to crystallize Nationalist sentiment in the country; the British attempt to impose conscription in 1918 was the final straw and the country was on the (rocky) road to partial independence. The rising has been both celebrated (as the birth of freedom) and damned (as a pointless and violent exercise). Even writers at the time were ambivalent about its meanings and purpose. W.B. Yeats wrote ambiguously of the horror unleashed in

"Easter, 1916" ("A terrible beauty is born") and Sean O'Casey's 1926 play *The Plough and the Stars* interrogated the whole notion of violent nationalism. Certainly the journey to independence is popularly seen to have started here and as a consequence many writers have been interested in the events themselves and the personalities involved. A recent revisionist account, Sebastian Barry's *A Long Long Way* (2005), presents the rebels as unpopular boys who had little effect on the people they were trying to liberate.
Jerome de Groot

Date April 1916

Place Dublin, Ireland

Why It's Key The Easter Rising had immediate impact on many writers, such as Yeats, and has continued to resonate in the Irish imagination.

Opposite An independent Irish republic is announced

Key Event
Dada is born

Disputes rage about the origin of Dada's name: is it a baby's first gurgle, Romanian for "yes, yes" or the French for "hobby-horse?" Many accounts suggest Hugo Ball, the movement's co-founder, just plucked it at random from the Larousse dictionary. If so, from that small absurdist act sprouted an (anti) aesthetic attitude that would become perhaps the most influential of the twentieth century, cited and practiced by everyone from André Breton to Damien Hirst.

Expressionist writer Ball pitched up in Switzerland with his lover and artistic collaborator, singer Emmy Hennings, in 1915, escaping a war that discredited the very idea of "civilized" Europe. By early 1916, aided by Marcel Slodki, they had started "Cabaret Voltaire," a venue for "musical recitals and readings," as their advert put it, in a backstreet Zurich bar called the Meierei. The Cabaret was a sort of insane vaudeville evening conducted six nights a week in a backroom hung with Arps and Picassos. Musical entertainments

including Dutch banjo players, a balalaika orchestra, and even Artur Rubinstein on piano vied for attention with Expressionist and Bruitist poetry, sound terrorism, experimental dancing, African mask performances, and much more, provided by artists like Richard Huelsenbeck, Janco and Tristan Tzara, and Hennings and Ball themselves. This, then, was Dada: painter Christian Schad wrote that "spontaneous incongruities, formulated anti-meaning, ebullient collisions of opinions created the atmosphere from which Dada gave birth to itself in spring 1916." "Dada means nothing," cried Tzara; maybe, but it still nevertheless helps define what we call modern art.
Doug Haynes

Date 1916

Place "Cabaret Voltaire," Zurich, Switzerland

Why It's Key More ink has been spilled over the Dada movement than probably any other single modern art movement. Its shadow is long, reaching to us today, but its beginnings were at the back of a pub during World War I in neutral Switzerland.

POBLACHT NA H EIREANN.

THE PROVISIONAL GOVERNMENT
OF THE
IRISH REPUBLIC
TO THE PEOPLE OF IRELAND.

IRISHMEN AND IRISHWOMEN : In the name of God and of the dead generations from which she receives her old tradition of nationhood, Ireland, through us, summons her children to her flag and strikes for her freedom.

Having organised and trained her manhood through her secret revolutionary organisation, the Irish Republican Brotherhood, and through her open military organisations, the Irish Volunteers and the Irish Citizen Army, having patiently perfected her discipline, having resolutely waited for the right moment to reveal itself, she now seizes that moment, and, supported by her exiled children in America and by gallant allies in Europe, but relying in the first on her own strength, she strikes in full confidence of victory.

We declare the right of the people of Ireland to the ownership of Ireland, and to the unfettered control of Irish destinies, to be sovereign and indefeasible. The long usurpation of that right by a foreign people and government has not extinguished the right, nor can it ever be extinguished except by the destruction of the Irish people. In every generation the Irish people have asserted their right to national freedom and sovereignty; six times during the past three hundred years they have asserted it in arms. Standing on that fundamental right and again asserting it in arms in the face of the world, we hereby proclaim the Irish Republic as a Sovereign Independent State, and we pledge our lives and the lives of our comrades-in-arms to the cause of its freedom, of its welfare, and of its exaltation among the nations.

The Irish Republic is entitled to, and hereby claims, the allegiance of every Irishman and Irishwoman. The Republic guarantees religious and civil liberty, equal rights and equal opportunities to all its citizens, and declares its resolve to pursue the happiness and prosperity of the whole nation and of all its parts, cherishing all the children of the nation equally, and oblivious of the differences carefully fostered by an alien government, which have divided a minority from the majority in the past.

Until our arms have brought the opportune moment for the establishment of a permanent National Government, representative of the whole people of Ireland and elected by the suffrages of all her men and women, the Provisional Government, hereby constituted, will administer the civil and military affairs of the Republic in trust for the people.

We place the cause of the Irish Republic under the protection of the Most High God, Whose blessing we invoke upon our arms, and we pray that no one who serves that cause will dishonour it by cowardice, inhumanity, or rapine. In this supreme hour the Irish nation must, by its valour and discipline and by the readiness of its children to sacrifice themselves for the common good, prove itself worthy of the august destiny to which it is called.

Signed on Behalf of the Provisional Government,

THOMAS J. CLARKE.

SEAN Mac DIARMADA. THOMAS MacDONAGH.
P. H. PEARSE. EAMONN CEANNT.
JAMES CONNOLLY. JOSEPH PLUNKETT.

Key Author
Henry James

"Try to be one of the people on whom nothing is lost." These words, from Henry James' (1843–1916) essay, "The Art of Fiction" (1884), serve as advice to prospective readers and as a description of the guiding principle behind his novelistic practice.

His novels frequently trace the cultural clashes between Americans and Europeans (or Europeanized Americans), contrasting American innocence with European experience and moral relativism. This "international" theme runs throughout his work, from his early novels, *The American* (1877) and *The Europeans* (1878), to the masterpieces of his late period, *The Wings of the Dove* (1902), *The Ambassadors* (1903), and *The Golden Bowl* (1904).

What makes James' writing unique is the depth of his psychological analysis and the corresponding complexity of his later style. His dense, convoluted sentences, accumulating detail with each subordinate clause, examine the inner workings of character and ultimately the operation of consciousness itself (his brother, William James, the philosopher and psychologist, first coined the term, "stream of consciousness"). The subtleties of his later prose make strenuous demands on the reader, but in his insistence on the subjectivity of experience and the limits to our ability to fully "know" others, James took the novel to the brink of modernism.

An extremely prolific author, James wrote over twenty novels, more than a hundred short stories, numerous plays, several books of literary criticism and travel writing, and three volumes of autobiography. Taken collectively, his prefaces to the revised New York edition of his novels (1907–09) constitute one of the most sustained analyses of the art of writing fiction ever produced by a single writer.

David Cross

Date 1916 (death)

Author Henry James

Nationality USA

Key Works *Portrait of a Lady* (1881), *The Bostonians* (1886), *What Maisie Knew* (1897), "The Turn of the Screw" (1898)

Why It's Key Following the enthusiasm of the modernists for his work, Henry James' reputation as one of the foremost practitioners of fiction increased throughout the twentieth century.

Opposite Henry James

Key Passage
"In a Station of the Metro"

"In a Station of the Metro

The apparition of these faces in the crowd;
Petals on a wet, black bough."

Like William Carlos Williams' comparably enigmatic "so much depends/upon/a red wheel/barrow," this little poem has become an emblematic moment of Modernism. It is also the exemplary poem of "Imagism." In 1915 Pound said that "the Image" was "a radiant node or cluster; it is what I can, and must perforce, call a VORTEX, from which, and through which, and into which, ideas are constantly rushing." The rush here comes from the disparity between the lines, requiring the reader's dynamic grasp of mind to bridge the gap. To make sense of the juxtaposition we have to perceive the human faces in the dark in a heightened way such that they are not just "appearance" but "apparition," to see them as these fragile petals lying flat on the wet tactile bough, illuminated by transience and delicacy. Pound is drawing here on a symbolist heritage of luminous but cryptic moments, but curbing the lushness of the symbolist tradition into a well-wrought verbal sparsity.

It took Pound a while to reach this final form. In April 1913 he published in the journal *Poetry* a first version with portentous typography:
The apparition   of these faces   in the crowd;
Petals   on a wet, black   bough.
Then in June 1913, in T.P.'s *Weekly*, he omitted the spaces, but substituted a colon at the end of the first line, suggesting that the second line in a way explicates the first; the book publication in *Lustra* restored the ponderably indirect semi-colon – one further non-grammatical element, incidentally, in this poem which is not grammatically a legitimate sentence.
Peter Swaab

Date 1916

Author Ezra Pound (1885–1973)

Nationality USA

Why It's Key This two-line poem, influenced by Japanese haiku, epitomizes Imagism and Pound's urge to "make it new."

Key Author **Mary Webb**
Gone to Earth

"In her schooldays boys brought maimed frogs and threw them in her lap, to watch, from a safe distance, her almost crazy grief and rage."

A woodland animal in human form, Hazel Woodus, heroine of *Gone to Earth*, is the beauty of the English countryside personified. So intense, however, is her sympathy with suffering nature that she can become an object of uncomprehending ridicule. The same might be said of Mary Webb's work as a whole – unforgettably sent up by Stella Gibbons in *Cold Comfort Farm* (1932).

Hazel Woodus is all innocence and grace, but there is a schematic clumsiness in the obvious symbolism of her name; she is full of spontaneity, but when she walks up the aisle to be married with her pet fox in tow, it seems incongruous. Her naïveté is so complete as to strain credulity. To the modern reader, her dialect-speech has a ring of Mummerset.

But Mary Webb (1881–1927) was unapologetic about an approach to writing which did not pretend to psychological verisimilitude: she was trying to engage poetically with the traditions of the countryside. Hazel is not supposed to represent the sort of sophisticated moral self that comes from scriptural ideas and civilization. Whilst Christian values and imagery do have a place in Webb's work, it harks back repeatedly to the pre-Christian past. As in Thomas Hardy's novels the apparent improbabilities are less a sign of authorial ineptitude than marks of a quasi-pagan worldview in which fate counts for more than human action. Where Hardy and D.H. Lawrence are concerned with the encroachments of modernity and urbanization, Webb takes the bucolic world on its own merits.

Better known because of an endorsement from Prime Minister Stanley Baldwin, *Precious Bane* (1924) takes a similarly sacramental view.

Kate Kerrigan

Date 1917 (publication)

Nationality UK

Key Works *The Golden Arrow* (1916), *The House in Dormer Forest* (1920),

Why It's Key Webb's 1917 novel seemed to capture the profound poetic spirit of the English landscape and rural existence. Only later would her untrammeled lyricism make her a figure of fun.

Key Character **David Levinsky**
The Rise of David Levinsky

Written during the years of growth of New York's Jewish East Side, this fictional autobiography chronicles the experience of twentieth-century America through the life of a Russian Jew – his poverty-stricken childhood, move to America, financial success in the textile industry, and arrival at a dubious, regret-filled maturity. It is about the process of becoming American by making money, and by shedding an older – and perhaps more valuable – identity.

Levinsky's physical growth, sexual enlightenment, and education reflect his gradual movement away from home and journey to America. The United States represents a liberation from traditional bonds of religion which degrades into promiscuity, and a promise of educational achievement which deteriorates into financial acquisitiveness. The experience of becoming American is problematic and conflicted.

Cahan was a Lithuanian immigrant to the United States who made his name with stories of the New York ghetto, and founded a successful Yiddish newspaper. A socialist and proponent of Herbert Spencer's theory of social evolution, Cahan saw that the immigrant experience of America could be read as a form of evolution – the unfolding of latent possibilities – but he saw too that adaptation could bring about loss.

Levinsky tries to tell the typical American capitalist romance: "The man who has built the greatest skyscrapers in the country, including the Woolworth Building, is a Russian Jew who came here a penniless boy." He is only dimly aware of the ironies of his own "rise," but Cahan's novel is the tragedy of a self-made man who loses his sense of self. In middle age Levinsky regards the new generation of Jewish Americans with disapproval. Many American Jews felt Cahan's novel was an attack on their respectability, largely because of the very volatility of their position, which Cahan was trying to describe.

Lucy Daniel

Date 1917

Author Abraham Cahan (1860–1951)

Nationality USA

Why It's Key David Levinsky is the archetypal Jewish immigrant made good, starting as a penniless Russian Jew and ending up a wealthy American businessman. But Cahan questions the criteria he uses to judge his own success. *David Levinsky* is one of the most important novels about the American immigration experience.

Key Event **W.B Yeats and his wife experiment with automatic writing**

Spurned by his long-time love and the object of his obsession, Maud Gonne, the Irish poet W.B. Yeats asked her daughter, Iseult to marry him in September 1917. Two weeks after she refused him, Yeats proposed to an old friend Georgina ("George") Hyde Lees and was accepted. From this unpromising background springs an extraordinary development that was to significantly shape Yeats' subsequent poetry. Things looked rocky for the newly married couple until George tried automatic writing, scribbling down words without thinking about what she was doing. Yeats was so impressed that he decided she was channelling supernatural spirits and began to pay attention. He put questions to these "spirits" through George and kept a record of their replies.

Cynics suggest that George's automatic writings were guided only by a desire to save the marriage. Whatever their origins, Yeats used them as the basis of *A Vision*, a work of spiritual theology which explains world history in terms of fluctuating cycles and the phases of the moon. He also began to write these theories into poems, such as "The Second Coming." The opening image of the falcon "turning" in a "gyre" – a widening circle – is taken from *A Vision*. The distinctive conical shape described by the bird's motion lies behind the cycles of creation and destruction that recur throughout history. Yeats thought that this process had reached a crisis with World War I and the poem ends with a mythical beast "slouch[ing] towards Bethlehem to be born." Apocalypse is on the way.
Matthew Creasy

Date 1917

Title "The Second Coming" (written in 1919), in *Michael Robartes and the Dancer* (1921), *A Vision* (1925)

Author W.B. Yeats (1865–1939)

Nationality Ireland

Why It's Key In 1888 Yeats helped to found a secret society, the Hermetic Order of the Golden Dawn. Symbols and allegorical figures can be found throughout his poetry.

Key Event **ee cummings is arrested and spends four months in prison**

The Enormous Room describes events which took place during ee cummings' (1894–1962) wartime stint as an ambulance driver with the Norton-Harjes ambulance company in Northern France in 1917. cummings left America, in defiance of his parents' wishes, to support the Allied armies on the Western front, and worked his passage across the Atlantic with his friend William Slater Brown, referred to in the book only as "B." *The Enormous Room* describes cummings' arrest by the French authorities, and his incarceration in military prison at La Ferté Macé along with a diverse collection of soldiers, engineers and other prisoners.

The story is remarkable as much for the playful tone cummings adopts throughout his ordeal as for the appalling privations he and his fellow prisoners suffer at the hands of the French authorities and the skill with which the author observes and lampoons the cruel absurdities of wartime bureaucracy. On publication, the book divided reviewers. Generally, those familiar with cummings' earlier modernist experimentation in poetry regarded it as a more or less successful work of imagination, while those who chose to read the book as a straightforward documentary text found it unsatisfactory.

The language of *The Enormous Room* has been much discussed by critics, especially cummings' frequent and unpredictable shifts of register, from the grandiose to the colloquial, and his exuberant and ironic phrasing. The narrative lacks any recognizable "arc," and the majority of the book contains detailed portraits of the characters who populate *The Enormous Room*, and isolated episodes from their lives together. Remarkably for a book which sold so few copies in the author's lifetime, it still provides an immensely vivid, provocative response to the inhumanity of warfare and resists attempts at classification.
Charles Beckett

Date 1917 (arrest)

Place France

Title *The Enormous Room* (1922)

Nationality USA

Why It's Key *The Enormous Room* sold only 2,000 copies in its first edition, but its unique aesthetic and political sensitivity has influenced authors such as Hemingway, and contributed a new approach to the portrayal of human spiritual progress in the most deprived conditions.

Key Event **Leonard and Virginia Woolf establish the Hogarth Press**

Leonard and Virginia Woolf set up the Hogarth Press to publish relatively unknown works by authors whom they felt important. It was named after the Richmond house to which they had retreated to escape the bomb-blasts of central London. The project was originally conceived by Leonard as a small hand printing business designed to distract Virginia from her periodic bouts of mental illness.

The first book published by the Press was a 32-page pamphlet entitled *Two Stories* containing Virginia's story "The Mark on the Wall" and one by her husband called "Three Jews." The dust jacket was illustrated by Virginia's sister Vanessa and, over the coming years, the Hogarth Press would provide commissions to many of the artists associated with the Bloomsbury Group.

The Woolfs continued hand printing until 1932, but in the meantime increasingly became publishers rather than printers. Additional equipment was installed at Hogarth House and some of the work was handled by outside firms. However, sixteen of the thirty-two books which were published during the years that the press was in Richmond (1917–24) were printed by the Woolfs' own hand, including works by T.S. Eliot, E.M. Forster, and Katherine Mansfield as well as the earliest translations of Freud. From 1921 Virginia Woolf always published with the Press, except for a few limited editions. In 1938 the Press was bought by Chatto & Windus.

Kathryn Hughes

Date 1917

Place UK

Why It's Key Thanks to the Hogarth Press "difficult" fiction – often non-linear and with a lack of sympathetic characters – found its way into print. The Press grew from being a cottage industry designed to distract Virginia Woolf from her psychological troubles into an important engine for driving some of the best writing of the modernist age into the mainstream.

Opposite Virginia Woolf

Key Book
Eminent Victorians

Eminent Victorians burst into a world where all the pieties and personalities of the previous age were under deep suspicion. The recently-ended war had made thinking Britons wonder whether the Victorian institutions with which they had grown up – the public school, church, and army – were not, in fact somehow to blame for the killing fields of France.

Lytton Strachey certainly thought so – in a letter to his friend Virginia Woolf in 1912 he wrote that their Victorian predecessors "seem to me a set of mouth bungled hypocrites." In *Eminent Victorians* he picks four titans of the previous century to belittle – sometimes literally. Thomas Arnold, the headmaster of Rugby, is described as having legs that were slightly too short for his body. Cardinal Manning is reduced, at the end of Strachey's mischievous essay, to nothing more than his hat. General Gordon is revealed as having a weakness for drink. And Florence Nightingale, who in her prime had made cabinet ministers quake, ends Strachey's essay as a fat, senile, old lady.

As Strachey made clear in his Preface, he was not interested in compiling one of those vast "Lives and Letters" that had typified biographical writing in the previous century. Depending heavily on secondary sources, his intention was to write an impressionistic essay of his subject's character rather than give chapter and verse. Also new was his bold irreverence towards his subjects, which contrasted strongly with the hagiographic tone of earlier biographical writing. As a key member of the Bloomsbury group, Strachey could be relied upon to think the unthinkable and say the unsayable about his parents' generation.

Kathryn Hughes

Date 1918 (publication)

Author Lytton Strachey (1880–1932)

Nationality UK

Why It's Key The reviews for *Eminent Victorians* were uniformly enthusiastic. In time the book took its place as one of the founding texts of twentieth-century biographical writing. Its conspicuous candor freed biographers to write honestly about the foibles as well as achievements of their subjects.

Key Book
Diary of a Madman

Baihua literature is the written form of the language that began to unify modern China during an era when cultural identity was congealing and promoting nationalism and social reform. Baihua, it transpired, became the People's language, debunking and eventually overthrowing the classical language of the elite. *Diary of a Madman* is a collection of stories that recounts the archaic, unjust, and corrupt social system that was being overrun by Imperialist nations of the East and West.

Such is the premise from which one must read *Diary of a Madman*. Even in its translated form, colloquialisms are forever immortalized in this book, refusing to relent to a modern translation so as not to dilute its original cultural meaning. Author Lu Xun consistently refers to ancient Confucian texts, reinforcing the virtues of core Chinese belief systems such as filial piety and respect for ancestors.

Many of Lu Xun's epigrammatic statements roll off a politically sharpened tongue, and yet he still manages to make his text accessible to the common reader – his target audience – explaining the complicated arteries of social and filial connections while recounting his moral tales of all that his society holds dear, and also what threatens it.

From this dynamic collection of short stories emerges another commentary, one that pointedly criticizes social realities that the Communist Party is actively attacking, such as the disparity of wealth and access to education. Lu Xun's breadth of social satire is impressive, managing to embed his dream for a better China deep within the growing consciousness of a collective that literally re-wrote Chinese history.

Alexandra Hamlyn

Date 1918 (publication)

Author Lu Xun (1881–1936)

Nationality China

Why It's Key One of the founders of the controversial China League of Left-Wing Writers, Lu Xun was part of the seminal reforms that represented a major victory for the Chinese Communist Party in 1930. He is considered by many as one of the leading forebears of Baihua, or vernacular, literature.

Key Book
The Return of the Soldier

Rebecca West was an important figure in the early women's movement, participating in the suffragette protests alongside the Pankhursts, later developing interests in Fabian socialism and other radical movements. She was a prolific writer in a wide number of fields. Her *Times* obituary suggested she would be remembered more "as a great reporter of our times" than as a novelist.

She reported on the Nuremburg trials and wrote extensively about the politics of the Balkans. Her literary reputation has endured, however, as successive waves of feminist readers have rediscovered her. *The Return of the Soldier* (1918) is West's first novel (written when she was 24) and one of the earliest to respond to World War I from a female perspective.

It concerns the return home from the trenches of a shell-shocked officer, Chris Baldry, whose memory has been so badly damaged that he has no recollection of his present marriage to the shallow and snobbish

Kitty. Instead he finds himself still deeply in love with his former sweetheart, a humble inn-keeper's daughter called Margaret, who is now herself married. In contrasting the narrow, superficial world of upper-class Kitty with the down to earth, "honest" values of Margaret, West offers a piercing analysis of human relationships beset and distorted by class distinctions and prejudices. As such it provides far-reaching insights into World War I's impact on class and social structures in Britain.

Gerard Woodward

Date 1918 (publication)

Author Rebecca West (1892–1983)

Nationality UK

Why It's Key One of the first novels to react to World War I from a female perspective.

Key Passage "The Dynamo and the Virgin"
The Education of Henry Adams

"The force of the Virgin was still felt at Lourdes, and seemed to be as potent as X-rays; but in America neither Venus not Virgin ever had value as force...."

Standing in the dynamo hall of the 1900 Paris Great Exposition, Henry Adams experiences an epiphany, mesmerized by the power of the machines before him. He realizes he is present at a crucial historical junction, a shift not just between centuries but between the vastly different perspectives of spirituality and science. Using the characteristic third-person narrative he adopts throughout his *Education*, he tells us that, "to Adams the dynamo became a symbol of infinity... he began to feel the forty-foot dynamos as a moral force, much as the early Christians felt the Cross."

Punning on words like "force" and "energy," he begins to equate the sublime mysteries of science and religion, marvelling at the way both can somehow generate incredible works: "no more relation could he discover between the steam and the electric current," he writes, "than between the Cross and the cathedral."

Ultimately, "The Dynamo and the Virgin" suggests the "old world" of spiritual power as a sexy, European, and feminine one, exemplified by Venus and Mary and creating beauty and order. It was, he says, the animating force of all previous civilization, "the greatest force the Western world ever felt." Now, though, he mourns its decline as the anarchic and brutal world of the machine takes over: "All the steam in the world," he laments "could not, like the Virgin, build Chartres." Boggling at the new science, his mind roves across the mysteries of the atom and invisible rays and he contemplates a chaotic, sexless, and violent American future.
Doug Haynes

Date 1918 (publication)
Author Henry Adams (1838–1913)
Nationality USA
Why It's Key Henry Adams was the great-grandson of John Adams, the second President of the United States, and grandson of John Quincy Adams, the sixth President. He was one of the founders of the American historical profession and wrote a nine-volume history of the country 1889–91.

1910–1919

Key Character **Ántonia Shimerda**
My Ántonia

Ántonia Shimerda, the Bohemia immigrant whose bright spirit animates Willa Cather's spare, lyrical novel of 1918, has within her much of what Cather most revered in the pioneering Western spirit: passion, determination, and courage. Though she struggles with personal hardship (her beloved father's suicide; later, an attempted rape), she prevails, eventually becoming a happy wife and mother herself, presiding over a large brood on a farm in Nebraska.

Ántonia is presented in the novel through the memory and perception of narrator Jim Burden, who befriended her and helped teach her English when they were growing up years before in "Black Hawk" (based on Willa Cather's *Red Cloud*). Taught the ways of the old country by her father, an intelligent man who never quite adjusts to the move, Ántonia tries in her life both to honour the old country and to take on the optimistic spirit of the new. In particular, Ántonia, along with Jim, forms a deep and lasting relation to the vast prairie landscape, achieving moments of transcendent happiness under the open, blue sky, and later achieving fulfilment living and working on the land with her family.

Lively and adventurous, defiant and affectionate, Ántonia remains a resonant figure in Jim Burden's life, even after he relocates to the east coast, where he practices law and inhabits a loveless, childless marriage. As Jim reflects with a friend he encounters on a train at the novel's beginning, Ántonia "seemed to mean to us the country, the conditions, the whole adventure of our childhood." As such, he recalls her with the wistful affection that brings her glowingly to life.

Of the novel in which Ántonia appears, H.L. Mencken wrote, "No romantic novel ever written in America, by man or woman, is one half so beautiful as *My Ántonia*."
Sylvia Brownrigg

Date 1918
Author Willa Cather (1873–1947)
Nationality USA
Why It's Key Cather's energetic, spirited teenager is a Bohemian immigrant who struggles to make a new life in Nebraska with her parents and siblings. Viewed through the memory of Jim Burden (like Cather, a Nebraskan who moved to New York), Ántonia embodies the optimism and energy of the pioneer spirit Cather so admired.

Key Event **W. H. Auden meets Christopher Isherwood**

A "small boy with enormous head and large eyes, carefully copying down the work of the boy at the desk next to his" was W.H. Auden's (1907–73) first impression of Christopher Isherwood (1904–86); Isherwood recalled a boy remarkable for "his naughtiness, his insolence, his smirking tantalizing air of knowing disreputable and exciting secrets." The two boys met at St Edmund's School in Hindhead, Surrey, and, although Auden was two and a half years younger, they enjoyed each other's company until the 14-year-old Isherwood left the school in 1918. They were reintroduced in 1925 when Auden had just started at Oxford and Isherwood, having left Cambridge, was struggling to write a novel.

Auden regarded Isherwood as his most important critic, and unquestioningly incorporated into his poems any alterations that he suggested. Isherwood owed his friend a debt too: it was on a visit to Auden that he first came to Berlin, the inspiration for his best work. The two traveled extensively together (a trip to China resulted in a book of prose and verse, *Journey to a War*) and enjoyed an intermittent sexual relationship. Their most important collaborations were the three plays they wrote in the 1930s, which addressed, through oblique fantasy, themes such as the rise of Fascism; Isherwood said that he wrote the "straight" parts while Auden did the "woozy" bits – that is, the verse and the more poetic stretches of prose. In 1939 they both emigrated to America, though many thought that they should have stayed in England to do war work.

Jake Kerridge

Date 1918

Place UK

Why It's Key W. H. Auden and Christopher Isherwood met at prep school, heralding a long friendship and a significant literary partnership. Of particular note are the plays they wrote together, *The Dog Beneath the Skin* (1935), *The Ascent of F6* (1936), and *On the Frontier* (1939).

Opposite Isherwood and Auden

1910–1919

129

Key Event
Arthur Cravan is lost at sea

Born Fabien Avenarius Lloyd, Arthur Cravan (1887–1918) was the nephew of Oscar Wilde's wife, Constance, and he proudly declared an affinity with his uncle, "although our chest measurement differs." In the tradition of his heroes Walt Whitman and Arthur Rimbaud, Cravan devoted his energies épater le bourgeois. As Mina Loy (1882–1966), the English poet who became his wife, later noted, "the instinct of 'knock-out' dominated his critique." From 1912 to 1915, Cravan published six issues of a polemical journal called *Maintenant* (insulting writers and painters about their physical as well as artistic shortcomings) which became a model for subsequent Dada magazines and Guy Debord's Situationism. Cravan enjoyed many adventures including, in 1916, a boxing match with black heavyweight champion Jack Johnson in Barcelona, which paid for the transatlantic steamer on which he encountered Leon Trotsky.

In 1918 he married Loy and tried to make a living by boxing in Mexico. At the end of the year the couple decided to go to Venezuela. Loy set off by steamer, with Cravan following in a sailboat. He never arrived, and speculation about his fate continued for years. Loy believed he had been murdered for his money; others claimed to have seen him alive and with a new name. He probably drowned. In 1929, when the *Little Review*'s "Confession-Questionnaire" asked, "What has been the happiest moment of your life?" Loy replied, "every moment I spent with Arthur Cravan." "Your unhappiest?" "The rest of the time." Her love for her lost "poet-boxer" became the stuff of myth, inspiring poems such as "Colossus."

Kasia Boddy

Date 1918

Place en route to Venezuela

Why It's Key No one has solved the mystery of the disappearance in 1918 of proto-Dadaist, and "the world's shortest-haired poet," Arthur Cravan. He inspired the work of fellow modernist poet Mina Loy.

Key Event F. Scott Fitzgerald falls in love with Zelda Sayre

Scott Fitzgerald (1896–1940) met Zelda Sayre (1900–48) in the last year of World War I, while he was in the army and stationed at Camp Sheridan in Alabama. She was the belle of society in the city of Montgomery, the archetypal flapper, daughter of a Supreme Court judge, with aspirations towards becoming a writer herself. Fitzgerald was disappointed that he never did get to go to war, but he had met the love of his life and they were married in 1920. The couple settled in New York City and when Fitzgerald's second novel *The Beautiful and the Damned* was published in 1922 he drew on their relationship in his portrait of the married life of a pair of alcoholic spendthrifts.

Scott's literary success enabled them to move to Great Neck, Long Island, where the extravagant drunken partying of this wealthy suburban enclave provided him with material that was to appear in *The Great Gatsby* (1925). However, the couple were living beyond their means and they moved to France, where the cost of living was lower, in 1924.

In 1930 Zelda suffered a nervous breakdown. Diagnosed as schizophrenic, she spent most of the rest of her life in institutions. Fitzgerald drew on this in his portrayal of Nicole, the wife and patient of the psychoanalyst Dick Diver, in *Tender is the Night* (1934). Zelda claimed that Fitzgerald actually used material from her diaries. She finally realized her own literary ambitions with the novel *Save Me the Waltz* (1932).

Michael Munro

Date 1918

Place USA

Why It's Key Zelda was the love of Fitzgerald's life, although their relationship became a troubled one. Her personality inspired many of his female characters and aspects of her life, including her descent into mental illness, informed much of his work.

Opposite F. Scott Fitzgerald and Zelda Sayre

Key Event
The Death of Wilfred Owen

News of the death of Lieutenant W.E.S. Owen (1893–1918), MC, while fighting on the Sambre-Oise Canal in northern France, reached his mother in his native town of Oswestry in the Welsh Marches on 11 November 1918, just as the church bells were ringing out a celebration of the newly declared peace.

Like many other Shropshire lads, Owen, the son of a station master, had joined up in 1915. He served with the Artists' Rifles and was soon commissioned. Owen had begun writing poetry before the war, but the experience of the monstrousness of modern warfare gave this technically innovative and gifted poet something to get his teeth into: "My subject is War," he wrote, "and the pity of War."

In June 1917 Owen was sent back to Britain with shellshock, and while recuperating in Craiglockhart Hospital in Edinburgh he met fellow officer and poet Siegfried Sassoon, who encouraged Owen to develop his poetry, and his strong anti-war stance. Friends said they could get Owen a safe staff job, but he saw it as his duty to return to the Front to bear compassionate witness to the horrors borne by his fellow men in the trenches. He was awarded a posthumous Military Cross for his courage and leadership during an attack in October 1918 on German strong points around the village of Joncourt.

Few of Owen's war poems were published in his lifetime, but they have subsequently helped to shape our view of the futility of the "Great War." It was Owen himself who condemned "The old Lie: Dulce et decorum est / Pro patria mori."

Ian Crofton

Date 1918

Place UK

Why It's Key The death of the finest of the English war poets in action just days before the Armistice bitterly confirmed his view of the waste of war.

Key Author **Guillaume Apollinaire**
Calligrammes

Apollinaire's (1880–1918) short life was not short of incident: he was at one time implicated in the (temporary) theft of the *Mona Lisa* from the Louvre; he had a number of significant romantic affairs which inspired some extraordinary love poems; and after enlisting in the army at the end of 1914, he saw considerable action in World War I and was invalided out after suffering a serious wound to the head. However, it is his work as a poet and critic that has ensured the longevity of his name. Exhilarating, resourceful and still strikingly modern, poems such as "Zone," "Les Collines," and "La Jolie Rousse" combine words and images in novel ways, using techniques gleaned from the art of montage and the aesthetics of dream-work, while managing to retain the traditional consolations of poetry in beautiful clusters of color, feeling, and mystery.

Apollinaire's poetry responds affirmatively to the social and technological transformations of the early twentieth century. It is also one of the most indispensable links between the work of the most forward-looking artists (Rimbaud, Mallarmé) of the previous century and the innovations of movements like Cubism and Surrealism. He was as much influenced by, and an influence on, visual artists such as Robert Delaunay and Pablo Picasso, as he was a crucial figure in the development of modernist literature.

Robin Purves

Date 1918 (death)

Nationality France

Key Works *Alcools* (1913), *Les peintres cubistes* (1913), *Le poète assassiné* (1916), *Les mamelles de Tirésias* (1917), *L'esprit nouveau et les poètes* (1918), *Calligrammes* (1918)

Why It's Key Apollinaire coined the word "surrealism." *Calligrammes*, a collection of poetry which used typographical innovations was published shortly after his death.

Opposite *Calligrammes*

Key Author **Heinrich Mann**
Der Untertan

Heinrich Mann's (1871–1950) best-known early work was *Professor Unrat* (*Small Town Tyrant*, 1908), the story of a tyrannical high-school teacher who falls hopelessly in thrall to the cabaret singer Rosa Frölich. This became the 1930 film *The Blue Angel*, which immortalized Marlene Dietrich's voice (and her stockinged-and-suspendered legs) as the siren Lola-Lola.

Mann's more ambitious novel *Der Untertan* (translated under various titles, but best known as *Man of Straw*, 1918) appeared at the end of World War I, though it had been completed before its outbreak. Diederich Hessling is the son of a paper manufacturer who rises to power in the fictional small town of Netzig by adopting and virtually embodying the militaristic, capitalistic and anti-intellectual values of late nineteenth century Germany. Outwardly supporting the conservative values of his class, Hessling is in fact totally unprincipled in his business dealings and private life, and his rise is satirised as a perfect example of bourgeois hypocrisy.

Like his older, and much more famous brother Thomas, Heinrich Mann chose exile after the Nazi takeover of 1933, and settled in Nice. A lifelong Francophile, he wrote two novels about Henry IV, whose tolerant attitude to religion helped end decades of religious war in sixteenth century France – Mann's literary rebuke to intolerant times.

He escaped to America in 1940, where he spent the war years, dogged by ill health and financial difficulties, but politically active – he denounced the Nazi atrocities against Czech civilians in his book *Lidice* (1943). He died in California in 1950, shortly before his intended return to (East) Germany.

Cathy Benson

Date 1918

Nationality Germany

Why It's Key Though a less subtle writer than his brother Thomas, Heinrich was arguably a more prophetic one.

Key Works *In the Land of Cockaigne* (1901), *The Little Town* (1909), *The Poor* (1917), *The Chief* (1925), *Young Henry of Navarre* (1935), *Henry, King of France* (1938), *Review of an Age* (autobiography, 1945)

Key Event **Sylvia Beach sets up Shakespeare and Company**

Sylvia Beach (1887–1962), an American devotee of modern French writing, was living in Paris when she decided to set up Shakespeare and Company, an English-language bookshop and lending library, in 1919. The idea was primarily to cater for her compatriots who were flocking to France, taking advantage of the weakness of the franc against the dollar to live more cheaply than they could at home. The shop became a meeting place for French as well as expatriate American writers, including Ernest Hemingway, F. Scott Fitzgerald, and Ezra Pound. Beach not only gave them encouragement, but held readings from which they could make some money, and provided hospitality for many.

In 1921 the shop moved to larger premises at rue de l'Odéon, where it remained until closed during the German occupation in 1941, and it was from here that Beach published James Joyce's *Ulysses* in 1922 after the Irish author had failed to find a publisher who would take a risk on it. Customers of Shakespeare and Company were also able to buy or borrow books that were banned in the United States or the UK, such as D.H. Lawrence's *Lady Chatterley's Lover*.

Beach never reopened her shop after the war, but in 1956 she published *Shakespeare and Company*, a memoir of life on the Left Bank that included her portraits of many leading literary figures of the interwar years. She gave permission for the name to be used again in 1951 but had no connection with it. This shop still exists, at rue de la Bûcherie.

Michael Munro

Date 1919

Place Paris, France

Why It's Key In the 1920s the cost of living in France was less than in the United States and among the Americans who came to Paris were several authors, who soon found a home from home at Beach's bookshop. She gave help and hospitality to many aspiring writers and published James Joyce's *Ulysses* when no publishing house would consider it.

Key Author **Ronald Firbank** *Valmouth*

Condensed, elliptical, and fantastic, Firbank's novels dazzle and unsettle. "I think nothing of filing fifty pages down to make a brief, crisp paragraph, or even a row of dots," he wrote. The result was writing which discards almost all of what E.M. Forster called fiction's "realistic lumber." What remains is a series of carefully arranged fragments: snatches of dialogue, brief passages of lush description, wittily acerbic observations, and ludicrous incidents (*Concerning the Eccentricities of Cardinal Pirelli* (1926) begins with the baptism of a dog and ends with the Cardinal scampering naked around a darkened cathedral in pursuit of a choirboy).

Densely and sometimes enigmatically allusive, Firbank's fiction seems to reject the very idea of major characters and central narrative in favor of a prolific array of interwoven subplots peopled with memorable eccentrics. *Vainglory* (1915) follows in part the attempts of Mrs Shamefoot to have a stained-glass window of herself put up in Ashringford Cathedral, while *Valmouth* (1919) takes places in a seaside health-resort whose air promotes remarkable longevity. The settings of his later fiction include exoticized versions of Spain, Cuba, and North Africa. Firbank's later novels are also increasingly open in their treatment of homosexuality.

Perhaps the most remarkable of Firbank's comic gifts is his ear for the absurdity of overheard conversation. Evelyn Waugh gratefully acknowledged Firbank's innovations in this area. Firbank also takes an infectious delight in naming: his characters include Mrs Thoroughfare, Miami Mouth, Sir Somebody Something, and His Naughtiness Prince Olaf. Despite his influence on subsequent writers, Firbank's work remains strikingly individual.

Paul Vlitos

Date 1919 (publication)

Name Arthur Annesley Ronald Firbank (1886–1926)

Nationality UK

Key Works *Inclinations* (1916), *Caprice* (1917), *Santal* (1921), *The Flower Beneath the Foot* (1923), *Sorrow in Sunlight* (1925)

Why It's Key Writers including Evelyn Waugh, W.H. Auden, V.S. Pritchett, Anthony Powell, and Alan Hollinghurst have admired Firbank's innovative fiction.

Key Book
Winesburg, Ohio

Concerned with pre-industrial American life and its movement away from a traditionally rural foundation, *Winesburg, Ohio* is a series of interlocking short stories focused on the small-town inhabitants of Winesburg. Their sadnesses and desires are reflective of a certain kind of simpler and more honest life which was dying away in the early twentieth century, when Anderson wrote the book.

Calling his characters "grotesques," Anderson sought to portray the missed opportunities, frustration, and lack of sophistication of the small town. His characters' imprisonment in lives of their own making, their unwillingness to pursue their hearts' desires, undermine the myths of the American Dream and progress which, by the time of its publication in 1919 after World War I, were already well under attack.

Winesburg, Ohio is about truth-seeking, both of a personal and a social kind. In the recurring image of Winesburg's denizens telling their heart-breaking stories to the young reporter George Willard, the novel poses questions with which the modernists of Anderson's day were concerned: How can we know the truth of ourselves? How can we represent and articulate this truth, even if we find it? What does it mean to be part of a human community? Are we truly alone, no matter where we are?

Anderson was a penpal of another ground breaking modernist, Gertrude Stein, with whom he often discussed experimental literary style. His collection of short tales challenged the notion of what a "novel" was and, though critically successful and garnering him a prestigious literary prize from *The Dial*, the most famous literary journal of its day, was not particularly a popular success. Today, it is considered a pivotal American modernist text.
Elizabeth Rosen

Date 1919

Author Sherwood Anderson (1876–1941)

Nationality USA

Why It's Key Considered alternately a critique of small-town American provincialism and a nostalgic longing for it, *Winesburg, Ohio* challenged received notions of the novel at the same time as it explored modernist ideas about "truth" and the human condition.

Key Book
The Motion Demon

A life-long invalid, Grabinski wrote of characters also hidden from the world, given to strange reveries and curious states of half-consciousness. The stories, pulsating with lurid and macabre detail, shun folklore and use technology as a medium for the supernatural. In *The Motion Demon*, his most popular work, the moving train becomes a symbol of compulsion – the "train neurosis" is a modern insanity, an unstoppable force, a harbinger of murderous libidinal fantasies. Characters are persecuted by several versions of themselves - doppelgangers, succubi, and demonic machines. Fireman and arsonist, sane citizen and madman, alive and dead, even male and female might share the same body. Grabinski called this kind of fantasy, indebted to contemporary psychoanalytic ideas, "psychofantasy." Appalled and fascinated by lewdness, he is sexually explicit.

His stories are about unwanted visitors, things "lured out of non-existence" – unspeakable thoughts made flesh. In "The Area" a writer is set upon by monstrosities conjured from his own imagination, pleading for life, and orgiastically sucking him of his own. Dread of the unknown reaches paranoiac levels in "The Glance." The main character shudders at open doors, then turning corners becomes a problem. Soon he sees all soft furnishings as potential hiding places, and finally is unable to turn round in his own home without announcing, "I am turning round now," for fear of what might be behind him.

Grabinski is most modern in his insistence that the supernatural works within us. There is always an unknown adversary who paces behind the walls of one's house; leaves "correspondence" hidden in the fire's embers; awaits you in a storm; inhabits the house across the street; spies you out, destroys you, seduces you – and yet, you eventually realize, has existed within you all along.
Lucy Daniel

Date 1919

Author Stefan Grabinski (1887-1936)

Nationality Poland

Original Title *Demo Ruchu*

Why It's Key Grabinski was one of the twentieth century's most original writers of fantasy and horror fiction, but died an obscure death, from tuberculosis. The 1950s saw a renewal of interest in his work.

Key Character **Zorro**
"The Curse of Capistrano"

Zorro is the nom-de-guerre of Don Diego de la Vega, a nondescript nobleman in the Spanish California of the early nineteenth century. Shocked by the repressive tyranny of the state governor, de la Vega takes the part of the people by donning a black cape, a mask, and his rapier. His trademark is a "Z" inscribed with the tip of his blade. The character first appeared in "The Curse of Capistrano" written by the pulp novelist Johnston McCulley for *All-Story Weekly*, and therefore he is one of many figures in the twentieth-century American imagination to have graduated from the pages of pulp magazines to full blown cultural archetype. The character has appeared in TV series and a number of films, most notably played by Douglas Fairbanks.

Zorro combines Western style stories with European swordplay, Robin Hood sentiments and Latin temperament. His mystery and secret identity is key to his appeal. The morality of the stories is not convoluted, and Zorro's swashbuckling is always in a good cause. Champion of the poor and the unfortunate, the masked vigilante hero living to an extent on the fringes of society provided the model for The Shadow and Batman.

The question of Zorro's ethnicity is complex – he is an American hero, forged post-World War I for a new generation of readers, but he is also Spanish and from a time when California was not American. Thus like his peers – Superman, Batman, Robin Hood – his difference is central to his characterization.

Jerome de Groot

Date 1919

Author Johnston McCulley (1883–1958)

Nationality USA

Why It's Key Zorro was the first mass culture non-Anglo-Saxon American super hero. In 2005 Isabel Allende wrote her version of *Zorro*, a novel in which she expanded on El Zorro's (The Fox's) life story.

Opposite **From the film adaptation of** *Zorro*

Key Character **Mary Olivier**
Mary Olivier: A Life

May Sinclair's semi-autobiographical novel *Mary Olivier: A Life* expresses Sinclair's frustration entailed in being born a woman in the mid-nineteenth century. It is a compelling narrative of Mary, youngest of five children and the only daughter; who, like the author, is intellectually gifted and emotionally sensitive. The novel is told mainly in the third person, but the point of view is consistently Mary's. The reader shares her struggle to achieve autonomous identity despite the various forces that conspire to frustrate her development and systematically cut off each opportunity that offers itself to her.

Close to Sinclair's own experience, her father starts the novel as a respectable head of household, but eventually loses his money, becomes alcoholic, and dies of apoplexy. He is a distant figure, who seems to resent his children coming between him and his wife. Mary's mother is anti-intellectual, and narrow-mindedly religious: She favors her sons and makes Mary give up all the opportunities that come her way since as the only daughter she must stay at home to look after her mother. Late in the novel she admits to Mary that she was jealous of her.

The novel gives an insightful account of the tensions in mother-daughter relationships, as Mary veers between filial desire, resentment, and belated, hard-won reconciliation. In the final sequence of the novel Mary writes in the first person as she achieves a heart-wrenching acceptance of living as a "real self" despite all her losses and disappointments. By charting the character of Mary from early childhood to late middle age, Sinclair examines unflinchingly the tragic experience of being born a woman in the mid-nineteenth century. The result is a powerful female Bildungsroman that impressively combines intellectual acuity, emotional intelligence, and self-reflective honesty. A must read for every woman!

Helen May Dennis

Date 1919

Author May Sinclair (1863–1946)

Nationality USA

Why It's Key Sinclair was the first to use the phrase "stream of consciousness" in a literary context, to describe Dorothy Richardson's prose style. She was influenced by her Imagist friends, her readings in philosophy, and by the psychoanalytic theories of Freud and Jung.

Key Event **The Algonquin Round Table meets for the first time**

The Algonquin is a hotel in New York. Between 1919 and around 1927 a loose collective known as the Algonquin Round Table met there informally for lunch. The Table was a loose consortium of playwrights, composers, novelists, agents, journalists, actors, and actresses. Several of the original members had met whilst writing for the U.S. military newspaper *Stars and Stripes*. Consciously political and liberal, it numbered key left-wing thinkers, writers and cultural movers. Important members included Harpo Marx, Dorothy Parker, George S. Kaufman, Ruth Hale, and Franklin Pierce Adams.

The Table reflected the new public presence and significance of women after World War I, with figures such as Parker, Jane Grant, and Hale campaigning on equality issues (Hale helped to pass the 1920 19th Amendment for women's voting rights). The activities of the members of the Algonquin Round Table provide a unique sidelight into the cultural moment of early 1920s New York, from the founding in 1925 of the *New Yorker* by Harold Ross and Jane Grant to the plays of Kaufman, Robert Sherwood, Edna Ferber, and Marc Connelly.

The Algonquin Round Table's fame is because of its function as cultural melting pot and, possibly more popularly, for the biting and caustic wit it became renowned for. Parker, darling of the Algonquin, set the bar high and the group was well known for its pithy, savage humor. Subsequently it has become a by-word for catty, intelligent, witty, cynical liberals. This reputation for fast-talking one-liners has often prevented real attention being paid to the political and literary work being undertaken.

Jerome de Groot

Date 1919

Place New York, USA

Why It's Key The Algonquin Round Table was a forum for wits and a focus for New York's thriving liberal intelligentsia in the Roaring Twenties.

Key Event **Ashford discovered and published her childhood novel**

Although it was published in the Edwardian era, the world of nine-year-old author Daisy Ashford's story is arch-Victorian. It concerns Mr. Salteena, "an elderly man of 42" and his young friend, Ethel Monticue, a lively seventeen-year-old addicted to "ruge." After a visit to an ostentatiously genteel acquaintance, Bernard Clarke, Mr. Salteena suffers from an anxiety that he is "not quite the right side of the blanket," and therefore travels to London where he hopes a friend of the Prince of Wales will "rub him up a bit in sociery ways." Somewhat surreally, he makes his way to the Crystal Palace, where measurements are immediately taken for plush knickerbockers and other essential gentlemanly accoutrements.

Mr. Salteena's romantic plan is to surprise Ethel with his newfound class, but it is his inevitable disappointment that led J.M. Barrie to remark in his Preface that Salteena "has a touch of Hamlet." Barrie was also very taken with his elation at being given tea in bed: "I say said Mr. Salteena excitedly I have had some tea in bed." Salteena has a great simplicity as well as an unwittingly piquant heroism. Most endearing is Ashford's flouting of all manner of codes of Victorian discretion, in particular Bernard Clarke's eagerness to take the unaccompanied Ethel to the "Gaierty Hotel" in London and compare the beds of their adjoining rooms. *The Young Visiters* triumphs through its appropriations of adult phrases, spliced with childish half-understandings, eccentric punctuation, a near-constant stream of malapropisms, and utter lack of tact. Against which all objections about its literary merit are "as piffle before the wind."

Lucy Daniel

Date 1919

Title *The Young Visiters* or *Mr. Salteena's Plan*

Author Daisy Ashford (1881-1972)

Nationality UK

Why It's Key A comic masterpiece, *The Young Visiters* (written in 1890) is one of the most well-known and best-loved pieces of juvenilia ever written.

Key Passage
Ten Days that Shook the World

"Day broke, and the pickets of Kerensky's Cossacks came in touch. Scattered rifle-fire, summons to surrender. Over the bleak plain on the cold quiet air spread the sound of battle, falling upon the ears of roving bands as they gathered about their little fires, waiting... So it was beginning! They made toward the battle; and the worker hordes pouring out along the straight roads quickened their pace... Thus upon all the points of attack automatically converged angry human swarms, to be met by Commissars and assigned positions, or work to do. This was their battle, for their world; the officers in command were elected by them. For the moment that incoherent multiple will was one will... "

This striking piece of reportage is typical of the vivid, politically committed writing in John Reed's firsthand account of the October Revolution. Reed had made a career in radical journalism, sympathetically covering the workers' side in a number of industrial disputes in the United States. During World War I he became a war correspondent on the Eastern Front, and found himself in Russia as the Bolshevik leaders began to plan the October Revolution. He forged a strong friendship with Lenin, and there are interviews with the Bolshevik leader in *Ten Days that Shook the World*.

After the Revolution, Reed returned to the United States, where he was instrumental in founding the U.S. Communist Party. Accused of treason, he fled back to Russia, where he died of typhus. He is the only American to have received the honor of burial in the Kremlin Wall.

Ian Crofton

Date 1919

Author John Reed (1887–1920)

Nationality USA

Why It's Key *Ten Days that Shook the World* became one of the century's most famous pieces of radical journalism. In 1929 the John Reed Clubs were set up, with chapters across the United States, to encourage "proletarian" writing.

Key Author
Olive Schreiner

The death of Olive Schreiner (1855–1920) in 1920 saw the loss of a remarkable woman who was arguably South Africa's first major fiction writer as well as a pioneering feminist and staunch opponent of imperialism. The daughter of an Evangelical English mother and a German Lutheran missionary father, Schreiner was raised on several South African mission stations, but rejected established religion at an early age in favor of more independent thinking. In 1881 she left South Africa and journeyed to Britain in order to publish her first novel, *The Story of an African Farm* (1883). Highly innovative and beautifully written, *African Farm* deals with many controversial issues of its day, including women's oppression, colonialism, religious doubt, sexuality, and the struggles for personal and political freedom.

In Britain, Schreiner became friends with, and acclaimed by, a group of advanced thinkers which included Havelock Ellis, George Bernard Shaw, and Eleanor Marx, and in 1894 she married the politician Samuel Cronwright. She continued to alternate periods living in South Africa and Britain, and subsequently produced a number of important political works. Her study *Women and Labour* (1911), for example, had a great influence on the contemporary women's movement (as did her 1891 collection of allegories and visionary writings, *Dreams*), whilst her hatred of colonial exploitation – and particularly the figure of Cecil Rhodes – was the focus of several other works. Passionate, eloquent, and dedicated to justice and equality throughout her life, Schreiner is now recognized as a major thinker of the late nineteenth and early twentieth centuries.

Simon Avery

Date 1920 (death)

Key Works *An English South African's View of the Situation* (1899), *Thoughts on South Africa* (1923), *From Man to Man* (1926), *Undine* (1927)

Why It's Key Olive Schreiner had a major influence on the emerging women's movement and contemporary thinking about imperialism in South Africa. Schreiner constantly sought to challenge established ideas and was admired by intellectual thinkers of the day.

Key Author
Benito Pérez Galdós

Spain's greatest nineteenth-century novelist, Benito Pérez Galdós (1843–1920) – a realist who has been compared to Dickens, Balzac, and Tolstoy – was born in Las Palmas, in the Canary Islands, on May 10, 1843. He went to Madrid in 1862 to study law and, from 1873, devoted himself exclusively to writing. He was prolific: he wrote 32 novels, 46 "National Episodes" ("Episodios nacionales"), 24 plays, as well as short stories and critical articles.

His series of novels known collectively as the "Contemporary Novels" ("Novelas contemporáneas") include many of his greatest successes, especially the four-part *Fortunata y Jacinta* (1886–87) – the turbulent story of two women, their husbands, and their lovers, told with sure-footed narrative and characterization – and *Misericordia* (1897). Like Balzac, Galdós' characters appear and reappear in several books, but unlike Balzac's, these characters are often depicted very differently depending on the narrator's viewpoint.

With the *Episodios nacionales*, Galdós undertook a critical analysis of the socio-political history of Spain, from the Battle of Trafalgar in 1805 to the Bourbon restoration in 1868.

In his fiction, Galdós often commented satirically and ironically on what he saw as the weaknesses of bourgeois life – particularly in Madrid. His 1901 play, *Electra*, turned him into a leading anti-clerical figure. In 1910 he was elected a deputy for the Republican Socialist coalition, but he suffered from progressive blindness and two years later – after completing *Cánovas*, the last of the *Episodios nacionales* – he lost his sight completely. He died on January 4, 1920.
Adam Feinstein

Date 1920 (death)

Nationality Spain

Key Works *Doña Perfecta* (1876) *Marianela* (1878),

Why It's Key Benito Pérez Galdós' chance of long-lasting international fame was sabotaged by jealous conservative countrymen, when they launched a slander campaign against him after learning that he would be nominated for the Nobel Prize for Literature.

1920-1929

141

Key Author
Knut Hamsun

The winner of the Nobel Prize in 1920, Hamsun (1859–1952) is credited with being the creator of the solitary outcast, the absurdist wanderer, filling a meaningless life with angry, pointless gestures. He was a leading writer of the Neo-Romantic revolt, rescuing the novel from excessive realism at the turn of the twentieth century. Hamsun was the son of a peasant farmer and he received almost no education. The first thirty years of his life were spent in wandering as a casual laborer in Norway and the United States.

His first great novel, *Hunger* (1890) features a writer enduring the struggle of life. The "action" is his hunger, cadging, cheating, and lies – some of which he seems to believe himself. In a literature overshadowed by Ibsen, in whose plays people work out the moral dilemmas of right conduct, always staying in character, Hamsun was an iconoclast. He wrote, "I dream of a literature with characters in which their very lack of consistency is their basic characteristic."

Further works of fierce individualism, including *Mysteries* (1892) and *Pan* (1894) made him the most celebrated Norwegian writer of his generation. In later life he rejected his early anarchism and embraced an anti-modern, back-to-nature philosophy in such books as *Growth of the Soil* (1920). Ever the irresponsible outsider, his flair for being the outcast, contemptuous of the world, led him to support the Nazis during their occupation of Norway. He was imprisoned after the war and put on trial but the charges were dropped.
Jad Adams

Date 1920 (Nobel Prize for Literature awarded)

Nationality Norway

Why It's Key "In Hamsun characters provoke apparently pointless encounters which they then disown or annul at whim. They are epistemological brawlers, always challenging meaning to a fight. They invent the scenes through which they move, and thus invent themselves afresh on every page" (James Wood, *The Irresponsible Self*).

Key Author **Edith Wharton**
The Age of Innocence

At age 11, Edith Wharton (1862–1937) showed a story to her mother that began with a character apologizing for the untidiness of a drawing room. She recalls the incident in her autobiography: "never shall I forget the sudden drop of my creative frenzy when she returned it with the icy comment: 'Drawing-rooms are always tidy'."

Wharton spent her literary career exposing the emotional chaos that tidy drawing rooms conceal. Brought up in the traditional environs of nineteenth-century "Old" aristocratic New York, Wharton was also a product of the new, Gilded Age America, whose technological, financial, and cultural frontiers were advancing faster than at any other time in the young country's history.

An insider's perspective on her society, along with a writer's feeling of alienation from it, shaped Wharton's first novel, *The House of Mirth* (1905). Its heroine, torn between a modern desire for self-sufficiency and the financial necessity of marrying well, observes, "The only way not to think about money is to have a great deal of it."

Old New York's men fare no better than its women in attempting independence, as Newland Archer of the Pulitzer Prize-winning *The Age of Innocence* (1920) discovers. Prevented from leaving his loveless marriage both by his upbringing and by the ruthless machinations of New York society, Archer is trapped forever in its narrow confines. *The Age of Innocence* interprets a sickening prelude to social exclusion as: "the tribal rally around a kinswoman about to be eliminated from the tribe." Wharton's anthropological dissections of high society's rituals are at once admiring and cautionary. Her fiction both mourns a culture too rarefied to breathe twentieth-century air, and heaves a sigh of relief at its passing.

Dinah Roe

Date 1920 (publication)

Nationality USA

Other Key Works *The Decoration of Houses* (1898), *Ethan Frome* (1911), *A Backward Glance* (1934)

Why It's Key Wharton broke new literary ground with her anthropological descriptions of the customs of nineteenth-century aristocratic New York. Her observations influenced contemporary chroniclers of high-society tribal behavior, such as Candace Bushnell and Bret Easton Ellis.

Opposite Edith Wharton

142

Key Book *Hungry Hearts*
Anzia Yezierska

Anzia Yezierska was born in Poland and grew up among the overcrowded tenements of New York's Lower East Side. She worked in a sweatshop and studied at night. In the stories she began writing her explicit intention was that a working immigrant woman – a cleaner or a sweatshop worker – should be allowed a narrative voice and the expression of her own world-view, rather than being the object of other people's philanthropy, and other people's stories.

Hungry Hearts is about both literal hunger for food ("Mamma! It's so empty in my stomach! Ain't there nothing?") and her female characters' hunger for self-expression ("this wild, blind hunger to release the dumbness that choked her"). Critics damned the emotionality of Yezierska's stories – her characters are given to melodramatic outbursts, which are (intentionally) both heart-rending and comic.

She wrote about immigrant girls' attempts to outgrow their families by education; to escape rent-collectors and matchmakers and live in their own houses and choose their own husbands. Her autobiographical characters are often attracted to "Anglo-Saxon" males based on John Dewey, the American philosopher, with whom Yezierska had a brief affair which she relived through her fiction. She is never less than keenly alert to the ironies of such stories of assimilation and "rise."

In "The Fat of the Land," Yezierska gives her typical twist to the American success story. At the beginning Hanneh Breineh is a poor tenement woman; years later she is decked out in silk and diamonds, desperately lonely in a big house, irrevocably distanced from her American children, and embarrassed in front of the servants. Her chief joy is going back to Hester Street and bargaining with the peddlers to "get the eating a penny cheaper," like in the old days.

Lucy Daniel

Date 1920 (publication)

Author Anzia Yezierska (1885–1970)

Nationality USA

Why It's Key *Hungry Hearts* was Yezierska's first story collection. In Hollywood, Sam Goldwyn gave her $10,000 to make a movie version, dubbing her "Queen of the Ghetto," and falsely publicising her "overnight" rags-to-riches story. Yezierska, ashamed that her new-found wealth stemmed from her stories of some of New York's poorest, left Hollywood.

Key Book
Chéri

To say that Colette thought a great deal about love would be an understatement. Her entire writing life grew from her desire to reveal her characters' romantic and erotic secrets. Her first bestseller was *Claudine* and that account of a teenage girl's adventures with men was greeted with both shock and delight. *Cheri*, her best novel, looks at those same adventures but this time from the perspective of an older woman. *Cheri* is a novel of experience.

Léa is 49 years old, a courtesan, and her lover, the Chéri of the title, is 25. He is the son of one of her friends and is capricious and demanding. Léa, proud and voluptuous, is still desirable but she is trying not to show how much she minds the prospects of losing her looks and her lover. Chéri loves his older mistress but declares his intention of marrying someone younger and more suitable.

There may be love here but it is a cruel kind. Colette was unsparingly truthful in her portrayal of the power struggles inherent in affairs of the heart. As well as a story of a doomed relationship, Cheri is also a portrait of a time and a place – pre-war Paris and the world of the *demi-mondaine* and the kept men and women. It crystallised for many people an image of Parisians as sophisticated sensualists, taking lovers without guilt and losing them without anguish. The people of France clearly took Colette to their hearts. She was the first woman to be given a state funeral.

Kathy Watson

Date 1920

Author Colette (1873–1954)

Nationality France

Why It's Key Colette once wrote that "whatever one writes, comes to pass." Shortly after finishing *Chéri*, at the age of 47, she began a love affair with her 16-year-old stepson.

Opposite **Colette**

Key Author **Katherine Mansfield**
Bliss

Katherine Mansfield was christened Kathleen Mansfield Beauchamp in Wellington, New Zealand, in 1888. Her youthful decision to change her name was one of many shifts of identity that marked her short life and intimate relationships. An English education provided her with her first opportunity to reinvent herself, and in London, far from her wealthy colonial family, the rebellious young New Zealander re-established herself as a passionate artist with a confident future. Her quest for life-experience to fuel her writing resulted in at least one miscarried pregnancy and the undiagnosed gonorhhea which would lead to tuberculosis. But whilst this simmered undetected, Mansfield was forging a reputation as an exciting new literary talent. Her stories are characterised by their freshness and spontaneity; the deceptive lightness and simplicity which belie the fastidiousness of their execution. She has a journalist's eye for detail, a playwright's ear for dialogue, and a cinematic ability to seamlessly shift her focus. Although she was sometimes accused of sentimentality, her finest stories are dispassionate and coolly sardonic. Mansfield's death at 34 and the posthumous image presented by her husband, literary critic John Middleton Murry, cast her finally as a suffering, almost saintly figure. But although her life made a tragically short story, the woman who lived it was spirited, duplicitous, and funny. In the words of Leonard Woolf: "By nature, I think, she was gay, cynical, amoral, ribald, witty… I don't think anyone has ever made me laugh more than she did in those days."

Admired in her lifetime for their originality and economy of style, her stories still shimmer with vitality, modernity and the revelation of the extraordinary within the everyday.

Amy Rosenthal

Date 1920

Author Katherine Mansfield (1888–1923)

Nationality New Zealand

Other Key Works *In a German Pension* (1911), *Prelude* (1918), *The Garden Party* (1922)

Why It's Key Although she aspired to move beyond the short story form and confessed towards the end of her life that "I am tired of my little stories like birds bred in cages," Mansfield's mastery of the genre changed its nature forever.

Key Character **Hugh Selwyn Mauberley**
Hugh Selwyn Mauberley

"Hugh Selwyn Mauberley" is the alter ego of Ezra Pound, an American poet who moved to London in 1908. After World War I, Pound became thoroughly disenchanted with English life and culture. He lost close friends, the sculptor Henri Gaudier-Brzeska and the philosopher T.E. Hulme, to the war and felt that the poetic principles he had set forth for the Imagist movement had become diluted. Pound voiced his feelings through a lengthy, satirical and, in places, cryptic dramatic monologue. The whole sequence starts with an Ode for the tomb of "E.P." that declares him "out of key with his time." Mauberley's acquaintance includes "Mr Nixon," a portrait of populist author and critic, Arnold Bennett, who advises him to "give up verse, my boy, / There's nothing in it." Pound's response is to write in short four-line stanzas (quatrains) with unusual rhymes on English, Latin, and Greek words.

Pound distanced himself from his creation, comparing his poem to T.S. Eliot's fictional speaker in "The Love Song of J. Alfred Prufrock": "I'm no more Mauberley than Eliot is Prufrock," he wrote, "Mauberley is a mere surface … an attempt to condense the James novel." Indeed, much of the poem finds Mauberley complaining about his inability to write: "Incapable of the least utterance or composition… Nothing, in brief, but maudlin confession." The final poem of the sequence, "Medallion," is sometimes seen as Mauberley/Pound's triumph – the creation of a "hard" poetic form like a sculpture.

Canadian author, Timothy Findlay's novel *Famous Last Words* (1981) draws on Pound's later involvement with Fascism and imagines Mauberley caught up in political intrigue during World War II.
Matthew Creasy

Date 1920

Author Ezra Pound (1885–1972)

Nationality USA

Why It's Key Pound left London for Europe in 1920 and spent the rest of his life working on an epic series of poems, the *Cantos*. *Hugh Selwyn Mauberley* represents a significant step towards the fragmentary style, full of complex literary allusion, that characterizes the poems in *Cantos*.

Key Character **Hercule Poirot**
The Mysterious Affair at Styles

SPOILER

Agatha Christie's most famous creation, Hercule Poirot, was inspired by Belgian war refugees evacuated to the south coast of England, near her home, during World War I. The former police detective with a brilliant mind and a borderline obsessive-compulsive disorder fascinated audiences around the globe. He appears in over 30 novels and more than 50 short stories, and Christie's books have been translated into over 100 languages. Poirot became the first fictional character to receive an obituary on the front page of the *New York Times*.

Unlike other writers of the Golden Age of detective fiction (Margery Allingham, Dorothy L. Sayers, Ngaio Marsh), Christie resolutely failed to have a crush on her hero, and spent much of her career wishing she could kill him off, calling him "a tiresome ego-centric little creep."

However, Poirot has proved more alluring to actors: he has been played by, among others, Albert Finney (grumpy), Peter Ustinov (urbane), and David Suchet (dapper). Poirot is involved in almost every variant of the murder mystery – ostensible victim as murderer (*Peril At End House*); policeman as murderer (*Hercule Poirot's Christmas*); narrator as murderer (*The Murder Of Roger Ackroyd*); everyone as murderer (*Murder On The Orient Express*); and even detective as murderer (*Curtain: Poirot's last case*).

Christie intended to write in the Sherlock Holmes tradition, and much like Holmes, Poirot's personal life can best be described as opaque. He does not, however, solve crimes with magnifying glass and learned monographs, but with psychological assessment and deduction – the little gray cells.
Natalie Haynes

Date 1920 (first appears)

Author Agatha Christie (1890–1976)

Nationality UK

Why It's Key Several elements of the plot of *The Mysterious Affair at Styles* became staples of detective fiction: the country house setting, the array of possible suspects, the twists, and the deliberately misleading details. Christie went on to write 66 detective novels.

Opposite Hercule Poirot

Key Characters **Elizabeth Mapp and Emmeline "Lucia" Lucas** *Queen Lucia*

Edward Frederick Benson was born in 1867, the fifth child of Edward White Benson, Headmaster of Wellington College and later Archbishop of Canterbury, and Mary Sidgwick Benson. He was hugely prolific, and produced dozens of books before his death in 1940 – novels, ghost stories, memoirs, and biographies.

He is best remembered for a series of books about Emmeline "Lucia" Lucas and Elizabeth Mapp. These fall somewhere between a comedy of manners and a war of attrition, and Benson pulls off the rare feat of writing achingly funny prose about an array of characters whose single unifying quality is a total lack of humor. Neither Mapp nor Lucia is remotely clever, cultured, or pleasant, yet their exploits are compelling. We revel in each humiliation heaped upon them, and delight in Lucia's minor victories. Perhaps our affection for them is the same as that shown by the urban sophisticates in *Lucia In London*, who initially despise her, then begin to indulge her almost as one would an ugly pet, so completely monstrous, yet entirely harmless do they find her.

After *Queen Lucia* the rivalling duo of society ladies continued to plot each other's humiliation and downfall in *Miss Mapp* (1922); *Lucia in London* (1927); *Mapp and Lucia* (1931); *Lucia's Progress* (1935); and *Trouble for Lucia* (1939). The later books are set in the town of Tilling, based on Benson's adopted home-town of Rye, in Sussex. Indeed, Lucia might be seen as Benson's alter-ego – his home, *Lamb House*, is the model for hers, *Mallards*. He became mayor of Rye in 1934, and Lucia became mayor of Tilling in *Trouble For Lucia*. Happily, the resemblance ends there, and E.F. Benson was not swept out to sea on a kitchen table.
Natalie Haynes

Date 1920 (first appear)

Author E.F. Benson (1867–1940)

Nationality UK

Why It's Key Benson's great comic creations Mapp and Lucia appeared throughout the 1920s and 1930s in a string of novels which satirized English provincial life.

1920–1929

149

Key Passage **The wrestling had some deep meaning** *Women in Love*

SPOILER

"'One ought to wrestle and strive and be physically close. It makes one sane.'
'You do think so?'
'I do. Don't you?'
'Yes,' said Gerald.
There were long spaces of silence between their words. The wrestling had some deep meaning to them – an unfinished meaning."

This exchange occurs after the scene made famous in Ken Russell's acclaimed film version of *Women in Love*, in which two men, Birkin and Gerald, wrestle naked together. Birkin is a self-portrait of Lawrence himself, and his friend Gerald is the son of a mine owner. The two have embarked on relationships with the sisters Gudrun and Ursula, who had already appeared in Lawrence's novel *The Rainbow*.

Gerald's character embodies all the flaws that Lawrence finds in men – a cruel strength matched by emotional weakness and spiritual barrenness. Gerald is associated with death: as a boy he had accidentally killed his brother; his sister accidentally drowns; and his father is dying. His affair with Gudrun is marked by mutual destructiveness, and, on a winter holiday in the Alps, he attempts to kill her in a jealous rage. Disgusted with himself, he wanders off into the snow to die: "… he slipped and fell down, and as he fell something broke in his soul."

At the end, Birkin – who has sought to achieve with Ursula a fuller union than the conventional one between sexes, based on equality and recognition of difference – mourns the fact that he has been unable to forge a similarly deep relationship with his dead friend. "I wanted eternal union with a man too: another kind of love," he says. Ursula will have none of it: "It's an obstinacy, a theory, a perversity," she says. But Birkin/Lawrence has the last word: "I don't believe that," he answered.
Ian Crofton

Date 1920

Author D.H. Lawrence (1885–1930)

Nationality UK

Why It's Key In this novel, written during World War I, Lawrence offers a revolutionary redefinition of the relations between men and women, and men and men.

Opposite D.H. Lawrence

Key Event *This Side of Paradise* makes F. Scott Fitzgerald a celebrity

This Side of Paradise established F. Scott Fitzgerald as both the leading voice and the leading exemplar of what is known variously as the Jazz Age or the Roaring Twenties. Published in 1920, at the outset of the decade it came to represent, the novel is both a barely disguised autobiography and a self-conscious portrait of the "lost generation" which emerged in the aftermath of World War I – although that conflict is no more than a distant rumble in the narrative. On the last page, Scott Fitzgerald sums up this "new generation… grown up to find all Gods dead, all wars fought, all faiths in man shaken…."

The first printing of *This Side of Paradise* sold out within 24 hours and made the author famous, its success enabling him to marry Zelda Sayre, a tempestuous Southern belle. He was only 23, and Zelda three years younger, and the pair threw themselves into a fast-living, self-destructive lifestyle that set a pattern for young celebrities. The tone and subject matter of *This Side of Paradise* – much of it written when Scott Fitzgerald was himself a student at Princeton – mark a break from the novels of the previous century, and prefigure such later American writers as J.D. Salinger and Bret Easton Ellis. Years of hard drinking took a toll on both Scott and Zelda: he died at the age of 44 in Hollywood, where he worked as a hack scriptwriter, and she suffered a series of mental breakdowns, dying in a fire at a mental hospital in 1948.

Bruce Millar

Date 1920

Author F. Scott Fitzgerald (1896–1940)

Nationality USA

Why It's Key Scott Fitzgerald was unable to match the commercial success of *This Side of Paradise* with his other novels, *The Beautiful and the Damned* (1922), *The Great Gatsby* (1925) – which is now regarded as a masterpiece of American fiction – and *Tender is the Night* (1934). *The Last Tycoon* was unfinished at his death.

Key Event *The Black Mask* magazine is founded

In 1920 the writer and satirist H.L. Mencken and his partner, drama critic George Jean Nathan, set up *The Black Mask* as a popular magazine to underwrite the literary publication *Smart Set*. The magazine initially offered a wide selection of pulp writing, including mystery, crime and the occult. The crime writing imitated English models of analytic detective fiction from Arthur Conan Doyle and G.K. Chesterton. After only eight issues Mencken and Nathan sold the title to their publisher, having used it to raise some quick funds and not foreseeing what the publication might become. The editorship was given to Joseph Straw, who began to turn it into a forum for innovative naturalistic crime fiction. Under his stewardship *Black Mask* transformed the way that detective fiction was written. The magazine began to commission work interested in a new, harder-edged style. It published what is considered the first tough detective story, "Three Gun Terry" by Carroll John Daly, in 1923. This writing was direct, violent, and ambiguous; the morality of the detective story became murkier. The magazine became immensely successful and, as a consequence, influential. The tone of the stories leached into film and television. Crime-fighters became street tough, illiterate, uncompromising, and ambivalent about their moral stance. They drank, and fought, and swore; the prose was pared down, "realistic," and muscular. Dashiell Hammett made his first appearance in 1922, and had a great influence on the house style; Raymond Chandler began writing for the magazine in 1933, and contributed stories which he later turned into *The Big Sleep* and *Farewell, My Lovely*.

Jerome de Groot

Date 1920

Nationality USA

Why It's Key *The Black Mask* became an influential forum for American crime writing, and eventually gave birth to the new hard-boiled style.

Opposite H.L. Mencken

Key Character **Kristin Lavransdatter**
Kristin Lavransdatter

Passion dominates Kristin Lavransdatter. "Wayward, unruly" and disobedient, Kristin resembled the heroines of Undset's previous novels, which focused on infidelity and the erotic life. What made Kristin's story exceptional was that it began in 1306. It was an epic story telling the domestic life of a woman: a completely new departure not just for Undset but for historical fiction anywhere. It told of love, adultery, murder, suicide and violence, through Kristin's life, birth to death. Physically, and in her appetites and actions, Kristin is the strongest of heroines. In a feudal world of lords and retainers, she is naturally rebellious.

But Undset was no New Woman; she was working from an earlier precedent. Perhaps the most extraordinary scene is Kristin's prolonged, tormented labour – described with brutal clarity – during which she reproaches her appalled husband for his previous infidelity to another woman, and has a vision of all life coming from pain. Realism mixes with something

magical, Undset's idea of the divine, which included deep attunement with nature, with womanhood part of nature's fertility.

Undset's characters live the same emotional lives as modern people, but in a world dominated by faith. At the edges of this world are Pagan forces. Schooled at a convent but learned in witch medicine, Kristin struggles with this dichotomy. In the astonishingly moving conclusion, she saves a prostitute's child from being buried alive as a sacrifice to the plague goddess, then fetches the mother's plague-stricken, filthy corpse. After a terrible, slippery journey with the body, as she kisses the dead woman's foot, blood gushes from her own mouth; the black death sweeps through all God's creation. Undset's unique imagination, preoccupied with spiritual corruption and salvation, shows us the world in an utterly different light from the one to which we are accustomed.

Lucy Daniel

Date 1920

Author Sigrid Undset (1882–1949)

Nationality Norway

Why It's Key Undset won the Nobel Prize in 1928 for the international bestseller, the *Kristin Lavransdatter* trilogy. One of Kristin's sons observes that "she bore her tall body as straight as a lance." "The bravest and most high-minded of women," she is a heroine of epic stature. Her story has been compared with *Madame Bovary* and *War and Peace*.

1920–1929

153

Key Event **Capek coins the word "robot" in *R.U.R.* (*Rossum's Universal Robots*)**

Anticipating by decades the dilemmas concerning work, freedom, and autonomy that vex, for example, Asimov's influential *I, Robot* stories (1950), Capek's seminal drama gave us the word and the concept "robot," derived from the Czech for "servitude." Robots recall the Jewish golem or the medieval homunculus but are as characteristically modern as Shelley's Frankenstein; immediately popular and performed in translation in the United States and Britain, Capek's play spoke to contemporary anxieties about Fordism, "big society," and the fate of the individual spirit. Indeed, in 1923 a public discussion about its meaning was held in London featuring luminaries like Shaw and Chesterton, in response to which Capek defended *R.U.R.* as a "struggle [between] equally serious verities."

The contest he indicates involves differing attitudes towards work and technology. In his play, robots are invented by nineteenth-century scientific

materialist Old Rossum (from "reason") as a Promethean disavowal of God; subsequently, however, they become the twentieth century's banal object of mass-production, manufactured for profit by the off-shore Rossum's Universal Robots company run by disenchanted Prospero, Young Rossum. The factory's manager, Domin ("master"), believes robots liberate humans from labour but Alquist, its engineer, thinks work defines humanity and creativity; Helena, the daughter of the company's president, rejects robotics as inhuman. All have a valid point. Significantly, when the robots (inevitably – this is sci-fi) rebel, it is because they work while humans do not. A prescient warning about rudderless, capitalist "progress," Capek's Hegelian humanoids question the possibility or even desirability of a toil-free utopia.

Doug Haynes

Date 1921

Author Karel Capek (1890–1938)

Nationality Czechoslovakia

Why It's Key A successor to writers like Jules Verne and H.G. Wells, Capek, by turns a philosopher, journalist, novelist and dramatist, personally disliked *R.U.R.*, but his legacy will always be dominated by his resonant contribution to science fiction and the popular imagination.

Opposite *R.U.R.* in performance

Key Author **Ramón Pérez de Ayala**
Belarmino y Apolonio

Pérez de Ayala (1880–1962) was born in the northern Spanish city of Oviedo (the "Pilares" of his novels). Oviedo was also the birthplace of the great nineteenth-century novelist Leopoldo Alas (1850–1901), who would be his university tutor in the faculty of law, and serve as one of his inspirations as a novelist. His early novels are autobiographical in varying degrees, as they chart the young life of Alberto Díaz de Guzmán. *A.M.D.G.* (1910) was a fiercely satirical depiction of Jesuit education, which caused a scandal – an even greater one was created by a stage adaptation in the early 1930s. News of the latter controversy reached Britain, where the conservative and Catholic press used it as a stick to beat the author, recently appointed as Spanish ambassador by the left-liberal Republican government.

His later novels became more symbolic and contrapuntal. In *Belarmino y Apolonio* (1921), for example, the two title characters are philosophically inclined shoemakers who have diametrically opposed worldviews. His final, and in many ways most accomplished, novels are sophisticated explorations of the Don Juan figure, *Tigre Juan* and *El curandero de su honra* (*The Healer of his Honour*), both published in 1926 (in fact they are essentially two parts of the same novel).

He wrote no more novels after 1926, and there has been much speculation about the reasons for this creative silence. He resigned as ambassador to London in 1936, and after the Spanish Civil War lived in exile in Argentina before returning to Spain in 1955.

Cathy Benson

Date 1921

Nationality Spain

Why It's Key Pérez de Ayala was a writer who spanned the realism of the nineteenth century and the experimentalism of the early twentieth. Few of his works are easily available in English (ironically, as he was an Anglophile, and his wife was American), but he is an elegant stylist and a major figure of Spanish modernist fiction.

Key Event *Six Characters in Search of an Author* premieres in Rome

They come in from the back, cross the stalls, climb onto the stage. They demand performance (they already have existence). They will interrupt whatever has got the former (as it happens, another play by Pirandello, being rehearsed).

The masks they wear mark them out as not exactly human. They are created stuff, a by-product of human creativity (but their author is missing, in either denial or refusal). That's why, despite having existence, they cannot be agents. Or rather, they do exist for all time (yes, they are indeed immortal), but only as part of a set story, and only if played out over and over again.

A different rehearsal gets going, among much disruption and misunderstanding from both casts (the invasive characters, the interrupted actors and their director). The hard, tragic core of the story of the Six emerges, is spent in this reasoning meta-theater, gets shockingly dispersed as the final curtain is lifted onto the revelation of the uncanny truth of the visitation.

The Roman premiere, in May 1921, turned into public riot, to the chant "Mad-house! Mad-house!" But already by the next major opening night, in Milan, in September of the same year, the Six had made it, if not their missing author, for Pirandello, by then destined to travel the world to check how his legend was doing.

Federica Pedriali

Date 1921

Original Title *Sei personaggi in cerca d'autore*

Author Luigi Pirandello (1867–1936)

Nationality Italy

Why It's Key The most innovative, ground-breaking play in twentieth-century Italian theater.

Key Book
Main Street

Main Street, set in small-town Minneapolis in the 1910s, is a thoroughly modern novel. It features a strong female protagonist, unusual for a book authored by a male, and favors characterization and description over plot, action, and other obvious narrative devices. Though it was published in 1920, many of *Main Street*'s characters give voice to the cultural attitudes and social values of the coming decade and, at times, it reads like it was written with the benefit of hindsight to the roaring twenties and the Depression. Lewis' use of archetypal characters and often humorous facsimiles of small town life made the book a bestseller on publication, particularly in America where it found an eager readership hungry for a novel which captured the flavor of their everyday experience. The scabrous depiction of small town in-fighting and double-dealing, and the controversy it provoked, only served to enhance the novel's popularity. Some thought the novel too bleak, unfairly depicting the denizens of small-town America as a bunch of back-stabbing oafs, but *Main Street*, like Lewis' other novels, is a response to the thick streak of uncritical idealism that runs through American culture. The fact that the novel is still poignantly relevant today should perhaps be a cause for concern, but at the very least *Main Street* serves as a sophisticated, entertaining and, at times, near-prescient attempt at redressing the balance in favor of a more skeptical evaluation of the mores, values, and institutions of the most powerful country on earth.

Christian Kerr

Date 1921

Author Sinclair Lewis (1885–1951)

Nationality USA

Why It's Key Lewis was the first American to win the Nobel Prize in literature, "for his vigorous and graphic art of description and his ability to create, with wit and humor, new types of characters."

Key Author **Hermann Hesse**
Siddartha

In *Siddartha* Hesse documents the spiritual journey of the eponymous hero, a young Indian nobleman who turns his back on his native Hinduism in a quest for further enlightenment. The story is set in the era when Gautama Buddha himself is believed to have lived, the sixth century BC. After many years of searching, including periods of immersing himself in worldly matters such as earning a living as a trader and fathering a son, Siddartha attains a measure of enlightenment. At the end of the novel he is a simple ferryman, seeing the ever-flowing, ever-renewed river as an allegory of the oneness of the universe.

The novel was translated from German into English for the first time in the 1950s and it was in the decade that followed that Hesse's work achieved its greatest international influence. Interest in mysticism and especially in eastern philosophies was widespread amongst young people in the west, from the time of the Beats, rising to a peak in the hippie counterculture of the later 1960s. Hesse's fiction was a way into this world for many who would have shied away from reading original religious or philosophical texts. In such novels as *Demian* (1922), *Steppenwolf* (1933) and *The Glass Bead Game* (1988) Hesse's exploration of the artist as philosopher proved to be required reading for seekers after enlightenment. In particular, rock music of the 1960s and 1970s is full of references to his work, with, for example, a band calling themselves Steppenwolf and "Abraxas" (from Demian) being the title of an album by Santana.

Michael Munro

Date 1922

Author Hermann Hesse (1877–1962)

Nationality Germany

Why It's Key Hesse's interest in mysticism and philosophy, especially in Buddhism, is the prevailing characteristic of his writing and *Siddartha* is his masterpiece in the genre of philosophical fiction. While Hesse was popular during his lifetime, and he won the Nobel Prize in Literature in 1946, his continuing fame is due to a revival of interest in his work in the 1960s.

Key Book
Amok

1920–1929

Zweig liked the convention of passengers meeting on a cruise liner as a pretext for telling a story. Like Somerset Maugham his persona, and to an extent his real person, was a wealthy traveller with a fondness for anecdotes. The framing device in his two greatest stories, *Amok* and *The Royal Game* (1941), however, has the real task of making extreme subject matter acceptable. The doctor who runs "amok" – a Malay expression which accentuates his "non-European" behavior – has allowed powerful, manipulative women to destroy his self-respect and position in life. Self-exiled to avoid shame, after eight isolated years in an Indian village he reacts hysterically when a beautiful Englishwoman asks him a favor. The story has a strange denouement in Naples harbor. The younger son of a rich, cosmopolitan Viennese family, Jewish but non-practising, Zweig was a passionate internationalist who began his career believing in the power of writers and intellectuals to build a world culture. The rise of Hitler, which forced him out of Austria, destroyed his vision and drove him to suicide. He wrote an engaging autobiography but mostly put aspects of his troubled psychology into stories and historical biographies. The artistic value of *Amok* is threatened by Zweig's tendency to suppose eroticism and hysteria can successfully convey the inner life of convincing human beings. But it is a cornerstone in understanding a moderate talent whose high-profile literary activity on the European stage earned him excessive attention. The stories are cinematic, but the erotic themes can seem simply lurid today.

Lesley Chamberlain

Date 1922

Author Stefan Zweig (1881–1942)

Nationality Austrian

Why It's Key Zweig became one of the most widely read authors in the world between the wars with tales of erotic obsession and suicide. *Amok*, a study in Freudian hysteria in a lonely doctor, also touched on the theme of exile from European civilization explored by greater writers like Mann and Conrad.

156

Key Passage
The Waste Land

"Unreal City,
Under the brown fog of a winter dawn,
A crowd flowed over London Bridge, so many,
I had not thought death had undone so many."

T.S. Eliot wrote *The Waste Land* while working as a clerk in Lloyd's Bank after World War I. Many parts of the poem, such as these lines, are located in the centre of London, the banking area where Eliot worked. At the same time, the poem depicts a composite "unreal city" and expresses a general sense of cultural and spiritual chaos. Eliot's notes to these lines explain that they draw on Baudelaire's poetic descriptions of Paris in the nineteenth century and the Inferno of the Medieval Italian poet, Dante Alighieri. The crowds crossing London Bridge are implicitly compared to miserable souls stuck in Limbo outside Heaven and Hell and beyond salvation. Under the "brown fog" in London, the masses seem to suffer a similar predicament.

When it was published in 1922, Eliot's contemporaries saw *The Waste Land* as the expression of a general cultural malaise after the war. However, as well as literary allusions, it mixes public events and private feelings. Parts of the poem were written while Eliot recovered from a nervous breakdown. He later dismissed it as "just a piece of rhythmical grumbling." But his biographer Lyndall Gordon sees in Eliot's description of misery and chaos a yearning for order and the seeds of his later conversion to Anglo-Catholicism, which guided his decision to take British citizenship.

Recently, Eliot's reputation has become controversial. Photographic reproductions of drafts of *The Waste Land* revealed the role of Ezra Pound and Eliot's wife, Vivienne in editing the poem, raising questions about the poem's authorship. Eliot has also been accused of anti-Semitism.

Matthew Creasy

Date 1922

Author T. S. Eliot (1888–1965)

Nationality Born USA, took British citizenship 1927

Why It's Key *The Waste Land* influenced twentieth-century poetry greatly. It contributed to a split between poets who chose to follow Eliot's difficult, fragmented, and allusive techniques and those who chose more accessible, open forms.

Opposite T. S. Eliot

Key Author
Giovannni Verga

Born too early or too late? Upon first meeting Pirandello, in 1904, Verga must have felt that the former was the case. After D'Annunzio, there was always one young pretender too many. One shouldn't spend a lifetime staving them off, better cave in.

But perhaps one shouldn't blame it on third parties either. Perhaps the caving in had taken place years earlier, at the height of one's powers. But then, where did the masterpieces come from? For there could be no doubt, there had been masterpieces: *The House by the Medlar Tree* (*I Malavoglia*, 1881) and *Master Don Gesualdo* (*Mastro-Don Gesualdo*, 1889) And more masterly still, those short stories: "Rosso Malpelo", "The She Wolf", "Cavalleria rusticana". As the latter especially had shown (having made Mascagni's operatic success), the material was almost too good, regardless of the medium, or the authorship.

Was then the method to blame? That French method, now called realism. It was surely quite straightforward to state what the method consisted in. Sincerity. Approach reality with sincerity and reproduce it. Yet with some topics it would simply be impossible to remove oneself from the scene as the method required: impossible to achieve that impersonality or absence of the author which was the demanding central tenet of the new school of thought.

So, one had to fake the removal and the absence. But invariably it showed. Worse still, it could bring one's art to a crisis, as it did soon after *Mastro-Don Gesualdo*, in the decade of *Cavalleria*'s greatest success on the stage, the 1890s. For some reason, the faking couldn't go beyond the primitive Sicilian repertoire of the masterpieces. Paradoxically, and this was the toughest lesson of all, it would also not take one to any other form of poetics. Stuck and influential, for all realisms to come. Or more historically put, the second best nineteenth-century Italian novelist, after Manzoni.
Federica Pedriali

Date 1922 (death)

Author Giovanni Verga (1840-1922)

Nationality Italy

Why It's Key Verga was the model for the revived Italian post-war realism.

Other Key Works Short Story Collection *Cavalleria Rusticana and Other Tales of Sicilian Peasant Life* (*Vita dei campi*,1880)

Key Book
Trilce

Trilce – one of the greatest, and most complex, collections of poetry of the twentieth century – was published in 1922 but its author, the Peruvian César Vallejo, began writing most of the poems in 1918 and 1919. Many of them mark a radical change from Vallejo's previous collection, *Los heraldos negros*. There is a dramatic break from all the norms of metres and versification. A constant tension arises from the poet's desire to safeguard unity of structure against the temptations of experimenting with language. Vallejo was fully aware of the danger that a drive for freedom could lead to chaos. But he felt compelled to seek a balance between the need to destroy or dismantle traditional poetic language and the need to recreate language in a voyage of self-discovery, rather than aesthetic communication. The collection also reveals the chasm between the quest for ideal unity and the force of empirical reality, with all its imperfections and restrictions. The abrupt and dissonant tone of many of the poems borders on exasperation – and sometimes anguish – in the face of this insoluble conflict. A further source of tension arises from Vallejo's struggle to integrate two irreconcilable cultures, the Incan and the Spanish. In general, the poems evoke Vallejo's obsessions at the time: home, mother and childhood, prison walls, erotic relationships. Longing for the mother, in particular, is a fundamental aspect of Vallejo's nostalgia for happiness. In presenting a kaleidoscope of confused, fleeting perceptions, his words exude an irresistible dynamic. Vallejo himself wrote of *Trilce*: "The book was born in a complete void. I am responsible for it. I assume all responsibilities for its aesthetics. Today, more than ever, I feel a sacred obligation, until now unknown, weighing upon me; that of being free! If I am not free today, I will never be."
Adam Feinstein

Date 1922

Author César Vallejo (1892–1938)

Nationality Peru

Why It's Key When *Trilce* was first published Peruvian readers may have been baffled by Vallejo's breaking new ground, putting him beyond the sensibilities of his times. As Clayton Eshleman put it, *Trilce* is "still today the most dense, abstract and transgression-driven collection of poetry in the Spanish language." But it is now recognized as a masterpiece.

Key Story
"In the Grove"

"In the Grove" consists of seven dramatic monologues by people who are concerned with a male dead body found in the grove. The witnesses' apparently coherent testimonies contain much speculation, while the confessions of the perpetrator and his victims differ radically....

This is one of Akutagawa's *ocho* (royal dynasty) stories, based on old Japanese legends, and deals with a tale about a highwayman's attack on a couple in Book 29 of *Tales of Times Now Past*. However, he revises the source from a robbery and rape into the rape of the wife and the death of the husband, foregrounding the psychological question of what could have caused a man to die in such a situation.

In his version of the story, the highwayman claims that there was a clean fight between the two men over the wife. The wife, now a nun, confesses that she killed her husband on his own instructions and then attempted suicide because neither of them could bear the humiliation. Finally, the man's ghost suggests that he killed himself, seeing his wife act kindly to the offender after the rape, even asking him to murder her husband. Akutagawa, who was versed in English literature, says in a letter that he wrote "In the Grove" with Robert Browning's dramatic monologues in mind. Unlike Browning, however, all the story's voices are equally untrustworthy, and even its supernatural powers are far from omniscient. "In the Grove" is a modernist investigation into the arbitrariness of what people think is "truth."

Miki Iwata

Date 1922

Author Ryunosoke Akutagawa (1892–1927)

Nationality Japan

Why It's Key Based on a Japanese folk tale, "In the Grove" explores the arbitrariness and unreliability of apparently objective truth, in an experimental narrative form. Akira Kurosawa based the film *Rashomon* (1950) on "In the Grove" as well as Akutagawa's story "Rashomon."

Key Character **George Babbitt**
Babbitt

Such was the impact of Lewis' portrait of the portly, middle-aged realtor George Babbitt that "babbittry" became a synonym in the 1920s for middle class conformity. The mid-American city of the novel, Zenith, may be "built for giants," its steel towers emblems of the brave new world of post-war prosperity and progress, but many Americans inhabiting it, Lewis implies, are intellectual and moral dwarfs. Indeed, Babbitt is a sketch of the new petite bourgeoisie of the era: white-collared and wealthy but relative arrivistes. Lacking sophistication, genuine self confidence and individual autonomy, Babbitt is a classic middleman, intensely dependant upon the approval of others and, consequently, the toy of the new discourse of advertising. Floral Heights, the suburb where he lives (in a Dutch Colonial, and thus mercantile, style of house, where he is "proud" to be awakened by the "best of nationally advertised [...] alarm-clocks") has been claimed only recently, for example, from scrubby woodland; his car is "poetry and tragedy, love and heroism" to him; he distrusts his neighbors as "Bohemians" because (during Prohibition) they drink and party; and he belongs to the Boosters Club alongside solid Republican burghers like himself. At work, Lewis writes, making the class relations clear, Babbitt is a "squire" among the "rustics" who service his building.

Of course, there is drama and discontent here. When his friend is imprisoned, Babbitt has a crisis, an affair, and gets drunk. But ultimately he learns to embrace his position, cheered by the possibility that his children may prove more imaginative than himself.

Doug Haynes

Date 1922

Author Sinclair Lewis (1885–1951)

Nationality USA

Why It's Key Described as a man who does not produce or create anything but whose talent is to sell houses to people "for more than they could afford," Babbitt typifies the burgeoning class of intermediaries that helped fuel the 1920s American economic boom. Lewis' satire shows him up as a shallow materialist who needs to be taught a lesson.

Key Character **William Brown**
Just William

"'He's mad,' said Mr Brown with conviction. 'Mad. It's the only explanation.'" This account of William Brown is a common refrain of his father's. Mr Brown, often felled by a William-induced headache, appeals to his wife for respite on a regular basis, usually after his son has broken something, enraged a neighbor, kidnapped a baby, or knocked him into a rhododendron bush by accident.

With a combination of endless curiosity and a desire to cast himself as a hero in whatever is taking place, *Just William* has become the twentieth century's most iconic naughty schoolboy. He has a wild and unchecked imagination and a bottomless font of well-intentioned, madcap schemes to get rich, drive away hated aunts, or entice some unwitting victim into falling in love with one of his long-suffering older siblings. Against all odds, these often backfire in such a way that the unintended outcome wins him undue praise – Mr Brown, for all his stern admonishments, often slips him a half-crown for ridding them of a houseguest.

William's cheeky, freckled face, regularly smeared with burnt cork from playing Injuns was immortalised in Thomas Henry's classic illustrations. In these and later images he appears in short trousers and a striped schoolboy cap, his knees scraped, tie askew, a penknife in one pocket and a white rat in the other. Together with his Society of Outlaws – Ginger, Douglas, Henry, and Jumble the dog, he terrorises their respective families, wages fierce battles with their archrivals the Hubert Laneites, and continues to bring delighted smiles to generations of children.

William has been adapted for film, television, radio and on stage, and has even been the subject of minor controversy when the RSPCA accused him of cruelty to animals – for painting his dog Jumble blue.

Francesca Segal

Date 1922

Author Richmal Crompton (1890–1969)

Nationality UK

Why It's Key Crompton was a prolific writer, and William Brown appeared in stories from 1919 until as late as 1970 (her final book was published posthumously). Although she wrote many short stories with other subjects, the volumes of William's scrapes and adventures are her best-loved works and William himself is one of Britain's most cherished rascals.

Key Passage
Ulysses

"Mr Leopold Bloom ate with relish the inner organs of beasts and fowls. He liked thick giblet soup, nutty gizzards, a stuffed roast heart, liver slices fried with crustcrumbs, fried hencods' roes. Most of all he liked grilled mutton kidneys which gave to his palate a fine tang of faintly scented urine."

This passage from chapter four of *Ulysses* introduced the world to "Mr Leopold Bloom," an ordinary man in one of the most extraordinary books of the twentieth century. James Joyce's novel depicts events in Dublin during 24 hours on 16 June 1904. As well as Bloom, the novel features Stephen Dedalus (from Joyce's previous novel, *A Portrait of the Artist as a Young Man*) and Bloom's wife, Molly Bloom. Not a lot happens in the book: Bloom goes to a funeral and wanders around Dublin; Stephen gets drunk and is rescued from a fight by Bloom; and Molly cheats on her husband. What distinguishes *Ulysses* is its style. It is a work of high realism that describes in minute realistic detail almost everything about Bloom's life and experience, from what he likes to eat for breakfast (kidneys) to what he reads on the toilet. But *Ulysses* is also a literary experiment that explores how ordinary events enter consciousness. Joyce employs a wide variety of techniques, from inserting newspaper headlines into his text to writing a chapter in the form of a play. The book concludes with Molly Bloom ruminating on the day's events in a long, unpunctuated monologue.

Ulysses influenced many writers from Samuel Beckett to John Updike and Marilyn Monroe was even photographed reading a copy in 1954.

Matthew Creasy

Date 1922

Author James Joyce (1882–1941)

Nationality Ireland

Why It's Key Joyce called the style he uses to get inside Bloom's thoughts "interior monologue" and credited its invention to French writer, Edouard Dujardin. *Ulysses* was banned in the United States until 1933 because of its sexual content. It still became one of the most famous novels of the twentieth century.

Opposite James Joyce

Key Book
Seven Pillars of Wisdom

Taking its enigmatic title from the Book of Proverbs, *Seven Pillars of Wisdom* comprises the memoirs of T.E. Lawrence, an account of the Arab revolt against the Turks (1916–18) and his heroic role in "those whirling campaigns." The product of various painstaking versions, its eventual publication by subscription in 1926 cemented Lawrence's reputation as one of the defining heroic personas of the early twentieth century – "Lawrence of Arabia." Amongst his many feats of stubborn fortitude may be counted the composition itself – having lost the entire manuscript whilst changing trains at Reading in 1919, Lawrence determinedly rewrote the whole from memory the following year.

With its evocation of vast desert terrains, exotic places, and lightning "do-or-die" sorties on camelback, it is easy to see why it held such appeal for a jaded post-war generation eager to find a beacon of individual heroism and honorable conduct amidst the collective nightmare of entrenched mutual annihilation. Powerfully redolent of the author's daily life in the desert and increasing identification with the people and cause for which he had been instructed to fight, the text is episodic and impressionistic, in E.M. Forster's assessment, "an unexampled fabric of portraits, descriptions, philosophies, emotions, adventures, dreams" all hung about "this tent-pole of a military chronicle."

The dedicatory poem is to "S.A.," often identified as Selim Ahmed, a young Arab consort of the English officer, although this enigmatic tribute might equally be to the nation he had grown to so admire. Richard Adlington's 1955 biography charged Lawrence with melodramatic self-aggrandisement. A notoriously lurid episode of *Seven Pillars* in which the hero is captured by the predatory Bey of Deraa and gang raped by his Turkish captors has been pounced upon by commentators seeking corroboration of Lawrence's imputed sadomasochistic tendencies.

Matt Birchwood

Date 1922 first published in a private edition

Author T.E. Lawrence (1888–1935)

Nationality UK

Why It's Key The ardent dedicatory poem fuelled conjecture of Lawrence's homosexuality. [To S.A.] – "I loved you, so I drew these tides of men into my hands/ and wrote my will across the sky in stars/ To earn you Freedom, the seven-pillared worthy house,/ That your eyes might be shining for me/ When we came."

Key Event **Publicity campaign for *The Devil in the Flesh* causes scandal and sensation**

Radiguet's literary career, like his life, was short and dazzling. A poet at fifteen, he was equally precocious in his many love affairs. His first novel, *The Devil in the Flesh* (*Le Diable au corps*), was written before he was eighteen. A fifteen-year-old boy has an affair with a nineteen-year-old woman whose husband is away fighting at the front. Because he is only twelve when it begins, all World War I means to this boy is "a four year holiday." This was distressing subject matter with the power to shock, even if the affair is doomed to end horribly.

The Devil in the Flesh was first published as *Coeur Vert* (Green Heart), which gives a sense of its true subject: a boy becoming a man. This boy is both conniving and inept, savage and tender. When his mistress throws her husband's letters from the front into the fire, he wishes the husband will be killed in the war. We follow his twisting conscience as, having ruined his lover and broken her husband's heart, he dictates the only loving letters the man ever receives from his wife. When she falls pregnant he commits an infidelity – reasoning that his "casual lusts" enrich his love "as the plundering bee enriches the hive." Finally she dies because of his ineptitude. His blend of cynicism and innocence is a fascinating attempt to rationalise the morality of love – "there is nothing more egotistical than happiness."

The novel is still a love story, limpidly told, its scenes of passion pierced through and rendered more truthful with the sweet incompetence of youth. Its several film adaptations have paid ample homage to this sensual honesty. Radiguet died of typhoid the same year, otherwise who can say to what stellar brilliance he might have lifted himself, or been hoisted?

Lucy Daniel

Date 1923

Author Raymond Radiguet (1903–23)

Nationality France

Why It's Key By sixteen Radiguet was existing at the frenetic heart of Parisian Cubist, Surrealist and Dadaist circles, and finding in Jean Cocteau an avid mentor. Cocteau and Radiguet spent holidays together, and Cocteau devotedly promoted Radiguet. It is said that Radiguet's death is what drove him to opium.

Key Event **Edith Sitwell performs the experimental entertainment *Façade***

Has there ever been a serious English avant-garde? Compared with related developments in France, Germany, Austria, Russia, and Italy in the 1920s and 1930s – Dadaism, Constructivism, Futurism, Surrealism – British modernism often seems a rackety and somewhat amateurish affair, more send-up than substance. No more so, perhaps, than in June 1923, when the aristocratic siblings Edith, Osbert, and Sacheverell Sitwell – arrogant, publicity-seeking, and deeply self-enamoured – presented the experimental entertainment *Façade* at the Aeolian Hall in London. Intended as shockingly "modern," the performance featured the epicene Edith (concealed behind a Picasso-style painted backcloth) intoning a series of supposedly "abstract" poems through a papier mâché megaphone to the rhythmic jazz-inflected music of the young English composer and Sitwell protégé William Walton.

The pretentiousness-quotient was no doubt high. To Edith's rage and mortification *Façade* was instantly lampooned – most drolly perhaps in "The Swiss Family Whittlebot," a short sketch Noel Coward wrote for his popular revue *London Calling!* In one of the show's comic high-points a sibylline poetess name "Hernia Whittlebot," draped in outlandish robes and played by the singing actress Maisie Gay, recited nonsense verse with her brothers "Gob and Sago."

But neither Sitwell nor *Façade* should be dismissed out of hand. Though not as complex or adventurous as Schoenberg's *Pierrot Lunaire* (1912) or the Cocteau/Satie *Parade* (1917), two obvious influences, *Façade* remains an authentic modernist artifact. Walton's music delights, but most cherishable of all are the sixty-six-year-old Sitwell's lurching, ungainly, yet mesmerizing recitations. Delivered as half-chanted, surreal nursery rhymes, poems like "Said King Pompey" and "Jumbo's Lullaby" reveal themselves as jaunty mini-masterpieces and Sitwell herself as one of the great avatars of hip.
Terry Castle

Date 1923

Author Edith Sitwell (1887–1964)

Nationality UK

Why It's Key *Façade* was a unique outcrop of English modernism, from the eccentric family of avant-gardists, the Sitwells. Its performance became legendary. In the historic 1953 recording made by Sitwell, the singer Peter Pears and the English Opera Group Ensemble, the whole bizarre enterprise holds up surprisingly well.

1920–1929

163

Key Event
Book-of-the-Month-Club is launched

Founded in 1923, the Book-of-the-Month-Club is a mail-order system for selling and circulating novels. The system works on a negative response model – the subscriber is offered a novel and if they do not refuse it is mailed to them. Members are often offered the books for a substantial discount on the publisher's price which is offset by the terms of their commitment to the Club (generally they will have to accept a minimum number of books in a time period). Using the postal system as a way of circulating cheap and popular fiction had been common practice since 1839 when Park Benjamin and Rufus Wilmost Griswold had started up the "story newspaper" *Brother Jonathan*, but with Book-of-the-Month-Club its popularity reached new levels. Coinciding with the development of more efficient presses this new type of distribution network radically changed the way that books were read, circulated and marketed in the United States and the world; it paved the way for subsequent developments such as Pocket Books, American Mercury Books and the UK's Penguin imprint.

The BOTM system is useful for publishers and marketing departments as it generally guarantees a particular size of readership for a work but similarly it skews the reading audience towards particular genres and types of writing. Whilst primarily and originally aimed at a popular market, today literary fiction published by quality presses is increasingly sold in this fashion.
Jerome de Groot

Date 1923

Nationality USA

Why It's Key The BOTM Club presaged the mass-marketing of books and instituted a new way of reading, publishing and selling books.

Key Passage **"Mass-Production Houses"** from *Towards a New Architecture*

"The house is a machine for living in."

Reiterating like a mantra the notion that "the house is a machine for living in," *Towards a New Architecture* is a manifesto for the "International Style" of architecture, conceived by Le Corbusier (Charles-Edouard Jeanneret, 1887–1965), Walter Gropius and others in the early 1920s and which exercises considerable influence still. Opposing all things decorative, Corbusier's text insists upon a strictly minimalist aesthetic for a school of building design aspiring to the sublime harmony achieved by the modern engineer, mathematically in touch with "universal laws." Primary shapes and Doric proportions resonate with their viewer, Corbusier says, because "this is [...] the axis on which man is organized in perfect accord with nature." Engineering is evolved but architecture, he opines, is in "an unhappy state of retrogression." Hence a sense of lean necessity permeates his constructions: surfaces, lines and masses are arranged not frivolously but with the rigour normally accorded to manufacturing aircraft, cruise liners, or automobiles.

Corbusier's interest in the potential of industrial methods is demonstrated in the passage "Mass-Production Houses," which socialises his notion of the "House-Machine." Sweeping aside the vagaries of nostalgic bourgeois styles, dwellings built in the "new spirit" are "healthy (and morally so too) and beautiful in the same way that the working tools and instruments which accompany our existence are beautiful," he suggests. Equating moral and physical health with the formal qualities of factory design, Corbusier imagines a functional utopia rolled out on an urban production line, its culture a product of "pruning, cleansing; the clear and naked emergence of the Essential."

Doug Haynes

Date 1923

Author Le Corbusier

Nationality France (born in Switzerland)

Why It's Key Like the short-lived Constructivist movement in post-revolutionary Russia, the Bauhaus, and architects like Ludwig Mies van der Rohe, Le Corbusier was a modernist visionary seeking to reconcile human needs with production methods in a way that might radically improve everyday life.

Opposite
Le Corbusier's villa Savoye

Key Character **Jeeves** *The Inimitable Jeeves*

He first appears, with a hangover cure, in "Jeeves Takes Charge":

"'If you would drink this, sir,' he said, with a kind of bedside manner, rather like the royal doctor shooting the bracer into the sick prince. 'It is a little preparation of my own invention. It is the Worcester Sauce that gives it its color. The raw egg makes it nutritious. The red pepper gives it its bite. Gentlemen have told me that they have found it extremely invigorating after a late evening'."

Duly swallowing it down, Jeeves' new employer, Bertie Wooster, is indeed violently invigorated – "as if someone had touched off a bomb inside the old bean" – and "then everything seemed suddenly to get all right." In many stories and novels for the next half century, Wodehouse would give a few hints about Jeeves' circumstances and connections, but he would retain this magical aura, more than a gentleman's gentleman, a wizard or genie, perhaps, a custodian of tradition, omniscient like Sherlock Holmes, even a sort of ideal mother (we never hear of Bertie's actual parents). With such a helper, who needs a helpmeet? Jeeves' task is often to preserve Bertie's idyllic bachelorhood from unsuitable matrimonial alliances, not to mention oppressive aunts bearing familial responsibilities.

Like many a comical master-servant pairing from Plautus and Menander on, Jeeves and Bertie make a deliciously odd couple, and also embody a running joke about the class system. Bertie's very existence – feckless, "exceedingly amiable," with a private income – is a provocation to all sorts of bullies and authorities, and an affront to contemporary earnestness. "Mr Wodehouse's idyllic world can never stale," wrote Evelyn Waugh: the Jeeves stories are its happiest expression.

Peter Swaab

Date 1923

Author P.G. Wodehouse (1881–1975)

Nationality UK

Why It's Key Jeeves and Wooster, the enduringly popular comedy double act, first appeared in the story collection *The Man with Two Left Feet*, and returned in a series including *My Man Jeeves* (1919); *Carry On, Jeeves* (1925); *Thank You, Jeeves* (1934) and many other novels and stories.

Key Character **Coleman**
Antic Hay

Theodore Gumbril, the central protagonist of *Antic Hay*, encounters characters including a bombastic artist, an over-refined writer, a world-weary socialite and an untrustworthy businessman. None stick in the mind as vividly as the deeply sinister Coleman: womaniser, blasphemer and philosopher of disgust. His extravagant beard or "beaver," Coleman explains, is both a tool of seduction ("It enables one to make such delightful acquaintances in the street") and a tribute to Jesus ("Christlike is my behaviour, / Like every good believer, / I imitate the saviour, / And cultivate a beaver"). Coleman's ingenious blasphemies belong to what Huxley called "an age which has seen the violent disruption of almost all the standards, conventions and values current in the previous epoch."

Even Coleman's live-in lover Zoe despises him, and towards the end of the novel she stabs him in the arm with a penknife. Coleman is still covered in blood as he simultaneously outlines his philosophy of transgression and aggressively seduces Rosie Shearwater, the wife of an acquaintance. Approvingly quoting the Church Fathers on the revoltingness of women and sex, Coleman asserts that "It's only when you believe in God, and especially in hell, that you can really begin enjoying life." Against a background of postwar pessimism and disenchantment, Coleman propounds and enacts his credo with virulent energy. "You're really horrible," Rosie protests, and it is hard to disagree. But like Rosie the reader finds it impossible to avoid "listening with a disgusted pleasure to his quick talk, his screams of deliberate and appalling laughter."

Huxley said *Antic Hay*, his second novel, was "written by a member of… the war generation for others of his kind." Critics called Huxley a "futilitarian" – a description his character Coleman would gleefully embrace.

Paul Vlitos

Date 1923

Author Aldous Huxley (1894–1963)

Nationality UK

Why It's Key "A young man with a blond, fan-shaped beard stood by the table, looking down at them through a pair of bright blue eyes and smiling equivocally and disquietingly as though his mind were full of some nameless and fantastic malice."

167

Key Event **Edna St Vincent Millay becomes first woman to win Pulitzer Prize for Poetry**

Edna St Vincent Millay, largely ignored today, was once America's most popular, and critically respected, poet. Thomas Hardy classed her with the skyscraper as America's greatest achievement. Edmund Wilson (who was smitten by her) considered her genius greater than F. Scott Fitzgerald's, and influential *Poetry* editor Harriet Monroe called Millay the greatest woman poet since Sappho. Millay's reputation has waned since her death, largely because her adherence to traditional forms, and her contempt for the deliberately cryptic writing of modernism (she wrote a poem ridiculing the belief that "straightforwardness is wrong, evasion right") means that a literary tradition which continues to favor the difficult has dismissed her as sentimental. This seems a surprising fate for someone viewed in her own time as avant-garde, the Bohemian poet incarnate. Millay produced an anthem for her age in "First Fig," which reads in its entirety: "My candle burns at both ends; /

It will not last the night; / But ah, my foes, and oh, my friends— / It gives a lovely light!" Millay's life was far more unconventional than her polished, formal poetry: her bisexual escapades, first at Vassar College, and then in Greenwich Village, formed an essential part of her celebrity. Having eventually married an older businessman, Millay soon fell in love with a much younger man and embarked on an affair that prompted the sonnet sequence *Fatal Interview*, an unlikely bestseller in the midst of the Great Depression. Her poetry supporting the Allied cause in World War II was dismissed as propaganda, and began the decline in her poetic reputation.

Sarah Churchwell

Date 1923

Author Edna St Vincent Millay (1892–1950)

Nationality USA

Why It's Key By far the most famous American poet, and one of the most famous women, of her generation, Millay was one of the few poets in the twentieth century whose work was at once immensely popular, financially successful, and critically respected.

Opposite Edna St Vincent Millay

Key Book *The Good Soldier Svejk and His Fortunes in the World War*

Cited by some as the first ever "anti-war" novel, *The Good Soldier Svejk* startled critics with its irreverence when it was first published in 1923: most of them felt that it belittled the seriousness of World War I and the heroism shown by Czech soldiers. They also objected to the fact that the dialogue was peppered with dozens of earthy Czech obscenities, the range of which it is impossible to recreate in an English translation. The book's massive popularity shows that the general public were more receptive to a work that ridiculed the conflict that had cost them so much.

The novel is a long, picaresque account of the adventures in the Austrian army of the Czech soldier Svejk, who has been certified as an "official idiot" by the authorities and appears to be naively loyal to the Austrians, but is in fact a shrewd observer of events. The book closely reflects Hasek's own experiences fighting for the Austrians, and many of the novel's characters are real people he encountered. There are no bloody battle scenes (Hasek died before he could finish the book, so Svejk never gets to the Front) but the novel's power lies in its portrait of the enervating bureaucracy found in both the army and the state: a typical character is Colonel Kraus, who devotes all his energy to ensuring that his men salute him properly. *Svejk* was hugely influential: Bertolt Brecht wrote a sequel and Joseph Heller claimed that it was a direct influence on *Catch-22*.
Jake Kerridge

Date 1923

Author Jaroslav Hasek (1883–1923)

Nationality Czechoslovakia

Why It's Key The first novel to portray war as tedious and futile rather than glamorous and heroic.

Key Book *Cane*

This 1923 work of high modernism by one of the Harlem Renaissance's most talented writers remains the cornerstone of Jean Toomer's reputation as an author and poet. *Cane* experiments with form as many modernist works do, collecting poetry, vignettes, and short stories under the same cover. One of the most powerful depictions of black American experience in the early twentieth century, *Cane* is full of exquisite, melodic, evocative writing. Its haunting images betray Toomer's roots in the Imagist movement, while its experimental attempts to fuse three literary forms into one work to express the African-American experience makes him a true peer of modernist authors such as Sherwood Anderson, Gertrude Stein, and Ernest Hemingway.

Toomer, who himself was light-skinned and could, and did, pass for Caucasian, claiming that his racial status was irrelevant, even when the society around him made it clear that it was not, was inspired to write about race in America after a stint living in the South. Many of the stories in *Cane* explore the conflict, both emotional and practical, which is engendered by the ability to "pass" as a white man. At the same time, *Cane* reflects the black experience by, for instance, replicating the "call and response" of the African-American church sermon.

Despite garnering favorable reviews when first published, *Cane* quickly went out of print and was only rescued from obscurity and reprinted in the late 1960s when interest in African American literature and the Harlem Renaissance was revived. Although it was lost for almost four decades, critics now acknowledge *Cane* as one of the masterpieces of both twentieth-century American and African American literature.
Elizabeth Rosen

Date 1923

Author Jean Toomer (1894–1967)

Nationality USA

Why It's Key Languishing in obscurity for nearly forty years, this beautifully written masterpiece of the Harlem Renaissance was "rediscovered" in the 1960s and its modernist struggle with both form and topic has sealed its author's reputation.

Opposite Jean Toomer and his wife Marjory Latimer

Key Character **Lord Peter Wimsey**
Whose Body?

Wimsey is a war veteran. His ennui conceals a deeper discontent. A life of luxury, even with intellectual pursuits, is not enough. The elegance of his London existence masks the confusions he feels within, just as it does the uglier side of modern society. Nightmares of the Front return to torment him, whilst crimes of greed or passion are a reminder of the barbaric impulses beneath the civilized veneer.

In creating a character like Wimsey, Dorothy L. Sayers was working within an established tradition. Following Sherlock Holmes' example, the gentleman-detective was often an amateur, extremely talented, but odd or in some way unsuited to normal life. Sayers completed most of the eleven full-length Wimsey novels in the 1920s and 1930s, the so-called Golden Age of mystery fiction, when Agatha Christie, Ngaio Marsh and Margery Allingham were also writing prolifically, featuring the same detectives in successive adventures.

Wimsey's bantering conversational style belies a serious mind. He has the self-knowledge to recognize that he is initially intrigued by a crime as an intellectual puzzle, but once involved feels the responsibility, since the murderer will almost certainly hang. His flair for detection is an aspect of his neurosis: he is, his fictional uncle says, "all nerve and nose."

Detractors have dismissed the Wimsey novels as "snobbery with violence," but they dramatize the difficult transition from the certainties of Edwardian England to the disorientating modernity of the 1920s. The "whodunit" element is increasingly subordinated in what are strongly character-driven novels to Wimsey's developing love for the independent-minded woman writer, Harriet Vane.

Wimsey also appears in *Strong Poison* (1930); *Murder Must Advertise* (1933); *Nine Tailors* (1934); and *Gaudy Night* (1935); among others.
Kate Kerrigan

Date 1923

Author Dorothy L. Sayers (1893–1957)

Nationality UK

Why It's Key Haunted by his experiences in the trenches of World War I, Lord Peter Wimsey, an aristocrat, investigates murders as a hobby. *Whose Body?* added Wimsey to the gallery of eccentric detective heroes.

170

Key Author **Italo Svevo** *Confessions of a Zeno (La conscienza di Zeno)*

One of the most important characteristics of Svevo's writing is his close knowledge of and connection with European psychology and psychoanalysis, and especially Freud. His interest in Freudian theories enabled him to study his fictional characters in their internal fights and monologues. All the protagonists of his novels represent different versions of the same type: modern contemporary man who has lost control of his life, who is a hypochondriac with all sorts of imaginary diseases, and who cannot make sense of his professional or private life, especially his emotions, except through the help of a psychiatrist.

Zeno Cosini, the main protagonist of *The Confessions of Zeno*, not only represents the end of the artist/intellectual's hopes of creation during the profound crisis of European society at the turn of the century, but also the artist's ineptitude for life. Nothing Zeno wants to do turns out the way he has planned, but instead the way others have wanted. His

confessions are implosive because they are confessions, and explosive because they are stolen from his doctor, Doctor S (Doctor Svevo?) and published out of revenge on the whole of society. His novel is a time bomb, a bitter social critique of the bourgeois Trieste (or urbanized Italy) of the time, and his confessed ultimate plan is that of planting this bomb in the centre of the Earth to watch the whole planet explode. Irony is the main ingredient in Svevo's writing, and, despite the seriousness of the issues, his effects are deeply and bitterly comical.

The profound drama of Svevo's characters, whose typology climaxes in Zeno Cosini, has been compared to the human drama of characters portrayed by Proust, Joyce, Kafka, and Musil.
Rossella Riccobono

Date 1923

Author Italo Svevo (pen-name of Ettore Schmitz, 1861–1928)

Nationality Italian

Other Key Works *Story of a Life (Una vita,* 1892); *Senility (Senilità,* 1898)

Why It's Key Svevo can be considered the "father" of the classical literature of his city: Trieste. His writing was recognized in its European importance and influence very late in his career, in connection with the publication of *The Confessions of Zeno* (1923).

Key Passage
Studies in Classic American Literature

"Always the same. The deliberate consciousness of Americans so fair and smooth-spoken, and the under-consciousness so devilish. *Destroy! destroy! destroy!* hums the under-consciousness. *Love and produce! Love and produce!* cackles the upper consciousness. And the world hears only the Love-and-produce cackle. Refuses to hear the hum of destruction underneath. Until such time as it will have to hear."

For years and years everybody thought those classics of nineteenth-century American literature – *The Last of the Mohicans*, *Moby-Dick*, *The Scarlet Letter*, *Leaves of Grass* – were children's adventure stories or sweet historical romances or harmless nature poems. That is, until dirty D.H.L., the miner's son with filth down his fingernails, came along and started scratching at the surface, determined to find the pus beneath the pretty pink cicatrix. Scratch scratch, went David Herbert, there's sin and sex and death in here somewhere, let's get digging.

Though Lawrence sometimes writes like a mischievous child set on outraging his elders (here's Walt Whitman in his giant automobile, hurtling across America, crushing Indians under his wheels), his purposes are always deadly serious. He was serious about art, and serious about life, and in these essays he sought to rescue the great American literature of the past from trivialization. Even if his judgements may sometimes be wildly wrong, he forced America to look again at its heritage, at its collective psyche, at its bland, blinkered uniformity. One might not want men like Lawrence drafting government policy, but one needs them now and again to give us all a hefty kick up the backside. "Had you ever thought of *that*?" he shouts, before running off with a laugh.
Ian Crofton

Date 1923

Author D.H. Lawrence (1885–1930)

Nationality UK

Why It's Key A provocative and highly entertaining series of essays that prompted a major reappraisal of the golden age of American literature.

1920-1929

Key Author **Rainer Maria Rilke**
Sonnets to Orpheus

Rilke (1875–1976) was born in German-speaking Prague and as a child was dominated by his emotional and possessive mother. A career is not the right word for his achievement. He led an utterly serious life in poetry, in which he looked to a succession of intelligent, creative and in some cases useful rich women to support him emotionally and materially. With the Russian-born writer Lou Salomé he travelled to Russia twice, in 1899 and 1900, and the deep effect Russian piety had on his makeup was reflected in *The Book of Hours* (1905). The Russian influence and his deep and constant inwardness, despite a rebellion from formal Roman Catholicism, also revealed Rilke as a mystical thinker whose work would inspire Heidegger and more generally prompt debate over his message for modern man. The two volumes of the *New Poems* (1907–8), with their vivid visual images and classical plasticity, and a poetic novel, *The Diaries of Malte Laurids Brigge* (1910)

marked the high point of his middle period, which was influenced by the six years he spent in Paris, including a brief stint as Rodin's secretary. The *Sonnets to Orpheus* and the *Duino Elegies* (1923), utterly different in tone and yet complementary, climaxed a short life that ended painfully. Rilke counts as a difficult poet, because the effort to communicate was subordinate to the intense exploration of his tremulous sensibility. But his work, which shows French symbolist influence and transforms German into a highly nuanced sculptural and musical medium, is elegant and seductive high art.
Lesley Chamberlain

Date 1923

Nationality Austria

Why It's Key Rilke is the best-known modern German poet in the world. His work has been widely admired and creatively translated by fellow poets seeking to transpose its unique spiritual delicacy and limpid form into diverse twentieth-century traditions.

Key Event *The Constant Nymph* becomes the British bestseller of the 1920s

*T*he Constant Nymph was the most popular British bestseller of its time, and one of the most popular romantic novels ever. Teresa, the fourteen-year-old nymph whose upbringing in the mountains of Austria has made her a free spirit, is in love with Lewis, a young composer whose artistic nature makes him equally untameable. But Lewis marries one of Teresa's cousins, and from this mismatch, and Teresa's claims on Lewis' wilder side, the passion of the plot evolves.

One of the most interesting things about *The Constant Nymph* now, although it is still a pithily well-written novel, is what it tells us about reading habits and what made a bestseller in those early days of bestsellerdom, the 1920s. Its glancing anti-Semitism for one thing probably fell beneath contemporary readers' radar. Loosely based on the circles of Augustus John, the artist, it painted a picture of a privileged bohemian world to which but few of its readers had access. In its portrayal of women, it gave us an appealing clan of disorderly, irreverent feral creatures, although charming and accomplished ones, and an intricate dissection of male and female attitudes to love, marriage and adultery, without sensationalism but with quiet psychological complexity. Here was a romantic novel equally admired by female and male readers (not least J.M. Barrie and A.E. Housman). One of its triumphs, as Anita Brookner noted in her introduction to the 1983 Virago reprint, is its transfer of a typical romantic hero and heroine into an entirely believable modern world. Romantic yet pragmatic, it is the perfect middlebrow entertainment. Given her huge influence in shaping that area of fiction, it is surprising that Kennedy is no longer very well known; she was one of the twentieth century's most successful British novelists.

Lucy Daniel

Date 1924

Author Margaret Kennedy (1896–1967)

Nationality UK

Why It's Key It provided a stage hit for Noel Coward in 1926, and was adapted for the screen in 1928 (in a version with Ivor Novello and Mabel Poulton), again in 1934, and then again in 1943, with Charles Boyer and Joan Fontaine in the lead roles. Kennedy was also a screenwriter and dramatist as well as a prolific, prize-winning novelist.

Key Event **Breton publishes the Surrealist manifesto**

*A*fter the demise of Dada, Breton, together with poets Paul Eluard and Philippe Soupault, began experimenting with literary techniques influenced by Freud: automatic writing, games of chance, works dictated from trance-states. The 1924 Manifesto (in the early twentieth century, every new idea needed a manifesto) brought these practices together as Surrealism. *Manifesto of Surrealism* (*Manifeste du surréalisme*) was at once a rallying cry, an exposition of Dada's anti-rational successor and an avant-garde text in its own right. Breton's document came complete with a list of impressive antecedents to prove its credentials, including Swift, Sade, Hugo, Baudelaire, and Reverdy. Every passage was penned with its author's customary sententiousness and memorably claimed the rights of poetry, imagination and dream over all other kinds of thought and activity. Indeed, Breton imagines "the future resolution of [...] dream and reality," as an "absolute reality, a *surreality*, if one may so speak."

While there were to be many further definitions of Surrealism as its practitioners explored its applications – to poetry, photography, walking in the city, falling in love – the one most often cited is surely the faux-lexicographical entry from the Manifesto: "SURREALISM, *n*. Psychic automatism in its pure state, by which one proposes to express [...] the actual functioning of thought." Satirizing rational categories, this designation neatly captures the surrealist desire for direct contact with the hidden, unconscious forces that might revolutionize a dry, ordered and bourgeois life. So, while it valorises poetry, Surrealism is maybe more anarchism than aestheticism, always exempt, as Breton writes, suggestively, "from any moral or aesthetic concern."

Doug Haynes

Date 1924

Author André Breton (1896–1966)

Nationality France

Why It's Key It introduced another avant-garde to the world, picking up where the scandal of Dada had left off. So pervasive that its influence was felt, even at the time, from high art to advertising and fashion, Surrealism became a conduit between intellectualism and mass culture.

Opposite Surrealist poets Eluard, Breton, and Desnos

Key Event **Kafka dies and his works are given to the world**

Kafka has a plausible claim to be the most influential author of the twentieth century, a fact which has a peculiar and ambiguous relation to the circumstances of his death since his last will instructed his close friend and literary executor, Max Brod, to destroy all of his writings ("preferably unread") and to allow no reprinting of the fairly small amount of work already published while Kafka was alive. Brod did not follow his friend's instructions and seems to have indicated to Kafka in advance that he would not.

Kafka died in a great deal of discomfort and pain, having contracted pneumonia while suffering from pulmonary fever. With a dedicated group of friends to comfort him, he struggled to cope with the knowledge and experience of his imminent passing, writing scribbled notes for his carers when he became unable to speak, but never once pronouncing from his deathbed on the need for the survival or destruction of his literary fiction. His lover, Dora, had once been told

to burn some of his manuscripts and carried out the order faithfully in his presence, but Max Brod refused to follow the terms of Kafka's testament and the great novels and stories survived into a secure canonical status. *The Trial*, *The Castle*, and "Metamorphosis" (as well as *Amerika* and "The Judgment") are perhaps the most talismanic titles in European fiction, works which delineate the awareness of man's existential abandonment and degradation like no others.

Robin Purves

Date 1924

Author Franz Kafka (1883–1924)

Nationality Czechoslovakia

Why It's Key The posthumous publication of Kafka's works, apparently against his wishes, by his friend Max Brod, made him one of the century's most influential writers.

Opposite Kafka's grave

Key Event *Billy Budd, Foretopman* is published in London

Melville's early South Seas fictions had enjoyed both critical acclaim and commercial success, but when later novels such as *Moby-Dick* (1851) were condemned as boring, badly written, and confusing, the disillusioned author abandoned his writing career and became a New York customs inspector. Melville faded so far into oblivion that when he died only one newspaper carried an obituary, and even this misprinted his name as "Henry Melville."

In 1919, the centenary year of Melville's birth, American scholar Frank Jewett Mather wrote that "to love Melville was to join a very small circle. It was like eating hasheesh." All this was about to change. The structural complexities and philosophical ambiguities that had made Melville's novels so unpalatable to an earlier age would now be rediscovered and celebrated by a generation of modernist readers who would catapult his complex works of fiction into the emerging American canon.

Billy Budd, Foretopman, written in Melville's final years and left unfinished at his death, was discovered and published in 1924. Set in 1797, the plot follows Billy Budd, a handsome and guileless young seaman aboard a British warship. Falsely charged with inciting mutiny, Billy lashes out at his vindictive accuser and inadvertently kills him with single blow. Billy is court-martialled by the Captain and sentenced to hang the following dawn.

For disillusioned, post-war readers of the 1920s, the dark complexities of *Billy Budd* demonstrated the monumental struggle between good and evil and the persistence of social inequities and institutionalised injustice. The impact of the novella extended well beyond the 1920s, inspiring Benjamin Britten to compose *Billy Budd* the opera, first performed in 1951, with a libretto by E. M. Forster.

Sarah Wood

Date 1924

Author Herman Melville (1819–1891)

Nationality USA

Why It's Key It played a significant part in the 1920s "Melville Revival," which transformed the author from a forgotten teller of South Seas tales into a major American novelist. According to Raymond Weaver, Melville's first biographer, *Billy Budd* was Melville's "last word upon the strange mystery of himself and of human destiny."

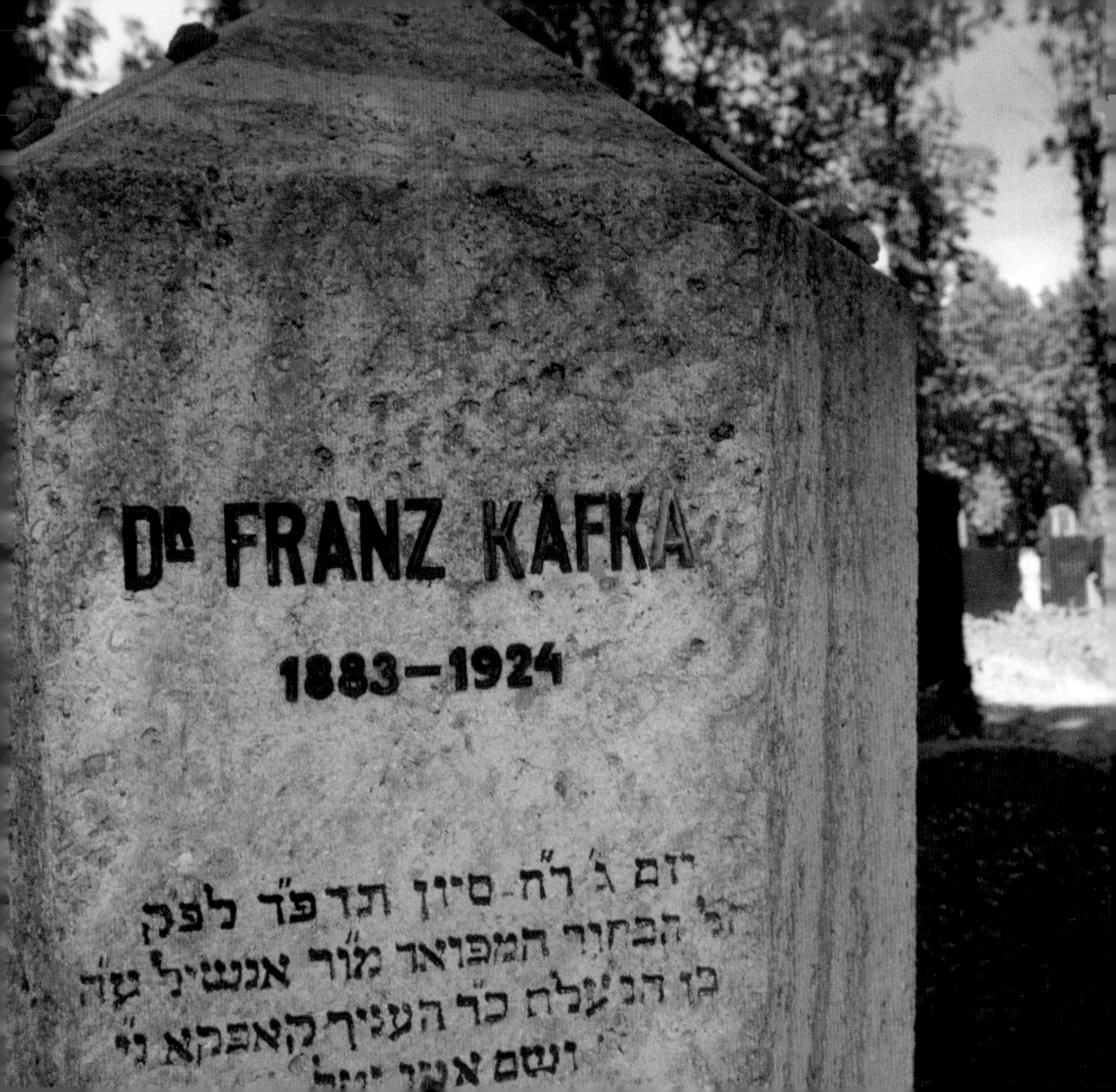
Dr FRANZ KAFKA
1883–1924

Key Book
The Magic Mountain

Conceived as a long short story, *The Magic Mountain* grew into a vast literary-philosophical exploration of Germany on the eve of the Great War. Mann moved on from the warm, unforced realism of *Buddenbrooks* and pioneered a trademark ironic realism which carried a rich cultural baggage: his fascination with German pessimism. Schopenhauer, Nietzsche, Wagner, and Freud lie just beneath the surface of this purportedly comic novel. Between the genesis and the execution of *The Magic Mountain* Mann wrote *Reflections of an Unpolitical Man*, which, in another attempt to understand the legacy of pessimism, directly explored the artistic distinctiveness but democratic deficit it brought to classical German culture. Not always to the advantage of his own art, but affording a powerful conspectus of a European civilization with a death-wish, he carried these themes over into this canonic novel.

How can the idea of death seduce the healthy young engineer Hans Castorp, originally only visiting his sick cousin in a sanatorium in the Swiss Alps? Mann subverted the traditional novel of personal development, the *Bildungsroman*, to portray Castorp's plunge into intellectual morbidity before he finally saw the light and returned to the common-sense "flatland." Castorp is an archetype. As characters the humanist man of letters Settembrini, the sanatorium director Behrens and even the near-silent cousin Joachim are perhaps more memorable. Mann's style in this novel has been described as musical and his own comments suggest he was inspired by Wagner's use of the leitmotiv, to keep the reader aware of constantly recurring thematic material.
Lesley Chamberlain

Date 1924

Author Thomas Mann (1875–1955)

Nationality Germany

Why It's Key Mann's monumental novel bound up his fate with twentieth-century Germany even before the rise of Nazism. His exploration of the tension between artistic decadence and political liberalism was autobiographical in origin, and lead to irony at the heart of his work.

Opposite Thomas Mann

Key Book
A Passage to India

SPOILER

E.M. Forster's most famous novel is also one of the first to be openly critical of the British in India. Like his earlier novels set in Italy, it contrasts the stifled, censorious and sexually inhibited English upper middle classes against a potentially liberating experience of "otherness," and in so doing upholds the value of personal relations and the fulfilled inner life of emotional connectedness that was a crucial element of Forster's liberal-humanist views.

The novel concerns Adela Quested's visit to Chandrapore to see the man she is likely to marry, Ronald Heaslop, the City Magistrate. In her determination to see the "real" India, however, she persuades Dr Aziz, an enthusiast of British rule, to organize a trip to the nearby Marabar Caves. It is at these caves that an incident occurs, never fully resolved, which results in Aziz's prosecution for insulting behavior. When Adela withdraws the charge Aziz is left disillusioned with the Colonial administration, and turns instead towards his own Indian heritage.

Forster's famous dictum "Only Connect" (the epigram to his earlier novel, *Howards End*) is shown to have its biggest challenge in British-ruled India. The stark conclusion that Aziz and his British friend Fielding cannot truly be friends until the British are driven "into the sea," foreshadows much of the post-colonial writing that emerged in the 1970s and after. Forster's own career as a novelist ended with this novel, and though active as a literary figure until his death in 1970, it was to remain his finest moment.
Gerard Woodward

Date 1924

Author E.M. Forster (1879–1970)

Nationality UK

Why It's Key *A Passage to India* was one of the first novels to be critical of British rule in India.

Key Book *The Counterfeiters (Les Faux-Monnayeurs)*

Cynicism, hypocrisy, duplicity: the echo of Gide's title resounds throughout the novel. Like the counterfeit coins which circulate through the narrative, nothing is what it seems. The outwardly respectable bourgeois families of the two young men at its centre, Bernard Profitendieu and Olivier Molinier, are being corroded from within by suppressed scandals. Alienated from their parents, Bernard and Olivier renounce their moribund value system, finding themselves drawn into the world of moral and literary experiment of Olivier's uncle Edouard, a writer at work on a new novel entitled… *The Counterfeiters*.

As in his previous novels, Gide was interested in anatomizing the corrupt and decadent reality underlying the immaculately mannered appearance of the Parisian salon society he inhabited. But what makes *The Counterfeiters* a crucial departure is the ingenious reflection of this theme in the novel's form. The author perpetually surfaces from his narrative to look askance at his characters and discuss his themes. Mid-way through the novel, he remarks that the "'deep-lying subject' of my book… is… no doubt, the rivalry between the real world and the representation of it we make to ourselves."

Through the brilliant, amoral Edouard's journal, whose pages punctuate the novel, Gide explores the literary and metaphysical possibilities opened up by this "rivalry" between reality and its representation. Edouard imagines a novelist who rejects "counterfeit" narrative and psychological conventions, and who embraces the possibilities the novel presents for remodelling reality. In putting reality so radically in question, *The Counterfeiters* proved startlingly contemporary with the postmodernist literary tendencies it preceded by half a century.
Josh Cohen

Date 1925

Author André Gide (1869–1951)

Nationality France

Why It's Key The novel married Gide's characteristic concerns with the decadence and moral nihilism of the French bourgeoisie to a tantalizing exploration of the nature of writing itself, anticipating many of the strategies of "postmodernist" literature.

Key Book
The Making of Americans

Stein was characteristically immodest about her own 925-page magnum opus: "It is tremendously long and enormously interesting and out of it has sprung all modern writing." It started as a traditional story about her German-Jewish family's progress in America – a paean to the middle class, in line with Stein's obsession with normality. But as she wrote the novel a momentous stylistic shift occurred. Stein, who famously studied psychology under William James, filled notebooks with sprawling categorizations of everyone she knew, according to type. As this story of matchmaking and moneymaking began to ask what really makes an American, Stein's system became all-encompassing.

The same words and phrases proliferate, with miniscule changes meant to represent the relationships between people. Attempting to convey a particularly American "space of time that is filled always filled with moving," Stein used monumental levels of repetition.

The novel honors no contract between author and reader. It continually predicts and rarely fulfils; exasperated interruptions from the narrator seem tantamount to novelistic suicide, tearing at the bonds that make novels what they are – character, time frames, authorial hindsight, dialogue. At one point the narrator is reduced to tears, as if Stein has driven her own narrator to the point of breakdown.

This was extraordinary for its time. By publication in 1925 the novel could still appal readers (or rather, non-readers, since many confessed to being unable to read it) with its stylistic strangeness, but it was completed in 1911, making it one of the first modernist literary experiments. It opened up paths of disruption and freedom that novels have been following ever after, not just in the avant-garde, of which Stein was the self-appointed queen, but in all the ranks that followed.
Lucy Daniel

Date 1925 (publication)

Author Gertrude Stein (1874–1946)

Nationality USA

Why It's Key *The Making of Americans* began as a fairly traditional story, and ended as a massive modernist experiment. It was started in 1905, finished in 1911 but not published until 1925 – it came out after *The Waste Land*, *Ulysses*, and *Jacob's Room*, but its composition preceded them all.

Key Character **Nick Adams**
In Our Time

There is a good case for saying that Nick Adams is the most important character in Ernest Hemingway's work. He is the protagonist of fifteen stories, written over a long period and included in various collections. We first see him as a child growing up in the woods of Michigan, then as an adolescent, encountering prostitutes and prize fighters on the road, then at war and as a veteran, and finally, as a young man travelling in Europe. While Hemingway pointed out that "Nick in the stories was never himself," Adams is closer than most to a self-portrait. Hemingway's first book *In Our Time* (1925) begins and ends with Nick. In the first tale "Indian Camp," he is taken by his doctor father to watch a birth and ends up also witnessing a suicide; in the fifth, "The Battler," he finds comfort at the camp of a white ex-fighter and his black companion (and perhaps lover). Such encounters disturb him greatly but he can't say why. In the book's final, two-part, story "Big Two-Hearted River," he leaves sex, death and war behind and makes his camp alone. The story explores the ways in which careful attention to the details of everyday tasks (cooking, casting, baiting his hook) just about holds trauma at bay. Consciousness (and the prose which expresses it) is rigorously limited, minutely and carefully adjusted.

In 1972 Philip Fisher collected Hemingway's Nick Adams stories (which had appeared in various books) and presented them in chronological order of his advancing age.

Kasia Boddy

Date 1925 (first appearance)

Author Ernest Hemingway (1899–1961)

Nationality USA

Why It's Key Lying on his back observing the pine trees and the sky, Nick sometimes seems as much like a latter-day Thoreau as the American Cézanne that his creator intended.

Key Character **Clarissa Dalloway**
Mrs Dalloway

SPOILER

Clarissa Dalloway is the middle-aged, middle-class wife of an MP living in London in the early twentieth century. The novel follows her experiences throughout a single day in June 1923 as she makes preparations for a party. Yet behind her assumed role as society hostess lies a sense of overwhelming isolation and an awareness of the seeming pretence of her life. As the narrative moves in and out of her thoughts, impressions, and memories, we come to understand how she has rejected potentially meaningful relationships in the past – with Peter Walsh and with Sally Seaton – because of a fear of being exposed and vulnerable. Instead, she has resigned herself to a life of repression, conformity, and conservatism, the cost of which is "the death of her soul."

Clarissa's sense of self is mirrored in the parallel narrative of Septimus Smith, a psychologically disturbed war veteran suffering from both shellshock and the effects of living in the alienating modern city environment. This connection is confirmed at Clarissa's party when news of Septimus' suicide breaks into Clarissa's social world and she identifies herself with him in an understanding that "death is defiance." Clarissa, however, realizes that her life must be "lived to the end" and the novel suggests that it is Elizabeth, her daughter, who will embrace the more revolutionary ideals which Clarissa left behind in her youth.

Mrs Dalloway was the inspiration for Michael Cunningham's 1998 Pulitzer Prize-winning novel, *The Hours*, which was itself made into a popular film directed by Stephen Daldry (2002).

Simon Avery

Date 1925

Author Virginia Woolf (1882–1941)

Nationality UK

Why It's Key One of Woolf's most popular works, it employs "stream of consciousness" narrative – where we follow the thoughts, sensory impressions and memories of the protagonist as they float through her mind. It had a major impact on the development of the novel form, as well as being highly influential on women's writing.

Key Character **Jay Gatsby**
The Great Gatsby

Fitzgerald originally wanted to call the novel Trimalchio, after a character in Petronius' *Satyricon*. Trimalchio is an old, fat, ugly, freed slave who spends his newly acquired wealth on ostentatious parties. Gatsby also throws lavish parties but he's young and handsome and remains wryly aloof from the debauchery around him. In fact the only reason Gatsby stages his parties is to impress Daisy Buchanan, the love of his early life who now lives in a house directly across the Long Island sound. Gatsby wants to rewrite history. In 1917 he was a poor soldier called Jimmy Gatz and "she was the first 'nice' girl he'd ever known." But Daisy married someone else. By 1922, with the help of the war, a month at Oxford, Prohibition bootlegging, and careful attention to the plots and idioms of popular fiction, he has reinvented himself. When Daisy sees his piles of silk and linen shirts in every color (a man in England sends them over every season) she sobs. She says he resembles the "advertisement of the man" (her

highest praise). He says her voice is "full of money" (his highest praise). Gatsby's doomed pursuit of the alluring but "careless" Daisy is narrated by another Midwesterner once keen on reinvention, Nick Carraway. Nick sees, and admires, Gatsby's "capacity for wonder" as uniquely American, even if Daisy was never going to be "commensurate" to its power. Gatsby's dreams, and by extension America's dreams, remain worthwhile even if "foul dust" often floats in their wake.

Kasia Boddy

Date 1925

Author F. Scott Fitzgerald (1896–1940)

Nationality USA

Why It's Key "If personality is an unbroken series of successful gestures, then there was something gorgeous about him, some heightened sensitivity to the promises of life, as if he were related to one of those intricate machines that register earthquakes ten thousand miles away."

Opposite *The Great Gatsby*

Key Event **Hemingway and Fitzgerald are introduced in a café in Montparnasse**

Two of America's greatest twentieth-century literary figures – Ernest Hemingway and Scott Fitzgerald – met for the first time at the Dingo American Bar (better known simply as the Dingo Bar) in Montparnasse, Paris, in late-April, 1925. Fitzgerald was the far better known at the time: he had already published three novels, including, just weeks earlier, *The Great Gatsby*, soon to be acknowledged as a masterpiece, as well as several volumes of stories. In contrast, Hemingway, working mainly as a journalist, had published only a handful of stories and poems in little magazines. His first American book, the collection of short stories, *In Our Time*, would not be published until October of that year. But Hemingway was by far the more successful drinker of the two: Fitzgerald passed out on this first evening together in Paris, a fact Hemingway never forgot. Neither did he forgive Fitzgerald for asking whether he had slept with his first wife, Hadley, before he married her.

The most famous friendship in American literature was a troubled one. Although Fitzgerald had a low opinion of Hemingway as a human being ("He was always willing to lend a hand – to those above him"), he continued to refer to Hemingway as "the greatest living writer of [his] time." He helped in the editing of Hemingway's first major novel, *The Sun Also Rises*. In contrast, however, two decades after Fitzgerald's death in 1940, Hemingway continued to defame Fitzgerald in stories and interviews, and even posthumously in his memoir, *A Moveable Feast*.

One of Hemingway's biographers has suggested that the drunken hypochondriac he depicted in *A Moveable Feast* represented an attempt to cut a rival "down to size" after a number of critics had reappraised, and praised, Fitzgerald's work following his death.

Adam Feinstein

Date 1925

Place France

Why It's Key Hemingway did try to encourage Fitzgerald during the desperate, discouraging nine years between *The Great Gatsby* and *Tender is the Night*. Nevertheless, he felt superior to Fitzgerald and tended to bully him. He despised what he saw as Fitzgerald's worship of youth, his sexual naivety, attraction to money, inability to hold his drink, self-pity and lack of commitment to his art.

Key Event *The New Yorker* is founded by Harold Ross

On February 17, 1925 a new magazine launched in New York with the announcement that "it is not edited for the old lady in Dubuque." *The New Yorker* has prided itself on its metropolitan sophistication, while remaining well aware that it depends on an out-of-town subscription readership. From the start, the magazine has been associated with many different forms: elusive cartoons (by Charles Addams or Saul Steinberg), hard-headed investigative journalism (such as John Hersey's "Hiroshima," James Baldwin's "The Fire Next Time" or Seymour Hirsch's "Chain of Command," on Abu Ghraib), whimsical pieces (by E.B. White, James Thurber or A.J. Liebling), film criticism (famously by Pauline Kael), anecdote ("The Talk of the Town") and the short story. While the magazine has published diverse work by many major writers over the years, the idea of the "New Yorker short story" is still largely associated with mid-century realist authors such as Irwin Shaw, J.D. Salinger and three Johns –

O'Hara, Cheever and Updike. Until recently, surrealism, experimentation or anything in "bad taste" tended to be rejected in favor of "moment of truth" tales of coming-of-age or adultery (or so the stereotype has it). The magazine has only had five editors: Harold Ross (1925–1951), William Shawn (1951–1987), Robert Gottlieb (1987–1992), Tina Brown (1992–1998) and David Remnick, who took over in 1998. For many *The New Yorker* will be forever associated with the image that appeared on its first cover, "Eustace Tilley" by Rea Irvin, a dandy looking at a butterfly though a monocle. The complete run is now available on CD-ROM.
Kasia Boddy

Date 1925

Place New York, USA

Why It's Key "*The New Yorker*" said Robert Warshaw in 1947, "has always dealt with experience… by prescribing the attitude to be adopted toward it."

Opposite
The New Yorker building

Key Event *Mein Kampf* is published

Mein Kampf, or *My Struggle*, was Adolf Hitler's manifesto for world order. He wrote the first volume, *Eine Abrechnung* (*An Account*), from notes dictated while he was in prison in 1925. In the two volumes he outlines many of the extreme views which he later enacted as Chancellor of Germany. These included the superiority of the "Aryan" or master race, and the demand for "lebensraum," or living space, for the German peoples. Hitler presents himself as an "übermensch," or super-human.

Anti-Semitism is an open and recurrent theme, with statements such as: "The personification of the devil as the symbol of all evil assumes the living shape of the Jew." Long before he came to power in 1933 – through a general election – Hitler had proclaimed his distaste for democracy: "There must be no majority decisions, but only responsible persons," he said. "The broad masses of a population are more amenable to the appeal of rhetoric than to any other force."

The writing in *Mein Kampf* is labored, convoluted, repetitive and, at times, almost unreadable. As such, the book became a symbol of Hitler's beliefs, rather than a concise manifesto of them. Nevertheless, many historians argue that European leaders and their advisors could have scrutinized this work more closely to see the threat that Hitler posed.

Despite the turgid prose, however, the book was popular even before Hitler came to power. By the end of World War II about 10 million copies of *Mein Kampf* had been sold; every soldier at the front and every newly-wed couple was given a free copy.
Rosie Blau

Date 1925 (volume 1), 1926 (volume 2)

Author Adolf Hitler (1889–1945)

Place Germany

Why It's Key This manifesto of Adolf Hitler's beliefs formed the core of Nazi Party policy from 1933 and is still brandished by neo-Nazis today as a symbol of fascism.

Key Passage "Haircut"
Haircut and Other Stories

"It's a cinch Doc went up in the air and swore he'd make Jim suffer. But it was a kind of a delicate thing, because if it got out that he had beat Jim up, Julie was bound to hear of it and then she'd know that doc knew and of course knowin' that he knew would make it worse for her than ever. He was goin' to do somethin', but it took a lot of figurin'."

It's a crying shame that Lardner's (1885–1933) fiction has fallen out of vogue, for he is the certain inheritor of satirist Mark Twain's mantle. Not only did Lardner love to deflate the egos and expose the foibles of the "average" American, but he also did it using the particular idiom and vernacular of the early twentieth century Americans. In fact, Lardner made his name because of his ability to recreate regional dialects, colloquial speech and slang. His wicked sense of humor didn't hurt him, either.

Lardner hit the big time when *The Saturday Evening Post* published a series of epistolary pieces collectively called *You Know Me, Al*, letters purportedly written by a bush league baseball pitcher to a friend describing life on the road. Using the *lingua franca* of the small-town American and semi-professional athlete, Lardner lets his narrator, Jack Keefe, expose himself as self-interested, undeservingly egotistic and a bit dim. But even though Jack is a bit of a blowhard, Lardner's satire did not turn edgy until after the real-life Black Sox Baseball Scandal, a disappointment which Lardner took personally when his home team, the White Sox, deliberately threw the championship.

Afterwards, Lardner set out to expose the greed, hypocrisy, and cruelty of people through his satire. Yet he never failed to be funny and his ear for the way real people talked never deserted him, even after his stories became more biting and satiric. His best, and most complicated, work was produced during this time.
Elizabeth Rosen

Date 1925

Author Ring Lardner

Nationality USA

Why It's Key Lardner's impeccable ear for rendering colloquial speech and talent for depicting average Americans and all their peccadilloes made him the twentieth century heir to the "local color" school of writing which originated with Mark Twain.

Key Passage *Gentlemen Prefer Blondes:*
The Illuminating Diary of a Professional Lady

"So when I got through telling Dorothy what I thought up, Dorothy looked at me and looked at me and she really said she thought my brains were a miracle. I mean she said my brains reminded her of a radio because you listen to it for days and days and you get discouradged and just when you are getting ready to smash it, something comes out that is a masterpiece."

Anita Loos (1888–1981) worked as a screenwriter, playwright, journalist and author, achieving mass acclaim with the novel, *Gentlemen Prefer Blondes*. Irritated by the fact that her friend, H.L. Mencken, "one of the keenest minds of our era," was always to be found in the company of a beautiful blonde who lacked intellectual acumen, she wrote a short story for *Harper's Bazaar*. Sales of the magazine doubled and then tripled upon the publication of a spoof diary of the blonde and beautiful Lorelei Lee, lacking in education, but possessing a keen financial cunning. The book became an instant bestseller, translated into 13 languages, described by George Santayana as the best book of philosophy written by an American, and by Edith Wharton as the great American novel.

Proving that it was precisely as easy to turn a hit book into a hit film in the early twentieth century as it is now, it took another 28 years to produce the Howard Hawks movie-musical of the same name, starring Jane Russell as the brunette Dorothy and Marilyn Monroe as the artless Lorelei, breathing her way through the film's most memorable song, "Diamonds Are a Girl's Best Friend."

Loos' genius was to catch the tone of Lorelei so completely that she became instantly, utterly real: "I thought that any girl who was a lady would not even think of having such a good time that she did not remember to hang on to her jewelry."
Natalie Haynes

Date 1925

Author Anita Loos

Nationality USA

Why It's Key Loos did much to develop a highly influential style of wise-cracking American comedy. In Lorelei Lee she created a heroine who seemed both instantly recognizable and unlike any other fictional young woman before her in her gleefully guilt-free party going, gold digging and, of course, diamond loving.

Opposite
Gentlemen Prefer Blondes

Key Passage
Manhattan Transfer

"Sunlight dripped in her face through the little holes in the brim of her straw hat. She was walking with brisk steps too short on account of her narrow skirt; through the thin china silk the sunlight tingled like a hand stroking her back. In the heavy heat streets, stores, people in Sunday clothes, straw hats, sunshades, surfacecars, taxis, broke and crinkled brightly about her grazing her with sharp cutting glints as if she were walking through piles of metal shavings. She was groping continually through a tangle of gritty saw-edged brittle noise."

The novel presents the story of metropolitan New York from the time of its incorporation (1898) up until the "Jazz Age" (1920s). It deploys a "collectivist" technique, which presents a series of discontinuous but meaningfully juxtaposed cinematic scenes, featuring a multitude of characters whose lives criss-cross Manhattan in a perpetual seethe of urban estrangement. The novel's strength lies in a carefully edited accumulation of "objectivist" detail. Even "stream of consciousness" passages read as observations of sense perceptions in someone's brain, rather than as romantic expressions of selfhood.

This passage describes the main female protagonist Ellen Thatcher as she walks through Central Park. It registers sense data, implying that this is how living in the condition of urban modernity affects human consciousness. Rather than character revealed through interiority, Ellen moves through the world sensing her personal identity in terms of her fashionable clothes and the constraints they impose. She perceives the city as "sharp cutting glints" of scenes, accompanied by the "gritty saw-edged brittle noise" that sounds as perpetual accompaniment to this accelerating, mechanical age.
Helen May Dennis

Date 1925

Author John Dos Passos (1896–1970)

Nationality USA

Why It's Key Born in Chicago, an illegitimate child of parents married to others, Dos Passos described his boyhood as being a "hotel child." He wrote *Manhattan Transfer* after reading *Ulysses* and *The Waste Land* (both 1922). In 1938 Jean-Paul Sartre acclaimed him "the greatest living writer of our time."

Key Book
Turbott Wolfe

William Plomer's first novel was written when he was only 19, and was published by Leonard and Virginia Woolf's Hogarth Press in 1925, after he sent it to them for perusal. The book was critically well-received in the UK and United States, but it was greeted with a deluge of opprobrium in Plomer's native South Africa. Laurens van der Post recalled that only three of the many reviews of the work were positive.

Plomer's novel constitutes a bitter attack on the complacency of white South African society. Outside the eponymous character's close circle, white characters in the book are almost universally presented as irredeemable racists. In contrast, black characters are presented in a somewhat idealized light. A key plot element is the formation of the "Young Africa" society, an organization dedicated to an "Africa for the Africans" policy. Inter-racial love and marriage not only form a central theme of the plot, but also are deliberately proposed by "Young Africa" as a means to racial equality. The book is also regarded as one of the first works of South African literature to include fully realized black characters.

Although the apartheid policy was enacted 23 years after the publication of *Turbott Wolfe*, Plomer's attack on the racism of white South African society, and his emphasis on racial equality, have led him to be regarded by many as the father of anti-apartheid literature.
Tim Lovering

Date 1925

Author William Plomer (1903–1973)

Nationality South Africa

Why It's Key *Turbott Wolfe*, with its themes of racial equality and integration, and its attack on white South African racism, led William Plomer to be seen as the father of anti-apartheid literature.

Key Book
The Sun Also Rises

Ernest Hemingway's first full-length novel catapulted its author into celebrity and has become one of the great classics of American literature. Focusing on a group of American and British expatriates in Europe during the 1920s, the novel dramatizes the physical, psychological, and emotional scars inflicted by World War I. The novel is narrated by Jake Barnes, who was wounded on the Italian front and rendered impotent, but is hopelessly in love with Lady Brett Ashley, a beautiful but promiscuous woman who loves Jake but cannot tolerate a relationship that can never be consummated. Brett is engaged to a bankrupt Scot but has an affair with a Jewish American writer who does not understand the rules of Brett's game and cannot accept that their liaison was meaningless to her.

The novel reaches a climax during the fiesta in Pamplona, to celebrate the running of the bulls, in a series of scenes that establishes that these characters are morally impotent and bankrupt, betraying their own values because of the emotional privations caused by the war. Corruption is everywhere, and only in the ritual of sports – fishing, bullfighting, boxing – can purity of meaning be rediscovered. The novel introduced Hemingway's hallmark style, a deceptively simple, declarative mode that made little explicit but was subtly rich in implication. In fact, this story about the traumas of war very rarely mentions war itself, focusing instead on aftermath: the characters can only helplessly drink, fight and fornicate as they try to escape the pain and despair created by the war that destroyed them just as effectively as if it had killed them.

Sarah Churchwell

Date 1926

Author Ernest Hemingway (1899–1961)

Nationality USA

Why It's Key The novel inaugurated the phrase – and the concept – of the "lost generation," who were struggling with anomie and despair after World War I. It also brought Hemingway instant fame and fortune, and was instrumental in transforming him into arguably the most influential twentieth-century writer of English.

1920–1929

187

Key Character **Lolly Willowes**
Lolly Willowes

Lolly Willowes, the unmarried protagonist of Sylvia Townsend Warner's beautifully written and witty first novel, spends 20 years of her life as a maiden aunt looking after her brother's children in London and resigned to the drudgery of domestic routine. In a moment of revelation, however, she comes to recognize the narrow-minded conservatism of the Willowes family and leaves to live on her own in the remote village of Great Mop. Here, in a world which comes to represent mythic rural England in the wake of World War I, she celebrates the beauty of nature, revels in her independence, and makes a pact with the devil to become a witch.

In her choice to be "a witch by vocation," Lolly is acutely aware of the need to escape the claustrophobic limitations of the life of the spinster (a figure on the increase after the war). Turning her back on family, home and tradition, she places herself on the margins of society so that she can claim a new power and forge an identity free from the pressures of convention. As Lolly tells the devil, a woman becomes a witch "to have a life of one's own, not an existence doled out… by others."

The work of Sylvia Townsend Warner has recently been undergoing a revival of interest, and *Lolly Willowes* in particular is now seen as an important precursor of much twentieth-century women's writing with its critique of male systems of control and celebration of female empowerment through nature and witchcraft.

Simon Avery

Date 1926

Author Sylvia Townsend Warner (1893–1978)

Nationality UK

Why It's Key *Lolly Willowes* has always been Warner's most popular novel. The story of a woman who escapes the conventions of society to start a new empowered life as a witch, the novel has been read as a feminist parable and prefigures many of the key concerns of women's writing later in the century.

Key Character **Winnie-the-Pooh**
Winnie-the-Pooh

Winnie-the-Pooh began life as Edward Bear, the favoured teddy of A.A. Milne's son, Christopher Robin. Joined by the other toys in the nursery, the stories of Pooh Bear have charmed and captivated both children and parents since they came to life more than 80 years ago.

All the animals that live with Christopher Robin in the Hundred Acre Wood have distinct and delightful personalities. Timid Piglet is in awe of his bigger friend Pooh; Owl is the thinker and philosopher; Eeyore is curmudgeonly and pessimistic, although always secretly thrilled to see the others when they visit. A.A. Milne's characters are all utterly charming, but it is Pooh who is the unquestionable favorite with his gentle disposition and never-ending willingness to set forth on a daring mission to help his friends (or sometimes to find some honey). These missions often end with unwitting or accidental triumph or sometimes, when his initial bravado fails him or he does something silly, a nervous retreat to Christopher Robin who makes everything alright again.

Pooh, as he often says himself, is a Bear of Very Little Brain, for whom the world is a wonderful and sometimes confusing place – although there is nothing that can't be fixed with a pot of honey. In *Winnie-the-Pooh*, Milne has captured perfectly the innocence and sweet hopefulness of early childhood. Pooh's best friend Piglet puts it best: "Pooh hasn't much Brain, but he never comes to any harm. He does silly things and they turn out right."

Winnie-the-Pooh himself has reached worldwide superstardom since Disney first adopted him and he is now king of one of their most successful franchizes. In 2006 Winnie was even awarded his own star on the Hollywood walk of fame, in honor of his 80th birthday.
Francesca Segal

Date 1926

Author A.A. Milne (1882–1956)

Nationality UK

Why It's Key A.A. Milne has been celebrated as a playwright and *Punch* contributor before the success of Winnie-the-Pooh, but it is for the Pooh stories and his two volumes of children's poetry that he is best remembered.

Opposite **Christopher Robin and Winnie-the-Pooh**

Key Event **The musical version of *Show Boat* begins modern U.S. musical theater**

"Three generations of women" has now become a tooth-hurting cliché of popular fiction, but it was not thus in the 1920s. Parthy Hawkes is a life-denying termagant, possessed of a good heart in the wrong place, endlessly at war with her bushy, sprightly husband, her wayward and talented daughter, Magnolia, and, above all, her own deepest desires. Magnolia adores everything: the river, the life of the actor, her father, the strange and motley troupe which forms her adoptive clan.

Life on the showboat has all the rich, tropical indolence of the Deep South, and all its blistering passions and medieval taboos. Julie, Magnolia's confidante and mentor, flees the boat after a rejected lover exposes her mixed parentage. Elly, the juvenile lead, talentless, racist and selfish, runs off with a man who later abandons her; her husband has in turn to abandon the boat when she falls sick. Magnolia can replace Elly, but who is to replace Shultzy? None other than Gaylord Ravenal, a handsome charming and remarkably talented young man who breathes new life into the showboat's performances. He falls in love with Magnolia, she with him, and all seems bright. Two problems quickly loom, however: he has too much of a past and, if that inconvenient gambling habit furnishes any clue, all too little future.

But there is more to Ferber's tale than a gentle, bucolic saga of love winning through and life winning out; it prophesied the eventual colonization of black music by whites and reminded America of that ooze of racism which can rise up to unseat even the most tolerant and bohemian communities. The Mississippi itself, "Father of Rivers," contrary, dark and savage, the bringer of wealth, the witness and abetter of injustice, remains the story's true protagonist.
Murrough O'Brien

Date 1926

Author Edna Ferber (1887–1968)

Nationality USA

Why It's Key *Showboat* remains Ferber's best-loved book. In it, she took the theme of the woman who must fight through thickets of prejudice and softened it in the cause of accessibility. In 1927 Jerome Kern and Oscar Hammerstein II's *Show Boat* the musical hit Broadway. Musical theater has never been the same since.

Key Event
Agatha Christie disappears

The celebrated mystery writer Agatha Christie disappeared from her comfortable Berkshire home on the evening of Friday December 3, 1926. The next morning her car was found abandoned several miles away and a huge publicity storm ensued. The police dragged a nearby lake and 15,000 volunteers searched the surrounding countryside.

11 days later, and following a tip-off, Mrs Christie was discovered living quietly in a hotel in genteel Harrogate, Yorkshire. She appeared to have no recollection of her real identity, nor of the events of the past few days. Doctors put out the story that she was suffering from amnesia brought about by the recent death of her mother. In fact, a definitive explanation for Christie's disappearance is still wanting. Some people thought that it must be a publicity stunt to boost the sales of her latest book – *The Murder of Roger Ackroyd*. This seems unlikely, since *Roger Ackroyd* was already a big commercial success and for many people remains her greatest work.

Far more likely is the theory that Christie was distraught over the affair of her husband, the handsome war veteran Archibald Christie, with another woman. The fact that she had checked into the hotel using the same surname as her husband's mistress suggests that the situation was playing heavily on her mind. Two years later Christie divorced her husband and eventually married the archaeologist Max Mallowan with whom she stayed until her death in 1976. Whether Christie consciously staged her disappearance to attract her errant husband's attention, or was genuinely suffering from a "fugue state," is something which continues to fascinate mystery buffs.

Kathryn Hughes

Date 1926

Place UK

Why It's Key In 1979 the events of December 1926 were dramatized in a film called *Agatha* starring Vanessa Redgrave and Dustin Hoffman. In order to make the story palatable to an international audience, Hoffman plays an entirely fictional American journalist assigned to investigate the Christie disappearance. The results were predictably disappointing.

Key Book
Dream Story (*Traumnovelle*)

Fridolin and Albertina are an almost ideally middle-class couple. He is a successful private practitioner, she a beautiful wife and devoted mother. They have a delightful daughter. But something strange, sinister, and never quite explained occurs one night after a masked ball. As they pore over that night's events, each begins to test the other's fidelity. The stakes rise, hurtful revelations emerge. Then the doctor is called away to attend a dying patient. And the strangest night ensues.

Sexual possibilities open up on the streets of Vienna for Fridolin, only to close as abruptly. He can't bring himself to sleep with a kind-hearted young whore, he can't quite indulge the love of the dead councillor. Then an old friend, Nachtigall, leads him to a secret ball, an eerie conclave of monks, cavaliers and naked nuns. Convinced that a woman has sacrificed herself to save his life, he returns home, only to hear that while he was living a dream his wife was dreaming of someone else and that he, her husband, appeared in that dream only as a martyr to be mocked. There is a kind of reconciliation.

The genius of *Dream Story* lies in the way it grafts a deeply sophisticated middle European sensibility onto one of the oldest folk traditions, the May Moon Tale, in which the unwary traveller, sure of his own strength and probity, is drawn by otherworld forces into dark and seemingly endless labyrinths, where nothing is but what should not be. Is it altogether coincidental that Nachtigall means "Mad Night"?

Murrough O'Brien

Date 1926

Author Arthur Schnitzler (1862–1931)

Nationality Austria

Why It's Key Schnitzler evinced a profound preoccupation with the double standards which attend the relationship between the sexes. *Dream Story* is the acme of this concern. Kubrick's film of the book, *Eyes Wide Shut* (1999), moved his story to New York, giving added edge to an already disturbing tale.

Key Character **Judith Earle**
Dusty Answer

Judith Earle is an only child whose solitude is occasionally broken by the family of cousins who come to stay next door. Captivated from childhood by beautiful Charlie and Mariella, brooding Julian, dependable Martin and elusive Roddy, Judith yearns for their visits and mourns their absences. When the cousins return after the War, however, their glamour has been touched by tragedy.

Re-encountering them as a young woman with a place at Cambridge University and a vestigial sense of her own attractiveness, Judith discovers, to her astonishment, that she has a new effect on her old playmates. But it is Roddy with whom she falls in love. At Cambridge, meanwhile, she forms an intense friendship with charismatic, sexually ambiguous Jennifer, who becomes the focus of her living world whilst her secret longings are reserved for the indifferent Roddy. Both relationships lead to disenchantment and rejection.

On the brink of sexual awakening, Judith remains beguilingly naïve, arousing complicated passions in others and fatally mistaking physical desire for love. She is a sympathetic heroine, whose composure masks a warm internal life and whose intelligence does not protect her from heartbreak; indeed, from the series of heartbreaks which mark her transition from girlhood to womanhood. *Dusty Answer* – once a *succès de scandale* – is a tender elegy to first love, friendship and lost innocence, and although the moral and sexual climate in which it was written is considerably changed today, Judith remains a character with whom anyone who has loved, lost and braced themselves to start again must surely identify.

Amy Rosenthal

Date 1927

Author Rosamond Lehmann (1901–1990)

Nationality UK

Why It's Key A single ecstatic review in *The Sunday Times* made *Dusty Answer* a bestseller and brought its author overnight notoriety. For the rest of her life she would receive letters from women readers asking how she could have described their personal experience so precisely.

191

Key Author
Jerome K. Jerome

Jerome Klapka Jerome (1859–1927) was born in Staffordshire in 1859 and came to London to be educated at Marylebone Grammar School. He left school early and after various jobs turned to literary work as a career. His first works were either plays or reflections on stage life, but it was with the publication of *Three Men in a Boat (To say nothing of the Dog!)* in 1889 that he found enormous public and widespread fame.

The brief description of a boat trip up the Thames undertaken by the narrator, J., and his friends George, Harris and the dog Montmorency, has charmed legions of readers with its innocence and light-hearted verve. Jerome himself suggested that the book had no real literary style or particular usefulness; rather it was the "simple truthfulness" of the work which was important.

This directness, a confiding tone and a sense of innocence are central to the book's appeal, as is the genial slapstick, silliness and buffoonery. The book's theme in many ways is Englishness – the geography of the nation is reflected in the gentle countryside and river, and the Thames journey allows J. to reflect on English leisure time and history.

Jerome's gift was for a gentle, inclusive humor. He helped to foster an institutionalized literary mockery of the seriousness of society, founding and editing *The Idler* magazine. He is an idiosyncratic writer, interested in the fatuousness and silliness of humanity. In 1900 he published a sequel in which the three (minus the dog) tour Germany on bikes, entitled *Three Men on the Bummel*.

Jerome de Groot

Date 1927 (death)

Nationality UK

Why It's Key The author of the much-loved *Three Men in a Boat*, Jerome was also a prolific journalist and prominent literary figure of the late nineteenth century, and founded *The Idler*.

Key Event **The execution of the two Italian-American anarchists Sacco and Vanzetti**

Nicola Sacco (1891–1927) and Bartolomeo Vanzetti (1888–1927), both Italian immigrants, were arrested in Massachusetts in 1920 on suspicion of having committed robbery and murder. This was against the background of the so-called "Red Scare" in the United States, in which there was widespread fear of a Communist revolt inspired by the Russian Revolution. As the two accused were admitted anarchists, it was felt by many that they were on trial more for their political convictions rather than any real involvement in the crimes. It was also believed that racist anti-immigrant feeling was playing an undue part in making sure that the two men would not have a fair trial.

When, despite liberal protests and legal appeals, the two were sent to the electric chair in 1927, the furore inspired several American writers. Upton Sinclair based his novel *Boston* on the case. The playwright Maxwell Anderson wrote *Winterset* in 1935, using the idea of a son of one of the executed men trying to clear his father's name, and it featured in Dos Passos' *U.S.A.* trilogy (1938). The poet Edna St. Vincent Millay was arrested the day before the execution for carrying a placard proclaiming, "If These Men Are Executed, Justice is Dead in Massachusetts."

The case continued to resonate throughout the twentieth century, often seized on as the archetypal example of the unfairness and prejudice against the Left and the ordinary worker that characterized the American justice system, and it featured in the protest songs of Woody Guthrie and Pete Seeger as well as in such works as Kurt Vonnegut's *Jailbird* (1979).

Michael Munro

Date 1927

Place Massachusetts, USA

Why It's Key This case was a *cause célèbre* in the United States. Ostensibly a criminal matter of robbery and murder, its political overtones were seen to dominate and for several years it aroused great controversy. The case inspired several authors and was a great rallying point for liberal opinion in Depression-era America and elsewhere.

Opposite
Protests on th[...]

192

Key Passage
The Bridge of San Luis Rey

"There is a land of the living and a land of the dead, and the bridge is love, the only survival, the only meaning."

The Bridge of San Luis Rey is now seen as a prototype of the modern "disaster story," in which various stories about a disparate group of characters run alongside each other until they are resolved in some way by a common catastrophe. Wilder's starting point is different: he begins with the catastrophe itself, in this case the collapse of a bridge in eighteenth-century Peru, killing five people. He then examines the lives of those five in a series of brief, exquisite character sketches that reveal what exactly are the stories that the disaster has brought to a resolution. He also tells the story of Father Juniper, an Italian priest who believes that because the disaster is a "sheer Act of God," an investigation into the lives of the victims will yield some clue as to what behavior God regards as punishable – or rewardable – by death.

This scientific approach to evaluating human worth earns Wilder's scorn. Juniper has been asking the wrong question: it is not the nature of God that the five life-stories reveal, but the nature of love, in its various forms. The book's closing lines became famous when Tony Blair quoted them after the terrorist attacks in the United States in 2001: "We ourselves shall be loved for a while and forgotten. But the love will have been enough; all those impulses return to the love that made them...." Throughout the novel Wilder mercilessly exposes human folly and weakness in cool prose, and this gives depth to his lyrical, uplifting conclusion.

Jake Kerridge

Date 192[...]

Author Th[...]
(1897–1975)

Nationality USA

Why It's Key Wilder's words provide comfort in troubled times.

Key Character **George Sherston**
Memoirs of a Fox-Hunting Man

Memoirs of a Fox-Hunting Man is, in effect, a partial biography of Siegfried Sassoon's (1886–1967) early years disguised as a novel. Sassoon himself appears as George Sherston while his mother is Aunt Evelyn. His real-life siblings, meanwhile, have disappeared. Sherston is an awkward, isolated boy who comes alive when he joins the local hunt during the years before World War I. Sassoon gives lyrical descriptions of the Kent and Sussex countryside, as well as some sharp-eyed caricatures of the bluff country squires who inhabit it. He also describes a local cricket match on the village green, where the well-mannered contest contrasts ironically with the savage slaughter which the reader knows awaits many of the young players on the killing fields of France.

The book ends with Sherston's enlistment in a local regiment and the first few weeks of fighting on the continent. The story is continued in two sequels: *Memoirs of an Infantry Officer* and *Sherston's Progress*.

Initially *Fox-Hunting Man* was written anonymously: Sassoon was worried that, if it flopped, it would harm his reputation as one of the best-known poets of the "Great War." As it turned out the book was a great success, won the Hawthorden Prize, and became a fixture on English Literature syllabuses around the world.

Sassoon later remarked that Sherston comprised only one-fifth of his actual personality. Certainly Sherston is resolutely un-bookish, nor does he give any hint of erotic feelings towards other men. Sassoon himself remained conflicted about his own homosexuality, and eventually married in middle age.
Kathryn Hughes

Date 1928

Author Siegfried Sassoon

Nationality UK

Why It's Key Early readers of Sherston's fictional memoirs enjoyed them because they described an England that had gone for good. Later readers, however, noted that the references to barbed wire, Boer War veterans and the listlessness of the present generation of young public school men hinted at the Armageddon that lay just around the corner.

Key Author
Thomas Hardy

Thomas Hardy's death saw the loss of both a great novelist and a great poet, who had been a major influence on the transition from Victorian to modernist aesthetics. Although his first love was poetry, Hardy (1840–1928) made his name from fiction writing between the 1860s and 1890s. With his first real success, *Far From the Madding Crowd* (1874), he established the semi-fictional rural world of Wessex, the setting for his following 10 novels. These tackle the great social and intellectual upheavals of the nineteenth century with their examination of the dynamics of rural life, class conflict, gender relations, history and the "ache of modernism."

Increasingly Hardy's questioning of established thought brought him into conflict with the conservative establishment. In particular, his final novels, *Tess of the D'Urbervilles* (1891) and *Jude the Obscure* (1895), were vilified for their explicit treatment of sexuality, attacks on the institution of marriage and criticism of religion in a post-Darwinian world. Following the attack on *Jude*, Hardy abandoned novel writing and returned to poetry for the last 30 years of his life. In all, he wrote nearly 1,000 poems, often characterized by a sparse, direct style, which explore the natural world, lost love and faith, alienation and the exile figure.

Hardy had a huge influence on the development of the novel in terms of form and content and was greatly admired by D.H. Lawrence and Virginia Woolf, amongst others. His poetry also had a major impact on a range of twentieth-century poets and helped establish a new tradition which was highly influential on subsequent poets such as W.H. Auden, Louis MacNiece, Philip Larkin and Seamus Heaney. He remains one of the most widely read and admired British writers.
Simon Avery

Date 1928 (death)

Nationality UK

Other Key Works
Under the Greenwood Tree (1872), *A Pair of Blue Eyes* (1873), *The Return of the Native* (1878), *The Mayor of Casterbridge* (1886), *The Woodlanders* (1887), *Wessex Tales* (1888), *Wessex Poems* (1898), *Poems of the Past and Present* (1902), *The Dynasts* (1908)

Why It's Key Hardy was both a major late-Victorian novelist and a major twentieth-century poet.

Key Author **Federico García Lorca**
Gypsy Ballads (Primer romancero gitano)

When Spanish fascists shot the 38-year-old Federico García Lorca (1898–1939) on the morning of August 19, 1936, and threw him into an unmarked grave, they silenced one of the twentieth century's greatest poets.

Lorca was born in the village of Fuente Vaqueros in the southern Spanish province of Granada on June 5, 1898. His first publication was an Andalusian travel book, *Impressions and Landscapes* (*Impresiones y paisajes*), which appeared in 1918. Shortly afterwards, he moved to Madrid where, in 1921, he published his first collection of verse, *Book of Poems* (*Libro de poemas*). His romantic historical play, *Mariana Pineda*, opened to great acclaim in 1927. By the following year, when his *Gypsy Ballads* (*Primer romancero gitano*) was published, he was already Spain's best-known poet and a leading member of a cultural grouping known as the Generation of '27.

At the end of the 1920s, he visited New York but found it spiritually sterile. His collection of poems, *Poet in New York* (*Poeta en Nueva York*), was published posthumously in 1940. He returned to Spain in 1931 after a happier trip to Cuba and wrote his three finest plays: the celebrated "rural trilogy" of *Blood Wedding* (*Bodas de Sangre*), a Greek tragedy-style love triangle; *Yerma*, about conflict in a barren marriage and *The House of Bernarda Alba* (*La Casa de Bernarda Alba*), written just months before his murder, a study of passion submerged under matriarchal repression.

He also wrote a superb four-part poem, "Lament for the Death of a Bullfighter," dedicated to his friend, Ignacio Sánchez Mejías, who had been killed in the ring.

Although the most "gitano" (gypsy) of poets, Lorca said: "I sing to Spain and I feel her to the core of my being, but above all I am a man of the world and brother of everyone."

Adam Feinstein

Date 1928 (publication)

Nationality Spain

Other Key Works
Mariana Pineda (1927),
The Shoemaker's Wonderful Wife (1930),
Poem of Deep Song (1931),
Blood Wedding (1933),
Yerma (1934), *Lament for Ignacio Sánchez Mejías* (1935), *The House of Bernarda Alba* (1945)

Why It's Key Lorca was a friend of Buñuel, Dalí, de Falla and Neruda and his creative work embraced verse, prose, drama, music, folklore, and painting.

Key Author **Ford Madox Ford**
The Last Post

As a pre-eminent editor and promoter of new writing, Ford Madox Ford (1873–1939) had a footing in two distinct literary periods. Before World War I, he published, among others, James, Hardy, Bennett and Yeats in *The English Review*, which he founded in 1910. In 1924, he founded *The Transatlantic Review* and further developed his instinct for discovering and promoting important new writers by publishing the likes of Joyce, Stein, Hemingway and Pound.

Prior to his career as an editor and proponent of new writing, Ford published two novels with his friend Joseph Conrad, *The Inheritors* (1901) and *Romance* (1903). The novels showed early signs of the innovative technique and experimentation that would come to characterize the modernist movement. Ford's later works reflected his aim to introduce into English fiction the objectivity and psychological realism of the great French novelists. In this sense, his novels do not confine themselves to the "realistic" depiction of

experience as it unfolds but are an exploration – as in his World War I-spanning tetralogy *Parade's End* – of the effects on the individual of a global and social catastrophe as experienced through the vagaries of memory, cognition and emotion. In these books, Ford eschews the third-person omniscient narrator in favor of positioning the protagonist as "the unreliable narrator," obscuring any impression of the author and raising interesting questions about authority and authorship.

Ford spent his last years living frugally in the south of France where he continued to support new writing until his death in 1939.

Christian Kerr

Date 1928 (publication)

Nationality UK

Other Key Works *The Good Soldier* (1915), *Parade's End* (published separately as *Some Do Not*, 1924; *No More Parades*, 1925; *A Man Could Stand Up*, 1926 and *The Last Post*, 1928)

Why It's Key *Parade's End* is regarded as one of the great works of twentieth century literature securing Ford's reputation as one of the leading figures of the modernist movement.

Key Book
Coming of Age in Samoa

Margaret Mead's most famous book also became one of the most widely read and hotly debated anthropological studies of the twentieth century. Written at a time when eugenics was a respectable field of study and biological determinism seemed to be gaining the upper hand in the nature/nurture debate, Mead's study of adolescent sexual behaviour on the Pacific island of Samoa appeared to strike an important blow for those who believed culture and socialization were the more important influence on human development.

Mead's depiction of young Samoan women as sexually relaxed and casually promiscuous shocked U.S. society at the time, particularly when the inference was that such behaviour patterns produced a more cohesive and less stressed society than was to be found in materialistic, sexually repressive Western cultures. The book's influence reached far beyond its own era and was an important factor in the movement towards sexual openness and female liberation that occurred from the 1960s onwards.

It was perhaps inevitable that such controversial material would be challenged. From the outset Mead's methodology – relying on informant testimony and observation rather than statistical analysis – was questioned, and in the 1980s the debate took a particularly fierce turn when fellow anthropologist Derek Freeman made the claim that Mead's research was seriously compromised, and that her primary informants were unreliable. The debate continues, with defenders claiming that Freeman's attack was ideologically driven. Mead died just before Freeman's book appeared, and so was unable to reply to the criticisms.

Gerard Woodward

Date 1928

Author Margaret Mead (1901–1978)

Nationality USA

Why It's Key A controversial anthropological study that questioned Western attitudes to sexual morality. Mead developed her arguments in *Growing Up in New Guinea* (1930) and *Sex and Temperament in Three Primitive Societies* (1935).

Opposite Margaret Mead

Key Book *Story of the Eye*
(Histoire de l'oeil)

SPOILER

An acknowledged erotic classic, *Story of the Eye* is Bataille's first and most successful attempt at fiction and his most widely read work, though he is primarily known for his unusual, hybrid contributions to the fields of philosophy, aesthetics and economics.

Bataille's first novel was published under the pseudonym, Lord Auch, until the first posthumous edition in 1967. It tells the picaresque tale of the narrator's wanderings around Europe in the company of two girls, Simone and the fragile Marcelle, and a "fabulously rich Englishman" called Sir Edmund. The novel begins with the narrator lying on the floor masturbating to the sight of Simone on a bench just above his face, soaking her genitalia in a saucer of milk; it ends with the happy band (apart from the now dead Marcelle) delighting in the rape, torture, and murder of a priest in the sacristy of his church, where they defile the Host and play sexual games with the priest's enucleated eye.

The structure of the narrative is constructed by a unique metonymic logic based on the resemblance between certain ovoid shapes (eggs, testicles, eyes) and the profound associations such shapes have in Bataille's own mind. The result is an incomparable work combining intense sexual excitement and violent frenzy with a solemn brand of silliness indicative of Bataille's previous allegiance to the Surrealist movement.

Robin Purves

Date 1928 (significantly revised 1940)

Author Georges Bataille (1897–1962)

Nationality France

Why It's Key Susan Sontag wrote about *Story of the Eye* in her influential essay "The Pornographic Imagination," which appeared in *Styles of Radical Will* (1969). She compared it with the work of the Marquis de Sade.

Key Event *Diamond Lil* conquers Broadway

Mae West started as a child actor in vaudeville and was writing and producing by the mid 1920s. She clearly wanted to be noticed – calling her 1926 play *SEX* (in capitals) was an early clue. It was hugely popular, and newspapers coyly referred to it as "That Certain Play" (though they'd been happy enough to accept the ads which displayed the proper title). Her next play, *The Drag* (in which she did not appear), dealt with male homosexuality, and was kept off Broadway by a moral panic in the press. West duly landed in jail for 10 days – a badge of honor she wore proudly for the rest of her life.

Her greatest success as a playwright was in 1928 with *Diamond Lil*. Just why she caused so much scandal, and why she has been seen by others as a champion of feminism, can be judged from what her character says about men's attitude to sex: "It's their game. I just happen to be smart enough to play it their way." Once the furore had died down (and the takings were carefully counted), she went on to conquer Hollywood. The play became what is probably her most successful film, *She Done him Wrong* (1933), in which she co-stars with Cary Grant (it made him a star). This is the film where she doesn't (quite) say her most famous line "Come up and see me sometime." What she actually says ("Why don't you come up some time and see me?") just doesn't sound quite as catchy somehow.

Cathy Benson

Date 1928

Author Mae West (1893–1980)

Place USA

Why It's Key Mae West was a lifelong provocateur and campaigner against censorship. In a series of taboo-busting plays which she wrote in the 1920s she gained nationwide attention, landed in jail and established the persona that she would make enduringly famous in films of the 1930s and 1940s.

Opposite Mae West

Key Character **Orlando** *Orlando*

Orlando is the main character of Virginia Woolf's 1928 novel of the same name. It was dedicated to her lover Vita Sackville-West and is, in effect, an extended love letter. Orlando is an Elizabethan nobleman who refuses to grow up. He remains a young man even when, in the reign of Charles II, he is sent as ambassador to Constantinople. It is at this point that he falls into a deep sleep and wakes up a woman, living in this female form for the next two and a half centuries.

As a woman Orlando is finally able to find love – with the equally sexually ambiguous Shelmerdine. She also finds a place at the literary salons of Pope, Addison, and Swift and learns, finally, how to write passable poetry (as a man her verse has been lamentable). However, in the public world Orlando's new gender turns out to be a liability: she is deprived of her ancestral property on the grounds of her gender (Vita Sackville-West had not been able to inherit Knole on the death of her father for just this reason).

In the character of Orlando, Woolf not only explores the pleasures and possibilities of trans-gendered living. She also questions the very underpinnings of the whole biographical genre. Woolf's father Leslie Stephen had been the editor of that monumental Victorian production, *The Dictionary of National Biography*, which was remarkable for its lack of entries on women. By changing into female form does Orlando forfeit the right to be commemorated? And what of the fact that she is not yet dead? By carefully subtitling her book "a Biography," Woolf pushes hard against the boundary that lies between fiction and non-fiction as well as that which separates male from female.

Kathryn Hughes

Date 1928

Author Virginia Woolf (1882–1941)

Nationality UK

Why It's Key *Orlando* remained uncensored on publication. In the 1970s it re-emerged as a favorite text amongst feminist and lesbian readers and remains a key text for "queer" critics writing today. In 1993 Sally Potter made a film based on *Orlando*, with Tilda Swinton in the leading role and Quentin Crisp as Queen Elizabeth.

Key Book
And Quiet Flows the Don

The broad sweep and moving humanity of Sholokhov's epic novel of Russia's Don Cossack south through the painful years of the Civil War (1919–1921) brought justified comparisons with Tolstoy.

First translated into English in 1934, and reprinted in 1967, after the Nobel award, it served to reassure a world readership that great Russian literature survived into the Soviet era. Sholokhov, whose formal education ended aged thirteen, early emerged as a storyteller of the Don region where he was born and, with a brief sojourn in Moscow, spent the rest of his life.

The novel was unusual for showing its hero Grigory Melekhov mistakenly choosing the "wrong," White, side in the Civil War against the Bolsheviks. It portrayed village life in fine detail, without sentiment, and was particularly attentive to the way women suffered in harsh times, both materially and intimately, with their men away. Sholokhov, who didn't join the Communist Party until 1932, escaped the fate of less fortunate contemporaries because Stalin admired his novel, despite the absence of an optimistic ending.

It seems to have been Sholokhov's huge success in the West that prompted the rumor, subsequently shown to be unfounded, that the novel was plagiarized from the diaries of a White Russian officer. His subsequent novel *Virgin Soil Upturned*, finally finished in 1960 after 28 years in the making, was less successful and showed signs of Sholokhov coming under ideological pressure to write the required version of the brutal early 1930s collectivization of agriculture as it affected the Don region.

Lesley Chamberlain

Date 1928

Author Mikhail Sholokhov (1905–84)

Nationality Russia

Why It's Key An obscure author in his own country, Sholokhov shot to worldwide fame when 37 years after publication of *And Quiet Flows the Don* he was awarded the Nobel Prize in Literature.

Opposite Mikhail Sholokhov

1920–1929

Key Event **Publication of *The Well of Loneliness* leads to a 20 year ban**

"I would rather give a healthy boy or a healthy girl a phial of prussic acid than this novel," wrote James Douglas in *The Sunday Express* in 1928. His words led to a trial for obscenity, the result of which was that *The Well of Loneliness* was banned in Britain for 20 years.

This novel is the story of Stephen – a girl whose aristocratic father wanted a son and whose mother is frightened by her boyishness. Stephen likes hunting and hates wearing dresses and, after a series of passionate crushes on older women, she declares herself an "invert," the term used by sexologist Havelock Ellis to describe homosexuality. The novel contained the first frank discussion of homosexuality in mainstream fiction.

Later, while driving an ambulance during World War I, Stephen finds love with Mary Llewellyn. When the war is over, the two women move to Paris and throw themselves into what would now be called gay and lesbian culture. Happiness is impossible for them – Hall depicts the homosexual demi-mondaine lifestyle as tragic and self-destructive.

The Well of Loneliness was Hall's fifth novel. She was a best-selling author who knew that to write such a book was to risk her reputation and her career. "I have put my pen at the services of some of the most persecuted and misunderstood people in the world" she said and she told her agent that she wouldn't change a word.

For decades, it was the best-known lesbian novel in the world. Attempts to ban it only increased its visibility and, by extension, created greater awareness of female homosexuality. Even today – when the book's attitudes and language seem dated and its message depressing – it still provokes discussion and academic debate and features in accounts of coming out.

Kathy Watson

Date 1928

Author Radclyffe Hall (1880–1943)

Place UK

Why It's Key Another lesbian novel, Compton MacKenzie's *Extraordinary Women* was published in the same year but not banned, much to the author's disappointment. Instead he cashed in on the controversy by claiming one of his characters had been inspired by Radclyffe Hall.

Key Book
Macunaíma

Macunaíma, the bewilderingly rich picaresque novel written by Mário Raul de Morais Andrade and first published in 1928, is considered one of the founding texts of Brazilian modernism. Andrade wrote the novel in an uninterrupted six-day burst of creative energy in 1926. It is an enormously perplexing work. Some early readers considered it too flamboyant, flippant and obscene. In his adventures to recover a magical amulet, Macunaíma, the libidinous protagonist – a "hero without a character," as the novel's subtitle dubs him – travels throughout Brazil and back in time, repeatedly outwitting his adversaries through his native cunning. This anti-hero is ethically ambivalent: positive actions and feelings like compassion and an urge to help or protect others are constantly interwoven with negative actions and feelings like envy, bitterness, deceit and manipulation.

In the book, Andrade sought to shatter the continental Portuguese tyranny over his country's written language by demonstrating the innate creativity of the Brazilian people as expressed in their folklore and indigenous mythology.

The novel's style is an extraordinary fusion of the avant-garde and the primitive, a mixture of classical Portuguese and colorful expressions from Brazil's blacks and Indians. Irony and satire are tempered by moments of tenderness. There is a clear link between what Brazilian critics call "aesthetic primitivism" and what became known three decades later as "magical realism."

Adam Feinstein

Date 1928

Author Mário de Andrade (1893–1945)

Nationality Brazil

Why It's Key Mário de Andrade was a poet, essayist, musician and novelist. His treatment of native myths in *Macunaíma* is significant because unlike fellow Latin American writers he did not want his protagonist to be exclusively identified with any region or tribe or with any pre-Colombian or colonial culture.

Key Passage **"The Ballad of Mack the Knife"** (*"Die Moritat von Mackie Messer"*)

"Oh, the shark has pretty teeth dear
And he shows 'em, pearly white
Just a jack knife has Macheath dear
And he keeps it way out of sight."
(trans. Marc Blitzstein)

Brecht's innovative and influential reworking of John Gay's *The Beggar's Opera* (1728) was conceived as a reaction to the polite predictability of bourgeois theater and opera, and as a means of reconnecting with audiences in a less formal, more immediate manner. An early high point in the career of one of the twentieth century's foremost political dramatists, the play is an iconic urban text.

Central to the play's intended effect is the use of music, composed by Kurt Weill in collaboration with Brecht, and the employment of songs designed to be sung by non-professional singers. The macabre humor and moral cynicism of these songs provide commentaries upon the story and reinforce the play's depiction of human greed and selfishness within a parody of capitalism. That said, this is only partly true of the "murder ballad" of the prologue, which introduces us to the dangerous charms of the businessman-gangster, Macheath; by establishing his "untouchable" reputation in a catalog of murders, robberies and rapes both his ruthlessness and his overconfidence are suggested.

Yet it is surely not the cautionary message but the appeal of the glamorous killer and the peculiar eroticism of the imagery – the concealed knife, the gloves covering the "shark" within – that have allowed this song to become independently famous in countless recordings by Frank Sinatra, Louis Armstrong, Robbie Williams and many others.

Jon Hughes

Date 1928

Original Title *The Threepenny Opera* (*Die Dreigroschenoper*)

Author Bertolt Brecht (1898–1956)

Nationality Germany

Why It's Key The most famous song from an iconic play of the 1920s which eroded traditional divisions between "high" and "low" culture.

Key Passage
A Room of One's Own

"so audaciously trespassing"

In the first part of *A Room of One's Own*, Woolf's narrator visits Oxbridge, a fictional university college. As she walks around the grounds, contemplating the relations between women and fiction, she is brusquely shooed off the grass by the college Beadle since only male scholars are permitted on the lawn. Having lost her train of thought, the narrator subsequently decides to visit the library. Upon opening the door, however, she is ushered back by the librarian who, "like a guardian angel barring the way with a flutter of black gown instead of white wings," insists that women cannot enter unaccompanied.

This initial passage, although humorously written, is crucial to Woolf's exploration of the ways in which women artists have been excluded from the worlds of male learning and opportunity, depicted here as fortress-like and impenetrable. The rest of the essay then develops this idea by emphasising the need to break with systems of oppression, to write women back into history, and to develop a tradition of women's writing. More specifically, Woolf argues that women require a room of their own (representing both physical and psychological space) and economic independence (valued by Woolf at a substantial £500 a year) if they are to achieve true freedom as thinkers and writers.

With its penetrating, insightful, and exploratory prose, *A Room of One's Own* has subsequently had a massive impact on twentieth-century thinking about women and writing, with Woolf often being cited as one of the most important foremothers of contemporary feminism.

Simon Avery

Date 1929

Author Virginia Woolf (1882–1941)

Nationality UK

Why It's Key Woolf's polemical essay, *A Room of One's Own*, is one of the most important works of twentieth-century feminism. Originally delivered as two lectures to students at the women's colleges of Cambridge University, it prefigures many later feminist concerns regarding women's writing.

1920–1929

203

Key Book *Grand Hotel* *(Menschen im Hotel)*

At Berlin's most expensive hotel, an aging Russian ballerina, a thief, a businessman, a doctor, a dying man and a secretary / nude model are all passing through. Like life, you "eat, sleep, lounge about, do business, flirt a little, dance a little" – and then you're on your way out again. This is Vicki Baum's hotel philosophy: "A hundred doors in one corridor and nobody knows a thing about his next door neighbours. When you leave another arrives and takes your bed."

In the great corridor of hotel literature, from Arnold Bennett's *Imperial Palace* and *The Grand Babylon Hotel* via Neil Simon's "Suite" comedies to *Hotel du Lac*, *Hotel World* and even *Hotel Babylon*, Baum's *Grand Hotel* is the grandest of them all.

This is the world of chance acquaintance – in the lift, in the bar, while dancing the Charleston – two main characters only know each other "for a few hours in the hotel bed of Room No 68"; a world of glittering surfaces, where people go to escape the poverty outside, where only the thickness of a wall separates prosperity and disaster; and in the end this is an almost Beckettian vision of people locked in their individual rooms with their secrets.

Cinematic in its concept, accomplished with choreographic élan, and with a magnificent finale, the novel was bound for the big screen and when it hit, became a sensation and an instant classic. Baum's novel pre-empted the ensemble piece. *Grand Hotel* is an arch comment on modernity – even down to the central image of the revolving door, that modern invention that seemed perfectly to express the constant motion of modern life, and individual people's dispensability within it, shovelling them in and out: "The revolving door turns and turns – and swings… and swings… and swings…."

Lucy Daniel

Date 1929

Author Vicki Baum (1888–1960)

Nationality Austria

Why It's Key *Grand Hotel* has been filmed several times; the first 1932 Hollywood film is a classic, starring Greta Garbo, Joan Crawford, Lionel Barrymore, and John Barrymore. After the film, Garbo's husky "I want to be alone" became her life motto. The novel was a bestseller making Baum one of the era's most widely read authors.

Key Book
A High Wind in Jamaica

A family of children on their way from their home in Jamaica to school in England are captured unintentionally by a pirate ship. Rather than an adventure in the mould of Peter Pan, or a presentation of barbarity meeting innocence, Hughes tells a tale which is much more subtle and subversive.

Away from the late Victorian and Edwardian fiction that portrayed childhood as a golden age and children as essentially innocent, Hughes shows the children's complex inner lives in the way they create a children's world on the ship. They are devious and manipulative, both naïve and calculating, while the pirates are seen to be merely hard-working men of limited imagination. Hugh Walpole said, "It has genius because it says something that a million people have seen before, but says it uniquely."

Rescued, the children are able to tell of their glorious deeds to a credulous adult world, and to be witnesses at the trial of the pirates, after which the men are hanged for a manslaughter that in fact was committed by one of the children.

A High Wind in Jamaica is a considerable work of imagination, as Hughes had not been to Jamaica when he wrote it so its descriptions of jungle and tropical climate were self-generated. It is tempting to analyze the preoccupations of the book in terms of Hughes' own childhood, which must have been darkened by the fact that by his sixth birthday his father and both siblings had died.

Jad Adams

Date 1929

Author Richard Hughes (1900–1976)

Nationality UK

Why It's Key *A High Wind in Jamaica* was the book in which children first lost their innocence, paving the way for Golding's *Lord of the Flies* and a bleak, twentieth-century view of humanity.

Key Character **Ellery Queen**
The Roman Hat Mystery

Dannay (1905–1982) and Lee (1905–1971) made an inspired decision in using the memorable name of their fictional amateur sleuth as their *nom de plume*. Ellery the character was an informed, educated and often sanctimonious bibliophile in the vein of Philo Vance. Lee and Dannay also made him a writer of detective stories, which added a layer of first-person narrative authority that became a distinguishing feature of the stories.

Exploiting the public's penchant for puzzles and formal playfulness, the first Ellery Queen novel, *The Roman Hat Mystery,* included a mock non-fictional preface, a floor plan of the crime scene and a list of characters from which readers could choose their most likely suspects. Towards the end of the book appears the Ellery Queen trademark "Challenge to the Reader" whereupon Ellery the writer invites the reader – who has been privy to the same series of clues as Ellery the detective – to solve the crime and name the murderer.

It was, perhaps, this invitation to actively participate in the solving of the crime to which the audience responded most enthusiastically, and the formula was used in many subsequent Ellery Queen stories.

Dannay and Lee wrote dozens of Ellery Queen books and hundreds of radio scripts, and the character was licensed to feature in theater, films and television. The stories became increasingly convoluted and variable in quality, but the plethora of cultural output did, at any rate, expand the Queen canon, increasing the character's stature to that of a logical successor to Sherlock Holmes.

Christian Kerr

Date 1929

Authors Frederic Dannay and Manfred Bennington Lee

Nationality USA

Why It's Key Ellery Queen was both a pseudonym used by writers Dannay and Lee and the name of the detective-hero of the novels written under that name.

Opposite Frederic Dannay and Manfred Bennington Lee

Key Book
Berlin Alexanderplatz

Stream of consciousness flows into the turbulent waters of urban life in this striking evocation of one man's experience of post-World War I Berlin. Franz Biberkopf, freshly released from prison after serving time for manslaughter, tries to make good against the odds. Biberkopf is "*l'homme moyen sensuel*," German style, and most memorable is Döblin's creation of a simple mind. The reader feels how the phenomenal world impacts on Biberkopf's consciousness while vividly experiencing the other protagonist, the city itself.

The impersonality of its ordinances, from tram routes to newspaper accounts of court cases, golden handshakes and new crimes, the richness and variety of chance acquaintance and the general daily struggle to survive, acts as a backdrop for the revelation of burning personal needs in Biberkopf, held up by the narrator as a specimen. The narrator, who introduces each of the nine sections of the novel, feigns scientific detachment. Beyond his dispassionate gaze lies an evident sympathy for the plight of the urban proletariat and the cruelty of the "system."

Döblin, a Jew, held strong socialist views and fled the Nazis on both counts in 1933. He began his prolific literary career as an Expressionist and *Berlin Alexanderplatz* radiates the energy, excitement and despair characteristic of the little man responding to the teeming cityscape. Here is also that rare example of what might have been a worthy but turgid document of social realism stimulating the creation of a highly sophisticated, discontinuous literary form, a stirring mix of texts and data that adds up to tragedy.

Lesley Chamberlain

Date 1929

Author Alfred Döblin (1878–1957)

Nationality Germany

Why It's Key *Berlin Alexanderplatz*, unique in the German tradition, has been compared to Joyce's *Ulysses*. Little-known to an English language readership, it is one of the great European novels of the 1920s.

Key Book
Passing

For a while, the Harlem Renaissance of the 1920s thrust a new generation of African-American artists, writers and intellectuals into the cultural limelight, a celebration of black American achievements before the Depression arrived to effectively end it. Some figures, like the poet Langston Hughes, achieved permanent places in the literary canon but others, including Larsen, faded along with the "new negro movement" itself. So, despite its contemporary success, *Passing* became one of those books by women writers "rediscovered" and popularized in the 1970s. The work has, however, remained a staple of university reading lists ever since, providing an intimate insight into the highly racially stratified world of 1920s black America.

At the heart of the novel is the practice of "passing," whereby a light-skinned black person secretly "passes" for white. Central characters Irene Redfield and Clare Kendry, girlhood friends reacquainted as adults, often do so. Irene, a bourgeois Harlemite, passes in order to enter spaces segregated for whites; Clare, a brasher, sexier, parvenu is actually passing in front of her white husband, a racist who jokingly calls her "Nig" because she is dark. In the novel's second chapter, when the women first accidentally meet again, some of the complexities of passing emerge. Scrutinizing one another before recognition, each assumes, with a touch of paranoia, the other is a white woman who suspects her observer of being black. *Passing* reveals "race" as a mobile, superficial construct. And along with their racial "transgression," the relationship between Irene and Clare starts to threaten other taboos.

Doug Haynes

Date 1929

Author Nella Larsen (1891–1964)

Nationality USA

Why It's Key A rediscovered classic of the Harlem Renaissance, Larsen's novel probes the boundary between black and white and was a unique exploration of black female sexuality.

Key Book
Les Enfants Terribles

Written under the "obsession of 'Make Believe' from [the musical] *Show Boat*," and while its author was receiving treatment for opium addiction, *Les Enfants Terribles* marked a shift in style for writer, filmmaker, ringmaster of French culture and leading surrealist Jean Cocteau. In a letter to André Gide, found in the book *Opium*, his "cure diaries," Cocteau wrote: "I owe you so much; there was a time when, had you not intervened, I would have gotten lost following the example of my counterfeit handwriting. Now I want to announce the true benefit of my cure: work is working me. I am disgorging the book I have meant to write (but couldn't) since 1912."

And disgorge he did. Dashed off in 19 days, the novel introduces the world to brother and sister Paul and Elisabeth, the doomed holy terrors of the title, "singular beings and their asocial acts are the charm of a pluralistic world which expels them," explains Cocteau. "It all begins with childhood things; at first all one can see of it are its games." The Game, objects stolen from the outside world; their room, a shrine to disorder, the setting in which most of the book takes place, and mostly at night.

Adapted by Cocteau – who also provides the voice-over – *Les Enfants Terribles* was turned into a haunting film by Jean-Pierre Melville (famous for *Le Cercle Rouge*) in 1950, the private mythology and obsessions of Paul and Elisabeth's damaged fantasy world celebrated in celluloid, though it has perhaps not aged well.

Susan Tomaselli

Date 1929

Author Jean Cocteau (1889–1963)

Nationality France

Why It's Key A published author by 1914, Cocteau's greatest creation was himself: novelist, playwright, critic, artist, filmmaker, set designer, boxing promoter, and social butterfly, Cocteau was the avant-garde celebrity of his time, brushing shoulders with Apollinaire, Proust, Picasso, Braque, and Stravinsky, and influencing French New Wave cinema.

Key Event **Writers rally in defence of James Joyce's *Work in Progress***

In 1929 James Joyce was seven years into the work that would become *Finnegans Wake*. His love of word games and riddles was such that he chose not to reveal his book's title, referring to it only as *Work in Progress*. He published sections of it as they were completed in avant-garde literary magazines, such as transition. Nevertheless, the linguistic experimentalism of his new writing came in for criticism from other writers such as Rebecca West, Sean O'Faolain, and Wyndham Lewis.

In response, Joyce secretly orchestrated this collection of essays defending his new work, selecting twelve writers and critics to write on different aspects of *Work in Progress*. He chose this number deliberately to match the number of Christ's apostles. The title makes a Joycean pun on separating sheep from the herd just as Christ separated the damned and the saved. Joyce chose friends such as Stuart Gilbert and Frank Budgen for his contributors, but also asked some of the brightest new lights amongst modern writers to help out. These included the American poet William Carlos Williams and the French writer, Eugene Jolas. The best essay is by another Irish writer, Samuel Beckett, criticising readers who want to skim off "the scant cream of sense." In Joyce's writing, Beckett explained, "words are not the polite contortions of 20th century printer's ink. They are alive. They elbow their way onto the page, and glow and blaze and fade and disappear." This essay became a significant defence of Joyce's experiments with language in his later works.

Joyce also planned a subsequent book of four essays (to match the number of gospels in the New Testament) that was never written.

Matthew Creasy

Date 1929

Place Paris

Title *Our Exagmination Round His Factification for Incamination of Work in Progress*

Why It's Key The book concludes with two letters of protest. Although he himself denied it, the second "litter" addressed to "Mister Germ's Choice" by "Vladimir Dixon" was for a long time believed to have been written by Joyce himself because it is so full of his characteristic puns.

Key Character **Benjy Compson**
The Sound and the Fury

The towering reputation of Faulkner's fourth novel owes much to the tour-de-force of the opening section, narrated by the severely retarded, perhaps autistic, Benjy Compson. The novel's title alludes to Macbeth's characterisation of human life as "a tale/ Told by an idiot, full of sound and fury/ Signifying nothing… " As we read the opening pages, we inevitably associate this "idiot" with their mentally impaired narrator, whose words seem at first so incoherent as to "signify nothing." As we read on, however, the fractured, discontinuous elements of Benjy's world gradually cohere, to be clarified by the chapters that follow (indeed, there are few novels that more richly reward a second reading).

The challenge for the reader of Benjy's section is to fill in the gaps opened up by his way of perceiving the world. Benjy does not have the means to perceive time, to grasp relationships between past and present. Moreover, he tends to relate to words as if they were themselves things, rather than means of representing things. The effect of these lacunae in comprehension is at once confusing and beautiful, capturing the world around him with a sensory immediacy lacking in ordinary perception, as in "I could smell the bright cold."

Benjy's narrative is our first glimpse into the tragic history of the Compsons that will unfold in the course of the novel. With Faulkner's characteristic tragic irony, it reveals him to have intuitive insight into the social and sexual malaise of his family entirely lacking in its other members.
Josh Cohen

Date 1929

Author William Faulkner (1897–1962)

Nationality USA

Why It's Key Faulkner's use of a severely retarded young man as the first of the novel's four narrators was remarkable both for its psychological insight and its radical modernist sensibility.

Key Event **De Beauvoir and Sartre meet, beginning a life-long collaboration**

Simone de Beauvoir (1908–1986) and Jean-Paul Sartre (1905–1980) met in 1929 while studying for the aggregation in Philosophy, an elite national graduate degree. At 21, Beauvoir was the youngest person ever to have taken the exam. Though examiners claimed she was the better philosopher, Beauvoir was placed second to Sartre. The two vowed to remain intellectual companions for life, acknowledging a "marriage of true minds." For most of their lives they saw each other daily.

Their unconventional relationship, underpinned by the belief that individuals should be free from society-imposed constraints, was an experiment in love from which existentialism was born. They would endlessly relate to each other details of their many secondary affairs; Sartre called this openness "transparency."

Though the two are remembered as much for the lives they led, the impact of their work cannot be overestimated. An anti-colonialist, pro-abortionist, and socialist, Beauvoir wrote novels, essays, biographies and an autobiography. She is best known for *She Came to Stay* and *The Mandarins*, which won her the prestigious Prix Goncourt literary prize, as well as her seminal account of woman's oppression, *The Second Sex*, which paved the way for contemporary feminism. She read and edited Sartre's work until his death.

A politically engaged activist and intellectual, Sartre was a prolific writer of philosophical treatises, novels, plays, and political pamphlets, *The Roads to Freedom* trilogy having broadest appeal today. In 1964 Sartre refused the Nobel Prize in Literature, stating he did not wish to align himself with institutions.
Elizabeth Whyman

Date 1929

Place Paris, France

Why It's Key The unconventional personal lives of de Beauvoir and Sartre challenged bourgeois conformity and are analyzed as much as their works. Despite being mother of the modern feminist movement, de Beauvoir declared that her greatest achievement was her relationship with Sartre.

Opposite **Simone de Beauvoir and Jean-Paul Sartre**

Key Book *All Quiet on the Western Front* (Im Westen nichts Neues)

The classic account of modern warfare from the point of view of ordinary soldiers, *All Quiet on the Western Front* was an instant international hit on publication in 1929: its English edition was reprinted seven times in a month, despite being about German soldiers during World War I, enemies only a decade earlier. All the horrors of industrial trench warfare are here, from the fear and carnage to the sheer boredom, but the author is careful not to leaven his narrative with glimmers of excitement or with intimations of poetic beauty in suffering. The reader is not even told which battle is taking place, and knows no more than the soldiers themselves.

In his short preface, the author makes clear that the book is "least of all an adventure… It will try simply to tell of a generation of men who, even through they may have escaped its shells, were destroyed by the war." The pointlessness of war may be a well-worn theme, but Erich Maria Remarque gives it a remarkable freshness through his evocative portrayal of a group of young farmers, tradesmen, and former students, their sufferings and their simple pleasures in bodily functions: they obey orders but have no real hatred of the enemy, reserving their enmity for the ever-present rats which steal their bread and for certain non-commissioned officers.

The English title was a mistranslation of the original German *Im Westen nichts Neues* (*Nothing new in the West*), which soon entered the language in its own right.

Bruce Millar

Date 1929

Author Erich Maria Remarque (1898–1970)

Nationality Germany

Why It's Key The Nazis banned Remarque's books for their anti-war sentiments in 1933, and he spent the rest of his life in the United States and Switzerland, where he died. In 1958 he married the Hollywood actress Paulette Goddard.

Opposite
All Quiet on the Western Front

Key Event **Robert Graves leaves England for Mallorca**

Born with a self-confessed rebellious nature, Robert Graves (1895–1985) was never likely to fit comfortably into the English middle-class society of the early part of the twentieth century. His recollections of battlefield service in the trenches of World War I occupy the largest part of the book and it is this element for which it is most remembered. Despite his "over-riding poetic obsession" Graves saw little poetry in the mud and slaughter of Flanders, preferring instead to approach his experiences with irony and the kind of gallows humor that prevailed in the ranks. This was a controversial stance in a Britain that was more concerned with idealising the generation of lost young men.

Belatedly taking up a university education that war service had postponed, Graves also dealt scathingly with a post-war England that was hardly "a land fit for heroes" but as class-ridden as before the great conflict. Wealthy industrialists and farmers had made substantial profits while their workers fought and died, and demobbed, often maimed, ex-servicemen were reduced to begging for a living. His espousal of socialism and support for the Russian Revolution brought him into conflict with his peers in the middle class.

Although blessed with children, Graves' marriage was unable to support the strain of the relative poverty into which his determination to pursue writing led them and he scandalised friends and family by leaving them all behind when he departed for Mallorca with the American poet Laura Riding. "So I went abroad, resolved never to make England my home again."

Michael Munro

Date 1929

Nationality UK

Why It's Key Graves' memoir *Goodbye to All That* chronicles his upbringing, his war service, ventures into the literary world and his marriage and children. Its critical assessment of English middle-class life and its puncturing of the romantic illusions about World War I, made it as controversial as his decision to abandon England to live with "another woman."

Key Book *Emil and the Detectives* (Emil und die Detektive)

The most famous of Erich Kästner's many successful children's novels, *Emil and the Detectives* has achieved lasting international popularity in translations and adaptations for film, television, and radio that is unusual in German literature, and it stands alongside Remarque's *All Quiet on the Western Front* (published the same year) as a landmark publication of the Weimar Republic. It is in many ways a pioneering text, adapting the detective genre for a young readership, and featuring a contemporary urban milieu, working class characters and the speech patterns of Berlin.

Its continued appeal in part derives from the employment of children as the "detectives"; the story of young Emil Tischbein, who is robbed on a train journey from provincial Neustadt to Berlin, and who in befriending a band of local children overcomes regional and social differences and catches the culprit, has influenced countless tales of "meddling" child adventurers, few of which – one thinks of the Famous Five or Harry Potter – are remotely as progressive, witty, or concise as Kästner's text.

Kästner was one of the outstanding satirical humorists of the Weimar Republic and the droll, self-conscious narrative voice employed to recount the adventure, combining a journalist's sensitivity to place and detail with the poet's joy in words and images, offers adult readers plenty to enjoy, as do the iconic illustrations by Kästner's long-term collaborator Walter Trier. A sequel, *Emil und die drei Zwillinge* (*Emil and the Three Twins*), in which the friends join up again for a seaside adventure, was published in 1935.
Jon Hughes

Date 1929

Author Erich Kästner (1899–1974)

Nationality Germany

Why It's Key One of the most influential children's novels of the 1920s, Kästner's tale of friendship and adventure in Berlin has achieved a popularity which transcends time and place.

Key Author **William Faulkner** As I Lay Dying

The author of twenty novels, dozens of short stories, and three volumes of poetry, as well as numerous Hollywood screenplays, William Faulkner's (1897–1962) prolificacy was fully matched by his imaginative range. Like Hardy's Wessex, Faulkner's Yoknapatawpha County, the recurring setting for his fiction, was an imaginative reinvention of his own region in Mississippi. Full of intricate narrative, historical and psychological interconnections, the Yoknapatawpha novels read as a kind of extended epic poem of the post-bellum Southern United States.

Faulkner's novels anatomize the painful social and psychological effects of the South's humiliating defeat in the Civil War, and the consequent breakdown of the pre-war South's feudal hierarchies; no other American writer has more vividly captured the chronic racial and sexual paranoia engendered by miscegenation, or racial mixing. One of the key authors in the "Southern Gothic" sub-genre, he also portrays the decay of the white Southern aristocracy, along with its fragile illusions of nobility and chivalry.

But Faulkner is equally significant for his restless spirit of formal innovation, perhaps most boldly displayed in his 1930 novel *As I Lay Dying*. His fragmentation of narrative perspective and linear time, his inventive use of popular genres (notably the "noir" thriller in *Sanctuary*) and his breathlessly long and dense sentence structures all placed him at the center of American literary modernism.

The winner of the 1949 Nobel Prize in literature, Faulkner's influence has spanned across great expanses of space and time, encompassing later American writers as different as Cormac McCarthy and Toni Morrison, as well as novelists from France to Latin America.
Josh Cohen

Date 1930 (publication)

Nationality USA

Other Key Works *The Sound and the Fury* (1929), *Sanctuary* (1931) *Light in August* (1932), *Absalom, Absalom!* (1936)

Why It's Key At once one of the greatest regional writers and formal innovators of modern literature, Faulkner's contribution to, and influence on, American and World literature is incalculable.

Key Passage
"To Brooklyn Bridge"

"O harp and altar, of the fury fused,
(How could mere toil align thy choiring strings!)"

In the early twentieth century, the accelerating pace of technological and social change in industrialised societies was revolutionising the ways in which people experienced the world. Much modernist writing is brooding and pessimistic in tone, articulating a sense of personal alienation and cultural crisis in this age of transformations. However, the opening section of Hart Crane's (1899–1932) epic poem *The Bridge* rhapsodically apostrophises New York's Brooklyn Bridge as a sublime symbol of the technological triumphs of the modern world.

In modernist poetry, urban landscapes are often seen as harsh, fractured, discordant and at odds with nature. In Crane's eleven beautiful stanzas, however, the sweeping arcs of the bridge mirror the arc of a seagull's wing in flight, and its cables are seen as the "choiring strings" of a great harp. Crane also shows us the bridge as an altar – a man-made wonder whose "curveship lend[s] a myth to God."

However, an altar may be a place of sacrifice as well as worship. Crane's visionary celebration of the bridge incorporates the quotidian and the tragic, acknowledging the casualties as well as the achievements of modern urban life. We see bored office workers in plummeting elevators, cinema audiences enthralled but ultimately unsatisfied by the "panoramic sleights" of the silver screen, and a suicide who leaps from the parapets of the bridge with his "shrill shirt ballooning." The speaker exclaims to the bridge that "we have seen night lifted in thine arms," and thus the scene becomes a twentieth-century pietà, encompassing both pity and awe.

Anna Tripp

Date 1930

Title *The Bridge*

Author Hart Crane

Nationality USA

Why It's Key When T.S. Eliot's poem *The Waste Land* was published, Crane pronounced it "good, of course, but so damned dead." "To Brooklyn Bridge" offers an alternative vision of early twentieth-century life, representing a departure from the brooding gloom of European modernism.

Key Author **Wyndham Lewis**
The Apes of God

For W.H. Auden, Wyndham Lewis was "that lonely old volcano of the right," an outsider amongst the writers he himself had called "the men of 1914," who published in the *Egoist* and included Eliot, Pound, and Joyce. Indeed, Lewis never quite fitted with modernism's Big Four (if we add Yeats), preferring to puff away noxiously from the sidelines, critical of what he regarded as "the social decay of the insanitary trough that lay between the two great wars," a decadence characterized for him by the transition from bourgeois sterility to socialist orthodoxy.

His harshly satirical novels reflect this view, most famously *The Apes of God* (1930), which pilloried the pseudo-intellectuals he thought were hastening national decline. A *roman à clef*, *Apes* reserves a special ire for the Sitwells and all things Bloomsbury; notoriously, following its publication, the social columns of English newspapers were filled with the cries of the slighted. Lewis was also of course a prodigious painter, trained at the Slade and the progenitor of perhaps England's only indigenous avant-garde, Vorticism, a geometrical visual style owing much to Marinetti's Futurism and first seen in the short-lived publication *Blast* (1914–15).

In both paint and prose, Lewis' focus is always the expulsion of interiority and the cultivation of "deadness," a mode mimicking the "rigid [...] articulations of the grasshopper." The "all-puppet cast" of *Apes*, for example – its goofy clowns, poseurs, and fall guys – are painfully reduced just to cumbersome "things" by the keen, chauvinistic wit Lewis thought of as objectivism.

Doug Haynes

Author Percy Wyndham Lewis (1882–1957)

Nationality UK (born Canada)

Other Key Works *Tarr* (1918), *The Art of Being Ruled* (essays, 1926), *Time and Western Man* (1927), *The Wild Body* (1927), *The Childermass* (1928)

Why It's Key Lewis has only relatively recently become regarded as a key modernist writer, artist and essayist. His political affiliations have hitherto been held against him.

Key Passage "Midnight orgies at No.10"
Vile Bodies

"'Midnight Orgies at No. 10.' My dear, isn't that divine? Listen, 'What must be the most extraordinary party of the little season took place in the small hours of this morning at No. 10 Downing Street. At about 4 AM the policemen who are always posted outside the Prime Minister's residence were surprised to witness' – Isn't this too amusing – 'the arrival of a fleet of taxis, from which emerged a gay throng in exotic fancy dress' – How I should have loved to have seen it. Can't you imagine what they were like? – 'the hostess of what was described by one of the guests as the brightest party the Bright Young People have yet given, was no other than Miss Jane Brown, the youngest of the Prime Minister's four lovely daughters. The honourable Agatha… ' Why, what an extraordinary thing… Oh, my God!"

Evelyn Waugh's *Vile Bodies* satirizes the Bright Young Things of London Society in the decadent inter-war years. Waugh himself described the novel as a "welter of sex and snobbery." V.S. Pritchett called it a hectic and savage satire. While it lacks a well-laid plot, the sense of a chaotic, hedonistic generation reeling from party to party while the edifices of society and government slowly crumble into the greater chaos of a new world war, is brilliantly, dazzlingly evoked. Often regarded as the English version of F. Scott Fitzgerald, chronicler of the American Jazz Age hedonism, Waugh went on to describe the same generation's experiences of World War II in the *Sword of Honour* trilogy.

Gerard Woodward

Date 1930

Author Evelyn Waugh (1903–66)

Nationality UK

Why It's Key Waugh's portrait of the Bright Young Things cemented his reputation as the supreme satirist of his generation.

Key Author **Langston Hughes**
Not Without Laughter

Langston Hughes (1902–67), born in Joplin, Missouri, is widely considered to be one of the most prolific writers of the twentieth century. His poetry, plays, fiction, essays, columns, and songs gave birth to the Harlem Renaissance and would later inspire the Négritude literary and political movement. Hughes made his literary debut at 19 with what would become his signature poem, "The Negro Speaks of Rivers," published in 1921 in the renowned African-American publication, *The Crisis*. This poem – in which Hughes proclaims "I've known rivers: Ancient, dusky rivers. My Soul has grown deep like the rivers" – would appear, five years later, in *The Weary Blues*.

Hughes' literature was intended to explain, uplift, and illuminate the African-American experience. Other issues Hughes explored, through stories of joy, struggle, and humor, were Africa, slavery, and communism. Hughes challenged racist stereotypes, confronted capitalism, and brought theoretical concepts such as pan-Africanism and black aesthetics to life. In 1926, Hughes published "The Negro Artist and the Racial Mountain" in the left-leaning journal *The Nation*. This essay, where Hughes announces, "We younger Negro artists now intend to express our individual dark-skinned selves without fear or shame," was adopted as a manifesto for the Harlem Renaissance as soon as it was published.

Over the course of Hughes' career, he wrote sixteen books of poems, two novels, three collections of short stories, four volumes of "editorial" and "documentary" fiction, twenty plays, children's poetry, musicals and operas, three autobiographies, a dozen radio and television scripts, and dozens of magazine articles. In addition he was the recipient of numerous distinctions including a Guggenheim Fellowship, the NAACP's Spingram Medal, and an induction into the National Institute of Arts and Letters in 1961.

M.K. Asante, Jr.

Date 1930 (publication)

Nationality USA

Why It's Key Hughes' play *Mulatto* was the longest-running dramatic work on Broadway by an African American until surpassed by Hansberry's *A Raisin in the Sun* (1959), which takes its title from the a line in Hughes' poem, "Montage of a Dream Deferred" where he asks "What happens to a dream deferred? Does it dry up like a raisin in the sun, or does it explode?"

Opposite Langston Hughes

Key Book
1066 and All That

1066 and All That, subtitled *A Memorable History of England, comprising all the parts you can remember, including 103 Good Things, 5 Bad Kings, and 2 Genuine Dates*, first appeared in serial form in *Punch*, the humorous magazine, to which Sellar and Yeatman were regular contributors.

The book is a parody of the style of history teaching then prevalent, with history Whiggishly presented as a series of kings, queens, battles, and dates, progressing through Good Things and Bad Things towards the largely superior present.

The authors strive for balance, hence their measured verdict on the English Civil Wars: "The Cavaliers (Wrong but Wromantic) and the Roundheads (Right but Repulsive)." There is astute analysis too: "Charles II was always very merry and was therefore not so much a king as a Monarch." The authors are *au fait* with more recent trends in historiography, such as examining underlying economic trends: "The National

Debt is a very Good Thing and it would be dangerous to pay it off, for fear of Political Economy." There is also advice on exam technique, for example, "On no account attempt to write on both sides of the paper at once." The book concludes with an anticipation of Francis Fukuyama's 1992 post-Cold War treatise, "The End of History": "America was thus clearly top nation, and History came to a."

Various writers have attempted sequels, for example Paul Manning's *1984 and All That* and Craig Brown's *1966 and All That*, and in 1938 there was even a musical version of the original book.
Ian Crofton

Date 1930 (publication)

Authors W.C. Sellar (1898–1951) and R.J. Yeatman (1898–1968)

Nationality UK

Why It's Key A much-imitated comic classic, (misre)presenting English history in the form of pedagogic questions and a muddled schoolchild's answers. According to the Compulsory Preface, "History is not what you thought. It is what you can remember."

Key Character **Miss Marple**
Murder at the Vicarage

Jane Marple solved her first crime in *Murder At The Vicarage*, published in 1930. Defying nature, she remained a frail old lady until her final appearance in *Sleeping Murder*, 46 years later. Her fondness for knitting, wearing tweed, and leaving sentences unfinished led to her routine underestimation by lower echelons of the police force. But her fierce intelligence combined with an absolute capacity to believe the worst in people enabled her to solve crimes which left them baffled.

Her deductive skills stemmed from a lifetime spent living in a village, observing human behavior. Over the years, she mustered a mental encyclopedia of every possible social deviancy, all previously exhibited by the second son of the late vicar, or occasionally a renegade milkman.

She battled juvenile delinquents (*They Do It With Mirrors*) murderous film stars (*The Mirror Crack'd From Side To Side*), homicidal prodigal sons (*A Pocket Full Of*

Rye), and train-robbing doppelgangers (*At Bertram's Hotel*), all without surprise or shock at what the human mind can devise.

Margaret Rutherford and Angela Lansbury brought their own interpretations to the role, but Joan Hickson is widely agreed to have given the definitive performance of Miss Marple in the BBC's adaptation, between 1984 and 1992. Sadly, this has not prevented ITV from producing a more recent pantomime-esque version, with inexplicable plotting, starring the otherwise excellent Geraldine McEwan.

The spirit of Miss Marple lives on, however, in *Midsomer Murders*, *Murder, She Wrote*, and other murder mystery shows with a disproportionately high rural body count.
Natalie Haynes

Date 1930

Author Agatha Christie (1890–1976)

Nationality UK

Why It's Key The original of Miss Marple appeared under the name Caroline Sheppard in the Poirot mystery *The Murder of Roger Ackroyd*; she was the murderer's sister. Marple became the archetypal amateur detective.

Opposite Agatha Christie

Key Passage
Swallows and Amazons

Decades before Harry Potter waved his wand, Willie Wonka exploited the Oompa-Loompa cheap labor and Enid Blyton's "Five" became "Famous", John, Susan, Titty, and Roger Walker (the Swallows) sailed into the public's affections thanks to Arthur Ransome's tale of innocent hi-jinks: where else could a name like "Titty" seem neither twisted nor worthy of titters?

Today, *Swallows and Amazons* stands as an innovative classic that redefined children's literature: Geoffrey Trease described Ransome as "[deflecting] the stream of fiction into new channels." First published between the two World Wars, the book is very British indeed, balancing vivid Wordsworthian memories of Ransome's own holidays in the Lake District against a Kiplingesque obsession with healthy, practical activities: like their friends the Blacketts (the Amazons), the Walkers can build huts and fix boats like marines.

This wholesome evocation of happy, middle-class family life struck instant chords which resound to the present: in 1937, Ransome won the first Carnegie Medal for children's literature; the book has been adapted for both the large and small screens; tourists flocked to Coniston and Windermere, a tradition kept alive today by fans from as far away as the United States and Japan.

In the twenty-first century, *Swallows and Amazons* is perhaps best read as an elegantly-constructed period piece: if the Walkers seem to lack an internal, emotional life, for instance, this reticence offers insights into the society that created them. In any case, with all that sailing and construction work to do, kids in those days simply didn't have the time.

James Kidd

Date 1930

Author Arthur Ransome (1884–1967)

Nationality UK

Why It's Key In Blackwell's *Guide to Children's Literature* (2001), Arthur Ransome is called "probably the most influential British children's writer of the twentieth century." If this surprises in a post-Dahl-and-Rowling universe, then it is to underestimate the enduring power of the twelve stories initiated by *Swallows and Amazons*.

Key Passage
The Maltese Falcon

"When a man's partner is killed he's supposed to do something about it."

At the climax of Hammett's genre-defining work of hard-boiled detective fiction, his hero, Sam Spade, must choose whether to betray his lover, the beautiful *femme fatale* Brigid O'Shaughnessy, or to risk being arrested himself for the string of crimes committed in the course of the novel. Spade's brutally pragmatic decision – "They'd hang me sure. You're likely to get a better break" – signals the triumph of self-interest over love. It exemplifies Hammett's rejection of the traditional moral and emotional imperatives of earlier crime fiction, and is perhaps the quintessential expression of the unsentimental approach of the hard-boiled hero.

Spade's decision is also rooted in a masculine ethos of professionalism and duty that entails an almost ascetic denial of emotion and desire – as he

ultimately puts it, "I won't because all of me wants to." The moment is extraordinary because it is so fraught with uncertainty; despite everything, Brigid and Spade might really love each other, and it is inherently painful to witness such an act of self-denial. The emotional cost to him is clear, as he holds a ghastly smile that gradually becomes a grimace as he speaks. But in Hammett's rather bleak and misogynistic world, relying on the love of a woman is a fatal weakness, and Spade cannot tolerate even the faint possibility that he is being manipulated. As he tells her repeatedly and doggedly: "I won't play the sap for you."

Rowland Hughes

Date 1930

Author Dashiell Hammett (1894–1961)

Nationality USA

Why It's Key Arguably the greatest of all hard-boiled detective novels, *The Maltese Falcon* established many of the features of the genre, developed by later writers such as Raymond Chandler. Adapted several times for the screen, most notably by John Huston in 1941, with Humphrey Bogart as the cynical and inscrutable Sam Spade.

Opposite **Humphrey Bogart**

Key Event W.H. Auden's *Poems* establish him as the "voice of a generation"

Poems, Auden's first full-length collection, was published by Faber and Faber in 1930. T.S. Eliot, then Faber editor, had rejected an earlier manuscript, also titled *Poems*, which Stephen Spender privately printed in 1928, but the later *Poems* showed a major development in Auden's poetry. This has been largely attributed to his nine-month stay in Berlin in 1928, and the influence of the European avant-garde and new theories of psychology, notably those of American psychotherapist and educator Homer Lane.

The book is modern not principally in form or language, but in its tone and sensibility, with a complex and unsentimental view of love that reflects Auden's experience of various relationships in the permissive atmosphere of Weimar Berlin, especially his intermittent friendship and sexual affairs with Christopher Isherwood. There is a restless intelligence in his best poems that disdains easy rhetoric, no matter how polished and complete his lines may first appear. It is this quality, and the political and sexual liberalism that lies beneath his metaphors that marks him out as the first of a new group of poets to emerge from the dominating influences of high modernism.

The politics of *Poems* is also free of the conservatism and philosophical abstraction that previous generations of poets used. It has an attractive openness to the reader unfamiliar with classical tradition and immediately engages us in the personal thoughts of the author. The influence of this direct voice can still be felt in much contemporary English poetry and he remains a massively influential figure. The enduring popularity of individual poems such as "Funeral Blues" will ensure his legacy continues.
Charles Beckett

Date 1930

Author W.H. Auden (1907–73)

Nationality UK/USA

Why It's Key *Poems* had a powerful influence on Auden's peers, including Spender, Cecil Day-Lewis, and Louis MacNeice. In subsequent generations the frankness of Auden's tone, the rhetorical complexity and the unsentimental descriptions of romance and love can be detected clearly.

Opposite W.H. Auden

Key Character Inspector Maigret *Pietr-le-Letton*

Commissioner Maigret stations his huge, lugubrious, pipe-smoking figure close to the scene of the crime and waits. Carefully nurtured intuition is the skill he shares with his creator, Georges Simenon, surely the finest crime novelist ever. In the weary Paris-based detective revered by his colleagues Simenon invented a connoisseur of wrongdoing, more interested in understanding the errors of his fellow human beings than bringing them to court. The technique was the man, and it was there from his debut, in *Pietr-le-Letton*. "It was a theory he had, which he had never elaborated and which remained imprecise in his mind, to which he gave the name, for himself, of the theory of the split. In every wrongdoer, in every outlaw, there is a man. But there is also and above all a partner in a game, an adversary, and it's this person that the police must try to see, it's usually this person they can tackle."

Maigret eats, drinks, and smokes. His technique is the opposite of detectives who try logically to deduce the cause of the crime. The moment when he approaches the truth he is physically overwhelmed. In Paris, but also in Antibes and New York, wherever he finds himself, he will be sweating and nauseous, the worse for drink, soaked to the skin or beset by violent dreams, as he feels his way to a solution. In his 75 short, pacy Maigret novels Simenon also invented "France" for millions of readers worldwide, through the commissioner's feeling for people and places.
Lesley Chamberlain

Date 1931

Author Georges Simenon (1903–89)

Nationality Belgium

Why It's Key By 1950 the Maigret novels were selling three million copies worldwide. A BBC television series followed a decade later. Simenon coupled a vast popular readership with high praise from the mandarins of the literary world.

Key Passage "Reflection on Ice-breaking"
Hard Lines

"Candy
Is dandy
But liquor
Is quicker."

This self-contained piece, "Reflection on Ice-breaking" from *Hard Lines*, epitomizes the poetry of Ogden Nash. It is short and to the point, and puts across its message with humor. The title is as much a part of the poem as its four short lines, giving the reader the essential concept when taken as a whole. Whereas a poem of preceding generations with "Reflection" in its title might have encompassed hundreds of lines, recollecting emotion in tranquillity, this is a twentieth-century poem; life moves too fast to reflect for very long. Yet brevity and immediacy of response do not necessarily mean lack of insight. Nash encapsulates in these few lines a truth about the efficacy of alcohol in removing human inhibitions.

Again typically of Nash, this is an American poem. The language, particularly "candy" and "liquor," is very much the vocabulary of the United States and is in contrast to the more "literary" turn of phrase usually associated with verse. Nash uses the vernacular to address everyday issues, mentioning Republicans and Democrats, the Bronx, the Lexington Avenue Express and a host of other references that would be as instantly familiar to the man in the street as the reader of *The New Yorker* magazine. His wordplay, shameless punning, deliberate misspelling to generate unlikely rhymes and, above all, his talent to amuse not only made Nash a contemporary hit but ensured that dozens of poets who followed him would recall his wit and linguistic dexterity as a formative inspiration.
Michael Munro

Date 1931

Author Ogden Nash (1902–71)

Nationality USA

Why It's Key Nash's humorous, often ironic, take on everyday life was immediately popular among a reading public to whom poetry was a stuffy pursuit. In particular, the highly quotable short poems struck a chord with the same audience that appreciated the wit and ingenuity of the popular Gershwin lyrics of the time.

Key Book
Living My Life

"Red Emma"'s autobiography *Living My Life* makes for a compelling read, despite its size, consisting of two hefty volumes. It starts with the Jewish immigrant Goldman's arrival in New York City in 1889, at the age of 20, and proceeds to detail her life over the ensuing decades, spanning her encounters with other anarchists, her travels and lecturing tours in Europe and North America, her repeated imprisonment in the United States, her deportation to the Soviet Union in 1919, and her meetings with the English socialist Edward Carpenter after her move to Britain.

Goldman saw her autobiography as a representative personal story and a quest for the realization of her political ideal of anarchism. The personal and the political indeed constantly intertwine in Goldman's account, which makes it so fascinating to read. For instance, there is the bitter falling-out with her friend Johann Most over a disagreement about the campaign for the eight-hour day. Thus, Goldman's

autobiography simultaneously conveys conflicting political viewpoints as well as the drama of people's everyday relationships.

Living My Life gives expression to Goldman's dynamic spirit and changing political views, ranging from the use of violence as a political tool, to her critique of Russian state communism, ultimately revealing a radical mind that demanded total human freedom: "I did not believe that a Cause which stood for a beautiful ideal, for anarchism, for release and freedom from conventions and prejudice, should demand the denial of life and joy. 'I want freedom, the right to self-expression, everybody's right to beautiful, radiant things.'"
Anne Schwan

Date 1931

Author Emma Goldman (1869–1940)

Nationality USA (citizenship revoked)/UK (born Lithuania)

Why It's Key *Living My Life* is the most comprehensive insight into the mind and revolutionary times of this flamboyant woman. Due to its conversational style, speckled with humorous anecdotes, it is also a highly entertaining read.

Opposite Emma Goldman returns to the USA after a 15-year exile

Key Book
Sanctuary

SPOILER

The story of *Sanctuary* concerns the rape and subsequent degradation of a young woman, Temple Drake, who is assaulted with a corncob by an impotent bootlegger called Popeye. The plot is complicated, as the story alternates between Temple's point of view and that of a lawyer, Horace Benbow, whose fate coincides with hers. Misadventure brings both Horace and Temple, at separate times, into the company of violent bootleggers living on the outskirts of Jefferson, the capital of Faulkner's famous fictional Yoknapatawpha County, and the setting of most of Faulkner's novels. A car accident brings Temple to the house, owned by a bootlegger called Lee, who is living with his common-law wife and baby; the sinister Popeye is one of his partners, and other menacing bootleggers are leering at her. Temple runs to a barn to hide from the men, asking Tommy, whom Faulkner describes as a "halfwit," to protect her. Popeye unceremoniously shoots Tommy and proceeds to rape Temple with a corncob. He then takes her to a brothel in Memphis, where her corruption takes hold. After Lee has been accused of Tommy's murder, Temple is brought back as a witness but perjures herself and swears that Lee killed Tommy; Lee is lynched and Temple escapes to Europe with her father.

The sensationalism of its action and characters – gangsters, prostitutes, bootleggers, and the bloody corncob waved in court – made *Sanctuary* Faulkner's greatest commercial success. He wrote a sequel many years later, *Requiem for a Nun*, which tells of Temple's unhappy marriage to a man who "forgives" her sordid past; it became the only play that Faulkner published.

Sarah Churchwell

Date 1931

Author William Faulkner (1897–1962)

Nationality USA

Why It's Key *Sanctury* was written deliberately as a "pot-boiler," according to the author, a cynical and calculated exercise in writing popular fiction. Faulkner scholars have disputed this claim, arguing that the book's themes of evil and corruption and its social critique of small-town Southern pieties make it an important achievement.

Key Passage "Little Miss Marker"
Guys and Dolls

"He not only spends plenty on Marky, but he starts picking up checks in Mindy's and other spots, although up to this time picking up checks is something that is most repulsive to Sorrowful.He gets so he will hold still for a bite, if the bite is not too savage and, what is more, a great change comes over his kisser. It is no longer so sad and mean looking, and in fact it is almost a pleasant sight at times, especially as Sorrowful gets so he smiles now and then, and has a hello for one and all, and everybody says the Mayor ought to give Marky a medal for bringing about such a wonderful change."

Damon Runyan's short story collection, *Guys and Dolls*, takes the reader on a journey through the American underworld of gamblers and petty criminals. Runyan found inspiration in the stories he reported on as a newspaper journalist. The prohibition era was fruitful matter, and his stories mostly took as their setting the murky morality of the gangster. However, there is often a sense of conversion and elevation in the lives of his characters.

In "Little Miss Marker," a child is placed as a bet by her gambling father. Hardened gambler Sorrowful Jones adopts her as his own, with other gangsters and Broadway misfits forming a kind of family around her. To the amazement of his friends, Sorrowful undergoes a transformation and softens, even his "kisser" becoming a "pleasant sight at times."

Runyan never allows the story to become too saccharine: the benefits the girl brings the gangsters are tempered with the uncomfortable notion that Little Miss Marker herself is spoilt by her new environment. The story is typical of Runyan's deftness with themes of salvation and corruption. When Little Miss Marker dies from pneumonia, Sorrowful returns to his former self. The jocular tone is muted, and quite suddenly becomes moving.

Thomas Dymond

Date 1932

Author Damon Runyan (1884–1946)

Nationality USA

Why It's Key The musical *Guys and Dolls* is based upon two of Runyan's short stories, "The Idylls of Miss Sarah Brown" and "Blood Pressure." The original production in 1950 ran on Broadway for over 1200 performances. Runyan's stories have been adapted into several films, and his writing is relevant to the work of directors such as Tarantino and Scorcese.

Key Author **Elizabeth Bowen**
To the North

Elizabeth Bowen (1899–1973) was an Irish-born writer who spent most of her adult life in England. In 1923 she married Alan Cameron, an educational administrator. The marriage, though strong, was unconsummated and Bowen began a series of affairs with a number of eminent men. This complicated personal life, in combination with her Anglo-Irish heritage (she continued to spend brief periods of time in Ireland throughout her life), and a strong sense of place and of the appearance of things (she had briefly trained as an artist), contributed to a distinct writing style that is as penetrating in its psychological insights as it is vividly descriptive.

She first achieved wider recognition with *To the North* (1932), a novel about two London society women, and their struggle to achieve a balance between independence and emotional conciliation in their relationships. Cecilia wills herself into marriage with the kind but passionless Julian, while her sister-in-law Emmeline is drawn towards the rakish Mark Linkwater. The novel has a characteristically violent undertone, a feature of Bowen's writing that found its full expression in her novels and stories of wartime London. These are generally regarded as her finest achievement. *The Heat of the Day* (1949) is regarded by many as the most detailed evocation of what it was like to live in London during the war years. The systematic yet random destruction that was wrought by the Blitz took on an almost mystical significance in Bowen's wartime fiction.

Bowen was deeply influenced by Jane Austen and Henry James, and her writing continues their tradition of social comedy into the middle of the twentieth century.

Gerard Woodward

Date 1932 (publication)

Nationality UK/Ireland (born Ireland)

Other Key Works *The Death of the Heart* (1938), *Collected Stories* (1980)

Why It's Key Writer of highly perceptive social observation who found her metier in depicting wartime London. Bowen also wrote over 80 short stories, and was a master of the form.

Key Book
Sunset Song

Sunset Song is a truly "glocal" twentieth-century novel in its examination of how international events increasingly structure the rhythms and textures of the most localized forms of living. It asks its reader to realize the inextricable relations between individual/home/community and region/nation/world. The narrative relates the cataclysmic effects of war, consolidated landowning, and international capital on a small farming community in Scotland during the time of World War I. At its center is Chris Guthrie, who heroically struggles within a dysfunctional family to farm their smallholding. On one level the vernacular narrative voice is hers, intimately detailing her conflicting beliefs and aspirations as she seeks to harmonize her identities as a maturing, ambitious young woman with some education ("English Chris") and as a member of the "folk" of Kinraddie ("Scottish Chris").

The novel's structure and perspective (Its use of a "self-referring you" was lauded as an innovation in narrative voice) never loses sight of its wider ambit. The "Song" consists of four sections: "Ploughing," "Drilling," "Seed-time," and "Harvest," establishing a cyclical and at times cosmic outlook. This is punctuated by powerful ruminations on myth, ancestry, local history, and the geological endurance of the land. Gibbon was determined to force Scotland into thinking about the future of its rural communities in their submission to the forceful process of modernization. Some characters advocate international socialism and pacifism, movements that would form the principal concerns of the following two novels in Gibbon's *A Scots Quair* trilogy, relating Chris' son Euan's reaction to the forces of industrialization and urbanization in a transformed landscape.

Graeme Mcdonald

Date 1932

Author Lewis Grassic Gibbon (1901–35)

Nationality UK

Why It's Key The key novel of the Scottish Literary Renaissance, the inter-war movement of writers (including Hugh MacDiarmid and Neil Gunn) who argued for independence from English Literature. Commonly regarded as one of the most significant works in Scottish Literature.

Key Book *Journey to the End of the Night (Voyage au bout de la nuit)*

Céline's landmark work opens on the battlefields of World War I and unfolds as a profound anti-humanist adventure taking in the author's experience as a doctor in French colonial Africa and the interwar Paris slums. An anti-war testament, it revels in the muck of the flesh. The colloquial first-person narrative and deep cynicism vis à vis human nature pave the way for many later French novels, loosely labelled "existentialist," like Camus' *The Outsider* and *The Plague*, and for the power of absurdity in the writing of Charles Bukowski and Samuel Beckett.

Céline's narrator Ferdinand Bardamu is licentious, hate-driven, and sensual, but appeals because of his frankness, clear-sightedness, and lack of cant. His sympathy for the exploited, downtrodden masses in a society fixated on bourgeois privilege is also remarkable, accompanied as it is by no particular political engagement. An ethic of voluntarism in the face of life's absurdity emerges from exceptionally

vivid, lurid pages whose energy never flags. Bardamu's unliterary language, which was to prove so influential, was a torrent of sharp observations and ferociously down-to-earth metaphors.

Journey to the End of the Night has been misread as simply misanthropic and Céline critically neglected because of his wartime anti-Semitism and collaboration with the Nazi-sympathizing Vichy government. But a close reading of Bardamu's fate shows it to be the story of an honest man compelled to fulfil and deride other people's worst expectations of him, in which respect it prefigures the life Céline later enacted.
Lesley Chamberlain

Date 1932

Author Louis-Ferdinand Céline (1894–1961)

Nationality France

Why It's Key A popular and critical success, this was the first great European novel to express the post-Great War disillusion which scarred the literature and philosophy of the twentieth century.

Key Event
William Faulkner goes to Hollywood

Soon after William Faulkner arrived in Hollywood for the first time in 1932, he was complaining about the monotony of the California weather – and he was fond of exaggerating his ignorance of movies. Yet the future winner of the 1950 Nobel Prize in Literature would soon find that he relied largely on his screenwriting, rather than his novels, to be able to provide for his extended family.

It was the director Howard Hawks who bought the film rights to Faulkner's World War I short story, "Turn About," and invited Faulkner to write the screenplay. The film, released as *Today We Live* in 1933 and starring Joan Crawford and Gary Cooper, was Faulkner's first screenwriting credit (the last was for Hawks' 1955 *Land of the Pharaohs*).

By the 1940s, Faulkner's novels, except for *Sanctuary*, gradually went out of print. Desperate for money but now notorious for his heavy drinking, Faulkner reluctantly signed a seven-year contract

with Warner Brothers in 1942 at a third of his previous salary. It was at Warner's that he wrote two of Hollywood's most memorable films of the 1940s, adapting Ernest Hemingway's novel, *To Have and Have Not*, and Raymond Chandler's detective novel, *The Big Sleep*. Both were once again directed by Hawks, with whom Faulkner would write five of his six credited screenplays.

Faulkner also contributed to United Artists' *The Southerner* (1945), directed by the great Jean Renoir. Faulkner, himself from the South, later said he considered this his best screenwriting work. However, he received no screen credit because technically he was under contract to Warner Brothers (thus barring him from working for another studio).
Adam Feinstein

Date 1932

Author William Faulkner (1897–1962)

Nationality USA

Why It's Key In their 1991 film, *Barton Fink*, Joel and Ethan Coen presented a drunken, raving character, W.P. Mayhew, who was Faulkner in very thin disguise. However, the portrait was misleading: although Faulkner was an alcoholic, he worked hard in Hollywood, writing unproduced scripts as well as contributing to 50 films.
Opposite William Faulkner

Key Passage
Brave New World

"But I don't want comfort. I want God, I want poetry, I want real danger, I want freedom, I want goodness. I want sin."

"In fact," said Mustapha Mond, "you're claiming the right to be unhappy."

"All right then," said the Savage defiantly, "I'm claiming the right to be unhappy."

*B*rave *New World* is Huxley's critical response to the notion that science can produce world stability and individual happiness. He shows what society could be like if scientists take over the world and if they control every natural human impulse and emotion.

Lives begin in the London Hatchery and end in the Park Lane Hospital for the Dying. The inhabitants are conditioned before birth and are kept conditioned for life. In the London Hatchery foetuses are chemically changed and artificially graded to produce the intelligence required for their chosen role in society –

from Alpha Plus at the top to Gammas and Epsilons and the bottom. Further control is achieved by "hypnopaedia" when the inhabitants are children, and by the drug Soma throughout their adult life. The novel critiques mass production and consumerism and emerging ideas about behaviorism and psychoanalysis – all of which were becoming increasingly topical at the time of writing. *Brave New World* measures time from the year of our Ford and the religious sign is that of a T, a clear satire on Henry Ford and the mass production of his Model T car in the United States. Mustapha Mond, one of the controllers of the World State, believes that art has to be sacrificed for the sake of stability and happiness, but John Savage from the Reservation outside the state claims the right of people to be unhappy. Huxley's pessimistic novel still has currency today and is one of the most widely read dystopias of the modern era.

Pat Wheeler

Date 1932

Author Aldous Huxley (1894–1963)

Nationality UK

Why It's Key Aldous Huxley's brilliant satire *Brave New World* is a seminal dystopian novel. With its pessimistic view of a rigidly ordered and controlled utopia and in its revolt against the Wellsian scientific utopia, it ushered in a new generation of science fiction dystopian writing.

228

Key Passage "what Aunt Ada saw in that woodshed" *Cold Comfort Farm*

"When you were very small – so small that the lightest puff of breeze blew your little crinoline skirt over your head – you had seen something nasty in the woodshed.

… Even now, when you were seventy-nine, you could never see a bicycle go past your bedroom window without a sick plunge at the apex of your stomach… in the bicycle shed you had seen it, something nasty, when you were very small."

The wittiest and most elegant parodic novel of the twentieth century, *Cold Comfort Farm* was the first foray into prose fiction for poet and journalist Stella Gibbons. It warm-heartedly mocks the romances of Mary Webb, mostly set beneath the leaden skies of remote rural shropshire. Her heroine, Flora Poste, is a practical and expensively educated young woman who finds herself orphaned on her 20th birthday with an annual income of only 100 pounds and no property.

So Flora decides to embark on a career as a parasite, living off her relatives until she marries. When distant cousins the Starkadders invite her to their Sussex smallholding, she packs her bags and sets about restoring order to their mouldering homestead, crouched on a bleak, flint-fanged hillside outside the village of Howling and presided over by the curse of ancient Aunt Ada Doom who once "saw something nasty in the woodshed."

Gibbons has fun converting the stereotypes of romantic fiction (the panther-ish young stud and the flighty beauty "wandering the indifferent bare shoulders of the downs") into sane and functional human beings. She briskly introduces contraception, smart dressing, and mops. But she never does find out what Aunt Ada saw in that woodshed, and the phrase has now passed into the language, humorously denoting an excessively dwelled-over childhood trauma.

Helen Brown

Date 1932

Author Stella Gibbons (1902–89)

Nationality UK

Why It's Key An immediate success, at least one reviewer thought it too funny to have been written by a woman and suggested that "Stella Gibbons" was really Evelyn Waugh. This is particularly ironic as one of the novel's characters is writing a book claiming that Branwell Bronte was the true author of *Wuthering Heights*.

Opposite Stella Gibbons

Key Book *The Radetzky March* (*Radetzkymarsch*)

One of the great elegiac novels of empire, *The Radetzky March* reflects, mournfully but not sentimentally, on a lost world: the multicultural, supranational, and ultimately unsustainable empire of the Habsburgs, at the periphery of which Joseph Roth had grown up. In the tradition of the great realist family sagas of the nineteenth century, the story focuses upon a single, declining dynasty, the Trottas, whose fortunes seem strangely tied to those of the empire. The last of the line, Carl Joseph, is a tragic, transitional figure, caught between tradition and modernity: his individuality crumbles in the shadow of his heroic grandfather, to whose reputation he can never live up, and under the stern gaze of the Emperor's ubiquitous portrait; the premature deaths of lovers and comrades anticipate his own, at the onset of the war that will bring about the Empire's end.

The novel is rightly admired for its evocation of physical and sensual detail, in, say, descriptions of uniform, or of the melody and rhythm of Strauss' famous march, both of which come to represent an almost abstract sense of national identity. It is equally powerful in suggesting a sense of place, with settings including the provincial swamps and forests of Galicia and the decadent pomp of Vienna, and in representing the rituals that gave life structure and meaning: formal meals, a fatal duel, the annual Corpus Christi procession in Vienna. This towering novel continues to serve as a springboard for readers to discover a prolific and significant European author.
Jon Hughes

Date 1932

Author Joseph Roth (1894–1939)

Nationality Austria

Why It's Key The prolific journalist and novelist Joseph Roth's major achievement, the international reputation of this epic novel of the end of empire, continues to grow.

230

Key Character **Conan the Barbarian** "The Phoenix on the Sword"

The first appearance of Robert Howard's best-known hero Conan the Barbarian was in a short story entitled "The Phoenix on the Sword" which appeared in 1932 in an issue of the American pulp fantasy and horror magazine *Weird Tales*. The story was an immediate success and Howard went on to write many more for publication in the magazine.

The author identified Conan as a Cimmerian, a native of a fictional barbaric land, and introduced him as "black-haired, sullen-eyed, sword in hand, a thief, a reaver, a slayer, with gigantic melancholies and gigantic mirth." Howard had studied various mythologies and it seems that the tradition he drew on most was that of the Celtic legends. Conan is immensely powerful and agile, a born fighter who wanders through dangerous and wonderful lands performing deeds of great courage and strength, usually for his own gain. He is no fool and can use cunning as well as brawn, but is not immortal or even superhuman. He can be temporarily defeated by magic or insuperable odds but is never bested in straightforward combat.

Howard died by suicide at the age of 30, but his creation has long outlived him. Other writers, such as L. Sprague de Camp, took up the character and featured him in many more stories as well as full-length novels. Marvel Comics used Conan as the hero of a series of comics that ran from 1970 to 1993, and he also inspired television cartoon series as well as several highly popular Hollywood films, the most successful being *Conan the Barbarian* (1982) which introduced the movie-going public to Arnold Schwarzenegger as the eponymous hero.
Michael Munro

Date 1932 (publication)

Author Robert Ervin Howard (1906–36)

Nationality USA

Why It's Key Robert Howard is often credited with being the father of the fantasy "sword and sorcery" genre and the powerful, irascible warrior Conan is the archetypal hero of this particular brand of fiction.

Key Character **Studs Lonigan**
Young Lonigan

Studs Lonigan is not the kind of "hero" readers aspire to be like. Neither is he anything as intriguing as an anti-hero. He's a non-hero. He was deliberately created as an image of what American society should try not to be like. Farrell's trilogy takes him from fifteen to early death at 30, and the stagnating, wasted life in between. Set in the poor Irish community of Chicago's South Side where Farrell grew up, these are books born of anger, written with bluntness, a great deal of evocative slang, and not much regard for stylistic niceties.

Vanguard Press, to avoid obscenity charges, strangely published *Young Lonigan* as a case study, with a preface by a psychologist, including the caveat that "it is not for children or for the unsophisticated." Readers were shocked by the sexual explicitness but not, apparently, the appalling racism Farrell depicted; the tension, exploding in the 1919 race riots, between Irish and African American communities, both disenfranchized. Studs' coming of age includes involvement in racial attacks and bombings. He loses his virginity at a gangbang and thereafter frequents "cathouses," always longing romantically for his true love, a nice Irish girl who's too pure to be with him. A drunken scene at a 1929 New Year's Eve party ends in a rape. This must have been shocking material at the time; it is still very uncomfortable, even soul-destroying.

The dangerous, seemingly more real, real life depicted in Farrell's work, without the intervening flourishes of much of a literary style – was something direct and new; Farrell's reputation, though he was prolific, later slumped, but his influence, through Studs Lonigan, was widespread. A young Norman Mailer was one of those influenced by Farrell's harsh, brutal story.
Lucy Daniel

Date 1932 (publication)

Author James T. Farrell (1904–79)

Nationality USA

Why It's Key One of the book's epigraphs was from Frank Norris, the pioneering U.S. naturalist writer, and suggested the American novel would have to turn to "vulgar" subject matter to become an authentic document of American life.

Key Author
Raymond Roussel

Raymond Roussel (1877–1933) was infamous rather than famous in his own lifetime, although this was as much a result of his conspicuous wealth and eccentricity as his innovative and complex writing. Roussel longed for literary fame throughout his life, and was, for long periods, convinced of its imminence: "I shall reach immense heights and I am destined for blazing glory." However, his works were either ignored or derided in his lifetime because of their obscurity and complexity. In 1932, just before his death, Roussel published "How I Wrote Certain of my Books" ("Comment j'ai écrit certains de mes livres"), a description of his "procédé," or method, which explained that his works were all based on differing forms of the pun. The change of meaning caused by various interpretations of the same or similar words provided the stimulus for explanatory digressions of extraordinary complexity, or as he describes it: "I sought new words… always to take them in a different direction than that which was presented first of all, and that provided me each time a creation moreover."

Although Roussel was defended by the Surrealists during his lifetime, it is only posthumously that his kinship with various avant-garde writers has earned him a more substantial place in literary history. He has been an influence on the work of Oulipo writers such as Georges Perec and Harry Mathews, who appreciated Roussel for the idea of literary production under arbitrary constraint, and more recently by Alain Robbe-Grillet and the poet John Ashbery. In this way, perhaps his most fervent desire has been realized: "and so I seek comfort, for want of anything better, in the hope that perhaps I will enjoy a little posthumous fame on account of my books."
Julia Jordan

Date 1933 (death)

Nationality France

Other Key Works Novels *Locus Solus* (1914), *Impressions d'Afrique* (1910), *Nouvelles Impressions d'Afrique* (1932) **Poems** "La Vue," "Le Concert," and "La Source" (1904) **Plays** *The Star on the Forehead* (1925), *The Dust of the Suns* (1927)

Why It's Key An experimental poet, novelist, and dramatist, Roussel's works influenced many avant-garde writers.

Key Passage **"Shangri-La"**
Lost Horizon

"He stood uncertainly on the threshold of the dark corridor; through a window he could see that the sky was clear, though the mountains still blazed in lightning like a silver fresco. And then, in the midst of the still encompassing dream, he felt himself master of Shangri-La."

Lost Horizon begins as a ripping yarn about "Glory" Conway, a British diplomat whose plane is hijacked en route to Peshawar. After landing in Tibetan wasteland with a dead pilot, the mist clears and the kidnapped party get their first glimpse of Shangri-La: a monastery carved from an impassable mountain, above a paradisal valley. Using a blend of Christian and Buddhist principles and indigenous narcotics, the resident lamas prolong their lives into their hundreds. There is a superbly well-stocked library, and eastern asceticism mixes with "good manners" and a collective stiff upper lip. "To be quite frank, it reminds me very

slightly of Oxford," says Conway. There is just one problem with Shangri-La: nobody is allowed to leave.

Conway is entranced by the docile way of life. But then Conway has been left shell-shocked after being blown up in World War I. He is, after that horror, "passionless," unable to cope in the world, without loved ones, perhaps delusional. The disappearance of his dream reflects a more general collapse – Wall Street, the British empire. The blazing mountains hint of approaching apocalypse in the world beyond the valley, the mounting threat of another world war.

Shangri-La has become known as an eastern paradise, but *Lost Horizon* is about lost innocence and lost possibilities. Nevertheless its appeal as a modern legend has been for audiences enchanted by the idea that there might still be places left on earth where such a paradise could exist, untouched by the horrors of the modern world.
Lucy Daniel

Date 1933

Author James Hilton (1900–54)

Nationality UK

Why It's Key Hilton's novel gave us the term Shangri-La to describe a utopia. The huge popular success of both the novel and Frank Capra's 1937 film version popularised the idea, now a modern myth. Several places claim to be the inspiration for the lost valley, but as one of its monks helpfully points out, "You will not find Shangri-La marked on any map."

1930-1939

233

Key Characters **Nick and Nora Charles**
The Thin Man

Has there ever been a more serendipitous piece of movie casting than Dick Powell and Myrna Loy as Nick and Nora Charles? Perhaps the fact that the film was made just a year after their first appearance in print accounts for the closeness in spirit, but Powell and Loy capture the essence of Nick and Nora brilliantly: witty and affectionate, competent and professional. The initial success of the 1934 film led to five screen sequals and a television series in the 1950s.

After the often brutal realism of his earlier work, Hammett tempered his pessimistic vision of American urban existence with the sparkling repartee of screwball comedy when he created Nick and Nora. Nick is a private detective, Nora his loving and yet far from downtrodden wife. In Prohibition-era America, they drift from speakeasy to cocktail party to nightclub – accompanied by Asta, their ever-present Schnauzer – downing scotch and martinis like they're going out of fashion, yet never less than urbane and utterly

charming. Somehow Nick manages to find clients and even to do some detecting – though it always seems more of a distraction than a vocation – while Nora drolly assists, indulges and restrains him, almost matching him drink for drink. Nora punctures the air of masculine bravado that usually accompanies Hammett heroes – when Nick refuses to stay in bed after being shot, she remarks "Alright, hard guy, get up and bleed on the rugs." Their world is just as violent and corrupt as Sam Spade's, but they refuse to take it too seriously, and they have each other to rely on.
Rowland Hughes

Date 1933

Author Dashiell Hammett (1894–1961)

Nationality USA

Why It's Key Hammett's last novel, and also his lightest and most witty, contains all the internecine plotting, authentic dialogue, and violent realism of his earlier work, and his most likeable protagonists, Nick and Nora Charles.

Opposite William Powell and Myrna Loy as Nick and Nora Charles

Key Book
Testament of Youth

This fascinating autobiography illuminated a corner of history which was being overlooked. Though there had already been many histories of the Great War from a military, masculine viewpoint, there was very little about life on the Home Front, and nothing at all detailing the difficulties and tragedies experienced by women. In addition, *Testament of Youth* revealed the making of a feminist, from the day when the eleven-year-old Vera was berated for impropriety after having stopped in the street to talk to her younger brother and his friends, to her adult resistance to the traditional role expected to be played by a wife in an early twentieth-century marriage.

Vera was more intellectually gifted than her brother, who wanted to be a composer and musician. Her father refused to spend money on further education for his daughter, while insisting that his son should go to Oxford. However, it was Vera who won a scholarship and went up to Somerville in the Autumn of 1914. Her brother, and his best friend, who became Vera's fiancé, joined up straight from school. Both were killed.

Testament of Youth describes the life of a provincial family in the early part of the century, and the changes in morality which resulted from the circumstances of the Great War. Vera Brittain gave up her place at Oxford and went to France as a nurse. The unimaginable intimacy of contact with male bodily functions in the hospital helped her generation of women develop much healthier attitudes to sex and marriage than had hitherto been allowed them.

Felicity Skelton

Date 1933 (publication)

Author Vera Brittain (1896–1970)

Nationality UK

Why It's Key In her foreword, Brittain writes that she wanted to "rescue something that might be of value, some element of truth and hope and usefulness, from the smashing up of my own youth by the War…. It is not by accident that what I have written constitutes, in effect, an indictment of a civilisation."

Key Book
The Autobiography of Alice B. Toklas

Gertrude Stein's life-long partner Alice B. Toklas is the narrator of this book, which describes their life together in Paris during the first part of the twentieth century. However, it quickly becomes clear that Stein has, in fact, written her own autobiography, disguised as an imaginary memoir by Toklas. Stein has Toklas giving an account of Stein's early life, making it clear that she is recalling and interpreting events which she has not witnessed herself. The book, then, becomes an extended meditation on the slipperiness of memory and factual accuracy.

However, *The Autobiography of Alice B. Toklas* is much more than a labored joke about multi-layered narrative. Stein packs her story with gossipy stories about the intimate lives of the famous painters and writers with whom she came into contact. Independently wealthy, Stein collected early work by Cezanne, Matisse, and Picasso. She also knew many of her fellow Americans who flocked to Paris between the wars, including Djuna Barnes, Ezra Pound, and Ernest Hemingway. All were invited to her famous Saturday evening salon at the flat in rue de Fleurus which she shared with Toklas.

The Autobiography of Alice B Toklas is also remarkable for its naïve style and its absence of commas (a key signature of modernist writing). The child-like stream of consciousness which Stein ascribes to Toklas – "It was about this time that Ezra Pound came, no that was brought about in another way" – allows her to make an important point about the fluidity of the documentary record. This neatly echoes, of course, some of the experiments in perspective and perception that were currently engaging painters such as Picasso.

Kathryn Hughes

Date 1933 (publication)

Author Gertrude Stein (1874–1946)

Nationality USA

Why It's Key Although Stein had previously published innovative poetry such as "Tender Buttons" (1914), it was not until *Toklas* that she became a commercial success. At the age of 59 she relished her newfound fame, "I bought myself a new eight-cylinder Ford car and the most expensive coat made to order by Hermes."

Opposite Gertrude Stein

Key Passage "Life is for living"
Design for Living

Otto: We should have principles to hang on to, you know. This floating about without principles is so very dangerous.
Gilda: Life is for living.
(Act 2, Scene 2)

Design For Living exposes a harsh side to the Bohemian lifestyle. Centring his comedy upon a *ménage à trois* between a painter, a playwright, and an interior designer, Coward presents his audience with a complex series of relationships. Gilda, the main character, has sexual relationships with two men but marries neither, the two men eventually accepting that she should not have to choose between them. Sense and morality are represented by Ernest, a family friend of Gilda: it is he she turns to when her other relationships overawe her. Gilda's eventual rejection of Ernest and their marriage provides us with a powerful final image in the play. Ernest's seriousness and pain is

the subject of derisive laughter from the trio, the curtain falling on their uncontrollable mirth.

One way of viewing the play is to see it as a stinging critique of infidelity and Bohemian sensibilities. Gilda's rejection of social convention should be stirring and admirable, but Coward tempers it with the pain of Ernest, a decent man who truly loves Gilda. At one point, he turns on her two lovers, telling them "You practically ruined her life between you, and you caused her great unhappiness with your egotistical, casual passions" (Act 3). Coward does not allow the aspirations of the trio, their essential message that "life is for living," to triumph completely.

The play was a huge success when first performed and influential to several other writers. In particular, Terence Rattigan's *The Deep Blue Sea* (1952) develops the themes of suppressed sexuality and the flouting of convention.

Thomas Dymond

Date 1933 (performance)

Author Noel Coward (1899–1973)

Nationality UK

Why It's Key Coward was an actor and playwright, with over 40 plays to his name. Coward's stylish, amoral, extremely popular plays often defied convention. *Design for Living* described an overturning of traditional moral values, and was a huge success – which helped him get away with such risqué material.

Opposite Noel Coward (middle) with *Design for Living* cast

1930–1939

237

Key Event
Black Mountain College is established

Exiled from Nazi Germany when Hitler's government closed down the Bauhaus, Josef and Anni Albers relocated to America and were hired by the founder of Black Mountain College, John A. Rice, to teach art in accordance with the most progressive pedagogical theories of the day. Black Mountain College attracted some of the most important and influential artists of the twentieth century as students or teachers, encouraging an inter-disciplinary and experimental approach to creativity that changed the stakes for cultural production in America. The artists and thinkers who passed through its portals included Kenneth Noland, Robert Rauschenberg, R. Buckminster Fuller, William and Elaine De Kooning, Clement Greenberg, John Cage, Merce Cunningham, Charles Olson, Robert Motherwell, and Cy Twombly, a by no means definitive list of now-hallowed names who cite Black Mountain as an unprecedented opportunity

to ignore convention and mix art with life, to accept what is, in a spirit of gently methodical openness to the material environment.

Black Mountain College in its idiosyncratic blend of European discipline and American freedoms utterly transformed the arts in America, including dance, painting, sculpture, music, and poetry, and exerted an influence which is still felt in secluded pockets of experimentation all over the world.

Robin Purves

Date 1933–1956

Place North Carolina, USA

Why It's Key In the 1950s Black Mountain College became a center for artistic rebellion and an avant-garde approach in all fields of the arts, but particularly in poetry. Writers who were involved included Charles Olson, Denise Levertov, and Robert Creeley.

Key Event **Bunin is the first Russian to win the Nobel Prize in Literature**

The award of the world's most important literary prize to Ivan Alekseyevich Bunin (1870–1953), a Russian writer in exile since the 1917 Bolshevik Revolution, honored possibly the most poetically accomplished prose writer Russia has ever produced. Bunin was a unique example of a Russian writer whose talent grew in emigration. But the citation commending "the strict artistry with which Bunin has carried on the classical Russian traditions in prose writing" left pundits in no doubt that East-West politics had entered literature in a big way by the early 1930s.

Bunin, born in 1870 to a gentry family in Voronezh, southern Russia, saw himself continuing the great traditions of literature written by Tolstoy and other Russian noblemen. Based in France, he set about preserving the soul of a vanished country. Saddled with an impoverished existence, for several years he and his wife let it be known that a Nobel Prize would rescue them. Bunin went down in Nobel Prize history as the first Laureate without a country but died destitute after helping many Russian exiles in similar trouble. Soviet critics suggested he was a reactionary writer. Even abroad, dissenting voices suggested the prize should have gone to the leading Soviet writer Maxim Gorky. These comments emphasized the split between a socially engaged form of literature encouraged by Communism and a more individualistic enterprise that the *engagé* Left outlawed. But they also reflected the enduring difficulty of describing Bunin's achievement. He evokes the delicate poetry of human sensibility in a style apparently belonging to no time or tradition.
Lesley Chamberlain

Date 1933

Author Ivan Alekseyevich Bunin (1870–1953)

Nationality Russia

Why It's Key Bunin's richly crafted short stories have attracted top-class translators including D.H. Lawrence and Leonard Woolf, who collaborated on a version of "The Gentleman from San Fransisco." His poetic masterpieces included "Mitya's Love" and the autobiographical *The Well of Days* (1933).

Opposite Ivan Bunin

Key Event **Publication of *People of the Cave***

The publication of Tawfiq Al-Hakim's play *People of the Cave* in 1933 signalled a significant turning point not only in the history of Modern Arabic drama, but also in Egyptian and Arabic theatrical art. The plot is based on a Qur'anic and Biblical story; that of the Sleepers of Ephesus, Christians who escaped prosecution by the Romans by hiding in a cave where they slept for more than 300 years. They awoke unaware of how much the world had changed.

Yet Al-Hakim wove this simple and familiar storyline into a complex philosophical dramatic structure full of symbolism and laden with social and political metaphors. Chief amongst these is how his fellow Egyptians needed to wake up to the changing world around them and deal with it in a more intellectually complex way. The play epitomizes Al-Hakim's attempt to take the genre beyond popular farce and melodrama that predominated during his time and develop it into a theater of ideas or, in his own words, "a theater of the mind." The play symbolizes the challenges that Egyptians faced at the time and prophesied the changes that would happen in Egypt two decades later.

Al-Hakim's exposure to western drama while studying in Paris was instrumental in his attempts to adapt the genre to the taste of Arab audiences who perceived the dramatic art according to a set of different values: either as a form of popular entertainment true to the indigenous Arab performing traditions of "Khayal Al-zill" (shadow performances) or "mhabbazatiyyah" (street performers); or a form of performed poetry as in the case of the verse plays of his predecessor Ahmed Sawqi.
Ashraf Eissa

Date 1933 (publication) (first performed 1935)

Title *People of the Cave* (*Ahl Al-Kahf*)

Author Tawfiq Al-Hakim (1898–1987)

Nationality Egypt

Why It's Key The archetypal modern Arabic play, *People of the Cave* was a watershed in the development of the drama of ideas in Arabic literature.

Key Event
Nazis in Berlin burn books

Nineteen thirty-three saw the Nazis take power in Germany and as a consequence implement a series of repressive measures. Joseph Goebbels, Nazi Minister for Popular Enlightenment and Propaganda, began a series of incursions which were meant firstly to bring cultural practices into line with Nazi goals and secondly to marginalize the Jewish community. Cultural organizations were purged, institutions such as publishers or newspapers shut down, and censorship became rife. In April the German Student Association announced a national "Action against the un-German spirit" which would climax with a purging, cleansing bonfire of all books suspected of being of a questionable nature (a "Säuberung" by fire). This was intended to purify Germany's culture and the students consciously echoed Martin Luther in their call to racial simplicity.

On May 10, 1933, accompanied by songs and anthems, the Nazis in Berlin made a large pile and burned the books of Jewish intellectuals and all manner of "un-German" writers. Authors whose work was thrown on the pile included leading German writers (Bertolt Brecht) or suspicious Americans (Ernest Hemingway). Marx, Freud, Einstein, Thomas Mann, and H.G. Wells were all included in the purge of "degenerate" work, although individual cases are hardly important given the scale of the event. In all between 20–25,000 volumes were burnt, and actions including bonfires, radio announcements, and torchlight marches took place in towns across the nation. Various key libraries and collections including that of the proto-sexological Institut für Sexualwissenschaft were also burnt during this time. The actions demonstrated to the world the anti-intellectualism of the Nazi movement, its virulent anti-Semitism, and the shocking cultural vandalism which was happily undertaken in the name of Fascism.

Jerome de Groot

Date 1933

Place Berlin, Germany

Why It's Key The Nazi burning of books became an important and enduring symbol of censorship, and of aggression towards Jewish people; it also hardened intellectual responses to the Fascist regime across Europe.

Opposite Nazis and students burn "anti-German" literature

1930–1939

241

Key Book
Midnight

Midnight is not the sort of book one picks up for some light entertainment. Populated as it is with more than 50 principle characters, Mao Tun provides a character list for the reader's reference should the names get too confusing – which for many it will. When embarking on this project, Mao Tun intended for it to be a social commentary on the whole of China, as a nation, but found himself limited by the vastness of China's domain. Instead choosing to focus the scope of his novel on Shanghai, what emerges is a locally specific epic tale that goes into labored detail about the social dynamic, movements, and realities of many characters that represent the myriad strata of Chinese society in the 1930s.

There are moments when Mao Tun's tone borders on controversy, but it is essential to bear in mind that he successfully assuaged censorship with a mask over his subtle political coloring – it requires critical observation to pick up on these nuances. Mao Tun laments his indirectness, calling it one of the book's "shortcomings," however the manner in which he seamlessly bridges the chasm between a metropolitan Shanghai that is steeped in western sensibility, and the encroaching dominant inevitability of the Communist Revolution, is captivating and detailed. Pulsing through this intricately structured text are Confucianist values, economics, and a sense of growing Nationalism. During a time when China is redefining her paradigm of thought and intent, comments such as, "A communist can change himself from a rat into a tiger," are discursive.

Alexandra Hamlyn

Date 1933

Author Mao Tun (1896–1981)

Nationality China

Why It's Key *Midnight* is accredited as instigating the seminal moments of Chinese vernacular literature and revolutionary realism. Significantly, Mao Tun also participated in the Kuomintang's Northern Expedition (1926–28) and supported movements such as "New Literature." He was awarded reign as the Minister of Culture in 1949.

Key Book
Banana Bottom

Banana Bottom, last of McKay's three novels (after *Banjo*, 1929), is the most accomplished, and although it did not have a wide readership when first published, it was critically well received and considered quite revolutionary for the way it dealt with issues of race, class, creed, and sexuality.

The title refers to the Jamaican village where some of the action takes place during the 1900s. A sort of Caribbean *Pygmalion*, it is the story of Bita Plant, who returns as a cultivated and beautiful black celebrity to the island of her birth after seven years' education in Europe, sponsored by white missionary benefactors, Malcolm and Priscilla Craig. Their plan for their protégée is that, having been groomed into this God-fearing paragon, she will marry appropriately within the church, then as a dutiful wife help to continue the work of the mission. But Bita's affinity for her own traditions, customs and beliefs has not been eradicated and she is drawn back into Jamaican culture and heritage, the festivals and superstitions and passions that do not befit a lady of her supposed refinement.

Central to the book is the conflict within Bita, whose time abroad, as well as broadening her knowledge, has awakened in her an innate need to belong. The tension between European and Jamaican values and ways of life emerges through her various relationships with the characters and situations she meets while seeking self-fulfilment. McKay uses directness, lyricism, humor, and melodrama to highlight important issues of social and political injustice.

Margaret Busby

Date 1933

Author Claude McKay (1890–1948)

Nationality Jamaica

Why It's Key Moving to New York in 1912, McKay became linked with the Harlem Renaissance. He won instant fame for his 1919 poem "If We Must Die" (recited by Churchill in a rallying wartime speech). His best-selling first novel *Home to Harlem* (1928) was reprinted five times within two months.

242

Key Passage
Frost in May

"Even when they practised receiving an un-consecrated wafer with closed eyes and outstretched tongues, it seemed to Nanda that at the moment of Communion itself, Theresa could not look more dazed with happiness."

Nanda's First Communion is one of major events of not only her schooling, but also of her spiritual life. Yet as this passage unfolds it becomes clear that the girl's preoccupation with her own spiritual moment prevents her from actually experiencing it. Her friends' "closed eyes and outstretched tongues" show the kind of experience Nanda covets. Yet "dazed with happiness" makes the experiences seem a little over-indulged.

"They walked into the chapel two by two, pacing slowly up the aisle like twelve brides, to the sound of soft, lacy music." When the day finally comes the girls are described as the brides of Christ, and the word "lacy" overstresses the intensity of the moment. "Nanda tried to fix her attention on the mass, but she could not." Of course, such a build up can only lead to disappointment.

"'This is the greatest moment of my life. Our Lord Himself is actually present, in the flesh, inside my body. Why am I so numb and stupid? Why can't I think of anything to say?'" Nanda's reverie, "in the flesh, inside my body," is dampened by self-reproach, "numb" and "stupid." This is typical of her experiences at her school. She is so captivated by ritual and symbolism that her own sentiments become lost. Her problem is perhaps that of the convert; Nanda wants to have an active role in her religious life and refuses to experience it at a distance. Such fervor does not sit well with the nuns and the passion we see here eventually leads to far greater and much more significant misunderstandings.

Royce Mahawatte

Date 1933

Author Antonia White (1899–1980)

Nationality UK

Why It's Key There are few literary girls' school novels and *Frost in May* stands out mainly because of the precise yet ambivalent way the school is represented. Nanda's ill-fated career at the Convent of the Five Wounds is recorded with such quiet clarity we get to see the innocence of the initiate and the harshness of the convent's strictures.

Key Character **Miss Lonelyhearts**
Miss Lonelyhearts

The title character of Nathanael West's novella, who works as an agony columnist for a city newspaper, is described this way: "Although his cheap clothes had too much style, he still looked like the son of a Baptist minister. A beard would become him, would accent his Old-Testament look. But even without a beard no one could fail to recognize the New England puritan. His forehead was high and narrow. His nose was long and fleshless. His bony chin was shaped and cleft like a hoof." Assigned as a joke to answer letters from anonymous sufferers seeking advice and consolation, Miss Lonelyhearts instead becomes overwhelmed by the desolation of their lives and is increasingly caught up in messianic attempts to save them. In a brief commentary on his work, West notes that Miss Lonelyhearts "became the portrait of a priest of our time" – a time defined by economic depression, Prohibition, and the post-war shattering of received belief systems. In keeping with its bleak urban setting,

Miss Lonelyhearts traces its hero's trajectory toward not salvation or transfiguration but complete delusion.

Especially notable in West's handling of the character is its alternation between psychological realism and the cartoon-like flatness of caricature, in line with the author's description of his work as "a novel in the form of a comic strip." This combination of realist and modernist modes, along with the cartoon quality of his hero's fundamentalist religiosity, makes West's rendering of Miss Lonelyhearts one of the most sharply memorable in twentieth-century fiction.

Nicholas Lawrence

Date 1933

Author: Nathanael West (1903–40)

Nationality USA

Why It's Key Miss Lonelyhearts is a male New York City agony aunt who faces a world of emptiness, alienation, and spiritual breakdown. West describes his plight, and that of Depression-era America, with black humor.

1930-1939

243

Key Author **Evelyn Waugh**
A Handful of Dust

Evelyn Waugh (1903–66) is probably best known for *Brideshead Revisited* (1945), a weirdly durable and potent fantasy of gracious living among the Roman Catholic landed gentry, written amid the austerity and ruination of the last years of World War II. *Brideshead* represents an elegiac and celebratory strain in Waugh's oeuvre which also finds expression in his biographies of Ronald Knox and Edmund Campion, and in his little early book on Rossetti (there would be an abiding aestheticism), and it gives intensity to his satires of lives which fail to take account of such – or any – ideals, never mind measuring up to them. The early novels take pleasure in visiting horrors on figures unconscious of the darker possibilities of life, as for instance in *Vile Bodies* (1930) on the feckless and infantilized set of Bright Young Things.

A Handful of Dust, from the middle of Waugh's life and writing career, may well be his best novel. In it the Church Father side of the author, deploring, excoriating

and retributive, is in an interesting tension with his comic energy, characterized by a brilliant relish of human folly and by satirical brio. Poor Tony Last, the protagonist, is betrayed maritally, disappointed in his dream of building a great good place, and is finally consigned to one of the most memorable hells in literature, stranded deep in the jungle of British Guyana, where his deranged captor requires him to read out the novels of Dickens, on an endless loop.

Peter Swaab

Date 1934 (publication)

Author Evelyn Waugh

Nationality UK

Other Key Works *Decline and Fall* (1928), *The Loved One* (1948), *The Sword of Honour* trilogy (1965)

Why It's Key Waugh's satirical style had a great influence on succeeding generations of writers. *A Handful of Dust* epitomizes the shifting moral values of Britain in the 1930s.

Key Author **Bruno Schulz**
The Street of Crocodiles

Bruno Schulz (1892–1942) was fifty when in 1942 he was shot in the head by a Gestapo officer on the streets of Drohobycz, a small town in Polish Galicia. He was born there, and apart from several years studying architecture in Lwów, remained there all his life. Schulz taught drawing at a local school and wrote the two slender volumes of stories that have given him a place in the front ranks of world literature. *The Street of Crocodiles* (1934) and *Sanitorium Under the Sign of the Hour Glass* (1937) are mythologies of childhood, a young boy's tales of life with his father. But these are no *shtetl* folk tales. Schulz saw them as constituting a "spiritual genealogy" and his debts to the modernist experiments of Proust, Mann, Musil, Rilke, and Kafka (to whom he is much compared) are evident. Drawn to "the cheapness, shabbiness, and inferiority of material" (his exemplary creations are tailor's dummies), Schultz inevitably transforms and animates matter.

After the war Schulz's work fell out of fashion, considered decadent and esoteric in a Poland dedicated to socialist realism, and it was not until 1957 that the books were republished. Schulz's influence on late twentieth-century fiction is considerable, with Danilo Kis, Bohumil Hrabal, Cynthia Ozick, Philip Roth, and David Grossman acknowledging their debt. Ozick, Roth, and Grossman have all "borrowed" details from Schulz's life in their fiction.
Kasia Boddy

Date 1934 (publication)

Nationality Poland

Why It's Key A major modernist who was discovered by English readers when Celina Wieneska's translations were published in 1963. During the 1970s Philip Roth included Schulz in his Penguin "Voices from the Other Europe" series.

244

Key Character
Mary Poppins

The character of Mary Poppins, the magical nanny who arrives out of the sky to put things right at Number 17 Cherry Tree Lane, first appeared in the 1934 novel of the same name. However, the great success of the later Disney film based on P.L. Travers' book has led to confusion about the nature of the "real" Mary Poppins.

Far from being a pretty, well-spoken young woman built along the charming lines of Julie Andrews, Mary Poppins is described (and illustrated in the original drawings by Mary Shepard) as looking like a Dutch doll. Her complacent satisfaction with her own appearance – "Practically Perfect" – is heightened by the reader's awareness that the nanny is, in fact, rather plain with a nose that resembles an old-fashioned clothes peg. Likewise, Travers gives Poppins the genteel cockneyfied speech of an upper servant, rather than the elegant RP conveyed by Andrews in the 1964 film.

Travers (born Helen Lyndon Goff), who was Australian by birth, had been hugely influenced by the writings of the Russian mystic Gurdjieff as well as the earlier work of the psychoanalyst Jung. Mary Poppins, with her gnomic utterances about the East Wind and her insistence on introducing her young charges to dancing cows, chimney sweeps, and talking dogs, is a classic figure from eastern philosophy. It is her job to save the Banks' household from the muddled and anxious materialism into which it has fallen (Mr Banks is a bank clerk, and the action is set at the height of the Great Depression).

After the modest success of her first outing, Mary Poppins reappeared in several sequels. However, it was not until the success of the Disney film – which had been twenty years in gestation – that the character became hugely famous. Travers, typically, hated Julie Andrews' interpretation, dismissing her as a "soubrette."
Kathryn Hughes

Date 1934

Author P.L. Travers (1899–1996)

Nationality Australia

Why It's Key In 2004 a new stage musical of *Mary Poppins*, developed by Cameron Macintosh, has sought to reclaim some of the darker aspects of the original character. The success of this interpretation suggests that Travers' original conception of the magic nanny had a greater resonance than anyone previously realized.
Opposite Mary Poppins

Key Author
Luigi Pirandello

Even the house itself, apparently, lacked personality. The celebrity living in Via Bosio 15, Rome, was clearly in no habit of leaving marks of his persona. Witnesses describe him as sheer energy. An energy that could impersonate any number of dramatis personae. But perhaps it is more correct to say that his art was haunted by incorporeal visitors forcing their personal histories onto his lack of one (or onto his creative absence: the plot of his best known play, *Six Characters in Search of an Author* [1921]).

Luigi Pirandello (1867–1936) takes center stage in a phenomenal career marked by exceptional quality and quantity of output (hundreds of irresistible short stories, an incredible feat of variation on the basic theme of personal inexistence; scores of thought-provoking, revolutionary plays; the several fundamental novels, for in fact who, to this day, can really do without reading those euphoric tales of insubstantiality, *The Late Mattia Pascal*, or *One, No One and One Hundred Thousand* [1926]). A career marked by controversy (over his supposedly apolitical fascism) and by public honors (the Nobel Prize in 1934), and yet unstoppable in its course.

A bit of a superhuman course, then. But with no cult of selfhood, unlike that of his arch-enemy D'Annunzio. He hoped he would still be busy working on his death, and death in this case obliged, in the middle of the unfinished Mountain Giants. Yet any recent biography, after the early hagiographies, will stress the thoroughly human Pirandello struggling with concerns, disease, his obtuse and calamitous times (trying to establish a new national theater wasn't exactly fun given the sponsors, Mussolini and his inartistic regime). A raw, tough, mean struggle, even though time, and space too, had seemed particularly well disposed when granting a special birth to an unknown Sicilian place called Chaos, of all names.

Federica Pedriali

Date 1934
(Nobel Prize awarded)

Nationality Italy

Other Key Works Plays *Right You Are, If You Think You Are* (1917) **Novels** *The Late Mattia Pascal* (1904)

Why It's Key Pirandello's prolific career reached its apex in the early to mid-1920s, following the global success of *Six Characters in Search of an Author* (1921) and *Henry IV* (1922).

Key Book
Seven Gothic Tales

Seven Gothic Tales was Karen Blixen's first published work. She published it under the name Isak Dinesen. Dinesen was her maiden name, and Isak she chose – in Hebrew Isak means "one who laughs." The collection of seven stories was published in the United States in 1934. The American Book-of-the-Month club chose to feature the work, ensuring a large commercial success for the first time author.

Blixen wrote *Seven Gothic Tales* in English, her second language. The tales are set in the mid-nineteenth century. Blixen said in an interview, "I moved my *Tales* back a hundred years to a really romantic time, in which people and relations were different from today. Only in that way could I be completely free."

"The Deluge at Normandy" features four aristocratic people trapped in a hayloft by a flood. They tell stories to pass the time until their rescue at dawn. Despite the situation, the story is crafted as if they are telling stories in a social setting. The stories reveal both their true identities and the roles that they play. The Cardinal, who is revealed in fact to be the Cardinal's valet and murderer, confesses that he has learned, "when the devil grins at me, to grin back."

The tales emulate the gothic traditions of writers such as Poe and Stevenson, yet the stories contain a humorous awareness of the traditions they represent. The opening of "The Deluge at Normandy" mocks the Gothic with the lines, "The romantic spirit of the age, which delighted in ruins, ghosts, and lunatics… "

Jennifer Young

Date 1934

Author Isak Dinesen (pen-name of Karen Blixen, 1885–1962)

Nationality Denmark

Why It's Key Blixen's first and most famous work, a series of highly crafted supernatural stories with multiple narrators and "story within a story" constructions.

Opposite Isak Dinesen

Key Book
The Postman Always Rings Twice

This is the novel that defined the darker side of hard-boiled fiction. It introduced all the characters that time and imitation has since made into clichés. Here is the sulky femme fatale, the passionate and greedy lover, and the foolish, unsuspecting victim-husband. There is also the no-time-to-waste pace of the story and the dialogue, sharp as a whip and just as cruel. It's a grim tale of no-hopers grabbing at a little money and wrestling with passions and events beyond their control.

The story – the eternal triangle – is simple and straightforward. Frank Chambers, a worthless drifter, wanders into a Californian diner and falls in love with sultry Cora Papadakis, the much younger wife of the owner. The two lovers concoct a plan to kill the husband and from then on, we are waiting to see how they will be punished. There is no whodunit element to this crime story. The morbid thrill of the book lies in wondering when and how retribution will come.

Full of sex (explicit enough to get the book banned in some states) and violence, this exciting, dirty, intemperate novella perfectly captured the downbeat atmosphere of the Depression era and inspired a score of imitators. Crime novelist Elmore Leonard is a direct descendant of James M. Cain and Albert Camus claimed that *The Postman Always Rings Twice* influenced his writing of the existentialist classic *L'étranger*.

The Postman Always Rings Twice has been filmed several times, memorably in 1946 (starring Lana Turner and John Garfield) and in 1981 (with Jessica Lange and Jack Nicholson, and screenplay by David Mamet).
Kathy Watson

Date 1934

Author James M. Cain (1892–1977)

Nationality USA

Why It's Key There has been much debate about the book's title. One thing's for sure, no postman ever appears. James M. Cain's first novel, like his later work, is more explicit and darker than the fiction of Chandler and Hammett. His work usually employs a femme fatale; it added to the popularity of this stock figure.

Key Event **Publication of *Novel with Cocaine* leads to an enduring mystery**

That *Novel with Cocaine* could be ascribed to Nabokov is hilarious in itself. But such rumors were common currency when confronted with whom to credit with authorship of this soi-disant "Dostoevskian novel of ideas," as the author concerned simply did not step forward. In any case, it was the novel's narcotic association and reputation years after the event which led to such speculation (emanating from an Updike comparison with Nabokov's style). Many consider the novel to be the work of Marc Levi, a Russian émigré working under a French identity, who either died in Paris in 1973 or returned to Russia only to suffer under Stalin, depending upon which version you prefer to believe.

What is known is that *Novel with Cocaine* was published by "M. Ageyev" in *Numbers*, a Russian émigré journal in inter-war Paris, as "Confessions of a Russian Opium-Eater." This immediately places the book in the De Quincey tradition of the picaresque

drugs confessional, both books being mined substantially in later years, most notably by the Beats. Furthermore, that book's frame of reference takes in the Russian Revolution of 1917 as only a minor facet rather than outright reality, as the young narrator Vadim is too hell-bent on his substance of choice or wilfully transmitting syphilis to every woman available to him. When Vadim turns away from his friends' revolutionary fervor, it is because the dictatorship of the proletariat cannot offer him "instantaneous happiness on a scale… never dreamed of before" in the same way that the substance referred to can.
Andrew Stevens

Date 1934

Author M. Ageyev (1898–1973)

Nationality Russia

Why It's Key *Novel with Cocaine*, an early twentieth-century drugs confessional, led the way for William Burroughs, among others.

Key Character **Julian English**
Appointment in Samarra

John O'Hara had made a name for himself with short stories, particularly in *The New Yorker* magazine, and journalism before he published *An Appointment in Samarra*, his first novel. It was an immediate success and was praised by, among others, Ernest Hemingway. Its protagonist, Julian English, is a car dealer who is part of the well-connected establishment in his home town. O'Hara shows English as a heavy drinker and womanizer who, over the course of three days, impulsively commits a series of self-destructive acts, culminating in his suicide. It is his excessive drinking that gets him into trouble but it is his dawning perception that he is not as widely respected as he believed that leads him to kill himself, fittingly for a car dealer, through carbon monoxide poisoning caused by running a motor in a closed garage.

The difficulties that English gets himself into are not necessarily insoluble. He fears his wife will find another man, but in fact she is ready to stick by him.

His drunken social gaffes are not terminally damaging. However, O'Hara clearly wants his character's death to be seen as inevitable, not least through his choice of title. This is taken from a traditional story in which a man in Baghdad sees the figure of Death gesturing at him. He tries to escape his fate by fleeing to the town of Samarra, only to meet Death there. The apparition explains that he had been surprised to meet the man earlier in Baghdad as he had an appointment with him in Samarra.

Michael Munro

Date 1934

Author John O'Hara (1905–70)

Nationality USA

Why It's Key O'Hara's first novel became known as one of the great works of inter-war fiction. English is a typical O'Hara character, sexually voracious, feeling frustrated by the artificial barriers of social class, but sensitive enough to be driven to commit suicide. The novel, despite its risqué style, was a great success and launched the author on his writing career.

1930–1939

249

Key Character **Claudius**
I, Claudius

Tiberius Claudius Drusus Nero Germanicus abandons the dry and dusty histories he has previously written to record the compelling story of his own life. In this first part of Claudius' "autobiography," Robert Graves guides us from Claudius' birth, through to his difficult adolescence, afflicted by a speech defect and a deformity of his feet. This unlikely boy, through many twists of fate, finally ascends to supremacy and becomes Emperor. From his point of view we witness Augustus Caesar's establishment of a new type of monarchy, the unpopular reign of Tiberius and the carnival chaos of Caligula.

Claudius reveals the political machinations behind the powerful Patricians of Rome, bringing to life his grandmother, the manipulative and cruel Livia. He portrays her as the true ruler of Rome, controlling events firstly through her husband, Augustus and then through her son, Tiberius. With an eye for irony and a touch of pomposity, Claudius shows a side of Rome left out of conventional history books, weaving hearsay and speculation with historical fact, reporting his version of reality behind the now mythic characters of Roman aristocracy.

Grave's achievement is to combine fact and fiction, leaving behind dusty, colorless biographies of historical figures. By giving Claudius his own voice, Graves engages with the reader and allows a greater empathy with the character of Claudius.

The chaos of Rome surrounds Claudius, seemingly the only sane member of a *dramatis personae* otherwise filled with madmen, betrayed brothers, and buxom prostitutes. His scorn for Rome, his reluctance for power and his physical unsuitability make him the ideal candidate for Emperor after the monstrous pageant of debauchery of Caligula's sovereignty. Claudius, more than any other man, knows what Rome is, and is not fooled by the glittering illusions of power.

Thomas Dymond

Date 1934

Author Robert Graves (1895–1985)

Nationality UK

Why It's Key Poet, novelist, and academic Robert Graves brought to life the unusual history of the Emperor Claudius, filling in the historical facts with personality and offering a unique viewpoint on the Roman world.

Key Book
Une Semaine de Bonté

Max Ernst (1891–1976) had already experimented extensively with collage by the time he created his pictorial novel *Une Semaine de Bonté*. He favored printed illustrations taken from old magazines in the form of wood or steel engravings, and developed an approach in which he added some disconcerting detail to an existing picture, transforming the mundane and the clichéd into something disturbing and subversive.

The "narrative" of *Bonté* is no clearer than that of a dream. Like the other Surrealists, Ernst was very much aware of the writings of Freud, and was concerned to unveil the secrets of the subconscious. He once said that his collages transformed "the banal advertisement page into a drama which reveals my most private desires." In *Bonté*, it is not just his own inner desires that are exposed, but also those of bourgeois society.

Thus we find recurring images of respectable Victorian gentlemen, whose heads are those of birds or beasts, toying sadistically with half-naked, chained women, or fleeing from unknown terrors. Elsewhere, two genteel ladies taking tea together might seem quite ordinary, were it not for the giant fish emerging from the hair of one of them. Some of the images are more abstract, for example an avenue of giant eyes, or a plane on which pairs of shaking hands recede towards the horizon. As Tristan Tzara, the Dada poet, wrote in 1951: "Max Ernst reverses the appearance of objects to the point of a direct attack on their essence." Ernst's subversion is thus not only satirical, but also challenges our assumptions about the nature of reality.
Ian Crofton

Date 1934

Author Max Ernst

Nationality Germany

Why It's Key A collage novel by one of the leading artists of Dada and Surrealism. It was first published as a series of five pamphlets in a limited edition of 1000 copies each. Ernst is credited as the most important practitioner of the collage novel, a precursor of the graphic novel.

Key Event **Maxim Gorky becomes the first president of the Union of Soviet Writers**

The modern world's first and only closed "system" of literature, Soviet socialist realism, was defined and written into law by Stalin in 1932. It required writers to eulogize working-class heroes and give life to healthy, optimistic social outcomes compatible with class-driven Communist ideology. The result was simple-minded, didactic fiction with cardboard characters and little artistry. Gorky was made to serve as its figurehead after he returned homesick to the Soviet Union in 1928. The imposition of socialist realism may be regarded as a tragedy in Russian culture, given the huge modernist impetus all the arts derived from the Bolshevik Revolution and the rich ferment of new ideas and critical schools that survived barely more than a decade, before Stalin suppressed any work of genuine power and either murdered, exiled, or silenced its authors. In Gorky's defence, the *Untimely Essays* he published after 1917, fiercely critical of Lenin and Bolshevik inhumanity, better indicated his true politics.

The autobiographical trilogy, his memoirs of Tolstoy, and the late novel *The Artymonov Business* showed his genuine strength as a writer, as opposed to the typecast moralizing of *Mother*. In the wake of the Revolution, both in Russia and from abroad, Gorky also helped many writers survive. His election as the first president of the Union of Soviet Writers in 1934 was an in-character compromise. He did worse things in his final troubled last years. But post-Soviet Russia has much enjoyed trampling on a fallen hero it never elected to prominence in the first place.
Lesley Chamberlain

Date 1934

Author Maxim Gorky (1868–1936)

Nationality Russia

Why It's Key Gorky's Soviet political masters adopted *Mother* (1906) to set the standard for politically correct "socialist realist" fiction which became the USSR's state policy in 1932. The Union of Soviet Writers was established to control the work done by writers; those who deviated from the rules were sent to labour camps.

Opposite Maxim Gorky

Key Event *Tropic of Cancer* is banned in the UK and United States

Henry Miller's depiction of his life in 1930s Paris ushered in a new way of writing about sex. Gone were the euphemisms and covert and peripheral references that had previously sufficed: now sex was a focus for discussion and a new language, direct and aggressive in tone, was evolving for the purpose.

This is a supremely misogynistic piece of writing and there is still something shockingly brutal about Miller's prose. His comments about his friend's wife, Ida Verlaine are indicative of his: "I didn't give a fuck for her as a person, though I often wondered what she might be like as a piece of fuck, so to speak." This reductive and objectifying attitude is characteristic of the narcissistic and egotistical narrative voice that seems implicitly to be addressing a male reader. Women are described as little more than the facilitators of male desires, animalistic and available, and sunk in a base physicality without agency.

Although originally published in 1934, the novel was prohibited for decades in the United States and the UK. After its release in the United States in the 1960s, charges of obscenity were brought against the publishers, Grove Press. It went on to develop a cult following and was particularly influential for the Beat generation. Their eagerness to shun convention spawned a desire to experiment with the extremes of experience and the licentious freedom of Miller's narrative appealed to this desire.

Despite the problematic gender politics, Henry Miller's work made an important contribution to the development of modernist fiction. With its experimental mixture of confessional autobiography and fiction, and passages where the narrative constitutes a "stream of consciousness" it was both innovative and dynamic.
Juliet Wightman

Date 1934

Title *Tropic of Cancer*

Author Henry Miller (1891–1980)

Nationality USA

Why It's Key *Tropic of Cancer* was a landmark publication that tested the boundaries between erotica and pornography. In the 1960s it became the focus of a famous and influential obscenity case.

Opposite **Henry Miller**

Key Event
Perelman joins *The New Yorker*

Sidney Perelman was a word-lover and a keen student of European literature who liked to pepper his work with foreign phrases and recondite references, making him eminently unsuitable for his early career as a Hollywood hack and jobbing magazine humorist – he even hated his successful period as a writer for the Marx Brothers because he was made to simplify his scripts. But he found his ideal outlet when, aged 30, he was hired to write regular pieces for *The New Yorker*, the only American humorous magazine to be aimed at an educated, metropolitan audience. Although the magazine already boasted James Thurber and E.B. White among its contributors, Perelman became, and remained for 30 years, its star humorist.

Perelman wrote comic essays which he mock-pretentiously called feuilletons, mining his boyhood memories for material (he wrote a fine series about the pleasures and pains of rewatching films he had loved as a boy) and scanning the newspapers for odd stories that might ignite his own bizarre imagination. He matched high style with low subject matter, laced his elegant prose with gutter slang, and constantly surprised his readers by interrupting his narratives with surreal flights of fancy, puns ("Diana turned on the radio. With a savage snarl the radio turned on her") and deconstructions of clichés. His acknowledged master was James Joyce (a picture of whom sat on his desk while he endlessly honed his work) and, by dragging the techniques of modernism into mainstream humor, he influenced comic writers in every medium.
Jake Kerridge

Date 1934

Author Sidney J. Perelman (1904–79)

Nationality USA

Why It's Key "I loathe writing but I'm a great believer in money": a brilliant humorist finds his spiritual home.

Key Event **Elizabeth Bishop meets Marianne Moore**

1930–1939

Elizabeth Bishop was introduced to poet Marianne Moore in 1934 by the Vassar College Library in New York. From then on their friendship blossomed. Moore, a major figure in the modernist movement, was a friend to T.S. Eliot, Ezra Pound, and ee cummings. As editor of the influential journal *The Dial* she encouraged new writers; her often-quoted advice was that poets should show "imaginary gardens with real toads in them."

As a result of Moore's encouragement, Bishop decided against a career in medicine to focus on poetry. Her early work appeared in the underground literary magazine, *Con Spirito* and in 1935 Moore published Bishop's poems in the anthology *Trial Balances*. Again, encouraged by Moore, Bishop submitted her work to the Houghton Mifflin Prize. Her manuscript, *North and South*, was chosen over 800 entries and published in 1946. Bishop's second book, *Poems: North and South – a Cold Spring*,

presenting her first two collections, won the esteemed Pulitzer Prize.

The two women's intensive correspondence continued until Moore's death in 1972, even though Moore, in later life a celebrity beyond literary circles, would occasionally write as many as fifty letters a day in response to "volumes of irrelevant mail." Bishop believed her mentor was "the world's greatest living observer," a title used in her contribution to the Marianne Moore issue of *A Quarterly Review of Literature* (1948). The description in Moore's writing clearly inspired Bishop, who used their correspondence to practise her own writing skills, develop her voice and test the response in preparation for public forums.
Elizabeth Whyman

Date 1934

Authors Elizabeth Bishop (1911–75), Marianne Moore (1887–1972)

Nationality USA

Place New York

Why It's Key The correspondence between Pulitzer Prize-winning poets Moore and Bishop provided the format for the young Bishop's literary expression. The mentorship was most crucial to Bishop, who went on to be considered one of the greatest twentieth-century poets.

Key Character **Mr Chips**
Goodbye, Mr Chips

SPOILER

Perhaps based on his father's experiences as a schoolmaster and on Hilton's student experiences at The Leys School, Cambridge, the novella tells the story of a much-loved retired schoolmaster, Charles Chipping, who is nearing the end of his life. "Mr Chips" spent his entire career at Brookfield, having arrived as teacher when he was 22. Never distinguished by intellect or personality, he nevertheless managed to gather a devoted following among generations of boys. At the age of 48 he surprised himself and delighted everyone else by marrying 25-year-old Kathie. The great tragedy of his life was Kathie's death a year later in childbirth; the baby also died. At retirement he moved only across the road, and continued to have the new boys to tea. As he lies on his deathbed he hears someone lament that he'd never had children, and replies that he had, "Thousands of 'em... all boys."

While it can be read as the simple story of an uneventful life, the novella goes further. It shows on

the one hand that even the quietest figure has been capable of great love and experienced great tragedy. On the other hand, it also stands as a microcosm of the rapidly changing modern world. It opens with memories of the mid-Victorian period, and by the time it closes at the end of Chipping's life, World War II is imminent. Chipping and Brookfield have survived, but been profoundly affected by, the ravages of the Great War, and seen great social change in popular culture, education, and women's rights. It stands therefore, for the great changes that affected Britain over nearly a century.
Gretchen Gerzina

Date 1934

Author James Hilton (1900–54)

Nationality UK

Why It's Key *Goodbye, Mr Chips* was written quickly after a flash of inspiration by James Hilton, already the well-known author of *Lost Horizon*, and made him into a bestselling author. Five years later the film version, based on his screenplay, also became a big hit.

Opposite Peter O'Toole playing Mr Chips in the film adaptation

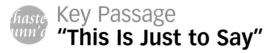

Key Passage
"This Is Just to Say"

I have eaten / the plums / that were in / the icebox and which / you were probably / saving / for breakfast forgive me / they were delicious / so sweet / and cold

One of Williams' maxims was "no ideas but in things," meaning that poetry should deal primarily with the concrete world, ideas should come second. With "This Is Just to Say," he seems to have achieved exactly this goal. The poem, sometimes thought to be a message to his wife, has the quality of a "found" object, a domestic note the poet has seized upon as art in the same way a painter might incorporate a newspaper scrap into a painting. Writing in the 1930s, such techniques were commonplace. And given Williams' fondness for the vernacular voice, one hears too how the poem catches the beauty of natural, everyday cadences. Somehow such ordinariness conjures the reality of objects; readers are often struck by the plumminess of these plums, their sweetness and coldness.

Yet Williams, whose literary acquaintances included arch-modernists like Pound, was sceptical of mimesis, or the capacity of words accurately to copy things. As much as the poem appears to perform a moment of intimate communication, it is also simply an object made of words. The "This" of the title, for example, refers to the poem itself as well as the fictional note it dramatizes. Thus Williams produces a particular tension, demonstrating poetic language as both a medium for human relationships and a strange, detached world of its own.

Doug Haynes

Date 1934

Author William Carlos Williams (1883–1963)

Nationality USA

Why It's Key This poem, among Williams' most widely anthologized, mixes imagistic enigma with an accessible subject-matter; it is hugely popular and yet its meaning remains undecideable.

Key Passage
Call it Sleep

"They rounded the corner – There they all were, sitting on the curb.
'See! I tol' ye.' Izzy shot ahead, shaking David completely. 'Hey, Geng!'
'Hey, Izzy!' they chorused.
'Let a reggiluh guy sid donn, will yuh?'
'Led 'im sid donn!' they ordered, and shoving against each other made room for him beside Kushy. Stranded, David hesitantly approached and stood up behind them.
'So w'ea wuz yuh?' Kushy asked.
'I went wid my modder.' Izzy basked in their gaze. 'an' we bought shoes – best kind onnuh Eas' Side. Waid'll yuh see 'em.'"

Call it Sleep is one of the Great American Novels, and the one that most successfully captures the rich, multi-lingual music of immigrant life in the slums of New York. Roth's characters – Jewish immigrants in the Lower East Side – slide effortlessly from Yiddish to German to Polish, with the children slipping occasionally into the English that they have mastered beyond anything their parents will achieve.

The contrast between the nuanced and sophisticated conversations that the adults hold in Yiddish and their struggle to buy groceries in broken English is conveyed by Roth's spectacular use of phonetic transcription. Roth's linguistic pyrotechnics are clearest in the street scenes he describes, when the children's All-American slang becomes almost unrecognisable in their heavily-accented English.

The novel's star, David, is a timid and desperately sensitive child. Roth's genius with idiom and dialect is matched only by David's fantastical and delirious stream of consciousness that swirls through the novel at fever pitch and turns many passages – and indeed all the final pages – into poetry.

Francesca Segal

Date 1934

Author Henry Roth (1906–95)

Nationality USA (born Austria-Hungary)

Why It's Key *Call it Sleep* was Roth's first novel, and it would be 60 years before he produced another – *Mercy of a Rude Stream*, which reached the public only a year before his death. In the interim Roth had all but abandoned writing and intermittently worked as a farmer, metal grinder, and teacher.

Key Book *A Universal History of Infamy* (*Historia universal de la infamia*)

These "exercises in narrative prose" openly plunder a wide and eccentric range of source texts including Mark Twain's *Life on the Mississippi*, Herbert Asbury's *The Gangs of New York*, and Sir Percy Sykes' *A History of Persia*. The stories exemplify Borges' talent, to be used to great effect in later writings, for what might be called creative plagiarism, whereby stories are appropriated and transformed by subtle shifts of emphasis and organization. Whilst the stories tell of all manner of shameless depravity, cruelty and duplicity, Borges' coolly impersonal, ironic tone lends them an irresistible urbanity and lightness.

Familiar legends such as Billy the Kid and his nemesis Sherriff Garrett sit alongside the Widow Ching, pitiless female pirate of the nineteenth century and Kôtsuké no Suké, fatefully impudent Japanese courtier of the eighteenth century. The last and most famous of the stories, "Man on Pink Corner," tells of a violent grudge match between two compadritos, knife-fighting toughs of the Buenos Aires slums. Narrated in the gritty language of the compadrito, the story showcases Borges' mastery of different idioms and perspectives.

The effect of these juxtapositions of different times and places is to convey a kind of bird's-eye or "universal" vision of deadly human vice or "infamy." The collection also anticipates Borges' abiding fascination for paradox, most notably in the story of "The Improbable Impostor Tom Castro," whose claim to be a grieving mother's dead son is made credible by his utter lack of likeness to the original man.
Josh Cohen

Date 1935

Author Jorge Luis Borges (1899–1986)

Nationality Argentina

Why It's Key These entertaining studies in human wickedness across the ages prefigure in both theme and style the great story collections that would establish Borges as a master of modern world literature.

Key Authour **Fernando Pessoa**

Fernando Pessoa (1888–1935) had already published 2 books of poetry, *35 Sonnets* and *Antinous*, when Alberto Caeiro (one of Pessoa's heteronyms) was created in 1914. Pessoa wrote over 30 poems in a single go. It was at this moment that he felt "an appearance of someone in me… my master appeared in me." This was the birth of Caeiro.

Fernando Pessoa considered the alternate personae he created, and whose names he published work under, to be "heteronyms." He differentiated between the concept of a pseudonym and a heteronym. He considered that a "heteronymic work is by an author writing outside his own personality: it is the work of a complete individuality made up by him, just as the utterances of some character in a drama would be."

Pessoa's most significant work is *The Book of Disquietude*. Pessoa published fragments of the work in journals during his lifetime, but after his death 350 fragments were found in an envelope marked *Book of Disquietude* (*Livro do Dessossogego por Bernardo Soares*, [1982]). The title page in this envelope lists Bernardo Soares as the author, yet autobiographical elements of Pessoa himself exist in the text, which has lead to Soares being termed a "semiheteronym."

Pessoa's heteronyms each wrote in different styles and on different subjects. Each had a completely realized biography. The heteronyms reviewed each other's works, usually disapproving of writing published by Pessoa himself. The creation of these literary lives is a remarkable achievement.
Jennifer Young

Date 1935 (death)

Nationality Portugal

Other Key Works *The Keeper of Sheep* (*Guardador de Rebanhos*, written in 1914), *English Poems* (1921), *Message* (*Mensagem*, 1933)

Why It's Key Pessoa's poetry was unique because of its heavy use of invented personae to write in different styles. Pessoa had at least 72 of these alternative personae.

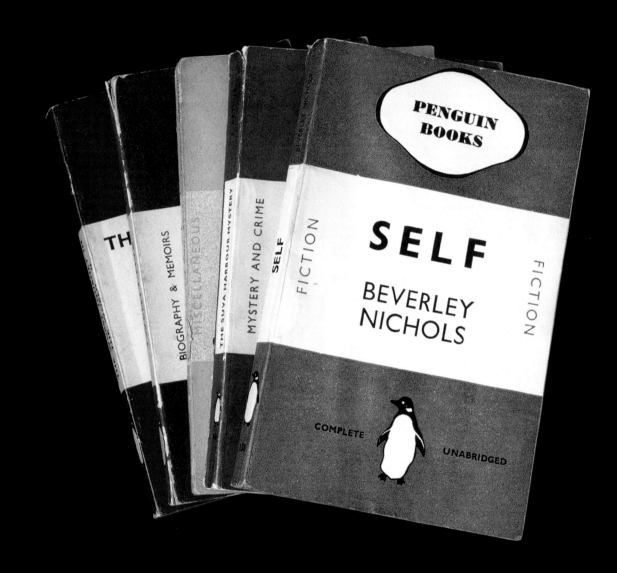

PENGUIN BOOKS

SELF

BEVERLEY
NICHOLS

FICTION

FICTION

COMPLETE   UNABRIDGED

MYSTERY AND CRIME

SELF

THE SUVA HARBOUR MYSTERY

MISCELLANEOUS

BIOGRAPHY & MEMOIRS

TH

Key Event **Penguin paperbacks are launched in the UK**

Browsing the station bookshop in Exeter having spent a weekend with Agatha Christie, Allen Lane (director of the Bodley Head press) found nothing but reprinted classics and pulp novels. He realized that there was a gap in the market for contemporary writing aimed at a wide audience; furthermore, he recognized that this market wanted books to be convenient and both easily accessible and readable. He therefore founded Penguin books to cater for this need, mass producing contemporary crime, biography, and fiction. The Penguin paperbacks had distinctive covers and were color-coded by subject (dark blue for biography, green for crime, orange for fiction). The public appetite was much as Lane thought, and the company sold one million books within ten months. In 1937 the Pelican imprint began to develop the list, particularly printing "educational" books of history, politics, or economics; in 1945 they began the Penguin Classics list. The paperbacks were light and small, making them easy to read, and printed very cheaply but with relatively high production values.

The introduction of these volumes revolutionized literary production and the book market in the UK. The books invited you to read them in unfamiliar spaces rather than in a chair, table, or study. They were sold in Woolworths, in corner shops, and on station platforms, as well as in traditional bookshops. In this way they attempted to change reading habits and enfranchise readerships. They marketed "quality" writing of all kinds in the way that most cheap print genre fiction had been presented – in effect making literary writing a mass-market commodity.

Jerome de Groot

Date 1935

Place UK

Why It's Key The publication of Penguin's cheap paperbacks in the UK made reading more convenient, affordable, and accessible.

Opposite A selection of Penguin paperbacks

1930-1939

259

Key Book
Untouchable

It is hard to imagine that the theorist behind the Indian Progressive Writers' Association had to endure the embarrassment of 19 rejections from various British publishing houses (at the time Anand was living in England, having obtained in 1928 a PhD in Philosophy from the University of London) before finally being able to publish *Untouchable* with Wishart Books. Yet not only had its acceptance to be mediated by the poet Oswell Blakeston, but as a condition for publication Wishart editor Edgell Rickword requested a Preface by E.M. Forster as a disclaimer to any potential accusation of "dirtiness" likely to be addressed to the novel by critics.

Untouchable was published a month before the World Conference of Intellectuals held in Paris in 1935. Its main subject, the humiliations and abusive remarks from higher Hindu castes suffered by outcaste protagonist Bakha during one day of his life, reflected the climate of widespread intellectual ferment against violence and oppression dominating this period. While in Europe intellectuals were fighting against Fascism, in India committed writers like Anand were opposing a system of caste divisions which separated the country internally creating, as Bakha feels in the novel, a "moral barrier" between human beings. Not surprisingly, the 1970 edition is dedicated to reformist writer K.S. Shelvankar and M.K. Gandhi (the latter also figures as a character within the story). *Untouchable* testifies to the vicissitudes unjustly endured by Bakha. Dressing like the Tommies in a nearby regiment, he hopes for a life devoid of discrimination and perpetual abuse….

Letizia Alterno

Date 1935

Author Mulk Raj Anand (1905–2004)

Nationality India

Why It's Key Written by the founding member of the Indian Progressive Writers' Association, a national intellectual movement that wielded considerable influence during India's freedom struggle, *Untouchable* is a modern classic denouncing for the first time the condition of untouchability suffered by outcastes in 1930s India.

Key Book
Swami and Friends

Swami and Friends was primarily meant as a novel for children but it went on to become popular with adult readers as well. On the surface, it explores the small world of the innocent, impulsive, and mischievous child protagonist Swaminathan (or Swami) and his band of friends – Somu, Mani, Sankar, Samuel, and the Europeanized Rajam – all studying at Albert Mission School.

But it can be read, and quite possibly was intended to be read, at several levels and from different perspectives. As children's literature, while exploring the world of a group of south Indian school children, complete with their little fears and anxieties, it universalizes their experience so that its young readers all over the world easily identify themselves with its characters and even adult readers find themselves mentally recreating the magical years of their childhood. As an anti-colonial novel it attempts subtle criticism of the British rule through such scenes as the nationalist demonstration that inspires Swami to break the windowpanes of the Head Master's room. As a commentary on the contemporary society it delves into the cultural confusion and social unrest which educated Indians suffered from during the British rule. Swami, for example, develops a divided self – he admires the western ways of his friend Rajam and loves the English game cricket, but hates the British model of education together with its cultural impositions, its hidden agenda of mass-producing clerks who might be of use in running the colonial administration, and above all the unkind teachers who administered it.

Rajeshwar Mittapalli

Date 1935

Author R.K. Narayan (1906–2001)

Nationality India

Why It's Key *Swami and Friends* launched R.K. Narayan as a novelist, and the subsequent novels secured his position as the most widely read Indian novelist in English. It also introduced the imaginary town Malgudi which served as the fictional locale of almost all Narayan's novels and short stories.

Key Event **Orwell's journey leads to the writing of *The Road to Wigan Pier***

The Road to Wigan Pier marked a turning point for Orwell in both style and subject matter. The book is split into two parts; Part 1 describes the social conditions he found on his journeys and Part 2 consists of Orwell's opinions of socialism. His powerful descriptions of the conditions under which people lived were well received but Part 2 was thought too controversial, given the strength of Orwell's comments. Victor Gollancz initially intended to publish Part 1 on its own, but after deliberation decided to publish both parts, with a critical introduction that commented on what followed. Orwell has been criticized for his portrayal of the working classes in that he resolutely ignored their attempts to improve their own lives and that he focused primarily on the working-class man, thereby diminishing the lives of working-class women. What is important about *The Road to Wigan Pier*, however, is Orwell's attempt at self-knowledge about the conditions of the working classes and his recognition of the social problems inherent in England at the time. In that respect Orwell's work differs considerably from Jack London's *The People of the Abyss* (1903) whose book covered similar ground but who saw himself as much more of a proletarian journeyman.

Bea Campbell's *Wigan Pier Revisited* (1984) takes up Orwell's journey in the 1980s and highlights many of same areas, but brings it up to date with emphasis on the lives of women. Orwell's work remains influential today, still widely studied and leading the way for similar works to be undertaken.

Pat Wheeler

Date 1936

Author George Orwell (1903–1950)

Nationality UK

Why It's Key In 1936 Orwell spent three months traveling around areas of mass unemployment in Yorkshire and Lancashire, most notably, Wigan, Sheffield, and Barnsley. *The Road to Wigan Pier* is the result of that journey and when it was published the following year by the Left Book Club it made a considerable impact in literary and political circles.

Key Author **Klaus Mann**
Mephisto

Klaus Mann was the talented author of intensely personal novels that explore the tensions between a life of bohemian decadence, to which he naturally inclined, and a commitment to political activism, to which he felt morally obliged. His turbulent life was shaped by circumstances beyond his control: by both the advantages and pressures associated with an extraordinary family – his father was the novelist Thomas Mann, his uncle the more consciously political novelist Heinrich Mann – and by the exile from Hitler's Germany into which the liberal, openly gay young writer was forced in 1933, the point at which he emerged as a tireless anti-fascist campaigner and publicist. In a life that was blighted by instability, depression, and drug addiction, Mann was never able quite to fulfil his potential as a novelist.

He is chiefly remembered for his passionate *roman à clef Mephisto* (1936), which was inspired by Heinrich Mann's influential exposé of the "subordinate" mentality of the German bourgeoisie, *The Subject* (*Der Untertan*, 1918). The novel is a thinly disguised, damning account of the career of the actor Gustav Gründgens, formerly Mann's friend (and brother-in-law), who stayed on and enjoyed a successful career in Nazi Germany, and, arguably, helped to legitimize Hitler. Other significant works by Mann include his epic, multi-layered portrayal of exile, *The Volcano* (*Der Vulkan*, 1939), and his moving memoir *The Turning Point* (*Der Wendepunkt*, 1942). From 1938 Mann was based in the United States, and he served in the U.S. Army in Europe in 1943–5. He died of an overdose of sleeping tablets in Cannes.

Jon Hughes

Date 1936 (publication)

Author Klaus Mann (1906–1949)

Nationality German (from 1937 a Czech citizen; from 1943 a U.S. citizen)

Why It's Key The talented but troubled son of the Nobel Prize-winning novelist Thomas Mann, Klaus Mann was both a significant novelist and a tireless anti-fascist campaigner.

Key Author **Lao She**
Rickshaw Boy (Luotuo Xiangzi)

SPOILER

In early twentieth-century China, most written material used classical Chinese, which only the educated elite of the country understood. With the rise of nationalism, particularly after the anti-imperialist, patriotic May Fourth Movement in 1919, cultural institutions were re-evaluated and vernacular Chinese became common.

May Fourth made possible the ensuing outpouring of authors such as Lao She (1899–1966) and Lu Xun. Though Lao She (whose real name is Shu Qingchun) wrote many novels and plays, he is best known for *Rickshaw Boy* (1936). The book traces the pitiful degradation and ruin of an industrious peasant who moves to 1920s Beijing, becomes a rickshaw puller, and works every day from dawn to night, until finally he dies in the snow.

The book stresses the futility of the individual's struggle against society, as Lao She said of the rickshaw workers: "It never occurred to them to stand together, each went his own way; each man's hopes and exertions obscured his vision." The story became popular even outside China, and was a bestseller in the United States in 1945 – though the ending was changed to a happy one.

Lao She's professional success was his own downfall, however. He toned his writing to the ideology of the Chinese Communist Party after 1949, and wrote plays with Marxist themes, such as *The Teahouse*. But along with other intellectuals he became a victim of the Red Guards during the Cultural Revolution and was paraded through the streets and publicly beaten. In 1966 he committed suicide by drowing himself in a lake in Beijing.

Rosie Blau

Date 1936 (publication)

Title also known as *Camel Xiangzi*

Nationality China

Why It's Key His popular novel *Rickshaw Boy* encapsulated the impossibility of bettering one's own life. Lao She suffered for his success during the Cultural Revolution, but his work found favor again after his death.

Key Author
Rudyard Kipling

Rudyard Kipling (1865–1936), the first English writer to win the Nobel Prize in Literature, was the most famous writer at the height of the British empire yet he was always a controversial figure. After a blissful early childhood in India Kipling was "boarded" in England from the age of five, and returned to India as a teenager to work as a reporter on a newspaper. The division between his "native" and "imperial" selves runs through his best work and gives his most thoughtful art its color.

The success of *Plain Tales from the Hills* (1888) and other stories of Indian life allowed Kipling to travel to London as a rising literary star where he was soon to distinguish himself also as a poet with his *Barrack-Room Ballads* (1892). These verses, rendered in the vernacular of common soldiers, led to his being fêted as the poet of imperialism, but many of his works (such as the story "The Man Who Would Be King" and the poem "Recessional") were not celebrations, but warnings of the hubris of empire. After Kipling the British Empire was no longer seen as a location of swashbuckling adventures or dutiful boredom that no serious writer would engage with, but now was a place of moral conflict, thoughtless cruelty and compromised ideals.

Kipling's *Jungle Book* (1894) made him an enduringly popular children's writer with Mowgli a dualistic character half-wolf, half-man (but rejected by both people and wolves) whose presentation led the way in the depiction of children of psychological complexity.
Jad Adams

Date 1936 (death)

Nationality UK

Other Key Works *Stalky & Co.* (1899), *Kim* (1901), *Just So Stories* (1902), *Puck of Pook's Hill* (1906)

Why It's Key With phrases like "east of Suez" and "the female of the species." Kipling added more expressions to common English speech than any writer excepting Shakespeare and the translators of the King James Bible.

Key Character **Scarlett O'Hara**
Gone with the Wind

When *Gone with the Wind* opens, 16-year-old Scarlett O'Hara, the spoiled daughter of a plantation slaveholder, is plotting how to win Ashley Wilkes, the man she thinks she loves. By novel's end, Scarlett has survived the Civil War, the burning of Atlanta, the near-destruction of Tara, the deaths of her mother, father, daughter, unborn child, and two of her husbands, and still doesn't have the right man. The heroine of the most popular romance in American history does not get her man; in fact, she doesn't get either of her men, pursuing Ashley through peace, war, and Reconstruction, only to realize when his saintly wife Melanie dies that she doesn't love him after all. Scarlett really loves Rhett Butler, her third husband, "scoundrel" and "scalawag," blockade-runner and self-made man, the black sheep with a heart of gold who mocks, manhandles and, ultimately, masters her. But Rhett refuses Scarlett her happy ending while delivering one of the most famous lines in American culture. When Scarlett asks him what she will do if he leaves her, he declares, "Frankly my dear, I don't give a damn," and walks out of the house and out of the story.

Scarlett can be an infuriating companion through the 12 years of epic conflict she endures: she is self-deceiving, pig-headed, frequently obtuse, amoral, a neglectful mother, and absolutely blind to the devoted love of Rhett Butler. But Scarlett has been beloved by generations of readers (particularly during the Depression, to whom she offered a model for survival) for her spirit, her determination, her fortitude, and her tenacity. She ends the novel as she began, plotting how to get the man she wants, "For tomorrow is another day!"
Sarah Churchwell

Date 1936

Author Margaret Mitchell (1900–49)

Nationality USA

Why It's Key Scarlett O'Hara instantly became the iconic Southern belle when she burst from the pages in 1936. With her trademark expressions, flashing green eyes, and obdurate determination, she epitomized the spirited and shrewd New Woman.

Opposite Vivien Leigh as Scarlett O'Hara in the film adaptation of *Gone*

Key Author **Munshi Premchand**
The Gift of a Cow

"In my opinion… literature has three aims – enrichment, entertainment and depiction." This is how Munshi Premchand (1880–1936) defined the objective of literature. He wanted literature to portray the truth, and only the truth, and be within the easy reach of common readers. He did not believe providence to cause human suffering. It is rather the exploitative forces – feudal lords, colonial rulers, moneylenders, and the priestly class – who preyed on the Indian peasants and other unprivileged people and rendered their life miserable.

Premchand's (1880–1936) novels and short stories deal with everyday heroes who regularly suffer exploitation but never sacrifice their dignity. His very first novel *The Service Home* (*Seva Sadan*, 1919) exposes the evils of the dowry system and institutionalized prostitution. Rangbhumi illustrates the terrible oppression perpetuated by the Indian rulers on the voiceless masses. *The Gift of a Cow* (*Godan*, 1936)

his last and most influential work, is an epic of rural India. Its long-suffering hero, the quintessential Indian farmer Hori, is an unequal match to the evil forces ranged against him. He literally "goes down" fighting the battle of life. Premchand's protagonists in other novels take on the tyrannical social order, offer the best resistance possible and, unlike Hori, often emerge victorious. That way they perhaps demonstrate their creator's undying optimism.

Being a people's writer Premchand wrote in a language they easily understood. He preferred to call it Hindustani. He was guided by the principle, "those who love the people also love the language of the people." It is no wonder then that even seven decades after his death his works continue to be read with keen interest.
Rajeshwar Mittapalli

Date 1936

Nationality India

Other Key Novels *The Abode of Love* (1921), *The Theatre* (1925), *Nirmala* (1926), *The Field of Action* (1932), *Embezzlement*, (1931)

Why It's Key Popularly credited with being the father of modern Hindi fiction, Premchand weaned Hindi fiction away from the treatment of romantic, magical, and religious themes, and employed it in the service of larger social causes.

Key Book
Nightwood

A lesbian novel, classic of "Sapphic modernism" that also sympathizes with heterosexual obsessive desire, *Nightwood* also constitutes a treatise on the shortcomings of Judeo-Christian morality, new-world sanctimony, and old-world decadence. Djuna Barnes spent more than six years writing *Nightwood*, during which time it was rejected by half a dozen major U.S. publishing houses and extensively revised at least three times before being championed by T.S. Eliot at Faber & Faber. Eliot's admiration for *Nightwood* derived from what he called its "great achievement of a style, the beauty of the phrasing, the brilliance of wit and characterization." The baroque flamboyance of its language and the rogues' gallery of misfits who wander helplessly in its chiaroscuro shadows guarantee this rather plotless short novel a continued place in many lists of great American novels of the twentieth century.

It tells the story of Barnes' tempestuous nine-year love affair with the American artist Thelma Wood on

Paris' Left Bank during the 1920s, dramatizing lost characters in search of refuge from themselves, seeking a remedy for immutable love and loss. Although dark, it is also luminous and penetrating, offering sardonic wit and aphoristic insight into the human condition, most of which is offered by the unforgettable Dr. Matthew Mighty-grain-o-sand Dante O'Connor, the transvestite abortionist raconteur who functions as the novel's Greek chorus and the characters' confessor; his monologues and speeches work as comic set-pieces, quite apart from their resonance with the novel's themes of betrayal, sin, exile, and wandering.
Sarah Churchwell

Date 1936

Author Djuna Barnes *(1892–1982)*

Nationality USA

Why It's Key This modernist masterpiece, sexual satire, and rhetorical tour de force was hailed by Dylan Thomas as "one of the three great prose books ever written by a woman" and by T.S. Eliot as having "a quality of horror and doom very nearly related to that of Elizabethan tragedy."

Opposite Djuna Barnes

Key Book
Minty Alley

C.L.R. James is less known as a creative writer than for seminal works of political theory, social commentary, history (such as his brilliant *The Black Jacobins: Toussaint L'Ouverture and the San Domingo Revolution*, 1938) and his cricket memoir *Beyond a Boundary*. Yet his one published novel *Minty Alley*, along with some earlier short stories, is undeniable proof of his talent for fiction.

Written in 1927 but not published for another nine years, the completed manuscript was in James' suitcase when he first arrived in Britain in 1932 (although, as he tantalizingly wrote in *Beyond a Boundary*: "Contrary to expected experience, the real magnum opus was to be my second novel"). Set in a working-class community of Port of Spain, Trinidad, the story is seen through the eyes of Haynes, an educated middle-class young bachelor, whose circumstances after the death of his over-protective mother lead him to take lodgings among the "ordinary" people in

Mrs. Rouse's boarding-house at number 2 Minty Alley. Initially, his servant Ella is a buffer between the pampered Haynes and the other residents until she becomes ill and goes to her own home for many months. Soon the privileged outsider finds himself inexorably drawn into the colorful lives and loves played out in *Minty Alley*, as both arbiter and participant. Key to the book's success is the wholly convincing depiction of Haynes, for which James undoubtedly drew on his own intellectual background – he had already read Thackeray's *Vanity Fair* several times by the age of nine.

Margaret Busby

Date 1936

Author C.L.R. James (1901–89)

Nationality Trinidad

Why It's Key A groundbreaking work by an intellectual giant of the twentieth century, this was the first novel to be published by a black Caribbean in the UK and is in the forefront of the tradition of writing about the "barrack-yard" that became increasingly popular in the Caribbean of the 1930s.

Key Event
The Spanish Civil War

Long considered "the last just cause," the Spanish Civil War was one of the most influential conflicts of the twentieth century in terms of the art and literature it inspired. Efforts to create and sustain a democratic republic in Spain after the fall of Alfonso XIII in April 1931 occupied many Spanish intellectuals and artists, from Miguel de Unamuno, to Ortega y Gasset, to Federico García Lorca. The latter embarked on a project to bring theater to the Spanish countryside as part of republican efforts to combat cultural ostracism and illiteracy.

As the most conservative sectors of the army tried to stage a coup in July 1936 against the democratically elected popular front – a leftist coalition of republicans, communists, and socialists – the people resisted and a long war ensued: its enduring marks are still visible in contemporary Spain.

Helped by Hitler and Mussolini, Francisco Franco famously declared a crusader's war on "intelligence"

and artists, teachers, and writers became only the most visible victims in every city and every town. If Picasso's *Guernica* (1937) depicted the horrors of German bombing over the Basque country years before they became a daily event in London and elsewhere, García Lorca's cold-blooded assassination in the summer of '36 soon became the symbol of the fascist attempt to erase the critical voice of culture. His last play, *The House of Bernarda Alba* (1936) investigated the tragic life of five daughters living under virtual house arrest by a mother whose defense of tradition and small town appearances sketched out the kind of backward morals upheld by local priests and fierce nationalists in their battle against equality and a tolerant version of modernity.

Pedro García-Caro

Date 1936–1939

Why It's Key As well as the generation of Spanish writers directly affected by the Civil War – including Hernández, Machado, and Lorca – many international writers lent support to the republican cause, including Orwell, Auden, Neruda, Hemingway, Paz, and Malraux. A recent popular novel by Javier Cercas, *Soldiers of Salamis* (2003) mockingly states that "Fascists won the war, but they lost the history of literature."

Opposite Spanish Civil War

Key Event *How to Win Friends and Influence People* becomes a bestseller

Dale Carnegie's evergreen and massively popular volume of tips for better "personal engineering" is a colossus in the canon of American self-improvement manuals, a genre that started with Benjamin Franklin's *Poor Richard's Almanack*. And given that it has so far spent eight decades in print, *Friends* must be doing something right, right? An early career in sales is perhaps perceptible in the vim with which Carnegie delivers his message: chapter titles promise to acquaint the reader with "How to Make People Like You Instantly," or "How to Spur People On to Success"; chapters seek to teach conversation, argumentation, and motivational skills through simple techniques like smiling or listening more carefully to others. The basic thesis here is that personal success depends on the way we make others feel and the book thus suggests ways to make them feel good. True to his own dictates, Carnegie writes in accessible, anecdotal prose and gleans authority through citations. He quotes, for example, Dr. Johnson on the hubris of over-judgementalism, Dewey on the desire to be important and Emerson's observation that "Every man I meet is my superior in some way. In that, I learn of him."

Friends derives much of its success of course from its Depression context: in the mid-30s, there was a trend among the unemployed and undereducated towards self-improvement through distance learning, of which Carnegie's how-to book (and its accompanying course) is a variety. Unlike conventional education, though, this text is not about "knowledge," he says, it is an "action book" turning life into management science.
Doug Haynes

Date 1936

Author Dale Carnegie (1888–1955)

Nationality USA

Why It's Key The author of a number of self-help manuals, Carnegie's flagship volume for his motivational course was initially only printed in a run of 5,000. Quickly, however, its popularity grew and the book remains in print today, the prototype for innumerable copyists.

Key Character **Horatio Hornblower** *The Happy Return*

Named for the character in *Hamlet* and for Nelson, Horatio Hornblower is a complex, solitary man. Plagued by anxieties and uncertain of his abilities, his ascent through the ranks is constantly prey to disappointment and accident (such as the near sinking of Nelson's coffin during the funeral procession up the Thames which Hornblower organizes). As is common in populist historical novels Hornblower has a series of fictional experiences on the edge of "significant" events – he foils an attempt to rescue Napoleon from St. Helena, meets Clausewitz, falls in love with Wellington's (fictional) sister. The series runs to eleven novels and various short stories, and through the sequence Hornblower rises to become Viscount and Admiral of the Fleet.

As a character Hornblower has proven uniquely attractive and well-loved, in contrast to many similar figures in historical series. This is as much down to his vulnerability as his heroism. The Hornblower novels are military historical romances; hugely successful, they demonstrated that the minutiae of military life was an important part of how audiences conceived of the past, and consequently they have had a great impact on how historical fiction is written. The setting of the novels – both the Napoleonic wars and the British navy – would influence subsequent novelists such as Bernard Cornwell and Patrick O'Brian. The Hornblower books also have a significant life in film and on television, too, and as such have dictated the way that Napoleonic history is imagined in the United States and the UK. Hornblower's brand of virtuous, noble loneliness was formative in writing the character of Captain Kirk in Star Trek.
Jerome de Groot

Date 1937

Author C.S. Forester (1899–1966)

Nationality UK

Why It's Key The Hornblower novels introduced a new, particularly military historical romance which was read by men and women.

Opposite Gregory Peck (right) as Horatio Hornblower

Key Book
"The Devil and Daniel Webster"

"The Devil and Daniel Webster" is a retelling of the classic German Faust tale, set in rural New Hampshire and centering round a farmer plagued by bad luck who sells his soul to the Devil in exchange for ten years' good fortune. In Steven Benét's retelling, the eminent real-life statesman, Daniel Webster, is persuaded by the farmer to argue his case with the Devil "when the mortgage falls due."

The story is rich with references to current and abiding concerns in American writing, cleverly weaving ironic commentary on themes such as patriotism and the treatment of native Americans into the dialogue between the eponymous characters. In one exchange, Webster denies the Devil's right to citizenship and therefore to the farmer's soul. The Devil, in reply, lists the many evils of America's brief history, saying "my name is older in this country than yours." Benét's tale refuses to let America off the hook and the Devil is ultimately held to be an intrinsic part of the nation's evolution. Webster, in the end, matches the Devil, but not before condemning slavery and racism as "evil" and then, curiously, saying no more on those particular subjects.

This has been taken as a condemnation of the real Daniel Webster for famously declaring his willingness to compromise on the matter of slavery in his famous speech of 1850. While "The Devil and Daniel Webster" at first seems a whimsical fantasy, it soon reveals itself to be both an acknowledgement of "necessary" evils and an affirmation of "real" American values. In Benét's telling, American folk are just too damn independent to be bothered much by Hell.

Christian Kerr

Date 1937

Author Steven Vincent Benét (1898–1943)

Nationality USA

Why It's Key Steven Vincent Benét was an American writer of poems, novels and short stories. He won the Pulitzer Prize in 1929 for his Civil War poem, "John Brown's Body," for which he is best remembered along with his short stories, "By the Waters of Babylon", and "The Devil and Daniel Webster."

Key Character **Joey Kowalski**
Ferdydurke

Joey Kowalski provides us with a thinly disguised portrait of the author as a young man. In the opening pages, we are even told that he has written an unsuccessful book bearing the very same title as Gombrowicz's 1933 debut. Although he is clearly the (anti-) hero and first person narrator, one is reluctant to describe Kowalski as the protagonist because he is constantly acted upon. In the most famous passage, this amorphous 30-year-old is visited by an eminent old professor who treats him like a kid before marching him off to school where – curiouser and curiouser – he fits in as naturally as a pupil half his age. *Ferdydurke* (1937) could be defined as a deformation, rather than a formation, novel.

If Kowalski embodies the notion (later popularized by Sartre) that identity is in the eye of the beholder, his own sense of immaturity reflects Poland's cultural inferiority complex which itself symbolizes the growing infantilism of society. Gombrowicz's first novel is not only an existentialist masterpiece, it also chronicles the emergence of the "new Hedonism" Lord Henry had called for in Oscar Wilde's *The Picture of Dorian Gray* as well as the shifting human relations Virginia Woolf had observed in the early years of the twentieth century. Outwardly, we strive for completion, perfection, and maturity; inwardly, we crave incompletion, imperfection, and immaturity. The natural progression from immaturity to maturity (and death) is paralleled by a corresponding covert regression from maturity to immaturity. Mankind is suspended between divinity and puerility, torn between transcendence and pubescence. Through Joey Kowalski – as well as the schoolgirl and the farmhand – Gombrowicz was able to diagnose this tantalizing tryst with trivia which characterizes the modern world.

Andrew Gallix

Date 1937

Author Witold Gombrowicz (1904–69)

Nationality Poland

Why It's Key Witold Gombrowicz's most famous character embodies the prescient idea that modernity is immaturity.

Key Book
The Blind Owl

The opium-drenched evocative quality of the writing of the seemingly landmark Persian novel *The Blind Owl* has seen it become not only a cult/countercultural classic but a serious contribution to the region's literature in the twentieth century. The slender volume, actually penned outside the region in Europe, represents both a serious commentary on daily life under the Shah and the social relations in Iranian society. Though the prose is largely solipsistic, where *The Blind Owl* transcends obvious countercultural repute is through the sheer force the author devotes to analyzing the hypnotic sway women have over every man present in the novel; the devotion to physical characteristics is magisterial.

Befitting the positively decadent subject matter and the attitudes of the era, it was printed in India and forbidden on sale in Iran, though Hedayat's death later saw it re-emerge. As if to testify to the fact that novels with troubled births unfortunately often endure similarly troubled lives, the book was re-banned by the Iranian regime in 2005, in a sweeping act of Islamist totalitarianism. A more obvious reason could be found in the book's "decadent" drug-induced state, which would mark it out for the censor's attention, were it not also for the Buddhist and Hinduist commentary. Hadayat, as someone who moved in the resolutely secular leftish intellectual circles of post-war Paris, would probably find some wry irony in the offence taken to his commentary. As with Azar Nafisi's memoir *Reading Lolita in Tehran* (2003), the book has become a marker for the struggle against literary repression.

Andrew Stevens

Date 1937

Author Sadegh Hedayat (1903–51)

Nationality Iran

Why It's Key One of the most important modern works of literature in the Persian language, *The Blind Owl* could not be sold in Iran at the time of its publication due to its graphic sexual and drug-themed content. It has also been banned in Tehran in 2005.

Key Character **Lennie Small**
Of Mice and Men

Lennie Small suffers from some kind of mental deficiency that is never specified, but we are told that he hears voices in his head. His major problem is that he doesn't know his own strength, and he is fated to kill or damage anything soft or vulnerable that he touches. He and his friend George Milton are itinerant farm workers who travel through Depression-era California, going from place to place and casual job to job with the dream of saving up enough money to buy a farm where they could settle down. George is able to look out for Lennie and keep him out of trouble most of the time while benefiting from his friend's capacity for sheer hard work.

The novel addresses issues arising from the plight of the rural poor in contemporary America, concerns that Steinbeck was to go on to develop further in *The Grapes of Wrath* (1939), which won a Pulitzer Prize. Lennie and George have no real home and little prospect of a permanent job. They are hired for busy times only, such as harvests, and are "let go" when no longer needed. Their enforcedly transient lifestyle allows them no opportunity to put down roots or develop relationships outside their own powerful association of mutual need. Their dream of owning a place of their own was never likely to be realized. It goes awry, just as the poet Robert Burns observed in his often-quoted line about "the best-laid plans of mice and men."

Michael Munro

Date 1937

Author John Steinbeck (1902–68)

Nationality USA

Why It's Key Lennie Small's innocence and lack of understanding allied to great physical strength is the root of the tragedy that informs *Mice*. His relationship with George Milton, small but bright, is almost archetypal in its pairing, in two separate individuals, of physical power with the intelligence needed to control it.

Key Character **Janie Crawford**
Their Eyes Were Watching God

*I*n *Their Eyes Were Watching God*, Hurston used her personal experience of a turbulent love affair with a younger man, but transformed the details, retaining its core emotional truth. The novel commences when Janie Crawford returns to Eatonville, Florida, having shot her third husband in self-defence. It is narrated as if Janie were telling the story of her life to her neighbor and best female friend, Phoeby. Critics have argued that Janie only achieves full selfhood and self-knowledge by telling her story and reflecting on it, since before this telling, she is often silenced by the men in her life, especially her second husband Jody Starks.

Janie is the mixed race grandchild of a female slave and a slave owner. She describes how her grandmother warned her that black women are "the mules of the world," but her story is one of holding on to her desire to be treated as an equal with the men of her community, despite many setbacks. When her second husband dies, she finally gets her chance with the much younger drifter, "Teacake." They become migrant workers on the "Muck," but she is happy – until they are caught in a flood and Teacake is bitten by a rabid dog. Janie shoots Teacake in self-defence, and finds herself in a hostile courtroom pleading for her life. Her eloquence convinces a white jury that she had to kill the "mad dog" in the husband that she adored, and she is set free.

The novel articulates compellingly both female erotic desire and an ordinary woman's aspiration for personal fulfilment and independence. Only two generations after slavery, the character of Janie depicts how black women craved personal autonomy, not just legal freedom.
Helen May Dennis

Date 1937

Author Zora Neale Hurston (1891–1960)

Nationality USA

Why It's Key Many of her male contemporaries in the Harlem Renaissance criticized her for not writing urban, social documentary realism. Zora Neale Hurston died in penury and was buried in an unmarked grave in Fort Pierce, Florida. Novelist Alice Walker found and marked the grave in 1973, sparking a Hurston Renaissance.

Key Book *A Dark Night's Passing (Anya Koro)*

A *Dark Night's Passing* offers the intense, if not fraught inner life of Tokito Kensaku, whom Shiga acknowledged to be a self-portrait. Kensaku, traumatized at discovering the family secret that he is the offspring of his mother's adultery with his paternal grandfather, later learns of the similarly adulterous behavior of his wife Naoko with her cousin, prompting him to retreat in devastation and self-abandonment to the isolated Daisen mountain in the remote Tottori prefecture. Alone with nature, Kensaku welcomes powerful, sublime emotions, which deliver him from life's defeats and agonies. However, the work concludes ambiguously, with its hero suspended between life and death, his fate unclear.

As with many of Shiga's short stories, this novel revolves around the intimate familial, romantic, or erotic experiences endured by the narrator, with reference to only a small circle of characters and their concerns. In its close, restrained description of private events, *A Dark Night's Passing* resists being easily placed in a particular cultural or historical moment, but, alternatively, presents a condensed but universal vision of acute human suffering. Shiga spent over a quarter-century writing his masterpiece, which was originally started in 1912 as a first-person semi-autobiographical novella entitled "Tokito Kensaku," and was finally completed as a third-person two-part novel in 1937, retaining the first-person voice in the introductory chapter, where Kensaku recounts his childhood. In its intermingling of fictional possibility with lived experience, *A Dark Night's Passing* is related to the major form of Japanese fiction known as the I-novel (*watakushi-shosetsu*).
David Taylor and Tomonao Yoshida

Date 1937

Author Naoya Shiga (1883–1971)

Nationality Japan

Why It's Key On the basis of this novel and a highly respected group of stories, Shiga has maintained his status as one of the most influential of Japanese authors. *A Dark Night's Passing*, much admired by contemporaries such as Hideo Kobayashi, is still considered one of the greatest works of twentieth-century Japanese literature.

Key Character **Bilbo Baggins**
The Hobbit

Tired to his prominent eartips of marking exam papers, Professor J.R.R. Tolkien was relieved to see that one of his examinees had had the humility, or consideration, to leave his entire answer paper blank. Contemplating the white sheet before him, Tolkien picked up his marking pen and wrote, "In a hole in the ground lived a hobbit." At the time he had no idea why.

But what are hobbits? Hobbits are the creatures of folklore forgotten by folklorists, and it's easy to see why. They are plump and little (rarely more than three foot tall) and live in holes in the ground; they don't do magic, they can't stand adventures, they like grub, booze, their family trees, books on things they already know about, pipe-smoking, and not to be bossed about. They have no killer instinct, and love giving presents. The hobbit, in short, represents a certain kind of Edwardian Englishman.

Bilbo Baggins, the hero of *The Hobbit*, is in most respects a typical hobbit, but there's something wilder in him which longs to be let out. Gandalf the wizard spots this trait in him and decides to draw it out by co-opting poor Bilbo in a quest to recover a hoard of dwarvish treasure from a dragon. Flustered over his missing handkerchiefs, hating the long gaps between meals, and feeling endlessly small and unimportant, Bilbo nonetheless discovers in himself unsuspected reserves of courage and selflessness.

The hobbit retains his hold on the imagination because, more than any other figure from folklore, he represents the child in all of us which must become an adult.

Murrough O'Brien

Date 1937

Author J.R.R. Tolkien (1892–1973)

Nationality UK

Why It's Key In Bilbo Baggins, Tolkien gave hope and humor to children of all ages from eight to eighty. A new kind of folk hero, unenterprising, stolid and set in his ways, Bilbo appeals to anyone who cannot take courage for granted.

Key Passage
Nausea

"The Nausea… is no longer an illness or a passing fit: it is me."

Nausea was Jean-Paul Sartre's first novel and arguably his best work of fiction. The protagonist Antoine Roquentin, a true anti-hero, is supposed to be writing a biography of the Marquis de Rollebon but is finding it harder and harder to write. Increasingly distracted by spells of dizzy nausea, he walks the streets of Bouville and kills time in its cafes. We follow his frank diary entries, as uncertain as their author about the cause of his malaise, until, about three-quarters through the book, we get to a section simply titled "Six o'clock in the evening": "The Nausea hasn't left me and I don't believe it will leave me for quite a while;… it is no longer an illness or a passing fit: it is me." Roquentin describes how he was sitting in a public square and began to stare at a tree root, analysing its appearance so closely that he fell into a kind of horrified trance. "Existence had suddenly unveiled itself… it was the very stuff of things, that root was steeped in existence. Or rather the root, the park gates,… all that had vanished. … This veneer had melted, leaving soft monstrous masses, in disorder – naked, with a frightening, obscene nakedness." Struggling to describe his experience, Roquentin draws together the fundamental vocabulary of existentialism: his abysmal sense of superfluity, the essential contingency of everything; he writes, "the word Absurdity is now born beneath my pen" – and so was born one of the most influential philosophical movements to come from twentieth-century France.

Sophie Lewis

Date 1938

Author Jean-Paul Sartre (1905–80)

Nationality France

Why It's Key If *Nausea* established Sartre as the high priest of the new philosophy of existentialism, then this is his credo. Here he gives words and rationale to the powerful sense of disaffection felt by thinkers around him, faced with the oppressive materiality of the world.

Key Author **Raja Rao**
Kanthapura

Raja Rao's (born 1908) death in July 2006 certainly did not go unnoticed, but it took some time for the general public to acknowledge him as one of the most prominent writers of our century, whose writing represents India as a powerful spiritual force uniting East and West. His novels are imbued with profound philosophical-religious significances which his Brahmin characters exploit to investigate themes like friendship, love, and cultural diversity. Indian by origin and sensibility, Rao lived most of his life outside India, between France and the United States. India however was always at the core of his writing and thought, apart from having shaped his intellectual spirit.

Entering the literary world (particularly the French milieu) as he put it, a "South Indian Brahmin, nineteen, spoon-fed on English, with just enough Sanskrit to know I knew so little, with an indiscrete education in Kannada, my mother tongue," the language problem was to him the first challenging issue to confront as an Indian author writing in English. His theorization of the necessity for Indian writers to express their emotional and intellectual world in a personally elaborated foreign language was published as the Foreword accompanying his first novel *Kanthapura*, today a classic text in Indian education curricula, portraying a village account of Gandhian anti-British movements preceding Indian independence. Exhorting Indian writers not "to write like the English" nor "only as Indians," Rao set up the premises for a challenge every future Indian author would have to face when writing in English: the dilemma of conveying "in a language that is not one's own the spirit that is one's own."

Letizia Alterno

Date 1938 (publication)

Nationality India

Other Key Works *The Serpent and the Rope* (1960), *The Cat and Shakespeare* (1965), *The Great Indian Way: A Life of Mahatma Gandhi* (1998)

Why It's Key A well-known figure in the politics of 1930s India, Rao was a philosopher and novelist exploring mysticism and Hinduism, and also a leader in the linguistic appropriation of English within the Indian context.

Key Book
In Dreams Begin Responsibilities

Who now has heard of poor Delmore Schwartz? The son of Jewish immigrants, he was born in Brooklyn in 1913 and, for a brief time, when he was in his twenties, he was perhaps the most celebrated young writer in America. Among his friends was Saul Bellow, who would in a career of long and hardened achievement have the success for which Schwartz always longed, even as he failed to fulfil his early promise as a poet and short story writer. Schwartz yearned for greatness, to be "the Lindbergh, Moses, Siegfried, Odysseus of America." But he ended up broken, twice divorced, drunken, and alone. He died largely forgotten in a midtown Manhattan hotel in 1966.

Bellow wrote about their friendship in his novel *Humboldt's Gift* (1975), which is narrated, in the high style, by a writer called Charlie Citrine. As a young man Citrine travels by bus from the Mid-West to New York to seek out Von Humbolt Fleischer, his hero, and author of the acclaimed *The Harlequin Ballads*. They become friends, but soon their fortunes are reversed: as Citrine excels, Humboldt withers, becoming increasingly mired in depression and self-pity, as did Schwartz himself.

Bellow once saw the ageing Schwartz emerge dishevelled and probably drunk from his New York apartment but ducked behind a car to avoid him. In the novel, this encounter is reimagined with considerable pathos as Humboldt, the Schwartz figure, is portrayed stumbling towards death. "He was gray stout sick dusty, he had bought a pretzel stick and was eating it. His lunch. Concealed by a parked car, I watched. I didn't approach him, I felt it was impossible."

Jason Cowley

Date 1937

Author Delmore Schwartz

Nationality USA

Why It's Key *Dreams*, Schwartz's masterpiece was published when he was 25. In the title story, a young man watching a film of his parents' courtship is moved to shout at the screen, "Don't do it. It's not too late to change your minds, both of you. Nothing good will come of it. Only remorse, hatred, scandal and two children whose characters are monstrous!"

Key Book
U.S.A.

One might fear hubris in an author calling his work after a country as huge, varied, and complex as the United States. But of all the twentieth-century writers who included the name in their titles, Dos Passos is the one most thoroughly to have conjured up an expressionistic, kaleidoscopic vision of an entire nation in the first thirty years of the century.

The three books which make up *U.S.A.* have few characters in common, but the fragmented structure continues throughout. Four different styles of writing intermingle in an expressionistic montage. "Newsreel" sections introduce headlines and snippets from actual newspapers and magazines. Sections titled in italics give partial biographies of historical American figures. Other sections consist of more conventional narration about fictional characters, and the "Camera Eye" shows the thoughts and experiences of a subjective character, assumed to be the author in autobiographical mode.

Dos Passos studied art, and developed his writing style in response to Cubism and Imagism. His left-wing politics made him keen to give an objective, truthful view of an increasingly capitalist society, where the gap between very rich and very poor was often ignored, and which eventually imploded in the crash of 1929. In a style possibly influenced by early cinema, the book delivers a huge slice of life, or lives, at the beginning of the last century. While the novel challenges the reader's assumptions about storytelling and characterization, it is never difficult to become involved in the different strands of the narrative. Its portraits of the modern city, sprawling, vibrant, and dirty are unbeatable.

Felicity Skelton

Date 1938 (published as *U.S.A.*) Previously published as three novels: *The 42nd Parallel* (1930), *1919* (1932), and T*he Big Money* (1936)

Author John Dos Passos (1896–1970)

Nationality USA

Why It's Key To a modern reader, this massive book, over a thousand pages long, reads like the most modern experimental fiction. At first publication, it was the political slant which particularly captured the public attention.

275

Key Book *Acquainted with Grief* (*La cognizione del dolore*)

Maradagal, 1934. An imaginary South American setting, with a villa and a double-widow. The place reeks of mourning. But there is the world out there, in all its promiscuous continuity. And in that, there may be chance. The lost one, the loved one, not so much the husband, long dead, but the younger son lost in the recent (imaginary, yet not so imaginary) war, may in fact return, if only in image.

But what of the other son, the survivor? Over those same circumstances his *Acquaintance with Grief* goes through rejection, dejection, vilification, rage, and disease.

The plot doesn't come to much in this book. A villa as symbol of a world truly upside down. Two major episodes, a medical visit and a return home, amounting to one intensely unreasoning yet furiously sound-minded dialogue with authority, parental, and cultural. It couldn't feel closer to home. Actually, it is home in the most disguised autobiographical sense.

And it is for this reason – because there can be no real distance from home and its fictions – that the writing can get truly red-hot here, in a series of phenomenal outbursts of philosophical bad temper.

Yet this prose, daring as it does to risk the extremes of abstraction out of the enraging banalities of life, is also magnificently embodied, corporeally engaged in a merciless account of the universal absurdity. As such, it marks a huge creative release and the final coming together of Gadda's many experiments with the novel form, thus preparing the way for his further masterworks of existential polemic, *L'Adalgisa* (1944) and *That Awful Mess on via Merulana* (1957).

Federica Pedriali

Date 1938–1941 (Originally published in part in *Letteratura*)

Author Carlo Emilio Gadda (1893–1973)

Nationality Italy

Why It's Key Unavoidable, unrepeatable model of contemporary anti-narrative fiction.

Key Character
Superman

Any true comic book fan will tell you that Superman is undoubtedly the archetypal superhero. Initially created as a villain by childhood friends Jerry Siegel and Joe Shuster in 1932, Superman (or Kal-El, to give him his birth name) did not appear in recognizable form until *Action Comics* Number One in 1938.

Born on the planet Krypton, which faced imminent destruction, Kal-El was placed into a small spacecraft which transported him safely to Earth, where he was adopted by a loving couple and given a new name: Clark Kent. Not long after this, he began to demonstrate a range of superpowers including almost limitless strength, x-ray vision and the ability to fly, his only weakness being a potentially fatal allergy to the mineral Kryptonite, derived from the remains of his homeworld.

The effect on popular culture of Siegel and Shuster's creation cannot be overestimated. Superman's adventures kick-started the entire superhero comic book genre, paving the way for later characters such as Batman, Spider-Man, and the X-Men.

Clothed in one of the most recognizable costumes of the twentieth century, Superman embodies all that we have come to expect from the superhero narrative: incredible powers which are tirelessly used in the fight against evil, the "average guy" alter-ego, an epic origin story and of course, the requisite arch nemesis, represented here by Lex Luthor. Superman has now been protecting the city of Metropolis, and indeed the entire world, for nearly 70 years. He was killed (and later resurrected) in 1992, and finally married his long-term girlfriend Lois Lane in 1996. His popularity has not diminished: Superman has indeed proven to be indestructible, achieving truly iconic status.
Tim Stafford

Date 1938

Authors Jerry Siegel (1914–1996, USA), Joe Shuster (1914–1992, Canada)

Why It's Key Superman has inspired radio serials, television series, and several movies. The myth continues to be reinvented for each new generation, most recently in Bryan Singer's 2006 film *Superman Returns*, which deals with the hero returning to Earth to find that Lois has a son and a new boyfriend.

Opposite *Superman* comic

Key Author
Pearl S. Buck

Acting as an ambassador of literary progression, Pearl S. Buck (1892–1973) was awarded the Pulitzer Prize for Literature in 1932 for her novel, *The Good Earth* (1931). Buck was born to missionary parents and was raised in provincial China, speaking Chinese, and playing with local children. Evacuated in 1900 during the Boxer Uprising, this existence was very rare in her time, and she would have been one of the few Caucasians to have lived in China, let alone to achieve mastery over the Chinese language. Throughout her life, Buck strove to achieve cross-cultural understanding, illuminating what many perceived to be both foreign, and cloistered to the outside world.

Buck writes with keen insight into the oddities of Chinese traditions and social decorum. In *The Good Earth*, she pits her tale of a newly-wed peasant farmer and his growing family against the backdrop of rural China, bringing to life an enigmatic social commentary through the deceptive simplicity of a bucolic existence. *The Good Earth* is emblematic of Buck's understanding of the local Chinese person's nationalistic attachment to their land and livelihood, one that later spawned the Communist uprising.

Thoughtfully considering the role of women in her experience of China, foot binding is a recurrent theme in her *House of Earth* trilogy (*The Good Earth*; *Sons*; *A House Divided*). Many of her female protagonists are strong, capable women, which is in itself a feminist statement against a misogynist culture. Buck's novels continue to echo the contemporary changes in China's recent history with regard to traditional rites, and form one of the first inquiries into the role of women in Chinese culture.
Alex Hamlyn

Date 1938 (Nobel Prize awarded)

Nationality USA

Other Key Works *East Wind, West Wind* (1930), *The First Wife and Other Stories* (1933), *All Men are Brothers* (a translation of the Chinese novel *Shui Hu Chuan*, 1933), *The Mother* (1934), *The Time Is Now* (1967)

Why It's Key Buck was a pioneer in promoting and documenting an understanding of Chinese culture in the West.

Key Event **Hermann Broch begins work on *The Death of Virgil* under Nazi arrest**

Arrested after the Nazi takeover of Austria in the Anschluss of 1938, and facing the imminent possibility of death, Hermann Broch worked on expanding a short story he had written for radio which recreated the last hours of the Roman poet Virgil. Thanks to international protests, led by fellow writers such as Joyce and Edwin Muir, he was soon released. During a short stay in Britain, and later in the United States, he developed the original dozen or so pages into the nearly 500 of *The Death of Virgil* (*Der Tod des Vergil*), which was published in 1945. Into it he poured the insights gained at the threshold of his own threatened death, and also his speculations on the nature and importance of literature, as Virgil debates whether to have the manuscript of his greatest work, *The Aeneid*, destroyed.

The palpably elevated intentions of the work haven't stopped people being extraordinarily rude about it. It has been widely dismissed as "unreadable,"

and even Aldous Huxley, no dumber-down, suggested to Broch that the novel asked too much of the reader. The earlier trilogy *The Sleepwalkers* (*Die Schlafwandler*, 1931–2) is considerably more reader-friendly, and tends to get a much better press.

Broch himself regarded the book more as a poem than a novel, and the reader who hopes to reach the farther shore must surrender to the rhythms and repetitions of its incantatory prose. These have been faithfully rendered in Jean Untermeyer's English translation, a four-year labor of love she undertook in close collaboration with the author.
Cathy Benson

Date 1938

Author Hermann Broch (1886–1951)

Nationality Austria

Why It's Key Last of the great European modernists, Broch confronted the horrors and cultural disintegration of the twentieth century fortified with an intimate knowledge of the great works of European high culture. He erected *The Death of Virgil* like a monument in rejection of the reality of growing Nazi power.

1930-1939

279

Key Character **Pinkie** *Brighton Rock*

Pinkie has inherited a business too big for him. His former boss has been murdered by a rival gangland leader – an Italian lounge lizard, no less, which makes it worse. His associates, all genial duffers, are rapidly revealing themselves to be less than equal to the task of holding his squalid little empire together. It is Brighton in the 1930s, a world in which lower-middle class gentility is pockmarked by unacknowledged gangland culture. The murder of a frightened renegade sets Ida, ruthlessly benevolent, on Pinkie's tail.

Many of Greene's books are informed by his adopted Catholicism, and they tend to stress the redemptive power of faith. But there is no redemption in, or for, Pinkie, the boy-man anti-hero of *Brighton Rock*: all hellfire has done for him is to bake his mind so hard as to leave no pores open for the access of human feeling. He nods to the notion of Heaven, but he can't bow to it: for him it's an abstraction. Hell is all he knows, all he believes in, and all he can offer the world.

This is what his poor, deluded girl bride and fellow believer acknowledges even in her love for him.

Greene was intrigued by the paradox that while faith can be the most saving force in the world, piety – or residual religion – often proves the most destructive. In the savage figure of Pinkie, driven to his doom by the very need to cover his tracks, Greene gives us a startling and immortal vision of darkest sin at work in sunniest suburbia.
Murrough O'Brien

Date 1938

Author Graham Greene (1904–91)

Nationality UK

Why It's Key *Brighton Rock* reminded readers that youth and innocence are not so much chalk and cheese as apple and serpent. Its bleak ending was deemed too upsetting by the makers of the film version, which gave Richard Attenborough his first great role.

Opposite Richard Attenborough as Pinkie in the stage adaptation of *Brighton Rock*

Key Passage
Rebecca

"Last night I dreamt I went to Manderley again."

So begins *Rebecca*, the 1938 best-selling classic novel by Daphne du Maurier. The speaker is the narrator of the book, who is never named. We know her only as the second Mrs de Winter, a young girl who marries a handsome, older widower and goes to live at his beautiful, gothic manor house on the Cornish coast.

The Girl – for that is how she is usually referred to by literary commentators – is dreaming of Manderley as it was when she first arrived as a young bride. As the story unfolds we discover that the house has since been burnt to the ground and that Mr and Mrs de Winter now live far away.

As this summary suggests, *Rebecca* bears startling similarities to *Jane Eyre*, published 90 years earlier. Indeed, the book can be read as a conscious re-working of Charlotte Bronte's classic novel. De Winter's dead first wife – Rebecca – is the brooding sexual presence which haunts the book, making the Girl feel gauche and virginal by comparison. Mrs Danvers is the sinister housekeeper who plays on the young woman's insecurities by constantly reminding her that Rebecca – whom she clearly adored – was a far more fitting mistress of a Manderley.

In the course of the book the house itself becomes as powerful as any character in the book. It was based on Menabilly, the beloved Cornish home where du Maurier spent much of her adult life. Obliged to follow her soldier husband to a posting to Egypt in 1937, du Maurier wrote her most famous novel as a love song to the Cornish idyll that she had left behind.
Kathryn Hughes

Date 1938

Author Daphne du Maurier (1907–89)

Nationality UK

Why It's Key In 1940 *Rebecca* was made into a film by Alfred Hitchcock, one of several du Maurier novels which he brought to the screen. The stand-out performance is by Judith Anderson who produces an almost demonic version of Mrs. Danvers. The film won Hitchcock his only Best Picture Oscar.

Opposite Fontaine and Anderson (right) in *Rebecca*

Key Passage
Finnegans Wake

"Riverrun, past Eve and Adam's, from swerve of shore to bend of bay brings us by a commodius vicus of recirculation back to Howth Castle and Environs."

The first sentence of James Joyce's final work *Finnegans Wake* also completes the last sentence of the book: "A way a lone a last a loved a long the." This is the first circular work of literature. It echoes the natural life cycle of a river as it is dispersed into the ocean only to be sucked up into the clouds (recirculated), falling as rain and becoming a river again. Joyce was strongly influenced by the cycles of history and world events described by eighteenth-century Italian philosopher, Giambattista Vico. *Finnegans Wake* reinvents English, incorporating puns on names, places and events from innumerable languages. The book is, however, firmly located in Ireland: "Eve and Adam's," for example, inverts the name of a pub just outside Dublin, as well as the mythical first couple in the Old Testament Book of Genesis.

There is no single plot in *Finnegans Wake*, just allusions to nearly every plot you can think of. The title is taken from a Dublin street ballad which tells of a builder who apparently falls from a ladder to his death. At his wake someone spills whiskey on his head, reviving him. Some readers see the book as Finnegan's dream ("riverrun" may be his revery), others see it as a revolutionary call to his Irish ancestors to wake up from the sleep of history.
Matthew Creas

Date 1939

Author James Joyce (1882–1941)

Nationality Ireland

Why It's Key While many have expressed admiration for the ingenious punning language of *Finnegans Wake* it remains one of the least read best-known books of the twentieth century. It became a favourite text for the postmodern theories of deconstruction proposed by Jacques Derrida, who wrote an essay based on only two words of the text.

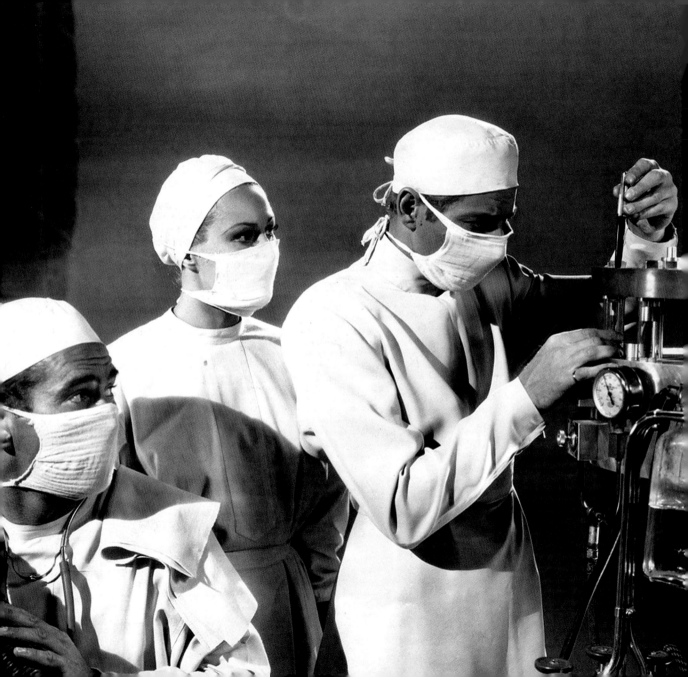

Key Author **Henry Green**
Party Going

The author of nine novels and one memoir, all produced between 1926 and 1952, Henry Green is credited with creating a style of writing that fused experimental techniques with basic realism. Despite the everyday setting of his novels, Green employed an energetic, idiosyncratic use of language and dialogue in order to emulate the speech patterns he heard around him. This distinctive quality is evident in Green's second novel *Living* (1929), which drew on his own experiences working in his father's engineering works for its depiction of life on the factory floor. With its colloquial language, removal of punctuation and verbs, and the absence of the definitive article, the novel attempts to vividly record the nuances of working-class dialogue.

The outbreak of war in 1939 initiated what would prove to be Green's most productive and creative period, despite his initial fears that there would not be enough time to write "before one is killed." His most admired novels *Party Going* (1939), *Caught* (1943), *Loving* (1945), and *Back* (1946) are all infused with the atmosphere of war, and demonstrate a broadening of his stylistic devices. Green's wartime work in the Auxiliary Fire Service also provided him with new social experiences, which are fictionalized most clearly in the portrayal of the fire station culture and relationships of *Caught*. In his final novels, *Nothing* (1950) and *Doting* (1952), Green moved towards an increasingly abstract style of writing, depending solely on dialogue to communicate both the novels' relationships and plots.

Laura Coffey

Date 1939

Author Henry Green (1905–1973)

Nationality UK

Why It's Key Green was a highly original artist who was celebrated in mid twentieth-century British literary culture for his unique prose style, influenced by modernism. Green's writing ended abruptly in 1952. After completing his last novel he claimed: "I find it so exhausting now that I simply can't do it anymore."

Key Character **Walter Mitty**
"The Secret Life of Walter Mitty"

Walter Mitty's secret life may only last about 2,500 words, but its influence has endured for some 28,500 days (and counting). In 2003, for example, Thurber's most famous creation hit the headlines after being embroiled in the tragic death of Dr. David Kelly: the weapons expert was dismissed as a "Walter Mitty" figure by spin doctor Tom Kelly at the height of the Hutton enquiry.

This year, cold on the heels of Danny Kaye's 1947 "musical," come reports of a new film adaptation, planned for 2009. James Thurber would be pleased, not least because he was "horror and struck" at Kaye's song-and-dance portrayal which popularised Mitty, but destroyed the delicate and poignant balance of the comedy. Stoic and distinctly middle-aged, Thurber's Walter Mitty withdraws into daydreams, nostalgically redolent of boy's own adventure stories, to escape the tedium of his existence, his nagging wife, and the relentless march of time: Mitty may look like an aging husband under the thumb, but actually he's nonchalantly facing a firing squad, as in the famous final image: "Walter Mitty, the Undefeated, inscrutable to the last."

This is the ridiculous and genial character who captivated readers in 1939 – male ones above all: 20 years after publication, Thurber recalled receiving letters from six different men ("including a Des Moines dentist") all asking "how I had got to know them so well." This ability to dissect the inner lives of everymen everywhere suggests Thurber as a forerunner of chroniclers of masculine experience like Woody Allen and Nick Hornby. Indeed, wherever men soothe the pain and tedium of their lives with dreams and fantasies, Walter Mitty will survive and prosper.

James Kidd

Date 1939 (first published in *The New Yorker*).

Author James Thurber (1894–1961)

Nationality USA

Why It's Key Mitty has sired dead-ringers like Billy Liar and Reginald Perrin, and is rumored to have illegitimate progeny in Charles M. Schulz's *Peanuts*. Residing in the OED, Walter has entered the language in his inimitable Mittyesque, Mittyish, and Mitty-like fashion.

Opposite Walter Mitty, surgeon

Key Author **H.P. Lovecraft**
The Outsider and Others

Tall, thin and spectrally pale, Rhodes Island author Howard Phillips Lovecraft (1890–1937) could have walked straight out of the pages of one of his own monstrous tales. Never widely published outside the pulp magazines of the 1920s, including *Weird Tales* (founded 1923), Lovecraft's unwholesome and blood-curdling prose, filled with bizarre creatures, unutterable horrors, and the blackest of terrors, brought to life the author's most vivid and fantastic dreams.

"Since Poe affected me most of all horror-writers, I can never feel that a tale starts out right unless it has something of his manner." An autodidact and a diligent reader – there exists a catalogue of his personal library which runs to over 1,000 titles – so intoxicated was Lovecraft with Edgar Allan Poe, and Irish fantasist Lord Dunsany, one critic went so far as to suggest a difficulty in determining what was Lovecraft and what was "some half conscious memory of the books he has read."

The Outsider and Others (1939), published two years after his death from intestinal cancer, as well as the Cthulhu Mythos, a Lovecraftian legend of prehistoric Earth, and his invented Necromicon tome, referenced throughout his richly crafted stories, ensured Lovecraft was better known posthumously than during his lifetime, bringing the wild hills of Vermont, "the outpost of a frightful cosmic race," more close in this "new dark age."

Though dismissed as a "hack" and purveyor of "bad taste and bad art" by Edmund Wilson, H.P. Lovecraft can count Borges, Stephen King, Joyce Carol Oates, and Michel Houllebecq amongst his disciples, and today is placed alongside his beloved Poe, Nathaniel Hawthorne, and Ambrose Bierce in the American macabre literary tradition.
Susan Tomaselli

Date 1939

Nationality USA

Other Key Works "The Rats in the Wall" (1924), "The Call of Cthulhu" (1928), "The Dunwich Horror" (1929), "The Shadow Over Innsmouth" (1936), "The Thing on the Doorstep" (1937)

Why It's Key "Perhaps one needs to have suffered a great deal in order to appreciate Lovecraft." (Jacques Bergier, co-creator of the fantasy realism magazine *Planète*).

Key Book
The Pit (El pozo)

Published on the eve of World War II, *The Pit* was largely ignored, even in Latin America, and was not republished for decades. Scarcely long enough to be called even a "short novel," its power and, in time, influence were all the greater for this.

Eladio Linacero is an ex-journalist who shares a seedy room with the dim but sincere political activist Lázaro. During a night when Lázaro is unaccountably absent Linacero writes what he wryly calls his "extraordinary confessions" on the back of political leaflets. He recalls the death of his marriage (a universal lament for the loss of love), and recounts one of the innumerable imaginary adventures which are now the only thing which give his life meaning. Attempts to communicate the importance of these daydreams – once to a prostitute and once to a poet – resulted in ridicule or incomprehension. He is, finally, "a solitary man smoking in a place that could be anywhere in the city." There are background rumbles

from the impending war in Europe, but though recognizing that Lázaro's faith gives him a purpose he himself lacks, Linacero remains an atomized individual, uncommitted, in the end, even to his own memories and dreams.

Mario Vargas Llosa has said this book marks the beginning of the modern novel in Latin America, and it certainly echoes through his own massive *Conversation in the Cathedral* (*Conversación en la Catedral*, 1969). Although his work is still only partially and irregularly available in English, Onetti's influence on his continent's literature is incalculable and enduring.
Cathy Benson

Date 1939

Author Juan Carlos Onetti (1909–94)

Nationality Uruguay

Why It's Key Onetti is one of the "undiscovered" Latin American writers who were the godfathers of the "Boom" in Latin American writing of the 1960s. Together with writers such as Roberto Arlt (1900–42) and Mario Benedetti (1920), Onetti brought the Latin American novel off the sierra and into the heart of the city.

Key Book
At Swim-Two-Birds

*A*t Swim-Two-Birds has been described as the first post-modern novel, and it is easy to see why. Prolifically intertextual (it contains extracts from over 40 other works), with multiple beginnings (three), it could be described as a novel about someone writing a novel about someone writing a novel. Its playful approach to language and the tropes of fiction-making (there is a character who materializes fully formed before the reader's eyes, foregoing, as most fictional characters do, the process of birth and growing up), it is a comedy that lays bare the creative process itself.

O'Brien, whose real name was Brian O'Nolan, wrote a satirical column for the *Irish Times* (under the name Myles Na Gopaleen). Born in county Tyrone, one of twelve children, he attended University College Dublin and had a brief spell in the civil service before becoming a writer. He is often compared to James Joyce, and although he was a great admirer of Joyce's work, and shared the older author's love of Dublin and its people, O'Brien's satirical imagination is so sharp that it is tempting to see *At Swim-Two-Birds* and his other novels as parodies of the modernist prose of *Ulysses* and *Finnegans Wake*. More importantly and surprisingly, perhaps, for a writer who never lived outside Ireland, he has closer parallels with European and South American writers such as Calvino and Borges than with his compatriots, and remains an important influence on younger writers today.
Gerard Woodward

Date 1939

Author Flann O'Brien (1911–66)

Nationality Ireland

Why It's Key Experimental comic novel regarded by some as the first work of postmodernism.

Key Book
The Day of the Locust

*T*he Great Depression of the 1930s coincided in the United States with the growth of the movie industry in California. Out of Hollywood came the films that were to provide a temporary escape from lives of drabness and poverty for millions of American cinemagoers. The West Coast was seen as a place where the American dream of rising from nothing to wealth and success could still be realized and thousands of would-be stars flocked there. Nathanael West (born Nathan Weinstein) made the journey himself from his native New York to work as a screenwriter in 1935.

West experienced at first hand the often squalid reality that was the underside of Hollywood, the hundreds of failures eking out a living while waiting for the big break that would never come. His main character, the struggling painter Tod Hackett, symbolizes all artists, including writers like West himself, forced to produce hack work to make a living.

West's characters are reminiscent of stock roles in films, from the ingenue trying to break into pictures to the pushy mother of a precociously-talented child. Where West differs from movies is in unflinchingly showing what contemporary Hollywood would leave out, such as the "starlet" having to use sex to get anywhere and the fact that the lovable would-be child star is actually a nasty brat.

West's Hollywood, like America itself, is populated by "locusts," unthinkingly devouring the illusions shown on the big screen, while easily roused to mob violence. Meanwhile the American dream is polluted and betrayed all around them.
Michael Munro

Date 1939

Author Nathanael West (1903–40)

Nationality USA

Why It's Key This novel was shocking in its exposure of the tawdriness and cynicism at the heart of America's dream factory. Although one of the characters is called Homer Simpson, Matt Groening, creator of *The Simpsons* cartoon series, denies that this is where he found the name for his paterfamilias.

Key Character **Sasha Jensen**
Good Morning, Midnight

Good Morning, Midnight is one of Jean Rhys' Paris novels, a city she inhabited in between the wars, and in which she spent a particularly desperate and confused period of her life. Living with her Dutch husband (who was imprisoned for what she called "currency irregularities"), experiencing extreme poverty and the death of one of her children, the loss to a care home of another, she suffered bouts of depression, breakdown, and alcoholism.

Sasha Jensen, the heroine of Rhys' novel, shares many of her author's problems, and the novel is a dark wander through a desolate and lonely urban landscape. At the same time there is something defiant about Sasha's exclusion from the conventional world of cocktail parties and Parisian soirees. She rails against the small-mindedness of the middle classes – "everything in their whole bloody world is a cliché. Everything is born out of a cliché, rests on a cliché, survives by a cliché. And they believe in the clichés.

There is no hope." She is bereft and isolated, but she is also libidinous, wilfully vulgar (there is a scene where her drawers fall down in public) and rebellious – a challenging and taboo-breaking role for a female character at that time. The novel is also, like all of Rhys' writing, stylistically sophisticated, blending a sometimes inebriatedly rambling prose with a stream of consciousness narrative style that continues the modernist tradition of Virginia Woolf.

Gerard Woodward

Date 1939

Author Jean Rhys (1890–1979)

Nationality Dominica

Why It's Key After initial success as a writer Rhys' reputation waned, becoming so removed from literary circles that in 1957 an advert was placed in the *New Statesman* asking for her whereabouts. She re-emerged from obscurity to enjoy a late flowering of literary acclaim.

Key Passage
The Big Sleep

"I was neat, clean, shaved and sober and I didn't care who knew it. I was everything the well-dressed private detective ought to be. I was calling on four million dollars."

When you think of hard-boiled crime writing (or its close relative, film noir), you probably hear a voice in your head – a dry, self-deprecating, first-person narrative, punctuated by artful, surprising imagery. That voice belongs to Philip Marlowe, the archetypal "private eye," and it was first heard in the opening pages of *The Big Sleep*, in which Marlowe arrives at the palatial home of a rich client, General Sternwood, and encounters his dissipated younger daughter, Carmen. Marlowe's creator, Raymond Chandler, was careful to include certain generic prerequisites – the urban setting, the general cynicism about modern society, the idiomatic dialogue. Perhaps less obvious are Chandler's refinements to the template – a more precise

evocation of the Los Angeles cityscape, and an allusive, literary tone communicated through Marlowe's distinctive voice. In these opening pages, we glimpse his sharp wit, and his knack for arresting similes – Carmen's teeth are "as white as fresh orange pith and as shiny as porcelain." Most crucially, we witness his instinctive chivalry: when Carmen deliberately falls into his arms, Marlowe catches her. Hammett's Sam Spade would have let her head crack on the floor. In Marlowe, Chandler created a hero with enduring appeal – a tough but vulnerable man who retains his independence and integrity despite the violence and corruption that surrounds him.

Rowland Hughes

Date 1939

Author Raymond Chandler (1888–1959)

Nationality USA

Why It's Key Chandler reinvigorated the genre of hard-boiled crime fiction, which, by the late 1930s, had become formulaic and trashy. His stories are rooted in a harsh realism, but in Philip Marlowe, Chandler created a modern-day knight errant, able to transcend the corruption around him.

Opposite Humphrey Bogart in *The Big Sleep*

Key Author **Eric Ambler**
The Mask of Dimitrios

Eric Ambler (1909–98) is best known for his popular thrillers which were written to a successful formula, usually involving an ordinary Englishman who unwittingly finds himself caught up in the world of international espionage and intrigue. His novels, such as *The Mask of Dimitrios* (published in 1939, made into a classic film noir in 1944) typically have fast-moving plots, though Ambler was skilful in his controlled use of suspense for maximum unnerving effect. His novels became known for having an air of authenticity, often alluding to current world events and political situations. A staunch anti-fascist, Ambler naturally looked to communist Russia as a foil for the rising tide of nationalism in Europe and often depicted Soviet characters in a balanced, often sympathetic way, particularly in his earlier novels.

His career as a novelist was interrupted by World War II, followed by a burgeoning career in films. He wrote original screenplays and also adapted the works of other writers for the screen, while his own novels – such as *The Light of Day* (1962) and *Journey Into Fear* (1940) – were made into highly successful films. He returned to novel writing in the 1950s, his work reflecting the new complexity of global power struggles that had replaced the simplistic ideologies of the pre-war era and, in doing so, Ambler further cemented his reputation as a writer of considerable sophistication. His novels are widely regarded as early models for subsequent writing in the genre, and his motifs and technique can be clearly traced through the history of the spy story in both literature and film.

Christian Kerr

Date 1939 (publication)

Nationality UK

Other Key Works *The Dark Frontier* (1936)

Why It's Key An influential writer of spy novels, his work helped shape the modern thriller. He fought in World War II, eventually becoming assistant director in the Army Film Unit. He continued with filmmaking post war, receiving an Oscar nomination for his work on the classic, *The Cruel Sea* (1953), as well as writing many more successful novels.

Key Event
Sigmund Freud dies

Detractors of Freud (1866–1939), who died in exile from Nazi-occupied Austria in London in 1939, often forget how his theory of the unconscious, which he began to explore in the 1890s, inspired much of the irony and anti-heroism that characterizes twentieth-century Western literature. The existence of unconscious motivation is difficult to prove scientifically and continues to cause lay offence because it denies human beings ultimate free will. The sexuality behind self-expression and Freud's fascination with forms of perversity can also seem to undermine dignity. Freudianism has been dismissed as a "bourgeois" science for the repressed and decadent upper class of his day. But we have a more indulgent view of humanity thanks to this medical genius who understood how the desires of early childhood for love and security underlie adult emotional life.

Freud's erotic reworking of our inner lives was often fanciful, as can be seen from case studies like "The Wolf Man"(1918) in which the writer took over from the scientist. When he invented psychoanalysis as a "talking" therapy designed to bring unconscious motivation to light through a re-examination of childhood Freud was partly driven by a need to understand his own sexuality, and the lack of scientific rigour entailed in psychoanalysis' foundations has detracted from its popularity in the last 30 years. But his understanding of humanity makes clear Freud was on to something. He remains one of the great definers of the modern and in France especially his influence has been marked in philosophy and cultural theory, right up to the present day.

Lesley Chamberlain

Date 1939

Place: London, UK

Nationality: Austria

Other Key Works *The Interpretation of Dreams* (1899), *Beyond the Pleasure Principle* (1920), *The Ego and the Id* (1923), *Civilisation and Its Discontents* (1930)

Why It's Key Freud's theories on the unconscious mind, sexuality, and the imagination had an incalculable influence on twentieth-century literature.

Opposite Sigmund Freud

Key Character **Sally Bowles**
Goodbye to Berlin

In 1929 Christopher Isherwood left his medical studies in London to join W.H. Auden in Berlin; he stayed for nearly a decade tutoring privately and enjoying a relatively louche émigré lifestyle. His experiences of the end of the Weimar republic and the ascent of Nazism are recounted in *Mr Norris Changes Trains* (1935) and *Goodbye to Berlin* (1939; this latter included the novella *Sally Bowles* that he had published in 1935). Isherwood wrote semi-autobiographically, and several of the key characters in the collections are modelled on real people (Bowles is based on Isherwood's friend Jean Ross, for example). He was also extremely interested in objectivity, and the stories strive for clarity and simplicity.

The American-born Bowles is flighty, naughty, self-obsessed, and vibrant; she drinks, sings cabaret, smokes, has sex and ignores or accepts the complex sexuality of the narrator (a thinly veiled Isherwood). Her eccentric commitment to personal freedom flies in the face of public events in Berlin, and she is in some ways (although not herself German) the last flowering of a society in decay. In Isherwood's writing and her subsequent manifestation in the film *Cabaret* (1972) Bowles is generally presented as emblematic of the decadence of Weimar Germany, but it is clear that Isherwood's concerns are as much with the early rise of fascism and ordinary people's experiences of this repressive ideology than with any *fin-de-siècle* portrait. Bowles is a free spirit of sorts but the sadness the narrator senses behind her is that of something lost.

Jerome de Groot

Date 1939

Author Christopher Isherwood (1904–1986)

Nationality UK

Why It's Key Sally Bowles is the embodiment of Weimar Republic Germany in Isherwood's classic account of the 1930s: seedily elegant, tragic, flamboyant, fragile, and doomed.

Key Event **Steinbeck gives a voice to the migrant farmers of the dust bowl**

After decades of over-grazing and over-farming, a prolonged drought during the 1930s turned the plain states of Oklahoma, Texas, Kansas, and Colorado into a dust bowl. Thousands of farms were foreclosed amidst a wider national economic depression, forcing hundreds of thousands of dispossessed sharecropper families on the largest American internal movement of whites, lured by the promise of work on the California fruit farms. John Steinbeck's epic *The Grapes of Wrath* follows the journey West of the migrant Joad family.

Titled after a line from the "Battle Hymn of the Republic," the unofficial anthem of the free North against the Southern slave states during the American Civil War, *The Grapes of Wrath* suggests that the United States is likewise split during the Depression between two competing worldviews: the selfishness of middle-class aspirations for private property and managerial authority versus the neighborly cooperation of laboring-class community. Harried, beaten, and belittled as little more than work animals, the "Okies" search for dignity as much as employment, food, and housing.

The Grapes debunks the "California myth" of the sunshine states as the new location for realizing the American dream. Echoing the biblical *Exodus*, the novel investigates the bitter roots for revenge by American "peasants" against a soulless market, and can be read as prophesying the peasant revolutions in China and Cuba. In an age when global rural populations are increasingly forced off the land in a time of environmental catastrophes, Steinbeck's tale of migrant workers has renewed relevance as a diagnostic warning.

Stephen Shapiro

Date 1939

Title *The Grapes of Wrath*

Author John Steinbeck (1902–68)

Nationality USA

Why It's Key *The Grapes* captures the moment when urban, coastal artists began to recognize the plight of the rural, non-immigrant poor as a worthy topic. With protagonist Tom Joad, Steinbeck creates a populist American icon.

Opposite From *The Grapes of Wrath* film adaptation

Key Event
Brendan Behan is sent to Borstal

In 1939 Brendan Behan (1926–64) was arrested for IRA activity. Although Behan was a committed Republican from a young age, opinion is divided as to whether his failed Liverpool bombing campaign was planned alone, or masterminded by the IRA. Too young for prison, the then 16-year-old Behan was sent to a progressive Borstal institution in Hollesley Bay, Suffolk.

Borstal Boy is Behan's autobiographical account of his journey from arrest in 1939 to release in 1941. The memoir is an honest and often shocking portrait of prison life. Behan's colorful recollections of the people and places encountered over the course of his time in prison also reflect the divisive issues of class, nationality, religion, and politics within contemporaneous British society as a whole. Behan's gift for capturing the nuances of dialect and individual speech is as evident in his memoir as it is in his plays. Borstal Boy presents a detailed and often wonderfully funny picture of the intricacies of prison society; Screws, Cockneys, Geordies, Paddys, Toffs, and Chinas are just a few of the many categories of person introduced along the way. The narrative is as much about the friendships forged amongst his fellow prisoners as it is about his personal experience as an IRA man within the English Penal system. Behan's personal story is at the heart of a larger collective experience. In many respects Borstal Boy is about a group of young boys growing up together in unusual circumstances.

Kate Harris

Date 1939

Title Borstal Boy (1958)

Nationality Ireland

Why It's Key The publication of Borstal Boy in 1958 followed the successes of his two most famous plays, The Quare Fellow (1954) and The Hostage (1958). His work was greeted with critical acclaim both in England and the United States and he became a celebrated literary figure. Behan was a brilliant performer, gifted in speech and song.

292

Key Character **Joey Evans**
Pal Joey

Pal Joey is an example of an epistolary novel, a genre that was becoming increasingly rare in the twentieth century. The story is told in a series of letters from Joey Evans to his friend Ted (the title coming from Evans' habitual sign-off as "Pal Joey"). These letters reveal Evans to be an amusing correspondent, always ready with a wise-crack. In his colloquial, often racy, frequently misspelled brand of American English, he also gives away the less endearing characteristics of a "man on the make." Like many of John O'Hara's (1905–70) characters, he feels that he is not being given his due by an unfair society. He is on a relatively lowly rung on the ladder of showbiz success but he aspires to the top and calculatingly uses his appeal to women to try to raise the money that will allow him to live in the style to which he would like to become accustomed.

Joey Evans is a memorable creation: unscrupulous, self-serving, and exploitative, but there's something about his undisguised ambition that allows him to win the reader's sympathy. The character was too popular to remain within the confines of a book and he was given new life in a Rodgers and Hart stage musical (1940) of the same name, for which O'Hara himself wrote the libretto and Gene Kelly played the lead. Evans was made more likeable for this adaptation and the process continued when a film version was made in 1957, starring Frank Sinatra, but the movie didn't repeat the success of the stage show.

Michael Munro

Date 1939

Author John O'Hara (1908–70)

Nationality USA

Why It's Key Joey Evans is an amoral nightclub entertainer. His venality is counterbalanced by charm, and this ensured that he became a minor cultural hero, or perhaps anti-hero, when the novel was published but even more so when it was adapted, first as a Broadway musical and then as a Hollywood film.

Opposite Evans and entourage in the film adaptation

Key Event *Mrs Miniver* is published in book form

Jan Struther was the pen name of Joyce Anstruther (1901–54), the daughter of a Scottish Liberal MP, who published volumes of verse in the 1930s. From 1937 she wrote a regular column for *The Times* about the everyday life of a fictional English middle-class family, the Minivers, based on the diary of the wife and mother, conceived as being an "ordinary" woman. The columns were at first humorous, although always well-observed, sketches of domestic tribulations but their atmosphere grew more sombre as the prospect of war with Germany became an inevitability. *Mrs Miniver*, the book based on the columns, became a No 1 bestseller in the USA, which in 1939 was still neutral and dominated by a powerful noninterventionist lobby that was determined not to let the nation become embroiled in another European conflict.

Unlike her fictional heroine, Jan Struther left Britain with her children for the United States in 1940, but she devoted much of her time to raising money for British war relief. She continued to popularize both her work and its message of civilization being forced to resist Nazi barbarity by undertaking an American lecture tour and numerous radio appearances. President Roosevelt believed that she had played a great part in changing the course of American opinion about the war, and Winston Churchill was said to have remarked that *Mrs Miniver* had done more for the Allied cause than a flotilla of battleships, or, in some versions of the quotation, six military divisions. Struther's granddaughter, Ysenda Maxtone-Smith, wrote about her life in *The Real Mrs Miniver* (2001).

Michael Munro

Date 1939

Nationality UK

Why It's Key The story of Mrs Miniver, at first appearing in newspaper columns before emerging in book form in 1939, is credited with helping to hasten the entry of the United States into World War II. The film version of 1942, starring Greer Garson, won several Oscars as well as even more American sympathy for the Allied cause.

Key Character **The Whisky Priest** *The Power and the Glory*

The protagonist is never named: he's only "the father," or "the man in the drill suit," or Montez, or just "the man." To the villagers who know him, he is, above all, "the whisky priest." Greene gives us a contemptible little creature, drunken, compromised, and cowardly and then shows how of such material saints can be made.

Our whisky priest is harried the length and breadth of Mexico in the late thirties, a land in which to be a priest is to be a traitor, in which, with the church bells gone, there is no way of telling the time. He encounters unexpected kindness (in prisons) and unsuspected contempt (in his home town): he meets his natural daughter, grown hard in a hard world, and feels the first breath of love. He realizes, as he sees hard-earned wine – for once more precious than brandy – disappear down the gullet of a corrupt official, that something has changed in him. Then the man who has been hunting him, the stern, atheistic lieutenant, gives him five pesos out of pity, not recognizing him. More and more he finds himself prompted to mercy: he can't leave an Indian woman behind with her dead child, he must go back for her. He returns the money some villagers have given him for masses and baptisms. He goes to give absolution to a dying American murderer knowing that he will be betrayed to his hunters. Such acts, ineffectual in themselves, become the saving of him, and the redemption of at least some of his former accusers. The whisky priest, unlikely and unwilling martyr, divides the sheep from the goats – much like the God he eventually finds himself serving.

Murrough O'Brien

Date 1940

Author Graham Greene (1904–91)

Nationality UK

Why It's Key An insult became a proverb. "Whisky priest" began as a term of contempt. In Greene's novel, replete with a wry compassion, a humorous religiosity, and a humanist optimism all his own, it grew into a term almost of affection.

Opposite Graham Greene

Key Character **John Singer**
The Heart is a Lonely Hunter

In *The Heart is a Lonely Hunter*, the central character is Mr. Singer, a deaf-mute who lives in a small Southern town with his friend, Anatonapoulos, another deaf-mute. The friendship is all consuming for Mr. Singer – Anatonapoulos is his only friend.

When Anatonapoulos is sent to an asylum, Mr. Singer is forced to look outside his narrow life. He takes a room in a boarding house and eats all his meals at the New York Café. Here he meets Jake Blount, a Marxist alcoholic who wants to create a social uprising, and the café owner, Biff Brannon. Through the boarding house he meets Mick Kelly, a teenager who dreams of music, and Dr. Copeland, an African American doctor. These four characters visit Mr. Singer regularly, and despite his deafness, they pour their hearts out to him.

McCullers called Singer's character "an emotional catalyst for all the other characters." He becomes the repository for all their dreams, ambitions, and hopes.

While Singer himself depends on their company, he is utterly necessary to their lives. The inability of the characters to connect highlights how social, racial and economic factors isolate people. The characters' individual voices combine to form a fugue, emphasized by Singer's musical name.

Richard Wright compared Mr. Singer to a priest, receiving confessions from the other characters. Others have seen him as a Christ figure. Singer commits suicide at the end of the novel, when he learns Anatonapoulos has died. While he is everything to his four visitors, Singer has always been lonely for his missing friend. The four visitors are left bereft after his death – each imprisoned in their own way. Talking to a deaf-mute has been their only escape.
Jennifer Young

Date 1940

Author Carson McCullers (1917–67)

Nationality USA

Why It's Key Mr. Singer, deaf-mute and the receptacle for the dreams of the other characters, ties the entire novel together. He draws out the best of the other characters, as is seen after he dies.

Key Book
Native Son

The story of the short, doomed life of Bigger Thomas was an immediate bestseller. The title draws ironic attention to the fact that there is no place but prison (either in the slums of Chicago's South Side or literally behind bars) for young black men. Rather than admit to being in his white employer's bedroom (no one would believe he was simply helping her), Bigger kills her and his life quickly unravels. The last third of the book is devoted to his trial and the efforts of his Marxist lawyer to understand his actions. This is impossible since, as Wright notes, "the telling of it would have involved an explanation of his entire life." In any case Bigger had already been condemned by the racist press – provoking commentators to describe Mike Tyson and O.J. Simpson (on trial in the 90s) as modern-day Bigger Thomases.

Native Son was also a riposte to the enduring influence of *Uncle Tom's Cabin*. If Harriet Beecher Stowe's protagonist is a long-suffering Christ-like slave, Wright's is a rapist and murderer. The two are so

perfectly opposed, James Baldwin thought, that Wright had merely created a "complement to that monstrous legend it was written to destroy."

Since 1940 African-American writers have often felt the need to respond to *Native Son*. "It's about time some Negro writer wrote a good novel about some good Negroes who do not come to a bad end," complained Langston Hughes in 1946. Percival Everett's *Erasure* (1999) includes a lengthy parody entitled "My Pafology."
Kasia Boddy

Date 1940

Author Richard Wright (1908–60)

Nationality USA

Why It's Key "'I didn't want to kill', Bigger shouted. 'But what I killed for, I am!'" *Native Son* was Wright's indictment of what he called "the moral horror of Negro life in the United States." It made him the most important, and wealthiest, African American writer of his day.

Key Book
For Whom the Bell Tolls

Hemingway experienced the Spanish Civil War (1936–39) at first hand as a war correspondent and his sympathy with the Republican side informs this, his longest novel. He was saddened by the loss of his beloved Spain to the victorious fascists and the novel celebrates the fortitude of ordinary Spanish people in their struggle to retain their freedom. The Republican government was famously assisted by thousands of left-leaning foreigners in the International Brigades of frontline volunteers and also by romantic and idealistic individuals like the book's hero, the American Robert Jordan, who sacrifices his life to save his comrades.

The title is an echo from the English Metaphysical poet John Donne (c. 1572–1631). In his Meditations Donne wrote: "Any man's death diminishes me, because I am involved in Mankind; And therefore never send to know for whom the bell tolls; it tolls for thee." By drawing his title from this well-known passage Hemingway was telling his readers that the world as a whole had lost by the fall of Spain to the forces of reaction. It was not possible to look on the Civil War as a purely Spanish affair, even if the intervention of German and Italian troops and aircraft on the fascist side were overlooked. The book was in part a warning to the rest of the world of what was likely to come. Of course, by the time of the novel's publication another world war had broken out, although the United States was not as yet caught up in it.

The novel sold over a quarter of a million copies in the year of publication and the film version in 1943, starring Gary Cooper and Ingrid Bergman, was nominated for an Academy Award.

Michael Munro

Date 1940

Author Ernest Hemingway (1898–1961)

Nationality USA

Why It's Key This novel, by a world-famous author at the height of his powers, brought home to thousands of readers a realistic picture of what life had been like in Spain during the Civil War, partaking equally of heroism and evil, loyalty and betrayal.

Key Event *Darkness at Noon*
exposes Stalin's show trials

This slim roman à clef was the first, devastating exposé of the Stalinist show trials that had taken place in Moscow in 1936–8, and its power to undo the sympathies of British socialists for Communist Russia subsequently turned it into a Cold War set text. More a political than a literary classic, much of its power lay with the authority of its Hungarian-born author, Arthur Koestler (1905–83), who had traveled in Russia and been an active member of the Communist Party. Koestler had also been imprisoned in Spain during the Civil War. He wrote the novel in Paris, in German, before fleeing to Britain.

The story of N.S. Rubashov, a loyal Party member arrested and condemned to death, was an interpretation (no longer considered factually true) of leading Bolshevik Nikolai Bukharin's fall from grace. But Koestler, accounting for his own past, also wanted to explain how Party loyalty could persuade a decent man to betray and murder his fellows. With an argument that would remain relevant for the duration of the twentieth century, he showed how a philosophy which pretended to altruism in fact amounted to a savage utilitarianism in the Party's interests. The dark, obsessive text, translated and improved by Koestler's then lover Daphne Hardy, who also supplied the title, has in places an impressive Biblical ring. Critics who insist it stands as a monument to the general power of totalitarian ideology overlook the unique humanitarian appeal that Communism exercised on young idealists after two decades of war and economic depression.

Lesley Chamberlain

Date 1940 (publication)

Nationality Hungary

Why It's Key *Darkness at Noon* exposed Stalin's purges of the Communist party in the 1930s. More of a veiled confession than a novel as such, it is probably the only fiction that will be remembered by a writer latterly better known for his interest in the paranormal. It remains essential reading for anyone interested in the power of Communism to inspire belief, and the disillusion that followed.

Key Event **Vladimir Nabokov arrives in the United States**

When Vladimir Nabokov arrived in the United States in 1940 he was fleeing the Nazis, but Nabokov's early manhood had also been spent as a refugee. He had been brought up in Russia where his father was a liberal statesman before the revolution. The family fled the Soviet Union and Nabokov went to Trinity College, Cambridge then started his literary career under the pseudonym V. Sirin while he was living in Paris and Berlin. All his work until he was over 40 was written in Russian though many of the early works such as *Despair* and *Laughter in the Dark* were later successfully translated into English. None gained him much money and it was as an obscure and impoverished writer that he arrived in America.

In the United States his mentor was Edmund Wilson who helped him to publish fiction and essays. *Lolita*, a long, literary defence of a paedophile's love for a girl was his third novel in English. He planned to publish it anonymously to protect his job at Cornell

University where he had already been castigated for teaching a "dirty lit" course including such classics as *Madame Bovary* and *Ulysses*. *Lolita* was to be offered to four U.S. publishers before being published by the Paris-based Olympia Press. A U.S. edition led to a furious debate between his puritanical accusers and his defenders in the literary establishment. The success of the book allowed Nabokov to leave his job at Cornell and he returned to Europe, settling in a hotel in Switzerland. He was to become known as one of the century's great prose stylists.
Jad Adams

Date 1940

Author Vladimir Nabokov (1899–1977) Novelist, poet

Nationality Russian, (naturalized USA)

Why It's Key After his move to the United States Nabokov wrote in English. With its penetrating depiction of American suburban life, its road trip across the USA through the cheap commercialism of the nation in the halcyon years of the 1950s, in *Lolita*, Nabokov wrote the Great American Novel.

Key Event **James Jones is present at the Japanese bombing of Pearl Harbor**

The title comes from "Gentleman-rankers," a poem by Rudyard Kipling:
"Gentlemen-rankers out on the spree,

Damned from here to Eternity"

The novel deals with the events that happen to a small group of characters in a company of the U.S. Army based in barracks in the great U.S. Naval base in Hawaii. Unknown to them, they are living through a period of transition. As professional military men rather than the draftees of later in the war, they are still caught up in the relationships of a peacetime army. Among the members of one particular group of servicemen, issues of dominance, rivalry which finds competitive sport (particularly boxing) as its only outlet, bullying, and sexual infidelity are the all-important concerns. What they don't know, while the reader, with hindsight, obviously does, is that their lives are about to be changed utterly by the surprise attack that will befall

them. The personal entanglements that seem to be what life is all about will be swept into the background.

Jones' novel was an immediate bestseller and won the National Book Award. Its realism and its presentation of American servicemen as human beings with the failings and self-interest of us all rather than as heroes inspired by noble ideals was representative of a new wave in American war fiction, that included such novels as Norman Mailer's *The Naked and the Dead* (1948). Jones was to continue this development in *The Thin Red Line* (1962). In 1953 a film version of the novel was made which won eight Oscars and famously gave the world the iconic image of Burt Lancaster and Deborah Kerr rolling in a passionate clinch in the surf.
Michael Munro

Date December 7, 1941

Title *From Here to Eternity* (1951)

Author James Jones (1921–77)

Nationality USA

Why It's Key *From Here to Eternity* (1951) came to be regarded as one of the classic novels of World War II soon after publication. Jones was present at the attack and it is his own experience of this and life in the U.S. Army immediately before the war that underpin the novel.

Key Author
Virginia Woolf

In popular literary consciousness, Virginia Woolf (1882–1941) is most famous for developing a style of writing known as "stream of consciousness." Her later detractors in the post-war period characterized this apparently formless interior narrative as the indulgent twittering of a privileged novelist who had few real concerns – poverty, hunger – to write about. From the 1970s, however, a new generation of literary critics and feminist scholars insisted on seeing Woolf as a key modernist whose pioneering novels and essays challenged traditional forms of narrative in both fiction and biography.

In 1904, Virginia and her sister Vanessa moved from Kensington to Gordon Square. There they came to know the loose-knit circle of writers and painters known as the Bloomsbury Group. One of these – the writer and political activist Leonard Woolf – later became Virginia's husband and nursed her through escalating bouts of mental illness.

In novels such as *Night and Day* (1919), *Mrs. Dalloway* (1925), and *To The Lighthouse* (1927), Woolf eschews plot-driven narrative in favour of exploring her characters' inner consciousness. The result is an intense lyricism, preoccupied with auditory and visual sensation rather than the record of mere events. Meanwhile, in cod-biographies such as *Orlando* (1928) and *Flush* (1933) Woolf attempts this same approach with apparently non-fictional subjects. For a generation raised on the solid realism of Victorian novel and biography, this amounted to revolution or desecration, depending on your point of view.

In March 1941, depressed by the way the war was going (if the Germans invaded the Woolfs would almost certainly become a key target), Virginia Woolf drowned herself by weighting her pockets with stones and walking into the river near her Sussex home.
Kathryn Hughes

Date 1941 (death)

Nationality UK

Key Works *Jacob's Room* (1922), *A Room of One's Own* (1929), *The Waves* (1931), *Between the Acts* (1941)

Why It's Key Woolf's playfulness with narrative form paved the way for many of the more extreme experiments of the postmodernist period. In the words of E.M. Forster, she pushed the English language "a little further against the dark."

1940–1949

299

Key Event **Underground Press *Les Editions de Minuit* is founded in Paris**

The *Editions de Minuit* were established in Paris as a clandestine publishing house for free-thinking works, without heed to the censorship and control of the German occupiers of France in World War II. The books were printed by a handful of small printers and distributed largely from person to person, by intimate acquaintance or through the resistance networks. First published was Vercors' *Le Silence de la mer* (1942), which became emblematic of the French literary resistance. Vercors was followed by other French literary eminences – Eluard, Aragon, Mauriac, Maritain – all publishing under their *noms de guerre*. On Liberation, the association of the *Minuit* authors with left-wing resistance was cemented when the publishing house was awarded the 1945 Femina Prize for literature, for its wartime clandestine work, republished in the collection "Under the Oppression."

Emerging from the underground after the war, *Minuit* under the direction of Vercors (pseudonym of Jean Bruller, 1902–91) found it hard to maintain its moral and intellectual high ground while balancing the books. It was only after Vercors' departure in 1948 and his replacement by Jérôme Lindon (1925–2001) that *Minuit* took on and sustained the mature form for which it has since become known: cutting-edge literature and thought, both original and translated, presented in uniform unadorned covers to turn all attention to content. Based in Paris' Left Bank since 1951, Lindon's *Minuit* went on to become the publishing home of Samuel Beckett and of the Nouveau Roman novelists, remaining a trailblazer in literary innovation.
Nimrod Ben-Cnaan

Date 1941

Founders Vercors, Pierre de Lescure (1891–1963)

Why It's Key Originally established as a clandestine publisher during World War II, *Editions de Minuit* has been inextricably linked with the French national mythology of resistance. Emerging from underground to great prestige after the war, *Minuit* went on to become a leading avant-garde publisher of fiction and thought, both original and translated.

Key Event *The Last Tycoon* is published by Edmund Wilson

After the great financial success of his first two novels and his short stories, which made him the highest paid American writer in the 1920s, F. Scott Fitzgerald had watched the two novels upon which he pinned his highest artistic hopes, and which he considered his greatest achievements, *The Great Gatsby* and *Tender is the Night*, dwindle into commercial failures. His own spendthrift habits (he wrote Edmund Wilson that he had $10,000 worth of liquor in his cellar that he intended to drink in 1922, a year when the average schoolteacher annually earned approximately $1,300) combined with the enormous medical bills created by his wife Zelda's mental breakdown and subsequent institutionalization, sent him to Hollywood to try to earn a living as a screenwriter.

Unlike his contemporary William Faulkner, Fitzgerald never acquired the knack for screenplay writing, but he used his insider's knowledge of Hollywood to provide the outline for his last novel. *The Last Tycoon: A Western*, loosely modeled on the life and early death of "boy genius" producer Irving Thalberg, represented Fitzgerald's last attempt to resuscitate his gift, his critical reputation, and his career. He completed about 60,000 words before he died, only half of the story he projected, although already longer than *The Great Gatsby* in its entirety. In Monroe Stahr, his hero, Fitzgerald created what many readers consider his most fully realized character, and the language of the surviving drafts demonstrates the intense lyricism and brilliant prose that characterizes Fitzgerald's literary genius.

Sarah Churchwell

Date 1941

Author F. Scott Fitzgerald (1896–1940)

Nationality USA

Why It's Key Fitzgerald's last, unfinished novel was edited and published in incomplete form along with his notes and outlines for it, by his friend and critical champion Edmund Wilson. In a 1941 review, *The New York Times* declared that "one would be blind indeed not to see that it would have been Fitzgerald's best novel."

Opposite F. Scott Fitzgerald

Key Passage
The Myth of Sisyphus

"There is but one truly serious philosophical problem and that is suicide."

Albert Camus' *The Myth of Sisyphus* opens with perhaps the most famous and important single statement in twentieth century philosophy: "There is but one truly serious philosophical problem and that is suicide." Judging whether life is or is not worth living, he asserts, is the fundamental question of philosophy. Life is essentially absurd; we are creatures who live in constant sight of our own death, but ones for whom this death can have no meaning. Camus uses the ancient Greek myth of Sisyphus to illustrate the absurdity of our condition. Sisyphus heroically defied the Gods and imprisoned Death so that humans could be immortal. In retribution, the gods devised a punishment whereby Sisyphus must eternally push a boulder up a hill, just to watch it fall back down again; walk down, and push it up again. Through an extraordinary imaginative recreation of Sisyphus' torment, Camus eventually concludes that "all is well," for him, and for us.

The essay remains a powerful and affecting piece of work, even when shorn of its context of mid twentieth-century existentialism. The belief in the possibility of liberation at its heart, that we can triumph over the "cold mathematics that command our situation," is perhaps the key to its continued vitality and relevance: after all, "there is no fate that scorn can't surmount." This polemical and deeply individual essay, written under the Nazi occupation in 1942, remarkably retains its ability to make sense of our individual freedoms today. Knowledge of our own absurdity is still, it seems, what will save us. Eventually, as Camus writes, we "must imagine Sisyphus happy."

Julia Jordan

Date 1942

Author Albert Camus (1913–60)

Nationality France

Why It's Key A concise and beautifully written treatise on the importance of individual freedom in the face of life's absurdity, *The Myth of Sisyphus* is Camus' finest philosophical work, and remains one of the twentieth century's most influential pieces of writing.

Key Book
The Seventh Cross

Seghers' panoramic novel set in Nazi Germany describes communist Georg Heisler's escape from a concentration camp. Whilst six other fugitives are eventually captured and returned to the camp, where seven crosses for the men have been erected, the seventh cross for Georg remains empty. Focusing less on the action of Georg's seven-day odyssey, the novel highlights the escapee's personal encounters during that week. Seghers paints a subtle portrait of life in a controlled society, describing the mindset of Nazi functionaries, collaborators, and opportunists, as well as very "ordinary" citizens. The skilful characterization weaves them all together into one big net, analyzing the structure of an entire people and showing how each and every person acts according to their own choice. Like *The Diary of Anne Frank*, *The Seventh Cross* is ultimately an optimistic book where courage and dignity triumph over the evils of an oppressive regime, but unlike *The Diary of Anne Frank*, Seghers emphasizes humanity as the result of a socialist politics of collective solidarity.

When Seghers, a Jewish communist, wrote this carefully researched book in the 1930s, she had already sought refuge from Nazi persecution in France. In 1941, she and her family emigrated to Mexico. Although the German version of *The Seventh Cross* was printed in Mexico in 1942, the work was not available to readers in Germany until after the end of World War II. After her return from exile, Seghers settled in communist East Germany, in accordance with her political ideals. The writer's seemingly uncritical attitude towards the German Democratic Republic's regime is one reason why her reputation in the West was limited during the Cold War period. Only more recently has her work attracted renewed attention and the recognition that *The Seventh Cross* in particular deserves.
Anne Schwan

Date 1942

Author Anna Seghers (1900–83)

Nationality Germany

Why It's Key This masterpiece of German exile literature brought Anna Seghers great fame when it was originally published in the United States. Adaptations in comic strip and Hollywood movie format contributed to the work's success in the English-speaking world at the time.

Key Book
The Man Without Qualities

Musil's masterpiece is an exploration of one year in the life of an introspective individual within the context of the decaying Austro-Hungarian society that preceded the outbreak of World War I.

With a deftly ironical touch, Musil weaves the inner journey of Ulrich, a man searching for meaning in a world increasingly ruled by empiricism, into the wider story of the imminent collapse of the Habsburg monarchy. As Ulrich's outer world disintegrates, so, in many ways, does his personality, as he comes to realize that the notion of objective "reality" is essentially a false one. Among the book's major themes is that abiding one of modernist literature: the attenuation of actuality. In Musil's own words, "I am not concerned with actual events… Events, anyhow, are interchangeable. I am interested in what is typical, in what one might call the ghostly aspect of reality."

In the book, Ulrich holds the same views, attitudes and opinions as Musil, who is in fact dramatising his own search for what he called "the hovering life," a synthesis between empirical fact and mysticism, which could be termed an escape from personality, perhaps even from personal identity. *The Man Without Qualities* is a cornerstone of literary modernism, representing the struggle to locate some ineluctable truth through the mode of fiction. With it, Musil moved the concept of the novel towards philosophical exploration, where it continues to probe the shifting, shadowy realms of human experience to this day.
Christian Kerr

Date 1942

Author Robert Musil (1880–1942)

Nationality Austria

Why It's Key Musil is frequently ranked with Proust and Joyce, largely due to the complexities of subtle observation and stylistic virtuosity of this, his major work. Despite the book's standing as one of the cornerstones of modernist literature, it brought Musil little commercial success in his lifetime.

Key Book
Embers

The setting is a dilapidated castle in the Carpathian Mountains, on a dark and stormy night. The year is 1940. Henrik, an ageing aristocrat, is expecting a visitor: his estranged friend Konrad. Over a prolonged candlelit dinner, 40 years after their last meeting, old grievances surface. There are long-standing scores to be settled.

The two men had once been inseparable. They attended the Viennese military academy together. They remained close even as Henrik rose through the ranks while Konrad sought a life of comfort. Until the day Henrik discovered Konrad's affair with his late wife, Krisztina. Now Henrik demands to know what other plans the illicit lovers had once harbored. "You killed something inside me… but we are still friends," he says. "Tonight, I am going to kill something inside you."

Sándor Márai's melancholy novel, published in Hungary during World War II, is as much about betrayal, jealousy, and revenge as it is about endings – the end of friendship, the end of trust, the end of an empire.

The disintegration of the Austro-Hungarian empire, which both men once served, weighs as heavily on Konrad as his ancient castle's oppressive atmosphere.

Translated into French and German in the 1950s, *Embers* – along with Márai's other novels – was mostly forgotten. The book's fortunes changed as, in the late 1990s, it became a posthumous bestseller in Italy and Germany. In 2001 it appeared in English to much critical acclaim. The literary world hailed the discovery of a long lost masterpiece.

Ángel Gurría-Quintana

Date 1942

Author Sándor Márai (1900–89)

Nationality Hungary

Why It's Key Márai's novel is emblematic of the turbulent times he lived through. He was educated – and began writing – in German and, whilst he tried to stay clear of partisan politics, Communism's ascendancy in Hungary finally forced him into exile. He spent time in Switzerland, Italy, and the USA, where he committed suicide in 1989.

Key Passage
The Land of Spices

"Two people were there. But neither saw her; neither felt her shadow as it froze across the sun."

The scene upon which the novel hinges is also that which led Irish censors to ban it. Mère Marie-Hélène Archer, Reverend Mother of an Irish Convent, has turned her back on love and is facing a spiritual crisis. "She is afraid of love," her own sometime Reverend Mother says, "even of the love of God. This makes me sad for her, for she has very high standards."

Marie fled into convent life following a scene which robbed her of her innocence. She had gone home to find roses for the convent altar; entering her beloved father's study, she surprised him in a homosexual "embrace" with a pupil. This was the delicate passage which caused the novel, such a moral novel, as it happened, to be banned.

Marie's salvation through love comes via her pupil, Anna Murphy, an autobiographical character for O'Brien, who was also placed in a convent aged six. Marie organizes Anna's education at University College, Dublin (where O'Brien herself studied), with the satisfaction of delivering her up to the real world. But Marie is a career woman, too. From the feminine society of the convent, the two heroines each achieve freedom and success, personal and professional power.

The Land of Spices took its title from a poem by George Herbert, and is about the longed-for gift of finding that spiritual other land. In the book religious understanding has affinity with the life of the imagination. Anna's spiritual victory comes when she realises the value of art. This extraordinary subject matter is only part of an insider's portrayal of a convent school, done with comedy. The book so ironically deemed immoral has become a classic of convent life.

Lucy Daniel

Date 1942

Author Kate O'Brien (1897–1974)

Nationality Ireland

Why It's Key Kate O'Brien was one of Ireland's greatest novelists and *The Land of Spices* remains the finest novel of convent life, a classic of the girls' school genre.

Key Event *The New York Times* Bestseller List is launched

While not all will admit it, there isn't an English language publisher who doesn't eagerly scour *The New York Times Book Review* magazine every Sunday to see if their latest production will be worthy of having the strap line "New York Times Bestseller" on its cover. And while some authors might rather have Pulitzer or Booker Prize Winner appended to their names, many must envy Danielle Steel her 390 consecutive weeks on the list, or Stephen King his 28 number 1 placings. There's nothing that signals success quite like the top spot on the essential chart for the biggest bookselling market in the world.

The first list appeared on 9 August 1942, with the number 1 slots on the fiction and non-fiction lists going to *And Now Tomorrow* by Rachel Field and *The Last Time I Saw Paris* by Elliot Paul respectively. Since then, every week the *Times* list has provided a barometer of publishing popularity, basing its figures on weekly sales reports from selected booksellers and wholesalers across the United States. In July 2000, in a bid to end the dominance by JK Rowling, whose first three Harry Potter books had held the top three placings on the fiction list for over a year, a separate children's list was created.

It would be hard to argue that one can equate success on the NYT list with literary merit. Few would count *The Power of Positive Thinking* by Norman Vincent Peale, which spent a total of 98 weeks at number 1 between 1953 and 1955, among the greatest books of the twentieth century, while critical heavy-weights such as Iris Murdoch, George Orwell, and Alexander Solzhenitsyn never topped the charts.

Frances Powell

Date 1942

Why It's Key *The New York Times* helped to change the perception of the publishing industry from a gentleman's profession to a multi-million dollar, unit-shifting behemoth with the introduction of their bestseller list in 1942.

Opposite *The New York Times*

Key Event Crucifixion novel becomes one of the best-selling novels of the 1940s

Lloyd C. Douglas (1877–1951) was as unlikely a candidate to become a best-selling novelist as his major work, *The Robe*, was to become a chart-topping piece of fiction. Douglas was the son of a Lutheran minister who was ordained as a minister himself and combined a career in the pulpit with a spell of religious teaching at university level. He didn't write his first novel until he retired from the ministry in his fifties. As might be expected from a clergyman, *The Robe*, like all of Douglas' work, carries a strong Christian message and is highly didactic. It tells the story of a Roman officer who, when given command of the detachment responsible for supervising the crucifixion of Jesus, wins Christ's robe in a game of dice. The robe has miraculous effects on the Roman, who eventually becomes a Christian himself and suffers blissful martyrdom.

For a historical novel of any setting to become a bestseller was very unusual, particularly as its brand of overt Christianity was more often seen as a potential turn-off for the mass popular market even in as strongly Christian a country as the United States. However, it is as much a testament to the timeless fascination of "the greatest story ever told" as it is to the writing abilities of Douglas that this novel captured the public imagination and held it for many years. *The Robe* is little read now, and more people will be familiar with the Hollywood film version of 1953 than with the text itself.

Michael Munro

Date 1942

Author Lloyd C. Douglas (1877–1951)

Nationality USA

Why It's Key Surprisingly to many, this novel written by a former Lutheran minister, based on events around the crucifixion of Christ became an instant bestseller. A few months after publication it reached number one on *The New York Times* Bestseller List and remained one of the highest-selling novels throughout the decade.

Key Event **Hernández dies while imprisoned after the Spanish Civil War**

The great Spanish poet, Miguel Hernández, who died of tuberculosis in prison in 1942 at the young age of 31, wrote some of the most heartrendingly beautiful verse of the twentieth century.

Hernández had fought for the Republican side during the Spanish Civil War and was condemned to death by the victorious fascists – a sentence commuted to 30 years' imprisonment. In 1938, while in jail, in poor health, and sorrowful after the death of his first son, Manuel Ramón, he began writing *Songs and Ballads of Absence*, a series of poems dedicated to his wife, Josefina. None of these poems were published until 1952 and as a collection not until 1958.

A sense of absence resonates in these brief songs rooted in a fragmented reality: the wind, clothes, a bed, blood, a kiss, a rose, the poet's son and wife, life, death. The poems read like an extraordinarily intense diary of the poet's heart, gentle confessions punctuated by lightning bolts of rage. In poems like "La libertad es algo," "Era un hoyo muy hondo," "Troncos de soledad," "Tan cercanos y a veces," "Escribí en el arenal," "En este campo" and "Llegó tan hondo el beso," he seemed to be thirsting for the simple traditions of Spanish poetry: the popular couplet, Antonio Machado's gnomic style, Gustavo Aldolfo Becquer's melancholy. And yet here, Hernández's melancholy is usually tempered by his natural pride. It is tragic that, at the time of his death, he was reaching the peak of his poetic powers.

Adam Feinstein

Date 1942

Title *Songs and Ballads of Absence* (*Cancionero y romancero de ausencias*, 1958)

Author Miguel Hernández (1910–42)

Nationality Spain

Why It's key This book is marked by profound personal sorrow. Hernández's first son, Manuel Ramón, was born in 1937 but he died just ten months later and Hernández never had the chance to see him alive.

Key Book
The Robber Bridegroom

Welty's first novel makes innovative use of fairytale to explore the American Deep South, whose culture thrived on romantic versions of the past, the historical novels of Sir Walter Scott being especially popular. The story is set on the Natchez Trace in the late eighteenth century. The place is wild and wooded, inhabited by notorious outlaws, by indigenous Natchez Indians, as well as by Clement, the naive, gullible father of the beautiful young heroine, Rosamond, and her wicked, ugly stepmother, Salome.

Legendary historical figures people the story, yet it reads like a fairytale, featuring a talking raven and a talking head, dangerous encounters in the forest, and repetitive quests. In particular the novel alludes to the Brothers Grimm folktale, also called "The Robber Bridegroom," and to the mythical story of Cupid and Psyche. The plot revolves around the concept of duality in all human experience (as Clement says: "All things are divided in half – night and day, the soul and body, and sorrow and joy and youth and age") – and around Clement's gullibility, Salome's bitterness, and Jamie and Rosamond's inability to recognize both aspects of each other's personalities. Its action depends on human frailty and flaws, on false recognition and misunderstandings.

Welty's style is both comic and disarmingly subversive, implicitly critiquing the Deep South for the way it mythologizes its past as "aristocratic" and its white women as "Southern Belles." She is particularly subversive in portraying a female heroine who is immediately attracted to the wild sexuality of the bandit Jamie Lockhart, even though he ravishes her. It takes the whole of the story, and many complications of the plot, for the lovers to reconcile their illicit passion with the propriety and respectability demanded by a civil society.

Helen May Dennis

Date 1942

Author Eudora Welty (1909–2001)

Nationality USA

Why It's Key Welty said of the novel: "The story is laid in actual place, traces of which still exist, and in historical times – which have been well recorded"; but "this is not a *historical* historical novel."

Opposite Eudora Welty

Key Passage *The Outsider* (*L'Étranger*)

"Mother died today. Or, maybe, yesterday; I can't be sure. The telegram from the Home says: Your mother passed away. Funeral tomorrow. Deep sympathy. Which leaves the matter doubtful; it could have been yesterday."

*T*he Outsider begins in the present tense, which establishes a sense that the first person narrator, Mersault, exists in a continuous present. In this first paragraph, narrated in a laconic, numbed tone, death announces itself suddenly in the middle of an ordinary day. It is a theme central to Camus' sense of the absurd. Human life is full of paradoxes, and the greatest of all is that we value our existence and our happiness, but at the same time we know we shall die, and that ultimately our aspirations are futile and our endeavors are meaningless. Mersault lives for sensual pleasures of the moment, and is unable to articulate his emotions, yet he ends up having to accept responsibility for an accidental killing.

A series of random circumstances draw him into a fight with an Arab, and the blazing heat of the African sun is the main reason he pulls the trigger rather than turn away. He is tried and judged guilty of murder, because he failed to cry at his mother's funeral and because he refuses to embrace Christianity and pretend repentence.

Like Camus, Mersault is a *pied-noir* Algerian. In post-war Algeria political tensions between the *pieds-noir* and the majority Muslim population were rising, and this is reflected when Mersault shoots and kills the Arab, against whom he bears no personal grudge. Readers focused on the novel's emphasis on unpretentious truth, the flaws in human justice, and on Mersault's final recognition and celebration of "the gentle indifference" of the universe.

Helen May Dennis

Date 1942

Author Albert Camus (1913–1960)

Nationality France

Why It's Key The original French text was innovative in using the colloquial compound past tense (*passé compose*), rather than the conventional past tense for literary texts (*le passé historique*). Camus is often associated with the French existentialist Jean Paul Sartre, yet both men denied that Camus was an "existentialist."

Opposite Albert Camus

Key Book
Two Serious Ladies

*B*owles wrote her one novel in the late 1930s in Paris, New York, and Mexico. She employs idiosyncratic style and subject matter, describing women in strange situations and perplexing states of mind. Structured as a triptych, it is full of love triangles, and is about women who resist conventional and comfortable roles, choosing instead to destabilize their lives in a number of deliberately perverse ways. Bowles was lesbian, which is reflected in the dedication to "Paul, Mother, and Helvetia," the latter being her lesbian lover whom she met in Mexico.

Although the two women's stories are strangely disjunct, they are acquaintances, and meet in parts 1 and 3; firstly at Miss Goering's party, and lastly in a seedy bar late at night. In the final encounter, Miss Goering remarks that Mrs. Copperfield has "gone to pieces" and Mrs. Copperfield's response is: "I have gone to pieces, which is something I've wanted to do for years." In different ways both women seek to go to

pieces, Miss Goering from an autoerotic masochistic perversion of moral sensibility, and Mrs. Copperfield in a self-destructive attempt to recover her freedom of desire in a dysfunctional marriage. Miss Goering challenges herself to enter increasingly dangerous encounters and situations, and in the process hurts everyone close to her, including her lesbian companion. Miss Goering deliberately abandons her class milieu, yet still uses her class status as an erotic mask. Mrs. Copperfield flirts with street women in the red-light district of Panama, before falling for Pacifica, who reappears in tow back in the United States in the final scene. Except she is now making her bid for freedom by asserting her right to visit her new boyfriend – yet another love triangle to end on as the two serious ladies contemplate one another in the late night bar.

Helen May Dennis

Date 1943

Author Jane Bowles (1917–73)

Nationality USA

Why It's Key Afflicted with severe writer's block, Jane Bowles' entire literary output consists of one novel, one play, and a few short stories. Nevertheless the poet John Ashbery called her "one of the finest modern writers of fiction, in any language," and for Truman Capote she was "one of the really original prose stylists."

Key Event *The Fountainhead* makes Ayn Rand a household name

It may be amusing to note today that drawing rooms across the United States in the late 1940s were in thrall to one work of fiction, whose much-maligned author was to enjoy the most temporary heights of celebrity. Rand fled the newly founded Soviet Union for the United States (in her view "the only moral country in the history of the world") in 1926 at the age of 21 to seek a career in Hollywood, where she did not prosper as she might have hoped.

Both her experiences of violent collectivism and of perceived failure in Hollywood were to inform her work until the end. Rand's espousal of Objectivism (ostensibly the refutation of altruism), which unusually for a form of philosophy enjoyed a brief popularity among the wider reading public, found much to rail against in New Deal America.

Rand's first two novels had dealt with her own experiences under collectivism in Soviet Russia but in her third, *The Fountainhead*, she turned her attention to her adoptive land. Rand reportedly based the novel on having heard a public lecture by English Fabian socialist Harold Laski and projected his shortcomings on her villain. Though Rand had tried to utilise literature as a means of getting her ideas across, having failed through film, as a book *The Fountainhead* hardly ranks as a classic. Where it does succeed (and it continues to sell well today) is the tinsel-town evocation of people and place, with its author once declaring "What other religion do we need?" of the New York skyline.

Andrew Stevens

Date 1943

Title *The Fountainhead*

Author Ayn Rand (1905–82)

Nationality USA (born Russia)

Why It's Key *The Fountainhead* was a huge commercial success; in it Rand put forward her libertarian philosophy of "Objectivism," which was taken up by many intellectuals.

Key Character **The Little Prince** *The Little Prince (Le Petit Prince)*

Saint-Exupery's beautifully crafted prose and famous accompanying water color illustrations have made the interplanetary traveling "Petit Prince" one of France's best known literary characters. The fairytale quality of the Little Prince's adventures, as recounted by the stranded airman who befriends him, continue to hold an appeal for adults and children alike. The Prince's perceptive and humorous account of the different planets and characters he has come across remind both narrator and reader of the extent to which we can lose the open honesty and optimism of childhood when we enter the adult world. Each planetary inhabitant comes to exemplify different adult failings, central among which are preoccupations with authority, time, money, drink, and vanity. The Prince leaves each planet saddened by the inability of its isolated adult inhabitant to enjoy the world they live in.

However, the burgeoning friendship between airman and boy bridges the gulf between adulthood and childhood and teaches the former to appreciate the importance of personal relationships and individual moments. Against the backdrop of the isolated Saharan desert both man and boy discover a new understanding and appreciation of the worlds they have come from. The spirit of Saint-Expury's classic story of self-discovery is encapsulated in one of the book's most oft-quoted lines, "It is only with one's heart that one can see clearly. What is essential is invisible to the human eye." Exupery's writing was often inspired by his experience as an aviator. *Le Petit Prince* is said to draw on his experience of a crash landing in the Sahara in 1935.

Kate Harris

Date 1943

Author Antoine de Saint-Exupery (1900–1944)

Nationality France

Why It's Key *The Little Prince* was imprinted on the French national consciousness by the fact that an image of Saint-Exupery and his most celebrated creation appeared on the 50 franc note until the launch of the euro. *Le Petit Prince* has sold in excess of 50 million copies worldwide.

Opposite Antoine de Saint-Exupery

Key Event **Raymond Chandler goes to Hollywood**

Look up "Raymond Chandler" in David Thomson's *Biographical Dictionary of Film*, and you won't find him. Or rather, you will, but only if you make like Philip Marlowe and grub around in other people's "lives" – Billy Wilder's, for example: "if [*Double Indemnity*] is unusually complete amid Wilder's work that may be because of Raymond Chandler's presence and the intrinsic tendency of the thriller form towards pessimism."

In many ways, Chandler's "presence" has made better films than Chandler himself ever managed. Watch films as diverse as *Bladerunner*, *Dead Men Don't Wear Plaid*, *Grosse Pointe Blank*, and *Collateral*, and you'll see Chandler writ large in the hard-boiled dialogue, atmospheric sense of place, troubled, but tough-talking loners, high sex-to-violence ratio, and infamously labyrinthine plots: not even Chandler could tell Howard Hawks who murdered Owen Taylor in *The Big Sleep*.

This is really Chandler of the novels, which added the *noir* into *film noir*; Chandler of the cinema was less influential. Having accepted Hollywood's dollar out of curiosity and financial need, he gradually realized that neither was sufficient reason to endure endless studio interference. Chandler quietly unraveled much like Faulkner, Fitzgerald, and Hammett before him: he literally drank the script for *The Blue Dahlia* into shape, then insisted on calling its female star "Moronica Lake."

These experiences did inspire Chandler's late novel, *The Little Sister*, and his candid essay, "Writers in Hollywood," for the *Atlantic* magazine. There he wrote: "The studio spends the money; all the writer spends is his time (and incidentally his life, his hopes, and all the varied experiences which finally made him into a writer)."

James Kidd

Dates: 1943–1950 in Hollywood

Author Raymond Chandler (1888–1959)

Nationality USA

Why It's Key With his hard-boiled novels a central influence on the emerging film noir genre, Chandler was a natural candidate for screenwriting. Having had a hand in some of the era's finest pictures (*Double Indemnity*, *Strangers on a Train*), the marriage of convenience descended into disarray and, by the end, mutual antipathy.

Opposite Raymond Chandler

1940–1949

313

Key Passage **"The Simple Art of Murder"** *The Simple Art of Murder*

"Down these mean streets a man must go who is not himself mean, who is neither tarnished nor afraid."

Chandler's essay is an appeal for realism in the detective story and he begins by laying into the implausible plots of some of the English classics of the genre with all the deadly power of Moose Malloy. He goes on to praise Dashiell Hammett, who "gave murder back to the kind of people that commit it for reasons" rather than used crime as merely the backdrop to a cunning puzzle. But even Hammett's work is "not quite enough": the truly realistic detective novelist must acknowledge the crooked world of which each crime is only a symptom, a world in which "gangsters can rule nations" and police and lawyers are corruptible.

Chandler ends by wondering whether a detective story can ever be "art." Even one that is scrupulously realistic must have "a quality of redemption" if it is to attain the level of art, and Chandler claims that this quality should be embodied by the detective, who must be to some extent a romantic, idealized figure: "a complete man and a common man and yet an unusual man… a man of honour, by instinct, by inevitability." This anticipates W.H. Auden's view that the detectives in aesthetically satisfying crime stories are figures of extraordinary virtue – "in a state of grace" – because they are playing a Godlike role, restoring a prelapsarian order. The essay is a fascinating insight into how Chandler created Philip Marlowe, a character whose presence can be felt in any modern story dealing with private eyes and "mean streets."

Jake Kerridge

Date 1944

Author Raymond Chandler (1888–1959)

Nationality USA

Why It's Key In his essay on the state of the detective story, published after the success of his classic novels *The Big Sleep* (1939), *Farewell, my Lovely* (1940), *The High Window* (1942), and *The Lady in the Lake* (1943), Chandler immortalized the creed of the private eye.

Key Book
Ficciones

The publication of *Ficciones* first introduced Borges' mature prose style to an audience beyond his immediate circle of admirers and fellow writers in Buenos Aires. First published in 1944, it is in fact a collection of two volumes of Borges' stories: *The Garden of Forking Paths* (1941), and *Artifices* (1944). Most of the stories from *The Garden of Forking Paths* were produced while Borges worked as a junior librarian, and some of them, most obviously "The Library of Babel," owe their genesis to his profession, and his professional surroundings. As he put it: "I have always imagined that paradise will be a kind of library."

Ficciones also introduces many of the philosophical themes and motifs that emerge again and again in Borges' later books; in particular, memory, and its relationship with the present, as in "Funes, the Memorious," the story of the man who forgets nothing, or the links between imagination, the unconscious,

and creativity, in "The Circular Ruins" and "Pierre Menard, author of Don Quixote." The combination of acute logical enquiry and narrative trickery, plus a dry sarcastic humor which characterizes Borges' unique style, has also been seen as the source of inspiration for many authors in the "Magical Realist" tradition.

Borges himself remains supremely absent from his stories, clues to authorial intent carefully removed from enigmatic texts that are a mixture of historiography, fiction, and existentialism. Despite the translation and widespread availability of many later works, Borges' reputation in the English-speaking world still rests largely on *Ficciones*.

Charles Beckett

Date 1944

Nationality Argentina

Author Jorge Luis Borges (1899–1986)

Why It's Key Writers as diverse as Salman Rushdie, Umberto Eco, Thomas Pynchon, and Gabriel García Márquez have all acknowledged their debt to the unique flights of imagination and the curious internal logic of Borges' fictional realities.

Opposite Jorge Borges

314

Key Passage **Animal Farm**
Animal Farm: A Fairy Story

"For once Benjamin consented to break his rule, and he read out to her what was written on the wall. There was nothing there now except a single Commandment. It ran:
ALL ANIMALS ARE EQUAL
BUT SOME ANIMALS ARE MORE EQUAL THAN OTHERS
After that it did not seem strange when next day the pigs who were supervising the work of the farm all carried whips in their trotters. It did not seem strange to learn that the pigs had bought themselves a wireless set, were arranging to install a telephone, and had taken out subscriptions to *John Bull*, *Tit-Bits* and the *Daily Mirror*."

The amendment to the seven commandments of animal farm – "all animals are equal but some are more equal than others" – appears on the farm wall one morning, and serves as a chilling illustration of the profound inequalities that are being perpetuated in the name of socialism.

By the end of Orwell's fable, the writing is truly on the wall for the non-porcine occupants of animal farm. The new regime has bedded in, the composition of the cohort of animals has undergone many changes, and only a few of the original number remain. The days of human rule are all but forgotten.

The steady distortion and erosion of the socialist values that gave rise to the revolution on the farm is reified in the bizarre human-like behavior adopted by the pigs. The pigs appear physically ridiculous as they try to walk on two legs and the spectacle functions as a metaphor, demonstrating that their conduct is totally at odds with their stated political aims. This is an astute allegorical representation of the gulf between the ideology and practice of Stalin's regime in the Soviet Union, which began with the promise of a communist state but came to be characterized by the appalling atrocities visited upon its people.

Juliet Wightman

Date 1945

Author George Orwell (1903-50)

Nationality UK (born India)

Why It's Key It is in this passage that Orwell uses the allegory of the animal farm to provide a succinct encapsulation of the way in which the Soviet Union's post-revolutionary communist regime eventually came to reproduce the very conditions it had originally aimed to overturn.

Key Character **Pippi Longstocking**
Pippi Longstocking

When Pippi looks up at the skies, imagining her mother in Heaven, she habitually calls out, "Don't worry, I can take care of myself!" When she parts company with the sailors who knew her father, she assures them, "Don't worry, I can take care of myself!" And she can take care of herself – magnificently. A sober assessment, of course, would lead one to the conclusion that the storm in which her father's ship was lost also made an end of him; but nine-year-old Pippi knows better. He is now living on a cannibal isle and the cannibals have made him their king.

Not only can she look after herself, she makes a point of looking after others, particularly the disgruntled, distressed, or lonely – and particularly other children. She befriends Tommy and Annika, two bored, restricted siblings who live next door to the house Pippi's father bought. Surely, you think, surely no one can get away with being "the strongest girl in the world," free of responsibility, endowed with infallible folk magic, relentlessly eccentric, with a witticism or anecdote for every occasion, before whom the dull, crushing power of adult authority must bow and bend – surely there has to be some comeuppance? Some? No. The charm and glory of Pippi lies above all in her ability to take on all comers, pompous, or bullying, and win: the genius of Astrid Lindgren ensures that Pippi's victories never become dull or predictable.

In some ways she is the warrior-poet: what she can't do herself she invents. All great children's stories are predicated on the conquest of fear. Pippi goes one further: she shows that there is nothing to fear.
Murrough O'Brien

Date 1945

Author Astrid Lindgren (1907–2002)

Nationality Sweden

Why It's Key The *Pippi Longstocking* books have sold over 40 million copies worldwide. She performed a valuable service for feminism: as an all-conquering heroine, she prompted generations of schoolboys to reflect that girls need not be quite as soft and silly as they had imagined.

Key Event **Colette is the first woman admitted to the Académie Goncourt**

The Académie Goncourt was founded in 1902, charged with awarding an annual prize for the best work of fiction in French. Its membership is restricted to ten, and admission to the select number is a sign of having become part of the French literary establishment. By 1945 Colette was already a prolific author but her career had been rather controversial. Her first novels, about a precocious young Parisian girl called Claudine, were published under the name of her older husband Henri Gauthier-Villars (known as "Willy"), and were a *succès de scandale* in belle-epoque France. She went on to appear in Paris music-hall shows, and her onstage kiss with a fellow female performer in one review almost provoked a riot in the audience. Having left her husband, she embarked on affairs with both men and women, but it was her open flaunting of a lesbian relationship that caused most outrage.

Her climb to respectability began in World War I, during which she converted a house belonging to her second husband into a hospital for wounded servicemen. For this she was awarded the Légion d'honneur in 1920. Her writing flourished after the war, her typical heroine struggling to reconcile feeling and moral discernment, and reached an even wider audience with *Chéri* (1920). By the time that her most popular novel, *Gigi* (the story of a young girl raised to be a courtesan), was published in 1945 Colette's reputation was secure. Not only did she become a member of the Académie Goncourt, she also became its president in 1949.
Michael Munro

Date 1945

Author Colette (1873–1954)

Nationality France

Why It's Key Sidonie Gabrielle Colette, who wrote under the *nom de plume* of Colette, had come a long way to achieve such respectability, having scandalized polite society with her music-hall appearances and open lesbian affairs. The publication in the same year of her most famous novel *Gigi* cemented her reputation as a writer.

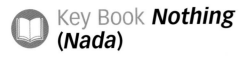

Key Book *Nothing (Nada)*

Carmen Laforet's *Nada* (*Nothing*) is one of Spain's finest – and most celebrated – modern novels. It caused a sensation on its publication in 1945 – when Laforet was just 24 – for its realistic depiction of the misery of a Barcelona just after the end of the Spanish Civil War. The manuscript of the novel had already won Laforet the very first Nadal Prize the previous year.

It is cited alongside Camilo José Cela's 1942 novel, *The Family of Pascual Duarte* (*La Familia de Pascual Duarte*), as a work which revitalized literature in Spain. Unlike most Spanish novelists of her time, Laforet wrote in short, clear sentences, and did not feel the need to present a moral message.

The narrator, Andrea, arrives in Barcelona in 1939, just after the end of the civil war, to begin her university studies. She is rapidly disillusioned by the physical violence, verbal abuse, and sexual repression she witnesses in her relatives' flat. An aunt has a lover, whose wife is in an asylum. Antonia, the filthy maid, has a foul-mouthed parrot. The family, living in idleness and fear of a return of what they see as the "red terror," represents the morally debased country which Spain has become after the cripplingly brutal conflict.

Laforet exerted an influence on Miguel Delibes and the Madrid realist writers of the 1950s. She paved the way for a generation of women novelists – such as Carmen Martín Gaite and Ana María Matute – who rebelled against the moral degradation of post-World War II Spain.

Adam Feinstein

Date 1945

Author Carmen Laforet (1921–2004)

Nationality Spain

Why It's Key Laforet wrote in 1983: "I write short, my words tight to the thread of the narrative." *Nada* has become a modern classic.

Key Character **Charles Ryder** *Brideshead Revisited*

Charles Ryder is the world-weary narrator of Evelyn Waugh's wistful masterpiece *Brideshead Revisited*. Ryder's realization that the country house site of his army billet is also the scene of his youthful association with the Flyte family, triggers a nostalgic recollection of pre-war days at Oxford as well as vividly evoked encounters in Morocco and Venice. Through his eyes we meet the members of this extraordinary Catholic aristocratic dynasty, representatives of a passing world of flamboyant decadence and effortless superiority which, like the baroque pile they inhabit, has all but fallen into obsolescence by the advent of World War II.

At Oxford, the earnest Ryder is hypnotized by Sebastian, the youngest of the Flytes, a charming socialite given to fits of whimsicality and alcoholic excess. Waugh's account of their first meeting – Sebastian vomits through the open window of his ground floor room – is characteristic of the light comic touch of *Brideshead*'s early sections. Charles is drawn into an exciting social circle and an intense friendship develops between these two whose "naughtiness high in the catalogue of grave sins" is left teasingly ill-defined by Waugh.

For many television viewers, Waugh's narrator will be forever associated with Jeremy Irons who played Charles Ryder against Anthony Andrew's Sebastian Flyte in the acclaimed 1981 adaptation by Granada Television. Memorable scenes of beautiful people cavorting against a backdrop of architectural grandeur have perhaps overshadowed the real subject of the novel as declared by Waugh – "the operation of divine grace" upon his characters and upon Charles in particular whose painful spiritual journey from casual agnosticism to heartfelt prayer, "an ancient, newly-learned form of words," in the chapel of the abandoned house lends a powerfully elegiac air to the epilogue.

Matt Birchwood

Date 1945

Title *Brideshead Revisited: The Sacred and Profane Memories of Captain Charles Ryder*

Author Evelyn Waugh (1903–1966)

Nationality UK

Why It's Key *Brideshead Revisited* represented a departure from the stringent satire of Waugh's earlier comic works and was judged overblown and sentimental by some of its first critics.

Key Event **Alexander Solzhenitsyn is sentenced to eight years in a labor camp**

Alexander Solzhenitsyn, a distinguished Red Army officer who made disparaging political remarks in a letter home from the front, was caught by military censors and sentenced to eight years' hard labor as the war ended. His subsequent tale of life in a prison camp, *One Day in the Life of Ivan Denisovich* (1962), had enormous repercussions both in Russia and the West. He showed that most of the inmates were innocent of any crime, and were treated with an inhumanity utterly at odds with the Soviet Union's professed humanist ideals. Solzhenitsyn's story of one decent and dignified man's survival under wretched conditions implicated Stalin's regime rather than the entire Soviet ethos, and even signalled hope. He just managed to get it published by the prominent literary journal *Novy Mir*, in 1962, before the thaw initiated by Khrushchev's anti-Stalin speech in 1956 ended with Khrushchev's own downfall as Soviet leader. The story became politically unmentionable.

Subsequently marginalized, and eventually expelled from the Soviet Writers' Union in 1969, Solzhenitsyn found his real form as a writer in the two great novels he published abroad, *Cancer Ward* (1968) and *The First Circle* (1969). His metaphorical titles (the second an allusion to Dante's Inferno) made his camp reminiscences stand in part for the entire imprisoned condition of Soviet life. The controlled surroundings of the camp's cancer ward and, in the second case, the special technical institute where imprisoned scientists worked, set the stage for rich conversations about the nature of Russia and illustrated the dilemma of moral choice under political oppression.
Lesley Chamberlain

Date 1945

Title *One Day in the Life of Ivan Denisovich* (1962)

Author Alexander Solzhenitsyn (born 1918)

Nationality Russia

Why It's Key This candid tale was published in Russia during the post-Stalinist Thaw. Once Brezhnev's regime plunged the country back into ideological stasis its revelations about prison camp life became above all a landmark in Western understanding of the "real" Russia.
Opposite Solzhenitsyn

Key Event **The affair between Elizabeth Smart and George Barker**

Elizabeth Smart led an eventful early life. She had completed a round-the-world journey while still a student, and was a frequent visitor to Europe. In the 1930s she had embarked on an affair with the painter Jean Varda, a friend of Anaïs Nin's. It was during a visit to London, however, that the event occurred that was to change her life, and to make her a writer. She was browsing the bookshops of Charing Cross Road when she happened on a copy of a book of poems by George Barker. By the time that she had finished the book, she was convinced that Barker was the man that she wanted to marry. Returning to North America at the outbreak of World War II, Smart was able to contact him, and Barker replied asking for her help in escaping Japan, where he had been sent as a teacher by the British Council. Smart was able to arrange and to pay for the passage of Barker and his wife to the safe haven of the United States. Within a month of his arrival, Smart and Barker had become lovers, and were

expecting a child, although he refused to leave his wife. Smart turned her heartbreak into one of the most breathtaking achievements in English prose of the twentieth century, *By Grand Central Station I Sat Down And Wept*. The book combines poetry, Biblical language, and a symphonic structure to portray Smart as the archetypal spurned lover. The book, first published in 1945, became a cult sensation, and achieved a wider impact when a revised version was published in 1966. Smart returned to England in 1942, and eventually bore Barker four children. They never married.
Neil Wallington

Date 1945 (publication)

Author Elizabeth Smart (1913–86)

Nationality Canada

Why It's Key Smart falls in love with a man she has never met through the power of the written word and begins an affair. When he refuses to leave his wife, she produces one of the most extraordinary memoirs in English, a book so candid that her parents persuade the Canadian prime minister to ban it for 30 years.

Key Book
The Pursuit of Love

The Pursuit Of Love was Nancy Mitford's fifth book, and the one which cemented her reputation as a gifted comic writer. The eldest sister of the celebrated Mitford clan (containing fascists, communists, and a Duchess), Nancy was the one to realize that their eccentric upbringing would make an excellent setting for comedy.

Although *The Pursuit Of Love* and its sequel, *Love In A Cold Climate*, are ostensibly fiction, she made ample use of her parents, Lord and Lady Redesdale, who became Uncle Matthew and Aunt Sadie, and her siblings (Jassy's running-away fund, for example, is based on Jessica Mitford's savings, which she indeed used to run away with her future husband, Esmond Romilly, to fight in the Spanish Civil War). Nancy's relatives reacted reasonably patiently to her often ungenerous caricatures of them – although the occasional friction between them can be read in *Love From Nancy: The Letters Of Nancy Mitford*.

The Pursuit Of Love captured its readers' imagination – the demented family of "Mad, mad Mitfords," with terrifying Uncle Matthew and dippy Aunt Sadie at their centre. There is an edge beneath the glittering prose, however – the girls may have grown up in a vast country mansion, but to them it was a prison – with no formal education, and isolated in the countryside, they were dependent on finding husbands who could take them away to new and more fulfilling lives.

The two books were adapted by Deborah Moggach for a successful BBC TV series in 2001, *Love In A Cold Climate*, starring Rosamund Pike.
Natalie Haynes

Date 1945

Author Nancy Mitford (1904–73)

Nationality USA

Why It's Key *The Pursuit of Love* and its sequel *Love in a Cold Climate* were thinly disguised accounts of the Mitfords' eccentric family life, and cemented the reputation of the sisters. Mitford also introduced the terms "U" and "non-U" in her comic study of the English aristocracy, *Noblesse Oblige*.

1940–1949

321

Key Event **Gabriela Mistral wins the Nobel Prize in Literature**

The Chilean poet, Gabriela Mistral (1889–1957), was living in Petrópolis, in southeast Brazil, when the Swedish Ambassador informed her that she had been awarded the 1945 Nobel Prize in Literature. It was the first time the prize had ever been granted to a Latin American writer.

It came as a welcome piece of good news following a bleak period for Mistral: her close friend, the Austrian-Jewish writer, Stefan Zweig, who was living in Petrópolis in flight from Nazi persecution, had committed suicide with his wife in 1942. The following year, tragedy struck again, when her 17-year-old nephew, Juan Miguel, nicknamed Yin-Yin, took his own life with arsenic.

At the age of 56, she boarded the steamer Ecuador bound for Stockholm to receive the Nobel Prize on December 10, 1945, from King Gustav V of Sweden. In its citation, the Swedish Academy declared: "It is in homage to Latin America's rich literature that

we turn today to its queen, the poet of Desolation, who has become the great songstress of compassion and maternity." Within months, more awards flowed in: she received France's Légion d'Honneur, an honorary doctorate from the University of Florence in Italy and the Enrique José Varona Medal from Cuba.

Born Lucila Godoy Alcayaga, she first gained renown as a poet in 1914 when she won the Chilean Society of Artists and Writers' prize for her collection, *Sonnets of Death* (*Sonetos de la muerte*). Her first book of poems, *Desolation* (*Desolación*), was published in New York in 1922. Among the best-known of her other collections are *Tala* (1938) and *Lagar* (1954).
Adam Feinstein

Date 1945

Nationality Chile

Why It's Key In 1932, Mistral became the first Chilean woman to be given a diplomatic posting abroad – as consul in Genoa – although she was unable to take up her duties there because the Mussolini regime placed her under house arrest. After that, she served as consul in Madrid, Lisbon, Guatemala, Nice, L.A., and New York.

Opposite Mistral receives the Nobel Prize

Key Passage *The Common Sense Book of Baby and Child Care*

"Trust yourself, you know more than you think you do…"

"Trust yourself," Dr. Spock urged anxious parents, "you know more than you think you do." By advocating a more intuitive approach to childcare, and insisting that common sense could and would enable new parents to make conscientious and judicious choices about the children's care, Spock radically challenged the conventional wisdom of pre-war experts. His austere predecessors seemed to detect malice and manipulation in the instinctive behaviors of newborns and young children, and urged parents not to pick up crying infants or display any kind of warmth or affection that may lead to "spoiling."

Although with the publication of *The Common Sense Book of Baby and Child Care* Spock undoubtedly broke new ground, his ideas were firmly of his time. The unflinching obedience that doctors such as Truby King deemed necessary assumed unwelcome connotations after World War II and from the turn of the century, Freudian psychoanalysis became hugely influential. As a result, there was a newfound sense of the psychological basis of children's behaviors and an understanding of key developmental processes. This was accompanied by a desire to recognize and engage with the fears and anxieties of children and to provide them with a loving and nurturing environment in which to grow to adulthood.

Spock's great achievement was that he assimilated these new ways of thinking and evaluated their collective implications for the way in which children were raised. What is more, he was able to present this advice in an authoritative yet accessible text.
Juliet Wightman

Date 1945

Author Dr. Benjamin Spock (1903–98)

Nationality USA

Why It's Key This passage is indicative of the relaxed, flexible, and confident parenting that Dr. Spock encouraged. The book's status as the best-selling non-fiction book after the Bible is testament to the enduring appeal of the common-sense approach to childcare that it espouses.

Opposite Dr. Spock

Key Event **The Bombing of Dresden is witnessed by the young Kurt Vonnegut**

"I thought it would be easy for me to write about the destruction of Dresden," writes Kurt Vonnegut in *Slaughterhouse Five*, "since all I would have to do would be to report what I had seen… But not many words about Dresden came from my mind…." That may have been true, but the words which did finally come from Vonnegut's mind about the fire-bombing of the German city of Dresden created a fire-storm of another kind. *Slaughterhouse Five* became Vonnegut's breakout novel and an anti-war classic.

Couched as science fiction, the novel is the story of Billy Pilgrim, an inept soldier taken prisoner by the Germans who survives the bombing of Dresden. Billy consequently becomes "unstuck in time," randomly traveling back and forth through parts of his life, including his future. In doing so, he learns a lesson from the alien Tralfamadorians who hold him captive in his future: because time has four dimensions and all moments are always happening, one is always living, and always dying. Billy's mantra – "And so it goes" – is the result of this lesson, and perhaps Vonnegut's most famous aphorism.

Vonnegut's inspiration was his experience as a prisoner-of-war. He was being held in Dresden during February 13–15, 1945 when Allied forces dropped over 3,000 tons of bombs on the city. Dresden, once considered the "Venice of the north," was largely destroyed. Haunted for years by his wartime experience, Vonnegut set out to write an anti-war book which would persuade people "that they are not under any circumstances to take part in massacres, and that news of massacres of enemies is not to fill them with satisfaction or glee."
Elizabeth Rosen

Date February 13–15, 1945

Place Dresden, Germany

Why It's Key The devastating aerial raid on the city of Dresden near the end of World War II inspired Kurt Vonnegut's 1969 novel *Slaughterhouse Five*. The novel's fiercely anti-war message touched a nerve with a young, idealistic population already suspicious of the military-industrial machine, and ultimately made the novel a classic in the anti-war genre.

Key Book
Comet in Moominland

Although the Moomins themselves first appeared in an earlier book entitled *The Little Trolls and the Great Flood*, *Comet in Moominland* is widely acknowledged as the formal beginning of the Moomin series. After the dark years of World War II, Jansson created these gentle, accepting, and noble creatures, who look after one another to the last and have a strong and unshakable sense of justice. The events that befall them, though dealt with lightly, often have a greater social significance however and *Comet in Moominland* has been seen by many as an allegory for nuclear warfare.

Moominpappa is engaged in writing his memoirs (these were later published as *The Exploits of Moominpappa*) and is busy tidying the garden and making jam, and so away from all this domestic activity, Moomintroll and Sniff set off to explore. They discover that a comet is headed straight towards Moomin Valley and they have a matter of days before it hits.

"'What would happen then?' whispered Sniff.

'Everything would explode,' said Moomintroll, gloomily.

There was a long silence.

'Then Snufkin said slowly: 'It would be awful if the earth exploded. It's so beautiful.'"

The only thing to do is to set off for the Observatory to talk to the Professors and so, with a packet of sandwiches and a pair of woolly stockings lovingly packed by Moominmamma they set out to save the world.

Witty and insightful, *Comet in Moominland* introduces characters who would later gain a world-wide cult following – inquisitive and philosophical trolls who set the world to rights.

Francesca Segal

Date 1946

Author Tove Jansson (1914–2001)

Nationality Finland

Why It's Key The Moomin family consists of Moominpappa, Moominmamma, and their son Moomintroll. They are joined in their adventures by many other strange creatures who have cameos throughout this enduring series, which gradually blurred the line between children's and adults' literature.

Opposite Moominland

Key Book
All the King's Men

It is often assumed that Robert Penn Warren based the protagonist of his novel, the political demagogue Willie Stark, on the populist Louisiana governor Huey P. Long (1893–1935) who, like Stark, was assassinated. While Warren himself denied this, there are some unmistakable parallels.

The story of Stark's rise to political power from ordinary beginnings is, on the face of it, utterly in keeping with the American ideal that any child born in the United States can grow up to be president. When he starts out, Stark is sincere in his desire to help the common people, specifically the poor farmers in the American South at the height of the Depression, but the corrupting effect of power soon tells on him and he ends by being interested only in furthering his own career at the expense of those he has supposedly been elected to represent. Stark acquires enemies, both through using blackmail as a means of his advancement and through his predatory sexual conquests, and one of these enemies will bring about his death.

The outright cynicism of Jack Burden, who becomes Willie's tool and narrates the novel, came as shocking to many American readers who at the time were still convinced that their political leaders were basically moral men, no matter what area of the political spectrum they occupied. *All the King's Men* had the effect of leading more Americans to question the motives and character of their politicians, a process that continued throughout the twentieth century, reaching its culmination, perhaps, in the Watergate scandal of the 1970s, whose revelations came as less of a surprise than would once have been the case.

It has been filmed twice: in 1949, winning Oscars but differing considerably from the novel, and again, more faithfully, in 2006.

Michael Munro

Date 1946

Author Robert Penn Warren (1905–89)

Nationality USA

Why It's Key This classic study of political corruption won the Pulitzer Prize (making Warren the only person to have won the prize for both fiction and poetry) and was a dramatic exposé of the cynicism at the heart of the American Dream and of the perversion of the great ideal of democracy.

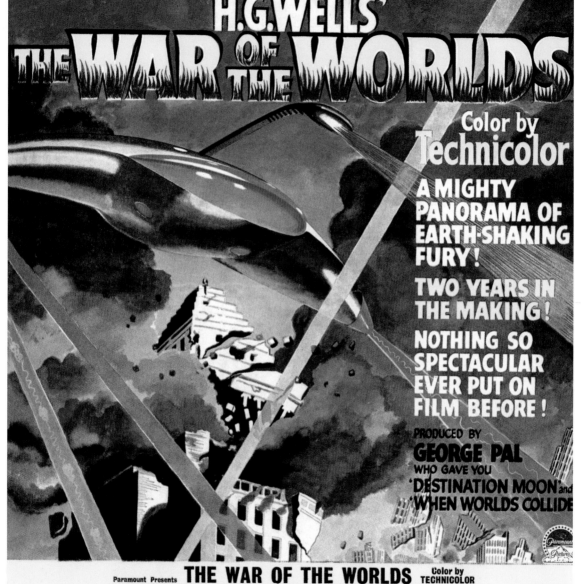

Key Author
H.G. Wells

Herbert George Wells (1866–1946) was one of the loudest voices in the world of letters in Britain during the first decades of the twentieth century. As a youth he worked as a draper's apprentice, but, having acquired a taste for reading and determined to improve himself, he found work as a teaching assistant, before winning a scholarship to study biology at the Normal School of Science in London.

Wells married his cousin in 1891, but ran off with the woman who was to become his second wife three years later. He never took to marriage, and became an advocate of free love. He also became a committed socialist, joining the Fabian Society in 1903, but soon fell out with his fellow Fabians, George Bernard Shaw and Beatrice and Sidney Webb.

Wells' first novels – such as *The Time Machine* (1895), *The Island of Doctor Moreau* (1896), and *The War of the Worlds* (1898) – were science fiction. He took the genre beyond the high adventure and technological speculation of Jules Verne, using it rather as a means to explore social and political issues, and to express his concerns about where science might lead humanity.

His next group of novels, such as *Kipps* (1905) and *The History of Mr. Polly* (1910), are comic yet realistic portrayals of lower-middle-class life. As Wells grew older, he became less concerned with literary values than with the necessity for social progress if humanity was not to destroy itself: "Human history becomes more and more a race between education and catastrophe," he wrote in 1920. The advent of World War II increased his pessimism, and he died shortly after its conclusion.

Ian Crofton

Date 1946 (death)

Nationality UK

Other Key Works *The Invisible Man* (1897), *A Modern Utopia* (1905), *Ann Veronica* (1909), *Tono-Bungay* (1909), *The Shape of Things to Come* (1933)

Why It's Key One of the pioneers of science fiction, who was also influential as a "straight" novelist, as a social and political polemicist, and as a popularizer of both history and science.

Opposite *War of the Worlds*

Key Event **Boris Pasternak first meets Olga Ivinskaya**

SPOILER

Boris Pasternak's life and work both occupy a prominent romantic position in twentieth-century Russian literature, where Pasternak is most celebrated as a poet. *Doctor Zhivago*, "The Doctor of Life," has a rough chronological structure but essentially its time frame is poetic, measured by chance meetings between Yuri Zhivago, his beloved Lara, and the Communist husband Antipov whom she abandons. Pasternak interweaves poems with moments of spiritual awakening while the Revolution and subsequent Civil War made daily life a struggle for survival. A huge cast of incidental characters comes and goes in a way reminiscent of the great nineteenth-century Russian novels, loose and baggy in form, as Henry James called them, but saturated with life and the quest for its meaning.

As a writer cum Russian-style philosopher Pasternak was steeped in the religious mysticism of the fin-de-siècle and his natural means of expression was symbolic. Some western critics objected, but the "universe," manifest in nature, time, and the power of coincidence, gave his novel all the continuity and coherence he thought necessary. The Russian Eternal Feminine, an essential aspect of that universe, was embodied in Lara, who, when she finally chose the weak Zhivago over the strong Antipov revealed Russia's true and tragic destiny. What added depth to Pasternak's portrait of his spiritual generation, and of the age Russia's Silver Age poets and philosophers shared with Lenin and the Red Army, was the respect Zhivago and Antipov showed each other, as two manifestations of the Russian dream, both demanding so much self-sacrifice.

Lesley Chamberlain

Date 1946

Title *Doctor Zhivago* (1957; 1987 in Russia)

Author Boris Pasternak (1890–1960)

Nationality Russia

Why It's Key For his only novel, an epic and poetic treatment of how the Russian intelligentsia experienced the Bolshevik revolution, Pasternak drew on his love for a young editor, Olga Ivinskaya. The result was one of the greatest love stories of all time.

Key Passage
America is in the Heart

"We are all Americans that have toiled and suffered and known oppression and defeat, from the first Indian that offered peace in Manhattan to the last Filipino pea pickers."

This much-cited statement from Bulosan's semi-fictionalized autobiography illuminates its central ideological message. Typically both passionate and didactic, he addresses his major concern of national identity by aligning the struggles of Filipino migrants in Depression-era California with an aboriginal American past, a move which makes the Filipino presence in the United States seem inevitable (which largely it is, given the countries' interrelationship). Simultaneously, he draws on the nation's multiracial heritage to contest ideas of American-ness as white, by excluding Caucasians (who violently oppress people of color throughout the text) both here and from the vision of America which directly follows.

Here, perhaps more than anywhere else in this work, Bulosan offers his own version of the Declaration of Independence, but conceptualizes it in specifically transnational terms. America is a utopian ideal as much as a literal place. It is "a prophecy of a new society of men: of a system that knows no sorrow or strife or suffering." Notwithstanding the gendered nature of this romanticised image – some critics have noted Bulosan's exclusive emphasis on men in this passage – and the text's wider tension between fact and fiction, this dream of America as a beacon of freedom and equality, as the sum of its founding principles, has continued to resonate with readers, lifting the memoir beyond its particular time and place.
Ruth Maxey

Date 1946

Author Carlos Bulosan (1913–56)

Nationality Philippines

Why It's Key A landmark work of Asian American letters, *America is in the Heart* gave impassioned voice to dispossessed migrant laborers, and particularly to the exilic lives of Filipinos, in America's West Coast states in the 1930s and 40s. Bulosan was one of the first Filipinos to produce a major literary work in English.

Key Event
Publication of "Hiroshima"

On August, 31, 1946, a year after the first atomic bomb was dropped, readers of *The New Yorker* opened their copies to find the entire issue devoted to a journalistic account of the bombing of Hiroshima, as seen through the eyes of six eye-witnesses. John Hersey's (1914–1993) even-handed and objective reporting was later republished as the book *Hiroshima* and became a profoundly influential bestseller.

With great restraint, and eschewing sentimentality, *Hiroshima* detailed the lives of two physicians, a poor widow with three children, a German Jesuit missionary, a young clerk, and a Japanese Methodist minister before, during, and after the attack. In addition to making the hundred thousand Japanese who died in the attack real human beings rather than statistics, *Hiroshima* was also a pivotal document because it, unlike much of what had been written in the year after the attack and in spite of government claims to the contrary, made it clear that radiation poisoning

from the bomb was in fact having a long-term and fatal effect.

Though the article was criticized by a few for not showing enough emotion in depicting the horrors of an atomic attack, Hersey's account largely received accolades from other critics and readers-at-large. Charles Poore of *The New York Times* wrote, "Nothing that can be said about the book can equal what the book has to say," and Louis Ridenour, writing for the *Saturday Review of Literature*, lauded Hersey's handling of the topic, saying, "It seems to me impossible for anyone to read 'Hiroshima' without drawing morals for himself… everyone able to read should read it, and go on to speak of the morals that I feel should be drawn from this superb bit of reporting."
Elizabeth Rosen

Date 1946

Title "Hiroshima" (*New Yorker*); later republished as a book *Hiroshima*

Author John Hersey

Nationality USA

Why It's Key Heralded as an objective and important piece of journalism which exposed the horror of the atomic bombing of Hiroshima and the subsequent radiation poisoning, Hersey's account was one of the first to put human faces to the statistics.

Key Book
If This Is a Man

"Our language lacks words to express this offence, the demolition of a man," Primo Levi wrote in *If This is a Man*, his extraordinary memoir of his ten-month long imprisonment in Auschwitz.

Levi was a chemist living in his native Turin when he was captured by the Nazis and sent to the German death camp. "It was my good fortune to be deported to Auschwitz only in 1944," Levi stated in the preface. The work's title pervades the whole book, as Levi asks what a man really is in a place such as Auschwitz; whether humanity or morality can survive in a world where the concentration camp exists. The power of this work lies both in the horrific story it tells, and in Levi's clear and unsentimental prose. He speaks neither of revenge nor hatred, though he always denied forgiving the Germans.

Although liberated by the Red Army in January 1945, Levi did not reach Turin until October of that year. He wrote the book "in order of urgency" after he returned to Italy, partly to tell the world what had happened and partly to write the experience out of his system. That he was unable to do the latter was attested by his suicide in 1987.

The book was brought out by a small publisher in November 1947, and only 1,500 copies were sold. Levi had to wait until 1958 before Einaudi published it, in a revised form. The book was first translated into English in 1959, and subsequently many other languages.

Rosie Blau

Date 1947

Author Primo Levi (1919–87)

Nationality Italian

Why It's Key This was one of the most important works of the twentieth century, drawing attention to the horror of the Holocaust and the questions these events raised for the whole of humanity. Levi's was one of the first books on the subject to reach a wide international audience.

Key Event
Gruppe 47 is formed in Germany

The founding members of Gruppe 47 were Hans Werner Richter (1908–93) and Alfred Andersch (1914–80), who set up the group when *Der Ruf*, the magazine they edited, was banned by the Allied occupation authorities (Andersch, a former Communist party member, was doubtless regarded with great suspicion). Their own work is relatively little known outside Germany, and they certainly never sought to form a "school" or gain literary disciples, but their influence has been all the greater for this. Though Group membership was "by invitation only," it was not a clique. Above all it sought to encourage young writers, and the Group prize became one of the most prestigious and coveted accolades a young writer could receive. It was awarded to many who later achieved worldwide fame, including two writers who later won the Nobel Prize: Heinrich Böll (1950), and Günter Grass (1958, awarded – pre-publication – for *The Tin Drum*). Böll, with his spare style and moralist's eye for the guilty traces of totalitarianism in the democratic Federal Republic, is in many ways representative of the Group's ethos.

The group was always unapologetically on the left, but undogmatically so, and it had wide influence on a generation and more of German writers. However, the Europe-wide political ructions of 1968 proved too much to avoid splits and open controversy, even for a group which had weathered two decades at the center of the country's literary life. The final meeting of the group was in 1967, and it was formally wound up a decade later.

Cathy Benson

Date 1947

Nationality Germany

Why It's Key In 1945 the German literary scene was a panorama of devastation. Many writers had emigrated to escape the Nazis, some had perished in concentration camps, and others had committed suicide. The German language itself seemed tainted by a dozen years of official Nazi rhetoric. Gruppe 47 engaged with this daunting context, and left a lasting imprint on modern German literature.

Key Event *I Will Spit on Your Graves (J'irai cracher sur vos tombes)* causes a scandal

The moral outrage concerning Boris Vian's novel *I Will Spit on Your Graves (J'irai cracher sur vos tombes)* made him a reluctant celebrity villain. At the time Vian was already known as a pillar of the bohemian Left Bank in Paris: a civil engineer by profession, the "prince of Saint-Germain-des-Près" was also a jazz trumpeter and singer, a magazine reviewer, and a satirical columnist in Sartre's periodical, *Les Temps modernes*. The novel resulted from a bet Vian had made with his publisher, to write an American-style hard-boiled thriller in two weeks. Set in the American South, it told the story of a black man, with skin so fair he passed for a white man, who avenges his brother's lynching by seducing and murdering white women. To enhance authorial credibility, Vian assumed the pseudonym "Vernon Sullivan," identifying himself as the "translator" into French.

The book sold well, but after a copy was found by the Parisian hotel bed on which a married man had shot his lover and then committed suicide, Vian was demonized by the tabloids and consequently prosecuted for causing an outrage to public morals. He was fined one franc for every copy sold – 100,000 by that time – but also suffered a gross misrepresentation of his writing style and abilities. The scandal reflected the post-war French fascination with American popular culture, tainted as it was with fear and moral ambivalence. Only posthumously, in the 1960s, was Vian's work rediscovered for its true innovative value, rather than by its association with American culture.

Nimrod Ben-Cnaan

Date 1947

Author Vernon Sullivan, pseudonym of Boris Vian (1920–59)

Nationality France

Why It's Key Public outrage was caused over a violent, American-style thriller novel crediting as its author the African-American alter ego of Boris Vian, a central figure in the bohemian Paris left bank. This resulted in the first French obscenity trial since that of Flaubert's *Madame Bovary*.

Key Author
Willa Cather

Willa Cather was born in 1873 (died 1947) in Virginia and brought up from the age of nine in Nebraska. After some years working as a teacher and then a journalist she turned to writing full-time, and in the course of four prolific decades wrote twelve novels of extraordinary range and material density. Together they make up a momentous imaginative reconstruction of North American history, at once celebrating the creative forces behind American expansion and lamenting a lost heroic past. The depicted locations include, among others, seventeenth-century Québec, New Mexico, Nebraska, Virginia, New York, and Chicago.

The important artistic principle she puts forward in her essay "The Novel Démeublé" – that "whatever is felt upon the page without being specifically named there – that, one might say, is created" – is suggestive of the underlying weight of her fictions and characters, often reminiscent of Turgenev, and suggestive too in relation to an often enigmatic sense of sexual dislocation in her work. In recent years Cather's work has begun to recover from a critical condescension once visited on it, perhaps on account of distaste for her seemingly old-fashioned taste for the elegiac and her dislike of modernity. She is now more frequently recognized as a complex and contemporary artist, modern in her sense of the complications of race and gender, and of the ways in which fantasy goes into the narrative making of cultures. She can be seen too as a writer of apparently traditional but in fact audaciously and subtly experimental narratives, most notably perhaps the sections of her masterpiece *Death Comes for the Archbishop* (1927), arranged like panels in the pictorial narrative of a saint's life.

Peter Swaab

Date 1947 (death)

Nationality USA

Key Works *O Pioneers!* (1913), *My Ántonia* (1918), *The Professor's House* (1925), *Lucy Gayheart* (1935), *Sapphira and the Slave Girl* (1940)

Why It's Key Cather's work explored a complicated modern understanding of race and gender through subtle experiment and wide-ranging subject matter. Her theme is America, but her narratives have universal scope.

Key Book
Doctor Faustus

Dr. Faustus reworked key aspects of the life of Nietzsche, and of the tragedy of German culture in making way for the rise of Hitler, into this story of an avant-garde composer, Adrian Leverkühn, who entered into a pact with the devil in pursuit of his art. Mann drew liberally on the history of turn-of-the-century German music, and figures like the composer Arnold Schoenberg and the conductor Bruno Walter to bring the contradictions of genius to life. Probably no great prose fiction writer has explored the metaphysics of music so profoundly, nor been able to bring literature and music formally so close.

Like the pre-war *The Magic Mountain*, and many of his smaller works, this novel once more gave life to Mann's own artistic obsessions. The explicit link it forged between Expressionist art and Nazism showed Mann at once – through the Faustian theme – taking on the mantel of Goethe as poet of the nation, and in a more personal sense accepting some blame for the German collapse. Yet the political equation was never so convincing as the extraordinary map Mann drew in *Dr. Faustus* of his own tormented and voluptuous inner landscape, where he lived in thrall to beautiful form while constantly doubting his capacity to feel true charity for another human being. Mann wrote a book-length afterword, published separately, *The Genesis of a Novel*, in which he tried to make clear his aims. To the end of his life the liberal activist commentator and the metaphysically-inclined artist were in conflict.

Lesley Chamberlain

Date 1947

Author Thomas Mann (1875–1955)

Nationality Germany

Why It's Key Difficult, dense and fascinating, this novel is Mann's last attempt to link Germany's twentieth-century disaster with the pessimism of its artistic tradition.

Key Book *The Path to the Spiders' Nests* (*Il sentiero dei nidi di ragno*)

Partisan warfare seen through the eyes of a child: a metaphor and a projection for the inadequacies of the self. After all, it is perfectly legitimate to feel inadequate when confronted with history. Cesare Pavese had had no doubts. It was a promising first book, a kind of fairy tale from the woods, told out of playfulness rather than fear, and he was ready to champion it.

Yet Calvino wasn't entirely at ease. Official excuses were indeed not hard to find. You couldn't be held responsible. You could barely be called an author, such were the times in post-war Italy. At best you were but the anonymous voice of the collective trauma, a witness and a survivor. And even if there was a responsibility of sorts (for you had to gamble on tales of war and resistance), you could still be excused on the grounds of having used up your creativity to satisfy the need for cathartic storytelling universally felt at the time.

Always one for editing his own work in some official, advertised capacity, and having reached the mid-point of his career, in 1964 Calvino re-prefaced his youthful *The Path to the Spiders' Nests* along such lines, for he still felt uneasy about that book, an unease bordering on remorse. Because if there can be excuses for the creative act, what about the fear it had left him with? In spending the times, the chance, the book, he had discovered his own engagement in dangerous games of desire, games involving life and death at their crudest. He was bound to find out that he couldn't really blame those games, as much as he would like to, on the power of stories to tell themselves regardless, the very tenet of his neorealism, soon exhausted, and, since that exhaustion, of his mature poetics also.

Federica Pedriali

Date 1947

Author Italo Calvino (1923–85)

Nationality Italy

Why It's Key Calvino's early novel established, and exhausted, one of the possible manners of neorealist fiction.

Key Event
First publication of Anne Frank's diary

Anne Frank's (1929–42) diary was first published in the Netherlands in 1947, under the title *Het Achterhuis*, or *The Secret Annexe*. An eloquent record of the two years which her Jewish family spent in hiding during World War II, it is written with courage, humor, and wisdom. In 1942, when thirteen-year-old Anne began her diary, her home town of Amsterdam was already under Nazi occupation. Weeks later, her family and four companions went into hiding in an unused apartment in Otto Frank's office. The entry to this "secret annexe" was concealed from the office by a moveable bookcase. Only a few trusted employees knew of their presence and, during business hours, the secret inhabitants were obliged to be still and silent.

Anne's diary expresses the frustration of confinement and the fear of being discovered, whilst chronicling the shifting emotions of any girl passing from childhood to adolescence, rebelling against her parents, and falling in love. The diary ends abruptly in 1944, when the family were betrayed and deported. After the war, when it was confirmed that Anne had died at Bergen-Belsen, her father, the sole surviving family member, was persuaded to publish it. The Dutch publication was followed by German, French, American, and English versions, but only when it was adapted for the New York stage did it achieve worldwide popularity. Today, the public imagination remains profoundly touched by the lively, intelligent, mischievous girl who wrote with such spirit and searching self-criticism in the face of persecution, danger, and death.

Amy Rosenthal

Date 1947

Place Netherlands

Why It's Key The publication of Anne Frank's diary provided the world with a face for the 1.5 million Jewish children murdered in the Holocaust. For future generations, her diary is a key to remembering the genocide as well as to honoring the dead, and her unmitigated faith in humanity is an inspiration.

Opposite Anne Frank at her desk, in hiding

Key Event
The "Black Dahlia" murder

The Black Dahlia case is America's equivalent of the Jack the Ripper killings – the gruesome unsolved murder of Betty Short, a failed but beautiful young actress whose mutilated corpse was discovered near the famous Hollywood sign in 1947. The murder garnered untold media attention at the time, and has proven a seemingly endless source of speculation ever since. More importantly, however, the case also provided James Ellroy (born 1948) (whose own mother had been murdered when he was ten years old) with grist for his imaginative mill. His novel takes the merest outline of "real" events and improvises freely – almost all of his characters are fictional.

The first-person narrator is Bucky Bleichert, a young cop whose partner becomes obsessed with the murder before disappearing; in turn, Bleichert is also irresistibly drawn into the investigation, to the detriment of his health, his marriage, and his career. Ellroy's remarkable talent for internecine plotting is showcased by the detailed web of connections that accumulates around the figure of the Black Dahlia herself. Equally typical of his writing is the richness of the language, a kaleidoscopic mixture of police procedural jargon and underworld slang. *The Black Dahlia* established the author's vision of post-war Los Angeles as an inferno of drugs, pornography, violence, and corruption – a vision of the city in which crime is an integral part of the political and economic system, and everything is connected, from highlife to lowlife. Ellroy takes us to dark places that Philip Marlowe never dreamed of.

Rowland Hughes

Date 1947

Place USA

Why It's Key Besides a slew of "true crime" books on the subject, the murder inspired James Ellroy's novel of the same name, the first of his *LA Quartet* also featuring *The Big Nowhere*, *LA Confidential*, and *White Jazz*. The novels elevated Ellroy from the status of talented popular novelist to the front rank of contemporary American writers. Ellroy's novel was adapted for the screen by Brian De Palma in 2006.

Key Passage
A Streetcar Named Desire

"Whoever you are – I have always depended on the kindness of strangers."

Blanche DuBois' reference to "the kindness of strangers" in the final scene of *A Streetcar Named Desire* serves to emphasize the extent of the emotional destruction that has been unleashed by the relationships most closely bound by ties of blood and marriage.

As in much of Williams' work, the unhappy past hangs over the present. In Blanche DuBois, one of post-war American drama's most famous female protagonists, Williams created a character whose troubled sexual past shattered traditional expectations of "respectable" female behavior. The genteel southern belle is exposed as an unstable fantasist with a drink problem and a sexual proclivity for much younger men. Yet this damning portrait of Blanche is tempered by the audience's knowledge of the tragedy of her first

marriage and her brutal treatment at the hands of her brother-in-law Stanley. The play's ending is brutally honest in its depiction of human desire and loss.

An unhinged Blanche is taken away by a doctor at the uneasy request of her beloved sister Stella. Husband and wife are left on stage, emotionally ravaged and divided by the events unleashed by Blanche's visit. Williams broke away from the constraints of traditional stage realism in the stage directions for this scene: "Lurid reflections appeared on the walls in odd, sinuous shapes. The 'Varsouviana' is filtered into weird distortion, accompanied by the cries and noises of the jungle." The nightmarish physical disintegration of the domestic setting gives an added tension to the dark emotional undercurrents that come to the fore at the end of this powerful piece of drama.
Kate Harris

Date 1947

Author Tennessee Williams (1911–1983)

Nationality USA

Why It's Key *Streetcar* established Williams' reputation as a major post-war American dramatist when it garnered multiple awards. Williams' open exploration of the powerful force of sexual desire shocked many theater-goers in the 1940s and 50s.

Opposite Marlon Brando playing the character of Stanley in the film adaptation

Key Character **Billy Bunter**
Billy Bunter of Greyfriars School

Claimed by the *Guinness Book of Records* to be the most prolific author of all time (thought to have had more than seventy million words published), Charles Hamilton wrote an astonishing number of stories for children's papers under more than twenty pseudonyms. His most notable work was for the *Magnet*, for which he wrote (as "Frank Richards") a 15,000-word story every week from 1908 to 1940. These were set in Greyfriars, a minor public school in Kent, and deployed a huge cast of characters. Billy Bunter, "the Owl of the Remove," started off as comic relief, but soon became by far Richards' most popular creation – George Orwell said he was "famous wherever the Union Jack waves." Bunter has no redeeming qualities: he is lazy, boastful, a compulsive but useless liar, constantly cadging money or stealing food while promising that everyone will be repaid when his long-awaited postal order arrives from the family home, "Bunter Court" (in reality a suburban villa). He is

a mini-Falstaff, but one who is treated indulgently by his creator: Bunter may frequently fall victim to the wrath of his teachers and fellow students (resulting in the famous cry of "yarooh!"), but certainly not as often as he deserves, and many of his adventures end with his being rewarded for unwitting acts of virtue. In 1947 Richards began a series of novels (two a year until his death) which reflected Bunter's popularity by promoting him to central character; he also wrote the scripts for a Bunter television series.
Jake Kerridge

Date 1947 (publication)

Author Frank Richards (pen name of Charles Hamilton, 1876–1961)

Nationality UK

Why It's Key The "fat owl" of *Greyfriars* became one of the most famous characters in children's literature.

Key Event
Aleister Crowley dies

Aleister Crowley (1875–1947) fancied himself as something of a Nietzschean superhero, styling himself "the wickedest man alive," and doing his best to live up to this sobriquet. His father was a wealthy brewer who became a member of the Plymouth Brethren. Crowley began to dabble in bisexuality and in assorted hocus pocus while an undergraduate at Cambridge, at the height of the fin de siècle infatuation with decadence and mysticism. He became a member of the Order of the Golden Dawn, a kabbalistic sect of which W.B. Yeats was also a member. Crowley was subsequently ejected from the Golden Dawn, founded his own order, the Silver Star, and called himself "the Great Beast," after the devilish monster of Revelation.

In 1904 Crowley wrote *The Book of the Law*, the basis of his philosophico-religious system called Thelema, whose watchword was "Do what thou wilt shall be the whole of the Law." He went on to set up a Thelemic community in Sicily, where he attempted to raise demons and unmercifully beat his lovers of both sexes, believing this to be liberating to all concerned. Crowley became hopelessly addicted to heroin after a doctor had prescribed it to treat his asthma, and died of a respiratory illness in a Hastings boarding house. According to one witness, his last words were, "Sometimes I hate myself." His "autohagiography," *The Confessions of Aleister Crowley*, was published posthumously in 1971. Since the 1960s Crowley has been a hero to the more gullible sort of heavy-metal rocker.

Ian Crofton

Date 1947 (death)

Nationality UK

Why It's Key The most famous occultist of the early twentieth century, a hero to generations of dabblers in magic, hedonism, and recreational drugs, especially in the United States, although in reality he was little more than a sociopathic charlatan. W. Somerset Maugham's 1908 novel *The Magician* was based on Crowley.

Opposite Aleister Crowley

Key Book
Under the Volcano

The novel narrates the last day in the life of Geoffrey Firmin, British Consul in Quauhnahuac, a small town in Mexico. It is the Day of the Dead in 1939, a day of celebration on which it is believed all dead souls return to visit. It is one year after the Consul's death. The story then moves back one year to the arrival of Yvonne, the Consul's estranged wife.

The novel's protagonists are exiled from a Europe that is about to plunge into the darkness of war. The Consul, tormented by impotence and remorse, is a reflection of the decay of western civilization. As we follow Firmin in his final, drunken descent towards the abyss, everything around him acquires symbolic significance. Mexico is Paradise and Inferno rolled into one. In his mezcal-induced state, the Consul appears to have passed into the world of the Dead. There is beauty in the absurdities of life. The narrative incorporates a stream of repeated images; runaway horses, peasants who resemble Sorbonne professors, a ferris wheel, a stray dog, a darkened cinema, along with passing thoughts, snippets of conversation, and signs along the way.

Using verve and a determination to break with tradition, Malcolm Lowry created a remarkable work of art. There are strong references to Dante and the Jewish Kabbalah, which provides the central image of a drunken man being akin to a magician who abuses his powers. To Lowry, mankind has been led astray and appears to be on the brink of destruction.

Jamal Mahjoub

Date 1947

Author Malcolm Lowry (1909–57)

Nationality UK

Why It's Key Lowry began writing the novel in 1937, ten years before the book was finally published. Surviving destitution, war, and the burning down of the author's house, *Under the Volcano* was initially resisted by his publishers in London but was an immediate success and has enjoyed cult status since.

Key Book *Exercises in Style* (*Exercices de Style*)

Raymond Queneau was co-founder of the Oulipo (Ouvroir de Litterature Potentielle), a group of mainly French novelists and poets dedicated to experimental writing. In particular they were interested in ways of generating new and unexpected material through the imposition of constraints on writing (George Perec's novel *La Disparition*, which excludes the letter "e," for example). Such writing often lent itself towards a playfully comic form, and the work of the Oulipo writers is often criticized for lacking depth and seriousness.

Queneau himself was a keen amateur mathematician, and once wrote a sequence of sonnets with interchangeable lines, enabling the reader to rearrange the poem into an almost limitless number of variations. The work was called "A Hundred Thousand Billion Poems." *Exercises in Style*, however, remains a tour de force of experimental writing. It takes a simple, inconsequential story of a man who notices another man on a bus, then notices him again two hours later sitting on a bench with a friend, talking about buttons. The story is then retold in 99 different ways. The first variation is called double entry, in which everything appears twice "I saw and noticed a young man and an old adolescent…" Other versions are in "Dog Latin" or operatic English, rhyming slang, haiku form, and so on. The language-specific nature of *Exercises in Style* and other works of the Oulipo make them uniquely difficult to translate, though English versions have appeared, and the work of Queneau and his followers is becoming more widely known outside France.

Gerard Woodward

Date 1947

Author Raymond Queneau (1903–76)

Nationality France

Why It's Key An unexceptional tale is retold in 99 different ways, a virtuoso performance that demonstrates how various the modes of storytelling are.

Key Author
Osamu Dazai

Three attempted suicides, two marriages, drink and drug addiction, and a conspiracy theory. Dazai's life reads like a novel itself. In turn, blurring the boundaries between autobiography and fiction, his most memorable works read like his life. This was no languorous literary conceit, simply Dazai's attempt at self-expression following one of the darkest periods in Japanese history. His departure from traditional Japanese aesthetics has seen him compared to Kafka, Dostoevsky, and Camus whilst his trademark first person narrative follows a long Japanese tradition.

For Osamu Dazai (1909–1948) the conflict started early, attempting to reconcile his personal and political values with those of his family and social class. Dazai dipped into Marxism, dropped out of university and dabbled with the banned Communist party of Japan. A member of the Buraiha ("undependable") group he represented a movement of seemingly irresponsible anti-heroes, known as "The Decadents" in the West.

1935 saw his second suicide attempt, followed by a curious suicide pact with his then wife Hatsuyo. It failed and they divorced. The dark exploration continued after the war. *The Setting Sun* (*Shayo*, 1947) depicts the decline of Japanese class etiquette through defeat: a Japan at a crossroads. Such was its influence a new word entered the Japanese lexicon – "shayozoku" ("poor aristocrats"), a reference to the war's destruction of Japanese society. Only a year later Dazai published the haunting *No Longer Human* (*Ningen Shikkaku*). A startling story of alienation and anomie, the title literally translates as "Disqualified as a Human." Whether his drowning in 1948 was suicide or, as some contend, murder at the hands of his lover, Dazai's legacy was far-reaching, but perhaps there was more to come. We are left wanting; the title of his final unfinished work was a simple yet enigmatic *Goodbye* (*Gutto Bai*).

Sarah Birchwood

Date 1948 (death)

Author Osamu Dazai

Nationality Japan

Why It's Key Troubled post-war "I-novelist" famed as much for his multiple suicide attempts as for his nihilistic yet moving works. His daughter Yukio Tsushima is also a celebrated writer and master of the first person shishosetsu novel.

Key Book
Cry, The Beloved Country

Stephen Kumalo, pastor of the village of Ndotsheni in the Umzimkulu valley of South Africa, embarks on the long journey to Johannesburg to seek his lost sister and his son, Absalom, who has followed his aunt and whose letters home have ominously ceased. The elderly man negotiates the bewildering metropolis and its shadier suburbs, his search for Absalom becoming increasingly urgent as he intuitively connects his son with the reported murder of a young white liberal. Kumalo's worst fears are confirmed as he finds Absalom in police custody, distraught and incommunicative.

The novel's simple, direct style powerfully conveys Kumalo's grief, shame, and anger. But *Cry, The Beloved Country* ultimately has wider concerns than the tragedy of individual families. As Alan Paton pointed out in his preface to the 1987 edition, he regarded "the land of South Africa itself" as one of the principal characters of his book. The narrative is interspersed with chapters featuring numerous disembodied voices, showing the fault-lines along which the country is divided: black, white, oppressed, privileged, liberal, racist, progressive, complacent. This device allows multiple perspectives on the country's social problems: the mass migration to urban centers, the emptying of rural communities, capitalist greed and exploitation, and the cultural vacuum left by the passing of tribal systems.

As an extraordinary bond of sympathy and compassion develops between Kumalo and the father of the murdered man, a note of tentative hope for the future of South Africa emerges. Sadly, fiction and reality diverged. Several months after the book was published, the National Party instituted the system of Apartheid. This brutal regime would last for 46 years.
David Cross

Date 1948

Author Alan Paton (1903–1988)

Nationality South Africa

Why It's Key Probably the single most important novel to come out of South Africa in the twentieth century, *Cry, The Beloved Country* compelled South African readers to face the racial hatred and fear which divided their country, and alerted the rest of the world to the oppressive measures of the white oligarchy.

Key Characters
The Glass family

While *The Catcher in the Rye*'s Holden Caulfield is Salinger's most famous creation, he wrote far more consistently on the Glass family, in several novellas, like *Raise High the Roof-Beam, Carpenters* (1955) and *Franny and Zooey* (1961), and short stories, like "A Perfect Day for Bananafish" (1948), which describes Seymour Glass' suicide. Precocious offspring of a Manhattan family of mixed Irish-Jewish descent, the Glass children, who appeared on a t.v. quiz show, combine cosmopolitan sophistication with an otherworldly innocence and psychic frailty.

Seymour's Eastern philosophical outlook both grounds and disorients his siblings, especially his college professor brother, Buddy, who narrates most of the stories. The younger siblings respond to their elder siblings with a variety of anger, depression, and a lingering sense of betrayal. Beatrice "Boo Boo" seeks normality as a suburban housewife, while Frances "Franny" and Zachary "Zooey" become actors.

Especially with Seymour's fascination with Zen, the stories stand as a more genteel introduction to Buddhism for Americans than that of Salinger's edgier contemporaries. Mainly published in *The New Yorker*, the Glass family's combination of introspective neuroticism and comfort with world cultures strikes a balance for liberal readers during the Cold War period. Although anxieties about the Atomic Bomb and McCarthy-era pressures to act "American" skirt the narratives, the Glass stories remain generally disengaged from public politics. Holden Caulfield is the more beloved of Salinger's imagination because he lacks the esotericism of the Glasses' attempt to "see more" beyond the "glass" or veil of illusion of everyday life. The Glass family saga captures a particular moment in the paradoxes of 1950s liberalism, at once democratic and uncomfortable with the unruliness of popular culture.
Stephen Shapiro

Date 1948–65

Author J. D. Salinger (born 1919)

Nationality USA

Appear in novellas: Seymour: An Introduction (1963), short stories: "Uncle Wiggily in Connecticut" (1948), "Hapworth 16, 1924" (1965)

Why It's Key The Glass family were the characters Salinger used most consistently in his fiction. He used them to express his philosophical beliefs in such classic stories as "A Perfect Day for Bananafish."

Key Book
The Naked and the Dead

Accepted as a classic in the extensive genre of war literature, Mailer's first published novel is an electrifying and ultra-realistic account of an American combat unit's devastating experiences fighting Japanese forces on the Pacific island of Anopopei. The author's determination to map the shockwaves of war from private experience to national political philosophy transforms this into a politically controversial novel. Its scope extends beyond the naturalistic, offering a study of the nature of power and its abuses in and beyond military contexts. It also considers the possibility of universal compassion through an involved portrayal of the limits of human endurance and sacrifice.

Commonly perceived as a sterling work of anti-fascism, the novel provides a critique of concentrated power: in both "foreign" imperialist ambition and certain corrupt features of American society. The aggressive nature of capitalism and the extent to which it will secure its own interests at home and (perhaps more significantly) abroad is chief among Mailer's many targets.

A series of flashbacks are sewn into the plot and characterization. Each member of the platoon is contextualized by his position in the American social and cultural fabric. Mailer's depiction of the severe divide between officer and regular soldier is intended to reflect the American class divide. In this manner the novel indicts the delusions of national brotherhood in wartime by ironically demonstrating the way in which acts of extreme loyalty and bravery by those at the front are diminished by merciless decisions on human expendability made by distant generals and politicians. Reading it in the present we are left to contemplate the extent to which General Cummings' typically forthright remark has come to pass: "Historically the purpose of this war is to translate America's potential into kinetic energy."

Graeme Mcdonald

Date 1948

Author Norman Mailer (1923)

Nationality USA

Why It's Key One of the first post-war novels to gain instant worldwide fame as a truly realistic account of the traumatic experience of the battlefield. A classic in war literature; adapted into a film in 1958.

Key Event
Dr. Alfred Kinsey causes a sensation

The collective jaw of America's chattering classes hit the floor when Dr. Alfred Kinsey published his extensive study, *Sexual Behaviour in the Human Male*, in 1948. Just when they had recovered from this first shock, Kinsey came out, in 1953, with *Sexual Behaviour in the Human Female*. Both books became instant best-sellers, and are said to be the top-selling science books of all time.

Kinsey, a professor of zoology at Indiana University, and director of its Institute for Sex Research from 1942, conducted a total of 18,500 personal interviews as the basis of his two surveys. The reports were a revelation. He found that sexual orientation was largely a matter of degree, and devised a scale to reflect this, by which 0 was completely heterosexual and 6 completely homosexual. Among his detailed findings was that 11.6% of white males between the ages of 20 and 35 scored 3, and the general drift was that homosexual behavior in both males and females was much commoner than had been believed. Kinsey also found that masturbation was practised by 62% of women and 92% of men, and that extramarital sex and sadomasochistic tendencies were widespread. The innocence of American pastoral life also came under scrutiny, when it transpired that that 40–60% of rural teenagers raised on livestock farms had had sex with animals.

Conservatives lambasted the Kinsey Reports as incitements to moral degeneracy, while statisticians criticized the fact that his samples were not randomly selected. Kinsey himself concluded, "The only unnatural sex act is that which you cannot perform."

Ian Crofton

Date 1948

Title *Sexual Behaviour in the Human Male*

Author Dr. Alfred Kinsey (1894–1956)

Nationality USA

Why It's Key Kinsey's detailed survey demonstrating the scale and range of sexual activity in America helped to lift the taboo on the subject, and paved the way for the "permissive society" of the 1960s.

Opposite The Kinsey report shocked the U.S. public

INS and AP Science Writers' Review—
KINSEY REPORT ON WOMEN

Key Book *The Tunnel* (*El túnel*)

This short novel consists entirely of the intensely introverted ruminations of the painter Juan Pablo Castel, who confesses in the first sentence that he is a murderer. In the hundred pages which follow, we learn that his victim, María Iribarne, was probably the only person who fully understood his art.

Sábato had trained as a physicist, and worked in the Curie laboratories in Paris, but gave up a life of scientific research to become a writer. Having rejected science just as it established, at Hiroshima and Nagasaki, its potential to destroy humanity, Sábato devoted his first novel to demonstrating how logic and apparent rationality can lead to an act of murderous insanity. Castel's obsessive ratiocination, and blistering contempt for humanity, give a hair-raising portrait of a man isolated in his own thoughts, quite cut off from any vital human contact. The title of the novel comes from his own metaphor for his existence – burrowing in complete isolation from another living soul.

The book was highly praised by both Graham Greene and Albert Camus (with whose *L'étranger* of 1942 it has significant parallels – indeed both books were originally translated with the same title *The Outsider*). This was not, however, quite the moment for Europe and the United States to "discover" Latin American literature. Sábato did not publish another novel for thirteen years. By then, with writers of a younger generation like Márquez, Fuentes, and Vargas Llosa unleashing the 1960s "Boom" in Latin American literature, more attention was paid to their precursors such as Sábato and Borges.

Cathy Benson

Date 1948

Author Ernesto Sábato (born 1911)

Nationality Argentina

Why It's Key This novel was one of several early indications, for those who wished to take note, that Latin American writers had their own stories to tell, which neither aped traditional Spanish themes and techniques, nor pandered to an appetite for the folkloric.

342

Key Book *All About H. Hatterr*

A novel widely considered as unclassifiable, *All About H. Hatterr*, by the Indian philosopher and man of letters, G.V. Desani, was first published in 1948. Often held up as a comic and linguistic masterpiece, it is routinely compared with the work of Sterne, Joyce, and even Shakespeare and has also been likened to the writings of Carroll and Kipling. Produced during the British phase of Desani's truly transnational career – he was born in Kenya, grew up in India, spent time in Burma and Japan, and eventually settled in the United States – the novel recounts the experiences of H. Hatterr, son of a white European father and a Malay mother, as he travels around India in a search for spiritual enlightenment.

Hatterr's fantastical, dreamlike journey brings him into contact with an assortment of philosophical teachings and a succession of fraudulent holy men, whose effects are countered by the ideas and behavior of his loyal friend, Banerrji. Hatterr's biracial status –

"his fifty-fifty Oriental mind" – arguably provides Desani with the perfect position from which to satirize religious charlatanism, the self-importance of British imperialism, and the language of legal, medical, scientific, and anthropological discourse.

Critics have praised Hatterr for its inventive, unique use of English. Desani's freewheeling, ludic, absurdist style incorporates neologisms, word play, vernacular usage, malapropisms, comic hyperbole, scripted dialogue, phonetic transcription, misspellings, syntactic games, changes in narrative tense, multiple literary allusions, metatextuality, and irony. This rich creativity leads to an exhausting, intense, distinctly weird reading experience, but also one which is ultimately rewarding.

Ruth Maxey

Date 1948

Author G.V. Desani (1909–2000)

Nationality India

Why It's Key Desani's comic and linguistic tour-de-force became a cult classic after it was enthusiastically endorsed by such writers as T.S. Eliot, Saul Bellow, and Anthony Burgess. The novel, itself often viewed as part of a dazzling literary lineage, has notably influenced and inspired later Indian writing in English.

Key Event **Césaire and Senghor introduce the term "Négritude"**

Négritude, which most closely means "blackness" in English, is a literary and political movement that was developed in the 1930s by poets and politicians Léopold Senghor from Senegal and Aimé Césaire from Martinique. Both Senghor and Césaire believed that Négritude, a concept which denounced assimilation and celebrated African ancestry, was the best weapon against the physical and ideological violence of colonialism. It would, according to Senghor, allow Blacks under French rule to pull up a "seat at the give and take table as equals."

Négritude was significantly influenced by the Harlem Renaissance of the previous decade. Langston Hughes and Claude McKay, in particular, would inspire Senghor, Césaire, and other Négritude writers to proudly address Blackness and confront racism. Senghor would even credit McKay as the "the true inventor of Négritude." The term Négritude was first printed in Aimé Césaire's 1939 poem, "Cahier d'un

retour au pays natal" ("Notebook of a Return to My Native Land"), published in the third issue of *L'etudiant noir* (*The Black Student*), a magazine he started with Senghor. The magazine, though short-lived, was influential in its disavowal of assimilation as a tool of resistance and its embrace of the word Nègre, which before had exclusively carried negative connotations.

Senghor's 1948 poetry anthology, *Anthologie de la Nouvelle Poésie Nègre et Malgache*, included a preface by French existentialist Jean-Paul Sartre which helped establish Négritude at the center of a Francophone dialogue about black identity and agency. Négritude, rooted in pan-Africanism, represents a collective identity, consciousness and aesthetic born from the African colonial experience. Senghor would later become president of Senegal from its independence in 1960 until 1979.

M.K. Asante, Jr.

Date 1939, 1948 (publications)

Authors Aimé Césaire (born 1913, Martinique), Léopold Senghor (1906–2001, Senegal)

Why It's Key Senghor and Césaire, who were first trained as poets, would delve into the world of politics, Senghor as President of Senegal from 1960 (Senegal's independence) until 1979 and Césaire as Mayor of Fort de France and a representative of Martinique in France's Parliament.

1940-1949

343

Key Passage *The Second Sex (Le Deuxième Sexe)*

"One is not born a woman: one becomes one."

Born in Paris, the French novelist, philosopher and critic, Simone de Beauvoir studied at the Sorbonne where she met her life-long lover and mentor, the philosopher Jean-Paul Sartre. Rejecting the conventional and religious ways of her lawyer father and devoutly Catholic mother, de Beauvoir eschewed traditional marriage and instead had several love affairs during her life, with both men and women. During her profound affair with novelist Nelson Algren, it is claimed that she was at last able to achieve a highly-charged, sexual orgasm and this experience partially inspired her to write her ground-breaking feminist treatise, *The Second Sex* (1949). Confusingly, her complex personal life contradicted the militant feminist viewpoint she held in public and in her publications. Beauvoir was an existentialist and therefore believed that "existence precedes essence." This belief,

combined with her awareness of society's oppressive male hierarchy, would eventually result in her theory that "one is not born a woman, but becomes one." Her argument that females are not born inferior to males may sound perfectly acceptable now, but prior to the publication of *The Second Sex*, it was widely believed that women were born inferior to men, and were even considered unstable deviants. Beauvoir also argued that females should never view males as the absolute archetype of the human species toward which women should aspire. She was an active member of the French women's liberation front and she is one of the famous women who by claiming (falsely it transpired) to have had an abortion, forced the French government into legalising abortion in 1974. She should be highly regarded as the godmother of feminism and initiator of equality for women throughout Western society.

Alice Goldie

Date 1949

Author Simone de Beauvoir (1908–86)

Nationality France

Why It's Key In her seminal work of militant feminism, *The Second Sex* (1949), de Beauvoir claimed that although born equal to men, women are living as second class citizens in the twentieth century as social constraints and conditioning consign women to their inferior position. Prior to this theory, many believed women were literally born inferior to men.

Key Event **Jack Kerouac makes a road trip**

"Whee. Sal, we gotta go and never stop going till we get there."
"Where we going, man?"
"I don't know but we gotta go."

The infamous road-trip Kerouac made in the company of the mercurial Neal Cassady is recounted in *On The Road*, the best-selling gospel of the Beat Generation, which had an influence way beyond the literary field to become a genuine cultural phenomenon.

On the 19th of January, 1949, Kerouac and friends set out from New York to New Orleans, heading for the home of William S. Burroughs in order to reunite Al Hinkle with his wife, who was Burroughs' uninvited and unwelcome guest. Having deposited Hinkle, Kerouac and the Cassadys explored the Southwest in Cassady's car, smoking marijuana and stealing food and gas, embarking on sprees through Texas, Arizona, California, before the gang temporarily went their separate ways and Kerouac took the bus back to New York. *On The Road* conflates this and other trips to tell the story of Sal Paradise (Kerouac) and Dean Moriarty (Cassady) as they invent a new kind of life in search of Whitmanesque emancipation and adventure, in an America which is rapidly clamping down on its most traditional forms of freedom.

Burroughs, addicted to heroin and unwilling host to the trippers, called the journey an exercise in "sheer compulsive pointlessness" but Kerouac's literary refashioning found an endless and invigorating delight in the sheer velocity of headlong travel and unplanned encounter.
Robin Purves

Date 1949

Participants Jack Kerouac, Neal Cassady, LuAnne Cassady, Al Hinkle

Place New York to New Orleans

Title *On the Road* (1957)

Author Jack Kerouac (1922–69)

Nationality USA

Why It's Key *On the Road* became the gospel of the Beat Generation.

Key Character **Willy Loman** *Death of a Salesman*

Arthur Miller's tragic antihero, the failing traveling salesman on the brink of breakdown, became one of the most enduring characters in twentieth century American theater, and along with Blanche DuBois, transformed the public perception of the kind of person a playwright could draw into the audience's sympathy. (Though the response elicited by Miller's play frequently goes beyond sympathy: from 1949 on theatergoers have been heard sniffling and sobbing by the play's end, grieving a death foretold in the play's very title.)

A salesman whose diminishing performance has put his position in peril, Willy Loman is a recognizable paradox of a man, at once pathetic and resolute, optimistic and devastated, loving and unkind. In Willy's confused mental state, he simultaneously inhabits a present tense troubled by his anxieties about work and the return home of his restless, angry son Biff; and a past that glows warmly, when business was good, the neighborhood was green, and Biff was a high school football player and was "well liked."

Willy Loman's eventual suicide has been seen as a critique of the capitalist American dream, but the play would not have the lasting power it has if it were mere polemic, and Willy would not haunt audiences' imaginations if he were only a symbol. That the character was loosely based on Miller's own uncle, a salesman suicide, may help explain the vividness of the portrait, but the latter is ultimately owed to the play's simply poetic language. There are few more painful moments than Biff's defiant, corrective assertion to his self-deluded father: "Pop! I'm a dime a dozen, and so are you!"
Sylvia Brownrigg

Date 1949

Author Arthur Miller (1915–2005)

Nationality USA

Why It's Key One of the great tragic figures of American theater, Arthur Miller's defeated, self-deceiving salesman was first brought to life by Lee J. Cobb in a Broadway production directed by Elia Kazan in 1949, and the play went on to win most major awards including the Pulitzer Prize.

Opposite *Death of a Salesman*

B owen's evocative novel of complex relationships in an ethereal, translucent wartime London remains one of the most intelligently rendered studies of the way in which war reveals a variety of shifting allegiances. At a significant point near the close, Stella Rodney confronts her lover Robert, who has been identified as an enemy spy by a sinister British agent. Her disbelief at this private and public act of betrayal is met with scorn by Robert's confession of admiration for the vision of order wrought by fascism. His counter-democratic argument is carried by a central question: "what country have you and I outside this room?" This opens out a key theme contained within the ambivalent, elusive narrative: the solidity of modes of belonging in matters of love, patriotism, and politics. Bowen places this within a knowing, literary frame of reference, where storytelling and the manipulations it commandeers become persuasive currency in a society at war.

It is fitting that in a world where flickering identities cloud authenticity, Bowen sets her story in a semi-real world: a haunting yet strangely luminescent London. It is a spectral city, where relations old and new can be deconstructed in the second it takes a bomb to whistle down. It is the perfect space for a novel that investigates the lacunae of war within the private battles of individuals.
Graeme Mcdonald

Date 1949

Author Elizabeth Bowen (1899–1973)

Nationality Ireland

Why It's Key "War's being global meant that it ran off the edges of maps; it was uncontainable." *The Heat of the Day* is one of the most atmospheric and distinctive literary accounts of the way in which war reaches beyond the front and transforms private domestic environments.

346

Key Passage **Appendix: the B Vocabuary**
Nineteen Eighty-Four

T his detailed and rigorous explication of Newspeak contained in "Appendix: the B Vocabulary" not only substantiates the main body of the novel but also stands alone as a cogent and insightful analysis of the ways in which language is always ideologically inflected. As an appendix to *Nineteen Eighty-Four*, Orwell provides a comprehensive explanation of the principles of Newspeak, the official language of Oceania. Although not yet used exclusively, the language evolved out of the ruling party's explicit aim of providing "a medium of expression for the world-view and mental habits proper to the devotees of Ingsoc." In doing so, it functioned as an all-encompassing tool for the eradication of dissident thought.

The B vocabulary, which is comprised of the parts of language that relate to politics in the broadest sense, sought to rid words of their connotations, reducing their referential capacity to a single signified. By constantly reducing the available lexicon and favoring compound words, Newspeak worked to eliminate the need, opportunity, and possibility of free thought by making speech an almost unconscious activity.

Although ostensibly a description of Big Brother's linguistic aspirations, Orwell is also offering a pithy deconstruction of the way in which totalitarian regimes manipulate language in order to influence perceptions and behaviors. Referencing familiar constructions such as "Comintern" (Communist International) and "Nazi" (Nationalist Socialist) he makes the case that language structures thought rather than thought structuring language. While Orwell argues in the appendix that "no word in the B vocabulary was ideologically neutral," he is really demonstrating that no language can be divorced from ideology.
Juliet Wightman

Date 1949 (publication)

Author George Orwell (1903-50)

Nationality UK (born India)

Why It's Key It is from the B vocabulary that we derive many of the Orwellian neologisms that have so captured the public imagination: "sexcrime," "doublethink," and "Newspeak" itself among them.

Opposite "Big Brother is watching you." From the film adaptaion

Key Book *The Thief's Journal* (*Le Journal du voleur*)

The publication of *The Thief's Journal* marked the end of Genet's first and most prolific creative period. The novel, Genet's fourth in six years, is a fictionalized autobiography that charts his progress in the 1930s through the length and breadth of Europe's underbelly as a formative voyage. The fictional protagonist's experiences generally repeat themselves: he has fleeting homosexual affairs with various criminal or otherwise contemptuous types; habitually betrays his big loves to follow new flames; and survives on theft, which sometimes gets him imprisoned and deported. In lionizing criminality and betrayal and in celebrating the state of incarceration, Genet's reflections cohere into a consistent alternative vision. This serves to challenge our understanding of issues like human relations, debasement, and beauty, making *The Thief's Journal* a philosophical novel, as well as a thematic key for his later works.

Due to its frankness and "amorality" it was nevertheless considered a hot potato, leading publisher Gallimard (not for the first time with Genet's works) to publish it under the counter, without the publisher's name. Yet however controversial, Genet's creative genius seemed clear to all, and was therefore taken as established by Sartre and Cocteau in their public petition to the French President to pardon Genet, then facing imprisonment for outstanding offences. Extraordinarily and unexpectedly, President Auriol concurred and in August 1949 pardoned Genet in advance. The presidential pardon was taken as official acknowledgment of Genet's literary importance and, together with *The Thief's Journal*, became a significant element in Genet's mythical reputation as "noble outlaw."
Nimrod Ben-Cnaan

Date 1949

Author Jean Genet (1910–86)

Nationality France

Why It's Key The surprising success of an intellectuals' petition to the French President to pardon Genet, who at the time was facing further imprisonment, served to shape Genet's public image as a lovable rogue. This image was reinforced by the account of his early life as a vagabond thief and prostitute.

Key Event **Nelson Algren wins inaugural National Book Award**

After studying sociology at university, Algren trained as a journalist and used his experience of riding the railroads in the South to gather material for his first novel, *Somebody in Boots* (1935). His last novel, *A Walk on the Wild Side* (1956), is a reworking of this first novel, and although Algren subsequently gave up writing fiction, Lou Reed immortalized it in his song of the same title.

Algren's fascination with life in Chicago's semi-slum neighborhoods is evident throughout his oeuvre; characters inhabiting the netherworld of his novels include addicts, gamblers, prostitutes, and criminals. Algren was not completely sentimental about the poor, often portraying them as mean-spirited and ignorant, although he also had compassion for the downtrodden and disenfranchised. Having been imprisoned for stealing a typewriter, and hospitalized after attempting suicide over a failed love affair, Algren once declared that he was comfortable living among people who claimed welfare, and befriended many prostitutes and junkies while working for the Federal Writers' Project.

Inspired by his love for Simone de Beauvoir, Algren immersed himself in writing his masterpiece, *The Man with the Golden Arm*, an intense novel about Frankie the Machine, a morphine-addicted card-dealer. When Frankie is released from prison, trying to stay clean in a bad, poverty-ridden underworld of desperate characters proves practically impossible. Further pressure from an emotionally dependent wife who fakes her disability to trap him in a dead marriage is the final force to push Frankie back into the nightmare world of addiction.

One of the most innovative novels of post-war American literature, *The Man with the Golden Arm* is regarded as Algren's greatest work and at last brought him first-rate critical praise as a masterly chronicler of society's dark side.
Alice Goldie

Date 1949 (publication)

Title *The Man with the Golden Arm*

Author Nelson Algren (1909–81)

Nationality USA

Why It's Key A group of publishers got together to launch the National Book Awards in 1950. The first ceremony was held at the Waldorf Astoria Hotel, New York, to "enhance the public's awareness of exceptional books" by Americans, and make reading more popular.

Key Passage *The Kingdom of this World* (*El reino de este mundo*)

"At every step I encountered the marvellous in the real. Yet I thought, also, that the presence and prevalence of that marvellous reality was not a privilege unique to Haiti, but a heritage of the whole of America, where the final reckoning of cosmogonies has yet to be accomplished… And the point is that, given the landscape's virginity, its formation, its ontology, the Faustian presence of Indians and Negroes, given the revelation of its recent discovery and the fertile miscegenation it fostered, America is far from draining its well of mythologies… But what is the history of all America if not a chronicle of the marvellous in the real?"

Thus did Cuban writer Alejo Carpentier describe his impressions of a journey to Haiti, carried out five years earlier, in the preface to the first edition of his novel *The Kingdom of this World*. He had witnessed voodoo rituals and had visited the citadel at La Ferrière,

built by a mad king. He had heard the stories of the escaped Haitian slave, François Mackandal, whose followers believed in his supernatural powers, and learned about the exploits of Dutty Boukman, whose execution sparked Haiti's liberation from France.

Unlike Europe, where the real and the fantastic inhabit different narrative spheres, Carpentier saw everywhere in Latin America's past signs of the supernatural embedded in the ordinary. By coining the term "lo real maravilloso" – the marvellous in the real – he articulated what many saw as a central characteristic of works of literature emerging from Latin America in the 1960s. Long before critics dreamt up the phrase "Magical Realism," Carpentier had provided a working definition.

Ángel Gurría-Quintana

Date 1949

Author Alejo Carpentier (1904–80)

Nationality Cuba

Why It's Key Carpentier's ambition for his second novel was to offer a panoramic view of Haitian independence. Well acquainted with Europe's vanguard movements, he was anxious to put some distance between surrealism's artificiality and "the marvellous in the real" as experienced in the Americas.

1940–1949

349

Key Event *The God that Failed* becomes a Cold War weapon

The shrewd decision of Richard Crossman (1907–74), a leading British post-war socialist intellectual and future statesman himself, to assemble an array of the intelligentsia capable of mounting the case against communism on intellectual rather than mere economic grounds was more than prudent in terms of the book's enduring weight. Rather than go for the usual suspects, the writers brought together in *The God that Failed* represent an array of viewpoints and experiences, from the anti-fascist combatant Ignazio Silone, to Richard Wright, still under surveillance at the height of McCarthyism, even after his relocation to Paris. Yet during the era in which the war was fought in obscure French journals as well as in jungles of former colonies, it was Wright's experiences at the hands of political barons in the Chicago slums that enabled him to denounce the communist technique more effectively than any study of Stalin's numerous flaws or body counts. Given the pressing weight of the era in which

they were writing, with Stalinism still in full sway in the Eastern side of the war-ravaged continent and the People's Republic of China newly victorious, the six writers not only defied the beliefs they once held so firmly but went against many of their intellectual peers and risked nailing their new colors to a very precarious mast. With the brutal suppression of events in Hungary and the death of Stalin still yet to happen, Crossman et al's prescient contribution still holds sway as a convincing case against totalitarian modes of thought today, be they pursued under seemingly benign objectives.

Andrew Stevens

Date 1949

Place UK

Why It's Key Six essays by disillusioned writers about their former communist beliefs became a formidable intellectual Cold War propaganda piece. The essays by Arthur Koestler, André Gide, Stephen Spender, Richard Wright, Ignazio Silone, and Louis Fischer flew in the face of a number of fellow-traveller tendencies in the artistic and literary communities.

Key Author
Cesare Pavese

Cesare Pavese (1908–50) was also known as the "man-book" ("l'uomo libro"). His writing activities stretched, artistically, from poetry to prose and professionally from literary criticism and translation, to being the main editor at Einaudi Publishing House, Turin. Pavese had believed in his ability as a writer since his late high school years. He graduated in American literature with a long dissertation on Walt Whitman, a poet whose books were to influence Pavese's own poetry to constant rebellion against the canonical Italian tradition, and a re-oxygenating of both poetry and prose – formally, linguistically, and with regard to content. Pavese's main merit was that of continually introducing foreign writers and fresh influences into the stale and conservative intellectual and cultural atmosphere of Fascist Italy, and continuing to support Italian engaged literature in post-war Italy. Some of the writers he translated were Herman Melville, William Faulkner, and James Joyce. Thanks also to his work, Italian literature received the energy to move from being provincial and marginal to having a more respected and international profile.

Although nationally and internationally Pavese's fame was mainly connected to his historical critique of Fascism and his political siding with the Partisans movement (mostly in connection with his novels *The Comrade* and *The House on the Hills*), his interest did not rest with politics, but rather with existential problems. To understand Pavese's characters it is necessary to read his poetry in preparation for his prose, as the mould of his characters lies in the opening poem in *Work is Wearing*, "Mari del Sud" ("Southern Seas"). Split as he was in his origins between Turin and the Langhe countryside in Piedmont, his novels and poetry deal with the city opposed to the hills as a symbol of Italian modernization, and irreparable loss of innocence.

Rossella Riccobono

Date 1950

Nationality Italy

Other Key Works *Il compagno* (The Comrade, 1947); *La casa in collina* (The House on the Hills, 1948); the trilogy *La bella estate* (The Beautiful summer, 1949), which earned the prestigious Italian *Strega Award* in 1950; *La luna e i falò* (The Moon and the Bonfires, 1950)

Why It's Key Both as an artist and as a critic/editor, his work was central and influential in Italy during the 1930s and 1940s.

1950-1959

351

Key Character **Aslan**
The Lion, the Witch and the Wardrobe

There has been much discussion of the function of Lewis's children's novels as Christian allegory. Aslan is seen creating the land of Narnia out of the darkness through the power of his voice in *The Magician's Nephew*. He offers himself as a sacrifice to redeem the traitor Edmund in *The Lion, the Witch and the Wardrobe*, then rises from the dead the following morning. He gives signs, tests faith, and seems to be omniscient. He appears as a lamb when tracked down beyond the Last Sea in *The Voyage of the Dawn Treader* – and oversees the end of the world and the passage of the righteous into paradise in *The Last Battle*.

Interest in Narnia was revived by the release of the Disney film, *The Chronicles of Narnia: The Lion, the Witch and the Wardrobe* in 2005, in which Aslan was voiced by Liam Neeson. However, certain aspects of Lewis's creation sit uneasily with twenty-first century sensibilities. Aslan presides over a world where kings rule by divine right, hierarchies are fixed, young men are taught to fight the good fight, and female characters tend to be domesticated (Mrs Beaver), evil (The White Witch), or prone to vanity and triviality (the unfortunate Susan is ultimately excluded from Narnia quite ruthlessly because of her interest in "nylons and lipstick and invitations"). Perhaps even more uncomfortable is the representation of the pseudo-Islamic Calormenes and their "false god" Tash, against whom Aslan's army wages holy war in *The Last Battle*.

Anna Trip

Date 1950

Author C.S. Lewis (1898–1963)

Nationality UK

Why It's Key Aslan is the embodiment of the divine in *The Chronicles of Narnia*. He appears as a great golden lion with "solemn, overwhelming eyes" and a terrible roar. He is not a tame lion: he does not come when called, is loving but stern, and has been loved by children for over half a century.

Opposite Aslan

Key Event **Gwendolyn Brooks is the first African American to win the Pulitzer Prize**

At the height of American apartheid, Gwendolyn Brooks (1917–2000) made history as the first African American to win the Pulitzer Prize, the nation's highest literary honor. With her second book of poetry, *Annie Allen*, Brooks established herself as a significant voice in American literature. The prize-winning book is a technically flawless volume of verse in which Brooks experimented with several new forms including the sonnet ballad. *Annie Allen* was a brilliant showcase of Brooks' ability to weave several realities into one intimate portrait, documenting the experiences and perspectives of black women in Chicago. Despite her focus on working class black women, Brooks' work had incredible mainstream appeal, appearing in both black and white newspapers, magazines, journals and publications. The granddaughter of a runaway slave, Gwendolyn Brooks' success was a testament to the tremendous progress that had been made over two generations, while still acknowledging through poignant social commentary that there was much work to be done. Gwendolyn Brooks was one of the most prolific writers of her time. She won hundreds of awards and honors, including an invitation by President John Kennedy to read at the library of congress poetry festival in 1962. A champion of the Black Arts movement, Brooks is not simply a great African American female writer. As a Pulitzer Prize winner, she began her journey to become an internationally respected leader and one of the most important poets of the last century.

Pierce Freelon

Date 1950

Place USA

Why It's Key Gwendolyn Brooks joined the staff of the *Chicago Defender* at just 17 years old in 1934 and continued her ascension, earning a Guggenheim Fellowship in 1945. Gwendolyn Brooks was an inspiration to countless African American women and remained politically active until her death in 2000. Her popular poem, "We Real Cool," is still used in classrooms throughout the world.

Key Author
George Bernard Shaw

Playwright, novelist, journalist, polemicist, critic, public speaker: George Bernard Shaw (1856–1950) was one of the most prolific and wide ranging writers of his day. In 1876 he moved to London, finding employment as a ghostwriter of music criticism. However, his early literary ambitions were slow to come to fruition. Shaw wrote five unsuccessful novels and received only a tiny income from his music, literature and art criticism. He famously obtained an informal university education at the British Library. By the late 1880s Shaw had emerged as a successful drama and music critic. He was also a leading light within the Fabian Society. During this period, as well as producing music, art and literature reviews, he published major critical works on Ibsen and Wagner, and edited *Fabian Essays in Socialism*. Over his lifetime Shaw campaigned for a diverse range of causes: women's rights, the inequality of the voting system, reform of the English alphabet, to name but a few. By the turn of the century Shaw was protesting against what he saw as the artificiality of the West End and arguing that Britain needed a theater of ideas which would present audiences with plays that dealt with contemporary moral and social issues. These ideas were to influence the generation of playwrights who followed him. Although Shaw's playwriting career began relatively late in 1892, he went on to write over fifty plays. He refused to shy away from controversial subjects. His 1893 play, *Mrs Warren's Profession* suggested commercial prostitution was the only viable choice of career for his protagonist, and was banned by the censor on the grounds of immorality.

Kate Harris

Date 1950 (death)

Nationality Ireland

Key Works *Mrs Warren's Profession* (1893); *Man and Superman* (1903); *Major Barbara* (1905); *Pygmalion* (1913); *Heartbreak House* (1919); *Back to Methuselah* (1921); *Saint Joan* (1923)

Why It's Key Shaw was awarded the Nobel Prize in 1925. His work is defined by his commitment to intellectual and moral debate. He firmly believed in the necessity of a theater of ideas.

Opposite G.B. Shaw

Key Author
George Orwell

George Orwell (1903–50) died from tuberculosis aged just 46. The publication of his two great novels, *Animal Farm* and *Nineteen Eighty-Four* in 1945 and 1949 respectively, elicited worldwide recognition and appreciation of Orwell as a powerful political novelist, whose allegorical exploration of soviet totalitarianism and dystopian depiction of life under a Fascist regime were both timely and supremely prescient. In addition to his fiction writing, Orwell was a respected journalist and pamphleteer. His journalism and works of political analysis and social criticism were extremely influential, as were his powerful satirical novels.

Undoubtedly he saw himself primarily as a political writer, but he remained uncomfortable with party political affiliations. He consistently tested and reconfigured his political principles throughout his career, and much of his writing pivots around the axis of democratic socialism. His experiences in Burma, where he served with the colonial police, engendered a profound anti-imperialism and a firm desire to escape "man's dominion over man" (*Burmese Days*, 1934). This commitment to social justice continued, and both *Down and Out in Paris and London* (1933) and *Keep the Aspidistra Flying* (1936) present bleakly realistic representations of living in abject poverty in the 1930s. Although lesser known than his later works, these accounts have been hugely influential, informing popular perceptions of the social conditions of the period.

No other writer has done more to provide a vocabulary with which to articulate the extremes of political experience or been able to do so in such a way as to reveal the linguistic apparatus of political oppression.
Juliet Wightman

Date 1950 (death)

Nationality UK

Key Works *The Road to Wigan Pier* (1937); *Homage to Catalonia* (1938); *Coming Up for Air* (1939); *Inside the Whale* (essays, 1940); *Animal Farm* (1945); *Nineteen Eighty-Four* (1949); *Shooting an Elephant* (essays, 1950)

Why It's Key Orwell demonstrated the all-encompassing power of language and how it structures our experience of the world.

1950-1959

355

Key Book
The Martian Chronicles

Ray Bradbury emerged from the golden age of American science fiction magazines, at a time when the space age and technology were seen as both romantically alluring and apocalyptically dangerous. Bradbury's short stories somehow managed to explore the new fictional possibilities of the technological age in a uniquely poetic and lyrical way.

The Martian Chronicles (published in the UK as *The Silver Locusts*) is a collection of stories linked together around the theme of the future colonization of Mars. The narrative loosely describes the initially successful resistance of the Martians, who eventually succumb to the Earthians' greater technological power. There are clear parallels with the European colonization of North America, particularly in stories like "The Settlers" and "The Musicians." One of the most distinctive features of *The Martian Chronicles* is their juxtaposition of a homely nostalgia for small town America with a futuristic vision of space travel and alien races. Nowhere is this more apparent than in "The Third Expedition" (first published as "Mars is Heaven"), a story in which the telepathic Martians fool the arriving Earthmen into believing that they are seeing scenes and people from their 1920s childhoods. This and other stories in the collection (Bradbury insisted that his future-set stories were fantasies, rather than science fiction) lend the book a strangely haunting, elegaic quality. "There will Come Soft Rains," a story about an automated house that carries on operating long after its occupants have died, is a particularly striking example.
Gerard Woodward

Date 1950

Author Ray Bradbury (1920)

Nationality USA

Why It's Key Highly original and influential collection of science-fiction short stories. Bradbury's influence is far reaching and can be seen in many later works, from *Star Trek* to *Blade Runner* to *The Matrix*.

Opposite **Ray Bradbury**

Key Passage **The "Three Laws of Robotics"**
I, Robot

"1. A robot may not injure a human being or, through inaction, allow a human being to come to harm.
2. A robot must obey the orders given it by human beings except where such orders would conflict with the First Law.
3. A robot must protect its own existence as long as such protection does not conflict with the First or Second Laws."

Before Isaac Asimov's "Three Laws of Robotics," man-made intelligences in popular fiction followed the Frankenstein model – that artificial beings were created only to then destroy their masters. Asimov first set out the "Three Laws of Robotics" to provide a framework for the conduct of intelligent creations not possessed of any innate survival – and therefore moral – instinct, while allowing for the advent of the "sympathetic and noble robot" in literature. The Laws were to become a unifying theme in his work, but

Asimov's robot characters have consistently struggled with the manifold permutations and interpretations of the "Three Laws," finding themselves in complex situations where they are forced to develop, through trial and metacognition, their own moral consciousness.

As human beings know, the complexities of life are not easily governed by simple laws. Later, Asimov added the Zeroth Law, which preceded the First Law and decreed, "A robot may not harm humanity, or, by inaction, allow humanity to come to harm." The other Laws were amended sequentially to accommodate the Zeroth Law, which served to add a more complex ethical dimension to the robots' struggle for self-consciousness. Asimov's "Three Laws of Robotics" have provided a wealth of material for discourse – a literary platform in a populist genre from which to explore the deeper moral themes that have preoccupied humans since the dawn of moral intelligence.
Christian Kerr

Date 1950 (published in *I, Robot*)

Author Isaac Asimov (1920–92)

Nationality USA

Why It's Key First published in 1942 in *Astounding Science Fiction* magazine, the "Three Laws of Robotics" became so established in the public consciousness that it influenced forever the way in which these man-made creations would be perceived both in fiction and in real life.

Opposite *I, Robot*

Key Author **Rosario Castellanos** *Sobre cultura femenina* (*On Feminine Culture*)

Rosario Castellanos (1925–1974) represents at once the concerned and activist middle-upper class intellectual, and the tortured feminist woman working in the midst of a patriarchal, (post)colonial society such as Mexico. Her death in strange circumstances while working as an ambassador for her country in Israel is usually accepted as a suicide after a long struggle with depression. The beginning of Castellanos's intellectual career coincides with the publication of Simone de Beauvoir's *The Second Sex* (1949), a milestone in twentieth-century feminism. Castellanos's commitment to women's rights and her denunciation of women's marginal role, and the treatment of their bodies as well as their intellects as commodities, puts her at the forefront of feminist voices calling for gender justice and equality. Her essay *Mujer que sabe Latín* (*Woman Schooled in Latin*) challenges the patriarchal construction of the female subject – the title itself dramatically echoes the male chauvinistic saying in

Spanish "Woman schooled in Latin, does not wed nor end well." She jokingly opened her poem "Self-portrait" with a contrast between the more prestigious social title "lady/miss" – "Yo soy una señora" (I am a lady/miss) – and the dearth of academic achievements, to conclude with an evocation of the solitude of women who devote themselves to the life of the mind. In her two novels *Balún Canán* and *Oficio de tinieblas* as well as in her collection of short stories *Ciudad Real* Castellanos complexly staged the multiple layers of physical and social repression of indigenous communities in southern Mexico and focused on the conflation of racial and gender violence. Through multiple episodes of sexual and social oppression against Maya women in Chiapas, Castellanos critically probed the state of exception in which native women in the Western hemisphere have lived – and died – for centuries and which epitomizes gender relations as a form of social colonialism.
Pedro García-Caro

Date 1950

Nationality Mexican

Other Key Works *Ciudad Real* (*City of Kings*, stories, 1960); *Poesía no eres tú* (*Poetry Is Not You*, 1972)

Why It's Key In 1950 Castellanos published her master's thesis on feminine culture. She went on to publish poetry, essays, and novels and was a leading figure in Mexican literature and feminism. In the early 1970s she became the Mexican ambassador to Israel, where she died by electrocution.

Key Book
The Grass Is Singing

Mary, a lonely, passive woman living a comfortable empty life in colonial Rhodesia, meets Dick who thinks nothing of marrying her and bringing her to his farm away from the city and friends. Tension, listlessness, boredom, and the heat take center stage. Dreams of a blossoming, successful farm clash with the harsh reality of the landscape – what are they really doing there? Is this where they belong? Control becomes the motivator, a reason for living. Dick attempts to control the land; Mary finds relief in controlling the servants, but not for long.

The novel piercingly and uncomfortably questions privilege, power, and human desire. As the farm rots, so too does Mary as she spends hours on the sofa feeling as if "she were going soft inside at the core, as if a soft rottenness was attacking her bones." As everything decays, the possibility of regeneration appears in the body of Moses, a black servant who asks "Why is Madame afraid of me?" And therein lies the core

obstacle of the tale – how can there be equality when there is fear and ignorance? A suffocating heat saturates the rooms in the small house, a reflection of Mary's suppressed passion for Moses. Who is in control now? The consequences of subordination and unequal servant/master interactions are fully played out in this tense, unnerving tale of hatred, lust, and desire. Lessing seeks to explore the unimaginable ruin of colonial action on both human relationships and the land itself.
Anastasia Valassopoulos

Date 1950

Author Doris Lessing (1919–)

Nationality UK

Why It's Key *The Grass Is Singing* revealed the destructive effects of colonialism on human relationships; explored interracial sexual desire, and opened up questions surrounding loneliness and madness.

358

Key Character **Jesse B. Semple**
The Simple stories

In the 1940s, African Africans were lukewarm in their endorsement of America's fight for democracy abroad. The U.S. government instituted a campaign to increase black support, recruiting newspapers including the *Chicago Defender*, which invited Langston Hughes to help with this effort. Although Semple was modelled on a young defense plant worker Hughes met one day in Patsy's Bar and Grill in Harlem, Semple was an archetype. In *The Best of Simple* Hughes states, "it is impossible to live in Harlem and not know at least a hundred Simples." As his name suggests, Jesse B. Semple (Just Be Simple), extols the virtues of common sense and keeping things simple. His self-given middle initial is a placeholder for classic interrogations of action and twentieth-century existentialism. In a climate where African Americans found it challenging to be themselves, or simply to be without the burdens of color and class, Jesse's name takes on added meaning. Semple is nicknamed Simple as a mark of acceptance

and endearment by the characters who interact with him, and to honour his "make it plain" approach to the truth. Semple is the kind of man whose voice, wisdom, and personhood goes unacknowledged by the larger society. He is persevering despite invisibility. In the last Simple collection, *Simple's Uncle Sam*, Jesse B. says, "My mama should have named me Job instead of Jesse B. Semple. I have been underfed, underpaid, undernourished, and everything but undertaken – yet I am still here." He is critical, insightful, and nobody's fool. Over two decades, Simple offered insights about living well, the war effort, love and marriage, McCarthyism, and enduring discrimination. Donna Akiba Harper has made immeasurable contributions to our understanding of Hughes' short fiction in general, and the Simple stories in particular. In addition to editing Hughes' fiction, she has published *Not So Simple: The Simple Stories by Langston Hughes*.
Monifa Love Asante

Date 1950 (published)

Author Langston Hughes (1902–1967)

Nationality USA

Why It's Key This popular, urban folk character was first created for Hughes' column in the *Chicago Defender*, the most influential and largest black-owned daily newspaper in the U.S. Semple's views and exploits were collected in a series of stories published between 1950 and 1965. The Simple stories continue to enjoy considerable appeal.

Key Author **John Wyndham**
The Day of the Triffids

John Wyndham (1903–69) was, in many ways, the natural successor to H.G. Wells. Largely self-educated, a restless early career saw him pass through a number of professions (farming, law, advertising), and a spell in the army during World War II, before settling on writing as a career. It was reading Wells's *The Time Machine* as a boy that first aroused his interest in science fiction.

Wyndham made his name with the *Day of the Triffids*, in which tall, sting-lashing mobile plants threaten to take over a world in which the human race is suffering from blindness caused by a passing comet. The mysterious triffids are the product of human biological experimentation, and Wyndham's best novels – *The Day of the Triffids*, *The Kraken Wakes*, *The Midwich Cuckoos*, and *The Chrysalids* – have in common a theme that responds to the post-war anxieties about the nuclear threat, in that they concern a potentially apocalyptic disruption to an established social order, the origin of which is often scientific or extra-terrestrial. This sense of threat is enhanced by an exaggerated representation of social stability and moral certainty. The changelings of *The Midwich Cuckoos*, for instance, work their alien menace on a sleepy English village. The portrayal of a tweedy middle England under threat from outside forces has lead some to criticize Wyndham for being cosily anti-intellectual, perhaps missing some of the ironies of these hauntingly powerful tales.

Gerard Woodward

Date 1951

Nationality UK

Key Works *The Kraken Wakes* (1953); *The Chrysalids* (1955); *The Midwich Cuckoos* (1957)

Why It's Key Leading science-fiction writer of post-war Britain, the author of several highly original novels, often warning of the danger of technological experimentation. Like H.G. Wells he grounded his stories in recognizably real, everyday settings.

1950–1959

359

Key Book
Fires on the Plain

SPOILER

Loosely based on the novelist's own wartime experiences and partly influenced by Christian ideas, *Fires on the Plain* takes place in the Philippines after the defeat of the Japanese army. Tuberculous Private Tamura has been forced out of his corps and wanders in the wilderness, frightened by fires which he assumes are made by locals who hate Japanese soldiers. Finding the rood spire of a church, Tamura takes the risk of going into a village, with a glimmer of hope of spiritual salvation. However, the village is deserted and the church has been ransacked. In desperation, inside the church Tamura kills a Philippine woman.

Roaming alone searching for food, Tamura meets a dying soldier who gives Tamura permission to eat him after he dies. But just as Tamura's right hand is reaching to cut off the dead man's arm, his left one automatically stops it, and he hears a voice say "don't let your left hand know what your right hand is doing."

This passage, from Matthew 6: 3, suggests Tamura's ironic destiny. His life is then saved by Nagashima, a fellow soldier, who feeds him dried "monkey" meat, which later turns out to have been human flesh. Tamura's efforts to preserve his human dignity are again thwarted and he shoots Nagashima, believing himself an angel carrying out God's vengeance. The novel ends with Tamura's confessions in a mental hospital. Paradoxically, the ending seems to be the author's own attempt to maintain his sanity after the horrors of the War.

Miki Iwata

Date 1951

Author Shohei Ooka (1909–88)

Nationality Japan

Why It's Key Dealing with cannibalism among the devastated Japanese Army during World War II, *Fires on the Plain* is one of the most influential Japanese novels of the postwar period.

Key Author **Camilo José Cela**
The Hive (*La colmena*)

Born in Galicia of a Spanish father and English mother, Cela (1916–2002) fought for Franco's forces in the Civil War. His first novel, *La familia de Pascual Duarte* (*The Family of Pascual Duarte*), was published in 1942, and is a first-person narrative of the life and murders of a dirt-poor peasant from the arid southern region of Estremadura. Its stark depiction of cruelty and poverty inaugurated the genre of *tremendismo* (what today would probably be called "extreme fiction"). The book was promptly banned. Ironically enough, Cela was himself then employed as a censor (of a poultry-breeders' journal, he would sardonically remark if anyone brought the subject up).

His 1951 masterpiece *La colmena* (*The Hive*) had to be published in Argentina. Cela's avowed ambition simply to offer "a slice of life told step by step," was in effect deeply subversive, and the book faithfully depicts the poverty, fear and hunger of Madrid in 1942. Its apparent artlessness hides the skilful orchestration of a huge cast of characters, and its episodic manner reflects the influence of both Cela's mentor Pío Baroja, and Sartre's trilogy of wartime France, *Les chemins de la liberté* (1945-49).

His later novels became more experimental (one consists of a single uninterrupted sentence), but most readers agree the early novels are his major works. Much of his later career consisted of various forms of erudite provocation. Elected to the prestigious Spanish Academy in 1957, Cela compiled his *Diccionario secreto* (*Secret Dictionary*) (2 volumes; 1968, 1971) from the taboo words traditionally banned from the official dictionary.

He maintained a cantankerous non-conformism throughout a career lasting over half a century, irritating right and left about equally. He is said to have been as astonished as anyone by the award of the 1989 Nobel Prize, but his early novels certainly merited it.

Cathy Benson

Date 1951

Nationality Spanish/ Galician

Other Key Works *Viaje a la Alcarria* (*Journey to the Alcarria*) (1948); *San Camilo 1936* (1969); *Mazurca para dos muertos* (*Mazurka for Two Dead Men*) (1983)

Why It's Key Cela was responsible for some of the first signs of significant literary rebirth within Spain after a Civil War during which many writers had fled into exile or been killed.

Opposite Camilo José Cela

1950-1959

361

Key Book *The Autobiography of an Unknown Indian*

"I have lived through contemporary events in a manner which has developed my understanding of the history of our country by sharpening my sensibility to it. In my student days I used to be specially drawn to those periods of history in which some great empire or nation, or at all events the power and glory of a great state, was passing away."

The Autobiography of an Unknown Indian (written 1947–49) "describes the conditions in which an Indian grew to manhood in the early decades of this century." Born to liberal, middle-class Bengali Hindus, Chaudhuri vividly evokes his semi-rural childhood: its buildings, landscape, people, weather, traditions, gossip, politics, flora, and fauna. Having moved to Calcutta in 1910, Chaudhuri depicts the city with an equally compelling attention to detail.

Despite the book's title, in just over 500 pages it covers only the first twenty-three years of Chaudhuri's life. Ambivalently dedicated "To the memory of the British Empire in India," Chaudhuri's text is one man's ambitious attempt to write a history of his times. For Chaudhuri this is a history of decline and "decadence." In particular he mourns the passing of "the modern Indian culture created by Indians during the British rule, under the impact of European civilization." Chaudhuri is a product of this culture as well as its eulogist, referring with equal ease to Bengali, English, French, Latin, and Sanskrit literature, not to mention biology and physics.

Clear-sighted about the injustices of British rule in India, Chaudhuri is a provocative critic of the turn taken by Indian nationalism in the twentieth century, and is particularly scathing of "Gandhism." In this, his first book, he unforgettably depicts the conditions which shaped his idiosyncratic and unsettling view of Indian history, as well as shaping Chaudhuri himself as a man and writer.

Paul Vlitos

Date 1951

Author Nirad C. Chaudhuri (1897–1999)

Nationality India

Why It's Key The hostile reaction in India to the book's criticism of aspects of the nationalist movement brought an abrupt end to Chaudhuri's career as a journalist there. The book has since attracted praise from such diverse figures as Winston Churchill, V.S. Naipaul, and Doris Lessing. A sequel, *Thy Hand, Great Anarch!* was published in 1987.

Key Character **Holden Caulfield**
The Catcher in the Rye

Like Twain's Huck Finn, Holden Caulfield is one of American literature's enduring portraits of youth and injured innocence. Both figures offer a candid commentary upon an often-fraudulent adult world and both are memorable for the vernacular voice in which they do it. "If you really want to hear about it," *Catcher* begins, "you'll probably want [...] all that David Copperfield kind of crap." Famously censored for the licence of Holden's language, Salinger's novel has a remarkable ear for the profanities, preppy slang, and, for the 1950s, uninhibited sexual references of a New York sixteen-year-old in the throes of expulsion from his third private school. But of course it is exactly this directness that has always charmed readers, persuading them of Holden's sincerity whilst ironically revealing his callow inconsistencies. Indeed, this dialect of adolescence even becomes a terse poetry: reacting, for example, to a teacher's assertion that life is really a game, Holden writes, "Game, my ass. Some game. If you get on the side where all the hot-shots are, then it's a game, all right – I'll admit that. But if you get on the other side, where there aren't any hot-shots, then what's a game about it? Nothing. No game."

Both the Beats and the 1960s counterculture identified with Holden's battle against the "phoney" world of his parents; less obvious kinds of pain are here too, though: his physical awkwardness around females, including his beloved younger sister Phoebe; the death of his brother three years before; his fear of maturity – all these intrude with obliquity and pathos into an otherwise rollercoaster narrative.

Doug Haynes

362

1950–1959

Key Event **The Guinness Book of Records is conceived**

The most popular annual ever has its origin in a shooting party in Ireland in 1951. During the course of the shoot, by the River Slaney in County Wexford, Sir Hugh Beaver, managing director of Guinness, the brewers of Ireland's favorite porter, became involved in an argument as to which is Europe's fastest game bird: was it the red grouse or the golden plover? Unable to find the answer in any reference book, Beaver came to the conclusion that every night in pubs across Britain and Ireland similar arguments must be raging concerning the fastest, biggest, longest, oldest, and so on. Perhaps Guinness -- known for its innovative and entertaining advertising campaigns – could provide the answer.

Beaver therefore approached Norris and Ross McWhirter, twin brothers with a background in sports journalism who ran a facts-and-figures agency in London. In August 1954 he asked them to compile a book of British and world records as a promotional giveaway. The first trade edition came out the following autumn and by Christmas had reached the top of the UK bestseller lists. The book became an annual, and editions began to appear in many other countries around the world.

As well as editing *The Guinness Book of Records*, the McWhirters also became involved in right-wing politics, and in 1975 Ross was assassinated by the IRA. Norris continued to edit the book until 1985. He died in 2004. The book is now sold under the title *Guinness World Records*, and these days is more focused on popular culture, with features on such things as computer games and celebrity gossip.

Ian Crofton

Key Author **Alberto Moravia**
Il conformista (*The Conformist*)

Alberto Moravia (1907–90) was one of the dominant literary voices to emerge from Italy in the twentieth century. His stature in his own country was great, both as a novelist and a political commentator, and, unusually for an Italian author, he was able to support himself solely by his writing. His first novel, *Gli indifferenti* (*The Time of Indifference*) examines the empty lives and intellectual malaise of Rome's middle classes with a characteristically stark realism. With its themes of existential anguish, the book struck a particular chord in France, and, upon his first visit to the country, Jean-Paul Sartre and Albert Camus greeted him as a hero. He spent much of World War II in hiding with his wife, the novelist Elsa Morante. *The Conformist* tells the story of Marcello Clerici, an outwardly normal civil servant sent to France as an assassin by Italy's fascist government, based upon the 1937 assassination in Paris of Moravia's cousins, Carlo and Nello Roselli. The novel was immediately translated into English. Its taut, thriller-like plot and political relevance helped the novel to confirm Moravia's reputation as one of Europe's most important fictional voices. In 1952 the Catholic Church added his complete works to the Index of Prohibited Books. Moravia also had a lifelong interest in cinema, and collaborated on film scripts for various directors, including Luchino Visconti. He was in turn a popular author with directors, and films such as Jean-Luc Godard's *Contempt* (1963) and Bernardo Bertolucci's *The Conformist* (1970) enhanced his already great international prestige. He continued to use fiction to explore the complex moral history of the twentieth century until his death in 1990.

Neil Wallington

Date 1951

Nationality Italy

Key Works *Gli indifferenti* (*The Time Of Indifference*, 1929); *La romana* (*The Woman Of Rome*, 1947); *Il disprezzo* (*Contempt*, 1954); *La ciociara* (*Two Women*, 1957); *La noia* (*Boredom*, 1960)

Why It's Key this antifascist novel cemented Moravia's reputation as Italy's political conscience for much of the twentieth century.

Opposite **Aberto Moravia**

1950-1959

365

Key Event **Samuel Beckett begins writing in French**

The first of Samuel Beckett's (1906–89) longer fictions to be written in French, *Molloy* was published by Editions de Minuit in 1951, to be followed the same year by *Malone Meurt* (*Malone Dies*), and in 1953 by *L'Innomable* (*The Unnamable*), the third part of what had by then taken shape as a trilogy. The books didn't appear in English until 1955, 1958, and 1959 respectively, translated by Beckett himself (*Molloy* in collaboration with Patrick Bowles). Beckett said that he wrote in French because it was easier to do so "without style," but he went on self-translating almost all his subsequent writings, so this Gallic austerity was evidently not the only effect he wished for. His comedy is often amplified in English, or perhaps we should say in Irish (Christopher Ricks persuasively relates Beckett's self-undercuttings to the "Irish Bull"), and *Molloy*, whatever else, is Beckett's funniest novel, a masterpiece in the traditions of literary misanthropy.

The narrators of the two parts of the book are Molloy and Moran. Molloy, beginning the narrative in quest of his mother, is characterized by morbid sloth, sexual dismay, and rancorous blasphemy, in a prose which takes pride in felicity of phrase and shapely syntax. Moran, sent on a mysterious mission by the unexplained Gaber, has a more socially directed misanthropy, issuing in gloating cruelty, tyrannical whim (especially to his son), and psychopathic violence. In the second book Malone says these two were both him, and the narrator of *The Unnamable* will in turn claim Malone. The narrators are one and many. "How little one is at one with oneself, good God," as Molloy laments, bringing philosophical and theological dismay together, along with a comedy of paradox. "Unfathomable mind, now beacon, now sea," as he puts it elsewhere, in a great six-word sentence.

Peter Swaab

Date 1951

Place Ireland and France

Why It's Key The trilogy had a seminal influence on the French *nouveau roman*, and more widely on a school of writing preoccupied with the operations of the language and the groundlessness of human knowledge. Beckett's novels redefined the purpose of the novel.

Key Book
Memoirs of Hadrian

From his deathbed, a Roman emperor surveys his life and grapples with his inevitable demise. "Like a traveler sailing the Archipelago who sees the luminous mists lift toward evening, and little by little makes out the shore, I begin to discern the profile of my death." Belgian-born Marguerite Yourcenar conceived the idea for an account of the life of Hadrian as early as 1924, while still in her early twenties. It would take more than a quarter century – and countless stops, starts, and discarded drafts – for her to complete this masterwork. "There are books," she wrote, "which one should not attempt before having passed the age of forty."

It is a luminous novel, steeped in the wisdom and profound humanity of the second-century emperor who brought peace and prosperity to the Roman world, set boundaries to empire, rebuilt antique cities, and revived the cult of Hellenism in the Latin sphere. Yourcenar's Hadrian is a man of action, but also a contemplative soul. He has enjoyed power, cultivated thought, and pursued sensuousness. Among the occurrences that mark Hadrian's life, none appears as fundamental as his passion for Greek youth, Antinous, whose premature death colors with sorrow the remainder of the emperor's reign. "I have been absolute master but once in my life, and over but one being." As the once powerful man comes to terms with his finitude, he prepares for one last and definitive act of greatness: "Let us try, if we can, to enter into death with open eyes…"

Ángel Gurría-Quintana

Date 1951

Author Marguerite Yourcenar (pen name of Marguerite Cleenewerck de Crayencour, 1903–88)

Nationality Belgium

Why It's Key In 1981, Yourcenar became the first woman ever to be elected a member of the Académie Française. The novel's English language version is by her long-time partner, American translator Grace Frick. *Memoirs of Hadrian* was a bestseller which brought Yourcenar worldwide fame.

Key Event **William S. Burroughs shoots his wife dead in a tragic accident**

A bullet, hard, on the side of the head killed Joan Burroughs instantly; William Burroughs was arrested and skipped bail before the case came to trial, heading back to North America as his first novel, *Junky*, was being prepared for publication. Burroughs would later claim that the accidental killing was the act of founding violence which created him as an author.

Living the life of dissolute expatriates, both in thrall to various dependencies and dependents (Joan had a young daughter from a previous relationship, and a son by Burroughs), William and Joan Burroughs were undoubtedly headed for some kind of catastrophe and on the day she died, according to his subsequent testimony (in a preface to his novel, *Queer*) Burroughs had been overcome by an intense but mysterious despair and apprehension. That day he had arranged to sell his .380 automatic pistol but the potential buyer hadn't turned up to make the sale. Joan and he attended a party at a friend's apartment and started to drink heavily. Burroughs said that he had taken out the gun and was playing around with it. He is supposed to have announced that it was time for their "William Tell act" and when Joan placed a cocktail glass on her head, Burroughs aimed, shot low, and killed his wife. In a way that remains relatively obscure, Burroughs claimed that this drunken act, which led him to the events outlined in *Queer*, and the permanent sense of guilt it left him with, formed him as a writer who had no choice but to write his way out of his sense of possession by a demonic force he called the "Ugly Spirit."

Robin Purves

Date 1951

Place Mexico City

Why It's Key Burroughs later stated that Joan's death made him a writer. He wrote about the incident in *Queer*, written at the time but published in the 1980s.

Key Character **Amelia Evans**
The Ballad of the Sad Cafe

Breaking the mould for the flouncing and flirtatious, whalebone-waisted dames of classic Southern U.S. literature, Amelia Evans is introduced to readers of the novella as "a dark tall woman with bones and muscles like a man."

When we meet Amelia, it is as the rich and capable owner of a store and a swamp distillery which runs out the finest liquor in the county. Good with her hands – she built her own brick privy in two weeks and is a skilled carpenter – Amelia has more difficulties with people, her manner being brusque at best. Improbably, she once attracted the attentions of charismatic criminal, Marvin Macy. The disastrous marriage lasts nine days after which she lives contentedly alone until a hunchbacked cousin comes to stay. Her other local relative makes Amelia spit in the street, but Cousin Lymon – who can turn on the tears at will – soon has her infatuated. "A most mediocre person," wrote McCullers, "can be the object of a love which is wild, extravagant, and beautiful as the poison lilies of the swamp." He turns the store into a popular café filled with laughter until Macy returns to form the third party of a destructive love triangle.

Amelia is one of many isolated, misunderstood but intensely moving characters McCullers created in her short and troubled life. A childhood prodigy, her first novel *The Heart is a Lonely Hunter* (1940) about a deaf-mute named John Singer, was published when she was just 22.

Helen Brown

Date 1951

Author Carson McCullers (1917–67)

Nationality USA

Why It's Key Arthur Miller dismissed McCullers (who contracted rheumatic fever at fifteen and became a practical invalid in her thirties after a series of strokes) as a "minor author," but Gore Vidal praised her work as "one of the few satisfying achievements of our second-rate culture."

367

Key Character **Astro Boy**
Astro Boy (Tetsuwan Atomu)

Astro Boy, an unlikely hero from an unlikely source. Osamu Tezuka, "the God of manga," began as a shy schoolboy living in the suburbs of Osaka who found that drawing comics could win him friends. He later adopted a pen-name, inspired by his favorite childhood insect, the humble ground beetle or "osamushi." The reluctant medical student, inspired by the wide-eyed innocence of *Fantasia* and the exaggerated style of Japanese *ukiyo-e* prints, translated the Disney motif into a bittersweet vision of the 21st century.

Although created in a lab on April 7, 2003, and imbued with extraordinary futuristic powers, Astro Boy's biography is a reflection of Tezuka's post-war environment. Echoes of Nagasaki and Hiroshima resound in the character's Japanese name and become even more explicit in the *anime* theme song: "atom-celled, jet propelled, Astro-boy bombs away". Tezuka's boy robot had ideals to match his equipment. Alongside an ability to translate over 60 languages and blessed with 1000x hearing, Astro Boy has a heart capable of detecting criminal intent, an invaluable weapon in the fight against crime, evil, and injustice. The longevity of Tezuka's creation is testimony to the universal themes the narrative addresses: morality, racism, and heroism. Perching on this platform, Tezuka poses a question still pertinent today: has a science-based civilization improved the human race?

Born in Shinjuku, Tokyo, Astro Boy remains a quintessentially Japanese creation, so esteemed that since 2003, Japanese Rail have played his signature tune for departing trains at Shinjuku and he has been granted citizenship of Niza in nearby Saitama. His legacy lives on in Japan's popular culture, in cartoons such as *Doraemon*, the time-travelling superhero cat and in the visionary technology of the Sony AIBO dog, with his influence extending from Nintendo Game Boy and Play Station 2 to *The Simpsons* and *Calvin and Hobbes*.

Sarah Birchwood

Date 1951–1968

Author/Creator Osamu Tezuka (1928–1989)

Nationality Japanese

Why It's Key With jet-powered limbs and machine guns at the rear, this boy robot has propelled himself into the stratosphere of manga iconography and beyond.

Key Event **Hellman appears before the House Un-American Activities Committee**

Lillian Hellman (1930–84) – who wrote the scripts for *The Little Foxes*, among other films – appeared before the House Un-American Activities Committee (HUAC) in Washington on May 21, 1952. Although she was not a member of the Communist Party, Dashiell Hammett, with whom she lived, was and she herself was under FBI surveillance: in 1938, she had spoken at a rally in support of the Abraham Lincoln Brigade volunteers during the Spanish Civil War.

The anti-Communist witch-hunt had begun in 1947. Some of the early victims were the so-called Hollywood Ten who refused that year to deny or confirm involvement in the Communist Party and were blacklisted. About 80 percent of those who did not cooperate with the Committee lost their jobs.

By 1952, when Hellman took the stand, Richard Nixon was the HUAC's vice-president. Hellman refused to incriminate herself or others, pleading the Fifth Amendment – the constitutional provision allowing American citizens to remain silent. She wrote a celebrated letter to the Committee saying: "To hurt innocent people whom I knew many years ago in order to save myself is, to me, inhuman and indecent and dishonourable. I cannot, and will not, cut my conscience to fit this year's fashions…".

Even though she was not a friendly witness, the Committee did not cite her for contempt. That did not save her from being blacklisted, however, until the 1960s. She was forced to sell her home when her income virtually disappeared. Hellman recounted her experience of standing before the Committee in her 1976 memoir, *Scoundrel Time*. Although no evidence of any Communist affiliation was uncovered, when she went abroad in 1963 she was still being tracked by the State Department, which kept the FBI informed of her whereabouts.

Adam Feinstein

Date 1952

Place Washington, D.C., USA

Why It's Key By the time the witch-hunt ended in the late-1950s, hundreds of people had been imprisoned and up to 12,000 had lost their jobs. In the film industry, more than 300 actors, directors and screenwriters were denied work in the USA through the unofficial Hollywood blacklist.

Opposite **Lillian Hellman**

1950-1959

369

Key Event **Janet Frame wins an award for *The Lagoon* while in psychiatric hospital**

At 21 Janet Frame (1924–2004), grieving for a drowned sister, attempted suicide and was wrongly diagnosed with chronic schizophrenia. That misdiagnosis led to years of hospitalization, and terrifying electro-convulsive therapy, later described in the novel *Faces in the Water*. Seemingly consigned to a life in the dubious custody of what that period called mental health care, Frame became an observer of people locked away from society's gaze. In 1952 Janet's sister brought her a copy of her first book, *The Lagoon*, which consisted of stories she had written five years earlier. Nine months later, hospital staff announced she was to undergo a lobotomy, an operation which removed anxiety, but could leave patients in a vegetative state. Only days before the planned surgery, newspapers across New Zealand announced she had won the Hubert Church Award, the country's most important literary prize. The operation was cancelled. In 1955 she left hospital for good.

In a prolific writing life these experiences gave her empathy with outsiders and dreamers. Mainly through first person narratives, she wrote about childhood, loneliness, and writing, as well as what society sees as derangement. It is characteristic of her to suggest people are sometimes better off sick than restored, that the imagination may be impaired by wellness. Writing of her own depression in *An Angel at My Table*, Frame stated that it gives, to those who survive it, "a unique point of view that is a nightmare, a treasure, and a lifelong possession." Strikingly, she continued that this "must be the best view in the world, ranging even further than the view from the mountains of love, equal in its rapture and chilling exposure." Exceptional words from a great twentieth-century writer who had to fight to prove her own sanity.

Lucy Daniel

Date 1952

Place New Zealand

Why It's Key Frame's autobiographical trilogy, *To the Is-land* (1982); *An Angel at My Table* (1984), and *The Envoy from Mirror City* (1985) is an important account of life in psychiatric hospital in the 1940s and 1950s. Frame's best works include the novels *Owls Do Cry* (1957), *Faces in the Water* (1961), *Scented Gardens for the Blind* (1963), and *Intensive Care* (1970).

Key Book
Invisible Man

"I am an invisible man," begins Ellison's unnamed narrator. At the start and end, he is "hibernating" in a Harlem basement, contemplating his next move. The rest of the book tells the story of how he got there. In doing so, Ellison creates both a picaresque portrait of the black American artist as a young man and an allegory of the nation's history since the Civil War. The tale begins with the teenage protagonist about to address the white leaders of his southern town with a speech borrowed from Booker T. Washington. Before he can talk, however, he is forced to participate blindfolded in a humiliating battle royal. Ellison described this scene as an initiation rite into the ways of white America, but its lesson – that black men are supposed to entertain, not speak – is one that his protagonist is slow to grasp. So the book repeats the ritual, as *Invisible Man* encounters the promises of accommodationism, Communism, and black nationalism. But until he enters the basement and tells

this story, there is no place where he can "say what I got up in my head." He challenges invisibility and ideology with virtuoso style, fusing dense allusion and vernacular, surrealism and naturalism, to reinvent the American novel. As he plans to re-enter the world, the narrator concludes that "even an invisible man has a socially responsible role to play." After all, "who knows but that, on the lower frequencies, I speak for you?"
Kasia Boddy

Date 1952

Author Ralph Ellison (1914–94)

Nationality USA

Why It's Key "To be unaware of one's form is to live a death." *Invisible Man* received immediate international acclaim, and has been seen as a reinvention of the American novel.

Key Event **The Roman Catholic Church bans the books of André Gide**

When in 1559 the Roman Catholic Church first published its Index Librorum Prohibitorum (list of forbidden books) the idea was essentially to prevent Catholics from reading heretical Protestant writings. The list soon expanded, however, to protect believers not only from works considered to be dangerous to faith but also from those that it was feared would lead to moral corruption. It was in the latter category that the Church placed the works of French writer André Gide (1869–1951) in 1952, the year after the author's death. Gide would have found himself in famous company: other writers on the list included Montaigne, Gibbon and Voltaire, and more recently, in 1948, Jean-Paul Sartre.

Gide's works were mostly concerned with the philosophical issues of personal and intellectual freedom, and with the absolute necessity of being true to oneself, despite internal ambiguities. It was Gide who, in *Les Caves du Vatican* (1914), coined the

phrase "L'acte gratuite (the unmotivated action)" that was to be a key term in existentialism, but it was primarily his defence of homosexuality, particularly in his autobiographical works, that led to his appearance on the Index. Gide recounted both gay and straight sexual experiences but his most controversial transgression was to claim that homosexuality was less destructive to people than heterosexual love. Despite the Church's ban, Gide continued to be widely read and is better remembered today for being awarded the Nobel Prize in Literature in 1947, while the Index has fallen into disuse and has not been updated since the 1960s.
Michael Munro

Date 1952

Place Rome

Why It's Key Although Gide had died the preceding year, in 1952 the Catholic Church still felt it important to ban his writings to Catholics on the grounds of immorality. However, the Nobel Prize-winning author's works were already established as part of the canon of French literature and the ban had little effect.

Key Passage
Junky (Junkie)

"Junk is a cellular equation that teaches the user facts of general validity. I have learned a great deal from using junk: I have seen life measured out in eyedroppers of morphine solution. I experienced the agonizing deprivation of junk sickness, and the pleasure of relief when junk-thirsty cells drank from the needle. Perhaps all pleasure is relief... I have learnt the junk equation. Junk is not, like alcohol or weed, a means to increased enjoyment of life. Junk is not a kick. It is a way of life."

B urroughs' first novel was published back-to-back with a more traditional true-crime pulp novel (by Maurice Helbrant) purporting to be the real-life adventures of a Narcotics Agent. *Junky*, however, is far from pulp's lucrative combination of sensationalism and sociology aimed at feeding a prurient public with titillating stories of a degenerate underclass. It is unusual in that the book stages a shift away from a pulp genre serving up "real" criminals and addicts and towards a critique of the representations of the addict which, until this novel, had meant the misrepresentations of the U.S. Narcotics Bureau. We get potted histories of a cast of characters: George the Greek, Fritz the Janitor, The Fag, Subway Mike, Herman, Joe the Mex… and along the way official propaganda is explicitly contradicted. Burroughs' practice refuted "common knowledge" so comprehensively and so controversially that the publishers inserted parenthetical disclaimers, interventions by a self-appointed Voice of Reason protesting at the author's subversion of regulatory codes. The author's congenital inability to avoid causing trouble for the authorities even in his earliest attempts at fiction foreshadows the censorship trials that would dog his most notorious work; *Naked Lunch*, as wonderful as that novel is, still overshadows the innovations of the works that preceded it.
Robin Purves

Date 1953

Author William S. Burroughs (1914–1997)

Nationality USA

Why It's Key Though *Junky* did not have the same impact on the public as the more immediately scandalous *Naked Lunch*, with his first novel Burroughs was already operating at the limits of the law in ways that have not yet been entirely appreciated.

Key Passage
The Go-Between

"The past is a foreign country: they do things differently there."

W ith one of the most famous opening lines in twentieth-century literature, L.P. Hartley's *The Go-Between* introduces its central concern with the nature of memory. The novel's protagonist, Leo Colston, comes across an old box filled with the objects of childhood, and is forced to confront the memories likewise located within it. Prompted by an old diary discovered within the box, Leo recalls the fateful events of a holiday spent with his school friend at Brandham Hall, and his role as a go-between in the love affair between his friend's sister and the local farmer. Leo looks back on the golden Edwardian summer of 1900 from his vantage point in the post-war austerity of 1952, and his memories reveal an undercurrent of social tension and unease behind the façade of a leisured Edwardian England. Hartley uses the events of 1900 as a foil to examine the uncertain nature of post-war Britain, and the novel reveals how recovery of the past is a necessary part of making sense of the present. Hartley's "foreign country" is a critique of national identity in the process of reconstruction after World War II. The emphasis on doing things "differently" suggests the emptiness of contemporary models for social and cultural reconstruction. Britain is a nation foreign to itself, estranged from the security of its history and traditions, and a victim of the unprecedented social upheaval wrought by the recent conflict.
Laura Coffey

Date 1953

Author L.P. Hartley (1895–1972)

Nationality UK

Why It's Key This passage remains one of the most evocative observations on the nature of time and memory. Its nostalgic appeal has ensured its continued popularity, but it also hints at the difficult recovery of lost memories. The novel is a key work in a genre of fiction exploring the process of moving from childhood into adulthood.

Key Passage **Vladimir's speech**
Waiting for Godot

VLADIMIR ...Astride of a grave and a difficult birth. Down in the hole, lingeringly, the gravedigger puts on the forceps. We have time to grow old. The air is full of our cries. [He listens.] But habit is a great deadener. [He looks again at ESTRAGON.] At me too someone is looking, of me too someone is saying, He is sleeping, he knows nothing, let him sleep on. [Pause.] I can't go on! [Pause.] What have I said?

Vladimir's speech at the end of *Waiting for Godot* is possibly the supreme expression of existential hopelessness. Like Colonel Kurtz's cry, "The horror, the horror," at the end of *Heart of Darkness*, this is life picked clean of meaningful distraction and reduced to its essential and intimate relationship with death: even comforting "habit" has caught Beckett's mordant tone to become a "great deadener." Ground down by Godot's persistent failure to arrive and trapped by an endless cycle of boredom and repetition that wastes his time away, Vladimir confronts the bleak reality of life, devoid of significance, joy, or humor: birth occurs over and directly into the grave; the gravedigger merely releasing the forceps.

These images deny any consolation: death may abound in life, but there is no religious promise of life after death. Yet Beckett refuses to let this be his final word on finality. Having reached the end of his rope, Vladimir is about to noose it around his neck – "I can't go on," he says quoting Beckett's own *The Unnameable* – when hope enters stage left pursued by a boy who reiterates Godot's intention to come tomorrow.

Beckett knows that it's the hope that (almost) kills you, and returns his protagonists to the stasis of their existential waiting. "Shall we go?" Vladimir asks once more, speaking his last words of the play. "Yes," Estragon replies, as he has to, "Let's go." Beckett's final stage instruction follows: "They do not move."
James Kidd

Date 1953 (first performed in French); first performed in English 1955

Author Samuel Beckett (1906–89)

Nationality Ireland

Why It's Key Nothing changed the theater more surely than *Waiting for Godot*, which challenged every convention the art form had to offer. Toying with time, place and plot, Beckett confused, bored and disoriented his audience even as he made it laugh, cry and think.
Opposite *Waiting for Godot*

1950-1959

372

Key Book
Go Tell it on the Mountain

James Baldwin was one of the key American writers of the century, exploring the complexities of being black and homosexual with grace and passion. *Go Tell it on the Mountain*, Baldwin's first novel, is a coruscating, challenging polemic as well as a moving piece of autobiographical writing. First drafts of what was originally entitled *In My Father's House* had gained Baldwin a Eugene F. Saxon memorial award in 1945, and Baldwin finished the manuscript in Switzerland accompanied only by his lover and Bessie Smith records. The novel allowed Baldwin to meditate on his complex emotions relating to his family and upbringing, and particularly his relationship with his violent preacher stepfather. Told mainly in flashback and from multiple perspectives the novel relates events on the birthday of John Grimes. The novel is set on a "Saturday in March, in 1935" and takes place mainly in the churches and on the streets of poverty-stricken Harlem. As well as John's coming-of-age narrative which mainly deals with the church and his troubled relationship with his father there are three sections entitled "The Prayers of the Saints." These relate the life stories of John's father Gabriel, his mother Elizabeth, and his aunt Florence. Their stories are full of racism, horror, and the possible salvation of religion. The experiences of all three are upsetting and present the consequences of slavery and segregation. Baldwin's purpose was to present the complexity of contemporary African-American identity by considering the varieties of events and influences on its formation.
Jerome de Groot

Date 1953

Author James Baldwin (1924–87)

Nationality USA

Why It's Key Baldwin's debut novel dealt with race, religion, and sexuality in challenging and profound ways.

Key Author
Julia de Burgos

Julia de Burgos (1914–53) is one of Puerto Rico's most cherished and defiant poets. She came from the rural, poor areas of Carolina, Puerto Rico, and after much sacrifice, she became a teacher. In 1938 she published some of her most famous poems in *Poema en veinte surcos*, where she challenges the conventional gender roles and redefines national aesthetics. In "Río Grande de Loíza," the speaker personifies the river and eroticizes her relationship with it. But at the end, the river as a national emblem becomes the "cry" of Puerto Rico, only smaller in comparison to the speaker's own cry – the poem itself for her enslaved people, "para mi esclavo pueblo." Through her poems, de Burgos is a voice for Puerto Rican independence and the women's liberation movement.

In "A Julia de Burgos," the speaker criticizes the duality of female roles in a patriarchal society, by dramatizing the conflict between the "I," the "essence" of poetry, the "flower of the people," the natural, free, and strong woman, versus the "you," who is the superficial, the "flower of the aristocracy," the materialist, selfish, and submissive woman. In 1939 she published *Canción de la verdad sencilla*, and fell in love with Juan Isidro Jiménez Grullón, who inspired most of her love poetry in *El mar y tú* (1940). She travelled and lived with him in New York and Cuba, but in 1942 they broke up and she returned to New York. She suffered many economic hardships, and her health problems intensified due to her alcoholism. Although she received many honors and recognition by the Puerto Rican community, she died in 1953 without any identification on the streets of New York.

Cecilia Enjuto Rangel

Date 1953 (death)

Nationality Puerto Rico

Key Works *Poema en veinte surcos* (1938); *Canción de la verdad sencilla* (Song of the Simple Truth, 1939); *El mar y tú* (The Sea and You, 1940)

Why It's Key Julia de Burgos was one of Latin America's major poets, as well as a campaigner for women's and Afro-Caribbean rights.

Key Book
In the Castle of My Skin

In his autobiographical story of a Caribbean adolescence in colonial Barbados – "Little England" – during the 1930s and 1940s, Lamming lyrically records the narrator's transition from childhood to manhood, as the old social order is challenged by the emergence of organized labor. The setting for this classic coming-of-age narrative is an island society that is gradually evolving into the modern world, still burdened by the legacy of colonization and enslavement: "An estate where fields of sugar cane had once crept like an open secret across the land had been converted into a village that absorbed three thousand people. An English landowner, Mr Creighton, had died, and the estate fell to his son through whom it passed to another son who in turn died, surrendering it to yet another." Lamming's language is marked by a leisurely musicality that is in perfect keeping with the pace of change in the community. At the heart of it all is the young hero, G., who says of himself: "My father who had only fathered the idea of me had left me the sole liability of my mother who really fathered me." (Edith Clarke's influential 1957 study of West Indian family patterns, *My Mother Who Fathered Me*, memorably borrowed its title from Lamming.) Through the sensitive eyes of G., whose exceptional intelligence marks him out for a different future from his peers, the effects of societal change are observed, the connections made between individual, mundane experience and the larger issues of capitalism, feudalism, racism, and emigration, which latter theme would feature large in Lamming's later work.

Margaret Busby

Date 1953

Author George Lamming (1927–)

Nationality Barbados

Why It's Key Lamming's first novel won the Somerset Maugham Award. It was described by one critic as the finest novel yet to appear in West Indian literature, and was an important statement in the anti-colonial movement of the 1950s, counting among its champions Richard Wright and Jean-Paul Sartre.

Key Book
The Adventures of Augie March

Saul Bellow's third novel was his first attempt at that all-encompassing genre, the Great American Novel of picaresque self-fashioning. Born "under the sign of the recruit," Augie March throws off a succession of domineering influences (largely a series of father figures and love interests) and deals with the implications of the historical events that accompany his growing up, notably the Depression and World War II. His response to the world is always that of "an American, Chicago born." Augie March was the first novel, Bellow later said, that he had written with an "authentic voice" rather than the voice of "an Englishman or a contributor to *The New Yorker*." Augie begins his narrative by announcing that he is going to "go at things as I have taught myself, free-style." That "free-style" is a kind of Joycean fusion of high and low registers – a colloquial narrative interrupted with huge swathes of similes and (often elaborately mixed) metaphors, with comparisons to Heraclitus,

Machiavelli, and everyone in between. "It was up to me," Bellow recalled, "to find ways to reconcile the Trojan War with Prohibition, major league baseball, and the Old Country as my mother remembered it." While the British critic Anthony West complained that Bellow was hustling for "literary promotion" in an unseemly fashion, Norman Podhoretz praised his "willed buoyancy" and championed the young writer as the Jewish intelligentsia's "White Hope." Since 1953 novelists from Thomas Pynchon to Martin Amis have testified to the novel's liberating influence.
Kasia Boddy

Date 1953

Author Saul Bellow (1915–2005)

Nationality USA

Why Its Key *The Adventures of Augie March* is the novel that made Bellow famous.

Key Author **Elmore Leonard**
The Bounty Hunters

The publication in 1953 of *The Bounty Hunters*, a Western genre novel by a young Detroit advertising copywriter, marked the launch of one of the most significant American literary careers of the second half of the twentieth century. It was followed by a prolific stream of novels, stories, and film scripts from Leonard in which he frequently updated the setting to contemporary urban America, but rarely departed from the territory of crime. *Up In Honey's Room*, Leonard's 41st novel, was published in July 2007.

His thrillers may be harder, faster, more ingeniously constructed than those of his competitors in the genre, but that is not the key to his importance. Leonard's genius lies in his ability to capture the voice of America – not just in his unmatched gift for dialogue, much of it outrageously funny, but in his use of the spoken idiom as narrator, regardless of the niceties of grammar. As he put it himself in a famous list of tips for writers: "If it sounds like writing, I re-write it."

Leonard's works trace the migration of one of America's key myths – that of a tough, self-sufficient people, independent of government control – from the frontier of the Wild West, where it had settled in the nineteenth century while the West was still being won, to the inner cities and trailer parks of the late twentieth century. For many years, it was said that Elmore Leonard's stories were un-filmable, despite their detailed plots and backdrop in the criminal underworld loved by filmmakers. None of his books were made into films of any distinction. That theory was torn up in 1995 with the success of Barry Sonnenfeld's film *Get Shorty*, followed two years later by Quentin Tarantino's *Jackie Brown* (from the Leonard novel *Rum Punch*).
Bruce Millar

Date 1953

Nationality USA

Key Works *Fifty-Two Pickup* (1974); *Unknown Man No.89* (1977); *Freaky Deaky* (1988); *Get Shorty* (1991); *Be Cool* (1999)

Why It's Key The stories' strength of plot, dialogue, and character paint a vivid picture of what it feels like to walk the streets on the frontier between law and order – as true a picture as any created by more self-consciously literary writers.

Key Character **James Bond**
Casino Royale

In *Casino Royale* Ian Fleming created one of the archetypes of twentieth-century cultural life: James Bond. This patriotic, womanizing, fast-talking and fast-punching, gadget-heavy defender of the "free" world has global appeal and reach; along with Disney and *The Simpsons*, Bond is one of the most recognizable cultural franchises on the planet. British spy Bond is associated with fast cars, casinos, exotic locations, evening dress, and elegant girls. He effortlessly travels the world foiling the best attempts of the enemies of civilisation. Many of the things that are most famous about him stem from the film versions, however. Bond the brand is quite different from Bond the literary character. The novels in the series are far more about defending empire by any means necessary than the later films, and are explicit in their racism, homophobia, and casual violence towards women. They are related generically to other dark, hard-boiled fiction which is concerned with the nasty things lurking in the shadows. *Casino Royale* sees Bond nastily tortured, violently kill, and dismiss his treacherous companion with the words "the bitch is dead now." In 2006 the novel was once again filmed and the results praised for returning to the original "spirit" of the books: nasty, violent, misogynistic. Fleming claimed that the Bond books were based in his own experiences of espionage; whatever the truth in this, the character he created has an enduring quality which has far outgrown his source material.

Jerome de Groot

Date 1953

Author Ian Fleming (1908–64)

Nationality UK

Why It's Key The most famous spy in the world has spent decades defending the free world whilst still finding time to womanize and drink.

Opposite James Bond

Key Event **The Rosenberg Trial leads to Coover's *The Public Burning***

Robert Coover's fantastical reconstruction of the Rosenbergs' trial and execution in 1953 consists of two narrative strands, each more outrageous than the other. In one, America waits breathlessly for the public electrocution of the communist hate figures in Times Square. The alternate chapters, related by Vice-President Richard Nixon, tell of the catalogue of mishaps to which he's subjected in his struggle to prevent a stay of execution by the Supreme Court. The radical tonal contrast between these strands is itself a source of comedy. The build-up to the execution is rendered in the overblown rhetoric of McCarthyite anti-communism as a chapter in the eternal conflict and the "Legions of Darkness." Nixon's chapters, in contrast, are a tour-de-force of neurotic insecurity and hapless slapstick, featuring a picaresque sexual encounter with Ethel Rosenberg and the subsequent exposure of his behind (on which Ethel has written "I AM A SCAMP" in lipstick) to the American people.

The Rosenbergs were not a new source of interest for American novelists. Their trial and execution haunts Sylvia Plath's autobiographical *The Bell Jar* (published in 1963), and was fictionalised by E.L. Doctorow in 1971's *The Book of Daniel* as a memoir by their traumatised son. But the sense of melancholy and irreparable loss expressed in these novels gives way in Coover's to a crazed exuberance of language and imagination. The execution, he seems to suggest, is best understood as the beginning of America's affliction by a grotesquely comic collective psychosis. Evoking the great eighteenth-century satirists of England, Coover reveals just how potent a political weapon humor can be.

Josh Cohen

Date 1953

Author Robert Coover (born 1932)

Place USA

Why It's Key The execution of the Rosenbergs inspired this experimental epic, *The Public Burning* (published in 1977), a ferocious satire on American anti-communism and the emerging culture of the media circus.

Key Event **Maurice Girodias launches Olympia Press, the avant-garde publisher**

Maurice Girodias set up Olympia press in 1953 partly as a pornographer who was in it for the money, but he can also be seen as a champion of the freedom of publication. Olympia published *Tropic of Cancer*, *The 120 Days of Sodom*, *The Story of O*, *Lolita*, *The Ginger Man*, and *Naked Lunch*.

Girodias' father, Frank Kahane, had published Anaïs Nin, Henry Miller, and Radclyffe Hall, and Girodias took over the family business; the influx of American GIs in Paris gave him the idea to publish "classics" of French erotica, such as the Marquis de Sade, in English translation. A loophole in French censorship laws allowed Girodias to publish erotic books in English when they could not be published elsewhere. He soon branched out into commissioning erotic fiction – "dirty books" or "dbs" – written under pseudonyms, with such titles as *The Whipping Club* and *Thongs* (the latter one of several Olympia titles penned by Alexander Trocchi). The books appeared under false jackets, with

the words "*Jane Eyre* by Charlotte Brontë" on the covers of the more outré material. British dealers were soon queuing up to smuggle them across the Channel.

Lolita transformed the press's reputation when it was published in the Traveller's Companion series in 1955. In 1956 obscenity charges were brought by the French government, and, as the *Times Literary Supplement* reported, "Girodias embarked on the long process of 'lolitagation.'" But Girodias had done his job, however much acrimony there remained between him and *Lolita*'s author, Vladimir Nabokov. By 1958, according to the *Daily Express* there was reportedly a waiting list for the novel at the public library in Tunbridge Wells, that "town of retired gentlefolk."

Girodias pushed the boundaries of decency and obscenity in print and made it possible for many works to be published that previously would have been banned.
Lucy Daniel

Date 1953

Place Paris

Why It's Key Olympia's first publication was the second part of Henry Miller's Rosy Crucifixion trilogy, *Plexus*. James Campbell wrote, "Many others played their part, and often Girodias's motives were anything but noble; but half a dozen years of Olympia publishing did more to challenge and destroy the fortress of literary censorship in the Western world than any other post-war enterprise or event."

1950-1959

379

Key Book
Fahrenheit 451

SPOILER

Fahrenheit 451 is "the temperature at which book-paper catches fire and burns" according to a note prefacing the novel. Bradbury's novel relates events in a future dystopia in which books have been banned. Taking advantage of social attitudes which see books as problematic and confusing, the government takes steps to outlaw all printed material. To this end they employ a group of "Firemen" who seek out books and torch them with kerosene. The populace is expected, instead, to watch TV and take drugs. Guy Montag, the protagonist, has no problem with his job as a Fireman (although he feels emotionally empty) until he meets Clarisse McLellan, a young girl who shows him there is more to life than destruction. Montag becomes radicalised and rejects the society he works for, finally escaping the inexorable manhunt to enjoy exile and possible salvation in a post-nuclear future.

Bradbury is part of a set of 1950s science fiction writers who began to use the dystopian mode to

explore political repression and modes of resistance (you might loosely collect him with Philip K. Dick, Thomas Disch, and Kurt Vonnegut). The novel is a clear comment on repressive times and was published during the most controversial period of the House Un-American Activities Committee (HUAC) hearings which investigated disloyal and subversive organizations. However the book has proved to have widespread application, as Bradbury believed it would: "I meant all kinds of tyrannies anywhere in the world at any time, right, left, or middle."
Jerome de Groot

Date 1953

Author Ray Bradbury (1920–)

Nationality USA

Why It's Key Bradbury's dystopian vision of a land where books are banned recalls Nazi book burning and warns against censorship.

Opposite *Farenheit 451*

Key Event **Sylvia Plath suffers the severe depression that will inspire *The Bell Jar***

In 1953 Sylvia Plath was hospitalised with severe depression. The ambitious young American had just finished her third year at Smith, the elite girls' college. During the summer, following what should have been a glittering internship at *Mademoiselle* magazine in New York, Plath attempted suicide. She was found in time and admitted to McClean Hospital where she was given the electro-convulsive treatment which was the standard treatment at the time.

The events of that terrible summer were recalled ten years later in *The Bell Jar*, a novel published several months after Plath eventually succeeded in killing herself in London, following the breakdown of her marriage to the poet Ted Hughes. *The Bell Jar* was initially published under a pseudonym in order to avoid giving offence to the characters on which it was so clearly based, including Plath's mother, Aurelia. However, as a published poet with a growing reputation, Plath also wanted to ensure that this

"pot-boiler," written with an eye to the increasingly popular confessional memoir market, would not interfere with the critical reception of her verse, about which she cared deeply.

How ironic, then, that Plath's iconic fame today rests as much on *The Bell Jar* as it does on her poetry. Her account of how a perfect A-grade student began to slip into a miasma of self-harming when confronted by the limited roles that society has to offer women has struck a chord with generations of young female readers. Indeed, Plath's depression in the summer of 1953 has come to stand for the resistance of all white middle-class women to the impossible burden of becoming both a perfect wife and mother, and a first-rate artist.

Kathryn Hughes

Date 1953

Place USA

Why It's Key *The Bell Jar* (1963) has become an iconic text. The image of the descending bell jar, cutting off the oxygen of intimate contact, remains a powerful and profound literary description of clinical depression. In the 1970s and 1980s the novel gained extra cultural resonance from being set alongside other key feminist texts such as Betty Friedan's *The Feminine Mystique*.

Key Event **Dylan Thomas collapses and dies while drinking in New York**

Had Dylan Thomas died quietly at home, a glass of warm milk in one hand, Bible in the other, it's doubtful whether John Lennon would have wanted him anywhere near the cover of *Sgt Pepper* (Thomas floats above Marlon Brando and just below Lenny Bruce). Nor, one suspects, would Robert Zimmerman have ever been suspected of using the Welsh poet's name to put the Dylan into Bob Dylan. While Thomas' work made his name, it was his life and death that turned him into a national, artistic, and counter-culture legend. It helped, of course, that Thomas was a poet of verbal flair and emotional passion; what is equally undeniable is that his final, desperate, and booze-soaked days carousing and collapsing around Manhattan have boosted both his reputation and his sales. Many of these late stories have passed into myth, whether it's Thomas' famous claim that he downed 18 straight whiskeys ("I think that's the record") or his final words, which offer just the right mix of despair, regret, and enlightenment:

"After thirty-nine years, this is all I've done." The fact that these facts are often closer to fiction is both apt (Thomas was a natural-born liar) and good for business. On one hand, they have helped attract an audience far broader and more broad-minded than modern poets are used to – just as well given Thomas' tenuous status within academia (F.R. Leavis was only the first of many to be sniffy about his work).

On the other, uncertainty about what killed Thomas (alcoholism, suicidal despair, the end of his marriage, medical incompetence, undiagnosed diabetes) has generated enough studies to fill several bookcases: there are three monographs about his death alone. Indeed, having begun as the "Rimbaud of Cwmdonkin Drive," Dylan Thomas lives on as that most modern of phenomena: the literary industry.

James Kidd

Date 1953

Place New York

Why It's Key Dylan Thomas' untimely death aged just 39 years (in the bar of the White Horse Tavern in Greenwich Village) puts a hedonistic, twentieth-century spin on the myth of the doomed Romantic poet. No laudanum or consumption for the "Rimbaud of Cwmdonkin Drive," unless by consumption you mean beer, whiskey and, so it's alleged, a variety of drugs.

Opposite Dylan Thomas

Key Event **Huxley's experimental drug-taking leads to *The Doors of Perception***

"To be shaken out of the ruts of ordinary perception, to be shown for a few timeless hours the outer and the inner world... as they are apprehended, directly and unconditionally, by Mind at Large – this is an experience of inestimable value to everyone and especially to the intellectual."

As opening gambits go, Huxley's is straightforward, if slightly surprising in its frankness: "one bright May morning, I swallowed four-tenths of a gram of mescalin dissolved in half a glass of water and sat down to wait for the results." He was researching the uses of hallucinogenic drugs as a route to visionary experience, and offered himself as a willing guinea pig. This short book is an account of Huxley's mescalin experience, prompted by tape recordings of his reactions to ordinary objects, which became charged with significance while the drug took its effect. These include "a chair which looked like the Last Judgment." The experiment was an outcrop of Huxley's late adherence to Eastern mysticism and interest in parapsychology. Looking for spiritual fulfilment and living in California, at the same time as the Beats, he experimented with various hallucinogens, including LSD. Although not of the same literary value as Huxley's satirical novels, *The Doors of Perception* and its companion piece, *Heaven and Hell* (1956), a further essay on psychotropic states, form an indispensable part of his reputation as a liberating thinker. Huxley is known as a novelist of ideas, a searing commentator on the morals of his age. Here, in fact, he is no less concerned with moral imperatives; he is looking for a revelatory self-transcendence, and for answers to religious conundrums, attempting to uncover "naked existence" and reveal things as they truly are – a concern which might also be said to have dominated his fiction. It also made him a hero to 1960s counterculture.
Lucy Daniel

Date 1953

Author Aldous Huxley (1894–1963)

Nationality UK

Why It's Key In *The Doors of Perception* Huxley discussed the value of mescalin as a route to visionary experiences. Jim Morrison named his band The Doors after the book's title, originally taken from William Blake's *The Marriage of Heaven and Hell*: "If the doors of perception were cleansed everything would appear to man as it is, infinite."

Key Book
A Spy in the House of Love

Sabina, whose name recalls rape, roams the streets of Manhattan, a latter-day Dona Juana; always in search of erotic fulfillment without love or attachment, consciously seeking an approximation of masculine sexuality. At the same time her emotional antennae and her psychological insight into the near strangers she enters into liaisons with attest to her deeply feminine responses.

Anaïs Nin was born in France and moved to New York, where, as a teenager she became a model. In her diaries, Nin wrote of her need to develop a female aesthetic that spoke from the "womb," and asserted: "I am not interested in fiction; I want faithfulness." Faithful to bohemian female experience, Nin describes Sabina's need to experiment with different men, each of whom elicits a different version of herself. After each affair she returns to her equable husband, Alan. Eventually she realizes she doesn't have a "core" personality, but like Duchamp's "Nude Descending a Staircase" she has several versions of herself, but only presents one of these to her husband.

The novel is framed by Sabina randomly phoning a "lie detector" who is so fascinated by her conversation that he seeks her out, and follows her throughout her restless peregrinations, not judging but noting her movements. He is both a projection of her own conscience, and an avatar of the reader, who starts by feeling censorious but is seduced by the lyrical beauty of the prose and the acuity of intimate insight. The final scene, worthy of Antonin Artaud, doubles the initial scene in which the lie detector first discovers her.

One major influence in this text is D.H. Lawrence; but what a difference it makes when the author is female and speaks with honesty and the authority of subjective experience about desire, sensuality, emotional needs, and multiple (not unified) personality.
Helen May Dennis

Date 1954

Author Anaïs Nin (1903–77)

Nationality USA

Why It's Key Nin is famous for her journals giving a female perspective on her male literary contemporaries, and for writing female erotica for pleasure and for income. She was friend, and, in some cases lover, of Henry Miller, Antonin Artaud, Edmund Wilson, Gore Vidal, James Agee, and Lawrence Durrell.

Opposite Anaïs Nin

Key Book
The Lord of the Rings

It began as a children's story, a continuation of *The Hobbit*, but grew into something far greater: an Heroic Romance, a classic coming of age fable, and a strangely modern myth. Tolkien was a masterly storyteller, but he was also a philologist (perhaps the greatest of his generation) and used his understanding of ancient Northern languages to tell of the things ancient writers had omitted.

The story begins with an apparently innocuous trinket, picked up by Bilbo Baggins, a plain but very beautiful golden ring. But it has this peculiarity: it renders its wearer invisible. However, it also turns the wearer into a hopeless addict. The reason? It is the "One ring to rule them all," fashioned by the Dark Lord, Sauron the Great, Lord of Mordor, to bind together all the magical rings of Middle Earth, originally forged to help and heal the world. It falls to Frodo, Bilbo's nephew and heir, to find a way to destroy the Ruling Ring before it destroys Middle Earth – and himself.

Tolkien's Middle Earth was unprecedented and is still unrivalled, peopled with creatures at once utterly original and profoundly traditional: the Ents, the shepherds of the trees; Tom Bombadil, a kind of spirit of the soil, who remembers "the first acorn and the first raindrop," the barrow wights, evil ghosts reanimating the corpses of good men; the orcs, ruined elves who hate their dark master even as they serve him; Gandalf, the deeply unangelic angel; the unforgettable ringwraiths, men reduced to spectres by their hunger for power.

It has enthralled and appalled in almost equal measure. Some dismiss it as a boy's own adventure which has slipped its moorings, others praise it as a philosophical and moral masterpiece. In one sense to call it an epic is misleading: it is Heroic Romance. But it is an epic of courage, and the first great myth of addiction.
Murrough O'Brien

Date 1954–55

Author J.R.R. Tolkien (1892–1973)

Nationality UK

Why It's Key Tolkien gave the fantasy genre new life and academic authority. *The Lord of the Rings* regularly appears at the top of favorite books polls. Peter Jackson's film adaptation is widely recognized as a classic. Tolkien's work has appealed to every sensibility and many political persuasions from the Viet Cong to nuclear protestors!

384

Key Book
Brother Man

Best known of the three major novels published in Mais' last years (the others being *The Hills Were Joyful Together*, 1953, and *Black Lightning*, 1955), *Brother Man* has a complex narrative with a host of supporting characters, but its central focus is the Christ-like progress of messianic Rasta John Power, better known as Brother Man, a shoemaker, healer, and visionary who is caught up in a web of intrigue and betrayal in Jamaica's tough West Kingston slums. Because of his ability to cure the sick and injured, people elevate him to the status of a prophet, and throngs trail him in the street as with each miracle his reputation spreads. Looking on enviously is the evil Papacita, a violent enforcer whose authority is threatened by Brother Man's message of peace and love. "'Love is everything,' he said, simply. 'It is what created the world. It is what made you an' me, child, brought us into this world.'" Papacita also covets the attention of an attractive young woman whom Brother Man has rescued from the streets. In the end, Brother Man's Christ-like gifts lead to tragic, biblical consequences. The novel has significance as being considered the first serious depiction in literature of Rastafarianism – the religious and cultural phenomenon that first appeared in Jamaica in the 1930s – and Mais foresaw the power it would come to command within Jamaican society, twenty years before the era of the Rastafarian reggae superstar Bob Marley. Full of drama and melodrama, *Brother Man* provided ideal inspiration for a play by Kwame Dawes, *One Love*, which premiered at the Bristol Old Vic in 2001, "a powerful parable of desire and denial."
Margaret Busby

Date 1954

Author Roger Mais (1905–55)

Nationality Jamaica

Why It's Key In the first novel to examine the emerging Rastafarian movement, the charismatic Brother Man personifies human goodness and love. The structure of the book is innovative: each of five sections is introduced by a "chorus of people in the lane" commenting on the action.

Key Character **Jim Dixon**
Lucky Jim

Before Kingsley Amis became a grumpy old man, he invented in his first novel a protagonist, Jim Dixon, who is sometimes said to be an angry young one (two years before John Osborne's Jimmy Porter). But Dixon's moment comes a little earlier: the book is clear that there is a Labour government, so it cannot be set later than 1951. Part of his frustration comes from encountering – in the provincial university where he is a probationary lecturer in history – the kind of stratified and stultified English world that the post-war dispensation had been meant to transform. Like his author, Dixon has a number of faces he can put on – Edith Sitwell, Evelyn Waugh, sex life in Ancient Rome – with which to express his exasperations at this and the other problems of his life, which include too little money, too many hangovers, difficulties with girls, lodging-house life. Many of his frustrations center on his Head of Department, Professor Welch, and Welch's variously loathsome family. In an exhilarating showdown with the snobby Bohemian son, Bertrand, Dixon "hit him very hard indeed on the larger and more convoluted of his ears" and wins the day. He wins Bertrand's girl, too, and finally succeeds in leaving his previous attachment, the neurotic Margaret, who turns out (happily for the ending) to have faked a suicide attempt in order to prevent Dixon from leaving her. There are intimations here of the questions of misogyny which Amis' later books so disconcertingly investigate, but Dixon is allowed to be Lucky Jim, and to go off with the girl and with an escape from the squalors of academe into a more promising job in literary London. Great comic high spirits make this perhaps the most enjoyable of all Amis' books (and to speak personally, it's one I regularly reach for whenever my spirits need lifting).

Peter Swaab

Date 1954

Author Kingsley Amis (1922–94)

Nationality UK

Why It's Key Sometimes seen as an early incarnation of the angry young man, *Lucky Jim* is probably Amis' best-loved creation.

1950–1959

385

Key Character **Rhoda Penmark**
The Bad Seed

Rhoda Penmark, the gap-toothed, dimple-cheeked eight-year-old with her impeccably braided hair, who "never gets anything dirty" and is, according to her teacher, "the neatest little girl I've ever encountered," is probably one of fiction's most surprising psychopathic serial killers. Her immaculate bedroom, her keen intelligence, "her repose, her *neatness*, her cool self-sufficiency," which all seem to make her such a charming, ideal daughter and schoolgirl, are in fact the hallmarks of her psychopathic nature. She is in one sense a parody of the gifted child, or an inverted Pollyanna who, instead of believing the best of everyone, understands – and commits – the very worst of human nature. But March's novel is not a joke. Apparently written as a pot-boiler, it nevertheless utilises many of the Freudian ideas that March had immersed himself in, and suggests that violence itself is the "bad seed" that is hidden in every human heart, only waiting for the correct circumstances to reveal itself. Rhoda's small town is rife with cases for analysis. Her neighbour Monica Breedlove, who has been personally analysed by Freud, blithely discusses her own penis envy and castration impulses. A suburban world of bridge parties and cocktails at noon is spliced with case studies of murderous children. Rhoda herself suffers no guilt or fear of recrimination, reasoning that the electric chair is too big for her. She carries on coolly enjoying her ice cream while watching her latest victim burn to death. But guilt and shame about heredity tear Rhoda's mother to pieces when she discovers her own mother (Rhoda's grandmother) was an infamous murderess. Here was a disconcerting but enormously popular contribution to the nature versus nurture debate. In an extraordinary climactic scene, fraught with an overdose of psychoanalytical wisdoms, the "carrier" of the bad seed is ironically forced to fulfil her own genetic destiny….

Lucy Daniel

Date 1954

Author William March (1893–1954)

Nationality USA

Why It's Key Rhoda Penmark was the child progenitor of all subsequent fictional under-age sociopaths and murderers, who now occupy a genre of their own (particularly in film – *The Omen's* Damian, Stephen King's Carrie, or the violently unhinged protagonists of the teen satire, *Heathers*).

Key Event **Obscenity charges brought against sadomasochistic *The Story of O***

An erotic novel detailing taboo sadomasochistic practices, *The Story of O* sparked a debate that still continues over the possibility of women engaging in BDSM behaviors without compromising their feminist principles. More than this, however, it raised the issue of whether women can indeed "choose" such a submissive role if one accepts that wider sexual politics position women in ways that are both implicitly and explicitly subordinate to men. Because of the controversial gender politics of Réage's work, there was an assumption that the true author must be male, and that the fiction of female authorship contributed to the problematic sense that the sexual submissiveness being described was actually desired by women.

Paris-based Olympia Press published the novel simultaneously in both French and English. This risqué publisher was a more recent incarnation of Obelisk Press which had published other controversial works such as Henry Miller's *Tropic of Cancer*. Widespread discomfort with the novel's graphic content led to a police investigation and charges of obscenity mounted against the publishers by the French government. These charges came to nothing but the novel's worldwide distribution was fraught with difficulties. Grove Press obtained the rights to publish an English edition in the United States. Copies despatched to the publisher were impounded, but eventually released. The work was finally published there in 1965. In Britain, censorship laws precluded publication of the work until five years later.

It is fascinating that despite undoubtedly positive changes in the relationship between the sexes, there is still great unease about the content of this text. Is it possible that there is true emancipation in the extremes of sexual behavior? It is, of course, one of the great ironies of sexual power play that the masochist who fully submits to their partner wields an unprecedented power.
Juliet Wightman

Date 1954

Author Pauline Réage (pen-name of Dominique Aury, born Anne Desclos, 1907–1998)

Nationality France

Why It's Key Réage broke new ground in her description of extreme sadomasochistic sexual practices. Such an unashamed treatment of one woman's subordination to her lover and apparent willingness to submit to male violence for sexual pleasure proved too risqué.

Opposite *The Story of O*

1950-1959

387

Key Event
Bloomsday

Every year fans of James Joyce's *Ulysses* (1922) gather to celebrate Bloomsday, 16 June (1904) – the day on which the novel is set. Festivities include dressing up as characters from the book, reading parts of *Ulysses* aloud, and holding international academic conferences devoted to Joyce's work. Celebrations of Bloomsday are international and can be found from New York to Japan. In Dublin, Joyce's home city and the setting of the novel, people regularly attempt to retrace the movements of central characters during the course of the day. In 2004 Dublin hosted a five-month long centenary festival, "ReJoyce Dublin." Events included an exhibition of *Ulysses* manuscripts, stagings of Joyce's work as street theater, and a breakfast served to 10,000 people on O'Connell Street in the center of the city.

The first celebration of Bloomsday is usually dated to 1954. A small group of writers and enthusiasts gathered outside Dublin at the Martello Tower in Sandycove – the location of the novel's opening.

Those present included the poet Patrick Kavanagh and the author and newspaper writer Myles Na Gopaleen, also known as Flann O'Brien. According to his biographers, Na Gopaleen arrived drunk, he nearly got into a fight with Kavanagh, and their tour of Joycean sites was cut short at a pub in the city center. The association between Bloomsday and the consumption of alcohol persists to this day. Indeed, for many, Bloomsday has little to do with Joyce or his writings: it is a welcome excuse to drink Guinness and celebrate Irish culture.
Matthew Creasy

Date 1954

Place Dublin, Ireland

Nationality Ireland

Why Its Key Joyce himself celebrated the twenty-fifth anniversary of Bloomsday in 1929 in a restaurant near Versailles in France. The meal was attended by famous writers and critics including Paul Valéry, Thomas McGreevy, and Samuel Beckett. Beckett got so drunk he had to be abandoned at a bar on the way home, setting clear precedent for later generations.

Key Event *Bonjour Tristesse* becomes a runaway success – and sparks a scandal

Having failed her first year exams at the Sorbonne in the summer of 1953, 18-year-old Kiki Quoirez, a spoilt child of upper-middle class parents, decided to write a novel. Borrowing her title from an Eluard poem and her pseudonym from Proust's fictional princess, Françoise Sagan (1935–2004) was herself surprised by the overnight success of her first novel, *Bonjour Tristesse*. In this cynically recounted story of summertime maturation, Cécile, a naive, hedonistic 17-year-old, competes with older women for the attention of her womanizing widower father. When he decides to settle down with the sophisticated Anne, Cécile plots with her young beau Cyril to sabotage the union. The novel's frank depiction of relations between the sexes and between generations scandalized readers, together with Cécile's casual amorality and professed enjoyment of sex for pleasure, without love, and out of wedlock. Stoking the scandal was Sagan's own flamboyance and much-publicised love of sex, drugs, gambling, and fast cars. "This charming little monster," as one commentator famously called her, fast became an icon of metropolitan radical chic but also, to some, a symbol of modern depravity, even provoking the Vatican's censure. Yet beyond the hype *Bonjour Tristesse* won both critical acclaim and popular success, becoming one of the first major beneficiaries of France's belated "paperback revolution." Its publication coincided with the emergence, for the first time, of teenagers as a distinct age group in society, and it voiced the disillusionment, boredom, and irreverence of a young, affluent postwar generation insistent on making their own way in life.

Nimrod Ben-Cnaan

Date 1954

Place France

Why It's Key Sagan became a new kind of literary celebrity on the strength of a novel reflecting a new kind of youth. Sagan and her protagonist Cécile were young women liberated by their affluent circumstances and insistent on living a life of leisure and pleasure without heed to tradition or their elders' expectations, and without a committed ethical creed.

Key Passage
Lord of the Flies

"'*Kill the beast! Cut his throat! Spill his blood! Do him in!*' The sticks fell and the mouth of the new circle crunched and screamed. The beast was on its knees in the centre, its arms folded over its face. It was crying out against the abominable noise something about a body on the hill. The beast struggled forward, broke the ring, and fell over the steep edge of the rock to the sand by the water. At once the crowd surged after it, poured down the rock, leapt on to the beast, screamed, struck, bit, tore. There were no words, and no movements but the tearing of teeth and claws."

In his classic novel, Golding provides a frightening depiction of the changing behavior of a group of young boys who become stranded on an island after a plane crash. Freed from the safety, structure, and social mores of their British upbringing, the boys are tested in their struggle to survive. Do they work together or go it alone? Do they institute new rules or embrace a lawless freedom? And perhaps most importantly of all, do they uphold what is morally right or abandon such codes in favor of the violent and instinctive?

In the shocking climax of the novel, the base and destructive instincts of the group prevail and Simon, one of their number, is murdered in an orgiastic frenzy of animalistic zeal. At once both vividly real and densely symbolic, Simon's death is the cathexis of the physical, emotional, and moral energies that the extreme isolation has forced every boy to confront.

Simon, who throughout the novel has been the very incarnation of "goodness," has a prescient experience before the "lord of the flies." Whilst hallucinating, he hears the fly-blown pig's head explain that the "beast" of the island is not an actual creature, but rather an inescapable phenomenon, as it is lurking within everyone.

Juliet Wightman

Date 1954

Author William Golding (1911–93)

Nationality UK

Why It's Key Golding's novel was a timely exploration of competing human impulses. In the post-war period, assumptions about the relationship between good and evil were revisited with a renewed urgency forcing people to question how they might react when confronted with an extraordinary situation.

Opposite *Lord of the Flies*

Key Event **Article in _Life_ magazine inspires Dr Seuss to write _The Cat in The Hat_**

In 1954, an article by John Hersey appeared in the May 24th issue of the American publication _Life_, suggesting that the worryingly high level of illiteracy in children was caused by the dullness of the books they were given to read. "Pallid primers," Hersey called them. An editor at Houghton Mifflin read the feature and then issued a challenge to the cartoonist, Dr Seuss (real name Theodore Geisel, 1904–91). "He sent me a list of about three hundred words and told me to make a book out of them," Seuss recalled in a later interview. The task took him nine months and the result was _The Cat in the Hat_ (published in 1957), a minor masterpiece that has become an enduring children's favorite.

The poem, written in a bouncing triple metre, tells the story of two bored children whose day is enlivened by the visit of a mischievous cat and his associates, Thing One and Thing Two. The result is what all children love – chaos, mess, excitement but everything cleared up before Mother comes home. It's pure guilt-free

pleasure. The voice of conscience (cheerfully ignored) is provided by the family goldfish. Dr Seuss's idiosyncratic artwork is vivid, in black, white, and red, and the sweeping lines convey a sense of energy and movement. The book was an instant success and went on to become one of the best-selling children's books of all time. Within three years of publication, it had sold about three million copies. It has been translated into several languages including Latin under the title _Cattus Petasatus_. The cat reappeared in several other books, including _The Cat in the Hat Comes Back_ and _I Can Read with My Eyes Shut_. Dr Seuss's anarchic feline also made it impossible for anyone to use the word "dull" to describe children's books.
Kathy Watson

Date 1954

Place USA

Why Its Key Dr Seuss wasn't a doctor, he left Oxford University without completing his doctorate. He is famed for such classics as _How the Grinch Stole Christmas_ (1957) and _Green Eggs and Ham_ (1960), in which famously he rose to the challenge of writing a book using only 50 words. At the time of his death his books had already sold some 200 million copies.

Opposite Dr Seuss and The Cat

391

Key Author
Ernest Hemingway

One of the finest of all American writers, Ernest Hemingway (1899–1961) was born in Illinois. After the United States entered World War I, he joined a volunteer ambulance unit in the Italian army and was wounded. His experience of being treated in a Milan hospital would inspire one of his greatest novels, _A Farewell to Arms_ (1929). During the 1920s, Hemingway became a member of the group of expatriate Americans living in Paris, an experience which he described in his first important novel, _The Sun Also Rises_ (1926). He particularly loved Spain and the Spaniards. His book about bullfighting, _Death in the Afternoon_, was published in 1932 and his role as a journalist in the Spanish Civil War, during which he supported the Republicans, fuelled the touching 1940 novel, _For Whom the Bell Tolls_. Hemingway believed that art should confront us with harsh truths about ourselves and the world around us – and nowhere did that apply more starkly than in war. His works were

burnt by the Nazis in 1933 for being a monument to modern decadence.

Among his later works, perhaps the most potent is the novel, _The Old Man and the Sea_, the story of an old fisherman's solitary battle with the sea. But his straightforward prose, spare dialogue, distrust of adjectives, and predilection for understatement are particularly effective in his short stories.

Hemingway was awarded the Nobel Prize in Literature in 1954. Biographical research has revealed that, behind the "hard-boiled," macho façade of boxing, bullfighting, big-game hunting, and deep-sea fishing, Hemingway was a deeply troubled man. He killed himself with a shotgun at Ketchum, Idaho in 1961. Several posthumous works and collections provided ample evidence of Hemingway's versatility – _A Moveable Feast_ (1964), _By-Line_ (1967), _88 Poems_ (1979), and _Selected Letters_ (1981).
Adam Feinstein

Date 1954 (Nobel Prize)

Nationality USA

Key Works _The Snows of Kilimanjaro_ (1936); _To Have and Have Not_ (1937); _The Fifth Column and the First Forty-Nine Stories_ (1938); _For Whom the Bell Tolls_ (1940); _The Old Man and the Sea_ (1952); _A Moveable Feast_ (1964)

Why It's Key Hemingway's popularity worldwide is immense. His terse style has influenced writers ranging from Jack Kerouac and J.D. Salinger to Elmore Leonard.

Key Event **The first performance of** *The Quare Fellow*

The Quare Fellow opened at the Pike Theatre Club in Dublin in 1954. Set in a prison, the plot focuses on the twenty-four hours before a prisoner named the "Quare Fellow" is to be hanged. At a time when judicial hanging was still allowed by both British and Irish governments, the play was challenging in terms of both its subject matter and its setting.

Behan had spent two years in Borstal and a further four in jail for political activities and the play's realism clearly owes much to his personal experiences. Behan's uncompromising treatment of difficult, political material and his ability to mix song and dialogue marked him out as an exciting new voice in Irish theater. However, a large cast and a small capacity theater made the first production of *The Quare Fellow* an expensive one and it closed after a four-week run. In 1954 the unknown playwright's jailbird background and the contentious subject matter discouraged other theater managements from taking the play on.

However, Behan's fortunes were reversed after the play was picked up by Joan Littlewood's Theatre Workshop Company in 1956. *The Quare Fellow*'s English premiere at the Theatre Royal Stratford East was greeted by widespread critical acclaim and subsequently transferred to the West End for a six month run. The play's implied condemnation of the death penalty and its large cast of largely working-class characters made it a perfect play for the left-leaning Theatre Workshop: a company who prided themselves on their commitment to new writing and ensemble playing. Publicity surrounding both Behan and the production of his play increased when the playwright turned up drunk to a BBC television interview with Malcolm Muggeridge.
Kate Harris

Date 1954

Place Ireland

Author Brendan Behan (1923–64)

Why It's Key The play publicized the debate surrounding capital punishment and introduced a new Irish voice to the stage. One of the most significant things about the play's dramatic style is the fact that the "Quare Fellow" of the title doesn't actually make an appearance in the play.

Key Author **Kamala Markandaya** *Nectar in a Sieve*

The remarkable care Markandaya (1924–2004) paid throughout her career not to disclose details of her private life to the public might be indicative of a provocative refusal as an open-minded intellectual of the idea of judging people by their social background and status. The fact that she belonged to a Hindu-Brahmin family (from Mysore in South India) did not prevent her intentionally sympathetic exploration and understanding of the world of low-caste peasants depicted in her novels, or her audacious investigation of the clash/encounter between Indians and British in pre-independent India in *Some Inner Fury* (1955). In her personal life too she was not discouraged by orthodox Hindu beliefs about the inauspicious venturing across the "black waters" when she decided to settle in London in 1948 to marry English journalist Bertrand Taylor. Markandaya's fiction is infused with an insightful concern for her suffering characters, who are often representatives of a much larger collective. Her

widely acclaimed first novel, *Nectar in a Sieve*, won the American Library Association's Notable Book Award in 1955. Here, the motifs of tradition and change function as ensnaring forces enticing the reader to an empathic response. Together with her contemporaries Raja Rao, Mulk Raj Anand, and R.K. Narayan she set up a unique style for the representation of India, Indians, and the West, which identifies her as a path-breaker of Indian writing in English. Her diasporic writing is an approach to India through the intervention of memory and history, fused together by conflicting sentiments of compassion, anger, and surrender.
Letizia Alterno

Date 1954

Nationality India

Other Key Works *A Silence of Desire* (1960); *A Handful of Rice* (1966); *The Nowhere Man* (1972); *The Golden Honeycomb* (1977); *Pleasure City* (1982)

Why It's Key Pioneer writer of the Indian diaspora, Markandaya achieved international fame through her novels dealing with issues of poverty and industrialization, gender, and sexuality.

Key Book
The Last Temptation

Christ is a carpenter, but he uses his craft to make crosses for the Romans; Christ is the messiah, so he wants to kill all the pretended ones; Christ is the son of God and God Himself, but his mission and his destiny terrify him. Having surmounted all the temptations proffered him before his Passion, Christ encounters one for which nothing had prepared him. On the Cross, in his death agony, he has a vision of how matters might have turned out had he accepted the lot of an ordinary man.

This is the Christ presented in *The Last Temptation*. Nikos Kazantzakis's avowed aim was to make his readers love Christ all the more through his eccentric, passionate, fusion of Greek Orthodoxy, Buddhism, and Heaven knows what else. His work rises above the rather crass genre of "real Jesus" stories in its desire not to subvert but to invert the Gospel story. It is as if, having accepted the orthodox teaching, he feels nonetheless impelled to present it from the inside.

If you're human you're going to find it tough to accept that you're also God.

Christ's vision on the cross famously includes sex with Mary Magdalene. It is not sensationally described, but it provoked a furore of pyrotechnic proportions. But there should have been nothing in this to shock the true believer. The church had long taught that Christ took on all aspects of our nature, including, of course, the sexual – in order to redeem them. Kazantzakis only suggested that the true temptation was not sex as such – in his view a rather lowly instinct within the hierarchy of human impulses – but the insidious yearning for comfort, domesticity, ease of spirit, and content of body, and that such yearnings must be set aside when higher matters call – like a cosmos to be saved.

Murrough O'Brien

Date 1955

Author Nikos Kazantzakis (1883–1957)

Nationality Greece

Why It's Key The book's publication produced fierce controversy and Martin Scorsese's film adaptation resulted in angry crowds in Greece smashing their way into cinemas showing the film; in Paris, a cinema was gutted by fire. Kazantzakis was denied full funerary rites by the Orthodox Church for his perceived heresy.

1950-1959

393

Key Author **Flannery O'Connor**
A Good Man is Hard to Find

Frequently categorised as "Southern" or "Catholic" writing, Flannery O'Connor's fiction exceeds such bounds. Using the language of sin, grace, and redemption and located entirely in the American South, especially Georgia, her short stories and two novels obliquely illuminate Southern decline, slavery's social legacy, and the impact of World War II. Mary Flannery O'Connor (1925–64) was born in Georgia, the only child of a Catholic family. She excels at painful, amusing, and sometimes grotesque Southern sketches, accentuating the Puritanical narrowness of her subjects and their propensity to self-delusion and violence. Any parochial view of her work stems perhaps from her life, spent uneventfully in her native state, devoted to literature, and punctuated by spells at college in Iowa, in an artists' community in Saratoga, and with literary friends in New York and Connecticut. Indeed, diagnosed in 1950 with hereditary lupus, she eventually became a semi-invalid living with her mother on the family's Georgian dairy farm, continuing to write nonetheless.

The stories in *A Good Man Is Hard to Find* exemplify the irony with which she exposes the Southern world to its ghosts. The title tale features a family automobile holiday led astray by the overweening power of the grandmother, whose desire to visit an old plantation house leads them towards an implacable evil. In "The Artificial Nigger," we see a shared, hostile perception of blackness bond, "like an action of mercy," a white child with his unsympathetic grandfather while "The Displaced Person" references the Holocaust to show Southern regression into a radically closed society. Everywhere, impairment and prejudice underwrite this Gothic, bleakly comic universe.

Doug Haynes

Date 1955

Nationality USA

Key Works *Wise Blood* (1952), *The Violent Bear It Away* (1960), *Everything that Rises Must Converge* (1965)

Why It's Key She has been ranked with McCullers, Welty, and Capote as a quintessentially Southern author. In many ways a "writer's writer" who published work piecemeal in journals and magazines, her fame has increased since John Huston filmed *Wise Blood* in 1979.

Key Author
Saadat Hasan Manto

Manto (1912–55) was part of an influx of Muslim writers and intellectuals from post-Partition India which contributed to a burgeoning literary and journalistic scene in Lahore, Pakistan. Controversial stories such as his masterpiece on the horrors of Partition, "Khol Do" (1949), and "Thanda Ghosht" (1950), led to one literary magazine being banned and to Manto's vilification at the hands of the conservative elite. "Thanda Ghosht" dealt with the subject of necrophilia and featured much violence, which shocked contemporary readers in his homeland Pakistan. Consequently, many commercially-minded publishers closed their doors to him for fear of social and financial ruin. Manto, however, appeared to revel in his role as *enfant terrible* of Urdu literature, seemingly depicting scenes of sex and violence between lowly members of society principally in order to shock the prudish majority. That, at least, is how it seemed to those who found his work objectionable. The uncomfortable truth

was that Manto was actually uncovering the hypocrisy of a society that would, on the one hand, deny these things while, with the other, create the circumstances by which they come about. Manto's writing is characterised by a Kafkaesque vividness of depiction, society's ills writ large on the small canvasses of people's lives. Latterly, Manto became a somewhat tragic figure, ravaged by drink and penury. He became touchy and sullen in public, tolerating no criticism. Where once he was welcomed into literary and social circles, many started to avoid the cranky, often aggressive man who at every opportunity would attempt to borrow money to feed his appetite for the sub-standard liquor that led to his death of cirrhosis at the age of only forty-three.

Christian Kerr

Date 1955 (death)

Nationality Pakistan

Key Works Khol Do (Open It) (1949), *Thanda Ghosht (Cold Meat)* (1950), *Yazid* (1951), *Pardey Ke Peechhey (Behind The Curtains)* (1953)

Why It's Key Regarded as the greatest Urdu short story writer of the twentieth century, Manto wrote about subjects considered taboo in traditionally conservative Indo-Pakistani society.

Key Author **William Gaddis**
The Recognitions

Two time National Book Award-winner William Gaddis (1922–98) may be the most critically acclaimed writer you've never heard of before. He's also the winner of numerous prestigious grants and fellowships, and the experimental form of his novels has inspired countless contemporary writers, yet his work remains largely unread by the general reader. In part, this is because his novels are so difficult to read. His most famous – and earliest – novels are satires of the artistic world and corporate America, respectively. But it is the form and complexity of his novels which make him a key contemporary author.

The Recognitions, like the novels which followed, rejected exposition in its traditional form. The book was so long and unwieldy, and the techniques it used were so new in 1955, a time when the dominant fiction mode was realism, that critics largely ignored Gaddis until the publication of his second – even more difficult – book, a decade later. *JR* is written almost entirely in

dialogue, and Gaddis refuses to give the reader any help in differentiating between the voices speaking or in filling in the blanks of the story.

This time, and perhaps because in the decade which had intervened, critics realized that Gaddis' avant-garde narrative techniques and black humor had anticipated by almost ten years other literary trends, and gave credit where due, recognizing the unique contribution of Gaddis and praising his novels, in spite of their difficulty, for imitating the way people really spoke, with all their pauses, cut-off sentences, and half-finished thoughts. He was recognized, as well, for the kinds of topics his novels addressed: entropy, corporate greed, authenticity, fragmentation.

Elizabeth Rosen

Date 1955 (published)

Nationality USA

Other Key Works *JR* (1975), *A Frolic of His Own* (1994)

Why It's Key Gaddis is now considered one of the most important post-war authors. His radical fiction techniques anticipated other postmodern literary experiments, while his satiric treatment of life in contemporary America made him the forerunner of the "black humorist" fiction of the late 1950s and 1960s.

Key Author
Halldór Laxness

To populate one of the world's most inhospitable landscapes with such memorable characters was, in itself, an achievement. To do so in the Icelandic tongue, while his contemporaries chose other Nordic languages as their medium, set Halldór Kiljan Laxness (1902–98) apart. He was born in Reykjavik, but moved to the country at an early age. He set out to be a musician, yet after World War I found himself seeking employment as a Hollywood scriptwriter. He converted to Catholicism and entered monastic life. Disillusioned by the experience, he embraced Communism, but was soon repelled by Stalin's totalitarian regime. He travelled extensively, but remained emotionally rooted in the Icelandic countryside. In later life he took an active interest in Eastern spirituality.

Laxness's fiction with its traces of Catholicism, surrealism, modernism, and Oriental philosophy mixed with the spirit of Iceland's medieval folk epics, reflects his life's wildly contrasting facets. *The Great Weaver from Kashmir*, his first significant novel, is about a young peripatetic writer who finds comfort in Catholicism amid Europe's inter-war chaos. *Salka Valka*, a dyptich portraying an idealist heroine in a fishing hamlet besieged by entrepreneurial greed, heralded his preoccupation with socialist themes. The celebrated *Iceland's Bell* trilogy drew on the country's traditional sagas to explore ideas of Icelandic nationalism, while *Under the Glacier* offered a sardonic sendup of Christian mysticism.

Irrespective of his immediate ideological or spiritual concerns, Laxness' characters are consistently compassionate and wryly humorous. On declaring him the recipient of the Nobel Prize in Literature in 1955, the Swedish Academy lauded his contribution to the renewal of Iceland's "great narrative art."

Ángel Gurría-Quintana

Date 1955 (Nobel Prize)

Nationality Iceland

Key Works *The Great Weaver from Kashmir* (1927); *Salka Valka* (1931, 1932); *Iceland's Bell* trilogy (1943, 1944, 1946); *Under the Glacier* (1968)

Why It's Key No modern writer has probed Iceland's soul as deeply. His novels portray men and women engaged in a perpetual struggle to preserve beauty, memory, and integrity in the midst of a relentlessly unforgiving environment.

Key Author
Thomas Mann

The greatest German writer of the twentieth century, who became perhaps the world's greatest living reminder of a "good" Germany in the years he spent in American exile from Hitler, Thomas Mann (1875–1955) was nevertheless traumatized by his nationality and cultural allegiance. Most problematic were the long years before the rise of Hitler in which Mann luxuriated in being an apolitical man and praised German culture in similar terms. His artistic solution to his own life was to project the tension he felt as the decadent, homosexual-leaning son of a respectable family of Hamburg bankers into a vision of the times. In the progression from *Buddenbrooks* (1901) via *The Magic Mountain* (1924) to *Dr Faustus* (1947) the tension between the artist and the bourgeoisie was gradually transformed into Europe's life and death struggle to preserve a decent world. But Mann could never relinquish his passion above all for Nietzsche and Wagner, which this decency seemed to entail.

Summaries of the contents of his fiction don't do justice to the richly musical construction of his German texts, always more or less in homage to these great and controversial figures. Mann assumed an equal position with the great German writers of the late eighteenth century, Goethe and Schiller, and like them suffered from being regarded as marginal in the Anglo-Saxon world. His diaries and letters have been used since his death to cut a self-proclaimed national figurehead down to size. He seems too difficult for an anti-elitist age that has forgotten the importance of art.

Lesley Chamberlain

Date 1955 (death)

Nationality Germany

Key Works *Buddenbrooks* (1901); *Death in Venice* (1912); *The Magic Mountain* (1924); *Dr Faustus* (1947)

Why It's Key Highly praised in the middle decades of the last century, Mann was an intellectual humanist. He wrote unique novels, notably *The Magic Mountain*, about the seductions of art and introspection, as well as short stories and essays.

Key Character **Lolita**
Lolita

"Lolita, light of my life, fire of my loins. My sin, my soul. Lo-Lee-ta: the tip of the tongue taking a trip of three steps down the palate to tap, at three, on the teeth. Lo. Lee. Ta."

An average American girl, "plain Lo... four feet ten in one sock," captures the heart of a middle-aged nymphophile (his word) or paedophile (the more usual term) called Humbert Humbert. Recognizing that she's "disgustingly conventional," a consumer of movie magazines, "sweet hot jazz" and "gooey fudge sundaes," he is nevertheless enchanted. She reminds him of his lost childhood love, the nymphic ("that is demoniac") Annabel. In Humbert's imagination, and more controversially on his "live lap" and then his bed, little Lo is transformed into a creation of irresistible desire called Lolita. Nabokov toyed with several other names (Virginia, Juanita) but finally decided that he needed a "diminutive with a lyrical lilt" and that "one of

the most limpid and luminous letters is 'L'." Michael Maar recently argued that he may also, albeit perhaps unconsciously, have been thinking of Heinz von Lichberg's 1916 novella of the same title. *Lolita* became so infamous that the town of Lolita, Texas, even considered changing its name. In 1992, Amy Fisher, the teenager who shot her lover's wife, was known variously as the "Long Island Lolita," "Laughing Lolita" and "Lethal Lolita." More recently, critics and novelists (such as Emily Prager and A.M. Homes) have challenged this image, stressing that the girl is a victim not a seductress, and offering revenge by rewriting Nabokov's novel from her point of view.
Kasia Boddy

Date 1955

Author Vladimir Nabokov (1899–1977)

Nationality Russia, naturalized US

Why It's Key In the years since Nabokov's novel was published, Lolita has become synonymous with sexual precociousness.

Opposite *Lolita*

Key Author **Pier Paolo Pasolini**
The Ragazzi

Pasolini (1922–75) was a novelist, poet, journalist, philosopher, actor, film director, and a painter. Born in Bologna into a fascist-oriented family, his political opinions soon turned towards the ideals of the Italian Communist Party; he would define himself a Marxist. Pasolini was a multifaceted artist, one of the most intriguing Italian intellectuals of the twentieth century. Outside Italy he is best known for his varied cinema production, which includes a latter-day neorealistic portrayal of the gritty reality of the Italian underclasses, as well as adaptations from such "controversial" literary classics as Chaucer's *Canterbury Tales* (1972) and Boccaccio's *Decameron* (1971). However, his work spans a multitude of genres, including poetry and painting, being infused throughout with what, as an atheist, he himself defined as "natural sacredness." Pasolini promoted the preservation of dialects, and supported the cause of the proletariat through his critique of bourgeois society, consumerism, and the

spread of economic globalization in Italy after World War II. His refusal of conformism and conventional behavior contributed to create his scandalous and visionary persona. From his very first novel, *The Ragazzi* (1955), which was defined as ideologically violent, Pasolini laid himself open to accusations of obscenity: a quality which, in his view, was intrinsic to a passionate artistic vision. That same artistic vision came to be enacted by his violent death in bleak surroundings on the outskirts of Rome, the murder being at the time confessed to by a rent-boy with whom he had had an assignation. Thirty years on the alleged murderer recanted, and Pasolini's death has now become emblematic of Italy's many unresolved (political?) mysteries.
Mariarita Martino

Date 1955 (published)

Nationality Italy

Other Key Works *The Best of Youth* (*La meglio gioventù* 1954); *A Violent Life* (*Una vita violenta*, 1959); Films: *The Gospel According to St Matthew* (*Il vangelo secondo Matteo*, 1964); *The Hawks and the Sparrows* (*Uccellacci e uccellini*, 1966)

Why It's Key One of the most versatile and controversial figures in twentieth-century Italian culture.

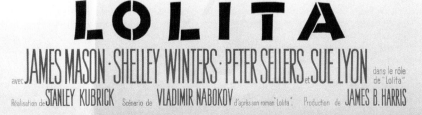

Key Author **Yashar Kemal**
Memed, My Hawk

Yashar Kemal, born in 1922, walks for inspiration, and writes his novels while standing up. That seems appropriate for someone who was drawn from an early age to the wandering storytellers who visited his village, and the oral traditions they brought with them. His most successful novels are based in the village life of southern Turkey. Memed is a folk hero who fights injustice. His is the action-packed story of a boy born under the oppressive rule of the local landowner, in the feudal regime which existed in Kemal's boyhood in rural Çukurova. Memed grows up a rebel and a bandit who takes revenge on the powerful and inspires the poor to fight for themselves. The four volumes of *Memed, My Hawk* took Kemal 39 years. Kemal began the first in his early twenties – Memed was 21; by the time he finished he was over 60, and Memed was still only 25.

Kemal has been the single most important influence on the development of modern Turkish literature, a committed writer who has deliberately stood for his country, and become a sort of national bard. A militant socialist, he became a prominent journalist. Kemal has been a member of the Turkish Labour Party, edited a Marxist publication, and has been president of the Turkish Writers' Union. He has been tried and briefly imprisoned for his political views. He has said that his early works were confiscated by the police without ever being published, and are now lost forever. In *Memed, My Hawk* he created a Turkish popular epic which also became a bestseller in English. It has been translated into 25 languages. His is an art that belongs in the world, and has a very strong sense of the particular region of the world from which he hails, a Faulknerian sense of place. He worked local legend into Memed's story, and his work has introduced to the language many local words that were previously unrecorded in written Turkish.

Lucy Daniel

Date 1955 (first English translation 1961)

Nationality Turkey

Key Works *Orta direk*, 1960 (as *The Wind from the Plain*, 1963); *Yer demir, gök bakir*, 1963 (as *Iron Earth, Copper Sky*, 1974); *Ince Memed II*, 1969 (as *They Burn the Thistles*, 1973); *Ölmez otu*, 1969 (as *The Undying Grass*, 1977)

Why It's Key This classic tale of Turkish village life brought Kemal worldwide fame, but his trilogy, *The Wind from the Plain*, may be his greatest work.

Key Book
The Man in the Gray Flannel Suit

With its portrayal of the small lives, staid careers, and large worries of the Rath family in 1950s Connecticut, *The Man in the Gray Flannel Suit* exposes the insecurity and unease behind the façade of suburban America. Tom and Betsy Rath feel under pressure to conform to the consumerist values of their social class, but struggle to keep up with the demands made on them by the materialist culture of a burgeoning post-war society. In an effort to improve their lot, Tom lands a PR job with a New York based TV network, but his initial enthusiasm and creative drive is crushed by the realization that he has been hired to be just another corporate yes-man. Despite Tom's apparent resignation to his role, Wilson reveals the grinding sense of disillusionment and frustration that wear away at Tom's sense of self. The novel's portrayal of contemporary America is contrasted with a series of flashbacks that Tom has of his army service during World War II, and Wilson shows Tom to be most alive and emotionally fulfilled in his wartime experiences. In particular, the wartime affair that Tom had with a young Italian woman, and the subsequent discovery of a child he has fathered from that relationship, provide the novel with its moral center. Wilson's unguarded representation of the nuances of sex, money, and class courted controversy upon the novel's first publication, but its real impact derives from its questioning of the values that form the core of post-war American society.

Laura Coffey

Date 1955

Author Sloan Wilson (1920–2003)

Nationality USA

Why It's Key Wilson's novel captured the mood of a generation in its portrayal of the discontented 1950s businessman. The title phrase rapidly became absorbed into common parlance as a by-word for the bland, spiritless social conformity of post-war urban America.

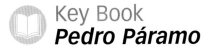

Key Book
Pedro Páramo

The greatest novel ever written by a Mexican author is also one of the shortest. In his writing, as well as in real life, Juan Rulfo was a man of few words. His entire published work adds up to no more than a handful of brooding stories, some minor film scripts, and his laconic masterpiece, *Pedro Páramo* (1955). After it, one critic said, Rulfo became the only Mexican whose fame grew with every book he didn't write.

The theme, set out in the opening sentences, is universal: "I came to Comala because I was told my father, one Pedro Páramo, lived here. My mother told me. And I promised her I would come to see him as soon as she died." So begins Juan Preciado's account as he sets out to find Comala, a place so hot that when its people die and go to hell they have to come back to fetch a blanket. What he encounters is a ghost town, overgrown with weeds and populated by whispers bringing tidings of past tragedies. In fact, Pedro Páramo, the great patriarch, has been dead for years, and the town of Comala has died with him. Yet his embittered offspring still roam his lands, once prosperous and now a barren dustbowl. As he listens to murmurs echoing through Comala's empty streets and emanating from its graves, Juan Preciado pieces together his father's brutal life, impossible love, and grim death. We are all, readers conclude, children of the same living rancour as he is. We are all *Pedro Páramo*'s children.

Ángel Gurría-Quintana

Date 1955

Author Juan Rulfo (1917–86)

Nationality Mexico

Why It's Key No other work of Mexican literature seems as timeless as *Pedro Páramo*. Rulfo's language is pared down to the point of almost lapsing into silence. The shattered strands of narrative connect it to modernist experiments, while the dialogue reflects the gruff mannerisms of peasants deep in the highlands of Jalisco, the author's place of birth.

1950–1959

Key Character **Sebastian Dangerfield**
The Ginger Man

It would be almost too easy to identify the character of Sebastian Dangerfield with his creator, J.P. Donleavy. Both are Americans, studying at Trinity College, Dublin in the first decade after the end of World War II, enjoying the bohemian literary life of booze and sex, fighting and philosophising while failing to keep up with their studies. However, while Donleavy undoubtedly drew on elements of his own experiences, he maintained that Dangerfield is loosely based on friend and fellow student, Gainor Stephen Crist.

Dangerfield is no mere two-dimensional creation but a portrayal of a complex and often contradictory character. He is married and a father, yet actively lusts after other women and behaves with insouciant irresponsibility as if free to do as he pleases. He is chronically short of money, often resorting to the pawnshop, but any funds he manages to acquire are quickly squandered on alcohol. He aspires to a life of wealth and luxury, yet lacks the will to work to achieve this and rejects with horror the conformity that he would have to submit to.

We should despise this person, but through Donleavy's comic gifts we come to sympathise with and almost admire him. He confronts life head-on and embraces it lustily. Though sometimes downcast and verging on despair, he always manages to find the courage to keep struggling in the face of a hostile and absurd universe. Donleavy did not invent the anti-hero, but his creation of Sebastian Dangerfield, the drunken artist, a misfit, truly belonging neither to the louche lower-class world or the comfortable bourgeoisie, was a new direction in fiction, one which inspired many other writers of the 1960s and 1970s.

Michael Munro

Date 1955

Author J(ames) P(atrick) Donleavy (1907–88)

Nationality Born USA; naturalized Irish citizen

Why It's Key Dangerfield was a new type of anti-hero. With his unflinchingly true-to-life, yet often poetic, prose Donleavy so stretched the definition of literary decency that the novel was first published in Paris under the imprint of a pornographer.

Key Character **Judith Hearne**
Judith Hearne

Judith Hearne is a powerful study of isolation and disappointment. Perhaps because of its bleakness, Brian Moore's first novel suffered numerous rejections by American publishers before finally being published in England, to excellent reviews. It won the Authors' Club First Novel award and was filmed in 1987 as *The Lonely Passion of Judith Hearne*, with Maggie Smith in the title role. The novel tells the story of an alcoholic Catholic spinster who lives in a Belfast boarding house. She is desperately lonely and harbors hopes of love. She meets a man, but the encounter does not bring the hoped-for happiness. With great deftness and tenderness, Moore depicts the disintegration of Judith Hearne's last illusions. Because Hearne is so vividly realized, the effect of this tale is devastating.

Moore's imaginative empathy with his main character is one of the novel's most striking and impressive features. Looking back to the time of its genesis, Moore said, "I was very lonely, I had almost no friends, I'd given up my beliefs, was earning no money and I didn't see much of a future. So I could identify with a dipsomaniac, isolated spinster." Moore's ambivalent relationship to Ireland (he emigrated to Canada in 1948), and his rejection of Catholicism, can be seen as contributing to the displacement and depression he speaks of here. Over the years, Moore became known as a male novelist with a rare talent for creating complex, sympathetic female characters; *I Am Mary Dunne* (published in 1966) offers an excellent example of this skill.
Emily Jeremiah

Date 1955

Author Brian Moore (1921–99)

Nationality Ireland (took Canadian citizenship)

Why It's Key Brian Moore's novel tells the story of a lonely spinster, the eponymous Judith Hearne: a memorable and moving creation. Moore wrote twenty novels in all, and was once described by Graham Greene as "my favourite living author."

Key Character **Auntie Mame**
Auntie Mame: An Irreverent Escapade

Witty, sophisticated, and impossibly glamorous, Auntie Mame is the 1950s American antidote to the fearsome and straight-laced battalions of Aunts who tormented P.G. Wodehouse's Bertie Wooster in 1920s England. Her philosophy (created for the Broadway adaptation of the book), "Life is a banquet, and most poor sons of bitches are starving to death. Live!," epitomizes the carpe diem mentality that helps her survive even the Great Depression.

When ten-year-old Patrick's father dies, he becomes a ward of the eccentric Auntie Mame, under whose tutelage he learns to socialize, decorate, and mix a mean martini. Packed with colorful characters and blue incidents, the book already seemed technicolor long before it hit the big screen in 1958. Rosalind Russell reprised her 1956 Tony Award-winning Broadway performance for the film version, while in 1966, Angela Lansbury collected a Tony Award for her role in the Broadway musical, *Mame*. Even an ill-fated attempt by a miscast Lucille Ball to bring the musical to the screen in 1974 failed to blight the Mame's reputation, and she remains a treasured American character.

Like a naughty relative adding liquor to the family punch, Auntie Mame spiked mainstream culture with a dose of high camp. Although the old-school, queeny flamboyance of Auntie Mame has made her a classic camp character, the secret of her success is her broader appeal, or rather her appeal to broads. Wealthy, fun-loving, and larger-than-life, Mame is more a playmate than a parental figure to her adopted nephew Patrick, who chronicles her fabulous New York lifestyle and adventures from 1929 to 1948. While many classic stories, such as *Oliver Twist* and *Jane Eyre*, explore the darker aspects of orphanhood, Auntie Mame positively revels in the absence of authority.
Dinah Roe

Date 1955

Author Patrick Dennis (pen-name of Edward Everett Tanner III, 1921–76)

Nationality USA

Why It's Key Mame helped prepare mainstream American audiences for more daring musicals like *La Cage Aux Folles*. But Auntie Mame also showed women that glamor and fun don't have to die out in middle age, and that maternal instincts come in all different shapes, sizes, and cocktail shakers.

Opposite *Auntie Mame*

Key Event *The Poems of Emily Dickinson* reveal one of America's greatest poets

In addition to cementing Dickinson's reputation as one of her nation's greatest poets, the 1955 release of *The Poems of Emily Dickinson* (1830–86) marked the resolution of one of the most notoriously messy publishing disputes in American literary history. While the poet's self-contained, socially isolated life had barely caused a stir, her death created a sensation. When hundreds of her poems were found in her desk after Dickinson's death, no one knew what to do with them. While it was hoped that they might appeal to contemporary readers, Dickinson's poems also exhibited unique, and commercially worrying formal innovations, such as long dashes, unexpected rhythms and startling rhymes, more at home in our century than in her own.

Editors Mabel Loomis Todd and Thomas Wentworth Higginson selected and significantly adapted the poems for *Poems by Emily Dickinson*, 1890. While these changes made her work more palatable to an enthusiastic late nineteenth-century readership, they meant that the full range of Dickinson's literary abilities remained unappreciated. Further editorial difficulties were created when her manuscript poems were divided between her sister Lavinia and Loomis Todd, following a land dispute and a battle over Loomis Todd's affair with Dickinson's brother Austin.

After a half-century of legal wrangling, Dickinson's entire body of work was made available to editor Thomas H. Johnson (1902–85), who restored the formal and thematic qualities of the original poems for a new readership. Johnson's definitive 1955 edition not only revived Dickinson's literary reputation, but enhanced it so that she now rivals Walt Whitman as the greatest American poet.

Dinah Roe

Date 1955

Place USA

Why It's Key "Publication — is the Auction/Of the Mind of Man — ," wrote Emily Dickinson, who remained unpublished in her lifetime. A heavily-edited volume of her poems was released in 1890, but it was not until Johnson's 1955 edition restored the poems to their original state that Dickinson took her rightful place in the American canon.

Opposite Emily Dickinson

Key Event A poetry reading marks the start of the San Francisco Renaissance

The reading took place at a small art gallery in San Francisco at the now-famous Six Gallery on 7 October, 1955. The event was organised by the established poet Kenneth Rexroth, to introduce to a wider public a handful of younger poets who were as yet essentially unknown. These included Alan Ginsberg, Gary Snyder, Michael McClure, and Philip Lamantia. Jack Kerouac (1922–69) had been invited to read but on the night preferred to remain in the audience, drinking wine and shouting encouragement to those on stage. The audience of around one hundred were wildly enthusiastic, especially when Ginsberg gave the first public reading of his seminal *Howl*, and word of mouth soon sealed the reputations of most of the new writers. Suddenly, it seemed, poetry was not the dull Victorian stuff learned by rote at school but as lively and free as jazz itself; it was a revelation to many that you could riff with words as well as music. The event was a defining moment in what would come to be known as the Beat Generation, not least by being recorded in a fictionalised form in Kerouac's *The Dharma Bums*. It was the beginning of California, and San Francisco in particular, being seen as the "happening" place in America, and this "San Francisco Renaissance" was to continue into the 1960s and 1970s with the counterculture hippie movement it inspired. In his novel Kerouac uses pseudonyms to thinly disguise the real writers, calling, for example, Gary Snyder "Japhy Ryder," and his drink-fuelled, larger-than-life version of the reading is better known than the actual details of the event itself.

Michael Munro

Date 1955

Place San Francisco, USA

Why It's Key These writers were the leading poets of what became known as the Beat Generation. Their work was characterized by freedom of style, the idea of poetry as performance, a flavor of Buddhist scripture, and the exuberant rhythms of jazz, and was to greatly influence the generation that followed in the 1960s and 1970s.

Key Passage
Howl

"I saw the best minds of my generation destroyed by madness, starving hysterical naked, dragging themselves through the negro streets at dawn looking for an angry fix…" begins the tirade of "Howl," a disarmingly open and capacious poetic text which pits the earthly "angels" of the nascent Beat Generation against the massed forces of "Moloch," capitalism figured as an Old Testament juggernaut-behemoth crushing the vulnerable outsiders of American life as it races ever onward in pursuit of surplus value. The poem is formed from a combination of prosaic or ecstatic incidents from his own unhappy existence in the "cold-water flats" of New York and flights of an imagination lit up by drugs and sex, by furious jazz and the great maverick canon of world literature.

It is difficult to overestimate the impact of "Howl" in its first public performances and its publication (by City Lights Books of San Fransciso). At Ginsberg's first public reading, with Jack Kerouac, Kenneth Rexroth, and other soon-to-be luminaries present, the audience was brought to an entirely unexpected pitch of excitement by the cumulative force of the poem's innovative and breath-based prosody, one of those singular moments in cultural life where there exists a general recognition that "things have changed." Its publication resulted in an obscenity trial which delivered Ginsberg enough publicity to make *Howl and Other Poems* one of the best-selling poetry titles of all time, to make himself an unprecedented kind of public presence in American culture, and to generate a landmark Supreme Court judgment that permitted a new sexual frankness in literature in the States and elsewhere.

Robin Purves

Date 1955

Author Allen Ginsberg (1926–97)

Nationality USA

Why it's Key Publication of Ginsberg's apocalyptic free verse vision of America led to a trial for obscenity; it became one of the best-selling poetry titles of all time and made Ginsberg a cultural icon.

Opposite Allen Ginsberg

Key Character **Tom Ripley**
The Talented Mr Ripley

SPOILER

Charming and nervously amoral "Mr Ripley" is always formally announced on the covers of the five novels Patricia Highsmith wrote about him over a 36-year period (*The Talented Mr Ripley* (1955); *Ripley Under Ground* (1970); *Ripley's Game* (1974); *The Boy Who Followed Ripley* (1980); *Ripley Under Water* (1991)). But the first word of each book in the "Ripliad" is always "Tom" and from the first line of *The Talented Mr Ripley* we empathize with him as the quarry of an unknown pursuant. Should he confront the situation or flee? This is a choice we continue making with him as he leaves New York for Europe and progresses from petty fraud to mass murder. Socially aspirant and with a keen sense of aesthetics, Ripley defines himself only by externals (clothes and interiors) constantly trying on the lifestyles and mannerisms of those he envies. His doubleness is wittily echoed by the house he eventually buys in France: "Belle Ombre" (Beautiful Shadow). When his façades crumble, he must kill to save his skin. "Would one thing after another come up to thwart him, murder, suspicion, *people*?" he frets after a couple of unplanned bludgeonings. "He hadn't wanted to murder, it had been a necessity."

Ripley is a twentieth-century Raskolnikov without a conscience: a murderer who traps his readers within the confines of his own psychology. He's often paranoid and insomniac, yet acknowledges that the risks he takes are what make his existence "fun" and he experiences exhilarating bursts of pure pleasure at his freedom from society's standard constraints. His crimes could all be easily avoided. But, as Graham Greene observed, Highsmith's characters "leap to life in their very lack of reason."

Helen Brown

Date 1955

Nationality USA

Why It's Key Patricia Highsmith disdained the cosy formulas of classic crime fiction, which indulged voyeuristic readers with a gawp at violent death before restoring moral order by identifying and punishing the guilty. "I think it is a silly way of teasing people, the 'who-done-it'," she said. "It is like a puzzle and puzzles do not interest me."

Key Event **Ted Hughes and Sylvia Plath meet for the first time in Cambridge**

At most college parties, even those given to celebrate a literary magazine, nothing much happens other than drinking, dancing, and some flirtation. At a party in Cambridge in February 1956 a romantic, dramatic encounter between two young poets – he tore off her hairband; she bit his cheek, drawing blood – led to one of the most significant partnerships in twentieth-century English poetry.

American Sylvia Plath was in Cambridge on a Fulbright scholarship when she met young Yorkshireman, Ted Hughes. They married four months later. It was a passionate union of two fiercely intelligent, ambitious writers, who shared a fascination with mythology and the natural world. By 1960 the couple had each published a volume of poems, and had their first child, a daughter. In 1962, soon after the birth of their son Nicholas, Hughes left Plath for another woman. Six months later she committed suicide in London.

Plath's posthumous volume *Ariel* established her reputation as one of the century's finest poets. Her suicide, and the subsequent publication of her journals and letters made her a tragic figure for a generation of feminist readers, who often condemned Hughes for his abandonment of her (and for his admitted destruction of one volume of her journals). Hughes refused to speak publicly about Plath, though he spent years diligently editing her collected poems. It wasn't until 1998 that Hughes, by then Poet Laureate, published *Birthday Letters*, a collection of poems written to and about Plath – a book that became a bestseller, and finally gave poetic voice to his side of the story. In one poem he wrote of the first meeting between himself and Plath: "The solar system married us." Hughes died later that year, thus closing the book, on a tempestuous relationship that has fascinated and moved generations of readers.

Sylvia Brownrigg

Date 1956

Place Cambridge, England

Author Ted Hughes (1930–98)

Author Sylvia Plath (1932–63)

Why It's Key The meeting of two young, passionate poets was the start of a literary love story that over fifty years has inspired biographies, films, and novels. Hughes and Plath together and separately went on to make indelible marks on English poetry.

Key Book *Cop Hater*

Ed McBain was a pseudonym used for crime fiction by an author who had been born as Salvatore Lombino but who later changed his name to Evan Hunter. *Cop Hater* was the first in a long line by McBain of "police procedural" detective novels. It introduces the reader to the police force of the fictional 87th precinct, in a city which is called Isola but is a lot like the author's native New York. Most of the books feature the detective Steve Carella and a recurring cast of fellow officers. In this case the investigation is into a series of killings of police officers in a city made even more edgy than usual by a heatwave.

McBain was a pioneer of the "police procedural" novel. Detective fiction that preceded this genre tended to center on an individual hero, whether an analytical genius like Sherlock Holmes or a hard-boiled "private eye" like Dashiell Hammet's Sam Spade or Raymond Chandler's Philip Marlowe. In most cases the regular police force was portrayed as incompetent, unable to solve cases without the help of the hero, and even as corrupt. The police procedural was to change this by describing the ways in which police officers actually went about combating crime in their day-to-day work. McBain's heroes are neither geniuses nor idiots but are recognizable human beings with their own virtues and failings. They have a difficult job to do and are often frustrated by the limitations that bureaucracy places on them. Rugged individualists are still stock characters in detective fiction, but the police procedural has become established as a popular form in books, films, and television series.

Michael Munro

Date 1956

Author Ed McBain (1926–2005)

Nationality USA

Why It's Key The book focussed on a realistic portrayal of the everyday work of police forces. McBain emphasized that, while the locale for the novels is fictionalized, "the police routine is based on established investigatory technique." Many of the books were made into movies, as was *Cop Hater* in 1958.

Key Book
Anglo-Saxon Attitudes

Angus Wilson's life and fiction reflected the displacement of the English middle class of the 1930s within the "affluent society" that Britain was becoming in the mid-1950s. Blossoming late as a writer but enjoying immediate and steady success, Wilson resigned his position as librarian at the British Museum just before beginning work on his second and most famous novel. *Anglo-Saxon Attitudes* a subtle and keenly observed social satire. Its title refers to the way certain upper-middle class liberals, influenced by the Bloomsbury circle, wallow in deliberations of the "right way." This self-torment is typical of the novel's protagonist, historian Gerald Middleton, who realizes at age 62 he is a "failure with a conscience." He stirs into action to remedy his personal failings as father, husband, and lover, and his longstanding professional acquiescence with an archaeological hoax bearing on English identity itself. Only partly successful, Gerald realizes that he cannot always rectify past mistakes,

and so must learn to live with them and to strive to improve as an individual.

Anglo-Saxon Attitudes stands on the cusp of a transformation of the ways English literature depicted social life. In the mid-1950s the Angry Young Men and their terse, blunt, accusative style of fiction became fashionable. Sharing many of their discontents, Wilson was an outspoken critic of the conservative, staid British society of the day. But he was of an older generation and the topics of his fiction reflected this; his self-conscious style – slower-paced, elaborate, and highly ironic – now looked outmoded.

Nimrod Ben-Cnaan

Date 1956

Author Angus Wilson, (Frank Johnstone) KBE (1913–91)

Nationality UK

Why It's Key The book was a critique of the old liberal middle class, whose time had passed. Yet it was also Wilson's literary style and preoccupation with the middle classes that were on their way out, in favor of the simpler and blunter style of the Angry Young Men, the predominant English literary current of the 1950s.

Key Book
Grande Sertão: Veredas

Grande Sertão: Veredas was originally conceived as a novella, part of a volume of short fictions set in the semi-arid backlands, or sertão, of the author's native state of Minas Gerais. As João Guimarães Rosa (1908–67) decanted his extensive knowledge of the region's folklore into every sentence and shred of dialogue, the simple story of two gunmen or jagunços crossing the sertão became a colossal work, a masterpiece of Brazilian regionalism that sizzles with inventiveness and captures like no other the spirit of a blighted landscape and its people.

Riobaldo is the garrulous narrator whose digressive monologue, as told to an unspecified listener, provides the novel's main flow. He tells of the sertão's myths and legends, of his intense friendship with fellow jagunço Diadorim, of their ride through the parched scrubland to avenge a blood feud. He is the archetypal backlands dweller: "I know almost nothing, but distrust many things."

Beyond the apparently simple plot and its surprising twist, the novel's triumph lies in turning into its central character the sertão itself, "this simple little universe of ours…You know how it is: the sertão is where the strong man rules, through cunning. God himself, whenever he comes, had better be armed!"

"Sertão: its emptiness," muses Riobaldo as he describes to his fireside listener the immensity surrounding them. The novel reflects that vastness. It also reflects the language of its inhabitants, dry and hard like the terrain. Sertão: not simply a setting, but a frame of mind. As Riobaldo warns: "The sertão is everywhere."

Ángel Gurría-Quintana

Date 1956

Nationality Brazil

Why It's Key Guimarães Rosa, a rural doctor-turned-diplomat, is credited with the imaginative reinvention of a region that had been mostly overlooked in Brazilian literature. His blend of folk and erudite references, seamlessly stitched together through bold linguistic experimentation, make him the twentieth century's most influential Brazilian writer.

Key Character **Cruella de Vil**
The Hundred and One Dalmatians

We first meet Cruella de Vil in Chapter I of *The Hundred and One Dalmatians*. A character composed of bizarre extremes, she wears her signature "absolutely simple white mink coat" in all weathers; addicted to heat, she serves all her dishes laced with pepper; her vampish clothes contrast with her "severely parted" hair, one half of which is naturally white and one black. Then there is her name: as Mr Dearly remarks, "If you put the two words together, they make 'devil'." Indeed, wicked Cruella plans to kidnap the Dearlys' cherished Dalmatians' puppies (and many others) and turn them into elegant spotted fur coats.

But the resourceful dogs trace their puppies to Cruella's country home, "Hell Hall," and sneak them all out disguised with soot. They troop home via Cruella's London house, where the dogs tear her precious furs to rags. The shock of finding her furs in tatters turns Cruella's black hair white and her white hair "a horrid shade" of green. She leaves the country and the Dearlys buy Hell Hall, whose façade they change from black to white and whose aspect is duly transformed from hellish to paradisal.

The success of Cruella and the dogcentric story inspired Smith to write a sequel, *The Starlight Barking* (1967), and Disney among others to adapt the books for the screen. In 2002, Forbes ranked Cruella as the thirteenth wealthiest fictional character, with a net worth of $875m. Was this taking things too far, given her grotesquely two-dimensional character? Perhaps. Cruella fulfils her role perfectly: a freakish embodiment of the clash of good and evil and a lesson in caring less for the surface and more for the heart of things.
Sophie Lewis

Date 1956

Author Dorothy Gladys Smith, known as Dodie Smith (1896–1990)

Nationality UK

Why It's Key Cruella is not a subtly drawn character. Her quasi-cartoonish black-and-white styling and infernal accessories formed the ideal complement to Smith's equally unsubtle anti-fur trade message, which captured the hearts of her young readers.

Opposite **Cruella de Vil**

Key Passage
The Lonely Londoners

"One grim winter evening, when it had a kind of unrealness about London, with a fog sleeping restlessly over the city and the lights showing in the blur as if is not London at all but some strange place on another planet, Moses Aloetta hop on a number 46 bus at the corner of Chepstow Road and Westbourne Grove to go to Waterloo to meet a fellar who was coming from Trinidad on the boat-train."

A cold, hostile, and disorienting environment is described in the opening sentence of Selvon's seminal novel, indicating the difficulties the first wave of the Windrush generation experienced in adjusting to this unfamiliar "Mother country." Selvon's archly named Moses is a pioneer of this arduous journey of displacement and assimilation. His knowledge of journeys and place names reflects a migrant's metropolitan savvy. Despite his position as an unofficial "liaison officer" for new arrivals, Moses never fully settles in an alienating city that ostracises its new community.

The passage's Dickensian trace (with a nod also to T.S. Eliot's "Unreal City") is intentional, presenting as it does a new vernacular narrative voice that would grow increasingly prominent in post-imperial British literature. Britain becomes "Brit'n" in Selvon's characters' world. Its languages and cultures expand in accordance with both the erosion of a standard syntax and singular, restrictive British idiom. This novel helped sew the seeds of that shift.
Graeme Mcdonald

Date 1956

Author Sam Selvon (1923–94)

Nationality Trinidad

Why It's Key A landmark in the canon of Black British Literature. One of the most significant novels of the experiences of the Windrush generation of Caribbean immigrants to Britain. Published two years prior to the infamous Notting Hill race riots in 1958, the year the Institute of Race Relations was established.

Key Character **Christopher Martin**
Pincher Martin

SPOILER

"Pincher"is the nickname of Christopher Martin, a cheat and rapist, whose negligence as a naval officer causes his own death and that of everyone else on his ship because he is preoccupied planning a rival's death while on watch duty. Martin is washed up on a rock in the Atlantic when his boat is torpedoed. Here, cold and starving, he clings to life for a few days, attempting to impose order on his harsh surroundings. Amid the scenes of eating limpets and attempting to build a sign visible to aircraft in seaweed, we see flashes of Martin's previous life as a student and an actor before he was called up to become a naval officer. The career stages mirror Golding's own, in university, the theater, and the navy.

Martin is already dead and the rock in the Atlantic does not exist. The cosmology of whether the "action" takes place in the moment before death, or after death and he is in hell or purgatory is not made clear. The book is the bleakest work of a contemporary prophet.

It is the closest an English novelist has come to the appreciation of the human condition that characterizes Samuel Beckett but, unlike Beckett, in his fiction Golding places perfectly normal characters in extreme situations, pushing them to their limits and beyond. "I am who I was" Martin insists, while his identity is stripped away as the world he has created disintegrates and "black lightning" cracks open the hollow shell of his constructed life.
Jad Adams

Date 1956

Author William Golding (1911–93) won the Nobel Prize 1983

Nationality UK

Why It's Key *Pincher Martin* saw the creation of a perfect anti-hero by whom others are judged: "He was born with his mouth and his flies open and both hands out to grab. He's a cosmic case of the bugger who gets his penny and someone else's bun."

410

Key Event *Look Back in Anger* introduces the "angry young man" to the world

The opening of *Look Back in Anger* at the Royal Court in May 1956 marked the arrival of the first of the so-called "Angry Young Men" of literature. The vituperative anger and world weary disillusionment of the play's protagonist, Jimmy Porter, was immediately linked to his creator when the theater's publicist described author John Osborne (1929–94) as "a very angry young man." Widely regarded as a watershed play in British theater history, Osborne's depiction of marital strife, generational conflict, and class division in 1950s Britain broke away from the staid upper middle-class settings which had dominated the British stage in the 1940s and early 1950s. The play's cramped and dingy bed-sit setting was the antithesis to the glamor and expense which typified contemporaneous productions in London's West End. Porter's vehement, emotional outbursts marked a radical departure from the formal diction and emotional concealment which had characterized the style of playwrights like Terence

Rattigan. The influential *Observer* theater critic Kenneth Tynan identified the play with the voice of a young post-war generation.

Critics have subsequently questioned *Look Back in Anger*'s revolutionary status, pointing out that the play adheres to a traditional three act structure. Today it is dated by the 1950s topicality that contributed to its original appeal and its depiction of women borders on sexist. Osborne himself later described it as "a formal, rather old fashioned play." Nonetheless the original success of *Look Back in Anger* on stage, television, and film secured the future of the fledgling English Stage Company and launched the career of one of Britain's most celebrated post-war playwrights.
Kate Harris

Date 1956

Place UK

Why It's Key Television was crucial to the play's success. Following an excerpt on the BBC and a screening of the play on ITV, box office takings almost doubled in a week. Osborne became a celebrated literary figure but the play's status as a watershed piece remains a contentious topic amongst critics. Today the text remains a fixture on university syllabuses.

Opposite *Look Back in Anger*

Key Event *The Outsider* initiates a rediscovery of Herman Hesse's works

For a time at least, it seemed that Colin Wilson would become the English dissenting intellectual of the familiar continental mode, having introduced himself spectacularly with *The Outsider* in 1956, the first English existentialist since Herbert Read a decade before. Dubbed a member of The Beat Generation and the "Angry Young Men," Wilson went on the run from the media following a public scandal involving a row with his future in-laws. Before his bizarre fall from grace (he was feted by a number of prominent post-war critics) and slide into needlessly prolific publication of books on the occult (which has made him an enduring household name in Japan), the Midlands autodidact penned his contribution to promoting the concept of the "outsider" who stands apart from conventional society from a London bedsit, deploying Kafka, Sartre, and Hesse to mount his case for an "English existentialism." It was the latter whom Wilson assisted in enjoying a small revival in England, with

Steppenwolf occupying a pivotal literary role in the counterculture that was to follow – unquestionably correct timing on Wilson's part giving a fortunate upturn to Hesse's reputation at the end of his life. Hesse's 1927 story of marginal Harry Haller, at odds with the world in which he finds himself but subjected to revelatory introspective highs through unfolding events, was a perfect metaphor for what was to follow in the next decade, though Wilson would struggle to define himself from hereon in.

Andrew Stevens

Date 1956

Place UK

Author Colin Wilson (1931–)

Why It's Key When *The Outsider* was published to massive acclaim it popularized the works of Herman Hesse, particularly *Der Steppenwolf*, in the UK, and initiated a rediscovery of Hesse's work.

1950-1959

Key Event *Peyton Place* becomes an instant bestseller

Emily Toth's biography of Grace Metalious, the author of the absurdly popular and critically mocked novel *Peyton Place*, quotes the author being badgered by a reporter about her childhood. She tried to wax poetic about herself, then stopped and smiled. "Actually," she said, "I was an awful pain in the ass." *Peyton Place*, which became a film and a popular primetime 60s soap opera, could not have been written by a nice girl. It hit so many nerves at once, exposing issues of class, gender, and small town hypocrisy, and salting the narrative with oh-so-much sex, that it became compulsory reading for much of America.

The novel is the story of three women, the beautiful, repressed Constance Mackenzie, her daughter Allison, and her poor employee Selena Cross. Constance is a widow with a secret: her affair with a married man gave her a child, Allison, who grows up under an altered birth certificate. Mackenzie will do anything to keep her secret safe, including rebuffing the

advances of attractive men like the new grade school principal, who ends up forcing himself on her (later, they marry). Allison wants to be a writer, and after enduring criticism from the town for being not girly enough, flees to New York City.

Selena is the most interesting character: she grows up in a shack with her crazy mother, and is abused and raped by her alcoholic stepfather. Eventually, she gets an abortion from the town doctor and the stepfather skips town – but when he returns, Selena kills him. In spite of the book's overwhelming popularity (or maybe because of it) critics decried Metalious as a "purveyor of filth," causing her to remark, "If I'm a lousy writer, then an awful lot of people have lousy taste."

Reyhan Harmanci

Date 1956

Place USA

Author Grace Metalious (1924–64)

Why It's Key *Peyton Place* revealed the sham behind the wholesome popular façade of "Leave it to Beaver" America, telling of rape, incest, abortion, abuse, class conflicts, and female sexual conquest in a small New England town. It was incredibly popular, selling millions, but also dismissed as simple smut.

Opposite Popular interest in *Peyton Place*

Key Book
That Awful Mess on via Merulana

Two crimes are committed in middle-class via Merulana, same block of flats, same floor, just a few days apart. Can there be a connection? Police officer Ingravallo would like to think so. But which is the link, given that links are only too easy to find?

Rome had to be the place: the seat of Power and Fascism as the seat of all evil. Yet, having got there, very little can be made of that vantage point. All notions, knowledge itself especially, are in fact queried in this book. For what is it exactly that we do when we perceive and organize a world (or disrupt it, as happens in crimes)?

But even so, investigative failure, if this is what *That Awful Mess on via Merulana* really comes to, turns quest and loss of quest into feast, a mighty satirical one, in which language (a number of languages, actually) is spectacularly fore-grounded to achieve maximum perception (and disruption) of the worlds we construct.

Extremely difficult to translate, and yet more successfully translated than other works by Gadda, this masterpiece of inquisitiveness, verbal flair, and ideological incorrectness comes invariably back to life, like the full-bodied wine it is, whenever given a chance – especially one involving large audiences, be it on the big screen (1959), the small screen (1982 and 1997), or at the theater (1996).

Federica Pedriali

Date 1957 (first published in part in *Letteratura* in 1946)

Author Carlo Emilio Gadda (1893–1973)

Nationality Italy

Why It's Key The ultimate ultra-modern point of reference in contemporary Italian prose.

Key Book
Homo Faber

Homo Faber is a novel about man's relationship to technology and about the questions of fate and chance. The plot concerns Walter Faber, an engineer who is caught up in a chain of events that overturn his rationalistic world-view. The airplane he is travelling on is forced to make an emergency landing; his former friend Joachim hangs himself; Faber meets and falls in love with a young woman – with unpredictable and tragic consequences. Finally, Faber develops cancer.

The novel's title indicates its main themes. "Homo faber" ("man the smith" or "man the maker") is a phrase found in the *Sententiae of Appius Claudius Caecus*, where it alludes to a view of human beings as in control of their destiny. The concept is also drawn on by such thinkers as Henri Bergson, Karl Marx, and Hannah Arendt. Frisch's Faber, however, is not in control: the book's central irony.

The novel's own fate has been considerable success. It has been translated into many languages, and has inspired a film (1991, directed by Volker Schlöndorff), starring Sam Shepard and Julie Delpy. This gripping novel is important because it charts the belief of modern man – and it is definitely masculinity that is at issue here – in technology, rationality, and mastery; and the misguided nature of that belief. The novel holds continuing relevance, given the speed of contemporary technological advances and the related (or competing) issues of nature and spirituality.

Emily Jeremiah

Date 1957

Author Max Frisch (1911–91)

Nationality Switzerland

Why It's Key Max Frisch is considered one of the most influential Swiss writers of the twentieth century. He wrote fiction, plays and diaries, and won numerous prizes for his work. *Homo Faber* is one of his most popular works.

Key Book
On the Beach

Later turned into an award-winning film version, *On the Beach* signalled a change for the normally phlegmatic author Nevil Shute. Having served in both World Wars and emigrated to Australia, the British novelist wrote one of the premier anti-Bomb novels of his generation in response to his disaffection with his native country.

On the Beach follows the last people on earth, a group of characters in Melbourne, Australia, who are awaiting the slow drift of radiation to reach their shores after a nuclear war in the northern hemisphere destroys all life there. The characters include the captain and crew of an American submarine docked in Melbourne as the nuclear war commences. After detecting a Morse code signal from the devastated U.S., the submariners decide to sail back to America to determine if any survivors exist. The novel alternately follows the submarine crew on its futile journey where they discover that the signal is being generated accidentally as a windblown soda bottle taps a telegraph key, and the characters left behind in Melbourne, where the submariners eventually return.

Alternately pathetic and quietly horrifying, Shute's novel refuses hysteria as its keynote and instead depicts a group of characters determined to live what remains of their lives as best they can, knowing that a ghastly death from radiation sickness is only a matter of time. *On the Beach* explored the psychology of those experiencing impending nuclear destruction, ending with the stoic but appalling scene of the Australian government handing out cyanide pills to its citizens as they file under a banner reading "There is still time, Brother."
Elizabeth Rosen

Date 1957
Author Nevil Shute (1899–1960)
Nationality UK, emigrated to Australia
Why Its Key One of the most famous anti-atomic bomb novels of its day, *On the Beach* was as notable for the matter-of-fact way its characters dealt with their impending nuclear death as it was for its sensational topic.

415

Key Character **Johann Ulrich Voss**
Voss

Despite being the first Australian to win the Nobel Prize, Patrick White's merit has been the subject of much debate within his country. He was a vicious critic of what he considered to be a society engrossed in a farcical and dangerous attempt to impose a misplaced foreign civility upon an unreceptive land; this, coupled with his unfashionable spiritual interest, has left this considerable writer somewhat in the margins, leaving him ripe for rediscovery. His most widely read book, *Voss*, is loosely based on the travels of nineteenth-century German explorer Ludwig Leichardt, who led a doomed mission into the then-unexplored wilderness of the Australian interior. The novel's fictional protagonist is Johann Ulrich Voss, whose unshakeable and egoistic drive to conquer the impossible landscape through the sheer force of will has a powerful effect on his cohorts, who begin to fear him as God, or, perhaps, the Devil himself. Whether genius, madman, savior, or demon, Voss is a powerful creation, as mysterious and unforgiving as the land he attempts to dominate. Through *Voss*, White offered an outsider's perspective on a nation grappling with its identity, and hesitant to accept the desolate grandeur of its inherited natural environment. Through his poetic depiction of Voss, this monomaniacal explorer, White offered an outsider's perspective on a nation grappling with its identity, and hesitant to accept the desolate grandeur of its inherited natural environment. In a 1958 letter, White explained his intentions, and lamented the reception, of *Voss*: "Above all I was determined to prove that the Australian novel is not necessarily a dreary, dun-coloured offspring of journalistic realism. On the whole, the world has been convinced, only here, at the present moment, the dingoes are howling unmercifully."
James Clements

Date 1957
Author Patrick White (1912–90)
Nationality Australia
Why It's Key White made a significant contribution to Australian literature by replacing the dry, patriotic realism that then pervaded the nation's fiction with a deeply stylized and lyrical voice that was unafraid to attempt to tackle the darker aspects of the national psyche.

Key Event **The crimes of Ed Gein become the inspiration for fictional serial killers**

Robert Bloch's (1917–94) early career saw him earn a living as a writer of "pulp" fantasy and horror, setting some of his tales in the fictional world of the Cthulhu Mythos, created by his literary hero and mentor, H.P. Lovecraft. Gradually, Bloch moved away from Lovecraftian imitation to develop his own unique style in science fiction and fantasy magazines such as *Amazing Stories* and *Fantastic Adventures*. One of his earliest stories to bear his distinctive mark was *Yours Truly, Jack the Ripper* (1943) which featured more factual detail than was customary in writing of that type. This lent the story an air of realism which augmented the already gruesome subject matter and presaged his most widely-acclaimed novel, *Psycho*, in 1959. The character of Norman Bates is reputedly based on serial killer, Ed Gein, who, just two years before publication of the novel, was arrested for multiple murder. On searching his home, police found furniture and clothing (including a part-made "woman suit") all made of human skin and body parts. Neighbours described Gein's deceased mother as having been puritanical and domineering. Bloch played down the influence of Gein on the genesis of the Norman Bates character, saying he had only vaguely heard of the case. Consciously or not, Bloch, in creating a character and events that mirrored so closely those in real life, produced a work of enduring, realistic horror that has served as the blueprint for nearly every psychopathic serial killer story since.
Christian Kerr

Date 1957

Place USA

Why It's Key Robert Bloch produced hundreds of short stories and more than 20 novels in the genres of crime fiction, science fiction and, most notably, horror fiction. He was a contributor to the pulp science fiction magazines of the 1950s and 1960s. The Gein murders also seem to have influenced the depiction of "Buffalo Bill," the serial killer in *The Silence of the Lambs*.

Opposite Ed Gein

417

Key Event **John Updike moves to Ipswich, Massachusetts**

Whatever they put in the water in Ipswich, it certainly agreed with John Updike, who moved there in 1957. The sixteen years he lived there was a period of astonishing creativity, by Updike's standards. Besides the usual mountains of non-fiction, he wrote three volumes of poetry, four children's books, and six short story collections. There were six novels, including the first of the "Rabbit" books.

After two years at the *New Yorker*, Updike had left the Big Apple with few misgivings: interviewed by Thomas Samuels in 1968, he spoke disparagingly of the "literary demimonde of agents and would-bes and with-it non participants." Just in case Samuels had missed the point, he added Hemingway's description of literary New York as "a bottle full of tapeworms trying to feed on each other."

Ipswich smashed this claustrophobic environment to pieces, opening up new horizons both personal and creative, and giving him the inspiration for his fictional town of Tarbox. An ideal place to raise a young family and a soothing environment for Updike's psoriasis, Ipswich was also an ideal place in which to write. "I was full of a Pennsylvania thing I wanted to say," he told Samuels. "Ipswich gave me the space in which to say it."

This was partly a practical consideration: Updike took an office in which to produce his variety of verse, fiction and criticism. Yet "space" also points towards an imaginative unshackling: Ipswich provided the characters, themes, moods and even the audience Updike wanted for his books. "When I write, I aim my mind not toward New York but toward a vague spot a little to the east of Kansas. I think of the books on library shelves, without their jackets, years old, and a countryish teen-aged boy finding them, and having them speak to him. The reviews […] are just hurdles to get over, to place the books on that shelf."
James Kidd

Date 1957–1973

Place USA

Why It's Key Ipswich, Massachusetts was more than just a place for John Updike's prolific writing. It was an inspiring location to write about: *Couples* is set in "Tarbox," a bourgeois, secular, and socially-enclosed suburb that bears more than a passing resemblance to Updike's adopted hometown.

Key Passage
Mythologies

"I am at the barber's, and a copy of *Paris-Match* is offered to me. On the cover a young Negro in a French uniform is saluting, with his eyes uplifted, probably fixed on a fold of the tricolor. All this is the meaning of the picture. But, whether naively or not, I see very well what it signifies to me: that France is a great Empire, that all her sons, without any color discrimination, faithfully serve under her flag, and that there is no better answer to the detractors of an alleged colonialism that the zeal shown by this Negro in serving his so-called oppressors."

In a politically quiescent age this magazine photograph might have been taken for granted but Barthes exposes it as having a powerful subtext supporting threatened establishment values. The power defending itself was the French empire embroiled in a colonial war in Algeria (1954–62). Most effective is the contrast between the magazine flipped through at the hairdresser's and bitter violence and injustice out of sight. The word "Negro" was acceptable at the time. Barthes was the political and cultural voice of the cool 1960s, with its radical new awareness of the sublimated mechanisms of social control. The essays in *Mythologies* explored the value systems behind everyday phenomena such as advertising, sport and fashion. After the student riots of 1968, Barthes declared himself dissatisfied with his "semiology." It lacked the political effectiveness to critique the hollow gestures of modern bourgeois society. Nevertheless postmodern iconoclasm was able to build on the foundations he laid.

Lesley Chamberlain

Date 1957

Author Roland Barthes (1915–80)

Nationality France

Why It's Key A pioneer structuralist critic, Barthes applied the tools of linguistics and psychoanalysis to social phenomena and uncovered a complex sign-language working to establish the myths by which the affluent, entertainment-oriented, post-war world lived.

Opposite Roland Barthes

Key Book *Season of Migration to the North (Muasim al hijra illa al Shimal)*

"I am the South that yearns for the North," declares Mustafa Sa'eed, the mysterious figure at the heart of Tayeb Salih's novel, published in English in 1964. Travelling to England in the 1920s to study, Sa'eed finds himself at sea in newly discovered freedoms. He becomes a fraudulent parody, playing to the naive and romantic notions of Africa that he encounters. Setting himself up as an orientalist cliché, Sa'eed becomes an arch seducer who preys on lonely women.

When we first meet Sa'eed, however, he has retreated to a remote village on the river Nile which has remained unchanged for centuries. The villagers, both pious and irreverent, are protective of their way of life. They pray, get drunk and tell lewd stories. It is here that the narrator of the novel, himself recently returned from England, meets Sa'eed and becomes fascinated by him.

Sa'eed then disappears in a flood. Presumed drowned, his body is never recovered. It is not clear whether he has killed himself. When his curiosity gets the better of him, the narrator finally opens the sealed room Sa'eed left behind. Inside, he discovers a recreation of an English study, complete with fireplace and a library of books in English: "A graveyard. A mausoleum. An insane idea."

Exceptional in many ways, Salih's novel addresses the complex legacy of colonialism and the consequences of crossing the cultural divides. It is also seen as a response to Joseph Conrad's *Heart of Darkness*, reversing the relationship between Africa and Europe. The style and approach of the novel create an enigma as powerful as the story it tells, though its ultimate conclusion is bleak and disconcerting.

Jamal Mahjoub

Date 1957

Author Tayeb Salih (1929)

Nationality Sudan

Why It's Key Declared the most important Arabic novel of the twentieth century, it has been described as "an *Arabian Nights* in reverse." Although little else has appeared in translation, the author has continued to publish in Arabic, over the years producing a body of work comprising novels, short stories, criticism, and travel writing.

Key Event **French novelists herald the Nouveau Roman**

The Nouveau Roman (New Novel) is the collective label attached in 1957 to a French literary current, also known at the time as *chosisme*, "the school of the gaze," or, after its publisher, "the school of Minuit." For the "New Novelists," the post-war novel was taken to reflect a new, pared down reality and so had to be different from its more opulent predecessors. It also had to stand its own ground against other media, in particular film. Yet while they shared common concerns, the New Novelists were not one group and had no single programme uniting them, as can be seen in the variety of their literary experimentation: Sarraute, for example, was looking to regain characters' credibility by exploring their interiority and the ways in which it was apparent as "sub-conversation"; meanwhile, Robbe-Grillet tried observing objects and situations from the outside, with no assumptions about them, so as to overcome the illusion of their meaningfulness.

The New Novel was not so much a literary revolution as a reassessment of novelistic tradition. Masters such as Flaubert and Proust were still treated respectfully, as pinnacles of their times; they were, however, seen as inadequate for conveying contemporary reality. The New Novel was not a bestselling phenomenon and was considered by many to be too academic and cerebral. It was nevertheless highly influential, broadening the definition of literary realism and inspiring further experimentation in literary fiction as well as in New Wave cinema.

Nimrod Ben-Cnaan

Date 1957

Place France

Authors Alain Robbe-Grillet (1922), Nathalie Sarraute (1900–99), Michel Butor (1926), Claude Simon (1913–2005)

Why It's Key This experimental literary current quickly became definitive of new French novels throughout the 1950s until the mid-1960s. Its beginnings can be traced back to the late 1940s, but the name "nouveau roman" was first used in a critical essay published in 1957.

420

Key Book *Memoirs of A Woman Doctor*

Saadawi's language is rebellious and violent. Language associated with the operating theater is used as a metaphor for the impact that her writing will have: "words written by a pen sharp as a scalpel that cuts through tissue to expose the throbbing nerves and arteries embedded deep in a body." A nameless protagonist, angry at being born a "girl" thinks she will overcome the uncertainty of being a woman through becoming a well-respected doctor. Womanhood means the smell of cooking, "the permanent reek or garlic and onions." Stereotypical images of women remind us that this is not just an Arab problem but also a universal one.

The promise of science, the medical profession, and the impenetrable language these fields rely on instil respect in the community. However, these are also found to be male-dominated arenas. In a memorable scene, a marriage certificate is called a "death warrant," warning us of the effects of a loveless

marriage, void of respect. Becoming a doctor, in its own right, proves not to be the road to success and esteem.

The most powerful passages in the novel describe a woman struggling with her identity, her vocation, and her gender limitations. Society is cruel, judgemental, and restrictive in its presumption that women are worth less than men. Moments of anger are juxtaposed with moments of reflection. Creativity and love are posed as potential ways out of this dead end. This work is inspirational to feminists globally and to anyone interested in human rights and gender equality.

Anastasia Valassopoulos

Date 1957 (first published in Egypt in serialized form. First English translation, 1985)

Author Nawal El Saadawi (1931–)

Nationality Egypt

Why It's Key This revolutionary feminist novel expresses, as El Saadawi herself says, "a reality which is still relevant today." It reveals "a lot of anger against the oppression of women" but also "a great deal of hope."

Key Event *A Taste of Honey* brings the "kitchen sink" to the stage

Shelagh Delaney is one of the few women to be associated with the "Angry Young Men" of the 1950s whose novels and plays examined the inherent class inequalities in British society at the time. Along with playwrights John Osborne and Arnold Wesker, she was instrumental in bringing innovative "kitchen sink drama" to the stage. The attempt to present the honest "realities" of working-class life was important to her; she said that she considered the drama of the era bland and trivial and that working-class people were misrepresented. Delaney wanted to present ordinary Northern people who were vibrant, "alive," and most of all, surviving. *A Taste of Honey*, written when she was just nineteen years old, was Delaney's rejoinder to the "well-made play," and it was a revelation to post-war theater audiences. The play was developed for the stage in theater workshops under the guidance of Joan Littlewood at the famous Theatre Royal, Stratford East. It controversially has two working-class women at its center, Helen, described as a "semi-whore" and her daughter Jo. It features a homosexual (Geof, an art school student) and a black naval rating (Jimmie, who fathers Jo's baby). Rather predictably given the play's controversial nature and subject matter it was not met with complete approbation. The critic from the *Daily Mail* is on record as saying "If there is anything worse than an Angry Young Man it's an Angry Young Woman," but renowned critic Kenneth Tynan gave it great praise. The play was seen to be "exhilarating" and Delaney was praised for bringing "real" people to the stage. The play's influence was wide reaching. Extracts from the play feature in Morrissey's song lyrics for The Smiths, in tracks such as "Hand in Glove," "Shoplifters of the World Unite," and "You've Got Everything Now."

Pat Wheeler

Date 1958

Place Theatre Royal, Stratford East, London

Author Shelagh Delaney (1939–)

Why It's Key The award-winning play was exceptionally successful and it transferred to the West End in 1959 and Broadway in 1960. The film adaptation was equally successful and won (amongst numerous other awards) the British Academy Award for best picture in 1961.

1950-1959

421

Key Author **José María Arguedas**
Deep Rivers (*Los Ríos Profundos*)

The work of José María Arguedas (1911–69) is one of the best instances of transcultural literature in Latin American fiction in particular, and in world fiction in general. Displaying a pioneering perspective, his fiction affirms the importance of interstices and threshold spaces where one perception blends or crosses over into another, showing how it is possible to stand by more than one culture and yet belong irrevocably to both.

Quechua was the author's mother tongue. Artistically, he faced the problem of translating into the alien medium of Spanish the sensibility of people who express themselves in Quechua. After some formal experiments, he opted for a correct Spanish skilfully reshaped to convey Andean thoughts and sensibilities, and this remains one of his triumphs.

In terms of scope and narrative complexity, Arguedas' work evolves from the small indigenous communities, villages and towns of the Andes to more complex geographical and cultural spheres, as shown by the spatial and narrative distance between *Water* (1935) and the posthumous *The Fox of Above and the Fox of Below*. In the stories of *Water* and the short novel *Diamonds and Flint*, the universe is perceived as an unavoidable dichotomy; in *Yawar Feast* and *Deep Rivers*, the Andean rural world is seen as opposed to the coastal white cities, but they are dialogically related; in *All Bloods* and *The Fox of Above and the Fox of Below*, Arguedas echoes the painful, contradictory and absolutely necessary meeting of these two worlds. Arguedas is considered one of the most important authors to speak out on issues such as the survival of native cultures and the dynamics between tradition and modernity. His work has acquired its full significance in today's multicultural and globalized world. A renewed critical appreciation of his work and legacy is ongoing.

Dora Sales

Date 1958

Nationality Peru

Key Works *Water* (*Agua*, 1935); *Yawar Feast* (*Yawar Fiesta*, 1941); *Diamonds and Flint* (*Diamantes y Pedernales*, 1954); *The Sixth* (*El Sexto*, 1961); *All Bloods* (*Todas las sangres*, 1964); *The Fox of Above and the Fox of Below* (*El zorro de arriba y el zorro de abajo*, 1971)

Why It's Key A key Peruvian writer, anthropologist, and defender of the dignity of the Quechua culture.

Key Author **Chinua Achebe**
Things Fall Apart

Things Fall Apart traces the downfall of Okonkwo, a strong man in a west African community who is destroyed by the arrival of white missionaries at the vanguard of the British colonial administration. Its author, Chinua Achebe (1930–), dramatised the fate of his forebears and painted a sophisticated picture of a complex society in elegant and spare prose that bears traces of an oral story-telling tradition. But he is also telling a story that – in broad brush – happened throughout the world, wherever European colonizers sought to replace indigenous cultures with their own. The novel gained weight through its publication in the era of decolonization, giving artistic voice to a global movement – and its title, from W.B. Yeats' *The Second Coming*, hints at the poem's next line: "Mere anarchy is loosed upon the world." Achebe's first novel, *Things Fall Apart* was followed by *No Longer at Ease* (1960) and *Arrow of God* (1964); together they form *The African Trilogy*, which is

regarded as a defining achievement in contemporary African fiction.

Achebe has been a very public man of letters, as an essayist, poet, editor, critic, and international academic; he also worked for the ill-fated government of Biafra during Nigeria's civil war. He has written, of *Things Fall Apart*, "I would be quite satisfied if my novels … did no more than teach my readers that their past – with all its imperfections – was not one long night of savagery from which the first Europeans acting on God's behalf delivered them" (*Morning Yet on Creation Day*, 1975).

Bruce Millar

Date 1958

Nationality Nigeria

Key Works *No Longer at Ease* (1960); *Arrow of God* (1964); *Beware, Soul Brother, and Other Poems* (1971); *Anthills of the Savannah* (1988)

Why It's Key Achebe's treatise "An Image of Africa: Racism in [Joseph] Conrad's *Heart of Darkness*" attacks the portrayal of black Africans in what is widely venerated as one of the key texts of twentieth-century literature.

Key Book
The Pledge

The Pledge is subtitled "Requiem for the Detective Novel" and was Dürrenmatt's response to those authors who were still in thrall to the rigid formulas laid down by the "Golden Age" mystery-writers of the twenties and thirties. It begins with Dr. H, former chief of the Zurich police, explaining that he dislikes detective stories because of their implication that all human behavior is explicable and that crimes can therefore always be solved by logical deduction. He tells the story of one of his own officers, Matthäi, who promises the parents of a murdered girl that he will find the killer – the "pledge" of the title – and becomes dangerously obsessed with the case.

H calls Matthäi a "genius" and his ratiocinative powers are certainly worthy of Poirot, Gideon Fell, or other Golden Age greats. Yet he fails, not because his deductions are incorrect but because they are incomplete – the master logician does not allow for the irrational act or the element of chance. Dürrenmatt

constantly teases the reader, offering up "clues" and following the usual detective story rhythms, but his "solution" shocks by having the randomness and banality of real-life crime. Although he is certainly not above using some of the old masters' familiar techniques to make his story exciting, Dürrenmatt is stringent in his exposure of the shortcomings of the traditional "detective story," and he anticipates the coming generation of writers who would transform the genre into the far more realistic, mercurial, and expansive form of the "crime novel."

Jake Kerridge

Date 1958

Author Friedrich Dürrenmatt (1921–90)

Nationality Switzerland

Why It's Key An exemplary thriller, *The Pledge* also questions the nature of the classic detective story.

Key Book
Night

As night descends in Elie Wiesel's novella, it plummets into the middle of the author's first night in a concentration camp, "that turned [his] life into one long night seven times sealed." This autobiographical account of survival begins in the Romanian town of Sighet. Poignantly, the languid grace of Wiesel's life in his hometown belies the vicious nature of the horror this pious teenager will endure. *Night* is the definitive text on the Holocaust, written by one of the few who survived. At the crux of this memoir, the question "Why do I pray?" is answered, and then renounced.

"Never shall I forget those moments that murdered my God and my soul," is Wiesel's haunting declaration of survival. Wiesel is spare in his descriptions of babies being tipped into mass graves, but it is through his reticence that other shocking truths are brought to the fore, and his understanding of relative pain allows him to vacillate between the suffering of mere thirst as he awaits evacuation, to etching his dying father's face into his memory in those precious final moments. Auschwitz is a place where reprieve can be bartered, and "work makes you free." Driven to desperation, as Jews struggle amongst themselves, and fight to the death for breadcrumbs in a "hermetically sealed" cattle cart, it becomes a battle fought by the darkest sides of human nature. *Night* is a lingering question mark poised at the end of the terms "faith," and "humanity."

Alexandra Hamlyn

Date 1958

Author Elie Wiesel (1928–)

Nationality Romania

Why It's Key A moment in literary history that ensures the survival of the Jews through the Holocaust in our collective voice and vision, as an event that not only should, but will, echo with meaning for mankind. Elie Wiesel was awarded the Nobel Peace Prize in 1986.

Key Book
The Once and Future King

The legend of Arthur has always been a fabulist's dream: it lent itself to any amount of chronological rearrangement. Anyone could score their mark on that mighty, weather-worn monolith. Even the earliest Welsh legends played fast and loose with dates and characters. In T.H. White's great sequence, *The Once and Future King*, the tendency to juggle periods and cultures hit its apogee. For White, Malory's *Morte D'Arthur* came as an unlooked-for benediction. He drew from that tale of doomed, illicit but ultimately noble love, of doomed idealism, and a doomed chivalric culture a powerful, perhaps surprising, lesson. Writing to a friend in 1940, he observed, "The central theme of *Morte D'Arthur* is to find an antidote to war."

Like all of his generation, White was deeply impressed by the peculiar horrors of twentieth-century war. In his witty, subversive but still tragic retelling of Arthurian Romance, man is not "homo sapiens" but "homo ferox," a creature born to evil, apt to savagery.

In *The Sword in the Stone*, the first of the series, White presents the young Arthur as needing the instruction of beasts: their social order is a better paradigm for morality than the one humans have invented. In this book, avowedly for children, Arthur is "Wart," and all too often, he's treated like one. As the series proceeds, Arthur discovers the principle of "Right for Might" – a brilliant inversion of the most erroneous maxim in history. His story confutes those who would maintain that trauma cannot be turned to good. Later still, Arthur learns compromise, or, as White puts it, "the seventh sense": the adult's pernicious notion that swift principle must learn to hobble at the pace of weakened conscience. In this, White shows what would have happened to the chivalric tradition had it been allowed to pass beyond adolescence.

Murrough O'Brien

Date 1958

Author T.H. White (1905–64)

Nationality UK

Why It's Key On its publication, *The Once and Future King* was widely recognized as a legitimate and original addition to Arthurian Romance, as well as a hugely provocative and stimulating tale in its own right. It is one of those rare books which can fascinate children and intrigue adults. It was made into a film by Disney, *The Sword in the Stone*, and a play, *Camelot*.

Key Author **H.E. Bates**
The Darling Buds of May

Herbert Ernest Bates (1905–74) published his first novel at the age of twenty, *The Two Sisters*, a story of a repressive family in the Midlands, that the author later felt was too heavily influenced by Conrad. More novels and collections of short stories followed, such as *The Woman Who Had Imagination* (1934) and *My Uncle Silas: Stories* (1939) but his real fame began only after World War II. He served in the Royal Air Force and wrote inspirational stories of service life under the pen-name of "Flying Officer X." These were published in collections such as *How Sleep the Brave* (1943) and his wartime experiences formed the basis of his most famous novel *Fair Stood the Wind for France* (1944), and the Burma-set *The Purple Plain* (1947) and *The Jacaranda Tree* (1949).

When he published *The Darling Buds of May* it was an immediate, if not critical, success. The Larkin family were described as living in rural Kent, anarchic, unconventional, lovers of the countryside, but above all happy. In the last volume of his autobiography, *The World in Ripeness* (1971) Bates claimed that the Larkins were inspired by a family he once saw eating crisps and ice-cream in a "ramshackle lorry that had been recently painted a violent electric blue." Pa Larkin (with his habitual assessment of things as "Perfick") along with Ma and their brood went on to feature in a popular series of novels, including *Hark the Lark* (1960) and *A Little of What You Fancy* (1970), living life to its sensual full. In the UK, *The Darling Buds of May* television series (1991–93), starring David Jason as Pa Larkin, brought new readers to Bates – as well as launching the career of Catherine Zeta-Jones.
Michael Munro

Date 1958

Nationality UK

Key Works *The Black Boxer: Tales* (1932); *Cut and Come Again: Fourteen Tales* (1935); *Something Short and Sweet* (1937); *The Watercress Girl and Other Stories* (1959); *The Vanished World: An Autobiography* (1969)

Why It's Key Bates was a prolific novelist and one of the great short story writers of the twentieth century, famous for his descriptions of rural England.

Opposite H.E. Bates

1950–1959

425

Key Book
Tom's Midnight Garden

Tom's Midnight Garden tells the story of Tom Long, who is sent to stay with his aunt and uncle in a flat without a garden. He is lonely and bored. One night, he hears the grandfather clock in the communal hall strike thirteen. He goes outside, to discover a large sunlit garden. Here he befriends a girl named Hatty from an earlier age. This story of time travel, growing up, and friendship holds enduring appeal. It evokes the child's rich imaginative world, which stands in opposition to dull adult truths. It probes the issues of reality and time; Pearce acknowledged her debt to J.W. Dunne, who argued that different periods of time can coexist and merge.

The themes of the story are universal. The idea of the secret garden recurs repeatedly in children's literature and is a potent image of fleeting, idyllic childhood. Tom's anguish at losing the garden and Hatty – who grows perceptibly older, at a rate which leaves Tom behind – recalls Peter Pan's attempts to persuade Wendy to stay with him in the timeless Neverland. Tom eventually grows "thin," ghost-like, when in the garden and finally he is unable to gain access to it. Childhood must pass.

The work has been televised three times, made into a film (directed by Willard Carroll), and adapted for the stage. This powerful and popular text has been described by the respected critic John Rowe Townsend (in his 1965 *Written for Children*) as a "masterpiece" and "an outstandingly beautiful and absorbing book."
Emily Jeremiah

Date 1958

Author Ann Philippa Pearce (1920–2006)

Nationality UK

Why It's Key The novel is widely acknowledged to be a masterpiece of English children's literature. It won the prestigious Carnegie Medal in 1958 and has been adapted numerous times. Pearce's other books include *The Battle of Bubble and Squeak* and *The Way to Sattin Shore*. She was awarded OBE in 1997 for her services to children's literature.

Key Character **Holly Golightly**
Breakfast at Tiffany's

Audrey Hepburn in a slim black dress. Audrey Hepburn flourishing a cigarette holder, Audrey Hepburn window-shopping at Tiffany's. Hepburn weeping into her drink at a New York bar: "You can't give your heart to a wild thing." This is one of those books that has been overshadowed by the famous film. Truman Capote wanted Marilyn Monroe to play the part of Holly Golightly. He complained that Paramount double-crossed him when they cast Audrey Hepburn.

The sly bittersweet novella marked a turning point for Truman Capote. In his creation of Holly Golightly and the men who love her, he left behind the overheated Southern Gothic writing of his earlier bestseller *Other Voices, Other Rooms* and developed the lean, sparse style that he deployed to such powerful effect when he later wrote his masterpiece *In Cold Blood*. On reading *Breakfast at Tiffany's*, Norman Mailer declared Capote "the most perfect writer of my generation."

Holly Golightly is a good-time girl – or call girl – whose story is told by an anonymous narrator who loves her and wants to save her. Only Holly runs away from men who want to save her. She's already run away from a husband and is fiercely resistant to the idea of owning or being owned. Golightly was free spirited, a charming user of people, un-domesticated – everything the 1950s American woman was not meant to be. Holly's restlessness, her determination to be herself makes her a 1960s feminist before that decade even began.

Kathy Watson

Date 1958

Author Truman Capote (1924–84)

Nationality USA

Why It's Key The book has become such a classic that it can sometimes be forgotten just how bold it was at the time it was published – with its independent, unconventional heroine, Holly Golightly.

Opposite Holly Golightly

Key Character **Arthur Seaton**
Saturday Night and Sunday Morning

Saturday Night and Sunday Morning is one of the groundbreaking British working-class novels of the late 1950s. Sillitoe (amongst others) began to question the long-accepted marginality of working-class men in British fiction. These writers attempted to present "new truths" about post-war Britain and to challenge what they saw as the sterility and complacency of middle-class society. Sillitoe was not initially part of the group of writers labelled the "Angry Young Men," but he is linked categorically to that movement of angry, social realist writing, and Arthur Seaton is forever connected with the social politics examined in this literature.

Arthur is one of the first young male, working-class protagonists in British fiction whose life is honestly and realistically portrayed. He represents an emerging youth culture that for the first time had money to spend. He has a job and the determination to live his life the way he wants. Materialism and self-gratification drive his ambition and his happiness is achieved in

terms of what he can buy. He spends his money on clothes, drink, and women, saying, "what I want is a good time" and "all the rest is propaganda."

The picaresque journey he undertakes encapsulates a particular time and place in British fiction and many readers strongly identified with his rebellion. He rants and rages against unseen and untouchable oppressors, and in a much-quoted passage says, "I'll be fighting every day until I die." However, unlike other literary characters of the period such as Joe Lampton in John Braine's *Room at the Top* (1957) Arthur does not reject his class roots. Sillitoe's later novel *Birthday* (2001) revisits the Seaton family and explores the relationship between Arthur and his brother Brian.

Pat Wheeler

Date 1958

Author Alan Sillitoe (1928–)

Nationality UK

Why It's Key Arthur Seaton rails against the dull, grey monotony of post-war England. His name became a byword for anger, disaffection, and youthful rebellion. The film adaptation (directed by Karel Reisz, 1960) was at the forefront of British New Wave films and received great critical acclaim.

Key Characters **Coffin Ed Johnson and Gravedigger Jones**

This hard-boiled, two-man African-American detective team is presented as a virtually inseparable work partnership in Chester Himes's Harlem cycle of crime thrillers, one rarely seen without the other. When first introduced they are peripheral characters, but by the second book they are fully developed, complex literary creations. Although their private lives are rarely mentioned, they are both married, middle-class family men with children, who live in Long Island and drive daily to their regular beat in Harlem. Gravedigger is described as having a lumpy face, reddish brown eyes that always seem to smoulder, and a big and rugged frame. He is more articulate than Coffin Ed, whose distinct feature is a badly scarred face, the result of acid thrown by a villain in *For Love of Imabelle*. Their nicknames indicate the legendary respect they command in the neighbourhood, despite working for the predominantly white NYPD, and give a clue to the brutal policing methods that they favor. Coffin Ed appears the more volatile of the pair, with Gravedigger sometimes having to restrain his excesses; none the less, Gravedigger's custom-made long-barreled nickel-plated .38 evokes universal dread. A law unto themselves, they reserve their trademark ultra-physical brand of enforcement for violent criminals, drug dealers, confidence tricksters, and pimps (according to their creator, "they never came down hard on anybody that was in the right"). As a counter-balance, their keen sense of injustice lets them show genuine compassion for innocent victims, and somehow the reader does not lose sympathy for them.

The pair also appear in *The Real Cool Killers* (1959), *The Crazy Kill* (1959), *The Big Gold Dream* (1960), *All Shot Up* (1960), *Cotton Comes To Harlem* (1965), *The Heat's On* (1966), and *Blind Man with a Pistol* (1969).
Margaret Busby

Date 1958 (revised as *A Rage In Harlem*, 1965)

First Appearance *La Reine des pommes* (*For Love of Imabelle*)

Author Chester Himes (1909–84)

Nationality USA

Why It's Key The first of Himes' "Harlem domestic detective stories" originally appeared as *La Reine des pommes* in France, where he had moved from the USA, and won the Grand Prix du Roman Policier.

429

Key Event **The Leopard becomes the best-selling novel in Italian history**

The appearance of *The Leopard* in 1958 brought posthumous fame to its author, who had died the previous year without publishing in his lifetime. The author, Giuseppe di Lampedusa, was an enigmatic aristocrat barely known beyond Sicilian literary circles. His only novel, written in his final years, traces the decline of his class in the half-century that followed Garibaldi's 1860 landing with 1,000 followers at Marsala in Sicily, a key event in the Risorgimento which overthrew the Bourbon Kingdom of the Two Sicilies and unified Italy for the first time since the Roman Empire. The dazzling novel evokes the baroque lifestyle of the old aristocracy through the Prince of Salina – family symbol the leopard – an attractive and highly intelligent figure whose dictum is the often-quoted paradox, "If we want things to stay as they are, things will have to change." Clear-sighted and ironical, Salina offers a summation of 2,500 years of Sicilian history in which the island had been colonized by a succession of rulers – ancient Greeks and Romans, medieval Arabs, Normans, Byzantines, northern Italians – to be met with a stubborn form of passive resistance by the native inhabitants. The clear implication is that progress and modernity – religious, political, cultural – continue to be met in the same way in the twentieth century, and perhaps beyond.

Five years after its publication, *The Leopard* was filmed by the Italian director Luchino Visconti, whose sumptuous visual style produced an unusually successful screen version of a novel. Like both Giuseppi di Lampedusa and his central character, the Prince of Salina, Visconti was an aristocrat by birth, although he was from Milan in northern Italy and a communist in his political convictions.
Bruce Millar

Date 1958

Title *The Leopard* (*Il gattopardo*)

Author Giuseppi di Lampedusa (1896–1957)

Nationality Italy

Why It's Key Hailed immediately as a masterpiece of contemporary Italian fiction, the book's stature has grown to the extent that it is now regarded as one of the great works of twentieth-century world literature.

Opposite *Il gattopardo*

Key Event **Boris Pasternak wins the Nobel Prize but is forced to reject it**

1950–1959

Boris Pasternak (1890–1960) was awarded the Nobel Prize in Literature following the sensational publication of *Doctor Zhivago* in the West the previous year, after the manuscript was smuggled out of Soviet Russia. The novel reinforced perceived Western values of individualism, freedom, and spiritual depth as opposed to the utilitarian and totalitarian ethic of the Soviet Union. The Kremlin's subsequent clumsy handling of the honor bestowed on Pasternak only strengthened an image of Nikita Khrushchev's Russia as an evil empire. Having already responded with enthusiasm and gratitude to the Swedish Academy, Pasternak was forced four days later to reject it, "considering the meaning this award has been given in the society to which I belong." In the ensuing campaign against him, he struggled not to be expelled from Russia, the classic Communist position of last resort. Pasternak, who polarized Russian literary circles with his spiritual but not overtly political dissent, continued

to write poetry concerned with love and immortality. When he died of lung cancer in 1960 thousands of people attended his funeral in the village of Peredelkino outside Moscow, in one of the earliest dissident manifestations in Soviet history. From the official side, Pasternak's neighbour Konstantin Fedin, President of the Writers' Union, refused to carry the coffin. Pasternak's grave became a place of pilgrimage for the remaining Communist years. *Doctor Zhivago*, whose spiritual and poetic ethos so profoundly rejected what the Soviet Union stood for, was not published in Russia until 1987. Three years later the house in Peredelkino was reopened as a museum.

Lesley Chamberlain

Date 1958

Place Russia

Why It's Key The West won a major victory in the Cold War when Russia's most spiritual writer was hailed a genius and his novel *Doctor Zhivago* made famous the world over, having been banned from publication in the author's own country.

Opposite Boris Pasternak

Key Character **Asterix**
Asterix the Gaul

Asterix the Gaul was born in 1959 in the French magazine, *Pilote*. The unconventional comic strip, created by René Goscinny and Albert Uderzo, was first published as a book in 1961.

It is around 50BC and all of Gaul is divided into three parts, but one small corner still holds out against the dastardly Roman invaders. The only thing these villagers are afraid of is the sky falling on their heads. But Julius Caesar wants rid of this defiant outpost.

Over the course of 33 books, the indomitable duo Asterix and his friend Obelix, the Menhir delivery man, defy and outwit those "crazy Romans," occasionally stopping to eat some wild boar. Asterix is the brains behind the pair, aided by a magic potion, supplied by Getafix the druid. Asterix and his crew have travelled across Europe, met Cleopatra in Egypt, visited North America, and sunk many a pirate ship on the high seas. Each book ends in the same way: with a banquet under the stars.

The humor in these comics is wry, intelligent, and visual. Anthea Bell and Derek Hockridge's superb English translations involve many jokes not in the French original, including changing the names of characters such as the elderly Geriatrix, Dogmatix the dog, and Unhygienix the fishmonger (and his wife Bacteria).

The books have now been translated into more than 100 languages, including Esperanto, Ancient Greek, and Serbo-Croat. Goscinny, who originally wrote all the words, died in 1977. Uderzo has continued the series, though at a slower rate.

Rosie Blau

Date 1959

First Appearance *Asterix the Gaul* (*Astérix le Gaulois*)

Author René Goscinny (1926–77) and Albert Uderzo (1927–)

Nationality France

Why It's Key The plucky Gaulish underdog gave his name to a resoundingly successful series that has entertained children and adults for decades, been translated into more than 100 languages and fuelled films, video games, and even a French theme park.

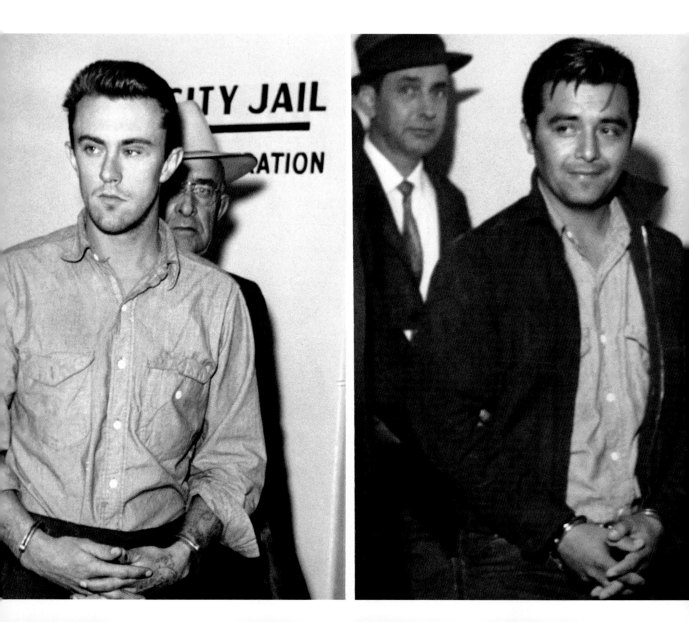

Key Event **The Clutter family murder leads Capote to write *In Cold Blood***

Part of the book's shocking impact was down to the gruesome nature of the crimes depicted. Along with Michael Harrington's *The Other America* (1962), *In Cold Blood* also exposed the image of 1950s America as a time of financial security and suburban well-being as a mythology, disguising the continuing presence of poverty and social exclusion long after the Depression.

During a 1959 winter night in the stereotypical small-town American heartland, the Kansas Clutter family were bound and shot for only a few dollars of stolen goods. Truman Capote's reportage of the murders practically created the genre of true crime fiction with its mixture of officially documented police and trial reports, and fictionalized conversation and thoughts by the individuals involved.

Capote describes the last days of the murdered and their killers' pursuit and capture by law officers in an anonymous narrative voice that makes no effort to judge or moralize the events. The shock for readers was not just the description of the pointless murders, but Capote's larger revelation that everything was not right in the post-war boom of suburbanization, white-collar, corporate employment, and wide-spread consumerism that Capote had earlier celebrated in his *Breakfast at Tiffany's*.

One of the killers, Perry Smith, ought to have been an American success story: the son of a small-business entrepreneur, Smith was highly intelligent and a Korean War veteran decorated for bravery. Instead he became addicted to painkillers and given to shiftless wandering through the maze of highways and bus routes. A product of a family damaged by alcoholism, bankruptcy, child abuse, racism (Smith is half-Native American), and connotations of homosexual rape, his inexplicable violence results from the frustration of exclusion from the mythology of good times in Eisenhower America.
Stephen Shapiro

Date 1959

Title *In Cold Blood* (1965)

Author Truman Capote (1924–84)

Place USA

Why It's Key *In Cold Blood* is the book in which Capote is said to have invented the genre of true crime fiction. His abandonment of the Beats' romanticism of the outsider laid the ground for a new mood of public anger during the 1960s.

Opposite Cutter family killers, Perry Smith and Richard Hickock

1950–1959

433

Key Author **Robert Lowell** *Life Studies*

Scion of a patrician Boston family, Robert Lowell (1917–77) rejected their interest in money-making, but could never quite shake off their presence in his poetry. He revolted against the Puritanism and naval tradition of his family during World War II by becoming "a fire-breathing Catholic C.O.," and was imprisoned for five months as a conscientious objector.

Lowell's second volume, *Lord Weary's Castle*, won the Pulitzer Prize in 1947. Perhaps its most celebrated poem is "The Quaker Graveyard in Nantucket," an extended elegy for his cousin Warren Winslow, lost at sea during the war. It has the measured lyricism of Eliot's *Four Quartets*, while drawing in imagery from both the biblical "Deluge" and that mythopoeic American classic, *Moby-Dick*. In *Life Studies* Lowell found a more individual voice, a voice that was to characterize his poetry for the rest of his life. Gone is the earlier formalism, replaced by looser structures and a more conversational style. There are elegiac memoirs of his uncle, his grandparents, his father, and the houses he was brought up in, seen through a gauze of descriptive detail, studded here and there with a sharp, brilliant image. There is also, in "Skunk Hour," a glimpse of the manic-depression that was to dog him for much of his life: "I myself am hell,/nobody's here."

In the 1960s Lowell became involved in the civil rights and anti-war movements, and reflected the intersection of politics with his personal life in *Notebook 1967–1968*. His private life remained in turmoil, not helped by bouts of heavy drinking. He left his second wife in 1970, and died of a heart attack in a cab in New York City.
Ian Crofton

Date 1959

Nationality USA

Key Works *Lord Weary's Castle* (1947)

Why It's Key Lowell's intimate, confessional poems, apparently casual but carefully wrought by a master craftsman, established a new register for younger poets in both America and Britain.

Key Event *Parinde* marks the start of the New Story movement in Hindi literature

Nirmal Verma (1929–2005) was both the initiator and the most revered practitioner of the New Story movement in Hindi literature. *Parinde* was his first story collection. The title story is an atmospheric, introspective, searching exploration of loss and memory. Its publication turned out to be a turning point in Hindi letters.

These new, realistic stories took as their focus the new social set-up in post-independence India, and the new relationships among the middle classes. They used a wider range of modern techniques than had characterized most previous Hindi literature; less rural, and less concerned with social reform, they reflected the dislocation of modern city life, the alienation of individuals from each other and from their environment, and universal concerns such as death and displacement through intimate renderings of states of mind and situations, rather than showy plots. Verma's stories are characterized by understatement and restraint. They contain no outwardly turbulent emotions, no great showdowns, but gradual revelations, delicate turnings-over of universal themes: relationships and the gaps between people, and between people's thoughts and their words and actions. In "The Short Story as a Pure Literary Form" Verma stated that Indian "emancipation from the past inevitably led to a state of alienation in the present – and it was the short story which reflected most powerfully this state of spiritual desolation."

Verma was also an esteemed translator of Czech fiction, and he brought writers such as Milan Kundera, Bohumil Hrabal, and Karel Capek to Hindi readers before most English readers discovered them. He lived for a time in Czechoslovakia and the UK as well as India. Several of his stories are set in Europe and deal with being an outsider or an exile. He also wrote novels, essays and travelogues.
Lucy Daniel

Date 1959

Place India

Title *Parinde* (translated as *The Hill Station and Other Stories*, 1962)

Why It's Key Nirmal Verma was one of the most important Hindi prose writers of modern times. Mohan Rakesh, Bhishma Sahni, Amarkant, and Kamleshwar were also exponents of the New Story movement.

434

Key Book
The Manchurian Candidate

At the height of the Cold War, a climate of fear was predominant in the West, not only of the looming threat of mutually-destructive nuclear war with the Soviet Union but also of subversion from within: the so-called "reds under the bed" theory. Condon's most successful and influential novel played on these concerns and also made use of the emerging idea that people could be brainwashed into performing actions that they would not normally even consider. Sergeant Raymond Shaw, feted as a Medal of Honor winner, has been programmed in this way in Manchuria after being captured by the Communists during the Korean War. His mother, a Communist agent, is able to "trigger" her son into becoming a cold-blooded assassin who will have no memory of his killings, clearing the way for her second husband, a McCarthy-like demagogue who is also a Communist agent, to become President.

The novel has been described as eerily prescient, as the 1960s was a decade that, politically, seemed to be characterized by assassination. Among the notable figures who died in this way were President Kennedy (1963), his brother Robert, a Presidential candidate (1968), and the great civil rights leader Martin Luther King (also 1968). Condon was among the first to popularize the ideas of brainwashing and "sleeper" agents and his exploitation of the conspiracy theory set the pattern that was to recur time and again in the political thrillers and spy stories that were all the rage in 1960s and 1970s fiction and film.
Michael Munro

Date 1959

Author Richard Condon (1915–96)

Nationality USA

Why It's Key This political satire tapped into the prevailing Cold War international tensions and helped create the 1960s vogue for conspiracy-theory plots. The film version made in 1962 was a favorite of U.S. President John F. Kennedy who allowed its director access to the White House during filming.

Key Book
The Magic Christian

"I started reading *The Magic Christian* and I thought I was going to go insane… it was an incredible influence on me." Hunter S. Thompson, a man infamous for shooting from the lip, was not the only writer impressed by Texan Terry Southern's satire on capitalism: Tom Wolfe lines up to doff his cap and Gore Vidal is on record saying *The Magic Christian* surpasses Flaubert's *Bouvard et Pécuchet*.

When *The Magic Christian* was published in 1959, Southern was already a fixture in the Parisian literary scene and had appeared in the inaugural issue of George Plimpton's *Paris Review*. The novel, about billionaire prankster Guy Grand who believes everyone has a price – "Grand's the name, easy-green's the game" – is a series of outrageous escapades concocted by Grand to expose human greed, buying people off for his own amusement.

Filmed in 1969, and transposed to swinging London, *The Magic Christian* starred Peter Sellers and other future stars of British comedy, though it deviated from the book to cast Ringo Starr as Guy Grand's adopted son. Southern's brush with Sellers led to him scripting *Dr Strangelove* (1964) for maverick director Stanley Kubrick, co-writing the counter-cultural classic *Easy Rider* (1969) with Peter Fonda and Dennis Hopper, touring America with the Rolling Stones in 1972 and writing for *Saturday Night Live* in the 1980s. But it was in the sixties that Terry Southern's flame burned brightest, propelled by the reception of *The Magic Christian* and immortalized on The Beatles' *Sgt Pepper* album cover, stood beside Dylan Thomas, the epitome of cool in his shades.

Susan Tomaselli

Date 1959

Author Terry Southern (1924–95)

Nationality USA

Why It's Key Hip godfather to the Beats – along with Gregory Corso he hustled William S. Burroughs' *Naked Lunch* into print – and purveyor of intelligent satire, Terry Southern is heralded as the inventor of New Journalism, the style of writing where the article is as much about the author as the subject, and is best known as a Hollywood screenwriter.

Key Book
Brown Girl, Brownstones

One of the few novels up until this time to deal authentically with the inner life of a black central female character, *Brown Girl, Brownstones* is also significant for its layered treatment of cross-cultural issues, with a skilful use of language to reflect the characters' diverse origins. It mirrors the author's own background in telling the story of a Barbadian girl searching for personal identity within New York's Bajan community; although Paule Marshall was born in Brooklyn, her parents were second-generation Barbadian immigrants. (She has been quoted as saying that she began to write *Brown Girl, Brownstones* "to unravel [her] knots.") The novel's main character is Selina, daughter of Barbadian immigrants Deighton and Silla Boyce, who grows up in the midst of family crises and tensions represented by her parents' differing values. Her hardworking mother wants to buy the brownstone building that they rent, but to do so would require the sale of the piece of land her father still owns in Barbados. Her feckless father, still dreaming of returning "home," is resistant to acquiring the New York property. The dilemma sums up the challenge of retaining identity or succumbing to a culture of materialism. Marshall writes engagingly about Selina's journey towards maturity, striving to sort out her parents' conflict at the same time as yearning for freedom. Within the panoramic context of black Brooklyn, Marshall gives a compassionate depiction of the immigrant experience – the challenge of retaining identity while succeeding in a materialist culture – and a nuanced portrayal of Caribbean womanhood.

Margaret Busby

Date 1959

Author Paule Marshall (1929)

Nationality African American

Why It's Key Usually cited as the beginning of contemporary African-American women's writing, and acknowledged by writers such as Alice Walker as important to their literary development, it heralded a new era of black women's fiction depicting the lives of Caribbean immigrants to the USA.

Key Book
Naked Lunch

Clichés and myths abound when it comes to Burroughs. Exotic uncle to the Beats, he was also a Harvard-educated, gun-toting, wife-slaying, queer junkie, American ex-pat sex-tourist who manufactured unreadable cut-up novels ("that's not writing, it's plumbing," said Samuel Beckett) and whose grumpy face peers lugubriously out from Peter Blake's sleeve for *Sgt Pepper*. Read his letters and there he is again: a pragmatic, misanthropic voice, part-Hammett, part-Swift, complaining about being grifted by his Beat houseguests and playing a desperate epistolary footsie with Allen Ginsberg.

Something of this implacable bloody-mindedness rubs off on *Naked Lunch*. Culled from thousands of pages of notes, some of which cannibalize parts of his earlier books, the novel is *not* "cut-up" but a series of perfected "routines" or cartoonish sketches in which characters like Dr Benway and the narrator William Lee play out the exhilarations and abjections of addiction and cure in a drifting, amoral lifestyle. All is rendered in that Burroughsian sawn-off, elliptical prose: "The old junky has found a vein... blood blossoms in the dropper like a Chinese flower... he push home the heroin and the boy who jacked off fifty years ago shine immaculate through the ravaged flesh," while the reader, like the "square wants to come on hip," either turns away or is caught in the vicarious pleasure of this smack-splattered ride. The themes here are all about control, manipulation, and need, both in the sense of the totalitarian society Burroughs satirizes and in the way he as a writer, relentlessly transgressive, never lets you off the hook.

Doug Haynes

Date 1959

Author William S. Burroughs (1914–97)

Nationality USA

Why It's Key In 1966 *Naked Lunch* was the subject of the last major literary censorship trial in the U.S. Authors such as Norman Mailer and Allen Ginsberg lined up in the Boston courtroom to defend the work against charges of obscenity. While the book is indeed profane, stylistically it treads strange new ground.

Opposite William Burroughs

Key Book
Cider with Rosie

"I was set down from the carrier's cart at the age of three; and there with sense of bewilderment and terror my life in the village began." So begins Laurie Lee's classic evocation of an English rural childhood in the remote Slad Valley, in the Cotswolds near Stroud. It was the early years of the twentieth century, and in this part of the country not much had changed for hundreds of years. Lee evokes his experiences of the small village school, the rhythms of the agricultural year, his first love, for Rosie Burdock, who, "having baptized me with her cidrous kisses, married a soldier, and I lost her for ever." But as he grows, the world shrinks, horses and carts are replaced by tractors and cars, and the fiddles and flutes with which the villagers entertained themselves are thrown out in favor of wireless sets. "The sun and moon, which once rose from our hill, rose from London now in the east."

Lee followed *Cider with Rosie* with two more volumes of memoirs. *As I Walked Out One Midsummer Morning* (1969) tells how he left the village to make his way in London, and then of his travels in Spain. *A Moment of War* (1991) deals with his service as a volunteer in the International Brigades during the Spanish Civil War. Lee also published several books of poems. Such was the enormous success of *Cider with Rosie* that Lee was able to buy his childhood home in Slad, where he lived out the rest of his days, and is buried in the village churchyard.

Ian Crofton

Date 1959

Author Laurie Lee (1914–97)

Nationality UK

Why It's Key An affectionate, lyrical childhood memoir of a rural way of life that has gone forever. It has been a perennial bestseller, and has become a standard exam text in schools.

Key Character **Titus Groan**
Titus Alone

Mervyn Peake was a celebrated artist before he became a writer. His first forays into literature were series of illustrations for *Alice's Adventures in Wonderland* and *Treasure Island*. In the first Titus book, *Titus Groan* (1946), he found a written style that perfectly complemented his gothic, almost Boschian artistic aesthetic. Although Titus is born and christened in this volume, and in its sequel *Gormenghast* (1950) takes possession of his kingdom, he doesn't really come into his own as a character until the third book, *Titus Alone*. From the start, Titus' impulses oppose the adherence to dust and tradition that characterizes Gormenghast. Literally enclosed in the castle's rulebook for his christening, "so that he is engulfed in the sere Text… and one with the inviolable Law," he later drops the "sacrosanct symbols" of his earldom into a lake. Despite a childhood spent learning "the language of dim stairs and moth-hung rafters," Titus eventually recognizes his deep longing to escape; at the end of *Gormenghast* he does just that. Outside the weird, rule-bound world of his kingdom, in time-honored picaresque style, Titus journeys and "discovers himself." He enters a world more recognisable to us as a dystopian sci-fi parallel to our own, and we see him as, in Peake's words "in a way, very ordinary."

While Peake's fantastical world anticipated the sci-fi subgenre "steampunk" (harking to an earlier future than that of cyberpunk) and led to numerous spin-offs including a hugely popular BBC TV series, Titus himself became something of a favorite character and alter ego to the sickening author. Before eventually succumbing to Parkinson's disease, Peake christened his grandson Titus.

Sophie Lewis

Date 1959

Author Mervin Peake (1911–68)

Nationality UK

Why It's Key Fans tend to be divided in their focus: is it Gormenghast, his Piranesi-esque fantasy kingdom, that they most admire? Or is it Titus Groan, 77th Earl of Gormenghast, both exemplary scion and disastrous catalyst of change? Peake's books gain steadily in critical appreciation.

1950–1959

439

Key Event *The Tin Drum* results in over 40 lawsuits against Günter Grass

Written from a hospital for the criminally insane, Oskar Matzerath, a monstrous man-child (he stops growing at age three, in protest at a sick world), narrates in the most idiosyncratic way the rise and fall of the Third Reich and his part in it. From childhood in Danzig to his present prison, Oskar is the eyewitness and personification of that regime's history. On his walls are portraits of Beethoven and Hitler, the twin poles of the "German character," artist and butcher, while his intellectual inspirations are Goethe and Rasputin. Taking in fabulist twists, his story unfolds to the constant, sinister beat of the drum he was given as a child. When he discovers he can shriek at sufficiently high pitch to shatter glass, we are reminded of Kristallnacht; when, in post-war Germany, we visit The Onion Cellar, where the patrons all peel onions – "the tears flowed and washed everything away" – we think of pseudo-guilt and Social Democracy.

For every literary prize the book garnered, lawsuits and scandal accrued too. Grass's scurrilous but sympathetic portrait of the gnomish picaroon Oskar, a libidinous egomaniac who compares himself to Christ, attracted accusations of child pornography and blasphemy, charges also made later of Schlöndorff's 1979 film of the book. In Bremen, for example, the city's literary prize was awarded to Grass but blocked by its liberal Social Democratic Municipal Senate. Behind such censoriousness, perhaps, lay the anxieties generated by a text that sets out to show, in satirical fashion, German petit-bourgeois complicity with Hitler's work.

Doug Haynes

Date 1959

Place Germany

Why It's Key Controversy surrounded the novel on publication, focusing on sexual and religious obscenity. Revelations that Grass was a member of the SS threaten to undermine his credibility as a critic of Nazi Germany. Perhaps such ethical difficulties reflect the finely poised satire of his work, wherein narrative identification is with a shocking, amoral protagonist.

Opposite *The Tin Drum*

Key Event **The first Broadway performance of a play written by a black woman**

In his 1951 poem, "Harlem," poet Langston Hughes questioned the impact of the unrealised dream on the soul of the dreamer and the community in which the dreamer exists. When he asked, "What happens to a dream deferred?" he was searching for a means to explain the anger, malaise, impulsiveness, explosiveness, sweetness, and absurd optimism found in the black community. Playwright Lorraine Hansberry (1930–65) replied to Hughes and extended the territory of his question in her play, *A Raisin in the Sun*, first produced in 1959. Hansberry took the title of her three act drama from one of the possible consequences of dream deferment that Hughes offered in his poem.

In Hansberry's realist exploration of the Youngers, a Southside of Chicago, working class family, she asks what dreams the modest death benefits of an overworked and subjugated man can fulfil for his family. Hansberry proposes that the money opens a small door through which the family escapes their confinement, only to enter another arena of race and class discrimination. In the play, Hansberry offers commentary regarding gender and oppression, matriarchy and the persistence of the black family, abortion, black masculinity, generational conflict, African American humanism, the guiding light of African liberation movements, responsibility and freedom, independence and interdependence, the relationship between spiritual and material wealth, the variety of black cultural expression, and the attainability of the American Dream.

The play was instrumental in the careers of the original cast, actors Sidney Poitier, Claudia McNeil, Ruby Dee, Lou Gossett, Jr., Glynn Turman, Diana Sands, and director Lloyd Richards. In 1974, Hansberry's husband, Robert Nemiroff produced *Raisin*, a musical based on the play.
Monifa Love Asante

Date 1959

Place USA

Why It's Key Now a classic of American theater, *A Raisin in the Sun* was a groundbreaking celebration of black life and courage; this Critics Circle award-winning play has been hailed for its honest depiction of working class life, observance of the wisdom of women, and synthesis of social and political issues. It has also been disparaged for its lack of belligerence and tilt towards integration.

Key Event **Quasimodo, anti-fascist poet, is awarded the Nobel Prize in post-war Italy**

"Italy is my country, o stranger, / It is of its people I sing, and of the sound / Of secret lamentation that comes from its sea, / I sing of its mothers' chaste grief, of all its life."

By the time Salvatore Quasimodo (1901–68) was awarded the Nobel Prize in 1959, the German fascists had long left Italy (as an antifascist militant, he had been temporarily imprisoned during World War II), and he was a prominent intellectual figure within Italian academia. Six years before the Nobel, he had shared the Etna-Taormina International Prize with Welsh poet Dylan Thomas. The Swedish Academy honored the poet "for his lyric poetry, which, with classical fire, expresses the tragic experience of life in our own times." This judgment results from Quasimodo's recurrent emphasis on the poet's fearless, uncompromising attitude towards life and its plagues, involving desperate loneliness ("Everyone stands alone on the heart of the earth / Transfixed by a sun-ray: / And it is suddenly night") and the awareness, at times, of being despised by the ones who choose to "serve" political power. The award marked a period in the history of the world haunted by terrible experiences of war and cruelty, the horrified silences and outspoken fears Quasimodo explores in his hermetic though daringly outspoken poems. It celebrated the poet's intellectual cry for a political regeneration in post-war Italy, where, as Quasimodo puts it in his Nobel lecture, "the politician wants men to know how to die courageously; the poet wants men to live courageously." Paradoxically, while glorifying a representative of the hermetic school the award also glorifies Quasimodo's ability to share, albeit from his ivory tower, the frightening experiences of war with millions in the world.
Letizia Alterno

Date 1959

Nationality Italy

Why It's Key Expatriated to the north of Italy, Quasimodo expressed a nostalgic longing for his native Sicily and a troubled remembrance of the hardship during the World Wars. His poetry is a witnessing and forewarning of man's solitude, and a form of resistance to foreign oppression.

Key Book
Hollywood Babylon

Kenneth Anger's *Hollywood Babylon* instantly became an international sensation. A leading light in the American underground, alongside Stan Brakhage and Bruce Conner, Anger himself made just nine short films – but they were enough to earn him praise from Martin Scorsese as "a unique filmmaker, an artist of exceptional imagination," as well as a personal invitation from Jean Cocteau to visit France. His use of jump cuts and sound exerted a huge influence on music videos and commercials.

When his money ran out, he decided to write a book of scandal. *Hollywood Babylon*, which was first published in France in 1959, describes the rise and fall of the movie star on the back of idol worship. He recalls Rudolph Valentino's predilection for submissive sex, Chaplin's misdemeanours with under-age girls, and a handful of starlet suicides. And he selected his photographs with a delicious sense of irony. It is perhaps significant that the publisher of the first,

French, edition, Jean Jacques Pauvert, also published the works of the Marquis de Sade. Asked how he had gone from filmmaking to writing *Hollywood Babylon*, Anger told one interviewer: "When I was living in Paris in the fifties, I told stories to people like François Truffaut before they were directing. They were writing. I told them stories about old Hollywood that they had never heard. And they suggested that I do a book."

A number of disputes with the publisher led to a delay of sixteen years before the English-language edition of *Hollywood Babylon* appeared in the United States – when it was published The *New York Times* called it "a delicious box of poisoned bonbons."

Adam Feinstein

Date 1959 (France); 1975 (USA)

Author Kenneth Anger (1930–)

Nationality USA

Why It's Key Volumes I and II opened the floodgates to a world of gossip, and the publication of its English-language edition in 1975 met a powerful post-Watergate drive to rip down icons.

1950–1959

441

Key Author **Ousmane Sembène**
God's Bits of Wood

Ousmane Sembène (often rendered as Sembène Ousmane) is one of sub-Saharan Africa's most renowned writers, and one of the most prolific from "Francophone" Africa. He has written ten major works since 1956. He has also reached a wide audience in Africa as a highly influential filmmaker. He has argued that high rates of illiteracy in African countries make film a much more important medium than literature.

Born in Senegal's Casamance region in 1923, Sembène's achievement's are all the more remarkable for his lack of a formal education beyond the age of thirteen. Many of his works are rooted in his personal experiences and political context. His first novel, *The Black Docker* reflected his time as a dock worker in Marseilles. *God's Bits of Wood*, set in the highly significant 1947 strike by workers on the Dakar-Niger railway, doubtless also drew on Sembène's memories of the 1946 general strike in Senegal which he experienced as a member of the construction workers'

trade union. After the 1960s Sembène became one of the first writers to shift his analysis from the relationship between colonisers and colonized to that between subject and state in independent African nations. In doing so, his work is notable for his early recognition of the perpetuation of social and political inequalities in post-colonial societies.

Tim Lovering

Date 1960 (published)

Nationality Senegal

Key Works *Le mandat, precede de Vehi-Ciosane* (1966), published in English as *The Money Order*, with *White Genesis* (1972); *Le dernier de l'Empire* (1981), published in English as *The last of the Empire: A Senegalese Novel* (1983)

Why It's Key Sembène is one of the most influential writers of anti-colonial, African nationalist literature, and of postcolonial African literature.

Key Author **John Betjeman**
Summoned by Bells

John Betjeman (1906-84) was, for his time, an unusual poet. He used traditional verse forms, and regular metre and rhyme when the fashion was all for loose structure and obscurity. He grabbed attention by being earthy and comic: "Keep me from Thelma's sister Pearl! / She puts my senses in a whirl, / Weakens my knees and keeps me waiting / Until my heart stops palpitating."

He extended the language of poetry with much use of brand names and place names: "I am a young executive. No cuffs than mine are cleaner; / I have a Slimline briefcase and I use the firm's Cortina. / In every roadside hostelry from here to Burgess Hill / The maîtres d'hotel all know me well and let me sign the bill."

Yet Betjeman was fundamentally serious; although devoted to the Anglican church, he was always troubled by doubt: "And is it true? And is it true / This most tremendous tale of all... / The Maker of the stars and sea / Become a Child on earth, for me?"

Betjeman made innovative use of television as a medium for his poetry, and had yet another prominent life as a conservationist – a passion which also broke into his verse, often savagely. Betjeman's poetry is amusing, moving, a joy to read. He summed up his career like this: "I made hay while the sun shone. / My work sold. / Now, if the harvest is over / And the world cold, / Give me the bonus of laughter / As I lose hold."

Robert Rollason

Date 1960 (published)

Nationality UK

Why It's Key To find a poet as popular as Betjeman, you have to look to Kipling, Tennyson, and Byron. His *Collected Poems* have sold more than 2.5 million copies – a staggering figure compared with any other twentieth-century poet in English. He was knighted in 1969 and became Poet Laureate in 1972.

Opposite John Betjemen

Key Book
Palace of the Peacock

Lauded for his lyrical prose, Wilson Harris communicates a highly sophisticated understanding of primordial questions and transcendental states of being. He muses provocatively on the conundrum of spiritual awareness and corporeal limitation, "I dreamt I awoke with one dead seeing eye and one living closed eye." Beyond what he refers to as the "womb of space," Harris explores a dreamscape through the topography of his native land, "The map of the savannahs was a dream. The names Brazil and Guiana were colonial conventions... They were an actual stage, a presence, however mythical they seemed to the universal and the spiritual eye." Harris speaks with authority on this matter, having explored the region of British Guiana in the 1940s as a Government surveyor.

Palace of the Peacock is one of those rare books that is a cultural melting pot of original and inspired ideas. Recalling Columbus' discovery of the Americas and the Enlightenment spurred on by the New World,

there is a sardonic aspect to the character of Donne, the main protagonist and spirit of a conquistador, who "had once dreamt of ruling them with a rod of iron and a ration of rum." Harris ebbs and flows between reality and dream, nestling complex philosophical ideas against keen psychological insight. Blithely swaying between binary metaphors, Harris frequently opposes form and experience to contradict one another. Harris explores themes such as original sin, and the darkness of human nature, in a quest to encompass greater spirituality by borrowing from the realms of the living and the dead simultaneously.

Alexandra Hamlyn

Date 1960

Author Wilson Harris (1921)

Nationality Guyana

Why It's Key After discarding three attempts at a first novel, it wasn't until *Palace of the Peacock* that Harris felt he had successfully embarked on a spiritual and imaginative journey into the heart of what was then British Guiana. He has since written more than 30 works of fiction, non-fiction, prose, and poetry.

Key Author **John Barth**
The Sot-Weed Factor

The title of John Barth's (1930–) *Lost in the Funhouse* (1968) aptly describes the experience of reading his work. Considered one of the premier American postmodernists, Barth's fiction has both anticipated and attempted to address several postmodern concerns. His third novel, *The Sot-Weed Factor* (1960), a sprawling, monster narrative, anticipated postmodern attempts to capture the complexity and totality of modern life in huge, encyclopedic novels. His explorations of the storytelling process and interaction between author and audience make him one of the first and best writers of metafiction.

While Barth's reputation as a "cerebral" and "academic" author has made him the object of scholarly study, Barth himself considers his work to be largely comic. His penchant, however, for dealing with philosophical topics such as nihilism – which his first three novels explore – or fiction-writing itself has continued to make him a darling of the academic world.

His 1967 essay "The Literature of Exhaustion" made him famous for arguing that the novel form had died, but, in fact, the essay argued that Modernism as an aesthetic approach was exhausted, not the novel. The essay was actually a survival guide for the novel, suggesting possible paths that novelists might take to give the genre continued relevance. As two of Barth's literary inspirations are *The Arabian Nights* and the Sanskrit *Ocean of Joy*, it is not surprising that one of the options he suggested in this essay – and which he himself has largely explored as a novelist – is to write fiction about fiction and fiction-writing, and, indeed, his metafiction *Chimera* won him the National Book Award in 1973.

Elizabeth Rosen

Date 1960 (published)

Nationality USA

Other Key Works *The Floating Opera* (1956)

Why It's Key Barth is one of the foremost writers of metafiction – fiction about fiction. Equally well known for his essays and critical work on literary studies, Barth is considered one of the fathers of American literary postmodernism. He was awarded the F. Scott Fitzgerald Award for outstanding achievement in American Literature in 1997.

Key Character **Atticus Finch**
To Kill a Mockingbird

SPOILER

Harper Lee wrote *To Kill a Mockingbird* in 1960 and in doing so created a moral hero for her times. Atticus Finch is a lawyer in Maycomb County, Alabama. To the consternation of the town's racist population Finch decides to act (for free) on behalf of a black man, Tom Robinson, accused of rape. Before the trial Finch shows great personal courage by facing down a lynch mob. During proceedings he demonstrates clearly that the father and daughter making the accusations are lying, yet despite this Robinson is convicted and dies attempting to escape. Finch's daughter Scout narrates the events that the family get caught up in during the late 1930s, and provides a nuanced, tender account of her father. Atticus is morally upright, gentle, proper, generous, and clear-sighted. He teaches Scout the value of tolerance, respect, and patience. In the opening sections of the novel he prevents her from mocking their slow neighbour, Boo Radley, and compels her to see things through others' eyes. This empathy is

key to his character. Finch's nobility and thoughtfulness throughout the book's events provide Scout, her brother Jem, and the reader with a moral compass despite the horrors that occur. The hagiographic account we have is of course inflected through Scout's eyes, but has been taken as gospel by legions of readers. Particularly as played by Gregory Peck in the 1962 film, Finch is the archetype of intelligent dissent against segregation and prejudice. Lee's novel won the Pulitzer Prize in 1961.

Jerome de Groot

Date 1960

Author Harper Lee (1926–)

Nationality USA

Why It's Key Harper Lee's upright lawyer who stands up against the ingrained racism of a small Southern town became a moral hero.

Opposite *Atticus Finch*

Key Book
The Open Door

Latifa Zayyat's novel *The Open Door*, published originally in Arabic in 1960, chronicles the memory of the recent triumphs, the obstacles, and the resolve that reflect this era of Egypt's modern history. *The Open Door* is of epic magnitude and is unique in its attempt to embody the spirit and ethos of the national project. There is no other novel in Egypt's literary history that attempts to represent the national collective spirit as *The Open Door* does.

The novel was considered daring at the time of its publication with its vivid descriptions of the sexual and political coming of age of a young middle-class Egyptian girl named Layla. The novel is about freedom and how young Layla and her older brother try to liberate themselves from the shackles of family control and society's expectations. Their fight for personal freedom is entangled with Egypt's own struggle for independence and their only means of succeeding is to challenge control imposed on them both on a personal and national level. Zayyat's use of colloquial Arabic was unprecedented, and the novel bubbles with the liveliest dialogue in modern Arabic literature. The brave conclusions that materialize through the narrative were both shocking and provoking. There are few women writers within this period of national consciousness who attempt to represent both the national narrative and the question of women's role within this movement. *The Open Door* is a landmark that helped shape a generation's political and social consciousness.
Maggie Awadalla

Date 1960 (Translated into English by Marilyn Booth, 2000)

Author Latifa Zayyat (1923–97)

Nationality Egypt

Why It's Key This novel is one of the first landmarks of national literature written by a woman in Egypt. The text constitutes a model of how, through national literature, new forms of literary language can emerge.

Key Event *Lady Chatterley's Lover* is the focus of a landmark obscenity trial

According to Philip Larkin, sexual intercourse began "between the end of the Chatterley ban and the Beatles' first LP." Although he was not the only person to credit D.H. Lawrence's most famous novel with kick starting a wave of sexual liberation, the book was actually first printed, privately, in 1928 in Florence. It was banned in many countries including Britain; some booksellers were imprisoned for selling it. When Penguin decided to print a cheap paperback edition in 1960, the Director of Public Prosecutions charged the publishers under the new Obscene Publications Act. The resulting trial became a testing ground for morality and art. Writers such as E.M. Forster argued that the book had considerable literary merit, a defence allowed under the act. The prosecuting barrister was judged hopelessly out of touch when he asked: "Is this a book you would wish your wife or servants to read?" The jury found Penguin not guilty.

What was all the fuss about? Firstly, there is the heroine, Constance Chatterley who has an affair with her husband's gamekeeper, Oliver Mellors. The story broke the taboos against extramarital sex and relationships outside one's class. Then there is Lawrence's use of four letter words to describe the sex act. Essentially though Lawrence's defenders were correct: his novel celebrates the sacredness of sexuality and the life-changing potential of an intimate connection between the right man and the right woman. Nevertheless, the title has never entirely shaken off its reputation as a byword for smut and the swinging sixties.
Kathy Watson

Date 1960

Title *Lady Chatterley's Lover* (1928)

Author D.H. Lawrence (1885–1930)

Nationality UK

Why It's Key The trial became a landmark in the history of censorship, as well as an emblem of the "swinging" sixties. Lawrence's original title for the novel was *Tenderness*.

Opposite Interest in *Lady Chatterley's Lover*

Key Book
The L-Shaped Room

Jane Graham is unmarried and pregnant and has been thrown out of the family home by her father. Having to face the stigma of being a single parent in the conservative 1950s, and lacking the emotional and financial support of her family, she takes a room in a dilapidated house in Fulham. The people she meets there renew her optimism and determination to face the future positively.

Reid Banks tackles social taboos frankly and unsentimentally and with an honesty that enabled many readers to empathise and identify with Jane's situation. As we have access to her story, we see that she does not conform to the stereotypes of women in her position: she is neither promiscuous nor uneducated, neither thoughtless nor irresponsible. Similarly, Jane must confront her own preconceptions when she shares a house with a Jewish writer, a black Jazz musician, and women who work as prostitutes. Her father's social conservatism, the very mindset that condemned her, is, after all, the same worldview that she was raised with. Such re-evaluation is liberating for Jane, and ultimately encourages her to develop confidence and a secure sense of self that remains unshaken by the narrow, judgemental outlook of others.

It is difficult now to fully appreciate how shocking the novel's subject matter was at the time of its publication. Reid Bank's sensitive treatment of controversial social issues is both affirmative and empowering, lauding the values of female independence and demonstrating the profound and wide-reaching impact that friendships can have.
Juliet Wightman

Date 1960

Author Lynne Reid Banks (1929–)

Nationality UK

Why It's Key For a generation of women, Lynne Reid Banks' novel served as an initiation into the adult world of prejudice, social inequality, the responsibilities of parenthood, and the possibility of female independence in a male-dominated culture.

Key Event **Harold Pinter achieves his first critical and commercial success**

Pinter's (1930–) ability to transform the patter of everyday life into powerful dramatic dialogue is one of the hallmarks of his innovative dramatic style, and *The Caretaker* is regarded as one of his greatest early plays. The plot revolves around the triangular relationship between two brothers, Mick and Aston, and their tramp lodger, Davies. The action is contained within a junk-filled room in Mick's flat and there is no real sense of the world beyond it. Both Aston and Mick make frequent but largely unexplained exits and both offer Davies the ill-defined role of Caretaker. The characters' backgrounds are sketchy, and the little that we do learn is cast into doubt by the emerging unreliability of all three characters. Aston claims to be doing up the flat in order for Mick to sell it but instead seems to spend his working days collecting more junk. Davies' repeated statement of his intention to travel to "Sidcup" to reclaim his belongings assumes a mythic quality in the face of his clear inability to leave the room. Mick's dream of the flat's "penthouse" potential is belied by the grim reality of the surroundings.

Pinter skilfully manipulates the nuances of everyday speech and behavior to expose the underlying power games at the heart of the characters' interactions. The relationships between the three men become increasingly unstable and a sense of the unknown pervades the play, leaving an audience teetering between laughter and fear. There is a dangerous edge to even the most comedic moments, of which it should be said, there are many. Early critics of Pinter's work were bewildered by the playwright's enigmatic dramatic style. However, Pinter has often rejected the idea of definitive interpretations or meaning. The fact that his work defies easy categorization can be seen as one of its strengths.
Kate Harris

Date 1960

Nationality UK

Why It's Key *The Caretaker* opened at the Arts Theatre in London on April 27th 1960 and a month later transferred to the Duchess Theatre in London's West End. In total the play ran for 444 performances. It is frequently revived and has been produced around the world. In time the adjective "Pinteresque" would be used to signify its atmosphere of restrained menace.

Opposite *The Caretaker*

Key Author **Yashpal**
Jhootha Sach

In 1929 Yashpal (1903–1976) detonated a bomb in an attempt to kill the Viceroy of India. He was hunted down, and in 1932, aged 28, sentenced to fourteen years' hard labor. While in prison this revolutionary man of violence became one of India's greatest fiction writers. He began writing in English, but soon vowed only to write in Hindi. The novel and short story were new developments in Hindi literature; their growth coincided with nationalism's growth, and nationalism was often their driving force – Yashpal's work is no exception.

Perhaps surprisingly, his direct and powerful stories often display quiet humor. With characters as seemingly remote as prostitutes in Delhi's red light district and Himalayan hill people, they focus on the lives of the poor and the need for reform, including women's freedoms (for example, "One Cigarette" (1955), "Purchased Happiness" (1959), and the novel *Divya* (1944), whose eponymous heroine becomes a prostitute in order to own her body).

One of his most scathing stories is "Sag," set in the August 1942 uprising. Two Indians are executed after killing an English family. The story is based perhaps on the execution of Yashpal's associate, Bhagat Singh. The English plant the revolutionaries' graves with fast-growing sag, or greens. The greens, nourished by Indian corpses, are harvested and sent to the Sahibs, and served at a banquet on crystal platters – by Indian servants who know where the greens have come from. This is a story about Indian abetting of British rule; the British government is run day-to-day by Indians; the executed men's jailors and guards are all Indian. But they are too wary of each other to voice their anguish. There is evidence that this story played a part in galvanising Indian nationalism.

Lucy Daniel

Date 1960 (published)

Nationality India

Other Key Works *Flights of a Caged Mind* (stories, 1939), *Post-mortem on Gandhism* (1941)

Why It's Key Also a key figure in Indian journalism, Yashpal founded the Hindi journal *Viplava* and its Urdu version, *Baagi*, in which political debate raged. Many considered his epic novel on partition, *Jhootha Sach* (*The False Truth*) Yashpal's masterwork.

Key Author **Attia Hosain**
Sunlight on a Broken Column

Educated in India before partition, Attia Hosain (1913–1998) belonged to a highly cultured and affluent Muslim family from Lucknow. She recalls her intellectual background to have been influenced by prominent figures of the Indian politics of the 1920–30s "who had two streams of thought at their highest level: their own indigenous culture and the western mind coming through their education, through their everything." Amongst these characters were important Muslim leaders and friends of her family such as Motilal and Jahwarlal Nehru, and M. A. Jinnah, who played a crucial role in the struggle for independence from British rule and strongly supported the partition cause. One other good friend of hers was Liaquat Ali Khan, Pakistan's first Prime Minister. The issue of partition strongly affected Hosain's life and work: after moving to London with her diplomat husband shortly before partition in 1947, she was later faced with the choice of following him back to Pakistan or of choosing her native – Indian – Lucknow. In a long interview which is published on her official website, Hosain explains she opted instead to settle down in London, supporting herself and her two children working part-time for the BBC before earning her life as a writer. Her first novel *Sunlight on a Broken Column* tells the story of three Indian generations sharing the same house and living in the midst of the political and economic turmoil resulting from partition. Yet it is also a reminiscent account of the country she belonged to, at times evoked melancholically through the eyes of teenage narrator Laila.

Letizia Alterno

Date 1961 (published)

Nationality India

Other Key Works *Phoenix Fled* (stories, 1953)

Why It's Key "…I grew up in an atmosphere where people spoke of what to do next, how to be involved, not only in the national movements but in the community, one had to be part of it." Hosain, a politically motivated, lyrical, and evocative writer about Indian society, has been a powerful influence on Indo-Anglian fiction.

Key Author
Junichiro Tanizaki

"Find beauty not only in the thing itself but in the pattern of the shadows, the light and dark which that thing provides." Tanizaki's words speak volumes. A product of his time, Tanizaki (1886–1965) was born in Tokyo and lived in the nearby port town of Yokohama, not long since opened for trade following Japan's two hundred years' seclusion. Surrounded by Western influences, Tanizaki's early ideals owe much to writers such as Poe, Wilde, and Baudelaire. However the Great Kanto Earthquake of 1923 was to shake the foundations of his home and of his cultural and artistic sensibilities.

With Tokyo in disarray, Tanizaki moved to Osaka, shifted his focus to the more traditional Kansai region and rediscovered old Japan. Early works such as *Manji* (1928) and *Some Prefer Nettles* (1929) reflect this change in attitude. The latter mirrors Tanizaki's own conflicts, as he pitches the cult of Western women against a rediscovery of the Japanese female. His essay *In Praise of Shadows* uses light and darkness to explore the differences between East and West, whilst Tanizaki's growing appreciation of the strong merchant class built upon traditional Japanese values shines through in his serial novel *The Makioka Sisters* (1943–48). Here he depicts a fading Japanese culture with rich characterization and fine storytelling. Surprisingly, Japanese military authorities deemed it too subversive for a wartime readership, left waiting until 1944.

Tanizaki's preoccupation with women surfaces again in his self-satirising tale of old-age fetishism – *Diary of a Mad Old Man* (1961). In keeping with his work, but diverging from traditional gender roles of Japanese literature, his male characters are mesmerised in masochistic worship of women. From feet to toilet habits nothing is too mundane for Tanizaki's erotic eye. But it is perhaps Tanizaki's softening of conflict and implicit acceptance of Western values that resonates most strongly today.
Sarah Birchwood

Date 1961

Nationality Japan

Why It's Key One of Japan's literary giants whose work covered themes as diverse as East meets West, man meets woman, and foot fetish meets coprophilia.

1960–1969

451

Key Book
The Wretched of the Earth

Frantz Fanon was born in Martinique, then a French colony, and became actively political as a teenager. He was part of the island's resistance which worked to undermine France's pro-Nazi Vichy government during the early years of World War II and when Martinique was liberated he volunteered to fight. Moving to France after the war to train as a psychiatrist, Fanon discovered that his war heroics (he received the Croix de Guerre) counted for little and that his color for much. His first book, *Black Skin, White Masks* (1952) related French racist attitudes as well as recounting the psychological effects of colonialism on the black population. He left France in 1953 to take a medical position in what was then French Algeria, becoming involved in the anti-colonial revolution of 1954 (the struggle would continue until liberation in 1962).

The Wretched of the Earth, published weeks before his death from leukaemia, is Fanon's rational and thoughtful critique of the colonial project. He is particularly interested in class, race, and culture in this text, arguing that to comprehend the effect of colony – and to have any chance of resisting it in an effective way – the complex relationship between these entities has to be understood. Jean-Paul Sartre wrote an introduction in which he suggested that the text advocated violence, despite the fact that Fanon was concerned throughout with the alienating and horrific effects of violent actions. For instance, he recounted the scarring effect of colonial policy in a key extract on the way in which repressive foreign powers practiced "cultural obliteration." This in particular was to be an influential way of theorising colonial practice, taken up by Homi Bhabha and Edward Said amongst others.
Jerome de Groot

Date 1961 (death)

Author Frantz Fanon (1925–1961)

Nationality France

Why It's Key Fanon was an influential anti-colonial writer whose work laid the basis for subsequent political struggle, and for postcolonial cultural theory.

Key Book
Stranger in a Strange Land

The science fiction of the late nineteenth and early twentieth century was very much for the enthusiast who revelled in flights to other planets and contact with aliens, whether hostile or otherwise. It was not until the publication of *Stranger in a Strange Land* that a work from within the genre was able to cross over into the mainstream and become a bestseller. The novel tells the story of Valentine Michael Smith, an orphan, the only survivor of an Earth mission to Mars. Smith has been raised by Martians, who have endowed him with paranormal abilities and attitudes that run counter to the human mores of the time. He returns to Earth and is perceived as a messianic figure, speaking of love and mutual understanding. Almost Christ-like, he is exploited, persecuted, and eventually killed, reappearing to devotees as an immortal spirit. Like Jesus, his message of love (and in Smith's case, very much of free sexual love) is contrasted with the intolerance, materialism, and urge to violence of the society in which he finds himself.

Heinlein was deeply interested in religion (the title is a Biblical reference, from Exodus), especially in the impact of the scientific advances of the twentieth century on Christianity. He sensed that in the early 1960s the times were indeed "a-changing," as Bob Dylan would have it, and saw that the use of a half-Martian hero would allow him to express ideas on morality and belief with a latitude that probably would not have been permitted in straight contemporary fiction. His novel became required reading among the "love generation" of the 1960s and 1970s.

Michael Munro

Date 1961

Author Robert A(nson) Heinlein (1907–1988)

Nationality USA

Why It's Key A classic of post-war science fiction, it was the first SF novel to break out of the genre's restrictions and become a bestseller. Apart from anything else, it is responsible for introducing the word "grok" to the English language as a "Martian" term meaning to understand on a deep and intuitive level.

452

Key Passage
Catch-22

"There was only one catch and that was Catch-22, which specified that a concern for one's safety in the face of dangers that were real and immediate was the process of a rational mind. Orr was crazy and could be grounded. All he had to do was ask; and as soon as he did, he would no longer be crazy and would have to fly more missions. Orr would be crazy to fly more missions and sane if he didn't, but if he was sane he had to fly them. If he flew them he was crazy and didn't have to; but if he didn't want to he was sane and had to."

Elevating paradox to new heights of philosophical, political, and even cosmic significance, *Catch-22* reads like *The Iliad* plagiarised by Groucho Marx. *Catch-22* very nearly wasn't *Catch-22* at all: having flirted with *Catch-18* (too similar to Leon Uris's *Mila 18*), *Catch-11* (too easily confused with Sinatra's *Ocean's 11* released in 1960), and even *Catch-14* (just simply not funny), Heller eventually decided that 22 was his magic number.

The vexed question of Orr's sanity expresses the "Catch-22" doctrine in its purest form: a nightmarish bureaucratic comedy where common sense is overwhelmed by nonsense, and issues of real import (life, death, survival) are relegated beneath petty rules and regulations. Yet, the concept suffuses almost every page of Heller's gloriously absurd and convoluted World War II novel. It is there in Yossarian's desire to "live forever or die in the attempt," in the ever-escalating number of missions the men have to fly, and in the rolling, surreal, parenthetical narrative structure of the plot itself.

Eventually, "Catch-22" expands to justify almost any belief system (whether military, governmental, patriotic, religious, familial) no matter how destructive, trivial or ridiculous. Naturally enough, Yossarian eventually concludes that "Catch-22" doesn't exist at all, save in the fevered imaginations of those around him. As he says: "Insanity is contagious… Everybody is crazy but us."

James Kidd

Date 1961

Author Joseph Heller (1923–1999)

Nationality USA

Why It's Key *Catch-22* initially received adulation and confused hostility. Now an acknowledged classic, it influenced wartime farces like *M*A*S*H* and comic writers like Howard Jacobson. The title has even become common currency: "Catch-22" best describes the absurd and destructive illogic that both causes wars and stems from them.

Opposite *Catch-22*

Key Book
Solaris

Solaris is Stanislaw Lem's best-known book and is widely considered, along with *The Ciberiad* (1965) and *His Master's Voice* (1968), his enduring masterpiece. It has been filmed twice: by the legendary Andrey Tarkovsky, and more recently Steven Soderbergh. It tells the story of astronaut and psychologist Kris Kelvin, who is sent to a remote research station orbiting the oceanic world of Solaris to investigate a series of strange occurrences there.

Apparently having a mind of its own, Solaris is capable of creating apparitions and independent physical beings. The philosophical crux of the book is in what it means to be fully human; the strange, mimetic envoys sent by Solaris to meet its human examiners allow Lem to explore this problem more or less directly.

Unusually in Science Fiction (a term Lem deplored – he was expelled from Science Fiction Writers of America in 1976 after being denounced as a Communist agent by none other than Philip K. Dick), *Solaris* describes an encounter between humans and an alien intelligence which is not humanoid. This meeting follows none of the conventions of "contact" in the way it is most often imagined. It allows for a much broader metaphysical or symbolic interpretation than had previously been the case in stories featuring encounters between humans and aliens, and consequently opened a whole new ground for SF writers. Solaris can only be documented, never explained, and its place in the universe, the implications it holds for human life and consciousness remain intangible, provocative.

Charles Beckett

Date 1961

Author Stanislaw Lem (1921–2006)

Nationality Poland

Why It's Key Its influence has extended beyond literature into philosophy, earning Lem the acclaim of Daniel Dennett and others, especially in the field of Artificial Intelligence. *Solaris* has also fired the imagination of filmmakers, famously, from the poetic critical interpretation of Tarkovsky, to Soderbergh's moody re-working.

Key Character **Miss Jean Brodie**
The Prime of Miss Jean Brodie

SPOILER

From the dialogues of Plato and Aristotle to *Goodbye Mr. Chips* (1932) and *A Separate Peace* (1959), the politics of the masculine classroom have long been a source of inspiration. But just when tales of maverick teachers and their pupils were becoming formulaic, Muriel Spark's Edinburgh schoolmistress Jean Brodie arrived to make the hackneyed genre sit up and pay attention.

A progressive teacher in a conservative 1930s school, Brodie insists on her methods because "there must be leaven in the lump." Like most memorable teachers, Brodie leads by example. She imbues her favorite pupils, the "Brodie set," with her passion for art, poetry, romantic love, and fascist politics, giving them colorful lessons from her own life story rather than the official curriculum. "I am putting old heads on your young shoulders," Miss Brodie says of her mission at Marcia Blaine School for Girls, "and all my pupils are the crème de la crème."

But inspiration can be a dangerous thing. Miss Brodie encourages a student to join Franco's army, and the girl dies when her train is attacked en route to Spain. Just as she is blind to the very real perils of fascism, Miss Brodie is equally unable to see dissent in her own ranks. She is dismissed from her position when she is accused of teaching fascism by a disgruntled member of the "Brodie set." Although she is defeated in the novel, the trail-blazing Miss Brodie has taken up a permanent position as one of pedagogical fiction's most iconic figures. Maggie Smith brought her to cinematic life in a 1969 Oscar-winning performance.

Dinah Roe

Date 1961

Author Muriel Spark (1918–2006)

Nationality UK

Why It's Key One of the most quotable heroines in twentieth-century fiction, Jean Brodie brings a fresh, female perspective to the well-explored territory of the classroom drama. "Give me a girl at an impressionable age," she says, "and she is mine for life."

Opposite *The Prime of Miss Jean Brodie*

Key Book
Revolutionary Road

A strong contender for bleakest novel ever written, *Revolutionary Road* is unsentimental, unremitting, and unbelievably well written. Constructed around the marriage of Frank and April Wheeler, it is a story of unfulfilled hopes and ideals torn apart. Set in a 1950s American suburb, it contains some of fiction's most gruelling scenes – from the opening amateur dramatics to the Wheelers' heart-rending final encounter over breakfast.

The book earned Yates rave reviews, not least from Tennessee Williams and Kurt Vonnegut, and a nomination at the 1962 American National Book Awards, where both it and *Catch-22* were beaten by Walker Percy's *The Moviegoer*. In an interview with *Ploughshares*, Yates later acknowledged that he failed to capitalize on this strong beginning: a decade after its publication, *Revolutionary Road* went out of print, and Yates's life spun out of control. A famously hard drinker, Yates once scandalized a writer's conference in

Vermont by running around naked and declaring he was the Messiah.

In this context, it was not entirely inappropriate that he was resurrected ten years after his death by a group of literary disciples who spread the word about his work in general, and *Revolutionary Road* in particular. Stewart O'Nan wrote a passionate panegyric in the *Boston Review*. Richard Ford added a eulogistic introduction to a 40th anniversary edition of *Revolutionary Road*, which was re-published in 2001 to a set of déjà vu rave reviews, not least from Julian Barnes and Nick Hornby. It now sits snugly as one of *Time* magazine's 100 Greatest Novels.

"Oh, sometimes, in my more arrogant or petulant moments, I still think *Revolutionary Road* ought to be famous," Yates said in 1971. Thanks to his talent and a few fairy godchildren, his wish has come true all over again.

James Kidd

Date 1961

Author Richard Yates (1926–1992)

Nationality USA

Why It's Key *Revolutionary Road* is so good that it is a classic of American literature twice over. Having fallen both out of fashion and print, *Revolutionary Road* was "rediscovered" in the twenty-first century when a pride of literary lions (Richard Ford and Russo chief among them) championed it back into life.

Key Character **George Smiley**
Call for the Dead

The character of George Smiley is one of Le Carré's most memorable creations. He is first introduced in *Call for the Dead* but reappears in many subsequent novels, particularly *Tinker, Tailor, Soldier, Spy* (1974), *Smiley's People* (1979) and *The Secret Pilgrim* (1991). He epitomizes the Cold War spy, being an experienced operative of MI6 (referred to throughout Le Carré's books as "The Circus"), but one who does not get to travel to exotic locations and romance beautiful women for Queen and Country. He is no debonair hero, but a rather short and plump middle-aged man with a notoriously unfaithful wife. He is a master of subterfuge, disinformation and dissimulation, which are the day-to-day weapons of the contemporary spy. He is not reckless but circumspect, living as he does in a world where double agents and the threat of betrayal are never far away, but he is courageous when he has to be. He is also ruthless enough to eliminate enemies himself, as when he kills the East German spy Dieter

Frey in this novel. He operates by means of his own formidable intelligence rather than depending on the gadgetry of the movie-style secret agent.

The James Bond brand of spy was and remains a popular type, but Smiley represents a more realistic portrayal of a counterintelligence agent. His world may be seedy and cynical rather than glamorous, but he too risks his life to defend his country against deadly enemies and he can never expect to be publicly rewarded for his services. The image that many people have of the character derives from the memorable portrayal by Alec Guinness in the BBC adaptation.

Michael Munro

Date 1961

First Appearance *Call for the Dead*

Author John Le Carré (pen-name of David Cornwell, 1931–)

Nationality UK

Why It's Key George Smiley made his first appearance in this novel, a new type of spy fiction which led a trend towards deglamorizing the genre. Smiley is not a slick, tough James Bond-like figure but a methodical, behind-the-scenes conspirator.

Key Character **Mr Biswas**
A House for Mr Biswas

Naipaul calls *A House for Mr Biswas* "the story of a man's search for a house and all that the possession of one implies." For Mohun Biswas, always Mr Biswas to the narrator, a house implies success, security, and independence (not least from the smothering embrace of his wife's family). We follow Biswas from his birth into a Hindu community in rural Trinidad early in the twentieth century to his death in the late 1940s, by which time he is at last a householder in Trinidad's capital and has fathered four children. Unlike his brothers, sent to work on the sugarcane estates, Biswas is propelled by a series of tragic and comic incidents into a variety of different occupations. He works in a rum-shop and as a sign-painter, trains to be a religious pundit, and runs a local store, before a brief period of satisfaction as an energetically inventive journalist.

Biswas marries into the extended Tulsi family, who pride themselves on their caste and wealth. While his irregular career frequently compels him to rely on the Tulsis for food and shelter, Biswas expends much wit at their expense, giving them nicknames, provoking them and mocking their pretensions to religious orthodoxy. Frustrated, not least in his literary aspirations, by the limitations of life in a restrictive family in a colonial society, Biswas is driven at times to irritability, despair and even breakdown. Although the house he finally acquires is shoddily jerry-built, the novel's clear-sighted but affectionate portrayal of Biswas poignantly conveys the significance of this achievement.

Paul Vlitos

Date 1961

Author V.S. Naipaul (1932–)

Nationality UK (born in Trinidad)

Why It's Key Like Naipaul's father, the writer Seepersad Naipaul (1906–1953), Mohun Biswas works as a journalist on a Trinidad newspaper. Naipaul gave the character Seepersad's wit and literary ambition, and drew heavily on the frustrations and achievements of his father's life.

1960–1969

457

Key Character **Binx Bolling**
The Moviegoer

Walker Percy's first novel, *The Moviegoer*, winner of the 1962 National Book Award, is arguably one of the most significant philosophical novels of the second half of the twentieth century. In Binx Bolling, the novel's protagonist, Percy provided a distinctly American counterpart to Albert Camus's Meursault by placing the existential hero within the steamy, vibrant, and profoundly religious backdrop of 1950s New Orleans.

Bolling is a successful Louisiana stockbroker suffering from alienation, which Percy felt was the condition of contemporary man. Bolling is so entrenched in the malaise of "everydayness" that he resolves to embark on a search to properly discover the reality that surrounds him. Bolling, however, is not a traditional questing knight; he engages in his mission with a disconcerting acquiescence and passivity, which suggests that, despite his desire for immersion, his search is initially mostly aesthetic; it potentially denies true interaction, and mirrors his experiences at the movies.

As Bolling is eventually forced into a position of responsibility towards his despairing and cynical cousin, and made to confront the loss of his stepbrother, he begins to understand that while a heightened perception of reality can help overcome malaise, true union with the world must move beyond aesthetic perception towards an ethical or spiritual involvement with other people. However, Bolling remains a disquietingly amorphous creation; his strange lack of agency causes the reader to look not at him, but through him, allowing one to share in Bolling's quest, and this provides the novel with its revelatory impact and moral impetus.

James Clements

Date 1961

Author Walker Percy (1916–1990)

Nationality USA

Why It's Key Percy initially studied to be a medical doctor, but eventually came to feel that "the more science progressed, the less it said about what it is like to be a man living in the world." He consequently decided he could be of more use as a "diagnostician" of the modern human condition.

Key Author **Katherine Anne Porter**
Ship of Fools

Porter (1890–1980) once declared that her "one fixed desire" in life was to be a good artist, which meant being "responsible to the last comma for what I write." Her stories reflect how seriously she took that responsibility: her luminous prose illuminates the problems of consciousness and conscience that are her chief preoccupations. Betrayal, illusions, the capacity of the mind to lie to itself: variations on the theme of truth, and its relationship to art, constitute Porter's great themes. "I shall try to tell the truth," she famously said, "but the result will be fiction." Her stories balance clear-sighted candor with sympathy for the characters poleaxed by her brutal honesty; her best stories tend to have a sting in the tail. Porter published only twenty-seven stories and short novels in the thirty years between her sudden authoritative arrival on the literary scene in 1930 with the publication of *Flowering Judas and Other Stories*, and the long novel, *Ship of Fools*, which she finally published 32 years later.

In 1939 she published *Pale Horse, Pale Rider*, which many readers consider her masterpiece. *Ship of Fools*, although popular, fared less well critically: its allegory of the moral failures that led to the catastrophes of Nazism and World War II is considered strained by many readers, and lacking in the subtlety that characterizes Porter's best work.

Sarah Churchwell

Date 1962 (published)

Nationality USA

Why It's Key Porter was nominated three times for a Nobel Prize in Literature, but never won. Primarily known for her short stories, Porter refused to publish much of what she wrote, judging it inadequate. At 72, she published her first novel, *Ship of Fools*, which became a bestseller; five years later Porter's *Collected Stories* won both the Pulitzer Prize and the National Book Award.

Opposite Katherine Anne Porter

Key Book
Pale Fire

The *Pale Fire* reader will confront a textual collision. On the page, there is "Pale Fire" – a 999-line poem in four cantos by a deceased (fictional) American poet, John Shade. Also on the page is the "commentary" by Charles Kinbote, Shade's neighbor, who has taken it upon himself to edit the poem. Rather than illuminating Shade's work, however, Kinbote's additions become their own perplexing narrative – one that intimates Kinbote's pathological narcissism and casts a sinister light upon the circumstances of Shade's death.

The peculiar clash of texts invites interpretation; indeed, Nabokov professed that *Pale Fire* "is full of plums that I keep hoping somebody will find." While Shade's poem is a relatively uncomplicated meditation on pivotal incidents in his life; Kinbote's commentary – his obscure footnotes that latch like parasites onto the text proper – becomes a textual labyrinth from which there seems to be no escape. One path in Kinbote's maze is a story about Charles II Xavier, the deposed

king of the "distant northern land" of Zembla, who escapes imprisonment by Soviet-backed revolutionaries. Thus, one of the novel's many disconcerting mysteries: is Kinbote actually Charles Xavier, living incognito – or is Kinbote's bizarre tale a product of his own delusional, paranoid mind?

In addition to its enigmatic content, Nabokov's fourteenth novel is remarkable for its formal inventiveness, which anticipates a hypertextual aesthetic. The layered, non-linear narrative is an intertextual tour de force, referencing writings by Coleridge, Eliot, Frost, Joyce, Proust, Sherlock Holmes, and countless others. Expressing the complexity and instability of experience, identity, history, and literary narrative itself, *Pale Fire* is a crossword puzzle in novel form – but without the definitive answer key.

Kiki Benzon

Date 1962

Author Vladimir Nabokov (1899–1977)

Nationality Russia, naturalized U.S.

Why It's Key The phrase "Pale Fire" is taken from Shakespeare's *Timon of Athens*: "The moon's an arrant thief, / And her pale fire she snatches from the sun" (VI, iii). Just as the moon assumes its brightness from the sun, Nabokov's Kinbote usurps the literary spotlight from the talented poet, Shade.

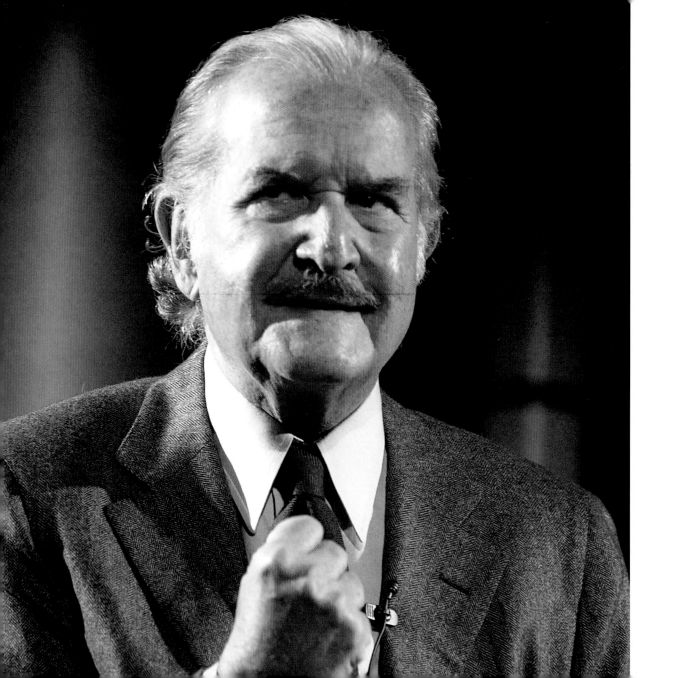

Key Author **Carlos Fuentes**
The Death of Artemio Cruz

Carlos Fuentes Macías (1928–) was born to a cosmopolitan Mexican family of diplomats stationed abroad, a fact that would mark his conflicting relationship with Mexican culture and identity during his entire career as a writer. Educated in Chile, the United States, Switzerland, and Mexico, Fuentes speaks English and French fluently, a determining factor in his efforts to internationalize Latin American literature during the sixties and seventies, the process known as the "Boom" of the Latin American novel. For a relatively short period Fuentes worked as Mexican ambassador to Paris (1973-1976) only a few years after having been declined entrance to the United States for his critical views of American imperialistic interventions in Latin America and elsewhere. His first novel, Where the Air is Clear (1958), a satire of industrialization and its effects on Mexico City – pollution, social marginalization, neo-colonialism, and cultural dependency on the U.S. – projected him as the enfant terrible of the Mexican

nationalist intelligentsia. Author of 30 novels, plays, essays, screenplays, and documentaries, he was the recipient of the Cervantes Award, the most prestigious award for Spanish language writers. His major novels *The Death of Artemio Cruz*, *Terra Nostra*, *The Old Gringo*, *Christopher Unborn*, and *The Campaign* intermingle history and fiction in carnivalesque ways to provoke a critical rewriting of official histories and sanctioned narratives. Similarly, some of his short stories – "Chac Mool," "The Crystal Frontier," and "The Orange Tree" – stage the cultural conflicts posed by modernity and the thorny relations among the different ethnic layers of Mexican identity. His novella *Aura* (1962) is perhaps his single most read work and offers a turn of the screw – following Henry James – in this exploration of the continued presence of history.
Pedro García-Caro

Date 1962

Nationality Mexico

Other Key Works *Terra Nostra* (1975); *The Old Gringo* (1985); *Christopher Unborn* (1987); *The Campaign* (1991)

Why It's Key One of the most influential Latin American writers of the century, Fuentes was a key figure in the Latin American literary "Boom."

Opposite Carlos Fuentes

Key Book
The Fire Next Time

The Fire Next Time (first published in *The New Yorker* as "Letter from a Region in My Mind") is a passionate plea for social justice that still carries resonance today. Written at a time when the U.S. was plagued by racial turmoil, the essay charts the author's personal development from the age of fourteen. Determined to avoid the drugs, poverty, and destitution around him in Harlem, Baldwin became a preacher. He soon became disillusioned with the sectarian Christian message which claimed God was white and that love extended only to those, "who believed as we did." Baldwin then turns his attention to the Nation of Islam, a movement which offered an alternative for those from whom "everything had been taken away, including hope." While he agrees with many of the moral arguments, Baldwin finds The Nation of Islam's solution to be no less problematic. God is black, whites are devils, and Islam is to rule the world: "The sentiment is old; only the color is new."

Struggling to make sense of the racial hatred that was tearing America apart, Baldwin argued for a complete rethink. In order to survive, he wrote, America needed to stop thinking of itself as a white nation. Unless it recognized its diverse nature the country risked destruction. Black and white had to accept they needed one another if they were ever "to achieve our country and change the history of the world."

The essay's title comes from a spiritual sung in the days of slavery: "God gave Noah the rainbow sign, no more water, the fire next time."
Jamal Mahjoub

Date 1962

Author James Baldwin (1924–1988)

Nationality USA

Why It's Key In addition to one of his most enduring and popular novels, *Another Country*, in 1962 Baldwin also wrote and published this essay, illustrating many of the ideas underlying that novel. The "other country" of the title is that which America needs to become if it is to avoid its own self-destruction through the continued persecution of its black population.

Key Book
Sex and the Single Girl

Forget *The Rules*. Put down *Women Who Love Too Much*. This is the original self-help relationship book for women. A 1962 bestseller by Helen Gurley Brown – who went on to become international editor-in-chief of *Cosmopolitan* – it is one of the defining books of 1960s women's liberation. It unashamedly asserted that it was okay to be single in your thirties and totally acceptable to have sex with a man you weren't married to. Clearly written in the days before sexual harassment in the office was identified as a problem with legal consequences, she assumes that many women would be having affairs with their (married) bosses.

The title is fabulously racy but the real message of the book is independence and self esteem and much of her advice is sound common sense. Buy good quality clothes, make the most of your looks but don't obsess over them (they vanish anyway), enjoy the company of men (but don't rely on them), and, above all, get a good job. "Nobody likes a poor girl," she warns, "She is just a drag." A man might leave a woman "like dishes in a sink" so it was important to work hard, get a broker and a portfolio of shares, and buy a nice apartment.

This remained Brown's message for the rest of her working life. For over 40 years and in more than 100 countries, the magazine she launched has preached the gospel of self-reliance and sound personal finance along with some dating tips and features on how to understand the male mind. Cosmo Girl was born in this book.

Kathy Watson

Date 1962

Author Helen Gurley Brown (1922)

Nationality USA

Why It's Key Brown's book was made into a 1964 film starring Natalie Wood and Tony Curtis. The script was written by *Catch-22* author, Joseph Heller.

Key Character
Spider-Man

Surely not even Stan Lee (1922–) and Steve Ditko (1927–), the joint creators of Marvel Comics' Spider-Man, could have foreseen just how popular and iconic the wall-crawling superhero would become in the latter decades of the twentieth century. First appearing in 1962 in *Amazing Fantasy Number 15*, Spider-Man was such a hit with comic book readers that he was granted his own title, *The Amazing Spider-Man*, a year later. Even to those who have never read a comic book in their lives, Spider-Man ranks alongside Superman and Hulk as one of the most instantly recognizable images in contemporary western culture.

When teenager Peter Parker is bitten by a radioactive spider at a science fair, he develops strange new powers including increased strength, the ability to climb walls, and the famous "Spidey-sense," which allows him to detect potential danger. After designing a blue and red costume and inventing web shooters which allow him to swing effortlessly from building to building, Peter is ready to fight crime as his alter-ego, Spider-Man, always reminding himself that "With great power comes great responsibility."

Spider-Man personifies the central tenets of the Silver Age of comic books: a young man whom teenagers could identify with, whose powers were often a burden as much as a gift and who had to contend not only with villains such as the Green Goblin and Doctor Octopus, but also with the demands of homework and a social life. His popularity shows no sign of abating in the twenty-first century.

Tim Stafford

Date 1962

Nationality USA

Why It's Key A poll of U.S. college campuses in *Esquire* magazine in 1965 showed that Spider-Man (in addition to Che Guevara) was considered a popular revolutionary icon. If there is any doubt as to his continuing popularity, one need look no further than the box-office takings for Sam Raimi's Spider-Man movie trilogy.

Opposite Spider-Man

Key Character **Randle P. McMurphy**
One Flew Over the Cuckoo's Nest

In 1959 Ken Kesey volunteered for a project entitled MKULTRA at the Menlo Park Veterans Hospital in California. The controversial project investigated the effect of hallucinogenic and psychoactive drugs on human subjects. Whilst participating Kesey worked the nightshift at the hospital and spent some time with psychiatric patients; he took the same drugs as them and underwent similar treatment (including electroconvulsive therapy) in order to understand them further. These two experiences profoundly influenced the writing of his first and most important novel, *One Flew Over the Cuckoo's Nest*, combining as it does an understanding of the potentials of the human mind with a clear sense that patients in psychiatric hospitals are not necessarily insane but merely cast out by a society which failed to understand them and was made uncomfortable by them.

The novel takes place in an unnamed asylum and concerns the events following the admission of Randle P. McMurphy, transferred from a criminal prison. McMurphy is a lazy, shambolic rebel who is shocked by the repressive rules instituted by the ward's director Nurse Ratched to control the men in her care. His dissent involves refusing treatment, gambling, drinking, and the smuggling in of women, and the consequences of this clash with authority are the eventual suicide of an inmate and the final lobotomizing of McMurphy himself. McMurphy is such a symbol of freedom for the inmates that the narrator, Chief Bromden, decides to kill him rather than let him live in a bleak, dead vegetative state. McMurphy is famously a rebel and a fighter but Kesey's impassioned call for freedom seems outdated now; and McMurphy's final attack on Nurse Ratched is an act of ugly sexualized violence that readers generally find disturbing.
Jerome de Groot

Date 1962

Author Ken Kesey (1935–2001)

Nationality USA

Why It's Key Randle P. McMurphy is a pivotal representation of 1960s rebellion against institutional repression.

464

Key Book
The Lovers' Forest

Yaoi refers to works of literature and art including manga and anime which focus on sexually explicit male homosexual relationships where the older man is often depicted as a masculine, powerful, and self-controlled figure who protects and spoils an extremely beautiful yet frivolous young man. Born of a French aristocrat and a daughter of a Japanese diplomat, Guido de Guiche is a fabulously wealthy man with physical beauty and literary gifts. One night at a bar he casually picks up Paulo, an ethereally beautiful novice pleasure-seeker whose "innocent vice or cunningness stings Guido… like the first thorn in pale red that a rose shoots out." Their relationship quickly deepens, to the great agony of Guido's 48-year-old mistress Mrs. Ueda, who eventually shoots her lover dead. When he discovers Guido's body, Paulo roams through a park in grief. In no time, however, he finds himself whistling a tune lightly to himself when he becomes aware of the amorous glances of Raymond, an older and darker alter ego of Guido, who we know has been waiting in the wings all along.

Like her father Ogai Mori, one of the leading writers of the Meiji period, Mori is an unflinchingly self-indulgent aestheticist, and her description of the two beautiful lovers is tinted all over with lush details of Occidentalist romanticism; Paulo would lazily sip his martini from "a gold-rimmed olive-colored Venetian glass" with a nonchalant air like that of "a Parisian courtesan." Guido can be seen as a projection of her father, in whom she saw such paternal virtues as we find in Guido; Ogai, however, was not in the slightest way "beau" as the lovers in her fictional world all are. Unlike Dorian Gray, Paulo is forever immune from decay, safely encapsulated in Mori's thick imaginary forest.
Mayako Murai

Date 1962

Author Mari Mori (1903–1987)

Nationality Japan

Why It's Key *The Lovers' Forest*, Mori's 1962 novella about the fatal relationship between Guido, a 38-year-old libertine, and Paulo, a beautiful 18-year-old slacker, anticipated a subcultural movement known today as *yaoi*, which originated in Japan in the late '70s and has spread throughout the world.

Key Event *Silent Spring* inspires the environmental movement

During the 1950s, Rachel Carson, a zoologist and marine biologist who had worked for the U.S. Fish and Wildlife Service, became increasingly concerned about the effects of new chemical pesticides on the environment. Insecticides such as DDT – used to eliminate the mosquitoes that carry malaria, the lice that carry typhus, and a whole host of insect "pests" that feed on agricultural crops – were being hailed as the saviors of humanity. But Carson realized that things were not that simple, and laid out her findings in a new book, *Silent Spring*. "Over increasingly large areas of the United States," wrote Carson, "spring now comes unheralded by the return of the birds, and the early mornings are strangely silent where once they were filled with the beauty of bird song." What was happening, Carson pointed out, was that chemicals like DDT were concentrating higher up the food chain, interfering with the ability of insect-eating birds, and the birds of prey that fed on these birds, to breed.

Exposure to the chemicals then being freely dumped into waterways and the atmosphere was also hazardous to human health, argued Carson.

Inevitably there was huge opposition to her arguments from the chemical industry and other vested interests, but Carson had the support of many scientists, and the whole issue became a matter of public debate. But Carson did not live to see the ban imposed in the 1970s in many countries on the use of DDT for agricultural purposes, nor the flowering of the environmental movement that she had inspired.
Ian Crofton

Date 1962

Author Rachel Carson (1907–1964)

Nationality USA

Why It's Key The book that kick-started the modern environmental movement.

1960-1969

465

Key Event **The attempted assassination of Charles de Gaulle inspires Forsyth**

In August 1962 Jean-Marie Bastien-Thiry and members of the French nationalist Organisation de l'armée secrète (OAS) attempted to assassinate President Charles de Gaulle in the Parisian suburb of Petit-Clamart. De Gaulle's government had overseen a referendum on the independence of Algeria in which the country had voted overwhelmingly to cede the colony its freedom. The OAS attempted to prevent this through a campaign of bombings and the attempt on de Gaulle's life (the president miraculously escaped). The assassination attempt inspired the English writer Frederick Forsyth to write *The Day of the Jackal* about an imagined further plot instigated by the OAS and undertaken by an anonymous mercenary. Forsyth has the unnamed man, codenamed "Jackal," create an elaborate back story for himself to foil police attempts to catch him; he forges documents and sets up a number of aliases. The novel is assiduously plotted, carefully thought out and, most importantly, realistic.

The long processes the Jackal goes through to steal an identity, gather information, distance himself from his funders, and particularly his practical, unemotional approach to the assassination became the model for political spy thrillers subsequently. Forsyth's novel introduced a procedural element to the genre, and this particularity clearly helped with the creation of suspense and the audience's belief in the plot. The novel was extremely influential on thriller writers around the world and its grim afterlife includes giving the nickname to the terrorist Carlos "the Jackal" Sanchez and being found in possession of Yigal Amir, the killer of Yitzhak Rabin.
Jerome de Groot

Date 1962

Title *The Day of the Jackal* (1971)

Author Frederick Forsyth (1938–)

Nationality UK

Why It's Key Forsyth was inspired by this event to write his masterly procedural thriller *The Day of the Jackal*.

Key Passage "Nadsat" slang from *A Clockwork Orange*

"We fillied round what was called the backtown for a bit, scaring old vecks and cheenas…. Then we saw one young malchick with his sharp, lubbilubbing under a tree so we stopped… we bashed into them both with a couple of half-hearted tolchocks… we were after the old surprise visit. That was real kick and good for smecks and lashings of the old ultra-violent."

A *Clockwork Orange* is a dystopia set in London some time in the immediate future. When it was published in 1962 there had been nothing like it in English fiction. In its narrator, Alex, Burgess has given the reading public a classic teenage anti-hero, who still has currency in today's society. He is just fifteen years old, a member of a gang and he tells the story of his youthful rebellion, his conditioning to be good, and his final renunciation of violence. To do this he uses "Nadsat," a slang that uses bits of cockney rhyming slang and Russian (amongst other varieties of language). Although initially difficult to read, the language is not impossible to understand as its meaning is derived in the context of the narration ("malchick" and "lubbilubbing," for example). The language works to draw the reader in to the private world of the teenager, and interestingly, it simultaneously distances them from the violence. Although often criticised for its violence, this is a very moral novel that engages in a debate on free will. Burgess shows that the violence perpetrated by Alex is a form of choice and that the state's crime in taking away Alex's free will (under conditioning to be a model citizen) is the same, if not greater, than Alex's crimes. That is why, in the final part of the novel, Alex, now free from conditioning, chooses to change his ways and settle down. This complex and demanding novel remains a classic of British fiction

Pat Wheeler

Date 1962

Author Anthony Burgess (1917–1993)

Nationality UK

Why It's Key The abolition of National Service in the '60s was blamed for the rise in juvenile delinquency and young people were demonized for their indiscretions. The novel taps into this period of moral panic, with "Nadsat" cleverly highlighting the "otherness" of the new youth culture that was sweeping Britain.

Opposite *A Clockwork Orange*

1960–1969

467

Key Author
Robert Frost

Robert Frost (1874–1963) was born in San Francisco in 1874 and moved to Massachusetts with his family after the death of his father. In 1894 his first poem, "My Butterfly: An Elegy," was published in the New York Independent. The following year he married Elinor White. They had six children, two of whom died in infancy.

From 1897 to 1899 Frost studied at Harvard, leaving without a degree. His many attempts at running farms were mostly unsuccessful and the family was poor. Frost moved the family to England, where, aged 39, he published his first book, *A Boy's Will*; his second brought international acclaim: "One of the most revolutionary books of modern times," wrote his friend, critic Edward Thomas in *The Daily Times*. Upon returning to America Frost worked as an English professor at Amherst college from 1916 to 1938. After a series of personal tragedies in the 1930s, Frost published *A Witness Tree* (1942) which included the darker poems he considered his finest.

Often regarded as an unofficial Poet Laureate, Frost continued to travel widely giving readings and lectures and representing the United States on official missions, including a meeting with Soviet leader Nikita Khrushchev. In 1961 he recited his poems at the inauguration of President John Kennedy. He published over thirty books of poems, and was awarded four Pulitzer Prizes – an achievement unequalled by any other poet. His many honorary degrees included those from Oxford and Cambridge.

Frost's broad and enduring appeal is that he used the language and experiences of everyday rural life, creating poems imbued with deeper, hidden meanings.

Elizabeth Whyman

Date 1963 (death)

Nationality USA

Other Key Works *Mountain Interval* (1916), *New Hampshire* (1923), *In the Clearing* (1962)

Why It's Key "Robert Frost… is more than a New England poet: he is more than an American poet; he is a poet who can be understood anywhere by readers versed in matters more ancient and universal than the customs of one country, whatever that country is" (*The Atlantic Monthly* Vol. 187, No.6).

Key Event **40 years after first publication**
The Prophet achieves massive success

Born in Lebanon, Kahlil Gibran (1883–1931) emigrated to the United States as a young teenager. He attracted attention as both an artist and poet before publishing *The Prophet* in 1923. Written in English, it is a collection of short pieces of poetical prose cast as philosophical observations by the prophet Almustafa. In Lebanon Gibran's family were Maronite Christians and he claimed that this influenced his beliefs as well as his familiarity with the Bahai faith. He also absorbed elements of the philosophy of Nietzsche and the poet William Blake.

The Prophet was only moderately successful when it was originally published and the author died in relative obscurity. However, when the work was rediscovered by the counterculture of the 1960s, it was seized upon as offering mystical guidance by many who had lost faith in traditional religion but still sought a spiritual dimension in their lives. Although the book was written and published in America, most of its

readers assumed it had been written by an "Eastern" mystic, and this chimed with other eastern philosophies that were being explored in the west at the time, including Zen Buddhism and Taoism. The following are among its most-quoted lines: "The soul walks not upon a line, neither does it grow like a reed. / The soul unfolds itself, like a lotus of countless petals." Also well-known are these lines, often used in "alternative" wedding vows: "Love gives naught but itself and takes naught but from itself. / Love possesses not nor would it be possessed; / For love is sufficient unto love."

Michael Munro

Date 1963

Author Kahlil Gibran

Nationality USA (born Lebanon)

Why It's Key One of the aspects of the counterculture that arose in the '60s was an exploration of mysticism, especially that of the East, with many people seeking spiritual truth from alternative sources. *The Prophet* was the most popular work to benefit from this trend.

Opposite **Kahlil Gibran**

Key Author **Julio Cortázar**
Hopscotch (*Rayuela*)

Born in Brussels, brought up in Argentina, but ultimately cosmopolitan, Cortázar (1914–1984) lived much of his adult life in self-imposed exile in Paris. Always politically engaged, he supported the Cuban revolution, Salvador Allende, and the Sandinista government in Nicaragua, to whom he donated royalties from his later books. He was conferred French citizenship by Mitterand in 1981, and died in Paris in 1984.

His most celebrated novel, *Hopscotch* (*Rayuela*) is the story of Horacio Oliveira, bibliophile, *flâneur*, and barroom philosopher, who we follow through the streets of Paris and then to his native Buenos Aires. The reader is offered two routes through the novel: to read the first 56 chapters in traditional linear fashion, or to follow an alternative sequence which interleaves a set of additional ("expendable") chapters. Often hailed as decades ahead of its time, and variously described as an "antinovel" or a "hypertext novel," it is its

intriguing experimental structure and creative use of language that make *Hopscotch* special, rather than the shaggy-dog plot or the often irritatingly pretentious and self-absorbed characters.

Cortázar's true genius, however, lies in his short stories – surreal, frequently disturbing, and always unforgettable. A wealthy landowner is murdered by his wife and her lover, themselves characters in the novel he is reading; an unnamed narrator finds himself metamorphosed into an exotic fish; a pullover turns homicidal; a peerless orchestral performance ends in an act of mass cannibalism by the haut-bourgeois audience. From innocuous, even humdrum, openings, we are whirled off into a dark world of obsession and nightmare. Antonioni's archetypal "Swinging London" film *Blow-Up* was loosely based on one of his many macabre and compelling short stories.

Cathy Benson

Date 1963

Nationality Argentina

Other Key Works *End of the Game and Other Stories* (*Final del juego* [1956]), *All Fires the Fire and Other Stories* (*Todos los fuegos el fuego* [1966]), *Ceremonias* (1968)

Why It's Key Cortázar was a major figure of the Latin-American literary "Boom" and was held in the highest esteem by fellow writers. Neruda famously claimed that "People who do not read Cortázar are doomed."

Key Book
The Ice Palace

Siss and Unn mirror each other: the same age (eleven), the same height, with the same hair. Fascinated, alone in Unn's bedroom, they stare at each other in the mirror, then undress. This narcissistic "game of enticement" has a strong sexual undercurrent but also powerful innocence, which combine to create emotional confusion.

As Siss runs home, spooked, through the frosted woods, at night, the atmospheric evocation of the elemental world of ice, cold, and fear of the dark begins, and so does an extended meditation on equally elemental, yet obscure, emotions.

The ice palace is a waterfall encased in ice that resembles a palace. In order to avoid Siss and drawn to the silent world of ice, Unn wants it to become thicker and thicker; "the more enticing it was, the more right it was." Lost in a forest of ice, she enters a room where the ice seems to be weeping, its walls running with water. It echoes her own voice back to her. Gradually paralysed by the cold, she dies in the ice palace.

Nobody knows where Unn has gone, and the rest of the book is a search for her until finally the ice palace melts, destroying itself in the night, without witnesses. The lure of the ice is danger and beauty and something unfulfilled. This extraordinarily enigmatic little book keeps its secrets, like the ice itself, and like the adolescent girls at its center. Written in 1955, and by a man, its subject is perhaps an encoded idea of lesbian love, kept hidden, frozen, and congealed within a world of ice, and yet that explanation does not fully satisfy; the ice palace has more twisting cavities that lead to deeper, darker psychic places.
Lucy Daniel

Date 1963

Author Tarjei Vesaas (1897–1970)

Nationality Norway

Why It's Key "Something strange had happened." In Vesaas' enigmatic work, this is the only thing of which the reader can be completely sure. The impreciseness of that something, and the power of that strangeness make *The Ice Palace* such a captivating and unforgettable novel.

Key Book
Where the Wild Things Are

Where the Wild Things Are is a richly atmospheric picture book which has endured through decades and generations and retained its singular power to intrigue and disturb. Rather than offering the gentle adventures in sunny idylls common to fiction for this age group, author and illustrator Maurice Sendak explores a darker side of childhood – to the extent that this book was warily received by many when it was first published in 1963, amidst concerns that children would find it too frightening. *Where the Wild Things Are* is a poetic, multi-levelled, libidinally-charged text which focuses on the anarchic energies and emotional intensities of the child, and demonstrates the importance of fantasy in the expression and exploration of these feelings. Anti-hero Max (whose very name signals exuberance and excess) is first seen running amok in a wolf suit, hanging his teddy bear, menacing the family dog with a fork, and threatening to devour his mother. Confined to his room, Max experiences a cathartic fantasy adventure in the land of the Wild Things – magnificent, toothy, yellow-eyed monsters whom he subjugates with a hard stare then leads in a "wild rumpus." Finally, with his energy spent and tempted by the smell of his supper, Max sails away from his fantasy world and returns to his room, wearing an apparently docile smile. The book won the prestigious Caldecott Medal in 1964, and has inspired many adaptations and tributes, including an opera, a ballet, an episode of *The Simpsons*, and a song by Metallica.
Anna Tripp

Date 1963

Author Maurice Sendak (1928–)

Nationality USA

Why It's Key "We'll eat you up we love you so": Maurice Sendak eschews cuteness and sentimentality in order to explore the fierce love, consuming rages, and vivid fantasy life of the young child in this revolutionary 1960s picture book.

Opposite *Where the Wild Things Are*

Key Book
The Grifters

Barring two disappointing late efforts, just about any of Jim Thompson's 50-something novels could convey his impact on twentieth-century writing. Composed rapidly for the pulp fiction market, stories like *The Kill-Off* and *Savage Night* combine the punchy prose, underworld settings and troubled outsiders that define much American hard-boiled fiction.

What distinguishes Thompson is the complexity of the characters' relationships, the macabre, even surreal action they inspire, and the inventive narratives that twist reader expectations around Thompson's trigger finger. "There are 32 ways to write a story," he once said, "and I have used every one, but there is only one plot – things are not what they seem." Little wonder that Stanley Kubrick hired Thomspon to write *The Killing* and *Paths of Glory*, or that Stephen King and Quentin Tarantino are fans.

Things not being what they seem is writ large across *The Grifters*, a novel shaped by the Oedipal love triangle surrounding Roy Dillon, his mother, Lilly (only 14 years his senior), and Moira Langtry, Roy's girlfriend and a dead-ringer for Lilly. Triple crosses abound in a tale of confidence tricks, murder, moral decay and sexual obsession that ends by destroying two of Thompson's main trio.

And yet, as Tim Willocks has noted, a strangely tender note sounds throughout this bleakest of novels, in a way that the film adaptation did not allow. This reversal of the norm means that while John Cusack's portrayal of Roy leaves no room for redemption, Thompson's does – or almost. "And for a moment, he almost relented," Thompson writes, describing a defining confrontation between Roy and his mother. "He almost pitied her."

James Kidd

Date 1963

Author Jim Thompson (1906–1977)

Nationality USA

Why It's Key Every genre giant from James Ellroy to Thomas Harris owes Thompson's fast-moving but psychologically profound stories a debt of gratitude. Comparable to Dostoevsky had he just read his Sherlock Holmes, *The Grifters* is probably the most famous of the lot, thanks partly to Stephen Frears's excellent 1989 film.

Key Character **Enderby**
Inside Mr Enderby

Like the early work of Evelyn Waugh, the Enderby novels rail against modern life by following the adventures of an innocent who is plucked out of a cosy existence and exposed to the cruelty and vulgarity of the wider world. But Enderby is a much more rounded character than any of Waugh's. Burgess presents him as the archetype of the dedicated poet, subsisting on meagre meals while he spends his life writing (mostly in the lavatory), refusing (in one memorable scene) the prizes offered by philistines, avoiding emotional entanglement. But then Enderby marries the beautiful, shallow Vesta Bainbridge and Burgess punishes him for this lapse from his devotion to the Muse by sending him on a series of misadventures that covers the globe and lasts for four books.

Enderby is an unattractive figure in many ways: heedless of other people's feelings, constantly trying to suppress unpleasant bodily noises. But his commitment to his unprofitable art earns him a sort of nobility, especially when he is compared with such undeservedly successful figures as the Lennonesque rocker Yod Crewsy (for the attempted murder of whom Enderby is framed) or the psychologist Dr Wapenshaw, who (in a seeming parody of Burgess's earlier book *A Clockwork Orange*) brainwashes Enderby into giving up poetry so that he can become a useful member of society – a barman. Burgess's ornate style, which can appear overblown in his other novels, seems perfect here for capturing the discrepancy between Enderby's high ideals and the petty humiliations he suffers.

Jake Kerridge

Date 1963

Author Anthony Burgess (1917–1993)

Nationality UK

Other Key Works *Enderby Outside* (1968); *The Clockwork Testament,* or *Enderby's End* (1974); *Enderby's Dark Lady,* or *No End of Enderby* (1984)

Why It's Key Burgess exposes the horrors of the modern world by allowing disaster to befall the meek poet Enderby.

Key Character **Mrs. Robinson**
The Graduate

Benjamin Braddock, the main character of *The Graduate*, is the epitome of an isolated young male worried about his future life. Having recently graduated, he returns to his parents' house and during their proud homecoming party, he meets one of their friends, a bored Brentwood housewife, Mrs. Robinson. As Dustin Hoffman, playing Benjamin in the iconic 1967 movie, seriously states to Anne Bancroft's superbly acted Mrs. Robinson, "I find you the most attractive of all my parents' friends."

Mrs. Robinson seduces the virginal Ben, and is adept at handling their subsequent adulterous affair. A heavy drinker and frustrated housewife who no longer sleeps in the same bedroom as her husband never mind having sex with him, she solely wants Ben for sex, as she finds him young and attractive. Her whole sexual attitude was shocking; although *The Graduate* was published in the so-called swinging sixties, the USA was still a very conservative country.

Mrs. Robinson is a sexual predator who seems to have an almost cold, indifferent attitude to sex. She certainly has no love for Ben, and uses him to distract herself from the boredom of routine marital duties such as making breakfast for her husband every morning. She is the product of middle-class married conservative America where her role is to be perfect wife, mother, and smiling cocktail party attendee. She does not have the freedom other women will have by the end of the 1960s when abortion is legal and the Pill is easily available. Mrs Robinson is a tragic figure, denied freedom from society's expectations for women, and drowning her sorrows in alcohol and distracting affairs with younger men. Yet she has become a prime example of a liberated, sexual female. She was created at an American crossroads between the conservative 1950s and the swinging sexual revolution of the 60s.
Alice Goldie

Date 1963

Author Charles Webb (1939–)

Nationality USA

Why It's Key In Webb's autobiographical novel, Mrs Robinson is the quintessential sexy, older woman who seduces a younger man, the disaffected and confused Benjamin Braddock. Mrs Robinson is now the perfect byword to describe older women with younger tastes.

1960-1969

473

Key Event **Friedan marks the beginning of the "second wave" of feminism**

The Feminine Mystique grew out of a survey of Smith College graduates conducted by Betty Friedan. The female respondents revealed their unease and unhappiness. Friedan wrote an article about her findings; it was submitted to women's magazines in 1958 and rejected by all the editors who received it. Friedan decided to rework and expand the article into a book. *The Feminine Mystique* explored the role of women in industrial societies, and in particular the role of full-time homemaker; and it attacked the popular notion that women could only find fulfillment through childbearing and housework. Friedan located her analysis in post-war, middle-class, suburban communities. She suggested that men returning from war turned to their wives for mothering. She examined the role of technology in shaping – and devaluing – housework, and the influence of Freudian thought on dominant debates about the family.

The book was a bestseller, and its publication a notable event. According to *The New York Times* in 2006, the book "ignited the contemporary women's movement in 1963 and… permanently transformed the social fabric of the United States and countries around the world." It is widely regarded as one of the most influential non-fiction books of the last century.

Critics have argued that Friedan's analysis does not apply productively to women of other economic classes or to women of color: a bias that is detectable in much second-wave feminist thought. But despite such blind spots in Friedan's text, its importance and impact remain indisputable, and its legacy can be felt today.
Emily Jeremiah

Date 1963

Title *The Feminine Mystique*

Author Betty Friedan (1921–2006)

Why It's Key *The Feminine Mystique* exposed the "problem that had no name" – women's entrapment and dissatisfaction – and in so doing inspired thousands of readers to reassess and transform their lives.

Key Event
Fanny Hill is published in the USA

John Cleland (1709–89) wrote Fanny Hill while imprisoned in Fleet Street for debt. The book was immensely popular, and despite the prosecution of Cleland and his publisher for "corruption," and the official withdrawal of the novel, *Fanny Hill* continued to circulate in pirate editions. The story follows the familiar eighteenth-century model of the "Harlot's Progress" (as in Hogarth's popular painting series from 1732), in which an innocent country girl arrives in the big city only to be sexually corrupted and lured into working in a brothel. Daniel Defoe had earlier achieved popularity with similar stories in *Moll Flanders* and *Roxana* but neither of these novels is written erotically, with apparent intent to titillate. Another important difference is that both Roxana and Moll Flanders repent their licentious pasts, but Fanny Hill does not regret her past, although she realizes that she was exploited. She remains a "woman of pleasure," who fully enjoys sexual gratification. Because Fanny was not punished by her author for her sexual freedom, many feminists have seen her as an early female role model. "Fanny's" narrative voice is spirited and playful, and the story itself asks satirical questions about gender roles, love, and sexual economics. Although it was banned in the United States on its first publication in 1821, it was published again by G.B. Putnam in 1963 and immediately banned for obscenity, but Putnam challenged the ban in court, and in 1966 the U.S. Supreme Court ruled that the novel was not obscene in a landmark decision that changed the face of contemporary American literature.

Sarah Churchwell

Date 1963

Title *Fanny Hill; or, The Memoirs of a Woman of Pleasure* (1748)

Nationality UK

Why It's Key First published in 1748, *Fanny Hill* is the most famous erotic novel in English and has come to emblematize struggles to overturn obscenity laws. Its author and publisher were arrested in 1749 and the book was withdrawn. This pattern would continue for the next two hundred years.

Opposite *Fanny Hill*

Key Passage
Up the Junction

"Sylvie pisses in the road. 'Quick Sylv, there's a car comin' in ter park!' The headlamps beam. 'Pull yer drawers up!'
'It's all right,' she jumps to her feet, 'I don't wear no drawers Friday nights – it's 'andy…'"

Nell Dunn's writing in *Up the Junction* lies firmly within the post-war British realist tradition. The novel comprises a series of vignettes, different scenes in the lives of young, working-class women. The passage comes towards the end of the novel as the young women are out on a Friday night after a hard week at work and it encapsulates their carefree attitude to their bodily functions and sex as they appear throughout the novel. They see it as part of normal living and they are both unashamed and unabashed. The narrative consists mainly of highly vernacular conversations that range back and forth between the young women and the men they meet.

This passage appears in "The Tallyman," who the women meet in a nightclub. Despite its carefree beginning the chapter goes on to describe the ways in which the tallyman earns his wealth through exploitation of the poor: "Once you've got yer foot in the door you keep it there… you hold on to 'em and you never let them go…"

The juxtaposition of good times and their consequences is a feature of the novel. Sex outside marriage leads to unwanted pregnancies and abortion, crime leads to imprisonment and motorbikes cause death for their young riders. All, however, are shown to be part of the fabric of life in this environment and are treated with the same level of acceptance. Dunn's descriptive narrative is memorable in that she is one of the first women writers of the period who allows working-class women to have some autonomy in their lives.

Pat Wheeler

Date 1963

Author Nell Dunn (1936)

Nationality UK

Why It's Key When published it caused considerable controversy, mainly because of its representation of unfettered female sexuality. Widely regarded as one of the first novels of the era to foreground the lives of working-class women, it is unusual in its use of colloquial language. The novel won the John Llewellyn Rhys Memorial Prize in 1964.

Key Event
Sylvia Plath commits suicide

On February 11, 1963, Sylvia Plath (1932–1963) put her children to bed, left the next day's breakfast out for them, and sealed off the kitchen to prevent fumes from escaping. She swallowed a bottle of sleeping pills and stuck her head in the gas oven.

Plath's death represents one of the great tragedies in literary history. The precise "reason" for her suicide, however, has been difficult to determine. Plath suffered from severe depression throughout her life and, around the time of her death, she had been experiencing the heightened energy and euphoria that can accompany a manic episode (and which for Plath often coincided with intense productivity). Plath's sundered marriage to poet Ted Hughes undoubtedly contributed to her emotional fragility – and some people have held Hughes responsible for her death. Others blame the tricyclic antidepressants she was taking, which have since been found to potentially increase suicidal feelings. Others still suggest that Plath's chosen method was a morbid reference to the gas chambers that her father may have operated during World War II; in her poem "Daddy," Plath connects the father's menacing presence with a sense of torment and self-annihilation – the final line fusing accusation with defeat: "Daddy, daddy, you bastard, I'm through."

Plath's writing was largely governed by the ebb and flow of her psychiatric condition. Suicide and mental illness are recurring themes in her poetry, particularly in her posthumously published collection *Ariel* (1965). Her subjects include self-loathing, spiritual bankruptcy, destructive relationships, the Nazis and the Jewish Holocaust. Known for its emotional intensity, macabre imagery, and formal control, Plath's poetry is infused with existential woe, as evinced in her "Poppies in October": "O my God, what am I/ That these late mouths should cry open/ In a forest of frost, in a dawn of cornflowers."

Kiki Benzon

Date 1963

Nationality USA

Why It's Key The controversy over Sylvia Plath's death persists – as does her legacy as one of the most important female voices in twentieth-century poetry. Plath produced two volumes of poetry – *The Colossus* (1960) and *Ariel* (published posthumously in 1965) – and one novel, *The Bell Jar* (1963); she also kept extensive journals, which were published in stages after her death.

Opposite Sylvia Plath

Key Event **Jessica Mitford prompts an investigation into funeral parlours**

The American Way of Death was an expansion of a piece, entitled "Saint Peter Don't You Call Me," written by Jessica Mitford for *Frontier* magazine. At the instigation of her husband, Bob Treuhaft, Jessica (almost universally known as Decca), produced a stingingly critical assessment of the American funeral industries – urn-makers, undertakers, embalmers, and so on. She exposed their underhand tactics, especially the way they took advantage of bereaved families – offering them more expensive funerals than they could afford, and tailoring the funeral's "minimum" costs to roughly whatever life insurance the deceased had, for example.

The book was an enormous success, and led to Congressional hearings about funereal malpractice. Funeral Societies were set up, where people invested small amounts of money to cover their own low-cost funeral, so that their families could not be emotionally blackmailed later on into spending more money than the deceased had wished. A coffin manufacturer, not to be outdone, named its cheapest, nastiest coffin, "The Jessica." Mitford was delighted.

The American Way of Death was Jessica Mitford's first foray into investigative journalism, or muckraking, as she liked to call it. She went on to write about the arrest and trial of Dr Spock, the dubious business of giving birth in an increasingly litigious U.S. (*The American Way of Birth*), and the prison system (*Kind and Usual Punishment*), and to become a visiting lecturer at California State University. Her journalistic attitude was best summarised by herself: "You may not be able to change the world, but at least you can embarrass the guilty."

Natalie Haynes

Date 1963

Title *The American Way of Death*

Author Jessica Mitford (1917–1996)

Nationality UK, naturalized U.S.

Why It's Key Jessica Mitford, one of the legendary Mitford sisters, had a prominent career in the U.S. as a muckraking journalist. *The American Way of Death* led to Congressional hearings about the funeral industry.

Key Passage **"The Man who was a Fool"**
Strength to Love

"The means by which we live have outdistanced the ends for which we live. Our scientific power has outrun our spiritual power. We have guided missiles and misguided men."

Strength to Love explains the development of Dr. Martin Luther King Jr's stance on non-violence. King's journey began with his discovery of the teachings and philosophy of Mahatma Gandhi, who sought to neutralize injustice by engaging in peaceful resistance. King expounded upon Gandhi's philosophy, introducing Christian love as a source of strength in the struggle for freedom. *Strength to Love* eloquently set the theoretical framework for King's perspective on passive resistance, and set forth a new strategy for revolutionary activism at the height of the Civil Rights Movement. The most recognizable passage from this book includes the quote, "our scientific power has outrun our spiritual power. We have guided missiles and misguided men." This passage epitomizes Dr. King's mastery of the sermon. His speeches and writings reflect his background as a Baptist minister as he skillfully utilized the English language to craft his message of non-violence. In the turbulent and violent days of the Civil Rights Movement, Dr. Martin Luther King, Jr. provided a penetrating argument for nonviolence, love and coexistence. *Strength to Love* was instrumental in dispersing this message to an international audience. In 1968 Martin Luther King Day was established as a United States holiday to commemorate Dr. King for his passionate activism and humanitarianism.

Pierce Freelon

Date 1964

Author Dr. Martin Luther King, Jr. (1929–1968)

Nationality USA

Why It's Key Dr. Martin Luther King, Jr. was the most influential leader of the Civil Rights Movement and in 1964, the year *Strength to Love* was published, became the youngest man to be awarded the Nobel Peace Prize.

Key Book
The Woman in the Dunes

"One day in August a man disappeared." It is a simple beginning to a simple tale, plainly told, in one of the key works of modern Japanese fiction. Niki Jumpei, an amateur entomologist, heads for the beach hoping to discover a new species of sand beetle. Engrossed in his pursuits, he misses the last train home and seeks shelter in a shabby seaside village. He is offered accommodation in a rotting house at the bottom of a pit in the sand dunes. Its only resident is a pale woman whose nights are spent shovelling the encroaching sand out of the house. When he tries to leave, he finds that he is trapped in the pit, subjected to the villagers' whims. To survive, he too will have to labor ceaselessly alongside the woman.

There are hints of Kafka in this parable about the drudgery of human toil. Man and woman are unable to do anything but fight back the sand, Sisyphus-like, only to begin anew the following night. The question is whether Abe's characters are crushed or liberated by their daily travails. Niki Jumpei's rage at being isolated from the outside world eventually gives way to a renewed sense of purpose. Amid the dunes the couple finds not only companionship but, even, intimacy. When freedom is finally at hand, the lost entomologist prefers to postpone his escape. The parched, claustrophobic universe Abe creates in *The Woman in the Dunes* is as beautiful as it is menacing. His triumph lies in rendering it with such economy of narrative means.

Ángel Gurría-Quintana

Date 1964

Author Kobo Abe (1924–1993)

Nationality Japan

Why It's Key Sand gets into everything in Abe's most successful novel, a milestone of post-war Japanese literature. Ever-shifting, all-eroding, sand becomes an apt symbol of life's irrepressible force, lapping away at mankind's inconsequential efforts. Abe's book is also a powerful allegory about the will to be free.

Key Book
Last Exit To Brooklyn

Selby Jr's prose is formed from a rough mix of Nelson Algren's polyphonic street slang, Kerouac's restless stylistic improvisations, and exploitative pulp fiction melodrama. The book is divided into several Parts with occasional overlap of character or incident, each prefaced by an Old Testament epigraph, including two taken from the Book of Job. Each episode, except for the Coda which ends the book in a riot of anguished voices from the Projects, focuses on the story of a sinner who has a plague of disaster visited upon them by their peers in a social world characterised by weakness and violence. One of the most memorable characters is Harry, a suggestible union organiser, married with a child, who begins an affair with a transvestite prostitute and is ruthlessly used and discarded by his lover and "her" friends; his story ends when he drunkenly fellates a ten-year-old boy and is brutally beaten on some waste ground in revenge for the assault. Tralala is the sex worker heroine of another section who, in intoxicated competition with other working girls for clients, exhibits herself shamelessly in a bar and ends up gang-raped, battered, abused, and left for dead. The enduringly horrible scene is utterly relentless, defying the reader to dismiss it as overdone or implausible.

Robin Purves

Date 1964

Author Hubert Selby, Jr. (1928–2004)

Nationality USA

Why It's Key Possibly the most extreme example of dirty realism to be imported from the USA as well as the target for a charge of obscenity, after a campaign by a group of MPs to have the book prosecuted. The charge led to a trial, which the publishers won, and a tumult of publicity which for some time distracted readers from the intrinsic merits of the novel.

1960–1969

479

Key Character **Moses Herzog**
Herzog

Failures are notoriously introspective, but Saul Bellow will not allow his hero, Herzog, to remain in a limbo of self-searching. It is not enough for Moses Herzog, twice-failed husband, struggling academic prophet, to ponder the hardness of his own life. He tries to use his head to heal his splintered heart, though his head is itself fragmenting daily. He must sort out the whole human tragedy, in letters. So he writes, obsessively, to everyone, those who have wronged him, those whom he has wronged, the influential living, the famous dead, sometimes on paper, sometimes in his head. His mind in meltdown will leave him no rest: the world's problems can be solved, if only he can just finish that letter, complete that thought.

He doesn't want for friends: the kindly couple in Martha's Vineyard he runs out on because he can't cope with kindness, his lover Ramona, whom he can't love because she won't hurt him, the various lawyers, psychiatrists, and in-laws who have, so they say, his best interests at heart (though he's never quite sure whose side they're on). But his hatred of his estranged wife, Madeleine, a woman who can somehow conjure moral authority out of the cruellest acts, bids fair to overwhelm his reason.

All of this might easily alienate those unaccustomed to such extremes, but Bellow saves the reader from the ennui which often results from over-exposure to intensity by endowing his character with humor. And it is humor, coupled with Herzog's final recognition of the futility of hatred, which at last saves him.

Murrough O'Brien

Date 1964

Author Saul Bellow (1915–2005)

Nationality USA

Why It's Key Herzog was only one of several Jewish characters to enter the international consciousness as an archetype: Portnoy of *Portnoy's Complaint*, is another example. Herzog, however, fixed forever in the common imagination the figure of the post-Holocaust Jew, seeking consolation everywhere but in the God who failed his people.

Key Character **Neddy Merrill** "The Swimmer"
The General and the Golf Widow

Neddy Merrill, a middle-aged, middle-class suburbanite, decides to swim the few miles from his friend's house to his own via the intervening swimming-pools, the symbol of wealthy middle-America. It is a lazy midsummer Sunday when he sets out, leaving a party of friends cheerfully bragging about their hangovers. But as he travels, the world darkens around him and an autumnal decay sets in. Gradually, he loses his confidence in who he is and his place in the world. He seems to leave the heart of his community and become an outsider, stripped bare of pretension. His increasing vulnerability is emphasised by his near-nakedness. A woman he has despised abuses him. His ex-mistress is unpleasantly surprised to see him. Others puzzle him by sympathising with him in his troubles. By the time he arrives at his own house, the world is cold and dark, and the house is locked up and deserted.

Those familiar with Dante's *Inferno* may find references to the circles of Hell. Neddy sees the string of pools as a river, which he names the Lucinda River, after his wife. Certainly, his journey explores middle-class, middle-aged unease – what if we lose it all? Neddy's journey can also be seen as the journey of mankind, from golden youth to impotent old age, the fading of the American dream, and as a vision of the degradation of human life on the planet. His is a story which stays with the reader, in its nightmare vision of a world whose reality can dissolve around us.

Felicity Skelton

Date 1964

Author John Cheever (1912–1982)

Why It's Key The story has remained one of Cheever's most popular and most anthologised, perhaps because it shows, as in a nightmare, the reversal of the American dream – the man who believes he has it all, and is found out.

Key Author **Roald Dahl**
Charlie and the Chocolate Factory

Parents always knew their children were in safe hands when they gave them Enid Blyton's Famous Five or Malory Towers books to read. They were less sure about Roald Dahl's (1916–1990) more lurid tales, however. It wasn't that the nice children didn't triumph over nasty adults in his books (a regular theme of the Famous Five, after all); it was just that the triumph came in such a gleefully horrid form, resulting in humiliation at best and unpleasant death at worst. Children, however, have always been delighted by Dahl's slightly warped imagination, vivid language, and strategic use of scatological humor.

Dahl began his writing career as an author of short stories for adults, and the dark humor and sense of macabre which infuses his famous *Tales of the Unexpected* collection is also clearly present in his children's books. In his best-loved work, *Charlie and the Chocolate Factory*, Dahl is at his most vindictive in the fates he metes out to the four grotesque children who join Charlie Bucket on his tour of Willy Wonka's magical factory. As the children show themselves to be alternately greedy, impulsive, or spoiled, they're dispatched in a variety of unpleasant ways reminiscent of Hoffman's *Der Struwwelpeter*.

However, Dahl also turns his flamboyant imagination to tremendous use when describing good things. What child's mouth hasn't watered at the descriptions of Wonka's Whipple-Scrumptious Fudge-Mallow Delight or the BFG's favorite burp-making beverage, Frobscottle? Who hasn't envied James his fantastic flight across the Atlantic on the giant peach? It's his ability to combine soaring flights of fancy whilst always leaving a sting in the tale which makes Roald Dahl such an enduring children's favorite.

Frances Powell

Date 1964

Nationality UK

Other Key Works *James and the Giant Peach* (1961); *The Twits* (1980); *Matilda* (1988)

Why It's Key Dahl inherited Enid Blyton's crown as the foremost British children's author, sweeping away her cosy realm of Toytown and lashings of ginger beer at the same time. In its place he created the darker worlds inhabited by Willy Wonka and the BFG, where revenge is sweet.

Opposite Roald Dahl

Key Event **Amiri Baraka's *Dutchman* opens in New York**

Amiri Baraka's *Dutchman*, an explosive, politically charged one-act play, debuted on March 24th, 1964, at Cherry Lane Theater in Manhattan. Garnering critical acclaim while simultaneously stirring up controversy, *Dutchman* was a poetic indictment of American racism and capitalism.

Set entirely on a subway train in New York City, the play centres round an interracial clash between Lulu, a white femme fatale, and Clay, a young, well-dressed black intellectual. The apparent random meeting of Clay and Lulu on the subway concludes with Lulu stabbing Clay in the back while bystanders simply watch, their silence a symbol of their approval.

Dutchman successfully integrates African and European mythical allusions, surrealistic techniques and cultural criticism. Widely considered to be a theatrical masterpiece, *Dutchman* thrust Baraka into the international spotlight and it may well be his most famous literary work.

After its debut, the play went on to receive a Village Voice Obie Award for Best Off-Broadway play of 1963-64. The play was also the last play Baraka wrote under his birth name, Leroi Jones. Soon after the debut of *Dutchman*, he would change his name to Amiri Baraka as a way to honor his African roots and reject his "slave name." Baraka would later pen the screenplay to the 1967 film adaptation of *Dutchman* which was directed by British filmmaker Anthony Harvey.
M.K. Asante, Jr.

Date March 24th, 1964

Author Amiri Baraka (1934–)

Nationality African-American

Why It's Key An explosive indictment of American racism and capitalism that *The New York Times* described as a "boxing glove jabbing at the malignancies of American capitalism."

483

Key Book *Understanding Media: The Extensions of Man*

Understanding Media made a celebrity of communications theorist Marshall McLuhan, and an industry of Media Studies. Written in a catchy, aphoristic style, it made complex, traditionally academic thinking palatable to a popular audience. Although this dense work is not an easy read, its portentous tone and epigrammatic flourishes make for a compelling narrative. For example, McLuhan observes, "after more than a century of electric technology, we have extended our central nervous system itself in a global embrace." As a result, "the globe is no more than a village."

Influenced by the Jesuit philosopher Pierre Teilhard de Chardin (1881–1955), who thought that electricity extended the central nervous system, and by his Cambridge mentor F.R. Leavis (1895–1978), who approached the study of contemporary culture as a serious subject, McLuhan examines the ways in which technology, "the medium," extends both our physical selves and our abilities. He examines the effects of mass media on the culture at large, observing that "the message of any medium or technology is the change of scale or pace or pattern that it introduces into human affairs."

Understanding Media provided both a methodology and a language for coming to terms with the electronic age, as well as foreseeing future advances. Although they predate the world wide web, McLuhan's theories could, for example, easily describe the internet: "In the case of electricity, it is not corporeal substance that is stored or moved, but perception and information," and "the instant speed of electronic information… permits easy recognition of the patterns and the formal contours of change and development." While his celebrity has faded, McLuhan's ideas survive in the phrases he coined such as "global village" and "the medium is the message."
Dinah Roe

Date 1964

Author Herbert Marshall McLuhan (1911–1980)

Nationality Canada

Why It's Key A revolutionary examination of the ways in which technology extends mankind's abilities, introducing phrases like the "global village" and "the medium is the message." McLuhan's work was the subject of a collection of essays, *McLuhan, Hot and Cool* (1967), with contributions by Susan Sontag and Tom Wolfe.

Key Event Chairman Mao's Little Red Book is published

The Little Red Book became an icon of Mao's rule in China and the pervasive influence of the Communist party. It was published by the Chinese government in April 1964 as *Quotations from Chairman Mao Zedong* – the "Little Red Book" referred to the pocket-sized edition later produced. As the name suggests, the book is a series of excerpts of the Chinese leader's many speeches and writings, laying out his take on Marxist-Leninist thought.

In Imperial times, China had been ruled through a sprawling hierarchy of civil servants; all information filtered down slowly from the Emperor of China through this network to the Chinese population. The Little Red Book, by contrast, represented the direct will and rule of Mao Zedong over the Chinese people.

More than 900 million copies have been printed – only the Bible has sold more. But this wasn't all about popular demand – at the height of Mao's power, all Chinese citizens were expected to own the book and carry it with them. The quotations are divided into topics such as "The Communist Party," "Class and Class Struggle" and "Patriotism and Internationalism." Although many of the subjects it discusses are explicitly political, Mao Zedong's thought extended to every layer of society and aspect of life, for example: "Literature and art are discussed with respect to communism, in an orthodox fashion."

After Mao died in 1976 the influence of the book declined. Although it is still on sale, most buyers are now foreign tourists seeking a souvenir of a period in history many Chinese would rather forget.

Rosie Blau

Date 1964

Author Mao Zedong (1893–1976)

Nationality China

Why It's Key The Little Red Book became a symbol both of Mao's thought and his power throughout China. The rhetoric in the volume was used to justify some of the most egregious acts of the Cultural Revolution from 1966–69, and all schools and workplaces set aside time to study and recite the readings.

Opposite Mao's "Little Red Book"

Key Event Latin America's greatest novelists collaborate *El Gallo de Oro*

Juan Rulfo published almost all of his fiction in the space of a few years in the mid-1950s. The rest of his life was filled with many activities, including his remarkable photographs of Mexican landscapes and people, and work for the cinema.

The many film versions of his stark, spare stories have mostly been scripted by others, but in 1964 he produced an original film treatment called *El gallo de oro* (*The Golden Cockerel*), which tells of a peasant who gains riches and love, then loses them, through the hazards of cockfighting and fate. The story was scripted by the then almost unknown Gabriel García Márquez (who cites Rulfo, with Kafka, as his greatest inspiration) and the Mexican Carlos Fuentes (then already gaining fame with his early novels. The resulting film has always been popular in Mexico, but is no masterpiece. Other versions have since been made; it was even adapted as a Colombian telenovela in 2000. However, no remotely faithful version could ever be released in the UK, as showing real cockfighting on screen is against British law.

Rulfo's vision is probably better represented by the experimental film projects he contributed to, including *La fórmula secreta* (*The Secret Formula*, 1965), a surreal satire on American imperialism (the formula in question is for Coca-Cola). He also acted in an adaptation of a Márquez story, *En este pueblo no hay ladrones* (1964, *There are No Thieves in This Town*) as part of an astonishing cast including Luís Buñuel and Leonora Carrington.

Cathy Benson

Date 1964

Author Juan Rulfo (1918–1986)

Nationality Mexico

Why It's Key Rulfo was one of the progenitors of "magic realism." He also did notable work for the cinema, providing the story for a film, which was turned into a screenplay by two of the most talented young writers of the 1960s "boom" in Latin American literature, Carlos Fuentes and Gabriel García Márquez.

Key Event **Jean-Paul Sartre refuses the Nobel Prize**

The history of the Nobel Prize in literature is not exactly littered with refusals. In 1958, Boris Pasternak, who was delighted to receive the honor, was eventually forced by the Soviet government to refuse. George Bernard Shaw, in 1925, was happy to accept the honor but could not bring himself to take the money. The first full and unqualified, and to this date, sole refusal was made in 1964 by Jean-Paul Sartre. Sartre turned down the money and the distinction, not, as he had it, as "an improvised act," but for reasons of principle. He wished to remain unfettered by any honors, and had previously refused the Legion d'honneur, and professorial entry to the Collège de France. His response to the nomination, which had been let slip by *Le Figaro Littéraire* on 14th October 1964, was swift and unequivocal: "It is not the same thing if I sign Jean-Paul Sartre or if I sign Jean-Paul Sartre, Nobel Prize winner. A writer must refuse to allow himself to be transformed into an institution, even if it takes place in the most honorable form." This position of uncompromising idealism was, perhaps short-sightedly on behalf of the Swedish Academy, met with a frigid response: "the fact that he is declining does not alter in the least the validity of the nomination"; but Sartre's commitment to freedom in his life as well as in his philosophy would perhaps have met with approval from the prize's founder Alfred Nobel, who once said of himself: "Greatest sin: Does not worship Mammon."

Julia Jordan

Date 1964

Author Jean-Paul Sartre (1905–1980)

Country France

Why It's Key Sartre's refusal of the Nobel Prize in Literature remains a unique event in the award's history. In fact he is, along with Le Duc Tho, who was the intended co-recipient with Kissinger of the peace prize in 1973, one of only two people to refuse any Nobel Prize.

1960-1969

487

Key Book *The Autobiography of Malcolm X*

Born Malcolm Little, Malcolm X became one of the leading spokesmen for militant black nationalism in America in the early 1960s. The book was based on interviews conducted with Malcolm by Alex Haley (who was later to achieve fame as the author of *Roots*), and did not appear until after its subject had been assassinated in New York City. Thousands of young black Americans were able to identify with the earlier part of the book, which dealt with Malcolm's childhood growing up amid racism. He describes how taking the path of becoming involved in drugs, violence, and pimping seemed the only way to "make it" in a society that oppressed his people. The book pulls no punches in revealing both the attractions of and suffering caused by such a life of criminality.

Where Malcolm's experience differed from that of many was his recruitment to the black Muslim organization the Nation of Islam while in prison. His new-found faith not only gave him something to believe in but inspired him to take action to improve the status of black people in the United States. The book describes how Malcolm eventually broke with the Nation of Islam and his conversion to orthodox Islam. He accused the NOI of being racist against whites and came to believe that cooperation with non-racist white people was the only way forward. The book is as outspoken as Malcolm X was himself, a trait that earned him many enemies in both white and black society, and it was at the hands of black assassins that he died.

Michael Munro

Date 1965

Author Malcolm X (1925–1965) and Alex Haley (1929–1992)

Nationality USA

Why It's Key This tale of a black youth drifting into a life of crime mirrored the experience of many, showing what it was like to be the victim of institutionalised racism, yet its account of the author finding new faith and struggling to better both his own lot and that of his people was inspirational.

Opposite Malcolm X

Key Book
Black Rain (*Kuroi Ame*)

As winner of the Noma Prize and The Order of Cultural Merit, Ibuse stands tall amongst contemporaries and readers alike. Hailing from the Hiroshima area himself, he presents a harrowing account of the atomic bomb survivors, cutting a swathe through political rhetoric and power play with dignity and poise. So numerous and substantial as to merit a title of their own, the *hibakushka* – atomic bomb survivors – are paid a moving tribute by Ibuse's fictional exploration of Little Boy's lethal impact on everyday village life in wartime Japan.

Adapted from historical records and beginning as a serial in *Shincho* magazine in 1965, *Black Rain* takes the form of a diary rewritten by a fictional character. Contaminated by the "black rain" and succumbing to radiation sickness, Shigematsu's niece is destined for a life of social isolation and discrimination. Juxtaposing excerpts from Shigematsu's own wartime diary, Ibuse successfully interweaves past and present, old and young, hope and despair in the search for a suitable husband for the young Yasuko.

Mentor to Osamu Dazai and acclaimed by Nobel Prize winner Kenzaburo Oe, Ibuse embarks on a quest for greater understanding, a depiction of the tenacity and courage of the human spirit. Through compassionate characterization and empathetic insight, composed some two decades after the event, Ibuse renders the horror comprehensible, the bitter historical truth palatable. For those willing to take a taste of Ibuse's sharp story, the satisfaction lies in the growth and progression depicted in the narrative. As his characters gain understanding and courage, so Ibuse urges us to do the same.

Sarah Birchwood

Date 1965 (Japanese edition, 1966 English language edition)

Author Masuji Ibuse (1898–1993)

Nationality Japan

Why It's Key A bold and compelling account of Hiroshima survivors, *Black Rain* lends a human face to a global tragedy.

Key Event **Frank Herbert's *Dune* wins the first ever Nebula award**

The Nebula prize is given every year by the Science Fiction and Fantasy Writers of America (in contrast to the other significant SFF prize, the Hugo, which is voted for by fans attending the World Science Fiction Convention). There are prizes in the categories of novel, novella, novelette, short story, and script. Although of no financial value, the award is seen to be more prestigious than the Hugo in some ways because it is voted for by the author's peers. Winners have included the crème of science fiction over the last four decades, including Ursula Le Guin, William Gibson, Neil Gaiman, Isaac Asimov, and Kim Stanley Robinson. The first award was presented to Frank Herbert for his novel *Dune* (it also received the Hugo). *Dune* is one of the biggest selling science fiction novels, and has produced five sequels and a multitude of other related products (games, films, prequels). Set some 14,000 years into the future the set of novels relates a galactic imperial power struggle between warring aristocratic houses.

The most sought after substance in the empire is the spice melange, used for interstellar travel and to extend human life. Melange can only be mined in treacherous conditions on the desert world Arrakis. The hero of the novel, Paul Atreides, emerges as the semi-divine chosen one and defeats the corrupt emperor of the galaxy through his leadership of the fierce native Fremen of Dune. The novels are ritualistic and portentuous, pseudo-philosophic epics.

Jerome de Groot

Date 1965

Author Frank Herbert (1920–1986)

Nationality USA

Why It's Key *Dune* was the first winner of this prestigious and influential science fiction award, and became one of the best-selling science fiction novels ever.

Key Event **Randall Jarrell champions** *The Man Who Loved Children*

In 1965 the American poet and critic Randall Jarrell was killed – perhaps committed suicide – in a traffic accident. He had dealt in his own work with the world of childhood and children's literature and had also written powerfully on the sufferings of combatants in World War II. One of his more unlikely legacies was the work of Christina Stead, for whose novel *The Man Who Loved Children* he had just written a new introduction.

"An Unread Book," he had called it. Now it is generally recognized as a modern classic although it is still apparently struggling to find its niche. Readers in the 1940s had found it difficult to accept this account of the traumas of family life as literature. Radicals found in Sam Pollitt an unflattering portrait of themselves.

Stead's characterization of Sam, a new kind of liberal patriarch, strikes the reader as astonishingly modern. He awards himself monikers bespeaking his own courage and strength ("Sam-the-Bold"); in his mateyness he allows his growing children no privacy;

he uses an attention-seeking and borderline-racist babytalk. The novel opens with his marriage already at an impasse, his wife Henny eaten up with impotent rage. Physically, she has been reduced to a "hag" while her husband still cuts a fine figure. Increasingly, we see the action through the eyes of erudite Louie, Sam's daughter by his first marriage, who is forced to take on adult responsibilities before her time.

Jarrell suggested that the space given to Henny's "tirades" was a weakness, but since that time a taboo has been lifted. We are now accustomed to reading accounts of abusive or neglectful parents in childhood memoirs. Henny's wrathful outpourings counterpoint Sam's complacent rhetoric to create a terrifying psychological space in which the fictional children have to survive.
Kate Kerrigan

Date 1965

Title *The Man Who Loved Children* (1940)

Author Christina Stead (1902–1983)

Nationality Australia

Why It's Key An idealistic self-deluded man is impervious to the state of abject poverty his sense of his own integrity brings his family to. An American marriage is dissected in a degree of unsparing detail that a 1940s readership was not ready for.

Key Author **Luis Valdez**

U.S. playwright, film director, and Chicano activist Luis Valdez (1940–) started his literary career in the mid-sixties working with Mexican-American farm workers in his hometown of Delano, California. Valdez has written, co-written, and directed many plays and films depicting the Chicano experience, including *La Carpa de los Rasquachis* (1973), *El Fin del Mundo* (1976), *Zoot Suit* (1978), and *Tiburcio Vasquez* (1980). Some of his best-known pieces (*Los vendidos* [*The Sellouts*]), were staged by the troupe of El Teatro Campesino, a cultural outlet of the United Farm Workers. Drawing from a mixture of *commedia dell'arte*, medieval religious plays and indigenous performances, Valdez infused El Teatro Campesino with its characteristic one-act plays. Often acting without stage, or script, farmer actors dramatized the conditions of migrant workers and set the foundations for *teatro chicano*. Valdez plays with the boundaries between stereotype and individual

development, heroic resistance to acculturation and the role of banditry or lawlessness in the Chicano's fight for equal rights in the U.S. His radically Brechtian approaches often break the boundaries between the stage and the public, showing a mirror back to the audience to reveal the continuities and ruptures of drama and everyday reality. Valdez's is clearly one of the most innovative and influential voices of the Chicano literary movement. He also wrote and directed the box office hit movie, *La Bamba* (1987), about the life of Ritchie Valens.
Pedro García-Caro

Date 1965

Nationality USA

Why It's Key Valdez is one of the most important and influential Chicano writers. In 1965 he formed El Teatro Campesino, which began as a company which put on short plays for striking farm workers, often performing in the fields, using music, improvisation, stock characters, and minimal props and costumes. Valdez went on to become the first Chicano writer to have a play on Broadway (*Zoot Suit*).

Key Event **Jacqueline Susann engineers the status of *Valley of the Dolls***

Jacqueline Susann (1918–74) is famous for her hugely popular romp, *Valley of the Dolls*, a story of immorality, sex, drug addiction, and death in Hollywood. It chronicles the rise and fall of three young women in their attempts to obtain successful careers in the sleazy world of entertainment. It is rumored that the three characters were loosely based on Judy Garland, Marilyn Monroe, and Grace Kelly.

This book was Susann's second novel and after record sales figures, a film adaptation, and TV series, it made her one of the world's wealthiest women writers. She was crowned the Queen of Pulp Fiction but the literary establishment had condemned Susann's style as too bombastic with unsuitable subjects resulting in a trashy, escapist novel. This was harsh, as although the glamorous characters inhabit the sordid entertainment world, and the novel contains sexually explicit scenes, swearing, and drug use (the "dolls" in question being various prescription drugs), Susann had penned a

cautionary tale with an absorbing plot that clearly highlights the lack of morality amongst characters living in life's fast lane. Susann was remarkably astute in the marketing of her book; she manipulated its sales in bookshops by befriending and flattering staff, ensuring that her novel was displayed in the most conspicuous areas of the shop. It is also claimed that she bought many, many copies of her own book to further manipulate its sales figures and secure the cult classic status of *Valley of the Dolls* early on in its best-selling publication life. Of course, the raunchy film adaptation (1967) did not hinder further sales either, and it is now judged as a camp classic.

Alice Goldie

Date 1966

Nationality USA

Why It's Key Prior to the publishing phenomenon that is J.K. Rowling, Jacqueline Susann's book, *Valley of the Dolls*, was among the top twenty all-time best-selling novels with an estimated nineteen million copies sold worldwide. Fantastic success for a woman who once declared that "Acting is glamour, but writing is hard work so I'm going to be an actress."

Opposite *Valley of the Dolls*

490

Key Book *Five Hours with Mario (Cinco horas con Mario)*

Five Hours with Mario – widely regarded as the finest novel by the Spanish writer and journalist, Miguel Delibes – begins in March 1966 with the death of Mario Díez Collado, a politically committed professor and journalist. During his wake, his widow, María del Carmen Sotillo (better known as Menchu), reads verses from the Bible which Mario had underlined and, plagued by guilt, launches into a five-hour interior monologue which dominates the book. Initially reproaching her husband for not understanding her ideas or meeting her needs, she ends on a note of self-accusation, revealing that she had once almost been unfaithful to him.

The abyss between the two protagonists, Menchu and Mario, can be seen as reflecting the centuries-old chasm between the "two Spains" – one, liberal and open, represented by Mario, and the other reactionary and closed, represented by Menchu. Significantly, it is Carmen – depicted by Delibes as an archetype of the

middle-class provincial Spanish woman with her blind submission to prejudice, dogma and social hypocrisy – who survives, a symbol of the Francoist regime still stifling Spain at the time. In contrast, there is a sense that it is both Mario's search for authenticity and a new, potentially dynamic Spain that have been suffocated.

Delibes explained the style of this book in an interview, saying: "I've always tried to say what I felt. I didn't feel totally gagged by censorship... But in *Five Hours with Mario*, my first idea was to present Mario alive. However, the censors would never have accepted Mario's condemning the society in which we were living. So I resorted to the sophistry of Mario being dead and having Menchu express Mario's credo in order to repudiate and reject it... At times, censorship was convenient in that it made us adopt subtle formulas and subtlety always has an aesthetic significance. We lost this subtlety when censorship disappeared."

Adam Feinstein

Date 1966 (English translation 1988)

Author Miguel Delibes (1920–)

Nationality Spain

Why It's Key Delibes uses changes of perspective, ambiguous contexts, word repetitions, puns, and proverbial echoes to weave an intimate relationship between ideological and formal concerns. An ironic style becomes the theme of the book: the reader must decode the text by rejecting a literal interpretation of Menchu/Delibes's words.

Key Book
The Master and Margarita

One summer's day in the 1930s the Devil makes an appearance in Stalin's Moscow in the guise of Woland, a magician seven-feet tall who wears a loud check jacket and a jockey cap. He is accompanied by a retinue that includes a naked girl and a mansize cat, who walks on his hind legs, smokes cigars, and uses his Mauser automatic pistol to deadly effect. Their principal target is the literary establishment, a bunch of careerist, spiritless deadheads, mere time-serving bureaucrats in the Writers' Union, a toadying organ of the totalitarian state. We are also introduced to the Master, a writer of great integrity, whose novel about the appearance of Jesus before Pontius Pilate (long sections of which are contained in the book), has been rejected for publication by the literary bureaucrats. The Master, in despair, has ended up in a lunatic asylum, but his beloved mistress, Margarita, makes a pact with Woland in order to achieve her lover's release…

Bulgakov, who trained as a doctor before becoming a writer, spent much of the 1930s drafting and revising *The Master and Margarita*, and was still polishing it when he died. He first ran into difficulties with the censors in the late 1920s, and in 1930 Stalin refused his request to be allowed to emigrate, and found him a job as an assistant producer and literary adviser at the Moscow Art Theatre. *The Master and Margarita* was not published in the Soviet Union until many years after his death, and that of Stalin.

There have been several adaptations of Bulgakov's masterpiece for stage, TV, and screen. In August 2006 news emerged that Andrew Lloyd Webber was considering turning the book into one of his musical confections.

Ian Crofton

Date 1966–67 (Published posthumously in serial form; published in English in 1967)

Author Mikhail Bulgakov (1891–1940)

Nationality Russia

Why It's Key A biting satire on the materialism of Soviet society combined with elements inspired by Goethe's *Faust*. Regarded by many as one of the finest Russian novels of the twentieth century.

Key Author **Jorge Amado**
Dona Flor and her Two Husbands

If Salvador, capital of the Brazilian state of Bahia, lingers in popular imagination as the country's throbbing melting pot – home to lusty mulatas, charming rogues, and enterprising down-and-outs – it is greatly thanks to the work of native Bahian Jorge Amado (1912–2001).

His first novel, *The Country of Carnival* (1931), written at nineteen, foreshadows Amado's preoccupation with Brazilian elites' lack of empathy towards the underprivileged. *Cacao* (1933) and *Sweat* (1934) were inspired by his political affiliations – he was a member of the Brazilian Communist Party, and represented it in the national assembly from 1945 to 1947, when it was outlawed.

He is more fondly remembered for later novels such as *Gabriela, Clove and Cinnamon* (1958), which celebrates the irrepressible exuberance of Bahia's women, or *The Two Deaths of Quincas Wateryell* (1959), which makes folk heroes out of Salvador's misfits.

Amado was already the country's most popular writer when he published *Dona Flor and her Two Husbands* (1966). Food and sex, two of Amado's favorite themes, come together in the comical tale of a strong-willed cookery teacher, prematurely widowed on Carnival Sunday. Dona Flor soon finds herself in a steady marriage to a reliable but dull man – until her first husband comes back to haunt her. The novel's large print-run (75,000 copies) was unprecedented in Brazil, as were the crowds queuing to buy the book and get his autograph.

Among the honorary titles Amado received, he was proudest of being named *obá* (spirit medium) of Xangó, a principal deity of the Afro-Brazilian Candomblé religion.

Ángel Gurría-Quintana

Date 1966 (publication)

Nationality Brazil

Why It's Key Amado remains his country's most beloved writer (nine out of ten Brazilians claim him as their favorite), and perhaps the Brazilian novelist best known abroad. He contributed more than anyone to perpetuating the romantic image of Bahia as an exotic land peopled by sensuous women, cuckolded colonels, inventive immigrants, and lovable scoundrels.

Opposite **Jorge Amado**

Key Book
Beautiful Losers

Leonard Cohen's *Beautiful Losers*, steeped in the atmosphere of 1960s Montreal, takes the form of a reflection upon an unusual love triangle between an unnamed academic, his best friend F., and his deceased wife, Edith, who unexpectedly committed suicide by sitting down at the bottom of an elevator shaft. Throughout the novel, the narrator attempts to come to terms with his overwhelming grief by obsessively researching the story of Catherine Tekakwitha, a seventeenth-century Iroquois saint who heralded from the same virtually extinct tribe as his late wife. The narrator's fascination slowly turns into an overpowering romantic and sexual obsession with the long-deceased martyred native, through which his desire transmutes into a longing for religious and personal redemption. Throughout, the narrator's drive to find meaning in a chaotic and disparate universe is challenged by F., his cynical but brilliant friend who eventually becomes entangled in the violence of French-Canadian

separatism. The fractured universe of this experimental novel is mirrored in its form; it is told through letters, monologues, lists, dialogue, prayers, historical documents, advertisements, phrasebooks, invocations, poetry, and annotation, and addresses themes as diverse as Canadian politics, 60s pop music, and Christian mysticism. Cohen has been unfortunately and inaccurately pigeonholed as the bard of melancholy and despair – one reviewer suggested that his albums should be packaged with razor-blades – but one read of this hilarious, absurd, filthy, and consistently brilliant novel will remedy any misapprehension.

James Clements

Date 1966

Author Leonard Cohen (1934–)

Nationality Canada

Why It's Key Before he even picked up a guitar Cohen was regarded as a major writer at home. His first three books of verse and one novel established his unabashedly dramatic voice, but it was with *Beautiful Losers* that Cohen gained recognition as one of the finest experimental novelists of his era.

Opposite Leonard Cohen

Key Characters **Rosencrantz and Guildenstern**
Rosencrantz and Guildenstern Are Dead

In *Rosencrantz and Guildenstern are Dead*, Stoppard takes two of the minor characters from Shakespeare's *Hamlet* and makes them into the unwitting stars of the show. The play is self-consciously theatrical and much of the humor is derived from the fact that the audience is aware of the famous dramatic context in which the two characters are operating. As befits minor players on the peripheries of a major tragedy, Ros and Guil have very little to actually do and spend a large part of the play hanging around pondering life and their purpose in it. Every now and again Shakespeare's plot and dialogue intrude on the action leaving the audience with the impression that the lives of the two courtiers are caught up in wider events of an importance that they will never fully grasp. Critics have suggested that there are strong parallels between the dramatic predicament of Rosencrantz and Guildenstern and that of Vladimir and Estragon in Samuel Beckett's *Waiting for Godot*. Stoppard

undoubtedly plays with dramatic styles in *Rosencrantz and Guildenstern*; this is seen most obviously in his conflation of techniques from both Renaissance and Absurdist theater. However, his dramatic manipulation of Shakespeare's material is highly original. The modern tone of Ros and Guil's dialogue contrasts with the fluid verse of Shakespeare's play, marking them as outsiders and highlighting their impotence in the world of the Elizabethan play. In the hands of Rosencrantz and Guildenstern, *Hamlet*, widely regarded as one of Shakespeare's greatest tragedies, becomes an absurdist farce.

Kate Harris

Date 1966

Author Tom Stoppard (1937–)

Nationality UK (Born Czechoslovakia)

Why It's Key *Rosencrantz and Guildenstern* was first produced by Oxford undergraduates as part of the "fringe" at the 1966 Edinburgh Festival. In April 1967 the play was produced to great critical acclaim by the National Theatre Company.

Key Character **Jacy Farrow**
The Last Picture Show

In fiction, television series, and films, it seems that every American high school has its most popular girl. Other, less pretty, girls want to bask in her reflected glory, while she is the object of adolescent lust to young men of every description, from the athletes to the nerds. Jacy Farrow fulfils this role perfectly in *The Last Picture Show*. She is blonde and beautiful and her parents are wealthy enough for her to be out of the league of ordinary boys but she is still happy to flirt with them and tease them by smiling as she passes in her convertible, and skinny-dipping at the local lake.

The novel captures a period of change throughout the USA. A generation of young men is growing up that didn't fight in World War II; they have more freedom and more money in their pockets, and they have rock 'n' roll. Things are changing for women too, and Jacy reflects this. She doesn't want to become like her mother, with nothing to do but drink and cheat on her rich husband. While the center of attention, she is bored and aspires to a wider world. However, while Jacy can be freer than the women of her mother's generation, the liberation experienced by many women in the 1960s and 1970s is as yet undreamed-of.

The character of Jacy rang true with many readers who had come of age a decade before the novel was published, whether as an evocation of their first love or best friend, and the 1971 film version played on the current wave of nostalgia for the 1950s.
Michael Munro

Date 1966

Author Larry McMurtry (1936–)

Nationality USA

Why It's Key For many readers, the flirtatious, teasing and often downright bitchy Jacy was the archetypal embodiment of adolescent girls of the period, moving towards an independence that their mothers never experienced. She was memorably played by Cybill Shepherd in the movie version of the story in 1971.

Key Book
Efuru

In a 1977 interview, Flora Nwapa said of her eponymous heroine: "I tried to present a dignified woman, who suffered in silence, who was good and understanding, but was badly rewarded by fate." Efuru, beautiful, well-born, independent-minded and respected as a trader, deserves to have better luck with men than is meted out to her in two unhappy marriages. First she chooses to elope with Adizua, who is from an undistinguished background – a choice that does not go down well with her family. After some years she has a much-wanted child; but her husband has begun disappearing and staying away from home for days. Even after their beloved daughter falls sick and dies, he is not there for the funeral, and the rumour is that he has taken another wife. Eventually Efuru realizes that she has no option but to leave him, and she returns to her father's house. Courted by a new young suitor, she marries again, happily at first until he too deserts her, failing to attend her father's funeral. Alone and childless, she turns to the lake goddess, Uhamiri, but the novel ends with an unanswered question: "She dreamt of the woman of the lake, her beauty, her long hair and her riches…. She gave women beauty and wealth but she had no child. She had never experienced the joy of motherhood. Why then did women worship her?" However, while *Efuru* is usually considered a feminist work, the way that its plot incorporates female circumcision remains deeply worrying.
Margaret Busby

Date 1966

Author Flora Nwapa (1931–1993)

Nationality Nigeria

Why It's Key With *Efuru*, Flora Nwapa became black Africa's first internationally published female novelist in the English language. She has been called the mother of modern African literature and forerunner to a generation of other African women writers. She brings a rare female perspective to the traditional Igbo culture that she depicts.

Key Book
Hell's Angels

In the first section of *Hell's Angels: The Strange and Terrible Saga of the Outlaw Motorcycle Gangs* – "Making the Menace" – Thomson reflects on his first few months in the year he spends in the company of the "notorious" motorcycle gang. He confesses: "By the middle of the summer I had become so involved in the outlaw scene that I was no longer sure whether I was doing research on the Hell's Angels or being slowly absorbed by them." In this admission can be found the embryonic gestures of Thomson's "Gonzo" writing that was to become globally infamous and much copied as his reporting became increasingly hip, outlandish, and fiercely provocative in equal measure.

Thomson's "embedding" authorizes his debunking of his subjects, demonized, and mythologized as degenerate "big city Huns." He scoffs at the threat they are perceived to pose to respectable society, revels in his revelation of their domesticity, and parallels their social compassion with their predilection for illegality

and "immorality." Thomson's journalistic investigation reveals their function as contemporary sideshow freaks; a tourist attraction for the American public. He not only asks why this is but also exposes the hypocrisy in prevailing ideas of American respectability.

As the narrative progresses Thomson frequently crosses the "neutral" line that distances a reporter from his subject. His eventual ejection after a brutal beating from this gang of "dog-eating, crotch busting fools" left him free to cultivate an alternative phenomenon in the world of reporting. This book demonstrates the "New Journalist" ethos and should be seen as a classic work in "deviance" studies as much as it is prototypically Gonzo – the full blown method, style, and persona that would come to fruition four years later with *Fear and Loathing in Las Vegas*.

Graeme Mcdonald

Date 1966

Author Hunter S. Thomson (1937–2005)

Nationality USA

Why It's Key One of the foundational texts of American "New Journalism"; the movement that changed the style, direction, and ethos of journalistic writing. Its alternative style of reporting greatly influenced the cultural expression of an America seeking to make sense of an emergent counterculture and the first incursions in Vietnam.

1960-1969

497

Key Author
David Goodis

After the publication of his first novel, *Retreat from Oblivion*, Goodis (1917–1967) moved to California where he had a brief, unremarkable career as a screenwriter. Disillusioned by the Hollywood grind, he moved back to his parents' house in Philadelphia in 1950 and a major turning point in his writing ensued. During the 1950s he wrote twelve of his eighteen crime novels, and became a mainstay of Fawcett's renowned Gold Medal imprint. While his style has elements of the classic detective fiction of Raymond Chandler and Dashiell Hammett, Goodis wasn't concerned with mysteries and solving crimes. His work was character-driven, and explored the psyche of society's castaways. The relentless despair in his work had more in common with Beatnik writers, such as Jack Kerouac.

Toward the end of his life, he was involved in litigation, claiming that his novel *Dark Passage* had been illegally used as the basis for the popular television show, *The Fugitive*. The lawsuit was settled

posthumously, in Goodis' favor. At the time of his death much of his work remained out of print, yet from the 1980s on, presses such as Black Lizard, Serpent's Tail, and Hard Case Crime have reissued his work. In January, 2007, an enthusiastic group of scholars, contemporary crime writers, and fans gathered for Goodiscon in Philadelphia. The event marked the fortieth anniversary of Goodis' death, and exemplified how his work continues to resonate and inspire.

Jason Starr

Date 1967 (death)

Nationality USA

Other Key Works *Cassidy's Girl* (1951); *The Moon in the Gutter* (1953); *Down There* (1956)

Why It's Key By penning gritty noir novels such as *Dark Passage* (filmed starring Humphrey Bogart and Lauren Bacall), Goodis was one of the major voices in 1950s American crime fiction. His work catapulted lowlifes and drunks into a prominent place in crime fiction.

Key Author **Milan Kundera**
The Joke

Born in Brno in what was then Czechoslovakia, Milan Kundera's (1929–) life and work have always been inextricably intertwined with the country's political fortunes. Indeed, one of the pivotal issues that his work continues to revolve around is the idea that the political is the personal.

From *The Joke*, his first and most overtly political novel, and the work which most closely adheres to our expectations of the form, his writing has become more experimental and meditative. His previous incarnation as a jazz musician is evident in the cadences of his writing and his extended digressions and philosophical ruminations lend his writing an abstruse and ethereal quality.

His own involvement in the public life of his country had tangible and far-reaching consequences, however. As a young man, he joined the Communist Party, but was expelled just two years later in 1950 for "anti-party" activities. He rejoined years later, but his prominent role in the failed attempts to reform the party during the Prague Spring meant that life became very difficult for him after the Soviet invasion of 1968. He was removed from his teaching post and his books were banned from the country's libraries, and subsequently from publication. Many of his most famous novels, including *The Book of Laughter and Forgetting* (1979) and *The Unbearable Lightness of Being* (1984), were written after his exile to France in 1975.

Kundera is a supremely important writer who has asked searching questions about the nature of the individual in relation to the state and vice versa. In doing so, he invites us as readers to question the distinctions we make between the public and the private.
Juliet Wightman

Date 1967 (published)

Nationality
Czechoslovakia

Other Key Works
Immortality (1990);
Ignorance (2000)

Why It's Key Writing in both Czech and French, Kundera explores the ways in which the most intimate impulses and relationships are informed by the broader workings of the political realm. His work explores the relationship between exile, identity, memory, and nostalgia.

Opposite Milan Kundera

Key Author
Dorothy Parker

Parker was born Dorothy Rothschild, a name she never liked. She always preferred to be known by her married name, Mrs Parker, even long after she and her first husband, Edwin Pond Parker, had divorced. She was a writer who consistently struggled with deadlines, battling writers' block, unhappy love affairs, alcoholism, and an enormous social circle in her attempts to put pen to paper.

Her work is consequently slight in scale – short stories rather than novels, brief stanzas of verse rather than epic poems. Her genius was to capture emotional turmoil, of which she knew a great deal, in comparatively few words – "The Lovely Leave" is only a few pages long, but tells the reader everything they will ever need to know about waiting for a lover. As Ogden Nash wrote, "The trick about her writing is the trick about Ring Lardner's writing or Ernest Hemingway's work. It isn't a trick." She was a vicious critic of both drama and literature, famously dismissing the cuteness of A.A. Milne with the putdown, "Tonstant Weader Fwowed Up."

Parker is a writer remembered almost exclusively for words she did not write. Her spoken *bons mots* were so widely reported and repeated that far more people know her response when challenged to use the word "horticulture" in a sentence ("You can lead a whore to culture, but you cannot make her think."), or her memorable rhyme, "Men seldom make passes at girls who wear glasses," than have read her O. Henry Award-winning short story, "Big Blonde."
Natalie Haynes

Date 1967 (death)

Nationality USA

Key Works *Laments for the Living* (1930); *After Such Pleasures* (1933); *Not so Deep as a Well* (1936); *Here Lies* (1939)

Why It's Key Parker was the drama critic for *Vanity Fair* and later literary and drama critic for the *New Yorker*, where many of her stories were also published. Her humorous verses also displayed her legendary biting wit.

Key Book
The Magic Toyshop

The Magic Toyshop exhibits many of the literary preoccupations found in Angela Carter's (1940–1992) subsequent works. Her use of mythology, fairy tale, gothicism, and magic realism begins to take root in this early novel where she explores many of the constrictive cultural stereotypes attributed to women. The novel is typically postmodern in its intertextuality; Carter uses the vocabulary of radical feminism here and alludes to other works of literature, myth, and film. The narrative is driven by fantasy and gothic conventions, including a "maiden" in peril and images of entrapment and incarceration. The novel focuses on a young protagonist Melanie, who is on the cusp of womanhood and who is aware of her growing sexuality. In a witty play on colonial exploration Carter uses America, a "new found land," as a metaphor for exploration and discovery. However, it is Melanie who is on a voyage of discovery, "exploring the whole of herself" and finding the "mountain ranges" and the "moist richness of her secret valleys" that emphasize her body as a site of pleasure and desire. The moment Melanie discovers herself sexually, she is orphaned – she is punished for forbidden knowledge and transgression. Throughout the novel Carter offers a sustained attack on patriarchal myths and power and her feminist stance is revealed as she explores Melanie's responses to the containment of her body in her new environment and her eventual journey to become an active female subject. The novel established Carter as a strong female erotic voice and it remains at the forefront of feminist writing in the twentieth century.

Pat Wheeler

Date 1967

Nationality UK

Author Angela Carter (1940–1992)

Why It's Key Carter was one of the most original British fiction writers, and one who helped to authenticate a voice for women in literature.

Key Book
A Grain of Wheat

This third novel by one of Africa's most significant writers and activist intellectuals offers acute insight into the messy difficulties of anti-colonial liberation struggle. The novel is primarily set in December 1963 in a small rural village in central Kenya during the four days leading up to the day of Kenyan Independence (Uhuru). It skilfully interweaves several characters' memories and resolutions of events during the State of Emergency lasting from 1952–1956. In doing so it expresses the crucial challenges facing Kenyans as they experience their autonomy from British colonial rule: historical honesty, the responsibility of freedom, and the necessity of just government.

An expertly framed political narrative relates the fraught relations between members of the peasant community affected by involvement with the Mau Mau movement. At the centre is the psychodrama of Mugo, considered a hero for his support of the martyred Kahika under detention in a British concentration camp.

Mugo's struggle with the public revelation of his actual role as an informer (albeit under extreme duress) informs Ngugi's themes and political aims, notably the arduous necessity of truth, confession, and communal solidarity.

The novel's powerful conclusion warns against the re-emergence of colonialist forms of oppression characterized by the delusional John Thompson. Ultimately, Ngugi's work speculates on the strength of post-imperial relations by pointing to the important connections between private and national forms of suture. It expresses the difficult task of political and cultural independence. A potent image of a pregnant woman induces a closing symbol of hesitant, creative expectancy. The reunion of an estranged partnership confirms the rehabilitation of the Kenyan past in the present, with a mind to the new Kenya of the future.

Graeme Mcdonald

Date 1967

Author Ngugi Wa Thiong'o

Nationality Kenya

Why It's Key Central novel of Kenyan decolonization and one of the most important works of postcolonial African literature.

Key Book
The Fixer

From a Jewish immigrant family in Brooklyn, Bernard Malamud won a Pulitzer Prize in 1967 for his fourth novel, *The Fixer*. Invoking life in a tsarist Russian prison and written in an uncluttered modern style, it confirmed Malamud's gift to create page-turners of moral horror. In eight novels and several volumes of short stories Malamud concentrated on small-time Jews in trouble. The rich Yiddish language and life in *The Assistant* (1957) gave way in *The Fixer* to a painful study of helplessness. This pacy novel is far removed from fiction about "issues." It starkly presents anti-Semitism and prison brutality in late nineteenth-century Russia. From the back-street criminals who frame the hero for a crime he didn't commit, to the unseeing warders, to Bok's estranged wife and the sympathetic investigating magistrate, Malamud's characters are richly drawn, as if painted in oils.

Malamud's youth was marked by suffering. His disturbed mother died when he was fifteen and to judge by the destructive women in his novels, like Bok's potential girlfriend Zina and his accuser Marfa, he felt she spoilt his life. His loveable but feckless father, a grocer who endured the Depression, and his grandfather, an immigrant from Russia, also left their mark. A college professor before he found fame as a writer, Malamud made good, but denied that privilege to his decent, downtrodden characters. He was an atheist who viewed his Jewishness as a curse, although the survival of Bok gave *The Fixer*, with its fabulous set-piece ending, a religious dimension.

Lesley Chamberlain

Date 1967

Author Bernard Malamud (1914–1986)

Nationality USA

Why It's Key *The Fixer* secured Malamud a reputation as one of the great American novelists of the 1960s. His rich mining of his Jewish background linked him with Saul Bellow and Philip Roth.

Key Book
The Confessions of Nat Turner

Nat Turner (1800-1831), the leader of a slave rebellion in Virginia in 1831, left his actual "confessions" in statements made to a lawyer before his trial. However, many historians have dismissed these statements as being invented or at least highly embellished by Turner, and by the lawyer, rather than as the literal truth. Styron provoked controversy by taking this material as the starting point for his fictional version of these events, presented from Turner's point of view. Many African-Americans objected to the idea of a white novelist presuming to document the black experience from within, especially in the setting of the slavery era. By emphasising Turner's violent sexual desire for white women, it was claimed, Styron was also playing up to racist stereotypes of the black male and white fears of rape and miscegenation.

Styron countered that he was essentially showing Turner as a hero struggling against white oppression, someone who in the end would rather die than continue to exist as a slave. He was supported by some black authors, particularly his friend James Baldwin, who felt that Styron's work was at heart sympathetic to its hero, and to black slaves in general, while avoiding making Turner out to be some kind of saint. In an era of growing interracial tension in the United States, with developments such as the Watts riots in 1965 and the formation of the Black Panther party in 1966, black opinion on the whole was not ready to accept a white interpretation of black history.

Michael Munro

Date 1967

Author William Styron (1925–2006)

Nationality USA

Why It's Key This novel aroused controversy because its author, a white man, presented an account of a historical slave revolt from the point of view of a black man. Not only was this considered presumptuous, it was also seen as reinforcing racial stereotypes. Despite this, the book won the Pulitzer Prize for fiction in 1968.

Key Book
Trout Fishing in America

Like many Americans who contributed to the counter-cultural melting pot that was the Californian west coast in the 1960s, Richard Brautigan was born in another part of the country, in his case the state of Washington. He had already established a small, local reputation as a poet before the publication in 1967 of his first novel *Trout Fishing in America* brought him international fame.

Its episodic, anecdotal style is characteristic of Brautigan's fiction as is its almost childlike openness to the senses and minutiae of daily life. On the surface it is an account of the narrator's fishing trips throughout the country, springing partly from a nostalgic attempt to recapture one particular spell on a river, idealized by cherished memory into the perfect piscatorial experience. As the narrator wanders through contemporary and remembered America, the uncaring and materialistic lifestyle that surrounds him is contrasted unsympathetically with the ideals he shares with his fellow members of the nascent counterculture. The novel articulates in prose, rather than the more pervasive rock and folk music of the day, the attitudes of the hippie movement, whose desire for peace and a more natural way of life led many to "drop out" of the current go-getting society, which they characteristically described as being driven by the "military-industrial machine." The novel's nostalgic approach to the past, combined with its concern for living intensely in the moment, perfectly encapsulated one of the contrasts inherent in the hippie dream, the kind of attitude that led to the latest electronic recording technology being used by musicians who preferred to dress like characters from the "Wild West."
Michael Munro

Date 1967

Author Richard Brautigan (1935–84)

Nationality USA

Why It's Key Considered the first important novel to articulate the ideals and aspirations of the nascent hippie movement, the novel's whimsical narrative nonetheless contains a damning critique of an uncaring and materialistic society that was highly influential on counter-cultural attitudes in the rest of the 1960s and 1970s.

Opposite Richard Brautigan

Key Event **The last *Boy's Own Paper* is published**

The *Boy's Own Paper* was first published in 1879. The ethos behind it was Christian, the aim being to encourage reading while at the same time inculcating proper values in the impressionable young. It featured puzzles and readers' letters, but it specialized in adventure stories, whether as self-contained tales or serials, and among its famous contributors were Arthur Conan Doyle, R.M. Ballantyne, and Jules Verne. It was highly illustrated, including comic strips and full-page reproductions of specially commissioned paintings. Also popular were stories of British heroes, especially winners of the Victoria Cross. A typical example of this was the January 1917 issue, which highlighted "The Boy Hero of the Chester," telling the story of Jack Cornwall, a young VC winner at the naval Battle of Jutland in June 1916. This issue even contained a letter from Admiral Lord Beresford to *Boy's Own* readers: "Cornwall has set an example of devotion to duty which will be an inspiration to British boys for all time … every boy can endeavour to live up to his example by practising discipline and being obedient in small things."

After World War II the *Boy's Own Paper* came to be seen as very old-fashioned, propounding jingoistic attitudes and celebrating British greatness in a way that was increasingly irrelevant to the nation's true status in the later twentieth century. It was not alone in this, however, but it was so typical of its type and era that its name lives on in describing a particularly boyish, somewhat naive, attitude to life.
Michael Munro

Date 1967

Nationality UK

Why It's Key The *Boy's Own Paper* is best remembered for its thrilling stories featuring upstanding young Anglo-Saxon heroes putting the world to rights in a plucky manner. By the time of its demise it had become associated with old-fashioned jingoism, but its lasting mark on British language is seen in the phrase "a *Boy's Own* adventure" still being used to describe feats of derring-do.

Joe Orton is murdered by his lover

Described by biographer John Lahr as a "modern Lord of Misrule," Joe Orton wrote gloriously sardonic plays that broke taboos and box office records with equal ease: *The Ruffian on the Stair*, *Entertaining Mr Sloane* and *Loot*. By 1966, Orton was so well known that he received the decade's highest accolade – an invitation to work with The Beatles.

A year later, Orton was more famous than ever thanks to his sensational and sensationalized death which was front page news the very next day. Killed by various loves that dared not speak their names at the time – long-suppressed rage, sexual jealousy, and artistic envy – the playwright seemed destined to be mythologized as a doomed hedonistic artist, a tragic "queer," or both.

That Orton is neither of the above owes much to Lahr's *Prick Up Your Ears* (adapted for the screen by Alan Bennett and Stephen Frears in 1987) and his own vivid *Diaries*. Ironically, while these have secured his

posthumous celebrity, their depictions of Orton's tragic death and scandalous life have eclipsed public perceptions of his art. More read about today than he is read or performed, Orton's star has dipped behind those of his luckier and more durable contemporaries, Tom Stoppard and Harold Pinter.

Interviewed by the *Evening Standard* in 1966, Orton spoke of fame in quite different terms. Asked to describe his "ultimate aims," Orton replied, "to write a play as good as *The Importance of Being Earnest*." But, he continued, "Unlike Wilde, I think you should put your genius into your work, not into your life."

James Kidd

Date 9 August 1967

Nationality UK

Why It's Key Orton's murder by his lover Kenneth Halliwell (who afterwards committed suicide) is a defining moment in the history of British culture, theatre, and sexuality. The ultimate impact on Orton is ambiguous: the tragic and gruesome circumstances of his death have helped make him one of Britain's most famous writers, but at the cost of his own work's reputation.

Opposite Joe Orton

1960-1969

505

Key Event **Harlan Ellison publishes New Wave sci-fi anthology *Dangerous Visions***

The arrival of the short story collection *Dangerous Visions*, edited by Harlan Ellison (1934–), injected a healthy dose of sex, violence, and psychedelia into a science fiction scene that was buckling under the weight of its own bloated pretensions. The timing was crucial to the book's status: Vietnam rolled bloodily on, as did the Civil Rights movement and, for many, there was the pervading sense that something was about to give. These young, new writers – among them, Philip K. Dick, Robert Silverberg, and Brian Aldiss – tended to be liberal, left-wing, and anti-war (in fact, broadly ambivalent about technology in general). The old school tended to be more conservative and pro-war. *Dangerous Visions* was seen as a divisive force, firmly demarcating the line between these two camps. The SF establishment wrote about the "hard," material aspects of the colonization of space and evoked a sense of wonder at humanity's noble quest and its technological marvels. The New Wave concerned itself

with humanity's "inner space" and the effects of the inexorable march of progress upon it. For them, the "sense of wonder" had been replaced with a sense of unease and uncertainty. Humanity's quest for the stars became an odyssey into the human soul by way of all-too-earthly delights. Many of the writers in *Dangerous Visions* have since become SF establishment figures themselves, and its legacy is that the themes and ideas expressed within have entered into common parlance, placing what was once the preserve of the experimental left-field firmly in the popular consciousness.

Christian Kerr

Date 1967

Nationality USA

Why It's Key *Dangerous Visions* heralded the end of "nuts and bolts" science fiction and the beginning of a more experimental and daring approach to the genre, notably depicting complex sexual themes for arguably the first time in mainstream SF. Ellison received a special citation at the 26th World SF Convention for editing "the most significant and controversial SF book published in 1967."

Key Event **Celan's introduced his influential idea of the "breath-measure"**

Celan (who adopted an anagram of the family name Ancel) survived the war in a Nazi labor camp. Both his parents died in Auschwitz. The poetry he wrote in German after he moved to Paris in 1948, until his suicide in 1970, challenged the dictum that there could be no poetry after the Holocaust. Celan, who claimed that words were all he had left, reinvented the basis for lyrical utterance. Titles such as "The Rose for No-one," "Speech Mesh," "String Suns," and "The Compulsion of Light" suggested a strange beauty left in the wake of man's ungraspable inhumanity to man. *Atemwende*, which meant the "turn" or "change" of breath, showed him exhuming, from under the buried surface of poetic speech, a voice almost silenced by shock. Jewish mystical thought schooled him in a theology of absence and helped configure his dense imagery. His early medical training may have suggested the "mesh" of words that, like the way the body heals a flesh wound, begins the healing process by forming a hard

scab. A learned student of the history of German, Celan created new compound words, or split existing words into their components, to convey extreme experience. The closeness of Yiddish to medieval German was a rich stimulus. Celan described his poems as a homecoming. But the paradox of his work was that the space behind words, beyond death, still loomed dislocated and empty. His place in modern literature is unique and has attracted the finest translators, above all Michael Hamburger.

Lesley Chamberlain

Date 1967

Title *Atemwende*

Author Paul Celan (1920–1970)

Nationality Romania

Why It's Key After publishing his first collection of poems in 1952 Celan became widely recognized as the finest poet in German of his generation. The extreme concision and mystery of his work has saved him from exploitation by the Holocaust industry.

506

Key Passage **The levitation of Remedios the Beauty** *One Hundred Years of Solitude*

"Fernanda felt a delicate wind of light pull the sheets out of her hands and open them up wide. Amaranta… tried to grasp the sheet so that she would not fall down at the instant in which Remedios the Beauty began to rise. Úrsula, almost blind at the time, was the only person who was sufficiently calm to identify the nature of that determined wind and she left the sheets to the mercy of the light as she watched Remedios the Beauty waving good-bye in the midst of the flapping sheets that rose up with her, abandoning with her the environment of beetles and dahlias and passing through the air with her as four o'clock in the afternoon came to an end, and they were lost forever with her in the upper atmosphere where not even the highest-flying birds of memory could reach her."

There are portents of wonder strewn throughout *One Hundred Years of Solitude* – indelible ash crosses, a tribe plagued by insomnia, buried suits of

armor, rains that last for four years, a plague of yellow butterflies, the skeleton of a ship on dry land – but nothing prepares the reader for the moment when Remedios the Beauty simply floats out of the story. The casual manner in which it is reported, almost in passing, is as surprising as the event itself.

Magical realism? As Gabriel García Márquez often explained, anyone who grew up listening to their old aunts' tales about the lives of saints would consider such an account strictly realistic. To Macondo's inhabitants, Remedios the Beauty's levitation is no more extraordinary than the discovery of ice.

Ángel Gurría-Quintana

Date 1967

Author Gabriel García Márquez (1928)

Nationality Colombia

Why It's Key Márquez borrowed the name of Macondo – the imaginary setting for the book – from an abandoned banana plantation passed while travelling by train to his birthplace, Aracataca, to sell his family home. The book brought magical realism, and Latin American literature, to the world's attention.

Key Passage
Snow White

"QUESTIONS:
1. Do you like the story so far? Yes ( ) No ( )
2. Does Snow White resemble the Snow White you remember? Yes ( ) No ( )...
15. In your opinion, should human beings have more shoulders? ( ) Two sets of shoulders? ( ) Three? ( )"

These self-parodying "QUESTIONS" are inserted right in the middle of Donald Barthelme's *Snow White*, a novel which shakes readers out of their conventional narrative expectations. In this postmodern parody of the classic fairy tale, Snow White lives with seven dwarves called Kevin, Edward, Hubert, Henry, Clem, Dan, and Bill, who do good business in building, cleaning and Chinese baby food. Barthelme's rewriting amplifies one aspect of the traditional fairy tale – Snow White's cohabitation with the dwarves – and recasts their relationship as a sexually overindulgent and existentially problematic one.

The narrative is fragmented into short sequences not more than three pages long which are told from different viewpoints and with different styles – the languages of politics, technology, comic books, etc. are collaged – so that any narrative or psychological development becomes difficult. The classic climax in which the stepmother figure poisons Snow White into a state of apparent death is replaced by an undramatic death of the prince figure who mistakenly drinks the poisoned vodka Gibson prepared for Snow White by her rival Jane. Snow White goes on living with her six alienated bourgeois dwarves (one gets hanged for causing a loss to their business). The novel ends with a hilarious parody of Disney's canonized version of Snow White: "REVIRGINIATION OF SNOW WHITE… THE HEROES DEPART IN SEARCH OF A NEW PRINCIPLE HEIGH-HO."

Mayako Murai

Date 1967

Author Donald Barthelme (1931–89)

Nationality USA

Why It's Key Barthelme has created a new form of fairy tale for our time where the characters do not communicate with each other except sexually, the narration is cut up into fragments which do not follow a linear narrative, and there is no happily ever after for the heroine; she tries to write a poem about freedom while she keeps house for the dwarves.

1960–1969

507

Key Event **A march on the Pentagon leads Mailer to pen *Armies of the Night***

In October 1967, an eclectic circus of 1960s peace activists marched on the Pentagon to exorcize the building by encircling and psychically levitating it, thus helping to end the war in Vietnam.

Using a first-person account of his own arrest in the march, novelist Norman Mailer's (1923–) *Armies of the Night: History as a Novel, the Novel as History* is as raucous and disorderly as the counterculture that he describes. Already a famous novelist and founding editor of the progressive *Village Voice*, Mailer's New Journalism style of mixing the facts and description of the narrator as a figure in these facts captures the chaotic energies and aspirations of the 1960s.

In his account, Mailer recorded the increasing role of black American militancy as a model for the white, middle-class dissidents in ways that foreshadowed the later turn by some to urban terrorism. Harvard-educated, Jewish Mailer also presented an ethnic struggle for cultural authority as

the children of immigrants were beginning to demand recognition by the older WASP elites, while also refusing to obey the polite mannerisms of this older ersatz American aristocracy.

Previously, left-wing writers looked to abolish the traditional institutions of education and media. *Armies of the Night* argues that the "barbarians," those who are not the children of the traditional white establishment, not only have the right to enter the gates, but are actually smarter and better equipped to run the institutions than a dying American gentry, typified by Secretary of Defense Robert McNamara's escalation of an imperial war that had never much chance of success.

Stephen Shapiro

Date 1967

Nationality USA

Why It's Key Mailer uses the description of an anti-Vietnam demonstration as an allegory for the failure of traditional power elites in charge of American domestic and foreign policy. In the midst of a 60s milieu that included other "non-fiction novels" such as Capote's *In Cold Blood*, *Armies of the Night* blended autobiographical and novelistic techniques to create a populist history for the anti-war left.

Key Author **Enid Blyton**
The Famous Five series

Enid Blyton was an immensely popular and prolific children's author – at one time she was the fourth most translated writer in the world, and her total output amounts to over 600 books. Unusually she worked right across the childhood age ranges, writing stories for "young folk" (such as the Noddy books), as well as adventure stories for older children (The Famous Five, etc.). Her works became so profitable that a company had to be set up to manage her business affairs, and Blyton became one of the first writers to be marketed as a "brand," the familiar freehand signature that appeared on all her books acting rather like a "logo."

The "production-line" rate of output, combined with a post-war reassessment of children's literature among tightly budgeted librarians, and changing social attitudes from the 1960s onwards, lead to Blyton's works being regarded with suspicion and unease among middle-class parents. At best her stories were regarded as bland, formulaic, with limited vocabulary and stereotyped characters, at worst she was regarded as racist and sexist. Whilst it is not clear that Blyton was ever "banned" from public libraries (as opposed to librarians simply choosing not to purchase her books), it is clear that a great many parents did impose their own disapproving bans on Blyton's works.

This along with an ongoing interest in the reality behind the idyllic lifestyle depicted by Blyton's publicity machine (in her autobiography her daughter, Imogen, describes her mother as "emotionally crippled") has failed to dilute Blyton's popularity, and she still sells in enormous numbers across the world.
Gerard Woodward

Date 1968 (death)

Nationality UK

Other Key Works *The Magic Faraway Tree* series (1939–51); The Adventure series (1944–55); *The Malory Towers* series (1946–51); *The St Clare's* series (1941–45); *The Secret Seven* series (1949–63)

Why It's Key One of the most popular children's authors of all time. Young people around the world adored her books while parents and librarians condemned them.

508

Key Event **Didion takes a trip to California, inspiring *Slouching Towards Bethlehem***

Joan Didion's first book of non-fiction (after an early novel, *Run River*, published in 1963) was a collection of essays that established its author as one of the keenest, most distinctive chroniclers of American social and political cultures. Didion's voice of cool intelligence, her eye for physical and historical landscapes, and her acute ear for ironies of speech and situation, have remained consistent in her other works of fiction, memoir, and non-fiction, but *Slouching Towards Bethlehem* remains a defining book for the author and for its time. Anyone seeking to understand 1960s culture in the U.S., specifically in California where the Western belief in self-reinvention has its deepest roots, would do well to begin by reading Didion's blade-sharp essays. "The center was not holding," is how Didion opens the title piece, her classic account of the nascent community of hippies in the Haight-Ashbury district of San Francisco. In it, Didion meets many young souls strung out on drugs and incoherent philosophies, and characteristically vanishes into the scene she describes: her art is to offer a curiously egoless account in a voice that is distinctively Didion. Her own personal history and her aesthetic are developed in pieces such as "On Keeping a Notebook" or "On Self-Respect," reflections in which the California native is both comical and skeptical about her younger selves. That Didion is as bracingly clear-eyed about her own flaws as she is about other people's helps her to earn our trust in her unsentimental, trenchant observations. She is both forgiving and unforgiving, a companion and a scold, and with these contradictions captures something crucial in the society around her.
Sylvia Brownrigg

Date 1968

Author Joan Didion (1934)

Nationality USA

Why It's Key *Slouching Towards Bethlehem* is a brilliant collection of essays from the sixties that introduced one of the most important voices of modern American letters.

Opposite Joan Didion

Key Book
The Naked Civil Servant

"If at first you don't succeed… failure may be your style."

And yes, Quentin Crisp was a failure, but only if a refusal to accept the conventional understanding of success can be counted as failure. Few have reinvented themselves quite so radically, or so rigorously, as Quentin Crisp. Then again, for anyone born Dennis Pratt ("my name before I dyed it") self-reinvention must represent less a career move than an aesthetic obligation. As he states in the opening pages of *The Naked Civil Servant*, his witty and poignant memoir of life as a gay man before the loosening of the laws, he was, at least from the '30s, not merely a self-confessed homosexual, "but a self-evident one," wearing mascara outdoors when even women dared not.

He tells us of the erotic possibilities offered by the Blackout during World War II, expatiates on the essential timelessness of Camp. Chased around a room by an elderly Czech smeared in fish oil, beaten up by gangs who leave him alone when they discover that he's from Chelsea, harassed by the police, endlessly rejected in love, Quentin Crisp retains throughout a wide-eyed, heavy-lashed mildness. Like all great epigrammatists, he understood that true wit springs from an appearance of innocence.

He attained two very different cultural crowns, which managed somehow to perch together on that remarkable bouffant sweep: that of gay icon, and, in his own words, "stately homo," the acceptable, because outrageous, face of late twentieth-century homosexuality.

Murrough O'Brien

Date 1968

Author Quentin Crisp (1908–99)

Nationality UK

Why It's Key *The Naked Civil Servant*, though published after the (partial) legalization of homosexuality, described a life lived in flamboyant defiance of sexual codes. Crisp's courage, humor, and utter lack of embarrassment inspired a whole generation of gay men to accept and proclaim their sexuality.

Key Character **Myra Breckinridge**
Myra Breckinridge

SPOILER

"I am Myra Breckinridge whom no man will ever possess" – thus Vidal's heroine, the ultimate bitch goddess of male nightmare and wet dream, introduces herself. Flaunting the improbable breasts and endless legs of the 40s movie stars she so admires, she becomes an avenging angel for her sex, driving men to slathering distraction.

Myra's mission is to smash the phallocracy that has dominated Western civilization since the time of the ancient Greeks. Her theater of operations is Hollywood, where she teaches Posture and Empathy at her uncle's acting academy. Here she determines to liberate one of her students, Mary-Ann Pringle ("so reminiscent of the early Lana Turner"), from her beau, the unremittingly macho Rusty Godowski, whom she succeeds in anally penetrating as he lies tied to a bed in the academy infirmary. "Once inside, I savored my triumph. I had avenged Myron. A lifetime of being penetrated had brought him only misery. Now, in the person of Rusty, I was able, as Woman Triumphant, to destroy the adored destroyer." It turns out, of course, that Myra was once Myron, and has had a gender reassignment procedure. Unfortunately for Myra, her passion for Mary-Ann is not reciprocated, the latter having "a horror of Lesbianism." Thwarted, Myra performs a volte face, regrets her "pretentious phase," and has her surgery reversed (as far as is possible) in order to set up in a "conventional" man-woman domestic arrangement with her adored Mary-Ann. The status quo is thus, ironically, restored.

Ian Crofton

Date 1968

Author Gore Vidal (1925)

Nationality USA

Why It's Key An exuberantly outrageous contribution to the sexual revolution of the 1960s. Himself a gay man, Vidal used his creation to subvert traditional gender roles, and in so doing upset conservative opinion and spawned a bestseller. A sequel, *Myron*, followed in 1975.

Opposite *Myra Breckinridge*

Key Event **Kawabata becomes the first Japanese to win Nobel Prize in Literature**

In his Nobel lecture, "Japan, the Beautiful and Myself," Kawabata, the last major writer to work in the "classical" Japanese tradition, and perhaps one of the few novelists successfully to combine a non-European aesthetic with a European art form, described the influence of Zen on his work. "The Zen disciple sits for long hours silent and motionless, with his eyes closed. Presently he enters a state of impassivity, free from all ideas and all thoughts. He departs from the self and enters the realm of nothingness. This is not the nothingness or the emptiness of the west. It is rather the reverse, a universe of the spirit in which everything communicates freely with everything, transcending bounds, limitless."

Kawabata was born in the industrial town of Osaka in 1899, the son of a doctor. He was orphaned in early childhood and went to live with his grandparents. He was profoundly affected by the catastrophic defeat of Japan in the war, prompting him to declare that he would write only elegies. Influenced by the formal austerity and fragile lyricism of haiku, he is a miniaturist: he compresses where others seek to inflate and enlarge. His is a fiction of extreme economy, even of emptiness. The dominant themes of his novels are male narcissism, the connection between sex and death, erotic obsession and the vulnerability of female purity. The preoccupation with mutability is acute.

In 1972, at the age of 72, suffering from insomnia and disturbed by the fame that the Nobel Prize had brought him, Kawabata put his head in a gas oven and killed himself.

Jason Cowley

Date 1968

Author Yasunari Kawabata (1899–1972)

Nationality Japan

Key Works *Snow Country* (1935–1947); *Thousand Cranes* (1949–1951); *The House of Sleeping Beauties* (1961); *Beauty and Sadness* (1965)

Why It's Key The award of the Nobel Prize in Literature to Kawabata has been seen as a movement away from western writers towards true cosmopolitanism.

Key Event
The Booker Prize for fiction is launched

There is no more successful or influential literary prize than the Booker, which is open to novelists from the Commonwealth published in Britain and writing in English. It was established in 1968 when Michael Caine, the then chairman of Booker plc (an international food distribution conglomerate with close links to the old Commonwealth), and various senior literary publishers, set out to create the British equivalent of the Prix Goncourt in France or the Pulitzer in the U.S. What they did not realize is that very soon the Booker would become the dominant book prize in the English-speaking world, even though American writers are excluded from entry. Its success would inspire an entire culture of imitation and reaction, both in the literary world and in the wider arts community. It would mean, too, that prizes would very quickly supplant reviews as our primary means of literary transmission, becoming the ultimate measure of cultural success and value.

In 1992, Caine set up a Russian Booker prize, which galvanised Russian publishing during the immediate post-Soviet period. Today, the Russian prize has a new sponsor but the Booker name continues. More recently, following Caine's death, his widow, the Liberal Democrat politician Emma Nicholson, created in his memory the Caine Prize for African Writing, which is generally known as the "African Booker."

In 2002, the Man Group, a financial services company, became the new sponsors. The winner's cheque was raised from £20,000 to £50,000, and the prize was renamed the Man Booker. Its influence remained undiminished.

Jason Cowley

Date 1968

Place UK

Why It's Key The first Booker Prize went to P.H. Newby, with *Something to Answer For*. In 1972 John Berger caused controversy when he donated half his prize money to the Black Panthers. Iris Murdoch is so far the most nominated author; she received six nominations and won in 1978 with *The Sea, the Sea*. In 1993 Salman Rushdie won the "Booker of Bookers" for *Midnight's Children*.

Key Passage
The Electric Kool-Aid Acid Test

'WE BLEW IT! …' '… it was perfect, so what do you do?' 'WE BLEW IT!'

At the end of the book all of the freaky Merry Pranksters have departed except for Ken Kesey and his friend Ken Babbs, who sit improvising stoned lyrics to the noodling of their guitars. The great travelling adventure is over and the old school bus, luridly painted in fluorescent colors, and with "Furthur" [sic] as its destination, is parked somewhere off-road. Kesey faces a jail sentence for possession of marijuana. It certainly has been a long strange trip but now it's over, and the dull reality of the everyday world is coming back to banish the LSD-fuelled visions of freedom, excess, and creativity. Tom Wolfe was able to document the beginnings of the "hippie dream" from inside, without becoming one of them himself, and as this passage shows, he saw that the movement carried within it the seeds of its own destruction.

Wolfe almost single-handedly created the "New Journalism," using the techniques of a novelist to replace straight reportage. Instead of cultivating objectivity, Wolfe and those he inspired became engaged with the story, incorporating long stretches of rambling conversation and spiralling off into vivid description and stream-of-consciousness narration rather than recounting the dry facts. A playful approach to typography was also characteristic of Wolfe's style, with much use of capitals and multiple exclamation marks. Song lyrics, poetry, imagined dialogues, jumping backwards and forwards in time… anything and everything was admissible, as long as it worked, and the new style became almost ubiquitous in the decades that followed.
Michael Munro

Date 1968
Author Tom Wolfe (born 1930)
Nationality USA

Why It's Key Wolfe was a leading light in the "New Journalism" movement of the 1960s, and this best-selling account of novelist Ken Kesey's psychedelic road trip is the archetypal example of his work and was highly influential both on the journalism of the time and the ensuing decades and on the development of the non-fiction book.

513

Key Author **Christa Wolf** *The Quest for Christa T. (Nachdenken über Christa T)*

The novelist Christa Wolf (1929–) was the most important writer of the German Democratic Republic, whose work was admired and discussed in both East and West. Always a committed socialist, Wolf was a prominent member of the ruling Socialist Unity Party from 1949 to 1989. Her work reflects her political commitment, but also displays a sensitivity to the dangers of utopianism and an awareness of fault lines at the heart of life in the communist East and, arguably, within modern life in general: the tension between duty and desire, public and private, and experience and hope. In her key texts through the 1960s and 1970s Wolf was able to develop a formally sophisticated method to articulate these themes. She employs forms of self-conscious and self-questioning narrative, and dispenses with linearity in favor of overlapping, multi-layered strands. Her writing is brave and unconventional, suggesting continuities between fascism and the present, critical of patriarchal

structures within GDR society, and psychologically acute. Wolf's career has always been subject to an extraordinary degree of moral scrutiny, and the belated publication of a fictionalized account of harassment at the hands of the Stasi (*Was bleibt* (*What remains*), [1990]), and the revelation in 1993 of her own brief period of activity as a Stasi informant, prompted huge controversy. Though her reputation may have been tarnished by the revelations, her status as a literary giant of contemporary German letters, matched only really by Günter Grass, is undeniable.
Jon Hughes

Date 1968 (published)
Nationality Germany

Other Key Works
Divided Heaven (Der geteilte Himmel [1963]), *Patterns of Childhood (Kindheitsmuster* [1976])

Why It's Key The most significant author of the GDR, Christa Wolf's controversial, formally sophisticated novels combine the moral, the political, and the psychological.

Key Book
Soul on Ice

At the end of a tumultuous decade of bloody civil right struggles, Eldridge Cleaver's radical book *Soul on Ice* was an immediate sensation. Cleaver's dark, psychosexual revolutionary blueprint struck a chord with white radicals, as it opened a rare door welcoming them to join in the fight for black liberation. The first section of *Soul on Ice*, entitled "Letters From Prison" was very different from his contemporary, Dr. Martin Luther King Jr's, "Letter From a Birmingham Jail." Cleaver's "Letters" expressed an awakening consciousness as a black man, resulting from a series of violent encounters with racism. Perhaps the most controversial and sadistic element to Cleaver's self-discovery was his open endorsements of rape. *Soul on Ice* depicts Cleaver's conscious decision to become a rapist after being emasculated by a white prison guard. "I arrived at the conclusion, that as a matter of principle, it was of paramount importance for me to have an antagonistic, ruthless attitude toward white women."

Cleaver decided to become a rapist, as he felt that his sexual dominance over white women was synonymous with political revolution. However, he did not begin his sexual terrorism on whites, he claims to have "started out practicing on black girls in the ghetto." *Soul on Ice* is an elaborate articulation of sexual perversions, blatant homophobia, misogyny, political commentary, and revolutionary rhetoric. It is a frightening and stimulating addition to the Black revolutionary canon of autobiographical texts, and was counted among the *New York Times'* ten best books of 1968.

Pierce Freelon

Date 1968

Author Eldridge Cleaver (1935–1998)

Nationality USA

Why It's Key Following the assassination of Malcolm X, *Soul on Ice* helped catapult Cleaver to the forefront of the Black revolutionary struggle. Cleaver was the spokesperson for the Black Panther party and helped orchestrate the Panthers' most compelling icon, the photograph of founder Huey Newton sitting with a rifle in one hand and a spear in the other.

Key Author **Maya Angelou**
I Know Why the Caged Bird Sings

Angelou's six volumes of memoir and many works of poetry have made her one of the founding mothers of black literary consciousness in post-war America. *I Know Why the Caged Bird Sings*, which was first published in 1969, spent over two years on *The New York Times'* bestseller list and is now a permanent fixture on school and university syllabi on both sides of the Atlantic. "Dr Angelou," as she likes to be known, has been given many honorary degrees and a lifetime chair at Wake Forest University.

In *The Caged Bird* Angelou tells of a dirt-poor pre-war childhood spent with her grandmother in Arkansas. Angelou's style is lyrical, as lush the steaming beauty of the southern landscape it describes. Later the mood darkens as Angelou tells of her move to the city and rape at the hands of her mother's boyfriend. When the man is lynched by outraged relatives, the seven-year-old Angelou refuses to speak for several years on the grounds that "I thought my voice had killed him."

In later volumes of memoir Angelou recounts her work as a cabaret artist as well as her involvement in the Civil Rights Movement and an extended stay in Ghana, searching for her spiritual homeland. Her intensely expressive and highly personal narratives struck a chord with all those people – especially African Americans – who were struggling with issues of gender, race, and nationality in the 70s and 80s.

Now approaching 80, Angelou continues to be a national institution in America. In 1993 she was invited to read her work at President Clinton's inauguration, only the second poet to have had that honor.

Kathryn Hughes

Date 1969

Nationality USA

Why It's Key The great triumph of Angelou's work was to break out of the ghetto of African-American liberationist writing and become a mainstream read. Her narrative of triumph over a sequence of tragedies spoke not just to black readers but to white women and gay men and women, all of whom were questioning their identity from the 60s onwards.

Opposite Maya Angelou

The French Lieutenant's Woman

Although Fowles' novel is firmly set in the mid-Victorian period, it contains twentieth-century sensibilities and perspectives. In particular he grafts onto a fairly conventional romance the possibility that his characters, far from being trapped in the oppressive inevitability of the novel's plot, might be able to avail themselves of the very modern (some would say post-modern) possibility of existential freedom.

The French Lieutenant's Woman, set largely in Lyme Regis in the 1860s, is the story of a love affair between wealthy amateur palaeontologist Charles Smithson and an enigmatic governess, Sarah Woodruff. While Woodruff seems to display many of the characteristics of a 1960s liberated woman, Charles' official fiancée Ernestina is a conventional, conforming Victorian. As Charles ricochets between these two women, Fowles deftly moves between past and present, adding footnotes, epigraphs, and quotations from Darwin, Marx, and the great Victorian poets.

Much influenced by the French *nouveau roman* (he had read Modern Languages at Oxford after the war), Fowles also tells us, in the guise of the narrator, that he has "cheated" by creating three different endings. As he coyly teases the reader, "These characters I create never existed outside my own mind." At one point Fowles even appears in an enigmatic disguise as an anonymous bearded character to turn back his watch and give us the final, existential ending.

The French Lieutenant's Woman was always considered to be an unfilmable novel. However, in 1981 it was brought to the cinema screen by Karel Reisz. Harold Pinter's script gets round the problem of the open ending by creating a parallel modern-day story in which the actors also embark upon an ambiguous love affair.

Kathryn Hughes

Date 1969

Author John Fowles (1926–2005)

Nationality UK

Why It's Key Influenced by the French school of the nouveau roman, Fowles' novels marked the beginning of a trend for a new kind of formal innovation in British novels.

Opposite John Fowles

517

The Unfortunates

In writing *The Unfortunates*, B.S. Johnson's objective was to represent the unpredictable workings of the mind. After experimenting with several typographical and structural formats, Johnson (to the chagrin of his publishers) decided upon a radical narrative strategy: to dispense with the conventional novel format altogether. Not bound like a typical codex novel, *The Unfortunates* comes in a box that contains twenty-seven discrete sections of text; two of the sections are marked as first and last, but the sequence of the remaining sections is left for the reader – or chance – to determine.

While its design is conceptually complex, *The Unfortunates* relates a fairly ordinary story. A football reporter is sent to cover a league game in Nottingham. During the proceedings, he becomes distracted by memories of an old friend – a lecturer from Nottingham who died of cancer. The narrator's attention thus darts and drifts between events of the present – the plays and progress of the football game – and those of the past, which are variously sorrowful and uplifting, trivial and momentous.

Although Johnson has been criticized for producing "gimmicky" fiction, whose audacious style functions only to conceal a lack of literary merit, the form of *The Unfortunates* is perfectly continuous with its themes. The unpredictable processes of memory and cognition are manifest in the random arrangement of the text itself. Ray Bradbury remarked that Johnson's contrivance becomes "a physical, tangible metaphor for randomness and the nature of cancer." *The Unfortunates*, as its title suggests, is particularly poignant as a depiction – and an enactment – of how despair, trauma, and disease are processed in the mind.

Kiki Benzon

Date 1969

Author B.S. Johnson (1933–1973)

Nationality UK

Why It's Key What is most unfortunate about *The Unfortunates* is that its untraditional format has made it a particularly expensive work to publish. The random, fragmentary structure of the novel not only reflects the nonlinear and disjointed nature of memory, but it also presages contemporary hypertext fiction.

Key Character **Alexander Portnoy**
Portnoy's Complaint

Date 1969

Author Philip Roth (1933–)

Nationality USA

Why It's Key Roth's most famous character, Portnoy is perhaps best known for his frank (and very funny) recollections of adolescent masturbation, leading Jacqueline Susann to famously tell Johnny Carson of Roth: "I'd like to meet him, but I wouldn't want to shake his hand."

Alexander Portnoy, Jewish son of Newark, New Jersey, sex-obsessed chronic masturbator, guilt-filled bearer of his parents' love and expectations, is in analysis, and if anyone has needed the analyst's couch more, his story has yet to be told. An unquenchable id warring with an authoritarian superego, a fixation on his mother compounded by an emasculated father, early sexual experience that seems the root of all of his behavior, Portnoy has it all. What's more, he's willing to talk about it: Portnoy's psychoanalytic monologue goes on for more than 250 pages, and at the end of this breathless, hilarious outpouring, his analyst is allowed a single line in response: "Now vee may perhaps to begin. Yes?"

Roth unleashed Portnoy on the world in 1969, and although he has created many memorable characters in over twenty books since, Portnoy remains his most famous invention. The book is a marvel of literary impersonation; it is Portnoy's voice – frantic, impassioned, and devastatingly hilarious – that more than anything else is the engine of the work. His life, as he tells it, has been the product of warring impulses: his stereotypically overbearing and meddling Jewish mother has given him the conscience (and the inhibitions) of the Nice Jewish Boy, while paradoxically provoking in him overwhelming desires to transgress, to "be bad," as he puts it. It is this bad behavior that most readers will remember; in a voice that seems equally inspired by the stand up comic as it is by Franz Kafka, Portnoy talked his way right into the center of late sixties (counter-)culture.

David Gooblar

1960–1969

518

Key Character **Vito Corleone**
The Godfather

Date 1969

Author Mario Puzo (1920–1999)

Nationality USA

Why It's Key A character whose courteous, stately manner is all the more frightening for the brutal intentions it conceals, mafioso Vito Corleone replaced the renegade cowboy as the ultimate American outlaw.

The Corleone family lawyer gives this euphemistic explanation of Vito Corleone's mafia power: "Italians have a little joke, that the world is so hard a man must have two fathers to look after him, and that's why they have Godfathers."

Ever since Francis Ford Coppola's film adaptation of *The Godfather*, it has been impossible to picture Vito Corleone as anyone other than the bulldog-faced Marlon Brando, who won an Oscar for his portrayal of the ruthless mafioso. Yet Vito Corleone charmed and terrified the reading public long before his transition to the silver screen. He began life as the creation of Mario Puzo, a commercially unsuccessful novelist who set out to write a cynical bestseller. But Vito Corleone transcended his pulp fiction origins, becoming one of American literature's greatest villains.

A chivalrous, old-fashioned, silver-tongued family man, he rules his urban empire in a self-consciously "Roman" mode, commanding his "soldiers" to do his bidding. Corleone's appeal is strongly related to his roots. The nineteenth-century immigrant experience built America as we know it, but, until *The Godfather*, the country's earlier, English-speaking arrivals dominated its mythology. The cowboys of Louis L'Amour and the cops and robbers of Raymond Chandler and Dashiell Hammett were the tough guys of the fiction landscape. A Sicilian immigrant who speaks Italian to his intimates, Vito Corleone brings an old-world class and credibility to career crime.

Despite his exaggerated good manners and commitment to the welfare of his family, Corleone is a thug, a hardened criminal who lies, steals, and murders, or at least persuades others to do so on his behalf. The embodiment of a capitalist ideology which promotes material wealth and personal power above all else, Vito Corleone is the dark side of the American dream.

Dinah Roe

Key Character **Flashman**
Flashman

Harry Paget Flashman originally appears as a character in Thomas Hughes' *Tom Brown's Schooldays* (1857). In that novel he is a bully, cad, and womanizer who is finally expelled from Rugby school for drunkenness. The *Flashman* novels follow his surprisingly successful trajectory after his expulsion. They are presented as the "Flashman papers," a set of newly-discovered manuscript memoirs in which an 80-year-old Flashman looks back over his glittering career and gloats about how it was all a sham. After Rugby he joins the army and through a mixture of good horsemanship, luck, and sycophancy gains the admiration of various important figures including the Duke of Wellington. This ability to impress his betters despite his selfishness, abject cowardice, and avariciousness (traits which he keeps well hidden from the authorities but parades proudly to the reader) means that he is continually advanced and regularly decorated. In *Flashman* he makes his name in

Afghanistan and India, and subsequent books see him despoiling the women and robbing the men of the United States, central Europe, and West Africa.

Flashman as a character is not attractive; he is a foul-mouthed criminal bully and a vicious misogynist not above rape and murder through negligence. The novels recount his drinking, gambling, sexual rapaciousness, and cowardice; they are sensationalist and scandalous, and in many ways Flashman's grubby ruthlessness is celebrated. However the books also introduce the reader to the seedier side of the nineteenth century, recounting with glee the grim reality of empire. In undermining heroic boy's own accounts of imperial achievement the series suggests that heroism is foolish and that history itself generally celebrates those who have blundered into success.
Jerome de Groot

Date 1969 (first appearance)

Author George Macdonald Fraser (1925–)

Nationality UK

Why It's Key Anti-hero and cad whose mischievous individualism has proven extremely popular with male readers of historical novels. There are currently twelve books in the *Flashman* series.

Key Book
Yellow Back Radio Broke-Down

Ishmael Reed's second novel (after *The Free-Lance Pallbearers*, 1967) is the first Hoo-Doo Western, a hilarious parody of the sort of pulp fiction that features formulaic tales of cowboys and Indians and outlaws. Our hero the Loop Garoo Kid is a cloven-hoofed, silver-tongued black gunslinger, one of an amazing cast of characters in a travelling circus whose adventures find them in the town of Yellow Back Radio in the Wild Old West. There is also the villainous Drag Gibson, a rich, slovenly cattleman; Mustache Sal, his nymphomaniac, mail-order bride; Bo Schmo and the neo-social realist gang; Chief Showcase, stand-in for Chief Cochise; Thomas Jefferson, third President of the United States; Big Lizzy of the Rabid Black Cougar Saloon; and many others. Along the way some diehard myths of American folklore are demolished, stereotypes turned on their heads; and not simply that in this town the adults have been driven out and the children are in charge. Reed's revolutionary achievement is to discard every rule of

polite fiction, bending genres and introducing a new improvisational, anti-realist aesthetic all his own: "Neo-HooDooism," a unique blend of Haitian voodoo, West African religious practices, and non-linear time. The book conforms to no expectations, down to punctuation and layout. Reed (who wearing other hats is poet, essayist, publisher, magazine editor, critic, anthologist, songwriter, playwright, television producer, and lecturer) is a controversial literary guerrilla and the author of several other novels, including *Mumbo Jumbo* (1972), *The Last Days of Louisiana Red* (1974), and *Reckless Eyeballing* (1986).
Margaret Busby

Date 1969

Author Ishmael Reed (1938–)

Nationality USA

Why It's Key "Folks. This here is the story of the Loop Garoo Kid. A cowboy so bad he made a working posse of spells phone in sick. A bullwhacker so unfeeling he left the print of winged mice on hides of crawling women. A desperado so ornery he made the Pope cry and the most powerful of cattlemen shed his head to the Executioner's swine."

Key Author
Ivy Compton-Burnett

In Ivy Compton-Burnett's (1884–1969) twenty novels, written between 1922 and her death, late Victorian England becomes the scene of a brilliant reworking of Greek tragedy. Upper middle class life, usually the story of two intertwined families passing through mixed fortunes, seethes with repressed violence, as large casts of characters compete for money and love. The plots that turn on birth, marriage, and death leave conventional Victorian melodrama behind thanks to the extraordinary language the characters speak. *Manservant and Maidservant* (1947) and *A House and its Head* (1935) are among the best titles. Compton-Burnett grew up in the milieu she described and found a unique way of evoking its passions and torments after studying classics. The spoken word in her work is a mask, concealing and revealing each character's fate. The country-house setting, reminiscent of Agatha Christie, ensures that at least two of the essential tragic unities, of manner and

place, hold the novels together. The church and its judgement also loom large.

Compton-Burnett, also like Christie, shows characters committing crimes in a conventionally genteel milieu. Men and women, masters and servants, lie and murder out of desperation for money and love. Often their lives and their sense of what is right has been disturbed by a tyrannical parent or head of household. Compton-Burnett's readers have to work to grasp the subtle horror of her narratives. But as a contemporary of Freud and a forerunner of Sartre she yields to no one in her hellish sense of family life a century ago.

Lesley Chamberlain

Date 1969 (death)

Nationality UK

Other Key Works *Brothers and Sisters* (1929); *A House and its Head* (1935); *A Family and a Fortune* (1939)

Why It's Key Compton-Burnett, who grew up in a troubled upper-middle class family and escaped from it to read classics, seems to set the scene one or two generations on for another unique dramatic manipulator of the English novel, Iris Murdoch.

Opposite Ivy Compton-Burnett

Key Passage
Ubik

"His stove had reverted. Back to an ancient Buck natural-gas model with clogged burners and encrusted oven door which did not close entirely."

At this mid-point in the novel, Joe Chip returns to his flat to find that familiar objects are regressing into older forms. Past is juxtaposed with present via a collision of language. "Conapt" for "apartment" is suddenly placed against the "burned grease" of an old-fashioned oven; the television is replaced by "a dark, wood-cabinet, Atwater-Kent, tuned radio-frequency oldtime AM radio"; the "homeopape," an electronic media port, had "vanished entirely."

Timeshifts and technologies, though, are not the focal point of this novel. As in most of his works, Dick is directly interested in the philosophical questions raised by science fiction idioms. When he sees the television Joe reflects on the nature of Forms and whether an ideal "TV" exists rather than an object made of

constituent parts: "…was there something inner not able to decay?" His thoughts move to reincarnation and the death of one of his colleagues. Will they be reunited at a future point?

The literary references in this passage range from Plato's *Republic* to *Winnie-the-Pooh*, via *The Tibetan Book of the Dead*. There is an irreverence in the way these texts are combined, and also a relish in the knowing that we can never be certain of the meanings in the world around us. The reflections in this passage exist only to be undercut by the interrogations and the explanations on later pages.

Royce Mahawatte

Date 1969

Author Philip K. Dick (1928–1982)

Nationality USA

Why It's Key The America of a futuristic 1992, which keeps finding itself back in 1939, is a humorous and chilling critique of hyper-capitalism, but, then again, none of it may be real at all. The multiple realities in this novel tap into 1960s drug culture and are now very much a staple of mainstream science fiction.

Key Book *Jacob the Liar* (*Jakob der Lügner*)

Jacob Heym, a Polish Jew, is ordered to report to the German ghetto police for curfew violation, and in the station he overhears a radio report of approaching Russian troops. The "violation" was a bored guard's cruel joke, so on release Jacob tells the good news to a friend, but as no one would believe the true story (freed by the police without punishment?) he claims he has a secret radio, and soon becomes the only source of hope for the entire ghetto. Possession of a radio was a capital offence for Jews, but he is constantly beset by requests for more news, so his well-intentioned lie has farcical consequences – and tragic ones, as some are emboldened to defiance as well as simple endurance.

The official GDR view of the end of the war – a liberation from Nazi tyranny by fraternal Soviet forces – was regarded with some irony at best by many East Germans. However, for the enslaved Jewish workers of Lodz the arrival of the Red Army offers their only (all too tenuous) chance of survival. This distant possibility is what gives the novel its power and poignancy.

Becker provided two endings to the novel. The 1975 film chose the bleaker of the two, while the 1999 version (on which Becker was also a consultant), chose the more optimistic (though not wholly saccharine) alternative, which ends with Jacob's death, but the final liberation of the city by Russian troops.

Cathy Benson

Date 1969

Author Jurek Becker (1937–1997)

Nationality Germany (born Poland)

Why It's Key 30 years before Roberto Benigni's *Life Is Beautiful*, the horror of the Holocaust is laid bare through comedy – by an East German writer; Becker had survived an upbringing in the Lodz ghetto where the novel is set. It is unique in having been filmed both in East Germany in 1975 and by Hollywood in 1999.

Opposite *Jacob the Liar*

523

Key Event **Albert Speer publishes a memoir of his life as a Nazi official**

Albert Speer (1905–1981) was Hitler's favorite architect, responsible for the immense parade grounds built at Nuremburg for the infamous Nazi rallies of the 1930s. In 1942 Hitler made him minister of armaments, responsible for war production. Speer succeeded in boosting output, at least partly by the extensive use of slave labor. After the war he faced trial at Nuremburg, where he was sentenced to twenty years' imprisonment.

Speer was forbidden to write his memoirs in prison, but succeeded in smuggling out extensive notes. The publication of *Inside the Third Reich* shortly after his release caused a sensation. It not only showed the Nazi leadership as a bunch of barely sane incompetents riven by petty court politics, but also gave a portrait of Hitler as a self-deluded, psychopathic megalomaniac, incapable of sustained work.

Inevitably, questions were asked about Speer's own role. He barely mentioned Nazi atrocities in his book, in which he denied knowledge of the Holocaust (as he had at the Nuremburg Trials). His attempts to justify his own role are not convincing: he claimed to have tried to improve conditions for slave workers, to have prevented Hitler from embarking on a scorched earth policy, and even to have planned Hitler's assassination in early 1945. But his testimony at Nuremburg, in his memoirs and in various interviews was inconsistent. Although Speer may not have been a raving Nazi ideologue, it became clear to many that he was a fellow traveller motivated by greed and self-interest.

Ian Crofton

Date 1969 (Published in German as *Erinnerungen* ("recollections"); the English edition came out the following year

Title *Inside the Third Reich*

Nationality Germany

Why It's Key The first insider's account from the Nazi elite who had led their country to disaster. Its failure to mention Nazi atrocities aroused furious controversy.

Key Event **For the first time, a Native American writer wins the Pulitzer Prize**

When N. Scott Momaday's first novel *House Made of Dawn* was awarded the Pulitzer Prize for Fiction in 1969, the event heralded the beginning of the Native American Literary Renaissance. It coincided with the rise of Pan-Indian political activism, commencing on Californian university campuses and soon spreading nationwide as the American Indian Movement (AIM). Momaday was not a political activist in the late 60s; rather he was commencing a prestigious career as university professor, poet, author, and artist. Nevertheless, his experience resonated with the spirit of AIM, since his own upbringing combined tribal and European-American heritage in a positive and creative fashion. Momaday's father, a teacher and artist, was Kiowa and his mother, a teacher and author of children's fiction, was mixed-blood Scottish, French, and Cherokee. Consequently Momaday was comfortable combining elements of traditional oral tribal cultures of the American Southwest with mainstream and modernist literary techniques. The novel appealed to Anglo-American readers, since they recognized its strategies of fragmentation and of poly-vocal narration, and its themes of alienation and identity crisis as universal to modern culture. Native American readers responded to its complex, allusive use of specific tribal cultural traditions, including those of Jemez Pueblo and of the Navajo. Momaday influenced younger authors, for example Leslie Marmon Silko, whose novel *Ceremony* (1978) also featured a World War II veteran as its central protagonist, and also used a Navajo "chantway" as a major structural device.

Helen May Dennis

Date 1969

Title *House Made of Dawn* (1968)

Author N. Scott Momaday (1934–)

Why It's Key *House Made of Dawn* takes it title from a Navajo "chantway" or healing song, sung by the singer/shaman during the traditional healing ritual that also involves symbolic sand-painting. With this novel, Momaday brought Native American fiction into the mainstream.

Key Author **Dario Fo** *Accidental Death of an Anarchist*

Although conventionally labeled, especially outside Italy, a left-wing playwright, there are many facets to Fo's creativity. He is a painter, performer, writer, and polemicist but is primarily actor-author in a country in which that combination has enjoyed a dominance unparalleled in other theatrical traditions. Fo (1926–) made his debut with radio monologues, before switching to farce, with some scripts inspired by the repertoire of the theatrical family of Franca Rame, his wife and stage partner.

The farce was his preferred genre, and perhaps his greatest achievement was to have forged, with co-operatives which caught the mood in Italy at the height of the post 1968 extra-parliamentary movement, a wholly new style of didactic, political farce. Fo was no superficial iconoclast, but both as writer and performer had his roots in the theater traditions of Italy, so astonished his comrades by staging such works as *Comic Mysteries*, a contemporary rewriting of medieval mystery plays. With this work, he also returned to the one-man shows with which his career began, compelling even his opponents to recognise his unique acting abilities. His international reputation as political playwright reached its peak in the 1970s, when his companies toured all over Italy bringing theater to communities unfamiliar with the stage, and when his work was published, performed, and adapted all over the world as a response to conflicts he was unaware of at the time of writing. Fo was awarded the Nobel Prize for Literature in 1997.

Encouraged by Rame, in the 1980s he turned his interest to the women's movement, with plays, sometimes co-authored, performed by her. He widened his own interests to include popular art of all genres, not only theater, and published books and presented TV programmes which gave an idiosyncratic viewpoint on some of the great masters of western painting.

Joseph Farrell

Date 1970 (published)

Nationality Italy

Other Key Works *Can't Pay? Won't Pay!* (1974); *Female Parts* (1977); *Tale of a Tiger* (1978); *The Pope and the Witch* (1989); *Johan Padan Discovers the Americas* (1991); *My First Seven Years* (*Plus a Few More*) (2002)

Why It's Key Fo is routinely described as the most frequently translated and performed of all post-World War II playwrights, from any country.

Key Author **Judy Blume**
Are You There, God? It's Me, Margaret

Judy Blume's (1938–) novels address social problems in realistic terms, particularly in their settings, and in their resolutions, which resist easy answers or simplistic value judgments in which good is rewarded and wrongdoing punished. Blume's refusal to compromise in these matters, to simplify or whitewash her characters and their actions, has made her one of the most banned children's authors in the United States; her books are consistently among the most challenged in America by censorship groups and the religious right. *Are You There God? It's Me, Margaret* was Blume's second book for children (her first, *Iggie's House*, concerned racism), but its success prompted her to continue writing stories about children and teenagers dealing with common problems in unsentimental ways. Margaret is a twelve-year-old girl trying to reconcile her parents' interfaith marriage – she has a Jewish father and a Christian mother – and establish her own sense of religion. Margaret also

struggles with the onset of puberty, including menstruation, and buying her first bra. Blume's next book, *Then Again, Maybe I Won't*, tells a similar story about a young boy coming to terms with adolescent sexuality. Because of its forthright attitude toward problems of religious and sexual identity, *Are You There God? It's Me, Margaret* continues to be one of the hundred most frequently challenged books in American school libraries.

Sarah Churchwell

Date 1970

Nationality USA

Why It's Key Judy Blume's books treat controversial subjects with sensitivity and realism. Blume's novels for young adults were among the earliest to confront contentious issues such as menstruation and sexual competition among young girls, masturbation and illness, divorce, social climbing and shoplifting, and teenage sexuality.

Key Book
Troubles

The novel relies heavily on metaphor, as the crumbling of the once-grand Majestic Hotel in Ireland's County Wexford symbolizes the breakdown of British rule in the country in the years following World War I. The hotel's owner, Edward Spencer, belongs to the Anglo-Irish Protestant "Ascendancy" and his apparent inability to maintain his property parallels the waning of his class's authority over the largely Catholic Irish people.

The gradual increase in the frequency and level of violence of the activities of the anti-British Sinn Fein impinge only slowly on Spencer and his long-term guests, including the hero of the story, Major Brendan Archer, obsessed as they are with their own "troubles," unaware that life as they have known it is changing utterly.

Farrell's wry humor is never far away, even though the story has its tragic elements. He is at once elegiac about the disappearance of the old order, which can be

seen to have virtues as well as faults, and satirical about the pretensions of people who have really lost any claim to power but fail to see it. The author tends not to apportion blame for the entrenched views and escalating violence of the various groupings, but sees all of them as caught in the impersonal and inexorable workings of history itself.

"Troubles" has always been the euphemistic term for the periodical flare-ups of civil strife in Ireland and the author's choice of title was both apt and opportune. Farrell would have been aware of a resurgence of sectarian violence in Ulster in the late 1960s but could not have envisaged how long these "Troubles" would last.

Michael Munro

Date 1970

Author J(ames) G(ordon) Farrell (1935–1979)

Nationality UK

Why It's Key *Troubles* was Farrell's first in a series of three novels, the "Empire Trilogy," that dealt with aspects of the decline of the British Empire from the period of the Indian Mutiny to World War II. *Troubles* won the Faber Memorial prize; *The Siege of Krishnapur* (1973) won the Booker prize; the last of the series, *The Singapore Grip*, appeared in 1978.

Key Book
Deliverance

James Dickey was already known as a poet when he published his first novel, *Deliverance*, and his story's raw violence came as surprising to many readers. The plot hinges on the contrasts between civilization and wilderness, and between the rule of law and a Hobbesian state of nature in which it is every man for himself. In many ways the journey undertaken by the four main characters is a voyage into the past. Their aim is to canoe down a section of river that is soon to be flooded as a consequence of the building of a dam, and they are keen to experience this wilderness before it is gone forever. This chimes in with the nascent environmentalist movement of the time, with many Americans beginning to see the value of conserving the natural world.

What doesn't occur to the protagonists is that when the country truly was wilderness it was inhabited by people who were a law unto themselves. Like an echo from the Wild West, gun-carrying natives confront them, who see them only as prey. The realization that such feral beings might actually exist was one of the major impacts of the book. It was a sobering thought to consider after the late 1960s period of hippie "love and peace" philosophy. The narrator of the story is only able to survive the ordeal by finding qualities within himself that have nothing to do with these values but spring from more primitive human qualities such as endurance and the refusal to surrender one's life without a struggle.

Although it was critically well-received, the book was really made famous by John Boorman's film version in 1972 for which Dickey wrote the screenplay and appeared in a cameo role as a sherrif.
Michael Munro

Date 1970

Author James Dickey (1923–1997)

Nationality USA

Why It's Key Dickey's novel about four suburban American businessmen who take a trip to the wilderness of northern Georgia which turns into a struggle for survival struck many as a resonance from the past. It seemed to hark back to the lawless frontier era.

Opposite **1972** film adaptation of *Deliverance*

Key Character **Crow**
Crow

Crow – lamb-killer, eye-pecker, carrion-gorger, black against the sun, the negation of light – the perfect hero for the age after Auschwitz. Ted Hughes had served up nature red in tooth and claw before, but with Crow he created a mythic, anthropomorphized persona to explore the human condition in all its grim hopelessness. But Crow's encounters with horror and despair are shot through with a sardonic black humor, for Crow is the eternal trickster – the god-slayer Loki in Norse mythology, the Raven of the Pacific Northwest, the shape-shifter Proteus of the ancient Greeks.

Crow outfaces Death at the womb-door, makes his Mama weep blood, plays a childish prank on Adam and Eve, eats the Serpent, retches when God asks him to say "Love," looks on as the sexes engulf one other, witnesses battles and apocalypse, scavenges the skulls and garbage that remain. Crow is dismembered, beheaded, eviscerated, castrated, paralyzed, but ultimately survives,

"Grown so wise so terrible
Sucking death's mouldy tits."

For years afterwards, spotty boys and girls with bad dreams and difficulty kissing sprinkled their verses with throbbing muscle and glints of severed bone. Crow laughed until his sides split. His innards fell out as royalty cheques. The Queen, impressed, made Mr Ted poet laureate. His muse, King of Carrion, squatted in his palace of skulls. "Sing," implored Mr Ted,

"Sing on my finger, sing in my ear, O littleblood."

But the last cry had flapped away, and all Crow had left to reign over was silence.
Ian Crofton

Date 1970

Author Ted Hughes (1930–1998)

Nationality UK

Why It's Key As the poet Peter Porter wrote in *The Guardian* when *Crow* was first published: "English poetry has found a new hero and nobody will be able to read or write verse now without the black shape of *Crow* falling across the page."

Key Event *Steal This Book* becomes the bible of the U.S. counterculture

Steal This Book reflects the anti-authority, DIY culture of the late 1960s in its explanations of how to subvert society from within; it also demonstrates the latent violence of the counterculture movement. Abbie Hoffman was one of the founders of the Youth International Party (also known as the "Yippies"), and was an activist during the Vietnam war – and thus well known for outlandish Situationist anti-war demonstrations.

He was arrested in Chicago during the violent demonstrations against the 1968 Democratic National Convention and subsequently became one of the "Chicago Seven." The group were charged with conspiracy and incitement to riot, and the trial became a focal point for the clashes between the government "fascist pigs" and the burgeoning youthful peace movement. Numerous counterculture figures testified, including Timothy Leary, Rev. Jesse Jackson, Norman Mailer, and Arlo Guthrie. After being acquitted Hoffman got thrown off the Woodstock stage by Pete Townshend for attempting to interrupt The Who's set and published *Steal This Book*, which went on to become the bible of the alternative movement.

An early form of culture jamming (humorously subverting from within), the book was banned by many shops because of its content. It combines tips on how to grow marijuana, make pipe bombs, live communally, steal credit cards, buy weapons, orchestrate riots, and snarl up the organization of the government. *Steal This Book* teaches the reader to resist all organized governance and corporate control with wit and intelligence, but also advocates armed resistance to a capitalist state which has let its youth down.
Jerome de Groot

Date 1970

Place USA

Author Abbie Hoffman (1936–1989)

Why It's Key "The Yippie bible," Hoffman's book made the political activist author a symbol of rebellion across the United States; as a manifesto of resistance it has influenced most western political critique since.

Key Event **Mishima commits "hara-kiri" after attempting to rouse army to mutiny**

SPOILER

No one who did not know him well foresaw Yukio Mishima's suicide. A revered author in post-war Japan, nationalistic though never racist, he was seen as both sage and clown, an exquisite writer and a faintly ridiculous self-publicist. "What will he do next?" was the half-affectionate, half-exasperated response of literary Japan to his antics. These included having himself photographed as St Sebastian, claiming to be heir to the samurai tradition though his own family was merely genteel, and ranting at western influence even as he embraced it in his own works. The smiles and smirks faded on the November 25, 1970.

Mishima had created a personal militia, the Tatenokai, whose avowed aim was to return to the pre-war imperialist dispensation. With their help, Mishima captured a Japanese general, hectored a crowd of indignant or indifferent soldiers on their duty to their fatherland, and then proceeded, disappointed but not altogether surprised, to open his stomach with a dagger. His friend (and lover) Morita then decapitated him (incompetently), to be decapitated in his turn. Mishima's end was as much a lover's suicide pact as an expression of loyalty to Old Japan.

But the tragicomic grandiloquence of his end is by no means its most remarkable aspect: evidence indicates that Mishima had not only planned his death but, in true artistic fashion, prophesied it – in a story. In *Patriotism*, Mishima shows a young lieutenant in the Japanese army caught between loyalty to his friends and loyalty to the emperor. Unable to resolve this dilemma, he commits suicide. His wife asks permission to do the same. So sparsely vivid is the description of the various stages of pain endured by the young man as he opens his stomach that it is almost impossible to believe that the author had not experienced it – except that we know he can't have.
Murrough O'Brien

Date 1970

Place Japan

Author Yukio Mishima (1925–1970)

Why It's Key Instead of inspiring his fellow countrymen to emulate the glories of Japan's imperial past, Mishima's attempt to reawaken Japan to its heritage merely reminded them of its horrors His friend and literary rival, Kawabata, was so haunted by Mishima's death that a year later he followed suit.

Opposite Yukio Mishima addressing Japanese military

Key Passage
The Female Eunuch

"The essential factor in the liberation of the married woman is understanding of her condition… Essentially she must recapture her own will and her own goals, and the energy to use them, and in order to effect this some quite 'unreasonable' suggestions, or demands, may be necessary."

A classic of second-wave feminism and international bestseller, *The Female Eunuch* caused a furore when it was published in 1970. Angry and revolutionary in tone, Germaine Greer scrutinizes the myth of female inferiority by taking apart supposedly scientific theories of gender difference. The book demonstrates how women are trained from an early age to be sexually passive, arguing that this repression of sexual desire and curiosity turns women into "female eunuchs." Greer challenges women to reject negative body images, to rediscover their libido and to let go of their confining role in the nuclear family. *The Female Eunuch* pairs its attack on patriarchy with a critique of capitalism, suggesting that consumerism contributes to female entrapment.

Some may be surprised that Greer's feminist classic ends with a conciliatory note towards the other sex, indicating that women's struggle for emancipation could serve as an inspiration for men once "they jumped off their own treadmill."

Although the position of women in western society has undergone significant changes since the publication of *The Female Eunuch*, Greer's irreverent musings about the pressures surrounding body hair and curves, and the roots of gender inequality have not become irrelevant. *The Female Eunuch* continues to divide its readers and remains a living testimony to the social movement of feminism that many would have liked to declare dead long ago.

Anne Schwan

Date 1970

Author Germaine Greer (born 1939)

Nationality Australia

Why It's Key A feminist classic that gave voice to the discontent and demands driving an emerging social movement. Deliberately subversive and polemic in style and message, *Eunuch* is an affront against the pillars of western patriarchal society, ranging from religion to ideals of feminine beauty.

Opposite Germaine Greer

1970–1979

530

Key Passage
Love Story

SPOILER

"I had forgotten my coat; the chill was starting to make me ache. Good. Good.
'Oliver,' said my father urgently, 'I want to help.'
'Jenny's dead', I told him.
'I'm sorry,' he said in a stunned whisper.
Not knowing why, I repeated what I had long ago learned from the beautiful girl now dead.
'Love means not ever having to say you're sorry.'

And then I did what I had never done in his presence, much less in his arms. I cried."

Until very near the end of the novel, Erich Segal's narrative remains almost irritatingly chipper. Oliver Barrett IV, a wealthy Harvard law student, and Jenny Cavilleri, a Radcliffe music major, who, in her own words is "smart and poor," fall in love. Despite his family's disdain for their relationship, they marry and decide to start a family. When they are unsuccessful and undergo fertility testing, they discover that Jenny is terminally ill. Oliver struggles to find the money for expensive medical treatments and is eventually forced to approach the father who disowned him for money. With the lack of any information to the contrary, Oliver Barrett III gives his son the money, assuming that he has got another woman pregnant. It is in this final passage that the situation becomes clear and estranged father and son finally reconcile at Jenny's deathbed.

Bringing together the two love stories of the novel, one romantic, one familial, this concluding moment sees Oliver and his father reach a new understanding.

The bouncy and colloquial style of Segal's prose contrasts sharply with the gravity of the plot and it is this disparity that heightens the emotional impact of the novel. In this passage, the language remains simple and uncluttered, and the sparing dialogue ensures that this ending is understated and poignant.

Juliet Wightman

Date 1970

Author Erich Segal (born 1937)

Nationality USA

Why It's Key This passage ends with the line immortalizsed in the film of the book as "love means never having to say you're sorry." The novel, does not, in fact, use this exact phrasing, but the tear-jerking effect remains the same.

Key Event **Allen's book causes outrage for encouraging skinhead violence**

Joe Hawkins is a teenage oik from Plaistow, East London. Joe solemnly hates and cannot abide hippies, social workers, school teachers, trade unionists, immigrants, do-gooders, and anyone who isn't exactly like himself. About all Joe does like is donning bovver boots and kicking other people's heads. The world he lives in is unchanging and bleak and the following passage appears in both *Skinhead* and *Skinhead Girls*: "If air was precious, a sentence spoken without four-letter emphasis was enough to bring a sudden silence, raised eyebrows and get the speaker an award for bravery in the face of obscenity. Even the two barmaids spoke with an anatomical descriptiveness and some of their suggestions were physical impossibilities except for a mechanical engineer."

Teachers were horrified to find these novels circulating under school desks, proving that they weren't in favor of everything that got recalcitrant teenagers reading. Laurence James who edited *Skinhead* for James Moffatt's (whose pen-name was Richard Allen) publisher New English Library says: "The research Jim did for the skinhead books was two hours in one pub talking to half a dozen skinheads. He hated skinheads, he hated kids. In his early days Jim was an extremely talented hack, but unfortunately, as it went on he began to believe that he was in touch with youth culture. He started putting masses of terrible racism in his books. I was labouring away trying to get rid of all this from his prose. In the end, after *Skinhead Girls*, I actually refused to deal with him any more."

Stewart Home

Date 1970

Title *Skinhead*

Author Richard Allen (1922–1993)

Nationality Canada (born Australia, died UK)

Why It's Key This pessimistic pulp novel appealed to British working-class youth, was a seminal influence on the punk generation, and was invoked by eighties pop star Morrissey in the song "Suedehead" as an object of nostalgia.

Key Author **Alice Munro** *Lives of Girls and Women*

Alice Munro is widely regarded as the doyenne of short story writers working in 2007. Her first collection, *Dance of the Happy Shades*, was published in 1968 and since then she has produced 10 further books, most recently *The View from Castle Rock* (2006). *Lives of Girls and Women* is the only one of Munro's fictions to be published as a "novel," largely because it is about a single town, Jubilee, Ontario, and has a central character, Del Jordan. But, like all of Munro's books, it is structured as a collection of interlinked stories about a variety of "dull, simple, amazing and unfathomable" people, "deep caves paved with kitchen linoleum." Del struggles to reconcile her identity as a woman and as a writer: "I wanted men to love me," she says, "and I wanted to think of the universe when I looked at the moon."

This dilemma remains Munro's central theme: romance and intelligence, "dorky" women and small towns, are never properly reconciled. But Munro is also fascinated by storytelling itself, and in particular the changing stories we tell ourselves about our lives. Since Chekhov, the short story has tended to focus on the single moment in a life that changes everything. Munro tends to push against this model. *Runaway* (2004) includes three stories about a woman called Juliet. In the first, we witness a pivotal moment and think we know the shape of her life. But other moments, in the second, and then the third, tale, change that shape.

Kasia Boddy

Date 1971 (publication)

Nationality Canada

Other Key Works *Dance of the Happy Shades* (1968), *Lives of Girls and Women* (1971), *The Beggar Maid* (1978), *The Progress of Love* (1986)

Why It's Key "Mostly in my stories, I like to look at what people don't understand... What we think is happening and what we understand later on."

Key Book
Collected Poems

Frank O'Hara has become known in the 40 years since his death as the quintessential New York poet, inheritor of a tradition of immersion in the details of urban life that stretches back to Whitman and Baudelaire. On a fence in Manhattan's Battery Park City one can find lines from the poet's "Meditations in an Emergency" (1971): "One need never leave the / confines of New York to get all the greenery one wishes – I can't / even enjoy a blade of grass unless I know there's a subway / handy, or a record store or some other sign that people do not / totally *regret* life."

But as his monumental yet intimate *Collected Poems* reveals across its 500 pages, the city for O'Hara was less a subject than an environment, a correlate for his own diverse and restless body of work. According to his friend and fellow poet John Ashbery, O'Hara's achievement was to create a new poetry "with something basically usable about it – not only for poets in search of a voice of their own but for the reader who turns to poetry as a last resort in trying to juggle the contradictory components of modern life into something like a livable space."

It is the graceful juggle of contrariety and conflict through urban flows that gives much of this poetry its distinctive character and lends it an infectious sense of the possibilities of freedom, movement, and inspiration. Far from the optimistic heyday of mid-century Manhattan, O'Hara's work continues to inspire readers with its daring and élan: "Grace / to be born and live as variously as possible."

Nicholas Lawrence

Date 1971

Author Frank O'Hara (1926–1966)

Nationality USA

Why It's Key O'Hara was the quintessential New York poet, whose work celebrated modern urban life.

Key Event *Maurice* is published, nearly 60 years after it was written

Now recognized as a classic of gay literature, *Maurice* has a complex publishing history. E.M. Forster was inspired to write a novel on a gay theme in 1913 although without any intention of publishing it due to fear of personal and legal repercussions. He showed the manuscript to a number of close friends and continued to revise it, reworking parts of it as late as 1960 when he wrote on the cover, "Publishable, but worth it?" In the end, the novel was only published in 1971, a year after Forster's death.

A kind of case history, the novel tackles the painful coming to sexual awareness of Maurice Hall, who first attempts to break out of his claustrophobic middle-class upbringing when he goes to Cambridge. Here he has a three-year platonic relationship with Clive Durham, a fellow student, although Clive eventually rejects Maurice for a socially acceptable, if seemingly joyless marriage. Maurice is left to deal with his sexuality alone until he meets Clive's handsome gamekeeper, Alec Scudder, who initiates a cross-class physical relationship which finally allows Maurice to break free of English restraint and hypocrisy and be true to himself.

On publication, reviews of *Maurice* were largely negative since it was seen as a dated period piece with little relevance to post-Stonewall gay politics. More recently, however, *Maurice* has been reread as an important work which broke new ground in writing about same-sex relationships and which took an early stand against the idea of homosexuality as being "unnatural" or a disease.

Simon Avery

Date 1971

Author E.M. Forster (1979–1970)

Nationality UK

Why It's Key *Maurice* was written in 1913, but only published posthumously in 1971, for fear of a critical and legal backlash. It is seen as a major work in the history of gay literature for its critique of homophobic oppression and its call for tolerance and acceptance. A film, directed by James Ivory, was released in 1987.

Key Character **Chauncey Gardiner**
Being There

"Chauncey Gardiner" – businessman, intellectual, political advisor and expert handler of the media in Jerzy Kosinski's satirical novel, *Being There* – does not, in fact, exist. He is merely Chance, a simple-minded illiterate gardener, who has lived all his life within the house and grounds of his employer and whose only interaction with the outside world has been his obsessive watching of television. Following his employer's death, he is evicted and, in a minor traffic accident, meets Elizabeth Eve Rand, wife of the millionaire businessman, Benjamin Rand. On asking his name, she mishears his stuttered response, "Chance...the gardener" as "Chauncey Gardiner" and, impressed by his impeccable clothes (his employer's) and reserved manner, assumes him to be educated, wealthy, and socially well-connected.

So begins a collective misreading of character. Befriended by the powerful Rands, "Chauncey" comes into contact with the business community, the media and even the President of the United States. His simple utterances about gardening are interpreted as political homilies or sagacious metaphors for future economic growth; his baffled silence in sophisticated circles is regarded as inscrutability; his stated lack of comprehension read as ironic commentary. With the intelligence services unable to discover any past indiscretions (or, indeed, anything of his previous history), he is the perfect public figure: a blank page onto which ideals, allegiances, and moral qualities can be limitlessly inscribed.

Kosinski's political fable of an accidental hero – a man who succeeds and rises simply by "being there" – wittily dissects the nature of media influence, public perception, and celebrity culture, retaining the same relevance today as it did when first published.
David Cross

Date 1971

Author Jerzy Kosinski (1933–1991)

Nationality USA (born Poland)

Why It's Key Kosinski defected to the United States from state-controlled Poland by inventing academic sponsors for his application to study at an entirely fictitious U.S. foundation. He became President of the American Center of P.E.N.

Opposite Peter Sellers as Chauncey Gardiner

Key Character **Henry Chinaski**
Post Office

Charles Bukowski left it a little late to become one of the most recognizable and widely imitated American literary voices of the twentieth century. He was fifty-one when he published *Post Office*, which he wrote in twenty-one nights, consuming a pint of whiskey and two six-packs of beer a night, after working for twelve years for the post office and living in poverty and drink-induced squalor. ("The poet laureate of skid row" was part of Los Angeles' literary underground throughout the 1960s.) Bukowski, the consummate alcoholic raconteur, had a gift for telling his own tale, and making its dirtiest, ugliest moments into compelling, shambolically beautiful prose.

In *Post Office* (1971), "presented as a work of fiction and dedicated to nobody," Hank Chinaski lurches from one crazy incident to another, one woman's bed to another. In *Ham on Rye* (1982), the best of the Chinaski novels, Bukowski revisited his childhood and youth – and first encounters with drink, women, and the written word, the three governing forces of his life. He describes how he began to write, holed up in his bedroom with his acne. Tough, hard drinking, womanizing, ingrained bachelordom is partly a front for unbearable sensitivity, a tenderness that shines through the obscenity, an appreciation of life that surmounts its unfairness. The sequence of Chinaski novels also has moment after moment of blistering comedy.

Bukowski claimed Chinaski's vein of misogyny was simply down to stumbling on "a bad run" of women. Although the women are treated badly, one has to note that so are the men. On the autobiographical elements behind Hank, Bukowski wrote, "I find it easier to attack myself, to be irreverent to myself than to others. I can take it." In his hapless alter ego he found the medium for his astonishing gift for dialogue. As Chinaski perfectly understated it of one of his heroes, Hemingway, "he knew how to lay down a line."
Lucy Daniel

Date 1971

Author Charles Bukowski (1920–94)

Nationality USA

Why It's Key Bukowski was a poet before he was a novelist – vigorously anti-academic and scabrously, profanely comic, powerfully individual. The alter ego first presented in *Post Office* was in some ways a blind, a tough, cool, and funny one, which masked his seriousness, just as the miraculous naturalness of the style seamlessly hid the hard graft behind it.

Key Character **Rabbit Angstrom**
Rabbit Redux

The tetralogy of novels that make up the *Rabbit* series were published at roughly 10-year intervals from 1960 onwards, each book acting as a snapshot of its particular era, and together forming an extraordinarily rich chronicle of small town U.S. life in the second half of the twentieth century. The Rabbit series opened with *Rabbit, Run* (1960), in which the restless Harry "Rabbit" Angstrom takes flight from his stifling marriage to Janice Springer and embarks on a series of encounters, which lead him back to his wife and his marriage with a grinding and tragic inevitability.

Harry's marriage turns out to be surprisingly durable however, and Janice is a prominent character throughout the series. With *Rabbit Redux* (1971) the political and social background becomes more prominent. Harry has long discussions about the Vietnam War and the Civil Rights movement with some sixties dropouts he takes in when Janice leaves to move in with her lover. The remaining novels see

Harry attain bourgeois respectability as part owner of his father-in-law's car dealership, and the final novel, *Rabbit at Rest* (1971), has the former basketball hero grow fat in late middle age.

As Harry blunders through his life, passing effortlessly from fool to hero and back again, a sort of small town Everyman ("he's neither Republican nor Democrat," Updike once observed of his character, "he just likes presidents"), the richness of Updike's prose and his extraordinary eye for detail make the *Rabbit* books as notable for their style and lyrical elegance as for the story they tell.

Gerard Woodward

Date 1971

Also Appears In *Rabbit, Run* (1960), *Rabbit Redux* (1971), *Rabbit is Rich* (1981), *Rabbit at Rest* (1990), "Rabbit Remembered" (novella in *Licks of Love*, 2001)

Author John Updike (born 1932)

Nationality USA

Why It's Key Harry "Rabbit" Angstrom emerges as one of the most important characters in twentieth-century U.S. fiction.

536

Key Author
Pablo Neruda

The man whom Gabriel García Márquez called "the greatest poet of the twentieth century in any language" was born Ricardo Eliecer Neftalí Reyes Basoalto in Parral, central Chile, in 1904. His first book of poetry, *Crepusculario*, published in Santiago in 1923, under his assumed name of Pablo Neruda, was followed in 1924 by the erotically charged collection which made his reputation, *Twenty Love Poems and A Song of Despair*. He wrote many of his finest poems, later to appear in the collection, *Residence on Earth* (1933), while serving as Chilean consul in the Far East.

In 1934, Neruda was posted, with his first wife, Maria Antonia Hagenaar, to Spain. The horrors he witnessed during the Spanish Civil War and the fascists' assassination of his great friend, the poet Federico García Lorca, changed his outlook from one of introspection to social and political commitment. Neruda joined the Chilean Communist Party in 1945.

As a senator, he furiously condemned President Gabriel González Videla's betrayal of the Left and, as a result, Neruda was forced into hiding for a year. Much of this anger went into his magnificent collection, *General Song* (1950). The next few years were spent in exile in Eastern Europe and Mexico, juggling life between his second wife, Delia del Carril, and his third wife-to-be, Matilde Urrutia. In the mid-1950s, now back in Chile, Neruda published three books of odes, followed by *Extravagaria* (1958), a collection of poems, some of which are gloriously self-mocking. Ill with prostate cancer, he was forced to renounce his Paris Ambassadorship and return to Chile in 1973. He died on September 23, 1973, just 12 days after Augusto Pinochet's military coup.

Adam Feinstein

Date 1971 (Nobel Prize in Literature awarded)

Nationality Chile

Other Key Works *Crepusculario* (1923), *General Song* (1950), *Elementary Odes* (1954), *One Hundred Love Sonnets* (1960), *Isla Negra Notebooks* (1964), *Memoirs* (1974)

Why It's Key Neruda's love poetry is still widely read. *Twenty Love Poems* remains the most reprinted collection of verse in Spanish.

Opposite Pablo Neruda

Key Book
The Dice Man

Launching a revolutionary nihilistic philosophy which states that true freedom can only be attained when life is governed by the throw of a six-sided cube, *The Dice Man* is also a brilliant satire on the psychological profession, whose claims to "save" souls have come to echo those of organized religion.

Cool-tongued "Luke Reinhart" is a hero in the tradition of Joseph Heller's Yossarian. He's a disillusioned psychologist painfully aware that the therapy he offers isn't making his clients (or himself) any happier. To shake his tired existence from its rut he rolls dice to determine his actions and liberate himself from the habits and expectations of accumulated personality. This unorthodox process leads him to break the moral and sexual taboos of mainstream American life.

Condemned by some feminists as a sexist work pandering to male fantasies of commitment-breaking, its author claims that he was inspired by Simone de Beauvoir's writings on the limited roles society offers to women. As a result of the hero's dicing philosophy, his wife breaks free of a confining marriage to become a lawyer.

Though the novel was banned in several countries where the authorities felt social responsibility might be eroded by those emulating the dicing lifestyle, George Cockcroft has always maintained that "people have been doing horrible things for as long as we know without the dice. And I have no doubt they will do evil things with them. The dice free you from pressure, and it is usually the people under enormous pressure who do the most dreadful things."

Helen Brown

Date 1971

Author George Cockcroft (born 1932) writing as "Luke Reinhart": also the name of the novel's protagonist.

Nationality USA

Why It's Key "Life is islands of ecstasy in an ocean of ennui, and after the age of thirty land is seldom seen." Controversy surrounded *The Dice Man*'s advocacy of living according to the roll of the dice.

1970-1979

539

Key Author **Hunter S. Thompson**
Fear and Loathing in Las Vegas

Fear and Loathing in Las Vegas was meant to be an account of the "Mint 400" motorbike race for *Sports Illustrated*. But something funny happened on the way to Vegas… "We were somewhere around Barstow on the edge of the desert when the drugs began to take hold… suddenly there was a terrible roar all around us and the sky was full of what looked like huge bats." Thus a straightforward assignment, under the influence of a range of recreational pharmaceuticals, becomes, as Hunter S. Thompson's subtitle has it, "A savage journey to the heart of the American Dream."

In his twenties Thompson had had a succession of jobs – both journalistic and menial – and had been fired from most of them. In the 1960s he became involved with the Californian counterculture, wrote a book about the Hells Angels, and then moved to the wilds of Colorado, where he unsuccessfully ran for sheriff on the "Freak Power" ticket. In 1970 he began his long association with *Rolling Stone*, and it was in this magazine that *Fear and Loathing in Las Vegas* first appeared in serial form, having been "aggressively rejected" by *Sport Illustrated*. Thompson's work became increasingly political, albeit from an off-beat, anarcho-libertarian perspective, and was often savagely illustrated by the British caricaturist, Ralph Steadman, a lifelong friend.

Thompson, a gun enthusiast, shot himself in the head on February 20, 2005. At his funeral his ashes were fired from a giant cannon, to the accompaniment of fireworks. "I hate to advocate drugs, alcohol, violence, or insanity to anyone," he used to say, "but they've always worked for me."

Ian Crofton

Date 1971 (publication)

Author Hunter S. Thompson (1937–2005)

Nationality USA

Why It's Key Thompson was a pioneer of "Gonzo" journalism, in which reportage is subjective – sometimes even fictionalized – and merged with the writer's own experience of the events described.

Opposite Hunter S. Thompson

Key Event **Philip Hobsbaum holds creative writing meetings at his Glasgow flat**

Tom Leonard, James Kelman, Liz Lochhead, Alasdair Gray, and Jeff Torrington are the most well known writers who, in the early 1970s, attended a peculiarly Glaswegian kind of salon at the home of Philip Hobsbaum, a lecturer at the University of Glasgow. Hobsbaum was a teacher, poet, and critic who had already studied under eminent literary critics F.R. Leavis and William Empson before he arrived in Glasgow. His reading group seems to have introduced a generation of extremely influential writers to each other, who have continued to associate in a spirit of solidarity and friendship.

Hobsbaum had convened similar groups before, most notably in Belfast, but the Glasgow group contained a remarkably high proportion of the most important novelists, poets, and dramatists of the 1970–1990 period. Most of these writers achieved their first real successes in the 1980s and most of them are still productive today; it is difficult, perhaps impossible, to decide just how big a part Hobsbaum's reading group played in this success because most of the writers had already formed their own very idiosyncratic styles and attitudes before they met here, but it seems to have been the only environment available in Glasgow where work in unfamiliar modes could be read and discussed in an atmosphere of mutual respect.

Robin Purves

Date 1971–1975

Place Glasgow, Scotland

Author Philip Hobsbaum (1932–2005)

Why It's Key Alasdair Gray, James Kelman, Liz Lochhead, and Tom Leonard all attended Hobsbaum's reading group, and it became the center of Glasgow's literary renaissance.

Key Book
Surfacing

Often referred to as an "ecofeminist" novel, *Surfacing* was recognized when it was published in 1972 as an important development of the post-modern feminist argument. The story of an unnamed young woman going back to the wild and remote island she grew up on to try and locate her missing father, having been forced to abort her child after having an affair with a married man, it is one of self-discovery through the psychological turmoil of the search and reveals a society that is rooted in suppression.

Surfacing is a book that encourages many critical approaches because of its complexity. As ecofeminism it makes a definite link between the two worlds of nature and femininity, exploring a duality and conflict brought about by the main character's struggle to exist in both the "masculine" world of logic and language and the "feminine" world of nature and emotion. It also approaches the question of colonialism through comparison of the oppression of a patriarchal system with the conflicts experienced by an English-speaking Canadian woman.

As one of Atwood's earliest novels, it lays the groundwork for many of her later themes concerning women's roles and their relationship with the patriarchal system, as well as issues of both gendered and national identity. It explores such ideas with an acute sensitivity to the details of a psychotic episode and demonstrates early on in her career Atwood's ability to immerse herself, and the reader, in a story with her distinctive, multi-layered, poetic style.

Sophie Baker

Date 1972

Author Margaret Atwood (born 1939)

Nationality Canada

Why It's Key *Surfacing*, Margaret Atwood's second novel, was key to the development of the post-modern feminist argument. It lays out the themes that Atwood revisits in her extensive, and continuing, career, and does so in a way that grounds feminist ideas in the story of acute mental breakdown.

Opposite Margaret Atwood

Key Author **Ira Levin**
The Stepford Wives

Date 1972 (publication)

Author Ira Levin (born 1929)

Nationality USA

Other Key Works *A Kiss Before Dying* (1952), *Deathtrap* (1978)

Why It's Key Levin's suspense novels combined the preoccupations of his era – feminism meets elements of science fiction in *Stepford* and in *Rosemary's* the modern psychological thriller confronts the age-old battle between good and evil.

Born in New York between the two world wars, Ira Levin (born 1929) has been a hugely popular author of many science fiction and suspense novels which have been made into famous films, notably *Rosemary's Baby* and *The Stepford Wives*.

In his satirical novel, *The Stepford Wives*, Levin cleverly questions the nature of human identity and its worth when the wives are replaced with highly photogenic, vacuous androids. He creates a frightening vision of a bland, sterile Connecticut town of the future, Stepford, where consumerism is the creeping evil and the robotic wives are beautiful but not sexy or loveable, as they all resemble those immaculate actresses found in adverts for floor-wax, detergents, and cleaning fluids. The term "Stepford Wife" is now used to indicate an uncannily perfect woman who is mindlessly devoted to domestic life.

In his bestselling thriller, *Rosemary's Baby* (1967), Levin demonstrates that evil is intrinsic to human society by introducing supernatural forces which invade the everyday life of a newly married couple living in a New York apartment. Levin is such a popular author because he is a first-class storyteller who writes inventive and innovative gems containing scientific and supernatural twists.

In *Boys from Brazil* (1976), the inherent evil is in the form of a Nazi scientist who is using his knowledge to create baby boys in Hitler's genetic image. Not only does Levin shrewdly question the Nazi idea of eugenics, but he is also one of the first authors to examine the possible consequences of cloning human beings (decades before Dolly the Sheep was cloned). Levin is also a master at creating realistic characters and good honest psychological suspense, which further enhances his enormous popularity with readers.
Alice Goldie

Key Event ***Pounamu, Pounamu* is the first story collection to be published by Maori**

Date 1972 (publication)

Author Witi Ihimaera (born 1944)

Nationality New Zealand

Why It's Key In 1973 Ihimaera wrote *Tangi*, the first Maori novel. Since then he has enjoyed international success, particularly with *The Whale Rider* which became a successful film. In 2003 he republished *Pounamu* in an "anniversary collection" having rewritten most of the stories.

Pounamu, Pounamu stood for a doubly significant event when it first saw the light in the early 1970s. It was not only the first story collection to be published by a Maori writer, but the first work of fiction to center on a Maori setting and Maori characters. It represented a seriousness about issues of Maori identity and culture that was most apposite at the time (when Maori people were beginning to become politically active in demand of their sovereignty), as well as an insight into ordinary lives within that community.

This collection of stories was a homecoming, an acknowledgement of the author's heritage as well as a breaking of new ground. "Pounamu" is the name for the precious New Zealand greenstone, a kind of jade, which Witi Ihimaera associated with the treasured things of life, such as the village life of his childhood. The early stories, set in the fictional (but largely autobiographical) village of Waituhi which Ihimaera was to repopulate again and again in later works, are not overtly political; they deal with romantic, family, and tribal relationships within a modern Maori setting.

Ihimaera's work has been instrumental in forming the perception of Maori culture for the world in general. He gained world renown for *The Whale Rider* (1987), the story of a young girl's relationship with a whale, linked to the survival of her community. He has since written historical novels and even a "Maori Western" (*Bulibasha*, 1994), and rewritten the works of New Zealand literary heroine Katherine Mansfield from a Maori point of view (*Dear Miss Mansfield*, 1989). In the 1990s he began writing about his experience of coming out as a married gay man, but it was his pioneering work of the 1970s that put Maori culture on the literary map.
Lucy Daniel

Key Book
Invisible Cities (Le città invisibili)

Take fifty-five cities, as good a number as any to make sixty-four. Or rather, settle for fifty-five cities and eleven series or themes. So, five cities to a theme. Pretty neat, for some reason. Or rather still, take fifty-four cities, the number of cities in More's *Utopia*, add one truly invisible city, Baucis, and place it at the center of the text. Break up the one frame into eighteen half-frames, that is nine entire frames; add fifty-five, and you have sixty-four, the number of squares in a chessboard. You can check it all in a diagram. But the result is not a square. It is better than a square because of a three-way interaction: nine chapters (firmly enclosed by the half-dialogues); eleven series (of five numbered items each: 1, 2, 3, 4, 5); fifty-five titled cities (with the title naming the series and the number within the series, but not the name of the city, as that is reserved for the text). Seven chapter structures (chapters 2–8) thus generate the sequence 5, 4, 3, 2, 1 from the ten-element chapter 1 establishing the proceedings. That is,

each new chapter after the first one opens on the closing item of a series and closes on the opening item of a new series, with the final chapter, again in ten elements, progressively exhausting the remaining materials. The resulting cities are all-contiguous, as well as categorized and sequenced. Definitely neat.

This may look like some very clever permutational wizardry carried out in the least textual space. Yet its incredible beauty lies in the constructed sense of it being a last poem to the city, any city, and, above all, one's own original city, though disguised through line and number.

Federica Pedriali

Date 1972

Author Italo Calvino (1923–85)

Nationality Italy

Why It's Key Outstanding non-French example of late twentieth-century combinatorial fiction; hugely successful in the English-speaking world. Received as a masterpiece of minimalist writing, *Invisible Cities* is arguably also the text where, in a real feat of technical virtuosity, Calvino, always reluctant to say it all, has achieved just that.

1970–1979

543

Key Event *Joy of Sex* breaks new ground in its exploration of adult relationships

First published in 1972, *The Joy of Sex*, which was originally to have been entitled *Cordon Bleu Sex*, emulated the style of popular cookery manuals with suggestions for starters, main courses and sauces, and pickles. Alex Comfort's seminal approach to lovemaking offered a realistic and affirmative discussion of sex that was lacking in earlier, more descriptive treatments of the topic. Its unashamed forays into all aspects of couples' sexual lives aimed to shift emphasis away from the purely functional, and, in doing so, to enable couples to experiment and share mutually-enjoyable and guilt-free sexual experiences.

Chris Foss' accompanying illustrations have become synonymous with the book but serve to date it firmly in the early 1970s. Indeed, Comfort's guide was both a product of and an agent in the sexual revolution that began in the 1960s. Promoting the values of liberation and tolerance, and insisting upon gender equality, *The Joy of Sex* reified a body

of changing attitudes into a practical and accessible illustrated manual.

The book has been updated since its original publication but it retains many of Comfort's own particular predilections, such as the rather subjective belief that the removal of a woman's body hair is an act of "vandalism." In addition, it remains decidedly heterosexist and contains no discussion of homosexual relationships. Although it now lacks the breadth and scope of more recent "how-to" sex guides, it is still a bestseller, perhaps because it appeals to a generation of one-time teenagers whose illicit consultation of the text marked an initiation into the more sophisticated world of adult relationships.

Juliet Wightman

Date 1972 (publication)

Place UK

Author Alex Comfort (1920–2000)

Why It's Key A groundbreaking sex manual that broke with the tradition of its austere predecessors by providing a joyful exploration of adult relationships.

Key Book *The New Sufferings of Young W. (Die neuen Leiden Des jungen W.)*

The publication of Ulrich Plenzdorf's novella in the German Democratic Republic produced a literary sensation. A phenomenal success with younger readers in both East and West Germany, the text's protagonist and narrator, Edgar Wibeau, became the GDR's first literary anti-hero, a teenage rebel who dies in an accident after running away to Berlin to escape the pressures of a conventional childhood, and whose grievances against a restrictive and prescriptive system are presented in a humorous postmortem narrative.

The success of the novella derives in large part from the employment of this distinctive narrative voice and from the playful adaptation of literary models; Edgar identifies with Holden Caulfield, the protagonist of Salinger's *The Catcher in the Rye*, whose mannerisms and voice he echoes, and his colloquial narration adds unique color. This and other enthusiasms such as American jeans, jazz, and – as implied in the title – Goethe's Werther, whose "sufferings" had inspired previous generations, are thematically integrated into the construction of a character whose attempt to find a purely individual identity raises questions about the stifling nature of a society concerned only with collective identity.

The publication of material such as this was only made possible by a brief period in the early 1970s of liberalization in the state's attitude to art and literature, and by a degree of ambiguity in the "message," permitted by the protagonist's premature demise. Despite this, it provoked an unprecedented degree of controversy in the GDR and is a landmark publication.
Jon Hughes

Date 1972

Author Ulrich Plenzdorf (born 1934)

Nationality Germany

Why It's Key A landmark work of fiction from the 1970s, Plenzdorf's witty intertextual narrative of teenage rebellion has proved a lasting success with young readers.

Key Author
Heinrich Böll

Heinrich Böll (1917–1985), who won the Nobel Prize in Literature in 1972, was the conscience of post-war Germany. The novels, stories, and radio plays he wrote between 1955 and 1965, even when typically humorous, struck a note of moral urgency, as he explored the humdrum lives of ordinary people. A non-judgemental sympathy for human weakness and a sparse, intense, almost biblical prose became characteristic of work highlighting post-war misery but also addressing a moral lesson to that mass of conformist Germans who had succumbed to Hitler.

Böll's Catholic background and his active war especially helped shape the early fiction which, exemplifed by *The Bread of Those Early Years* (1955), was not so much realism as magic moralism. This short masterpiece, which for almost 40 years lacked an English translation, was a love story. But its real quality lay in the way the narrator transformed events like lighting a cigarette or buying flowers into critical moments of spiritual value or worthlessness. The text was rich in poetic metaphors, and the compressed time scale, and the way life-changing inner events occurred in outwardly routine circumstances set the pattern for later work.

In the 1960s critics began to find Böll's work sentimental, although novels like *Billiards at Half-Past Nine* (1959) and *The Clown* (1963) gave him a world following. His sense that spiritual values were endangered by post-war prosperity led to him to support the radical politics of the 1968 generation. *The Lost Honour of Katharina Blum* (1974) was turned into an excellent film by Volker Schloendorff.
Lesley Chamberlain

Date 1972 (Nobel Prize in Literature awarded)

Nationality Germany

Other Key Works *The Clown* (1963), *Group Portrait with Lady* (1971)

Why It's Key Böll established himself in the 1950s as West Germany's most representative writer, stylistically simple and unerringly democratic, although retaining a deep German concern with the individual inner life.

Key Author **Bessie Head**
A Question of Power

Bessie Head (1937–1986) was born in Pietermaritzburg as the daughter of an unknown black man and a wealthy white woman who had been committed to a mental asylum by her own family as a result of the affair. Head's own accounts suggest that these circumstances, and the "colored" status arising from them, had a profound effect on her relationship with the country of her birth. It was this situation which formed the focus of Head's third and final novel, the semi-autobiographical *A Question of Power*.

Head's racial ambiguity, in a South Africa where government policy insisted that racial identity be regarded as an absolute, informed her enduring concern with liminality. A further layer was added to her own marginality in 1964, when she left South Africa on an "exit permit," rendering her essentially stateless, and with the certainty of immediate arrest should she return to the country of her birth. She settled in the village of Serowe in Botswana, where much of her fiction is set. Here, she found herself an equally liminal figure as a South African colored woman, and recoiled at a new kind of racial stratification in the antipathy of her black Tswana neighbors towards the San people.

Eventually coming to terms with Serowe, Head's work became increasingly concerned with rural life in Botswana. Her writing changed the landscape of South African literature by rejecting the conventional sites of black and white identities, and by shifting focus to the rural experience.

Timothy Lovering

Date 1973 (publication)

Nationality South Africa

Other Key Works *When Rain Clouds Gather* (1968), *The Collector of Treasures and Other Botswana Village Tales* (1977), *Serowe: Village of the Rain Wind* (1981)

Why It's Key Bessie Head's writing addressed a new set of concerns in South African literature, dealing with the tensions between rural and urban life, and with the complexity of racial identities.

Key Author **Sidney Sheldon**
The Other Side of Midnight

Sidney Sheldon (1917–2007) came relatively late to novel-writing, publishing his first, *The Naked Face*, in 1970, but he had already established himself as a writer of screenplays in Hollywood, stage musicals on Broadway, and highly popular television shows, including the long-running comedy series *I Dream of Jeanie* (1965–1970). He repeated the commercial success of *The Other Side of Midnight* with a stream of bestselling novels, such as *Rage of Angels* (1980) and *If Tomorrow Comes* (1985), but he never won critical acclaim. His books were often dismissed as sensationalist, dominated by an over-romantic view of the world, more concerned with making the reader turn the page than constructing believable plots and realistic characters: the archetypal "airport novel."

However, Sheldon was happy to be a popular bestseller, and worked hard at his craft, claiming that he never described a place he hadn't personally visited, relishing the personal control that had been all but impossible in his writing for the big and small screens. He deliberately created page-turners, saying in 1982: "I try to construct them so when the reader gets to the end of a chapter, he or she has to read just one more chapter. It's the technique of the old Saturday afternoon serial: leave the guy hanging on the edge of the cliff at the end of the chapter." He was well known for portraying strong women, struggling to succeed in a world dominated by powerful, often ruthless men, and his work was especially, but never exclusively, popular among female readers.

Michael Munro

Date 1973 (publication)

Nationality USA

Why It's Key *The Other Side of Midnight* was an immediate success, rising to the top of *The New York Times* bestseller list, and established Sheldon's trademark style of cleverly plotted, sensational and suspenseful writing. It was made into a film in 1977.

Key Event
Reinaldo Arenas is arrested

He was arrested on false charges of seducing two teenage boys. By the time he was tried in the summer of 1973, Reinaldo Arenas had become an enemy of the state, guilty of publishing his work abroad without consent of the censorious Cuban Writers' Union. Among his accusers were some of his own colleagues and former friends. He had stepped outside the boundaries set by Fidel Castro's infamous "Words to the intellectuals" of 1961: "Within the Revolution, everything; against the Revolution, there is no right." Arenas was not only homosexual – a crime in itself under Castro's regime – but counter-revolutionary.

He escaped during the trial, and for some time lived a fugitive life in Havana's Lenin Park. There, in the margins of a dog-eared copy of *The Iliad*, he began scribbling his memoirs. He was re-arrested in 1974 and imprisoned at El Morro castle. He survived by composing letters for inmates' families and lovers. Severely beaten when his attempts to smuggle work

out of prison were discovered, he recanted his "ideological deviations" and was released in 1976.

Arenas was among the 120,000 Cubans who arrived in the United States on the Mariel boatlift of 1980. He settled in New York and was diagnosed with AIDS seven years later. Only then did he continue the book of memoirs he had begun in hiding. Its title, *Before Night Falls* (1992), referred to the urgency of writing while daylight was available in Lenin Park. It also referred to the need to set down his story before his imminent death.

Ángel Gurría-Quintana

Date 1973

Place Cuba

Author Reinaldo Arenas (1943–1990)

Why It's Key Arenas had published a single novel, *Celestino Before Dawn* (1967) before his arrest. His openly gay lifestyle and criticisms of the Revolution had attracted censors' attention and incurred the wrath of a repressive police state.

Opposite **Reinaldo Arenas**

1970-1979

547

Key Book
The Rachel Papers

The Rachel Papers, published when Martin Amis was 24, is a work of aggressive exhibitionism: slick, confident, and stylistically inventive. It is narrated by the smart-talking Charles Highway. He is 19 and, while preparing to go up to Oxford, he amuses himself by seducing and then spurning young women. He keeps fastidious records – his papers – of his conquests and couplings. He is an auditor of the carnal. The novel has a young man's dread of and disgust for the middle-aged, for what time does to us all. "The skin had shrunken over her skull," Highway writes of his mother, "to accentuate her jaw and commodious cellarage for the gloomy pools that were her eyes; her breasts had long forsaken their natural home and now flanked her navel; and her buttocks, when she wore stretch slacks, would dance behind her knees, like punch balls."

Everything that would define Amis as an atrocity-minded comic novelist and stylist was here in microcosm: the grotesque humor and revolt against

pulchritude ("her breasts had long forsaken their natural home"), the cruelty, the ironic knowingness and allusions, the baroque phrase-making. It was clear that from the beginning of his career Amis knew exactly what he wanted to say and how to go about saying it, and in his own exalted voice. Later novels – notably *London Fields* (1989) and *The Information* (1995) – would deepen and harden in their preoccupation with decay and disaster, but the striving for original effect, for what he called the High Style, remained the same.

Jason Cowley

Date 1973

Author Martin Amis (born 1949)

Nationality UK

Why It's Key *The Rachel Papers*, Martin Amis' first novel, foreshadows several aspects of his mature style. It catapulted him into the literary limelight, where he remained as one of the most influential British writers of the 1970s, 1980s, and 1990s.

Key Event **Rolando Hinojosa publishes the first book in Klail City Death Trip series**

Rolando Hinojosa is the granddaddy of the Chicano movement, and his Klail City Death Trip series is unlike anything else in modern literature. In 15 installments (to date in 2007) not only has Hinojosa created a fictional county in the Río Grande Valley of southern Texas and populated it with over a thousand characters; he has done so in two languages, with genre-defying versatility – one volume is an epistolary novel; one a short novel in verse; another a war diary; one pastiches a 1980s telenovela; and some are murder mysteries.

The first, *Estampas del valle* (1973), drew on Spanish literary tradition both in its "Estampas" (sketches), based on medieval Spanish character portraits, and its protagonist Jehú's picaresque journey. Ten years later Hinojosa first translated one of his own books into English, taking liberties forbidden any other translator, reworking it so much that the translation stood as a new novel in its own right. His bilingual ability to recast his material is particularly useful for transferring humor.

Despite radical adventures into new territories, the series entertains both as separately enjoyable novels and one coherent entity. This supposed "death trip" of Chicano culture is mirrored in the books' journey from Spanish to a blend of English and Spanish, and finally (in *Rites and Witnesses*, 1982) the first installment written originally in English, seemingly sealing the loss of Spanish-language identity within the Chicano community. But while they address racism and cultural divides, these are success stories, spanning a period beginning in racial segregation and ending in integration. The most acclaimed is *Klail City y Sus Alrededores* (1976), along with its English recasting *Klail City* (1987), written 11 years later, and, in an astonishing feat of self-translation, both the same story and a different book.

Lucy Daniel

Date 1973

Author Rolando Hinojosa (born 1929)

Nationality USA

Why It's Key The Klail City Death Trip series is the grandest achievement of Chicano literature and consists of 15 volumes. The background is the centuries-long story of the Spanish-Mexican population of Texas.

548

Key Passage *Fear of Flying*

"My response… was not (not yet) to have an affair and not (not yet) to hit the open road, but to evolve my fantasy of the Zipless Fuck."

Erica Jong, young, beautiful, and blonde, appeared in her publicity photographs to be the antithesis of the 1970s feminist. In fact, *Fear of Flying* could with hindsight be read as the first "chick-lit" novel; at the height of the women's lib movement its cheerful raunchiness certainly came as a shock. But it is a book which is more serious than titillating. To those women who were coming of age at the time of its publication, taking the newly-available contraceptive pill, enjoying – if that's the right word – "free" love, and struggling to be granted the same respect and freedoms as men, *Fear of Flying* and its heroine, Isadora Wing, told it like it was.

Isadora, attending a conference abroad with her emotionally cold psychiatrist husband, muses on the situation of women, the drawbacks of marriage, the nuisance of menstruation, and books, politics, travel, and sex. John Updike compared the novel to Philip Roth's *Portnoy's Complaint* for its sexual honesty.

Jong defined the famous "Zipless Fuck" as "more than a fuck… Zipless, because when you came together zippers fell away like rose petals, underwear blew off in one breath like dandelion fluff… For the true, ultimate zipless A-1 fuck, it was necessary that you never got to know the man very well… anonymity made it even better."

The serious point of the book lies in its attempt to discover a post-liberation way of living with men, while managing to retain a separate identity. In fact, it is worth reading if only as a social document which describes women's experiences in the 1960s and 1970s.

Felicity Skelton

Date 1973

Author Erica Jong (born 1942)

Nationality USA

Why It's Key *Fear of Flying* treated women's liberation with humor – a rarity at the time. It is also famous for the frankness of the descriptions of bodily functions, especially sex.

Opposite Erica Jong

Key Book
Crash

In the introduction to the 1995 edition of his most controversial novel, J.G. Ballard writes that he would "like to think that *Crash* is the first pornographic novel based on technology. In a sense, pornography is the most political form of fiction, dealing with how we use and exploit each other in the most urgent and ruthless way."

The novel tells of a character (named Ballard after its author) who survives a violent collision after losing control of his car at 60mph on the anonymous network of roads on the outskirts of London. The novel takes on a hallucenogenic atmosphere as Ballard is drawn into the extreme crash fetishizing cult of Vaughan, a former TV-scientist, turned "nightmare angel of the expressways." Vaughan's ultimate fantasy is to die in a high-speed chrome-and-flesh mangling union with the actress Elizabeth Taylor. The pair become obsessively aroused by "the mysterious eroticism of wounds: the perverse logic of blood-soaked instrument panels, seat-belts smeared with excrement, sun visors lined with brain tissue." In their "autogeddon," human beings are opened up to greater sexual possibilities by their injuries. They are moving towards a future dystopia in which humanity becomes more desirable where it intersects with metal.

Although Martin Amis panned *Crash* as "heavily flawed" reviewing it in 1973, he later recanted, saying that the novel "scintillatingly succeeds" and arguing that "readers should always be wrestling with the writers who feel intimate to them." There is no doubt that *Crash* had a huge impact on Amis and other writers of his generation whose work attempts to understand modern society's exhilarating and often destructive relationship with technology.
Helen Brown

Date 1973

Author J.G. Ballard (born 1930)

Nationality UK (born China)

Why It's Key Simon Sellars, the editor of the "Ballardian" online magazine argues that *Crash* sees "the first appearance of Ballard's fully blown 'catalyst figure,' Vaughan, an archetype which Ballard seems to refine in every one of his latter-day novels...."

Opposite From the film adaptation of *Crash*

551

Key Character **Kilgore Trout**
Breakfast of Champions

The very definition of curmudgeon, Kilgore Trout is a failed science fiction writer who has great ideas and a complete indifference to being published. This is just as well, since he hasn't a jot of literary talent, and his main publisher is a distributor of pornographic magazines which use his short stories as "filler" in girlie magazines and thus relegates the author's work to the kind of store where the average reader is not likely to discover him.

Kurt Vonnegut's most famous character, Trout first appears in *God Bless You, Mr. Rosewater* as the favorite author of that novel's protagonist, Eliot Rosewater, who is also Trout's only fan. Trout reappears as a character throughout Vonnegut's oeuvre and Vonnegut writes of him that the grouchy writer is the only character he ever created who has the intelligence and imagination to suspect he might be a character in someone else's novel. It is this intelligence and imagination which ultimately makes Trout an off-the-wall but wise figure in Vonnegut's novels. In addition to *Breakfast of Champions* (1973), where he is actually the main character, Trout also appears in *Slaughterhouse Five* (1969), *Jailbird* (1979), *Timequake* (1997), and *Galápagos* (1985), in which his son, Leon, is the narrator.

Trout's views are almost always pessimistic and cynical, and he has often been regarded as representing Vonnegut's own views on the human race. Indeed, Vonnegut recently "reported" that Trout committed suicide on October 15, 2004 after learning from a psychic that George W. Bush would win the presidential election in a 5–4 vote by the Supreme Court. Ironically, though a complete unknown within Vonnegut's fictional world, Trout is extremely well known in our own, so much so that in 1975, a successful science fiction novel called *Venus on the Halfshell* appeared under his name.
Elizabeth Rosen

Date 1973 (publication)

Appears in *God Bless You Mr. Rosewater* (1965), *Slaughterhouse Five* (1969), *Jailbird* (1979), *Galápagos* (1985), *Timequake* (1997)

Author Kurt Vonnegut (1922–2007)

Nationality USA

Why It's Key Often regarded as Vonnegut's mouthpiece, Kilgore Trout is a failed writer whose pronouncements about the human race have endeared him to Vonnegut's readers.

Key Event **Virago Press is set up to publish women writers**

Virago Press was founded in 1973 by Carmen Callil, Rosie Boycott, and Marsha Rowe to publish "books by and about women." Their first publication was *Fenwomen* by Mary Chamberlain. A "Virago" originally meant a strong or warlike woman; through use it developed to mean a shrewish scold. This double meaning therefore suited the press, which was interested in being strong but also reminding the patriarchal literary establishment that their stranglehold over publishing was at an end. This celebratory reclamation of what was a term of insult figures the purpose and activity of the press well.

Virago Press was particularly influential during the 1970s and 1980s in reprinting the works of key forgotten or marginalized women writers; it was an important part of second-generation Anglo-American feminist attempts to reclaim literary history. Elaine Showalter's *A Literature of Their Own* and Sheila Rowbotham's *Hidden History* influenced the press'

introduction of particular lists such as Virago Modern Classics and the Virago Reprint Library. With distinctive cover art and the solid "brand" of the Virago press supporting them these lists gave a readership to books forgotten by mainstream audiences for decades.

Virago has also circulated the work of some of the most important female writers of the last 30 years: Angela Carter, Margaret Atwood, Sarah Waters, Pat Barker, and Maya Angelou. It has given a true international voice to women as one of the largest publishing companies in the world, and is still defiantly political despite now being a subsidiary of Little, Brown.
Jerome de Groot

Date 1973

Place UK

Why It's Key World leader in the publishing of writing by and about women, Virago Press was a key feminist icon as well as being an influence on the international literary scene.

552

Key Event **Solzhenitsyn is deported after his book exposes the Soviet police state**

Alexander Solzhenitsyn's massive history of the Soviet prison system was based on first-hand accounts by hundreds of the millions of victims, including himself, who passed through the labor camp system that began under Stalin. When it began appearing in the West in 1974, such was the moral authority of Solzhenitsyn, who had won the Nobel Prize in Literature in 1970, that it finally destroyed the lingering western hope that Soviet Communism was a decent attempt at socialism.

Given the size and Russian orientation of the original volume most Westerners read the one-volume abridged edition of 1986. The officially-sanctioned inhumanity, but even more the devastatingly careless attitude to human life which Solzhenitsyn's collective memoir revealed, made it an agonizing text, brought vividly alive by the narrative skill of a great writer.

Yet if Solzhenitsyn's anti-Soviet message was unequivocal, and turned him overnight into a free-

world hero, his attitude to Russia proved uncongenial and often unfathomable to many western liberals. For his 20 years abroad he lived in Vermont, where, to continue writing, he simulated the harsh conditions of Siberia in his own backyard and delivered stinging criticisms of western decadence. When he returned to Russia in 1994, after a brief honeymoon period, his wrathful Christian denunciations of post-Soviet ways were equally unwelcome. In 1995 he wrote that "We must build a moral Russia or none at all," and his place in history looks likely to be amid the ranks of the great nineteenth-century intelligentsia, asking the impossible of a tragic country.
Lesley Chamberlain

Date 1974

Place Russia

Title *The Gulag Archipelago* (1973–78)

Author Alexander Solzhenitsyn (born 1918)

Why It's Key Solzhenitsyn brought the concept of the Gulag – the brutal network of state correction camps – to light, when he published the history *The Gulag Archipelago* in 1974. He was then stripped of his Soviet citizenship and deported.

Opposite Alexander Solzhenitsyn

Key Event *Gravity's Rainbow* – the Pulitzer Prize's most controversial candidate

Thomas Pynchon's epic novel *Gravity's Rainbow* is a notoriously "difficult" work. Spanning over a thousand pages and set in Europe at the end of World War II, the novel is a dense constellation of events, characters, and institutions surrounding a mysterious rocket called the 00000. U.S. Army lieutenant Tyrone Slothrop – whose sexual encounters in London uncannily predict the locations that V-2 rockets will strike – becomes embroiled in a complex and often absurd mystery involving the 00000, its component part, the S-Gerät, and its constituent polymer, Imipolex G. Slothrop's obsession with the missile takes him all over Europe, where he is variously pursued, waylaid, and assisted by bizarre figures and forces such as Operation Paperclip, IG Farben, Standard Oil, the Phoebus cartel and the Illuminati.

By the end of the escapade, Slothrop's very identity splinters into shards; he discovers that a Captain Blicero means to fire the S-Gerät with his

sex slave Gottfried strapped inside the capsule. The spiraling and frenetic narrative comes to an abrupt end, as if the text itself is destroyed when the 00000 impacts its target.

The critical reception of *Gravity's Rainbow* has been acutely divided because, on one hand, the novel is blisteringly cerebral, erudite, and inventive, while on the other hand, it is unreservedly subversive. No behavior or issue is too contentious to be countenanced – from Pavlovian conditioning and parapsychology to conspiracy theories and sexual depravity. Pynchon's characters – whose musings traverse a spectrum of scientific, mystical, artistic, pop-cultural, political, and philosophical topics – are conduits for the controversial debates that render *Gravity's Rainbow* a compendium of postmodern concerns.
Kiki Benzon

Date 1974

Author Thomas Pynchon (born 1937)

Nationality USA

Why It's Key The Pulitzer Prize jury on fiction unanimously agreed that *Gravity's Rainbow* should win the prize; members of the Pulitzer board, however, unanimously disagreed, calling the book "unreadable," "turgid," "overwritten," and "obscene." In the end, no award was given that year.

554

Key Event
Philip K. Dick experiences a theophany

In late February 1974, Philip K. Dick experienced the first of a series of visions, an experience he later described as being struck and blinded by a beam of pink light. These episodes typically lasted several hours, after which Dick experienced prolonged phosphene interference, like the after-image of a bright bulb. Apparently, inexplicably, the beams planted large amounts of information in his brain: information that he could not have acquired from any other source. In particular, he became convinced that his newborn son Christopher was suffering from a potentially fatal, undiagnosed condition. He persuaded sceptical doctors to examine the boy and they found an inguinal hernia, a protrusion of the intestine through the abdominal wall, life-threatening if left uncorrected.

This experience directly inspired Dick's most ambitious work, the trilogy made up of *VALIS* (acronym for Vast Active Living Intelligent System) (1980), *The Divine Invasion* (1981), and *The Transmigration of*

Timothy Archer (1982). The true significance of *VALIS*, in particular, has been little understood. Although apparently disowning his/Horselover Fat's radical cosmogeny and theology, Dick nevertheless conducts one of the twentieth century's most erudite, original, and searching studies of religion.

VALIS is considered a cryptic, secondary work, but its full impact and influence has yet to be felt. The hero Horselover Fat's radical speculations are dismissed, both by the character Philip K. Dick, and seemingly by the author himself, but the originality of what he imagines, and the intensity with which he pursues this intellectual course, is unmatched in science fiction.
Charles Beckett

Date February–March 1974

Place Los Angeles, California

Author Philip K. Dick (1928–1982)

Why It's Key Dick's experience had a profound effect on the writing of generations of science fiction authors. *VALIS* demonstrated a fluidity of character, voice, and tone that massively expanded the SF writer's fictional horizon and frame of reference.

Key Character **Saeed** *The Secret Life of Saeed, the Ill-Fated Pessoptimist*

Saeed is a comic hero and his "pessoptimistic" story one of the greatest comic novels in Arabic. This was a satirical book which broke the mould in Arab fiction, was immediately recognized as a fresh voice, and became as popular as it was innovative. The story is told in the form of letters from Saeed to an unknown recipient, recounted from somewhere in outer space. Through all the adventures he relates, Saeed reveals himself as stupid and a coward, as well as an informer for the Zionist state and a failure with women.

In a series of very short chapters, through the medium of scorching wit, and a faux-naif voice, Habibi discusses some of the most pressing concerns of the Arab-Israeli conflict taking in two wars in the state of Israel and twenty years of Saeed's life. Saeed's gullibility and obedience have the effect of highlighting the viciousness of events surrounding him; he is a naïve figure who casts the world around him into an even darker light. Saeed, in fact, has to play it dumb to save his own life, until finally an extra-terrestrial saves him the bother. This unique contribution to modern Palestinian literature was perhaps the most effective in describing the absurd horror of the chronic violence of the world Saeed inhabits.

He owes his life to the fact that an ass stepped in front of a bullet intended for him, from the same aggressors who shot his father in 1948. He claims he is one of "the rest" – the unnoticed, the ordinary people who are everywhere – and therefore, in a typical paradoxical turnabout, "I truly am remarkable."
Lucy Daniel

Date 1974

Author Imil Habibi (1922–96)

Nationality Arab Israeli

Why It's Key One of Israel's most esteemed Arab journalists and novelists, Habibi was the editor of the leading Israeli Arab periodical, *Unity* (*Al-Ittihad*). He was also a founding member of the Israeli Communist Party and elected three times to the Israeli Knesset.

Key Passage **"To the Sea"** *High Windows*

To step over the low wall that divides
Road from concrete walk above the shore
Brings sharply back something known long before –
The miniature gaiety of seasides.
Everything crowds under the low horizon:
Steep beach, blue water, towels, red bathing caps,
The small hushed waves' repeated fresh collapse
Up the warm yellow sand, and further off
A white steamer stuck in the afternoon –

Still going on, all of it, still going on!

So begins the first poem of what turned out to be Philip Larkin's final collection, *High Windows*, with assured poetic skill and an immediately recognizable authority and poignancy. A delayed successor to *The Whitsun Weddings* (1964), the book confirmed Larkin's position as the most widely admired and celebrated contemporary poet in the British Isles.

This pre-eminence was disputed in the 1990s, following the publication of letters and a biography which revealed that Larkin's socio-political views were often ugly and bigoted, and that he was in his life frequently reactionary about race, gender, and politics. There was plentiful evidence of a not always benign conservatism in Larkin's previously published works. *High Windows* includes a truculent engagement with public affairs – for instance in "Going, Going," about the spoliation of rural England, and in "Posterity," a crassly anti-American and anti-Semitic poem about U.S. academia. Against these and more personal prospects of gloomy decline, the collection sets various versions of redemptive pastoral. "Still going on!" Larkin writes in "To the Sea," and the enigmatic tone of this exclamation is both pleased and saddened by these leisured rites which will outlast the "repeated fresh collapse" of Larkin's and others' selves.
Peter Swaab

Date 1974

Author Philip Larkin (1922–1985)

Nationality UK

Why It's Key Larkin's poetry emphasizes solitude, transience and the provincial, mixing melancholy and anger, colloquialism and a higher style. In poems like "To the Sea" Larkin depicts a Britain endeared by custom and continuity.

Key Character **Carrie**
Carrie

When readers recall the heroine of Stephen King's first full-length novel it is not as the telekinetic mass-murderer that she becomes, but as an excluded, overweight teenager terrified by the sight of her own menstrual blood striking the tiles of her high school shower block in "dime-sized drops." "Plug it *up*," chant her classmates as they pelt her with tampons. Carietta White was raised by her widowed mother in an abusive and extremely repressive Christian atmosphere which condemns female sexuality as the devil's work.

King tells Carrie's story in rapid-fire documentary form. The events of "Prom Night" at Ewen High School, Maine, are revealed in a series of psychologist's reports, inquest transcripts and survivor memoirs. Although less polished than King's later works, *Carrie* showcases his pitch-perfect ear for the vernacular and his ability to lure out the terrors that dwell beneath the seemingly safe and often sentimentalized communities of small town America.

The plot of *Carrie* is a fantastical re-imagining of the true persecutions of "witches" in Christian cultures. Often outsider women, they were reviled and ultimately murdered by their own communities. The twist in King's tale is that Carrie really does have the superhuman power to fight back.

Carrie's story is a tragedy: a cautionary fable about the devastating consequences of bullying. She only ever wanted love and acceptance. But the fear and hatred of her peers turns her into "Lady Macbeth," "unaware that she was scrubbing her bloodied hands against her dress," weeping as she laughs, thinking "o momma I'm scared momma MOMMA."
Helen Brown

Date 1974

Author Stephen King (born 1947)

Nationality USA

Why It's Key Though more people may know Carrie from Brian De Palma's 1976 film, the novel launched a mainstream literary career for King who went on to write over 60 enormously popular novels. He was honored with the Lifetime Achievement Award by America's National Book Awards in 2003.

Opposite Scene from the 1976 film adaptation of *Carrie*

Key Event **Bruce Chatwin's telegram to employers at *Sunday Times Magazine***

In late 1974, Bruce Chatwin (1940–1989) threw up his job as a feature writer on *The Sunday Times Magazine* and headed for the far south of Argentina – an event marked by the legend of the telegram he sent to his editor: "Have gone to Patagonia." The legend is typical of Chatwin's storytelling: an elegant and concise formulation that contains a poetic truth. What is incontestable is that this break – his third, after quitting his job as a Sotheby's art expert and then dropping out of an archaeology degree at Edinburgh University – heralded a dazzling literary career cut short by his death from AIDS in 1989.

In Patagonia was published in 1977, bringing Chatwin immediate fame and transforming travel writing into one of the most fashionable literary genres. Comprising 97 short, sometimes loosely connected chapters, the book opens as a quest for the origin of a piece of brontosaurus skin from Patagonia displayed in Chatwin's grandmother's glass cabinet.

The theme of wandering and exile runs through *In Patagonia*, as it does through Chatwin's own life. It reached its apogee 10 years later in *The Songlines*, his account of traveling with Aborigines in the central Australian desert, in which Chatwin explores a theory that had haunted him since his twenties – that man is by nature nomadic, and settled civilization a mistake. Although he is known as a travel writer, the three other books Chatwin published in his lifetime were novels: *The Viceroy of Ouidah* (1980), *On the Black Hill* (1983) and *Utz* (1988).
Bruce Millar

Date 1974

Place UK

Author Bruce Chatwin (1940–1989)

Why It's Key Bruce Chatwin may have breathed new life into travel writing, but he was also a throwback to an earlier model of literary adventurer stretching back to Lord Byron. An impeccable prose stylist, he had an art expert's eye for description and breathtaking powers of concision.

Key Passage *Zen and the Art of Motorcycle Maintenance*

"What is in mind is a sort of Chautauqua… like the traveling tent-show Chautauquas that used to move across America… intended to edify and entertain… "

Early in his novel, Robert Pirsig sets out his stall in terms of what he wants to communicate and of where he wants the reader to follow him. In the 1970s many Americans were looking backwards rather than forwards in their quest for purpose. Contemporary society seemed to be on the verge of breakdown, with the "generation gap" at its widest yet, student-led protest against the war in Vietnam, rioting in the city ghettos, and racial tension at its height. Pirsig reaches back into the collective memory to identify with the nineteenth-century *Chautauqua*, the show combining entertainment and education named after Lake Chautauqua in New York State. He wants to talk about the idea of quality in everything, not "What's new?" but "What is best?" However, he is not content to sit and philosophize; rather, like the restless Kerouac and the Beat Generation, he would prefer to be "on the road." By couching his meditations as stops along the way in a travelogue, a journal of a trip through modern America observing and commenting on what he sees, Pirsig carries the reader with him on both his actual and philosophical journeys.

Although comparatively little-read in the twenty-first century, when it was published the book was considered to be "life-changing" in its insights and had great influence on the thinking of the later 1970s, with its search for meaning and insight into what had gone wrong with contemporary society.

Michael Munro

Date 1974

Author Robert Maynard Pirsig (born 1928)

Nationality USA

Why It's Key A highly unusual bestseller: a philosophical discussion on quality and value, using the vehicle of a fictionalized motorcycle journey across the United States carried out by the author and his young son. It captured the mood of the 1970s, that slightly more cynical decade that followed the expansive and idealistic 1960s.

Key Book *A Dance to the Music of Time*

"A hundred per cent bastard" is how one victim describes him. Of *Dance*'s vast crowd of close to 500 characters – good, bad, dim, brilliant – Widmerpool is the worst. He begins as a gauche, unpopular schoolboy in *A Question of Upbringing* but in later books soon makes his mark as a crafty, totally unscrupulous operator. With his view of our existence as an elaborate dance, where people enter each other's lives, slip out, reappear, and keep reappearing, Powell created a fascinating narrative that moves and surprises continually through its near-3,000 pages.

Each of the 12 books may be read separately, but for the long-distance reader Powell's alter ego, Nicholas Jenkins the narrator, holds the multiple threads together through the decades and the worlds of Eton, Oxford, big business, the wartime Army, the London Blitz, post-war politics, and the arts, particularly literature, painting, and music. Powell's writing is moving, exact, and witty: promiscuous Pamela Flitton is a monster but still amuses, Jenkins' discovery that his first love, Jean Templer, was not as sweet as she seemed is both sad and funny. Powell's achievement is to have blended black themes – duplicity, betrayal, ruthless egotism, death – with much laughter. Was Powell a snob? He writes about the upper classes but not always – the naked maid Bilson, soldiers from the Valleys, salesman Odo Stevens, angry proletarian intellectual J.P. Quiggin, even ogre Kenneth Widmerpool's genteel mother – all argue *Dance* is a true wide-ranging comédie humaine of the twentieth century.

Robert Rollason

Date 1975 (A sequence of 12 novels beginning with *A Question of Upbringing* [1951] and ending with *Hearing Secret Harmonies* [1975])

Author Anthony Powell (1905–2000)

Nationality UK

Why It's Key Readers and critics alike have an intense appreciation of Powell's great work. "A complete civilisation… here in the midst of London… it altered my perception of the world." (Michael Frayn)

Opposite Anthony Powell

Key Book *Ecotopia: The Notebooks and Reports of William Weston*

1970–1979

Ernest Callenbach's utopian novel details the journey of the American journalist William Weston to the republic of Ecotopia – formed through the secession of three U.S. states. Weston's mission is to report back to the U.S. public in regular newspaper columns. The Ecotopian state has strong green credentials, combining these with cooperative structures in industry, new models of education and health care, and alternative human relationships, emphasizing radical democracy on all levels. Initially sceptical, New Yorker Weston is gradually drawn into Ecotopian concepts of living. The sexual assertiveness of Ecotopia's women particularly puzzles macho Weston, but he soon discovers the delights of egalitarian relationships.

Ecotopia is built on feminist principles, yet the book simultaneously perpetuates essentialist ideas about gender: the country's Ritual War Games are presented as a necessary valve for man's supposedly inherent physical competitiveness. What is similarly controversial is *Ecotopia*'s outlook on race relations. Rather than imagining racial egalitarianism, Callenbach portrays a divided country, with segregation enforced by its black minority. This could be read as a concession to the radical, separatist wing of the 1970s U.S. black power movement, or as a self-critical comment implying that even progressives fail to realize harmonious race relations.

Ecotopia is not one of the static societies and distant lands that can be found in other utopian texts; it is dynamic ("full of contradictions") and close to home, located in former U.S. territory. As Callenbach's website suggests, this makes the book "politics fiction," rather than "science fiction," resisting "far-out assumptions about either technology or human nature," but challenging its readers to think about implementing Ecotopian ways of living in their here and now.

Anne Schwan

Date 1975

Author Ernest Callenbach (born 1929)

Nationality USA

Why It's Key Published within the socially revolutionary context of the 1970s, *Ecotopia* drew on extant experimental living practices. Together with its "prequel" *Ecotopia Emerging* (1981) it inspired ensuing models of alternative social organization across the world.

560

Key Book
Heat and Dust

SPOILER

Heat and Dust vastly differs from other Indian novels, especially those in the national languages, which often demonize the British characters, and Anglo-Indian novels which invariably treat Indian characters with condescension or contempt. It presents an objective fictional appraisal of the influence of India on the European consciousness. Its author has the ideal credentials for the purpose – Polish-German parentage, British education, and a 24-year sojourn in India.

Heat and Dust, which won the Booker Prize in 1975, tells the story of the sensitive, passionate Olivia, who comes to live in India as the wife of a British colonial officer in the early 1920s. Having been thoroughly bored and disillusioned with the secluded life of the small British community in a town called Satipur, and yielding to the attraction held out by the East, she begins a romantic relationship with the charismatic, young Nawab of Khatm. The resulting pregnancy causes a scandal. She terminates the pregnancy and goes to live, alone and for the rest of her life, in a village at the foothills of the Himalayas. Olivia has been soft and vulnerable and allowed India to inexorably change her.

Paralleling Olivia's story is the story of her step-granddaughter. This unnamed young narrator of the novel comes to India, 50 years later, tracing Olivia's life but ironically goes through the same experience as the older woman. She gets pregnant by her landlord Inder Lal, but decides against abortion. India changes her too, as it has done everybody who ever came in intimate contact with it.

Rajeshwar Mittapalli

Date 1975

Author Ruth Prawer Jhabvala (born 1927)

Nationality USA

Why It's Key Major Minnies concludes : "It is all very well to love and admire India – intellectually, aesthetically… but always with a virile, measured European feeling. One should never allow oneself to become softened by an excess of feeling; because the moment that happens, one is in danger of being dragged over to the other side."

Key Book
The Great Railway Bazaar

This is the book that instigated a rediscovery of travel writing in the mid-1970s. Paul Theroux was a successful novelist when he embarked on his four-month journey across Asia. He was also a train enthusiast, and convinced that "if a train is large and comfortable you don't even need a destination" he determined to take every eastbound train from Victoria Station in London, as far as Tokyo. The book reinstated the romance of travel in the modern world: "railways are irresistible bazaars." He rode the "trains with bewitching names" through Turkey, Iran, and Afghanistan to India, Burma, Thailand, and Japan, and headed back on the Trans-Siberian Express.

Every landscape is filtered through the lens of chance acquaintance, droll vignettes of traveling companions – from junkies, hippies, scholars, and "an unlikely tycoon," to the unnerving Mr. Pensacola who recounts tales of opium smuggling, and Duffill, left stranded on a platform, whose name consequently becomes a verb. He avoids tourist sites, visits insalubrious quarters (particularly drawn to brothels), and finally is himself "duffilled" in Moscow. Theroux's routes have since been taken by legions of backpackers, though some are no longer possible, such as those in Vietnam, where he arrived at the tail end of the war.

The image of himself he conjures at the end, scribbling the book's last paragraphs on the final leg back to London, as if all this were just an impromptu sketch that he has barely troubled to extricate from his stained and weather-beaten notebooks, was an evocative example to thousands of would-be travel writers. It is somewhat disingenuous; he shapes, characterizes with novelistic flair, consciously fashions the book's feeling of serendipity. He awakened readerly longings which were fulfilled and perpetuated by other Titans of modern travel writing such as Bruce Chatwin, William Dalrymple, and photojournalist Nick Danziger.

Lucy Daniel

Date 1975

Title *The Great Railway Bazaar: by train through Asia*

Author Paul Theroux (born 1941)

Nationality USA

Why It's Key This book helped inspire a contemporary rediscovery of travel writing. Theroux followed it up with books that detail his travels by tain to North and South America, Pakistan and Bangladesh, and China.

1970–1979

561

Key Character **Coalhouse Walker, Jr.**
Ragtime

This jazzy, playful novel includes historical characters such as Harry Houdini, Sigmund Freud, and Henry Ford. However, the hero is probably the fictional Coalhouse Walker, a pianist who plays Scott Joplin rags in early twentieth-century United States. He doesn't appear until just over halfway through the book, but he quickly engages the reader's sympathy when he is attacked and his Model T Ford vandalized by racists. Coalhouse is one of those flawed tragic heroes for whom disaster seems inescapable when chance places them at the wrong place at the wrong time. His insistence on his rights as a citizen, whatever his color, and his implacable demands for restitution, turn to violence when he is treated by the authorities with indifference.

Ragtime is considered to be an early example of the postmodern novel, but it is an easy joy to read. Doctorow describes a United States where industrialization coupled with mass immigration, especially from Europe, is changing the country rapidly into the modern multicultural nation which we now recognize.

Between the abolition of slavery and the start of the Civil Rights movement, African Americans often found themselves treated with suspicion, regarded by the white community as a'n inconvenient reminder of the past. Unbowed, Coalhouse holds out for an equal place in society under the law. After his fiancée is killed while trying to help him, Coalhouse becomes more and more intent on obtaining justice and revenge. Other young men gather round him, as the fight grows more bloody. When the gang take hostage the library belonging to the financier J.P. Morgan, which contains the artefacts collected on his worldwide travels, the outcome becomes inevitable.

Felicity Skelton

Date 1975

Author E. L. Doctorow (born 1931)

Nationality USA

Why It's Key The novel, set in the first 15 years of the twentieth century, includes a dazzling mix of historical and fictional figures; one of the latter is Coalhouse Walker, Jr., an African-American, who becomes both a hero and a terrorist.

Key Character **Howard Kirk**
The History Man

It is 1972, and Howard Kirk is a radical sociologist working at the University of Watermouth. With a Zapata moustache, and sweatshirts with "rousing symbols on the front, like clenched fists," he encapsulates the free-spirited mood of university life during the early 1970s, being essentially anti-everything. Manipulative, oversexed, and arrogant, Kirk considers all structure – political, social, sexual – abhorrent and consequently revels in his own amorality.

Kirk's preening pomposity was used by Malcolm Bradbury to attack the opaqueness of much contemporary academic life, both undermining the alleged political radicalism (Howard is really pretty conservative) and the theoretical developments being worked on in various fields of the humanities (Howard splices together Freud, Marx, Weber and all manner of other philosophers into an unholy mess). The key issue is personal; Howard presents himself as an open man but has no time for ideas or people that do not square with him. He ignores lonely colleagues, mocks talented students and sexually humiliates women who reject him. As such he reveals himself as a tin-pot petty fool with no empathy. He cannot seduce the lovely and pragmatic English lecturer Miss Callendar because she actually believes in people and beauty, things that have passed him by and therefore left him only half a man, no matter how "now" he is.

As a symbol for the introspective self-absorption of the radical intelligentsia Kirk suggests that the left has become so absorbed with rejection that it cannot ever foment revolution; that as a movement it is more interested in saying "no" and indulging in pleasure than actually changing anything or communicating to anyone outside a select clique.
Jerome de Groot

Date 1975

Author Malcolm Bradbury (1932–2000)

Nationality UK

Why It's Key Howard Kirk's appearance inaugurated the idea that the campus novel could be an aggressive satire and paved the way for subsequent fictional critiques of academic life during the 1980s and 1990s.

Opposite Malcolm Bradbury

Key Character **Reginald Perrin**
The Death of Reginald Perrin

SPOILER

Reginald Iolanthe Perrin is a classic British dour anti-hero in the vein of gloomy Tony Hancock or hopeless Billy Liar. Nobbs' dark examination of the horrors of suburbia, contemporary middle-class maleness, and middle age has Perrin becoming increasingly frustrated and unable to cope with his life. He lives in Climthorpe, on the outskirts of London, traveling every day to work at the ironically titled Sunshine Desserts. Perrin's fragile mental state is generally due to the day-to-day dullness of existence and the numbing regularity of his life. He begins to fantasize of escape and his dreams begin to crowd into his actual life, and send him slightly crackers.

Nobbs' subject is similar to much American fiction of the period – John Updike particularly was writing comic novels about suburban issues – but the misery and grinding grayness of the novel is peculiarly British, as is the gleeful pricking of pomposity. In order to escape Perrin fakes his own death by leaving his clothes at the side of the sea. Eerily John Stonehouse, Labour MP, enacted a similar pretence of suicide in Miami in 1975 although the two acts are not related (at that point the book was finished but not published). The book was turned into a hugely successful and significantly lighter television series in which Perrin was played to glum perfection by Leonard Rossiter.
Jerome de Groot

Date 1975

Also appears in *The Return of Reginald Perrin* (1977), *The Better World of Reginald Perrin* (1978), *The Legacy of Reginald Perrin* (1995)

Author David Nobbs (born 1935)

Nationality UK

Why It's Key Most well known for the subsequent tv series, Reggie is an icon of British comedy, and Jonathan Coe has called Nobbs "probably our finest post-war comic novelist."

Key Author **Ian McEwan**
First Love, Last Rites

Nineteen seventy-five saw the arrival of a startlingly new voice in British fiction. *First Love, Last Rites*, the first collection of stories by Ian McEwan (born 1948), revealed a young writer who spoke directly to readers in a country that was soon to witness the birth of punk.

The stories explore various forms of depravity and perversion, including castration, sadism, incest, paedophilia, rape, and murder, usually committed by outcasts from "normal" society, who inhabit the edges of an urban, post-industrial wasteland. Almost as shocking as the subject matter are the deadpan voices of the narrators, who are in most cases the perpetrators of the hideous acts described. This technique suggests an author withholding judgement, who instead portrays these events as extreme examples of "ordinary" human nature.

McEwan was the first graduate of the MA program run by Malcolm Bradbury at the University of East Anglia (later graduates include Rose Tremain, Kazuo Ishiguro, and Clive Sinclair), and, unusually for a British author, he established a literary reputation as a writer of short stories. His second collection, *In Between the Sheets* (1978), still shocks in its focus on abnormal and delusional behavior. He continued to explore similar themes in his first novel, *The Cement Garden* (1978), a tale of incest among orphaned children.

Subsequent novels have moved him closer to the literary mainstream, although he has frequently returned to subjects of violence and madness. He remains an important and influential figure, not least because he encouraged other British authors to explore the darker aspects of life, and as an author who retains the ability to provoke and to disturb.
Neil Wallington

Date 1975 (publication)

Nationality UK

Other Key Works *The Child In Time* (1985), *Enduring Love* (1997), *Atonement* (2001), *Saturday* (2005)

Why It's Key A debut collection of short stories that broke new ground in its willingness to explore the more macabre aspects of existence and launched the career of one of the most important novelists in the UK.

Key Event **Romain Gary becomes the only person to win the Prix Goncourt twice**

The Prix Goncourt is the most prestigious French literary prize. Its small monetary value belies the life-changing effect it can have. Romain Gary first won it in 1958, for *Racines du Ciel*. The writer and war hero had already published several novels, but the Goncourt win catapulted him into the literary big time. Gary became a feted literary figure, although little was known about his background.

In fact, Gary was born Romain Kacew, in Vilnius, though some claim Moscow. He changed his name to Romain Gary on coming to France. After the win he continued to write but it seemed his star had faded (and his Gaullist political allegiances gone out of fashion). He began to write under a plethora of pseudonyms, publishing four novels as Emile Ajar, one as Fosco Sinibaldi and one as Shatan Bogat. None of this was known when in 1975 Ajar was awarded the Goncourt for his second novel, *The Life Before Us* (*La Vie Devant Soi*). However, a furore followed. Ajar refused to appear and sent his cousin Paul Pavlovitch to receive the prize, first posing as the writer himself, then instead of him. The book sold more than one million copies.

In 1979, Gary's wife committed suicide. Gary shot himself the following year, leaving a short testament for posthumous publication: *The Life and Death of Emile Ajar (Vie et Mort d'Emile Ajar)*. Here he revealed that he and Emile Ajar were one and the same, and explained his subterfuge: "as a writer, I was… pigeon-holed and categorized," a lesson in "how a writer may be imprisoned by the face we give him." However, his last, cheeky words were "Je me suis bien amusé" ("I have really enjoyed myself"), and it's true that his multiplication of writing identities has finally guaranteed his place in literature.
Sophie Lewis

Date 1975

Place France

Title *The Life Before Us*

Author Romain Gary (1914–1980)

Why It's Key Consternation that the author could be so reclusive he preferred not to receive his prize in public was followed by uproar after his death, when it was revealed that Gary's pseudonym had so hoodwinked the judges that they had not recognized the veteran author's work.

Key Event **The murder of Canadian poet Pat Lowther inspires Carol Shields' novel**

In late September of 1975, the Canadian poet Pat Lowther disappeared; her body was discovered three weeks later. Her second husband Roy Lowther was later convicted of the murder.

Lowther's collection *A Stone Diary*, which the poet had submitted for publication before her death, was published in 1977, and three years later a collection of her early and unpublished poems, *Final Instructions*, appeared. In 1980, the League of Canadian Poets established the Pat Lowther Award, a prize awarded annually to a book of poetry by a Canadian woman.

Lowther's life and death have inspired a number of literary works, including her daughter Christine Lowther's first poetry collection, *New Power* (1999), and the novel *Mary Swann* by Carol Shields. Shields' novel describes the impact of an obscure poet, Mary Swann, upon four characters: a feminist literary critic, the poet's biographer, a small-town librarian, and a newspaper editor. The book is divided into five sections, the first four each focussing on one of the characters, and the last detailing what happens when all meet at a conference on Swann.

The novel is a witty examination of the production and reception of texts, of gender, and of knowledge. It is a self-aware work that is also moving and gripping. While offering no clear "solution" to any of the mysteries it probes – not least that of Swann's violent death – it nonetheless satisfies and inspires. A later novel by Shields, *The Stone Diaries*, evokes Lowther's work through its title, confirming the poet's impact on Canadian literature.

Emily Jeremiah

Date 1975

Place Canada

Author Carol Shields (1935–2003)

Why It's Key *Mary Swann* (1987) established Carol Shields as a significant voice in Canadian fiction. The novel was inspired by the life and death of the poet Patricia Louise Lowther (née Tinmuth), who was born in 1935 and murdered in 1975. Lowther is the author of *This Difficult Flowring* (1968), *Milk Stone* (1974), and *A Stone Diary* (1977).

1970–1979

565

Key Passage **"Nicholas Hawksmoor, His Churches"** *Lud Heat*

SPOILER

"I spoke of the unacknowledged magnetism and control-power, built-in code force, of these places; I would now specify… the ritual slaying of Marie Jeanette Kelly in the ground floor room of Miller's Court, Dorset Street, directly opposite Christ Church… the Ratcliffe Highway slaughter of 1811, with the supposed-murderer, stake through heart, trampled into the pit where four roads cross to the north of St George's-in-the-East… the battering to death of Mr Abraham Cohen, summer 1974, on Cannon Street Road, one spoke of the quadrivium: £110,000 in old bank-notes in the kiosk behind him, stuffed in cocoa-tins & cigarette packets; three ritualistic coins laid at his feet, as they were in 1888 at the feet of Mary Ann Nicholls, the first Ripper victim."

Lud Heat's opening section, "Nicholas Hawksmoor, His Churches," opened up an obscure 1711 Act of Parliament (to designate 50 churches for the burgeoning metropolis) to literary scrutiny, examining the lines which manifest themselves when marking the alignment of Hawksmoor church locations in East London. *Lud Heat* begins the examination of the government architect's motives for aligning the six churches into what Sinclair considers to be a pentagram, an allusion to Satanism.

These ideas subsequently found their way into *Hawksmoor* (1985) by Peter Ackroyd. The novel ran with the Satanic motif transposed onto modern London through a series of murders occurring within the pentagram's reach. Unsurprisingly, Alan Moore, a writer closer to Sinclair's milieu but distinctly non-London in outlook, also found inspiration in the Hawksmoor alignment and used it to elucidate upon the possible motives of another Whitechapel villain, Jack the Ripper in the graphic novel *From Hell*.

Andrew Stevens

Date 1975

Author Iain Sinclair (born 1943)

Nationality UK

Why It's Key Iain Sinclair's section on architect Nicholas Hawksmoor's churches inspired Peter Ackroyd's *Hawksmoor*, which appeared 10 years later. Sinclair's book is a blend of factual information and imaginative material.

Key Event **Ashbery wins multiple prizes for** *Self-Portrait in a Convex Mirror*

In 1976, John Ashbery's sixth book of poetry *Self-Portrait in a Convex Mirror* won three major literary prizes: the National Book Award, the National Book Critics Circle Award, and the Pulitzer Prize. This hat trick ushered in official recognition of an avant-garde tendency in post-war American poetry that had largely been ignored by the literary establishment. Ashbery's poetry became the most prominent example of an experimental, counter-cultural poetics (first anthologized in Donald Allen's *The New American Poetry* in 1960) that combines modernist disjunctiveness with the casual rhythms of the American vernacular. The book's title poem, a meditation on the painting of the same name by Renaissance Mannerist Parmigianino, is on the surface atypical of Ashbery's writing: addressed to a singular specified object, discursively continuous, sober in tone. Yet the poem, along with others in the collection, shares with earlier work a playful scrambling of poetic registers, a combination of mock bathos and charged emotion, and a searching, quasi-Romantic interplay between interior and exterior states. The experience that the poet recounts of meeting Parmigianino's enigmatic gaze in his self-portrait might well serve as a description of the poem's address to its readers: "there is in that gaze a combination / Of tenderness, amusement and regret, so powerful / In its restraint that one cannot look too long. / The secret is too plain. The pity of it smarts, / Makes hot tears spurt: that the soul is not a soul, / Has no secret, is small, and it fits / Its hollow perfectly: its room, our moment of attention."

Nicholas Lawrence

Date 1976

Title *Self-Portrait in a Convex Mirror* (1975)

Author John Ashbery (born 1927)

Nationality USA

Why It's Key Ashbery's hat trick of awards was an unprecedented achievement, and marked the official recognition of U.S. avant-garde poetry.

566

Key Author
Saul Bellow

Saul Bellow (1915–2005) was born in the old Jewish part of Montreal to immigrant Russian parents. A precocious child, he was already fluent in English, French, Hebrew, and Yiddish at the age of nine, by which time Bellow and his family had relocated to Chicago. Many of his novels have Chicago as a backdrop and also echo Bellow's Jewish heritage as the main protagonists search for identity, while experiencing social isolation and spiritual dissatisfaction.

Bellow wrote his extraordinary first book, *Dangling Man* (1944) using his experience as a Merchant Marine during World War II. This is a philosophical journal of a frustrated young man living in Chicago who is waiting to be drafted and hoping that army life will ease his suffering. In Bellow's first full-length novel, *The Adventures of Augie March* (1953), the narrator is once again a young Jewish man growing up in Chicago during the Great Depression. The youth travels across the United States, losing his girlfriend along the way and experiencing random events in this picaresque novel. Although searching for his raison d'être, it always escapes him. The panic-stricken scholar in *Herzog* (1964) is trying to find his sense of psychological identity by analyzing his past, thus treating the reader to an extravagant travelogue through Chicago. The isolation of an elderly survivor of the Holocaust dominates *Mr. Sammler's Planet* (1970), as this poor man cannot understand the American society he now reluctantly inhabits. The masterly comic novel, *Humboldt's Gift* (1975), has the street-wise, self-mocking but failed writer, Charlie Citrine as its hero.

Bellow's rich, imaginative prose always has leading characters who feel alienated from the world, the outsiders of society. Bellow was one of the fundamental influences on American literature after World War II.

Alice Goldie

Date 1976 (Nobel Prize in Literature awarded)

Nationality Canada/USA (born Canada)

Other Key Works *Seize the Day* (1956), *Henderson the Rain King* (1959)

Why It's Key Bellow won the Nobel Prize for the "human understanding and subtle analysis of contemporary culture" present in his work. He was awarded the Pulitzer Prize for *Humboldt's Gift*.

Opposite Saul Bellow

Anne Rice's 1976 *Interview with the Vampire* started out as a cult favorite and eventually became a cultural phenomenon without which the morose, self-aware vampires of *Buffy the Vampire Slayer*, *Blade*, and numerous other contemporary vampire-centered novels and films would not exist. Written in part as a way to cope with her own child's death – the child vampire Claudia is partially based on her – Rice's novel is a meditation on immortality, Catholic morality, and sexuality.

Interview with the Vampire's protagonist is Louis, a 300-year-old vampire who began life as a southern plantation owner and is, when we meet him, an immortal who is highly conflicted about his need to take human life. Indeed, Louis is highly conflicted about almost everything, including his maker, the charismatic Lestat, star of many of the other novels in Rice's *Vampire Chronicles*, with whom he has co-habited, hunted, and mulled over immortal existence for centuries. Framed by the story of an eager boy interviewing him, *Interview* allowed a vampire to speak in his own voice for the first time – a voice uninflected by Transylvania and the literary precursor of *Dracula*. Accused by Lestat of thinking too much instead of enjoying his predatory nature, Louis is a vampiric philosopher, an immortal observer and narrator who is simultaneously both inside and outside the human race, and whose metaphysical ruminations reveal a profound, sometimes existential despair about human transience and foibles.

Equally notable for the way it sexualized vampires, *Interview* differs from Bram Stoker's *Dracula* in the way its sexual currents are as homoerotic as hetero-erotic. The novel began a trend which continues today of taking the lowbrow subject matter of supernatural creatures and using them to address topics which have typically been in the purview of highbrow texts.

Elizabeth Rosen

Date 1976

Author Anne Rice (born 1941)

Nationality USA

Why It's Key Told from the perspective of the vampire, rather than his victims, *Interview with the Vampire* allowed readers to consider the immortals and their predicament for the first time, and subsequently began a trend to treat "trash" subjects such as vampires as serious literary vehicles.

Opposite Brad Pitt in the film adaptation of *Interview*

1970–1979

569

Key Book *The Woman Warrior: Memoirs of a Girlhood Among Ghosts*

Subtitled a *Memoir*, *The Woman Warrior* rejects the linear plot of the conventional Bildungsroman, preferring to tell its story more indirectly, in a mode that seamlessly blends realism and fantasy. Kingston divides *The Woman Warrior* into five sections, each of which is organized around stories about mothers and daughters.

The first story, "No Name Woman," which her mother tells Maxine when she begins menstruating as a cautionary tale, concerns her father's aunt who gave birth to an illegitimate child and then drowned herself and the baby in the family well; because of the shame she brought to the family, they condemn her to oblivion and refuse to talk of her or even to say her name. In "White Tigers," Maxine imagines her childhood as if she were the mythical Chinese warrior woman, Fa Mu Lan. "Shaman" tells the story of Maxine's mother's struggles to become a doctor in China, battles that are symbolically rendered as fights with ghosts and spirits.

"At the Western Palace" concerns Maxine's aunt, who has a mental breakdown after emigrating from China to the United States.

The final chapter, "A Song for a Barbarian Reed Pipe," begins with Maxine's struggles learning English, and her determination never to be a slave or a wife, the two roles she associates with her mother's stories, before returning to a famous Chinese legend, of Ts'ai Yen, a renowned artist captured by barbarians. She introduces the story of Ts'ai Yen by saying, "Here is a story my mother told me… The beginning is hers, the ending mine." The book thus ends on an image of reconciliation and a shared heritage, of translation and reinvention in new forms. According to the Modern Language Association, it is the most frequently taught text in U.S. universities, appearing on American literature syllabi, but also in anthropology, Asian studies, education, psychology, and sociology.

Sarah Churchwell

Date 1976

Author Maxine Hong Kingston (born 1940)

Nationality China/USA

Why It's Key A semi-autobiographical account of growing up a Chinese-American girl in San Francisco's Chinatown, refracting problems of gender and ethnic identity through the prism of fantasy, memory, and family stories. It won the National Book Critics Award for Non-fiction in 1976.

Key Book
The Selfish Gene

When *The Selfish Gene* turned 30 in 2006, it required a wide variety of parties to celebrate the full range of its impact. An essay collection, *Richard Dawkins: How a Scientist Changed the Way We Think*, brought together intellectuals as varied as John Krebs, Steven Pinker, A.C. Grayling, Matt Ridley, and Philip Pullman. A special event held at the London School of Economics ("The Selfish Gene: Thirty Years On") added contributions from Daniel Dennett, Melvyn Bragg, and Ian McEwan.

In other words, since its publication in 1976, *The Selfish Gene* has touched the worlds of evolutionary biology, philosophy, broadcasting, psychology, literature, science, logic, politics, and religion, to name but nine. Terms coined in the book, such as "meme," have entered the language: Malcolm Gladwell used it in *The Tipping Point*, so it must be cool if nothing else.

In the beginning, however, *The Selfish Gene* simply investigated "The gene's eye view of Darwinism" (as Dawkins writes in 1989) and did so for as broad an audience as possible. Written like "science fiction," it was published to universal acclaim. It took time and popularity for Richard Dakwins' ideas and metaphors to attract controversy and misinterpretation: later editions clarified Dawkins' figurative use of "selfish" (not a moral statement), analogies to Chicago gangsters and the mating habits of the caddis fly among other misconceptions.

One final side-effect of the book's success was to thrust Dawkins himself into the public spotlight, a role he has embraced *con* impressive *brio*, never more so than as "Darwin's Rottweiler" exposing the evils and illogic of Creationism.
James Kidd

Date 1976

Author Richard Dawkins (born 1941)

Nationality UK

Why It's Key A seminal work of popular science to rival Stephen Hawking's *A Brief History of Time*, *The Selfish Gene* manages to explore complex ideas without confusing the layman or boring the expert. The book's merits as "serious" science and its place in the debate between evolution and religion have come into question.

570

Key Book
Roots: The Saga of an American Family

What gripped the world's imagination was that Alex Haley was purportedly the first African-American who managed to trace his genealogy to a specific named African ancestor from an exact location, impressively chronicling his ten-year search in *Roots*. Beginning with memories of his grandmother's stories about an African ancestor, Haley relentlessly scoured international archives, talked to scholars, and ultimately traveled to the Gambia, where in a dramatic revelation he learned from a *griot* (a traditional oral historian) the narrative of the Kinte family, including the disappearance in the late eighteenth century of one Kunta Kinte.

Haley termed his book "faction," a fictionalized version of the true story, spanning the journey from his ancestral homeland to the United States. Captured in 1767 in the Gambian village of Juffure, Kunta Kinte survives the "Middle Passage" to the United States and is taken to Virginia, enslaved and renamed Toby. To deter him from persistent escape attempts, his foot is amputated; but eventually he settles down with Bell and they have a daughter, Kizzy. When Kizzy is sold to North Carolina, she carries with her the stories her father told of his origins, which she eventually passes on to her son, Chicken George (a gamecock trainer), who in his turn tells his children, so that generations later they reach Alex Haley himself.

Despite accusations of historical inaccuracy and of plagiarism, *Roots* was a critical success, won the Pulitzer Prize and the National Book Award, and has had a lasting effect on the teaching of African-American history.
Margaret Busby

Date 1976

Author Alex Haley (1921–1992)

Nationality USA

Why It's Key *Roots* had enormous international success and the television mini-series based on it was a phenomenal hit (shops and restaurants reported drops in takings whenever it was on air). *Roots* instilled new pride in black Americans about their African ancestry.

Opposite Alex Haley

Key Book *Kiss of the Spider Woman* (*El Beso de la Mujer Araña*)

Kiss of the Spider Woman, an Argentinian novel charting the growing affection between cellmates, marks a radical departure from the adventure stories of conventional prison fiction like *The Great Escape* (1950) or *Papillon* (1970). Written in the mode of Jean Genet's *The Miracle of the Rose* (1946) and Oscar Wilde's *De Profundis* (1962), Manuel Puig's novel is more interested in effecting an escape through imagination rather than over prison walls. Its two main characters, Valentin and Molina, learn to free their minds through storytelling, conversation, and human connection.

On the surface the men have little in common; Valentin is a political prisoner while Molina is a gay window dresser arrested for "corruption of minors." But confinement forces each man to explore a world outside the limits of his own experience. A modern-day Scheherazade, Molina charms Valentin with his detailed retellings of the storylines from movie melodramas. That these entertaining movies are also Nazi propaganda films highlights the potential dangers of the unfettered imagination.

This novel pushed social and formal boundaries, not only exploring taboo subjects like homosexual love and revolutionary politics, but also testing the conventions of storytelling. Written mostly in dialogue, the novel draws us into the characters' conversation in a manner more familiar to cinema-goers than readers. Puig assures us that this strategy is deliberate: "I write for somebody who has my own limitations. My reader has a certain difficulty with concentrating, which in my case comes from being a film viewer. That's why I don't request any special efforts in the act of reading."

Dinah Roe

Date 1976

Author Manuel Puig (1932–1990)

Nationality Argentina

Why It's Key This formally experimental novel broke free from the conventions of traditional prison fiction. Puig's celebration of homosexuality and political freedom was radical for its time, while the novel's use of dialogue, montage, and footnotes distinguished his storytelling technique.

1970–1979

Key Event **Songwriter and poet Wolf Biermann stripped of his GDR citizenship**

By the end of 1976, the East German songwriter and poet Wolf Biermann had been banned from public performance and publication of his work for over 11 years. Biermann was a convinced socialist, and had moved to the Communist East out of conviction in 1953, where he emerged as a talented writer, composer, and performer of poems and songs in the direct, simple style of Brecht and Hanns Eisler. With time, however, his work had become increasingly critical of the gulf between the theoretical "workers' and farmers' state" and the reality of totalitarianism.

The regime saw him as a threat and had repeatedly offered him what most GDR citizens were denied: the opportunity to leave the country. Biermann refused these offers, and when he accepted the invitation to perform at a series of concerts in the Federal Republic, he did so only on the express understanding that he would be allowed to return to the East. However, just three days after his first concert in Cologne, on November 16, 1976, it was announced that Biermann was to be stripped of his GDR citizenship and refused re-entry.

This proved a highly counterproductive step, for the Politbureau had not reckoned with the wave of protest that followed, which raised Biermann's profile in both East and West Germany. Numerous prominent cultural figures in the GDR signed a protest petition, though without effect; the consequent tightening of censorship and state control certainly diminished levels of trust in the regime, which was never fully to recover from this crisis.

Jon Hughes

Date 1976

Place German Democratic Republic

Author Wolf Biermann (born 1934)

Why It's Key The resulting widespread protest boosted Biermann's profile and led to a crisis of confidence in the GDR's leadership; further cultural figures and intellectuals left the GDR as a consequence.

Key Book
My Story

Controversy may be said to have been the key accompanying feature of author Kamala Das' unconventional lifestyle and writing. A very public figure within Indian literary academia, a syndicated columnist, and an activist concentrating on humanitarian work, Das' reputation has at times suffered from too much publicity. Her autobiography – *My Story* – narrates her life as an Indian woman as it had never before been exposed by any other woman writer from India. The reader is presented with an unabashed, ultra-detailed account of her social and sexual life as an ordinary woman "ready for love, ripe for a sexual banquet." As she explains in an interview though, the book is more about love than it is about lust: "I may have written about love affairs, but I have not glorified lust. There was nothing obscene about love."

Apart from poetry, for which she has been awarded several prestigious literary prizes (such as the Kent Award for English Writing from Asian Countries and the Sahitya Academi Award) her artistic range of works also includes nude painting and the writing of short stories, mainly in Malayalam. Indeed, she is known as Madhavikutti to Malayali readers and Kamala Das to her English public. Short-listed for the Nobel Prize in Literature in 1984 along with Doris Lessing and Nadine Gordimer, she shocked the world – particularly her Hindu fans – with her conversion to Islam in 1999 (which she considers as the only religion loving and protecting women), changing her name from Kamala Das to Kamala Suraiya.

Letizia Alterno

Date 1976 (publication)

Author Kamala Das (born 1934)

Nationality Indian

Why It's Key Outstanding poetess from India who challenges those "not willing to accept the fact that a Hindu woman could be unconventional and not-so-traditional." Das is outspoken and straightforward about all aspects of life, particularly those silencing women into shamefulness and discomfiture.

1970-1979

573

Key Author
Ann Beattie

Nineteen seventy-six was a red-letter year for Ann Beattie: she published both her first collection of short stories (*Distortions*) and her first novel (*Chilly Scenes of Winter*). These debuts showcased the spare prose, dry sense of humor, and way with uncovering the inherent in everyday life that has characterized much of Beattie's body of work.

Often described as a spokesperson for the post-hippie generation (rather too often for her own liking), Beattie injects a certain narrative chaos into the realism of writers such as Updike and Cheever: like Richard Ford, she has been mentioned in the same (bad) breath as the "Dirty Realist" movement.

Set largely on the East Coast of the United States, her world is populated by the disaffected, the dissatisfied, and (increasingly) the disconnected, drifters who seem singularly unable to do anything about their drift. Charles in *Chilly Scenes of Winter* (1976) may be in pursuit of happiness (a married woman named Laura), but he never seems likely to catch up with it.

As the hippies have turned into yuppies, Beattie has kept watch, dissecting their failing relationships, their failing jobs, their failing children. For some, this intense focus has limited the emotional scope and depth of her work, criticism that rather misses the playful wit of her writing: for example, the satire on Hollywood soap operas in *Love Always* (1986). It also downgrades the integrity of her humane, if melancholy writing. As Margaret Atwood writes: "A new Beattie is almost like a fresh bulletin from the front: We snatch it up, eager to know what's happening out there on the edge of that shifting and dubious no man's land known as interpersonal relations."

James Kidd

Date 1976 (publications)

Author Ann Beattie (born 1947)

Nationality USA

Other Key Works Short Stories *The Burning House* (1982), *What Was Mine* (1991), *Park City* (1998), *Perfect Recall* (2000), *Follies* (2005)

Why It's Key One of America's finest writers of the second half of the twentieth century, Beattie's speciality is the short story, but she has also written many acclaimed novels.

Key Event **Gary Gilmore's execution prompts an explosive account by Mailer**

Based on exhaustive interviews with Gary Gilmore, his friends, and his victims, *The Executioner's Song* (1979) was a fascinating departure for a writer caricatured as a self-promoting "bad boy" and pilloried for the florid excesses of his prose, misogyny, and romanticizing of violence. Although Gilmore's killing spree might seem obvious territory for a writer long obsessed with existential violence, the book is remarkable for Norman Mailer's withdrawal of his authorial presence. The book gives us the thoughts and feelings of the key characters in their own, unadorned language. The hauntingly spare prose, evocative of Hemingway, amplifies the bleakness and horror of the story it tells.

The Executioner's Song, however, is more than a mere documentary reconstruction. Divided into two parts, the book's first part chronicles Gilmore's early criminal career, focusing especially on the months before his serial murders. At all times, Mailer scrupulously avoids the temptations to explain, sentimentalize, or moralize Gilmore's horrific crimes. The book's second half explores the media circus surrounding Gilmore's trial and execution, and the consequent transformation of private tragedies into public property. It also details Gilmore's refusal to appeal his death sentence, a refusal that deepens the already very complex dilemmas the book opens up around the morality of capital punishment.

Published to both acclaim and controversy, *The Executioner's Song* proved a major contribution to the debate sparked by the revival of the death penalty in 1976. It was later adapted for television by Lawrence Schiller, whose attempts to secure exclusive rights to Gilmore's story are central to the last part of Mailer's book.
Josh Cohen

Date 1977

Place USA

Author Norman Mailer (born 1923)

Title *The Executioner's Song* (1979)

Why It's Key Based on exhaustive interviews and research, Norman Mailer's epic reconstruction of Gary Gilmore's serial killing spree, trial, and execution helped spark an impassioned debate about capital punishment in the United States.

Key Passage
The Women's Room

"Whatever they may be in public life, whatever their relations with men, in their relations with women, all men are rapists, and that's all they are. They rape us with their eyes, their laws and their codes."

The Women's Room follows the story of Mira, an obedient 1950s American housewife, who describes the harsh realities of living within a strictly patriarchal system through her experiences of marriage, childbirth, divorce, and as a Harvard graduate student. Though she surrounds herself with strong groups of women, their experiences are often more painful than her own, and despite the other characters' political awareness and feminist ideas there is a sense of inevitability to the pain and suffering which they eventually experience at the hands of men and which they cannot escape – something that has often been used to criticize the novel.

Though arguably now out of date on many counts and sometimes described as being cartoon-like in its interpretations, *The Women's Room* was hugely influential at the time of publication and still has resonance not just for the western world, where the feminism movement of the 1970s has been largely successful, but for many developing countries where the role of women has not been so radically altered. Though the book gained notoriety for the passage containing the oft-quoted "all men are rapists," this is often misquoted as French's own direct view, or more generally the view of all feminists. It was in fact spoken by a fictional character within the novel, after the brutal rape and trial of her daughter, and in one of the book's many monologues on the state of society; and it does not go unchallenged by the main character of the book.
Sophie Baker

Date 1977

Author Marilyn French (born 1929)

Nationality USA

Why It's Key As a bestseller of the feminist movement of the 1970s, *The Women's Room* addressed many key issues to arise out of the debate in a popular format that sent the critics into a frenzy and earned the book oft-quoted notoriety, with the infamous passage that claims "all men are rapists."

Opposite Marilyn French

Key Character **Milkman Dead**
Song of Solomon

Date 1977

Author Toni Morrison (born 1931)

Nationality USA

Why It's Key *Song of Solomon* won the National Book Critics Circle Award. It was the first novel by a black writer to be chosen as main selection for the Book-of-the-Month Club since Richard Wright's *Native Son* in 1940.

Toni Morrison's third novel, *Song of Solomon* traces the personal development of the young, urban, male protagonist, Milkman Dead from a self-preoccupied young man to an individual more aware of his roots and of the value of his community. Milkman grows up in Michigan, in the family of an upper-class northern black businessman who tries to forget about a past rooted in the shameful experiences of slavery and the Great Migration from the poor rural south to affluent northern cities. However, Milkman learns the hard way that he needs to understand his family's history in order to achieve a responsible and compassionate adulthood. He journeys back down south, thinking he is on the track of hidden gold, only to discover that his quest is not for gold but for self-knowledge. He is re-immersed in his family's past and only then does he understand and properly value the remnants of black culture – the blues, riddles, and folktales, which have surrounded his childhood.

Milkman's series of discoveries about the hidden layers of his and his ancestors' past changes his outlook by the end of the novel. However the ending – and whether there is a future for Milkman – remains ambiguous, as along the way he has destroyed the life of his cousin and one-time lover, Hagar. The novel was innovative in its focus on the importance of African-American history, and represented a new approach in Morrison's work in its attention to a central male character.

Helen May Dennis

Key Book
Elbow Room

Date 1977

Author James Alan McPherson (born 1943)

Nationality USA

Why It's Key When McPherson won the Pulitzer Prize for fiction for *Elbow Room* he was the first black writer to do so, and only the second black recipient in any category. Although he continued to write stories and essays it was 20 years until he published another book, the memoir *Crabcakes* (1998).

In his autobiographical essay "On Becoming an American Writer" James Alan McPherson recalls a youthful visit to the World's Fair in Seattle, where the theme of the U.S. exhibit was taken from Walt Whitman's *Leaves of Grass*: "Conquering, holding, daring, venturing as we go the unknown ways." The idea of becoming a "representative American" by encompassing diversities and contradictions became central to McPherson's work.

McPherson writes about ordinary people and relationships with a deceptively easy conversational touch, and an impeccable ear for dialogue. Race is one of this funny, thoughtful, painful, and touching collection's important themes, particularly in the title story, a complex meditation on a mixed-race marriage, where McPherson described his own frustration at being expected to write from a racially motivated perspective. It expressed his view of the deep subtleties of the race question in the United States, and how this was fundamentally tied in with the country's forms of narrative expression. The United States would have no true, honest literature without its people becoming free – and both black and white still were not, despite the hard-won victories of the Civil Rights Movement.

"Elbow room" is what the black woman at the story's center tries to find, in her globe-trotting and international raconteurism – the mental "elbow room" not to look at the world from a white or a black perspective, but to "relate to white and black and everything else in the world from a self as big as the world is." Without offering an easy fix, this is McPherson's moral vision of the U.S. writer, indeed traceable to Whitman (as well as Ralph Ellison, a more direct mentor), and a U.S. literature defined in terms of integration of extremes and diversities.

Lucy Daniel

Key Author **Mario Vargas Llosa**
Aunt Julia and the Scriptwriter

Mario Vargas Llosa's (born 1936) life-long vocation as a writer arose, as he reveals in his 1993 memoirs, *A Fish in the Water*, almost as an act of rebellion against his father's authority. Now one of Latin America's greatest novelists, Vargas Llosa was born in the Peruvian city of Arequipa on March 28, 1936. In 1959, he moved to Paris and then to Madrid, where that same year he published *The Cubs and Other Stories*. His first novel, *The Time of the Hero* (1963), brought him instant fame. It is a tense and sometimes extremely violent retelling of his own experiences at the Leoncio Prado military college in Lima.

His brilliant *The Green House* (1966), set in a brothel, shows the influence of William Faulkner's formally inventive tales of violence, greed, and unrestrained instincts. The equally accomplished *Conversation in the Cathedral* (1969), was Vargas Llosa's first attempt at what he calls a "total novel,"

portraying all levels of a society – in this case under the Peruvian dictatorship of Manuel Odría in the 1950s.

In 1977, Llosa published *Aunt Julia and the Scriptwriter* (*La tia Julia y el escribidor*), based on his own relationship with his aunt, whom he married in 1955. *The Feast of the Goat* (2000) is a fictional account of the final days of the Dominican Republic's dictator, Leónidas Trujillo, who was assassinated in 1961. Vargas Llosa's most recent novel, *Mischiefs of the Bad Girl* (2006), impressively relates a Peruvian expatriate's passionate obsession with a woman he first met decades earlier as a teenager.

Adam Feinstein

Date 1977 (publication)

Nationality Peru

Other Key Works *Captain Pantoja and the Special Service* (1973), *The War of the End of the World* (1981)

Why It's Key After his failed campaign for the Presidency of Peru in 1990, Vargas Llosa has dedicated himself exclusively to writing fiction, literary criticism, and journalism. He writes a regular column for the influential Madrid daily, *El País*.

1970–1979

577

Key Book
Dispatches

While Michael Herr was sent to Vietnam as a war correspondent, he actually sent back relatively few reports to *Esquire* magazine and much of the material that he eventually used in *Dispatches* was previously unseen. The book is a product of the New Journalism movement of the late 1960s and 1970s, in which many of the techniques previously associated solely with fiction were used to create a more vivid and imaginative narrative.

The result is a picture of an experience that was at times nightmarish and hallucinatory, not least because of the roles played by drugs and rock music in the lives of the "grunts" in the field, but is always grounded in the immediate, brutal, day-to-day realities of contemporary warfare. The soldiers described are rarely professional military men but for the most part unwilling conscripts who often don't know why they are there. However, Herr is at pains to convey the sense of identity with their

comrades in arms that is often the only thing that makes sense to them.

In the United States, public opinion about Vietnam has gone through various phases, from the 1970s backlash of disillusion and contempt for veterans to a belated recognition of the courage and sacrifice of the soldiers on both sides. There can be no doubt that it is Herr's vision of an anarchic and deadly confusion that largely informs the enduring popular view of the Vietnam War, especially as portrayed in Coppola's *Apocalypse Now* and other films that his work inspired.

Michael Munro

Date 1977

Author Michael Herr (born 1940)

Nationality USA

Why It's Key One of the first books to give a graphic account of the experiences of ordinary American soldiers in the Vietnam War. John le Carré called it "The best book I have ever read on men and war in our time." Herr also drew on his first-hand knowledge in writing for the films *Apocalypse Now* (1979) and *Full Metal Jacket* (1987).

Key Author **Iris Murdoch**
The Sea, The Sea

Iris Murdoch (1919–1990) brilliantly caught a certain mood of middle-class England in the 1950s and 1960s, when it was chic to be neurotic. Many of her heroes and heroines, vaguely aspiring to be moral, suffer from religious hang-ups which affect their sex lives. She has been accused of descending to the level of women's magazines because of her preoccupation with "relationships," but she found a ready public in the secretly bewildering days of the new post-war permissiveness. Like the protagonist in *A Word Child* (1975), she spun words with facility and supplied a new vocabulary of faintly comic self-examination to the first British generation for 150 years to worry about being uptight.

Murdoch led a dual career as a novelist and a philosopher, and the quirkiness of the latter affected all she did. Her preoccupation with "metaphysics as a guide to morals," the title under which her deeply unfashionable philosophical essays later appeared, translated into a genuine seriousness in *The Bell* (1958). *The Flight from the Enchanter* (1956) wove a young woman's readiness to be sexually dominated into a rich evocation of the social possibilities of post-war London.

Murdoch, an unashamed intellectual, drew on worlds she knew – the universities, the Civil Service, and the arts – and the familiar foibles of snobbishness, whimsy, and passion. She failed to change with the changing times. Increasingly her fictional world was unrecognizable as contemporary UK. Meanwhile her mystical obsessions forced her stories into repetitive melodrama. Her husband's posthumous biography, and an ensuing feature film, have not helped her serious reputation.

Lesley Chamberlain

Date 1978 (publication)

Nationality UK

Other Key Work
Under the Net (1954)

Why It's Key Iris Murdoch's reputation as a highly enjoyable novelist, at once highbrow and grippingly readable, was already on the wane by the time *The Sea, The Sea* won the Booker Prize in 1978. Her earliest work is the best.

Opposite Iris Murdoch

Key Character **Anna Madrigal**
Tales of the City

Mrs. Madrigal is the landlady of 28 Barbary Lane, an old apartment building in which she houses at various stages of their fictional lives the central characters of Armistead Maupin's six *Tales of the City* novels – which, prefiguring Helen Fielding's *Bridget Jones's Diary*, first appeared as newspaper columns (in the *San Francisco Chronicle*). She greets each new arrival with a large spliff, taken from the home-grown marijuana plants which she tends and nurtures alongside her mainly deviant tenantry, and names honorifically after notables of queer or queer-friendly America (Tallulah, Lennon, Sigourney).

We first encounter her in a rustle of plum-colored silk, gracefully uttering transsexual-of-the-world wisdoms: "If you're going to be degenerate, you might as well be a lady about it, don't you think?" A young father and wartime GI before becoming something else, Mrs. Madrigal sweetly and urbanely embodies the possibility of remaking your own life and identity.

She is a kind of fairy godmother and ideal house-parent, giving her charges freedom to roam but watching out for them too. Her romance with the businessman Edgar Halcyon in the first book tentatively suggests a marriage of alternative and corporate America. The love between them is partly a sexual fulfilment – quite boldly given that neither is young and one is transsexual – but, with the emotional delicacy which accompanies Maupin's sometimes outrageous plotlines, it also expresses a deeper and more general human need for affinity.

The melodious name Anna Madrigal is an anagram. I won't spoil it here for you.

Peter Swaab

Date 1978

Author Armistead Maupin (born 1944)

Nationality USA

Why It's Key Anna Madrigal is the eccentric landlady in Maupin's comic stories of sexual liberation in San Francisco.

Key Character **Garp**
The World According to Garp

T. S. Garp, like his creator John Irving, is a novelist, wrestler, and father. His life and career are influenced by a string of strong, independent women: his mother, Jenny Fields, "lone wolf" (to use Garp's own words), nurse and feminist icon; his faithful friend, Roberta Muldoon, transsexual and ex-football player for the Philadelphia Eagles; and Helen Holm, daughter of his wrestling coach, his first, most trusted reader, and later his wife and mother of his three children.

A storyteller and prose stylist of rare talent, Garp works hard to establish himself as a writer of literary fiction, only to suffer the indignity of having his books fitfully appreciated by critics but vastly overshadowed by the popularity of his mother's timely and polemical (if poorly written) autobiography, *A Sexual Suspect*. Becoming a public figure by dint of his central place in someone else's narrative is a frustrating and unpleasant experience for Garp, who increasingly

finds himself the focus of anger for the United States' more militant feminists.

Garp keenly feels the burden of early success and the novelist's vulnerability to critical reappraisal, with the publication of each new work as likely to diminish, as enhance, literary reputation. The pressures of work and childrearing, along with his and Helen's infidelities, intermittently threaten his marriage, but he remains a devoted father, ever anxious for the safety of his children. His fears prove sadly well-founded as violent events bring death and injury to his family. Grief and anger are channelled into his fourth novel, which takes a provocative stance on sexual violence, and Garp edges toward a calmer acceptance of the world, even as his writing provokes alarming public reaction.
David Cross

Date 1978

Author John Irving (born 1942)

Nationality USA

Why It's Key Irving's fourth novel won the National Book Foundation's award for paperback fiction in 1979. *The Hotel New Hampshire* (1981), *The Cider House Rules* (1985), and *A Prayer for Owen Meany* (1989) secured his place in the affections of a generation of readers.

581

Key Event **I.B. Singer receives the Nobel Prize in Literature**

I.B. Singer began his Nobel lecture by evoking Oswald Spengler and his fellow prophets of doom in diagnosing the malaise of the modern West: "his loneliness, his feeling of inferiority, his fear of war, revolution and terror." Not coincidentally, these are abiding themes of Singer's fiction. Again and again, he portrays men and women hopelessly estranged by the pious certainties and social narrowness of traditional Jewish life, yet yearning for spiritual solace and meaning. Singer goes on to suggest that the writer might prove a source of such meaning for modern society.

In the second part of his lecture, Singer spoke of the emotional richness and plasticity of Yiddish, "a language of exile, without a land, without frontiers...." He points to its infinite resources for expressing both ordinary human reality and sublime spiritual longing – and in so doing indirectly defines the key elements of his own writing.

There was a peculiar appropriateness to Singer's use of this Nobel lecture to extol the spiritual and human virtues of Yiddish. Not simply the language in which his fiction was originally published (largely in the New York-based *Jewish Daily Forward*), Yiddish is central to its spirit and themes. Whether as citizens of Yiddish-speaking communities in Poland or as exiles in the United States, his characters live a complex, often tormented relationship to their mother tongue and its cultural and religious associations. Annihilated as a living language along with the bulk of Eastern European Jewry itself, Yiddish persisted for Singer as a haunting token of its murdered speakers.
Josh Cohen

Date 1978

Author Isaac Bashevis Singer (1902–1991)

Nationality USA (born Poland)

Why It's Key The award of the Nobel Prize in Literature sealed I.B. Singer's reputation as a literary master, and sparked a broader interest in the language and cultural traditions of Yiddish.

Opposite I.B. Singer

Key Book *A Contract with God and Other Tenement Stories*

By the time of *A Contract With God*'s publication, Will Eisner had enjoyed a successful career as a creator of what were still known at the time as "funny books." The medium had hitherto operated in a cultural ghetto whereby writers and artists garnered little respect outside their largely teenage fan base. The stories rarely rose above the level of standard adventure fare or, as Eisner put it, "two supermen, crashing against each other."

Regarding the medium as "an art form in itself... with a structure and gestalt all its own" and inspired by the events of his own life in Depression-era Brooklyn, Eisner conceived of an extended "comic book" that would use the instantly recognizable format of sequential panels of artwork, speech bubbles, and expositional captions to tell the stories of real people in real situations coping with life's struggles and calamities.

In the title story, Eisner dramatizes the loss of his own teenage daughter to leukemia and his subsequent railing against the God with whom he had assumed he had made a contract decades before. Not such a "funny book," then, though the story is ultimately a redemptive one, Eisner seemingly coming to terms with his God over the course of his protagonist's struggle. Thanks to Will Eisner, and those he inspired (Frank Miller, Alan Moore et al), it is no longer a shameful thing to say that you are, as Eisner himself would have it, a connoisseur of sequential art. Since 1988, the comic book industry's highest accolades, The Will Eisner Comic Industry Awards, have been awarded to those writers and artists who continue to advance the medium into groundbreaking new themes and concepts.
Christian Kerr

Date 1978

Author and Illustrator Will Eisner (1917–2005)

Nationality USA

Why It's Key Regarded by many as the first graphic novel, *A Contract With God* moved the comic strip medium into the realm of literate, socially-intelligent graphic storytelling, and directly influenced the boom in "sequential art" that continues today.

582

Key Author **Georges Perec** *Life: A User's Manual (La Vie mode d'emploi)*

Georges Perec (1936–1982) was an important member of Oulipo (Ouvroir de littérature potentielle, or "workshop of potential literature"), a France-based group of experimental writers who, beginning in the 1960s, used formal constraints to govern the style and content of their literary work. Along with Oulipo members such as Raymond Queneau and François le Lionnais, Perec used rigid systems of organization – such as lipograms, palindromes and other "story-making machines" – as means to generate new kinds of narratives.

Perec's writing is riddled with catalogs, wordplay, and measurements. His obsession with data and classification may have been influenced by his job as an archivist at a neurological research laboratory, where he worked for nearly 20 years. Perec parodies scientific inquiry in "Cantatrix sopranica L. et autres écrits scientifiques" (1991), which "documents" an experiment in which sopranos are pelted with rotten tomatoes. Perec used mathematical theories to devise the structure of *Life: A User's Manual* (*La Vie mode d'emploi*, 1978), a 600-page novel about the inhabitants of a 10 x 10 Parisian apartment block and a wealthy Englishman who spends his life trying to complete an insanely complex project (involving puzzles, watercolor painting, and global circumnavigation); the narrative plays out according to the Knight's Tour (where a knight piece tours the chessboard, touching every square only once) and a complicated series of lists (42 lists with 10 objects each) that Perec "processed through" a mathematical array called a Graeco-Latin square.

While some critics dismiss Perec's texts as little more than elaborate crossword puzzles others consider Perec a literary innovator and ascribe to the author a creative dexterity comparable to the Metaphysical Poets.
Kiki Benzon

Date 1978 (publication)

Nationality France

Other Key Works Film *L'Homme qui dort* (1973) **Novels** *Species of Spaces and Other Pieces* (1974), *W, or the Memory of Childhood* (1975), *53 Days* (1989)

Why It's Key Perec might best be considered a literary "engineer." *A Void* (1969), is a 300-page novel written without the letter "e," followed by *Les revenentes*, in which the only vowel used is "e."

Key Book
The House of Hunger

Dambudzo Marechera's first book, *The House of Hunger* won him the Guardian Fiction Prize in 1979. The book had attracted immediate attention in the UK, where Marechera had lived and studied since leaving Rhodesia (now Zimbabwe) in 1974. The book was controversial in Zimbabwe itself, however, where the work was criticized as un-African. The Zimbabwean poet Musaemura Zimunya regarded *The House of Hunger* as too self-indulgent, and too European in style to be considered as a work of African fiction.

The book consists of a novella and a collection of nine short stories, all of which share a protagonist whose biography appears to mirror that of Marechera. Marechera's experimental approach in *The House of Hunger* eschewed direct narrative. He adopted a style of language that is almost astonishing in its representation of the extreme violence and poverty of existence under Ian Smith's Rhodesian regime.

The book has been widely praised as originating a new direction in Zimbabwean and African literature, embedded in a wider, more personal and introspective concept of freedom than the political definition that had provided the focus of African nationalist writing. The end of the Rhodesian regime in 1980 undoubtedly enhanced the significance of this, heralding a new political era to coincide with Marechera's new Zimbabwean literature. Marechera's influence has been identified in the work of a number of notable Zimbabwean writers, including Shimmer Chinodya, Nevanji Madanhire, and Charles Mungoshi.
Timothy Lovering

Date 1978

Author Dambudzo Marechera (1952–1987)

Nationality Zimbabwe

Why It's Key *The House of Hunger* raised awareness of conditions in Rhodesia at a moment of great political importance, and initiated a new direction in Zimbabwean literature.

Key Character **Sophie Zawistowska**
Sophie's Choice

SPOILER

Sophie Zawistowska makes several important choices in this novel. She chooses her Jewish lover Nathan, even though he is plainly mentally unstable, over her young admirer, Stingo, who narrates most of the story. In the end she chooses to die in a suicide pact with Nathan rather than live. However, the most crucial choice she has to make is when a sadistic Nazi at Auschwitz tells her she can keep only one of her two children. Forced to lose one or both, Sophie chooses to save her son and watches her daughter being taken away to certain death. It is the guilt she bears from having taken this appalling decision, even though it was forced on her, that informs the rest of her life. The fact that she subsequently loses all trace of her son only adds to her burden of grief.

The Nazis imprison Sophie and her family for smuggling food. She is not Jewish but a Polish Catholic, whose family had been anti-Semitic, and this aroused controversy. Styron believed that in portraying her he was illustrating the historical fact that the Nazi persecution was not confined to Jews alone, but he was accused of devaluing the Jewish experience of the Holocaust by treating it as the background to the story of a Gentile. Sophie's suffering, however, is undeniable and she is as much a victim of World War II as any fallen soldier. While she survives the physical effects of incarceration in a concentration camp, she eventually cannot live with the moral and psychological damage she has sustained.
Michael Munro

Date 1979 (publication)

Author William Styron (1925–2006)

Nationality USA

Why It's Key By making the eponymous Sophie a non-Jewish survivor of the Nazi concentration camps, Styron attracted fierce criticism from Jewish readers. The novel was a bestseller and the film version of 1982 won a Best Actress Academy Award for Meryl Streep in the title role.

Key Character **Nathan Zuckerman**
The Ghost Writer

Nathan Zuckerman is Philip Roth's favorite creation, a character who has featured prominently in so many novels that many readers and critics regularly confuse Zuckerman's voice with Roth's own. Roth has certainly invited such confusion, as Zuckerman is, in many ways, Roth's alter ego, his stand-in, his Roth-like mask. A Jewish novelist born in New Jersey in 1933, Zuckerman shares many biographical details with his creator, and over the course of eight books, Roth has used Zuckerman to sharpen, refine, and transform many of his own experiences into fiction.

In *The Ghost Writer*, Zuckerman's first appearance as protagonist, Roth's early battles with Jewish readers and critics are transmuted into a conflict between the young Zuckerman and his father over what a Jew can and cannot write about other Jews. Subsequent books see Zuckerman propelled up to the heights of literary celebrity with his *Portnoy's Complaint*-like bestseller, crippled by a series of mysterious physical ailments and writer's block, and sent on an ill-fated trip to Prague to attempt to rescue an unpublished masterpiece written by a victim of the Nazis.

Roth's "American Trilogy" – *American Pastoral*, (1997), *I Married a Communist* (1998), *The Human Stain* (2000) – of the late 1990s saw Zuckerman return from a long absence, this time to tell other peoples' stories, each of which commented on a different era of U.S. history: the radical politics of the 1960s, the Communist witch-hunts of the 1950s, and the sanctimonious political correctness of the 1990s. It all adds up to a monumental fictional autobiography, a vehicle through which Roth is able to show the comedy, the trials, and often the absurdity of a life as a writer in the United States at the end of the twentieth century.
David Gooblar

Date 1979 (publication)

Author Philip Roth (born 1933)

Nationality USA

Also Appears in *Zuckerman Unbound* (1981), *The Anatomy Lesson* (1983), *The Prague Orgy* (1985), *The Counterlife* (1986)

Why It's Key *The Facts* (1988) is prefaced by a letter written by Roth to Zuckerman, asking for his opinion on the autobiography. In reply Zuckerman tells Roth how bad he is at telling the truth.

Key Author **V.S. Naipaul**
A Bend in the River

V.S. Naipaul's work fiercely divides opinion. Throughout his writing Naipaul denounces political and cultural "corruption," "fantasy," and "decline," whether in India, South America, the Caribbean, or Africa. Particularly controversial have been his analyses of political Islam. While few would deny the elegance of his prose, Naipaul has been called both an unflinching scrutinizer of the processes of decolonization and an apologist for colonialism.

Vidiadhar Surajprasad Naipaul was born in 1932 in Trinidad (then a British colony), into a family who had come to the island from India in the nineteenth century as indentured laborers. In 1950 he won a government scholarship to study at Oxford. Naipaul's early fiction, culminating in his best-loved novel *A House for Mr Biswas* (1961), depicts the Indian community in Trinidad with a mixture of mockery and affection. Naipaul's subsequent novels have largely eschewed the humor of his early work. His novels of the 1970s, including the Booker Prize-winning *In a Free State*, are bleak portraits of social collapse and increasing violence in formerly colonized states, a vision shared by his non-fiction. Naipaul's often pessimistic and sometimes brutal conclusions about the societies he depicts are combined with striking evocations of character and material detail.

His later work has often blended fiction, travel writing, and autobiography in a search for ways of writing that are true to his own experience. When choosing subjects to write about, Naipaul has claimed that: "The people I was attracted to were not unlike myself. They too were trying to find order in their world."

V.S. Naipaul was awarded the Nobel Prize in Literature in 2001. He was knighted in 1990.
Paul Vlitos

Date 1979 (publication)

Nationality UK (born Trinidad)

Other Key Works *The Mystic Masseur* (1957), *In a Free State* (1971), *India: A Wounded Civilization* (1977), *Among the Believers: An Islamic Journey* (1981), *The Enigma of Arrival* (1987)

Why It's Key Author of over 25 books, including novels, travel writing, autobiography, and history.

Opposite V.S. Naipaul

Key Book
The Book of Laughter and Forgetting

Based upon the events of the Soviet invasion of Czechoslovakia in 1968, *The Book of Laughter and Forgetting* is Kundera's first post-exile novel. In this idiosyncratic work, Kundera makes new demands of the novel form, asking it to contain various sub-genres, narrative fragments, and fractured personal testimony. The structure of this novel resembles variations upon a musical theme, constructed as it is from seven separate sections that do not represent a coherent or linear narrative. The result is a trenchant exploration of the human condition, and the transient glimpses we are all occasionally afforded of our own true situation. The forces of laughter and forgetting are, Kundera suggests, two of the most powerful tools we have for self-preservation.

More than this, however, this unconventional novel looks at the ways in which we try to make sense of our own stories and our own emotional lives. What are the processes through which we produce, retrieve, and utilize personal and historical narratives? Kundera's contention here is that it is by forgetting that we truly shape our memories and identities. Moreover, forgetting is a supremely political act: as he contends, "the struggle of man against power is the struggle of memory against forgetting." The importance of remembering, and the vexed nature of any attempt to do so, is a concern than runs through Kundera's work.
Juliet Wightman

Date 1979

Author Milan Kundera (born 1929)

Nationality Czechoslovakia

Why It's Key In his first novel since leaving, his native Czechoslovakia Kundera offers an analysis of the events that led to his exile and of the political and emotional strategies that can be deployed as coping mechanisms during times of crisis.

Opposite Milan Kundera

1970-1979

587

Key Book
A Dry White Season

André Brink's most well-known novel, telling the story of an Afrikaner teacher's investigation into the death in police custody of a black schoolboy and his father, had an immediate impact upon its publication in 1979. The book was published both in English and in Afrikaans (*'n Droë Wit Seisoen*), and was banned in both versions by the South African Director of Publications on the grounds that it undermined the role of the Security Police. Significantly, the ban was rescinded in November 1979 following criticism by the weekly *Rapport* and other Afrikaans language publications, although the government maintained its strong criticism of the work's political and moral perspectives.

As a work of anti-apartheid literature, *A Dry White Season* is notable as the product of an Afrikaner writer. Brink began writing in English as well as Afrikaans following the banning in 1973 of his novel *Kennis van die Aand*, which was the first Afrikaans work to be banned by the South African government. The work is highly significant in its own right for its portrayal of the injustices of the apartheid regime. The novel was published in the wake of the Soweto riots of 1976 and the beating to death in police custody of Steve Biko in 1977, events which provided inspiration for Brink's story. *A Dry White Season*, with its powerful account of police brutality in a totalitarian South Africa, provided an important literary framework for understanding these events.
Timothy Lovering

Date 1979

Author André Brink (born 1935)

Nationality South Africa

Why It's Key Brink's work was highly influential for its presentation of a powerful piece of anti-apartheid literature from a white Afrikaner perspective.

Key Character **Ford Prefect**
The Hitchhiker's Guide to the Galaxy

The Hitchhiker's Guide to the Galaxy began life as a science fiction comedy radio series in 1978 and the urbane universe-trotter Ford Prefect was involved from the start. Those of a certain age would immediately recognize his name as a marque of, it has to be said, fairly mundane British motor car of the 1960s and 1970s. The joke is that this alien has so misinterpreted Earth society that he thinks that automobiles are the dominant form of life on the planet. This type of wit is typical of Douglas Adams' (1952–2001) style, managing to be both satirical about familiar things and matter-of-fact about the outlandishly fantastical. The series quickly became a cult hit and appeared in book form in 1979. It also successfully made the transition to television (1981) and eventually the big screen (2005).

Ford is an extraterrestrial posing as a human being while researching the planet Earth for the Guide. The story arises from the fact that when he resumes his traveling across space, researching and writing as he goes, he takes the somewhat ineffectual hero, Arthur Dent, along with him. It is through Ford's explanation of situations, environments, and events to the clueless earthling Arthur Dent that the reader learns about the wild and wonderful universe in which Ford moves and is introduced to a myriad of bizarre characters such as Prefect's "cousin," the two-headed Zaphod Beeblebrox. He is a wanderer both by profession and circumstance, having lost his home planet in a catastrophe which is never made entirely clear. A louche observer of the folly of all denizens of the universe, he regards the life-threatening and the ridiculous with the same level of detached amusement, and his aspirations rise no higher than to find a really good party.
Michael Munro

Date 1979 (publication)

Author Douglas Adams (1952–2001)

Nationality UK

Appears in *The Restaurant at the End of the Universe* (1980), *Life, the Universe and Everything* (1982), *So Long, and Thanks for All the Fish* (1984), *Mostly Harmless* (1992)

Why It's Key Ford Prefect is the pivot on which turns the whole edifice of *Hitchhiker's Guide*.

Opposite From the film adaptation of *Hitchhiker*

Key Author **Italo Calvino**
If on a Winter's Night a Traveller

Italo Calvino (1923–1985) was one of the twentieth century's greatest constructors of imaginary fictional worlds – the equal, in many respects, of Jorge Luis Borges. Born in Cuba in 1923, he and his family moved to Italy two years later. During the German occupation, he was forced to become a member of the Young Fascists but in 1943 he joined the Italian Resistance and fought the Nazis in the Ligurian mountains. He joined the Communist Party the following year. Calvino's first novel, *The Path to the Spiders' Nest*, written in just 20 days, is the neo-realistic story of a boy from the slums who joins the resistance movement.

In 1957 – in response to Nikita Khrushchev's revelations of Stalin's atrocities and the Soviet invasion of Hungary the previous year – Calvino abandoned the Italian Communist Party. By now, he had inaugurated a new literary style, somewhere between fable and fantasy, which earned him international acclaim. In 1957, Calvino wrote one of his most dazzlingly brilliant and witty works, *The Baron in the Trees*. In it, the son of an eighteenth-century baron, rebelling against his father's authoritarianism, climbs a tree and ends up spending his life in various treetops. The novella explores allegorically the relationship between individual conscience and the course of history.

Invisible Cities (1972) is a surreal fantasy in which Marco Polo invents dream-cities to amuse Kubla Khan. Calvino's remarkable 1979 novel, *If on a Winter's Night a Traveller*, is a parody of the genres of contemporary fiction. Calvino died of a cerebral haemorrhage at the age of 61 in Siena on September 19, 1985.
Adam Feinstein

Date 1979 (publication)

Nationality Italy

Other Key Works *The Cloven Viscount* (1952), *The Nonexistent Knight* (1959), *Marcovaldo* (1963)

Why It's Key Calvino wrote: "Having grown up in times of dictatorship, and being overtaken by total war when of military age, I still have the notion that to live in peace and freedom is a frail kind of good fortune that might be taken from me in an instant."

Key Book
The Bloody Chamber and Other Stories

Angela Carter's exploration of women's sexuality is most evident in her collection of short stories, *The Bloody Chamber and Other Stories*. The fairy tale, according to Carter, carries an outmoded form of encoded misogyny that perpetuates stereotypical assumptions about women. The stories in *The Bloody Chamber*, however, are not mere "reworkings" of fairy tales as some critics deem. Carter takes the original content of such tales as "Bluebeard," "Sleeping Beauty," "Beauty and the Beast," "Snow White," and "Little Red Riding Hood," and presents it in new stories that explore female desire. The blending of narratives, texts and styles is innovatively used to examine sexist ideology and to present new sexual mythologies for women. Carter allows what she calls "the limited trajectory of the short narrative" to concentrate her discussion of women's sexuality.

The resultant stories are luxuriant and sensuous in their imagery, symbolism, and sexual energy. The strength of *The Bloody Chamber* lies in the fact that Carter presents empowered women as sexually active and sensual beings, with each story conveying complex variations of sexuality – they become active participants in the sexual act. In an often reported quotation Carter said, "I am going for the testicles… It's dirty work, but someone's got to do it."

Many of the stories have been adapted for theater and film, most notably Neil Jordan's *The Company of Wolves* (1984). Carter's influence has been far reaching and the legacy of her work can be found in many contemporary novelists, including Jeanette Winterson.
Pat Wheeler

Date 1979

Author Angela Carter (1940–1992)

Nationality UK

Why It's Key In *The Sadeian Woman* (1979) Carter argues that women are the victims of a clever confidence trick that keeps their sexuality firmly under control. *The Bloody Chamber* is her response to that notion and to this day it remains a powerful force in women's fiction. The collection is widely taught in universities and colleges worldwide.

590

Key Book
Black Tickets

Often associated, alongside the likes of Raymond Carver and Tobias Wolff, with the "dirty realist" tendency in American fiction, Jayne Anne Phillips' first major collection shares those writers' focus on the forgotten and disenfranchized: street people, prostitutes, and petty criminals as well as ordinary working men and women. But where Carver's prose is distinguished by a quiet minimalism, Phillips' stories are remarkable for their lush, hypnotic lyricism, a stylistic signature that would carry over to her later fiction. What she shares with Carver, however, is an insistent concern with loss – of hope, of faith, and above all, of love, a concern that echoes across the collection's array of stories and characters.

In a brief prefatory note to the collection, Phillips writes that "these stories began in what is real, but became, in fact, dreams." It proves an uncannily precise description: eschewing traditional social realism, she imagines the often cruel and desperate lives of her protagonists from the inside rather than observing them "objectively" from the outside. Whether a child prostitute ("Lechery"), a betrayed convict ("Black Tickets"), or a stripper ("Stripper"), Phillips always gives her narrators a rich and complex inner life, revealing layers of emotional meaning in even the most brutal and debased acts. In so doing, she manages to reveal the singular humanity of each of her characters without descending into either moralizing or sentimentality. Through their eyes, the most mundane trappings of ordinary life – the feel of a room, the sound of a water pipe, the smell of another person – are endowed with a dense sensuality and strangeness.
Josh Cohen

Date 1979

Author Jayne Anne Phillips (born 1952)

Nationality USA

Why It's Key This acclaimed collection of stories, published when Phillips was just 26, brought a surprising lyricism to the portrayal of sexuality and violence at the social margins of the United States.

Key Book
The Transit of Venus

The Transit of Venus tells of a group of characters born between the wars who reach adulthood after World War II. It focuses on two sisters, born in Sydney and orphaned at a young age, together with the significant people in their lives. This impressive novel is extraordinary in its power, richness, impeccable novelistic skill, humor, and sense of life's tragic absurdity. Set in Sydney, England, New York, and Sweden, it accurately describes the nuances of mid twentieth-century experience. It traces the effects of war, of atomic power, of the break-up of the British Empire, the advent of second-wave feminism, and the ascendancy of the United States, not as inert historical phenomena but through the ways in which they affect characters' lives.

Hazzard subtly writes through differing points of view; sometimes suggesting the perspective of her major female protagonist, Caro – and note how the diminutive of Caroline gives a masculine ending for this strong female protagonist's name, sometimes narrating episodes from the male point of view, when a lesser writer of that period might have been tempted to go for the easy feminist polemic. Repeatedly, Hazzard intimates through the use of skilful restraint layer upon layer of feeling in a variety of social situations. She writes bravura chapters, which scintillate with authorial wit and aesthetically stunning use of wordplay and leitmotifs. She judges with perfect accuracy her final scene, knowing that she has given her reader all the necessary information earlier in the novel for her to end with eloquent understatement that creates a resonating impact.

I advisedly refrain from being more explicit. Read and discover for yourself how compelling, poignant, and agonizing this novel is right up to the last, devastating simile!

Helen May Dennis

Date 1980

Author Shirley Hazzard (born 1931)

Nationality Australia

Why It's Key In 1981 *The Transit of Venus* won the National Book Critics' Circle Fiction Award (USA). The title pun is characteristic of Hazzard's wit. *The Transit of Venus* refers both to the scientifically observable astronomical event and to the effects of erotic love and desire on people's lives.

Key Book *The Story of Zahra (Hikayat Zahra)*

Al Shaykh writes of the co-existence of love and brutality, sex and death. Depression, self-loathing, and fear result in a masochistic relationship that however allows for a personal rebirth. Setting: the Lebanese war, Palestinian refugees form the backdrop of war, cruelty and suffering. In the midst of this, Zahra learns to recognize her self-worth though aware of the paradox that the war has been crucial to the process. She says: "The war has been essential. It has swept away the hollowness concealed by routines. It has made me more alive, ever more tranquil." Controversially, the relationship with a sniper is the reason for this very tranquillity.

This work was hailed as introducing a new voice in Arab literature as it confronts issues of sex, abortion, and divorce. Al Shaykh is prominent in her vocalization of the concerns of Arab women and has been hailed as a bold author. Sexual pleasure is a crucial factor in *The Story of Zahra* and is juxtaposed to the death that permeates the country at war. Danger, risk taking, and intense internal struggles are at the heart of this compelling investigation into one woman's fight to retain sanity in the midst of insanity. Vivid descriptions and tense conversations point up brutality, rage, the force of war and its ability to blow apart dreams. The novel forms part of an ongoing preoccupation that Lebanese women novelists have with depicting the war and its influence and effects on women who fought their battles on the domestic and private front.

Anastasia Valassopoulos

Date 1980

Author Hanan Al-Shaykh (born 1945)

Nationality Lebanon

Why It's Key A consideration of female sexuality, women and war, and love in the midst of violence; Al-Shaykh was branded as a "reluctant feminist."

Key Book *The Name of the Rose* (*Il nome della rosa*)

The Name of the Rose is the first novel from the Italian professor of semiotics, Umberto Eco, and quickly became an international bestseller following publication in 1980. Sales were boosted again when Eco's novel was given the Hollywood treatment in the 1986 film with Sean Connery and Christian Slater in the lead roles as William of Baskerville and his apprentice monk, Adso of Melk. Purportedly derived from a fourteenth-century manuscript, the story is framed as Adso's memoir of the events of 1327, recollected "in the last or next-to-last decade of the fourteenth century." Eco's convoluted imaginary provenance makes much of the scholar as sleuth, a paradigm clearly central to the story proper, a medieval murder mystery in which the shrewd but world-weary Franciscan monk with a weakness for recreational substances investigates a series of grizzly monastic deaths with the aid of his baffled but inadvertently helpful side-kick, the young Benedictine narrator.

Lacking only a deerstalker hat, William performs deductive feats, applying the elementary methods of Roger Bacon and his fellow scholastics, in order to detect the corporeal causes of the murders initially blamed on demonic possession.

Equally knowing allusions abound throughout and Eco deftly interweaves his story with historical reference points: the offices and routine of monastic life, contemporary controversy over the heresy of Apostolic poverty, the judicial processes of powerful inquisitors are all vividly evoked. At the heart of the monastery, and the novel itself, is a labyrinthine library which holds the key to the mystery – a copy of Aristotle's fabled second book of *Poetics*, destroyed in the apocalyptic destruction of the monastery. Taken together, these elements set new standards of erudition and ingenuity for the historical novel, which have not been surpassed by Eco's many imitators.
Matt Birchwood

Date 1980

Author Umberto Eco (born 1932)

Nationality Italy

Why It's Key "I started to write *The Name of the Rose* in March of 1978, moved by a seminal idea. I wanted to poison a monk." (From the translator's note to the French version of the novel).

Opposite Sean Connery in the film adaptation of *Rose*

593

Key Book *Clear Light of Day*

"Isn't it strange how life won't flow, like a river, but moves in jumps, as if it were held back in locks that are opened now and then?" comments Bim in *Clear Light of Day*. Her observation helps explain the novel's unusual chronological structure, which begins and ends in the present, but shifts backwards in its central sections to focus on its characters' childhood and adolescence in the 1940s. As it does so, the novel delicately explores the complex, shifting relationships between four siblings who grew up together in a large but claustrophobic house in Old Delhi. Two have moved away: Raja, the eldest brother, has married a Muslim neighbor and moved to Hyderabad, while Tara, the youngest sister, has married a diplomat and lives abroad. In contrast Bim, a historian, has remained at home to care for her mentally-challenged youngest brother and her alcoholic aunt.

The dramatic events of 1947 (Independence, the riots in Delhi during the Partition of India and Pakistan) take place offstage, but nevertheless form for Bim "the great event of our lives." While rarely venturing outside a single house and garden, the novel's playful moves back and forth in time unsettle our initial assumptions about the siblings, juxtaposing their different perspectives on their shared past and registering the contrasts between their lives and their childhood expectations of adulthood. Bravely, the novel offers no final answers to the questions it raises: What is the relationship between public and private history, between the past and the present? What makes a "hero"?
Paul Vlitos

Date 1980

Author Anita Desai (born 1937)

Nationality India

Why It's Key Anita Desai has described *Clear Light of Day* as "the most autobiographical of all my works because it's the house and garden and neighborhood that I grew up in."

Key Author **Russell Hoban**
Riddley Walker

Russell Hoban (born 1925) is one of the most inventive and versatile writers in English today. He had a long career illustrating and writing children's books before turning to adult fiction in the early 1970s, with highly original novels such as *The Lion of Boaz-Jachin and Jachin-Boaz* (1973) a complex allegory about fathers and sons that combines map-making with Mesopotamian mythology, or *Pilgermann* (1983), a historical novel narrated by a ghost. *Riddley Walker* remains his finest achievement to date, however. Set 2,000 years after a nuclear holocaust, Hoban's novel is as much about the power of language as it is about the politics of a semi-feudal demechanized society in which storytelling and mythmaking have reemerged as the primary forms of historical discourse.

In a novel that cleverly weaves several narrative elements (the legend of St. Eustace, *Punch and Judy*) around a reworking of contemporary metaphors for nuclear energy, it is the language Hoban devises for Riddley Walker's narrative voice that is the book's most striking feature. It is an astonishing blend of distorted contemporary language that half recalls the forgotten technological age ("Adam" for "Atom"), regurgitated old English, neologisms, and bitingly satirical malapropisms – The Prime Minister and the Archbishop of Canterbury become the Pry Mincer and the Ardship of Cambry respectively. The overall effect strongly conveys the sense of a broken society struggling to reestablish its identity.

Gerard Woodward

Date 1980

Title *Riddley Walker*

Nationality USA

Other Key Works *Turtle Diary* (1975), *Amaryllis Night and Day* (2001)

Why It's Key Highly inventive and original author whose novel *Riddley Walker*, using an invented language to describe a broken society 2000 years after a nuclear holocaust, became a cult classic.

Opposite **Russell Hoban**

Key Author **Ngugi wa Thiong'o**
Devil on the Cross

Ngugi wa Thiong'o's (born 1938) debut novel, *Weep Not, Child*, became in 1964 the first English-language novel by an East African to be published; the last novel he wrote in English was *Petals of Blood* (1977). Ngugi's whole literary output is indivisible from its political ramifications. A month after his play *Ngaahika Ndeenda* (*I Will Marry When I Want*) opened in a community theater in October 1977, using peasants and workers as actors, the theater licence was revoked on the grounds that the play was subversive. Ngugi was imprisoned without charge from December 1977 to December 1978. While imprisoned, he wrote *Detained: A Writer's Prison Diary* (1981), and vowed to write his creative works only in Gikuyu. The novel that became *Devil on the Cross* was written on sheets of prison-issue toilet paper. On one occasion the manuscript was discovered and confiscated; Ngugi recalls in his prison memoir: "It was as if I had been drained of blood…. With this novel I had struggled with language, with images, with prison, with bitter memories, with moments of despair, with all the mentally and emotionally adverse circumstances in which one is forced to operate while in custody." It was returned on his release. Later translated into English, the novel is a scathing attack on modern Kenyan society and the alienation of people from their land. Visiting Britain for its launch, Ngugi learned of a plot to eliminate him on his return to Kenya, so he remained in self-imposed exile, not to return until 2004.

Margaret Busby

Date 1980

Original Title *Caitaani Muthara-Ini*

Nationality Kenya

Other Key Works *A Grain of Wheat* (1967), *Matigari* (1989)

Why It's Key *Devil on the Cross* was the first modern novel written in Ngugi's mother tongue – Gikuyu. Ngugi argued that African writers who do not use their native languages are writing "Afro-European literature," not African literature.

Key Book
Rama and the Dragon

Rama and the Dragon is written in a style akin to that of the modernist era, and contains large portions of stream of consciousness, internal monologues, and classical allusions; and does not proceed in a clear linear storyline. The novel presents the protagonist Mikhail through a series of scenes, memories, and dialogues that are juxtaposed to the point of view of his beloved, Rama. Mikhail and Rama represent two very different ways of approaching life; Mikhail is a puritan and idealist whilst Rama is an easy-going cosmopolitan girl from the city. The backdrop of this epic love story is Cairo in the 1960s, with occasional flashbacks and flash forwards to the 1950s and 70s. The passion of the two lovers is paralleled with the turmoil of Egypt's history.

Rama and the Dragon is a moving novel that reflects some of the deepest concerns of humanity, the meaning of life itself, and the struggle between passion and indifference. The pleasure of reading the novel lies in the challenge of mastering its text and piecing together the various parts: the internal musings of Mikhail and Rama, the evocative poetic epiphanies, and the often elusive conversations. The novel's greatest impact is derived from its innovative poetic style, which conjures the legacy of classical Arabic, and its juxtaposition with colloquial everyday spoken language; it also succeeds in amalgamating Egypt's Islamic tradition with its Coptic and Ancient Egyptian heritage.

Maggie Awadalla

Date 1980

Author Edwar al-Kharrat (born 1926)

Nationality Egypt

Why It's Key This book constitutes a new and innovative modernist approach to Egyptian writing. Since its original publication in 1980, Arabic Literature has not been the same.

596

Key Character **Ignatius J. Reilly**
A Confederacy of Dunces

The sixth-century philosopher Boethius probably did not predict that his most famous disciple in the twentieth century would be one of fiction's great monsters: Ignatius J. Reilly of New Orleans, thirty-year-old medieval scholar and serial hot-dog thief, whose recreations include visiting the ladies' art guild show in order to castigate the exhibitors for their lack of talent. Mountainous, flatulent, moustachioed, Ignatius lives with his mother whom he perpetually abuses and tries to shame if she ever wants to go out and leave him alone: "I shall probably be misused by some intruder!" Ignatius is unable to get a decent job owing to a fear of leaving New Orleans (due to an unpleasant experience on a Scenicruiser bus), but when his mother forces him to go out to work, he endures a succession of menial jobs, each one escalating into high farce because of his laziness and ineptitude – though he is more likely to blame disaster on the malevolence of the goddess Fortuna ("that strumpet!").

He constantly laments the lack of a "proper geometry and theology" in the modern world – the rot started with the Renaissance – but although his hatred of twentieth-century life borders on madness, there is something weirdly heroic about it. American literature had never seen anything quite like Ignatius and the critics were bulldozed by his personality in much the same way as the unlucky citizens of New Orleans. The novel received the Pulitzer Prize in 1981, twelve years after Toole committed suicide at the age of 31.

Jake Kerridge

Date 1980

Author John Kennedy Toole (1937–69)

Nationality USA

Why Its Key A great comic character who rails against all aspects of modern life (except doughnuts).

Key Author **Raymond Carver** *What We Talk About When We Talk About Love*

When Raymond Carver (1938–88) died the obituaries lamented the loss of an "American Chekhov." It was not unusual for their grief to extend to the fact that he had not written a novel, "only" short stories and poems. For Carver, a writer could only attempt a novel if he believed in "a world that makes sense... a world that will, for a time anyway, stay fixed in one place." Since he was writing about a world "that seemed to change gears and directions, along with its rules, every day," he wrote short stories and, it is widely acknowledged, revitalized the form. The standard history of Carver's work begins in 1976 when he published *Will You Please Be Quiet Please*, the product of thirteen years' writing. Five years later came the bleak minimalist vision of *What We Talk About*; then, the story goes, Carver tired of minimalism, finding it "gimmicky," and re-wrote many of the stories. These were published, along with new "more generous" fiction, in 1983 in *Fires*

and *Cathedral*. Since Carver's death, a different history emerges. The later published versions were those he originally wrote; the minimalist versions were the product of radical pruning by his editor at the time, Gordon Lish. Like Carver, his characters are masters of revision, torn between a compulsion to tell their tales of one "cruel turn of circumstances, and then the next," and an acknowledgment that no single telling will be enough. "I just want to say one more thing," says one man, "but then he could not think what it could possibly be."

Kasia Boddy

Date 1981

Nationality USA

Other Key Works *Will You Please Be Quiet Please* (1976), *Fires* (1983), *Cathedral* (1983), *Where I'm Calling From* (1988)

Why It's Key "There was more to it, and she was trying to get it talked out. After a time, she quit trying." Carver's stories were highly influential in both style and subject.

1980–1989

597

Key Book
Lanark: A Life in Four Books

Alasdair Gray's *Lanark* is an absorbing and challenging novel. Written over a period of around 25 years, the novel charts the life of Lanark, a man living in a strange town, his subsequent suicide attempt, and his time in UTHANK, where he awakes after he attempts to drown himself. The novel has six parts: it begins with BOOK THREE, followed by PROLOGUE (telling how a nonentity was made and made oracular), INTERLUDE (To remind us that Thaw's story exists within the hull of Lanark's), BOOK TWO, BOOK FOUR, and finally, EPILOGUE (annotated by Sidney Workman, with an index of diffuse and embedded Plagiarisms). It is postmodern in its intertextuality and self-referentiality and it has a number of extra-linguistic devices embedded within the text. There are drawings of motorway signs, diary or report entries, and a long list of footnoted authors, poets, and philosophers that do not appear to have any relevance to the story.

These appear in the EPILOGUE, which also contains a long discussion between the character Lanark and the author. Throughout the novel Lanark appears in various guises and incarnations, one being Thaw. Lanark says, "I seem to remember passing through several deaths," to which he is told, "they were rehearsals." The final death is one where nothing will remain. The final word of the novel is "GOODBYE." However, it is not an end – it seems to point back to the beginning. This extraordinary, surreal novel is in many ways unclassifiable, but it is one of the most powerful dystopias of the late twentieth century.

Pat Wheeler

Date 1981

Author Alasdair Gray (born 1934)

Nationality UK

Why It's Key *Lanark* was hailed as the best work of fiction written by a Scottish author for decades and has been compared to Dante's *Divine Comedy*, while Gray's illustrations and artwork have been compared to the work of William Blake. For many critics, *Lanark* is the book that changed the landscape of British fiction.

Key Event *HERmione* is published more than half a century after it was written

Hilda Doolittle's novel *HERmione* concerns a young woman, Her (Hermione) Gart, who has failed her college degree and is now languishing at her parents' home in Pennsylvania. She gets engaged to George Lowndes, believing their union will give her form and substance – "She wanted George to define and make definable a mirage" – but eventually realizes that this is the wrong path, and that her true mirror image, and love, is a woman, Fayne Rabb: "She is Her. I am Her. Her is Fayne. Fayne is Her." Her's self-discovery also involves starting to write. Female self-definition is thus affirmed, and the male gaze rejected as the source of women's worth and identity.

In recounting a young woman's awakening to sexuality and creativity, the work constitutes a Bildungsroman, a novel of development. The text is intensely lyrical and intricately woven; the effect is hypnotic. It possesses, too, a mythical, mystical quality. Names are deeply significant, and words in general highly charged; language and identity are linked. This is a demanding but compelling book.

In writing *HERmione*, H.D. drew on her brief, broken engagement to Ezra Pound (Lowndes), and her relationship with Frances Josepha Gregg (Rabb), her first great love and lifelong friend. H.D.'s involvement with both prefigured other bisexual triangles of which she would later form part. The rediscovery of H.D.'s work from the 1970s onwards coincided with, and owed much to, the emergence and development of feminist literary criticism. Feminist critics have now established H.D. as a significant figure in literary modernism.

Emily Jeremiah

Date 1981

Place USA

Author Hilda Doolittle (1886–1961)

Why It's Key The publication in 1981 of Imagist poet H.D.'s novel *HERmione* was a significant event in feminist literary history. The novel's celebratory exploration of lesbian love makes it particularly subversive and interesting.

Opposite Hilda Doolittle

599

Key Book
Raja Gidh

In Bano Qudsia's *Raja Gidh* (loosely translated as "The King Vulture"), the hero suffers a gradual loss of identity while wavering between ruminations on his rural background, and the vicissitudes of his immediate urban environment. The novel explores Qudsia's pet theory of transmission of Haraam genes, implying that the pursuance of "that which is not Holy" leads to the degeneration of a person's mind, soul, and self that is then transferred down through the generations. The symbol of the vulture features strongly, both as motif and metaphor, its lifestyle and feeding habits representing the moral and, by implication, physical degeneration of those who indulge in Haraam. The notion of the cycle of consumption – to eat and to be eaten – is suggested here, too, for are we not all, at the same time, both the consumers and the consumed?

The main themes of *Raja Gidh* are human intolerance, greed, and selfishness, to which Qudsia attributes life's trials and conflicts, both personal and national. The theme of genetic transmission of such traits and characteristics is a radical one for a novel published in 1981, and Qudsia has been acclaimed for her application of then-contemporary scientific thinking to a spiritual concept, and for lending credence to notions of faith in an age increasingly in the thrall of empiricism. Above all, *Raja Gidh* depicts the fits and convulsions of a developing society struggling to find its place in the world; a society which ultimately crushes individuals under the weight of its huge and inhuman socio-economic machinery.

Christian Kerr

Date 1981

Author Bano Qudsia (born 1927)

Nationality Pakistan

Why It's Key Bano Qudsia was born in Ferozepur, India and attended school in Dharamsala before moving with her family to Lahore, Pakistan during the Partition. She is regarded as a major writer in the Urdu language, her most famous work being the novel *Raja Gidh*, though she is also well known for her television and stage plays.

Key Character **Hannibal Lecter**
Red Dragon

When we first meet Hannibal Lecter, in *Red Dragon*, he is incarcerated at the Chesapeake State Hospital for the Criminally Insane. He has murdered nine people, and revealed himself to be an enthusiastic cannibal. Yet Lecter is not your standard serial killer. For a start, he is a voracious and obsessive reader – a lecteur, no less – and his conversation is rich in arcane allusion and even humor. He is a snob, a gourmand, and oenophile, and he values courtesy above all else.

In person, he is small and neat, with arms of "wiry strength." His eyes are maroon, and "they reflect the light in pinpoints of red." The profound mystery of the first two Lecter novels, *Red Dragon*, in which the doctor appears only as a minor character, and *The Silence of the Lambs*, the best of the series, was that no psychological explanation was offered for his extreme cruelty. He was the epitome of motiveless malignance. "Nothing happened to me," he says. "I happened. You can't reduce me to a set of influences."

Later, in *Hannibal*, in which Lecter has escaped from prison and is free once more to murder, and *Hannibal Rising*, much of his past is explained. It turns out that he is from an aristocratic Lithuanian family, and his childhood was marked by trauma and loss. Worst of all, he witnessed the murder and torture of his beloved sister, Mischa, by Nazi deserters. These early shocks made him the person he became: without conscience or remorse, enacting a terrible revenge on the world.

Each of Harris' Lecter novels have been adapted for the screen, with *Red Dragon* being filmed twice, the first time as *Manhunter*. Three different actors have played Lecter, though the character is most closely associated with Anthony Hopkins, who plays him with a diabolical menace and macabre humor.
Jason Cowley

Date 1981

Appears in *The Silence of the Lambs* (1989), *Hannibal* (1999), *Hannibal Rising* (2006)

Author Thomas Harris (born 1940)

Nationality USA

Why It's Key Before Lecter, serial killers were portrayed in literature as outcasts with little cultural sophistication. Since Lecter, it has become almost obligatory for them to have a PhD.

Opposite Anthony Hopkins as Hannibal Lecter

Key Character **Saleem Sinai**
Midnight's Children

Born on the stroke of midnight that ushered in India's independence, Saleem Sinai is, from birth, fated to lead an extraordinary life. From August 15, 1947, Saleem's life and the history of India are forever inextricably bound together. Like the 1,001 other "midnight's children" who share this propitious time of birth, he is imbued with extraordinary gifts. In addition to his superlative sense of smell, he is able to tune into the thoughts of others which, as he explains it, involves "consumed multitudes jostling and shoving inside."

Switched at birth, Saleem is raised in a family that is not biologically his own, but the novel pivots around a number of such complications. All the factors that would normally shape and inform identity are, for Saleem and for India, fragmented, disrupted, rearranged, and compromised – but ultimately reaffirmed. Rushdie weaves an inordinately intricate and meanderingly expansive narrative that serves to demonstrate that the most intimate personal experiences cannot be divorced from wider social, political, and religious considerations, but rather, are stratified at all levels by these concerns. Just as Saleem's telepathy suggests, the boundaries between the public and the private are tenuous at best, and at worst artificial. Saleem's story, recounted to his fiancée as the sense of his own mortality becomes increasingly difficult to ignore, is both supernatural and fantastical, but more than anything else poignantly political.
Juliet Wightman

Date 1981

Author Salman Rushdie (born 1947)

Nationality UK (born India)

Why It's Key Saleem's highly unpredictable and often intriguingly unreliable narrative guides us through Rushdie's epic depiction of a complex period in India's history. *Midnight's Children* is a major work of postcolonial fiction which won the Booker Prize in 1981, and in 1993 was awarded the Booker of Bookers.

Key Event **Thomas' Holocaust novel sparks a controversy**

D.M. Thomas was already well known as a poet and translator, especially of Russian literature, before he began writing fiction, and *The White Hotel* quickly became his most famous and best-selling work. It explores the twin concerns of psychoanalysis and the Holocaust by concentrating on the story of Lisa Erdman, a Jewish opera singer who is also a patient of Sigmund Freud. The character is fictional, but can be seen to be drawn from elements of cases documented by Freud. Controversy was aroused by the novel's explicit depiction of sex in the sexual fantasies that Anna recounts in her sessions of analysis, which, as the reader finally realizes, eerily foreshadow the circumstances of her death in the infamous massacre of thousands of Jews and other citizens of Kiev by the Nazis at Babi Yar in 1941. Thomas does not flinch from going into detail of the cruelties inflicted on these victims, particularly the obscene way in which Anna is eventually killed.

The fact that Thomas used material taken more or less directly from the novel *Babi Yar* (English translation 1969), by the Soviet writer Anatoly Kuznetsov (1929–79), also drew criticism. Thomas has always denied plagiarism, however, claiming that he is perfectly open about his use of such found materials, as well as his own poetry, in building up a many-stranded work of literature. His defenders have said that in *The White Hotel* Thomas anticipated some of the techniques later to be considered typical of postmodern writing.

Michael Munro

Date 1981

Place UK

Author D.M. Thomas (born 1935)

Why It's Key Its publication sparked controversy not just through its subject matter, especially graphic descriptions of sex and the horror of Nazi persecution of Jews, but also through its inclusion of passages from another novel, *Babi Yar* by Anatoly Kuznetsov.

602

Key Event **Elias Canetti wins the Nobel Prize in Literature**

The Nobel Prize brought international fame to Elias Canetti, a writer who had remained remarkably hidden from the public eye for most of his long and prescient career. He even wrote his diary in code to shield it from the prying eyes of critics, and his work detailed a lifelong obsession with isolation and communication. His own first language was Ladino, the Sephardic Jewish language, though he wrote in German, his fourth language. Kien, the main character of his only novel, *Auto-da-Fé* (*Die Blendung* [1936]) is a scholar of ancient languages who lives in his library, fears human contact, and is obsessed with books. Set in an unnamed Middle-European city based on Vienna, it was a major work of modernism, seen as a satire on the rise of mercantilism, and collective madness. Its surreal plot, through grotesquerie and caricature, is a fascinating comment on the situation that gave rise to national socialism. When his housekeeper

and fascistic caretaker invade Kien's inner sanctum, he burns down the library, with himself in it.

Much of Canetti's work, including the monumental *Crowds and Power* (*Masse und Macht* [1960]), is about the relationship between the individual and society. The work of two decades, this anthropological/psychological/philosophical study of crowds is one of the greatest works on human behavior, inspired by the burning of the Palace of Justice in Vienna in 1927 by an angry crowd, in which Canetti was caught up. He discussed the crowd instinct and violence, with evidence from many cultures and disciplines. A common theme in Canetti's work is that of belonging, and its opposite. That he lived in England but wrote in German contributed to his own position outside the literary fray, but also meant his reputation suffered until Nobel recognition.

Lucy Daniel

Date 1981

Nationality UK (born Bulgaria)

Author Elias Canetti (1905–94)

Why It's Key Canetti was a novelist, playwright, essayist, memoirist, and translator. His plays foreshadowed the theater of the absurd.

Key Book
Housekeeping

Housekeeping is a dark, sad, singular story of loss, displacement, dislocation: two sisters are orphaned when their mother drives into the same lake in which her own father drowned. The girls are left in the dubious care of an itinerant aunt, who makes a noble but futile stab at keeping house for the orphans. "Clearly our aunt wasn't a stable person," the narrator, Ruth, dryly observes at one point, in a piece of masterly understatement. Sylvie's instability is so fundamental, and literal, that she destroys the house and divides the sisters. Lucille yearns for a conventional life, but Ruth shares her aunt's inability to conform to ordinary patterns. She skips school, wanders the woods, and eventually she and Sylvie set the house on fire and walk off into an uncertain future.

It is a hauntingly lyrical book, full of condensed, dark poetry, structured around elemental antagonisms: inside and out; light and dark; fire, wind, and water. *Housekeeping* is also a story about hope and despair, suffused with the language of religion and spirituality, and intensely Biblical cadences. For the sheer gorgeousness of its prose, *Housekeeping* is considered by many one of the finest novels in English published in the last century.

In the 25 years since, Robinson quietly taught creative writing at the Iowa Fiction Writer's program and produced two non-fiction works. Many assumed that Robinson would be the Harper Lee of her day, and never produce another *To Kill A Mockingbird*, but in 2004 she published the Pulitzer Prize-winning *Gilead*.
Sarah Churchwell

Date 1981

Author Marilynne Robinson (born 1943)

Nationality USA

Why It's Key Hailed as an instant classic, *Housekeeping* was a finalist for the Pulitzer Prize and won the prestigious PEN/Faulkner Award for best first novel. It is often more poetry than prose; the plot is skeletal, providing simply the frame for the dense, dark language of loss, and memory.

603

Key Event **J.H. Prynne's *Poems***
would inspire generations of poets

J.H. Prynne has been a fellow of Caius College, Cambridge, since the early 1960s, and *Poems* collects all of his previously published work between *Kitchen Poems* (1968) and *Down Where Changed* (1979), together with a number of uncollected poems, with the exception of his first booklet of verse, "Force of Circumstance" (1962). The poetry is both unmistakably singular and extraordinarily various. It synthesizes the most up-to-date scientific knowledge with pre-scientific mythologies, reinterpreting human experience and history in a genuinely poetic and astoundingly original way. The first lines of the first poem ("The Numbers") announce "The whole thing it is, the difficult/matter," alerting the reader to an epic scale of enquiry couched in condensed and elliptical formats. The arc of the entire book begins in the necessity of adventurous thought, with a purity of aspiration expressed in sentences turned by exquisite enjambments, and ends in wild despondency and fractured protest: "sick and nonplussed/by the thought of less/you say stuff it."

J.H. Prynne's *Poems* offered the first concerted attempt to present the totality of his poetic writing, by reprinting the texts of his fugitive small press publications in a single, striking volume. This publication has since been superseded by a more up-to-date Bloodaxe collection but in its phenomenal and enigmatic appearance, this first edition had an indescribable influence on at least two generations of poets.
Robin Purves

Date 1982

Place UK

Author J.H. Prynne (born 1936)

Why It's Key In this collection, Prynne, one of the leading voices in post-war British poetry, brought together all the most important poems from his twelve previous collections, and his uncollected works.

Key Book
When The Wind Blows

While *When The Wind Blows* was not the first strip cartoon to tackle a grim subject, Raymond Briggs' established reputation as a children's author provided a broad audience for this politically subversive and harrowing work. This darkly humorous creation, set during the Cold War, follows Jim and Hilda Bloggs, an elderly couple living in the English countryside, in their attempt to comply with an absurd government pamphlet on how to prepare for an imminent nuclear strike, and their slow and tragic deaths from radiation poisoning after the attack. Briggs illustrates the dramatic change in the nature of global warfare by juxtaposing the unimaginable magnitude of the present threat against Jim and Hilda's fond reminiscences of their days buckling down in air raid shelters and waiting for the "all clear"; the couple are unable to understand the sheer scale of nuclear destruction or the threat of an invisible and harmful enemy.

Briggs' use of the strip form is virtuosic: he uses tiny, meticulous panels to emphasize the sheltered and intimate life of the loving couple, and punctuates these pages with double-page spreads of the gathering threat. He adorns the early panels with a bright and distinct palette, which slowly degrades into a filthy smudge as the couple succumb to the fallout. The book's staunch criticism of the British government's nuclear propaganda had a wide-reaching political impact, and was a subject of discussion in the House of Commons, where it was described as "a powerful contribution to the growing opposition to nuclear armament."

James Clements

Date 1982

Author Raymond Briggs (born 1934)

Nationality UK

Why It's Key Raymond Briggs declared that he "hoped *When the Wind Blows* might strike a blow for the much-despised medium of strip cartoons. It showed that it could deal with a profoundly serious subject in a straightforward way and make a serious point."

605

Key Passage
A Boy's Own Story

"'Well, yeah, but since there aren't any girls around…' I felt as a scientist must when he knows he's about to bring off the experiment of his career: outwardly calm, inwardly jubilant, already braced for disappointment."

Sixteen pages into the novel two boys "cornhole" each other. This scene is primarily concerned with taking us into the central character's alienated perspective, but it clearly establishes the directness that characterizes Edmund White's writing. At fifteen years of age, the protagonist is wise beyond his years, and far too nostalgic for his own good. His self-monitoring awareness, especially when it comes to words and masculine gestures, gives the language its preciseness. Yet it is also a way of stifling his own expression. On being asked if he has any Vaseline, he replies: "'No, but we don't need it. Spit will' – I started to say 'do', but men say 'work' – 'work'."

The protagonist is a narrator blinded by his self-loathing: his vision is poignant and self-judging. The other boy "whose words were so flat and eyes so without depth or humor" appears to be having all the fun and little trepidation. The narrator is alone with his pity, even when being intimate and he is constantly in search of gratification, which generally seems to be muted.

"…I was peaceful and happy because we loved each other. People say young love or love of the moment isn't real, but I think the only love is the first."

Reminiscent of Proust, the novel oscillates between a fraught present and a lamenting sense of loss and mutability. This is, arguably, the novel that brought literary gay fiction into the mainstream.

Royce Mahawatte

Date 1982

Author Edmund White (born 1940)

Nationality USA

Why It's Key Known for its sensitive observations and explicit sex scenes, *A Boy's Own Story* forms a trilogy with *The Beautiful Room is Empty* (1988), and *The Farewell Symphony* (1998). Together, they made White into a social documenter of gay lives in America.

Opposite Edmund White

Key Author
Gabriel García Márquez

Gabriel García Márquez (born 1928) chose not to wear the customary white tie and tails as he stepped up to accept the Nobel Prize in Literature in December 1982. Instead, he sported a guayabera, the traditional long-sleeved shirt used on formal occasions by men around the Caribbean. The message was crystal clear: the Colombian tropics, in all their overpowering lushness, had arrived for good on the literary world scene.

In fact the arrival had occurred earlier, with the worldwide success of his most famous novel, *One Hundred Years of Solitude*. Even before then, the writer from Aracataca had dazzled readers with his heady blend of sensuous prose and effortless storytelling. While works such as *Leaf Storm* (1955) and *No One Writes to the Colonel* (1961) prefigured the rain-soaked melancholy of the imaginary town of Macondo, *The Autumn of the Patriarch* (1975) and *Chronicle of a Death Foretold* (1981) dissected political power and violence, two of the author's recurrent themes.

Later novels, notably *Love in the Times of Cholera* (1985), confirmed his standing as one of the world's master storytellers. In the meantime, books like *News of a Kidnapping* (1996) were a reminder of his earliest vocation – journalism. Presenting him with the award, the Swedish Academy praised him for writing fiction "in which the fantastic and the realistic are combined in a richly composed world of imagination." The laureate countered this common but simplistic interpretation in his Nobel lecture: in Latin America, he said, even the strictly accurate accounts of reality resemble ventures into fantasy.
Ángel Gurría-Quintana

Date 1982 (Nobel Prize in Literature awarded)

Nationality Colombia

Why It's Key The Colombian writer's fiction injected new life into world literature at a time when European critics considered the novel an exhausted, sagging genre. His Nobel award was widely hailed as belated recognition of the uniqueness of Latin America's "Boom" generation of the 1960s and 1970s.

Opposite Gabriel García Márquez poses with novel

Key Book *The House of the Spirits*
(*La Casa de los espíritus*)

The House of the Spirits, the Chilean writer Isabel Allende's first novel – and still her best-known – started out life as a "spiritual letter" to her dying grandfather which she began writing in 1981 from her exile in the Venezuelan capital, Caracas.

Narrated by the granddaughter of the Trueba clan, Alba (who pieces together her family's past from numerous notebooks written by her grandmother, Clara), and making use of Allende's own childhood memories, the novel traces the history of Chile (although the country is not named) through four generations of the family, from the early twentieth century up to the aftermath of Augusto Pinochet's military coup (which overthrew Isabel's uncle, President Salvador Allende, in 1973).

The personal and the historical blend together in what is both a family saga, wracked by ideological conflict, and an account of the tragic fate of a country under the tyranny of military rule. In it, as in so many of Allende's novels, it is the independent-minded women who challenge traditional male authority.

The fusion of the magical and the real provokes powerful echoes of Gabriel García Márquez's great 1967 novel, *One Hundred Years of Solitude*, although these similarities may arise either as a result of piracy (Allende's own word) or parodic intertextuality. But it has been rightly pointed out that, while Allende's novel begins in the tradition of magical realism, it becomes less and less like García Márquez's book until finally "there is no longer magic but only realism."
Adam Feinstein

Date 1982

Author Isabel Allende (born 1942)

Nationality Chile

Why It's Key *The House of Spirits* was rejected by several Spanish-language publishers, but became an instant bestseller on its publication in 1982. Today, Allende is one of the most widely recognized voices in Latin American literature. She always begins writing her novels on January 8, the date she started writing her first.

Key Character **Adrian Mole** *The Secret Diary of Adrian Mole Aged 13¾*

Sue Townsend's Adrian Mole came to represent a generation of awkward youths longing to escape the tedium of Thatcher's Britain; for while not every teenager shared his ambition to become an intellectual, most shared his anxieties about spots, being under-endowed, and dying an "unqualified virgin."

We first meet Adrian on New Year's Day 1981 resolving to help the poor and ignorant, and to stop squeezing his spots. Over the 15 months covered in the *Secret Diary* he survives his parents' separation and reconciliation, his father's redundancy, victimization by school bully Barry Kent, not to mention the headaches caused by irascible pensioner Bert Baxter and his wayward dog. Most memorably, he falls for the alluring Pandora Braithwaite when they are thrown together during a protest about the right to wear red school socks.

Deciding to become an intellectual, he starts writing poetry (for example, displaying his political conscience with a verse addressed to the Prime Minister, which he feels sure will "bring the government to its knees": "Do you weep, Mrs Thatcher, do you weep?/Do you wake, Mrs Thatcher, in your sleep?/Do you weep like a sad willow/On your Marks and Spencer's pillow?/Are your tears molten steel?/Do you weep?") Unfortunately, Adrian lacks the intellect to succeed in this field, and it's his unintentionally hilarious misinterpretations which provide the real comedy; for instance, on being given a copy of *The Ragged-Trousered Philanthropists* he writes that he'll read it because he's "quite interested in stamp collecting."

The first instalment of Adrian's diary became the biggest-selling fiction book of the 1980s, and led to five subsequent volumes, which see him into middle age, when, one hopes, he has finally stopped worrying about the size of his "thing."

Frances Powell

Date 1982–2005

Appears in *The Secret Diary of Adrian Mole Aged 13¾*

Author Sue Townsend (born 1946)

Nationality UK

Why It's Key Like Holden Caulfield 30 years before him, Adrian Mole provided a poignant insight into the inner workings of the male teenage brain, while at the same time holding up a mirror to the drab realities of life in Britain in the early 1980s.

1980-1989

609

Key Passage
The Color Purple

"Well, us talk and talk bout God, but I'm still adrift. Trying to chase that old white man out of my head. I been so busy thinking bout him I never truly notice nothing God make. Not a blade of corn (how it do that?) not the color purple (where it come from?)…"

On its publication in 1982, *The Color Purple* immediately found itself both a bestseller and a highly controversial talking point. There were many who attacked the book, claiming it showed age-old stereotypes of violent, stupid, and abusive black masculinity. For many readers though, this was one of the most life-affirming and empowering novels of the late twentieth century.

It tells the story of Celie, a young, uneducated, black American girl raped by her stepfather, and then sold to her husband who deprives her of her beloved sister, Nettie. Ironically, it is when her husband brings his mistress, Shug, home to live with them, that Celie's life is transformed. She is fascinated by Shug, a beautiful, glamorous singer who commands attention and expects adoration. The two women become lovers and, with Shug's support, Celie finds the strength to leave her husband and begin an independent life. Celie's story is entwined with that of other women – her friend Squeak, her long-lost sister Nettie, and the powerfully built Sophie who is sent to prison for knocking a white man to the pavement.

Celie is doubly abused, firstly for her color and then for her gender. Yet the quality that made this book a bestseller was the tenderness of the writing. It's written in the form of letters giving the story directness and a distinctive voice, and Walker infuses the black folk English with a lyric quality. The novel captured the harshness of early twentieth-century black American rural life, as well as offering one of the most welcome happy endings ever.

Kathy Watson

Date 1982

Author Alice Walker (born 1944)

Nationality USA

Why It's Key In a later novel, *Possessing the Secret of Joy* (1992), Alice Walker revisited some of the characters created in *The Color Purple,* and explored the taboo of African female genital mutilation. Walker became the first African-American woman to receive the Puitzer Prize for this best-selling novel.

Opposite Alice Walker

Key Event *Akira*, the pioneering manga classic, is first published

Take youth alienation, corruption, and a nuclear bomb. Throw in a selection of superhuman powers, a heady dose of psychokinetic energy, and a group of cyberpunks on motorbikes – and you have a sci-fi comic strip to inspire a generation. *Akira* follows a complex tale of teenage friendship, loyalty, and gang warfare set against the chilling futuristic backdrop of Neo-Tokyo circa 2030.

Beginning life as a serial comic published in Japan's *Young Magazine*, *Akira* was subsequently released by Japan's key publisher, Kodansha, in six volumes. Global popularity ensued with a 1988 release in America, followed by an English version in 2000, combining both cultural and commercial impact. Leaving the international readership to play catch-up, *Akira*'s dark, dynamic depiction of World War III in Tokyo has long ignited the imagination of Japanese high-school students with a turbulent tale of teenage delinquents Shotaro and Tetsuo. All the while, the foreboding power of *Akira* draws the reader into an explosive pictorial narrative, famed as much for its groundbreaking stylistics as for its controversial themes. Absorbed by the sheer technical mastery of the artwork and engaged by the drama of the cinematic style, complete with fade-ins, voice-overs, and slow motion, the reader is treated to a renaissance not only of a futuristic Tokyo but also of the manga tradition itself.

Akira's brave new world addresses many of the taboos of Japanese society, and as a startling counterpoint to Japan's *kawaii* ("cute") culture, it presents a great escape into an imaginary world of assassination, psychotropic drugs, sex, and political corruption. A friendship torn apart, a metropolis imploded, *Akira* is an emblem of rapid social change and rebellion – and for as long as there is a new generation to appreciate it, so will it remain.
Sarah Birchwood

Date 1982

Place Japan

Why It's Key Created by Katsuhiro Otomo (born 1954), this epic manga classic is celebrated by Otaku (obsessive fans) the world over for its pioneering vision of a fast-paced post-war Asian future.

Key Author
Philip K. Dick

Philip Kindred Dick (1928–82), despite the complexity and bleakness of his books, became the most important and most widely admired science-fiction writer of the twentieth century before his death in 1982. His books generally involved a dystopian vision of life in thrall to faceless corporations, repressive totalitarian states, and amoral technology. Even though Dick was a genre writer, his work is among the greatest American writing of the 1960s. Dick was born in Chicago in 1928, but moved to Berkley, California when a young boy. In his late teens he was diagnosed with schizophrenia, and he was prey to disturbing mental fragility throughout his adult life (although his prodigious consumption of hallucinogens hardly helped). Late in life he fell prey to paranoid delusions and god-complex visions which colored his writings.

His fiction arises from a desire to explore the formation of reality, and the make up of humanity. Dick's work challenges the received ideas of reality, generally suggesting that the way we perceive the world is influenced, and constructed for us technologically. He also explored in great depth science fiction's concern with humanness, particularly writing about cyborg and proto-human robot forms.

He won the 1963 Hugo award for *The Man in the High Castle*, a dystopian novel about a future in which America lost the war with Germany and Japan, and is kept in slavery. Dick's bleak sense of a technologically mediated future has been extremely attractive to filmmakers, in particular, and movies of varying quality from *Total Recall* (adapted from *We Can Remember It for You Wholesale* [1966]) to *Blade Runner* (from *Do Androids Dream of Electric Sheep?* [1968]) have been based on his work.
Jerome de Groot

Date 1982 (death)

Nationality USA

Other Key Works *The World Jones Made* (1956), *The Three Stigmata of Palmer Eldritch* (1965), *Ubik* (1969), *Flow My Tears, The Policeman Said* (1974), *A Scanner Darkly* (1977)

Why It's Key The most influential science-fiction writer of the twentieth century, his impact can be found throughout genre writing, contemporary fiction, and film.

Opposite *Blade Runner*

Key Author
William Golding

William Golding (1911–93) won the Nobel Prize in Literature in 1983, the first English novelist since John Galsworthy in 1932. The Nobel committee considered that his novels "with the perspicuity of realistic narrative art and the diversity and universality of myth, illuminate the human condition in the world of today," highlighting his commitment to realism in style, as well as his ability to consider profound moral questions in an often extremely abstract and symbolic fashion. *Lord of the Flies*, for instance, his most famous work, sustains a variety of mythical and allegorical readings as well as being simply the relation of a series of traumatic events. The novel tells the story of a group of schoolboys shipwrecked on an island and forced to attempt to govern themselves. Their descent into primitive violence demonstrates the thin veneer of civilization, and the book's situation has become axiomatic. *The Spire* (1964) details the attempt of Dean Jocelin to build a huge tower in praise of God during the Middle Ages. Jocelin's single-mindedness descends into hallucinatory monomania, allowing Golding to meditate on the effects of religious fantasy and obsession. The spire itself becomes a multivalent symbol for pride, madness, and eventual disillusionment.

Rites of Passage, which won the Booker prize in 1980, is set on a sea voyage to Australia in the late eighteenth century. It considers again issues of savagery, shame, and social class. Golding's books deploy a variety of styles and formal elements and this versatility is key to his multiplicity of viewpoint.

Jerome de Groot

Date 1983 (Nobel Prize for Literature awarded)

Nationality UK

Other Key Works *Pincher Martin* (1956), *To The Ends of the Earth: A Sea Trilogy* comprising *Rites of Passage* (1980), *Close Quarters* (1987), and *Fire Down Below* (1989)

Why It's Key Golding was a serious, moral novelist whose range and versatility demonstrated that the form was still able to innovate.

Opposite William Golding

1980–1989

613

Key Book
Hollywood Wives

Hollywood Wives raised the game for romance fiction in terms of conspicuous consumption, label consciousness, and sexual explictness. Collins' series of steamy novels – *Hollywood Wives*, *Rock Star*, *The Stud*, *The Bitch* – concerned a self-obsessed moneyed set drinking, shopping, and sleeping with each other in California, and around the world. The novels reflect the romantic genre's take on the flamboyance and sheen of the 1980s – more sex, more beefcake, more glamorous locations, and much, much more money. They are big on adultery, excess, melodrama, bodily perfection, tanning, bitchiness, decadent scandal, and sensation. *Hollywood Wives* is the fictional equivalent of the U.S. television series *Dallas* and *Dynasty* (in which Collins' sister Joan starred), gleeful raunchy nonsense fascinated with the minutiae of the life of the rich. As Scott McCracken and Janice Radway amongst others have argued, romance is a genre in which the primary function is wish fulfilment. As such *Hollywood Wives* demonstrated the key concerns of the decade far more clearly than any more self-professedly august piece of writing.

It was a runaway bestseller – selling around 15 million copies worldwide, and being turned into a popular TV mini-series. Over the next 20 years it spawned – *Husbands*, *Kids*, the *New Generation* and, inevitably, *Divorces*. The books also paved the way for a new type of romantic "blockbuster" (essentially the novelistic equivalent of the "high-concept" gloriously dumb Hollywood movie) such as those by Jilly Cooper or Joanna Trollope; and for cultural phenomena like the UK television series *Footballer's Wives* or the vapid celebrity of Paris Hilton, wherein the self-regarding pursuit of glamor, fame and fortune has become an end in itself. ,

Jerome de Groot

Date 1983

Author Jackie Collins (born 1937)

Nationality UK

Why It's Key Collins' racy, aspirational epics unleashed a fleet of imitators, and changed the landscape of popular fiction.

Key Author **Nora Ephron**
Silkwood

If the main course Nora Ephron (born 1941) is serving up in *Heartburn* (1986) is cold revenge on her ex-husband, it comes with plenty of non-metaphorical side-dishes: lima beans with pears, bacon hash, and perfect vinaigrette; for while the novel is an elegy to her marriage, it's also a love-letter to a more satisfying and constant companion – food. *Heartburn* is a thinly disguised account of the break-up of Ephron's marriage to the Watergate reporter, Carl Bernstein, following his affair with the British journalist Margaret Jay, but it's also a cookbook of a sort. A passage on the joy of eating mashed potatoes when you're feeling low comes with specific instructions, and when the book's heroine, cookery writer Rachel Samstat, finally exacts messy revenge on her erring husband with a key lime pie, the recipe is included.

For Ephron, food is shorthand for warmth and pleasure. It's a theme she has also used in her hugely successful screenplays. In *When Harry Met Sally* (1989),

there's much comedy to be had from Sally's fastidious food ordering (a trait which the character apparently shares with Ephron herself) – she might be slightly uptight, but she knows how to enjoy at least one sensual pleasure. In *Sleepless in Seattle* (1993), the heroine, Annie, dumps her fiancé minutes after he's handed her the ring, but we shouldn't feel too bad for him: he's a mass of food allergies, so he's bound to be passionless and neurotic.

Unlike many of her screenplays, Ephron's *Heartburn* doesn't have a happy ending. She writes with heartbreaking poignancy and ruefulness about the break-up of a marriage, but we know that Rachel, like Nora, will survive as long as she has pot roast and peach pie.

Frances Powell

Date 1983

Nationality USA

Why It's Key As one of America's most successful female screenwriters and directors, Nora Ephron has created some of the best-loved "chick flicks" of the 1980s and 1990s. *Silkwood* was Ephron's first screenplay (co-written with Alice Arlen). The screenplay was nominated for an Academy Award. She adapted her only novel, *Heartburn*, for the screen as well.

Key Book
A Measure of Time

Better known as a writer of books for young people, Rosa Guy won critical acclaim and reached a new audience with *A Measure of Time*, which was a number-one bestseller in Britain. One reviewer said it was "in the tradition of Claude McKay, Ralph Ellison, and James Baldwin… a sharp and well written meld of storytelling and sociology." Maya Angelou was so overcome by it that she "fell to weeping." Dealing with the African-American experience of social change from the 1920s onwards, it is the story of sassy Dorine Davis, born into a poor Alabama family and molested by her boss while working as a maid. She leaves behind the racism of the south and flees to New York, where she is introduced to the glamorous black community in a Harlem that is a kingdom of tree-lined avenues, glittering nightclubs, and luxury apartment buildings. Dorine wants it all and, increasingly streetwise, makes her way on the fast track as a "booster," one of the most skilful upmarket shoplifters in the country. While

she heads towards becoming a self-made millionaire, she takes as lovers the dreamers and schemers of Harlem. For all the heady highs, however, there are also the lows, including the emotional tug of home and a spell in prison. Rosa Guy captivatingly recreates the life of New York City from the 1920s to the 1950s. The story of her central character was based on that of her step-mother who, arriving in Harlem in the 1920s, also worked as a "booster."

Margaret Busby

Date 1983

Author Rosa Guy (born 1925)

Nationality Trinidad/USA

Why It's Key Using the historical backdrop of race relations in the north and south of the United States from the 1920s onwards, *A Measure of Time* deals movingly with the African-American experience of social change, chronicling the "education" of a black woman. An ambitious book, it blends fictional and real characters and events.

Key Character **Cal**
Cal

Cal's rejection of a slaughterhouse job at the beginning of this powerful, morally complex novel signifies his refusal of the cycle of bloodshed and killing that has engulfed Ulster. Nineteen, Catholic, unemployed, and motherless, his immediate aversion from involvement in routine violence seems morally courageous. The eventual revelation that this solitary, sensitive young man has been accomplice to a cold-blooded IRA murder is a masterstroke by MacLaverty. As victim and perpetrator, Cal's ambivalent situation embodies the absurdity, difference, and contradiction typical of the province. His romantic entanglement with the wife of the RUC man he helped kill amplifies the tragic irony of his situation. The psychological trial induced by his ethnic persecution and his inner guilt drives resonant themes of confession, retribution, and potential absolution. Religious imagery portrays him as a suffering soul requiring redemption. The novel transforms these into secular issues that need to be addressed in order for wounded political and social relationships to heal and prosper.

It is crucial that Cal is not "neutral" in his beliefs. He encapsulates a national situation where everyone is inextricably and forcibly "involved" in the surrounding violence and despair. His development from inertia to action – from withholding information to providing it for greater and individual good – demonstrates the arduous requisite of forgiveness and reconciliation in healing fractured relations. Ultimately Cal's courage displays a human responsibility in recognition of his "sins" and their causes. His partially unresolved fate suggests the general challenge of transcending difference, and confronting the past towards future understanding. In this manner his private fate implied the public challenge for the Irish peace process.
Graeme Mcdonald

Date 1983

Author Bernard MacLaverty (born 1942)

Nationality Ireland

Why It's Key One of the seminal novels of the Northern Irish "Troubles." Its central concern – the necessity of honesty, confession, and apology – is embodied in the moral dilemma borne by its eponymous central character. In investigating grounds for the cessation of violence and hostility in Northern Ireland the novel was ahead of its time.

1980–1989

615

Key Character **Ruth Patchet**
The Life and Loves of a She-Devil

In what has been called an "inverted fairy tale" Weldon charts the self-destructive acts women will undergo to fulfil expectations of "feminine" beauty. In this satirical take on the romance novel, Ruth (memorably brought to life by Julie T. Wallace in the 1986 UK TV adaptation) is not a traditional heroine of fantasy or romance literature; in fact her husband, Bobbo, tells her "you are not a woman at all." She loses him to the petite and "feminine" romance writer, Mary Fisher. But she fights back saying, "I want revenge. I want power. I want money. I want to be loved and not love in return." In pursuit of her goal to ruin Mary Fisher, and win back her husband she undergoes painful plastic surgery to recreate herself in Mary's image. She is an extremely compelling character, and the novel charts her progress from passive victim to quintessential revenge daemon, a she-devil.

Ruth draws our attention to the role women are expected to play in marriage: "I assume I love Bobbo because I am married to him. Good women love their husbands." Somewhat ironically she believes in romantic love, and this aspect of her character evidences Weldon's satirical take on the consumers of romantic fiction. At the end of the novel she says, "it's not a question of being male and female, after all, it's just all about power." For Weldon everything is about power and gender, and in this darkly humorous novel she not only draws on women's oppression and the feminist struggle to overcome it, but also highlights women's complicity in such oppression by their pursuit of beauty and femininity.
Pat Wheeler

Date 1983

Author Fay Weldon (born 1931)

Nationality UK

Why It's Key At the time it was published the novel was hugely important for feminist critics. Patricia Waugh claimed that it "reveals the subversive potential of fantasy for decentring concepts of gender and identity" The film adaptation *She-Devil* (directed by Susan Seidelman, 1989) starred Roseanne Barr as Ruth and Meryl Streep as Mary Fisher.

Key Author **Terry Pratchett**
The Colour of Magic

Terry Pratchett (born 1948) is the foremost comic-fantasy writer of his time and one of the most popular authors ever (five of the BBC's Big Read "best loved books" were by him, equalled only by Dickens). His novels, particularly the *Discworld* series of books (of which there are over 40), are huge sellers and have been adapted for TV, film, theater, radio, and graphic novel. Pratchett began the series in order to gently mock the genre, but his work was so wildly successful it instead created its own new model of fantasy writing. Discworld travels through space on the back of four elephants which themselves stand on the back of a huge turtle. The biggest city is Ankh-Morpork, a seething cauldron of crime, stench, and terrible policing. There are various mini-series within *Discworld* as a whole and characters who recur (particularly Death and the City Watch). The books are heavy on slapstick, silliness, and light comedy, but the series even now retains the original irreverence and the

desire to prick pomposity that characterized the early books. They lampoon science fiction, classical myths, new age mysticism, the occult, and fantasy writing; they also gently mock contemporary political and social issues, particularly relating to the Middle East.

Pratchett's *Discworld* is an important phenomenon as it caters to a readership generally ignored by more literary writers; with J.K. Rowling and the resurgence of Tolkien it demonstrates that the role of the fantastic in contemporary culture is too lightly and easily ignored. He has also written series for children and young adults.

Jerome de Groot

Date 1983

Nationality UK

Other Key Works *The Colour of Magic* (1983), *The Light Fantastic* (1986), *Mort* (1987), *Truckers* (1988), *The Hogfather* (1996)

Why It's Key Terry Pratchett's particular brand of humorous fantasy now runs to over 40 books with TV, film, and radio spin-offs.

Opposite **Terry Pratchett**

Key Character **Michael K**
The Life And Times Of Michael K

Michael K is, from the outset, a figure who wishes to exist in isolation. He is born with a harelip, and is removed from school at an early age, and sent to a special boarding school. He later becomes a gardener in Cape Town, because he enjoys the solitude, and lives with his mother. When she becomes ill, she expresses a wish to return to the farm where she was born. Reluctantly, Michael agrees to take her, but their journey begins as a civil war breaks out, and his mother dies en route.

As Michael journeys across a war-torn South Africa, he moves between extremes, from imprisonment to liberty. At one point, he is reduced to eating insects to survive, while in captivity he refuses to eat, awing his captors. His behavior invites comparison with the central character in Kafka's story *A Hunger Artist* (1922), while his name recalls the hero of another of Kafka's novels: Joseph K in *The Trial* (1925). Like Joseph, Michael does not fully understand his situation and

struggles against an incomprehensible state bureaucracy. Coetzee later described South African writing as "a less than fully human literature, unnaturally preoccupied with power… it is exactly the kind of literature one would expect people to write from a prison." Michael is the kind of character you would expect to emerge from a prison, mute and slow (perhaps as a survival tactic), concerned with only his own liberty, but who, through his struggles, expresses an essentially human desire for freedom.

Neil Wallington

Date 1983

Author J.M. Coetzee (born 1940)

Nationality South Africa

Why It's Key The eponymous hero of the first of Coetzee's novels to win the Booker Prize, who in his passive resistance to suffering calls to mind the heroes of Kafka's fiction, and who stands at the center of an allegory that expresses the political realities of apartheid-era South Africa.

Key Event **Bill Buford coins the term "dirty realism" in** *Granta*

In 1983, Bill Buford put his name to an editorial in *Granta 8*, in which postmodern writers of the 1960s and 1970s, such as John Barth, William Gaddis, and Thomas Pynchon, were described as "pretentious in comparison" with: Jayne Anne Phillips, Richard Ford, Raymond Carver, Elizabeth Tallent, Frederick Barthelme, Bobbie Ann Mason, and Tobias Wolff. In a couple of pages, Buford characterized this new, new American writing. When he wrote: "This is a curious, dirty realism about the belly-side of contemporary life" he coined the exact term to define a new literary school. The term describes perfectly this type of U.S. writing. Dirty realism is above all about the ordinary lives of ordinary Americans. It describes in a minimalist style the lives of ordinary people who don't make it anywhere. It is not about "making the large historical statements"; instead it is about "low-rent tragedies" as Buford put it. Buford's endorsement validated a sparse, stripped-down style, a choice of unexceptional characters and subject matter,

and an implicitly political sympathy for the little guys, the ordinary folk, the failures and "drifters in a world cluttered with junk food and the oppressive details of modern consumerism."

Major "dirty realist" publications include Raymond Carver's *Short Cuts: Selected Stories* (1993), which included the short stories that inspired Robert Altman's film of that name, Richard Ford's *Independence Day* (1995), that has nothing to do with the film of the same name, Tobias Wolff's *This Boy's Life* (1989), made into a film in 1993, Jayne Anne Phillip's *Shelter* (1995), and Bobbie Ann Mason's *In Country* (1989), which was also made into a film.

Helen May Dennis

Date 1983

Place USA

Why It's Key When Buford started as editor of *Granta,* the magazine was limited to a few hundred readers. By the time he left in 1985, it had an international circulation of over 100,000 readers. The eighth issue was entitled "Dirty Realism: New Writing from America." *Granta 19* (Fall 1986) was a companion volume to "Dirty Realism" entitled "More Dirt: The New American Fiction."

1980-1989

619

Key Author **Hergé**

Hergé (1907–1983) was the pen-name of Belgian comic artist Georges Remi ("R. G." – his initials as pronounced in French and reversed). Between 1929 and his death in 1983, he produced 24 episodes of *The Adventures of Tintin*, the series which threw his most famous creation, intrepid boy reporter Tintin, into intrigues across the world. He also published 12 books in the lesser-known series Quick and Flupke, detailing the adventures of two young street kids.

In creating Tintin, Hergé was heavily influenced by the ethics of the Scout movement. The be-quiffed journalist is a model of physical courage, quick thinking, and unfailing steadiness of character. Around this somewhat blank center orbit the series' great comic characters – his wisecracking dog Snowy, the rambunctious Captain Haddock, and mad scientist Professor Calculus. In the course of his travels, Tintin embroils himself in gangland Chicago, military coups in Latin America, oil wars in the Middle East, a

mountaineering expedition in Tibet, and perhaps most famously, the first lunar landing.

Hergé has been justly praised for sparking the curiosity of his young readers with his meticulously detailed renderings of other cultures. More controversially, the early adventures, most notoriously *Tintin in the Congo*, displayed an offensively colonialist attitude towards native peoples. Deeply sensitive to such criticisms, Hergé later revised these episodes, and sought increasingly to nurture his readers' cultural sensitivity. The years following Hergé's death have seen Tintin become a merchandising phenomenon across the globe, and one of the most iconic faces in contemporary culture.

Josh Cohen

Date 1983 (death)

Nationality Belgium

Why It's Key When the creator of Tintin died of bone cancer, the world of comics and the graphic novel lost one of its greatest innovators.

Opposite *Tintin in Tibet* in Tibet

Key Book *Distant View of the Minaret and Other Stories*

In *Distant View of the Minaret and Other Stories* Alifa Rifaat unveils what it means to be a woman living in a traditional Muslim society and questions many of the norms and attitudes relating to women and their place. The book discusses women's sexuality, desires, dreams, and deprivation in a predominantly patriarchal society.

In a straightforward linear narrative, Rifaat's collection portrays women from different walks of life who have endured both emotional and physical hardships. For example, the short story "Distant View of the Minaret" portrays the frustration a wife feels in a loveless relationship, in which her husband intentionally denies her sexual fulfilment. The only solace the woman finds is in following the five daily prayers "which were for her like punctuation marks that divided the day and gave meaning to her life." In the distance she longingly gazes on the view of an ever-vanishing minaret behind the sprawling Cairo skyline. The minaret within this context functions as a phallic symbol and is embedded with Freudian connotations. The final twist in the tale is when the husband dies suddenly in bed after intercourse and the wife cannot find any compassion to mourn his departure. However the ultimate retribution for the husband lies in the fact that he died without purifying himself, an Islamic ritual that requests both parties to wash after intercourse.

Alifa Rifaat herself was brought up in a traditional manner and, due to an early arranged marriage, did not complete her education. Her work possesses a fresh and unadulterated approach which is both fascinating and moving. If there is a feminist tone to her writing, it is one that is derived from within an Islamic tradition, combined with a deep belief in what is fair, rather than one inspired by Western feminist movements.

Maggie Awadalla

Date 1983

Author Alifa Rifaat (1930–96)

Nationality Egypt

Why It's Key This collection of short stories is unique in its fresh and frank approach towards the nature of the relationship between men and women within the traditional Egyptian Muslim society.

620

Key Author **J.G. Ballard**
Empire of the Sun

One of the most influential of all post-war British writers, J.G. Ballard, who was born in Shanghai in 1930, began publishing his early stories in science fiction magazines, even though, against the conventions of the genre, he never wrote about space travel or the far future. What preoccupied him, rather, was the present and near future, and the ways in which our inner lives were being shaped and altered by our emerging media landscape, in which the image was all-pervasive, and by the hard technology of modernity and progress: motorways, Hollywood movies, high rise estates, science parks, airports. There is little that is realistic in his work; influenced by painters such as Salvador Dali, Max Ernst, and Giorgio de Chirico, Ballard is a prose surrealist, less interested in character, psychology and motivation than in the stylized effect.

His many admirers consider him to be a kind of seer; certainly early novels such as *The Drowned World* (1962) and *The Drought* (1965), in which he wrote about the effects of global warming, have a profound prescience. Again and again in his fiction Ballard creates closed, artificial communities – a business park, a fortress community of expatriates on the Costa del Sol, a high-rise apartment block, a gated resort hotel – then shows how they collapse under the strain of their own psychopathologies and contradictions.

His best novels are *Crash* (1973), about the erotic fascination of road accidents, and *Empire of the Sun*, in which he imaginatively recasts his boyhood experiences of internment under the Japanese in wartime Shanghai.

Jason Cowley

Date 1984

Nationality UK

Other Key Works *The Atrocity Exhibition* (1970), *Vermilion Sands* (1971), *High Rise* (1975)

Why It's Key Voyaging into the most disturbing reaches of "inner space," Ballard's influential style has become synonymous with a bleak dystopian vision of modernity.

Key Passage
Bright Lights, Big City

"You are not the kind of guy who would be at a place like this at this time of the morning. But here you are, and you cannot say the terrain is entirely unfamiliar, although the details are fuzzy."

S o begins Jay McInerney's satirical portrait of the early 1980s Manhattan social scene. Depicting the day jobs and night lives of twenty-something pleasure seekers, the novel presents a world of professional neurosis and sexual excess driven by "Bolivian marching powder," or cocaine. Funny, ironic, and Nabokovian in its linguistic virtuosity, *Bright Lights, Big City* is also a powerful account of the unnamed hero's alienation from his shallow milieu and his yearning for lasting love.

McInerney's inventiveness with simile and metaphor is matched by the acuteness and resonance of his wordplay. But the most distinctive feature of this novel is its use of second-person narrative. Combining the roles of narrator and protagonist, but also open to interpretation as an address to the reader and a generalizing pronoun, "you" in this work is at once the specific hero of this particular story and anyone who identifies with him. By referring to the subject through an object pronoun, this technique captures "the feeling of being misplaced, of always standing to one side of yourself, of watching yourself in the world even as you were being in the world." Thus the form of *Bright Lights, Big City* mirrors its themes: a displaced narrative voice recounts the exploits of a late twentieth-century American everyman whose sense of estrangement from himself and his surrounding culture is typical of the times.

Alison Kelly

Date 1984

Author Jay McInerney (born 1955)

Nationality USA

Why It's Key McInerney's novel encapsulated the pressures of career building, and the hedonistic pursuit of sexual and chemical pleasure among New York socialites. It was notable in literary terms for its use of second-person narrative.

1980–1989

621

Key Author **Louise Erdrich**
Love Medicine

O ne of the most popular Native American writers, Louise Erdrich (born 1954) has reached a wide audience with works of fiction exploring the position of Chippewa and mixed-blood Indians in contemporary American society. Of mixed German and Chippewa descent, Erdrich grew up in North Dakota, and it is here that she sets her novels and stories, following the lives of successive generations of linked families on and off reservation.

Like earlier writers in the movement for cultural recovery known as the Native American Renaissance (N. Scott Momaday, James Welch, and Leslie Marmon Silko), Erdrich dramatizes the tensions between traditional arts, myths, and legends, and the religions and ideologies introduced by white society. She also imbues her writing with a powerful sense of place and landscape, often linked to a political commitment to exposing the injustice experienced by Native Americans, particularly with regard to land rights.

Erdrich's works incorporate storytelling techniques from Chippewa oral tradition, achieving a blend of traditional and post-modern forms characterized by polyphony of narrative voices, overlapping storylines, disrupted time-schemes, provisionality and ambiguity, and a highly figurative style. Her strong sense of the interconnections in human experiences is reflected in the links within and between her works. The well-known quartet of novels *Love Medicine* (1984/1993), *The Beet Queen* (1986), *Tracks* (1988), and *The Bingo Palace* (1994), for instance, recounts Chippewa tribal history throughout the twentieth century, and intersects with stories in the popular collection *Tales of Burning Love* (1996). As an elder in *Tracks* puts it with a fishing metaphor, the stories in his head are "all attached, and once I start there is no end to telling because they're hooked from one side to the other, mouth to tail."

Alison Kelly

Date 1984

Nationality USA

Other Key Works Poetry *Baptism of Desire* (1989), **Autobiographyy** *The Blue Jay's Dance* (1995), **Children's** *The Birchbark House* (1999)

Why It's Key Erdrich has achieved critical acclaim and commercial success with fictional chronicles of the Native American struggle for cultural and economic survival in a predominantly white society.

Key Book
The Lover

Marguerite Duras' semi-autobiographical novel offers subjective and impressionistic reflections upon a precocious childhood. At 15, the narrator has an intense sexual relationship with a wealthy 27-year-old Chinese man. Set during the inter-war period in Sa Dec, French Indochina, their relationship is, on many levels, taboo. The intoxicating sensuality of their heady affair transcends and disturbs the boundaries of cultural acceptability, but even in its own terms, the relationship is transgressive and disturbing. It subverts traditional assumptions about the dynamics of sexual, racial, and monetary power, which are shown to be in a state of continual flux, endlessly subject to subtle realignment. Through this unorthodox love affair, and in her depiction of a family deeply troubled by a mother's divisive behavior, Duras provides a timely exploration of France's colonial past, and subjects the nebulous notion of "otherness" to renewed scrutiny.

This short novel is demonstrably a product of Duras' association with the Nouveau Roman, or "new novel," a French literary movement that sought to break the traditional dependence on plot, characterization, and conventional narrative modes. Critics have been divided on the novel's status as autobiography but she undoubtedly makes self-conscious use of the form, questioning the constructedness of memory, its luminescent quality, and the inevitable investments we all make, at both conscious and unconscious levels, in the process of remembering the past. The most commercially successful of Duras' works, it won the coveted Prix Goncort in 1984.
Juliet Wightman

Date: 1984

Author Marguerite Duras (1914–96)

Nationality France

Why Its Key Remarkable for the frankness with which one of France's most respected – but difficult and avant garde – writers offers access to a sensational aspect of her past, this novel catapulted Duras from left-wing intellectual to bestselling author.

Opposite Scene from the film adaptation of *The Lover*

Key Book
Small World

David Lodge was an academic at the University of Birmingham for nearly 30 years and his novels satirize the mores and pomposities of university life, particularly in the Humanities. *The British Museum is Falling Down* (1965), *Changing Places* (1975), *Nice Work* (1988), and *Thinks…* (2001) all take as their subject the follies of academics (particularly those who teach English literature of one kind or another) and the complexities of their relationship to the "real" world.

Changing Places introduced Philip Swallow, hapless member of the University of Rummidge (Birmingham) English department and conservative scholar. In that novel he participates in an exchange with Morris Zapp from Euphoria (Berkley), ambitious cigar-chewing theorist supreme and academic fixer (generally taken to be based on the scholar Stanley Fish). The point of the novel, and of its sequel *Small World* (1984), is to analyze the differences between the United States and the UK university systems, and to lampoon academic life in general. *Small World* widens the focus and introduces all manner of Eng. Lit. types, climaxing at the 1979 Modern Languages Association conference in New York. The novel articulates various live debates within the discipline, not least the value of studying literature and the significance of theoretical approaches (including deconstruction). At the same time Lodge plays an elegant structuralist game with the audience as most of his characters discuss the genre of romance (from Orlando Furioso to Mills & Boon) which, of course, *Small World* is in some ways an example of. His campus novels are extremely influential in presenting academia to the public in all its dynamic, strange, and self-absorbed oddness.
Jerome de Groot

Date 1984

Author David Lodge (born 1935)

Nationality UK

Why It's Key *Small World* is the key work of the modern master of the English university campus novel.

Key Character **Frank Cauldhame**
The Wasp Factory

Frank, the adolescent narrator of Iain Banks' darkly humorous novel, *The Wasp Factory* introduces himself as Frank, but informs the reader of an unfortunate "accident" in which he lost his genitalia. He is therefore marginalized physically, geographically (through living on a remote Scottish island), and socially (there is no record of his birth and no state documentation of his existence). He is isolated from social pressures and he is without the process of social maturation. Frank is shown to be in a natural state which Banks presents as amoral. He constructs his own reality without the constraints of society; he colonizes the island with power and destruction, and he appears to be untainted by justification and guilt.

Frank's motto is "all our lives are symbols. Only death itself is real." This notion expresses itself throughout the text through his use of rituals. Frank's daily routine is to tour his domain, checking and maintaining (among other things) the sacrifice poles, the bomb circle, and the skull grounds, and predicting the future through the sacrifice of wasps in his "factory." In carrying out these rituals Frank blows up and burns all manner of creatures. He is obsessed with violent images and casually informs the reader about the manner in which he has killed three people. These violent traits are linked to Frank's performance of masculinity. Eventually we learn that Frank has been the subject of an experiment by his/her father and that he is in fact female. The natural drives, instincts, and impulses that are allowed free expression in the novel are linked to the human condition; Banks shows that being male or female is of no consequence.

Pat Wheeler

Date 1984

Author Iain Banks (born 1954)

Nationality UK

Why It's Key Iain Banks' first novel immediately made a great impact on critics and readers. Although highly acclaimed by many critics as innovative and clever, it was also deemed to be highly controversial in its portrayal of murder and violence at the hands of its young protagonist Frank Cauldhame.

Key Event *Blood and Guts in High School* is banned in Germany and South Africa

In fairness, the controversy that raged over Kathy Acker's *Blood and Guts in High School* appears tame by the standards of more recent literary purges over depictions of sex and violence on the page, be it in Bret Easton Ellis' *American Pyscho* (1991) or A.M. Homes' *The End of Alice* (1996). In 1984 *Blood and Guts in High School* was banned in South Africa, hardly the apogee of an open and liberal society, but significantly by the authorities in West Germany, who took the view that Acker's breakthrough novel glorified incest. A ten-year-old protagonist who openly refers to her father as her lover, and leaves him because he can't satisfy her was never likely to secure an easy ride.

Acker's approach to writing was profoundly non-literary, employing art-inspired techniques in her own distinct craft, borrowing heavily from both pre-modernist literature and modernist art, disturbing the narrative via a number of pictorial and poetical devices. Acker, the unashamed plagiarist, was content to cut and paste entire sections from others' work, not least Jean Genet, who ends up becoming a central character later in the book. There is also the homage to Alexander Trocchi, whose *Helen and Desire* (1954), a novel in the form of the diary of a young girl enslaved by an Arab trader, is played out here. The sly tragedy in hindsight is how the novel moves from Mexico to the United States, almost mirroring Acker's own life in reverse, given how she died south of the border seeking an alternative medicinal cure for cancer.

Andrew Stevens

Date 1984

Place USA

Author Kathy Acker (1947–97)

Why It's Key Kathy Acker's first novel includes pornographic sexual elements and violence, and blends them with classical and literary allusion, including outright plagiarism. A highly controversial figure, she was regarded as a sex-positive feminist and therefore disowned by other feminists.

Opposite Kathy Acker

Key Character **John Self**
Money

The irony of John Self's name lies in the fact that he has little sense of who he is: Self is the poster-child of a global culture driven by money, a mid-Atlantic product of a transatlantic marriage, drowning in a sea of corporate branding. Self narrates the story of his own dissolution in a fragmentary, often hallucinatory monologue, as he struggles to find a cultural foothold in the modern world of which he is so emphatically a product.

Despite his creative, visual talent (he has "a screening room" in his head) he is afflicted by a catastrophic literal-mindedness and ignorance; unable to read, unable to concentrate, unable to understand what is happening to him. As he shuttles between New York and London in a futile effort to secure a film deal, we witness Self's world unravel, as his body and mind disintegrate. Society has conditioned him, stripped him of his defenses against the material temptations of the twentieth century. Trapped in a carnivalistic cycle of consumption and indulgence, addicted to drink, drugs, and pornography, Self is a comic grotesque, a bestial alter-ego of author and reader alike, simultaneously repulsive, hilarious, and pitiful. But despite his extraordinary decadence and corruption, he is nevertheless an innocent, frustrated by his inability to express himself. Self is ultimately the victim of a motiveless crime, a trick with no point, from which he somehow emerges, not only alive, but with a more coherent sense of his own identity.

Rowland Hughes

Date 1984

Author Martin Amis (born 1949)

Nationality UK

Why It's Key *Money* was the novel that firmly established Amis as one of the most talented and provocative writers of his generation, and in John Self he created a monstrous caricature, embodying the orgiastic excess of the 1980s, and the damage inflicted by capitalism on the postmodern consciousness.

Key Author **William Gibson**
Neuromancer

If all his writings were erased from reality tomorrow, William Gibson (born 1948) would retain a place in the popular imagination thanks to three syllables: cyberspace, the phrase he coined a quarter of a century ago. This famous little word is also partly responsible for Gibson's own all-but omnipresent epithets – the father or godfather of Cyberpunk, the hip off-shoot of science fiction that mixes imaginative dystopian fantasy with hi-tech literary noir. Much of Gibson's importance can be traced to *Neuromancer*, an acknowledged sci-fi classic which sold like a rock album (almost seven million copies), won every major science-fiction prize going, and inspired everything from *The Matrix* to U2, who toyed with the notion of scrolling the text above their live shows.

Despite its bleakly futuristic setting, *Neuromancer* confronted issues of vital contemporary importance (even if few people realized it in 1984) all expressed in vivid prose and page-turning plots. The more Gibsonian topics included: the interaction between humans and machines, the pervasive influence of the broadcast media on our minds, and a sharply developed awareness of far eastern culture (especially Japan). The more time passes, the more his prophetic work seems to be borne out by actual events.

"I felt that I was trying to describe an unthinkable present," Gibson told CNN in 1997. "I actually feel that science fiction's best use today is the exploration of contemporary reality."

This exploration has become increasingly explicit in Gibson's work, first in the *Bridge* trilogy, and then *Pattern Recognition* (2003). Set in a recognizable here and now, this post 9/11 tale of product branding, the internet, and globalization was Gibson's most conventional and mainstream novel to date – a trend *Spook Country* (2007) looks set to continue, albeit in his own inimitable style.

James Kidd

Date 1984

Nationality USA

Other Key Works The *Sprawl* trilogy (1984–1988), the *Bridge* trilogy (1993–1999)

Why It's Key One of the most influential science fiction writer of the last 50 years. His impact extends far beyond the literary, to embrace music, film, technology, philosophy, morality, and politics.

Opposite William Gibson

Key Character **Ricardo Reis**
The Year of the Death of Ricardo Reis

Ricardo Reis, an imaginary poet who advocates detachment from the world, is one of the "heteronyms" or multiple selves created by the Portuguese writer Fernando Pessoa. Reis, doctor, monarchist, and neo-classicist, is the supposed author of Pessoa's collection *Odes of Ricardo Reis* (composed 1914–33, and published posthumously in 1946). In 1984, Portuguese novelist José Saramago, who is a firm believer in the engaged intellectual, published *The Year of the Death of Ricardo Reis* (*O Ano da Morte de Ricardo Reis*). In this novel, set against a backdrop of fascist entrenchment in Portugal under the Salazar dictatorship, Reis returns to Lisbon in 1935 from exile in Brazil, talks to the ghost of the just-dead Pessoa, contemplates a series of Portuguese spectacles that turn sinister as politics itself becomes spectacle, and (disastrously) seduces Lídia, a chambermaid bearing the name of Reis' beloved in Pessoa's odes. Reis, who is no Catholic believer, visits Portugal's famous Fátima

shrine, lunches on mackerel near the station, and returns to Lisbon as skeptical as ever. In 1994 Pessoa and Reis were revisited once more by the Italian writer Antonio Tabucchi, whose play *The Last Three Days of Fernando Pessoa* (1994, *Gli ultimi tre giorni di Fernando Pessoa*) brings a dying Pessoa face to face with all his heteronyms, including Reis. The surprisingly tenacious literary afterlife of Pessoa's character points to the continued interest to creative writers of a figure that might be thought obsolete, the poet as the epicurean, non-engaged observer who declares, with Pessoa and Reis, that "wise is he who contents himself with the spectacle of the world."

Christopher Rollason

Date 1984

Authors Fernando Pessoa (Portugal, 1888–1935), José Saramago (Portugal, born 1922), Antonio Tabucchi (Italy, born 1943)

Why It's Key Ricardo Reis is a modern non-engaged intellectual and poet who has been revived in works by José Saramago and Antonio Tabucchi.

Key Passage
The House on Mango Street

"Only a house quiet as snow, a space for myself to go, clean as paper before the poem."

Sandra Cisneros uses vivid, abstract images to express the poverty, shame, and joy that the main character Esperanza experiences living on Mango Street. This passage is from the penultimate episode, "A House of My Own." The episode is only seven lines long, and simply explains how Esperanza will escape into her own house, a house that belongs just to her – not a father or a husband. Her house will not be derelict, and she will be proud to live there. The first episode in *The House on Mango Street* vividly portrays Esperanza's feelings of shame about her current home by relating a conversation that she had with a nun, who cannot believe she lives in a ramshackle house. This conversation sparks Esperanza's desire to gain a space of her own, in best Virginia Woolf style.

The House on Mango Street is told completely in Esperanza's voice, evoking a young woman's dreams and her struggle to grow up with those dreams intact. Sometimes the sections read like complete short stories, at other times they are short character sketches or observations. Cisneros has said the pieces add up "to tell one big story, each story contributing to the whole – like beads in a necklace." The richness of the language becomes poetic, yet the words remain the simple words of a teenage girl. The novel apparently moves randomly through observations and events, yet the progression highlights themes of isolation, otherness, the individual versus the community, escape and return. The novel also poignantly brings light to the Chicano experience in America. Despite the challenges facing Esperanza, the reader is left with no doubts that she will take her books and her writing and escape the confines of Mango Street.

Jennifer Young

Date 1984

Author Sandra Cisneros (born 1954)

Nationality USA

Why It's Key Cisneros' novel is a series of interconnected episodes about life in a Mexican-American community from the point of view of a teenage girl. The novel deals with growing up in urban poverty and gave a voice to a community which was under-represented in American literature at the time.

Key Author **Marguerite Duras**
La Douleur

Marguerite Duras (1914–96), originally Marguerite Donnadieu, made her literary reputation first in the 1950s. Her writing became associated with the highly influential nouveau roman school, which sought to portray characters' mental life using techniques such as stream of consciousness and disrupted chronology to get beyond the clutter of realist narrative. Duras' work is characterized by an insistence on the power and tricks of memory; she repeatedly returned to incidents from her own life, giving her narrators truncated versions of her own and her lovers' names, obsessively reconfiguring her experiences of war, intense love, and death. She also wrote screenplays and directed several of her own films, notably *Hiroshima mon amour* (1959), again working her life into her art and distrusting the surface of her story, allowing only a voice-over to speak, rather than the figures shown in the film.

Despite her long career as a writer, her moment of glory really came in the literary year of 1984–85. Following on the huge success of her Goncourt-winning novel *The Lover* (1984, *L'Amant*) came a vitriolic critical backlash at the end of the year. Then she published *La Douleur* (1985), stories and extracts from her wartime journals in Paris, the writing of which she claimed to have completely excised from her memory. In the main story, she waits in terrible suspense for her husband to return from the concentration camps. When he returns, she describes the horror of nursing his living skeleton back to health, and then she leaves him for another man. She says, "The war emerged in my shrieks," and her readers responded. In the moment that Duras acknowledged having no conscious hand in her account, she offered writing that literally told her life, without interference from her writing self. At last she had reached "the heart of the absolute pain of thought."

Sophie Lewis

Date 1985

Nationality France (born in Indochina, now Vietnam)

Other Key Works *Moderato Cantabile* (1958), *The Ravishing of Lol V. Stein* (1964)

Why It's Key Reading the manuscript discovered and published 40 years after it was written, Duras described herself as "confronted with a tremendous chaos of thought and feeling… beside which literature was something of which I felt ashamed."

1980–1989

629

Key Character **Jeanette**
Oranges Are Not the Only Fruit

Oranges Are Not the Only Fruit interweaves fiction with extracts from the Bible and fairy tales to explore a young girl's journey to self-knowledge and understanding. The novel charts Jeanette's progression from childhood to adolescence and in doing so explores her relationships with her mother, the church, and the wider community. Jeanette is adopted by her evangelist mother and is groomed by her to become a missionary. She says, "I cannot recall a time when I did not know I was special." However, as she grows up Jeanette realizes that she desires other women. This isolates her from her family and from the church community of which she is an integral part. After her sexuality is discovered her mother insists she is converted by the church into accepting heterosexuality. But Jeanette is a positive character who refuses to be subordinated by her lesbianism and although she initially lies about her conversion, she refuses to give in to threats from

the church. She sees her sexuality not as her problem but other peoples' problem. Jeanette exposes her church's hypocrisy and remains defiant in her sexuality. She rejects those who reject her and in so doing learns to accept herself.

Winterson derives much humor from Jeanette's situation. While the novel criticizes women who are complicit in promulgating patriarchal and theological orthodoxies, Jeanette remains a likeable, if somewhat awkward character throughout. Jeanette, the defiant lesbian was hugely popular with mainstream audiences, which was unusual at the time of publication.

Pat Wheeler

Date 1985

Author Jeanette Winterson (born 1959)

Nationality UK

Why It's Key Winterson's groundbreaking novel brought lesbianism to the center stage of British fiction. The novel examines the supposed normality of heterosexuality and challenges the sacred nature of "family" and the church. Winterson's novel is a great success story; a witty and affectionate love story that has a lesbian heroine.

Key Author **Grace Paley**
Later the Same Day

Largely set within the same small close-knit community in New York's Lower East Side, and featuring a recurrent set of characters, the stories of Grace Paley (born 1922) are often faintly praised as containing the "makings of a novel" in them. Reading her three collections chronologically we can trace the progress of these characters from the domestic concerns of their cramped apartments and "sexy playgrounds" in the 1950s to political engagement in the wider world as the 1960s turn into the 1970s and beyond. Cumulatively, however, these stories add up to something quite different from a novel. Taken together, the titles of Paley's first two books – *The Little Disturbances of Man* (1959) and *Enormous Changes at the Last Minute* (1974) – highlight the paradoxical powers of the short story collection, suggesting both littleness and enormity, change and monotony. And in the meantime, there is storytelling and poetry. The biggest compliment a character can pay another is to tell her that she's "a first-class listener." But these are no mere anecdotes. Information is compacted in laconic wisecracks and elaborate conceits within which abstractions and colloquialisms, facts and fictions, intermingle and are juxtaposed. Sentimentality never gets a look in. Many stories are structured around arguments – between friends, between parents and children, and, most often, between men and women. These arguments address small and big issues, questions of life and literature, but ultimately they come down to a dialectic between tragic inevitability (usually male) and comic possibility (usually female). Every ending is simply a pause. The argument will be continued "later the same day."

Kasia Boddy

Date 1985

Nationality USA

Why It's Key "I don't like writers who cut their characters off when if they'd let them live another half day it would have all been different. It's manipulative and I don't like it." Paley's stories are known for their rich use of New York vernacular.

Opposite **Grace Paley**

1980–1989

631

Key Book
White Noise

White Noise anatomizes the major concerns of late-twentieth century American life – namely, consumerism, environmental contamination, media ubiquity, and the fragmentation of the family unit. DeLillo remarked that *White Noise* was his attempt "to find a kind of radiance in dailiness." The "dailiness" he depicts involves Jack Gladney, Chair of Hitler Studies at the College-on-the-Hill, and his family, a patchwork tribe that includes Babette (Jack's fourth wife), and their children from former marriages. The "radiance" emanates from television screens, medical equipment, photoelectric doors, supermarket aisles of cellophane and plastic, and, finally, an "airborne toxic event" that threatens the small Midwestern town where Jack and his family reside.

While the context of *White Noise* is poignantly contemporary, the central theme in the work is ancient: fear of death. DeLillo's characters confront mortality in various ways – from Babette's addiction to Dylar (an experimental pharmaceutical touted to relieve "fear of death") to Jack's frantic displacement activities after he is exposed to the poisonous cloud. In the face of a possible "nebulous mass" growing inside his body, Jack buys a gun, clears out his home, fakes his way through hosting a Hitler Studies conference (he doesn't speak German), and carries on long discussions with his colleague Murray, who advises Jack to put his faith in technology: "It got you here, it can get you out." In depicting America's technological idolatry, synthetic fetishism, and spiritual vacancy, DeLillo achieves a profound absurdist satire whose critique is counterbalanced by humor and compassion.

Kiki Benzon

Date 1985

Author Don DeLillo (born 1936)

Nationality USA

Why It's Key With the critical and commercial success of *White Noise*, DeLillo's readership shifted from a predominantly academic set to a general base of literary enthusiasts. The title refers to the "white noise" in which we live – the undifferentiated drone of televisions, appliances, crowds, fluorescent lights, and our own inner murmurings.

Key Author **Russell Banks**
Continental Drift

Banks (born 1940) is the natural inheritor of the proletarian fiction of the 1930s. As a young man he knew Nelson Algren; he was also on the fringes of the Beat movement, and was influenced by 1970s postmodernism, which is tempered by realism in his later work. *The Book of Jamaica* (1980) was his breakthrough novel, based on a period living in Jamaica. *Trailerpark* (1981) consisted of thirteen connected stories that dealt with American poverty, and took Sherwood Anderson's *Winesburg, Ohio* as inspiration. *Continental Drift* (1985) brought together his two thematic strands of Caribbean and U.S. blue-collar lives. The novel also perfectly fused his gritty realism with metafictional impulses. Its compelling narrative includes a level of indirect discourse; the omniscient narrator comments on the action, and intervenes to draw moral conclusions. Two main characters, Bob Dubois, a working-class American who moves from New Hampshire to Florida looking for work, and Vanise

Dorsinville, a much poorer Haitian refugee, are given alternate chapters, until their stories eventually, tragically intersect. It's about human migration and ordinary broken lives, told in emotionally precise and uncompromising terms. It's also extremely readable, and sold well, taking Banks into the mainstream. He continued to experiment; *The Sweet Hereafter* (1991) told of the aftermath of a school bus crash, from the different viewpoints of four narrators; *Rule of the Bone* (1995) was told by its fourteen-year-old protagonist.

Banks' work remains preoccupied with race and class. He is a staunch social critic. *Continental Drift* begins with an invocation to the muse (a Voodoo deity) and ends, unfashionably, with an envoi which describes "sabotage and subversion" as the book's motives: "Go, my book, and help destroy the world as it is."
Lucy Daniel

Date 1985

Nationality USA

Other Key Works *The Relation of My Imprisonment* (1983), *Success Stories* (1986), *Affliction* (1989), *Cloudsplitter* (1998), *The Angel on the Roof* (2000), *The Darling* (2004)

Why It's Key In a long career in the front rank of American novelists, Russell Banks has written about ordinary lives with a fusion of experiment and compelling narrative.

Opposite **Russell Banks**

Key Character **Jean-Baptiste Grenouille**
Perfume: The Story of a Murderer

Jean-Baptiste Grenouille – hideous, inhuman, parasitic – is surely one of the most unpleasant protagonists in modern literature. Gifted with a supernatural sense of smell, but with no odor of his own, Grenouille works his way from an abominable orphanage to a revolting tannery, before landing a position as an assistant to Giuseppe Baldini, a struggling perfumer on Paris' Pont au Change. But Grenouille has no desire to use his sensory gift for the benefit of others; he wishes to master the art of scent manufacturing in order to capture an odor that he had, up until then, encountered only once: the fragrance of beauty and innocence that inspires love. Grenouille's amoral obsession leads him to a horrific murder spree, in which he takes the lives of 25 virgins, capturing their scent in order to mask his own odorlessness. Disgusted by the smell of people, but selfishly obsessed with the rare beauty of sexual innocence, Süskind's protagonist manages not only to embody human depravity, but also to expose it within

other characters in the novel and, perhaps, within the unsuspecting reader – providing insight into the relationship between sex, violence, death, and the nature of carnal desire.

Süskind's output has been disappointingly meagre since this novel's publication in 1985, but *Perfume* has gone on to inspire a popular film (despite being pronounced unfilmable by none other than Stanley Kubrick), as well as a song by Nirvana's Kurt Cobain, who claimed sympathy for Grenouille's misanthropy and desire for solitude.
James Clements

Date 1985

Author Patrick Süskind (born 1949)

Nationality Germany

Why It's Key The heightened and grotesque style of Süskind's fable brings to mind both Kafka and Poe, but it is the utterly original character of Grenouille, *Perfume*'s repulsive but unnervingly sympathetic protagonist, which has provided the novel with its enduring popularity.

Key Passage **"Disappear Here"**
Less Than Zero

"Disappear Here" is a billboard slogan for a travel agency that is first glimpsed through the designer sunglasses of Clay, the novel's narrator, as he drives along the L.A. freeway. It is descended from the billboard eyes of Dr. T.J. Eckelburg, whose gaze presided, unmoved, over the struggles of the 1920s elite in Fitzgerald's *The Great Gatsby*. The catchphrase plays on the dangers, and attractions, of a material American culture which promises more than it can deliver.

On vacation from college, Clay meets with his friends, young socialites perfecting their own disappearing acts. Tranquilized yet far from tranquil, these denizens of 1980s L.A. cruise the freeway, taking the occasional exit to score drugs, sell drugs, or engage in listless sex. Like a fairytale curse, "Disappear Here" is at once sinister and enchanting, luring Clay through increasingly disturbing episodes which include snuff pornography, drug addiction, and prostitution.

"People are afraid to merge on freeways in Los Angeles," Clay tells us at the beginning of the novel, and by its end, we realize that people's fear is well founded. Attempted mergers can have severe emotional consequences, or even fatal results, an idea which Ellis pushes further in *American Psycho* (1991), whose murderous narrator jokes that he works in "Murders and Executions" rather than Mergers & Acquisitions.

Summing up the prosperous, yet morally bankrupt spirit of the Reaganite 1980s, "Disappear Here," like Ellis' novel itself, simultaneously critiques and celebrates the urge to escape. It is an apt refrain for a novel whose privileged inhabitants are on permanent vacation.
Dinah Roe

Date 1985

Author Bret Easton Ellis (born 1964)

Nationality USA

Why It's Key *USA Today* aptly summed up the novel as "*Catcher in the Rye* for the MTV Generation."

Opposite Bret Easton Ellis

1980-1989

635

Key Author **Margaret Atwood**
The Handmaid's Tale

Atwood's (born 1939) first novel *The Edible Women* (1969) explores the construction of women's identity, through their body image, linked here to women's relationship with food, and the female body as fit for consumption in a phallocentric society. She followed this with *Surfacing* (1972) and *Lady Oracle* (1976), both widely recognized as among the most important feminist fictions of their day. In *Lady Oracle* the protagonist, Joan, is a fat woman and a writer of Gothic romances who sees herself, through the eyes of the people around her, as a "female monster." The alienation of the female body, and the recognition that the construction of femininity is capable of change is an important motif in this and all Atwood's work. *Bodily Harm* (1981) focuses on women's role as victim of male aggression and a woman's body as a site of sexual exchange. The novel explores women's role in pornography and male violence. However, *The Handmaid's Tale* (1985) still

resonates as her most politically motivated novel. Atwood draws on the growing moral conservatism in North America and increasing fears of its influence on social and political life. The Christian right stages a violent takeover and establishes Gilead, a repressive theocratic society. The story is a terrifying portrayal of a religious state where life is wholly regulated, and it is one of the foremost feminist dystopias, a highly political novel that presents a future where women's hard-won freedoms are overturned.

Atwood's later novels include *Cat's Eye* (1988), the story of a woman painter, *The Robber Bride* (1993), *Alias Grace* (1996), about a young girl who murdered her employer, and *The Blind Assassin* (2000), whose protagonist, Iris, is 82 years old, and which won the 2000 Booker Prize. She continues to produce highly inventive, political novels, including the memorable *Oryx and Crake* (2003).
Pat Wheeler

Date 1985

Nationality Canada

Why It's Key *The Handmaid's Tale* was nominated for a number of awards and won the Arthur C. Clarke Award in 1986. It has found its way onto school, college, and university courses throughout the world. The book was adapted by Harold Pinter and made into a film in 1990. Atwood has published poetry and short stories as well as novels.

Key Character **Florentino Ariza**
Love in Times of Cholera

The telegraph operator's apprentice was not much to look at – lanky, hair plastered with pomade, myopic eyes. He suffered from constipation and owned a single black suit. Yet he could serenade girls with his violin, recite romantic poetry, and dance the latest dances, so he remained the most sought after bachelor. Then, while delivering a telegram, Florentino Ariza noticed a schoolgirl looking distractedly his way. That casual glance, writes Gabriel García Márquez, "was the beginning of a cataclysm of love that still had not ended half a century later." The roll-call of literature's great lovers – Tristan, Abelard, Romeo – is incomplete without Florentino Ariza, whose passion for Fermina Daza survives ridicule, distance, and the passage of time, only to burn brighter in old age.

At the turn of the nineteenth century, in an unnamed town on Colombia's Caribbean coast, the turmoil of love resembled "the devastation of cholera": sleeplessness, anxiety, green vomit, diarrhoea, and "an urgent desire to die." Love-sick, Florentino swallows gardenia petals "so that he could know the taste of Fermina Daza," and takes swigs from bottles of cologne water to become drunk on her overwhelming aroma. His youthful ardor unrequited, he sets out to make fame and fortune while discovering the languid pleasures of the flesh. And he waits. For 51 years, 9 months and 4 days he waits. Until the day when Fermina Daza, suddenly widowed, is once again a free woman. No character in the history of the modern novel has been as doggedly and as unfashionably amorous.

Ángel Gurría-Quintana

Date 1985

Author Gabriel García Márquez (born 1928)

Nationality Colombia

Why It's Key Florentino Ariza and Fermina Daza are loosely based on the author's parents. His father, Gabriel Eligio García, was the humble telegraph operator in the small Colombian town of Aracataca. His mother, Luisa Santiaga Márquez, was the daughter of a colonel who vehemently opposed their affair.

Key Book
Hawksmoor

The narrative of Nicholas Dyer, told in authentic-seeming seventeenth-century prose, describes his early existence of suffering and squalor, in which he loses his family to the plague, contrasting this with his later life as an architect, designing churches to be built in London to replace those destroyed in the Great Fire of 1666. Ironically, this builder of Christian places of worship is a follower of satanism: "…that Satan is the God of this World and fit to be worshipp'd I will offer certain proof." Among the unholy practices followed by Dyer is the use of human sacrifice and blood to dedicate new buildings, and this is echoed in the twentieth century as the policeman Hawksmoor investigates murders with satanic overtones that appear to be linked with the same churches.

While it was not Ackroyd's first work of fiction, *Hawksmoor* established his name as a novelist of great originality. The parallels between the two periods are made clear, often surprisingly, as in the idea that the relative precariousness of London life in the seventeenth century is mirrored in the ease with which an apparent serial killer in the modern city is able to murder with impunity. Ackroyd's command of both historical and contemporary narrative allows the concept of evil to resonate across the centuries. Not the least disturbing element of the book is the fact that the churches referred to are real and unmistakably located. Anyone who, after having read this novel, happens to pass any of them will look at them in an entirely different light.

Michael Munro

Date 1985

Author Peter Ackroyd (born 1949)

Nationality UK

Why It's Key This novel has a striking narrative technique. It takes the life of the English architect Nicholas Hawksmoor (died 1736) and "splits" it between two storylines. A blend of horror, crime story, and historical fiction, it brings a sense of mystery and the uncanny to familiar landmarks on the streets of London.

Key Author **Paul Auster**
City of Glass

In his essay collection, *The Art of Hunger* (1982), Paul Auster (born 1947) claims a fascination with "the presence of the unpredictable, the utterly bewildering nature of the human experience." Chance, synchronicity, and the mysteries of existence: Auster's work is indeed charged with these themes.

Ever eluding expectation and certainty, Auster's fiction is populated by characters who find themselves in bizarre situations, where reason and the calculus of cause and effect no longer provide a framework for understanding. We read about a young man meandering unknowingly toward his long-lost father (1989, *Moon Palace*), an unlucky gambler forced to build a purposeless stone wall in the middle of a field (1990, *The Music of Chance*), and an author trying to make sense of a terrorist bomber's death (1992, *Leviathan*).

The inscrutable nature of identity and reality is most memorably rendered in Auster's *The New York Trilogy* (1987), which consists of three so-called "anti-detective" stories that examine solitude and obsession. In the most famous of these tales, *City of Glass* (1985), a crime writer named Daniel Quinn receives a phone call for "Paul Auster," and becomes embroiled in a complex yarn of urban surveillance that is replete with femmes fatales, doppelgangers, and a host of disintegrating personae. The more Quinn searches for truth, the more remote truth becomes.

Perhaps the most remarkable aspect of Auster's oeuvre is its formal diversity: in addition to 12 novels, Auster has produced four volumes of poetry, five collections of essays, and six screenplays. He has translated works by Stephane Mallarmé, Joseph Joubert, and Jean-Paul Sartre, contributed lyrics and spoken-word to rock and electronic music recordings, and recently directed a feature film, *The Secret Life of Walter Frost*.

Kiki Benzon

Date 1985

Nationality USA

Why It's Key Auster got the USA writing in his National Story Project, which began with radio broadcasts of stories by unknown writers, and grew into a collection, *I Thought My Father Was God: And Other True Tales* (2002). Auster's highly inventive prose deals with the fractured, mutable nature of the self.

Key Author **Richard Ford**
The Sportswriter

It took Richard Ford (born 1944) over a decade to make any real impact on the literary scene: after two well-reviewed novels failed commercially, he threw in his fiction writer's towel and became a sports journalist. When the magazine he worked for folded, and *Sports Illustrated* failed to hire him, Ford returned to fiction with a story, spookily enough, featuring a sports journalist who once wrote novels and short stories.

The Sportswriter made Ford's name, becoming one of *Time*'s best books of 1986: a sequel, *Independence Day* (1995), was the first novel to win both the PEN/Faulkner Award and the Pulitzer Prize. However, it was Ford's acclaimed short story collection, *Rock Springs* (1987), that earned him his seat among the vanguard of the influential "dirty realist" movement.

In many respects, the fit is cosy enough; in others, it is perhaps a little too cosy. True, Ford admires the bleak realism of Richard Yates, Raymond Carver, and Tobias Wolff. True, his own prose is spare and wry, his characters frequently dispossessed, grieving, and struggling: at the beginning of *The Sportswriter*, Frank Bascombe is all three, mourning his son, alienated from his wife (known only as "X"), and divorced from his youthful literary ambitions.

But, as Ford himself has noted, Bascombe may be scarred, but he is also in pursuit of happiness, however hard it is to find. As he notes in *The Sportswriter:* "I had written all I was going to write, if the truth had been known, and there is nothing wrong with that. If more writers knew that, the world would be saved a lot of bad books, and more people — men and women alike — could go on to happier, more productive lives."

James Kidd

Date 1986

Nationality USA

Other Key Works *A Piece of My Heart* (1976), *The Ultimate Good Luck* (1981), *Wildlife* (1990), *Women with Men: Three Stories* (1997), **Short Stories** *A Multitude of Sins* (2002), *Vintage Ford* (2004)

Why It's Key Ford's novels and stories chronicle the emotional and spiritual disappointments and crises of everyday people, such as Frank in *The Sportswriter*.

Key Book
Maus: A Survivor's Tale

In *Maus* Art Spiegelman recounted his father's experiences as a Polish Jew from the 1930s through the war and his eventual incarceration in Auschwitz. The key choices that Spiegelman makes are firstly to tell the story in graphic novel format and secondly to present each different race in the novel as an animal (Jews are mice, Germans cats, Swedes are deer, Americans are dogs). This latter innovation somehow allows the novel to be innocent and childlike whilst articulating great horror. The caricatures associated with the animals are also undermined by the book, which suggests that such a classificatory approach prevents people from seeing common humanity: "Ultimately what the book's about is the commonality of human beings" said Spiegelman.

The Holocaust story is alternated with moments showing the contemporary lives of Spiegelman and his father in New York and Florida. The use of his father's biography allows Spiegelman to explore a "normal" Jew's experience rather than generalize (his father is endearingly and annoyingly human, and he himself finds it difficult to accept racial difference). The novel draws on such forbears as Keiji Nakazawa's 1970s *Barefoot Gen* (about Hiroshima) as well as more obvious comic-strip tropes such as Tom and Jerry. The narrative and thematic complexity of *Maus* demonstrated that the graphic novel form was capable of emotional and conceptual depth. In 1992 it was awarded a Pulitzer Prize special award, stunningly underlining the entry of the format into the western mainstream.
Jerome de Groot

Date 1986

Author Art Spiegelman (born 1948)

Nationality USA

Why It's Key Prize-winning graphic novel about Auschwitz and the Holocaust, which demonstrated that the format could deal with serious and complex issues.

Key Author
Jorge Luis Borges

Jorge Luis Borges (1899–1986) is one of the most paradoxical twentieth-century writers – a universalist whose works are all in miniature; an absurdist whose most distinctive trait is his seriousness; an Argentinian raised on European literature; a writer who celebrates instability but whose works are amongst the most minutely ordered in literature.

Born to an Argentinian family of middle-class intellectuals, Borges was home-taught, and started writing his own fiction at the age of six. His first collection of short stories, *The Garden of Forking Paths*, was published in 1941, and this was followed by a burst of intense literary creativity that resulted in his finest short fiction, which was published in the volumes *Ficciones* (1945), and *El Aleph* (1949). Borges the writer of fiction is inseparable from his vast scholarship – his works included essays, several screenplays, literary criticism, prologues, numerous reviews, and some poetry. The themes of his major works reflect this sense of expansive erudition. The idea of infinity, libraries, maps, encyclopedias, games – recurring again and again in his fiction, these key Borgesian motifs all share a preoccupation with taxonomies of knowledge. Borges suffered from encroaching blindness for most of his life, which perhaps contributed to his desire to pin down the elusive ideal of universality that would make sense of the world.
Julia Jordan

Date 1986 (death)

Nationality Argentina

Other Key Works *A Universal History of Infamy* (*Historia universal de la infamia*, 1935)

Why It's Key Borges' lack of fixity is at the heart of his genius: "I am not sure that I exist, actually. I am all the writers that I have read, all the people that I have met, all the women that I have loved; all the cities that I have visited, all my ancestors."

Opposite Jorge Luis Borges

FRIDAY, JUNE 3
11:00 - NOON

FRANK MILLER

WILL SIGN COPIES OF

THE DARK KNIGHT RETURNS

DC COMICS BOOTH 4955

DC

Key Book
Batman: The Dark Knight Returns

Credited along with *Watchmen* with being the first postmodern comic book, Frank Miller's 1986 graphic novel *Batman: the Dark Night Returns* forever re-imagined an iconic superhero whose image and story had become part of the popular imagination. Gone were the "BAM!" and "POW!" of the cartoony Adam West television series. Instead, Miller gave comic fans a morose and no-longer young Bruce Wayne. Grown stiff with age and battle, and stiff-necked in his cynicism and barely suppressed anger, the Batman of *The Dark Knight Returns* is a scarier and more militant character than any of the various incarnations of the millionaire-turned-crime-fighter. Batman's nemesis, The Joker, is also more frightening and psychotic, literally the stuff of Bruce Wayne's nightmares.

Set in a future beset by violent criminal gangs, and filled with characters whose pain, both physical and psychological, is explored in detail, *The Dark Knight Returns* was considered one of the first adult-oriented comics. Along with Alan Moore's *Watchmen* (1986–87), it began a trend of depicting comic book heroes in darker, more psychologically realistic ways, but it stands above most of these imitators, in part because of its literary treatment of the myths of violence, which underpin both the origins of the Batman and the Western civilization that spawned him. Often accused of propounding a right-wing ideology, especially as regards crime and violence, Miller – who is also the author/illustrator of the ultra-violent *Sin City* – shot to fame with *DKR*, which was heralded not only for maintaining the previous continuity of the character, but also for its gritty, emotive illustration.
Elizabeth Rosen

Date 1986

Author Frank Miller (born 1957)

Nationality USA

Why Its Key Largely responsible for ushering in the "dark" age of comic book heroes, in which superheroes are portrayed in more realistic ways, *The Dark Knight Returns* gave the world a psychologically-battered and edgy middle-aged Batman who comes out of retirement to fight crime.

Opposite Frank Miller

1980–1989

641

Key Book
The Old Devils

"'If you want my opinion,' said Gwen Cellan-Davies, 'the old boy's a terrifically distinguished citizen of Wales. Or at any rate what passes for one these days.'"

After decades living in London, the writer, TV personality and "professional Welshman" Alun Weaver (CBE) has decided to go home. The return of Alun and his wife Rhiannon to South Wales reawakens long-dormant friendships, passions, and animosities, not least since Alun refuses to allow his age to prevent him from embarking or re-embarking on a series of affairs with his friends' wives. Rhiannon too has unfinished romantic business in Wales, the legacy of a youthful scandal that is unraveled as the novel progresses.

At odds with the modern world and frequently with each other, the novel's hard-drinking "oldsters" – including soppy Malcolm, wine-sodden Dorothy, overweight Charlie, and even-more-overweight Peter – are a rich source of both social and physical comedy. In contrast to the protagonists' frequent befuddlement and exhaustion, *The Old Devils* includes some of Kingsley Amis' most inventive and minutely-observed comic set-pieces. The key to these is in the writing's painstaking attention to detail, whether the focus is Alun's convoluted deceptions and self-deceptions, the absurd public unveiling of a statue of the local poet Brydan (a mercilessly-debunked version of Dylan Thomas), or Peter's hilariously complicated attempts to get his socks and underpants on in the morning.

The novel's most striking achievement is its refusal of both bleakness and sentimentality, the balance it maintains between mockery of the old devils and sympathy for them. Equally unsparing in its depiction of the follies of age and those of contemporary life, the novel nevertheless ends on a tentative note of hope and redemption.
Paul Vlitos

Date 1986

Author Kingsley Amis (1922–95)

Nationality UK

Why Its Key Winner of the 1986 Booker Prize, *The Old Devils* was described by Kingsley Amis' son Martin as "the book he will be remembered for."

Key Event **Wole Soyinka is the first African to win the Nobel Prize in Literature**

Winning the Nobel was a mixed blessing, Wole Soyinka (born 1934) claimed: "[E]verybody wants something as a result of that prize. It has such a prestige and such a hold on people's imagination in all corners and on all levels that you become the property of the world." His acceptance lecture ended with the following affirmation: "[O]f those imperatives that challenge our being, our presence, and humane definition at this time, none can be considered more pervasive than the end of racism, the eradication of human inequality, and the dismantling of all their structures. The Prize is the consequent enthronement of its complement: universal suffrage, and peace."

His work has been informed by an outspoken political activism, as a result of which he has suffered imprisonment (solitary confinement in 1967, during the Nigerian civil war), and exile. Inspired as a child by a tax revolt that his mother led, and by Nigeria's fight for independence, he later wrote in his classic memoir

Aké (1981): "Young as I was, it all took place around me… I'd listened to elders talking, and I used to read the newspapers on my father's desk. This was a period of anti-colonial fervor, so the entire anti-colonial training was something I imbibed quite early, even before the women's movement."

An influential international dramatist, he is also acclaimed for his poetry, life-writing, and essays, but has attracted criticism from some African contemporaries for his grandiloquence and linguistic obscurity. Nigerian critic Chinweizu controversially dismissed Soyinka's Nobel as: "the undesirable honouring the unreadable."

Margaret Busby

Date 1986

Place Nigeria

Author Wole Soyinka (born 1934)

Other Key Works *The Interpreters* (novel, 1965), *The Man Died* (prison journal, 1972)

Why It's Key The Swedish Academy described Soyinka as "one of the finest poetical playwrights that have written in English," citing his plays *Death and the King's Horseman* (written 1974) and *A Dance of the Forests* (1960).

Opposite Wole Soyinka

Key Book
Watchmen

A blue man who can rearrange the molecular structure of any object. An impotent bird-watcher turned crime-fighter. An ultra-conservative vigilante who eats sugar cubes right out the box. These are all characters from the 1986 Alan Moore/Dave Gibbons graphic novel *Watchmen*. In deciding to write a comic about what would happen if superheroes really existed, Moore and Gibbons changed the comic book world forever. The story of a group of former superheroes who have fallen on bad times, become cynical government operatives, or walked away from the crime-fighting business in disgust, *Watchmen* is credited – along with Frank Miller's *Dark Knight Returns* – with being the first postmodern graphic novel.

Watchmen tread where other comics had failed to go: into the bruised, battered, and sometimes warped psychology of superheroes. Its portrait of its superheroes was dark and discomforting, but was perhaps most radical in its treatment of them

as if they were real. In the *Watchmen* universe, caped crusaders get shot trying to foil crime because their capes get stuck in revolving doors, noir-inspired vigilantes are hunted down by the police, and gay heroes are "outed" with dire results. Its plot is no less pessimistic. Drawn to work together again in order to find out who is murdering them, the heroes discover an apocalyptic plot being perpetrated by one of their own: Ozymandias, the Smartest Man in the World. Not only are they unable to stop Ozymandias from carrying out his plan, but they cannot even reveal that such a plan existed, nor bring Ozymandias to justice for his crimes after the fact. *Watchmen* thus depicted a comic book world just as morally complicated and psychologically real as our own.

Elizabeth Rosen

Date 1986–87 (Originally published in single magazine form)

Author Alan Moore (born 1953, UK)

Illustrator Dave Gibbons (born 1949, UK)

Why It's Key Considered the first postmodern graphic novel, *Watchmen* inspired the trend to depict superheroes in dark and psychologically complex ways.

Key Passage **"Safe Love"**
Break It Down

The complete short story, "Safe Love":

"She was in love with her son's pediatrician. Alone out in the country—could anyone blame her.

There was an element of grand passion in this love. It was also a safe thing. The man was on the other side of a barrier. Between him and her: the child on the examining table, the office itself, the staff, his wife, her husband, his stethoscope, his beard, her breasts, his glasses, her glasses, etc. "

While other short story writers of the period, such as Tobias Wolff or Ann Beattie, rely on character development to drive their narratives, Davis enlists grammar to do the heavy lifting. Her tightly controlled writing imposes a formal restraint over the messiness of human drama. The effect is at once comic and tragic, as in "Safe Love," where the splendid absurdity of a crush is communicated through grammar as

much as event. The mood shifts between resignation and excitement, echoing the rhythms of infatuation itself. It is written like a joke, but, like the best jokes, it is also in earnest. While the suburban nature of this "safe love" undercuts its "element of grand passion," its safety also makes the relationship compelling. The barriers to this love are both profound: "the child," "her husband," "his wife," and banal: "his stethoscope," "his beard," "her glasses."

The neutral listing of the things "Between him and her" creates the potential for comic instability: "his stethoscope" is as much a barrier to the woman's passion as "his wife." The concluding "etc." hovers like an unspoken threat, or possibly a punchline.

Written like a parable or a fable, but without any clear moral or fixed meaning, Davis' story is ground-breaking in its resistance to the realist trend in American short story-writing of the mid 1980s.

Dinah Roe

Date 1986

Title "Safe Love" from the collection *Break It Down*

Author Lydia Davis (born 1947)

Nationality USA

Why It's Key An award-winning translator of the writing of Proust and Maurice Blanchot, among others, Lydia Davis brought an anti-realist, continental flair to U.S. short story writing of the 1980s. *Break It Down* was a finalist for the PEN/Hemingway Award.

1980–1989

645

Key Author **Carl Hiaasen**
Tourist Season

Anyone who has seen *Striptease*, the 1996 movie starring Demi Moore (though rather more in body than in spirit), could be forgiven for adjudging Carl Hiaasen (born 1953) a second-rate author whose pulp fiction fuses vulgarity and farce with kindergarten sex and politics. It's just possible Hiaasen believes this himself, but it would do his sharp, satiric, and entertaining novels a disservice.

He began writing as a journalist, joining *The Miami Herald* in 1976, and specialized in exposing property schemes that placed profit above preserving Florida's natural landscape. Still producing a weekly column for the paper to this day, Hiaasen's scathing attacks on everything from the Disney Corporation to the death of Anna Nicole Smith have, according to his website, "pissed off just about everybody in South Florida, including his own bosses."

In collaboration with colleague Bill Montalbano, Hiaasen wrote his first novel (a thriller called *Powder*

Burn) in 1981, going solo five years later with *Tourist Season*. Hybrids of barbed topical comedy and crime fiction, his stories are almost always set in Florida and are populated with the sorts of scheming politicians, corrupt businessmen, and naive tourists that Hiaasen encountered as a journalist. Many of the subjects are similarly idiosyncratic as well: as Hiaasen notes himself, *Double Whammy* (1987) may just be "the first novel ever written about sex, murder, and corruption on the professional bass-fishing tour."

If tackling this long-neglected topic wasn't impact enough, Hiaasen has recently broadened both his appeal and his readership by publishing two novels for "young adults" *Hoot* (2002) and *Flush* (2005). Essentially the same as his adult fiction but with a PG certificate, these successful books should ensure that Hiaasen's reputation will endure for many decades to come.

James Kidd

Date 1986

Nationality USA

Other Key Works *Skin Tight* (1989), *Strip Tease* (1993), *Stormy Weather* (1995), *Sick Puppy* (2000), *Nature Girl* (2006)

Why It's Key While Hiaasen the journalist exposes corruption through exhaustive investigation, Hiaasen the novelist employs satire, sharp characterization, and page-turning plots to achieve much the same end.

Opposite Carl Hiaasen

Key Event **Adam Mars-Jones and Edmund White collaborate on *The Darker Proof***

In 1987 the extent of the devastation caused by AIDS was becoming widely known, but there was still a taboo surrounding its discussion. Adam Mars-Jones and Edmund White, two outstanding writers who had themselves seen the effects of the disease and lost loved ones to it, decided to combine their energies in stories about the epidemic's desolating effect on the gay communities in London, Europe, and the United States. This was a book which although it contained very personal responses and exceptional artistry, was also a book with a "message"; the point was partly to broaden people's perception of HIV, at a time when there was a great deal of prejudice and misunderstanding, and sufferers were often ostracized.

The stories gave unflinching accounts of the reality of living and dying with the disease, and also reached towards a metaphysical interpretation of it. "Running on Empty," one of White's atmospheric stories, typical of his elegiac strain, was added in the 1988 edition.

The protagonist, thinking about how his own life has been curtailed by chance, puts the rhetorical question, "But then what did anyone ever have… the impermanence of sexual possession was a better school than most for the way life would flow through your hands…." More resigned to the hard truth than wondering about the answer, there is still the possibility here, as in all the stories, that the answer might be love. But the stories themselves, read individually, resist sentiment as much as breast beating. Mars-Jones' "An Executor," for example, while broaching unbearable sadness, contains some wickedly comic funereal moments. *The Darker Proof: Stories from a Crisis* still stands as a testament to a particular time of sadness within two literary communities, as well as a fine example of its authors' literary and sympathetic powers.
Lucy Daniel

Date 1987 (republished in 1988 with two further stories added)

Authors Adam Mars-Jones (born 1954, UK), Edmund White (born 1940, USA)

Why It's Key The word AIDS is deliberately not used in the collection, as a way of de-stigmatizing the disease; the characters are people, rather than victims. Mars-Jones also went on to write another story collection, *Monopolies of Loss* (1992), about characters living with the HIV virus.

Key Character **Inspector Rebus** *Knots and Crosses*

The tough, worldly, even cynical, Edinburgh police detective John Rebus is the protagonist in a best-selling and award-winning series of novels by Ian Rankin. Such characters have been something of a tradition in post-war Scottish fiction, whether on television (such as in the long-running series Taggart) or in novels such as William McIlvanney's *Laidlaw* (1977). One of the original aspects of Rebus, however, is that he is based in Edinburgh, rather than the more common crime-story location of Glasgow. With Edinburgh being better known to most of the public as a tourist destination, with its castle, Festival, and Tattoo, Rebus' excursions into the Scottish capital's dark underside have proved to have a fascinating lasting appeal.

Over the series, Rankin has taken pains to create a rounded, believable character. The reader knows about his military background, his failed marriage, his taste in music, and even the (real) pub that he prefers to do his serious drinking in. Rebus champions the underdog and has little respect for those in authority. He can be tough, but we warm to him for his kind heart and concern for his fellow human beings.

When Ian Rankin named his protagonist, he was deliberately alluding to the dictionary definition of rebus as a puzzle. In interviews he has stated that he was surprised to be addressed once by a reader whose actual surname was Rebus and who claimed it was Polish. Rankin was happy to incorporate an Eastern European immigrant origin into the backstory of his hero's family.
Michael Munro

Date 1987

Author Ian Rankin (born 1960)

Nationality UK

Why It's Key The hard-drinking, tough but vulnerable policeman soon became a popular hero, transcending being pigeonholed by the detective genre, and finding his way onto television in several adaptations of the novels.

Key Event **British government tries to ban _Spycatcher_, former M15 autobiography**

In the second term of Margaret Thatcher's government, the public were treated to the spectacle of the UK government's attempts to ban the memoirs of a former senior intelligence officer in MI5, Peter Wright (1916–95). The central allegation of the book was that Roger Hollis, Director General of the service during the 1960s, had been working for the Russians for 30 years. Tracing Wright's career from his recruitment in 1955, _Spycatcher_ exposes the skulduggery of the counter-espionage business, including the bugging of diplomatic talks, plans to assassinate President Nasser during the Suez Crisis and, most controversially, a CIA-inspired plot to undermine the British Prime Minister, Harold Wilson.

No matter that most of Wright's allegations were impossible to prove and, in the case of a widespread conspiracy against the Wilson government, later retracted under cross-examination on the _Panorama_ television program. In 1985, the Attorney General began proceedings to ban publication in Australia, thus initiating the media frenzy known as the "Spycatcher affair." The prosecutors soon found themselves in the ignominious position of having to justify their suppression of the memoirs, and gag British press reports of its contents, whilst the book remained widely available overseas with sales inevitably boosted by the free publicity. Court action finally failed in 1988, but not before _Spycatcher_ had become the number one hardback bestseller in the United States with a 20-week stay on the _New York Times_ list. Wright himself cut a rather ludicrous figure, appearing in court with his trademark Aussie-style hat and openly admitting that the memoirs had been motivated by the meagre pension offered by the British government. Nevertheless, the _Spycatcher_ furore became a cause célèbre, and an object lesson in how not to keep official secrets.
Matt Birchwood

Date 1987 (first attempt at publication 1985)

Place UK

Why It's Key From the _New York Times_ (1 August, 1987): "'I've never seen a book by an unknown author take off with such a roaring start," said Marvin Brown, the publisher of Viking Penguin… Mr. Brown denied reports in the London press that Viking had set up special airport displays for British tourists."

1980–1989

647

Key Book **_The Lost Language of Cranes_**

SPOILER

The title comes from the sub-plot of the novel, which tells of research student Jerene's interest in a study of infant twins, who after being isolated, acquired a language derived from the movements of the building machinery outside their window. The motif is carried throughout the novel, which explores language, and then emotions, as things that are constructed primarily from circumstance.

When Philip decides to come out to his parents, he is startled by his father's adverse reaction. It turns out that his father is also gay, and has been leading an undercover life of illicit encounters and silent crushes on the university students he teaches. Philip has to firm up his own quite openly gay identity against the breakdown of his parents' marriage and the loss of their New York apartment. The depiction of the mother is particularly affecting as the nature of her marriage slowly becomes clear to her and there is a memorable scene in which she finally realizes the truth about her husband's sexuality. This is a novel about what people will opt for, not as the best choice, but as the easiest of difficult options.

This is a work primarily concerned with the nature of the family. We see a range of characters, including single-parent, foster, and gay (one gay character has been raised by two gay men). Structurally, the novel is intricate as it contains not only Philip's interior life, and isolated youth, but also that of his family and his roommate, Jerene, and her own family difficulties. This is a rich and thoughtful debut that tackles the complexity of modern life in 1980s New York, where easy solutions are not always forthcoming.
Royce Mahawatte

Date 1987

Author David Leavitt (born 1961)

Nationality USA

Why It's Key This first novel marked a departure for gay fiction, by placing gay identity not within the solitary individual, but very much within the family. The intergenerational gay identities Leavitt explores are touchingly written and this novel earned him the reputation, then, as an assimilationist and pro-family gay writer.

T om Wolfe was already extremely famous as innovative journalist, controversialist, and dandy well before the arrival of *The Bonfire of the Vanities*, his first work of fiction, in 1987. His journalism of the 1970s and early 1980s had sought to prick left-wing pomposity and in particular was concerned with race. His targets were misguided bleeding heart liberalism (*Radical Chic*), the ludicrous excesses of modern art (*The Painted Word*), and the self-centeredness of modern life ("The Me Decade and the Third Great Awakening"). The eye for revealing detail and ruthless illustrating of hypocrisies developed in these writings meant that *Bonfire*'s social satire was sharp and unrelenting.

The book relates the class and racial conflicts of contemporary New York, a city in which huge money was being made just blocks from grinding poverty. The plot revolves around a fatal hit-and-run accident in the Bronx in which Sherman McCoy, Wall Street's

"Master of the Universe," is involved. The event becomes a huge trial, the means for a journalistic witch-hunt, and leads to rioting and political machination. Wolfe's presentation of the city is as mean, dirty, and thoroughly grasping. *The Bonfire of the Vanities* was a massive success and was thought of as a key state-of-the-nation text; as a consequence the film rights were sold for a then record amount of US$5 million. For all this, the film missed the detail and the sensationalism of the original, and was released to an underwhelmed public.

Jerome de Groot

Date 1987

Place USA

Author Tom Wolfe (born 1930)

Why It's Key Wolfe's sensational blockbuster novel highlighted the vanity and self-obsessed nature of the contemporary United States.

Opposite **Tom Wolfe**

Key Author **William T. Vollmann** *An Afghanistan Picture Show*

W illiam Tanner Vollmann is the black sheep of contemporary American letters. As is often the case with bold and challenging literature, Vollmann's work is a source of controversy among the critical and popular readership alike; some find his fearless tenor offensive, his interest in prostitution perverse, and his intricate prose style arrogant. Others are persuaded by Vollmann's intelligent, researched writing that disrupts traditional boundaries between fiction and non-fiction, autobiography and journalism.

In the same way that a "method actor" draws on personal experience to develop a character, Vollmann – a kind of "method novelist" – immerses himself in the environments about which he writes, acquiring and refining his material through first-hand experience. Before writing *The Rifles* (1994), Vollmann actually spent two weeks in the North Pole, reliving the hardships of the Franklin Expedition. In order to properly represent the underclass in *The Royal*

Family (2000), Vollmann mingled with prostitutes and smoked crack.

Referring to himself as a "former hack journalist," Vollmann has contributed to *Spin* magazine, *Esquire*, *The New Yorker*, *Granta,* and the *New York Times Book Review*. His serious reportage has stemmed from epicenters of violence, such as Cambodia, Somalia, and Iraq. Vollmann's travels with the mujahideen through Afghanistan became the subject of his first non-fiction book, *An Afghanistan Picture Show* (1987).

Violence continues to fuel Vollmann's imagination. In his seven-volume series of historical novels, *The Seven Dreams*, the narrator called "William the Blind" recounts clashes between native North Americans and settlers. In 2004, he published *Rising Up and Rising Down*, a seven-volume, 3,300-page, illustrated treatize on violence. Monstrous books and monstrous themes.

Kiki Benzon

Date 1987

Nationality USA

Author William T. Vollmann (born 1959)

Other Key Works *You Bright and Risen Angels* (1987), *The Atlas* (1996)

Why It's Key "William T. Vollmann is a monster: a monster of talent, ambition and accomplishment" according to the *Los Angeles Times*.

Key Book
Beloved

Based loosely on a true story, Toni Morrison's fifth novel tells the story of Sethe, an ex-slave who has been ostracized for murdering her baby daughter. It is set during the Reconstruction, the years immediately following the abolition of slavery in the southern states of America. Essentially, this is a novel about interior landscapes not historical periods. Through a series of layered narratives, each taking us closer to the heart of the story, Morrison presents a vivid and memorable cast of characters, all deeply scarred in some way by their experiences.

An extraordinary achievement, *Beloved* is reminiscent of nineteenth-century slave narratives and a powerful evocation of a historical period. It is also a ghost story with the dead baby returning as a young woman, *Beloved*, to haunt Sethe.

Beloved won the Pulitzer Prize for fiction in 1988 and in May 2006, the *New York Times* called it the best American novel of the last 25 years. One American critic reckoned it now featured in more PhD theses than Shakespeare.

When *Beloved* was published, Morrison was already critically acclaimed and commercially successful, but this book was declared almost immediately to be her best. Nothing she has written since has had quite the same impact. *Beloved* established her as a mainstream cultural icon and a writer whose work was rooted in the American black experience but was nonetheless universal. The book's evocation of slavery and slavery's legacy makes it the missing part of the jigsaw in America's literary view of itself.

Kathy Watson

Date 1987

Author Toni Morrison (born 1931)

Nationality USA

Why It's Key Morrison's most famous novel met with extraordinary critical and popular success, winning the Pulitzer Prize, and almost immediately being taken up on university reading lists. It continues to top lists of great American novels.

Opposite Oprah Winfrey playing Sethe in the the film adaptation of *Beloved*

1980–1989

651

Key Passage
Borderlands (*La Frontera*)

The publication in 1987 of *Borderlands* (*La Frontera*) is a key moment in the long struggle for cultural recognition of Hispanic people in the United States. Drawing from discussions of Mexican identity that sought to define its mestizo condition (mixed-race/cultural identity) Anzaldúa established a spiritual manifesto "La conciencia de la mestiza: Towards a New Conscience" (Chapter 7) to try and deal with the different layers of cultural and sexual oppression of dark-skinned lesbians living in the United States "borderlands." Rather than a mere administrative or political division, a line, the "borderlands" itself is perceived as a spiritual or cultural state – an "open wound." And this wounded self needs a curative narrative, a discourse about itself that will allow it to heal: this is Anzaldúa's ambitious and charismatic spiritual project. The "second class" condition of indigenous populations is in part created by their acculturation under several layers of European settling waves – Spaniards, English – and trapped in a complex field of loyalties and customs, linguistic, ethical, and ethnic codes. But from this seeming hotchpotch of contradicting and opposed discourses and identities, Anzaldúa embraces that which makes the mestiza strong: her diversity, her radical differences, and particularly her identity as an Anglicized Chicana (Mexican, Native American, and Hispanic) lesbian. By reclaiming and rejecting certain aspects of the self, she redefines her identity, accepts her multiplicity, and is able to return to her place in the world.

Pedro García-Caro

Date 1987

Author Gloria Anzaldúa (1942–2004)

Nationality USA

Why It's Key Anzaldúa's autobiographical work used an innovative mixture of Spanish and English as a way of showing the author's own and the Chicano people's mixed heritage.

Key Author **Haruki Murakami**
Norwegian Wood

Accidentally occidental. With one foot in the East and another planted in the West, Haruki Murakami (born 1949) is now a household name across the globe. Once a key player in a new generation of Japanese writers holding cult status in his native Japan, Murakami now finds himself part of the Japanese establishment of celebrity. With his childhood spent in the port town Kobe, one of the first in Japan to open to the West, Haruki Murakami has a lifetime's experience of traversing cultures.

As a graduate of Tokyo's prestigious Waseda University, Murakami's foundations lie in the conventions of the Japanese establishment, yet for a time he was comfortably installed in the United States, teaching at Princeton in the early 1990s. Western stylistic traits and cultural references abound throughout his work, possibly a reflection of his exposure to Western writers such as Raymond Chandler and Jack Kerouac during his formative years.

Casting the critical eye of an outsider, Murakami tackles challenging topics such as social isolation and the alienation of the individual amidst the consumerism of modern Japan – themes at odds with the harmonious social mechanisms of his native country. Murakami hit upon a winning combination with readers with *Hard-Boiled Wonderland and the End of the World* (1985), fusing the detective genre with science fiction, packaged in a postmodernist dream form. A decade later, he produced his magnum opus, *The Wind-Up Bird Chronicle* (1995) and, with it, a departure from earlier apolitical works in his exploration of Japanese culpability during the Pacific War. *Norwegian Wood* is his best-selling novel at home and abroad. The Japanese literary establishment has not always been appreciative, despite Murakami's frequent first place on prestigious award lists, including the Kafka, Tanizaki, Yomiuri and, most recently, the Kiriyama Book Prize.
Sarah Birchwood

Date 1987

Nationality Japan

Other Key Works *After Dark* (2004)

Why it's Key Tremendously popular contemporary Japanese writer; his works have been translated into 34 languages. At the height of his celebrity he was forced to flee Japan, seeking refuge overseas.

Opposite **Haruki Murakami**

Key Book
Closing

A novelist, short story writer, and journalist since 1968, Fairbairns was an important commentator on feminist issues who used traditional modes of storytelling to explore untraditional elements of the lives of women, and the political and passionate problems they encounter. After writing her first novels on the topics of social responsibility, Fairbairns concentrated on non-fiction dedicated to environmental and social concerns.

After 1979, and the publication of *Benefit* in which she pre-empts the futuristic view of women's role in society echoed later in Margaret Atwood's *The Handmaid's Tale*, she returned to writing fiction concerned with feminist issues. *Stand We At Last* (1983) manages to span the history of women's struggles for emancipation from the mid-nineteenth century through to the 1970s by tracing five generations of women. *Here Today* (1984) explores feminist themes within a conventional "crime" setting.

Closing is the story of four women who go on a training course in sales and the men they leave behind. Though not overtly feminist, its entertaining take on women caught between Thatcherism and feminism draws attention to Fairbairns' themes of working women and power politics. Fay Weldon writes of *Closing*: "Such a pleasure to read, such fun, so intelligent, so perspicacious, so well-plotted, so unobtrusively moral, so elating" – this characterizes Fairbairns' talent of making popularly political stories that address the overtly disturbing struggles that women continue to experience.
Sophie Baker

Date 1987

Author Zoë Fairbairns (born 1948)

Nationality UK

Why It's Key *Closing* is an entertaining study of the power politics and passionate lives of a small group of women in Margaret Thatcher's 1980s. It consolidated Fairbairns' return to writing fiction concerning women's issues, and has also been seen as an ironic, feminist take on 1980s blockbuster fiction and its heroines.

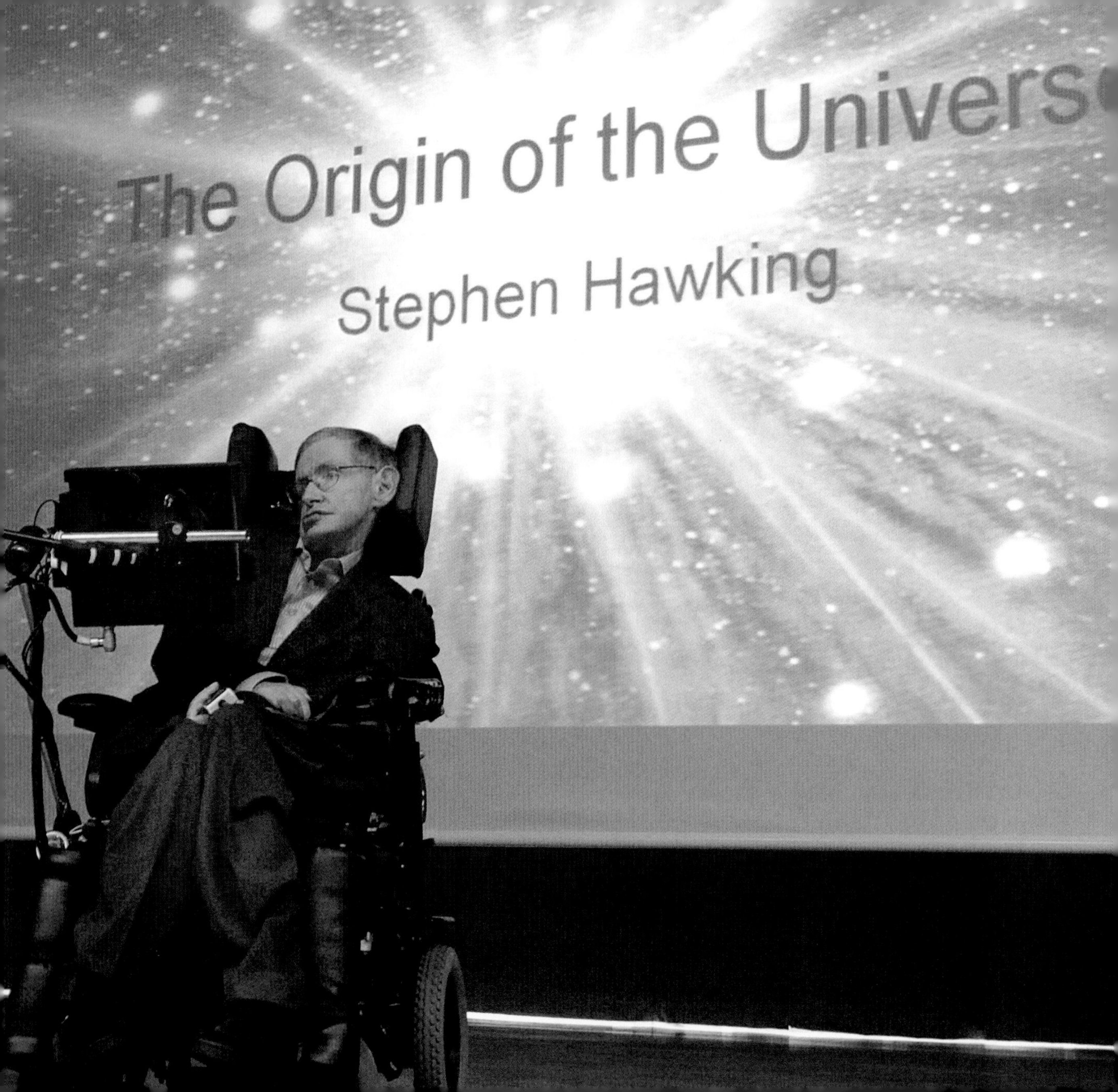
The Origin of the Univers
Stephen Hawking

Key Character **Mikage Sakurai**
Kitchen

Published at the height of Japan's economic boom, Banana Yoshimoto's debut is a quirky tale of the trials and tribulations of Japan's youth and their survival in the city. Seeking refuge from this disorientation, Yoshimoto's adolescent narrator Mikage states: "The place I like best in this world is the kitchen." Offering a vision of domestic security, Yoshimoto begins her most popular work with this intriguing contrast to the strident capitalism of "Ambitious Japan."

What follows is a depiction of the personal struggles of an often overlooked and overtaxed Japanese generation. Mikage, an orphan, is further disenfranchised when her grandmother dies, leaving her alone and bewildered amid the high-rise apartments of a sprawling Tokyo metropolis. Her new "family," a boy who works in a flower shop and his transvestite father, are the atypical characters that commonly populate Yoshimoto's contemporary Japan. Through these characters, against the backdrop of a comforting kitchen and the intricacies of food, Mikage embarks upon a journey of self-discovery, forging a path through her adolescent angst.

As Mikage proceeds to "feed her soul," we too are treated to an array of Japanese dishes – invited to join the young woman in her quest to satisfy her existentialist cravings for greater understanding and fulfilment.

The burgeoning connection between Mikage and her contemporary Yuichi is reinforced by Yoshimoto's use of dreams, an ethereal contrast to the hard-edged reality awaiting Mikage outside the warmth of the kitchen. With this dash of escapism, Yoshimoto deftly allows her heroine, and indeed her readers, to ponder the bigger questions: love, life, death, and of course the perfect *katsudon* (pork and rice dish).
Sarah Birchwood

Date 1987

Author Banana Yoshimoto (born 1964)

Nationality Japan

Why It's Key Sparking "Bananamania" in Japan, and often considered as the natural forbear of Japanese chick lit, this novella presents a narrator whose naivety belies the craft of the writer. Winner of the Umitsubame First Novel Prize, this touching story has also inspired two films and TV movies both in Japan and Hong Kong.

Key Event *A Brief History of Time* brings cosmology to the bestseller lists

Subtitled "From the Big Bang to Black Holes," *A Brief History of Time* is a report back to Planet Earth from the wilder reaches of cosmology, by one of the world's most brilliant physicists, Stephen Hawking. It deals with the origin of the universe, plus such questions as "Why does the universe go to all the bother of existing?" and the apparently paradoxical nature of black holes, hyper-dense fissures in space-time that suck in matter and which apparently let nothing escape, not even light. In the course of all this, Hawking introduces some inordinately difficult mathematics – but, having been warned by an editor that "Each equation… in the book would halve the sales," Hawking restricts himself to just one, Einstein's $E = mc^2$ (energy equals mass times the square of the speed of light).

This concession, plus the awe-inspiring subject matter, helped to keep *A Brief History* on the UK bestseller lists for a remarkable three years. It was the book that many began, but few finished – even Hawking's concessions to his publisher fail to make it an easy read. The whole phenomenon was enhanced by the extraordinary figure of Hawking himself, the youngest ever member of the Royal Society, successor to Isaac Newton to the Lucasian Chair of Mathematics at Cambridge, a genius confined to a wheelchair by a degenerative neuromuscular disease, unable to speak without a voice synthesizer. With all his afflictions Hawking seemed the embodiment of the striving human spirit, a modern Prometheus who, in his own words, sought to "know the mind of God."
Ian Crofton

Date 1988

Place UK

Author Stephen Hawking (born 1942)

Why It's Key The work of popular science by a leading physicist was a surprise bestseller.

Opposite Stephen Hawking

Key Book *Foucault's Pendulum (Il pendolo di Foucault)*

The most plot-ridden of plots and the conspiracy theory that one might have thought would end all conspiracy theories, though we know that of course it didn't…. Eco's novel about a conspiracy theory concerning the Knights Templar and a winding spiral of other associations, cults, and mysteries predated Dan Brown's 2003 bestseller *The Da Vinci Code*, displayed radical ingenuity and erudition, and was eventually about the nature of conspiracy theories, and the suggestibility of their theorists.

Eco's protagonists are a rackety bunch of intellectual mischief-makers and bibliophiles who design their own conspiracy theory, beginning as a game, entitled "The Plan." The conspirators feed data into a computer program which in turn churns out plausible sounding plots – all of which amounts to great fun until they begin believing their own mystical inventions – along with some shadowy and potentially dangerous figures.

Eco is a broad ranging and prolific academic, a professor of semiotics whose *Opera Aperta* (*The Open Work*), first published in 1962, was a major work of critical theory which influenced ideas of postmodernism. In *Foucault's Pendulum* he combined his academic brilliance not only with his preoccupation with medieval subjects, but also with the modern world of information technology, through 120 chapters of internecine plotting, which itself provokes multiple interpretation and decoding.

One of the novel's overarching subjects, disregarding all the myriad esoteric facts and allusions thrown in along its densely allusive way, is the ludic process of constructing plots, and the multiple possibilities for interpretation of all texts. It was about the nature and attraction of creativity itself, and a sense of puzzle and play in all its forms.

Lucy Daniel

Date 1988

Author Umberto Eco (born 1932)

Nationality Italy

Why It's Key Anthony Burgess called the book "an intellectual triumph, if not a fictional one." Although less popular than *The Name of the Rose* (1980) *Foucault's Pendulum* led the way for an erudite and intellectual school of modern fiction that played with historical facts, scientific theories, and complicated plotting.

Opposite Umberto Eco

Key Book
The Swimming Pool Library

Alan Hollinghurst's elegantly written debut novel, *The Swimming Pool Library*, focuses upon the sexual exploits of the rich, young, gay Will Beckwith in London in the early 1980s. Hedonistically self-absorbed in picking up men whilst swimming at the Corinthian Club and cruising around the capital, Will revels in his promiscuity during what Hollinghurst terms "the last summer of its kind" – an indication that the onset of the AIDS virus would bring an end to much of this excessive lifestyle. The gay subculture of Will's London is vividly portrayed by Hollinghurst in terms not only of the locations, meeting places, and highly graphic descriptions of sexual encounter (for which the novel has been both praised and condemned), but also in terms of the attendant threats of violence, homophobia, and police entrapment.

This episodic plotline of Will's pleasure-seeking is intertwined with his developing relationship with the aristocratic Lord Charles Nantwich, who Will rescues when Nantwich collapses whilst cottaging in a public toilet. Nantwich subsequently gives Will his personal diaries to read with the idea that Will might ghost-write his memoirs, a plot device which allows Hollinghurst to incorporate a fascinating version of gay history from the early twentieth century to the 1970s. A final shocking revelation in the diaries brings Nantwich's own history and that of Will's family together in disturbing ways.

A highly literary novel, beautifully written, and comic, sad, and sexy in turns, *The Swimming Pool Library* is a compelling novel that has helped transform the landscape of contemporary gay literature.

Simon Avery

Date 1988

Author Alan Hollinghurst (born 1954)

Nationality UK

Why It's Key A bestseller in both Britain and the United States, it won the Somerset Maugham Award in 1989 and gave a strong new drive to gay writing. Hollinghurst has subsequently developed his concern with gay cultures in *The Folding Star* (1994), The Spell (1998), and *The Line of Beauty* (2004).

Key Author **Amitav Ghosh**
The Shadow Lines

A polymathic character (a social anthropologist, journalist, novelist, and essayist), Ghosh (born 1956) has become one of the most recognized writers within postcolonial studies mainly for the exploration in his fiction of the element of space and its geographical territories outside the once colonial border. He reported for the *Hindu* on the devastation caused by the tsunami in the Andaman and Nicobar Islands in December 2004: "At these moments it seems that nothing is of value other than to act and to intervene in the course of events: to think, to reflect, to write seem trivial and wasteful." Ghosh has also been attentive to the issue of identity and to the problems of translation and language. In the specific context of India he identifies a rather "complicated relationship" with language, which results from the confrontation between the language one is born into and the language one has learned, viewing English as a "neutral territory." Amongst his novels, which have

been widely translated in several languages, the second, *The Shadow Lines* (1988), is a personal history of a family's experience of Partition in Bengal and the latest, *The Hungry Tide* (2004), is a hymn to the beauty of our world. The author comments that it "grew into a response to 9/11. I started reading Rilke then, and began to learn what he meant when he spoke of praising the world, its splendor and glory, despite the despair." Critic Pankaj Mishra defines Ghosh as one of few postcolonial writers "to have expressed in his work a developing awareness of the aspirations, defeats and disappointments of colonized peoples as they figure out their place in the world."

Letizia Alterno

Date 1988

Nationality India

Other Key Works *The Circle of Reason* (1986), *The Calcutta Chromosome* (1996), *The Glass Palace* (2000)

Why It's Key A writer whose fiction has been defined by postcolonial critic Homi Bhabha as "messing up" modernity, technology, and the local. In Ghosh's words, he has tried to weave together "the resolutely panoptical and the irreducibly local."

658

Key Character **Lenny Sethi**
Cracking India

Cracking India (*Ice-Candy-Man* in the UK) is the third novel by Bapsi Sidhwa, often described as Pakistan's finest English-language novelist, and draws on her memories of growing up in the Parsi community in 1940s Lahore. The terrifying events that accompanied the division of the sub-continent into India and Pakistan are seen in the novel through the wise yet innocent eyes of its narrator, Lenny Sethi. "My world is compressed," she announces. Four years old when the book begins, with one leg severely weakened by polio, Lenny's narrative rarely takes us further than a few streets from her affluent Lahore home.

Lenny belongs to the city's Parsi community, which anxiously awaits the future during the turbulent end of British rule and the violence of Partition. As the Parsi doctor who treats Lenny says: "We are the smallest minority in India… Only one hundred and twenty thousand in the whole world. We have to be extra wary, or we'll be neither here nor there."

Lenny is well-informed about political events, from eavesdropping on adults and listening to the news. She is equally curious about sex, watching at the local park as her attractive *Ayah* (nanny) is courted by a circle of admirers. Lenny looks on helplessly as these admirers divide themselves antagonistically into Hindus, Sikhs, and Muslims, with devastating results. Neither Lenny's age nor her relative privilege can cushion her from the effects of inter-communal violence, as a friend barely escapes the massacre of his village, her beloved *Ayah* is kidnapped, and the house next door to hers becomes a refuge for abducted women. Lenny describes the events she witnesses with "a child's boundless acceptance and curiosity." Her youthful inability to lie makes Lenny an unforgettable narrator.

The novel was filmed by Deepa Mehta in 1998, under the title *Earth* (*1947* in India).

Paul Vlitos

Date 1988

Author Bapsi Sidhwa (born 1938)

Nationality Pakistan

Why It's Key "India is going to be broken. Can one break a country? And what happens if they break it where my house is?" Lenny is a clear-sighted and inquisitive observer of the effects that Partition has on her world.

Key Characters **Oscar and Lucinda**
Oscar and Lucinda

Oscar and Lucinda won Peter Carey the first of his two Booker prizes (the second was for *True History of the Kelly Gang* in 2001). Set in the mid-nineteenth century, it can be read both as a pastiche neo-Victorian novel and as a postcolonial rewriting of history. The Reverend Oscar Hopkins and Lucinda Leplastrier are an "odd couple," two friends who never become a couple in the full sense yet whose destinies are intimately bound up with each other and with Australia's colonial history. Oscar is brought up in a remote English coastal village by a puritanical father (the historical model is Edmund Gosse's father Philip, of the Plymouth Brethren), who believes Christmas puddings are an abomination. He studies theology at Oxford, where he is nicknamed "Odd Bod," and acquires his lifelong gambling habit with surreptitious visits to the races. On the boat to Australia he meets fellow gaming addict Lucinda, heiress and owner of a glass factory. Their vicissitudes in the colony of New South Wales expose them to the stultifying conservatism of Sydney society – Oscar stays at Lucinda's house and the two are believed to be lovers which they are not – and culminate in Oscar's last gamble, a bizarre, half-deranged expedition to the outback to construct a monumental folly in the shape of a church made of glass. Through the twists and turns of Carey's dexterous narrative, the shy, nervous Oscar, and the extroverted Lucinda fascinatingly complement each other as a kind of couple-that-never-was, whose union, doomed to be only partial, is emblematic of wasted human potential under Australia's colonial dispensation.

Christopher Rollason

Date 1988

Author Peter Carey (born 1943)

Nationality Australia

Why It's Key The adventures of these two gambling friends and "odd couple" make up one of the most compelling historical novels of the late twentieth century.

Key Event **Nobel Prize in Literature is won by Naguib Mahfouz, a writer in Arabic**

Awarding the Nobel Prize for the first time to an Arab writer of novels rather than poetry – generally seen as the root of Arabic literature – was bound to cause contention. Naguib Mahfouz, however, remains one of Egypt's most popular authors. He was also no stranger to controversy.

For decades Naguib Mahfouz published his work without falling foul of either the Islamic clergy or successive regimes. A civil servant for most of his life, Mahfouz first ran into trouble in 1959 with the newspaper serialization of *Awlad Haritna* (*The Children of Gebelawi*). The novel's religious allegory provoked outrage and it was never published as a book in Egypt.

Mahfouz's work is unsurpassed in Arabic literature in terms of its range. From contemporary social realism to Islamic history, and the universe of the Ancient Egyptians, he also immortalized the street life of old Cairo. His writing contains mystical searching on the one hand and the difficulties faced in life by ordinary people on the other. He dealt with sexual and political matters, describing defeatism as well as state repression and the effects of privatization. A one-time cinema censor, several of his works have been made into films.

Mahfouz, who remained a columnist on the *Al Ahram* newspaper almost up to his death, was a respected institution in Egypt. His writing showed a willingness to push the limits of literature, experimenting with style and the mixing of Standard and spoken Arabic, as well as a keen talent for popular storytelling.

Jamal Mahjoub

Date 1988

Place Egypt

Author Naguib Mahfouz (1911–2006)

Why It's Key Mahfouz was awarded the Nobel Prize in 1988, the same year that Salman Rushdie's *The Satanic Verses* was published. Winning the prize reopened the controversy surrounding *The Children of Gebelawi*, 30 years earlier. Mahfouz was accused by extremists of being an apostate, and was stabbed on the streets of Cairo in 1994.

Key Event **Tsitsi Dangarembga's**
Nervous Conditions is published

Written in 1985, *Nervous Conditions* immediately came to international attention on its publication in 1988, and was highly praised by Alice Walker and others. The book won Dangarembga the Africa section of the Commonwealth Writers Prize in 1989. The semi-autobiographical work focuses on the female protagonist Tembu's struggle to obtain an education in white-dominated colonial Rhodesia (Zimbabwe). The book is highly significant for its consciously feminist approach. Tembu not only faces the violence of a colonial regime, but must also overcome the strictures of a highly patriarchal African society. The importance of this feminist perspective can be judged from Dangarembga's own struggle to publish *Nervous Conditions*, which was rejected by a number of Zimbabwean publishers on the grounds that it was unrepresentative of African women and their interests. The book was eventually published by The Women's Press in London, a fact which, combined with its English language medium, helped to ensure access to an international audience.

In winning her battle to publish *Nervous Conditions*, Dangarembga blazed a trail for African women writers to follow, and the international recognition that she received demonstrated the validity of her feminist approach in an African context. Dangarembga's own novel, however, remains the most significant work of Zimbabwean women's fiction to date.

Timothy Lovering

Date 1988

Place Zimbabwe

Author Tsitsi Dangarembga (born 1959)

Why It's Key *Nervous Conditions* is the first English language novel published by a black Zimbabwean woman.

1980–1989

661

Key Author **Anne Tyler**
The Accidental Tourist

In the era of the celebrity author, Anne Tyler (born 1941) is famous for avoiding the spotlight. She seldom gives interviews, and never lectures or goes on book tours. Yet neither is she celebrated for conspicuously not appearing, like Salinger or Pynchon. Perhaps this inclination toward modesty is a remnant of Tyler's Quaker upbringing, or a reflection of her unassuming Midwestern background, or a relic of her former career as a librarian. Tyler herself says, "what I hope for from a book – either one that I write or one that I read – is transparency. I want the story to shine through. I don't want to think of the writer."

Like their author, Tyler's books have a reserved, self-contained allure. Her best characters exist at one remove from their lives, like Macon Leary in *The Accidental Tourist* (1985) whose childhood is described as "a glassed-in place with grown ups rushing past, talking at him, making changes, while he himself stayed mute." Her books tell traditional stories about ordinary families, and their conflicts are human-scale. Tyler's mid- to late-1980s novels exerted a quiet influence in a decade notable for ambitious fiction like Toni Morrison's epic *Beloved* (1987) and Margaret Atwood's feminist classic, *The Handmaid's Tale* (1985). Though she became a bestselling author in the 1980s, Tyler resisted the cult of celebrity by avoiding public appearances as much as possible.

Tyler's character-based storytelling signalled a return to the work of half-forgotten Southern writers like Eudora Welty and Harper Lee. Although dismissed by some critics as formally unadventurous and middle-brow, her novels have survived because they maintain the delicate balance between popular appeal and literary merit. As is her custom, Tyler achieves this equilibrium so quietly that it looks effortless.

Dinah Roe

Date 1988 (film adaptation)

Nationality USA

Other Key Works *If Morning Ever Comes* (1964), *Breathing Lessons* (1988), *The Amateur Marriage* (2004), *Digging to America* (2006)

Why It's Key Although *Breathing Lessons* won Tyler the 1989 Pulitzer Prize, *The Accidental Tourist*, made into an Oscar-nominated film in 1988, is her most famous novel.

Opposite Scene from *The Accidental Tourist*

Key Author **Javier Marías**
All Souls (Todas las Almas)

"It's very possible that one part of my life... will forever be determined and ruled by a fiction, or by what this novel has brought me so far and what it has yet to bring." So says Javier Marías (born 1951) as narrator in *Dark Back of Time*, a "false novel" in the form of a memoir recording the extraordinary afterlife of *All Souls*.

On the face of it, *All Souls* could hardly have been less momentous: a finely crafted, elegant comedy of manners, its good humor tinged with a certain melancholy. A visiting professor at Oxford University, its unnamed narrator, goes to libraries, takes tea, gives the odd lecture, and has an affair, musing meanwhile on the evanescence of experience, the elusiveness of reality.

Since Marías had himself spent two years at Oxford as a visiting professor, his novel inevitably prompted rumor and speculation. This was in turn bound to catch the imagination of an author always haunted by a sense that memories may be more substantial than the individuals and events they recall. We are, for Marías, our residues, outlasted by our incidentals: remembered snatches of writing or conversation; photos or possessions; overheard remarks or sightings from afar. These chance impressions are not only more enduring than we ourselves, but also more influential, through the actions they may instigate in others.

The *All Souls* narrator seems a dissociated self, his moral direction not forgotten but apparently held at one remove. Habits of secrecy and self-presentation formed in Franco's Spain equip him well for a university society that runs on confidence and gossip – and for a postmodern culture in which surface is all. These preoccupations were to be developed in subsequent works like *A Heart So White* (1992) and *Tomorrow in the Battle, Think on Me* (1994).

Michael Kerrigan

Date 1988

Nationality Spain

Other Key Works *Dark Back of Time* (*Negra espalda del tiempo*, 1998)

Why It's Key *All Souls* explored the relation between lived experience and fiction. Marías presented a new kind of narrator, poised and ironic, yet self-absorbed and ultimately isolated.

Key Event **Ayatollah Khomeini pronounces a fatwa on Salman Rushdie**

In 1989, following the public burning of the novel in Bradford and protests in which several people died, the Iranian leader, Ayatollah Khomeini, pronounced a fatwa declaring that Salman Rushdie's *The Satanic Verses* was against Islam, the Prophet, and the Qur'an. While not a law, a fatwa is a religious decree that carries the weight of a legal pronouncement. The author and anyone involved in its publication were condemned to death.

The Satanic Verses, Rushdie's fourth novel, had proved controversial ever since its publication in September 1988. Literary critics complained it was difficult to follow. The fantastical novel opens with two characters falling through the air after a hijacked airplane explodes. One of them, Gibreel Farishta, is a Bollywood actor who has lost his religious faith. In a series of dreams he imagines the early days of Islam and the life of the prophet Muhammed.

The "satanic verses" are a matter of debate among Muslim scholars. The prophet is alleged to have dictated that three pre-Islamic deities be recognized as intermediaries between God and man, only to retract his words later, believing that Satan and not the Archangel had whispered them to him.

Bomb threats and attacks on publishers and translators, one of whom was killed, followed, prompting fear and the cancellation of some editions of the book. The British government rejected calls for blasphemy laws to be extended to Islam. Rushdie was afforded Special Branch protection, and effectively remained in hiding until 1998 when the Iranian government stated that the fatwa no longer applied.

Jamal Mahjoub

Date 1989

Place Iran

Author Salman Rushdie (born 1947)

Why It's Key The case triggered a debate about a possible conflict between western values such as freedom of speech, and the rights of Muslims to defend their beliefs. This issue has found echoes in a number of cases including a series of caricatures published in a Danish newspaper in 2005.

Opposite Rushdie protesters

SATAN RUSHDY
ซาตาน ซัลมาน รุสดี

ขอประทานโทษเถิดครรชิต
ขบวนการเดินขบวนต่อต้าน
MORAL MARCH AGAINST SACRILEGE

SATAN RUSHDY
ซาตาน รุสดี

SATAN RU
ซาตาน ซัลมา

Key Character **Keith Talent**
London Fields

Keith Talent is called many things in *London Fields*: a "cheat" (his profession), "The Pickoff King" (his darts nickname), "The Murderer" (his literary character). Yet perhaps the last word on the darkly comic heart of Martin Amis' seventh novel is best expressed by the first words written about him: "Keith Talent was a bad guy. Keith Talent was a very bad guy. You might even say that he was the worst guy. But not *the* worst, not the very worst ever. There *were* worse guys."

Thus writes Samson Young, Amis' slipperiest of narrators. Although Keith is bad – devious, calculating, depraved, and self-important – Young's opening joke is that Talent really isn't as "bad" as all that: far from being the worst villain in Amis' oeuvre (see the Nazis in *Time's Arrow* or Stalin in *Koba the Dread*, Keith is not even the worst "guy" in *London Fields*).

Instead, obsessed by his ever-imminent place in the big-time (of darts, crime, sex, and life), Talent never suspects his true role: as the overly-earnest stooge in a novel by Martin Amis where he plays fourth fiddle to our heroine, Nicola Six, our hapless "Foil", Guy Clinch, and even our unreliable and death-ridden "author."

So, while *London Fields* elegizes the grand narratives of a dying century (apocalypse by nuclear war, environmental collapse, not to mention those Amis staples – art, history, sex, and death), Keith fritters the millennium away with dreams, schemes and, above all else, darting glory: "'You're looking at that treble 20,' whispered Keith direly. 'Nothing else exists. *Nothing*.'"

James Kidd

Date 1989

Author Martin Amis (born 1949)

Nationality UK

Why It's Key Keith Talent was an anti-hero for a postmodern age who inspired a literary vogue for darts and saying "innit." He was formed by the low-life media voices he venerates – late-night television, tabloid sports reports, and porn. In the 1990s, when "Laddism" glorified all he held dear, a bit of Keith was visible in British men across the class divide.

665

Key Book
The Joy Luck Club

The Joy Luck Club is a novel about identity, in particular Chinese-American identity, and about the rich and complicated ties that bind us to our national and family histories. It focuses on four Chinese-American immigrant families who start a club known as "the Joy Luck Club," at which they play *mahjong* and eat together. In particular, the novel is concerned with the women in these families, and with mother-daughter relationships. The work is divided into four sections, each containing four chapters; and each chapter is narrated by one of seven female characters. According to Tan, the novel began life as a series of short stories – a number of these were published separately in magazines prior to the book's publication – and its structure reflects that genesis.

The numerous narrative strands also illustrate and illuminate the variety of perspectives given here on Chineseness and Americanness; neither is a homogenous or simple state. Identity in the novel is complex and shifting; it represents a struggle, and an adventure. Language is a key concern of the novel, with varieties of Chinese being set alongside American English, to surreal, comical, or lyrical effect. In this way different languages, and the cultures they reflect and shape, are relativized, in a way that is both playful and thought provoking. Tan's storytelling is vivid and her characters – particularly the mothers – are memorable: exasperating and moving by turns. The publication of this highly engaging book signified the emergence of a fresh and original voice in American fiction. Tan's other works include *The Kitchen God's Wife*, *The Bonesetter's Daughter*, and *Saving Fish From Drowning*.

Emily Jeremiah

Date 1989

Author Amy Tan (born 1952)

Nationality USA

Why It's Key Amy Tan's first novel, *The Joy Luck Club*, tells the stories of four first-generation Chinese-American women and their daughters. The book was an enormous popular success and was the basis of a 1993 film directed by Wayne Wang.

Opposite Amy Tan

Key Author
Leonardo Sciascia

Leonardo Sciascia was Sicilian in every fibre of his being, who dealt with Sicilian themes, notably the mafia, in virtually every book, yet who attracted the attention of readers and critics in other European and South American countries, who saw reflections of their political and moral dilemmas in Sciascia's treatment of contemporary problems. Sciascia made his biggest impact with a series of detective stories starting with *The Day of the Owl* (1961) which respected the traditions of the genre by opening with a crime and continuing with an investigation, only to undermine that tradition by refusing a neat solution that sees the criminal handed over to justice. The crime story gave Sciascia an outlet for his core creed: a tenacious trust in reason as that term had been understood in the France of the Enlightenment, a belief in justice balanced by a despair over the prospects of seeing justice done in a Sicily dominated by the mafia. "I hoped that someone would have said of me that

I had introduced Pirandellian categories into the detective story," he stated in *Sicily as a Metaphor*.

Sciascia was profoundly pessimistic, and as the mafia became in successive novels a metaphor for the exercise of power in modern society, his novels came to seem more like moral tracts for his time, and their appeal and strength was felt far away from the Sicily of their setting.

Side by side with these works, Sciascia produced a series of books in a genre which was his alone, and which can only be called "investigative essays." These were quasi-historical works, positioned at an indeterminate point on a spectrum whose extremes were fiction and chronicle. They allowed Sciascia to conduct an enquiry into some mystery or malpractice, such as the assassination of the statesman Aldo Moro by the terrorists of the Red Brigades.

Joseph Farrell

Date 1989 (death)

Nationality Italy

Other Key Works *The Council of Egypt* (1963), *Death of an Inquisitor* (1964), *One Way or Another* (1974), *Candido* (1977), *A Straightforward Tale* (1989)

Why It's Key He was the father of what has subsequently become known as "Mediterranean noir," a style of detective novel which has freed itself from its Anglo-American predecessors.

666

Key Character **Owen Meany**
A Prayer for Owen Meany

Physically stunted and cerebrally overgrown, Owen's story is told by his best friend, John Wheelwright. He is the son of the Meany Granite Quarry, petted by all the girls because of his doll-like stature, and with a mesmerizing effect on adults, too. With his best ever shot at a Little League game he also kills his best friend's mother, whom he idolizes, with what he ever after calls "THAT FATED BASEBALL." (Owen speaks in capital letters, to indicate the strange glitch in his vocal cords that has made his voice a permanent nasal scream.) Owen's many other idiosyncrasies, aside from his freakish, uncanny voice, include translucent skin, moral seriousness even as a child (most of the book deals with John and Owen's childhoods), and a strange attachment to a terrifying stuffed armadillo.

The set piece of the Nativity in which Owen plays baby Jesus, with disastrous results, is both comic and obscurely horrific, but also part of a theological theme which resonates throughout the book. Owen is

convinced he has seen the date of his own death, and that he will be an "instrument of God," about which he is completely right, through both a heroic death and his effect on his best friend; he is the reason John Wheelwright believes in God.

He aids John in other ways, notably the sawing off of one of John's fingers, to prevent him from having to fight in Vietnam (despite joining up himself); a similar single-minded moral purposefulness leads to his inevitable martyrdom and eventual status as an ideological hero, in an age that needs them. *A Prayer for Owen Meany* is set against the Vietnam War, but also in John's Owen-less present, the Reagan administration of the 1980s. If you read it now, it still has disturbingly topical applicability to United States foreign policy.

Lucy Daniel

Date 1989

Author John Irving (born 1942)

Nationality USA

Why It's Key Owen Meany is perhaps Irving's most profound creation, a small boy with a strange voice who becomes an ideological hero. His story has become a hugely well-loved bestseller.

Key Author
Thomas Bernhard

Plagued by lung disease for most of his life, Thomas Bernhard (1931–89) lived in Obernathal, a tiny village in Upper Austria, where he bought a house in the 1960s. He appeared to relish his status as Austria's greatest living writer, while flaying his country, and especially its middle class, with pitiless single-mindedness. A classic case of the "Nestbeschmutzer" (literally, "someone who fouls his own nest"), Bernhard's final play, *Heldenplatz* (*Heroes' Square*), was commissioned to mark the 50th anniversary of the Anschluss with Hitler's Germany. The play attacked Austrian self-delusion about the country's complicity with Nazism. It was condemned by then president Kurt Waldheim – whose murky wartime activities rather underlined the play's point.

The prose of his novels, consisting as it does of extensive interior monologue, has intimidated many readers, as has their unblinking searching out of some of the most unpleasant aspects of character and reality.

None of this precludes a savage, bleak humor in his portraits of obsessive characters: the architect of *Corrections* (modelled on Wittgenstein), the endlessly procrastinating writer of *Concrete* (1982), or the final (self?) portrait of a misanthropic loner in *Extinction* (1986).

Die Ursache (*The Cause*), the first of five volumes of autobiography, appeared in 1975 (they were collectively translated as *Gathering Evidence*, 1985). Here Bernhard revealed the roots of his disgust at human cruelty and hypocrisy in his childhood experiences, but also his great tenderness for his grandfather, himself a writer, who encouraged his interest in music, and was one of the most important influences on his life.

Cathy Benson

Date 1989 (death)

Nationality Austria

Other Key Works *Frost* (1963), *Gargoyles* (*Verstörung*, 1967), *The Lime Works* (*Das Kalkwerk*, 1970), *The Loser* (*Der Untergeher*, 1983), *Woodcutters* (*Holzfällen: Eine Erregung*, 1985), *Old Masters* (*Alte Meister*, 1985)

Why It's Key Bernhard won every Austrian literary prize, in a career of unrelenting literary harassment of the bourgeoisie, its pieties, and face-saving myths.

1980–1989

667

Key Book
Like Water for Chocolate

SPOILER

Laura Esquivel's first novel was a worldwide phenomenon which brought magic realism to blockbuster fiction. At the time of the Mexican Revolution, Tita and Pedro are in love, but forbidden to marry – instead she must care for her ungrateful mother until she dies. So Pedro marries Tita's sister to be close to her, and they spend 22 years mutually enthralled, stoking and stirring each other just below simmering point, until finally coming to the boil. The foregoing summary is a shoddy emulation of Esquivel's intricate intertwining of food, sex, and magic. From its opening scene, in which the narrator, Tita's great-niece, tells us the problem with crying when chopping onions is that "the next thing you know you just can't stop," this is a tale of compulsion, which plays out the universal truth of the book's epigraph: "To the table or to bed/You must come when you are bid."

Written as a monthly serial, recipes head the chapters, marking important feasts. Tita's tears flavor her sister's wedding cake, instigating a bout of general vomiting; her other sister ingests Tita's sublimated passion, and becomes a nymphomaniac prostitute (and later a general in the revolutionary army). Tita enters Pedro, gives him exquisite pleasure through the medium of food. But the phrase "like water for chocolate" in the text refers not to erotic passion, but Tita's sheer rage at her enslavement. Her bitter sister Rosaura dies of epic flatulence, while after all that time pent up, the release of Pedro and Tita's desire is so powerful it brings them to the brink of death. It's a mythic, fantastic love that inspires fertility and indiscriminate mating far and wide. A magical cookery book, a unique culinary-historical romance which tells through each of its recipes "the story of a love interred," it caught the public imagination, and capitalized on the book-buying public's insatiable erotic and culinary cravings.

Lucy Daniel

Date 1989

Author Laura Esquivel (born 1950)

Nationality Mexico

Why It's Key Esquivel's historical novel about a Mexican girl who shows her emotions through her cooking was the number one bestseller in Mexico for two years. In 1993 the book was released in the United States, and was also made into a film, creating a joint runaway success.

Key Character **Mr Stevens**
The Remains of the Day

While on a motoring tour across England in 1956, ageing butler Mr Stevens reflects on his life in service in the years preceding World War II. His emotional repression, tragic self-deceptions, and persistent self-justifications make him an intriguingly unreliable narrator. Throughout the novel he skirts fastidiously around painful or difficult issues; nevertheless, the reader is able to build up a picture of his heartbreakingly mismanaged personal relationships, and is prompted to reflect on the wider political implications of his attitudes and actions.

Lord Darlington, the English aristocrat whom Stevens serves with unquestioning loyalty, is seen associating with Oswald Mosley, of the British Union of Fascists, and Joachim Von Ribbentrop, Hitler's ambassador to Britain. Stevens puts absolute trust in his master's judgement and refuses, even with the benefit of hindsight, to speak or hear ill of him. When challenged on his failure to question Darlington's instruction to sack two Jewish housemaids, Stevens responds that he was only following orders.

The self-effacing Stevens hovers on the margins of twentieth-century history, refusing to acknowledge that he has any part in what he calls "the great debates of the nation." However, the values he represents – of knowing one's place in a social hierarchy, unquestioning deference to authority, and belief in strong leaders – all serve the anti-democratic political tendencies of the time. Thus this novel might be read as exploring the relationship of the "ordinary" person to politics, and diagnosing the social and psychological conditions in which fascism can take root and thrive.

Anna Tripp

Date 1989

Author Kazuo Ishiguro (born 1954)

Nationality UK

Why It's Key Ishiguro's skilful portrayal of Stevens' emotional and moral blindspots make this a profoundly moving and thought-provoking account of what the butler didn't see – or didn't allow himself to see.

Opposite Anthony Hopkins portrayed Mr Stevens in the film adaptation of *Remains*

668

Key Book
A History of the World in 10½ Chapters

With its innovative narrative strategies and generic frame-breaking, *A History of the World in 10½ Chapters* is a masterpiece of postmodern game-playing. However, this is a game with high stakes and a serious purpose, designed to challenge and unsettle the reader. Barnes asks profound and pressing questions about myth, history, and art, about cultural patterns of exclusion and persecution, and about what happens to human beings at moments of crisis or revelation.

The first voice we hear is that of a woodworm stowing away on Noah's ark. With engagingly mordant and iconoclastic wit, he speaks on behalf of those "Not Wanted on Voyage," and gives an alternative perspective on the familiar Biblical story: Noah is seen as an incompetent tyrant who mismanages the logistics and terrorizes the animals he is supposed to be saving. This woodworm narrator is a brilliantly conceived deconstructive device: he is a parasite released into one of the founding myths of western culture, to eat away at its framework.

The remaining nine and a half chapters range from a fictionalization of the hijacking of the Achille Lauro to a critique of Gericault's painting *The Raft of the Medusa*, from a personal meditation on love to an unsettling vision of heaven. Ultimately this book is about the functions of storytelling in human cultures. Barnes shows how stories are used to categorize, justify and control, to construct truths and exercise power – but also to explore, to ask questions, and to consider alternatives.

Anna Tripp

Date 1989

Author Julian Barnes (born 1946)

Nationality UK

Why It's Key *A History of the World in 10½ Chapters* is a novel that is not a novel. Barnes constructs a collection of tantalizingly interlinked narratives, which draw from the conventions of the novel, the short story and the essay, but which ultimately represent a new and unclassifiable literary form.

Daphne du Maurier (1907–89) was one of the best-selling novelists of the early and mid-twentieth century, and her later influence encompasses film, thriller writing, and historical fiction. She came from a cultured family – her father was a successful actor-manager, and her grandfather a famous novelist (George du Maurier, author of *Trilby*). She was a master of suspense and sensation, with a virtuosic understanding of the psychology of fear.

Rebecca (1938) is generally taken to be her masterpiece, a dark romantic novel of intrigue and horrible passion. It recounts the tale of an innocent (never named) who finds it difficult to shake off the ghost of her new husband's first wife (Rebecca). The moral ambiguity of the novel demonstrates du Maurier's complexity and challenge to genre – whilst Rebecca ends (probably) happily, the couple are compromised by murder, arson, and jealousy. The book is indebted to the work of the Brontës (in later

life she wrote a biography of Branwell Brontë). Its success made du Maurier one of the most famous and read writers in the world. Further thrillers set in Cornwall were lean, sharp pieces of writing. The narrative drive of her writing led to her work being successfully adapted for the cinema, including famous films of *Rebecca* and the short stories "Don't Look Now" (1973) and "The Birds" (1963). These three key works demonstrate the eeriness and almost gothic nature of her writing; certainly the threat of the unknown and repressed anxieties figure highly in her work.

Jerome de Groot

Date 1989 (death)

Nationality UK

Other Key Works *Gerald: A Portrait* (1934), *Jamaica Inn* (1936), *Frenchman's Creek* (1941), *My Cousin Rachel* (1951)

Why It's Key Daphne du Maurier was one of the twentieth century's most successful writers of popular novels and period novels of sensation.

Opposite **Daphne du Maurier**

1980–1989

671

Key Character **Jasmine Vijh**
Jasmine

The Bengali-American writer Bharati Mukherjee had already received critical recognition before she published her third novel, *Jasmine*, in 1989. Its eponymous protagonist is born into a Hindu family in a brutal, backward Punjab. Blessed with quick intelligence and strong self-preservation instincts, Jasmine eventually leaves India and enters the United States as an illegal immigrant.

In keeping with Mukherjee's customary preoccupation with lurid events, Jasmine survives a series of violent episodes and commits her own crimes. A fugitive from justice, she is portrayed as a woman in constant flight, moving westward in Mukherjee's conscious reworking of America's pioneer-settler ideology.

Leaving behind a dystopian India, a grimly industrial Florida, and the ghettoized Indian communities of New York in favor of Iowa and assimilation into the (white) American mainstream,

Jasmine finally heads west again – to California – but her crimes never catch up with her. Self-interested, tough, and morally ambiguous, Jasmine works her way through a succession of adoring men. She is young, beautiful, and confident that her sexuality – rather than natural abilities, hard work, or platonic relationships – constitutes her fastest route to American success. Although she endures numerous vicissitudes, Jasmine (birth name Jyoti) is usually defined by men, who variously name her Jasmine, Jase, and Jane.

Jasmine epitomizes a key phase of Mukherjee's unfolding immigrant dream, presenting an unsympathetic protagonist whose exceptionalism and individualism are continually stressed. This bold novel, with its paean to liminality and the frontier, allows South Asians, exemplified by Jasmine, to take their place in the longer history of immigrant America.

Ruth Maxey

Date 1989

Author Bharati Mukherjee (born 1940)

Nationality USA

Why It's Key A literary breakthrough for Calcutta-born writer Bharati Mukherjee, the most well-known chronicler of South Asian American experience, *Jasmine* proved controversial since its amoral protagonist's American assimilation is achieved on the basis of her sexual desirability and conscious rejection of ghettoization.

Key Book *The Ages of Lulu* (*Las edades de Lulú*)

After the death of long-time dictator Francisco Franco in November 1975, Spanish culture exploded like a can of condensed gazpacho that had been boiling for too long. Obviously, neither Spain nor gazpacho were intended for that kind of recipe. The period known as *la movida* (the rave) and its associated *destape* – literally "taking off clothes" – were part of the generalized youthful celebrations after such a long period of state-enforced Catholic prudery. In this context, the erotic novel by Almudena Grandes, *The Ages of Lulu*, made its appearance. It sent ripples through the Spanish literary scene, partly because it was authored by a woman, partly because it uncovered the new sexual mores embraced by Spaniards. The story of a woman's coming of age, and of her sexual initiation as the Francoist regime is trying to keep its grip on moral and political power is narrated from the vantage point of the more tolerant and mature present.

At 30, the narrator reminisces her sexual memoirs, a story of increasing participation in all kinds of sexual experiences with a strong preference for threesomes and cunnilingus. Voyeuristic and lurid, the numerous sex scenes are the intimate landscape of what goes unseen in the Almodóvar films of the period (particularly *Laberinto de pasiones* [1987] and *Átame* [1990]) which should accompany the reader at all times to understand the celebration of the kinky yet still provincial Madrid of the 1980s. A good though restrained film adaptation came out the following year (directed by Bigas Luna), after the novel had been awarded the 11th Vertical Smile prize, the highest erotic literature prize in Spain. Note that the prize's age, like Lulu's sexual life, parallels the new democratic period.

Pedro García-Caro

Date 1989

Author Almudena Grandes (born 1960)

Nationality Spain

Why It's Key The popularity of the erotic novel *The Ages of Lulu* fed into the new freedom associated with the Spanish cultural movement known as *la movida*.

672

Key Event
Rose Theatre is rediscovered

Every summer, theatregoers brave the London weather to watch performances at Shakespeare's Globe, a reconstruction of the Elizabethan theatre on the south bank of the Thames. Many, however, are unaware that a real Elizabethan theatre lies just a few yards away, beneath the headquarters of the Health and Safety Executive. In 1989, Museum of London archaeologists working on the site discovered the foundations of the Rose – a playhouse built by Philip Henslowe in 1587 where some of the most important plays of Shakespeare's time were performed. A fierce campaign was waged to preserve the foundations: in his final public speech, Laurence Olivier paraphrased Shakespeare's *Henry V* in proclaiming, "Cry God for Harry, England, and the Rose!". The campaign was ultimately successful, and the remains of the Rose still lie in a specially built chamber at the base of Rose Court office block. The structures are protected by sand and concrete until they can be safely displayed, and lighting is used to indicate their location.

Part of the interest of the Rose lies in its being our most tangible clue to what the outdoor Shakespearean playhouses were actually like: their layout, their dimensions, their materials. On a more emotional level, the site is charged with significance for anyone who cares about drama. It was here that Shakespeare's *Titus Andronicus* and *Henry VI* were probably staged, that Edward Alleyn confronted audiences with the "high astounding terms" of Marlowe's *Tamburlaine*, and that Hieronimo in *The Spanish Tragedy* bit out his tongue rather than speak to his tormentors. The foundations of much more than a playhouse lie hidden under that building in Southwark.

Tom Rutter

Date 1989

Place UK

Why It's Key The remains of one of London's first theaters lie underneath a Southwark office block. It was the stage for the plays of some of England's most famous writers: William Shakespeare (1564–1616), Christopher Marlowe (1564–93), Thomas Kyd (1558–94), and others.

Key Author **Walter Mosley**
Devil in a Blue Dress

In his noir novels Walter Mosley (born 1952) presented us with an unseen, previously pretty marginalized Los Angeles. Mosley sets his stories in Watts and around, reclaiming a black noir experience, and along the way reinvigorating a genre that has generally been, in the mainstream at least, fairly color-blind.

The hugely successful *Devil in a Blue Dress* introduced us to Easy Rawlins. Part Chester Himes' flawed hero, part Raymond Chandler's maverick private eye, Rawlins is a complex, engaging and lean creation. *Devil* presents his initiation into the murky criminal interface between white and black worlds. Rawlins aspires to be his own man, to own property, to have a good job, but is constantly undermined by outside social forces beyond his control. The only way to shirk the implacable definition America has prepared for him is to go outside normal social interaction, to live beyond the law whilst appearing to be the very model of propriety.

The sequel *A Red Death* (1991) continues Mosley's reinvigoration of the genre, but it also extends and develops the noir novel, moving from the relatively simple genre paradigms and moral simplicity of *Devil* to consider communism, civil rights, espionage, government corruption, and an increasingly complex sense of national/racial identity.

Whilst *Devil* gestured towards a preoccupation with wider issues than the genre novel was able to deal with (racism, government corruption, paedophilia, interracial relationships, mortgages), it was still in thrall to its formal plot concerns. *A Red Death* eschews such a generically narrative-led approach for a wide-ranging meditation on Americanness (and un-Americanness). Along with James Ellroy, Walter Mosley can reasonably claim to have reinvigorated the noir genre in the early 1990s.
Jerome de Groot

Date 1990 (publication)

Nationality USA

Other Key Works *A Red Death* (1991), *White Butterfly* (1992), *Black Betty* (1994), *RL's Dream* (1995)

Why It's Key Mosley's hard-boiled detective fiction reinvigorated the genre for the 1990s.

Key Author
Octavio Paz

Few writers explored and expanded their country's canon while engaging the world's literary traditions as comprehensively as poet and essayist Octavio Paz (1914–1998), winner of the 1990 Nobel Prize in Literature. Born in the midst of Mexico's revolutionary turmoil, he was initiated in literature while browsing through his grandfather's library. Poetry became his vocation and diplomacy his chosen career. He embraced the fight against fascism during the Spanish Civil War, but was repelled by Republicans' fratricidal violence. In Paris, he romped with the surrealists. In the United States, he imbibed the lessons of Anglo-American modernism. His discovery of India, and of traditions more ancient even than Mexico's pre-Hispanic cultures, led to one of the great adventures in critical thought.

Paz resisted political convenience as strongly as he resisted populist literary formulations. He opposed authoritarianism in whatever shape it took, famously resigning from his ambassador's post in New Delhi after the Mexican army opened fire on students, and falling out with old friends over the persecution of Cuban intellectuals. Through his editorship of key supplements and magazines – notably *Vuelta* – he became Mexico's most influential writer.

His youthful poetry, sensuous and earthy, revels in the contemplation of simple pleasures. Later poems reflected a sharp, omnivorous intellect. It was as an essayist, however, that he had the greatest impact. *The Labyrinth of Solitude* (1950) remains the most highly regarded meditation on the essence of Mexican culture. In awarding the Nobel, the Swedish Academy rewarded his success in combining, within an extraordinary body of work, modernity and tradition, the native and the cosmopolitan.
Ángel Gurría-Quintana

Date 1990

Nationality Mexico

Other Key Works *Under Your Clear Shade* (1937), *The Labyrinth of Solitude* (1950), *A Tree Within* (1987)

Why It's Key Paz was one of Latin America's most incisive intellectuals. The previous year's Nobel had also been given to a Spanish language author (Camilo José Cela), but the Prize underlined Paz's importance as a prose essayist and as boundary-pushing poet.

Key Author **A.S. Byatt**
Possession

With over 20 novels to her name, A.S. Byatt (born 1936) is one of the most acclaimed authors of post-war Britain. A distinguished academic, Byatt left education behind to become a full time writer, often contributing columns and articles to newspapers. Controversy arose when, in her *New York Times* column, she criticized the Harry Potter novels, and especially the adults who read them, claiming their imagination was stunted by reading such uninspiring prose. Her own writing is multi-layered and she has described her own work as web-like, illustrating the delicate strands linking her themes and imagery.

Byatt's sister is Margaret Drabble, another author, though their relationship is supposedly fraught with rivalry. Suggestions for this sibling squabbling are as diverse as envy over university degree results, to Drabble's unsympathetic portrayal of their mother in her own novels.

In *Possession*, the influence of earlier writers on her own work can be seen: D.H. Lawrence and Henry James in particular. *Possession* called for Byatt to pastiche the poetry of the early nineteenth century, the fictitious poets in the novels writing verses to one another. Her novels imbibe the culture of the times, alluding to philosophical ideas and political nuances of the age, creating work of depth and richness that can be both exhilarating and thought provoking.

Thomas Dymond

Date 1990 (publication)

Nationality UK

Other Key Works The Shadow of the Sun (1964), The Virgin in the Garden (1978), Possession (1990), Angels and Insects (1992), The Biographer's Tale (2000)

Why It's Key Dame Antonia Susan Byatt is a leading British post-modern novelist. Her novel *Possession* won the Booker Prize in 1990.

Opposite A.S. Byatt

674

Key Book
The Mambo Kings Play Songs of Love

Born in New York City to Cuban immigrants, Oscar Hijuelos was well placed to depict the lives of his two main characters, the brothers Cesar and Nestor Castillo, jazz musicians who leave Cuba for America in 1949. While they can't help but be homesick for their native island and loved ones left behind, the new world has so much to offer the brothers. It is a land of plenty (especially of food, booze, sex, and fancy cars) compared to pre-Castro Cuba, especially for those with money, and to those with talent, it is still a land of opportunity. Latin American-tinged jazz is all the rage and the brothers' mambo sound takes them to places they would never have dreamed about, to playing to adoring audiences in the dancehalls and nightclubs of 1950s America, to radio and television appearances, to making hit records. The downside is the hard work involved, especially the strains of touring, and the casual anti-Hispanic racism that they encounter almost everywhere outside their circle of fellow musicians.

Nostalgia informs the novel; not only in terms of the brothers reminiscing about their lives in Cuba, but as Cesar in particular looks back on their 1950s glory from a rather lonely old age. But it is also full of the energy of the irresistible music itself, of the ambition, arrogance and drive to "make it" common to the Latin American immigrant experience in postwar America. Hijuelos uses the brothers' relationships and their new families to give a vivid picture of the process of change from immigrant, to "hyphenated American," to native New Yorker.

Michael Munro

Date 1990

Author Oscar Hijuelos (born 1951)

Nationality USA

Why It's Key Hijuelos was the first writer of Hispanic descent to win the Pulitzer Prize for fiction. His novel opened a window onto the lives of Latin American immigrants in New York, exposing this world to a wider American audience as well as readers elsewhere. It inspired a film, *The Mambo Kings*, in 1992, starring Antonio Banderas.

Key Book
I Was Dora Suarez

Derek Raymond brought a new metaphysical intensity to what is nominally a crime thriller, set in an unglamorized London underworld as the AIDS epidemic took hold in the late 1980s. It is a frankly disgusting and disturbing book, in which the physical details of violence and injury, illness and death are dwelt on – not simply to further the plot, but repeatedly revisited – with what seems an appalling relish. The original publisher is said to have rejected the manuscript when it moved him to vomit.

Raymond's unnamed hero is a cynical police detective typical of the genre – an obstreperous maverick who insists on working alone and is recalled to duty after a brush with authority only because of a staff shortage. Austere and straight as a die, he finds himself surrounded by fools and madmen; but he is also a romantic figure, and falls deeply in love with his abused victim as he sets out to avenge her death. Eschewing the genre's usual attractions – excitement,

glamor, the thrill of the chase – the author presents us with a bleak and despairing worldview, and conjures a meditation on life and death, good and evil, which can be compared with Jacobean tragedy or Dostoevsky.

In his autobiography, *The Hidden Files* (1992) Raymond described *I Was Dora Suarez* as "my atonement for fifty years' indifference to the miserable state of this world; it was a terrible journey through my own guilt, and through the guilt of others."
Bruce Millar

Date 1990

Author Derek Raymond (1931–1994)

Nationality UK

Why It's Key Raymond was the son of a wealthy textiles manufacturer who dropped out of Eton for a rackety life in the criminal and literary underworlds of England and France. His first literary success, *The Crust on its Uppers*, set in London's gangland, was published in 1962. *I Was Dora Suarez* was his masterpiece.

Key Character **Dr. Kay Scarpetta**
Post Mortem

It's difficult to imagine now how different the world of crime fiction would be today without Dr. Kay Scarpetta. In a world where the popularity of television shows such as *Crime Scene Investigation* have made everyone into an expert in forensic science (to the extent that lawyers have complained that members of the public have unrealistic expectations of its accuracy), it's easy to forget that in 1990, when the first Kay Scarpetta novel was published, DNA testing was barely understood and few people had any idea what happens to a murder victim once they're on the pathologist's slab.

Patricia Cornwell's unflinching and often gut-wrenching descriptions of crime scenes and autopsies captured the imagination of readers. Kay Scarpetta always retains a strong empathy with the victims, allowing her outrage at their suffering to drive her to a resolution.

Away from the morgue, Scarpetta's interests are wholly domestic. When she visits the homes of the killer's victims, she's as likely to comment on their choice of soft furnishings as their injuries. She spends much of her spare time cooking and the all the novels are filled with lovingly described scenes of food preparation (to such an extent that two spin-off recipe books have been published to go with the novels). It's this mix of humanity and our morbid fascination with the dead which has kept Scarpetta at the top of the crime fiction charts for so long.
Frances Powell

Date 1990

Author Patricia Cornwell (born 1956)

Nationality USA

Why It's Key Scarpetta's impact on crime fiction, on screen as well as in publishing, is almost impossible to quantify. Her toughness and vulnerability as a woman in a man's world blazed a trail for dozens of other fictional female crime fighters. However, it's her brilliance as a pathologist that really makes her stand out.

Opposite Patricia Cornwell

Key Character **Karim Amir**
The Buddha of Suburbia

After the international success of his 1985 screenplay, *My Beautiful Laundrette*, British writer Hanif Kureishi published his prize-winning first semi-autobiographical novel, *The Buddha of Suburbia*, in 1990. Its protagonist, Karim Amir, a streetwise Londoner of Pakistani and white English parentage, relates in humorous, painful detail his sentimental and sexual education from suburban teenager to twenty-something in the heart of the capital.

The novel immediately establishes the biracial Karim's complex relationship with national belonging and later, whites, blacks and Asians all try to position him within an increasingly multicultural 1970s Britain. Restless, independent, and ambitious, he recognizes the absurdity of much rhetoric on race and resists this definition by others.

Karim's protean ability to adopt and reject identities leads naturally to his chosen profession of acting and his desire to thrive in this stems, in part, from his need to carve a place for himself in Britain. His energetic hedonism – the drug-taking and casual sex so often practised by Kureishi's male characters – is, moreover, a means of numbing much of the pain and confusion he experiences.

Karim consistently makes use of other people in his bid to achieve success, only to find himself exploited in turn. He remains essentially passive and selfish, and lacks the political commitment of his childhood friend, Jamila, an anti-racism activist. But his youthful amorality is also part of his fascination and appeal, with much of the narrative's tension generated by a readerly curiosity about whether Karim's conscience will eventually get the better of him.

Kureishi satirized, by turns, the pretensions and gullibility of affluent suburbanites, and the latent prejudices and cold-hearted pomposity of putatively liberal theater producers.

Ruth Maxey

Date 1990

Author Hanif Kureishi (born 1954)

Nationality UK

Why It's Key Through Karim, Kureishi articulated the difficulties – and celebrated the possibilities – of growing up mixed-race in Britain. Karim's brutally honest, first-person confessional narrative proved influential on later writers, thanks to its vibrant, humorous expression of a certain kind of second-generation British Asian experience.

678

Key Event *Afternoon, a story*
is the first hypertext novel

Before its publication by Eastgate Systems in 1990, *Afternoon, a story* appeared at the 1987 Association for Computing Machinery Hypertext conference, where author Michael Joyce (born 1945) and hypertext theorist Jay David Bolter demonstrated their electronic writing software, Storyspace. The software allows writers to create hyperlinks between sections of text (called lexias) so that the story develops according to what narrative thread the reader pursues. This "networked" structure means that one literary work will produce many different readings – multiple storylines of various lengths. The narrative itself is unstable because, unlike the codex novel, a hyperfiction is not "fixed" to the printed page.

Afternoon may be appreciated not only as a groundbreaking technical feat, but also for its haunting mystery and lyrical prose style. Joyce tells the story of Peter, a recently divorced technical writer who witnesses a car crash that may or may not have involved his ex-wife and their son. In an early lexia, Peter states: "I want to say I may have seen my son die this morning." This curious and weighty comment opens up into a narrative web whose very indeterminacy reflects the fluidity and frailty of memory and knowledge.

The first of its kind, *Afternoon* frequently appears in academic discussions of hypertext and postmodern literature. Some critics examine the narratological effects of a hyperlinked, flexible form, while others speculate about the demise of print texts in the digital age. While *Afternoon* and its electronic siblings may not immediately succeed paper-based fiction, the literary landscape is clearly changing: *Afternoon* has become a standard text in undergraduate literature classes, and is included in the *Norton Anthology of Postmodern American Fiction*.

Kiki Benzon

Date 1990

Place USA

Why It's Key In his *New York Times Book Review*, Robert Coover deemed the work "utterly essential to an understanding of this new art form." Considered to be the first hyperfiction, *Afternoon* established a technological and literary precedent for the stream of electronic and multimedia narrative work that would follow.

Key Author
Yusif Idris

A physician by training, Yusif Idris (1927–1991) possessed the ability to diagnose the nation's social and political ills and cast them into a dense, but brief and polyphonic, narrative. His use of various levels of the Arabic language (from the erudite and elevated to the mundane vernacular) broke with the formal Arabic tradition of his predecessors and contemporaries. The variety of linguistic forms and the ease with which he switched between them enhanced the semantic breadth of the language and endowed it with fresh possibilities for expression. Through a combination of his affirmative character, an unsure belief in the post-1952 Revolutionary regime, and a Kafkaesque outlook, Idris depicted a range of controversial topics that broke both literary and social canons. Homosexuality and the impact of social deprivation on women are among his thorny subjects. *A House of Flesh* (1971) and *The Cheapest Nights* (1954) are representative of his story collections, which have all been translated into English.

Political satire is at the center of Idris' dramatic output. *Al-Farafir* (1964) and *The Striped Ones* (1969) are classic examples of committed literature. Their depiction of the relationship between a dictatorial regime and its oppressed subjects has an Orwellian quality. Again, Idris' use of the vernacular represents a milestone towards the creation of the "third language" for theater that was sought and advocated by Tawfiq Al-Hakim and his contemporaries.

Idris was nominated for the Nobel Prize in Literature several times, but was beaten to it by fellow Egyptian Naguib Mahfouz in 1988. This was Idris' greatest disappointment of which he made no secret. A media war erupted between the two on TV, radio, and in the press. Idris' fiery temperament fuelled the debate over who most deserved the prize. Many critics and writers conceded both in public and in private that Idris was the better writer.

Ashraf Eissa

Date 1991 (death)

Nationality Egypt

Why It's Key Translated into over 20 languages, Idris is the undisputed master of the Arabic short story. Purported to be the Gogol of Arabic literature, Idris' contribution to the language, form, and subject matter of the Arabic short story remains the most significant to date.

1990-1999

679

Key Book
How the García Girls Lost Their Accents

Carla, Sandra, Yolanda, and Sofía are the four sisters who lose, among other things, their accents and discover, as immigrants to the USA, homesickness, discrimination, men, marijuana, university, love, babies, divorce, mental breakdown, poetry…. Good and bad, loss and gain are mixed up in their growing up.

Several of these 15 stories had previously appeared separately, but here they work together to novelistic effect, telling of the García family's move from the Dominican Republic to the USA, fleeing Trujillo's dictatorship. The story is told in reverse from 1989 to 1956, through the shifting viewpoints of the sisters, and their Mami and Papi. It begins with Yolanda's trip back to the island as a grown woman (mistaken for a tourist who speaks no Spanish), with all her family's scandals and squabbles to look back on, and ends with the family's arrival in the U.S. 30 years earlier, and their island life before that.

Alvarez writes in English, but her work is extremely popular in Latin America. In this, her first book, her greatest feat was to convey – wittily, movingly – both the process of immigrant acculturation and the universal experience of gaining a foothold in the world through language; for example, the girls' mother speaking in mixed metaphor, which shows she is still "green behind the ears"; Carla, after seeing a "pervert," attempting to explain what she has seen to a policeman, with the two barriers of imperfect English and the embarrassing delicacy of the knowledge she has just gained. Yolanda becomes a poet, and her relationships fail or succeed according to how free she is able to be with her language and her men. Both thematically within the book and literally beyond it, Alvarez gave us new accents to listen to, and new voices for telling the classic immigrant story.

Lucy Daniel

Date 1991

Author Julia Alvarez (born 1950)

Nationality USA

Why It's Key Alvarez was one of the four Latina writers marketed as "Las Girlfriends" in the early 1990s (along with Sandra Cisneros, Denise Chavez, and Ana Castillo). This label did much for their reputations at a time when "multicultural fiction" was often regarded as of more sociological than literary interest.

Key Author
Nadine Gordimer

In 1991, Nadine Gordimer (born 1923) became the first South African winner of the Nobel Prize in Literature. She was also only the second writer from sub-Saharan Africa, and the seventh woman to win the award. The award reflected a literary career which was intimately tied into the anti-apartheid struggle. She had already won the Booker Prize for her novel *The Conservationist* in 1974.

Born in Spring, Transvaal to a Jewish father and English mother, Gordimer's writing career began in 1937 at the age of fifteen; since then she has produced thirteen novels and hundreds of short stories. Gordimer's work has always been embedded within her South African environment, but through the 1950s, and especially following the Sharpeville massacre of 1960, her writing increasingly engaged with the South African government's racial policies. The impact of the racial laws on individual experience and identity emerges powerfully through her work.

Gordimer became close to Chief Luthuli, the President of the African National Congress (ANC) in the late-1950s, and from that time was intimately involved in white liberal networks of support for the anti-apartheid movement. This involvement continued and intensified, and she officially joined the ANC in 1990. Internationally, Gordimer came to be seen not just as a literary chronicler of life under the apartheid regime, but also as a powerful voice for South Africa's oppressed black population. Gordimer's position as an observer and critic of South African society was greatly strengthened by the fact that, unlike other writers, she refused to go into exile.

Timothy Lovering

Date 1991 (Nobel Prize in Literature awarded)

Nationality South Africa

Other Key Works *The Lying Days* (1953), *A Guest of Honour* (1970), *Burger's Daughter* (1979), *The House Gun* (1998)

Why It's Key South Africa's first winner of the Nobel Prize in Literature, Gordimer became acknowledged as one of the most influential commentators on the apartheid regime.

Opposite Nadine Gordimer alongside Nelson Mandela

Key Event *Generation X*
defines the post-baby boomers

Although its first recorded occurrence dates back to the early 1950s, "Generation X" gained currency as the name of a 1976 English punk band lifted from the title of an early study on youth culture. Billy Idol's group was later namechecked by Douglas Coupland in one of his zeitgeist-defining articles (1987–1989) that developed into a comic strip and, eventually, a book, published in 1991 (the same year as indie film *Slackers* and another Gen-X classic, *American Psycho*). Paradoxically, *Generation X* gave visibility to a nameless "X generation" of post-baby boomers which, according to Coupland, was "purposefully hiding" – not so much a lost generation, then, as one bent on losing itself. Thereafter, the expression became ubiquitous – supplanting "twentysomething" – and the Canadian author was hailed as the poet laureate of grunge (a phenomenon which also went mainstream in 1991).

St Martin's Press had envisaged an updated version of the *Yuppie Handbook*, but Coupland penned a bittersweet novel about the search for meaning in a world devoid of grand narratives. The result – a kind of *Arabian Nights* for slackers – accounts for the book's instant-classic status and enduring impact. Andy, Claire, and Dag all experience mid-twenties crises when they realize their existence has become "a series of scary incidents that simply [aren't] stringing together to make for an interesting book." In a bid to become latter-day Scheherazades, they "[q]uit everything," relocate to the Californian desert where they take on McJobs (another neologism popularized by this book) and transform their lives into "worthwhile tales" through storytelling. Their radical take on downshifting can be seen as a quest for the inscription of absence that points to a prelapsarian Neverland called America. It also happens to be one of the oldest, and indeed greatest, themes in American literature.

Andrew Gallix

Date 1991

Title *Generation X: Tales for an Accelerated Culture*

Author Douglas Coupland (born 1961)

Nationality Canada

Why It's Key The book that defined a generation.

Key Character **Patrick Bateman**
American Psycho

Lurking at the heart of Ellis' blood-soaked satire of 1980s America is yuppie king, Patrick Bateman, corporate raider, bon viveur, and sometime serial killer. Immaculately groomed and sporting a platinum American Express card, Bateman is never the most reliable of narrators because he is utterly mad, but it is he who guides us through the upscale, Dantesque Manhattan that comprises the novel's milieu and supplies its cast of "hardbody" females and identikit money men. The chill begins when, spliced into his monotonous catalogues of designer hardware, clothes and toiletries (a six-page, brand-heavy soliloquy on his personal hygiene routine is both numbing and hilarious), are at first snippets and then detailed accounts of his extra-curricular activities as butcher of derelicts, prostitutes and, eventually, particularly hated colleagues. His inner life, which juxtaposes the moribund concerns of wealth with violently pornographic fantasies, seems to be exploding into

reality. The parallel is obvious: as he himself puns, alongside the "mergers and acquisitions" of his profession, really, he is into "murders and executions."

What "redeems" Bateman for the reader is that he is unintentionally very funny. Undermining his pomposity are developed critiques of favorite groups – laughably, he admires Phil Collins, Whitney Houston, Huey Lewis – and often his gory adventures tend towards the absurd. Attempts to cook and eat one of his victims, for example, tread a line between horror and farce. Ultimately, however, he is a cipher, an anxiety-driven monster of capitalism, frighteningly aware of his own vacuity and that, as he suggests, "there is no real me."

Doug Haynes

Date 1991

Author Bret Easton Ellis (born 1964)

Nationality USA

Why It's Key Few can boast the notoriety of Ellis' cult work; originally to be published by Simon and Schuster, the company dropped it, anticipating protests. Pornographic and hard to read, *Psycho* is the emblematic text of what was dubbed "blank fiction."

Opposite Christian Bale as Patrick Bateman in the film adaptation *American Psycho*

1990–1999

683

Key Author **Rohinton Mistry**
Such a Long Journey

Rohinton Mistry's (born 1952) reputation rests on his three novels, all of which have been short-listed for the Booker Prize. He has lived in Canada since 1975, but his books are set in his native India, and the first two hark back to the period of his youth and early manhood. Consequently, his work has attracted the label "Indo-nostalgic," but although it is true that he brings great warmth to his vignettes of everyday life in 1970s India, his version of the subcontinent is also a dark place. His characters may be loveable, but they suffer: acts of violence, gory disasters, and mutilations abound in his pages. The 1970s saw great political and economic upheaval in India, and one of Mistry's themes is the devastating effects that "history" has on ordinary people, though he also explores the idea of how far people shape their own destinies through the choices they make.

This approach is reminiscent of the work of Salman Rushdie, although Mistry's admirers are often

critical of Rushdie; the cover of the paperback of *A Fine Balance* (1995) proudly reproduced one reviewer's opinion that the novel would "displace once and for all the idea that *Midnight's Children* is a good book about India." One difference between the two writers is that Mistry focuses on poor and dispossessed people; another is that he eschews technical experiment (or "magic-realist midnight muddles" as a character in *Family Matters* [2002] puts it) and writes traditional realistic fiction in transparent, unobtrusive prose – though his dialogue, like Rushdie's, is often hilarious.

Jake Kerridge

Date 1991 (publication)

Nationality Canada (born India)

Why It's Key The publication of *Such a Long Journey* marked the start of the career of one of the most important South Asian authors writing in English.

Key Author **Richard Powers**
The Goldbug Variations

What do you call a scientist who is in love with poetry? Call him Richard Powers (born 1957).

The brainy former physics major never met a scientific discipline he didn't like, or didn't want to take a swing at writing about, either. Dense both in terms of sentence construction and information, Powers' novels are considered by many to be more trouble than they are worth. Yet at its heart, his work is often about human relationships, either romantic or familial, and despite the coldness of the scientific framework of his stories, Powers has the ability to make you feel the ache of a lost love or astonishment at the human capacity to think or feel.

Intensely private and often referred to as brilliant, Powers' appearance on the American literary scene in the 1980s sent critics scurrying to find both literary precursors and a category in which to neatly store his work. There are, however, few novelists working today who are so committed to joining the literary

and scientific disciplines which he likes to fuse in his stories, a tendency which has led the Contemporary Authors reference series to remark that his fiction is "part story-telling, part textbook." Equally at home explaining virtual reality or artificial intelligence as he is rhapsodizing about art or elegizing the need for human companionship, Powers may not be a fast – or even fun – read, but his ability to combine such topics in his fictions makes him an author to be reckoned with in an age when such scientific endeavor is within reach.

Elizabeth Rosen

Date 1991 (publication)

Nationality USA

Other Key Works
Prisoner's Dilemma (1988),
Gain (1998)

Why It's Key Buried beneath their prodigious cerebral-ness and scientific topics, Powers' novels are philosophical inquiries into age-old questions such as what is art, and what does it mean to think? His use of science as both metaphor and subject matter in his novels makes him an important literary voice in a technological age.

Key Event *Sophie's World*
becomes a philosophical bestseller

Jostein Gaardner's novelistic guide to European philosophy was a publishing phenomenon, selling some 30 million copies in translation worldwide. The book recounts the intellectual journey of the fifteen-year-old Sophie Amundsen. Sophie receives mysterious messages which ask "Who are you?" and "Where does the world come from?"; in short order she becomes the student of Alberto Knox, sender of the messages, and a philosopher who teaches her the history of the discipline. He also helps her to outwit a shadowy nemesis called Albert Knag, who seems to be out to get her and her family. Together Knox and Sophie tour European philosophy from the Greeks to Sartre, covering figures such as Locke, Descartes, Hume, Berkeley, Kant, Hegel, Marx, and Darwin as well as general chronological periods (the Baroque or the Renaissance) and concepts (the Big Bang) on the way. Knox allows his pupil (and the readership) to learn at her (or their) own pace whilst making things fun with

site-specific pedagogy (dressing as a monk, reading *Alice in Wonderland*, visiting French cafes) as well as more traditional Socratic methods.

Bizarre and convoluted at times, the book is interested in practical demonstrations of concepts and the straightforwardness of explanations; it eschews complex jargonizing in order to deliver its message that philosophy is simply a means of understanding our – or Sophie's – world. The use of a child as the philosopher-explorer was key to the novel's charm and purpose: "The only thing we require to be good philosophers is the faculty of wonder."

Jerome de Groot

Date 1991

Place worldwide

Author Jostein Gaardner (born 1952)

Nationality Norway

Why It's Key *Sophie's World* was a huge-selling popular philosophy metafiction which addressed key questions in thought through the naïve figure of Sophie Amundsen.

Key Passage
The Famished Road

"These are the myths of beginnings. These are stories and moods deep in those who are seeded in rich lands, who still believe in mysteries.

I was not born just because I had conceived a notion to stay, but because in between my coming and going the great cycles of time had finally tightened around my neck. I prayed for laughter, a life without hunger. I was answered with paradoxes."

Vibrant with surreal imagery and timeless symbolism, yet unmistakably set in the Nigerian capital of Lagos in the early 1960s, this novel is narrated by Azaro, a spirit child, or *abiku*. According to Yoruba tradition, such infants are destined for a perpetual cycle of early death and rebirth. But, this time, Azaro is determined to experience life and make his mother smile, while the spirits keep trying to lure him back. Okri's style makes skilful use of the tension between the "real" world of violence and political conflict, the land of the living in which Azaro's

impoverished family struggle to survive, and the temptations of the carefree kingdom of the spirits. "I began to feed on my hunger. I fed well and had a mighty appetite. I dipped into myself and found other worlds waiting… A world of famine, famishment and drought… I listened to the music of famine." Although Okri has not himself embraced the label of magic realism, parallels have been drawn between his narrative technique and that of Rushdie's *Midnight Children* and Garcia Marquez's *One Hundred Years of Solitude*. *The Famished Road* was the first in a trilogy that continued Azaro's story with *Songs of Enchantment* (1993) and *Infinite Riches* (1998). Okri's childhood experience of the Biafran civil war has clearly influenced his work, which is much concerned with social conditions in Africa, while conjuring up uncommon characters and enchanted scenarios that are unforgettable – indeed a heady mix of hope, despair, vitality, and sheer poetry.
Margaret Busby

Date 1991

Author Ben Okri (born 1959)

Nationality Nigeria

Other Key Works *Incidents at the Shrine* (1986), *Stars of the New Curfew* (1988)

Why It's Key Awarded the Booker Prize, this novel became a bestseller for its 32-year-old author, the youngest ever winner. Its title derives from Wole Soyinka's poem, "Death in the Dawn": "And the mother prayed, Child/ May you never walk/ When the road waits, famished."

1990–1999

685

Key Author **Frank Chin**
Donald Duk

Donald Duk marked a turning point not only in the critical appreciation of Asian-American literature (which Frank Chin [born 1940] enthusiastically and tirelessly promotes) but also in Chin's own development as a writer. His stories up until then had largely revelled in masochistic self-loathing, his anti-heroes only gaining brief respite when able to articulate their inner struggle through elaborate and lengthy monologues or through a tenuous connection to a near-mythologized version of Chinese-American history. As is the case with his non-fiction, Chin has been criticized for the streak of misogyny and homophobia that seems, at times, to drive his polemic, and also for his bold assertions that many of his contemporaries in Asian and Asian-American literature are guilty of a falsification of Asian and Asian-American culture.

He is, however, widely praised for his pioneering work as a literary historian. *Donald Duk* is more transformative than Chin's previous works, featuring an

eponymous twelve-year-old protagonist who moves beyond the self-loathing that plagues the characters in his earlier stories by discovering the heritage of the Chinese-American laborers who helped build the railroads, and by exploring the rich traditions of Chinese mythology.

The book dramatizes the search for a Chinese "real" which, according to Chin, is, in essence, a martial view of the world. His recent works feature characters who embrace the view that "Life is War," frequently alluding to the heroic tradition in Chinese folklore. *Donald Duk* constitutes Chin's first major step in forging a new vision of Asian-American literary and cultural authenticity.
Christian Kerr

Date 1991 (publication)

Nationality USA

Other Key Works *Aieieee: An Anthology of Asian American Writers* (1974), *Gunga Din Highway* (1994)

Why It's Key Chin received an American Book Award in 1989 for a collection of short stories and another in 2000 for Lifetime Achievement. He is best known for *Donald Duk* and has also written plays and numerous essays.

Key Character **Francie Brady**
Butcher Boy

Patrick McCabe's novel is a chilling depiction of a young boy whose socially disadvantaged upbringing, sexual abuse at the hands of a priest, and progressive mental illness conspire to produce a strangely charming but ultimately murderous character. Francie Brady, the disturbed and disturbing narrator of *The Butcher Boy* begins his extraordinary tale by explaining, "when I was a young lad twenty or thirty or forty years ago… they were after me on account of what I done on Mrs Nugent." Born into a troubled Catholic family, with an alcoholic father and a mother who struggled with severe mental health problems until her eventual suicide, Francie's own psychological decline is played out in the claustrophobic confines of a small town life in the 1960s.

Mrs Nugent, the matriarch of a respectable Protestant family, becomes the object of Francie's obsessive hatred and bullying. The Nugents represent everything that is lacking in his life: parental responsibility, a reliable household income, good education and, most importantly, stability. Envious of their lifestyle, and influenced by the latent sectarian tensions of Northern Ireland at the time, he begins a darkly comic campaign of blackmail and violence against them. Mrs Nugent is eventually dispatched by Francie, who by this stage has found his vocation working in an abattoir.

The convincing dialect and the sparing use of punctuation lends depth and vibrancy to the narrative voice which is at times a stream of consciousness and at others that of a seasoned and compelling storyteller. Such is the power of Francie's narrative that we as readers become almost complicit in the events he relates, and able to follow, to some extent at least, the twisted logic of his damaged mind.

Juliet Wightman

Date 1991

Author Patrick McCabe (born 1955)

Nationality Ireland

Why It's Key McCabe's unforgettable rendering of a deeply troubled young boy provides a dramatic illustration of the ways in which environmental factors conspire to plunge an impressionable mind into insanity.

Opposite From the film adaptation of *Butcher Boy*

1990–1999

687

Key Book
Omeros

"a cloud hung from a branch in the orange hour / like a shirt that was stained with poetry and with blood."

Imagine – intricate invisible histories of inner and outer worlds emerging slowly out of language – like lost-to-ourselves, submerged islands. A poet's deep-lined, hollow palm caresses the planet, inhaling it, breathing gently upon it, leaving it purely impure – "some sorrows are like stones, and they never melt."

In *Omeros* "language carries its cure, / its radiant affliction." In its soundscape children's "voices are surf "; trees possess "vined bodies," speak in "green vowels," write with the "alphabet of scribbling branches"; Nature is a sacred being with a consciousness longer, deeper than man's officious, occluding histories and geographies, "the bitter history of sugar." The narrator "peels his sunburnt skin in maps of grey parchment / which he scrolls absently between finger and thumb." The poem is searing of soul-stealing cameras and of exploitative tourism, "the gold sea / flat as a credit-card." The stars of *Omeros* are poor black-skinned St Lucian fishermen with the names of Greek heroes: Philoctete, Hector, Achilles, Omeros. Hector's "chariot" is a sixteen-seater passenger van with "furred leopardskin" seats and "Coiled tongues of flame leapt from its sliding doors." A bewitching St Lucian waitress weaves through the narrative, turning heads and burning the hearts of men – her name a mythic echo – Helen, her presence "oblique but magnetic," her "sinuous neck / longing like a palm's." In one poignant moment, seeing his frail mother amongst other aged women, the poet says self-reflexively, "I no longer raged / at the humiliations of time"; "Time was that fearful friend / they talked to, who sat beside them in empty chairs, / as deaf as they were; who sometimes simply listened."

Nuzhat Bukhari

Date 1992

Author Derek Walcott (born 1930)

Nationality West Indies

Why It's Key Poetic language which is incantatory, expressionistic, demotic, lyrical *bel canto*, intensely metaphorical, daringly surreal, compulsively erotic, sublime, spiritual, metahistorical, prismatic, pantemporal – *Omeros* is the greatest verse epic of modern times. Walcott received the Nobel Prize in Literature in 1992.

Key Book *Men Are From Mars, Women Are From Venus*

Men Are From Mars, Women Are From Venus is a self-help bestseller which attained cultural significance due to its widespread popularity. The unexpected visibility of the book revealed a self-help generation, interested in quick fix books with snappy motifs and not a great deal of in-depth analysis. Subtitled *How to get what you want in your relationships*, the central tenet is that men and women are essentially on different planets to one another, and this leads to a set of fundamental differences. If each sex understands this dissimilarity they will be able to manage relationships far more effectively. Gray is interested in the things that make the sexes individual rather than looking at the similarities; by studying difference we can better gauge why individuals do certain things in relationships. The sexes communicate in particular ways, and if each one realizes this then common ground can be found faster as can the solution to problems. A famous example of this is the "cave" into which men withdraw when they are stressed, in contrast to women's desire to share and discuss worries.

MAFM,WAFV is the poster book of the self-help boom of the late 1980s and 90s, its cod-philosophy and relationship advice offering "Answers" and therefore understanding. The promise and premise of self-help writing is to furnish the reader with tools with which to live their life better. *MAFM,WAFV* suggests that men and women can live in harmony, so long as they are aware that they are fundamentally different beings from one another.

Jerome de Groot

Date 1992

Author John Gray (born 1951)

Nationality USA

Why It's Key Huge selling book which sought to explain the difference between the sexes.

Key Character **The English Patient**
The English Patient

He fell out of the sky and emerged from the wreck of a burning plane. Bedouins masked his face with oasis reeds and smothered his body with soothing ointments. A healer rubbed ground peacock bones into his charred skin. He was left at a British base at the edge of the Libyan desert. He found himself on a train to Tunis, then on a boat to Italy, and finally in an abandoned villa in the Tuscan hills. He responds to no name and bears no identity tag. His only possession is a weary copy of Herodotus' *Histories*. He speaks of the desert as a man would describe a lover. When overwhelmed by memories he looks "the way Duke Ellington looked and thought when he played 'Solitude'."

At the heart of Michael Ondaatje's beautiful and devastating novel, co-winner of the 1992 Booker Prize, is the mystery of the title character's identity. His carers refer to him as "the English patient," though he may be Hungarian expatriate Ladislaus de Almásy (loosely based on real-life explorer Lázló Almásy). He had joined a geographic mission charged with finding a lost oasis as Europe hurtled into World War II. What he had discovered, instead, was a woman he could love as much as he had loved the North African landscape. Their passion was forbidden and consuming. While he lies dying, the disfigured patient sums up the knowledge gleaned from pain: "There are betrayals in war that are childlike compared with human betrayals during peace."

Ángel Gurría-Quintana

Date 1992

Author Michael Ondaatje (born 1943)

Nationality Canada (born Sri Lanka)

Why It's Key *The English Patient* brought Ondaatje's blend of poetic observation and fragmented narrative to a worldwide readership. Anthony Minghella translated the stunning written imagery into a film in 1996.

Opposite Ralph Fiennes plays the eponymous English Patient in the film adaptation

Key Author **Cormac McCarthy**
All the Pretty Horses

Cormac McCarthy's (born 1933) work has always been distinguished by its evocative sense of place (Appalachia in his early novels, the American Southwest and Mexico in his later work); an ear for regional language; and its interest in outsiders (drifters, prostitutes, orphans, and ex-cons). His novels are often described as apocalyptic in their presentation of aberrant and extreme human nature in landscapes of austerely beautiful desolation. In its eschewal of conventional syntax, McCarthy's prose style owes much to Faulkner; he can switch effortlessly from the lean to the baroque, as passages of description slide ineluctably into philosophical rumination. A sense of history pervades his writing, a sense that the voices of the past inhabit the landscapes of the present. McCarthy's mythopoeic and metaphysical tendencies perhaps reached their apogee in the uncompromisingly violent and bleak historical novel *Blood Meridian* (1985). *All the Pretty Horses* tempers the nihilism of its predecessor with a patina of nostalgia for the "old West," but the novel remains anti-romantic in many ways. Set in the 1940s, it tells the story of John Grady Cole, a sixteen-year-old ranch-hand who crosses the border into Mexico after the death of his grandfather deprives him of his family's ranch. The preternaturally mature Cole is an uncannily skilled cowboy, and a taciturn, covert romantic, instinctively attuned to the natural environment. But he is a man out of time, fleeing from modernity towards a violent world he cannot control.

All the Pretty Horses brought popular success to go with critical acclaim. It is the first part of the Border Trilogy, continued in *The Crossing* (1994) and completed in *Cities of the Plain* (1998).
Rowland Hughes

Date 1992 (publication)

Nationality USA

Other Key Works *The Orchard Keeper* (1966), *Suttree* (1979), *Blood Meridian* (1985), *No Country for Old Men* (2005)

Why It's Key McCarthy is certainly one of the most important U.S. writers of the last forty years. His rich body of work has established him as one of the most distinctive and powerful voices in contemporary American writing.

690

Key Book
Snow Crash

Neal Stephenson's third work, a complex and dazzling novel of ideas that weaves Sumerian myth, Californian skate culture, and breathless technophilism into a beguilingly dystopian vision of a hyper-consumerist twenty-first century society, is best known for popularizing key concepts of virtual reality. Its "metaverse" is an exceedingly well-realized, though relentlessly spatial, commercial cyberspace that has been tremendously influential on subsequent real-world implementations, such as Uru, Active Worlds and, more recently, Cyworld and Second Life. The success of the book also popularized the use of the Sanskrit term "avatar" to describe virtual bodies, a use that has now become pervasive.

In a slightly *Boy's Own* atmosphere, the novel's protagonist, Hiro Protagonist – yep! – world's greatest hacker, outsider, drifter, and improbably good samurai sword-fighter, loses his job as a pizza delivery driver for the Mafia, and partners with hip valley-girl and skateboard courier Y.T. to speculatively gather information about, well, whatever. In the course of the novel, they discover that Snow Crash is a malicious computer virus targeted at the knowledge-elite in the metaverse, a real-world drug distributed by a network of Pentecostal churches run by fiber-optics monopolist L. Bob Rife, and, on top of all that, an ancient Sumerian spell, an intellectual meme responsible for the sundering of human language at Babel.

The play of ideas is rich and satisfying and the cultural and economic backdrop – globally distributed, branded nation states, gated suburban enclaves protected by private police forces, vestigial, irrelevant governments, and ruthlessly rational flows of information and cash – is coherent and convincing.
Scott Button

Date 1992

Author Neal Stephenson (born 1959)

Nationality USA

Why It's Key Invented the metaverse and popularized the term "avatar." Home to probably the best pizza delivery scene in modern fiction.

Key Event *Fever Pitch* – meaningful literary sportswriting with cultural significance

Nick Hornby's first book recounts his obsession since the age of 11 with Arsenal Football Club. A series of "match-report" chapters from the late sixties to the early nineties interweave intimate biographical detail with descriptions of a period of enormous transition in the culture and infrastructure of this most popular of British sports. The book's critical and commercial success established its position in the international canon of sportswriting. It has also had a major impact on British culture, being routinely described as a key artifact in the embourgeoisement of football in Britain. Its publication year coincided with the inauguration of the English Premier League, which in conjunction with support from satellite television has become one of the most successful global sports franchises (where Arsenal occupy a powerful role).

Fever Pitch examines how emotional and social emptiness can be filled by the passion and identity generated by sport's imagined community. The nature of that fixation and its influence on personal (especially masculine) instability lies at the core of Hornby's narrative. The book vaults beyond the personal in its description of the changing lifestyles, key events, intricacies, and social movements in British football since the late sixties. Its publication and subsequent high profile in cultural consciousness coincided with the conclusion of a decade-long attempt to erase the problem of hooliganism, racism, and unsafe stadiums. The traditional working-class male ethos and image of British football was eclipsed at its highest levels. The growth of football as a publicly acceptable pursuit for families and the middle classes has been a central feature of its commercial and cultural success since the 1990s. *Fever Pitch* can be seen as a productive factor in that shift.

Graeme Mcdonald

Date 1992

Author Nick Hornby (born 1957)

Nationality UK

Why It's Key Horby's bestselling autobiography is generally perceived as the quintessential book about the capricious experience of being a football supporter. A film in 2005 transported the object of fixation to the Boston Red Sox, proving that the concept of *Fever Pitch* – the extent to which fandom reaches unhealthy levels of obsession – is globally transferable.

Key Character **Smilla Jasperson** *Miss Smilla's Feeling for Snow*

When Greenland became a Danish colony in the early nineteenth century the indigenous inhabitants faced a number of brutal social changes which affected their way of life forever. Those Inuits who settled in Denmark suffered discrimination and were frequently marginalized. In *Miss Smilla's Feeling for Snow*, Peter Høeg placed this issue center stage by creating a heroine who is half-Greenlandic Inuit and half Danish.

The independent-minded Smilla is drawn to investigate the death of a neighbor's son, Isaiah, a young Greenlandic boy who dies when he falls from a snow-covered rooftop. It appears to be an accident, but Smilla believes otherwise. To uncover the truth she has to rely on her expertise and natural instincts, as well as her understanding of both Danish and Greenlandic cultures. To solve the mystery, Smilla is forced to undertake a dangerous voyage back to the Greenland she left behind as a child and uncovers a conspiracy that has remained hidden for decades.

The novel's great triumph, along with Smilla herself, is its creation of atmosphere. Copenhagen, buried in snow and darkness, is rendered a silent stage upon which the drama plays itself out. The novel's spare prose conveys the character of an intelligent young woman whose introversion is a means of protecting herself from society. Smilla's quest is more than a simple murder enquiry, it is also a personal bid to come to terms with her own identity. Smilla, who has always been torn between her two halves, sees in Isaiah the possibility of reconciling the Greenlandic and the Danish worlds.

Jamal Mahjoub

Date 1992

Author Peter Høeg (born 1957)

Nationality Denmark

Original Title *Frk. Smillas fornemmelse for sne*

Why It's Key It was the international acclaim for *Miss Smilla* which gave Høeg his unique status in Danish literary history. The following year *The Woman and the Ape* did not meet the same success and Høeg withdrew from publishing for a decade.

Key Event **Serb forces burn Sarajevo library's collection**

During the Bosnian Civil War (1992–1995) the former Bosnia and Herzegovina region was torn apart by contending nationalist forces. Sarajevo, the capital city, was subjected to a four-year siege. In 1992, at the height of the siege, Serb nationalist forces specifically targeted both the Institute for Oriental Studies and the National Library with incendiary grenades and mortar shells. The besiegers had cut the water before the latter shelling, forcing firemen to draw from the River Miljacka; they also swept the site with artillery fire to prevent emergency services attending to the blaze.

The attack was not simply on learning but clearly intended to destroy Bosnian cultural artifacts. The libraries between them contained manuscripts, periodical literature, and thousands of rare printed books. Some 1.5 million books were eventually lost. This cultural vandalism was the largest book-burning of modern times, although unlike that of the Nazis in 1933 and other regimes, was not an organized putsch of material but an act of aggression. The attempt to destroy a nation's culture was also more wide-ranging than the Nazi's mere destruction of "un-German" books. The burning of the library was part of a broader program of conscious destruction of cultural and religious heritage (mosques, churches, libraries, and religious archives) by many groups during the complex conflict; in 1993 the Council of Europe called it "a cultural catastrophe in the heart of Europe." The deliberate obliteration of cultures without military objective is a war crime and, whilst the damage in the region has been thoroughly audited, to date no case has been prepared.

Jerome de Groot

Date 1992

Place Bosnia

Why It's Key The largest single act of book burning in recent history was part of a wider programme of cultural destruction.

Key Event *Wild Swans* gives the world a new perspective on Chinese history

In 1989 the world caught a glimpse of political life behind the Bamboo Curtain, in the indelible image of a lone protestor defying government tanks in Tiananmen Square. The convulsive history leading up to that moment – the rise of Mao Zedong, the violence of the Cultural Revolution, and the Party's stranglehold on Chinese life and culture – is the backdrop for Jung Chang's family saga, telling the story of "Three Daughters of China," grandmother, mother, and author herself. Appearing only two years after the Tiananmen Square uprisings, *Wild Swans* brought twentieth-century Chinese history to the popular Western consciousness and was a runaway bestseller, selling 10 million copies and translated into 30 languages, including Chinese despite the fact that the book remains banned in Chang's native country. Feted by critics and award panels and read in coffee shops everywhere, *Wild Swans* seemed as ubiquitous as Mao's notorious Little Red Book.

Chang's epic opens in feudal Manchuria, where the author's grandmother, concubine to a warlord general, must suffer the traditional practice of feet binding, an image of female repression which resonates throughout the book. Charting the Japanese invasion, the collapse of the interim Kuomintang regime, and the Communist takeover of 1948, Chang describes her mother's involvement in the newly formed People's Republic. With the Cultural Revolution of 1966, Chang's parents fall foul of frenzied denunciations of Party officials as the new "class enemies" culminating in her father's imprisonment and descent into insanity. In the midst of such trials the young author is seduced by the cult of Mao, thrilled at receiving the red armband "at the very time the Cultural Revolution had brought disaster on my family." Despite this, Chang has been accused of glossing over her own involvement in the Red Guard and of embroidering the documented facts in the service of good storytelling.

Matthew Birchwood

Date 1992

Author Jung Chang (born 1952)

Nationality UK (born China)

Why It's Key *Wild Swans* inaugurated a string of popular successes treating Chinese history and the female experience aimed at a Western audience (*Falling Leaves, Farewell my Concubine*). With her husband, the historian Jon Halliday, Chang has gone on to write a controversial biography of Mao Zedong.

Opposite Jung Chang

Key Author
Isaac Asimov

We have Isaac Asimov (1920–1992) to thank for the word "robotics" and any ideas we harbor that robots will, by necessity, be programed not to hurt humans. One of the most prolific writers in the world, Asimov is not only one of the towering figures of the sci-fi genre, but can also be credited with ensuring that the science in the genre was real, rather than pseudo-science.

Trained as a biochemist, Asimov's true talent lay in being able to translate complicated or dull scientific concepts into understandable and exciting reading. He prided himself on the logic and good science in his stories, and his "Three Laws of Robotics," which laid out the principles by which any robot would need to be programed in order to interact with the human world, ultimately became a mainstay of the genre, in part because they allowed him, and those who came after him, to explore the ethics of both human and robot existence and co-existence.

In addition to his robot stories, Asimov is perhaps the best-known writer of "future history" fictions. His Foundation series imagines a future society and chronicles its history over the course of many books. Though written in the 1940s, the series is as popular today as it was then. Author of hundreds of books, Asimov wrote in the fields of popular science, history, humor, and autobiography, in addition to fiction.
Elizabeth Rosen

Date 1992 (death)

Nationality USSR (naturalized USA)

Other Key Works I, Robot series; Foundation series

Why It's Key Highly regarded as one of the grandfathers of the science fiction genre, in particular, his ideas about robots have gradually become a mainstay not merely of the sci-fi genre, but also of the larger culture which owes the words "robotic" and "positronic" to the author's imagination.
Opposite Isaac Asimov

1990–1999

Key Author **Rose Tremain**
Sacred Country

In over a dozen short story collections and novels published since the late 1970s, this highly intelligent and subtle English novelist has proved herself unafraid of the many varied terrains of the imagination. Though Rose Tremain (born 1943) has written books with contemporary settings – The Way I Found Her (1997) is the story of an English boy trying to solve a mystery in Paris, while 1992's Sacred Country is an extraordinarily vivid tale of a transgendered girl growing up in 1960s Suffolk – she is best known as a writer who helped bring literary respectability back to historical fiction.

With the publication of Restoration in 1989 – the boisterous, Pepys-inflected story of the rise and fall of Robert Merivel, a physician at the court of Charles II – Tremain established her ability to write novels rich in historical detail that were vibrant, modern, complex, and engaging, rescuing the genre from its shabby reputation. In doing so she helped open the way for a new generation of English writers tackling historical

settings, including Lawrence Norfolk, Andrew Miller, and Iain Pears.

Tremain returned to the seventeenth century with *Music and Silence* (1999) set in the Danish court of Christian IV, which won the Whitbread Award for best novel. *The Colour* (2003) was set in nineteenth-century New Zealand and had two bold, adventurous characters pursuing the folly of the gold rush there. All of Tremain's work displays a deep empathy and moral curiosity, her wry humor, and a persuasive sense both of life's hardships and of its glories, whether grand or small.

In an interview Tremain has said, "I'm not very interested in charting a day-to-day familiar reality. I'm always looking for territory in which to explore the big subjects, the life-or-death stories. All of these stories will have 'harsh moments' but they also have moments of transcendent happiness and wonder."
Sylvia Brownrigg

Date 1992 (publication)

Nationality UK

Other Key Works *Sadler's Birthday* (1977), *Evangelista's Fan* (1994)

Why It's Key A prize-winning novelist best known for novels whose colorful, deeply felt fictions often travel to other times and places.

Key Character **Quoyle**
The Shipping News

Quoyle, the singularly-named protagonist of *The Shipping News*, is one of life's great failures, drifting through life with a series of dead-end jobs. He is unattractive, "a great damp loaf of a man" with a "monstrous chin," about which he is intensely self-conscious. And he is emotionally damaged: abused and abandoned by his promiscuous wife, Petal, who dies in a car crash, leaving Quoyle to raise their two daughters, Bunny and Sunshine. But Quoyle is "good-hearted" in the words of his aunt, Agnis Hamm; his love for his daughters defines him. Having nothing left to keep him in New York, where he works as a "third-rate newspaperman," he agrees to accompany Agnis to Newfoundland, his ancestral home, where he begins to reconstruct his life, with a job as a reporter on the local newspaper, *The Gammy Bird*. Quoyle is genealogically connected to the landscape and people of Newfoundland, and yet totally unfamiliar with them. The novel traces his attempts to assimilate into the tight-knit community, to find a place for himself and his family in the world, and even to accept the fact that "love sometimes occurs without pain and misery." His quiet reticence encourages others to talk, and Quoyle becomes the silent heart of the novel around which Proulx weaves a rich tapestry of oral history and individual eccentricity, intensely evocative both of the place and its rhythm of life, showcasing her ear for regional speech and anecdotal storytelling.

She has consolidated her status as a major contemporary American writer with her subsequent novels, *Accordion Crimes* (1996) and *That Old Ace in the Hole* (2002), and with her remarkable collection of short stories, *Close Range* (1999), including the story "Brokeback Mountain," which was adapted in 2005 into a successful film of the same name. *The Shipping News* was also adapted for the screen in 2001.
Rowland Hughes

Date 1993

Author E. Annie Proulx (born 1935)

Nationality USA

Why It's Key Proulx's second novel earned the author the Pulitzer Prize for Fiction, and established her as one of the most distinctive and original of contemporary American writers.

Key Author
Toni Morrison

Toni Morrison, one of the most celebrated writers of our time, was born Chloe Anthony Wofford on February 18, 1931 in Lorain, Ohio. Morrison earned a degree in English and Classics from Howard University. She received her Master's from Cornell University where she wrote her thesis on the literary works of Virginia Woolf and William Faulkner. After graduation, Morrison taught literature at several universities and worked as an editor at Random House before making her literary debut in 1970.

The Bluest Eye (1970) Morrison's first novel, tells the story of Pecola Breedlove, a young black girl growing up in Lorain, Ohio. The story, told from five perspectives (Pecola's, her mother's, her father's, her friend Claudia's, and Soaphead Church's), deals with themes of identity, child molestation, and racism. Subsequently, Morrison published the novels *Sula* (1973), *Song of Solomon* (1977), *Beloved* (1987), *Jazz* (1992), and *Paradise* (1998). When asked who she wrote for during a lecture at Princeton University where she holds the Robert F. Goheen Professorship in the Humanities, Morrison replied "I want to write for people like me, which is to say black people, curious people, demanding people – people who can't be faked, people who don't need to be patronized, people who have very, very high criteria."

Morrison's literary career has been marked with honors, including the National Book Critics Circle Award, the American Academy and Institute of Arts and Letters Award, the Pulitzer Prize, and the Robert F. Kennedy Award. In 1993, Morrison was the first African-American woman to be awarded the Nobel Prize in Literature.
M.K. Asante, Jr.

Date 1993 (Nobel Prize for Literature awarded)

Nationality USA

Why It's Key In 2006 *The New York Times Book Review* called *Beloved* the best American novel published in the previous 25 years. Oprah Winfrey produced an award winning, critically acclaimed film adaptation of *Beloved* which starred Winfrey and Danny Glover.

Key Book
Farewell My Concubine

Written after the Tiananmen Massacre of 1989 and before the reunification of Hong Kong with the mainland in 1997, the central motif of a culture relinquished during the time of revolution rankled beyond artistic fantasy, as a powerful political message of impending doom. In the novel, the vanquished decadent art of opera represents the effects of the Cultural Revolution and the dissolution of the Qing Dynasty. When this book was published in 1992, there was a powerful sense of foreboding in Hong Kong with regard to communism, and what this could mean for society and for cultural expression.

The core sentiment of Lilian Lee's novel takes flight with the statement, "life is just a play. Or an opera." It is essentially a narrative that is doomed from the start; Lee states that "Prostitutes have no heart, and actors have no morals." Both Dieyi and Xiaolou, the main protagonists, are inextricably linked to these marginalized sectors of society; they represent both the vice and pretence of imagination. Dieyi, the abandoned son of a prostitute, is deeply in love with Xiaolou, and this complex theme is brought around full circle when Xiaolou abandons Dieyi to marry a prostitute. The operatic play of the novel's title weaves the tale of a concubine's fatal devotion to her doomed emperor; this is echoed by Dieyi's devotion to Xiaolou and draws a parallel with their complicated love triangle. *Farewell My Concubine* is a tale of symmetry just as it is a story of unrequited love.

Lilian Lee is the author of more than 30 works of horror, fantasy and mainstream fiction, as well as 15 screenplays.
Alexandra Hamlyn

Date 1993

Author Lilian Lee (pen name of Lee Pi Hua)

Nationality Hong Kong, China S.A.R.

Why It's Key An enigmatic portrayal of 20th-century Chinese history, from the 1930s to the 1980s, and the impact of the Cultural Revolution on so-called "decadent art." The indictment of the revolution caused controversy when the book was transferred to the big screen in 1993, so much so that the film was banned in China.

1990–1999

697

Key Author
Anthony Burgess

"PFFFRRRUMMMP.
And a very happy New Year to you too, Mr Enderby!"

Thus with a terrific fart starts Enderby (1963), following up before long with "Perrrrrp" and "Querpkprrmp." We may from the start suspect that Enderby, the semi-autobiographical poet-protagonist of four of Burgess' (1917–1993) novels, will not be entirely a man of the spirit. Himself a man of prodigious creative energy, the lapsed Catholic Burgess had a Rabelaisian pleasure in the body's unruly energy, one of the many forms of human vitality which his fictions generously represent. In more than 30 novels (and 60 books) written between 1956 and his death in 1993, Burgess managed an unusual combination of the attributes of realist and experimental fiction. Together with a broad fascination with character and event, he had a self-conscious and often avant-garde concern with techniques of narrative and with the nature of language itself. The cat in *Ulysses* which went "mrkrgnao" (not just "miaow") presides over Enderby's flatulences, and Burgess – who wrote two books on Joyce, a useful abridgement of *Finnegans Wake*, and a musical based on *Ulysses* – was the heir to Joyce's interest in how to put the things of the world into words and fictional shape. His output is so vast and varied that summary is difficult. His magnum opus? Perhaps the three novels of The Malayan Trilogy (1956–9), a relatively traditional post-war fiction about the end of empire; or the four exuberantly hilarious Enderby novels (1963–1984); or *Earthly Powers* (1980), in which the gay narrator's life touches and parallels the great events of the twentieth century. But this leaves out *A Clockwork Orange* (1962), a *cause célèbre* when filmed, and the historical novels, and the two sparkling volumes of autobiography, not to mention the reviews, poems, and symphonies… Truly a wonderful talent, and still underrated.
Peter Swaab

Date 1993 (death)

Other Key Works *Time for a Tiger* (1956), *The Enemy in the Blanket* (1958), *Beds in the East* (1959), *Inside Mr Enderby* (1963), *Enderby Outside* (1968), *The Clockwork Testament* (1974), *Enderby's Dark Lady* (1984)

Why It's Key Burgess was a versatile and inventive writer of satire, science fiction, comic novels, thrillers, essays, works of criticism, and historical fiction.

Key Book
My Idea of Fun: A Cautionary Tale

My Idea of Fun was greeted with the kind of vein-popping indignation Will Self had probably anticipated when he chose the title. One reviewer famously described it as the "most loathsome" book he had ever read (on the strength of a couple of *American Psycho*-style scenes) – a verdict the *enfant terrible* of British letters must have relished. Self's debut novel was so much more, however, than just another *succès de scandale*.

Under the tutelage of a gargantuan Svengali called The Fat Controller, Ian Wharton comes to see himself as a "towering superman" whose gratuitous outrages are beyond good and evil. The protagonist's "divided personality" (marketing executive/serial killer) enables Self to tap into the rich doppelgänger tradition which he revisited more than a decade later in *Dorian* (2002).

The plot revolves around a Nietzschean struggle between Apollonian and Dionysian forces. Wharton is an eidetic who can "replicate" anything he sees "with near-photoreal accuracy" – a gift which also turns out to be a curse. The Faustian bargain he strikes with the Mephistophelean Fat Controller ("the Dionysian other") stipulates that penetrating a woman would result in the immediate loss of his penis. Fearing that he may be "suffering from an excess of imagination" – a charge often levelled at Self himself – he attempts to leave behind the world of magic (but also of incest, masturbation, and autism) in order to become "generic." The whole novel is an account of how this plan fails. The pleasure principle seems about to prevail, but Ian's desire to destroy his suburban idyll can also be seen as the impotent rage of the alter deus unable to bridge the gap between fun and the retrospective "idea of fun" which is only a "tired allusion" to the real thing. Replication (read: realism) cannot grasp the essence of things.

Andrew Gallix

Date 1993

Author Will Self (born 1961)

Nationality UK

Why It's Key The *enfant terrible* of British letters lives up to the hype.

Opposite Will Self

698

Key Character **Donald "Sully" Sullivan**
Nobody's Fool

True to his nickname, "Sully" has a talent for making a mess of things. An injured knee has left him unable to carry on with freelance construction, forcing him to retrain as an air-conditioner repairman. We meet him just as he quits community college in an ill-advised attempt to return to outdoor work.

This "case study underachiever" is a lifelong resident of North Bath, a small town in upstate New York which has seen better days. It is the sort of tree-lined village that inspires city people to fantasize about buying a country house before they drive away forever. Like his hometown, Sully has a weathered charm which could be mistaken for folksy, country contentment by outsiders. Yet he is as far past his prime as North Bath itself, part of an America that time and progress have rendered obsolete.

At age 60, Sully is "divorced from his own wife, carrying on half-heartedly with another man's, estranged from his son, devoid of self-knowledge, badly crippled and virtually unemployable – all of which he stubbornly confused with independence." This novel's silver lining of sentimentality surrounds a considerable cloud of cynicism. Neither the setting nor the man is new territory for Richard Russo, who specializes in depressed small towns and characters. Sully provides a 1990s literary counterpoint to the earnest, blue collar folk mythology of Steinbeck's Tom Joad. Both Sully and his town are too finely drawn to invite nostalgia; the more time we spend with them, the more we realize that the past is not necessarily a nicer place to be. The scarred survivor of a violent alcoholic father, Sully is an absent parent and neglectful husband, whose redemption comes only with his refusal to be graceful in his decline.

Dinah Roe

Date 1993

Author Richard Russo (born 1949)

Nationality USA

Why It's Key As infuriatingly fatalistic as Dickens' Mr Micawber, and as gleefully anarchic as *Huckleberry Finn*'s Pappy, Richard Russo's Sully is a significant literary update of the American working class hero. Paul Newman played Sully in the 1995 film version.

Key Character **Paddy Clarke**
Paddy Clarke Ha Ha Ha

In *Paddy Clarke Ha Ha Ha* Roddy Doyle uses first person narrative, interior monologue, thoughts, memories, personal information, facts gleaned from books, stories, and parables – a never-ending variety of narratives that evoke the vocabulary and emotional responses of a boy to his immediate environment. Doyle captures the world of a ten-year-old boy and sustains it throughout the novel. Sometimes that world is hilariously funny, sometimes violent and very frightening. Paddy's gradual sense of isolation seeps into the narrative with the realization that his parents are fighting more and more. In the scene in which Paddy first realizes his father hits his mother, Doyle uses language sparingly – there is no need for details – showing the child's sense of wonder at the event: "I watched. I listened. I stayed in. I guarded her" seems to say so much with such little effort.

Paddy moves from a sense of belonging (to a family – to a gang) to a sense of isolation. There is a feeling of loss at the end of the novel but there is also hope. He finds out about the realities of life at a very young age and has to grow up quickly, but what he feels in the novel – the freedom, the fear and cruelty – is all part of the process. Childhood is a time of both freedom and fear, and Paddy's nuanced voice captures both elements exceptionally well.

Pat Wheeler

Date 1993

Author Roddy Doyle (born 1958)

Nationality Ireland

Why It's Key Paddy has one of the most distinctive young voices in contemporary fiction, and he has been compared favorably to the youthful narrators in both J.D. Salinger's *The Catcher in the Rye* and Harper Lee's *To Kill a Mockingbird*. The novel was awarded the Booker Prize in 1993.

Opposite Roddy Doyle

1990-1999

Key Event **Maya Angelou reads at the Inauguration of U.S. President Bill Clinton**

When President-Elect Bill Clinton invited Maya Angelou to write an inaugural poem for his swearing-in in January 1993, it seemed an indication of the changes Clinton might bring to his country after more than a decade of conservative Republican leadership. (The previous president to have bestowed such an honor had been John F. Kennedy, who tapped Robert Frost in 1961.) That Clinton chose an African-American woman was a piece of symbolism employed deliberately by a Southerner well-versed in the complex sexual and racial politics of a nation still grappling with its history of slavery and the civil rights upheavals of the 1960s.

Angelou was well known for a series of memoirs, including *I Know Why the Caged Bird Sings* (1969) in which she chronicled the transformations she went through as a poet, a dancer, and a single mother. The performance of her poem, "On the Pulse of Morning," a work incorporating American angers and American optimisms, was an inspirational piece of political theater – Angelou's training as an actor doubtless aided in her magnificent stage presence – though opinion was divided on the poem itself. Before writing it Angelou steeped herself in the writings of Frederick Douglass, W.E.B. Du Bois, and black preachers, and the poem speaks in powerful, repetitive cadences of the hardships of slavery and the damage inflicted on the earth by humanity, though it closes with an exhortation for unity and hope. President Clinton pronounced himself pleased with the poem and said he would hang it in the White House; the poem sold widely afterward, in published and recorded form, and assured Angelou a place in the rarefied group of American poets known to and cherished by a wider audience.

Sylvia Brownrigg

Date 1993

Place Washington, D.C.

Author Maya Angelou (born 1928)

Nationality USA

Why It's Key An African-American poet writes and performs a poem celebrating American diversity and condemning the cruelties of American history, in a work commissioned by an incoming U.S. President who intends to challenge certain fundamentals of the political establishment.

Key Passage
Trainspotting

"Society invents a spurious convoluted logic tae absorb and change people whae's behaviour is outside its mainstream. Suppose that ah ken aw the pros and cons, know that ah'm gaunnae huv a short life, am ay sound mind etcetera, etcetera, but still want tae use smack? They wont let ye dae it, because it's seen as a sign ay thir ain failure. The fact that ye jist simply choose tae reject whit they huv tae offer. Choose us. Choose life. Choose mortgage payments; choose washing machines; choose cars; choose sitting on a couch watching mind-numbing and spirit-crushing game shows, stuffing fuckin junk food intae yer mooth. Choose rotting away, pishing and shiteing yersel in a home, a total fuckin embarrassment tae the selfish, fucked up brats ye've produced. Choose life. Well, a choose no tae choose life. If the cunts cannae handle that, it's thair fuckin problem."

In its use of Leith vernacular, in its sociological thesis and in its moral challenges, this passage exemplifies the uncompromising nature of Welsh's spectacular novel debut. A paradox here is that these are the words of a junkie intellectual Mark Renton, whose struggle against heroin addiction and social deprivation brings competing notions of choice and compulsion into stark relief. Renton and his associates reject one form of consumerism expressed in material goods and bourgeois conformity for another super-addictive form of consumption: heroin. The passage reflects the irony that the drug market parallels the "mainstream" commodity structure. A further irony is that the popularity of Welsh's fiction has ensured a place for such characters and their predicaments within the mainstream of British consumer culture where the "choose life" mantra proved a popular logo.
Graeme Mcdonald

Date 1993

Author Irvine Welsh (born 1958)

Nationality UK

Why It's Key Commercially successful, morally shocking, stylistically challenging, and utterly of its time, this seminal work was also a crucial text of the second wave of the new Scottish writing. Its catalogue of the horrors of AIDS and heroin addiction in a ravaged Edinburgh ensured enduring notoriety.

Opposite Irvine Welsh

702
1990–1999

Key Author **Antonio Tabucchi**
Declares Pereira (*Sostiene Pereira*)

Antonio Tabucchi is the most important Italian novelist of the last three decades. Following a chance encounter with a book of poems by Fernando Pessoa, he became a life-long admirer of Portuguese literature, on which he lectures at the University of Siena. Several of his books have a Portuguese setting (one, *Requiem: a Hallucination* [1991] was originally written in that language), and throughout his work Tabucchi adeptly captures the melancholy mood the Portuguese call *saudade*, a sense of the simultaneous beauty and inescapable sadness of life. But while the terms "elusive" and "flitting" have been used to describe his work, Tabucchi, who in the 1990s was a founding member of the International Parliament of Writers, believes that authors can, and must, change the world for the better.

The hero of his ultimately upbeat masterpiece, *Declares Pereira*, a widowed and overweight cultural editor in late 1930s Lisbon, does finally make a stand against the oppressive Salazar regime – thus becoming for many Italians, on the eve of the momentous 1994 general election, a symbol of the opposition to media tycoon, and soon-to-be Prime Minister, Silvio Berlusconi. In the same way, in *The Missing Head of Damasceno Monteiro* (*La testa perduta di Damasceno Monteiro* [1997]), based on a real-life murder, Tabucchi prophetically denounced the involvement of the Portuguese National Guard. The author of some 30 works of fiction (several of which have been made into films) and non-fiction, which have brought him prestigious national and international accolades, Antonio Tabucchi is tipped to become Italy's next Nobel prize winner.
Elisabetta Tarantino

Date 1993

Author Antonio Tabucchi (born 1943)

Nationality Italy

Why It's Key The most celebrated Italian novelist of the past decades. His work unites a postmodern philosophy of doubt with a call for intervention in social and political affairs: "Doubts are like stains on a shirt... when I'm given a shirt that's too clean... I immediately start having doubts. It's the job of intellectuals and writers to cast doubt on perfection."

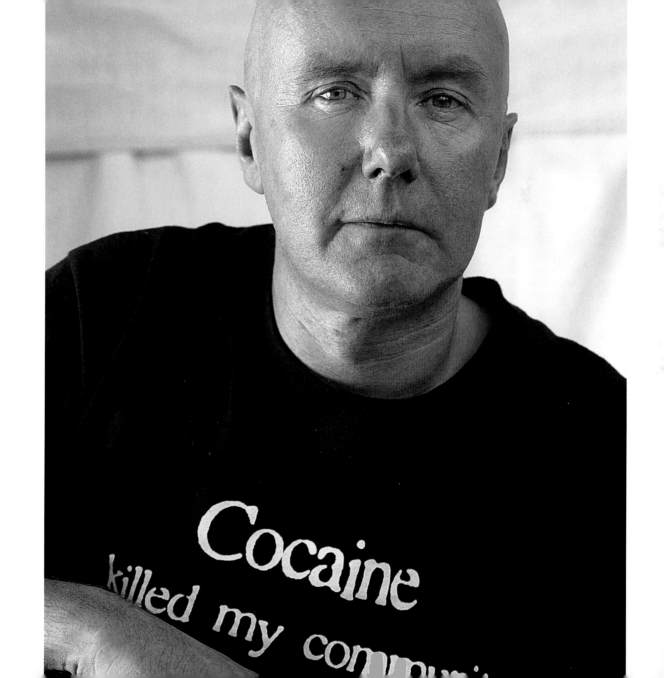

Key Book
A Suitable Boy

"You too will marry a boy I choose," says Mrs Rupa Mehra to her daughter right at the start of *A Suitable Boy*. On the surface, the novel is a sprawling family saga – almost a soap opera – revolving around that age-old plot motivator: the search for a husband. It is one of the longest novels ever published in English, with over half a million words – in paperback it runs to nearly 1,500 pages. But it is also one of the most engaging of novels, involving us in a richly realized world that we are, by the end, reluctant ever to leave. As one reviewer put it, "Not since Dickens has there been such a lively and idiosyncratic cast crowded into one novel."

Set in India in the years shortly after independence, the novel revolves around four families, the Mehras, the Kapoors, the Chatterjis – all middle-class, educated Hindus – and the aristocratic, Muslim Khans. Seth follows various interweaving plot lines that combine domestic with political concerns, and works in a host of ancillary characters, including cameos of some real historical figures, such as Indian prime minister Jawaharlal Nehru.

From the stench of the foetid pools where the tanners do their foul work to the sublime singing of a beautiful diva, from descriptions of the shoe industry and discussions of land reform to spectacular set pieces – a tiger hunt, intercommunal violence, the Great Kumbh Mela festival – in the end it is the story of ordinary people caught up in the tide of history that makes *A Suitable Boy* such a compelling read.
Ian Crofton

Date 1994

Author Vikram Seth (born 1952)

Nationality India

Why It's Key *A Suitable Boy* was a great popular success, winning the Commonwealth Writers Prize and the W.H. Smith Literary Award, although somewhat controversially it failed to be short-listed for the Booker Prize.

Opposite Vikram Seth

Key Book
Omon Ra

The title combines the Russian word for "special police forces" with the name of the Egyptian sun god. The result is a wonderfully disruptive and amusing post-Soviet fantasy of space exploration. Victor Pelevin himself had trained as a cosmonaut when Communism collapsed. After the change he began writing in a terse, humorous style completely at odds with the old socialist realism. The combination of hard science in *Omon Ra* with Eastern religion and commonplace Russian cruelty and absurdity brings to light imaginative currents that had lain under the Soviet surface for several decades. The symbols of the title pitch military coercion against imaginative infinity and the whole text is symptomatic of Soviet Russia's isolation from the rest of the world and its skewed, often fantastic perception of its own ambitions.

A major theme of the story is the relation of a happy, credulous childhood, in which imagination is nurtured with wonderful toys, to a grown-up world that turns out to be unbelievable: simply faked. The pilot puzzles over the gruesome preparation of his body for space flight in contrast to his once innocent dream to fly. *Omon Ra* revived a distinguished vein in Russian literature, that of the anti-totalitarian satire. It celebrated the deviant and the grotesque. But it proved not to be a herald of a great new Russian literature, in a country which has remained culturally bewildered without its old ideology to set the measure of things.
Lesley Chamberlain

Date 1994

Author Victor Pelevin (born 1962)

Nationality Russia

Why It's Key Pelevin, already a prize-winning author in Russia, won instant praise from critics round the world when this unique satirical cum mystical narrative was published, but with hindsight the story explained more about Soviet life than the new Russia it helped to put on the literary map.

Key Author
Kenzaburo Oe

In 1958, while still a 23-year-old student, Oe (born 1935) became one of the youngest ever winners of the prestigious Akutagawa Prize, and began a lifetime's literary celebrity, which was to include the 1994 Nobel Prize in Literature. Over the last half century he has produced a major though highly controversial body of work, covering a broad range of contemporary issues of international significance, extending beyond his initial appeal to post-war Japanese radicals, whose political awareness had heightened during the turbulent period after the 1960 Japan-U.S. Security Treaty.

Oe's early stories "Lavish Are the Dead" ("*Shisha no Ogori*" [1957]) and "Prize Stock" ("*Shiiku*" [1957], Akutagawa Prize) are clearly influenced by the existentialist novels of Jean-Paul Sartre, a key figure in Oe's general francophilia. In his youth, Oe established his commitment to problematic, even dangerous fictional subject matter, as in "Death of a Young Politico" ("*Seiji Shonen Shisu*" [1961]), an inflammatory short story about ultra right-wing influence on youth, based on the actual high school student who assassinated the Chairman of Japan's Socialist Party. Oe has gained renown for a series of distinguished if idiosyncratic forms of literary Japanese, transforming his style after the birth of his mentally disabled first child, the unhappy but crucial event which drives the confessional and semi-autobiographical *A Personal Matter* (*Kojinteki na Taiken* [1964]), possibly his finest novel. Oe's distinguished literary career continued to draw inspiration from private or national crises, and the resultant alienated or victimized individuals, such as in his 1965 tribute to the survivors of the Hiroshima atomic bomb. His further contributions to literature include the theoretical work *A Method for the Novel* (*Shosetsu no Hoho* [1978]).

David Taylor and Tomonao Yoshida

Date 1994 (Nobel Prize in Literature awarded)

Nationality Japan

Other Key Works *The Pinch Runner Memorandum* (1976), *A Quiet Life* (1990)

Why It's Key Novelist, left-wing humanist, pacifist, ecologist, and social critic, Oe remains one of the most important intellectual figures in Japan, his statements always galvanizing public opinion.

Opposite Kenzaburo Oe

706

Key Author **Jáchym Topol**
City Sister Silver

Already a central figure in the underground literary movement, in 1985 Topol co-founded *Revolver Revue*, a *samizdat* or underground magazine publishing contemporary Czech fiction, which continued until 1989 illegally. After the Velvet Revolution, the non-violent revolution that took place that year, it was published legally. Topol had been briefly imprisoned for his publications. But it was as a poet, a moulder of spoken Czech into new and radically beautiful literary contortions and configurations, as well as a lyricist for his brother's rock band, that he was best known until *City Sister Silver* (*Sestra*), his fictional debut.

City Sister Silver is an anarchic dissection of the situation after the fall of Communism. Through disconcerting shifts in register and voices, it captures the exhilaration of that time and its new freedoms, through a carnival of the senses mediated by its young narrator, Potok. The novel was both a response to political events and an explosion of bottled up energies, a way of confronting the history as it was being made – but not by relating events in sequential fashion, more by summoning up the spirit of the times: a thriller, a love story, a spewing forth of social criticism, a new way of looking at Czech literary language itself, as well as Czech society. Erotic, horrific, poetic, mythic, it is not primarily a piece of sociological reportage, though it has straightforwardly descriptive passages; but it expressed the ideological jolt experienced by Topol's generation after the revolution, a revolution and disarray reflected in the text itself. Elaborate and ambitious, it alternates fantasy with a portrait of contemporary corruption. Topol was hailed as the guiding spirit of the Czech new wave and was seen to be reinvigorating Eastern European literature in general.

Lucy Daniel

Date 1994

Author Jáchym Topol (born 1962)

Nationality Czechoslovakia

Other Key Works Poems *I Love You Madly* (1988), *The War Will Start on Tuesday* (1993) **Novels** *A Trip to the Train Station* (1994), *Night Works* (2001)

Why It's Key Topol has published commercially successful, stylistically radical poetry and novels. *City Sister Silver* has been translated into several languages.

Key Author **Edna O'Brien**
House of Splendid Isolation

In *House of Splendid Isolation* Josie O'Meara is a typical Edna O'Brien heroine. She is an Irish woman who has seen something of the wider world, having worked for a time in the United States, but has been drawn back to Ireland even though its social mores are particularly repressive to women. She has struggled to achieve happiness in a difficult marriage, and in this she is not unusual. Where O'Brien courts controversy is that, unlike many other Irish wives, her heroine has not only had an abortion but a passionate affair with a priest. As an elderly woman she is held hostage in her crumbling home by McGreevy, an IRA terrorist on the run and this obliges her to relive memories from her past. Through McGreevy, O'Brien brings in the world of contemporary Irish politics, and she risks alienating readers by showing the fugitive as a human being beset by fear and danger rather than as a mindless sectarian killer.

Her early works were banned for their sexual frankness, although they would seem mild to twenty-first-century readers. O'Brien continues to engage with controversial issues in present-day Ireland in her novel *In the Forest* (2002), which takes as its basis a real-life murder case that scandalized the country. She plays off the two main characters, a criminally insane youth and his older female victim showing how very different their lives have been but how fatally linked they ultimately are. Many people felt not only that the real murder case was too recent but that the author uses it to give too raw and damning a picture of rural Ireland.

Michael Munro

Date 1994 (publication)

Author Edna O'Brien (born 1932)

Nationality Ireland

Other Key Works
The Country Girls (1960), *Girl with Green Eyes* (1962), *Girls in their Married Bliss* (1963)

Why It's Key O'Brien's fiction has always been controversial, mainly for portraying the women of Ireland as unfulfilled and repressed by the society into which they are born.

Key Book
Reef

Through flashbacks, and beautiful lyrical prose, the novel tells of Triton, a Tamil servant in Sri Lanka. After a wayward youth, he is brought into the employment of Mister Salgado, a biologist, and becomes a revered chef. As Triton becomes more and more involved in Salgado's life, Sri Lanka is undergoing, post-Independence, civil disturbances and in particular the Tamil uprising of the early 1970s. Eventually, Salgado and Triton go to England and make a life for themselves there, and they are followed by disturbances of a more subtle kind.

Never leaving the intimate and the domestic, *Reef* shows the harrowing effects of nationalism on personal lives and more widely, on the fragile nature of identity. As Salgado falls in love with Miss Nili, Triton can do nothing else but do the same. The novel's social setting is the Christian educated elite who, after Independence, found it increasingly difficult to find a place for themselves in Sri Lanka. Through Triton's eyes, Gunesekera captures the indolence, cliquishness, and the powerful dialogue of this group as they try to maintain their status in a changing society.

The ending is ambivalent as political solutions become invariably personal. Mr Salgado returns to Sri Lanka for an uncertain future. Triton has to face his own independence in Great Britain. *Reef* is a bittersweet and original novel.

Royce Mahawatte

Date 1994

Author Romesh Gunesekera (born 1954)

Nationality Sri Lanka/UK

Why It's Key Short-listed for the Booker Prize in 1994, *Reef* is Gunesekera's first novel and a quiet and sensitive exploration of devotion, loyalty, and the love of food, English and Sri Lankan. Exquisitely observed, this novel made its mark by demonstrating that politics could be written about via the personal and domestic.

Key Event **Kelman wins the Booker Prize sparking a row among the judges**

"My culture and my language have the right to exist," James Kelman claimed in his Booker Prize acceptance speech, "and no-one has the authority to dismiss that right." Such strong assertions were typical from this acclaimed yet controversial author, committed as he has been throughout his career to the breaking down of class barriers and regional hierarchies Kelman believes characterize the history of English literature. Lauded for formal innovation and for its representation of the lives of the working classes in modern Glasgow, Kelman's work has inevitably been contentious. His speech anticipated the predictable furore that his novel's victory caused. Following the announcement one of the judges, Rabbi Julia Neuberger publicly disavowed the decision, calling it "disgraceful" and the book "inaccessible." Like some others she was offended by the novel's consistent use of swear words. The narrative renders the monologue of an embattled Glaswegian Sammy Samuels and his courageous attempt to gain official recognition and compensation after being blinded by a police beating. Neuberger's dissent was seized upon and magnified in a wider media debate galvanised by controversy. It confronted the cultural role, moral compass, and political direction of the Booker Prize as a world literary institution. It also exposed the class-bound formations of contemporary British society and its metropolitan literary culture. In this context and in its revelation of an emergent underclass failed by a post-Thatcher Welfare State, Kelman's novel stands as a key text in the culture wars of the 90s. The prize confirmed a contemporary "renaissance" in Scottish Literature and exemplified the new direction that "British" literature had begun to take to catch up with the breakthroughs of the "new literatures in English" that formed the cutting edge of global fiction writing since the 1960s.
Graeme Mcdonald

Date 1994

Title *How Late It Was, How Late*

Author James Kelman (born 1946)

Nationality UK

Why It's Key A critical storm surrounded Kelman's controversial winning novel. One prominent critic infamously labelled it an act of "literary vandalism." Many others queued up to defend this rich, challenging narrative of contemporary British underclass experience.

1990–1999

709

Key Character **Daisy Goodwill** *The Stone Diaries*

Carol Shields wrote with extraordinary intensity about ordinary lives, was fascinated by the interplay between history, biography, and fiction, and was a supreme prose stylist with a highly developed visual imagination. *The Stone Diaries* combines all these characteristics as well as taking some unusual, experimental leaps with the narrative form of the novel.

The Stone Diaries tells the life of Daisy Goodwill, daughter of a stonecutter, and his "solid" wife Mercy, who dies in childbirth. Daisy's life spans the twentieth century; she was born in 1905 and we follow her through to her fragile old age and death in the 1990s. The novel is remarkable for the varieties of narrative techniques it employs – there is a whole chapter in letters, for example; the narrative viewpoint changes from first person to third person; there are newspaper clippings and observations from minor characters. There is even a series of photographs of some of the principal characters, as though these were "real" people, and this a "real" biography (though there are no photographs of Daisy herself).

What emerges from Daisy's life is a question about what constitutes a life at all. Is any one individual the most reliable narrator of their own lives? If not, then who is? Shield's novel tells us that perhaps there is no such thing as an objective life story, and that what we think of as our own life stories are written by the people we know and by the people who observe us as much as by ourselves
Gerard Woodward

Date 1994

Author Carol Shields (1935–2003)

Nationality Canada

Why It's Key Shields was a leading Canadian novelist whose experiments with narrative form and concern with what she called "the arc of human life" produced nine novels and several short story and poetry collections. *In Larry's Party* (1997) she looked at the arc of life from a masculine perspective.

Key Character **Walter Rawley**
Mr. Vertigo

In keeping with the frenetic pace of Auster's previous novels, Walter Rawley's bizarre odyssey begins on the very first page, when the enigmatic Master Yehudi pulls the young beggar off the street with the promise that he'll learn to fly. Without relinquishing his hard-bitten cynicism, Walt gives in to his curiosity about the Master, and so is gradually drawn into compliance with a clandestine and very extreme training process in the flatlands of Kansas.

Walt's narrative voice, replete with wisecracks and obscenities, evokes the tough street argot of Depression-era America. The language of the street boy and child star, however merges into the more reflective, mature perspective of the adult narrator, telling his story from the distance of decades. This perspective casts the story of the flying boy sensation in the light of Auster's recurring themes and motifs. Walt's descriptions of the ecstatic, disembodied experiences of levitation and flight exemplify the author's abiding fascination for extreme physical and psychological states. Moreover, Yehudi's transformation of Walt from the abject, semi-feral child he calls "nothing," into a sublime, transcendent creature of the air can be read, like many of Auster's novels, as an allegory of the writer and his work. The wonder of Walt's spectators is mirrored in us as Auster's readers.

Walt's sublimity, however, is short-lived. Like many Auster protagonists, his reaches the heights only to crash inexorably down to earth. Nonetheless, his exuberant storytelling suggests that the spirit of flight lives on in him.

Josh Cohen

Date 1994

Author Paul Auster (born 1947)

Nationality USA

Why It's Key A Depression-era street kid who learns to fly and becomes a national sensation, the tough, wisecracking Walt was a departure from the cerebral and melancholic protagonists of Auster's previous novels.

Opposite Paul Auster

1990–1999

711

Key Event **One of the most popular non-fiction books of all time**

Southern Gothic in tone and depicting a plethora of eccentric and ambiguous Savannah personalities, *Midnight in the Garden of Good and Evil* centers round the murder of a local hustler by a respected art dealer and the four murder trials that ensued. While the work is categorized as non-fiction, Berendt presents a highly subjective version of real events whereby timelines are re-jigged and certain personalities become archetypal, larger-than-life, serving at times as peculiar decoration or light relief. While a degree of embellishment and supposition is expected of non-fiction, Berendt boldly acknowledges the work as a mélange of fact and fiction. By placing himself at the heart of events as they unfold, he gave the book the feel of a thriller, thereby enhancing immeasurably its populist appeal. In an interview by *Entertainment Weekly*, Berendt said, "People in Savannah don't say, 'Before leaving the room, Mrs. Jones put on her coat.' Instead, they say, 'Before leaving the room, Mrs. Jones put on the coat that her third husband left her before he shot himself in the head.'" It is this underlying, darkly humorous morbidity that Berendt, by effectively blending his own first-hand research with established versions of events, captures brilliantly in the novel, casting himself as the New York journalist feeling strangely out of place and time, compelled by the peculiar nature of the people and the place to expose the truth, but knowing in his heart that the truth is not absolute, particularly in a town like Savannah.

Christian Kerr

Date 1994

Title *Midnight in the Garden of Good and Evil*

Author John Berendt (born 1939)

Nationality USA

Why It's Key Berendt's "non-fiction" novel *Midnight in the Garden of Good and Evil* spent 216 weeks on the *New York Times* bestseller list and is set around a real-life murder case in Savannah, Georgia.

Key Book *The Wind-Up Bird Chronicle* (*Nejimaki-dori kuronikuru*)

Toru Okada is at home one evening, cooking spaghetti and listening to the London Symphony Orchestra, when he receives the first of a series of mysterious phone calls. His cat is missing and his wife fails to come home. A number of encounters with strangers, including a teenage neighbor and a pair of attractive twins, lead Okada on the journey to find his missing wife, Kumiko.

The Wind-Up Bird Chronicle resembles a modern epic, interweaving alienation, philosophical searching, shared dreams, love, and sex into a hypnotic narrative. The story takes in murder, gangsters, and abandoned houses along with a number of episodes that lead back into history and the atrocities committed by the Japanese army in Manchuria during World War II.

In Murakami's world, contemporary American culture fills a gap left by the absence of traditional Japanese values in modern life. Cut off from the past, his characters, who have odd names like Nutmeg and Malta, have no real sense of who they are. They drink beer, play baseball, and listen to western music. Toru Okada climbs down into an empty well to get to the essence of his being. It is only when he loses his wife that he begins to see the complexity and richness of the world around him.

In the meaningless void created by discontinuity Murakami's characters wrestle with existential angst as they try to make sense of their lives. In his depiction of a society orphaned by history Murakami creates a very distinctive world.

Jamal Mahjoub

Date 1994–5

Author Haruki Murakami (born 1949)

Nationality Japan

Why It's Key Murakami is the most successful author in Japanese history. His books have sold millions, both at home and abroad, despite accusations of his being too westernized. *The Wind-Up Bird Chronicle* was originally published as three volumes and is widely believed to be his best novel. It won the Yomiuri prize in Japan.

712

Key Event *Prozac Nation* kick-starts a trend for confessional writing

Elizabeth Wurtzel's *Prozac Nation* inaugurated a genre of confessional trauma writing about a host of psychological distresses ranging from depression to childhood abuse and eating disorders. Wurtzel's account of her severe depression throughout her teen years and decision, while a student at Harvard, to be an early adopter of Prozac appeared on the cusp of public recognition of depression's prevalence and the widespread prescription of antidepressants. But it counters the celebratory air surrounding these newly available treatments by questioning their actual benefit.

Wurtzel tentatively sees her depression as the manifestation of anxieties about the failure to achieve her family and friends' expectations. While Wurtzel acknowledges that Prozac may give some relief, she also speculates that it only responds to the bodily results of social pressures, and consequently these pressures, if left unresolved, will respond by having the body building up resistance to drugs. Depressed individuals face the paradox of treatments that may offer some immediate help, but at best only as a means of long-term management, rather than a cure.

Though its theme is depression, *Prozac Nation* is also an intellectual journey of 1990s post-feminism, where female writers explore the crushing pressures that contemporary women face, but in ways that part from (or are actively hostile to) the feminism of their mothers' generation. *Prozac Nation* is the calling card of Generation X writers, born after the American baby boom, who are unhappy with society, but lack a political language to articulate their complaints in anything more than tones of narcissistic anomie.

Stephen Shapiro

Date 1994

Author Elizabeth Wurtzel (born 1967)

Nationality USA

Why It's Key *Prozac Nation* opened the gates for public discussion of depression and mental illness for a post-baby-boom generation facing the increased pressures to succeed, and inaugurated the era of the "crisis memoir."

Opposite Elizabeth Wurtzel

Key Author
Seamus Heaney

Seamus Heaney (born 1939) was brought up a Catholic and a Nationalist on a farm in County Derry, and the everyday detail of rural life – digging potatoes, cutting turf – informs much of his early work. "By God, the old man could handle a spade," he remembers his father in "Digging." "But I've no spade to follow men like them," he says, determining instead to dig with his pen. The writer as artisan, and the poem as artifact, are constant themes in his work, as is the exploration of words at work in the world beyond literature.

No poet living in Ireland can be immune to the sectarian gashes that divide the island, and Heaney, though never a man to mount a soap box, found his "heart besieged by anger" after Bloody Sunday. A decade later he famously rebuked (in verse) the editors of *The Penguin Book of Contemporary British Poetry* for including him in their collection. His move from the North to the Republic in 1972 was not without significance.

But Heaney's rootedness in his Irishness allows him to transcend narrow nationalisms. In his "Requiem for the Croppies" killed in their thousands at Vinegar Hill in 1798, it is more than Irish national aspirations for which he mourns: it is the heartlessness of blind historical forces, pitting farm boys with scythes against cannon. Heaney is a man whose heart is as open as his mind, and it is this generosity of spirit that has found him a following far beyond the confines of his island.
Ian Crofton

Date 1995 (Nobel Prize in Literature awarded)

Nationality Ireland

Why It's Key When Heaney, the greatest Irish poet since Yeats, was awarded the 1995 Nobel Prize in Literature, the Swedish Academy praised his "works of lyrical beauty and ethical depth, which exalt everyday miracles and the living past."

Opposite **Seamus Heaney**

714

Key Author **Salman Rushdie**
The Moor's Last Sigh

An endlessly inventive, challenging, and political novelist and essayist, Salman Rushdie (born 1947) has been hugely influential for Indo-Anglian writing specifically, and late twentieth and early twenty-first century fiction more generally. His prose is dense, playful, mesmerising and at times exasperating, but his inimitable style has earned him high critical acclaim including the Booker prize, the Whitbread Novel Award, and the "Booker of Bookers."

In his teens, Rushdie and his family joined the many Muslims who moved from India to Pakistan. His fiction often examines the tensions between the two countries and explores the contradictions that constitute cultural identity. Writing in the magical realist tradition, which blends elements of the real with the fantastical, he has been able to explore the fractured identities and sense of divided loyalty engendered by the political situation.

Rushdie will forever be associated with the struggle for true freedom of expression. Worldwide controversy erupted after the publication of his fourth novel, *The Satanic Verses* (1988). Many Muslims considered the depiction of Islam blasphemous and in 1989 Iran's Ayatollah Khomeini issued a fatwa against him. Millions of pounds were offered as a bounty and consequently he was forced into hiding, living under tight security for years. While in hiding, he wrote the children's novel, *Haroun and the Sea of Stories* (1990), a parable, which explores the affective power of storytelling. The so-called "Rushdie Affair" focused attention on the effects of the written word and the issue of freedom of speech and forced a confrontation with the potentially violent implications of such freedom. As Rushdie himself was at pains to point out, however, "the attack against me and my work is only one battle in a larger war."
Juliet Wightman

Date 1995 (publication)

Nationality UK (born India)

Other Key Work *Midnight's Children* (1981)

Why It's Key A purveyor of magical stories, a writer of unparalleled imagination and complexity, Rushdie has come to represent the struggle between the freedom and suppression of expression.

Key Author **Penelope Fitzgerald**
The Blue Flower

Penelope Fitzgerald did not take up her literary career until she was nearing age 60, with a biography of pre-Raphaelite painter Edward Burne-Jones (1975). This was followed by a biography of her father Edmund Knox, editor of *Punch* magazine, and his three eminent brothers, *The Knox Brothers* (1977). Told with detached affection, her biographies offer scholarly yet engaging portraits of these imaginative individuals and their milieux.

Her earlier novels draw heavily on her own varied life experiences. *The Bookshop* (1978) recalls her years working in a struggling bookshop in Suffolk; *Offshore*, which won the Booker Prize in 1979, is based on her life on a houseboat on the Thames, while *Human Voices* (1980) is a humorous account of her wartime years working at the BBC. Her experience as an English teacher at a drama school is reflected in *At Freddie's* (1982), a novel about a theater school for children run by the eponymous woman of indomitable energy.

In her later works, Fitzgerald combines her succinct narrative style with her effortless skill in reconstructing the past with meticulous, almost tangible, details of everyday life. *The Beginning of Spring* (1988) and *The Gate of Angels* (1990) are cool and accurate observations of the daily lives of those who happened to live at a time when revolutionary changes in history were about to take place. Her final novel *The Blue Flower* (1995) is a fictionalized account of the life of German Romantic poet and philosopher Novalis. His slightly absurd passion for a rather banal twelve-year-old girl is dealt with in a delicate way that is at once unsentimental and moving. Her work received international recognition after *The Blue Flower* won America's National Book Critics' Circle Award in 1997.
Mayako Murai

Date 1995 (publication)

Author Penelope Fitzgerald (1916–1987)

Nationality UK

Other Key Works *The Golden Child* (1977), *Innocence* (1986)

Why It's Key Novelist and biographer, Fitzgerald's writing is characterized by its elliptical beauty and immaculate precision in constructing ironic social comedies which are filled with sensuous details of the mundane, yet have a peculiar surreal quality.

1990–1999

717

Key Book
Northern Lights

In the last years of the twentieth century, *Northern Lights* became notorious for its appeal to both children and adults. If adults are reading the same books as children, what does this say about adults in our society? What does it say about children? It is interesting, then, that one of the central preoccupations of Pullman's novel is the nature of the transition between child and adult. It is a fantasy adventure set in a vividly realized world existing in parallel to our own – a world both strangely familiar and intriguingly different. In this world, the soul of every person is externally manifested in animal form, and is known as their daemon. Children's demons can shape-shift freely, taking on different forms to suit the situation; however, when a person reaches maturity, the shape of their demon becomes fixed. The evil Gobblers (General Oblation Board of London) carry out monstrous experiments on children and their demons in order to ascertain the significance of this change.

Comparisons have been made to Rowling's roughly contemporaneous Harry Potter novels, which are also read by both children and adults. However, Pullman's trilogy is a great deal more philosophically complex. Although the sinister Mrs Coulter tells her daughter Lyra that children shouldn't worry about "big, difficult ideas," this is precisely what Pullman encourages them to do. *Northern Lights* involves its readers in metaphysical questions, encouraging them to think about the relationship between body and soul, good and evil, destiny and free will – and to ponder on the nature of the human.
Anna Tripp

Date 1995

Author Philip Pullman (born 1946)

Nationality UK

Why It's Key *Northern Lights* is the first book in Pullman's *His Dark Materials* trilogy. On publication in 1995, this beguiling fantasy novel became one of the most famous British examples of the publishing phenomenon known as "cross-over fiction."

Opposite Philip Pullman

Key Book
The Black Album

Kureishi's second novel received a mixed critical reception after his acclaimed and influential *The Buddha of Suburbia* (1990). This has dramatically shifted as critics have reconsidered the book's anticipation of key issues that preoccupy twenty-first-century British politics, society, and culture. *The Black Album* is a remarkably prescient examination of emergent conflicts surrounding multiculturalism in contemporary western societies. From the beginning it sets up oppositions and ambivalences: between alienation and socialisation; individuality and communality. It investigates divergent ideas of respectability and "immorality"; virtue and indecency. Such oppositions are found in the student Shahid's political and emotional involvement with a group of militant young Muslims and his liberated college lecturer. He is simultaneously attracted to and repulsed by the code of values exerted by both "decadent" secular Western consumerism and liberalism and "extremist" religious forms of fundamentalism. In an evocative London setting, Shahid is caught between cultures and ethnicities: between religion and secularism; love and politics.

In presenting such ambiguities of belonging and origins the novel engages with pressing, complex questions of assimilation, change, and tolerance. In confronting terrorism and violence in the capital and beyond it rejects absolutisms. Ultimately it advances the potential of hybridity to create new forms of Britishness. For Kureishi, "there must be a fresh way of seeing Britain and the choices it faces: and a new way of being British after all this time. Much thought, discussion and self-examination must go into seeing the necessity for this, what this 'new way of being British' involves and how difficult it might be to attain."
Graeme Mcdonald

Date 1995

Author Hanif Kureishi (born 1954)

Nationality UK

Why It's Key Extraordinarily prescient, the conflict between liberalism and fundamentalism among young second generation British immigrants was relevant to the time – the book is set in the shadow of the fatwa against Salman Rushdie. The extraordinary events of the 2005 terrorist attacks on London propelled the novel back into public focus.

Key Character **Lieutenant Billy Prior**
The Ghost Road

In the Ghost Road trilogy Barker explores issues of masculinity, militarism, and the conflicts inherent in the demands placed upon men in wartime. Lieutenant Billy Prior (along with Siegfried Sassoon and Wilfred Owen) is sent to Craiglockhart Hospital under the care of W.H.R. Rivers, the eminent doctor, to be cured of mutism. He is rather different from the other officers there, in that he is working class and as such is seen as a "temporary gentleman." Prior is therefore positioned at the center of class politics of the period. With Prior, Barker eschews the stultifying middle-class perspective that is firmly attached to some World War I fictions. He is a vigorous character, fueled by an awareness of class discriminations, but equally determined to make the most of the social and sexual opportunities war affords men such as him.

With Billy Prior, Barker introduces a modern perspective on masculinity and class; he is a bright and intelligent young man, sexually ambivalent, headstrong and at times wilfully disobedient. In *The Ghost Road* a conclusive irony is portrayed. Prior, the temporary gentleman is finally, on his return to the front, a fully paid up member of the "club to end all clubs." Not only is he "a fairly phoney gentleman," he goes into battle with a "phoney gentleman's gentleman" by his side. Prior is one of the most demandingly complex and engaging characters in contemporary fiction, and, unusually, he is working class. This is most telling and one of the reasons he made such an impact.

The trilogy, the most commercially successful of Barker's novels, won a number of awards including the Guardian Fiction Prize (*The Eye in the Door* [1993]) and The Booker Prize (*The Ghost Road* [1995]). In 2000 Pat Barker was award the CBE.
Pat Wheeler

Date 1995

Also Appears in *Regeneration* (1991), *The Eye in the Door* (1993)

Author Pat Barker (born 1943)

Nationality UK

Why It's Key Billy Prior is a working-class, bisexual officer in the highly regarded World War I trilogy. Throughout, Barker synthesizes fact and fiction to explore the unresolved psychological conflicts in men emotionally affected by the horrors of war.

Key Event **Camus' *The First Man* is published for the first time**

Discovered in a mud-spattered briefcase beside the wreckage of the car in which Albert Camus died in 1960, the manuscript of *The First Man* was not published for over thirty years because of his family's fears that the political ideas expressed in the book would provoke attacks on his reputation from the French left. It is Camus' most autobiographical novel, the story of Jacques Cormery, the son of a blind single-mother in colonial Algeria, and closely mirrors the author's own upbringing. Camus had not finished the book at the time of his death, and it is thought he intended it to be much longer.

The First Man is written in a much more descriptive, sensual style than Camus' previous work. It shows a greater concern with realist narrative than his other books, but nevertheless concentrates, as before, on the racial and social tensions of Algerian society. It is an exploration of the complicated links between a colonial power and the colonized society. There are

three pivotal relationships in the book: Jacques' tender care for his mother, his deep friendship and respect for his teacher Monsieur Bernard, and his struggle to lay the ghost of his dead father to rest.

The manuscript is published uncorrected, including Camus' often cryptic notes for revisions and new sentences. It captures something of the writer at work, and offers tantalizing glimpses into his method. Critics have speculated feverishly about how *The First Man* aligns with, or completes, Camus' existentialist schemes of singularity and solidarity, oblivion and absurdity. But without the finished text, these theories can never be definitively resolved.
Charles Beckett

Date 1995

Place France

Author Albert Camus (1913–1960)

Why It's Key It contributed an important dimension to critical understanding of Camus. It shows a major development in his fictional style, submerging philosophical and political concerns deeper beneath the richly detailed surface of the novel and invoking the realist tradition of nineteenth-century writing.

1990-1999

719

Key Passage
The Reader (*Der Vorleser*)

"The geological layers of our lives rest so tightly one on top of the other that we always come up against earlier events in later ones, not as matter that has been fully formed and pushed aside, but absolutely present and alive. I understand this. Nevertheless, I sometimes find it hard to bear."

At fifteen Bernhard Schlink's lucid and melancholy narrator Michael Berg fell in love with an older woman whom, years later he witnessed put on trial as a former concentration camp guard. Berg's retrospective story of his love for Hanna Schmitz peeled back some of the historical layers on which German post-war life was resting uncertainly. Rejecting the politically correct solution that evil can be reliably identified and punished and thus dealt with forever, Schlink's narrator refused to condemn without understanding. He was tormented to discover Hanna was crippled by illiteracy and in her own way a victim.

Schlink reopened the Holocaust wound and suggested that, beyond the power of the courts to deliver their verdict, it was always a human possibility that past horror might reoccur because moral dilemmas repeat themselves. Hanna tellingly asks those who judge her: "What would you have done?" and receives no answer. Through the device of the educated boy reading German literature aloud to the deprived ethnic German immigrant, the novel can also be read as an allegory of the fate of German culture, although Schlink's critics have found the portrait of Hanna as a victim and the troubled eroticism of Berg's love morally unacceptable.
Lesley Chamberlain

Date 1995

Author Bernhard Schlink (born 1944)

Nationality Germany

Why It's Key This novel was internationally hailed as a work of art finally able to evoke the universal moral burden of the Holocaust upon later generations. But its special pleading for a cruel woman has left many readers uncomfortable and it remains controversial.

Key Event *Longitude* starts a new trend in non-fiction writing

Dava Sobel's book recounts the story of John Harrison, who in the mid-eighteenth century had discovered an accurate way to measure longitude whilst at sea by using clocks. In so doing he won the British "Longitude Prize" and solved a problem which had bedevilled navigation for centuries. Being able to measure one's longitude (location on the earth east or west of the Prime Meridian, now taken as Greenwich in London) and latitude (location on the earth north or south of the equator) is key when sailing long distances and when drawing maps. Harrison, a "man of simple birth and high intelligence," invented a highly accurate chronometer to allow mariners to calculate their exact position. He managed, against the wishes of the scientific and naval establishments, to prove that his inventions worked and the consequences of this were immense.

Harrison's story is one of obsession and drive, but it also manages to encompass politics, empire, and economics; it was rich with possibility for the talented narrative writer, and extremely attractive to an audience hungry for scientific success stories. Written simply and directly, Sobel's book was an astonishing worldwide publishing phenomenon. As such it was widely imitated, inaugurating a new style of popular narrative history and biography which was generally focused upon science or a cultural artifact. Sobel demonstrated that the public were interested in reading about the untold stories of human progress.

Jerome de Groot

Date 1995

Author Dava Sobel (born 1947)

Nationality USA

Why It's Key *Longitude* created a new market for popular narrative history.

Key Event **Martin Amis receives a huge advance for his novel *The Information***

In 1995 Martin Amis was still the *enfant terrible* of British writing and at the top of his game after *London Fields* (1989) and *Time's Arrow* (1991). To secure what he thought was a fit reward for his new book he left his agent of many years (Pat Kavanagh) for Andrew Wylie, through whom he obtained an advance of £500,000 for his new book, *The Information* (1995). The action sparked what Amis called "an Eisteddfod of hostility" which certainly affected his reputation. Reactions ranged from personal enmity and annoyance at Amis' arrogance to more cerebral debates about whether authors should receive such sums. Amis had every right to ask for more: he had influenced an entire generation of novelists; he was regularly celebrated by critics whilst also selling well; he was a talented literary star with an excellent reputation. He was, however, seen as greedy. The key result of Amis' advance was that literary fiction writers became big stars in their own rights and were treated much more as players in the cultural game. The problems with this are twofold. Firstly, advance negotiation and bidding wars surrounding first-time books perceived to be winners can lead to massive sums being thrown at novelists, and the ensuing hype does not always help the writer's cause. This was the case with, for instance, Monica Ali's *Brick Lane* (2003) Hari Kunzru's *The Impressionist* (2002) and Gautam Malkani's *Londonstani* (2007). The sums and the media attention involved lead to press backlashes as books are held up to more than literary account, and the process often gives agents more power than publishers. Secondly, a book has to perform despite its quality; this has led to the arbitrary mass-marketing of literary fiction in a bid to move units and justify the financial investment.

Jerome de Groot

Date 1995

Author Martin Amis (born 1949)

Nationality UK

Why It's Key Amis' advance for *The Information* was by some way the biggest given a literary novelist to this point and ushered in an era of big cash contracts.

Opposite **Martin Amis**

Key Event
Execution of Ken Saro-Wiwa

Ken Saro-Wiwa's execution, along with eight of his fellow activists, in November 1995, caused international outrage, despite the failure of the Commonwealth Heads of State to impose sanctions against the regime of Sani Abacha before the sentence was carried out, or to condemn the behavior of Shell plc, whom Saro-Wiwa had famously accused of "genocide against the Ogoni people." The trial of the "Ogoni Nine" was later condemned as "judicial murder" by British Prime Minister John Major and denounced by the United Nations.

Saro-Wiwa first rose to prominence in Nigeria as a writer after his radio play *The Transistor Radio*, broadcast in 1972, won widespread critical acclaim. He went on to write a series of satirical novels, and, for young people, the hugely popular *Basi and Company* television series. He believed that the role of the writer included political activism; that he could not merely be a chronicler of change, but must actively try to effect it. It was this belief which gave rise to a series of increasingly polemical articles in various magazines, and essays, later collected in *Nigeria, the Brink of Disaster* (1991).

Wole Soyinka, Saro-Wiwa's friend, fellow writer, and activist, campaigned internationally for his release. On the day before the execution was carried out, Soyinka traveled to Auckland, New Zealand, to press heads of state for action against Abacha's regime, but without success. Saro-Wiwa's name has become synonymous with the struggle between the world's poorest tribes and the multinational companies and complicit governments who steal their resources. In a wider sense, he is remembered for his commitment to the ideal of literature's, and the writer's, participation in political and social causes.

Charles Beckett

Date November 10, 1995

Author Ken Saro-Wiwa (1941–1995)

Nationality Nigeria

Why It's Key Saro-Wiwa's death, and the statements he made during his trial have had global repercussions, and continue to haunt the exploiters of indigenous peoples around the world. His son now chairs the Saro-Wiwa Foundation, and continues his campaign against the destructive activities of oil companies.

1990–1999

723

Key Book *Blindness (Ensaio Sobre a Cegueira)*

José Saramago was, in 1998, the first Portuguese writer to win the Literature Nobel. His fiction may be divided into two chronological phases – one concerned with issues of Portuguese history and identity, the second centering on allegorical narratives of universal import. Saramago sees his writings as playing a part in the struggle against dehumanization in the era of globalization. *Blindness* belongs to the second phase.

It is located in the unnamed capital of an unnamed country; the characters too are all anonymous. A driver, "the first blind man," suddenly and inexplicably goes blind as his car stands at the traffic lights: from that moment an epidemic of "white blindness" slowly but inexorably spreads until the entire population – with one sole exception – has gone blind. The authorities respond with harshly repressive measures; a small group of people struggle to retain their humanity, in an environment that becomes ever more dehumanized as the bases of civilization crumble. The group is headed by an ophthalmologist's wife, the one person never to go blind, and is accompanied by a seeing dog. Saramago's novel is a chilling exploration of the thesis that at the heart of democracy there lies a latent totalitarianism, and it has been compared to George Orwell's *Nineteen Eighty-Four* (1949). In 2004 Saramago published *Seeing* (*Ensaio sobre a Lucidez*), an even darker sequel which continues his concerns over dehumanization into the twenty-first century.

Christopher Rollason

Date 1995

Author José Saramago (born 1922)

Nationality Portugal

Why It's Key *Blindness*, one of the best-known novels by Portugal's Nobel-winning José Saramago, is a major contemporary exploration of totalitarianism, starting out from a "what would happen if... " scenario, as an imaginary country goes blind.

Opposite José Saramago

Key Character **Morvern Callar**
Morvern Callar

Death, art theft, nihilism, and cool opportunism are established from the outset in this resonant piece of Highland noir from one of Scotland's most prominent contemporary novelists. The unfazed manner in which Morvern discovers the corpse of her writer boyfriend is reflected in a pristine prose that establishes her as a deeply alluring yet ambivalent character. She disposes of the body, empties his account, and appropriates his unpublished novel to generate funds allowing her to escape from the drudgery of life in "The Port": the depressed West Coast Highland town where several Warner novels are set. Drink, drugs, clubbing, and sex prove some respite from Morvern's vacuous life as a checkout girl, though it is her Mediterranean trip that releases her from going through the motions of the average unexpected windfall.

Morvern's esoteric attitude and actions ensure her iconic status as a memorable character. Beyond the tourist zone she reaches an epiphany of sorts that disproves the thesis advanced by some critics that this is a character exemplifying the amoral choices and lassitude of the nineties blank generation. This is no grunge novel and she is no grunge girl. Her character is much more complex: reactive and reflective of her deprived social and political environment. Ironically, she is in fact one of Scotland's "Thatcher children"; mixing genuine social concern with individualist abandon. She epitomizes an ethos borne from the informal economy of the rave generation: take what you can get and enjoy it while it lasts…

Graeme Mcdonald

Date 1995

Author Alan Warner (born 1964)

Nationality UK

Why It's Key Prominent debut novel by one of Scotland's most celebrated novelists, establishing Warner as a key figure alongside Irvine Welsh and A.L. Kennedy in the "second wave" of the new Scottish writing. The novel was adapted into a stylish film in 2002 by the award-winning director Lynne Ramsay.

724

Key Character **Captain Alatriste**
El capitán Alatriste

The adventures of Captain Diego Alatriste have bounded their virile way into feature film, graphic novel, and even a walking tour of Madrid which navigates the dark alleyways and rowdy taverns where he plies his mercenary trade – probably leaving out most of the bloodshed, and the more picturesque action from the brothels.

Courageous Captain Alatriste, a charismatic seventeenth-century Spanish "sword for hire," became a publishing phenomenon throughout the Spanish-speaking world in the late 1990s. His work is calculated, in *Purity of Blood*, "at so much per swordthrust. A slash across the face, slicing off the ear of a creditor or of a bastard dallying with one's wife, a pistol shot at point-blank range, or a handspan of steel in a man's throat" – all this has a price. But Alatriste also has a code of honor, and his stories plunge him into various shapes of derring-do involving pirates, political intrigue, and the Spanish Inquisition.

Arturo Pérez-Reverte draws on the authors he loved as a child – particularly Alexandre Dumas père – for his historical romances of the Spanish Golden Age, but also uses the genre to address ideas of Spanish nationhood, bringing in facets of the modern literary thriller. He both revels in the swashbuckling swagger and brings it a more circumspect modern gait. Invigorated by the flash of naked steel, the novels celebrate the dash and vigour of what was a glamorous and important time in Spain's history, but also an extremely bloody one. Before he became a novelist, Pérez-Reverte was a war reporter; his merry sword thrusts are often combined with realistic, darker violence. As a fantastical embodiment of Spain's glorious past, infused with a modern morality, Alatriste has become an iconic national character.

Lucy Daniel

Date 1996

Author Arturo Pérez-Reverte (born 1951)

Nationality Spain

Why It's Key Pérez-Reverte, one of Spain's most popular living novelists, writes historical fiction about Spain and Spanish colonial history. Captain Alatriste is his most popular character, and has appeared on a commemorative stamp and a board game.

Key Passage
Fight Club

"My tiny life. My little shit job. My Swedish furniture. I never, no, never told anyone this, but before I met Tyler, I was planning to buy a dog and name it 'Entourage.' This is how bad your life can get."

*F*ight Club diagnoses a crisis of masculinity and sadomasochistic desires for violence in late-twentieth-century America. The unnamed narrator is a financially successful middle-class professional. Worn out and disillusioned by a world that offers flat-pack consumer goods as the best reward for the tedium of constant business travel, an empty life in an anonymous apartment block, and service for an unethical capitalist company, the narrator unconsciously slips into the role of his alter ego Tyler Durden. Tyler – irreverent, aggressive, in control of his surroundings, and a sexual predator – founds the nocturnal "Fight Club" where bare-chested men wrestle each other to reclaim a sense of masculine self outside the constraints of the labor market. Subsequently, the "Fight Club" recruits men into "Project Mayhem," a fascistically organized group that plays anarchist tricks on the rich and plots terrorist attacks on corporate buildings. Project Mayhem's goal is to convince each bruised male ego "that he had the power to control history."

Feminists take issue with the exaggerated idea of male victimization and disempowerment in contemporary western society, as this is empirically not the case. But the fact that the novel offers a platform for such masculine fears around the loss of control, be they real or imagined, has contributed to its massive success. The book shockingly anticipates the terrorist events of 9/11 by giving voice to home-grown destructive fantasies targeted at America's corporate buildings. As the author himself suggests in his Afterword to the 2006 edition of the novel, *Fight Club* merely encapsulated already existing cultural anxieties and tendencies.

Anne Schwan

Date 1996

Author Chuck Palahniuk (born 1962)

Nationality USA

Why It's Key This apocalyptic novel casts a disturbing look at the damaging effects of late capitalism on the male psyche. *Fight Club* became a cultural phenomenon, capturing the spirit of a whole generation of men; actual fight clubs opened in America, and Donatella Versace presented a men's clothing line on the fight club theme.

1990–1999

725

Key Event **The first Orange Prize for women's fiction is awarded**

*D*o women write, or read, differently from men? Ever since it was first awarded, the Orange Prize for women's fiction has provoked such questions. Some have expressed doubt as to the need for or wisdom of a prize just for women writers. But no one now can contest the Orange's status and significance in the contemporary literary scene.

The impulse behind the Prize's establishment was its founders' concern that women writers were being wrongly overlooked when it came to the granting of literary awards. The Prize was intended to remedy this situation. It was announced at the ICA in January 1996 and the first Orange Prize was awarded to Helen Dunmore the following May for her third novel *A Spell of Winter*. The novel, which is set during the early years of the twentieth century, tells the story of siblings Catherine and Rob, who have been abandoned by their parents, and their passionate, forbidden love.

Since then, the Prize – which comprises £30,000 and a limited edition bronze figurine called the "Bessie" – has been awarded annually, with recipients including Carol Shields, Kate Grenville, Andrea Levy, Lionel Shriver, and Zadie Smith. Honorary Director of the Prize is Kate Mosse, author of the best-selling *Labyrinth* (2005). The Orange has become a highlight of the literary calendar, significantly boosting the reputation, and sales, of the writers on its shortlist. The Orange Award for New Writers, whose aim is to recognize and nurture emerging literary talent, was presented for the first time in 2005.

Emily Jeremiah

Date 1996

Place UK

Author Helen Dunmore (born 1952)

Why It's Key The Orange Prize for Fiction, established to promote and celebrate the work of women writers, has had a major impact on the literary landscape. Helen Dunmore, its first winner, is the author of nine novels, including *Burning Bright*, *The Siege*, and *House of Orphans*. She has also written short stories, children's books, poetry, and a radio play.

Key Character **Bridget Jones**
Bridget Jones' Diary

Bridget Jones was first introduced as a character to British readers in the form of a mock-diary published as columns in the newspapers *The Independent* and *The Daily Telegraph* in the 1990s. They chronicled the comic misadventures of Bridget Jones, a "thirtysomething" young professional woman who lives in London and tries to make something of her life, particularly focusing on the happy ending of conventional romance. The columns satirized the self-absorption and anxiety fostered by women's magazines such as *Cosmopolitan*, the "smugness" of married couples who pity Bridget's single state, the efforts of her parents and friends to help her find the right man, and her entanglement with the wrong man. Bridget's resolutions for breaking her bad habits – eating too much, drinking too much, smoking – inevitably fail, with comic results. She also struggles with her parents' separation, as her mother leaves her father for another man. *Bridget Jones' Diary*, which combined the columns into a novel, updated and spoofed *Pride and Prejudice*, as Bridget falls in love with Mark Darcy, named after the famous Mr Darcy of Austen's novel, while also fantasizing about the popular BBC adaptation of *Pride and Prejudice*, which starred Colin Firth as Mr Darcy and included a notorious scene in which Mr Darcy has been swimming. The film version of *Bridget Jones' Diary* continued this playfulness by casting Colin Firth as Mark Darcy, which helped ensure that the film was as commercially successful as the bestselling novel.

Sarah Churchwell

Date 1996

Author Helen Fielding (born 1958)

Also Appears In *Bridget Jones: The Edge of Reason* (1999)

Why It's Key The success launched the "chick lit" revolution, as a generation of women identified with Bridget Jones' anxieties about being a "singleton," struggling with professional ambitions, her self-image, and most importantly, her desire to find "Mr Right."

Opposite Renée Zellweger as Bridget Jones in the film

Key Book
The God of Small Things

Small things, ordinary events in routine life in Ayemenem (Kerala), the daily management of a family-run pickle factory, and the accidental death by drowning of English cousin Sophie Mol seen through the eyes of "two-eggs" twins Rahel and Esthappen Yako: these are the incidents which make up Arundhati Roy's novel, told through a clever narrative technique of both flashing back and forward to earlier points in the story or to future moments. A novel, Roy informs us, which is the result of "an inextricable mix of experience and imagination" (amongst the biographical references, Roy's own mother, a divorcee and social activist, apparently inspired the model for rebel Ammu in the novel, while the pickle factory in the book still exists today, owned by Roy's uncle). The particular touch impressed by the author on every page is her deft use of the English language, at times infused with irony (for instance in her mocking inversion of Conrad's novel: "Dark of Heartness tiptoed into the Heart of Darkness"), with anti-colonial sentiments of rebellion and anger, or with a meticulous psychology shaping events (such as Ammu's "lofty sense of injustice and the mulish, reckless streak that develops in Someone Small who has been bullied all their lives by Someone Big"). For what effectively captivates the reader's attention throughout the novel is not the narrated events in themselves, but rather the way these events have managed to affect the lives of all the characters involved in the story.

Roy says about her novel: "To me the god of small things is the inversion of God. God's a big thing and God's in control. The god of small things... whether it's the way the children see things or whether it's the insect life in the book, or the fish or the stars – there is a not accepting of what we think of as adult boundaries."

Letizia Alterno

Date 1996

Author Arundhati Roy (born 1961)

Nationality India

Why It's Key Roy's best-selling novel, awarded the Booker Prize in 1997, has been translated into 40 languages and has sold more than 6 million copies. She became the first non-expatriate Indian woman author to win the Booker Prize.

Key Passage
Infinite Jest

"At 2010h. on 1 April Y.D.A.U., the medical attaché is still watching the unlabeled entertainment cartridge."

In the near future of *Infinite Jest*, even time is commodified. It is Y.D.A.U.: Year of the Depends Adult Undergarment. The "entertainment cartridge" is "Infinite Jest," an experimental film shot from the point of view of a baby. Whoever watches the film becomes transfixed – unable to do anything but watch – and consequently dies in his or her own excrement. The lethal "Infinite Jest" cartridge is coveted by terrorist groups and political organizations, whose intrigues constitute one of the many narrative strands in Wallace's encyclopedic novel. Like the addictive, recursive film, *Infinite Jest* depicts its subjects ensnared in the toxic cycles of commerce, drug-use, competition, pollution, and filial neurosis that define citizenry in late-postmodern America.

At the center of the novel are the Incandenzas, a hyperbolic version of The American Family that includes Joe Incandenza – auteur of the "Infinite Jest" film, nuclear researcher, and tennis school headmaster – his wife Avril, a fabulously capable ex-professor-cum-neatfreak, and their three sons: Mario, the "hideously deformed" cameraman-child; Hal, the tennis champ-cum-lexical genius; and Orin, the cynical footballer. Their domain is the Enfield Tennis Academy, where sporting excellence is paid for in personal and psychic agony. Down the hill sits the Ennet House Drug and Alcohol Recovery Facility, presided over by the physically enormous ex-addict Don Gately. Inmates at both institutions are governed by the same addictive cycles and existential gravitas – a condition epitomized by the "Infinite Jest" cartridge that claims the lives of the "medical attaché" and, by turns, every person who is exposed to the film while trying to save him.
Kiki Benzon

Date 1997

Author David Foster Wallace (born 1962)

Nationality USA

Why It's Key A sprawling, ambitious and often hysterically funny novel, *Infinite Jest* is a dizzying network of plotlines, voices, and literary styles. Its cultural and psychological complexity is rendered in an equally baroque narrative fabric. After the acclaim came the backlash – notably Dale Peck's acid review reproduced in *Hatchet Jobs* (2004).

728

Key Character **Jack Maggs**
Jack Maggs

Jack Maggs is a fiction within a fiction. With his huge frame and "hooded hungry eyes" he is a recreation of Magwitch, the convict-benefactor in Dickens' *Great Expectations*, who returns to London from Australia to find Pip, his protégé. Explaining his creative re-imagining of this character, Carey said *Great Expectations* is to Australians a "prison," "a way in which the English have colonized our ways of seeing ourselves."

Maggs is a revised embodiment of Australian national identity. Orphaned and abandoned, he was cast out by Ma Britten, his abortionist foster mother, who delivered him up to a life of crime. He had a glimpse, when shoved down chimneys as a child thief, of the opulent England that novelists write about; this becomes his fictional homeland when transported. "I am not of that race," says Maggs, meaning Australians. But by novel's end he has multiplied "that race."

Maggs' Pip is Henry Phipps, ungrateful imperial beneficiary of his "convict gold." Carey's ingenious,

pacy pastiche also involves a writer, Tobias Oates – a version of Dickens himself. Oates cures Maggs of a terrible tic by mesmerism, and plunders his secrets, writing a novel, *The Death of Jack Maggs*. But Carey's novel is an act of appropriation; Maggs borrows Oates' quill to write his own story. Further, he makes Oates his subject, writes about him, and eventually shackles him.

Dickens' novel was a study of inheritance; of guilt and shame about origins and "the return of the repressed." Carey adds a postcolonial twist. Maggs' homecoming is a colonized subject's search for identity. But he can only discard his shackles by becoming Australian. Maggs writes his story in invisible ink, visible only to readers of Carey's novel; it disappears from the page as Maggs writes it, a vanishing text. Stories can be wiped out, but also rewritten; history can be repossessed.
Lucy Daniel

Date 1997

Author Peter Carey (born 1943)

Nationality Australia

Why It's Key The prisoner becomes the writer; the writer becomes the thief. *Jack Maggs* was part of Carey's revisionist approach to Australian literary history, which continued in his next novel *True History of the Kelly Gang*. Carey was also one of the first to succumb to an attack of Victoriana sweeping through modern fiction such as Sarah Waters' *Fingersmith*.

Key Author **Don DeLillo**
Underworld

Characterized by its descriptive intensity and satirical tenor, Don DeLillo's oeuvre includes fourteen novels, three plays, two screenplays, and several essays published in cultural periodicals. DeLillo's novels countenance diverse cultural zones from remarkably disparate points of view, showing the author's exceptional versatility and breadth of scope. His narratives are set in war zones, research laboratories, stand-up comedy venues, and garbage dumps; his protagonists are performance artists, child prodigies, waste technologists, and reclusive authors. While his fiction resonates with the epic themes of Faulkner, Joyce, and Pynchon, DeLillo claims to be most keenly inspired by European movies, jazz, and Abstract Expressionism.

DeLillo's writing has attracted attention from literary scholars since the publication of his first novel, *Americana* (1971), a frenetic picaresque about the effects of a media-saturated, celebrity-crazed environment upon individual behavior and identity. Popular recognition came later, with DeLillo's dark comedy, *White Noise* (1985), which chronicles the unraveling of a college town that is beset by a "toxic cloud" caused by a nearby railway accident. His other major success is *Underworld* (1997), a polyphonic and chronologically disordered historiography of Cold War America. In DeLillo's most structurally intricate novel, *Libra* (1988), historical detail and conspiracy theory surrounding the assassination of John F. Kennedy form the narrative backdrop for a complex psychological portrait of Lee Harvey Oswald. A cerebral and personally remote literary figure, DeLillo is widely regarded as one of the most important voices in contemporary American letters. A shrewd social commentator and master of the novel form, DeLillo told an interviewer: "We're all one beat away from becoming elevator music."

Kiki Benzon

Date 1997

Author Don DeLillo (born 1936)

Nationality USA

Other Key Works *Great Jones Street* (1973), *Ratner's Star* (1976), *The Names* (1982), *Mao II* (1991), *Cosmopolis* (2003)

Why It's Key Paranoia, terrorism, baseball, waste, art, television, suburbia, the CIA, commodity culture, global economics, the American Dream: such are the components of DeLillo's formidable literary landscapes.

729

Key Author **Philip Roth**
American Pastoral

Philip Roth (born 1933) is one of the most important American authors of the twentieth century. In almost 30 books written over nearly 50 years, he has shown an extraordinary range of talents and a virtuosic command of the novel form. Beginning with 1959's *Goodbye, Columbus*, which won the National Book Award, Roth has been awarded almost every literary honour except for the Nobel Prize.

A third-generation Jewish-American from Newark, New Jersey, Roth is best known for his fictional depictions of American Jews like himself and his family – and for the controversies his early books stirred up amongst the Jewish-American community.

An incredibly prolific author, Roth's continued focus on American Jews has certainly been the main thread that has united his work from the late fifties until the present day. Although his most common modes are comic and realist, Roth has made a career out of confounding critics and expectations, creating an œuvre so vast and varied that it is no longer possible to pin him down as any one sort of writer. His other abiding preoccupations have included the writing life in America, male sexual desire, psychoanalysis, and, most recently, American history.

Many readers and critics have identified a late career resurgence in the series of ambitious books Roth has published since the mid-nineties. With a ferocious energy perhaps surprising in a writer in his sixties, Roth launched himself headlong into the highest rank of American writers with such contemporary classics as *Sabbath's Theater* (1995), *American Pastoral*, and *The Human Stain* (2000).

David Gooblar

Date 1997

Nationality USA

Why It's Key Although *Portnoy's Complaint* (1969) will forever define Roth as a Jewish writer, he has always seen his subject as America: "I'm an American writer in ways that a plumber isn't an American plumber or a miner an American miner or a cardiologist an American cardiologist. Rather, what the heart is to the cardiologist, the coal to the miner, the kitchen sink to the plumber, America is to me."

Key Author **Iain Sinclair**
Lights Out for the Territory

Iain Sinclair (born 1943) is a writer based in Hackney, East London whose work in a range of media has been interested in the possibilities of place. He is the most innovative contemporary writer on the city of London, in particular. Sinclair's work in fiction, poetry and, most famously, his non-fictional accounts of roaming the city, is infused with a dynamic sense of the multiple meanings of place. This approach has some sympathy with the avant-garde or situationist theories of psychogeography, or the study of the effects of the physical environment on human beings.

Lights Out for the Territory, subtitled "9 Excursions in the Secret History of London," reveals the unknown places and meanings of the city through a series of expeditions and incursions into the city's fabric. As he says of the first walk in East London, his notion is to "vandalise dormant energies by an act of ambulant signmaking." For Sinclair, the walker re-inscribes the various meanings of the place as well as adding their own. He is an exceptional guide and passionate investigator of the meaning of things many people walk past without a glance: war memorials, cemeteries, road signs, detritus, second-hand book stalls. His interdisciplinary approach, melding geography with travel writing, fiction with magus-like divining of meaning, or walking and photography, has had wide influence upon a range of people from contemporary novelists to the graphic artist Alan Moore. His prose is dense with layered meaning and eccentric fact.

Jerome de Groot

Date 1997

Nationality UK

Other Key Works *Radon Daughters* (1994), *London Orbital* (2002), *Dining on Stones* (2004)

Why It's Key Key popular psychogeographer, historian, and recorder of graffiti and the hidden myths and meanings of London.

730

Key Event *Sex and the City*
becomes a chick-lit phenomenon

When Candace Bushnell was asked by the *New York Observer* to write a regular column, she was quite clear as to its subject. The 37-year-old blonde wanted to use her experiences, and those of her friends, to fill the rest of the city in on what it was like to be looking for love in post-AIDS New York.

Bushnell's "Sex and the City" column caused an immediate storm, with its frank, funny, but often desolate account of what it's like to be a single woman in a city where eligible men feel they don't have to try too hard. Among other memorable phrases coined by Bushnell were "modelizer" – a man who will only go out with professional models, or at least women who look like them – and "toxic bachelor" – a psychologically messed-up man who can spread misery simply by buying someone a drink.

In 1998 HBO started airing a show, *Sex and the City*, that was based on, although not exactly the same as, Bushnell's column. The central character, played by Sarah Jessica Parker, is a columnist who writes a lifestyle/relationship column for a New York paper whose initials – C[arrie] B[radshaw] – just happen to be the same as Bushnell's.

Much ink has been spilled on whether Bushnell's portrayal of women behaving as powerfully (and as badly) as men in the sexual arena represents a post-feminist triumph or something darker. Often the women mentioned in her columns seem to be hungering after the traditional goals of a marriage and a family. The only difference is that, this time around, they will do – and screw – anything to get it.

Kathryn Hughes

Date 1997

Author Candace Bushnell (born 1958)

Nationality USA

Why It's Key Often cited as one of the founding mothers of "chick-lit." In fact chick-lit is a highly variegated species, as a glance at the differences between *SATC* and *Bridget Jones' Diary* shows. *SATC* breaks down any lingering sense that women don't think, talk, and write about sex as explicitly and selfishly as men.

Opposite Candace Bushnell

HARRY
POTTER
and the Order of the Phoenix

Key Character **Harry Potter**
Harry Potter and the Philosopher's Stone

In a much-repeated anecdote, Harry Potter first appeared to J.K. Rowling in 1990, on a train journey from Manchester to London. She recalls: "I had never been so excited about an idea before... all the details bubbled up in my brain, and this scrawny, black-haired, bespectacled boy who didn't know he was a wizard became more and more real to me." She went on to plan the seven novels which would follow Harry through each of his seven years at Hogwarts School of Witchcraft and Wizardry – and then introduced him to the world in 1997. Since then, as the star of a global publishing phenomenon and multi-million pound merchandizing industry, Harry has sold upwards of 300 million novels and been credited with getting the children of the electronic age reading for pleasure again.

However, despite the fact that Harry champions ideals of courage, love, and loyalty, certain religious factions have condemned the books for their representations of witchcraft. In 2002, an American publication ranted that "the Potter books open a doorway that will put untold millions of kids into hell" – a sentiment echoed by the cartoon Christian, Ned Flanders, in *The Simpsons*, who is seen burning a Harry Potter novel. J.K. Rowling is proud of the fact that her work appears yearly on international lists of most banned books, putting her into the company of writers like Harper Lee and J.D. Salinger.

Anna Tripp

Date 1997

Author J.K. Rowling (born 1965)

Nationality UK

U.S. Title *Harry Potter and the Sorcerer's Stone*

Why It's Key Harry Potter is the orphan boy who discovers he is a wizard – and who has allegedly made his creator, J.K. Rowling, the richest writer in history.

Opposite J.K. Rowling

Key Author
Bohumil Hrabal

Bohumil Hrabal (1914–1997) is best known as the author of *Closely Watched Trains* (1965). Banned from publishing after the "Prague Spring" of 1968, he continued to write prolifically and had his work produced by underground and exile presses. His writing is humorous and profound in equal measure. Hrabal was a stylistic experimenter and allied this with a baroque tone. He celebrates the popular and the mawkish. Such innovations and complexities were deployed to critique repression and dogma.

I Served the King of England, written in 1971 and published secretly, is a fine example of his light, allusive style. It is a picaresque novel, although the protagonist's journey is not so much towards enlightenment as a tale of "how the unbelievable became true." Ditie, the narrator, works as a waiter in a series of fantastic hotels, telling tales of the various intriguing visitors. The opening section relates stories of inter-war elegance and excess. *Closely Watched Trains*, which Hrabal helped to become an extremely successful (and Oscar-winning) film, concerns the coming of age of Milos Hrma. The novel is slight but devastating. Hrma is, like Ditie, one of Hrabal's idiot savant "holy" fools whose naivety and openness can lead to revelation and salvation. Hrabal's influence in this sense over writers like Milan Kundera is obvious, as is the importance to Czech writing of his absurdist sense of humor. An example of this is the fact that he died falling from his hospital's fifth-floor window whilst feeding pigeons; a suitably illogical end which many Czechs assumed was intentional (his apartment was on the fifth floor and various of his novels include fifth-floor suicides).

Jerome de Groot

Date 1997 (death)

Nationality Czechoslovakia

Other Key Work *Dancing Lessons for the Advanced in Age* (1964)

Why It's Key Hrabal is one of the giants of post-war Czech fiction and a key critic of the Communist regime.

Key Author **Thomas Pynchon**
Mason and Dixon

Thomas Pynchon (born 1937) is the novelist every autograph hunter wants to meet and every journalist would sell their grandmother to interview. Famously publicity shy, Pynchon is widely regarded as one of the greatest writers currently working: his latest book generated miles of analysis, a testament to the enduring power of books like *The Crying of Lot 49* (1966), *V* (1963), and his masterpiece, *Gravity's Rainbow* (1973).

The archetypal Pynchon novel comprises characters with outlandish names (Oedipa Maas, Tyrone Slothrop), the grandest of grand narratives (paranoia, imperialism, racism, war), verbal fireworks that fuse colloquial voices with high literature, and labyrinthine plots that Homer would struggle to follow. While this idiosyncratic mix annoys some, it has captivated many more including Salman Rushdie, Don DeLillo, and William Gibson, who nominated Pynchon as a precursor of "Cyberpunk." Contrary to popular myth, Pynchon does venture into the public sphere, albeit largely through the written word: he supported Salman Rushdie after the fatwa, and in 2006 backed Ian McEwan against accusations of plagiarism. His reluctance to become a celebrity writer has not prevented him becoming world famous – quite the opposite, many believe. As with many enigmatic figures, Pynchon has been saturated with conspiracy theories, ranging from the bizarre (he is a collective of famous novelists) to the even more bizarre (he was the Unabomber). The *Soho Weekly News* even hypothesized that Pynchon was a J.D. Salinger *nom de plume*. "Not bad. Keep trying." was the only response. Thankfully, the rumor that Pynchon appeared on *The Simpsons* was absolutely genuine. Pynchon has thrilled, baffled, and challenged audiences for over half a century. His latest novel, *Against the Day* (2006), is a case in point. While *The New York Times* called it "bloated… pretentious [and] elliptical," "Pynchonistas" couldn't find a bookshop quickly enough.

James Kidd

Date 1997 (publication)

Nationality USA

Other Key Work
Vineland (1990)

Why It's Key Pynchon has gained as much fame for the so-called reclusive nature of his life as the wit and all-encompassing intelligence of his art. He is regularly mentioned in dispatches for the Nobel Prize in Literature.

Opposite **Thomas Pynchon**

1990–1999

734

Key Passage
Atomised (*Les Particules Elementaires*)

SPOILER

"Just as determining the apparatus for an experiment and choosing a method of observation made it possible to assign a specific behaviour to an atomic system… so Bruno could be seen as an individual or as passively caught up in the sweep of history."

Atomised had an immediate impact, winning the Prix Novembre, and becoming a bestseller translated into over 20 languages. The book traces the lives and origins of two half-brothers. The sexually driven Bruno, a brilliant reactionary whose misanthropic rants often mirror the author's views, is finally driven to madness by the death of the woman he comes to love. Michel Houellebecq's narrative aims to distinguish between sexual desire on the one hand as an incessant and capitalistic pursuit of pleasure, and on the redeeming other hand as a quest for care, kindliness and recognition by another. Michel, almost incapable of feeling, loses to cancer the woman he comes closest to loving – a parallelism of fraternal afflictions which may fictionally be clumsy, but at the level of ideas demonstrates the author's conviction that all attachments are destined to severance and grief. Michel is a biologist and in the book's sci-fi outcome he plays the crucial part in evolving the human race away from its contemporary situation towards a tranquillized future race. There is an often exhilarating way that *Atomised* moves from particular scenes to loftier views of the human animal, mingling compassion and scorn for these creatures caught in the toils of their historical moment.

The Possibility of an Island (2005) returns to the theme of a future race genetically modified beyond desire and distress, but it lacks the penetrating eye for the modern world and the fictional creation of a range of believable characters in *Atomised*, which seems likely to remain Houellebecq's best novel.

Peter Swaab

Date 1998

Author Michel Houellebecq (born 1958)

Nationality France

Why It's Key Cloning replaces sexual reproduction in Houellebecq's bestseller. Its pornographic scenes caused controversy.

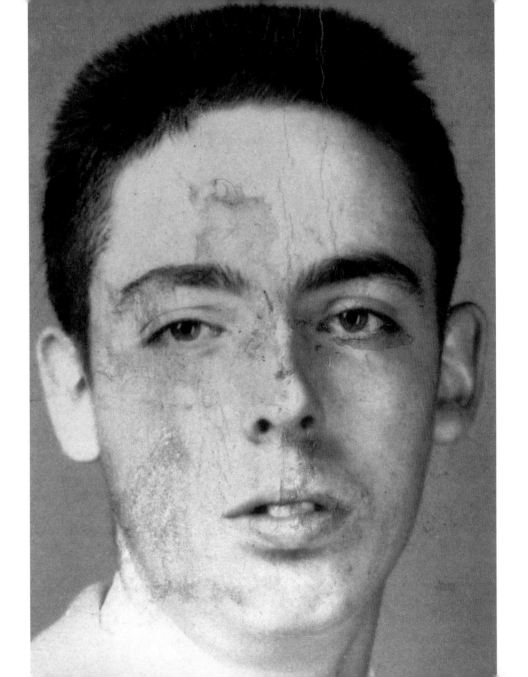

Key Author
Martha Gellhorn

Martha Gellhorn was a leading journalist, travel writer, and novelist, and one of the finest war correspondents of the twentieth century. She was one of the first women to be assigned to cover combat – and undoubtedly one of the best war writers, regardless of gender. "I followed the war wherever I could reach it," she said, and during her career she covered conflicts in Spain, Vietnam, the Middle East, Panama (aged 81), as well as writing on World War II from Finland, Hong Kong, Burma, and Singapore. She was in Czechoslovakia in 1938 and covered the hegemony of Adolf Hitler in late 1930s Germany. She went to Europe with the D-Day landings (famously impersonating medical personnel to get there) and was the first to report from Dachau concentration camp. Her journalism is taut, direct, and oftentimes compassionately interested in the collateral damage of war, focussing on the human consequence of actions rather than tales from the front. She would often visit

hospitals, orphanages, and refugee camps to assess the real damage: "hearts and minds, after all, live in bodies" she wrote damningly of U.S. policy in Vietnam (in stories which the American media refused to publish). Gellhorn also wrote important official reports about the impact of the Depression in the U.S. in the 1930s for the Federal Emergency Relief Administration; her research for this project gave her material for the novel *The Trouble I've Seen* (1936). Gellhorn's personal courage, swashbuckling vim, passion for the story, and glitzy domestic life (relationships with Ernest Hemingway, Bertrand de Jouvenel, and possibly H.G. Wells) have led to a cult of personality which takes away from her pioneering exploits and the exceptional quality of her writing.

Jerome de Groot

Date 1998 (death)

Nationality USA

Other Key Works Novels *What Mad Pursuit* (1934), *The A Stricken Field* (1940) **Journalism** *The Face of War* (1959), *The View from the Ground* (1988)

Why It's Key A brave and pioneering war correspondent and novelist, Gellhorn was one of the most important journalists of the century.

1990–1999

737

Key Author **J.M. Coetzee**
Disgrace

SPOILER

J.M. Coetzee is a writer of deep intelligence, drawn to symbol and allegory. He has perfected a kind of prison literature: his lonely characters are often afflicted by a nameless menace, guilty of no crime except that of being alive. David Lurie, the protagonist of *Disgrace*, written with thrilling urgency and concision, is a disaffected middle-aged academic who believes the high European cultural tradition – Romantic poetry, opera, philosophy, and Greek tragedy – has no place in Africa. He begins a disastrous affair with one of his students; the affair is discovered by the authorities and, when he refuses to apologise, Lurie is sacked. This is his disgrace. He travels to the Eastern Cape to stay with his daughter, Lucy, on her isolated farmstead; one afternoon, Lurie is attacked and his daughter gang-raped by black men. Too neatly – Coetzee is a programmatic writer, and his novels can be rigidly schematic – Lucy becomes pregnant. But she refuses to have an abortion, because she believes

humiliation is the fate she most deserves as a once privileged white woman in Africa. In despair, Lurie withdraws further, and ends up working with sick and dying animals. Not even his books can save him.

Disgrace, which won the Booker Prize, was received with dismay and anger in South Africa; the austere, reclusive Coetzee was accused by leading members of the African National Congress of disloyalty. In 2002, he resigned as a professor of literature at Cape Town University and emigrated to Australia, where he is an honorary fellow at Adelaide University. In 2003, he won the Nobel Prize in Literature.

Jason Cowley

Date 1999

Author J.M. Coetzee (born 1940)

Nationality South Africa (now an Australian citizen)

Other Key Works *Waiting for the Barbarians* (1980), *Life and Times of Michael K.* (1983), *Foe* (1986)

Why It's Key *Disgrace* was greeted with anger by the ANC. Coetzee has since won several major international literary prizes, including the Nobel (2003).

Opposite J.M. Coetzee

Key Author **Jim Crace**
Being Dead

Jim Crace (born 1946) is one of the world's living literary heroes, comparable to William Golding in his versatility. His settings range from a Stone Age village (*The Gift of Stones* [1988]) to an imaginary continent (*Continent* [1986]) to the West Coast of England in the nineteenth century (*Signals of Distress* [1994]) to the Judean desert (*Quarantine* [1997]) as well twentieth century cities. Crace has opened up new vistas for storytelling in the contemporary novel. The subject matter is equally eclectic and challenging; in *Being Dead* Crace begins with the dead bodies of his murdered protagonists, spinning backwards to weave in the events which led to their deaths, but also continuing the story of that death, which Crace, an unflinching atheist, sees as a complicated organic post-existence, a detailed decomposition within nature, as well as an afterlife in the mind of their daughter.

In *The Gift of Stones*, the central figure is a one-armed storyteller, an exalted figure through whom the isolated community, on the cusp of technological change from flint to bronze, gains a sense of the outside world. Crace perhaps sees himself as akin to this guiding figure, and storytelling is a central theme.

Crace has described his books as "hard companions"; they are tough and exacting but they have humor, and their striking note is plausible and beguiling invention. In *Being Dead* there are, for example, invented insects; in *The Devil's Larder* (2001) (which is made up of 64 short pieces about food) all the books' quotations and epigrams are invented, including ones from fictitious books of the Bible. His work does not belong to the realm of fantasy, more a hyper-imagined reality, with breathtakingly powerful descriptive exactness and a searching philosophical vision. His broad historical and geographical territory has become known as "Craceland."

Lucy Daniel

Date 1999

Nationality UK

Why It's Key *Quarantine* and *Being Dead* catapulted Crace into the front ranks of modern storytellers. *Being Dead* seemed to usher in a morbid trend for dead protagonists and narrators (Alice Sebold's *The Lovely Bones* [2002], or Percival Everett's *American Desert* [2004], for example), but was by far the most complex, serious, and accomplished of such works.

Key Author **Luther Blissett**
Q

Q is a chronicle of the Reformation told from multiple perspectives, chiefly those of an Anabaptist who becomes an armed rebel and his opposite number, a papal agent called Q. Deliberately crude depictions of comradeship and battle in the earlier parts of the book attributed to Anabaptist rebels are cut against the sophisticated Machiavellianism of Q's letters to his spy masters. The action includes explicit depictions of the machinations of nascent capitalism in the Italian city states and the political plotting accompanying it. All of which reflects the avowedly anti-capitalist politics of *Q*'s multiple authors.

During the late 1990s hundreds of people across the globe were involved in perpetrating pranks using the name Luther Blissett (the name of a British football player) but the project was originated in Bologna by *Q*'s authors. *Q* was Luther Blissett's first novel but it was preceded by a series of non-fiction books. The most important of these is *Mind Invaders*, which begins with quotes from Ray Johnson (Andy Warhol's favorite artist), Walter Benjamin (Marxist theorist), and Stewart Home (British novelist). Another book *A Ruota Libera* was attributed to the American anarchist Hakim Bey but consisted largely of writing by the Russian dictator Stalin. That *A Ruota Libera* was accepted as genuine demonstrated how far much of what passed itself off as the anti-parliamentary left in Italy had moved from revolutionary positions. Picking up on both artistic avant-gardes and the political currents Lenin denounced in *Left-Wing Communism, an Infantile Disorder*, Luther Blissett went beyond these influences to forge a twenty-first century revolutionary praxis.

Stewart Home

Date 1999 (publication)

Author Luther Blissett (collective pen name)

Nationality Italy

Why It's Key The Luther Blissett Project began with a 1995 prank which tricked a prime time Italian TV show into chasing a non-existent missing person. Their novel *Q* fooled many into believing Umberto Eco had written it. *Q* was actually the collective work of four young unknowns from Bologna who now publish books under the moniker Wu Ming.

Key Book
The Map of Love

The Map of Love is really two romantic stories which unfold in parallel. The first takes place at the birth of Egyptian nationalism. Lady Anna Winterbourne travels to Cairo after her husband is killed in the British conquest of the Sudan at the end of the nineteenth century. The second takes place in contemporary New York, where Isabel Cabot falls in love with the charismatic Omar al Ghamrawi, an acclaimed Egyptian conductor and intellectual.

Isabel discovers an old trunk that once belonged to her great grandmother, containing Anna's letters and journals. She hands it over to Omar's sister, Amal, in Cairo. It falls to Amal to piece together the story of Anna's encounter with Sharif, and their subsequent love affair and marriage, a hundred years earlier.

As in her previous novel, *In The Eye of the Sun*, which was hailed as an extraordinary contribution to contemporary fiction, Soueif manages to supply the reader with a detailed account of political events in Egypt's modern history. In the telling of what is otherwise an engaging romantic drama, real figures and events interact with fictional characters. The strength of the book lies in its marriage of contrasting elements. Sharif al-Barudi is a committed nationalist, determined to free his country of its colonial rulers. By falling in love with an Englishwoman he puts his political ambitions as well as his life in danger.

In her depiction of the difficulties faced by her characters, Soueif takes the reader beyond simple, stereotypical images of East and West to shed light on the contradictions that make us all human.
Jamal Mahjoub

Date 1999

Author Ahdaf Soueif (born 1950)

Nationality Egypt

Why It's Key *The Map of Love* was shortlisted for the Booker Prize and was a great commercial success. It was translated into Arabic by Fatma Moussa; a distinguished professor of English literature at Cairo university and one time translator of Naguib Mahfouz, she is also Soueif's mother.

739

Key Book
Waiting

SPOILER

Ha Jin was born and raised in China, joining the People's Liberation Army in 1969 to serve with the Red Guard at the tail end of the Cultural Revolution. Adaptation to and integration into Western culture and literary theory resonates through Ha Jin's prose, which is a unique blend of Asian reticence and western emotional insight.

Interwoven with Ha Jin's portrayal of the intricacies of attraction and human emotional longing is a strong social commentary that documents the changes in the communist influence. The central protagonist, Lin Kong, is a law-abiding comrade of Mao's China, and a dutiful doctor. Many complexities in Chinese beliefs are expressed through Lin, as he is well read in western literature and learned in western medicine, yet he turns to traditional Chinese medicine and habit during his times of greatest need.

Lin's relationship to his wife is portrayed with a keen psychological insight, and loaded with irony. Through the decades, Lin attempts to divorce his wife once every year. Initially repulsed by his wife's bound feet, Lin finds this previous symbol of beauty and aristocracy old-fashioned and ugly; he does not discover the nuances of attraction until he meets Manna who is a nurse at the hospital where he works.

Waiting is a tale of the long wait that Lin endures to be with Manna, and finally the sense of waiting that remains once their marriage is consummated. What lingers is the revelation that the binds that restrain him exist only in his mind, manifested as manacles of tradition, custom, and convention.
Alexandra Hamlyn

Date 1999

Author Ha Jin (born 1956)

Nationality USA (born China)

Why It's Key Spanning two decades, *Waiting* is set against the backdrop of Mao's Cultural Revolution and observes the evolution of the communist manifesto as it is expressed through various sectors of society. Winner of several awards, *Waiting* was notably awarded the PEN/Faulkner Award and The National Book Award.

Key Author **Günter Grass**
My Century

Günter Grass (born 1927) was born and raised in what was then the free city of Danzig. The city had been a part of the German Empire until the Treaty of Versailles, and is now the Polish port of Gdansk. Danzig before, during and after the war – during which it was utterly devastated – became the setting of Grass' great trilogy, *The Tin Drum* (1959), *Cat and Mouse* (1961), and *Dog Years* (1963). These novels – notable from a literary point of view for their innovative magic realism – played a key role in the German movement in the 1960s to recognize the guilt of the German people for the atrocities of the war. Such a coming to terms with the past was resisted by many of an older generation, who preferred to forget the Nazi era and their role in it, and to get on instead with achieving the "German economic miracle."

Grass is a committed democratic socialist, and was a prominent supporter of Chancellor Willi Brandt and his Ostpolitik – the policy of reconciliation with the Soviet Eastern Bloc. At the same time, in *Diary of a Snail* (1972), he argued for slow, evolutionary change, as opposed to the violent revolution urged by many young radicals. Grass initially opposed the reunification of Germany in 1990, fearful that a reunited Germany would return to war-mongering expansionism. In 2006 it emerged that Grass had been recruited in 1944 into the Waffen-SS. Some accused him of hypocrisy, while others pointed out that at the time he was little more than a boy, and had no choice but to serve.

Ian Crofton

Date 1999 (publication)

Nationality Germany

Why It's Key The giant of postwar German letters, a politically committed novelist who won the Nobel Prize in 1999, and in the same year published *My Century*, which includes a story for every year of the century.

Opposite Günter Grass

Key Character **Lionel Essrog**
Motherless Brooklyn

Motherless Brooklyn draws liberally on the conventions of classic hard-boiled crime fiction – sinister gangsters, fatal femmes, and wisecracking dialogue abound. But it's the central character of Lionel "Freakshow" Essrog, one of the Brooklyn orphans recruited by Frank Minna for his limo service and detective agency, that lifts the novel above mere pastiche.

The plot centers on Lionel's hapless and ultimately heroic efforts to track down Minna's killer. But the real source of comedy and pathos is Lionel's Tourette's syndrome. In less inventive hands, the idea of a detective with Tourette's might have been little more than a gimmick. Certainly there are many laughs to be had from his random obscenities, obsessional rituals, and inappropriate touching, often in situations of mortal danger. For crime fiction fans well versed in the unflappable coolness of Philip Marlowe and Sam Spade, Lionel's uncontrolled spasms of speech and gesture are made all the funnier by contrast.

But this is a novel that finally laughs with, rather than at, its hero. Its richness lies in the gap between Lionel as narrator of and as character in the plot. We see him simultaneously through the prism of his inner world, offering fascinating insights into his own condition ("It's sort of like talking about telephones over the telephone…"), and as the world sees him, stumbling loudly and chaotically through the action. This double vision is our insight into his peculiar success as a detective – no one suspects the acute perception and skill concealed behind the all too conspicuous façade.

Josh Cohen

Date 1999

Author Jonathan Lethem (born 1964)

Nationality USA

Why It's Key The great popularity and critical success of Lethem's groundbreaking crime novel was due largely to the detective, orphan, and Tourette's sufferer at its center.

Key Event **The republication of *Desperate Characters* "rediscovers" Paula Fox**

Paula Fox has written one memoir, and only six novels for adults. For many years she made her living as a children's writer, author of more than twenty books. In her award-winning *The Slave Dancer* (1973), a thirteen-year-old white boy is press-ganged in 1840 onto a slave ship and forced to see the miseries of slavery at first-hand. He is told by one of the men on the ship: "You'll see some bad things, but if you didn't see them, they'd still be happening so you might as well." This is also the theme of her second novel for adults, *Desperate Characters* (1970), which satirizes a smug, affluent couple in New York who are forced to confront the dangers of the world against which they thought they had safely insulated themselves. The book opens with a symbolic act of violence and betrayal: Sophie Bentwood is giving milk to a stray cat, which promptly bites the hand feeding it. Her fear that she might have rabies incites a growing paranoia that is reflected in her husband's raging at

the garbage and excrement that impinges on their sanitized world; a series of petty mishaps become exaggerated into a sense of impending doom, an overweening sense of their own importance. Fox's vision is excoriating and ruthless, which makes reading her books frequently an uncomfortable experience. David Foster Wallace has called *Desperate Characters* "a towering landmark of postwar realism"; it is also a presciently grim little parable of disintegration, urban anomie, and self-delusion. Like most of Fox's books, it went quickly out of print; partly because of the advocacy of Jonathan Franzen, Fox's books were reissued in the first years of the twenty-first century and launched a literary renaissance.
Sarah Churchwell

Date 1999

Author Paula Fox (born 1923)

Why It's Key *Desperate Characters*, first published in 1970, was hailed as an instant classic by Lionel Trilling, Alfred Kazin, and Irving Howe, who called it "grueling and brilliant," and compared it to *Billy Budd*, *The Great Gatsby*, *Miss Lonelyhearts*, and *Seize the Day*.

Key Characters **Joseph Kavalier and Sam Clay** *The Amazing Adventures of Kavalier and Clay*

Kavalier and Klayman are unceremoniously thrust together in New York as World War II breaks out in Europe. Joe has managed to flee Nazi-occupied Prague and has come to stay with his cousin Sammy. Their initial encounter is the start of what is to become a lifelong bond between the two young Jewish men who go on to co-create one of the most famous comic book superheroes of all time – *The Escapist*.

The Amazing Adventures of Kavalier and Clay is an affectionate tribute to the Golden Age of the comic book industry and the superheroes it produced. As *The Escapist* comics become increasingly successful and Joe tries desperately to save the family that he left behind from the Holocaust, the novel articulates the realities of the American dream and the horrors of a world at war.

Chabon propounds the notion that true heroism is defined by seemingly small acts of bravery as much as great ones, and deftly demonstrates the relevance

of the superhero myth to real life, exploring ideas of freedom, oppression, and the metaphorical "secret identities" which people hide behind everyday. Ultimately, both Kavalier and Clay learn that some things in life are easier to escape from than others and that real life can in fact be as bewildering, as dangerous and as incredible as anything printed in the pages of a comic book.

The meticulously researched narrative inter-weaves fiction with fact: Sammy and Joe's battle for the ownership rights to *The Escapist* parallels that of Siegel and Shuster, Superman's creators, and they also interact with a number of real people including Dr. Fredric Wertham and Stan Lee, the creator of Spider-Man.
Tim Stafford

Date 2000

Author Michael Chabon (born 1963)

Nationality USA

Why It's Key Coinciding with the renewed interest in comic books resulting from Bryan Singer's "X-Men" film in 2000, Michael Chabon's novel went on to win the Pulitzer Prize in 2001.

Key Book
Moth Smoke

Moth Smoke proved an eye-opener for many Western readers: a provocative, noirish tale of Lahore's rich elite. Perhaps it was such a critical success in the U.S. and UK because it was so unexpected; partly due to the lingering parochialism of those literary markets, *Moth Smoke* was seen as a great rarity. Pakistan was seeing a flourishing of artistic and literary activity.

1998, the year of Pakistan's nuclear standoff with India; Lahore is a city waiting for an explosion. That tension, and a steamy atmosphere, both sexy and malevolent, looms over the plot. It's about things pent up and about to detonate, from the lead character's upset stomach, which can instigate a metaphoric flight ending in a "nuclear fart," to the murder trial he faces, and an equally explosive relationship with his best friend's wife. Daru loses his bank job, and his downward trajectory takes a fatal spin when he falls in love with the wrong woman; Ozi, his childhood friend, represents a corruption Daru cannot stomach. Daru haphazardly becomes a drug dealer, starts smoking heroin, and is roped into violent robbery.

The book's female lead, Mumtaz, is strong, intelligent and funny, a bad wife and worse mother, but still the heroine. She is also a writer whose pseudonym is Manto, another Pakistani writer, who set a certain precedent for Hamid when he wrote about "Lahore's underbelly." Mumtaz, named after a romantic icon (Shah Jahan's queen, for whom the Taj Mahal was built), and whose surname is Kashmiri – representing the region India and Pakistan are fighting over – is also, like the other characters, an allegorical figure. In the end her rejection of both Ozi's corruption and Daru's violent reaction to it works on both a personal and political level.

Lucy Daniel

Date 2000

Author Mohsin Hamid (born 1971)

Nationality UK/ Pakistan

Why It's Key Hamid grew up in Pakistan, was based for several years in the USA and now lives in Britain. *Moth Smoke* is set in the "nuclear summer" of 1998. One character, the wordy Murad Badshah, says: "It was a summer of great rumblings in the belly of the earth, of atomic flatulence and geopolitical indigestion."

Key Book
A Friend of the Earth

There are many strands to Boyle's literary heritage. He would probably like to be seen as one of Mark Twain's contemporary satirical descendants; he was once a pupil of John Irving and John Cheever at the Iowa Writers' Workshop; he is also preoccupied with cults and utopian ideas. In *A Friend of the Earth* he gives us a thoroughly modern, ultra-topical dystopia which might be filed under "eco-fiction," but also offers his characteristic allures of comedy and a great story.

Tyrone Tierwater was once an eco-warrior with an environmental group, Earth Forever! Aged 75, he now manages a private menagerie of endangered beasts in the grounds of an aging pop star's California mansion. Ty's story is told in the first and third person as it switches between the not too distant future, where the world is falling apart, and the "ecoterrorism" and "ecotage" of 80s and 90s California's environmental movement, which idealistically tried to hold it together. Boyle's eighth novel references several well-known environmentalists, in the manner of his earlier penchant for writing about historical figures (Dr Kinsey in *The Inner Circle*, Dr Kellogg in *The Road to Wellville*).

Boyle has used Darwinian themes throughout his career (his first story collection was called *Descent of Man*). *A Friend of the Earth* fits neatly into the oeuvre; it follows *Tortilla Curtain* (also with a background concern about the environment and overpopulation), and feeds into the concerns of his next novel, *Drop City*, which focused on a utopian hippie movement which embraced nature. In a previous incarnation Ty was known as the "Human Hyena," and this idea of humans as mere hubristic, destructive animals is also one of Boyle's most important themes, a central tenet of his social satire.

Lucy Daniel

Date 2000

Author T. Coraghessan Boyle (born 1948)

Nationality USA

Why It's Key Boyle is known for his comic and often bizarre reinvigoration of the historical novel – he uses historical events as the basis for humorous stories. In *A Friend of the Earth* he uses real figures from the environmental movement but the outlook is bleaker; it is set in 2025, when the earth is being destroyed by global warming.

Key Event **Jhumpa Lahiri wins the Pulitzer Prize for Fiction**

In April 2000 Bengali American writer Jhumpa Lahiri accomplished a remarkable literary feat when she collected the Pulitzer Prize for Fiction for her debut work, *The Interpreter of Maladies*, an anthology of short stories. To win for a first book was considered unusual, but Lahiri, who had been producing fiction since childhood, was also the first ever Asian American – and the first writer of South Asian descent – to receive the award. Her Pulitzer success came after beating the longer-established novelists Ha Jin and Annie Proulx, and placed her amongst the ranks of such august laureates as John Steinbeck, Ernest Hemingway, and William Faulkner.

The Pulitzer is given to fiction "preferably dealing with American life" and Lahiri's understated, finely-observed, Chekhovian tales bring to mainstream attention the lives of South Asians, claiming their American status in nuanced, but unmistakable, terms. At the same time, Lahiri – herself the child of Bengali parents who emigrated to the United States in the wake of 1965 immigration reforms – uses the nine stories to relate the bewilderment, loneliness, and feelings of estrangement experienced by some first-generation Indian immigrants. And she handles India itself – both as a site of second-generation journeys and as a permanent homeland – with subtlety and confidence. Although one might argue that *Interpreter of Maladies* has been somewhat over-praised, it is undoubtedly impressive, particularly in its cast of characters who range from spoilt, Bengali American princesses to neglected, love-starved Indians to more stock figures, who include tough, resourceful, immigrant professionals, and shrewish, small-town Indian wives.

Ruth Maxey

Date 2000

Author Jhumpa Lahiri (born 1967)

Nationality USA (born UK)

Why It's Key Lahiri made history when she became the first Asian American to win the Pulitzer Prize for Fiction. *Maladies* brought the lives of first- and second-generation South Asian Americans to renewed popular and critical attention, placing them – and the short story as a contemporary form – on the literary map.

Opposite Jhumpa Lahiri

Key Character **Coleman Silk** *The Human Stain*

SPOILER

Coleman Silk, eminent professor of classics at Athena College, 69 years old, nearing the end of a brilliant career as an educator and adminstrator, says the wrong thing at the wrong time. And that, as little as that, Roth's intense and emotional novel suggests, is enough to undo a whole life, albeit a life seemingly constructed by force of will. Silk's mistake was to refer to two absent (and, unbeknownst to him, black) students as "spooks," and the subsequent uproar and public scandal over his supposed racism leads to his resignation, his wife's death, and eventually his own death. The novel takes place in 1998, with the backdrop the impeachment of President Clinton, providing a neat parallel for Roth's inquiry into America's passion for sanctimony and punishment.

But *The Human Stain*, and Coleman Silk himself, soon become more than that. Coleman, it turns out, has a secret: he is a light-skinned black man who has, since his early twenties, been passing as white. Based, at least in part, on Anatole Broyard, the *New York Times* book critic whose own passing remained, for the most part, a secret until his death in 1990, Silk is a fascinating figure who points up all the attractions and limitations of the American dream – the old canard that says that anyone can be whomever he wants to be. What Silk wants to be is free: of history, of race, of responsibility to anyone but himself. Roth's book suggests just how doomed such a project is.

David Gooblar

Date 2000

Author Philip Roth (born 1933)

Nationality USA

Why It's Key "He recognized that to conventional people for whom everything was ready-made and rigidly unalterable what he was doing would never look correct... The objective was for his fate to be determined not by the ignorant, hate-filled intentions of a hostile world but, to whatever degree humanly possible, by his own resolve."

Key Book
London: The Biography

Having written the lives of some of its most celebrated literary sons in biographies of Dickens and Blake, and copious fiction steeped in its mythology, Peter Ackroyd turned to London itself to produce the definitive history of the capital at the turn of the millennium. Combining wealth of detail with audacious scope, *London: The Biography* brought a new kind of historical writing to the bestseller lists. Like many a "biographer," Ackroyd is clearly besotted with his subject, producing not so much a chronology of the city as a sustained love letter to a familiar yet tantalizingly unknowable master/mistress (London, we learn, has characteristics of both genders, lending "a strange ambiguity" to the architectural phalluses of the city skyline).

Rejecting "orthodox historiographical survey" as inadequate to the task, Ackroyd sets out to map the "wilderness of alleys and passages, courts and thoroughfares, in which even the most experienced citizen may lose the way." This approach has exasperated some readers, frustrated by Ackroyd's indifference to providing a well-lit pathway through the jumble of folklore, anecdotes, and elliptical storytelling making up the body of *London*. But this is not intended to function as anything like a conventional guidebook, indeed the thrill of being lost is at the heart of its liberating spirit.

Besides, *London* is not without its ordering principles. Presenting a vast sweep of history, beginning with the agglomeration of clay and limestone which form the city's bedrock, Ackroyd overlays countless sub-histories – sewage management, madness, plague, riot, and suburbia, a story charting the rise of effluence and affluence. The author guides us through these fascinating side streets which open up periodically into unexpected vistas, vital conduits between then and now: "the ancient city and the modern city literally lie beside each other; one cannot be imagined without the other."

Matthew Birchwood

Date 2000

Author Peter Ackroyd (born 1949)

Nationality UK

Why It's Key "London goes beyond any boundary or convention. It contains every wish or word ever spoken, every action or gesture ever made, every harsh or noble statement ever expressed. It is illimitable. It is Infinite London." Ackroyd will take you around the capital, but not necessarily by the most direct route.

Opposite Peter Ackroyd

Key Event *Jimmy Corrigan* is hailed as a masterpiece among graphic novels

Chris Ware's graphic novel is in fact a collection of six years' worth of weekly comic strips, which appeared in the Chicago paper *New City*. The epic narrative focuses on one middle-aged man, the titular Jimmy Corrigan, who lives a solitary existence, retreating into his vivid imagination when reality becomes too threatening. Out of the blue, he is contacted by the father who abandoned him as a child and Jimmy agrees to meet him. As we observe their often painful attempts to forge a relationship, Ware interweaves a second story, that of Jimmy's grandfather's childhood in Chicago 1892.

Jimmy Corrigan: The Smartest Kid on Earth is, quite simply put, a masterpiece. The intricate plot and beautifully subtle characterization would be impressive in any medium, but the fact that Chris Ware tells such a sophisticated story using pictures and minimal dialogue instead of highly descriptive prose makes the book even more of an incredible achievement. While there have certainly been other milestones in the history of the graphic novel, such as Spiegelman's *Maus* in 1986, *Jimmy Corrigan* provides undeniable proof of how complex and emotionally powerful comic books can be. Employing a visually stunning and deceptively simple style of artwork reminiscent of early twentieth-century Americana, the book exploits the medium's potential to combine visual and written narratives in order to create fully-rounded characters and emotionally true situations with which we can identify. Heartbreakingly sad and at times almost unbearably poignant, *Jimmy Corrigan* is a landmark text, which sets new standards for the graphic novel.

Tim Stafford

Date 2000

Author Chris Ware (born 1967)

Place USA

Why It's Key *Jimmy Corrigan* received widespread critical acclaim in the United States and went on to win several awards within comic book industry circles. It also won the Guardian First Book Award in 2001, becoming the first graphic novel to win a major British literary prize.

Key Event **Dave Eggers bursts on to the literary scene with *Heartbreaking Work***

With the publication of *A Heartbreaking Work of Staggering Genius* in 2000, Dave Eggers made his loud, important entrance onto the American literary landscape. Eggers had since 1998 been the editor of *Timothy McSweeney's Quarterly Concern* (Timothy McSweeney being, like Monty Python, an invented character) – a witty, adventurous journal of distinctive retro-chic design, which published writers including Lydia Davis and Michael Chabon. The great success of *A Heartbreaking Work* helped cast a brighter light on *McSweeney's*; when Eggers moved operations from New York to San Francisco he was adding a significant publishing entity to northern California.

Its bombastic title notwithstanding, *A Heartbreaking Work* was a rich, fascinating memoir, recounting the loss of both Eggers' parents to cancer and his subsequent assumption of responsibility for raising his young brother. Eggers' prose was wry, intelligent, and self-knowing, and editorial quirks that seemed surprising would become recognizable as the *McSweeney's* house style: footnotes, ironic asides, and the wordy deconstruction of certain authorial choices (like the bombastic title).

Such was the appeal of Eggers' style, and such the forum he created with *McSweeney's*, that he helped create a literary aesthetic for a whole cadre of young American writers. Simultaneously ironic and enthusiastic, jaded and yet sincere, *McSweeney's* became a tone, an attitude, and a sense of humor as well as, in more pragmatic terms, a publishing venture, a thriving website (or "internet tendency"), and even a charity, in the form of 826 Valencia, where Eggers organized writing workshops for underserved teenagers. His own writing took an impressive turn with the publication in 2007 of *What is the What*, a novel about the lost boys of the Sudan.
Sylvia Brownrigg

Date 2000

Author Dave Eggers (born 1970)

Why It's Key A maverick writer, publisher and cultural figure in the United States whose journal *McSweeney's*, founded in the late 1990s, expanded in influence to become a literary style as well as an arbiter of "cool" for a generation of young American writers.

Opposite **Dave Eggers**

2000–

749

Key Event **Xingjian is first Chinese writer to win the Nobel Prize in Literature**

Author of *Soul Mountain* (1999) and *One Man's Bible* (2000), Gao Xingjian (born 1940) has also written numerous works that severely divided his mainland Chinese audience. So much so that Gao had to seek political asylum. Looking at some of Gao's paintings might be a good place to start when it comes to unlocking the secrets of his contorted and agile prose. Gao explains this somewhat cryptically: "Among the objects I looks at, we find I; among the object he looks at, we also find I; and among those you look at, we find I again; I and these objects exist concomitantly." Amidst Gao's prolific body of artwork, it is immediately obvious how vast his scope of imagination and emotion is; his panache as an artist draws on Asian tradition and his sensibility is steeped in Western logic and understanding.

Gao's writing is no different. Awarded the Nobel Prize for his "bitter insights and linguistic ingenuity," particularly in *Soul Mountain*, Gao's lofty ideals mimic the heights of "Lingshan," *ling* meaning spirit or soul, and *shan* meaning mountain. Gao's nomadic wanderer is in fact wandering through his soul and self, rather than just making a pilgrimage to the top of the mountain.

In *One Man's Bible*, Gao speaks with tenacious verve about the political climate he grew up in, asking, "Enemies had to be found; without enemies, how could the political authorities sustain their dictatorship?" Speaking from personal experience as one who is marginalized by society, Gao's central figures are often lone wanderers, philosophically exploring the wide-reaching effects of the Cultural Revolution, using locally specific symbols of Chinese culture as a medium to channel highly politicized messages and observations of the proletariat.
Alexandra Hamlyn

Date 2000

Nationality China

Why It's Key Playwright, novelist, poet, and artist, Gao Xingjian is perhaps one of China's best known dissidents. Emerging out of obscurity, he has lived in Paris since 1987 and is now a French citizen. His books are banned in China.

Key Passage
White Teeth

"'Do you hear that, mister? We're not licensed for suicides round here. This place halal. Kosher, understand? If you're going to die round here, my friend, I'm afraid you've got to be thoroughly bled first.'"

This passage appears in the first section of the novel, Archie's story. It is spoken by Mo Hussein-Ishmael, owner of a "celebrated" Halal butchers. Archie Jones has decided to kill himself after his marriage has ended and (rather fortuitously) he has chosen to gas himself in his car outside Mo's shop. Archie survives, has a moment of personal epiphany, and from that moment says "yes to life." He goes to a party where he meets Clara, his next wife who is "beautiful… magnificently tall, black as ebony and crushed sable." The passage is illustrative of Smith's multicultural approach, as well as the inherent humor and irony of her narrative style.

The novel proceeds to explore the relationships between three families: Archie Jones, who is a white, working-class Londoner and his Jamaican wife Clara; Samad Iqbal, a Bengali Muslim and his wife Alsana; and the Chalfens who are a middle-class Jewish family and whose children are friends of the Iqbal twins Magid and Millat and Archie's daughter Irie. Archie and Samad met during World War II, and their actions there have resonance in the future – but before this denouement is reached, the novel takes a long, loquacious journey through the interlocking experiences of these groups of people. *White Teeth* received almost rapturous reviews and Smith was hailed as a new voice, a significant new talent in British fiction. The novel draws many parallels with epic family tales of the past. It is, however, very modern in its subject matter, drawing on multicultural London for both its milieu and its debate about the changing face of the British family. Its success was seen to usher in a new period of "multiculturalism" in British publishing.

Pat Wheeler

Date 2000

Author Zadie Smith (born 1975)

Nationality UK

Why It's Key Zadie Smith burst onto the literary scene with *White Teeth*. Smith was listed in *Granta 2003* as one of the 20 best young novelists in Britain. The novel won numerous literary prizes including the Whitbread, the Guardian First Fiction Award, the Betty Trask Award, and the James Tait Black Memorial Prize for Fiction.

Opposite Zadie Smith

Key Event **Critic James Wood coins the term "hysterical realism"**

We know about "magical realism," but what comes next? According to James Wood, the British critic turned stateside literary guru, the "next stop" is "hysterical realism," in which "the conventions of realism are not being abolished but… overworked, exhausted."

In his essay "The Smallness of the 'Big' Novel," originally published in *The New Republic* magazine and subsequently included in the essay collection *The Irresponsible Self: On Laughter and the Novel* (2004), he cites novels by Americans Pynchon, DeLillo, and Foster Wallace as well as British writers Rushdie, and Zadie Smith above all, on whom his essay concentrates. He argues that these writers pursue a post-Dickensian kind of "vitality at all costs." They strive, in Smith's own words, to tell "how the world works rather than how somebody felt about something."

Wood was responding specifically to Zadie Smith's bestseller *White Teeth*, which he demolishes ultimately as authorial "problem-solving," though not without some emotional depth. Smith conceded that "hysterical realism" is a "painfully accurate term for the sort of overblown, manic prose to be found in novels like my own." The term then gained extra significance with Wood's suggestion that the genre might "look a little busted" after 9/11. Could the "essential silliness of [anglophone novelists'] lunge for multiplicities" survive this shocking collision?

Sophie Lewis

Date 2000

Author James Wood (born 1965)

Nationality UK

Original Title "The Smallness of the 'Big' Novel: Human, All Too Inhuman"; subsequently titled "Hysterical Realism"

Why It's Key Wood's concept and razor-sharp analysis are unique in showing a common ground on which to understand and criticize today's "big" English language novels on both sides of the Atlantic.

Key Book
The Rotters' Club

Jonathan Coe's period novel of Britain in the 1970s begins in the sleek, transformed Berlin of 2003. From the epitome of modern Europe we are then taken back to 1973; date of Britain's entry to the European Common Market and "a world without mobiles or videos or Playstations or even faxes." The central story spans 1973–79, commonly acknowledged as a turbulent time of major, irreversible change. As an anti-nostalgia novelist Coe is interested in the way in which historical events evolve and mutate; how public and private events interweave and shape our perceptions of the national past.

Key events such as industrial strife, racial tension, class conflict, and IRA terrorism are tracked from the perspective of the members of a lower middle-class Birmingham family: The Trotters. Schoolboy Ben Trotter is the principal narrator and Coe uses his mixture of naivety and evolving experience to explore how much we can know of the structuring forces of the world.

Ben's transition from schoolboy idealism to an informed cultural and political awareness is paralleled by a musical shift from indulgent rock symphonies to the anarchic energy and cynical rejections of punk and the revolutionary protest of reggae. With the beginning of Thatcherism (which looms over the novel) Ben's ominous closing reflection that "the country hangs in the balance" hints at what is to come: the rise to power of the middle classes; the erosion of monarchism; the power of popular and tabloid culture, the influence of European culture; the grip of individualism and rampant consumerism. It's a world away from Blue Nun with hors d'oeuvres of Salt 'n' Vinegar crisps in Tupperware boxes…

Graeme Mcdonald

Date 2001

Author Jonathan Coe (born 1961)

Nationality UK

Why It's Key *The Rotters' Club* was published when the 1970s was the focus of a nostalgia industry in British and American culture. Its sequel *The Closed Circle* was published in 2004. Both novels ask the present day reader to think about how twenty-first century Britain has (d)evolved to the present moment.

2000–

753

Key Event **Jonathan Franzen is involved in a public row with Oprah's Book Club**

Oprah Winfrey's Book Club, a regular feature of her immensely popular television talk show, was a rare instance of literature, in any form, taking up significant amounts of prime time television in the United States. Oprah's monthly selections gave large boosts to the sales of the books concerned. Single-handedly, it appeared, she had re-interested the American public in reading, and had done so via what is so often regarded as reading's nemesis – television. Book clubs and reading groups sprang up all over America.

Jonathan Franzen's decision to express his unease at his novel, *The Corrections*, being selected for Oprah's Book Club sparked an extraordinarily intense and protracted debate in the media. It was fueled in part by the words Franzen used to explain himself – "I feel I am solidly in the high art literary tradition, but I like to read entertaining books, so maybe this helps bridge that gap…." It seemed that Franzen was doing the unforgivable thing of setting himself above the common

mass of writers and readers. Some applauded his championing of highbrow values, others accused him of snobbery and elitism. Perhaps most surprisingly, it was Oprah herself who seemed to take the greatest offence. Franzen never rejected his selection, and even recorded an interview for the show. It was Oprah who "disinvited" him from the program. She abandoned her book club in its regular form shortly afterwards.

In many ways the dispute was between two media – television and the printed word – and is perhaps a rare example of the newer medium going into a sulk because it didn't get the older medium's respect.

Gerard Woodward

Date 2001

Place USA

Title *The Corrections* (2001)

Author Jonathan Franzen (born 1959)

Why It's Key Franzen's remarks about his award of an Oprah Book Club Sticker for *The Corrections* sparked an intense media debate about the highbrow and the lowbrow in modern fiction.

Opposite Jonathan Franzen

Key Book *The Shadow of the Wind (La Sombra del Viento)*

The Shadow of the Wind is a title of another book in Carlos Ruiz Zafón's gothic tale. A young man named Daniel Sempere finds the book one day, and its discovery changes his life. He quickly learns that he has the only known copy of the work – for another individual has systematically destroyed every other copy. The reader follows Daniel as he begins to uncover the mysteries of the book, and the shadowy figure of its author, Julian Carax. Jeopardizing his investigations is Inspector Fumero, a man with a vested interest in the whereabouts of the elusive author.

Amid the ruins of once wealthy houses and bullet-holed walls, Zafón captures the faded beauty of 1950s Barcelona and depicts a European setting still scarred from both World and civil wars. The gothic figure of Carax haunts the pages, his remarkable story entwining around Daniel's teenage life. *The Shadow of the Wind* is also a more traditional story of growing up. Daniel experiences the pains of unrequited love and betrayal, also battling to control his emerging sexuality. The course of the novel sees Daniel leave behind boyhood and face the trials of becoming a responsible adult.

Influenced by many other Gothic tales, in particular Ann Radcliffe and Matthew Lewis, Zafón takes earlier conventions of the genre but often provides a postmodern twist on his narrative. With plot turns that are often astonishing, rising suspense, and flickers of ghostly horror, Zafón updates gothic fiction for the twenty-first century, reusing standard characters and themes but refreshing the genre for the modern reader.
Thomas Dymond

Date 2001

Author Carlos Ruiz Zafón (born 1964)

Nationality Spain

Why It's Key Carlos Ruiz Zafón's bestselling book has sold over three million books worldwide and has been published in over thirty different languages.

2000–

Key Book *Erasure*

Erasure is narrated by Thelonius "Monk" Ellison, a black American writer – one who, according to his agent, is "not black enough." His latest novel has been rejected by 17 publishers, because the industry is only interested in black writers if their books have titles like *We's Lives in Da Ghetto*. Incensed, he writes a parody "ghetto novel" (under the pseudonym Stagg R. Leigh) in order to show up the tawdriness and insincerity of the genre, and is amazed when publishers and filmmakers start clamoring for the rights – even when he insists on entitling the novel *Fuck*. It is published to rave reviews; one (white) writer calls it "the truest novel I've ever read." Percival Everett includes the whole text of his parody in *Erasure* so that readers can ponder over whether they would have been fooled.

However, Everett's satire has a more controversial target than the gullible and condescending literary establishment. He suggests that black literary icons such as Richard Wright and Alice Walker have, in giving a "voice" to black people, been the unwitting means of forcing this voice on to all subsequent black writers; Monk thinks of their work and starts "screaming inside, complaining that I didn't sound like that." Their influence prevents him from developing his own literary identity, a fact that is mirrored in the bizarre scenes in which he has to disguise himself as "Stagg R. Leigh" for meetings and talk shows. The critics praised *Erasure* highly, each no doubt thinking it was all the other critics who were being satirized.
Jake Kerridge

Date 2001

Author Percival Everett (born 1956)

Nationality USA

Why It's Key A controversial satire about the pigeonholing of black writers that makes readers reassess their prejudices.

Key Character **Briony Tallis**
Atonement

SPOILER

Briony Tallis is the 13-year-old daughter of a well-to-do English family in 1935. She is blessed (although some might say cursed) with a fertile imagination and a drive towards being a writer: "… the Tallises began to understand that the baby of the family possessed a strange mind and a facility with words." Indeed, when we first meet her she is wrapped up in trying to stage a play she has written, *The Trials of Arabella*. She is the kind of child for whom ordinary life is too banal and has to be transformed by her own romantic creativity.

In later life, she has indeed become a writer and it is revealed that she is in fact the author of earlier parts of the book. She has been haunted throughout her life by the guilt caused by her false accusation, which blighted the lives of her sister and her lover. In her fiction she tries to make amends by giving the separated lovers a happy ending that Briony's actions denied them in real life. By presenting Briony in this double-faceted way McEwan is able to illustrate through a single character the different perspectives of childhood and old age. It also allows him to juggle the concepts of real life and art, in particular the "made reality" of fiction. At the end of her life Briony hopes that through her novelized version of what happened she can somehow change the past. The woman in her seventies is, in a way, still living in her imagination as she did as a child.

Michael Munro

Date 2001

Author Ian McEwan (born 1948)

Nationality UK

Why It's Key Briony Tallis is the pivot not only of the story but also of McEwan's characteristic playing with the nature of fiction and reality. The novel was short-listed for the Booker Prize in 2001.

2000–

755

Key Author **W.G. Sebald**
Austerlitz

Difficult to describe and almost impossible to classify, W.G. Sebald's (1944–2001) writings shift fluidly across the boundaries between fiction and non-fiction. His books incorporate photographs, diagrams, and pages from existing documents. Some of these have been altered to suit his purpose and many bear no explanation of what exactly we are looking at or why. A walking trip around the coast of East Anglia that takes in local history, the anatomy of the herring, Joseph Conrad's life, and much more makes up *The Rings of Saturn* (1998). It is at once a travelogue and a profound meditation on existence. The title figure in *Austerlitz* emerges like a shining angel, leading us backwards into European history, from the architecture of railway stations to Theresienstadt.

Sebald's books are not guided by any tangible plot, but rather develop as imaginative explorations that follow a line of thought wherever it might lead. The result is an encyclopedic array of anecdotes and histories that are linked in a chain of stories within stories. Images and characters, real and imagined, are drawn together into the weave. Although it appears to be assembled almost at random, the narrative follows a very precise structure.

In replacing the need for a driving narrative thread with an apparently rambling course, Sebald challenges our sense of what literature is. The documentation – diagrams, postcards, amateur photographs, often poor in quality – forces us to examine closely what is being presented to us. In this he captures the disconcerting spirit of modern existence.

Jamal Mahjoub

Date 2001

Nationality Germany

Other Key Works *The Emigrants* (1996), *Vertigo* (1999)

Why It's Key By the time of his death in 2001 Sebald's work had received almost universal acclaim. Although he had settled in Britain for over 30 years his work was also recognized in his native Germany where his awards included the Berlin Literature prize, the Heinrich Böll and Heinrich Heine prizes, and the Joseph Breitbach prize.

Key Event **Michael Moore's**
political satire becomes a bestseller

Subtitled *And Other Sorry Excuses for the State of the Nation*, Moore's indictment of the administration of President George W. Bush was a massive seller and demonstrated that political satire was still capable of being popular as well as impassioned. Moore completed *Stupid White Men* shortly before the September 11, 2001 terrorist attacks. As a consequence HarperCollins, his publisher, initially refused to publish certain sections and then did not advertise the book. Despite this, *SWM* became a huge bestseller, and this then led to it (and its author) becoming emblematic of the bitter split in U.S. political and cultural life between the left and the right.

Moore's guerrilla documentary-making and book writing is part of a committed campaign against big corporations, U.S. gun culture and, in particular, the Bush administration's foreign and domestic policy. *Fahrenheit 9/11*, which analyzed the reaction to the 2001 attacks, won the Palme D'Or at Cannes in 2005 and is the highest-grossing documentary of all time (surpassing Moore's Oscar-winning 2002 *Bowling for Columbine*, about guns). *SWM* was the first international salvo in this ongoing struggle, and does not pull its punches. Chapter 11 is "A Prayer to Afflict the Comfortable" calling for various ironic hardships to befall figures such as senators, white political leaders, Hollywood producers, and Catholic bishops (Moore argues this would speed up political change). The audience for Moore's brand of slapstick satire is huge and is attracted to his quizzical, little-guy-against-the-corporations style of direct action. *SWM* was followed in 2003 with *Dude, Where's My Country?*
Jerome de Groot

Date 2001 (publication)

Place USA

Title *Stupid White Men*

Author Michael Moore (born 1954)

Why It's Key Moore's controversial bestselling political satire attacked the Bush administration and showed the United States as a country divided.

Opposite **Michael Moore**

2000–

756

Key Character **Pi**
Life of Pi

SPOILER

Piscine Molitor Patel, otherwise known as Pi, is the young protagonist of Yann Martel's beautifully written novel, *Life of Pi*. The son of a zoo-owner in 1970s India, he is brought up with a great love of animals, admiring their beauty and respecting their behavior and needs. Imaginative, open-minded, and inquisitive, he is also drawn to religion at an early age. Rather than choosing one faith, however, as his parents and spiritual leaders would have him do, he embraces Christianity, Hinduism, and Islam and joyfully and eclectically celebrates all three.

This intellectual flexibility and understanding of animal behavior subsequently serve Pi well: following the death of his family in a shipwreck, he is cast out to sea in a small boat, accompanied by a 450-pound Bengal tiger named Richard Parker. Pi grippingly describes how he survives this scenario through his ingenuity in sourcing food and water and by his great determination in the face of physical suffering and fear.

In particular, Pi's caring for Richard Parker demonstrates his considerable compassion, ability to be understanding, and empathy.

Two hundred and twenty-seven days later, having finally reached land, Pi recounts his fantastic adventures to two disbelieving officials who subsequently ask him to produce a blander, more "realistic," and official account. Yet this reductive version makes us want to believe the original story all the more, and to hold onto the central tenets of Pi's character: a belief in the power of the imagination and an open mind.
Simon Avery

Date 2001

Author Yann Martel (born 1963)

Nationality Canada

Why It's Key *Life of Pi* became a bestseller after winning the Man Booker Prize in 2002. Comparisons made with Moacyr Scliar's 1981 novel, *Max and the Cats*, are acknowledged in Martel's Preface, yet the combination of adventure narrative, fantasy, and philosophical speculation makes *Life of Pi* an innovative and often intriguing work.

Key Passage **Introduction to** *Notable American Women*

"… how can a single word from Ben Marcus' rotten, filthy heart be trusted?"

Notable American Women is a work of baffling originality which reads like a user's guide to some weird-but-wonderful contraption that does not exist. Ostensibly, it is a dystopian family drama set on a farm in deepest Ohio, USA. Jane Marcus joins a feminist cult that aims to achieve total silence and stillness. As a result, her son (Ben) is subjected to the mother of all child-rearing experiments while her husband (Michael) is confined to a deep hole in the backyard.

The female Silentists' decision to suppress their own voices is primarily a political act, but it is also reminiscent of the aesthetics of silence which – from Rimbaud's agraphia to Cioran and beyond – has cast a shadow over contemporary literature. The first part of the novel is an "introduction," attributed to Michael, that aims to "mute all that follows." In a bid to pre-empt the symbolic killing of the paterfamilias (the author plays upon this Oedipal dimension by lending his own name to the protagonist), Michael pens this "disclaimer" to discredit his son's credentials both as a writer and a human being. Ben, we are told, is ugly, weak, neurotic, mentally disabled, and – worse still – an unreliable narrator whose book he invites us to burn: "How can a single word from Ben Marcus' rotten, filthy heart be trusted?" For good measure, he exploits the anxiety-of-influence motif by explaining that a father is "the first author" of his offspring's work anyway and that the latter's voice is simply the product of "sheer ventriloquism." The struggle to reassert authority which lies at the heart of these notes from underground could be construed as a deranged revenge – beyond the Barthesian grave – of the author over the scriptor.
Andrew Gallix

Date 2002

Author Ben Marcus (born 1967)

Nationality USA

Why It's Key The book that sealed Ben Marcus' reputation as one of the most singular voices in contemporary fiction.

2000–

759

Key Author **William Trevor** *The Story of Lucy Gault*

Those who enjoy melancholy with a comic tinge love the writing of William Trevor (born 1928). An Irishman, he prides himself as a storyteller, in the great tradition of James Joyce and Frank O'Connor. For almost 50 years, he has published prize-winning novels and short stories; his most recent book is a collection of stories, *A Bit on the Side* (2004). His earlier work was often cruelly comic, but his tone has darkened with time.

The Story of Lucy Gault is a novel permeated with his trademark yearning for what might have been. A young girl disappears while her parents are leaving their home in Ireland, and they come to believe, mistakenly, that she is dead.

Trevor's characters frequently suffer from awareness of the road not taken. The second wife, in *The Piano Tuner's Wives*, will never forgive the fact that she is the second; Bridie, the protagonist in *The Ballroom of Romance*, will always ache for what might have been; and the readers of *The Story of Lucy Gault* long for the fractured family to be reunited. He frequently employs unreliable narrators, who give his characters a hinterland which glimmers through the lucid prose.

Trevor's earlier books were set in England, and in London in particular. Later, though living in England, he turned to exploring Irish lives. A Protestant, he has sometimes been called a "big house" novelist, in the same vein as Elizabeth Bowen, but he writes as much about the poorer Catholic population as about wealthy landowners. In 1997 he was awarded an honorary CBE for services to literature. He has been awarded countless prizes and in 2002 was shortlisted for the Man Booker Prize for *The Story of Lucy Gault*.
Felicity Skelton

Date 2002

Nationality Ireland

Other Key Works *The Old Boys* (1964), *The Children of Dynmouth* (1976), *The Collected Stories* (1992), *Felicia's Journey* (1994), *The Hill Bachelors* (2000)

Why It's Key Trevor is a prolific Irish writer, widely regarded as one of the best – if not the best – living short story writers in English.

Opposite **William Trevor**

Key Book
Everything is Illuminated

For *The Times*, *Everything is Illuminated* has literally illuminated everything: a "work of genius," "a new kind of novel," the book has ensured that "things will never be the same again." Unsurprisingly, these gushing words feature prominently on the back-cover of the paperback edition. Yet, quite what "things" the reviewer had in mind is not clear: certainly, Foer's bank balance was irreversibly altered, as was his ability to pop unnoticed into his local bookshop.

Over time, the media scrum surrounding Foer's debut has dispersed, though not entirely, to reveal the book itself. What is left is an ambitious, funny, and moving first novel about a 19-year-old Jewish American called "Jonathan Safran Foer" (where do they get these names?) searching for Augustine, the woman who saved his grandfather from the Nazi Holocaust.

Taking its title from *The Unbearable Lightness of Being*, *Everything is Illuminated* has become a key text of a voguish literary "movement" featuring writers like Dave Eggers, Jonathan Lethem, and Nicole Krauss. What unites these admittedly different talents is ornate verbal and structural playfulness and a slippery use of autobiography: like "Safran Foer," Safran Foer went to Ukraine in search of his grandfather; unlike character "Safran Foer," author Safran Foer left empty-handed until he re-configured the experience in art.

Such was the book's cultural prominence that it easily outshone an enjoyable movie adaptation starring Elijah Wood and directed by Liev Schreiber. "One of the things I could never have known was how a book gets better after it's published," Foer told *The Guardian*. "Before, it was just my set of intentions[…].The best books are the ones that ask the most questions."
James Kidd

Date 2002

Author Jonathan Safran Foer (born 1977)

Nationality USA

Why It's Key This debut novel became a sort of literary litmus test which (con)fused novel and novelist: either you loved Foer's smart, playful form-bending fictionalized memoir (as Salman Rushdie and John Updike did) or condemned it as flash and superficial.

Key Character **Susie Salmon**
The Lovely Bones

Susie Salmon, the 14-year-old narrator of Alice Sebold's compelling bestseller *The Lovely Bones*, set in 1970s small-town America, is already dead when the novel opens. Having been brutally raped and murdered, Susie now speaks from heaven – which takes the form of a high school playground with "intake counsellors" rather than the conventional theological realm of God and angels – as she watches the search for her murderer and the ways in which her family and friends try to come to terms with their loss. Intriguingly, this narrative perspective, which accounts for much of the novel's originality, allows Susie to grow posthumously as she develops deeper understanding of her family members and experiences the trials of growing up vicariously through her friends and siblings.

The Lovely Bones has been hugely popular and has received much attention for its emphasis on the dead still being near us. It also appears to have been particular meaningful in the wake of both the September 11 attacks in America and increased concerns about child abduction and sexual violence (Sebold's earlier book, *Lucky*, published in 1999, is a memoir of her own experiences as a rape victim). Certainly in its intricate exploration of the processes of grieving and healing, the novel highlights the need for compassion and support and the subsequent possibilities of moving through trauma to some degree of acceptance and renewal. Elegantly written and intelligent, *The Lovely Bones* is a powerful and moving work which has helped reshape conventional fictional representations of the afterlife.
Simon Avery

Date 2002

Author Alice Sebold (born 1963)

Nationality USA

Why It's Key Alice Sebold's debut novel has been a bestseller on both sides of the Atlantic and widely acclaimed by critics for its innovative use of a young murdered girl in heaven as the narrator. The novel's exploration of grieving and the possibilities of healing and transformation have been particularly resonant in the wake of 9/11.
Opposite Alice Sebold

Key Character **Christopher Boone**
The Curious Incident of the Dog

Mark Haddon's (born 1962) brilliant, internationally bestselling novel, first published in 2003, has a memorable narrator: a 15-year-old boy, Christopher John Francis Boone, who has Asperger's syndrome (although his condition is never named in the book) and knows all the countries of the world and their capital cities and every prime number up to 7,057 (as he puts it: "Prime numbers are like life. They are very logical but you could never work out the rules, even if you spent all your time thinking about them").

His carefully constructed world falls apart when he finds his neighbor's dog impaled on a garden fork and is initially blamed for the killing. Christopher is determined to track down the real killer and turns to his favorite fictional character, the impeccably logical Sherlock Holmes, for inspiration. His investigation leads him down some wonderfully unexpected avenues.

Extremely perceptive and telling in its depiction of living with Asperger's syndrome – Christopher relates well to animals but has no understanding of human emotions, and cannot stand to be touched – the book is also poignant, comic, and suspenseful. His disorder plays a specific role in his detective work, especially when it comes to his association with others. Like many people on the autistic spectrum, Christopher is a visual thinker, and must have explicit visual stimulation to understand a situation. Accordingly, maps, charts, and mathematical equations – produced by Haddon himself after hours of doodling on his computer – are scattered throughout the book.

Adam Feinstein

Date 2003

Appears in *The Curious Incident of the Dog in the Night-time*

Author Mark Haddon

Nationality UK

Why It's Key Haddon says that one of the most pleasant, if eccentric, responses came from a publisher who said: "I didn't realize there was actually anything wrong with Christopher." "I've always treasured that reaction. It's kind of naive but perfect," said Haddon.

2000–

762

Key Event *Brick Lane* becomes a controversial bestseller

Monica Ali was claimed as one of the Best Young British Novelists by *Granta* magazine on the basis of the manuscript for her first novel that details the divergent lives of two Bangladeshi sisters from 1967 to the present. The book's depiction of a Bangladeshi family's struggle to settle in a notorious London housing estate was widely acclaimed. Its prominent position in British culture has been further amplified by the controversy it has generated since publication. As it was lauded it was also being described as "insulting" and even "racist" from an indignant but prominent vocal minority of the Brick Lane Asian community who attacked its depiction not only of Brick Lane and Tower Hamlets but also Bangladesh, where a significant portion of the narrative is set. This group accuse the novel of distortion and caricature at a time when the image of immigrants and ethnic minorities in Britain is extremely sensitive. Ali's own class and ethnic credentials have also

been questioned in the argument over the novel's ultimate authenticity.

The controversy publicly reignited in 2006 when proposed filming of the novel in Brick Lane locations was prevented by opposition groups. This was a salient echo of the text's own investigation of the dividing lines of ethnicity, religion and gender galvanised by passionate local politics. Opposition to the novel has produced robust defence from writers such as Salman Rushdie and Brick Lane residents supportive of its aims. It will continue to stimulate passionate discussion about national identity, immigration, and race and racism in a Britain transformed by increasing global diaspora. *Brick Lane*'s status as an integral text of the British immigrant experience at a complex and significant time in the composition of Britishness is assured.

Graeme Mcdonald

Date 2003

Author Monica Ali (born 1967)

Why It's Key "I cannot think of another novel in which the politics of our times are caught with such easy vividness," wrote Natasha Walter in *The Guardian* of *Brick Lane*. One of the most critically and commercially successful 21st century British novels, it has generated controversy in its depiction of the Bangladeshi community in London's East End.

Opposite Monica Ali

Key Book
Persepolis: The Story of a Childhood

A young girl visited by God. A grandmother who puts jasmine flowers in her bra. Throwing homemade wine down the toilet. Smuggling a Kim Wilde poster back to Iran! These are just some of the unexpected delights of Marjane Satrapi's *Persopolis*. From her earliest memory of being given a veil to wear at school and not knowing quite what to do with it (turning the veil into a skipping rope, a hood, and reins are all attempted in the school yard) to the evocative summary of 2,500 years of Persian history (all on half a page), Satrapi retells the history of Iran through the story of her family.

Rich comparisons make light of tense political realities such as when Marx is likened to God (though Marx has curlier hair) and the chaos of Iran's war with Iraq is represented through cars trying to escape a maze of directionless flames. Plastic keys painted gold provide entry into paradise in Satrapi's description of martyrs, depicted floating in the air with keys hung round their necks. Marjane's quirky comments and the clever placing of herself in the drawings remind us that we too are looking, questioning, and judging just like she is. That there is a black market for pop music such as "Yazoo, Abba and Pink Floyd" reminds the reader that after all, Marjane is a teenager, looking to identify with other teenagers around the staples of jean jackets and pop music, even if many around her think these are "symbols of decadence."

Anastasia Valassopoulos

Date 2003 (originally published in France in two volumes as *Persepolis 1* and *Persepolis 2* in 2000 and 2001 respectively)

Author and Illustrator Marjane Satrapi (born 1969)

Nationality Iran

Why It's Key Bringing graphic novels to a new audience, the bestselling *Persepolis* is an account of a girl's childhood in post-revolutionary Iran, told using vivid black and white only drawings.

Key Character **Henry DeTamble**
The Time Traveler's Wife

Time travel is nothing new in fiction, especially in science fiction, but Audrey Niffenegger gives the concept a new slant by portraying Henry DeTamble as someone who cannot control his sudden journeys through the years. The author ascribes this to a mysterious genetic disorder (which Henry will eventually pass on to his daughter), the nearest comparison perhaps being to epilepsy, with time-traveling episodes occurring to Henry instead of fits. Whatever is the cause of these incidents, Henry has to learn to cope with them and he becomes a highly resourceful character. In particular, he always arrives, whether in his past or his future, completely naked and he has to be able to do something about this quickly.

His wife, Clare, also has to learn to deal with her husband's abrupt disappearances and manifestations, as they have a series of encounters at different respective ages before finally meeting in "real time." The fact that the book's title refers to her rather than her husband is an indication that hers is the worse side of the relationship; Henry at least has exciting experiences to keep him occupied, while Clare has to endure being periodically abandoned, left to wonder when she will see the man she loves again. It is at once a consolation and a heartbreak that she knows she may meet Henry at any moment, even after in "real time" he has died. Above all, the novel is a love story; for Henry and Clare the idea of loving one another "forever" is not just a romantic cliché.

Michael Munro

Date 2003

Author Audrey Niffenegger (born 1963)

Nationality USA

Why It's Key Henry DeTamble's character provides the premise for the novel. The story of his abrupt temporal comings and goings in the life of Clare (his eventual wife) allows the author to interweave a conventional love story with a sci-fi thread that plays with the concepts of past, present and future.

Key Character **Cal Stephanides**
Middlesex

At the center of *Middlesex*, Jeffrey Eugenides' Pulitzer Prize-winning second novel, is Cal Stephanides, an unusual protagonist who is neither entirely male nor female and possesses an omniscient first-person voice. As he immediately informs us, Cal is born in 1960s Detroit, apparently female, to upwardly mobile, second-generation Greek American parents. Known as Calliope or Callie, the character lives as a girl, enjoying an untroubled childhood before hitting puberty when she is forced to navigate the painful, complex territory of hermaphroditism or intersexuality. From his current vantage point as a career diplomat in Berlin, Cal also narrates the tale of his grandparents' journey from Asia Minor to the American Midwest (arguably inventing their experiences), and later tells his parents' story before relating his own coming of age and the decision at 14 to identify as male.

Cal handles his epic family memoir and his own life story through a range of tones – tragicomic, satirical, lighthearted, ironic – and he is portrayed as clever, sardonic, and shy. Ultimately, however, he appears strangely opaque and unknowable. In classic Bildungsroman fashion, Eugenides focuses on Cal's early years, while the period between the ages of 15 and 41 remains a noticeable blank. Cal implies that the pain of bearing his secret as an adult, and his largely unsuccessful attempts at emotional and sexual intimacy with women, have made him wary about divulging too much information about himself. But there is a sense in which his creator stops short of fully imagining the implications of Cal's condition.

Ruth Maxey

Date 2003

Author Jeffrey Eugenides (born 1960)

Nationality USA

Why It's Key Through *Middlesex*, Eugenides presented Cal as a universal figure, emblematic of the gender ambiguity in everyone, and brought the subject of intersexuality, a commoner medical condition than one might think, to a wider audience.

Key Character **Oryx**
Oryx and Crake

SPOILER

Oryx and Crake is a work of what has become known as "extrapolative fiction": it is set in a disturbingly plausible future, in which a number of the new technologies and cultural tendencies of our present are taken forward to chillingly logical outcomes. Human trafficking, internet pornography, the exploitation of children by adults and of the poor by the rich all mark Oryx's life, but are taken almost entirely for granted in the high-tech, desensitized society in which Jimmy grows up. The natural world has been polluted and plundered (Oryx takes her name from the now-extinct antelope), and genetic engineering has progressed to the point where man-made species are common, factory-farmed for experimentation or consumption.

A virtual Oryx is glimpsed a number of times before Jimmy actually meets her: somebody who might or might not be Oryx appears on a child pornography site, and in a news story about a man who imports her and keeps her prisoner in his garage. She is finally encountered in the flesh as assistant to the sardonic genius, Crake, who was once Jimmy's school-friend and is now head of a top-secret project at the prestigious Paradice compound. Oryx is mentor to the Crakers, a new breed of humans engineered by Crake – and ultimately becomes the unwitting accessory to his devastating attempt to wipe out the human race. Her final manifestation is posthumous, as one of the ghosts that haunts Snowman in his struggle for survival in the post-apocalyptic world, and as a gentle deity to the Crakers.

Anna Tripp

Date 2003

Author Margaret Atwood (born 1939)

Nationality Canada

Why It's Key Oryx is an enigmatic character at the heart of this gripping dystopian novel. Neither her true origins, nor her real name, nor her complete life story are ever known. Her character is reconstructed solely through the anguished memories of Snowman, a.k.a. Jimmy, a man who loved her but never understood her.

Key Event **Demonstrations against Iraq war inspire McEwan's novel *Saturday***

February 15, 2003 was designated a global day of protest against the United States' planned war on Saddam Hussein's Iraq. Major demonstrations were held in around 600 cities worldwide. The gathering of three million in Rome is thought to be the largest anti-war rally in history. In London an estimated one million people gathered to protest against George W. Bush's proposed invasion.

The London demonstrations provide a backdrop to Ian McEwan's novel, *Saturday*, which takes place entirely within the 24 hours of that day. McEwan was one of the first writers to respond to the attacks on the World Trade Center in print, writing an article for *The Guardian* newspaper within two hours of the attacks taking place. *Saturday* is a longer response to that event and its aftermath, and is the most successful of the first wave of novels that have dealt with the so-called "War on Terror." The novel centers on brain surgeon Henry Perowne's preparations for a family

reunion, which are interrupted when he has a minor car accident with a violent criminal, who later disrupts the family gathering. Part of *Saturday*'s success is to do with the ways in which McEwan addresses wider issues through the English novel's more traditional subject matter of family relationships and day-to-day suburban domestic life. The random cruelty and the obsession with scientific minutiae are familiar McEwan themes, but here they add a special insight into the greater violence of political struggle and warfare. McEwan's achievement was to show that the English novel was capable of dealing with issues of global insecurity.

Gerard Woodward

Date 2003

Place London

Title *Saturday*

Author Ian McEwan (born 1948)

Why It's Key McEwan uses the conventions of the English novel to address issues surrounding George W. Bush's "War on Terror."

Key Event ***The Da Vinci Code* becomes a worldwide bestseller**

The Da Vinci Code has quickly become one of the most debated and widely read thrillers of the twenty-first century. Focusing on Robert Langdon, an American Professor of Religious Symbology, and Sophie Neveu, a French cryptologist, the narrative plunges the reader into a world of religious and political conspiracies, mysterious societies, and a fight over information which threatens to shake the Church to its core. The novel suggests that the "true" history of Jesus has been covered up by the Catholic Church and that the Holy Grail is in fact the bloodline springing from Christ and Mary Magdalene, his wife.

The Da Vinci Code's controversial ideas concerning the relationship between Jesus and Mary Magdalene, the "sacred feminine," early Christian history, the Priory of Sion, and the Knights Templar, are not original – indeed, Dan Brown was (unsuccessfully) taken to court for plagiarism by the authors of the 1982 study *The Holy Blood and the Holy Grail* – yet the novel has

subsequently been pilloried by religious groups, historians, and art historians for popularizing them.

The Da Vinci Code has had a massive impact on the publishing world and has led to numerous spin-offs, including non-fiction texts on the ideas raised (for example, Simon Cox's *Cracking the Da Vinci Code*, Laurence Gardner's *The Magdalene Legacy,* and Carl Olsen's *The Da Vinci Hoax*); other novels similarly dealing with grail quests, codes, and conspiracies (for example, Raymond Khoury's *The Last Templar* and Jim Hougan's *The Magdalene Cipher*); and humorous parodies (for example, Toby Clements' *The Asti Spumante Code*).

Simon Avery

Date 2003

Author Dan Brown (born 1964)

Why It's Key A worldwide publishing phenomenon with more than 60 million copies sold. Generating great controversy over its suggestions of religious conspiracy, the novel has spawned a subgenre of imitations as well as documentaries, numerous websites both supporting and denying Dan Brown's claims, and a 2006 film directed by Ron Howard.

Opposite *The Da Vinci Code*

Key Event
Shelley Jackson creates a "mortal novel"

In 2003, writer and artist Shelley Jackson launched *Skin*, a short fictional work "published" on human flesh. Volunteers are assigned one word from the text, which they have tattooed on their bodies. Only the participants will have access to the full text of the piece, which will not be broadcast, adapted, or published in any medium other than the original single-word tattoos. At the time of writing, 1,850 volunteers have been provisionally accepted to participate in the project, and 470 words have been tattooed. The total number of words to be tattooed is 2,095.

On *Skin* website, Jackson explains that participants "are not understood as carriers or agents of the words they bear, but as their embodiments." In fact, once tattooed and photographed, participants are referred to as "words." Jackson's "words" are encouraged to interact with one another and post messages on the project website, which, in effect, constitutes another narrative layer of the project.

In addition to this innovative textual performance – a "mortal work of art" – Jackson has made significant contributions to electronic literature and hypertext fiction. Her writing, which often concerns the politics of gender and the body, is characterized by generic fusion and formal experimentation. Jackson's hypertext *Patchwork Girl* (1997) integrates text and image towards a re-imagining of Mary Shelley's *Frankenstein*; her print novel *Half Life* (2006) countenances the puzzles of sexual, individual, and national identity through the experiences of conjoined twins. Jackson teaches in the graduate writing program at The New School University.

Kiki Benzon

Date 2003

Place USA

Title *Skin* (2003)

Author Shelley Jackson (born 1963)

Why It's Key Jackson jokes: "People have written to me saying that if two Words met, fell in love and had a baby, would that offspring be a footnote?" The project is an innovation in textual performance, expanding the nature of how we look at the written word.

2000–

768

Key Event **The first novel written in English by an Afghan, *The Kite Runner***

Amir and Hassan are fast friends. Both lost their mothers, and were nursed by the same midwife. They grow up in 1970s Afghanistan, a place now unrecognizable: a monarchy; a must-visit for any self-respecting hippy; a place as yet unmolested by the extremes of communism and Islamic fundamentalism which would later pull the country apart and into the abyss.

While Amir is the cosseted child of the Pashtun ruling class, Hassan, born with a harelip and a capacity for love to shame a saint's, belongs to the despised Hazara tribe. Hassan does whatever Amir suggests or demands, and shields him against the savagery of the streets. Amir tries to reciprocate, tries to wave away the world's taunts from Hassan's face. More effectually, he shows Hassan the wonders of Afghan heroic literature. But heroic tales do not always turn boys into men, and so it proves for Amir. When it comes to the testing point, at a grand kite-flying competition, when

Amir finds himself wedged between the claim of caste and family on the one hand and that of a loyal and loving playmate on the other, he makes the wrong choice, and that choice is to haunt him throughout the long years of an unpredicted exile. Afghanistan convulses, and Amir and his seemingly invincible father must flee to America.

Though they carve out an existence there, Amir's conscience leaves him no rest. He returns to Afghanistan – now under Taliban rule – to make what amends he can to Hassan. At once an intriguing, unconventional tale of immigrant struggle and a heart-piercing fable of atonement, *The Kite Runner* subverted every prejudice about Afghanistan. Its undeniably folkloric elements have proved a stumbling block for some, yet they are surely the point. "Real life" is heroic, and villainous; and betrayals, however great, are redeemable.

Murrough O'Brien

Date 2003

Author Khaled Hosseini (born 1965)

Nationality Afghanistan

Why It's Key *The Kite Runner* came as a revelation to readers unaware of an innocent, tolerant, peaceful Afghanistan. It reminded the world that refugees are as likely to be respected professionals as helpless peasants, and it reminded readers of the uncountable wealth in central Asian storytelling.

Key Author
Abdul-Rahman Munif

Abdul-Rahman Munif's (1933–2004) experiences of his time in the Iraqi oil ministry provided much material for his novels, which are often scathing in their parodying of Middle Eastern elites such as Saudi Arabia, the country of his father's birth, which perhaps unsurprisingly has banned many of his books.

His most famous work, the *Cities of Salt* quintet, chronicles the "evolution" of the Arabian Peninsula from a largely traditional Bedouin society to a rich and powerful kleptocracy. Munif became prominent not only for his contentious subject matter, but for his use of modernist narrative techniques. He invented the towns of Thebes and Wadi al-Uyoun as backdrops for the wider story of *Cities of Salt*, and wrote the narrative portions entirely in classical Arabic, whereas his characters speak in the colloquial Arabic of the tribe to which he or she belongs.

The narrative moves fluidly backwards and forwards through time, deepening the context and ultimately shedding new light on contemporary and historical events, while acknowledging the tradition of Arabic storytelling, which also employs a non-linear narrative approach, presents differing versions of the same events and indulges in lengthy, though illuminating, digressions.

In using these techniques, Munif deftly portrays a region utterly transformed in just a few short decades by the discovery of oil, exposing the hypocrisies and lies of the Middle East oil business and of the cast of nefarious characters that run it, as well as detailing how this transformation has intrinsically altered the lives of millions in the region.

Christian Kerr

Date 2004 (death)

Nationality Jordan

Other Key Works *Cities of Salt: Cities of Salt, Vol 1* (1984), *The Trench: Cities of Salt, Vol 2* (1985), *Variations on Night and Day: Cities of Salt, Vol 3* (1989), *Endings* (1991), *Story of a City: A Childhood in Amman* (1994)

Why It's Key Abdul Rahman Munif is recognized as one of the most important Arabic novelists of the twentieth century.

2000–

769

Key Book
Maps for Lost Lovers

Following his debut work, *Season of the Rainbirds*, published to critical praise in 1993, British Pakistani writer Nadeem Aslam underwent 11 years of seclusion before finishing his ambitious and wide-ranging second novel, *Maps for Lost Lovers*. The result is a deeply felt, unusually rich piece of writing and a powerful reading experience. *Maps for Lost Lovers* begins with the murder of Jugnu and Chanda, an unmarried Pakistani immigrant couple, living in a largely South Asian, working-class community, composed of Muslims, Sikhs, and Hindus, in an unspecified, northern English town. The rest of the novel explores the impact of the two "honor killings" on Shamas, Jugnu's elder brother, and his wife, Kaukab.

The text is many things at once: a condemnation of certain ancestral Pakistani practices, treacherously intact despite their transplantation to British soil; a feminist work concerned with social justice; a thriller driven by the unsolved murders; a love story which suggests that inevitably passion cannot be suppressed even when, chillingly, it carries the risk of death; a history of immigration; and a theological novel examining Islamic piety and Qur'anic interpretation.

Through a lyrical literary style, Aslam fashions dense poetry from the tragedy of the killings, Shamas' painful marriage, and Kaukab's exilic disappointments. Largely resisting a didactic tone, he angrily exposes the destructiveness of a particular British Asian community and its internecine obsession with appearances, tradition and social control. But Aslam also expresses deep respect for Pakistani culture through his sensitive characterisation of Shamas and Kaukab and their competing worldviews.

Ruth Maxey

Date 2004

Author Nadeem Aslam (born 1966)

Nationality UK

Why It's Key Poetically written work of British Asian fiction which risks re-inscribing some harmful stereotypes, while providing an important exposé of misogyny and sexual double standards in a Pakistani community in northern England.

Key Book
Small Island

Andrea Levy's father was one of the pioneers who in 1948 sailed from Jamaica to England on the *SS Empire Windrush* in search of a better life. The arrival of those Caribbean migrants, hopeful children of the British Empire, was a turning-point in British history. "Immigration is a dynamic process," Levy has said, "the people who come are as changed by it as the people they come to." Set in that time of change, *Small Island* draws on the experiences of the Windrush generation, for whom post-war London, emerging from five years of privation, was characteristically cold, prejudiced, and hostile, rather than being the welcoming haven of migrant dreams and expectations. Levy portrays the effect of that era on two "small islands," Jamaica and the UK, addressing varied experiences of race, class, gender, and identity. A collective history is played out in the interaction between four central characters: Gilbert (who joined the RAF to save Britain from fascism) and Hortense, a Jamaican couple trying to make a new life for themselves in the "mother country"; the English Queenie Bligh, who takes in lodgers when her husband does not return from his posting in India; and Bernard, the bigoted ex-serviceman. Through their poignant stories, *Small Island* depicts a pivotal episode in England's past. Linton Kwesi Johnson has called the novel "A work of great imaginative power which ranks alongside Sam Selvon's *The Lonely Londoners*, George Lamming's *The Emigrants*, and Caryl Phillips' *The Final Passage* in dealing with the experience of migration."

Margaret Busby

Date 2004

Author Andrea Levy (born 1956)

Nationality UK

Why It's Key Following *Every Light in the House Burnin'* (1994), *Never Far from Nowhere* (1996), and *Fruit of the Lemon* (1999) Levy won multiple prizes for *Small Island*. She is among several successful British-born Black and Asian novelists who have redefined the notion of Englishness.

Opposite Andrea Levy

Key Event *The Line of Beauty*
wins the Man Booker Prize

Alan Hollinghurst's fourth novel returned to the 1980s setting of *The Swimming-Pool Library*, and resembled it in dealing a spectacularly punitive shock to its main character, who is wealthier, brasher, and more of a hedonist in the earlier book, but similarly possessed of a snooty cultural style and a sexual taste for black men (which runs up against English racism as well as English homophobia). The endings shock the heroes and maybe the readers too into a realization that in the 1980s there was a war going on in the politics of homosexuality, with the governing classes as the villains.

A comparison to the panorama of urban energies and social change in *The Swimming-Pool Library* (1988) and *The Spell* (1999) makes it apparent that Hollinghurst is working on a different canvas here (wider in terms of gender, but narrower in class). The real subject is the tension between two kinds of conservative culture which joined forces, up to a point, in the 1980s: a traditional one, landed, affluent, Oxbridge-educated, and a newer, Thatcherite one, less tactful and humane, more impatient and violent for change. The protagonist of *The Line of Beauty*, the suggestively named Nick Guest, aspires to find a place for accepted gayness in the conservative world he's so drawn to, represented by the Fedden family. In its measured nuances and habits of restrictive irony the book is partly an admiring meditation on the works of Henry James, a predecessor also susceptible to the romance of affluent manners and male intimacy.

Peter Swaab

Date 2004

Author Alan Hollinghurst (born 1955)

Nationality UK

Why It's Key When *The Line of Beauty* won the Booker Prize in 2004, it caused some controversy for its scenes of gay sex and drug use; the book was later serialized in three parts by Andrew Davies for the BBC.

Key Event **Irène Némirovsky's** *Suite Française* **is finally published**

Irène Némirovsky (1903–1942) was already an established novelist, with two books to her name, when the German army invaded France in June 1940. As she fled Paris with her young family, she recorded the terror and confusion of the rush from the advancing Wehrmacht. After the fall of France, she was arrested, interned, and eventually sent to Auschwitz, where she was murdered in 1942. It wasn't until 62 years later that the manuscript that became *Suite Française* was brought to light.

Originally planned as the first in a series of five novels, *Suite Française* is actually the first two books *Storm in June* and *Dolce*. *Storm in June* describes the flight from Paris of several families. As it unfolds, it expertly and unsparingly reveals the different layers of French society, and exposes the absurdity of social etiquette in a time of war when every class, race, and creed are thrown together. *Dolce* focuses on the remote village of Bussy, during the first days of the Vichy regime, and describes the ways in which some members of the community begin to collaborate with the occupying forces.

Suite Française caused a sensation on its publication in France, with critics arguing the author should be posthumously awarded the Prix Goncourt. It has been sold to 17 countries and sold millions of copies worldwide. This success is a tribute not only to the author's remarkable courage and skill, but to the immediacy with which this contemporary novel captures the terror of war, and the honesty with which the writing penetrates the facades that support class systems.
Charles Beckett

Date 2004

Place France

Why It's Key It is too soon to judge the lasting influence of *Suite Française*, but its popularity has been enormous, and seems set to ensure its author a place in the canon of great twentieth-century novelists. The circumstances of the book's creation make its achievement even more remarkable.

2000–

772

Key Event **Takami's** *Battle Royale* **causes controversy over mimic murder**

A brilliantly brutal tournament where the prizes are people. *Battle Royale* encapsulates a moment of self-reflection, a ruthless critique of cultural malaise and the machinations of contemporary Japan.

As popular as it is controversial, the foundations of the *Battle Royale* cult lie in the arresting and intricate novel which has spawned two box office hit movies (one directed by Kinji Fukasaku), a manga series, and even a board game. It has since achieved international recognition, not least due to its graphic nature and a knowing nod to an outsider's perception of Japanese society. The premise is nothing short of shocking: under the dictates of a totalitarian state, a class of Junior High School students are left on a deserted island to establish a winner by a terrifying process of elimination and assassination. Pitched against each other, a violent and bloody battle naturally ensues.

Rich in social commentary, this dystopian rite of passage leaves the audience pondering the clash of conformity and individualism. We watch the spectacle of violence helplessly as the members of class 3B struggle to reconcile their natural instincts of self-preservation and survival with the social obligation to maintain the *wa* (harmony) of their *kumi* (class), both concepts crucial to survival in Japanese society.

This complex creation from the dark imagination of first-time writer Koushun Takami holds a macabre appeal for a diverse audience. Older readers may draw parallels with the allegorical exploration of the darker side of human nature found in *Lord of the Flies*. Above all, however, *Battle Royale* speaks to a generation immersed in the graphic fast-paced violence of computer games, anime and manga, East and West.
Sarah Birchwood

Date June 2004

Place Okubo Elementary School, Japan

Title *Battle Royale* (1999)

Author Koushun Takami (born 1969)

Why It's Key Puts the "mania" in Japanomania. A chilling interpretation of modern day Japan which scratches the superficial veneer of Japanese society to reveal a sinister vision of a nation with a noose around its neck.

Key Event **Elfriede Jelinek wins the Nobel Prize in Literature**

Despite the fact that it is the most famous literature prize in the world the process of awarding the Nobel is not particularly transparent. The Nobel foundation seeks the nominations of the 18-strong Swedish Academy, academics, and presidents of literary societies worldwide and previous winners. These nominations are then voted on by the Academy and the prize-winner must receive more than half the votes cast.

Elfriede Jelinek is an Austrian novelist and playwright who in 2004 became only the 10th woman to win the prize for literature. Her work is interrogatively feminist, austere, and bleak. Her key novel, *The Piano Teacher*, concerns a twisted love affair between pianist Erika Kohut and her student Walter Klemmer. This pessimistic work explores a dark female sexuality, voyeuristic and brutal. Jelinek is agoraphobic and accepted the award by video message.

A year later, Knut Ahnlund resigned from the Swedish Academy due to Jelinek's award; he described her work as "whining, unenjoyable public pornography" and "a mass of text shovelled together without artistic structure." His reactionary comments hardly showed him in a good light, although he was echoing certain uninformed critical concerns about her direct exploration of violence and sexuality; he further demonstrated the innate conservatism of the Nobel academy when he later claimed that Jelinek's prize "has not only done irreparable damage to all progressive forces, it has also confused the general view of literature as an art." Ahnlund's resignation attached a whiff of controversy to an unexpected but not undeserved award. Jelinek is a distinguished novelist and outspoken political activist; her writing is uncompromising and nihilistic.

Jerome de Groot

Date 2004

Nationality Austria

Why It's Key A controversial award which prompted the later resignation of a judge; the incident brought into focus the secretive nature of the Nobel.

2000–

773

Key Character **Amber** *The Accidental*

The Accidental is a book about how individuals break down, and about what they might subsequently become. It is about reality and how we avoid it. In the novel, the figure of Amber acts as a catalyst for disintegration, transformation, and confrontation.

The Smarts have retreated to their holiday cottage. Eve is the bestselling author of a series of "autobiotruefictinterviews," or autobiographies written from the point of view of people who have died. Her husband Michael is a lecherous academic. Astrid, 12, filters the world through the lens of her digital camera, and Magnus, 17, is a talented mathematician and the bearer of a terrible secret. All of these characters are in different ways self-obsessed and in denial.

Into this world, Amber arrives with no explanation, and the following words: "Sorry I'm late. I'm Amber. Car broke down." Before long, she has bewitched Michael, unsettled Eve, captivated Astrid, and seduced Magnus. Amber tells the truth. In so doing, she exposes the delusional fictions of the middle classes, revealing identity as shifting and experience as constructed and covered in cliché. Authenticity is a rare and fleeing thing. Through the figure of Amber, the novel critiques postmodernist cynicism, exploring the dangerous power of technology and of imagery, and the vacuity and falsity of Blair's Britain.

The book's style is dazzling, dizzying, and innovative, involving stream-of-consciousness technique, shifting perspectives, even poetry to enact the fissures and cataclysms provoked by Amber's presence.

Emily Jeremiah

Date 2004

Author Ali Smith (born 1962)

Nationality UK

Why It's Key Amber is a mysterious and complex character in *The Accidental*, which won the 2005 Whitbread Novel Award and was short-listed for the 2005 Man Booker Prize. Amber has been described as "a brilliant creation, her every speech and action completely unpredictable." (Paul Bailey, *The Independent*)

Key Author **Joyce Carol Oates**
The Falls

An extremely prolific and celebrated writer, Joyce Carol Oates (born 1938) is known primarily for her "proletarian" novels that divulge the complexities and violence of life in America, but has also written collections of poetry, short stories, and works of essay and criticism. She has been publishing since 1963 and writes with varying styles, her most striking combining elements of gothic fiction with a questioning approach to social realism, sexual ambiguity, and feminism.

Brought up on a farm in New York, and not a stranger to hard work, Oates was educated in the same one-room schoolhouse as her mother and pursued literature entirely under her own steam, writing, she divulges, since she was 14. She has taught at Princeton University since 1978, and runs a small press and literary magazine, *The Ontario Review*, with her husband. She leads a low-key life which belies her sheer productivity and influence, often cited as a favorite for the Nobel Prize in Literature

and as one of the most important and influential storytellers in the modern world. She has reworked entire swathes of American history in novels such as *Bellefleur* (1980) and her books have been nominated for innumerable awards. Her highly anthologized short story "Where Are You Going, Where Have You Been?" (1966) was dedicated to Bob Dylan.

The Falls (2004), her novel telling the story of a woman whose husband commits suicide by throwing himself over Niagara Falls, which is juxtaposed with the man-made "Love Canal" of toxic and nuclear waste, became a *New York Times* bestseller, and won the 2005 Prix Femina Etranger.

Sophie Baker

Date 2004 (publication)

Nationality USA

Other Key Works *A Garden of Earthly Delights* (1967), *them* (1969), *You Must Remember This* (1987), *Blonde* (2000)

Why It's Key Joyce Carol Oates' 32nd novel *The Falls* won the 2005 Prix Femina Etranger. It marked a critically acclaimed career of novel, poetry, short fiction, and critical writing that continues to grow and develop.

Key Book
Gilead

Marilynne Robinson's second novel takes the form of a single, sprawling letter from the Reverend John Ames to his young son. Writing in 1956, the elderly Ames is suffering from a life-threatening heart condition, lending great poignancy to his lyrical, meditative expressions of love for the mortal world he will soon be leaving.

Ames' letter weaves nimbly between the past and present of Gilead, the small Iowan town in which he serves as one of a handful of ministers. Gradually, the contours of both his and his forebears' lives come into focus, woven into the charged political history of this apparently unremarkable patch of middle America. In some of the novel's most vivid passages, he tells of his grandfather, a visionary preacher whose visions once fired Gilead's fervent abolitionist activism. These motifs of racial and economic injustice are mirrored in the present-day story of the return to Gilead of his godson and namesake. Without contrivance or intrusion,

Robinson's narrative ingeniously illuminates the links between the most intimate personal and most dramatic public histories.

Gilead is a rare experiment in contemporary fiction, an attempt to convey the close texture of human decency and religious devotion. It is replete with contemplative digressions on the nature of moral courage, the mysteries of divine grace and the spiritual pleasures of natural beauty. And yet it never lapses into easy piety or sentimentality. Ames' narrative voice is tender, wry, at times tormented, at others unwittingly pompous, giving us a potent sense of the psychological complexity of goodness.

Josh Cohen

Date 2004

Author Marilynne Robinson (born 1947)

Nationality USA

Why It's Key Published 23 years after Robinson's now classic debut *Housekeeping*, *Gilead* was published to similarly wide acclaim, though its overtly religious sensibility surprised some.

Key Event **Harold Pinter accepts the 2005 Nobel Prize in Literature**

There was much that was remarkable about Harold Pinter winning the 2005 Nobel Prize in Literature. For one thing, the 75-year-old playwright was not even rumored to be in the running for the laureateship – the favorites being Orhan Pamuk and the Syrian poet, "Adonis."

Then there was Pinter himself: critically ill with cancer of the oesophagus, he was rushed to hospital before he was due to pre-record his acceptance speech, and was only released to deliver his words. These he recited in a husky rasp while sitting in a wheelchair, his legs covered by a rug. As Michael Billington noted in *The Guardian*, there was something Beckettian about Pinter's somber fusion of "moral vigor with forensic detail."

The speech, entitled "Art, Truth and Politics," was no less astonishing than the speaker. Pinter offered a rare public glimpse inside his private imagination and its "exploration of reality through art." While Pinter the artist makes "no hard distinctions between what is real and what is unreal, nor between what is true and what is false," Pinter the citizen must ask: "What is true? What is false?"

These questions led into an excoriating critique of the "systematic, constant, vicious, remorseless […] crimes" of American (and British) foreign policy – in Nicaragua, Guatemala, El Salvador, and Iraq. "[Unflinching], unswerving, fierce intellectual determination, as citizens, to define the real truth of our lives and our societies is a crucial obligation which devolves upon us all," Pinter concluded. Prime Minister Blair and President Bush could not help but hear; whether they paid any attention is another matter entirely.

James Kidd

Date 13 October, 2005

Author Harold Pinter (born 1930)

Nationality UK

Why It's Key The Nobel Academy described the playwright as "generally seen as the foremost representative of British drama in the second half of the twentieth century." While his body of work is more than enough to qualify Pinter as a great artist, his outspoken views of world politics are fast gaining him a global reputation as a great man.

Key Event **Ismail Kadare wins the first Man Booker International Prize**

Whoever won 2005's inaugural International Man Booker was bound to earn a few headlines. An expansion of the already world-famous prize for British and Commonwealth writing, the International Booker was designed to honor a giant of world literature. The resulting shortlist was suitably stellar including Philip Roth, Doris Lessing, Muriel Spark, Gabriel García Márquez, and Ian McEwan.

So brightly did these literary stars shine that hardly anyone noticed the presence of an unheralded 69-year-old Albanian called Ismail Kadare. Hardly anyone, that is, apart from Professor John Carey, Chairman of the Judging panel who duly awarded Kadare the £60,000 prize. Newspapers spoke of an upset to rival David's defeat of Goliath: "Albanian Beats Literary Titans" trumpeted *The Guardian*.

In fact, Kadare had been writing for almost half a century in the most trying of political conditions. While his first book, *The General of the Dead Army*, earned him plaudits in Albania, subsequent novels (*The Castle*, *The File on H*, *The Pyramid*) placed him at odds with the Stalinist regime of Enver Hoxha. "I did something entirely normal," he would say in 2005. "I just did it in an abnormal country."

After years of walking Hoxha's dictatorial tightrope, Kadare was smuggled from Albania in 1990 living as an exile in Paris and relative obscurity until the International Booker intervened. Speaking about the possible impact of the Prize, Kadare hoped it would show the Balkans was not just "notorious exclusively for news of human wickedness," but could be the home of "achievement in the […] arts, literature, and civilization."

James Kidd

Date 2005

Author Ismail Kadare (born 1936)

Nationality Albania

Why It's Key Kadare's unexpected win put Albanian literature and Balkan culture on the map. An example of the power of the modern literary prize, it was a story worthy of Kadare himself: an unknown Albanian writer who has been producing novels and poems for 42 years becomes an overnight success.

Key Author **Kazuo Ishiguro**
Never Let Me Go

Kazuo Ishiguro's (born 1954) initial impact on the literary scene was rapid and profound. An early star of the University of East Anglia's creative writing course, he published his first short stories in 1981 and his debut novel a year later: the award-winning *A Pale View of the Hills*. In 1983, he was named as one of *Granta*'s best young writers alongside the "Fab Four" of Martin Amis, Ian McEwan, Salman Rushdie, and Julian Barnes.

It is not fanciful to argue that Kazuo Ishiguro's subsequent career has been more than a match for even these much-heralded contemporaries. *The Remains of the Day* (1989) put a very English spin on the Japanese-flecked themes of his first two books thanks to the unreliable narration of a starchy, self-deluding butler named Stevens. This exploration of public worlds impinging upon private selves and memory distorting past and present won Ishiguro the Booker Prize and his largest audience to date, thanks in part to a Merchant-Ivory film adaptation.

This success represented a creative watershed as Ishiguro's work has grown increasingly ambitious and experimental ever since. *The Unconsoled*'s (1995) hallucinatory narrative baffled as many critics as it impressed: James Wood stated that it "invents its own category of badness," an assessment reversed reviewing Ishiguro's next book, *When We Were Orphans* (2000) which "invents its own category of goodness."

2005's *Never Let Me Go* is possibly Ishiguro's finest work yet. Part science fiction, part boarding school memoir, it balances his artistic need to experiment with a heartfelt appeal to his reader's emotions. Having published only 3 books in the last 17 years, Ishiguro's next novel may be some way off; it is sure to be worth the wait.
James Kidd

Date 2005 (publication)

Nationality UK

Other Key Work
An Artist of the Floating World (1986)

Why It's Key Ishiguro's novels, translated into over 30 languages, have earned him a global audience and a regular berth on the shortlists for major literary awards.

Opposite **Kazuo Ishiguro**

Key Author **John Banville**
The Sea

A self-proclaimed artist in a sea of scribblers, John Banville (born 1945) produces novels that divide readers across the world. For many, he is the allusive and playful master of beautiful writing: extolling the fluid elegance of Banville's prose is now practically *de rigeur* when reviewing his latest. For some, however, his books are dense, indulgent, and obscure, while his highly praised prose paints the color purple a shade too deeply.

Both reactions were in evidence after Banville's split-decision win at 2005's Man Booker Prize. As with previous works, *The Sea* showed that Banville is as much an heir of Samuel Beckett as Henry James. Mixing realism with metaphysics, Banville's elaborately structured novel evokes the individual's struggle to perceive and represent the universe around him. While Banville writes frequently about writing as a result, he has also explored science some time before his peers (Martin Amis, Kazuo Ishiguro) made it fashionable.

In recent years, the scope of Banville's impact has broadened. His book reviews, which were best known for championing challenging writers like W.G. Sebald, made headlines in 2005 when Banville savaged Ian McEwan's *Saturday*: having called *Saturday* "dismayingly bad," he poured scorn on the literary culture that extolled such "fucking nonsense" (*The South China Morning Post*). Scurrilous rumours spread that he had deliberately knobbled a rival's bid for Booker glory.

In a move that many deemed just as shocking, Banville's next trick was to publish a terse and readable thriller written under the pseudonym Benjamin Black. It is increasingly fascinating to see what he will do next.
James Kidd

Date 2005 (publication)

Nationality Ireland

Other Key Works *Long Lankin* (1970), *The Newton Letter* (1982), *The Book of Evidence* (1989), *The Untouchable* (1997), *Shroud* (2002), *Christine Falls* (2006)

Why It's Key Arguably the finest Irish writer of the last 30 years, Banville's controversial victory in 2005's Man Booker Prize gained him the large audience his capacious talents have long deserved.

Key Event **Foer's *Extremely Loud and Incredibly Close* is published**

For most of 2005, you couldn't move without seeing the words Jonathan, Safran, or Foer up in lights, or at least up in headlines. Having wowed the literary world with *Everything is Illuminated*, New York's hottest literary star was set to repeat the trick with that difficult second novel, and the publishing world was readying itself for an "EVENT" – a sure sign being all the commemorative, limited editions of *Extremely Loud and Incredibly Close* that were being sold at twice the normal price.

In those heady days, you didn't actually need to read Foer to have an opinion about him: for many it was enough that he was young, talented, good-looking, successful, and recently married to the equally young, talented, good-looking, successful Nicole Krauss ("My idea of beautiful," as Foer writes in the dedication to *Extremely*). Upping the ante was the realization that both newly-weds had written novels in that hippest of twenty-first century genres: the "young-and-prodigiously-clever-and-possibly-autistic-child-creates-private-mythology-to-face-personal-and-global-tragedies" (cf. Mark Haddon).

In *Extremely Loud and Incredibly Close*, the tragedy that grabbed the headlines was 9/11; Foer also writes about the bombing of Dresden, but it was the September 11th plot narrated by nine year-old Oskar that captured the media's imagination. Nowhere is this more evident than in one of the novel's many form-expanding innovations: the flip-cartoon of the final pages, which famously reverses a 9/11 suicide to show a man flying up the World Trade Center. Not only is this conclusion to the book extremely moving, it also guaranteed that practically every copy, no matter how "new," would be ever-so slightly dog-eared.

James Kidd

Date 2005

Author Jonathan Safran Foer (born 1977)

Nationality USA

Why It's Key Firstly, *Extremely* was the second novel by the enfant terribly-good of the time, fifty percent of the hottest literary couple. Secondly, it was one of the first fictional attempts to capture the tragedy of 9/11. Lastly, for those intimidated by the words, there were pictures and cartoons.

Opposite Safran Foer

779

Key Event **Rumi is named USA's most popular poet**

Rumi (1207–1273), or Mawlana Jalal ad-Din Muhammad Rumi, is today regarded as the greatest of all Sufi mystic poets. *The Essential Rumi*, published in 1995 by Harper Collins, has sold over 250,000 copies in the United States, while *The Soul of Rumi* (2001) with translations by Coleman Barks, has also been immensely popular, making Rumi by far the best-selling poet in America. Partly this popularity is due to the successful adaptation of Rumi's verses to a natural English diction and phraseology, but it also has to do with the broad image of Islam that Rumi presents, and the appeal of a non-prescriptive spirituality. Sufi tradition in Islamic theology proposed the closer unity, or "Tawheed," of man with Allah through sacred experience, the belief that a man could approach knowledge of the almighty during periods of elevated spiritual consciousness, particularly through meditation, dance, and poetry. This radicalism allowed for a wider artistic, and particularly literary, celebration of Allah than was otherwise acceptable to orthodox religious teaching.

Rumi takes full advantage of this freedom in his most famous writing, notably the *Mathnawi,* or *Masnavi*, whose importance in some Islamic schools is thought to be second only to the Qu'ran itself. The whole work comprises 6 books of poetry, approximately 25,000 lines, all in rhyming couplets. It combines penetrating philosophy, theology, and allegorical fable in one massively versatile poetic work. Rumi also completed many speeches and sermons, collected in the *Fihi-Ma-Fih* and the *Majalis-i Sab'a* which continue to have a profound influence on spiritual discourse. Rumi is now one of the most widely read poets in the United States, and his writings enrich the lives of millions of readers across the globe.

Charles Beckett

Date 2005

Nationality Khorasan/Konya (modern Afghanistan/Turkey)

Why It's Key Rumi's work has been translated into all major languages and his poems continue to inspire innovation and experimentation in poetic traditions worldwide. UNESCO declared 2007 to be International Rumi Year, to commemorate the 800th anniversary of his birth.

Key Author **Stephen King**
Cell

In the pantheon of imaginative horror writing, Stephen King (born 1947) ranks alongside his own heroes Bram Stoker and Edgar Allen Poe: his eye for detail, instinctive way with narrative structure and ability to make the everyday seem uncanny and petrifying (a car in *Christine* [1983], a teenage girl in *Carrie*, a hotel in *The Shining*, a fanatical reader in *Misery*) have earned him devotees and imitators across the planet.

King excels in many other forms and genres besides that of the horror novel. In addition to comic books, science fiction, short stories, and screenplays, he has written on everything from The Ramones (penning the sleeve notes to "We're a Happy Family") to popular culture (his "The Pop of King" column for *Entertainment Weekly*). His "guides" to writing fiction (*On Writing* and *Secret Window*) are also remarkably successful.

In recent years, King has even become a Hollywood brand, albeit in the most unexpected of ways. While few of his major books have succeeded on the big screen (*Carrie* (1974), *Misery* (1987), and *The Shining* (1977) notwithstanding), adaptations of his lesser-known work have become cinematic classics: *Stand by Me* (1982), *The Shawshank Redemption* (1982), and *The Green Mile* (1996).

Despite his popularity, and possibly because of it, King has struggled to be taken seriously by critics and academics: his Lifetime Achievement Prize at the 2003 National Book Award prompted a storm of protest led by Harold Bloom, who accused him of publishing "penny dreadfuls." Perhaps Bloom's response only highlights King's true impact: that for the last thirty years, he has terrified, disturbed and (apologies Harold) entertained more readers than any other author.
James Kidd

Date 2006 (publication)

Nationality USA

Other Key Works *The Dead Zone* (1979), *Cujo* (1981), *Pet Cemetery* (1983), *It* (1986), *Dolores Claiborne* (1993), *On Writing: A Memoir of the Craft* (2000), *Cell* (2006)

Why It's Key King is arguably the world's most popular author. Few bestsellers sell better than him, and even those that do cannot match the sheer longevity, diversity, or quality of his career.

Key Author
Muriel Spark

Muriel Spark (nee Camberg, 1918–2006), spent her first 19 years in Edinburgh where she attended the James Gillespie School for Girls in an affluent part of the city. Her father was Jewish and her mother Christian, while Muriel herself was predominantly raised as a Scottish Presbyterian. Her character and social attitudes were shaped by these confusing religious influences as well as her Edinburgh education.

In 1937, she emigrated to Rhodesia (now Zimbabwe) to marry Sydney Spark, a schoolteacher. They had one son but the disastrous marriage collapsed after seven years, and Muriel Spark returned to England to work for the political intelligence department of MI6 during World War II.

Her conversion to Catholicism in 1954 was a catalyst in creating a stable, intellectual force in her life. Her first novel, *The Comforters* (1957), is an acerbic black comedy combining a ghostly tale and a caustic portrayal of Catholic bigotry, while commenting on the main character's problematic writing of her first novel. Given the dominating realism in British fiction of the 1950s, it was highly unusual.

Spark's most famous work is *The Prime of Miss Jean Brodie* (1961), in which a strong-willed schoolteacher dominates her pupils but her own arrogance leads to her betrayal by a pupil. With dialogue as precise as any poet, Spark's novels often center on social misfits or loners such as those in *The Ballad of Peckham Rye* (1960) and *Loitering with Intent* (1981). Her masterpiece, *Memento Mori* (1959), is an insightful meditation on human morality, ageing and mortality where a mysterious caller (God or Death perhaps) harasses a set of elderly friends by anonymously whispering the unpleasant truth, "Memento Mori" (roughly translated as "Remember you must die").
Alice Goldie

Date 2006 (death)

Nationality UK

Other Key Works *Child of Light: A Reassessment of Mary Shelley* (1951), *The Mandelbaum Gate* (1965), *The Abbess of Crewe* (1974), *Symposium* (1990), *Curriculum Vitae* (1993), *The Finishing School* (2004)

Why It's Key Dame Muriel Spark was an influential and unique writer. She was awarded an OBE in 1967 and DBE in 1993.

Key Author **Vikram Chandra**
Sacred Games

Vikram Chandra (born 1961) is one of the main voices of today's Indian literature in English. As an artist, he has always been deeply interested in the juxtaposition of ways of telling, expanding his thoughts about how forms model the world and help us to represent it. In his recent novel, *Sacred Games*, a remarkable contribution in the genre of noir fiction, and also in his previous works, *Red Earth and Pouring Rain* (1995) (a novel) and *Love and Longing in Bombay* (1997) (an organic short-story collection), the interaction of narrative branches subsumes an encounter of diverse languages, styles, values, identities, forms, and textures. Chandra does not anchor his viewpoint in simple dichotomies or straight polarizations. He conveys how people manage to live out their daily lives, relating to fellow human beings in all their flawed humanity in spite of historical and political forces not of their own making.

This is especially so in *Sacred Games*, internationally acclaimed as a masterpiece. Set in the Bombay (now Mumbai) of the 1990s, it tells the story of a notorious Hindu gangster, Ganesh Gaitonde, and a police inspector, Sartaj Singh, whose lives unfold and eventually intersect with unexpected consequences. Bringing to vivid life a profusion of characters and milieus, Chandra's extraordinary thriller-cum-detective novel depicts India with an unsurpassed richness of detail: its complexity and violence, the worlds of the poor and the wealthy, the heroes of Bollywood movies and the striving of human beings from every walk of life. This novel shows how, in a certain sense, there is no such a thing as the underworld, but simply the world, next to us and part of us – or, to echo the closing words of *Love and Longing in Bombay*: "Only life itself."

Dora Sales

Date 2006 (publication)

Nationality India

Why It's Key Chandra displays an untiring ability as storyteller, paying particular tribute to the Indian tradition of oral storytelling he appreciates so much. His literary project as a whole takes in a deep understanding of the multiplicity of the socio-cultural life of India, past and present.

Key Author **Sarah Waters**
The Night Watch

Nominee and winner of a number of literary awards, including two nominations for the Man Booker Prize and the winner of Somerset Maugham Award for Gay and Lesbian Literature, Sarah Waters (born 1966) has carved out a very clear niche for herself as a writer of literary lesbian historical fiction.

Her first work *Tipping the Velvet* (1998) is a picaresque novel set in the late 1800s and tells of Nancy Astley's journey through society as a male impersonator, a "boy" prostitute and finally as a political speech coach. When adapted for BBC television, it attracted a great deal of attention in the press.

Waters' inventiveness lies in the way that she writes about sexualities of the past without forcing psychological modernity onto her characters. Her influences are fascinating, the plots and character types are reminiscent of Victorian writers and they combine with the dark and sexualized awareness of Virginia Woolf, Jeanette Winterson, and Angela Carter. The effect is often striking. *Tipping the Velvet* has all the unpredictability and barefaced melodrama of a Dickens' novel and works both as politicized writing and as highly enjoyable page-turning fiction. *Affinity* (1999), set in Millbank women's prison, is a mystery story about spiritualism and fakery.

In *Fingersmith* (2002), Sue Trinder goes undercover as a maid to cheat an heiress out of her fortune. With a plot reminiscent of Wilkie Collins' *The Woman in White* (1860), Waters takes the reader inside the lunatic asylum and to the horrors of falsified identities. The novel also has some of the most staggering plot twists in recent years. Her most recent *The Night Watch* (2006) is set in London during World War II and draws on the popular lesbian romances of the period.

Royce Mahawatte

Date 2006 (publication)

Nationality UK

Why It's Key An acclaimed writer of historical fiction who combines period settings and storylines with lesbian themes. Combining impeccable historical research with the pace and feel of past literary forms, Waters has proven herself to be both a popular and experimental writer.

Key Author
John McGahern

John McGahern (1934–2006) first made himself widely known in the early 1960s when his second novel, *The Dark* (1965) was banned for its explicit content and anti-clericalism. A famously slow and careful writer, his prose style is sparse but particular.

His masterpiece, *Amongst Women* (1990) concerns former IRA officer Michael Moran who fought in the War of Independence and the Irish civil war. Moran tyrannizes his wife and daughters and the novel looks unflinchingly at this twisted, violent man through flashbacks narrated by the women in his life. Moran's unyielding control of his family is used to reflect the various kinds of violence that Ireland has had visited upon it but has also been somehow complicit in. Significantly his only son has left, unable to take the bullying any longer, but even after Moran's death his wife and daughters are under his influence, and this inability to break from the past denotes a terrible poignancy and bleakness.

The novel suggests that Ireland's women are constantly supporting a violent male (and Catholic) impetus to introspection and self-absorption; even giving the women the agency of narration is compromised by their obsession with making Moran happy.

McGahern's books were concerned with the rural life of Ireland and meditating through that existence on the nature of Irish national identity. *Amongst Women* and *That They May Face the Rising Sun* (2001) both explore nationhood and history through analysis of repressive close-knit rural communities, all of which are flawed in some way. He is also a masterly short-story writer and his command of this form demonstrates his ability to express profound concepts in his characteristic terse style.

Jerome de Groot

Date 2006 (death)

Nationality Ireland

Other Key Works *The Leavetaking* (1975), *Amongst Women* (1990), *Collected Stories* (1992), *Memoir* (2005)

Why It's Key John McGahern was, by the time of his death, the most respected and influential novelist in Ireland.

2000–

783

Key Event **Orhan Pamuk wins the Nobel Prize in Literature**

"Most honoured Orhan Pamuk! You have made your native city an indispensable literary territory, equal to Dostoyevsky's St Petersburg, Joyce's Dublin or Proust's Paris."

So said the Permanent Secretary of the Swedish Academy, Horace Engdahl, upon announcing Orhan Pamuk's Nobel win. The city is Istanbul, where Pamuk (born 1952) was born into a westernized bourgeois family. Educated at Robert Academy, an American-owned lycee on the European shore of the Bosphorus, he put himself through a long and arduous literary apprenticeship, delving into history, art, and literature from both western and eastern traditions and writing his first novels while his mother warned him he would never succeed.

His first novels to be published in European languages attracted the interest and admiration of western literary elites, though it is the literary readers

of countries as marginalized as Turkey that appreciate his gifts most keenly. He is, as Horace Engdahl pointed out, a writer "who in the quest for the melancholic soul of his native city has discovered new symbols for the clash and interlacing of cultures."

However, he is perhaps best known amongst those without a taste for literary fiction for having told a Swiss journalist in 2005 that a million Armenians and 30,000 Kurds had been killed in his country, and that it irked him that no one else talked about it. He was soon reminded why: following an extended hate campaign, he was prosecuted for insulting Turkishness. Though the charges were later dropped, the ultranationalists who brought the case against him and the rightwing media that aided and abetted them did succeed in convincing many gullible people that he was a traitor. But anyone who reads his books will know that the center of his world will always be his beloved Istanbul.

Maureen Freely

Date 2006

Nationality Turkey

Why It's Key "… My confidence comes from the belief that all human beings resemble each other, that others carry wounds like mine – that they will therefore understand. All true literature rises from this childish, hopeful certainty that all people resemble each other."(From Pamuk's Nobel Lecture, *My Father's Suitcase*)

Opposite Orhan Pamuk

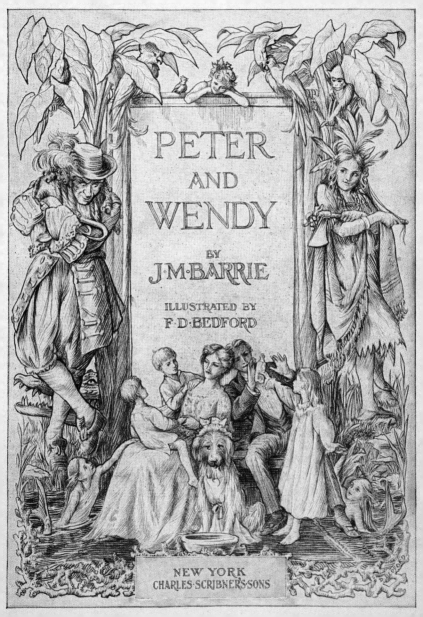

PETER AND WENDY

BY
J·M·BARRIE

ILLUSTRATED BY
F·D·BEDFORD

NEW YORK
CHARLES·SCRIBNER'S·SONS

BOOKS TITLE INDEX

AUTHOR INDEX

793

796

GENERAL INDEX

ACKNOWLEDGMENTS

Indices compiled by
Ann Barrett

Proofread by
David Price

Picture Credits
© -/epa/Corbis 586; © Alex Gotfryd/CORBIS 580; © Allen Ginsberg/CORBIS 624; © Andreea Angelescu/Andreea Angelescu /Corbis 744; © Andreu Dalmau/epa/Corbis 777; © Andrew Fox/Corbis/Corbis 648; © Archivo Iconografico, S.A./CORBIS 132; © BARBIER RENN PRODUCTION/CORBIS SYGMA 622; © Barnabas Bosshart/Corbis 382; © Barry Lewis/Corbis 114, 174; © BASSOULS SOPHIE/CORBIS SYGMA 492; © BBC/Corbis 152; © Bettmann/CORBIS 4, 18, 21, 30, 40, 47, 51, 55, 56, 91, 97, 98, 110, 119, 125, 128, 138, 143, 147, 151, 157, 160, 169, 180, 185, 188, 196, 200, 204, 216, 222, 226, 239, 246, 250, 252, 255, 262, 267, 294, 300, 304, 310, 312, 320, 334, 336, 340, 352, 354, 363, 390, 402, 404, 412, 416, 430, 432, 466, 469, 476, 482, 486, 510, 515, 527, 528, 537, 549, 571, 598, 608, 612, 639, 694, 735; © Blue Lantern Studio/Corbis 79, 784; © Bo Zaunders/CORBIS 325; © Caroline Penn/CORBIS 674; © Chris George/CORBIS 594; © Christopher Felver/CORBIS 13, 567, 630; © CLOSE MURRAY/CORBIS SYGMA 82; © Colin McPherson/Corbis 699, 703, 730, 763, 770; © Colita/CORBIS 360, 606; © Columbia Pictures/ZUMA/Corbis 376; © CORBIS 24, 113, 166, 176, 215, 288, 368; © CORBIS SYGMA 88, 137, 408, 522, 550, 650, 686, 689; © Dave Bartruff/CORBIS 485; © David J. & Janice L. Frent Collection/CORBIS 29; © David Lees/CORBIS 656; © Digital Domain/20Th Century Fox/Bureau L.A. Collection/Corbis 356; © Douglas Kirkland/CORBIS 322; © E.O. Hoppé/CORBIS 63, 85, 92; © Edifice/Corbis 165; © Eric Robert/CORBIS SYGMA 682; © Eudora Welty/Corbis 306, 454; © Fabian Cevallos/CORBIS SYGMA 418; © Filip Singer/epa/Corbis 653; © Forrest J. Ackerman Collection/CORBIS 15; © FOUGERE ERIC/CORBIS KIPA 704; © François Duhamel/Sygma/Corbis 568; © Frank May/epa/Corbis 790 © Gail Albert Halaban/Corbis 712; © Georges Pierre/Sygma/Corbis 208, 386; © Granada/Arts Council/Film 4 / The Kobal Collection/Buitendjik, Jaap 52; © Handout/Reuters/Corbis 332; © HELLESTAD RUNE/CORBIS SYGMA 350; © Ho/epa/Corbis 516; © Horacio Villalobos/Corbis 314; © Hulton-Deutsch Collection/CORBIS 5, 43, 71, 106, 109, 148, 228, 234, 240, 278, 308, 319, 347, 380, 410, 424, 446, 448, 454, 475, 481, 495, 504, 520, 530, 552, 558, 585, 670; © Issei Kato/Reuters/Corbis 706; © James Leynse/CORBIS 721; © Jan_Delden/epa/Corbis 796 © Jean Louis Atlan/Sygma/Corbis 437; © Jeffery Allan Salter/CORBIS SABA 632; © Jerry Cooke/CORBIS 220; © John Garrett/CORBIS 443; © John Springer Collection/CORBIS 105, 210, 218, 232, 268, 280, 282, 286, 291, 344, 378, 400, 438, 452, 491, 534; © John Van Hasselt/Corbis 618; © Juan Carlos Ulate/Reuters /Corbis 722; © Keystone/Corbis 144; © Laurie Sparham/Universal Studios/Bureau L.A. Collection/Corbis 726; © Louie Psihoyos/Corbis 538, 626; © Louise Gubb/CORBIS SABA 680; © Lynsey Addario/Corbis 782; © MACLELLAN DON/CORBIS SYGMA 716; © Manjunath Kiran/epa /Corbis 766; © MC PHERSON COLIN/CORBIS SYGMA 751; © Melissa Moseley/Sony Pictures/Bureau L.A. Collection/Corbis 460; © MGM/Corbis 556, 600; © Micheline Pelletier/Corbis 736; © Mike Segar/Reuters/Corbis 700; © Najlah Feanny/CORBIS SABA 575; © Nancy Kaszerman/ZUMA/Corbis 640, 748; © Neville Elder/Corbis 778; © Nicolas Asfouri/epa/Corbis 758; © NOGUES ALAIN/CORBIS SYGMA 714; © Odile Montserrat/Sygma/Corbis 364; © Orjan F. Ellingvag /Corbis 752; © Orjan F. Ellingvag/Dagbladet/ELLINGVAG/ORJAN/Corbis 634; © Oscar White/CORBIS 264; © Paul Colangelo/CORBIS 182;

© Peter Foley/epa/Corbis 710; © Philip Gould/CORBIS 470; © Randall Fung/Corbis 48; © Reuters/CORBIS 444, 643, 662, 664, 732 © Richard Melloul/Sygma/CORBIS 592; © Robbie Jack/CORBIS 35, 66, 373, 388; © Robert Estall/CORBIS 258; © Roger Ressmeyer/CORBIS 502; © Rune Hellestad/Corbis 459, 616, 644, 676, 692; © Smithsonian Institution /Corbis 120; © Sophie Bassouls/CORBIS SYGMA 498, 540, 546, 562, 578, 604, 746; © SPRIO GINO/CORBIS SYGMA 740; © Stapleton Collection /Corbis 74; © Stefano Bianchetti/CORBIS 172; © Steffen Kugler /epa/Corbis 654; © Sunset Boulevard/Corbis 293, 426, 428, 462; © Swim Ink 2, LLC/CORBIS 277, 397; © Sygma/Corbis 669; © Ted Soqui/Corbis 760; © Ted Streshinsky/Corbis 509; © Touchstone Pictures/ZUMA/Corbis 588; © Underwood & Underwood/CORBIS 131, 193; © Underwood & Underwood/CORBIS 198; © VAUGHAN STEPHEN /CORBIS SYGMA 610; PARAMOUNT/THE KOBAL COLLECTION 326; WALT DISNEY PICTURES/THE KOBAL COLLECTION 244; WARNER BROS/THE KOBAL COLLECTION 10, 660